9.85

AMERICAN
History : : :

A Survey

AMERICAN
History : : :
A Survey

RICHARD N. CURRENT *University of Wisconsin*

T. HARRY WILLIAMS *Louisiana State University*

FRANK FREIDEL *Harvard University*

: 1 9 6 3 :

New York   Alfred·A·Knopf

L. C. catalog card number: 60–16705

THIS IS A BORZOI BOOK,

PUBLISHED BY ALFRED A. KNOPF, INC.

Published 1961; reprinted 1961 (2), 1963

TO

W. B. H.,

As Always

PREFACE

History is life, the life of the past (and "the past" includes the whole of time up to this very moment). It provides the opportunities for, and sets the limits to, our lives in the present and the future. As Abraham Lincoln once said, "We cannot escape history."

History also means the *study* of life in the past, or of some part of it, and the *story* that is derived from such study. Our conceptions of the past (quite apart from the actualities of the past) have a significant bearing upon our attitudes toward the present. The reverse also is true. Our attitudes toward the present have a significant bearing upon our conceptions of the past.

Thus a totalitarian regime, imposing upon its writers a ready-made set of historical "laws" and conclusions, attempts to create a picture of the past that will favor its own present aims. In the totalitarian state, as satirized by George Orwell in his novel *1984*, all accounts of bygone events, even the back files of newspapers, are carefully altered every time there is a change in official policy. The government, regardless of its twists and turns, is made to appear all-wise and perfectly consistent. The people have no way of knowing what the old days were really like—what comforts and freedoms have been lost.

In a truly free society, historians have the right to seek to know the past as it actually was. They have the right (perhaps the most precious) even to make mistakes. They are limited only by their own infirmities and biases; they are obligated only to the impartial standards of historical scholarship. A society is likely to remain free so long as historians are thus allowed to write as they please.

The study of history, then, is no mere idle pastime. It is essential to intelligent life. It contributes to the successful working of a democracy.

American historians, in writing as they please about their own country, have come to agree upon most of the "facts." But there are countless facts, and with regard to some of them historians have disagreed as to which are the most important and which should be picked out and emphasized. Hence there are differences in the interpretation of certain phases of American history.

This textbook (based upon the same authors' two-volume *History of the United States*) is intended as an introduction and a guide to a complex and, in part, a controverted subject. Of necessity, the book has been written from the researches not of its authors alone but of hundreds of historical scholars. In deciding upon the inclusion of material and the handling of controversial issues, we have tried, wherever possible, to reflect the consensus of contemporary historical scholarship. At points where there is no clear consensus, we have relied upon our own tentative judgment.

The student should bear in mind that the whole of American history is not contained in this or in any other book. This one, indeed, is intended to open the subject, not to close it. The book will have succeeded if, with the indispensable aid of the instructor, it arouses a desire to learn more about American history than is included between these covers.

The student is urged to make himself familiar, at the outset, with the book as a whole and with all its special features. Chapter bibliographies and a general bibliography provide selected lists of books for further reading. Maps, conceived with a view to simplicity and clarity, are numerous. Graphs and charts reduce some of the statistical data to a form easily comprehended. Pictures, chosen not as ornaments but as aids to understanding,

are placed near the text material they illustrate, and they are accompanied by rather full explanatory captions. A number of "boxes" contain supplementary information, including excerpts from contemporary documents; these selections make the volume to some extent a book of readings as well as a textbook. Appendices embody additional documentary and statistical matter. The student should consider all these features—and of course the table of contents and the index also —as essential and integral parts of the book, to be used in his study of American history.

Though we have put this book together with considerable care, and have incorporated a number of changes suggested by users of our two-volume text, we are under no illusion that we have managed to get rid of every error of fact or interpretation. We shall continue to be grateful for suggestions of corrections or other improvements to be considered in future revisions.

R. N. C.

T. H. W.

F. F.

CONTENTS

ILLUSTRATIONS

MAPS

DRAWN BY THEODORE R. MILLER

CHARTS

AMERICAN
History : : :
A Survey

I

BACKGROUNDS AND BEGINNINGS

The story of the American people is fairly short if it be dated from the first enduring English settlement, at Jamestown in 1607. Since then, only some three and a half centuries have gone by—a period that can be spanned by the overlapping lives of no more than five or six men! But, of course, the American story actually begins in Europe. To see how the New World came to be discovered and colonized from the Old, it is necessary to review certain European developments of early "modern" times.

The Quickening of Europe

During the Middle Ages (roughly from A.D. 500 to A.D. 1500) the civilization of Western Europe was in many ways inferior to that of ancient Greece or Rome. After Germanic barbarians had overrun the Roman Empire, the dream of Roman peace and unity lingered on. The countries of medieval Europe were thought to form a single whole, under the spiritual authority of the Roman Catholic Church and the political authority of what was called the Holy Roman Empire. But kings often asserted power independently of the emperor, and nobles asserted power independently of the kings. Ordinary people, the serfs, tied by custom to the soil, worked the fields while their lords engaged in desultory warfare and chivalric games. Merchants and craftsmen were handicapped by the disorders that prevailed much of the time. Except within the Church, art and learning had few practitioners, and it was left to the monasteries to keep alive the memory of past greatness.

Forces leading to the awakening of Europe and the discovery of America were set in motion around A.D. 1000 by an outpouring of the Norsemen from Denmark, Norway, and Sweden. These Vikings made conquests as far east as Russia, as far south as France and the British Isles, and as far west as Iceland and Greenland. Two of them, Biarni Heriulfson and Leif Ericsson, on separate voyages, even touched upon the coast of North America, but later attempts at colonization failed, and neither of these men is generally considered the effective discoverer of the New World. Indirectly, however, the Norse did contribute to the subsequent discovery or rediscovery by Columbus. They pioneered in the construction of ocean-going ships, stimulated trade over the area of their widespread conquests, and infused into the life of Europe much of their own energy and daring. Their descendants in France, the Normans (who set up kingdoms in England, Italy and Sicily, and northern Africa), provided outstanding leadership in the Crusades.

The Crusades further encouraged shipbuilding and commerce. In Syria and Egypt the Crusaders got acquainted with a number of exotic goods—spices, perfumes, drugs, silks, china, glassware, gems —which were brought by land and by sea all the way from the Orient. In the Near East some Europeans, especially the Italians, set up trading posts where they exchanged for Oriental commodities the gold, silver, copper, lead, and tin from the mines of Western Europe. These traders sent their imports on to such wholesaling centers as Pisa, Genoa, and Venice, which distributed the goods among merchants from other towns and ultimately among the consumers, remote from the original sources of supply in China, India, or the "Spice Islands" of the East Indies.

This commerce fostered the growth of towns and gave a new importance to town life in Europe. The townsmen or bourgeoisie came to form a substantial "middle" class between the nobles and the clergy above them and the serfs below. They accumulated capital in larger and larger amounts, making possible trading ventures of increasing size and profit. Desiring peace and security, such as would be good for business, the merchants breathed a spirit quite out of harmony with feudalism and its disorders. In the contests between kings and turbulent nobles, the bourgeoisie came to the support of the kings and thus aided in the rise of centralized national governments.

Increased wealth, leisure, and security, by making possible a greater cultivation of the things of the mind, prepared the way for the Renaissance in Europe. The Renaissance was marked by a changing outlook on life. Formerly, preoccupied with their own sinfulness and weakness, men had viewed their earthly lives as contemptible and had tried to concentrate their thoughts upon eternity. Now, with increasing human self-confidence, they began to show more and more interest in the world about them. Formerly they had relied for their ideas mostly on the authority of the Bible and the works of Aristotle as expounded by the churchmen. Now many became willing to observe, experiment, and test truths for themselves. This changing attitude was involved both in the renewed study of Greek and Roman classics and in the creation of vernacular literatures. It was related also to the multiplication of efforts to control the natural environment by applied science and technology rather than by prayer or magic.

Among the inventions coming into use after the twelfth century were guns and gunpowder, bellows and blast-furnaces, various machines powered by water or wind, movable type and the printing press, the mechanical clock, improvements in ship design and construction, and several devices intended to aid the art of navigation. The compass, at first only a needle magnetized with lodestone and floated in water, told the navigator his direction. He could obtain his latitude by sighting a fixed star with the quadrant, the cross staff, or the astrolabe; and the clock together with certain astronomical data theoretically enabled him to calculate his longitude. But in actual practice he found it next to impossible to make accurate observation from the deck of a rolling ship. So he continued to follow the coasts when feasible, and when he ventured out of sight of land he proceeded (as Columbus did) mainly by dead reckoning, setting his course by the compass and finding his position by elapsed time and estimated speed.

Geographical knowledge was still, as in ancient times, a mixture of fable and fact, even though map-making improved remarkably. Mariners, foremost among them the Italians, carefully charted the shore lines along which they sailed, until the coastal areas of almost all the known world had been accurately mapped. On the high seas away from the familiar routes, however, everything remained a matter of speculation. Practical sailors and educated men believed that the earth was a sphere, but many of them underestimated its size. The first globe ever made, the work of a Nuremberg cartographer in 1492, showed an unbroken ocean stretching westward from Europe around to Asia and occupying only about a third of the earth's surface.

On the European edge of this sea of darkness stood the rising nation-states of England, France, Holland, Portugal, and Spain, each with a strong government and a consciousness of national unity. These countries, while the most powerful in Europe, were also the most distant from the rich sources of the Oriental trade. In the process of this trade, Italian and Arab merchants added their profits and commissions, and various rulers added their tolls and taxes, so that by the time Oriental wares reached the Atlantic nations the price was outrageously high, and excessive amounts of money were drained away to the eastward. If the middlemen somehow could be by-passed, the western merchants could gain larger profits for themselves and the western nations could end the troublesome loss of specie. Here was an adequate motive for finding new routes, entirely by sea, which could be controlled from home. The search for new approaches to the East led to the discovery of new lands in the West, in that presumably empty ocean which lay at the back of Europe.

Westward to the East

Without the wealth of the merchants and the organizing power of the nation states, the glorious age of exploration would have been unthinkable. But it would also have been inconceivable without patriotic and religious zeal, skillful seamanship, bold imagination, and courageous leadership.

Portugal early took the lead as an exploring nation. Its maritime supremacy owed a great deal to one man, Prince Henry the Navigator, who devoted his life to nautical studies and to the promotion of exploration. Concentrating upon the western coast of Africa, with the visionary aim of establishing a Christian empire to aid in war against the Moors, and with the more practical object of finding gold, Prince Henry sent out expedition after expedition, some of his mariners going as far south as Cape Verde. After his death in 1460 his work was carried on by intrepid explorers advancing still farther south. At last, in 1486, Bartholomeu Diaz went clear around the southern tip of the continent, and in 1497–8 Vasco da Gama proceeded all the way to India. In 1500 the next fleet bound for India, that of Pedro Cabral, was blown off its southward course and happened upon the coast of Brazil. So America would have been discovered within a decade even if Columbus had never made his famous voyage of 1492.

Christopher Columbus (1451–1506), born and reared in Genoa, got most of his seafaring knowledge and experience in the service of the Portuguese. He was not the first man to think of reaching the East by sailing west, but he was the first to do anything about it. Though an industrious student of geography, he was convinced of the feasibility of his plan as a result of errors rather than special insight. From his reading of Marco Polo's wondrous travel book, from his correspondence with the Florentine geographer Toscanelli, and from other studies and his own calculations, he gathered that the world was smaller than it actually is and that the Asian continent extended farther eastward than it actually does. So he concluded that the western ocean was narrow enough to be crossed on a relatively brief voyage. But he failed to convince the King of Portugal, and as the Portuguese progressed with their own route to the East around Africa, they completely lost interest in the idea of a westward crossing.

Columbus then turned from Portugal to Spain. Though not a maritime people

of the Moorish stronghold of Granada, the Mohammedans were practically eliminated from Spanish soil, and during that same year the Jews who rejected conversion were forced to leave the country. At last Isabella granted Columbus his request. He was to be admiral of the ocean sea, governor of all the lands he might discover, and owner of a tenth of the wealth to be produced therein.

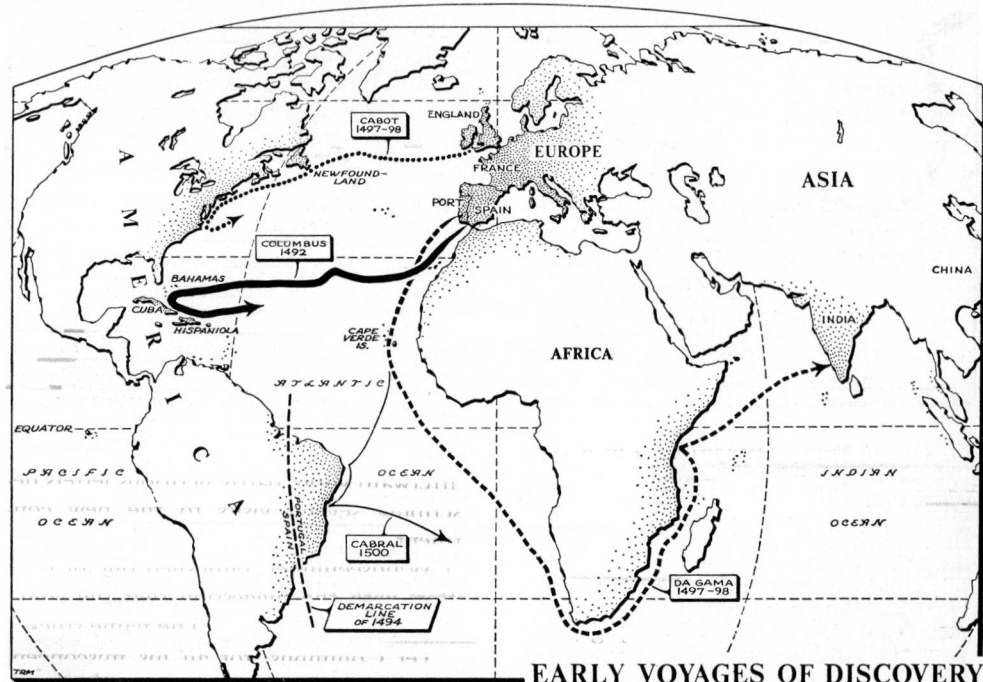

EARLY VOYAGES OF DISCOVERY

like the Portuguese, the Spaniards were proud, energetic, and zealous. They were being unified under the strongest monarchy in Europe after the marriage of Ferdinand of Aragon and Isabella of Castile. To Queen Isabella the importunate Columbus appealed for money, men, and ships with which to carry out his project and thereby extend the sway of Christianity and the power and glory of Spain. For several years the Queen withheld her aid, partly because her advisers doubted Columbus' theories and partly because she was busy with Christianizing and conquering Spain itself. In 1492, with the fall

On his first voyage, with the *Pinta*, the *Niña*, and the *Santa Maria* and with ninety men, Columbus steered as straight as he could for Japan. He thought he had arrived there when, ten weeks after embarking, he landed on Watling Island in the Bahamas, and he thought he had reached the China coast when he pushed on to Cuba. He returned to Spain with a few natives—he called them "Indians"— but he brought no news of the great Khan's court in China and no samples of the famous wealth of the Indies. The next year, with a much larger expedition, he discovered other islands and left a colony

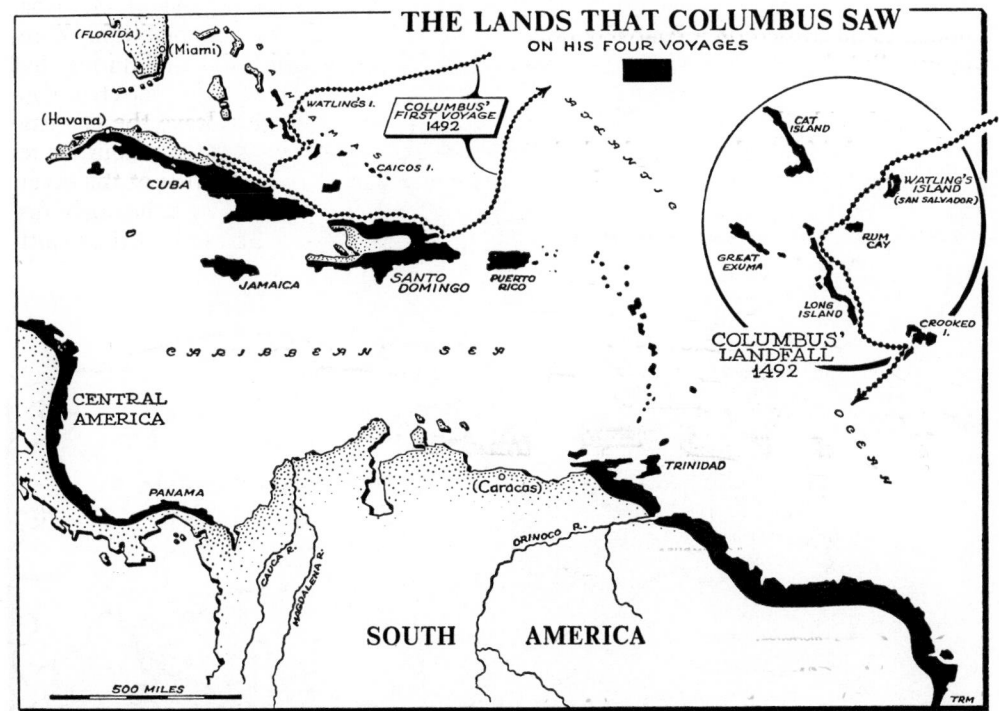

THE LANDS THAT COLUMBUS SAW
ON HIS FOUR VOYAGES

(FLORIDA)
(Miami)
WATLING'S I.
COLUMBUS' FIRST VOYAGE 1492
(Havana)
CAICOS I.
CUBA
JAMAICA
SANTO DOMINGO
PUERTO RICO
CAT ISLAND
WATLING'S ISLAND (SAN SALVADOR)
GREAT EXUMA
RUM CAY
LONG ISLAND
CROOKED I.
COLUMBUS' LANDFALL 1492
CARIBBEAN SEA
CENTRAL AMERICA
PANAMA
TRINIDAD
(Caracas)
ORINOCO R.
CAUCA R.
MAGDALENA R.
SOUTH AMERICA
500 MILES
TRM

on one of them, Hispaniola. On a third voyage, in 1498, cruising along the northern coast of South America, he passed the mouth of the Orinoco River and surmised that such a large fresh-water stream must emerge from a continent, one separate from Asia. On his last voyage, in 1502, he tried to sail around the northwestern end of the continent so as to find the rich and civilized part of the Indies, but he was blocked by the Isthmus of Panama and succeeded only in exploring the Caribbean coast of Central America. He died still thinking he had been in at least the fringes of the Far East.

At first a hero, then a man in disgrace, Columbus was not even honored in the naming of the land he had discovered. Disregarding his promised monopoly, Spain itself licensed numerous explorers after him, and rival governments sent out expeditions of their own. The Portuguese, who claimed the whole region of his discoveries, promptly dispatched a fleet to the scene (1501). A Florentine merchant,

Americus Vespucius, who was aboard, afterward wrote partly fictitious letters describing several visits to the new continent, and a German geographer, Martin Waldseemüller, published one of the letters with the suggestion that the land be named for Americus. The name stuck.

Yet Columbus, for all his misconceptions, deserved the fame that ultimately came to him. He dispelled the terrors of the unknown ocean and led the way to the New World. The explorers of many nations who followed him were but carrying on the work he had begun. Just as he had done on his final voyage, they concentrated their efforts mainly on the search for a water passage which would lead through or around the new lands and on to the riches of the Far East. They never found the kind of passage they sought (because it did not exist—until 1914, when the Panama Canal was opened) but they revealed the outlines of both continents and made known the vastness of the territory available for European use.

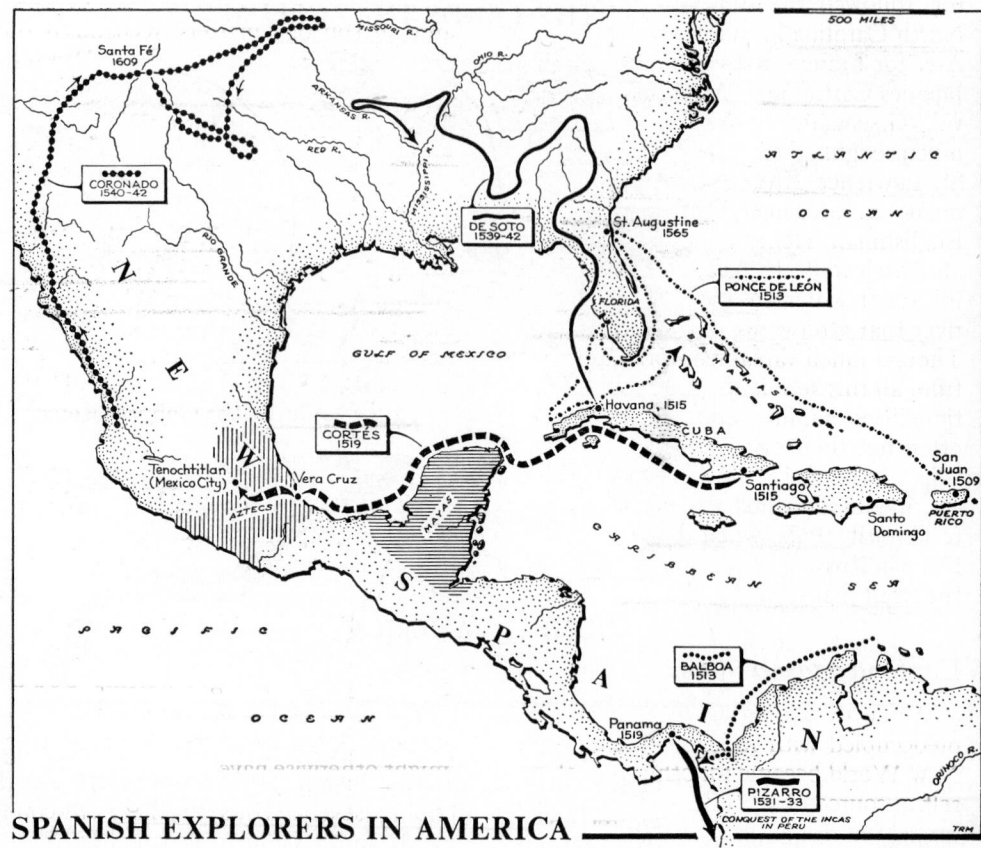

SPANISH EXPLORERS IN AMERICA

Spain, turning to the sea as a result of Columbus' initiative, replaced Portugal as the foremost exploring nation. Vasco de Balboa fought his way across the Isthmus of Panama (1513) and gazed upon the great ocean that separated America from China and the Indies. Seeking access to that ocean, Ferdinand Magellan, a Portuguese in Spanish employ, found the strait which now bears his name at the southern end of South America, struggled through the stormy narrows and into the ocean, so calm by contrast that he christened it the Pacific, then proceeded to the Philippines. There Magellan himself fell at the hands of natives, but his expedition went on to complete the first circumnavigation of the globe (1519–22). By 1550 the Spaniards had explored the coasts of North America as far up as Oregon and Labrador.

England followed Spain as a sponsor of voyages westward in search of the East. John Cabot, Genoa-born like Columbus and inspired by the latter's unsuccessful efforts to reach the Orient, sailed twice to the northwestern coast of North America under the auspices of King Henry VII, the first time in 1497. Much later, after failing to find a northeast passage around Europe, Englishmen began to look for a northwest passage around North America. Martin Frobisher made three trips, the last one in 1578, and discovered Frobisher's Bay, Baffin's Land, and the Eskimos, but not the strait he was after. Year after year, other Englishmen kept up the search.

Meanwhile, under Francis I, the government of France promoted a series of expeditions to the New World. In 1523–4 Giovanni Verrazano, a Florentine navigator, followed the shore northward from North Carolina in quest of an opening to Asia for France. Between 1534 and 1541 Jacques Cartier and Jean François Roberval, on separate voyages, tried to find the much-sought passage by pushing up the St. Lawrence River. The Dutch government, a latecomer, commissioned the Englishman Henry Hudson to find an all-Dutch route to Asia, and he was looking for it when, in 1609, he entered the river that afterwards was named for him. Though much valuable information came from all this activity by men of several nationalities sailing under diverse flags, often not their own, the precise relationship of the Asian and North American continents remained something of a mystery until 1728, when Vitus Bering, a Dane in Russian employ, voyaged through the strait that separates the two.

England against Spain

While remaining an obstacle to those preoccupied with routes to the East, the New World became for others a goal in itself, a source of wealth rivaling and even surpassing the original Indies. The Spaniards, busy making known the configuration of the American continents, were also getting acquainted with their interior and building an American empire. On the basis of Columbus' discoveries and a papal decree, they at first claimed the whole of the New World, but in the Treaty of Tordesillas (1494) they agreed to a demarcation line which left a great chunk of it (Brazil) to the Portuguese. Even so, the area open to Spanish exploitation was so vast and varied that it challenged the human and physical resources of Spain.

While Spain was building her American empire, the religious unity of Western Europe disappeared, with profound consequences for the colonization of America. As of 1500, the Christian world already was divided between East and West, between the Church of Constantinople and the Church of Rome. But virtually all of Western Europe was Roman Catholic and, in spiritual matters, recognized the supremacy of the Pope. Soon Western Europe itself was divided, between Catholics and those who protested, or Protestants, of whom there came to be many sects. The Protestant leaders intended to reform the Church, and so their movement is known as the Reformation. While losing many lands to Lutheranism, Calvinism, or Anglicanism, the Church of Rome undertook to reform itself and win back as much of the world as possible. This undertaking is known as the Catholic Reformation or the Counter Reformation.

These religious developments of the sixteenth century affected the colonization of America in several ways:

1. Minority groups opposing the state religion—such as the Puritans in England and the Mennonites and Moravians in Germany—looked to the New World as a place where they might worship God according to their lights. Thus the number of willing colonists was larger than it might otherwise have been.

2. Protestantism encouraged business enterprise by emphasizing the virtues of thrift and hard work, and permitting loans at interest, which in Catholic doctrine was usury, a sin. Overseas trading ventures often required loans and in many cases led to the founding of colonies. Colonization, from the point of view of many colonial promoters, was big business, and such business thrived as never before in a Protestant atmosphere.

3. The rise of national religions, in which the church was subordinate to the national sovereign, strengthened the nation-states. And the interests of the state, as well as the lure of private profit, provided a motive for the foundation of colonies.

4. Besides personal and national aggrandizement, the spread of religion was an object of colonization. The religious motive was sharpened by the contest between the forces of the Protestant Refor-

mation and those of the Counter Reformation. The contest was extended from the Old World to the New. Catholics sought to keep America Catholic, and Protestants tried to frustrate Rome and win America, or at least a part of it, for their own particular faith.

In the sixteenth century Spain acquired vast dominions in Europe as well as America, and her fate in the international politics and religious wars of the time, with England as her nemesis, had tremendous consequences for the future of the New World. Through a series of royal marriages a grandson of Ferdinand and Isabella inherited a large part of Western Europe and was elected emperor of the Holy Roman Empire as Charles V. When Emperor Charles V retired (1556) his son King Philip II of Spain did not receive the emperorship of the Hapsburg possessions in Germany. But Philip II retained extensive territories, including the American colonies, parts of Italy, and the Netherlands, and (1580) he made himself King of Portugal as well as Spain. He also assumed the task of leading the Roman Catholic forces of the world against the Protestant Reformation.

The great power of the sixteenth-century world, Spain monopolized America, North and South. She denied to foreigners, with few exceptions, the right to trade or settle within her overseas domain. But other nations, too, had American claims. Eventually these nations—the Dutch, English, French (and, much later, the Russians)—challenged the Spanish monopoly of North America.

In 1568 the Dutch revolted against Philip II, their Spanish overlord. They fought, as Dutchmen, for national independence, and, as Calvinists, for religious freedom. They were an industrial and maritime people, noted for their linen and woolen cloth, their ships, their fisheries, and their trade. Holding an advantage upon the sea, they robbed the galleons bringing treasure from the New World to Spain. When Spain agreed to a truce (1609), the Dutch turned to planning American colonies of their own.

In their forays against Spanish shipping the Dutch received encouragement and aid from England. Queen Elizabeth had to fend against the machinations of Philip II as he sought to enhance the power of Spain and win back to Rome the areas of Christendom that had been lost. English Catholics were ready to collaborate with a foreign king in forwarding this presumably holy work. With Philip's encouragement they plotted to get rid of Elizabeth and put Mary Stuart, "Queen of Scots," on the throne. Elizabeth, foiling them, had Mary executed.

In this undeclared war England did not remain on the defensive. Seamen loyal to the Queen—urged on by patriotism, piety, and plunder—struck at the colonial sources of Spanish strength in every way they could. Roving the waters of Spanish America, these "sea dogs" smuggled slaves, pirated treasure ships, and robbed unprotected towns. The greatest of them all, Francis Drake, followed Magellan's route into the Pacific, looted his way northward along the American coast, went on around the world, and returned a profit of several thousand per cent to the Queen, who secretly had backed his venture. When she knighted him, instead of rebuking him as the Spanish ambassador demanded, she indicated plainly enough that England was ready to challenge Spain upon the sea.

The decisive test soon came. After England had made an alliance with the rebels of the United Netherlands, Philip II declared war. Determining to invade and conquer England he assembled an unprecedented fleet of his best and largest warships, an "Invincible Armada." But the Spaniards thought of themselves as soldiers more than sailors, and they applied their ideas of land warfare to naval combat, loading troops on their unwieldy vessels to board the enemy craft and grapple at close range with the latter's men. The English, islanders that they were, relied upon their navy and their privateers, not upon an army. They had fast, maneuverable ships which could sail into the Spanish fleet, fire destructive broadsides, and escape to return and fire again. When, in 1588, the Armada appeared in the English Channel, the new naval tactics did not have a chance to show fully their superiority, for a terrible storm helped to scatter the invaders and destroy most of their ships.

England, having become the world's foremost sea power, could not be kept from colonial enterprises of her own on the other side of the Atlantic. Already Englishmen had made their first, rather tentative efforts to start settlements in the New World. Soon the English were to people the Atlantic coast of North America with colonies which eventually would grow into a great continental nation.

Englishmen Look Overseas

The dream of America as a place of unique opportunity—for liberty, abundance, security, and peace—appeared in England soon after Columbus' discovery. This dream found a classic expression in *Utopia,* a book written by Sir Thomas More and published in Latin in 1516 (translated, 1551), which described society on an imaginary island supposedly discovered by a companion of Americus Vespucius in the waters of the New World. Life in Utopia was as nearly perfect as human beings guided by reason and good will could make it. Though the Utopians lived comfortably enough, they scorned the mere accumulation of material things, and while all were expected to keep busy, none was oppressed or overworked. They enjoyed complete freedom of thought but were careful not to offend one another in the expression of their beliefs. True lovers of peace, they went to war only to defend their neighbors and thereby insure their own ultimate safety. In presenting such a picture of an ideal community, the book commented by in-direction upon the social and economic evils of More's England.

The Tudor age, for all its literary glory and its swashbuckling spirit, was not a happy time for most of the common people, who suffered not only from war and religious strife but also from the effects of economic change. While the population of England grew steadily—from three million in 1485 to four million in 1603—the food supply did not increase proportionately. Landowners concentrated on the production of wool. Neither cotton nor silk being yet in general use, wool was in great demand for making cloth. Land tilled at one time by serfs and later by rent-paying tenants, much of it better suited to sheep-raising than to the production of crops, was steadily enclosed for sheep-runs and taken away from the farmers on it. Thousands of evicted tenants roamed the countryside in gangs, to the alarm of more fortunate householders, whose feelings are preserved in the nursery rime: "Hark, hark! The dogs do bark: the beggars are coming to town." The Elizabethan government passed rather ineffectual laws for halting enclosures, relieving the worthy poor, and compelling the able-bodied or "sturdy beggars" to work. Relatively few of these could find re-employment in raising or manufacturing wool. All the while the cost of living rose, mainly because of an increased money supply arising from the output of Spanish gold and silver mines in America. England, it seemed, contained either too many sheep or too many people.

Amid the widespread distress, a rising class of merchant-capitalists prospered from the expansion of foreign trade as they turned from the export of raw wool to the export of woolen cloth. These merchant-capitalists gathered up the raw material, put it out for spinning and weaving in individual households, and then sold the finished product both in England and abroad. At first each exporter did business on his own, though he might belong to the Company of Merchant Adventurers.

This company regulated the activities of its members, secured trading privileges for them, and provided protection for their voyages. In time chartered companies sprang up, each with a monopoly from the sovereign of England for trading in a particular region, among them the Muscovy Company (1555), the Levant Company (1581), the Barbary Company (1585), the Guinea Company (1588), and the East India Company (1600). Some of these were regulated companies, similar to the Merchant Adventurers, each member doing business separately. Others were joint-stock companies, much like modern corporations, with stockholders sharing risk and profit either on single ventures or, as became more common, on a permanent basis. These investors often made fantastic profits from the exchange of English manufactures, especially woolens, for exotic goods, and they felt a powerful urge to continue with the expansion of their profitable trade.

To further this drive, spokesmen for the merchant-capitalists developed a set of ideas about the proper relation of government and business—ideas supporting the argument that (notwithstanding the sufferings of the dispossessed) the whole nation benefited from the activities of the overseas traders. The trade of England as a whole, it was said, was basically like that of any individual or firm: transactions were worthwhile if sales exceeded purchases in value. The difference in value would have to be paid in money (gold and silver), and the inflow of money into England would stimulate business and strengthen the national economy by raising commodity prices and lowering interest rates. Merchant-capitalists depended upon loans to carry on their business, and interest was considered now as a cost of production, whereas in medieval times it had been regarded as sinful usury. According to their theory, the government should act to encourage a "favorable" balance of trade—that is, an excess of exports over imports. This economic philosophy,

restated by Thomas Mun in his book *England's Treasure by Forraign Trade* (1664), came to be known in the eighteenth century as "mercantilism." It guided the economic policies not only of England but also of Spain, France, and other nation-states.

Colonies would fit well into this mercantilistic program, would also alleviate poverty and unemployment, and would serve other useful purposes, or so it seemed to a number of thoughtful Englishmen in the late sixteenth and early seventeenth centuries. The Oxford clergyman Richard Hakluyt, who published a series of explorers' narratives and an essay (1584) on "western planting," made himself the outstanding propagandist for the establishment of colonies. He and others argued that colonies would provide an additional market for English manufactures, and that the colonial demand would give employment in the mother country to the poor who lived there "idly to the annoy of the whole state." Colonial commerce, while yielding profit for shipowners and customs duties for the government, would bring from the colonies products for which England previously had depended upon foreigners—products such as tobacco, lumber, naval stores, and, above all, silver and gold. Colonies might also serve as bases for finding and controlling a westward passage to Asia, attacking the Spanish Empire, and converting the Indians to Protestantism.

The actual pioneers of English colonization were Sir Humphrey Gilbert and his half-brother Sir Walter Raleigh, both of whom were friends of Hakluyt and of the Queen. Gilbert obtained from Elizabeth a patent conferring upon him the exclusive right "to inhabit and possess at his choice all remote and heathen lands not in the actual possession of any Christian prince." In 1583 Gilbert planted on Newfoundland an abortive colony, then was himself lost at sea. Raleigh, receiving a grant similar to Gilbert's, sent out in 1585 an expedition which left colonists on

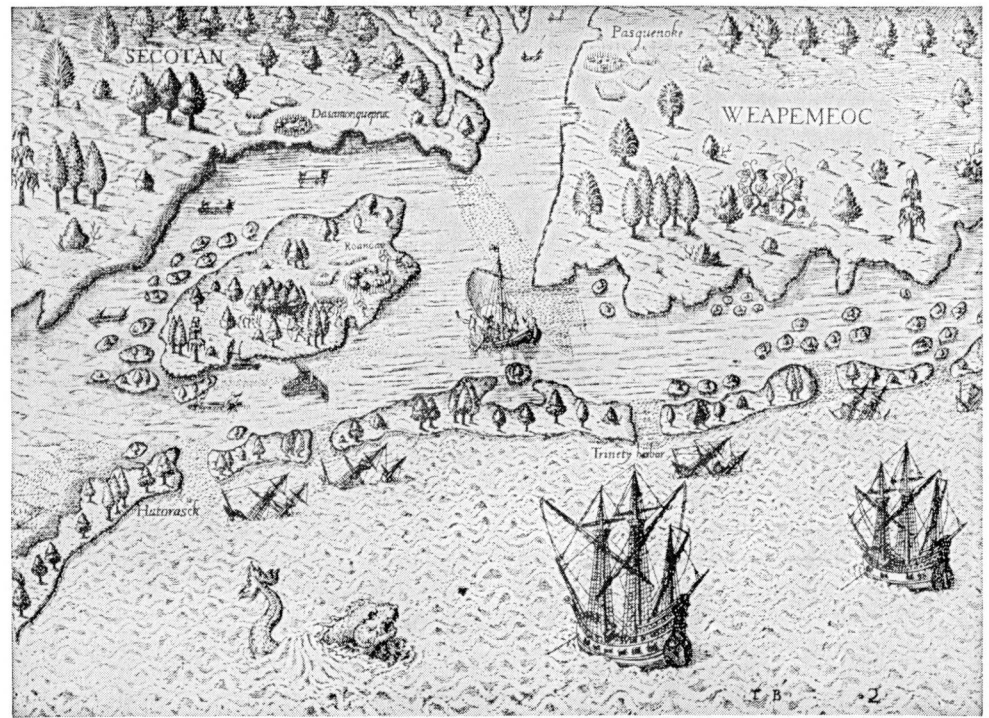

ARRIVAL AT ROANOKE. John White, a "skillful painter," sailed with the first colonizing expedition to Roanoke Island, in 1585. He recorded the country and its inhabitants in a series of pictures which Thomas Hariot, another member of the expedition, published in a *Briefe and True Report of the New Found Land of Virginia*. The illustration reproduced above was entitled "The Arrival of the Englishmen." It shows the sheltered position of Roanoke Island behind the Outer Banks of the North Carolina coast. After the failure of the first colonizing attempt, White went to Roanoke as governor of the second colony, in 1587. Returning to England for supplies, he was unable to get back to Roanoke again until 1590. He then could find no trace of the colonists, including his daughter and his granddaughter, Virginia Dare.

Roanoke Island, off the coast of what afterwards became North Carolina, but the entire group returned to England after only a year. After a second failure Raleigh in 1587 sponsored a third voyage, and against his orders the settlers, including women and children, disembarked at the same place. Here was born Virginia Dare, the first American-born child of English parents. A relief expedition, delayed till 1591 by the hostilities with Spain, found Roanoke Island utterly deserted. What became of the "lost colony" is still a mystery.

The colonizing efforts of Gilbert and

Raleigh taught lessons and set examples for later and more successful promoters of colonization. After sending out his ill-fated settlers, Raleigh sought financial aid from merchants to whom he sold rights of trading with his proposed colony. He realized that the undertaking was too big for the purse of one man alone. Some of the colonizers after him raised funds for their ventures by forming companies and selling stock, but others as individuals or unincorporated groups depended on their own resources. After the accession of James I, Raleigh was accused of plotting against the King. Raleigh was deprived of his monopoly, imprisoned, and eventually executed. None of his successors received grants so vast and undefined as both his and Gilbert's had been. Thereafter the crown, in theory the owner as well as the sovereign of lands to be occupied by Englishmen, granted and regranted territory

forts. There were two groups of interested merchants, the one residing mostly in Plymouth and the other in London. In 1606 the Londoners obtained from James I a charter giving them the exclusive right to colonize between the thirty-fourth and the thirty-eighth parallels. Taking the

---

SUFFERING AT JAMESTOWN

1607–1608

An expedition under Captain Christopher Newport began the Jamestown settlement in May, 1607. In June, Captain Newport sailed for England, leaving behind 104 settlers. In September only 46 of these were still living. One of the survivors, George Percy, wrote an account of the terrible time at Jamestown:

"There were never Englishmen left in a foreign country in such misery as we were in this new discovered Virginia. We watched every three nights, lying on the bare cold ground, what weather soever came; and warded all the next day; which brought our men to be most feeble wretches. Our food was but a small can of barley, sodden in water, to five men a day. Our drink, cold water taken out of the river; which was at a flood very salt; at low tide full of slime and filth, which was the destruction of many of our men. Thus we lived for the space of five months [from August, 1607, to January, 1608] in this miserable distress, not having five able men to man our bulwarks upon any occasion. If it had not pleased God to put a terror in the savages' hearts, we had all perished by those wild and cruel pagans, being in that weak estate as we were; our men night and day groaning in every corner of the fort most pitiful to hear. . . .

"It pleased God after a while to send those people which were our mortal enemies, to relieve us with victuals, as bread, corn, fish, and flesh in great plenty, which was the setting up of our feeble men; otherwise we had all perished."

---

to companies or proprietors, on terms that imposed varying conditions, and with boundaries that had limits but often were conflicting and vague.

Virginia and Maryland

Virginia was the name that—in honor of herself, the Virgin Queen—Elizabeth gave to an indefinite stretch of the North American mainland bordering the Atlantic coast. Along these shores Raleigh's investors aimed to renew his colonizing ef-

East India Company as their model, they intended to found not an agricultural settlement but a trading post. To it they expected to send English manufactures for barter with the Indians, and from it they hoped to bring back American commodities procured in exchange or produced by the labor of their own employees.

Their first expedition of three small ships carrying 120 men sailed into Chesapeake Bay and up the James River in the spring of 1607. The colonists—too many of whom were adventurous gentlemen and too few of whom were willing laborers —ran into serious difficulties from the moment they landed and began to build the palisaded settlement of Jamestown. When the men in Jamestown should have been growing food, they were required to hunt for gold and to pile up lumber, tar, pitch,

sued the horrible "starving time" in the winter of 1609–10, when famine and disease reduced the population of Jamestown from about five hundred to only sixty. The nearly crazy survivors were taken off on relief ships which arrived in the spring. Jamestown seemed about to be abandoned.

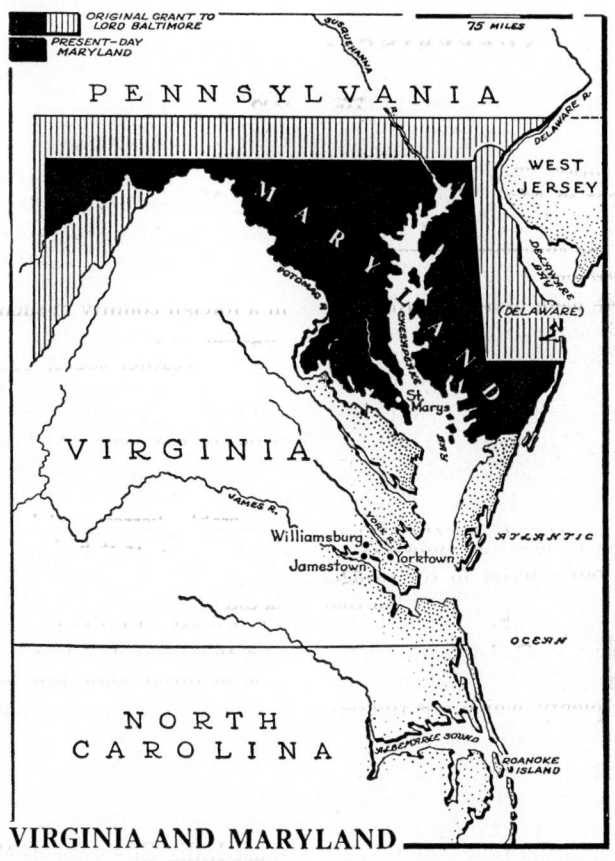

VIRGINIA AND MARYLAND

and iron ore for outgoing vessels. Inbound ships brought new colonists but insufficient supplies. Leadership in the colony was divided among the several members of a council, who quarreled continually until one of them managed to assert his will. This was Captain John Smith, hero of his own narratives of hairbreadth escapes from both Turks and Indians but a sensible and capable leader nevertheless. After Smith returned to England for treatment of a serious powder burn, there en-

It was saved, however, by steps which the promoters in London already were taking. To add to their funds, they created the Virginia Company, the stock of which they sold to "adventurers" willing to hazard money and gave to "planters" willing to migrate with private capital—that is, tools and other equipment. The company began to plan for an agricultural community as well as a trading post and, while continuing to send its own employees to Virginia as laborers, no longer

tried to feed them from a common storehouse to which all contributed their crops. As a profit-making venture the colony proved a failure, yet in a larger sense it was a success, for it demonstrated that English men and women could survive and prosper in America.

One of the stockholders of the Virginia Company, George Calvert, Lord Baltimore, conceived the idea of undertaking a new colony on his own. Himself a convert to the Roman Catholic faith, Calvert had in mind primarily a gigantic speculation in real estate and incidentally the establishment of a refuge for Roman Catholics, victims of political discrimination in England. From Charles I he obtained a patent to a wedge of Virginia's territory which lay north of the Potomac and east of Cheseapeake Bay, and which the King now christened Maryland in honor of his Roman Catholic wife, the Frenchwoman Henrietta Maria. George Calvert having died before the grant was made official, it was issued (1632) to his son Cecilius, the second Lord Baltimore.

Since the Virginia Company (which still claimed its land rights) objected to the Calvert grant, Lord Baltimore remained at home to defend his interests at court while he sent two of his brothers, with one of them, Leonard Calvert, as governor, to see to the settlement of the family's province. In March of 1634 the *Ark* and the *Dove*, bearing two or three hundred passengers, mostly Roman Catholics, entered the Potomac and turned into one of its eastern tributaries. On a high and dry bluff these first arrivals laid out the village of St. Mary's, while the neighboring Indians, already withdrawing to avoid native enemies, assisted by providing stocks of corn. The early Marylanders knew no massacres, no plagues, no starving time. Their most serious trouble arose from border disputes with the Virginians, disputes which provoked some bloodshed but finally were ended by the King's decision in favor of Maryland.

New England

New England got its name from Captain John Smith, who explored its coast and published a descriptive account, including a map. The right to colonize this area had passed to the Plymouth group of merchants at the same time (1606) the London group obtained colonizing privileges farther south. After an unsuccessful planting effort at the mouth of the Kennebec River, the Plymouth enterprisers reorganized as the Council for New England, a corporation dealing in real estate rather than promoting trade. The Council transferred its lands to individuals and companies in a series of overlapping and confusing grants. These, confirmed or altered by new grants directly from the King, provided the basis for all the colonies that emerged in New England—Massachusetts (including Plymouth and Maine), Connecticut, Rhode Island, and New Hampshire.

Many of the New England colonizers and almost all the colonists were Puritans, who had a religious as well as an economic interest in leaving England for settlements beyond the sea. The Puritans, influenced in varying degrees by the teachings of John Calvin, differed considerably among themselves, but most of them were alike in being mere Nonconformists, while a small minority were out-and-out Separatists. Detesting what they considered "popish" forms and practices, the Nonconformists aimed at first to "purify" the Church of England from within, though in America they were to break away completely. The Separatists, who were more radical, were determined from the beginning to worship as they pleased in their own independent congregations. Like all subjects of the King, however, they were forbidden by law to absent themselves from regular Anglican services, to hold unauthorized religious meetings, or to leave the realm without the King's consent.

Slipping away a few at a time, the members of a Separatist congregation from

Scrooby, in Nottinghamshire, crossed the English Channel and began their lives anew in Holland. Some of them decided to move again, this time across the Atlantic, where they might find opportunity for living more happily and also for propagating "the gospel of the Kingdom of Christ in those remote parts of the world." These Pilgrims made arrangements with English merchants for financing their venture, and they got permission from the Virginia

posure, but the rest managed to put their colony on its feet.

Since Plymouth lay outside the Virginia Company's possessions, its legal status as a colony was dubious from the start. Before leaving the ship forty-one of the first arrivals, to deal with threats of disobedience, signed the Mayflower Compact. This Compact was like the church covenant by which the Separatists formed congregations, except that it bound its

THE MAYFLOWER COMPACT

1620

"In the name of God, Amen. We, whose names are underwritten, the Loyal Subjects of our dread Sovereign Lord King *James*, by the Grace of God, of *Great Britain, France,* and *Ireland,* King, *Defender of the Faith,* &c. Having undertaken for the Glory of God, and Advancement of the Christian Faith, and the Honour of our King and Country, a Voyage to plant the first colony in the northern Parts of Virginia; Do by these presents, solemnly and mutually in the Presence of God and one another, covenant and combine ourselves together into a civil Body Politick, for our better Ordering and Preservation, and Furtherance of the Ends aforesaid; And by Virtue hereof do enact, constitute, and frame, such just and equal Laws, Ordinances, Acts, Constitutions, and Offices, from time to time, as shall be thought most meet and convenient for the general Good of the Colony; unto which we promise all due Submission and Obedience."

Company to settle as an independent community on its land. They tried, and failed, to get from James I a guarantee of religious freedom, but they learned "that he would . . . not molest them, provided they carried themselves peaceably." This was a historic concession on the part of the King, for it opened English America to settlement by dissenting Protestants.

From Plymouth, England, the *Mayflower* took its 102 passengers to Plymouth in New England, where on a bleak December day in 1620 they disembarked, though they had not reached their intended destination. During the first winter half of them died from scurvy and ex-

signers to observe the ordinances of a civil rather than a religious society, and it professed their allegiance to the King. The colonists soon cleared their land title with a patent from the Council for New England but never secured a royal charter giving them indisputable rights of government. As citizens of a virtually independent republic they went their way for over seventy years, until Plymouth was annexed to the much larger colony of Massachusetts Bay.

Massachusetts had its earliest beginnings in the English fisheries along its coast. From these a plan developed for establishing a permanent fishing and trad-

ing station and then a missionary outpost at Salem. A corporation, formed to
raise funds for putting the struggling colony on a sounder basis, was reorganized
in 1629 as the Massachusetts Bay Company, with a royal charter which granted a

High Church policies of the new king,
Charles I. Now a number of wealthy and
prominent Puritans among the stockholders, desiring to create a refuge for their
faith, expressed their willingness to go to
America if they were given control of the

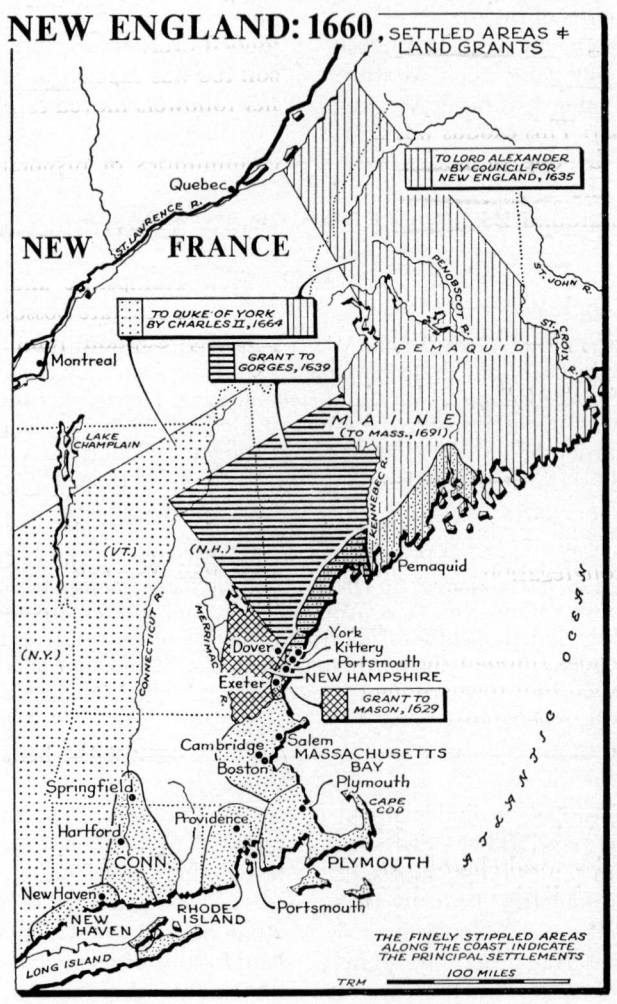

NEW ENGLAND: 1660, SETTLED AREAS +
                        LAND GRANTS

strip of land lying between lines three
miles south of the Charles River and three
miles north of the Merrimack and extending westward to the Pacific. The Massachusetts Bay Company at first intended to
maintain and develop the Salem settlement as a commercial enterprise, then
changed its plans because of the stern

company. By the Cambridge Agreement
they were given such control, and the corporation's headquarters were transferred
from Old to New England. The stockholders elected John Winthrop as governor of the company and hence of the colony also. A gentleman of means, with a
university education, a deep but narrow

piety, a cool and calculating temperament, and a remarkably forceful if stubborn character, Winthrop became the father of Massachusetts. The refounded Puritan colony got off to an auspicious start in 1630, when eleven ships and about a thousand settlers, many of them well-to-do, ventured across the Atlantic.

There soon began an outpouring from Massachusetts Bay to various parts of New England (and to other places in English America). This exodus was motivated generally by one or both of two considerations: the unproductiveness of the stony farms around Boston, and the oppressiveness of the Massachusetts government. Governor Withrop and a handful of assistants and freemen (stockholders in the company) ruled as if they were agents of God.

The Connecticut Valley, a hundred miles beyond the settled frontier, had fertile meadows which invited pioneering despite the presence of warlike Indians and the claims of the already fortified Dutch. In 1635 and 1636 several entire Massachusetts congregations, impelled by the strong bent of their spirits, as the Reverend Thomas Hooker said, drove their cattle and hogs through the wilderness and established four towns along the Connecticut River. A separate colony, the project of a Puritan minister and a wealthy merchant from England, grew up around New Haven on the coast. Eventually (1662) the governor of Connecticut obtained a royal charter extending his colony's jurisdiction over the New Haven settlements.

Rhode Island was founded by Roger Williams, a sensitive and likeable but troublesome young minister of Massachusetts Bay. Styling himself only a "seeker" after truth and salvation, Williams believed in a complete separation of church and state and in absolute freedom of conscience. He argued that the land belonged to the Indians and that the Massachusetts Bay Company had no valid title to it! Banished from the colony, he took

refuge among the Narragansett Indians during a bitter winter, and then with a few of his friends established the town of Providence, in 1636. Soon afterward Mrs. Anne Hutchinson, the Samaritan-minded wife of a substantial Bostonian, attracted many followers with her heretical doctrine that the Holy Spirit dwelled within and guided every true believer. Mrs. Hutchinson too was expelled, and she and some of her followers moved to Narragansett Bay, not far from Providence. In time other communities of dissidents arose in that vicinity and were combined under a royal charter (1663) as Rhode Island and Providence Plantations.

New Hampshire and Maine had become the separate possessions of two proprietors, Captain John Mason and Sir Ferdinando Gorges, when (1629) they divided along the Piscataqua River their grant from the Council for New England. Despite lavish promotional efforts, especially on the part of Gorges, few settlers were drawn to these northern regions until the religious disruption of Massachusetts Bay. In 1638 John Wheelwright, a disciple of Anne Hutchinson, led a party of his fellow-heretics to Exeter, in New Hampshire. The Massachusetts Bay Company extended its authority to the whole territory to the north but ultimately lost its cases against the heirs of both Mason and Gorges in the highest courts of England. New Hampshire then (1679) was set up as a separate royal province. Maine, the Gorges family having sold their rights to it, remained a part of Massachusetts from 1691 until admitted to the Union as a state in 1820.

The Carolinas and New York

Six of the eventual thirteen colonies had originated before the civil war in England during the 1640's, which temporarily halted colonizing activities from abroad. Then (1660) Charles II returned from his wandering exile to reign as the Merry Monarch and reward his faithful courtiers with truly regal gifts of land in the New World. He not only acknowledged with royal charters the various colonies which had broken off from the detestable (to him) Puritan commonwealth of Massachusetts, but he also gave rise within a quarter of a century to six additional colonies: North and South Caro-

tremendous estates for their own development, selling or giving away the rest in smaller tracts, and collecting annual payments as quitrents from the owners. There developed two widely separated areas of settlement, the one north and the other south of Cape Fear. After treating these areas for a while as parts of a single

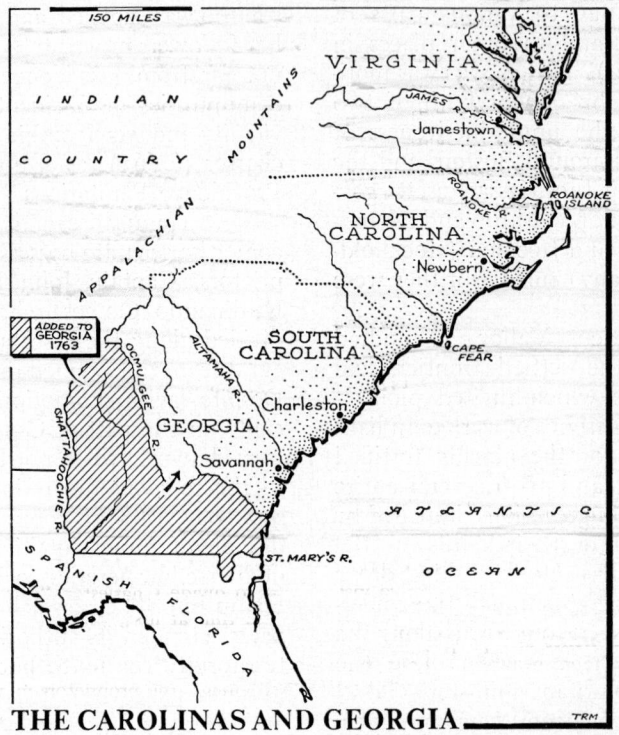

THE CAROLINAS AND GEORGIA

lina, New York, New Jersey, Pennsylvania, and Delaware.

Carolina (after the Latin *Carolinus*, meaning Charles), partly taken like Maryland from the Virginia domain, was awarded by Charles II to a group of eight of his favorites, all prominent politicians, of whom the most active in Carolina affairs was Anthony Cooper, Lord Ashley. In successive charters (1663, 1665) these eight received a joint title to the whole of the wide territory between the latitudes of 29° and 36° 30'. Like Lord Baltimore in Maryland, they expected to profit as landlords and land speculators, reserving

colony, with the same governor, the proprietors at last (1712) made them separate colonies, each with a governor of its own.

North and South Carolina already possessed distinct characteristics and quite different histories. The first settlers of North Carolina came mostly from other mainland colonies—a few from New England, the majority from Virginia. These pioneers showed the marks of neglect by the proprietors, who gave most of their attention to the southern half of their property. In South Carolina the proprietors saw to the founding of the city of Charles-

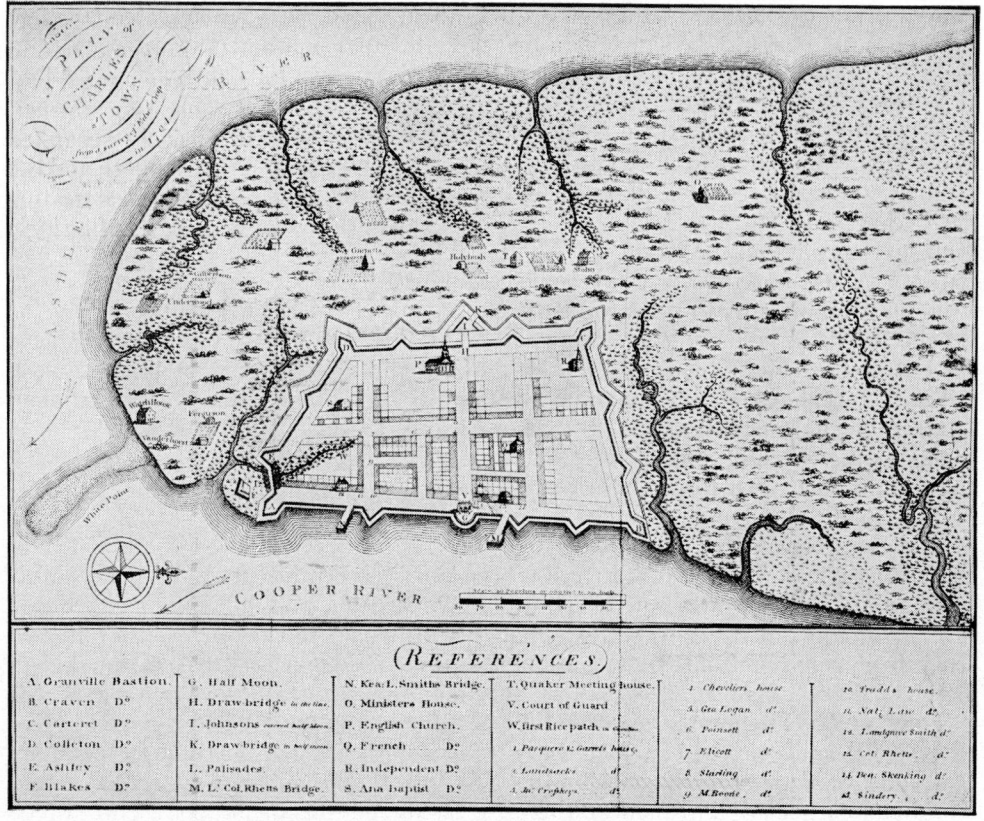

A. Granville Bastion.	G. Half Moon.	N. Kea. L. Smiths Bridge.	T. Quaker Meeting house.	1 Chevaliers house.	10 Tradds house.
B. Craven Dº.	H. Draw bridge in the line.	O. Ministers House.	V. Court of Guard.	5 Geo Logan dº	11 Nat. Law dº.
C. Carteret Dº.	I. Johnsons covered half down.	P. English Church.	W. first Rice patch in dº.	6 Poinsett dº	12 Landgrave Smith dº.
D. Colleton Dº.	K. Draw bridge in half moon.	Q. French Dº.	1 Parquars & Garrels house.	7 Elicott dº	13 Col. Rhetts dº.
E. Ashley Dº.	L. Palisades.	R. Independent Dº.	2 Landstocks dº	8 Starling dº	14 Ben. Skenking dº.
F. Blakes Dº.	M. Lt Col. Rhetts Bridge.	S. Ana baptist Dº.	3 Mr Crossleys dº.	9 M. Boone dº	15 Sindery dº.

A City in the Wilderness: Charleston in 1704. Lord Ashley, the most active of the Carolina proprietors, gave instructions to divide Charleston "into regular streets, for be the buildings never so mean and thin at first, yet as the town increases in riches and people, the void places will be filled up and the buildings will grow more beautiful." Thus, from the beginning, Charleston grew according to an orderly, rectangular plan. To hasten settlement, the proprietors in 1694 directed the Carolina governor to fortify the town. This map of 1704 shows Charleston (population, about 2,000) with its completed fortifications. Inside the walls were four churches, a few warehouses and shops, and several fine houses in addition to more modest dwellings. Outside were a Quaker meeting house and several rice plantations.

ton, with wharves, fortifications, fine houses, and wide streets. Several of the colony's early leaders and many of its first inhabitants came from the declining sugar plantations of the British West Indies, especially Barbados. Prosperous plantations developed on the mainland, and population grew much faster here than north of Cape Fear.

The year after making his Carolina grant Charles II bestowed (1664) upon his brother the Duke of York (afterwards King James II) all the territory lying between the Connecticut and Delaware rivers. A large part of this land presumably belonged to the Massachusetts Bay Company by virtue of the company's sea-to-sea grant. The whole region was claimed by the Dutch, who occupied strategic points within it.

The Dutch Republic, after winning independence from Spain, had launched upon its own career of overseas trading and empire building in Asia, Africa, and

America. On the basis of Hudson's explorations the Dutch staked an American claim and proceeded promptly to exploit it with a busy trade in furs. To add permanence to the business, the Dutch West India Company began to encourage settlement, transporting whole families on such voyages as that of the *New Netherland* in 1624, and later offering vast feudal estates to "patroons" who would bring over immigrants to work the land. So developed the colony of New Netherland. It centered around New Amsterdam with its blockhouse on Manhattan Island, and included thinly scattered settlements on the Hudson, the Delaware, and the Connecticut, with forts for their protection. In 1655 the Dutch extended their sway over the few Swedes and Finns settled along the lower Delaware. In the Connecticut Valley, however, they had to give in to the superior numbers of the English moving out from Massachusetts Bay.

Three Anglo-Dutch wars arose from the commercial and colonial rivalry of England and The Netherlands throughout the world and particularly in America, where the English resented the foreign stronghold which wedged apart their own northern and southern colonies and provided smuggling bases for the Dutch. During the second of these wars, in 1664, troop-carrying vessels of the English navy put in at New Amsterdam and extracted a surrender from the arbitrary and unpopular governor, the peg-legged Peter Stuyvesant. During the final conflict the Dutch reconquered and briefly (1673–4) held their old provincial capital, then lost it again for good.

New York, formerly New Netherland, already the property of the Duke of York and renamed by him, was his to rule as virtually an absolute monarch. Instead of going to America he delegated his powers to a governor and a council. He confirmed the Dutch patroonships already set up, the most notable of them being Rensselaerswyck with its 700,000 acres around Albany, and he gave away comparable estates to Englishmen so as to create a class of influential landowners loyal to him. The early settlements were confined to the immediate valley of the Hudson.

The Duke gave what became New Jersey to a couple of cronies, both Carolina proprietors, Sir George Carteret and Lord John Berkeley. The latter sold his half interest to two enterprising members of the Society of Friends, thus bringing the Quakers into the colonization business. And the Duke gave what became Delaware to another Quaker, the greatest of all the colonizers, William Penn.

The Quaker Colonies

The Society of Friends originated in mid-seventeenth-century England in response to the preachings of George Fox, a Nottingham shoemaker, whose followers came to be known as Quakers from his admonition to them to "tremble at the name of the Lord." The essence of Fox's teachings was the doctrine of the Inner Light, the illumination from God within each soul, the divine conscience which when rightly heeded could guide human beings along the paths of righteousness. Of all the Protestant sectarians of the time, the Quakers were the most anarchistic and the most democratic.

Like the Puritans earlier, George Fox and his followers looked to America for asylum. A few of them went to New England, but there (except in Rhode Island) they were greeted with fines, whippings, and orders to leave, and three men and a woman who persisted in staying were actually put to death. Many migrated to North Carolina, and there, as the first and fastest growing religious community, they soon predominated in colonial politics. Yet the Quakers desired a colony of their own, and Fox himself visited America (1671–2) to look over the land. As the head of a sect despised in England, however, he could not get the necessary grant without the aid of someone influential at the court. Fortunately for his cause, his teachings had struck the hearts of a number of wealthy and prominent men, one of whom in particular made possible a large-scale effort to realize the Quaker dream.

East and West Jersey, Carteret as one of the original proprietors keeping the East, and the Quakers the West. West Jersey soon began to fill up with Friends from England while East Jersey was being pop-

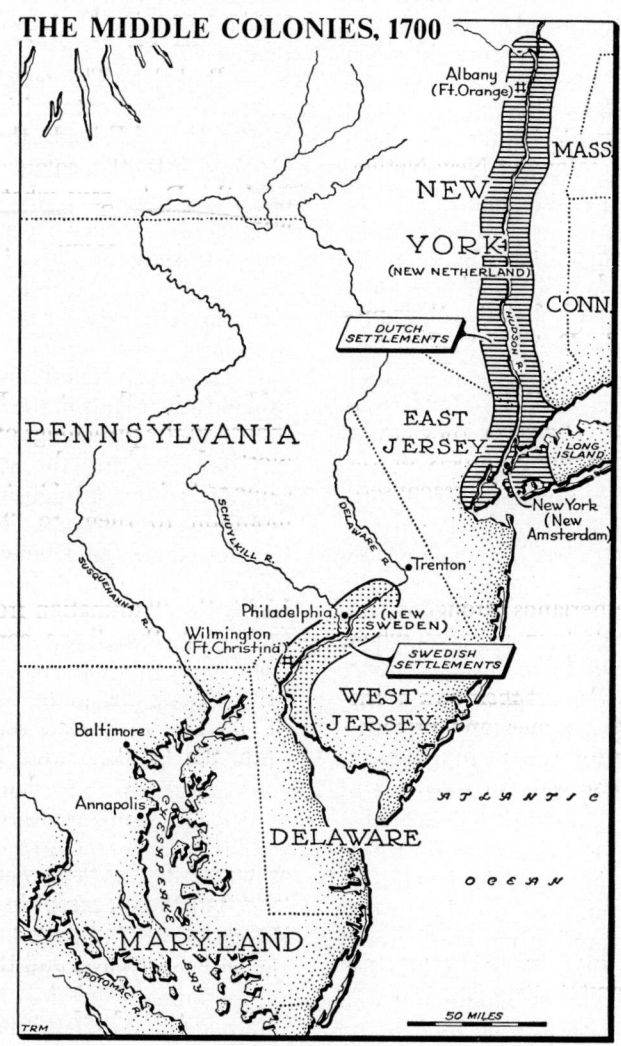

THE MIDDLE COLONIES, 1700

Albany
(Ft.Orange)
MASS.
NEW
YORK
(NEW NETHERLAND)
CONN.
DUTCH
SETTLEMENTS
EAST
JERSEY
LONG
ISLAND
New York
(New
Amsterdam)
PENNSYLVANIA
SCHUYLKILL R.
DELAWARE R.
SUSQUEHANNA R.
Trenton
Philadelphia
Wilmington
(Ft.Christina)
(NEW
SWEDEN)
SWEDISH
SETTLEMENTS
WEST
JERSEY
Baltimore
Annapolis
DELAWARE
ATLANTIC
OCEAN
MARYLAND
POTOMAC
CHESAPEAKE BAY
TRM
50 MILES

This was William Penn—whose father was an admiral in the Royal Navy and a landlord of valuable Irish estates.

New Jersey, half of which two of his fellow Quakers owned, received Penn's attention when he was asked to assist them with their debts. In their behalf he helped to see to the division of the province into

ulated mostly by Puritans from New England. Before long (1682) Penn together with other wealthy Quakers purchased the eastern property from Carteret, and eventually (1702) the two Jerseys were reunited as one colony, second in Quaker population only to Pennsylvania itself.

Pennsylvania—which Charles II in-

sisted on naming for his old ally, the admiral—was based on the King's grant of
1681. Penn, reconciled with his father,
had inherited the latter's Irish lands and
also his claim to the equivalent of $80,000
owed by the King. Charles II, possessing
more real estate than ready cash, paid the
debt with a grant of territory, between
New York and Maryland, which was
larger than England and Wales combined
and which (unknown to him) contained
more value in soil and minerals than any
other province of English America.

Like the Calverts, the Carolina proprietors, and the Duke of York, Penn intended to make money from land sales
and quitrents and from private property
to be worked for him. He promptly sold
several large tracts to rich Quaker associates and one tract of 15,000 acres to a
group of German immigrants led by Francis Daniel Pastorius.

Much more than a mere real estate promoter, Penn was interested in Pennsylvania most of all as what he called a Holy
Experiment. Colonies, he said, were the
"seeds of nations," and he proposed to
plant the seeds of brotherly love. He personally voyaged to Pennsylvania (1682)
to oversee the laying out, between the
Delaware and Schuylkill rivers, of the city
he appropriately named Philadelphia
("Brotherly Love"). He believed, as had
Roger Williams, that the land belonged
to the Indians, and he was careful to see
that they were reimbursed for it. His colony prospered from the outset because of
his thoughtful planning and also because
of the mildness of the climate and the fertility of the soil, the well-to-do and well
equipped class of settlers he brought in,
and the assistance they received from the
people of other colonies and from the Hol-
landers and Swedes and Finns already on
the ground—for Pennsylvania as Penn
first saw it was not the wilderness Virginia
had been when John Smith arrived.

Delaware, after its transfer to Penn
from the Duke of York (1682), was
treated as a part of Pennsylvania (and

was known as "the lower counties") but
was given the privilege of setting up its
own representative assembly. The three
counties did so in 1703, and thereafter
Delaware was considered a separate colony, though until the Revolution it continued to have the same governor as
Pennsylvania.

Georgia

Georgia, the last of the mainland colonies, was unique in its origins. It was
founded by neither a corporation nor a
proprietorship, and its guiding purpose
was neither to make profits nor to create a
sectarian refuge. In the beginning Georgia
was the work of trustees serving without
pay. Their main purpose was twofold: to
provide a new start in life for Englishmen
imprisoned for debt, and to erect a military barrier against the Spaniards on the
southern border of English America.

The charter from George II (1732)
transferred the land between the Savannah and Altamaha rivers to the administration of General James Oglethorpe and
his fellow trustees for a period of twenty-
one years. In their colonization policies
they were to keep in mind the needs
of military security. Landholdings were
limited in size so as to make settlement
compact. Negroes free or slave were excluded, and Roman Catholics also, to forestall the danger of wartime insurrection
and of collusion with enemy coreligion-
ists. And the Indian trade was strictly
regulated, with rum prohibited, to lessen
the risk of Indian complications. Oglethorpe himself led the first expedition,
building in 1733 a fortified town at the
mouth of the Savannah, and later constructing additional forts south of the Altamaha. Debtors released from imprisonment in England and refugees from the
religious conformity of Switzerland and
Germany were brought to Georgia and
outfitted at the expense of the trustees,
who raised funds from charitable individuals as well as from Parliament.

Before the twenty-one years of the trusteeship were up, the rule against big plantations, slaves, and rum was elimi- nated, and after 1750 Georgia developed along lines similar to those of South Carolina.

BIBLIOGRAPHY

On the European background of American history, see W. C. Abbott, *The Expansion of Europe* (1938) and E. P. Cheyney, *The European Background of American History* (1904). On early exploration: J. E. Gillespie, *A History of Geographical Discovery, 1400–1800* (1933); H. Hermannsson, *The Problem of Wineland* (1936); S. E. Morison, *Admiral of the Ocean Sea* (2 vols., 1942), a classic biography of Columbus. On the English backgrounds of settlement in America: Wallace Notestein, *The English People on the Eve of Colonization, 1603– 1630* (1954); Alan Simpson, *Puritanism in Old and New England* (1955); K. E. Knorr, *British Colonial Theories, 1570– 1850* (1944); J. U. Nef, *Industry and Government in France and England, 1540– 1640* (1940); J. A. Williamson, *Sir John Hawkins* (1927) and *The Age of Drake* (1938).

T. J. Wertenbaker, *The First Americans, 1607–1690* (1927) is a general account of the beginnings of settlement. Among the better regional studies are the following: T. J. Wertenbaker, *The Middle Colonies* (1938), *The Old South* (1942), and *The Puritan Oligarchy* (1947); C. M. Andrews, *The Fathers of New England* (1919); W. F. Craven, *The Southern Colonies in the Seventeenth Century, 1607–1689* (1949); and V. W. Crane, *The Southern Frontier, 1670–1732* (1929). Studies of individual colonies: G. F. Willison, *Behold Virginia* (1951) and *Saints and Strangers* (1945), which deals with Plymouth; S. E. Morison, *Builders of the Bay Colony* (1930); M. P. Andrews, *The Founding of Maryland* (1933); J. S. Bassett, *The Constitutional Beginnings of North Carolina* (1894); R. L. Meriwether, *The Expansion of South Carolina, 1729–1765* (1940); and S. G. Fisher, *The Making of Pennsylvania* (1932). The founding of colonies may also be approached through biographies of leading founders, among which are Bradford Smith, *Captain John Smith: His Life and Legend* (1953); E. S. Morgan, *The Puritan Dilemma: The Story of John Winthrop* (1958); O. E. Winslow, *Master Roger Williams* (1957); S. H. Brockunier, *The Irrepressible Democrat: Roger Williams* (1940); Edith Curtis, *Anne Hutchinson* (1930); and W. W. Comfort, *William Penn, 1644– 1718* (1944). William Bradford tells his own story in his *History of Plymouth Plantation*, which is available in several editions.

On colonial beginnings and institutional development, a work of exhaustive scholarship is C. M. Andrews' *The Colonial Period of American History* (4 vols., 1934–8).

2

GROWTH OF
AMERICAN WAYS

At the time of the discovery and settlement of America, the center of Western civilization was shifting from the Mediterranean to the North Atlantic. The people of the thirteen colonies, living as they did on the farther rim of that ocean, continued to participate in the growing Atlantic civilization and to be influenced by new currents of thought coming from abroad. Yet they did not remain merely European in their outlook, though they were representatives of a branch of European culture, nor did they remain purely English, though the great majority of them were of English stock. Wherever they came from, they clung at first to their accustomed ways, trying to make themselves feel at home in their new and strange environment. But that environment (including the wilderness surroundings, the generous economic basis of life, the presence of a variety of nationalities) led the colonists to depart from many of their customs. During the century and a half from 1607 to 1763 they developed variations of their own from the English way of life. They showed signs of becoming distinctively "American"—a term

which had been applied to them even before 1700 but did not come into general use till after 1750.

Land and Labor

The geographical setting of the English colonies, along the Atlantic seaboard from Maine to Georgia, conditioned the life that developed in them. Three thousand miles and more from England, they were separated from the mother country, and yet connected with it, by the Atlantic Ocean. The overseas crossing took from four to eight weeks in close-packed and often disease-ridden ships which sailed at irregular intervals depending on wind and weather. The distance and the difficulty of ocean travel put the colonists very much upon their own resources once they had landed on the American shore. Nevertheless, the nature of the shoreline and of the terrain behind it inclined them toward the sea, and they kept in touch with the homeland by means of the same ocean they had crossed.

To the first colonists, America was trees. From the Atlantic to the Appalachians and beyond stretched a great forest, unbroken except for occasional small clearings made by the elements or by the Indians, and thick with tall pines, maples, oaks, and countless other varieties of trees as well as shrubs. Even before sighting land the early voyagers to America could sometimes smell the fresh and invigorating forest scent, and once they had disembarked they found themselves in a veritable Garden of Eden, full of birds and beasts for game; flowers, berries, and fruits; and infinite resources of wood. All this made a refreshing contrast with comparatively treeless England, rapidly being deforested to meet the needs of industry. And yet the friendly forest—so green and beautiful, so rich in materials for food and shelter and manufactures of many kinds —also had its uninviting and even hostile aspects. In its shadows lurked the wolves and panthers that devoured the settler's livestock, lurked also the redmen who often threatened his and his family's lives. It stood in the way of the frontiersman eager to cultivate the soil, and he had to convert forest into fields by the slow and laborious effort of girdling or else chopping down the trees, burning the dead or downed timber, and eventually uprooting the stumps.

Apart from the great forest, the geographical fact that most distinguished the new from the old country and most influenced the economic development of the colonies was sheer space, the vast extent of land. Not that all the land was readily accessible. The need for clearing the forest, the presence of hostile tribes, the dependence upon water transport, and ultimately the difficulty of crossing the mountain barrier—all these considerations hindered the actual occupation of the land, and they operated more and more effectively in proportion to remoteness from the seaports. Hence the English settlements, scattered though they might seem, remained on the whole fairly compact throughout the colonial period, at least in comparison with the Spanish and

French settlements in the New World, though not in comparison with the crowded towns and countryside of the Old World. There populations teemed and lacked sufficient room. Here land was plentiful and people relatively scarce.

If the colonies were to be a source of profit for proprietors and companies and a source of economic strength for England, ways must be found to bring over a part of the excess manpower of the Old World to exploit the natural riches of the New. The enterprisers of colonization encouraged settlement by means of advertising campaigns, religious tolerance, and generous grants of land.

Thus attracted, many of the early settlers possessed sufficient wealth to pay their own way over and even to bring with them some capital (in the form of tools, supplies, or money), but others among the prospective emigrants from Europe and the British Isles were too poor to finance a voyage across the ocean and a new start in life on this side. To facilitate the immigration of people such as these, Virginia and some of the other colonies offered "headrights"—land grants of fifty acres or more per head—for each new laborer brought in from abroad. The person financing the laborer's voyage received not only the land but also the laborer's services for a period of years.

A system of temporary servitude grew naturally out of existing practices in England, such as that of apprenticeship, by which a man bound himself to a master for seven years to learn a trade. The men and women, English or foreign, who bound themselves to a master in America in return for their passage over were known as "indentured" servants. The period of service varied in the different colonies, ranging from four to seven years, and so did the conditions of work, which were regulated by colonial custom and law. Upon completing his term the servant was entitled to certain benefits— clothing, tools, occasionally land—in addition to his freedom and the privilege, if

This Indenture MADE the *Thirteenth* Day of *May* in the Year of our Lord one thousand, seven hundred and *eighty-four* BETWEEN *Alexr. Beard of Broughshane in the County of Antrua Taylor by Consent of his Father* of the one Part, and *John Dickey of Gullyboekey in the said County* ——— *Gentleman* ——— of the other Part, WITNESSETH, that the said *Alexandr. Beard* doth hereby covenant, promise and grant, to and with the said *John Dickey* ——— *his* ——— Executors, Administrators and Affigns, from the Day of the Date hereof until the first and next Arrival at *Philadelphia* ——— in America, and after for and during the Term of *Three* ——— Years to serve in such Service and Employment as the said *John Dickey* ——— or *his* Affigns shall there employ *him* according to the Cuftom of the Country in the like Kind. In Confideration whereof the said *John Dickey* doth hereby covenant and grant to and with the said *Alexr. Beard* to pay for *his* Paffage, and to find allow *him* Meat, Drink, Apparel and Lodging, with other Neceffaries, during the said Term; and at the End of the said Term to pay unto *him* the usual Allowance, according to the Cuftom of the Country in the like Kind. IN WITNESS whereof the Parties above-mentioned to these Indentures have interchangeably put their Hands and Seals, the Day and Year firft above written.

Signed, Sealed, and Delivered,
in the Prefence of

Peter Dillon

John Weir

Alexr Beard

John Dickey

AN EIGHTEENTH CENTURY INDENTURE. This contract, dated May 13, 1784, was made late in the history of indentured servitude and typifies the standardized form that developed. Note that it is printed, with spaces left blank to be filled in. In this particular case, the contract was made between the master and his servant before either of them sailed for America. Originally, a contract was written in two identical parts on a single sheet, which was torn in two, leaving an indented or indentured edge—hence the term "indenture."

he could afford it, of acquiring indentured servants of his own.

Not all such servants came of their own free will: some were sent by force. From time to time, beginning as early as 1617, the English government dumped shiploads of convicts in America, though according to Captain John Smith "some did chuse to be hanged ere they would go thither, and were." The government also transported prisoners taken in battles with the Scots and with the Irish in the 1650's. Likewise it got rid of other groups deemed undesirable: orphans, vagrants, paupers, and those who were simply "lewd and dangerous." Still other involuntary emigrants were neither dangerous nor dependent but were victims of kidnaping or "impressment." In some cases the government itself paid for the transportation of its exiles. More commonly the authorities avoided this expense through arrangements with shipowners or captains who reimbursed themselves by selling the services of their passengers in America. Unlike the exiles, most of the servants came willingly, eagerly.

They went in the largest numbers to Pennsylvania, after its founding late in the seventeenth century, for opportunities and working conditions were most attractive there, and they continued to go to Pennsylvania and New York, though in dwindling numbers, until long after the American Revolution. Relatively few landed in New England, where the economy was not such as to create much of a demand for them. In the seventeenth century they flocked to the tobacco colonies of Virginia and Maryland. Afterwards some continued to go there, but more and more the white servants were supplemented and replaced by Negro slaves.

The first Negroes in the English mainland colonies arrived in Jamestown in 1619. "About the last of August," the Jamestown planter John Rolfe noted, "came in a Dutch man of War that sold us twenty negars." The local planters bought these people not as slaves, it seems, but as servants to be held for a period of years and then freed, like the white servants with whom the planters already were familiar. Gradually permanent bondage for Negroes took the place of temporary servitude in Virginia, and the number of black slaves increased slowly—until about 1700. Then the importation of slaves began to rise very rapidly while the arrival of servants declined even more rapidly.

There were two main reasons for this change. In the first place, slavery gave the master a constant labor supply and practically complete control over it. Slaves, identifiable by their color, could not run away and merge themselves with the mass of free humanity so easily as white servants could. Slaves, moreover, could not rise out of their bondage to compete with their masters for wealth and political influence as the servants sometimes did. In the second place, slaves (considering the length of their service) were cheaper than servants, especially with the fall of slave prices after 1697, when the monopoly of the Royal African Company was broken and the slave trade was opened to English and colonial merchants on a competitive basis.

Slavery in colonial times, of course, was not confined to Virginia, nor was it confined to Negroes. Numerous attempts were made to enslave the Indians, and while a few of them lived out their lives in bondage, they were in general rather difficult to catch and to hold. Negro slavery came to the rice country of South Carolina and Georgia from the West Indies and took the place of white servitude from the outset. Slaves labored as domestics and occasionally as farmhands for wealthy families in the North. As of 1763, there were in all the colonies about 230,000 Negroes, most of them slaves. About 16,000 lived in New England, 29,000 in the Middle Colonies, and the rest in the South.

Population Growth

Besides the Africans, other non-English peoples came in large numbers to the colonies after the end of the seventeenth century, while immigration from England itself fell off. Recovering from a prolonged depression in the 1630's, England thereafter began to develop more and more industries which demanded workmen, so that the talk of overpopulation ceased to be heard. Instead of encouraging emigration from its own shores, the government tried to check the loss of English manpower by prohibiting the departure of skilled artisans, while continuing to unload the unemployable or the undesirable upon the defenseless colonies. Although during the eighteenth century the colonies received relatively few newcomers from England, the populations of several of them were swelled by vast numbers of arrivals from France, Germany, Switzerland, Ireland, and Scotland.

Of these immigrants the earliest though not the most numerous were the French Calvinists, or Huguenots. Under the Edict of Nantes (1598) they had enjoyed liberties and privileges which enabled them to constitute practically a state within the state in Roman Catholic France. In 1685 the edict was revoked, and singly and in groups the Huguenots took the first opportunity to leave the country, until a total of about 300,000 had left for England, the Netherlands, America, and elsewhere, only a small minority of them going to the English colonies. These émigrés were mostly artisans, merchants, and men of letters and science who enriched their new homes with both their talents and their wealth. In America they settled in the towns along the coast from Charleston to Boston, to become the ancestors of Americans like Paul Revere (Rivoire).

Like the French Protestants, many German Protestants suffered from the arbitrary enactments of their rulers, and German Catholics as well as Protestants suffered even more from the devastating wars of the Sun King of France, Louis XIV. The Rhineland of southerwestern Germany, the area known as the Palatinate, was especially exposed to the slaughter of its people and the ruin of its farms. For the Palatine Germans, the unusually cold winter of 1708–9 came as the last straw, and more than 12,000 of them sought refuge in England. The Catholics among them were shipped back to Germany and the rest were resettled in England, Ireland, or the colonies. Arriving in New York, approximately 3,000 of them tried to make homes in the Mohawk Valley, only to be ousted by rapacious colonial landlords. Some of the Palatines moved farther up the Mohawk, but most of them made their way to Pennsylvania, where they received a hearty welcome. After that, the Quaker colony was the usual destination of Germans, who sailed for America in growing numbers, largely Moravians and Mennonites with religious views similar to those of the Quakers. But quite a few of the German Protestants went to North Carolina, especially after the founding (1710) of New Bern by a company of 600 German-speaking Swiss. All together, the Germans comprised the largest body of eighteenth-century white immigrants except for the Scotch-Irish.

The Scotch-Irish, the most numerous of the newcomers, were not Irishmen at all, though coming from Ireland, and they were distinct from the Scots who came to America directly from Scotland. In the early 1600's King James I, to further the conquest of Ireland, had seen to the peopling of the northern county of Ulster with his subjects from the Scottish Lowlands, who as good Presbyterians might be relied upon to hold their ground against the Irish Catholics. These Ulster colonists —the Scotch-Irish—eventually prospered despite the handicap of a barren soil and the necessity of border fighting with the Irish tribesmen. Then, after about a century, the English government destroyed their prosperity by prohibiting the export of their woolens and other products, and at the same time threatened their religion by virtually outlawing it and insisting upon conformity with the Anglican Church. As the long-term leases of the Scotch-Irish terminated, in the years after 1710, the English landlords doubled and even tripled the rents. Rather than sign new leases, thousands upon thousands of the ill-used tenants embarked in successive waves of emigration. Understandably a cantankerous and troublesome lot, these people often were coldly received at the colonial ports, and most of them pushed out to the edge of the American wilderness. There they occupied land with scant regard for ownership, believing that "it was against the laws of God and nature that so much land should be idle while so many Christians wanted it to labor on and to raise bread." There also they fought the Indians as earlier they had fought the Irish. Among their illustrious descendants was the characteristically Scotch-Irish Andrew Jackson.

The Scots and the Irish, as migrants to America, had no connection with the Scotch-Irish. Scottish Highlanders, some of them Roman Catholics frustrated in the rebellions of 1715 and 1745, went with their tartans and kilts and bagpipes to more than one of the colonies, but mostly to North Carolina. Presbyterian Lowlanders, afflicted with high rents in the country and unemployment in town, left in largest numbers shortly before the American Revolution. These Scots, Lowlanders and Highlanders alike, with few exceptions became loyalists after the outbreak of the Revolutionary War, but the Scotch-Irish were patriots almost to the man, as were the Irish. The Irish had migrated in trickles over a long period and yet, by the time of the Revolution, were about as numerous as the Scots, though less conspicuous, many of them having lost their Roman Catholic religion and their identity as Irishmen.

All these various immigrants contributed to the remarkable growth of the colonies. In 1700 the colonial population totaled a quarter of a million or less; by 1775 it was nearly ten times as large, more than two million. The number practically doubled every twenty-five years, as Benjamin Franklin observed, leading the English clergyman Thomas Malthus to his pessimistic conclusion (1798) that any population, if unchecked, would increase in a geometrical progression while the means of subsistence (except in a new and favored country like America) could not be increased nearly so fast. Important as the continuing immigration was, the rapid growth of the colonial population was mainly due to natural increase, to the excess of births over deaths. In the colonies, with their abundance of land and opportunity, large families were an asset rather than a liability, and husbands and wives heeded the Biblical advice: "Be ye fruitful and multiply."

Hence the colonists of English origin, those who had arrived earliest and had had the longest time to multiply, continued greatly to outnumber those of non-English origin. Yet the proportion of non-English ancestry increased year by year, from a tenth in 1700 to a third (including the people from Africa) in 1760. There was a good deal of intermarriage between the different nationalities, and even before the Revolution thousands of Americans could trace their ancestry to

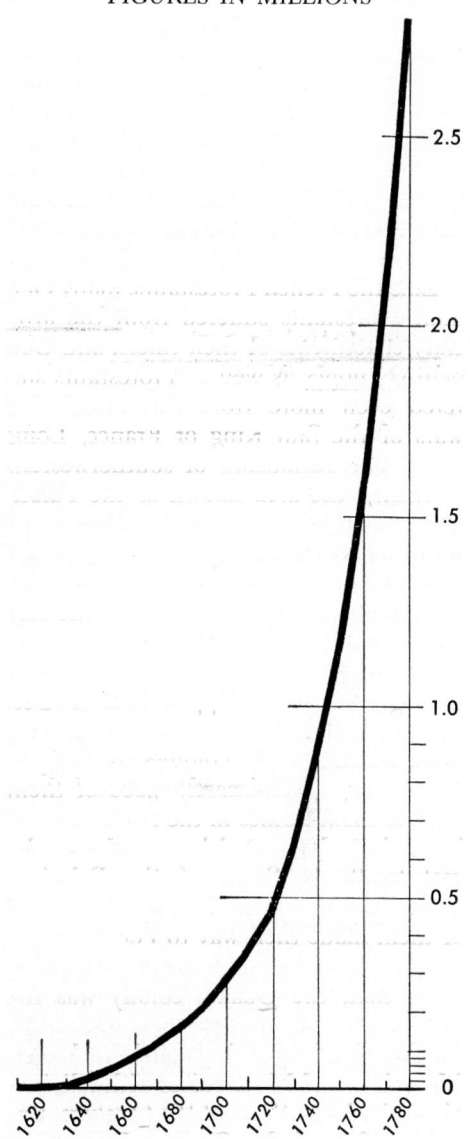

ESTIMATED COLONIAL POPULATION
ENGLISH MAINLAND COLONIES
FIGURES IN MILLIONS

two or more nations of the Old World.

As compared with the population of England, that of the colonies was not only mixed but also youthful and masculine, containing somewhat fewer old persons and women, especially along the frontier. And the colonial population was surprisingly mobile, New Englanders resettling in New Jersey and other colonies to the south, Pennsylvanians (Scotch-Irish and Germans) swarming up the Shenandoah Valley to emerge upon and people the back country of the Carolinas. In all the colonies men and women pushed upstream toward the unsettled wilderness, until with Daniel Boone leading the way into Kentucky (1769) they began here and there even to occupy the land beyond the mountains.

Along the seacoast a number of villages grew into small cities. For more than a century after its founding, Boston remained the largest town, but eventually it was overtaken by both Philadelphia and New York. In 1760 Philadelphia had more than 23,000 people, New York about 18,000, and Boston nearly 16,000. Next in order were Charleston, S.C., with approximately 8,000 and Newport, R.I., with 7,500. After 1700 these colonial towns increased more rapidly than most English cities, yet not always so rapidly as the American population as a whole. Eight out of a hundred Americans lived in towns in 1720, and only about five or six out of a hundred in 1742. The rest of the people—the overwhelming majority throughout the colonial period—were scattered over the countryside and lived upon farms of one description or another.

Agriculture and Industry

Though there were regional differences, farming throughout the colonies had certain characteristics in common. In all the colonies it was a matter of adapting European plants and animals to American conditions or applying European techniques to the cultivation of native crops. The ground was broken with hoe and mattock or with a crude wooden plow, usually drawn by oxen because of their slower and steadier pull than horses could provide, and often requiring two men to hold and guide it. Harvesting was a back-breaking work with sickle or scythe. Grain was threshed with a flail or by the trampling of oxen, and it was winnowed by being tossed in the air for the breeze to carry away the chaff. In George Washington's time these processes were not much advanced beyond what they had been in the day of the Pharaohs, and in colonial America there was even less care of the soil than there had been in ancient Egypt. Most of the colonists gave little thought to conserving their land by rotating crops, applying fertilizers, or checking erosion. Their attitude was reasonable enough in their circumstances: it paid them to economize on labor, not on land.

In New England the early settlers usually took up land in groups, each member receiving a village lot of his own, sharing the "common" as pasture and timberland, and tilling the strips assigned to him in the outlying fields. This township system was a relic of the manorial system, but here the town proprietors took the place of the feudal lord, and the farmers themselves planned their interdependent labors at their town meetings. After 1700 the commons were divided into private property and the strips were consolidated into separate farms. The typical farm became one that was small enough to be worked by the farmer, his sons, and perhaps an occasional hired hand, with the aid of neighbors at harvests and at house or barn raisings. It was bounded by fences made of stones that had been laboriously cleared off the fields. A fairly self-sufficient unit, producing mainly for use rather than for sale, it contained a variety of scrawny livestock, apple and other orchards, and fields devoted chiefly to hay and corn, the prevalence of the "blast" or black-stem rust having discouraged the cultivation of wheat.

In New York, despite the abundance of excellent soil, agricultural productivity lagged because of the engrossment of the land in great estates, running to thousands and even hundreds of thousands of acres, on which few people were willing to work as tenants when they could get

TOBACCO PREPARATION, EIGHTEENTH CENTURY. When tobacco was harvested, the stalks were hung in a well-ventilated barn to cure. After several months, in damp weather when the leaves were pliable, they were stripped from the stalks, sorted, and tied into "hands," then packed tightly in hogsheads. These were stored in public warehouses until examined by official inspectors. Eventually the hogsheads were carried by boat or wagon or were rolled to the nearest ship landing. Ships from England ascended the rivers of the tobacco country to pick up cargoes. From William Tatham, *An Historical and Practical Essay on the Culture and Commerce of Tobacco* (London, 1800).

farms of their own in other colonies. The Dutch and their descendants set examples of careful tillage on the freeholds they had acquired at an early date. In Pennsylvania, of all the colonies the most favored by nature for farming, the Germans likewise applied the intensive cultivation they had learned in the old country. Their neat and substantial barns were their pride, but the work of their womenfolk in the fields was sometimes shocking to non-Germans. With fairly large holdings, these farmers needed all the labor they could get, and in addition to their wives and daughters they employed indentured servants, women as well as men. In New York and Pennsylvania the farmers concentrated upon the production of staples to be sold abroad and at home. After ceasing to produce enough food to feed all its own people, New England depended upon these "bread colonies" for its wheat. So, to some extent, did those Southern colonies that were preoccupied with the growing of tobacco.

Tobacco came into use in Europe and Asia soon after Columbus's first return from the West Indies, where he had seen the Cuban natives smoking small cigars (*tabacos*) which they inserted in the nostril. In England Sir Walter Raleigh popularized the smoking habit, and the demand for tobacco grew despite the early objections of both moralists and mercantilists. Moralists denounced tobacco as a poisonous weed, the cause of many diseases. King James I himself led the attack with *A Counterblaste to Tobacco* (1604), in which he urged his people not to imitate "the barbarous and beastly manners of the wild, godless, and slavish Indians, especially in so vile and stinking a custom." Mercantilists at first were horrified because England's imports of tobacco came from the Spanish colonies and payment for them resulted in the loss of English gold.

Tobacco fitted well into the mercantilistic scheme of England, however, after John Rolfe had succeeded (1612) in domesticating the plant in the English colonies, at Jamestown. The growing of tobacco was so profitable that it soon spread all around Chesapeake Bay and became the economic mainstay of Virginia, Maryland, and part of North Carolina. Overproduction ensued, and the price fell repeatedly during the eighteenth century. Again and again, without much success, the planters tried various methods of crop control. Both falling prices and soil exhaustion (tobacco being very hard on the soil) stimulated the formation of larger and larger plantations, so that some of the economies of large-scale production could be gained and fresh lands could be continually brought into use. On these plantations slave labor was easily adapted to the simple and repetitive round of tasks which tobacco required—sowing, transplanting, weeding, worming, picking, curing, stripping, and packing.

Slave labor was fairly well suited also to rice culture along the Georgia and Carolina coasts. Here dikes and ditches leading from the tidal rivers permitted the necessary flooding and draining of the paddies, while care was taken to see that no salt water reached the rice with the incoming tides. To cultivate the growing rice, men had to stand knee-deep in mud, their bare backs exposed to malarial mosquitoes and to the broiling sun. Since white men could not be hired to do it, Negroes were compelled to perform this torturing and unhealthful work. But the rice plantations were smaller than the tobacco plantations and did not provide a similar year-round routine which would utilize slave labor to the full.

Indigo supplemented rice after the successful cultivation of the dye plant (1743) by Eliza Lucas, the daughter of a West Indian planter. Grown on high ground, the indigo did not get in the way of the rice on the river bottoms, and it occupied the slaves at times when they were not busy with the rice. They tended the indigo fields, cut the leaves, soaked them in vats, and extracted the residue as a blue powder. Glad for a chance to be freed from foreign sources of the dye, Parliament granted a bounty of sixpence a pound.

The early colonists were manufacturers as well as farmers. In the 1600's families produced nearly all their necessities within the household. To the end of the colonial period, household manufacturing continued to prevail on ordinary farms, though not in the rising towns.

In the towns artisans of many kinds appeared—carpenters, chandlers (candlemakers), coopers (barrel-makers), cordwainers (shoemakers), weavers, tailors, wheelwrights, and dozens of others. Except in such lines as millinery and dressmaking, women artisans were rare, though now and then a widow took over her husband's work and succeeded as a cobbler, tinworker, or even blacksmith. By 1750 almost a third of the people of Philadelphia owed their living to a craft of some kind.

The craft usually was a family enterprise, and the shop was on the ground floor of the master craftsman's home. The master was assisted by his sons and by one or more journeymen and apprentices, who lived as members of his household, and who aspired eventually to become masters with shops of their own. In some ways the craftsman was like the small businessman of the present. He had to procure and train workers, provide materials, supervise the work (while taking an active part in it), and find a market. When possible, he made goods to order, or, as he called them, "bespoke" goods, but in slack times he might produce a stock of articles for general sale.

Colonial craftsmanship became notable for quantity as well as quality. As late as 1700, all but a tiny fraction of the manufactures which the colonists bought were made in England. Before the Revolution, more than half of the manufactures were made in America. The rise of the colonial craftsman was watched with concern by men in London who took seriously the doctrines of mercantilism.

Water power was widely used in various kinds of colonial mills. At the rapids of streams small enough to be easily dammed, grist and fulling mills were set up to take some of the heavier labor out of the household, grinding grain and fulling cloth (shrinking and tightening the weave by a process of soaking and pounding) for the farmers roundabout. The millowner was usually a farmer himself in his spare time. He frequently used his water wheel to power a sawmill for cutting his neighbor's logs. Other and busier sawmills accompanied the lumber industry which followed the retreating forest.

Both fishing and fur trading became big businesses employing what were, by colonial standards, large amounts of capital. It was expensive to provide fur traders with goods for bartering with Indian trappers—guns, knives, blankets, looking-glasses, and beads to exchange for furs and hides—and most of the business came to be controlled by English merchants in London and colonial merchants in Albany, Philadelphia, and Charleston. It was costly also to outfit fleets for the fishing industry, which concentrated mainly in New England waters, though almost every farmer near a stream or pond was at least a part-time fisherman.

The fisheries led to shipbuilding, the first colonial-built ships being put together on the New England coast for the use of fishermen, and the abundance of timber and naval stores enabled the industry in the colonies to expand to the point of outdoing that of England itself. So cheap and yet so seaworthy were the materials that, despite the high wages of colonial labor, excellent ships could be produced at as little as half the cost of those built in English yards.

From the beginning of colonization, the home government encouraged the colonial production of iron in a crude form, as a raw material for English mills and foundries. When colonial iron-makers began to produce more than merely the crude metal, their competitors in England induced Parliament to pass the Iron Act of 1750, which removed the English duty on pig and bar iron but forbade the colonists to engage in the secondary processing of iron or steel. This prohibition was in line with other acts intended to prevent the rise of advanced manufactures in America. The Woolen Act (1699) prohibited the export of wool or woolens from a colony to any place outside its boundaries, and the Hat Act (1732) similarly prohibited the export of hats, which could be cheaply made in America because of the availability of beaver skins. But the colonists usually disregarded such legislation when it was to their interest to do so.

Money and Commerce

Though the colonists produced most of what they consumed, they by no means achieved economic self-sufficiency. They could not supply their entire wants from their own agriculture and industry. To maintain and raise their living standards they had to have the benefits of trade with one another and with people overseas.

Foreign trade provided indispensable consumer and capital goods which the colonists could not manufacture for themselves in suitable quantity or quality. From abroad the millowner had to get his machinery, the shipwright his hardware and navigating instruments, the farmer his spades and other tools, the Indian trader most of his supplies. Even a modest home included kitchen utensils, tableware, needles and thread, lanterns, and other equipment of European make. Wealthier families bought additional imports, luxury items such as mirrors, paper, books, fine furniture, and fancy cloth.

The central problem in the overseas commerce of the colonies was to find the means of payment for these imports. Money was scarce in the colonies. They did obtain a motley collection of Spanish and other European coins from their dealings with pirates and from certain routes of overseas trade. Massachusetts, alone among the colonies, coined its own money, the "pine-tree shilling," but only for about three decades (1652–84). Generally, in their transactions with one another, the colonists resorted to barter or else used money substitutes, though always calculating in terms of pounds, shillings, and pence. Beaver skins circulated widely as a medium of exchange and so did tobacco, not the leaves but warehouse certificates representing tobacco in storage. All the colonies experimented at one time or another with paper currency, often securing it with land, but Parliament suppressed this expedient by legislating against the Massachusetts land bank in 1740 and by outlawing paper money in New England in 1751 and in the rest of the colonies later on. Anyhow this kind of paper was not acceptable in payment for imported goods and services, which had to be bought with specie or with bills of exchange arising from colonial exports. In short, the colonies had to sell abroad in order to buy from abroad,

but British policy attempted to limit and control their selling opportunities.

Though the tobacco planters had an abundant staple for export, they were not allowed to dispose of it to the highest bidder in the markets of the world. According to a series of Trade Laws first enacted in 1660, tobacco was one of the "enumerated items" which must be exported only to the British Isles, whence more than half of it was re-exported to other places. The laws also prohibited the growing of tobacco in the British Isles, but protection against competition in the mother country did not quite offset the disadvantages of the colonial planter. He usually sold his annual crop to an English merchant, and the merchant credited him with its value, after deducting charges for shipping, insurance, and a merchant's commission. Through the merchant he bought slaves and manufactured goods, and the merchant deducted the cost of these from the planter's credit on the books. After tobacco prices had begun to fall, the planter often found at the end of a year that his crop did not pay for all the goods he had ordered in return. The merchant then carried him until the next year and charged interest on the extension of credit. As the years went by, the planter went more and more deeply into debt, eventually leaving his indebtedness to his heirs.

The colonial merchant in such ports as Boston, New York, and Philadelphia did not have the same difficulties as the tobacco planter, though he had others of his own. He was favored by the Navigation Acts, passed in 1650 and after, which excluded foreign ships from practically all of the colonial carrying trade. And he found a market in England for the furs, timber, naval stores, and vessels produced in the Northern colonies. But, according to the Trade Laws, he could not export fish, flour, wheat, or meat to the mother country, for he would thereby compete with her own producers. He had to dispose of these prohibited items in other markets if he was to obtain adequate means of paying for his imports from England.

In the English island colonies of the Caribbean the Northern merchant found a ready outlet for mainland products. In the French, Dutch, and Spanish islands of the Caribbean he also got eager customers—and often better prices. Responding to pressure from English sugar planters, who wished to monopolize the mainland trade, Parliament in the Molasses Act of 1733 put a high duty on foreign sugar taken to the continental colonies. The molasses duty was intended to discourage commerce with the foreign islands. But the Northern merchant could evade the tax by smuggling, and he often did. From the ports of New England and the Middle Colonies went cargo after cargo of lumber, horses, wheat, flour, biscuit, corn, peas, potatoes, beef, pork, bacon, and fish. From the West Indies were obtained sugar, molasses, rum, dyewoods, cotton, ginger, coffee, Spanish coins, and bills of exchange. Sometimes West Indian products were carried directly to England; more commonly they were brought back to American ports, where part was sold in the domestic market and the rest exported to England. These exports, together with bills of exchange and Spanish money, helped to pay for the English goods imported into the thirteen colonies.

To and from England, to and from the West Indies—these were much the most important routes of trade for the Northern merchant. He also worked out a number of routes of indirect trade with the mother country, some of them complex and frequently changing, others fairly stable and somewhat "triangular" in their simplicity. Thus he might direct his ships to Catholic southern Europe with fish, then to England with wine and other proceeds in cash or bills of exchange, and then back home with manufactured goods.

The most famous or infamous of the triangular trades by-passed England it-

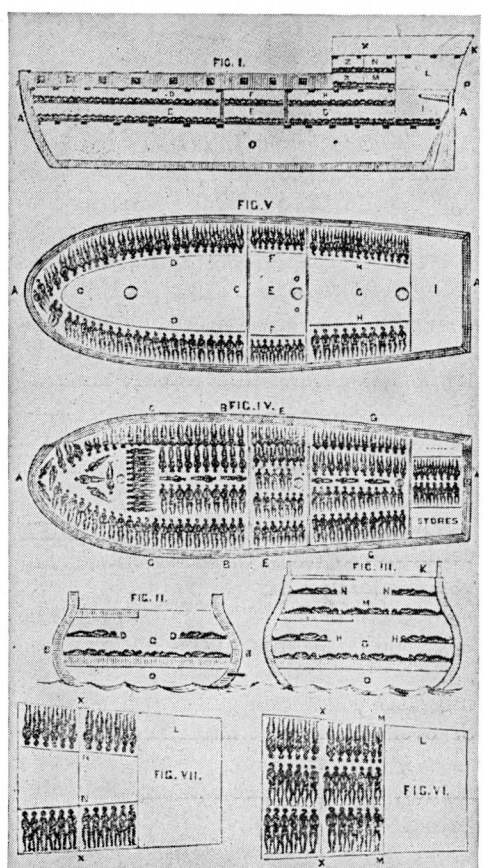

A SLAVE SHIP. This plan of the *Brookes*, an eighteenth-century vessel built especially for the slave trade, shows how little space was wasted. The slaves were packed in so tightly that they had no room to stand or even to sit. During part of the day (except in bad weather) they were allowed on deck to get food, air, and exercise. They usually were shackled. Their misery was intensified by seasickness and frequently by epidemics of dysentery and other diseases. Despite the high losses from death en route, more Negro than white colonists crossed the Atlantic before 1800. From first to last, five million or more slaves were shipped from Africa.

self. In this trade a ship took rum and other items from a New England port to the Guinea Coast of Africa, slaves from Africa to the West Indies, and sugar and molasses as well as specie and bills from the West Indies to the home port. There some of the cargo would be distilled into rum for another voyage of the same kind.

On the African coast the slave marts were kept supplied by native chieftains who made a business of capturing enemy tribesmen in warfare and bringing them, tied together in long lines known as "coffles," out of the jungle. Then, after some haggling on the seashore, came the horrors of the "middle passage." Those slaves who died en route were thrown overboard, and the losses from disease were generally high. Those who survived were "seasoned" for a time in the West Indies before being shipped on to the mainland.

Provincial Society

In England, as in Europe, class lines were sharply marked during the seventeenth and eighteenth centuries. The chances for any Englishman to rise above the station of his father and grandfather were rather slim—unless he went to America.

In the colonies the English class arrangement was not reproduced. Few or none of the nobility became colonists, though some of them were colonial enterprisers. To Virginia, as to Massachusetts and other colonies, there migrated a relatively small number of untitled gentlemen and a great many members of the middling and lower orders. Some of these arrivals doubtless hoped to reconstruct in America something like the social system they had known in England, only here they hoped to occupy the higher levels themselves. A fortunate few did acquire extensive landholdings and proceeded to mimic the aristocrats back home, but no true aristocracy was transplanted to the colonies.

Social mobility—the movement of individuals up and down the social scale—was much greater in colonial America than in contemporary England or in the twentieth-century United States. All except the slaves could aspire to a higher place for themselves or at least for their children. Once a man had made a fortune, he was accepted readily by those who theretofore had considered him their social inferior. The colonists, believing in enterprise and material success, honored the self-made man. Afterwards his descendants were inclined to forget the humble and even grubby origins of the family fortune and to think of themselves as thorough-going aristocrats.

Class consciousness and class distinctions came to be quite noticeable in colonial America. Usually a person's place in society was obvious from his appearance and dress. An ordinary farmer in his coarse linen homespun or a town craftsman in his leather apron made a sharp contrast with a planter or merchant in buckle shoes, knee breeches, colorful waistcoat, starched ruffles, and powdered wig. A farm girl, her face parched by winter fire or summer sun, her buxom figure clothed in homemade linsey-woolsey, was not likely to be mistaken for a planter's or merchant's daughter, whose delicate form was clad in imported silks and satins, and whose complexion was protected by a dainty parasol.

As some of the rich grew richer, some of the poor became more impoverished. There was a widening of extremes. If many of the early indentured servants acquired valuable land and respectable status after completing their servitude, many of the later ones either took up subsistence farming on the frontier or sank to the level of the "poor whites" on worn-out lands in the neighborhood of the planters. Yet, especially in New England, the vast majority of the people came to form a self-respecting, property-owning middle class. Throughout colonial America the benefits of physical well-being were more widely diffused than anywhere else in the world.

Domesticity was a keynote of life in the English colonies. They—unlike the Spanish and French colonies—were peopled predominantly by home makers, by married men who brought their wives and children with them or sent for their families after first preparing the way.

THE JOHN WARD HOUSE. The left-hand portion of this house in Salem, Massachusetts, was built in 1684. The right-hand portion, with another gable, was added later, and the lean-to in the rear still later. Note the second-story overhang. This was characteristic of many seventeenth-century dwellings in New England. It was copied from medieval English houses, but its origin and purpose are uncertain. The most likely theories are these: (1) it was a technical matter of construction: separate, offset posts for the two stories made possible a stronger framing than did one long post; (2) it was a matter of aesthetics: people liked the way the overhang looked. Note too the casement windows with their diamond-shaped panes, also typical of the time. (ESSEX INSTITUTE, SALEM, MASS.)

From the beginning, the family shelters of the colonists were fairly close imitations of those already familiar to them, yet houses (like almost everything else) were more or less altered by Americanizing trends. The first English pioneers built thatched huts rather than log cabins of the kind now considered peculiarly American. Introduced by the early Swedish settlers along the Delaware, the log cabin did not become the typical frontier dwelling until the eighteenth century. By that time a variety of building materials and architectural styles had appeared in the older settled areas. Though a higher proportion of colonial than of English houses were built of wood, a considerable number were built of stone or brick, some of which was imported. In New England a common type of farmhouse was the "salt-box," two stories high in front and one in back, and sided with unpainted clapboards. In the Middle Colonies the red-brick house with a Dutch gambrel roof and the substantial farmhouse of native stone were characteristic. In the South the more prosperous planters erected Georgian mansions, which as a

WESTOVER. In 1688 William Byrd I began the construction of a house on land he had bought along the James River, not far from the place where Richmond, Virginia, later was to be located. His son, the brilliant William Byrd II, lived here during much of his life (when he was not in England). In 1749 the house burned down, and William Byrd III had it rebuilt. He failed, however, to maintain the fortune his father and grandfather had accumulated, and eventually the estate passed out of the family's possession. A French traveler, the Marquis de Chastellux, who was a guest at Westover in 1782, wrote: "There are magnificent houses at every view, for the banks of the James River form the garden of Virginia. That of Mrs. Byrd surpasses them all in the magnificence of the buildings, the beauty of its situation, and the pleasures of society." Westover is one of the finest examples of the Georgian style, as applied to domestic architecture, in America. (PHOTOGRAPH BY THOMAS T. WATERMAN, LIBRARY OF CONGRESS)

rule were copies of English models, reduced in size and simplified in ornament.

Crowded into the generally small houses were comparatively large families. A family as a rule included not only numerous children but also a varying number of dependent relatives, such as elderly grandparents or unmarried aunts. The household was further enlarged in many cases by the presence of servants, domestic slaves, or hired hands living under the same roof. As head of the household, the father wielded strong authority over its members. He was entitled to whatever property his wife had owned before her marriage to him, but he was responsible also for her debts and misdeeds. The position of women, however, was somewhat higher in the colonies than in the homeland. Since they were relatively scarce, colonial women were proportionately val-

ued for reasons of supply and demand. They were, for instance, more free than Englishwomen to travel about without male escorts or female chaperones, though Sarah Knight's journey from Boston to New York by herself (1704) was rather exceptional, at least in regard to distance.

Religion: Decline and Revival

Though originating abroad, religions developed a new and distinctive pattern in America. With the immigration of diverse sectarians from several countries, the colonies became an ecclesiastical patchwork made up of a great variety of churches. Toleration flourished to a degree remarkable for the time, not because it was deliberately sought but because conditions favored its growth. No single religious establishment predominated in the colonies as the Church of England did in the British Isles and as other state churches, Lutheran or Roman Catholic, did in Western Europe.

By law, the Church of England was established in Virginia, Maryland, New York, the Carolinas, and Georgia. In these colonies everyone regardless of belief or affiliation was supposed to be taxed for the support of the church, and only Anglicans were supposed to vote or hold public office. Actually, except in Virginia and Maryland, the Church of England succeeded in maintaining its position as the established church only in certain localities.

Even in Virginia and Maryland, Anglicanism ceased to be quite the same thing that it was in England. To watch over the far-flung American parishes, the King and the Bishop of London depended upon the colonial governors. Most of the time the governors were preoccupied with political affairs, and the parishes worked out relatively democratic and independent church organizations of their own. Local vestries (governing boards of laymen) appointed pastors and provided for the payment of salaries. As tobacco prices fell, salaries were not increased. Hence not enough able and well-qualified men were attracted to the ministry. Some were further discouraged by the fact that they had to cross the ocean to be ordained by a bishop in England. Maryland became notorious for its idle and profligate "fox-hunting parsons." Even the most conscientious parsons in the South found it next to impossible to give adequate care to the souls of their parishioners, so far apart did the farmers and planters live and so extensive were the parish boundaries. Often the elaborate rituals of the church had to be simplified or omitted altogether.

To strengthen Anglicanism in America, the Bishop of London began in 1689 to delegate the supervision of the colonial churches to his personal representatives, or commissaries. When the first commis-

sary, James Blair, was appointed in Virginia, more than half of the parishes in the colony had no minister. When Blair died in 1743, after more than fifty years of devoted labor, there were only two unsupplied parishes.

To further strengthen Anglicanism, in America and elsewhere, the Church of England in 1701 set up the Society for the Propagation of the Gospel in Foreign Parts. Missionaries of the S. P. G. founded a number of new Anglican communions in the colonies, especially in Massachusetts and Connecticut. Seeing that Anglicanism in America was handicapped by the lack of a bishop, the missionaries agitated for the appointment of one. But Congregationalists and Presbyterians opposed this as a step toward tyranny, and the Anglican clergy of Virginia and Maryland agreed with them. No bishop was appointed.

Neither in England nor in America were Anglicans and Puritans quite so different as has often been thought. The Puritan fathers of Massachusetts intended at first only to transplant a purified branch of the Church of England. They proceeded, however, to create a separate tax-supported church-state, with the congregation in each town managing its own ecclesiastical affairs under the leadership of its minister. Thus they became Separatists, much like the settlers at Plymouth. And the Puritan church came to be called the Congregational, because of the more or less independent, autonomous nature of each congregation. Yet the Puritans continued to feel that they had a kind of spiritual kinship with the Church of England.

In theology the Puritans were somewhat more rigid, more grim, than the Anglicans, yet a little less so than the Calvinists of Europe. John Calvin had expounded his religious views in his *Institutes of the Christian Religion* (1536), one of the great theological works of all time. The main points, much simplified, were these: God is all-knowing, all-powerful. Man is weak, helpless, born in sin. He cannot save himself by his own efforts: he must rely upon God. Since God knows everything, God knows the future of every soul from the beginning of things, long before the soul is born. God knows whether it is to be saved, or damned. No man can do anything to save his soul, for at birth he already is one of God's chosen, God's elect, or else he is

not, and that is that. Though accepting these beliefs, the Puritans were more rational and less dogmatic about them than Calvin himself had been.

Originally the Puritans believed that only God's elect should belong to the church, but it was hard to know in every case exactly who was eligible for membership, exactly who had been chosen for eternal happiness. If a person underwent

a religious experience in which he felt an infusion of God's grace, and if he thereafter led an upright life, that person probably was one of the elect. Many were confident that they had undergone a satisfactory experience, but many others could never be sure. So people searched their own hearts and consciences, and those of their neighbors as far as possible, to find a reassuring sign of the desperately needed grace of God.

The Puritans also strove to lead a useful, conscientious life of thrift and hard work. They honored material success. As they prospered and life became a little easier, many lost the inner spirit of their religion and retained only the outward forms. Often the children of church members were unable to testify that they had experienced God's grace. To maintain church membership, a conference of ministers in 1662 approved a plan to ad-

CHRIST CHURCH, CAMBRIDGE, MASSACHUSETTS. Peter Harrison, who designed Christ Church, has been called "America's first professional architect." Born in England, Harrison became a ship captain when only twenty-three. He married an American woman with considerable property and prospered as a merchant of Newport, Rhode Island. In versatility though not in genius he rivaled Benjamin Franklin. He was not a jack of all trades, according to his biographer Carl Bridenbaugh, but was "rather a master of ten—ship-handling, navigation, shipbuilding, woodcarving, drafting, cartography, surveying, military engineering and construction, commerce, and the new agriculture," in addition to architecture. He acquired the largest and best selected architectural library in colonial America. Among the notable structures he designed were King's Chapel in Boston, Touro Synagogue in Newport, St. Michael's in Charleston, and Christ Church in Cambridge. The building committee for Christ Church insisted upon the most simple and inexpensive construction. Though he did not manage to keep within the cost limit, Harrison succeeded in creating a charmingly original design, in the spirit of the late Georgian style, at a remarkably low cost (see photograph on opposite page). On the interior, he produced an effect of considerable spaciousness for so small a church by leaving out the usual gallery, or balcony, on each side. (LIBRARY OF CONGRESS)

mit as partial members, with the right to vote but without the right to partake of communion, those members' children who merely professed a belief in Christian principles. Strict Puritans ridiculed this "Half-Way Covenant," and it did

the period, they believed in witches. In one of the many learned books he wrote, *Illustrious Providences* (1684), Increase Mather undertook to show that God had a special concern for New England and that the people should note carefully any

---

CONFESSION OF A WITCH

1692

Mrs. Mary Osgood, of Andover, Massachusetts, was examined for witchcraft, September 8, by a group of judges. They reported:

"She confesses that, about 11 years ago, when she was in a melancholy state and condition, she used to walk abroad in her orchard; and upon a certain time she saw the appearance of a cat, at the end of the house, which yet she thought was a real cat. However, at that time, it diverted her from praying to God, and instead thereof she prayed to the devil; about which time she made a covenant with the devil, who, as a black man, came to her and presented her a book, upon which she laid her finger, and that left a red spot: and that upon her signing, the devil told her he was her God, and that she should serve and worship him, and she believes she consented to it. She says, further, that about two years agone, she was carried through the air, in company with deacon Frye's wife, Ebenezer Baker's wife, and Goody Tyler, to five mile pond, where she was baptised by the devil, who dipped her face in the water and made her renounce her former baptism, and told her she must be his, soul and body, forever, and that she must serve him, which she promised to do."

About six weeks later, on October 19, she was visited by Increase Mather, who reported:

"Mrs. Osgood freely and relentingly said that the confession which she made upon her examination for witchcraft, and afterwards acknowledged before the honourable judges, was wholly false, and that she was brought to the said confession by the violent urging and unreasonable pressings that were used toward her; she asserted that she never signed the devil's book, was never baptised by the devil, never afflicted any of the accusers, or gave her consent for their being afflicted."

---

little to stop the growth of a worldly outlook. Sabbath after Sabbath the ministers preached sermons deploring the signs of waning piety.

None of the seventeenth-century ministers labored harder to keep up the old faith than did Increase Mather and his son Cotton. Puritanism demanded a well-educated ministry, and the Mathers were intellectual giants. Like most scientists of

evidence of "Witchcrafts, Diabolical Possessions, Remarkable Judgements upon noted Sinners," and the like. There later arose a widespread hysteria, which went to its greatest extremes in the Massachusetts town of Salem, where it was stimulated by the mumbo-jumbo of two West Indian slaves who were steeped in voodoo lore. Hundreds of people were accused as witches, many of them sentenced to die, and nineteen actually hanged before the witchcraft trials were stopped, in 1692. Afterwards almost all the witch-hunters publicly repented their part in the affair. The Mathers often were blamed for it, though in fact they had pled for moderation during the trials and had helped to bring them to an end.

Not all the Puritans were Congregationalists: some of them became Presbyterians. In belief, these two groups were essentially the same, but they differed in ecclesiastical organization, the Presbyterians having a more highly centralized government, with a governing body of presbyters (made up of ministers and lay elders) for the churches of each district. In the early 1700's many of the Puritan churches of Connecticut, and most of those founded in other colonies by emigrants from New England, adopted the Presbyterian form of government. The number of Presbyterians in America was greatly increased by the immigration of the Scotch-Irish. At first, most of these people lacked churches and pastors. Francis Makemie, often called the father of Presbyterianism in America, organized the first American presbytery (1705) and for twenty years traveled up and down the coast from New York to South Carolina to set up churches for the churchless.

Originally the American Baptists, of whom Roger Williams is considered the first, were also Calvinistic in their theology. Then, in Rhode Island and in other colonies, a bewildering variety of Baptist sects sprang up. They had in common a belief that infant baptism did not suffice and that rebaptism, usually by total immersion, was necessary. Some remained Calvinists, believers in predestination, and others came to believe in salvation by man's free will.

With the westward movement and the wide scattering of the colonial population, many of the frontiersmen lost touch with organized religion. With the rise of towns and the multiplication of material comforts, the inhabitants of the more densely settled areas were inclined toward an increasingly secular outlook. With the appearance of numerous and diverse sects, some people were tempted to doubt whether any particular denomination, even their own, possessed a monopoly of truth and grace. And with the progress of science and free thought in Europe, culminating in the Enlightenment of the eighteenth century, at least a few Americans began to adopt a rational and skeptical philosophy.

For thousands of the colonists, the trend away from religion was reversed by a revival movement known as the Great Awakening, which reached a climax in the 1740's. Wandering exhorters from abroad did much to stimulate the revivalistic spirit. John and Charles Wesley, founders of Methodism, which began as a reform movement within the Church of England, visited Georgia and other colonies in the 1730's with the intention of revitalizing religion and converting Indians and Negroes. George Whitefield, a powerful open-air preacher from England and for a time an associate of the Wesleys, made several evangelizing tours through the colonies.

The Puritans were divided on the issue of revivalism. A majority of the Congregational ministers of Massachusetts denounced the "errors" and "disorders" arising from revival meetings. Among the errors was the prevalent idea that a person could be saved by his own efforts, through conversion. Among the disorders was the practice of uneducated men "taking upon themselves to be preachers of the word of God," creating confusion and tumult, and leading members away from their regular churches.

Yet the outstanding preacher of the Great Awakening in New England was a Puritan of the Puritans and one of the most profound theologians in the history of American religious thought. This preacher was Jonathan Edwards. From his pulpit in Northampton, Massachusetts, Edwards attacked the new doctrines of easy salvation for all. He called upon his people to return to the faith of their fathers. He preached afresh the old Puritan ideas of the absolute sovereignty of God, the depravity of man, predestination, the necessity of experiencing a sense the largest number of people, prevailed the longest, and had the most lasting consequences. The Presbyterian church was split by the formation of a large and rapidly growing group of revivalistic, "New Light" Presbyterians. New mem-

---

"SINNERS IN THE HANDS OF AN ANGRY GOD"

1741

Jonathan Edwards (1703–1758) was the most original and systematic theologian of colonial America. A mystic who counterposed the horror of eternal damnation against the joys of eternal paradise, Edwards argued that God's grace is the only way that any man can be redeemed from the original sin committed by Adam (although he sometimes implied, as in this sermon, that poor sinners could yield themselves up to God's grace if their hearts were "filled with love to him who has loved them"). Edwards's aim of purifying Calvinism was far less representative of his era than was the religious liberalism of his contemporary, Benjamin Franklin. But the extremes of terror and salvation that he posed were undeniably effective: when he preached this sermon at Enfield, Connecticut, in 1741, it produced great "breathing of distress, and weeping."

"Your wickedness makes you as it were heavy as lead, and to tend downwards with great weight and pressure towards hell; and if God should let you go, you would immediately sink and swiftly descend and plunge into the bottomless gulf . . .

"O sinner! Consider the fearful danger you are in: it is a great furnace of wrath, a wide and bottomless pit, full of the fire of wrath, that you are held over in the hand of God . . . You hang by a slender thread, with the flames of divine wrath flashing about it, and ready every moment to singe it, and burn it asunder . . .

"And now you have an extraordinary opportunity, a day wherein Christ has thrown the door of mercy wide open, and stands in the door calling and crying with a loud voice to poor sinners . . .

"And let every one that is yet out of Christ, and hanging over the pit of hell, . . . now hearken to the loud calls of God's word and providence. This acceptable year of the Lord, a day of such great favours to some, will doubtless be a day of as remarkable vengeance to others. . . ."

---

ot election, and election by God's grace alone.

The Great Awakening spread over the colonies like a religious epidemic. It was most contagious in frontier areas and among the comparatively poor and uneducated folk, especially in the South. In the Southern back country it affected bers flocked to various free-will Baptist sects; the Baptists were on the way to becoming eventually one of the two most numerous denominations in the United States.

At the end of the colonial period, despite the successful work of many revivalists, English America contained fewer church members for its population than did any other Christian country of the time, and fewer than does the United States today. Even in New England, which was better churched than either the Middle Colonies or the South, probably no more than twenty persons in a hundred belonged, in 1760, to any religious body. This low proportion of membership, however, is not necessarily a fair measure of the importance of religion to eighteenth-century Americans. Many of them failed to join a church simply because there was no acceptable one within reach.

Literature and Learning

As an American variant of English culture developed in the colonies, it was reflected in the partial Americanization of the English language. New words originated in borrowings from the Indians (such as *skunk* and *squash*), from the French (*portage, prairie*), and from the Dutch (*boss, cooky*). Americanisms also arose from the combining of words already in the English language (*bullfrog, snow-plow*), from the formation of new adjectives based on existing nouns (*handy, chunky*), from the adoption of unfamiliar uses for familiar words (*branch*, meaning *stream; fall*, meaning *autumn*), and from the retention of old English expressions which were being dropped in England (*cater-corner; bub,* for *boy*). After 1700 English travelers in America began to notice a strangeness in accent as well as vocabulary, and in 1756 the great lexicographer Dr. Samuel Johnson mentioned the existence of an "American dialect."

Dr. Johnson thought of Americans as barbarians, and some no doubt were, but from the beginning many were concerned lest civilization be lost in the wilderness. They took pains to provide schooling for their children. At no time, however, did any of the colonies possess a system of free public education in quite the modern sense of tax-supported, compulsory schools. Massachusetts came the closest to it. That colony had the advantages of fairly compact settlement, a comparatively large number of university graduates among the early settlers, and a religion that strongly emphasized the ability to read the Bible. By a Massachusetts law of 1647, designed to circumvent "that old deluder Satan," each town of 50 householders was required to hire a schoolmaster to teach reading and writing, and each town of 100 householders was required to set up a Latin grammar school (high school). This law was not always enforced, but other colonies did not even adopt such legislation. Instruction in reading and writing was generally left to "dame schools" conducted in private houses, to church schools operated by the Quakers and other sects, to privately endowed "old field" schools (on worn-out plantation lands), to private tutors in the mansions of merchants and planters, and above all to mothers and fathers at the family fireside.

Far more people learned to read than ever attended school, yet a great many never learned to read at all. The literacy rate, which is unknown, must have varied a good deal from place to place. It seems to have been very low in some of the thinly settled areas, especially in the South. It was highest in the towns, especially in New England. On the whole, literacy doubtless improved during the eighteenth century, and by the time of the Revolution probably a majority of Americans could read.

The urge to read grew with the improvement in lamps and candles, which made reading a feasible way to spend long winter evenings. Reading tastes, in books, ran mostly to the Bible and theological works but also to the classics of Greece and Rome and to contemporary scientific and practical treatises. Much the largest proportion of all these books was printed abroad and imported, but the American towns of Cambridge and Boston were active book-publishing centers. Over two hundred titles came from their presses between 1640 (when the first edition of *The Whole Book of Psalms*, known as the "Bay Psalm Book," appeared) and 1700.

Periodical publications thereafter supplemented books and pamphlets as reading matter. Founded in 1704, the first regular newspaper in the colonies, though it was not very newsy, was the weekly Boston *News-Letter*, a small folded sheet of four pages with two columns to a page. By the 1760's one or more weekly papers were being published in each of the colonies except New Jersey and Delaware, both of which were well enough supplied by the presses of New York and Philadelphia. At first the papers contained much literary matter as well as news, the news being mostly of local interest. But more and more the journals concentrated upon public occurrences, and the coverage of a single paper was broadened to include the colonies as a whole through republication of items from exchange subscriptions. Several monthly magazines, notably the *American Magazine* of Philadelphia, were started after about 1750, with hopes of wide circulation. One after another they appeared for a year or two and then expired. More successful and more widely read were the yearly almanacs. Originally mere collections of weather data, these turned into small magazines of a sort, containing a great variety of literary fare. *Poor Richard's Almanac*, now well remembered, was only one of many, though a superior one.

Its publisher, Benjamin Franklin, was one of a few colonial-born men of letters who wrote works of lasting literary merit. His still widely read *Autobiography* was written after the colonial period (1770–8), but before that he had a number of published essays to his credit, including *Advice to a Young Man on Choosing a Mistress* (1745), *Reflections on Courtship and Marriage* (1746), *Observations Concerning the Increase of Mankind*

(1755), and *Advice to a Young Tradesman* (1762). These titles suggest the pragmatic and worldly-wise outlook of Franklin. Quite different was the sternly logical and other-worldly view of Jonathan Edwards, whose treatise *On the Freedom of the Will* (1754) is considered, by those who can understand it, as perhaps the most brilliant of American theological studies. The New Jersey Quaker John Woolman in his *Journal* (published in 1775, after his death) related a life as spiritual as Edwards' and as humanitarian as Franklin's but more humble and sensitive than either. A writer rivaling Franklin in charm, though not in productivity, was the Virginia planter William Byrd II, whose breezy *History of the Dividing Line* (not published till 1841) recounted his experiences as one of the commissioners who in 1728 marked off the boundary between Virginia and North Carolina. The *History* is full of sly and sophisticated comments on the Carolina mores.

If early Americans did not produce much that is remembered as great literature, the reason is not that they wrote little or wrote poorly, but rather that they were most interested in kinds of writing which are not especially popular today. As a rule, colonial authors had no time for belles lettres, for fiction, poetry, drama, and the like. Writers concentrated upon sermons, religious tracts, and subjects of urgent, practical concern. When poets did take up the pen, as a few able ones did in New England, they usually found their inspiration in religious themes.

Of the six colleges in actual operation by 1763, all but two were founded by religious groups primarily for the training of preachers. Harvard (1636) was established by Congregationalists, William and Mary (1693) by Anglicans, and Yale (1701) by conservative Congregationalists who were dissatisfied with the growing religious liberalism of Harvard. The College of New Jersey (1746), later

HARVARD COLLEGE, ABOUT 1740. At the left is Harvard Hall, built in 1675; in the center Stoughton Hall, 1699; at the right Massachusetts Hall, 1720. In 1641 an anonymous writer put down the essential facts regarding the beginnings of higher education in America, as follows: "After God had carried us safe to *New-England*, and wee had builded our houses, provided necessaries for our liveli-hood, rear'd convenient places for Gods worship, and settled the Civill Government: One of the next things we longed for and looked after was to advance *Learning* and perpetuate it to Posterity; dreading to leave an illiterate Ministry to the Churches, when our present Ministers shall lie in the Dust. And as wee were thinking and consulting how to effect this great Work, it pleased God to stir up the heart of one Mr. *Harvard* (a godly Gentleman and a lover of Learning, there living amongst us) to give the one halfe of his Estate (it being in all about 1700. l.) towards the erecting of a Colledge, and all his Library: after him another gave 300. l. others after them cast in more, and the publique hand of the State added the rest: the Colledge was, by common consent, appointed to be at *Cambridge* (a place very pleasant and accommodate) and is called (according to the name of the first founder) *Harvard Colledge*."

known as Princeton, was set up by Presbyterians in response to the Great Awakening. At any of these institutions a student with secular interests could derive something of a liberal education from the prevailing curricula, which included logic, ethics, physics, geometry, astronomy, rhetoric, Latin, Hebrew, and Greek. From the beginning Harvard was intended not only to provide an educated ministry but also to "advance learning and perpetuate it to posterity." King's College (1754), afterwards Columbia, had no theological faculty and was in-

BENJAMIN FRANKLIN, by J. S. Duplessis. (NEW YORK PUBLIC LIBRARY)

terdenominational from the start. The Academy and College of Philadelphia (1755), which grew into the University of Pennsylvania, was a completely secular institution, founded by a group of laymen under the inspiration of Benjamin Franklin. It offered courses in utilitarian subjects as well as the liberal arts—in mechanics, chemistry, agriculture, government, commerce, and modern languages. Though the colonies thus were well supplied with colleges, at least in comparison with other countries at the time, some Americans continued to go to English universities. But the great majority of colonial leaders, after 1700, received their entire education in America.

The greatest of colonial scientists and inventors, Benjamin Franklin, gained worldwide fame with his kite experiment (1752) which demonstrated that lightning and electricity were one and the same. Showing their respect for experimental science, Harvard, Yale, and William and Mary honored themselves by honoring Franklin as a Master of Arts. The University of St. Andrews in Scotland and Oxford University in England conferred doctoral degrees upon him. Thereafter he took satisfaction in being known as "Dr. Franklin." He interested himself in countless subjects besides electricity, and he was a theoretical or "philosophical" scientist as well as a practical one. He also was a promoter of science. In 1727 he and his Philadelphia friends organized the Junto, a club for the discussion of intellectual and practical matters of mutual interest. In 1744 he led in the founding of the American Philosophical Society, the first learned society in America.

Not only a scientist, philosopher, and inventor, but also a craftsman, public-spirited citizen, humanitarian, essayist, and later a statesman and diplomat, Franklin did more things superbly well than any other American of his time, or any time. Prudent yet daring and original, genial and witty yet serious in his devotion to the truth, he was as likable as he was admirable. In his pragmatism he typified the emerging American, or at least one prominent American, ideal. Other ideals were well represented by some of his notable contemporaries—Puritanism by Jonathan Edwards, mysticism by John Woolman, gentlemanliness by William Byrd. All these have left their traces on the American mind, but none so conspicuously as the attitude of Franklin. Hence he seems always "modern," timeless in his appeal.

Concepts of Law

As with social and intellectual life, the legal and political institutions inherited from England also were more or less modified in their transmission to the colonies. Changes in the law resulted in part from the scarcity of English-trained lawyers, who were almost unknown in America before 1700. Not till a generation after that did the authorities in England make a deliberate effort to impose the common law and the statutes of the realm upon the provinces. By that time the legal standards on this side of the ocean had become pretty well fixed, and a confusion of thirteen variant legal systems had come into being through lack of acquaintance or sympathy with English law, though all these systems embodied many of its essentials, including such ancient rights as trial by jury.

Pleading and court procedure were simplified in America, and punishments were made less severe. Instead of the gallows or the prison, the colonists more commonly resorted to the whipping post, the branding iron, the stocks, and the ducking stool (for gossipy women). Crimes were redefined. In England a printed attack on a public official, whether true or false, was considered libelous. In the colonies, at the trial (1734) of the New York publisher John Peter Zenger, who was powerfully defended by the Philadelphia lawyer Andrew Hamilton, it was held that criticisms of the government were not libels if factually true—a verdict which meant a long stride toward freedom of the press. Legal philosophy itself was changed as colonists came to think of law as a reflection of the divine will or the natural

order, not as an expression of the power of an earthly sovereign. Colonial lawyers, who became an influential class during the eighteenth century, were less closely attached to English tradition than the legal profession in the United States was afterward to be.

BIBLIOGRAPHY

The people of the colonies are viewed statistically in S. H. Sutherland, *Population Distribution in Colonial America* (1936), and in E. B. Greene and V. D. Harrington, *American Population before the Federal Census of 1790* (1932). Important studies of nationality groups coming to America include I. C. C. Graham, *Colonists from Scotland* (1956); F. Klees, *The Pennsylvania Dutch* (1950); A. H. Hirsch, *The Huguenots of Colonial South Carolina* (1928); H. J. Ford, *The Scotch-Irish in America* (1914); and A. B. Faust, *The German Element in the United States* (2 vols., 1909).

Authoritative treatments of labor in the colonies: R. B. Morris, *Government and Labor in Early America* (1946); M. W. Jernegan, *Laboring and Dependent Classes in Colonial America, 1607–1783* (1932); C. A. Herrick, White Servitude in Pennsylvania (1926); S. McKee, *Labor in Colonial New York, 1664–1776* (1935); U. B. Phillips, *American Negro Slavery* (1918); J. C. Ballagh, *A History of Slavery in Virginia* (1902); and L. J. Greene, *The Negro in Colonial New England* (1942).

Manufactures are treated by Carl Bridenbaugh, *The Colonial Craftsman* (1950); R. M. Tryon, *Household Manufactures in the United States, 1640–1880* (1917); A. C. Bining, *British Regulation of the Colonial Iron Industry* (1933) and *Pennsylvania Iron Manufacture in the Eighteenth Century* (1938); K. Bruce, *Virginia Iron Manufacture in the Slave Era* (1931); and E. N. Hartley, *Ironworks on the Saugus* (1957). A good introduction to colonial farming is L. Carrier, *The Beginnings of Agriculture in America* (1923). Other industries are described in R. McFarland, *A History of the New England Fisheries* (1911), and by R. G. Albion, *Forests and Sea Power* (1926).

On commerce, see L. H. Harper, *The English Navigation Laws* (1939); Bernard Bailyn, *The New England Merchants in the Seventeenth Century* (1955); F. B. Tolles, *Meeting House and Counting House* (1948), on Philadelphia Quaker merchants; C. P. Nettels, *Money Supply of the American Colonies before 1720* (1924); and K. Scott, *Counterfeiting in Colonial America* (1957).

Colonial civilization as a whole is ably discussed in D. J. Boorstin, *The Americans: The Colonial Experience* (1958), and in L. B. Wright, *The Cultural Life of the American Colonies, 1607–1763* (1957). Cultural relations between colonies and homeland are revealed in L. B. Wright, *The Atlantic Frontier: Colonial American Civilization* (1947); M. Kraus, *The Atlantic Civilization* (1949); and W. L. Sachse, *The Colonial American in Britain* (1956). A brief, introductory survey is C. M. Andrews, *Colonial Folkways* (1919).

Carl Bridenbaugh has contributed a great deal to our understanding of colonial society, culture, and politics in *Cities in the Wilderness: The First Century of Urban Life in America, 1625–1742* (1938); *Seat of Empire: The Political Role of Eighteenth Century Williamsburg* (1950); *Myths and Realities: Societies of the Colonial South* (1952); and (with Jessica Bridenbaugh) *Rebels and Gentlemen: Philadelphia in the Age of Franklin* (1942).

W. W. Sweet, *Religion in Colonial America* (1942), summarizes the subject. See also Perry Miller, *The New England Mind: The Seventeenth Century* (1939), and *The New England Mind: from Colony to Province* (1953); M. L. Starkey, *The Devil in Massachusetts* (1949), on the witchcraft craze; E. C. Gaustad, *The Great Awakening in New England* (1957); O. E.

Winslow, *Jonathan Edwards, 1703–1758* (1940); Janet Whitney, *John Woolman, American Quaker* (1942); and David de Sola Pool, *Portraits Etched in Stone: Early Jewish Settlers, 1682–1831* (1952).

Aspects of science and learning are treated in Brook Hindle, *The Pursuit of Science in Revolutionary America, 1735–1789* (1956); O. T. Beall, Jr., and R. H. Shryock, *Cotton Mather, First Significant Figure in American Medicine* (1954); John Duffy, *Epidemics in Colonial America* (1953); and Paul Monroe, *The Founding of the American Public School System* (1949). The greatest colonial scientist is the subject of many biographies; the most thorough is Carl Van Doren, *Benjamin Franklin* (1938); a compact life is V. W. Crane, *Benjamin Franklin and a Rising People* (1954). On houses and public buildings, see Hugh Morrison, *Early American Architecture from the First Colonial Settlements to the National Period* (1952).

3

THE EMPIRE: SUCCESS
AND FAILURE

During the sixteenth and seventeenth centuries the English had to contend with the Spaniards and the Dutch for room in North America. In the eighteenth century, however, the greatest threat to English America came from the French. By their final defeat of France in 1763, England and the English colonies gave new and convincing evidence of their capacity to survive and grow in international competition. For the moment the British Empire, victorious and prosperous, seemed an imposing success. Yet it was about to prove a failure, at least so far as its ability to hold the thirteen mainland colonies was concerned.

The Old Colonial System

Until the end of the colonial wars with the French, the British government in its treatment of the colonies was guided, at least roughly, by the long-standing ideas of mercantilism. The mercantilist philosophy valued colonies primarily for their trade. Supposedly the home country would be benefited if English mer-

chants were given, so far as feasible, a monopoly of colonial commerce. To carry out this policy, Parliament from 1651 on passed a series of Navigation Acts and other laws decided to inhibit direct trading between the colonists and foreigners and to discourage the rise of colonial manufactures which might compete with those of England. For more than a century, however, the laws were not rigorously and consistently enforced. The British Empire remained a rather vague concept in theory and a rather loose organization in practice, though from time to time attempts were made to centralize and rationalize the administration of the colonies and to tighten the control of the home government over them.

As early as 1624 King James I took a step toward centralization when he deprived the Virginia Company of its powers of governance and himself assumed the management of Virginia as a royal province. Then the mid-seventeenth-century struggle between Kings and Parliament, culminating in civil war, checked the development of a systematic royal administration of the colonies. Left to themselves, they took advantage of the turmoil in England by flouting the kingly prerogatives. Massachusetts even went so far as to exercise the sovereign power of coining its own money, the pinetree shilling. After the Restoration in England, Charles II was slow to discipline this worst offender, Massachusetts, even though an investigation showed a good deal of smuggling and a rather independent spirit there. Finally, in 1684, the King acted with determination, revoking the charter which had made Massachusetts a corporate, virtually self-governing colony.

Charles II did not intend to stop with that. Both he and his brother and successor James II admired the absolutist ways of Louis XIV, who in Canada had but one colony, which he ruled directly through his appointed officials, without having to contend with an elected assembly. Taking the Dominion of Canada as his model, James II set up a Dominion of New England which eventually included also New Jersey and New York. Over all these colonies, their legislatures having been abolished, ruled a single royal governor, the stern and unpopular Sir Edmund Andros. When James II was deposed in the English Revolution of 1689 the Andros regime collapsed, amid mob demonstrations in New England and Leisler's Rebellion in New York. So ended the first attempt at colonial unification from above.

But the trend toward increasing royal control of the colonies was resumed, though it did not go as far as some English officials desired. Despite the lobbying of Increase Mather and the protests of the Puritans, Massachusetts was not given back its old corporate charter but was made a royal colony (1691). So also were New York (1685), New Jersey (1702), the Carolinas (1719–29), and Georgia (1752). Only Pennsylvania-Delaware and Maryland continued as proprietary colonies, and only Connecticut and Rhode Is-

land as corporate ones. Some of the English experts in colonial affairs wished to see these colonies brought directly under the King's control like the others and a governor-general put in charge of all thirteen, with a deputy governor responsible to him in each one. But Parliament could not be persuaded to approve such a plan.

Though the colonies continued to be governed in the King's name, Parliament asserted its supremacy in colonial as well as domestic and foreign affairs after the Glorious Revolution of 1689. Theoretically Parliament represented the interests of the whole kingdom and indeed the whole empire. Actually it represented best the interests of the great merchants in England. Most of them objected to any ambitious scheme for imperial reorganization that would require large expenditures, increase taxes, and diminish the profit of the colonial trade. During the reigns of George I (1714–27) and George II (1727–60), both of whom were German-born, the real executive in England came to be the prime minister and his fellow cabinet ministers, who held their places not by the King's favor but by their ability to control a majority in Parliament. The first of the prime ministers, Robert Walpole, believed that a relaxation of trade restrictions against the colonies would enable them to buy more English goods and would thus benefit England and its merchants. Under Walpole was begun a policy of "salutary neglect" that was followed until after the outbreak of the French and Indian War.

Meanwhile the day-to-day administration of colonial affairs remained decentralized and inefficient. There was in England no separate and full-fledged colonial office. The officials of the various departments—treasury, admiralty, and so forth—had the responsibility of administering the laws overseas as well as at home. Among the departments there was much overlapping and confusion of authority, and within them there were few men or none who had visited America and obtained first-hand knowledge of American affairs. To provide information about colonial conditions and opinions, the assemblies in the colonies sent to London their own agents or lobbyists, among them Benjamin Franklin, who represented not only Pennsylvania but also Georgia, New Jersey, and Massachusetts. To coordinate the colonial business of the different government agencies in England was the function of two bodies, the Privy Council and the Board of Trade. Both were, however, essentially advisory groups with little power to take decisive action.

The conflicts of administrative authority in London, together with the deliberate ministerial policy of "salutary neglect," weakened the hold of England upon the colonies, and so did the character of the officials who were sent to America. These included the officials placed in charge of each royal colony—governor, councillors, secretary, attorney general, receiver general, surveyor general, supreme court justices—and the agents of the London administrative departments, such as collectors of customs and naval officers, who were located in all the colonies. Some of these officeholders were able and devoted men, but the majority were not. There being no merit system, appointments often were made on the basis of bribery or favoritism rather than ability or integrity. Many an appointee remained in England and, with part of his salary, hired another man to take his place in America. Such a deputy, poorly paid as he was, found it hard to resist opportunities to augment his income with bribes. For example, a customs collector seldom hesitated, for a fee smaller than the duty itself, to pass the goods of a smuggling colonial merchant. Even honest and well-paid officials, desiring to get along with the people among whom they had to live, usually found it expedient to yield to popular resistance in the colonies. This resistance to imperial authority centered in the colonial assemblies. By

1700 they had established the right to levy taxes, make appropriations, and pass laws for their respective colonies. Their legislation was subject to veto by the governor and to disallowance by the Privy Council, but they could force the governor to approve laws by withholding his salary and they could get around the Privy Council by repassing disallowed laws in slightly altered form. The assemblies came to look upon themselves as little parliaments, each practically as sovereign within its colony as Parliament itself was in England.

Toward Self-Government

The colonial charters had provided a basis for certain rights of self-government in America. These charters, while affirming the King's sovereignty, conferred governing powers upon colonial promoters (companies and proprietors) and guaranteed to settlers the liberties of English subjects. Eventually there developed thirteen representative assemblies.

The first appeared in Virginia, in 1619. Previously the stockholders of the Virginia Company, residing in England, had chosen officials and made laws for the colony. Then, with the rise of a class of well-to-do Virginia landholders, these men were allowed to elect their own representatives, who met at Jamestown in what was known as the House of Burgesses.

In the case of Massachusetts, as in that of Virginia, the powers of government were at first confined to the stockholders, or "freemen." These freemen, however, lived in the colony itself after the transfer (1629) of the Massachusetts Bay Company's headquarters from old to New England. Once a year they met in an assembly called the General Court, where they approved the laws by which the colony was to be governed. The rest of the settlers, those who owned none of the company's stock, demanded political rights, and Governor Winthrop finally agreed to increase the number of freemen. From 1634 on, the freemen having become too numerous and too widely scattered to attend personally to lawmaking, they sent representatives to the General Court, two or three from each town.

In all the colonies—royal, proprietary, and corporate—the colonial governments took the same general pattern. In each colony there was a governor and a two-house legislature, as in England there was a King and a two-house Parliament, though this rough similarity did not result from deliberate imitation. In England the title of "governor" originally was given to the executive head of a business corporation, and in America it came to have political significance when trading companies were transformed into political communities. The governor was appointed by the King in the royal colonies and by the proprietor in the proprietary colonies, and he was elected by the people in the corporate colonies. A governor's council, its members chosen in the same way as the governor (except in Massachusetts, where they were elected by the General Court), served as the upper chamber of the legislature. The lower house consisted of elected members. Executive, legislative, and judicial powers were somewhat mixed, for the governor and his council sat as the supreme court. Nevertheless, there was a separation of powers between the governor and the elected assembly, and the colonists took for granted the principle of separation which ultimately was to be embodied in the Federal Constitution. The very idea of a written constitution seemed natural to them because of their familiarity with colonial characters.

The colonial governments, as they had evolved by 1700, were not entirely democratic even with regard to the elected assemblies. The right to vote was limited by religious qualifications in some places and by property qualifications everywhere, the size of the property requirement varying from one colony to another.

On the whole, since ownership of real estate was widely diffused, the electorate was fairly broad, considerably broader than in England. In Massachusetts and other New England colonies the great majority of adult males had the franchise, though they did not always bother to exercise it. In Virginia and other Southern colonies there was a much smaller proportion of voters, and the assemblies were more oligarchic than democratic. By law, an assemblyman had to own more property than a mere voter, and by custom (already in force by 1700) he had to reside in the district he represented. So arose the peculiarly American idea of geographical representation, as in the United States Congress, which is quite different from the British Parliament, whose members have always been allowed to represent any constituency in the country, no matter which one they might happen to live in.

Political parties, as they developed in England during the eighteenth century, did not arise in the colonies, yet there was "politics" in the sense of struggles for office and for control of government. The assemblies, conceiving of themselves as little parliaments, persistently contended against the governors, not only in the royal colonies, where the governors were agents of the King, but even in the corporate colonies, where the governors were elected.

On several occasions political conflict led to violence. In some cases relatively democratic elements, identified with the frontier, aligned themselves against the governing cliques of the seaboard, but there is no single pattern that fits all the colonial rebellions. In Virginia the frontier followers of Nathaniel Bacon, exasperated at the government's neglect of Indian defenses, in 1676 marched on Jamestown and defeated the troops of Governor William Berkeley. After Bacon died of fever, his rebellion came to a sudden end, and Berkeley took a bloody revenge, seeing to the execution of thirty-seven of the leading rebels. "That old fool has hanged more men in that naked country," remarked Charles II, "than I have done for the murder of my father." In New York, at the time of the bloodless revolution of 1688–9 in England, Jacob Leisler led an uprising against the Stuart regime. With the backing of the common people, Leisler proclaimed himself lieu-

was averted only by concessions from the government.

Such strife was a disruptive force within the colonies, but other factors offset it and made for intercolonial unity. The growth of population, producing an almost continuous line of settlement along the seacoast, brought the people of the various colonies into closer and closer

---

ADVANTAGES OF THE FRENCH THREAT

1748–1749

Peter Kalm, a university professor in Swedish Finland, toured some of the English colonies during 1748–1749. He concluded:

"It is . . . of great advantage to the crown of England that the North American colonies are near a country under the government of the French, like Canada. . . . For the English colonies in this part of the world have increased so much in their number of inhabitants, and in their riches, that they almost vie with Old England. Now in order to keep up the authority and trade of their mother country, and to answer several other purposes, they are forbidden to establish new manufactures which would turn to the disadvantage of the British commerce: they are not allowed to dig for any gold or silver, unless they send them to England immediately: they have not the liberty of trading to any parts that do not belong to the British dominions, excepting some settled places, and foreign traders are not allowed to send their ships to them. These and some other restrictions occasion the inhabitants of the English colonies to grow less tender for their mother country. . . .

"I have been told by Englishmen . . . that the English colonies in North America, in the space of thirty or fifty years, would be able to form a state by themselves, entirely independent of Old England. But as the whole country which lies along the sea-shore is unguarded, and on the land side is harassed by the French, in times of war these dangerous neighbors are sufficient to prevent the connection of the colonies with their mother country from being quite broken off. The English government has therefore sufficient reason to consider the French in North America as the best means of keeping their colonies in due submission."

---

tenant-governor, but his enemies among the colonial ruling classes put down his revolt and had him hanged. In Pennsylvania a band of frontiersmen know as the Paxton Boys descended on Philadelphia in 1763 to demand defense money and changes in the tax laws, and bloodshed

contact, as did the gradual construction of roads, the rise of intercolonial trade, and the improvement of the colonial post office. In 1691 the postal service operated only between Massachusetts and New York and Pennsylvania; in 1711 it was extended to New Hampshire on the north, in 1732 to Virginia on the south, and ultimately all the way to Georgia. After 1753 Franklin as deputy postmaster improved the service, providing weekly instead of biweekly posts and speeding them up so that, for example, mail was delivered from Boston to Philadelphia in about three weeks instead of six. Post riders carried newspapers as well as letters and thus enlarged and unified the colonial reading public. Still another influence toward cohesion among the

Powhatan's brother and successor, Opechancanough, broke the peace (1622) with a massacre of more than three hundred and fifty unsuspecting Virginians. Thereafter, Indian wars were endemic along most of the frontier, and they were especially bitter and wasting in New England.

With a few exceptions like Roger Williams and John Eliot, a saintly missionary who translated the Bible into the Indian language, the Puritans viewed the red-

---

THE NEW ENGLAND CONFEDERATION

1643

"The said United Colonies [Massachusetts, Plymouth, Connecticut, and New Haven] for themselves and their posterities do jointly and severally hereby enter into a firm and perpetual league of friendship and amity for offence and defence, mutual advice and succor upon all just occasions both for preserving and propagating the truth and liberties of the Gospel and for their own mutual safety and welfare."

The United Colonies further agreed:

1. To provide men and provisions and to share in all costs in proportion to their abilities.

2. To send immediate aid to any of their confederates that might be invaded or in danger.

3. To appoint two commissioners apiece for managing the affairs of the confederation.

4. To begin no war, and to involve the confederation in no war, without the consent of at least six of the eight commissioners.

---

colonists was the presence in the neighboring wilderness of dreaded enemies, the French and their Indian allies.

On the whole the Indians had been well disposed toward the first English arrivals. In early Plymouth the Pilgrims discovered friends—Squanto, Samoset, Massasoit—who showed them how to gather seafood and cultivate corn, and thus enabled them to survive. When Jamestown was new, a truce was cemented by the marriage of John Rolfe with Chief Powhatan's daughter Pocahontas. But

men as "pernicious creatures" who deserved extermination unless they would be willing to adopt the white man's ways. In 1637 the exasperated Pequots went on the warpath in the Connecticut Valley. The Connecticut frontiersmen marched against a palisaded Pequot stronghold and set it afire. About five hundred of the Pequots were burned to death or killed when trying to escape, and most of the survivors were hunted down, captured, and sold as slaves. The Pequot tribe was wiped out.

The New England colonies faced danger not only from the Indians but also from the Dutch, who claimed the territory on which some of the outlying settlements were made. The colonies could not expect help from England at the time when the mother country was distracted by the civil war between Cavaliers and Roundheads. To provide frontier protec-

pired to annex them and objected to recognizing them as equals.

By 1675, when King Philip's War began, the New England Confederation had deteriorated so much that it could no longer be relied upon for organizing frontier defense. King Philip and the Wampanoags, with their Indian allies, destroyed or depopulated twenty towns

---

THE ALBANY PLAN

1754

At the call of the British government, delegates from seven colonies met in Albany, New York, to consider ways of dealing with the perennial Indian danger. War with France was about to break out. Benjamin Franklin was interested in the overall problem of colonial unity and defense, and with the aid of other delegates he devised a plan for intercolonial government. This plan was not approved by the colonial assemblies, for they did not wish to give up any of their own powers, and so it never went into effect. But the plan is evidence of the serious thought that, even before the Revolution, some colonial leaders gave to the question of American federation. The main provisions were as follows:

1. Parliament was to set up "one general government" in America, including all the thirteen colonies, each of which was to "retain its present constitution" except for the powers to be given to the general government.

2. The King was to appoint a President-General for the general government, and the colonial assemblies were to elect representatives to a Grand Council.

3. The President-General, with the advice of the Grand Council, was to have the following powers: (a) to handle Indian relations, making treaties and deciding upon peace or war; (b) to raise troops, build forts, and provide warships; (c) to make such laws and levy such taxes as would be necessary for the foregoing purposes.

---

tion, to adjust boundary disputes among themselves, and to further their mutual interests in other ways, four of the colonies joined (1643) in "The Confederation of the United Colonies of New England." These four were Massachusetts, Plymouth, Connecticut, and New Haven. The other settlements—those of Rhode Island, New Hampshire, and Maine—were excluded, since Massachusetts as-

and caused the deaths of a sixteenth of the white male population in three years of gloom and terror for New England.

Thereafter, in the more serious conflicts between English colonists and the Indians, the latter had the instigation and support of a European power—France (and at times also Spain). The ever-present danger gave the various colonies a sense of belonging together and of needing one another as well as the mother country. As late as 1754, however, the colonists had not yet acquired a feeling of common destiny strong enough to prepare them for a general intercolonial government. In that year delegates from Pennsylvania, Maryland, New York, and the New England colonies, meeting in Albany to negotiate a peace with the Iroquois, remained to discuss colonial federation. War with the French was imminent. Benjamin Franklin proposed to his fellow delegates a plan for coöperation among the colonies to provide for the common defense. But this Albany Plan could not get the approval of the provincial assemblies. They were not to be ready for united action on a permanent basis until after the climactic struggle with the Indians and the French.

JOIN, or DIE.

THE NEED FOR COLONIAL UNITY. Probably the first American editorial cartoon, this sketch appeared in Benjamin Franklin's newspaper, the *Pennsylvania Gazette* of Philadelphia, for May 9, 1754. The cartoon was intended to illustrate the need for colonial unity and, in particular, for the adoption of Franklin's Albany Plan.

The French in America

The French founded their first permanent settlement in America at Quebec in 1608, less than a year after the English had started their first at Jamestown. The earliest pioneers of New France, unprepared for the terrors of the Canadian winter, suffered losses comparable to those of the Virginians during the starving time. The founder of Quebec, Samuel de Champlain, one of a series of truly heroic French agents of empire, aimed to establish a base for finding a waterway to the Orient, carrying on the fur trade, and converting the natives to Christianity. He made a beginning, but for many years New France grew in population very slowly. Few Roman Catholics felt any inclination to leave their beloved homeland, *la belle France*, and the discontented Protestants who desired to emigrate were excluded from the colony.

The French greatly extended their sway in America after the Grand Monarch, Louis XIV, took the government into his own hands (1661) and, with a program of centralization at home and

expansion abroad, proceeded to live up to his supposed remark, "I am the state." His finance minister and economic planner, Jean Colbert, conceived of an integrated empire consisting of four parts: France itself as the center and the source of capital and manufactured goods; her West Indian islands (especially Martinique and Guadeloupe) as suppliers of sugar and other exotic products; posts along the African coast as aids in carrying on the slave trade; and the settlements in Canada as a market for exports from France and a granary for provisioning the West Indies. The colonies were to be governed directly from Paris, pretty much as if they were local subdivisions of France itself. New France was to have a governor, an intendant, and a bishop, each to be appointed by the King and each to serve as a check upon the other two. In practice this arrangement led to jealousies and cross-purposes which often frustrated the colonial administration—except when some individual official in America had the character and will to assert his preeminence. Such a man was Jean Talon, the first of the intendants, and even more outstanding was Count Frontenac, the greatest of the governors (1672-98).

Though Colbert intended to make

Canada a compactly settled agricultural province, the aspirations of Talon and Frontenac for the glory of France caused them to expand New France beyond Colbert's limits, and other forces also tended to disperse the colonial population. The lure of the forest and its furs drew immigrant peasants into the wilderness, where they often married Indian squaws and adopted tribal ways. Another group, the Jesuits, were impelled onward by their missionary zeal in the search for savage souls to save. And the bottom lands of the Mississippi attracted farmers dis-

couraged by the short growing season in Canada.

The nature of the Illinois country had been made known by adventuresome explorers. In 1673 Louis Joliet and Father Marquette journeyed together by canoe from Green Bay along the Fox, Wisconsin, and Mississippi rivers as far as the mouth of the Arkansas, then returned with assurance that the Mississippi empties into the Gulf of Mexico, not the Gulf of California as previously thought. The next year René Robert Cavelier, Sieur de la Salle, a supremely romantic and at the

CHAMPLAIN FIGHTS THE IROQUOIS. Samuel de Champlain—a veteran of the French army and navy, a friend of King Henry IV, and a hardy navigator and explorer—is considered the founder of New France. In 1603 Champlain set out upon the first of several explorations of the New World. In 1608 he led the expedition which founded the settlement at Quebec. In 1609 he discovered the lake that is named for him. At Lake Champlain he met a band of Iroquois; some of his men fired, and the terrified Indians fled. Thus began a historic enmity between the Iroquois and the French. While the French were allied with the Hurons and other enemies of the Iroquois, the Dutch and later the English in New York cultivated Iroquois friendship and trade. After 1700 the Iroquois adopted a policy of neutrality as between the English and the French. The loss of the traditional Iroquois tie was a handicap to the English in the French and Indian War. The sketch of the first encounter with the Iroquois was made by Champlain himself and was published in his book about his voyages (1613).

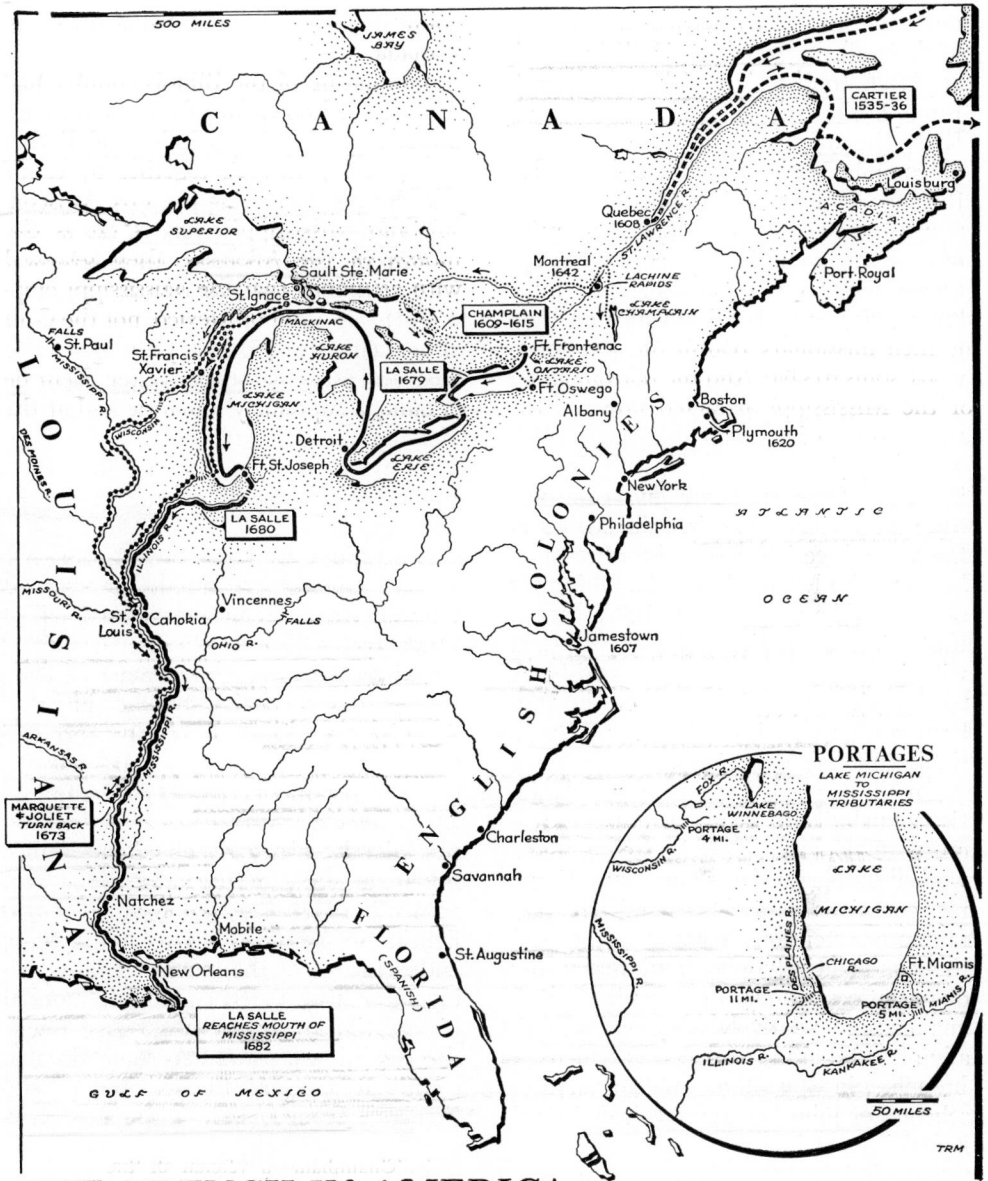

THE FRENCH IN AMERICA : EXPLORATIONS & SETTLEMENTS

same time a shrewdly practical man, began the explorations which finally, in 1682, took him to the delta of the Mississippi, where he took possession of the surrounding country for the King of France, naming it Louisiana in the King's honor. Eventually Frenchmen revealed the outlines of the whole continental interior and marked its boundaries with the cross and the *fleur de lis*.

To secure their hold upon the territory thus staked out, they founded a string of widely separated communities, strategically located fortresses, and far-flung missions and trading posts. On Cape Breton Island they established Fort Louisbourg, one of the most redoubtable strongholds in all the New World, to guard the approach to the Gulf of St. Lawrence. From both banks of the St. Lawrence River the strips of land ("seigneuries") of would-be feudal lords stretched away to the edge of the clearings. On a high bluff above the river stood Quebec, the pride of the French empire in America. Farther up the river was Montreal, even more "provincial" and less sophisticated than Quebec. Hundreds of miles to the northwest, near the juncture of Lake Superior with Lakes Michigan and Huron, was the tiny outpost of Sault Sainte Marie. Hundreds of miles to the southwest, at the juncture of Lakes Huron and Erie, was the well-fortified Detroit. Still farther in the same direction, along the Mississippi between the Missouri and the Ohio, was a cluster of hamlets—Cahokia, Kaskaskia, Fort Chartres, Sainte Genevieve—each with its outlying common-fields of black earth under cultivation. Over on the Wabash was the fifth tiny settlement of the Illinois country, Vincennes.

On the lower Mississippi were plantations much like those in the Southern colonies of English America, plantations worked by Negro slaves and supporting a race-conscious class of "creoles," who had far more pretensions to grandeur than did the comparatively poor and necessarily democratic seigneurs of Canada. Louisiana became relatively populous, especially after thousands of settlers had been brought in by the land-speculation schemes of John Law, whose "Mississippi Bubble" burst in 1721, to the ruin of investors in Europe and the disillusionment of recently arrived Louisianans. Founded in 1718, New Orleans soon grew into a city comparable in size with some of those on the Atlantic seaboard but quainter than most, with its houses built of cypress logs and bark roofs and set upon stilts above the swampy ground. To the east of New Orleans, along the Gulf of Mexico, were the towns of Biloxi (founded 1699) and Mobile, completing the string of mainland settlements which stretched all the way around from Fort Louisbourg.

The Great War for the Empire

Spacious though it was, the continent of North America seemed too small to contain both the English and the French. The English, as Protestants, and the French, as Roman Catholics, eyed each other with suspicion and fear. As fishermen and fur traders they competed for the profits of the forest and the sea. Each national group began ultimately to feel that its very survival in America depended upon the elimination of the other's influence.

No serious warfare between the two sets of colonists occurred, however, so long as their homelands remained at peace. In the Treaty of Whitehall (1686) the kings of England and France pledged themselves to refrain from hostilities in America even if ("which God forbid") they should find themselves at war with one another in Europe. This attempt to keep America out of Europe's wars soon proved a dead letter. England and France fought a series of three wars (1689–97, 1701–13, 1744–8), each of which led to fighting in America. The second of these ended in one of the great and far-reaching international settlements of modern history, the Treaty of Utrecht. At Utrecht the English were awarded some sizeable territorial gains at the expense of the French: Acadia (Nova Scotia), Newfoundland, and the shores of Hudson's Bay. In the third of the wars New Englanders captured the French bastion at Louisbourg, but to their bitter disappointment they had to abandon it in accordance with the peace arrangement, which provided for the mutual restoration of conquered territory.

This war and the two preceding it had arisen from European causes primarily, and only a small fraction of the people in the English colonies had taken any part.

To the colonists these were foreign wars —King William's, Queen Anne's, King George's—rather than their own. But the next conflict was different. Known to the colonists as the French and Indian War, it recently has been renamed the "Great War for the Empire," which in fact it was. Unlike the preliminaries, this climactic struggle originated in the interior of North America.

country across the Alleghenies as a profitable field for their operations, and the British government, aroused to the defense of its territorial rights, gave instructions to the colonial governors to resist French encroachments. Acting on these instructions, the governor of Virginia sent George Washington, then only twenty-one, to protest to the commanders of the French forts newly built be-

---

THE FRENCH CLAIM THE OHIO

1751

The French government sent the following instructions to its officials in New France:

"The River Ohio, otherwise called the Beautiful River, and its tributaries belong indisputably to France, by virtue of its discovery by Sieur de La Salle; of the trading posts the French have had there since, and of possession which is so much the more unquestionable as it constitutes the most frequent communication from Canada to Louisiana. It is only within a few years that the English have undertaken to trade there; and now they pretend to exclude us from it.

"They have not, up to the present time, however, maintained that these rivers belong to them; they pretend only that the Iroquois are masters of them, and being the sovereigns of these Indians, that they can exercise their rights. But 'tis certain that these Indians have none, and that, besides, the pretended sovereignty of the English over them is a chimera.

"Meanwhile 'tis of the greatest importance to arrest the progress of the pretensions and expeditions of the English in that quarter. Should they succeed there, they would cut off the communication between the two colonies of Canada and Louisiana, and would be in a position to trouble them, and to ruin both the one and the other, independent of the advantages they would at once experience in their trade to the prejudice of ours."

Within the American wilderness a number of border disputes arose, but the most serious of them concerned the ownership of the Ohio Valley. The French, desiring to control this direct route between Canada and Louisiana, began to build a chain of fortifications to make good their claim. Pennsylvania fur traders and Virginia land speculators, the latter organized as the Ohio Company, looked to the

tween Lake Erie and the Allegheny River, but these commanders politely replied that the land was French. While Washington was on his fruitless mission, a band of Virginians tried to forestall the French by erecting a fort of their own at the strategic key to the Ohio Valley—the forks of the Ohio, where the Allegheny and Monongahela rivers join. A stronger band of Canadians drove the Virginians

START OF THE **FRENCH & INDIAN WAR**

the ways of European warfare but unused to the American woods, Braddock wore out his men by having them cut a long military road through the forest toward Fort Duquesne, and he exposed them to attack from the tree-hidden enemy by marching them in the accepted European formation. Seven miles from the fort (July 9, 1755) he ran into a French and Indian ambush; he himself and large numbers of his men were killed, and the survivors fled all the way back to Fort Cumberland in Maryland. The frontier from Pennsylvania to Virginia was left exposed to Indian raids, and many frontier settlers withdrew to the east of the Allegheny Mountains.

After about two years of fighting in America, the governments of France and England finally declared hostilities, and a world war (known in Europe as the Seven Year's War, 1756–63) began. France and England now changed partners, France allying herself with her former enemy, Austria, and England joining France's former ally, Prussia. Henceforth battles were fought not only on the American mainland but also in the West Indies, in Europe, and around the world in India.

In this global contest the British had the advantage of the mightiest navy on the seas and, with Frederick the Great on their side, the finest army in Europe. In America the people of the English colonies outnumbered those of the French colonies by approximately 15 to 1, but were by no means that much stronger militarily. The French had numerous and powerful Indian allies, many of them newly attracted to the French by the latter's early victories in the war. The English had few such allies; the Iroquois, traditionally friendly to the English and hostile to the French, now remained firmly neutral. Furthermore, the French government kept its colonists in a fairly good state of military discipline and readiness, and could count upon the loyal services of a high proportion of its colonial

away, completed the work, and named it Fort Duquesne. Arriving with the advance guard of a relief force from Virginia, Washington met a French detachment in a brief but bloody skirmish, then fell back to a hastily constructed stockade, Fort Necessity, where he was overwhelmed by troops from Fort Duquesne and compelled to surrender (July 4, 1754). The first shots of the French and Indian War had been fired.

For the English colonists, the war had begun inauspiciously, and it continued to go badly for them during the next few years. They received aid from the home government, but this aid was inefficiently and unintelligently applied. The British fleet failed to prevent the landing of large French reinforcements in Canada, and the newly appointed commander-in-chief of the British army in America, General Edward Braddock, failed to retake the forks of the Ohio. Brave but aged, wise in

THE TAKING OF QUEBEC. In 1759 the capture of Quebec was the main objective of the British campaign in America. General James Wolfe, only thirty-two, commanded an army that proceeded up the St. Lawrence River on navy transports. General Jeffrey Amherst, commander in chief of the British armies in America, was to take forts Crown Point and Ticonderoga, then join Wolfe before Quebec. Amherst was delayed, and Wolfe decided to go ahead alone, though his army was smaller than that of the French at Quebec, under the Marquis de Montcalm. The Quebec defenses were too strong for a direct attack from the river. After a few months' siege, Wolfe daringly landed his troops above the town, led them up an insufficiently guarded ravine, and reached the heights known as the Plains of Abraham. Now the cautious Montcalm had no choice but to fight. He attacked without waiting to assemble all his available forces, and in about fifteen minutes he was compelled to retreat. The contemporary English engraving portrays in the one scene a whole succession of events—the landings, the climb up the ravine, and the battle itself. (LIBRARY OF CONGRESS)

manpower. The British government, on the other hand, exercised much less control over its thirteen colonies, which often acted as if they were autonomous. Only where and when they were exposed to immediate danger did the English colonists wholeheartedly support the war effort.

At first the overall direction of British strategy was weak. Then (1757) William Pitt as Prime Minister was allowed to act as practically a wartime dictator of the empire (much as Winston Churchill was in 1940 and after). Pitt reformed the army and the navy, replacing bureaucratic deadwood with young and eager officers. He gave generous subsidies to Frederick the Great, who thus was enabled to keep the French fairly busy in Europe. And he turned from the defensive to the offensive in America, with a determination to drive the French out of the continent.

With Pitt as organizer, the British regu-

NORTH AMERICA IN 1700

NORTH AMERICA AFTER 1713

lars in America, together with colonial troops, proceeded to take one French stronghold after another, including Fort Duquesne in 1758. The next year, after a siege of Quebec, supposedly impregnable atop its towering cliff, the army of General James Wolfe struggled up a hidden ravine, surprised the larger forces of the Marquis de Montcalm, and defeated them in a battle in which both commanders were slain. The fall of Quebec marked the climax of the American phase of the war, and the decisive battle was afterward remembered as a romantic and tragic encounter between two highminded and able men.

Some other phases of the war were less romantic, less high-minded. In the course of it the British resorted to such expedients as population dispersal. Fearing trouble from the French inhabitants of Nova Scotia, the British uprooted several thousand of them and scattered them throughout the English colonies; some of these Acadians eventually made their way to Louisiana, where they became the ancestors of the present-day Cajuns. Meanwhile the French and their savage allies were committing worse atrocities, and hundreds of defenseless families

NORTH AMERICA AFTER 1763

along the English frontier fell before the hatchet and the scalping knife.

Peace finally came after the accession of the peace-minded George III and the resignation of Pitt, who disagreed with the new King and wished to continue hostilities. Yet Pitt's aims were pretty well realized in the treaty signed at Paris in 1763. By its terms the French ceded to Great Britain some of their West Indian islands and all their colonies in India except two. The French also transferred Canada and all other French territory east of the Mississippi, except the island of New Orleans, to Great Britain, and New Orleans and the French claims west of the Mississippi to Spain. Thus the French gave up all their title to the mainland of North America.

The New Imperialism

So strong had grown the colonial feeling against direct legislation by Parliament that, during the French and Indian War, the English government did not attempt to tax or draft the colonists directly but called upon the assemblies to provide quotas of soldiers and supplies. This requisition system, itself a concession to provincial prejudice, heightened the self-importance of the assemblies, and most of them further asserted their autonomy by complying in a slow and niggardly way. Some of them, unwilling to be taxed by Parliament, also refused to tax themselves; they issued paper money instead.

In Virginia the legislature not only issued paper money but, when the resulting inflation raised the price of tobacco, also passed a law to deprive the Anglican clergy (who were paid in tobacco) of the benefits of the price rise. When this law was disallowed (1760), one of the ministers sued his vestrymen for his full pay. At the trial of the "parson's cause" the young lawyer Patrick Henry, defending the vestrymen, denounced the Privy Council for its tyranny and told his fellow Virginians to ignore its action. Roused by Henry's oratory, the jurors awarded the parson damages of only one penny. Thus did they defy the authority of the British government.

In Massachusetts the merchants disregarded the laws of the empire even more flagrantly than did the planters in Virginia. Throughout the war these merchants persisted in trading with the enemy in Canada and in the French West Indies. British officials resorted to general search warrants—"writs of assistance"—for discovering smuggled goods and stamping out the illegal and unpatriotic trade. As attorney for the Massachusetts merchants, James Otis maintained that these searches violated the ancient rights of Englishmen and that the law of Parliament authorizing the warrants was therefore null and void. With eloquence as stirring as Henry's, Otis insisted that Parliament had only a limited power of legislating for the colonies.

As the war ended, the London policy makers faced a dilemma, though they were not fully aware of it. On the one hand, they could revert to the old colonial system with its half-hearted enforcement of the mercantilist program, but that would mean virtual independence for the colonies. On the other hand, the men in London could renew their efforts to reform the empire and enforce the laws, but that would lead to revolt and absolute independence.

The thirteen mainland colonies were only a part of the British possessions scattered throughout the Americas and the world, and before 1763 they were not considered (except in their own eyes) as the most valuable part. Some of them, such as Virginia and Maryland with their tobacco production, fitted in fairly well with the aims of mercantilism, but on the whole the island colonies contributed a great deal more than those of the mainland to the profits of English merchants and the prosperity of the English homeland. The "sugar islands" in particular—Barbados and the Windward Islands, the Leeward Islands, Jamaica—yielded remarkable opportunities for the investment of English capital. They also complemented the economies of some of the mainland colonies by providing a market for the output of fisheries, farms, and forest industries.

Believing in a kind of commercial imperialism, most English merchants opposed the acquisition of territory for its own sake. But some Englishmen and Americans began to believe that land itself should be acquired for the empire because of the population the land would support, the taxes it would produce, and the sense of imperial greatness it would confer. Both William Pitt and Benjamin Franklin were among the advocates of this new territorial imperialism. Franklin wrote powerfully upon the future greatness of the British Empire in America, stressing the need for vast spaces to accommodate the rapid and limitless growth of the American people. Old-fashioned mercantilists, however, continued to think of trade as the essence of empire, and of island and coastal possessions as bases for trade. The issue came to a head with the peacemaking at the end of the French and Indian War. Commercial imperialists urged that Canada be returned to France in exchange for the most valuable of her sugar islands, Guadeloupe. Territorial imperialists, Franklin among them, argued in favor of keeping Canada. The decision to retain Canada marked a change in the emphasis of imperial policy.

With the acquisition of Canada and the other fruits of war in 1763, the area of the British Empire was more than doubled and the problems of governing it were made many times more complex. The war had left the British government with a staggering burden of debt, and English landlords and merchants objected violently to increased taxes. The rather halfhearted war effort of the colonists had shown the cumulative evils of "salutary neglect." And, by giving Great Britain undisputed title to the transmontane West as well as Canada, the peace had brought new problems of administration and defense. British statesmen feared that France, by no means crushed, might soon launch an attack somewhere in America for the recovery of her lost territories and prestige.

Responsibility for the solution of these postwar problems fell to the young monarch George III, who had come to the throne in 1760. Unlike his father and his grandfather, George III was thoroughly British and proud of it, and he was determined to follow the advice of his mother to be a King in fact as well as name. Shrewdly, he took care not to upset the recently developed constitutional practice according to which the party controlling Parliament made and unmade ministries. Instead, becoming a politician himself, the King created a party of his own through patronage and bribes and thus took control of Parliament away from the Whigs. Though not at all the ogre he was once pictured in American schoolbooks, George III achieved his aim of personal government and therefore deserves much of the credit or blame for the acts that followed.

More immediately responsible was George Grenville, whom the King made prime minister in 1763. Grenville, a brother-in-law of William Pitt, did not share Pitt's sympathy with the colonial point of view. He agreed with the prevailing British opinion that the colonists should be compelled to obey the laws and to pay a part of the cost of defending and administering the empire. He fancied himself something of an efficiency expert, and he was indeed an able administrator. Furthermore, as Chancellor of the Exchecquer and First Lord of the Treasury, he was well acquainted with matters of public finance. Promptly he undertook to impose system upon what had been a rather unsystematic aggregation of colonial possessions in America.

The Western problem was the most urgent. With the repulse of the French, frontiersmen from the English colonies had begun promptly to move over the mountains and into the upper Ohio Valley. Objecting to this intrusion, a federation of Indian tribes under the remarkable chieftain Pontiac raised the war cry. The British government issued, as an emergency measure, a proclamation for-

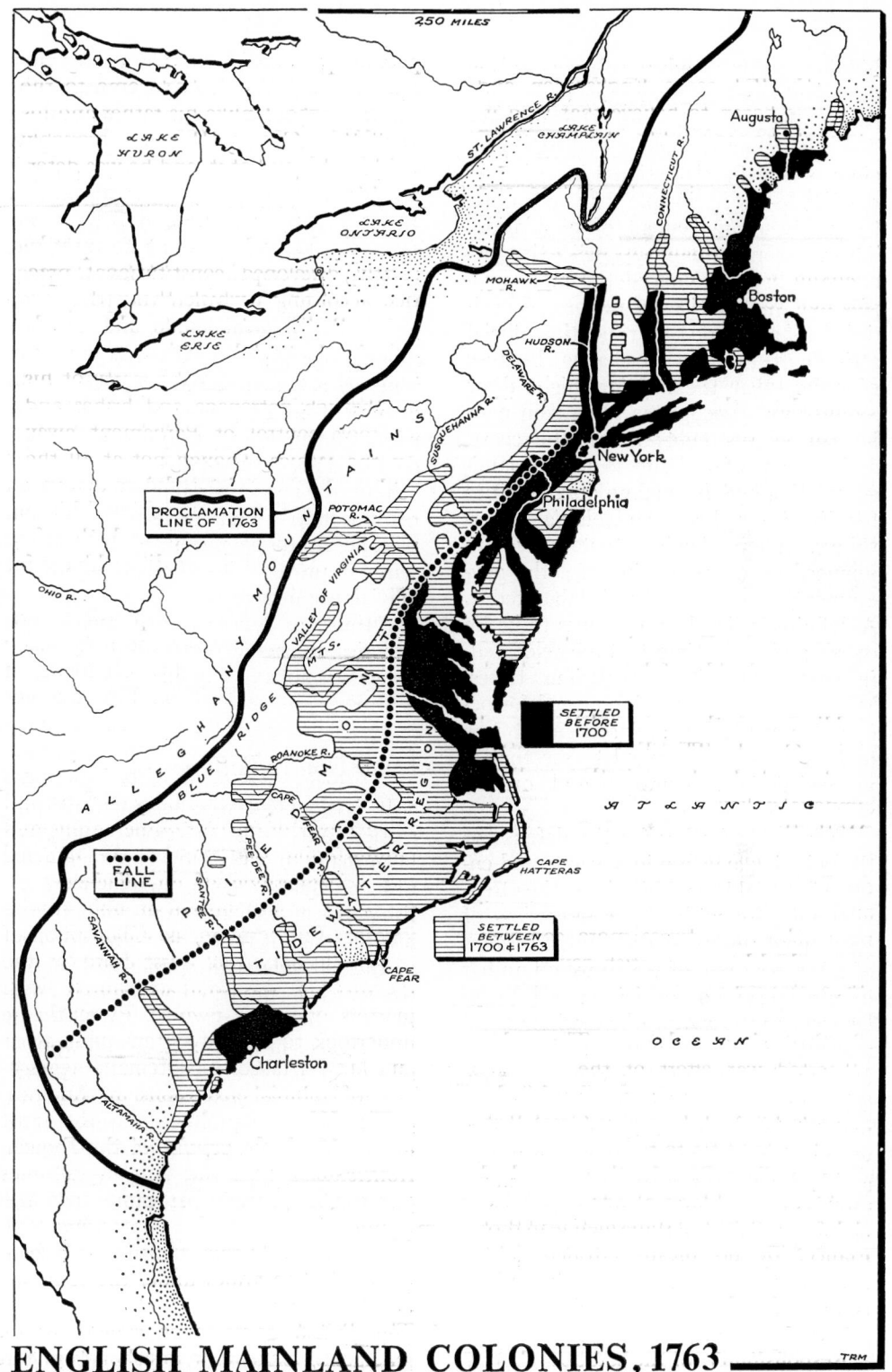

ENGLISH MAINLAND COLONIES, 1763

Map labels:

250 MILES

LAKE HURON

LAKE ONTARIO

LAKE ERIE

ST. LAWRENCE R.

LAKE CHAMPLAIN

CONNECTICUT R.

Augusta

MOHAWK R.

HUDSON R.

Boston

DELAWARE R.

SUSQUEHANNA R.

New York

PROCLAMATION LINE OF 1763

POTOMAC R.

Philadelphia

OHIO R.

ALLEGHANY MOUNTAINS

VALLEY OF VIRGINIA

BLUE RIDGE MTS.

SETTLED BEFORE 1700

ROANOKE R.

CAPE FEAR R.

PIEDMONT REGION

PEE DEE R.

SANTEE R.

ATLANTIC

CAPE HATTERAS

FALL LINE

SAVANNAH R.

TIDEWATER REGION

SETTLED BETWEEN 1700 & 1763

CAPE FEAR

ALTAMAHA R.

Charleston

OCEAN

TRM

bidding settlers to advance beyond a line drawn along the mountain divide between the Atlantic and the interior. Though the emergency passed, the principle of the Proclamation Line of 1763 remained—the principle of controlling the westward movement of population. This was something new. Earlier the government had encouraged the rapid peopling of the frontier for reasons of both defense and trade. In time the official attitude had begun to change, because of a fear that the interior might draw away so many people as to weaken markets and investments nearer the coast, and because of a desire to reserve land-speculating and fur-trading opportunities for English rather than colonial enterprisers. Then, having tentatively announced a new policy in 1763, the government soon extended and elaborated it. A definite Indian boundary was to be located, and from time to time relocated, in agreement with the various tribes. Western lands were to be opened for occupation gradually, and settlement was to be carefully supervised to see that it proceeded in a compact and orderly way.

To provide further for the defense of the colonies, and to raise revenue and enforce imperial law within them, the Grenville ministry with the cooperation of Parliament meanwhile instituted a series of measures some of which were familiar in principle and others fairly novel. Regular troops were now to be stationed permanently in the provinces, and (by the Mutiny Act, 1765) the colonists were called upon to assist in provisioning and maintaining the army. Ships of the navy were assigned to patrol American waters and look out for smugglers. The customs service was reorganized and enlarged, and vice-admiralty courts were set up in America to try accused smugglers without the benefit of sympathetic local juries. Royal officials were ordered to take up their colonial posts in person instead of sending substitutes. The Sugar Act (1764),

designed in part to eliminate the illegal trade between the continental colonies and the foreign West Indies, lowered the high molasses duty of the Molasses Act of 1733, but imposed new duties on a number of items and made provision for more effective collection. The Currency Act (1764) forbade the colonial assemblies to issue any more paper money and required them to retire on schedule all the paper money issued during the war. And, most momentous of all, the Stamp Act (1765) imposed a tax to be paid on every legal document in the colonies, every newspaper, almanac, or pamphlet, and every deck of cards or pair of dice.

Thus the new imperial program with its reapplication of old mercantilist principles began to be put into effect. In a sense it proved highly effective. British officials soon were collecting more than ten times as much annual revenue in America as before 1763. But the new policy was not a lasting success.

Inner Contradictions

It is doubtful whether mercantilism, carried to its logical extremes, could have been made to work. How could the colonists provide a growing market for English goods, as well as a source of cash and raw material, if they were to be deprived of the (illegal) trading and other activities which in the past had made it possible for them to pay? Mercantilism, it would seem in retrospect, would work at all only when it did not work very well, only when it was not pushed to extremes and its inner contradictions thereby exposed. Very likely, time would have shown the British leaders the unwisdom and indeed the impracticability of their course.

But most of the leading colonists were unwilling to wait patiently to find out whether the measures of the new imperialism were economically feasible. The experience of the French and Indian

War, while convincing prominent Englishmen of the need for tighter imperial control, had exerted an opposite effect on the attitude of colonials. Rightly or wrongly, they had gained a heightened sense of self-confidence in their own military prowess, along with a certain contempt for British regulars and especially their officers, such as the unfortunate General Braddock. The French threat having been removed from the frontier

forest, many of the colonists felt a new surge of expansive energy and daring. In short, they concluded that they needed not more but less of imperial guidance and protection than before.

Precisely through its different influences on the thinking of Englishmen and continental colonists, the grand victory of the empire was to lead directly to the empire's dismemberment in the American Revolution.

BIBLIOGRAPHY

Volumes 7 and 8 of L. H. Gipson's *The British Empire before the American Revolution* bear the title *The Great War for the Empire* and deal with the conflict from the point of view of British imperial policy makers. Other important works are C. M. Andrews, *The Colonial Background of the American Revolution* (1924); G. L. Beer, *The Old Colonial System, 1660–1754* (2 vols., 1912); O. M. Dickerson, *American Colonial Government, 1696–1765* (1912); C. M. Andrews, *Colonial Self-Government* (1904); and E. B. Greene, *Provincial America* (1905).

Nathaniel Bacon is described as the leader of a democratic movement in T. J. Wertenbaker's *Torchbearer of the Revolution* (1940) and as a rather unprincipled troublemaker in W. E. Washburn's *The Governor and the Rebel: A History of Bacon's Rebellion in Virginia* (1958).

The rise of New France and the Franco-British struggle are interestingly told in the classic writings of Francis Parkman, among

them *Pioneers of France in the New World* (1865), *La Salle and the Discovery of the Great West* (2 vols., 1879), and *A Half Century of Conflict* (2 vols., 1892). Some of Parkman's works have been skillfully condensed in *The Parkman Reader* (1955), edited by S. E. Morison. Important modern studies are H. I. Priestley, *France Overseas through the Old Regime* (1939); and G. M. Wrong, *The Rise and Fall of New France* (2 vols., 1928).

On the clash of frontiers and the French and Indian War, see also A. T. Volwiler, *George Croghan and the Westward Movement, 1741–1782* (1926); J. E. Bakeless, *Daniel Boone, Master of the Wilderness* (1955); C. H. Ambler, *George Washington and the West* (1936); the first two volumes of D. S. Freeman's multi-volume biography, *George Washington* (1948–57); A. B. Hulbert, *Braddock's Road* (1903); and H. H. Peckham, *Pontiac and the Indian Uprising* (1947).

4

GETTING READY

FOR REVOLT

The policy of George III's government, beginning with the measures of 1763–5, provoked resistance in the colonies and led to a decade of discontent that culminated in armed revolt. War came in consequence of a real clash of interests, economic and political, between the groups dominant in England and those dominant in the colonies. This conflict was the end result of a century and a half of divergence in the development of English and American ways. As an outstanding historian (Charles M. Andrews) has said, "New soil had produced new wants, new desires, new points of view, and the colonists were demanding the right to live their own lives in their own way."

Colonial Self-Interest

Self-interest generally led the colonists to be loyal subjects before 1763, and even after that time they had much to gain from maintaining their imperial connection. They enjoyed access to the markets of the empire, bounties on the production of certain goods, the protection af-forded by British naval and military forces, and the pride of belonging to the most powerful aggregation of peoples on the globe. In some respects the colonists had more in common with Englishmen than with one another.

Serious disputes continued to pit colonist against colonist. In 1771 a small-scale civil war broke out as a consequence of the Regulator movement in North Carolina. The Regulators were farmers of the Carolina upcountry who organized to oppose the extortionate taxes which the sheriffs collected. These sheriffs, along with other local officials, were appointed by the governor; there was no local self-government in the colony. At first the Regulators tried to redress their grievances peaceably, by electing their leaders to the colonial assembly. The western counties were badly underrepresented in the assembly, and the Regulators were unable to get control of it. They finally armed themselves and undertook to resist tax collections by force. To suppress the revolt, Governor William Tryon raised an army of militiamen, mostly from the eastern counties. The militiamen met and defeated the Regulators, some 2,000 strong, in the Battle of Alamance, in which nine on each side were killed and many others wounded. Afterward, six Regulators were hanged for treason. Though such bloodshed was exceptional, the people of the colonies were divided by numerous conflicts of interest.

After 1763, however, the policies of the British government increasingly offset the divisive tendencies within the colonies

ready burdened with debts to English merchants, would not only have to pay additional taxes but would also be deprived of the chance to lessen their debts by selling Western land, in which George Washington and others were much interested. Professional men—preachers, lawyers, and professors—considered the interests of merchants and planters to be identical with their own. Small farmers, much the most numerous group in the

DISUNITY IN THE COLONIES

During the French and Indian War the Englishman Andrew Burnaby visited America. Afterwards he wrote a book entitled *Travels through the Middle Settlements in North America in the Years 1759–60*. The book was published in London in the critical year 1775. Burnaby's readers must have concluded that the colonists were in no condition to put up an effective resistance to British authority, for he wrote:

"Fire and water are not more heterogeneous than the different colonies in North America. Nothing can exceed the jealousy and emulation which they possess in regard to each other. The inhabitants of Pennsylvania and New York have an inexhaustible source of animosity, in their jealousy for the trade of the Jerseys. Massachusetts-Bay and Rhode Island are not less interested in that of Connecticut. The West Indies are a common subject of emulation to them all. Even the limits and boundaries of each colony are a constant source of litigation. In short, such is the difference of character, if manners, of religion, of interest of the different colonies that I think if I am not wholly ignorant of the human mind, were they left to themselves, there would even be a civil war, from one end of the colony to the other; while the Indians and Negroes would, with better reason, impatiently watch the opportunity of exterminating them all together."

and caused Americans to look at the disadvantages of empire more closely than at its benefits. These policies threatened, in some degree or other, the well-being of nearly all classes in America.

Northern merchants would suffer from the various restraints upon their commerce, from the closing of the West to their ventures in land speculation and fur trading, from the denial of opportunities in manufacturing, and from the increased load of taxation. Southern planters, al-

colonies, stood to lose as a result of reduced markets and hence lower prices for their crops, together with an increase in their taxes and other costs, not to mention the difficulty of getting paper-money loans. Town workers faced the prospect of narrowing opportunities, particularly because of the restraints on manufacturing and paper money.

Already, at the end of the French and Indian War, the colonists were beginning to feel the pinch of a postwar depression.

Previously the British government, pouring money into their midst to finance the fighting, had stimulated a wartime boom. Now the government was going to take money out of the colonies instead of putting it in. If the government's measures should be strictly enforced, the immediate effect would be to aggravate the hard times. The long-run effect would be to confine the enterprising spirit of the colonists and condemn them to a fixed or even a declining level of living.

Grievous as were the economic consequences of George III's program, its political consequences would be as bad or worse. While colonial democracy was far from all-inclusive, the colonists were used to a remarkably wide latitude in self-government. Nowhere else in the world at that time did so large a proportion of the people take an active interest in public affairs. The chief centers of American political activity were the provincial assemblies, and here the people (through their elected representatives) were able to assert themselves because the assemblies had established the right to give or withhold appropriations for the costs of government within the colonies. If, now, the British authorities should succeed in raising extensive revenues directly from America, the colonial voters and their representatives would lose control over public finance, and without such control their participation in politics would be very nearly meaningless.

Home rule was not something new and different that these Americans were striving to get. It was something old and familiar that they desired to keep. They would lose it if the London authorities were allowed to carry out the program of raising revenues from colonial taxation and providing unconditional salaries for royal officials. The discontented Americans eventually prepared themselves to lay down their lives for a movement that was both democratic and conservative— a movement to conserve the liberties they already possessed.

The Stamp Act Crisis

If Prime Minister Grenville had wished deliberately to antagonize and unify some of the most influential groups in the colonies (which, of course, he did not) he could have chosen no means more effective than the Stamp Act. The tax fell upon all Americans, of whatever section, colony, or class. In particular, the stamps required for ship's papers and legal documents offended merchants and lawyers. Tavern owners, often the political oracles of their neighborhoods, now were supposed to buy stamps for their licenses; and printers, for their newspapers and other publications. Thus the tax antagonized those who could play most effectively upon public opinion.

Nevertheless, it occurred to few colonists that they could do more than grumble and buy the stamps, until the Virginia House of Burgesses sounded a "trumpet of sedition" that aroused Americans to action almost everywhere. In the House of Burgesses a group of young aristocrats aspired to exert themselves against the oligarchy of tidewater planters who, with the royal governor, dominated Virginia politics. Foremost among these young malcontents was Patrick Henry, who was ambitious to enlarge the fame he had gained in the "parson's cause." Henry made a fiery speech in the House (May, 1765), concluding with a hint that George III like earlier tyrants might lose his head, and to shocked cries of "Treason!" Henry is said to have replied: "If this be treason, make the most of it." Then he introduced a set of resolutions declaring that Americans possessed all the rights of Englishmen, especially the right to be taxed only by their own representatives; moreover, that Virginians should pay no taxes except those voted by the Virginia assembly, and that anyone advocating the right of Parliament to tax Virginians should be deemed an enemy of the colony. The House of Burgesses defeated the most extreme of Henry's resolutions, but all of them were printed and circulated as the "Virginia Resolves," thus giving the impression in other colonies that the people of Virginia were both more daring and better unified than was the fact.

Stirred by the Virginia Resolves, mobs in various places began to take the law into their own hands, and during the summer of 1765 riots broke out in various places, the worst of them in Boston. Men belonging to the newly organized "Sons assembly, James Otis proposed to his fellow legislators in Massachusetts that they call an intercolonial congress for concerted action against the new tax. In October, 1765, the Stamp Act Congress met in New York with delegates from nine of the colonies present. They divided into moderates and extremists. The extremists argued that a petition should be addressed only to the King, on the ground that Parliament had nothing to do with colonial rights. But the mod-

---

THE STAMP ACT CONGRESS: RESOLUTIONS

"I. That His Majesty's subjects in these colonies owe the same allegiance to the Crown of Great Britain that is owing from his subjects born within the realm, and all due subordination to that august body the Parliament of Great Britain.

"II. That His Majesty's liege subjects in these colonies are intitled to all the inherent rights and liberties of his natural born subjects within the kingdom of Great Britain.

"III. That it is inseparably essential to the freedom of a people, and the undoubted right of Englishmen, that no taxes be imposed on them but with their own consent, given personally or by their representatives.

"IV. That the people of these colonies are not, and from their local circumstances cannot be, represented in the House of Commons in Great Britain.

"V. That the only representatives of the people of these colonies are persons chosen therein by themselves, and that no taxes ever have been, or can be constitutionally imposed on them, but by their respective legislatures. . . ."

---

of Liberty" went about terrorizing stamp agents and burning the stamps. The agents, themselves Americans, hastily resigned to save their skins, and very few stamps were sold in the continental colonies. In Boston the mob got out of hand and proceeded to harry pro-British "aristocrats" such as the Lieutenant Governor, Thomas Hutchinson, wrecking his house even though he had opposed the passage of the Stamp Act.

At about the time that Patrick Henry presented his resolutions to the Virginia erates were in the majority, and the congress petitioned both the King and the two houses of Parliament. Though admitting that Americans owed to Parliament "all due subordination," the congress denied that they could rightfully be taxed except by their provincial assemblies.

If the British government had tried to enforce the Stamp Act, possibly the Revolutionary War would have begun ten years earlier than it actually did. The government was not deterred by resolves, riots, and petitions, but the Americans also used something more persuasive than any of these. That was economic pressure. Already, in response to the Sugar Act of 1764, many New Englanders had quit buying English goods. Now the colonial boycott spread, and the Sons of Liberty intimidated those colonists who were reluctant to participate in it.

himself finally was convinced that the act must be repealed. Opponents of repeal, and they were strong and vociferous, insisted that unless the colonists were compelled to obey the Stamp Act, they would soon cease to obey any laws of Parliament. So Parliament passed the Declaratory Act, asserting parliamentary authority over the colonies in "all cases whatso-

---

THE DECLARATORY ACT

1766

While repealing the Stamp Act, Parliament denied the arguments put forth by Americans at the meeting of the Stamp Act Congress and on other occasions. The constitutional issue was sharply drawn, as may be seen by comparing the resolutions of the Stamp Act Congress with these words of Parliament's "declaratory" act:

"Whereas several of the houses of representatives in his Majesty's colonies and plantations in America have of late, against law, claimed to themselves, or to the general assemblies of the same, the sole and exclusive right of imposing duties or taxes upon his Majesty's subjects in the said colonies and plantations; and have, in pursuance of such claim, passed certain votes, resolutions, and orders, derogatory to the legislative authority of parliament, and inconsistent with the dependency of said colonies and plantations upon the crown of Great Britain: . . . be it declared . . . That the said colonies and plantations in America have been, are, and of right ought to be subordinate unto and dependent upon the imperial crown and parliament of Great Britain; and that the King's majesty, by and with the advice and consent of the lords spiritual and temporal and commons of Great Britain in parliament assembled, had, hath, and of right ought to have full power and authority to make laws and statutes of sufficient force and validity to bind the colonies and people of America, subjects of the crown of Great Britain, in all cases whatsoever."

The merchants of England, feeling the loss of much of their colonial market, begged Parliament to repeal the Stamp Act, while stories of unemployment, poverty, and discontent arose from English seaports and manufacturing towns.

Having succeeded Grenville as prime minister, the Marquis of Rockingham used his influence in favor of appeasing both the English merchants and the American colonists, and King George III

ever," and then repealed the Stamp Act (1766). In their rejoicing over the repeal, most Americans paid little attention to the sweeping declaration of Parliament's power.

The Townshend Program

The appeasement policy of the Rockingham government was not so well received in England as in America. English landlords protested that the government had "sacrificed the landed gentlemen to the interests of traders and colonists." Soon the King dismissed the unpopular Rockingham and called upon William Pitt to form a new ministry. A critic of the Stamp Act, Pitt had a reputation in America as the colonists' friend, though his reputation suffered somewhat when he accepted a peerage as Lord Chatham. He continued as prime minister after gout and mental illness had laid him low, and the actual leadership of his administration fell to the Chancellor of the Exchecquer, Charles Townshend, "Champagne Charlie," a brilliant man but a sort of playboy of British politics.

Townshend had to deal with imperial problems and colonial grievances still left over from the Grenville ministry. Now that the Stamp Act was gone, the worst of these grievances was the Mutiny Act of 1765, which required the colonists to provide quarters and supplies for the British troops in America. The Massachusetts assembly, refusing to vote the supplies, was the first to defy the Mutiny Act, but the New York assembly, when it did the same thing, presented a more serious challenge to imperial authorities, since the army headquarters were in New York.

To enforce the Mutiny Act and raise a revenue in the colonies, Townshend proposed two measures to Parliament. First, New York was to be punished by the suspension of its assembly until the law was obeyed there. By thus singling out New York, Townshend thought he would avoid Grenville's mistake of arousing all the colonies at once. Second, duties were to be laid upon colonial imports of glass, lead, paint, paper, and tea. Townshend reasoned that the colonists could not logically object to taxation of this kind. At the time of the Stamp Act, some Americans had made a distinction between "internal" and "external" taxes and had denounced the stamp duties as internal taxation. While Townshend laughed at this distinction he took the colonists at their word and proposed duties which, without question, were to be collected externally. Parliament (1767) approved the Townshend duties and suspended the New York assembly.

To the colonists, however, the Townshend duties were scarcely more acceptable than the stamp tax, and the suspension of the one assembly threatened the annihilation of all. Taking up New York's cause as well as its own, the Massachusetts assembly sent out a circular letter urging all the rest to stand up against every tax, external or internal, imposed by Parliament. At first the Massachusetts circular evoked little response in some of the legislatures and ran into strong opposition in at least one of them, that of Pennsylvania. Then Lord Hillsborough, in the new office of Secretary of State for the Colonies, issued a circular letter of his own in which he warned that assemblies endorsing the Massachusetts letter would be dissolved. Promptly the other colonies, even Pennsylvania, rallied to the support of Massachusetts.

Besides inducing Parliament to lay import duties and suspend the New York assembly, Townshend also took steps to enforce commercial regulations in the colonies more effectively than ever. The most fateful of these steps was the establishment of a board of customs commissioners in America. Again, Townshend was giving the colonists what they had said they wanted, but they had been interested only in avoiding delays arising from the referral of important decisions to London, while he intended to stop the leaks in the colonial customhouses. His commissioners, with headquarters in Boston, virtually ended the smuggling at that place, though smugglers continued to carry on a busy trade in other colonial seaports.

Naturally the Boston merchants were the most indignant, and they took the lead in organizing another boycott. In 1768 the merchants of Philadelphia and New York joined those of Boston in a

SAMUEL ADAMS. In 1771, the year after the Boston Massacre, the wealthy John Hancock commissioned John Singleton Copley to paint a portrait of Hancock and another of Samuel Adams. Then a widower of forty-nine, Adams was prematurely old and was afflicted with palsy. Careless of his clothes, he usually wore a badly worn, rusty suit. Dressed up for his portrait, he is shown protesting to the lieutenant-governor of Massachusetts against the presence of the British troops in Boston, before the Massacre. At the time of this painting, Copley, of Boston, was an outstandingly busy and successful American portraitist. He was, for a while, a Patriot and an admirer of Adams; indeed, he testified against the British soldiers at the Massacre trial. Later Copley became a Loyalist and in 1774 he left America, to continue his artistic career in England for the rest of his life. (COURTESY, MUSEUM OF FINE ARTS, BOSTON)

nonimportation agreement, and later some of the Southern merchants and planters also agreed to cooperate. Throughout the colonies, crude American homespun became suddenly fashionable while English luxuries were frowned upon. Some enthusiasts, advocating the development of colonial manufactures of all kinds, looked forward to the creation of a self-sufficient America, with an economy independent of the Empire's.

Before the consequences of his pro-gram were fully apparent, Townshend himself died, leaving the question of revising his import duties to his successor, Lord North. Hoping to break the non-importation agreement and divide the colonists, Lord North secured (1770) the repeal of all the Townshend duties except the tea tax.

Meanwhile the presence of the customs commissioners in Boston led to violence. The Boston mob had the most aggressive leader of all, Samuel Adams. The impoverished son of a once wealthy brewer, Adams had taken to politics after he himself had failed in business. As a rabble-rouser he had no equal in the colonies, and from the time of the Stamp Act troubles he was the guiding spirit of Massachusetts radicalism, even outdoing James Otis. Adams' success as a politician depended upon his finding suitable topics for agitation, and the British government, having repeatedly supplied him with topics, obliged him again by locating the customs commissioners in Boston and then stationing troops there.

To the Boston "liberty boys," the presence of the customs commissioners was a standing invitation to violence, and before long the terrified officials were driven to take refuge in Castle William, out in the harbor. So that they could return safely to their duties, the British government placed four regiments (afterwards reduced to two) within the city. The presence of the redcoats antagonized Samuel Adams and his followers more than ever. While his men ragged the soldiers and engaged them in brawls, Adams filled the newspapers with imaginary stories of rapes and other atrocities committed by the troops, and he spread throughout Boston a rumor that the soldiers were preparing for a concerted attack upon the citizens. On the night of March 5, 1770, a mob of dockworkers and other "liberty boys" fell upon the sentry at the customhouse. Hastily Captain Preston lined up his regiment in front of the building to protect it. There

The "Bloody Massacre." This broadside, "Engrav'd Printed & Sold by Paul Revere, Boston," pictures the Patriot version of the Boston incident of March 5, 1770. At the extreme right, Captain Thomas Preston, in command of the Custom-House guards, leers as he orders his grinning men to fire on the unarmed citizens. The Custom House, Preston's headquarters, is sarcastically labeled "Butcher's Hall." (COURTESY OF THE METROPOLITAN MUSEUM OF ART, ROGERS FUND, 1923)

was some scuffling, and one of the soldiers was knocked down. Other soldiers then fired into the crowd, killing five of its members.

These events quickly became known as the "Boston Massacre" through the efforts of Samuel Adams and his adherents, who published an account bearing the title *Innocent Blood Crying to God from the Streets of Boston* and giving the impression that the dead were victims of a deliberate plot. The soldiers, tried before a jury of Bostonians and defended by Samuel Adams' cousin John Adams, were found guilty of no more than manslaughter and were given only a token punishment. Nevertheless, through newspapers and pamphlets, Samuel Adams convicted the redcoats of murder in the minds of many contemporary Americans, and year after year on March 5 he revived the people's memory with orations recalling the events of 1770. Later generations accepted his version of the "massacre" and thus, without knowing it, honored his skill as the foremost propagandist of the pre-Revolutionary decade.

The Philosophy of Revolt

Though America quieted down for a while after 1770, Americans did not abandon their principles, and these principles were revolutionary, at least in implication. "The Revolution was effected before the war commenced," one of the greatest of the Revolutionary leaders, John Adams, afterwards remarked. "The Revolution was in the minds and hearts of the people." Of course, very few of the people thought of outright independence till after the war had begun, and even those few (among them Samuel Adams) considered it best not to admit that independence was their ultimate aim. For the time being, most politically conscious Americans desired no more, and no less, than autonomy within the Empire. They argued that the English Constitution, correctly interpreted, supported their claims

to individual liberty and colonial self-rule, and that the laws of nature and of God justified them in resisting infringements upon their rights.

In the course of the argument the Americans came to the conclusion that they were better Englishmen than the English themselves, better acquainted with the Constitution and more devoted to the liberties it guaranteed. Some of the Whig politicians in England, such as William Pitt and above all Edmund Burke, who spoke eloquently in favor of conciliation, were more or less inclined to agree. But other Englishmen, like the famous lexicographer and literary critic Samuel Johnson, looked upon the Americans as a deluded and indeed a barbarized offshoot of the English people. The majority in England were outraged rather than convinced by all the speech-making and pamphleteering on the other side of the Atlantic.

To Englishmen the Constitution, though worthy of the highest respect, was an assortment of laws and usages that had developed through many centuries and that were rather elastic and vague. To Americans, on the other hand, it was a fixed and definite body of principles, which ought to be written down so as to avoid disagreements. Americans believed the colonies did have written constitutions—the colonial charters, which supposedly guaranteed to Americans all the traditional rights of Englishmen.

Of these rights the most fundamental, according to the colonists, was the right to be taxed only with their own consent. But the colonists were not consistent in all things, nor were they in this matter of taxation. At first some of them objected only to "internal" taxes such as those imposed by the Stamp Act. Most colonists hesitated to assert that all imperial taxation was unconstitutional, since they long had been taxed at least indirectly by the various trade laws. When Townshend levied his "external" duties, the Philadelphia lawyer John Dickinson maintained in the *Letters of a Pennsylvania Farmer* that even external taxation was legal only when designed to regulate trade and not to raise a revenue. But Americans did not like trade regulations, either, when the regulations began to be enforced. Eventually the discontented colonists took an unqualified stand upon the slogan "No taxation without representation."

This clamor about "representation" made little sense to Englishmen. Only about one in twenty-five of them was entitled to vote for members of Parliament, and many populous parts of England had no representatives at all. According to the prevailing English theory, however, Parliament did not represent individuals or geographical areas. Instead, it represented the interests of the whole nation and indeed the whole Empire, no matter where the members happened to come from. The unenfranchised boroughs of England, the whole of Ireland, and the colonies 3,000 miles away—all were represented in the Parliament at London. That was the theory of "virtual" representation, but Americans believed in actual representation. They felt they could be represented in Parliament only if they sent their quota of members to it. For a time some of them, even James Otis, considered proposals for electing American representatives, but most of the colonists realized that if they should participate in the action of Parliament they would be bound by that action, even though they were outnumbered and outvoted. So they fell back upon the argument that they could be fairly and properly represented only in their own colonial assemblies.

According to the American view of the Empire, and according to actual fact, these assemblies were little parliaments, as competent to legislate for their respective colonies as Parliament was for England. The Empire was a sort of federation of commonwealths, each with its own legislative body, all tied together by common loyalty to the King (much as in the British Commonwealth of Nations to-

day). This being their conception of the Empire, the Americans protested bitterly against the pretensions of Parliament but had nothing except kind words for George III—until they decided to cut their imperial ties completely and declare for independence. According to the English view, the Empire was a single, undivided unit, and everywhere within it the King and Parliament together were supreme.

The American doctrine of resistance to unconstitutional and tyrannical laws was based chiefly upon the Bible and the writings of John Locke. For generations the preachers of New England had taught that no man need obey a government when it violated the will of God as set forth in the Scriptures. Now, to show that rebellion against tyranny was lawful in God's sight, they retold such Bible stories as the one about a King of Israel who burdened his people with unjust taxes and was overthrown.

John Locke (1632–1704) had much the same relation to the American Revolution as Karl Marx later had to the Communist Revolution in Russia, though Locke (a conservative rather than a revolutionist like Marx) would probably have been shocked if he had lived to see the use that Americans made of his doctrines. In his *Two Treatises of Government* (1690) Locke attempted to justify a revolution that had already occurred, the English revolution of 1688–9 by which Parliament had won supremacy over the King. According to Locke's theory, men originally lived in a state of nature and enjoyed complete liberty, then agreed to a "compact" by which they set up a government to protect their "natural rights," especially their right to the ownership and enjoyment of private property. The government was limited by the terms of the compact and by "natural law." It was contrary to natural law for a government to take property without the consent of the owners, Locke wrote, and Americans noted in particular his sentence: "If any one shall claim a power to lay and levy taxes on the people by his own authority, and without such consent of the people, he thereby invades the fundamental law of property, and subverts the end of government." To Americans of the 1760's and 1770's it was clear that the British government was flouting the law of nature as well as the will of God. And, according to Locke, if a government should persist in exceeding its rightful powers, men would be released from their obligation to obey it. What was more, they would have the right to make a new compact and establish another government.

The Tea Excitement

From time to time after 1770 Americans resisting British law broke the comparative stillness in America with such deeds as the seizure of a revenue ship on the lower Delaware, the burning of another (the *Gaspee*) in Narragansett Bay, and the tarring and feathering of a customs officer on the streets of Boston. Not till 1773, however, did Americans reassert their revolutionary principles with anything approaching the unity and vigor of former years.

Tea revived the dispute. The East India Company, with a large stock of unsalable tea on hand, was nearly bankrupt, and Lord North induced Parliament to go to the company's relief with the Tea Act of 1773. This law permitted the company to retail its product in America without paying any of the usual taxes except the tea tax still remaining from the original Townshend duties. With these privileges the company could by-pass the middlemen and sell directly to colonial consumers at a price so low that even smugglers could not compete.

Lord North, like others in his office before him, was surprised by the reaction of the Americans. Not that he expected the tea-importing merchants in the colonies to like the new law, for it threatened to drive them out of business and replace them with a giant monopoly. But the colonists—especially the women—were excessively fond of tea. Lord North thought they would be so glad to get it cheap that they would swallow the hated tea tax along with it. Instead, they renounced their beloved beverage and turned for the time being to substitutes such as coffee and chocolate.

Meanwhile, with strong popular support, leaders in various colonies made plans to prevent the East India Company from landing its cargoes in colonial ports. In Philadelphia and New York determined men kept the tea from leaving the company's ships, and in Charleston they stored it away in a public warehouse. In Boston, having failed to turn back the three ships in the harbor, the followers of Samuel Adams staged a spectacular drama. On the evening of December 16, 1773, three companies of fifty men each, masquerading as "Mohawks," passed between the protecting lines of a tremendous crowd of spectators, went aboard, broke open the tea chests, and heaved them into the water. As the electrifying news of the Boston "tea party" spread, other seaports followed the example and held tea parties of their own.

When the Bostonians refused to pay for the property they had destroyed, George III and Lord North decided upon a policy of coercion, to be applied not against all the colonies but only against one, the chief center of resistance, Massachusetts. In four acts of 1774 Parliament proceeded to put this policy into effect. One of the laws closed the port of Boston, another drastically reduced the local and provincial powers of self-government in Massachusetts, still another permitted royal officers to be tried in other colonies or in England when accused of crimes, and the last provided for the quartering of troops in the colonists' barns and empty houses.

These Coercive Acts were followed by the Quebec Act, which was separate from them in origin and quite different in purpose. Its object was to provide a civil gov-

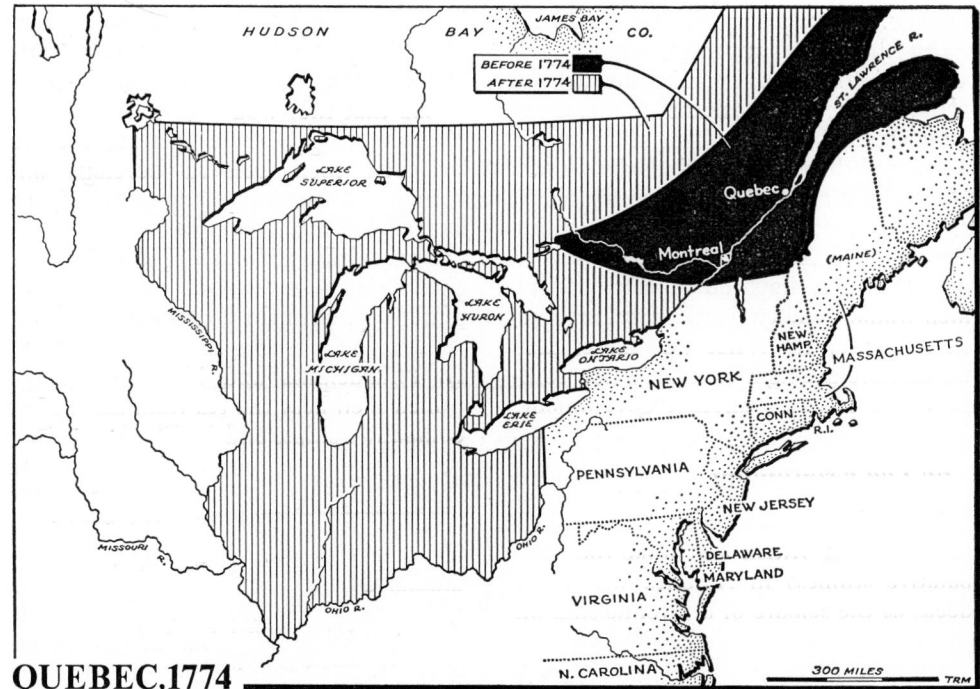

QUEBEC, 1774

ernment for the French-speaking, Roman Catholic inhabitants of Canada and the Illinois country. The law extended the boundaries of Quebec to include the French communities between the Ohio and Mississippi rivers. It also granted political rights to Roman Catholics and recognized the legality of the Roman Catholic Church within the enlarged province. In many ways it was a liberal and much-needed piece of legislation.

To the Protestants in the thirteen colonies, however, the Quebec Act was anathema. They were already alarmed by rumors that the Church of England schemed to appoint a bishop for America with the intention of enforcing Anglican authority upon all the various sects. To them the line between the Church of England and the Church of Rome always had seemed dangerously thin. When Catholics ceased to be actively persecuted in the mother country, alarmists in the colonies began to fear that Catholicism and Anglicanism were about to merge,

and at the passage of the Quebec Act they became convinced that a plot was afoot in London for subjecting Americans to the tyranny of the pope. Moreover, those interested in Western lands believed that the act, by extending the boundaries of Quebec, would reinforce the land policy of the Proclamation Line of 1763 and put an additional obstacle in the way of westward progress.

Had it not been for the Quebec Act, Lord North might have come close to succeeding in his effort to divide and rule the colonies by isolating Massachusetts. As it was, the colonists generally lumped the Quebec law with the Massachusetts measures as the fifth in a set of "Intolerable Acts." From New Hampshire to South Carolina the people prepared to take a united stand.

The Continental Congress

Revolutions do not just happen: they must be led and organized. From 1765 on, colonial leaders provided a variety of organizations for converting popular discontent into action, organizations which in time formed the basis for an independent government.

Some of these organizations were local, some colony-wide, and some intercolonial. In many cases the provincial assemblies themselves served as centers of resistance, and sometimes they were replaced or supplemented by extralegal meetings, as

level, a network of them connecting Boston with the rural towns, but Virginia was the first to establish committees of correspondence on an intercolonial basis. These made possible cooperation among the colonies in a more continuous way than had the Stamp Act Congress, the first effort at intercolonial union for resistance against imperial authority. Virginia took the greatest step of all toward united action in 1774 when, the gov-

---

DECLARATION AND RESOLVES
(*First Continental Congress*)

1774

". . . That the foundation of English liberty, and of all free government, is a right in the people to participate in their legislative council: and as the English colonists are not represented, and from their local and other circumstances cannot properly be represented, in the British parliament, they are entitled to a free and exclusive power of legislation in their several provincial legislatures, where their right of representation can alone be preserved, in all cases of taxation and internal polity, subject only to the negative of their sovereign, in such manner as has been heretofore used and accustomed. But, from the necessity of the case, and a regard to the mutual interest of both countries, we cheerfully consent to the operation of such acts of the British parliament as are bona fide restrained to the regulation of our external commerce, for the purpose of securing the commercial advantages of the whole empire to the mother country, and the commercial benefits of its respective members excluding every idea of taxation, internal or external, for raising a revenue on the subjects of America without their consent. . . ."

---

when (in 1768) Sam Adams called a convention of delegates from the Massachusetts towns to sit in place of the General Court, which the royal governor had dissolved. Adams and others in various places organized mobs as Sons of Liberty, and also set up committees of prominent citizens for a number of specific objects. The most famous and most effective were the committees of correspondence. Massachusetts took the lead (1772) with such committees on the local

ernor having dissolved the assembly, a rump session met in the Raleigh Tavern at Williamsburg, declared that the Intolerable Acts menaced the liberties of every colony, and issued a call for a Continental Congress.

Variously elected by the assemblies or by extralegal meetings, delegates from all the thirteen colonies except Georgia were present when, in September, 1774, the Continental Congress convened in Philadelphia. The delegates divided into moderates and extremists, as those at the Stamp Act Congress nine years earlier had done, but this time the more extreme members seized the upper hand. At the outset they showed their strength by designating Carpenter's Hall as the meeting place. This was the headquarters of the Philadelphia Carpenters' Company, and some members complained that its selection was an unseemly attempt to curry favor with the city's artisans. In the ensuing sessions of the Congress, however, the extremists were unable to carry through a program quite so thorough as some of them would have liked.

A majority of the delegates in Carpenter's Hall agreed upon five major decisions. First, in a very close vote, they defeated the plan of Joseph Galloway for a colonial union under British authority, a plan which included a legislative council made up of representatives from the colonial assemblies and a president general to be appointed by the King. Second, they drew up a somewhat self-contradictory statement of grievances, conceding to Parliament the right to regulate colonial trade but demanding the elimination of all oppressive legislation passed since 1763, and they addressed a petition to George III as their "Most Gracious Sovereign." Third, they approved a series of resolutions from a Suffolk County (Massachusetts) convention recommending, among other things, that military preparations be made for defense against possible attack by the British troops in Boston. Fourth, they agreed to nonimportation, nonexportation, and nonconsumption as means of stopping all trade with Great Britain, and they formed a "Continental Association" to see that these agreements were carried out. Fifth, the delegates adjourned to meet again the next spring, thus indicating that they conceived of the Continental Congress as a continuing organization.

Through their representatives in Philadelphia the colonies had, in effect, re-affirmed their autonomous status within the empire and declared economic war to maintain that position. The more optimistic of the Americans supposed that economic warfare alone would win a quick and bloodless victory, but the more pessimistic had their doubts. "I expect no redress, but, on the contrary, increased resentment and double vengeance," John Adams said to Patrick Henry; "we must fight." And Henry replied, "By God, I am of your opinion." During the winter of 1774-5 the enforcement of the non-importation, nonexportation, and non-consumption agreements proved increasingly difficult as people in the Middle Colonies and in the South, viewing the Continental Association as more tyrannical than the British government, began to complain against the sacrifices they were compelled to make—all for the sake of those troublemakers in Massachusetts!

During the winter the Parliament in London debated proposals for conciliating the colonists. Lord Chatham (William Pitt) urged the withdrawal of troops from America, Edmund Burke urged the repeal of the Coercive Acts, but in vain; and not even Chatham and Burke thought of renouncing parliamentary authority over the colonies. Lord North, conceding less than Burke or Chatham, introduced a set of proposals of his own, and Parliament approved them early in 1775. The essence of these so-called Conciliatory Propositions was that the colonies, instead of being taxed directly by Parliament, should tax themselves at Parliament's demand. With this offer Lord North intended to redivide Americans by appealing to the disgruntled moderates. But his offer was too grudging, and it came too late. It did not reach America till after the first shots of war had been fired.

Lexington and Concord

For months the farmers and towns-people of Massachusetts had been gathering arms and ammunition and training as

TAKING THE PLEDGE. This British caricature, entitled "A Society of Patriotic
Ladies, at Edenton in North Carolina," was published in London in March,
1775. It ridicules the American buy-at-home movement. The women are emptying their tea canisters and signing a pledge, which reads: "We the Ladies of
Edenton do hereby Solemnly Engage not to Conform to that Pernicious Custom
of Drinking Tea, or that we the aforesaid Ladies will not promote the Wear of
any Manufacture from England untill such time that all Acts which tend to Enslave this our Native Country shall be Repealed." (COURTESY OF THE METRO-
POLITAN MUSEUM OF ART)

"Minute Men," ready to fight on a minute's notice. The Continental Congress had approved preparations for a defensive war, and these citizen-soldiers only waited for an aggressive move by the British regulars in Boston.

In Boston, General Thomas Gage, commanding the British garrison, knew of the orders to arrest the rebel leaders Sam Adams and John Hancock, known to be in the vicinity of Lexington, he still hesitated, but when he heard that the minutemen had stored a large supply of gunpowder in Concord (eighteen miles from Boston) he at last decided to act. On the night of April 18, 1775, he sent a detach-

THE BATTLE OF LEXINGTON. A contemporary engraving by Amos Doolittle. It pictures the American version of the affair of April 19, 1775, at Lexington. In the center is shown "the party who fired first," at the command of Major Pitcairn, on horseback. In the foreground are some of the fallen and the fleeing members of the "Provincial Company of Lexington" (Minute-Men). The more prominent buildings on the edge of the square, or green, are the Public Inn at the left of the large tree and the Meetinghouse at the right of it. Behind the Meetinghouse are companies of British Regulars marching along the road to Concord. (COURTESY OF THE NEW YORK PUBLIC LIBRARY, STOKES COLLECTION)

warlike bustle throughout the countryside but thought his army too small to do anything until reinforcements should arrive, though some of his less cautious officers assured him that Americans were cowards, and Major John Pitcairn insisted that a single "small action" with the burning of a few towns would "set everything to rights." When General Gage received ment of about 1,000 men out from Boston on the road to Lexington and Concord. He intended to surprise the colonials with a bloodless coup.

But during the night the hard-riding horsemen William Dawes and Paul Revere warned the villages and farms, and when the redcoats arrived in Lexington the next day, several dozen minutemen awaited them on the common. Shots were fired and some of the minutemen fell, eight of them killed and ten more wounded. Advancing to Concord, the British burned what was left of the powder supply after the Americans hastily had removed most of it to safety. On the road from Concord back to Boston the 1,000 troops, along with 1,500 more who met them at Lexington, were harassed by the continual gunfire of farmers hiding behind trees, rocks, and stone fences. Before the day was over, the British had lost almost three times as many men as the Americans.

The first shots had been fired, but who had fired the first shot? According to the Lexington minutemen, Major Pitcairn upon his arrival had shouted, "Disperse, ye rebels!" and when this command was disregarded he had given the order to fire. According to the British officers and soldiers, one of the American guns had flashed first. The truth is still unknown, but the fact remains that the rebels succeeded in circulating their account well ahead of the British version, and they adorned it with horrible tales of redcoat atrocities. The effect was to rally to the rebel cause thousands of colonists, North and South, who previously had been lukewarm in its support. A war was on, and most Americans believed the enemy had started it.

BIBLIOGRAPHY

General surveys are L. H. Gipson, *The Coming of the Revolution, 1763–1775* (1954); J. C. Miller, *Origins of the American Revolution* (1943); C. H. Van Tyne, *The Causes of the War of Independence* (1922); and C. L. Becker, *The Eve of the Revolution* (1921). The American case is defended in C. H. McIlwain's *The American Revolution: A Constitutional Interpretation* (1923) and is attacked in R. L. Schuyler's *Parliament and the British Empire* (1929).

Becker and others view the Revolution as a kind of civil war—a struggle for power between radicals and conservatives in America —as well as a war for independence from Great Britain. This view is challenged by R. E. Brown, *Middle-Class Democracy and the Revolution in Massachusetts, 1691–1780* (1955), and it is upheld by E. P. Douglass, *Rebels and Democrats: The Struggle for Equal Political Rights and Majority Rule during the American Revolution* (1955). Different patterns from state to state are shown in T. Thayer, *Pennsylvania Politics and the Growth of Democracy, 1740–1776* (1953); R. P. McCormick, *The History of Voting in New Jersey* (1953);

C. A. Barker, *The Background of the Revolution in Maryland* (1940); and Oscar Zeichner, *Connecticut's Years of Controversy, 1750–1776* (1949). E. S. Morgan finds widespread agreement among Americans in *The Birth of the Republic, 1763–1789* (1956).

Phases of the prewar conflict are authoritatively treated in O. M. Dickerson, *The Navigation Acts and the American Revolution* (1951); A. M. Schlesinger, *The Colonial Merchants and the American Revolution, 1763–1776* (1917); E. S. and H. M. Morgan, *The Stamp Act Crisis* (1953); Clinton Rossiter, *Seedtime of the Republic* (1953); and Carl Bridenbaugh, *Cities in Revolt: Urban Life in America, 1743–1776* (1955).

Agitation that whipped up a revolutionary spirit is well handled in the following: A. M. Schlesinger, *Prelude to Independence: The Newspaper War on Britain, 1764–1776* (1958); Philip Davidson, *Propaganda and the American Revolution, 1763–1783* (1941); J. C. Miller, *Sam Adams, Pioneer in Propaganda* (1936); and Jacob Axelrad, *Patrick Henry, The Voice of Freedom* (1947).

5

BIRTH OF
THE UNITED STATES

In the American Revolution a war for autonomy on the part of the united colonies soon turned into a war for independence on the part of the United States. This new nation, with a population less than a third as large as the nine million of Great Britain, and with military and economic resources proportionately still smaller, finally secured not only the recognition of its independence but also the title to a vast territory in the West. The Americans had the advantage of fighting on their home terrain, far from the centers of British might. They profited from the mistakes of an enemy, long afterward famous for "muddling through," who at this time only muddled his campaigns and did not see them through. Above all, they had the benefit of tremendous foreign aid, especially after the American war merged with a world contest in which Great Britain faced the strongest powers of Europe as actual or potential foes. But the success of the Americans was due also to their own patriotic effort. Effectively, if imperfectly, they rallied their resources, human and material, in response to the inspiration of civilian leaders like Thomas Jefferson and Thomas Paine. Though losing battle after battle, they avoided catastrophes and gained at least a few decisive victories through the exertions of thousands of armed men under the majestic generalship of George Washington. And, having held their own in war, they won the peace because their diplomats—Benjamin Franklin, John Adams, John Jay—shrewdly made the most of the opportunities that the world situation offered.

War Aims: Independence

When, three weeks after the battles of Lexington and Concord, the Second Continental Congress met in the State House in Philadelphia, the delegates (again from every colony except Georgia, which was not represented until the following autumn) agreed in their determination to support the war but disagreed about its objects. At one extreme the Adams cousins, John and Samuel, leaned toward independence though they did not yet avow it, and at the other extreme John Dickinson hoped for an early reconciliation with Great Britain. Most of the delegates, holding views that ranged between those of Dickinson and the Adamses, disregarded Lord North's Conciliatory Propositions as insincere but voted reluctantly for one last appeal to the King in the Olive Branch Petition. Then, July 6, 1775, they adopted a Declaration of the Causes and Necessity of Taking up Arms, announcing that the British government

gagement of the entire war and one of the most sanguinary anywhere in the eighteenth century, that their original war aims seemed incommensurate with the cost. For another thing, they lost much of their lingering affection for the mother country when she made ready to use savage Indians, Negro slaves, and foreign mercenaries (the hated "Hessians") against them. And, most important of all, they felt that they were being forced into independence when the British gov-

---

DECLARATION OF THE CAUSES AND NECESSITY OF TAKING UP ARMS

1775

". . . Lest this declaration should disquiet the minds of our friends and fellow-subjects in any part of the empire, we assure them that we mean not to dissolve that union which has so long and so happily subsisted between us, and which we sincerely wish to see restored. Necessity has not yet driven us into that desperate measure, or induced us to excite any other nation to war against them. We have not raised armies with ambitious designs of separating from Great Britain, and establishing independent states. . . .

"In our own native land, in defence of the freedom that is our birthright, and which we ever enjoyed till the late violation of it—for the protection of our property, acquired solely by the honest industry of our forefathers and ourselves, against violence actually offered, we have taken up arms. We shall lay them down when hostilities shall cease on the part of the aggressors, and all danger of their being renewed shall be removed, and not before. . . ."

---

had left the American people with only two alternatives, "unconditional submission to the tyranny of irritated ministers or resistance by force," and that the people had decided to resist.

So, for the first year of the war, the Americans were fighting for a redress of grievances within the British Empire, not for independence. During that year, however, many of them began to change their minds, for various reasons. For one thing, they were making sacrifices so great, as in the battle of Bunker Hill, the bloodiest en-

ernment replied to the Olive Branch Petition with the Prohibitory Act, which closed the colonies to all overseas trade and made no concession except an offer of pardon to repentant rebels. The Americans desperately needed military supplies to continue the war, and now they could get them from abroad in adequate amounts only if they broke completely with Great Britain and proceeded to behave in all respects as if they comprised a sovereign nation.

These feelings in America were not

caused, but were clarified and crystallized, by the publication in January, 1776, of the pamphlet *Common Sense*. Its author, unmentioned on the title page, was Thomas Paine, who with letters of introduction from Benjamin Franklin had emigrated from England to America less than two years before. Though long a failure in various trades, Paine now proved a brilliant success as a revolutionary propagandist. In his pamphlet he argued with flashing phrases that it was plain common sense for Americans to sep-

Despite the persuasions of *Common Sense*, the American people were far from unanimous, and they entered upon a bitter debate over the merits of dependence and independence. While the debate raged, the Continential Congress advanced step by step toward a final break. Congress opened the ports of America to all the world except Great Britain, entered into communication with foreign powers, and recommended to the various colonies that they establish governments without the authority of the Empire, as in

---

DECLARATION OF INDEPENDENCE

1776

Major Premise: "We hold these truths to be self-evident, that all men are created equal, that they are endowed by their Creator with certain unalienable Rights, that among these are Life, Liberty and the pursuit of Happiness. That to secure these rights, Governments are instituted among Men, deriving their just powers from the consent of the governed, That whenever any Form of Government becomes destructive of these ends, it is the Right of the People to alter or abolish it. . . ."

Minor Premise: "The history of the present King of Great Britain is a history of repeated injuries and usurpations, all having in direct object the establishment of an absolute tyranny over these States."

Conclusion: "We, therefore, . . . solemnly publish and declare, That these United Colonies are, and of Right ought to be Free and Independent States. . . ."

---

arate from an England rotten with the corrupt monarchy of George III, brutal as an unnatural parent towards her colonies, responsible for dragging them in to fight her wars in the past, and no more fit as an island kingdom to rule the American Continent than a satellite was fit to rule the sun. "O! ye that love mankind! ye that dare oppose not only the tyranny but the tyrant, stand forth!" Month after month the pamphlet was reprinted until several hundred thousand copies were in circulation, passing from hand to hand and being read and reread.

fact they already were doing. Congress also appointed a committee to draft a formal declaration and, on July 2, 1776, before approving the declaration, adopted a resolution "That these United Colonies are, and, of right, ought to be, free and independent states; that they are absolved from all allegiance to the British crown, and that all political connexion between them and the state of Great Britain is, and ought to be, totally dissolved." Two days later Congress approved the Declaration of Independence, which gave reasons for the action already taken.

The 33-year-old Virginian Thomas Jefferson wrote the Declaration of Independence, his fellow committeemen Benjamin Franklin and John Adams revised the wording a little, and Congress made more drastic changes, striking out passages which condemned the British people and the slave trade. As the jealous Adams afterward complained, Jefferson said nothing new in composing the document. Its very virtue, in fact, lay in his noble phrasing of beliefs already widespread in America. He planned the document in two parts. In the first he restated the familiar compact theory of John Locke, who had held that governments were formed to protect the rights of life, liberty, and property, but Jefferson gave the theory a more humane twist by referring instead to the rights of "life, liberty and the pursuit of happiness." In the second part he listed the alleged crimes of the King who, with the backing of Parliament, had violated his compact with the colonists and thus had forfeited all claim to their loyalty.

Once adopted, the Declaration of Independence exerted an incalculable influence upon later history. With its democratic principle that "all men are created equal," it stimulated humanitarian movements of various kinds in the United States, and abroad it helped to inspire the French Revolution with its Declaration of the Rights of Man. More immediately, it led to increased foreign aid for the struggling rebels and prepared the way for France's all-out intervention on their side. It steeled American patriots to carry on without regard to offers of a peace short of the stated goal. And at the same time it divided Americans more cruelly and more extensively than they ever had been divided before.

At the news of the Declaration of Independence, crowds gathered to cheer, fire guns and cannon, and ring church bells in Philadelphia, Boston, and other places, but there were many people in America who did not rejoice. Some had disapproved of the war from the beginning, and others had been willing to support it only so long as its aims did not conflict with their basic loyalty to the King. These people, numerous but in the minority, refused to cross the new line that had been drawn. Either openly or secretly they remained Loyalists, as they chose to call themselves, or Tories, as they were known to the Whig or Patriot majority. Among the Loyalists were rich familes and poor ones, highly educated men (like the scientist Benjamin Thompson) and illiterates, townspeople and backwoodsmen. Among the Loyalist leaders were royal officials and Anglican clergymen who had sided with the British government throughout the prewar decade of controversy, plus a few of the wealthy merchants and large planters who earlier had belonged to the Patriot party but who seceded from it after the Declaration of Independence.

The remaining Patriots continued to be divided among themselves. On the one hand were men like John Adams and George Washington who wished to see independence achieved with comparatively little social change in America, but whose ranks were thinned by the loss of their former allies, now Loyalists. On the other hand were men like Thomas Jefferson who desired to accomplish democratic and humanitarian reforms along with independence. Thus (as in other wars, including World War II) patriotic Americans held different as well as common aims, some intending only to smite the foreign enemy, others aspiring also to lead a popular crusade at home.

New States and Confederation

While waging war, the Patriots also busied themselves with providing government for the new nation. With the outbreak of war they set up provisional governments based upon existing assemblies or emergency conventions as the royal officials fled from their positions in one colony after another. When the colonies became states, the Patriots formed permanent governments with written constitutions. The constitution-making procedure varied from state to state. In Rhode Island and Connecticut the legislatures merely revised the old colonial charters, and in most of the other states the legislatures, though not elected for that purpose, took it upon themselves to draft new constitutions. Thomas Jefferson, for one, insisted that the fundamental law should come from the people of each state, who should elect constitutional conventions and then vote on ratification. Actually, conventions were held in only three states, referendums in only five, and both a convention and a referendum in only one—Massachusetts.

The new constitutions, all pretty much alike in general outline though different in detail, were both conservative and democratic. They were conservative in retaining essentially the same structure as the old colonial governments. Except in Georgia and Pennsylvania, both of which experimented with a unicameral legislature, each constitution provided for a two-house legislature, with an elected senate taking the place of the former governor's council. All the constitutions continued the office of governor, though most of them denied the holder of this position the bulk of the executive powers he had enjoyed in colonial days. All of the new documents confirmed and extended the ideas of popular rule which long had been put into practice; every one of them included a bill of rights, and some had preambles stating that sovereignty (the ultimate power of government) resided in the people. To vote in any state a man had to own only a modest amount of property, in some states just enough so that he could qualify as a taxpayer. To hold office he had to meet a somewhat higher property requirement, essentially as in pre-Revolutionary times. Only in New Jersey were women allowed to vote, and eventually they were deprived of the suffrage even there. But, considering the widespread ownership of property, something approaching universal manhood suffrage existed from the beginning in all the states.

Once in operation, the new states proceeded to make advances in social as well as political democracy. In one way or another they multiplied opportunities for land ownership and thus enlarged the voting population. For instance, they eliminated the legal rights of primogeniture and entail, which before the war had helped to maintain a landed aristocracy by transferring an entire estate to the oldest son (when a man died without a will) and by keeping the estate intact from generation to generation (when a man by entailment willed that the property never be sold). The new states also made considerable progress toward religious freedom, though some retained religious tests for officeholding. New York and the Southern states, in which the Church of England had been tax-supported, soon saw to its complete disestablishment, and the New England states stripped the Congregational Church of some of its privileges. Virginia, in its Declaration of Rights, boldly announced the principle of complete toleration and, under the leadership of Jefferson as governor, enacted the principle in the Statute of Religious Liberty (1786). And the new states took steps toward personal as well as religious freedom. All of them except South Carolina and Georgia prohibited the importation of slaves, and even South Carolina laid temporary wartime bans on the slave trade. After the first antislavery society in America (founded in 1775) began its agitation, and prominent Southerners including Jefferson and Washington declared their opposition to slavery, Virginia and other Southern states changed their laws so as to encourage manumission, Pennsylvania passed a gradual-emancipation act (1780), and Massachusetts through a decision of its highest court (1783) held that the state's

Bill of Rights outlawed the ownership of slaves. Besides all this, five of the new states put provisions into their constitutions for the establishment of public schools, and all soon began to revise their criminal codes so as to make the punishment more nearly fit the crime.

While the separate states were fashioning constitutions and recasting their legal systems, the Second Continental Congress tried to create a written form of government for the states as a whole. No sooner had the Congress appointed a committee to draft a declaration of independence than it appointed another to draft a plan of union, and after much debate and many revisions the Congress, in November, 1777, adopted the committee's plan, the Articles of Confederation. The Articles of Confederation pro-

vided for a central government very similar to the one already in actual operation, though it increased the powers of Congress somewhat. Congress was to have the powers of conducting war, carrying on foreign relations, and appropriating, borrowing, and issuing money, but not the powers of regulating trade, levying taxes, or drafting troops. For troops and taxes it would have to make requisitions upon the states. There was to be no separate, single, strong executive (the "President of the United States" was to be merely the presiding officer at the sessions of Congress), but Congress itself was to see to the execution of the laws through an executive committee of thirteen, made up of one member from each state, through *ad hoc* and standing committees for specific functions, and through such

---

THE END OF SLAVERY IN MASSACHUSETTS
(*Decision of the State's Chief Justice*)

1783

"As to the doctrine of slavery and the right of Christians to hold Africans in perpetual servitude, and sell and treat them as we do our horses and cattle, that (it is true) has been heretofore countenanced by the Province Laws formerly, but nowhere is it expressly enacted or established. It has been a usage—a usage which took its origin from the practice of some of the European nations, and the regulations of British government respecting the then Colonies, for the benefit of trade and wealth. But whatever sentiments have formerly prevailed in this particular or slid in upon us by the example of others, a different idea has taken place with the people of America, more favorable to the natural rights of mankind, and to that natural, innate desire of Liberty, which with Heaven (without regard to color, complexion, or shape of noses) has inspired all the human race. And upon this ground our Constitution of Government, by which the people of this Commonwealth have solemnly bound themselves, sets out with declaring that all men are born free and equal—and that every subject is entitled to liberty, and to have it guarded by the laws, as well as life and property—and in short is totally repugnant to the idea of being born slaves. This being the case, I think the idea of slavery is inconsistent with our own conduct and Constitution; and there can be no such thing as perpetual servitude of a rational creature, unless his liberty is forfeited by some criminal conduct or given up by personal consent or contract."

1. [Article II] "Each state retains its sovereignty, freedom and independence, and every Power, Jurisdiction and right, which is not by this confederation expressly delegated to the United States, in Congress assembled."

2. [Article IV] The free inhabitants of each state "shall be entitled to all privileges and immunities of free citizens in the several states," and "full faith and credit" shall be given by each state to the judicial and other official proceedings of other states.

3. [Article V] Each state shall be represented in Congress by no less than two and no more than seven members, shall pay its own delegates, and shall have one vote (regardless of the number of members).

4. [Article VI] No state, without the consent of Congress, shall enter into diplomatic relations or make treaties with other states or with foreign nations, or engage in war except in case of actual invasion.

5. [Article VIII] A "common treasury" shall be supplied by the states in proportion to the value of their land and improvements; the states shall levy taxes to raise their quotas of revenue.

6. [Article IX] Congress shall have power to decide on peace and war, conduct foreign affairs, settle disputes between states, regulate the Indian trade, maintain post offices, make appropriations, borrow money, emit bills of credit, build a navy, requisition soldiers from the states, etc.—but nine states must agree before Congress can take any important action.

7. [Article X] A "Committee of the States," consisting of one delegate from each state, shall act in the place of Congress when Congress is not in session.

8. [Article XIII] No change shall be made in these Articles unless agreed to by Congress and "afterwards confirmed by the legislatures of every state."

administrative departments as it might choose to create. There were to be no Confederation courts, but disputes between the states were to be settled by a complicated system of arbitration. The states were to retain their individual sovereignty, each of the legislatures electing and paying the salaries of two to seven delegates to Congress, and each delegation having only one vote no matter how numerous. At least nine of the states (through their legislatures) would have to approve any important measure, such as a treaty, before Congress could pass it, and all thirteen would have to approve before the Articles could be ratified or amended.

Ratification was delayed by differences of opinion about the proposed plan. Some Americans were willing enough to accept a relatively weak central government, but others preferred to see it strengthened. The people of the small states insisted upon equal state representation, but those of the large states thought they should be represented in proportion to their population. Above all, the states claiming Western lands wished

STATE CLAIMS TO WESTERN LANDS, 1781

to keep them, but the rest of the states demanded that the whole territory be turned over to the Confederation government. The "landed" states, among which Virginia had the largest and best claim, founded their claims upon colonial charters, with the exception of New York, which based its rights upon a protectorate over the Iroquois Indians. The "landless" states, particularly Maryland, maintained that as the fruit of common sacrifices in war the Western land had become the rightful property of all the states. In this dispute selfish interests as well as high principles were involved, for rival groups of land speculators schemed to secure the cancellation or confirmation of private grants already made. At last New York gave up its rather hazy claim, and Virginia made a qualified offer to cede its lands to Congress. Then Maryland, the only state still holding out against ratification, approved the Articles of Confederation, and they went into effect in 1781.

The Confederation government came into being in time to conclude the war and make the peace. Meanwhile, during the years of fighting from 1775 to 1781, the Second Continental Congress served as the agency for directing and coordinating the war effort of the people of the thirteen states.

Mobilizing for War

Congress and the states faced overwhelming tasks in raising and organizing armies, providing the necessary supplies and equipment, and paying the costs of war.

Supplies of most kinds were scarce at the outset, and shortages persisted to the end. Though America, being a land of hunters, contained numerous gunsmiths, they were not able to meet the wartime demand for guns and ammunition, nor were they able to produce heavy arms. Some of the states offered bounties for the encouragement of manufactures, especially for the production of guns and powder, and Congress in 1777 established a government arsenal at Springfield, Massachusetts. Even so, the Americans themselves managed to manufacture only a small fraction of the equipment they used. They supplemented their own manufactures with matériel which fell into their hands upon the seizure of forts like Crown Point and Ticonderoga (in 1775), the surrender of British armies, and the capture of supply ships by American privateers. But they got most of their war materials through importations from Europe, particularly from France.

In trying to meet the expenses of war, Congress had no power to tax the people, and the states had little inclination to do so. Indeed, cash was scarce in the country, as it always had been. When Congress requisitioned the states for money, none of them contributed more than a tiny part of its share. At first Congress hesitated to requisition goods directly from the people, but finally allowed army purchasing agents to take supplies from farmers and pay with certificates of indebtedness. Congress could not raise much money by floating long-term loans at home, since few Americans could afford war bonds and those few usually preferred to invest their funds in more profitable ventures, such as privateering. So Congress had no choice but to issue paper money, and Continental currency came from the printing presses in large and repeated batches. The states added sizeable currency issues of their own.

With goods and coin so scarce and paper money so plentiful, prices rose to fantastic heights and the value of the paper money fell proportionately. There quickly appeared all the usual evils of wartime profiteering, and more too. One reason why Washington's men suffered from shortages of food and clothing at Valley Forge during the terrible winter of 1777–8 was that American farmers and merchants preferred to do business with the British forces occupying near-by Philadelphia, since the British could pay in gold or silver coin. To check the inflationary trend, Congress advised the states to pass laws for price control, but soon saw the futility of such measures and recommended that they be dropped. Eventually, in 1780, Congress decided that the states should accept continental currency from taxpayers at the rate of forty paper dollars to one silver dollar, then send it to Congress to be destroyed. If the currency was not turned in for taxes at a fortieth of its face value, it became utterly worthless; hence the expression, "Not worth a Continental." By this time Congress was able to meet the most pressing of its financial needs by borrowing from abroad.

The states added to their financial resources by seizing lands belonging to the Crown and to colonial proprietors. In 1777 Congress recommended that the states also confiscate and sell the property of Loyalists active in the British cause, then lend the proceeds to the central government. The states were eager enough to expropriate the Loyalists, though not to make the requested loan. Already Patriots were punishing Tories in various ways, taking from them the rights of citizenship, barring them from certain occupations, and imposing special taxes and heavy fines upon them. The seizure and sale of Loyalist property, resulting incidentally in a widened distribution of land ownership among the buyers, netted the states a total of several million pounds, in value if not actual cash. Around 100,000 of the Loyalists themselves, either voluntarily or because of banishment, left the country during the course of the war, the most numerous group going to Quebec and laying the foundations of English-speaking Canada. If the sorrows of the expropriated and the exiled seem heartrending, it must be remembered that the Patriots were engaged in a life-and-death struggle with Great Britain and that the Loyalists, comprising what in later years would be called a "fifth column," were eager to aid the enemy whenever they got the chance.

While thousands of Tories enlisted and fought in the British ranks, only a small proportion of the Patriots were willing to volunteer for the American armies, once the first surge of patriotism at the start of the war had passed. The states had to resort to persuasion and force, to bounties and the draft, the bounties being commonly in the form of land scrip, since land was an asset with which the states were well supplied. Thus recruited, militiamen remained under the control of their respective states. The recruits were, many of them, expert marksmen and on the average they were physically bigger and stronger than the British regulars, yet man for man they were no match for the redcoats in battle since they lacked the regulars' fine training, discipline, and *esprit de corps*.

Foreseeing some of the disadvantages of separately organized militias, Congress early called upon the states (while they were still colonies) to raise troops for a regular force, the Continental army, and agreed that it should have a single commander in chief. George Washington, forty-three years old, sober and responsible by nature, possessed more command experience than any other American-born officer available. And he had political as well as military qualifications. An early advocate of independence, he was admired and trusted by nearly all the Patriots. A Virginian, he had the support not only of Southerners but also of Northerners who feared that the appointment of a New Englander might jeopardize sectional harmony. As the unanimous choice of the delegates, he took command in June, 1775.

Congress chose well. Throughout the war Washington kept faithfully at his task, despite difficulties and discouragements that would have daunted a lesser

GEORGE WASHINGTON. [OPPOSITE] From 1772 to 1795 the Maryland-born artist and taxidermist Charles Willson Peale painted from life more than a dozen portraits of George Washington, under whom he served as a soldier during the Revolutionary War. This portrait, which conveys something of the moral as well as the physical grandeur of Washington, shows him in the uniform of commander in chief at his Princeton headquarters in 1776. Here is a more realistic likeness of Washington than the far more familiar unfinished portrait by Gilbert Stuart. Peale founded the Pennsylvania Academy of the Fine Arts and also the Peale Museum in Philadelphia. In the museum were displayed stuffed animals against a realistically painted background, skeletons of prehistoric monsters, objects brought from the West by the Lewis and Clark expedition (1804–1806), and scientific curiosities of various kinds. (THE PENNSYLVANIA ACADEMY OF THE FINE ARTS)

STEUBEN AT VALLEY FORGE. Many foreigners served as officers in the Continental Army—too many, it seemed to General Washington. Most of them received their commissions from Congress, not from the commander in chief. Once he referred to the foreigners as "hungry adventurers." But he deeply appreciated the assistance of a few of the volunteers from abroad, especially the Marquis de Lafayette and the Baron von Steuben. A veteran of the Prussian army, Steuben came to the United States in 1777, and Washington appointed him inspector general, with overall charge of military discipline, instruction, and supply. Steuben reorganized the Continental Army, provided for improved training and drill of soldiers, and wrote a manual of army regulations. The painting by Edwin A. Abbey, which hangs in the Pennsylvania House of Representatives, shows Steuben instructing troops in Washington's camp at Valley Forge, near Philadelphia, during the winter of 1777–1778. After the war he settled in New York. (COURTESY OF THE PENNSYLVANIA DEPARTMENT OF COMMERCE)

man. With the aid of foreign military experts such as the Marquis de Lafayette and the Baron von Steuben he succeeded in building and holding together the Continental army, though at no time did it number as many as 10,000 men (not counting the militia of the separate states). The morale of the soldiers, who were getting short rations and low pay, became so bad that mutinies broke out (in 1781) among the Pennsylvania and New Jersey troops. Meanwhile, during the dark winter of Valley Forge, some congressmen and army officers, conspiring together in the so-called Conway cabal, hinted at replacing Washington as commander in chief. He, on the other hand, complained often and bitterly against his employers, the delegates in Congress, who seemed to do too little in supplying him

with manpower and equipment, and too much in interfering with his conduct of military operations. The faults were not all on the side of Congress, which had its difficulties too. Washington had his shortcomings as a military commander and he lost more battles than he won. Yet he was a great war leader. For all his faults and failures, he led the army and the nation to ultimate victory with his supreme steadiness and courage, his sacrificial devotion to the cause of independence.

The Fighting, to 1777

For about the first year of the fighting (1775–6) the colonial armed forces took the offensive. After the British retreat from Concord and Lexington, the Americans besieged the army of General Gage in Boston, and though suffering severe casualties in the battle of Bunker Hill (actually fought on Breed's Hill, June 17, 1775), they inflicted even greater losses upon the enemy and thereafter they continued to tighten the siege. Far to the south, at Moore's Creek Bridge in North Carolina, a band of Patriots crushed an uprising of Tories (February 27, 1776) and thereby discouraged British plans for invading the Southern states with Loyalist aid. Far to the north the Americans themselves undertook an invasion of Canada. The fearless Benedict Arnold, assuming command on the death of Richard Montgomery, threatened Quebec after a winter march of incredible hardship, but in the end met frustration and defeat. In the spring a civilian commission headed by the seventy-year-old Franklin returned from the north without success in its efforts to secure the allegiance of Canada as the fourteenth state. Already, however, General Gage had given up his attempt to hold Boston and had departed with his troops and with hundreds of Loyalist refugees (March 17, 1776) for Halifax. Within a year from the firing of the first shots, the enemy had been driven from American soil.

The enemy soon returned, to put the Americans on the strategic defensive for the remainder of the war. During the summer of 1776, in the weeks immediately following the Declaration of Independence, the waters around the city of New York became filled with the most formidable military force Great Britain ever had sent abroad. Here were hundreds of men-of-war and troopships and a host of 32,000 disciplined soldiers under the command of the tall and affable Sir William Howe. Having no grudge against the Americans, Howe would rather awe them into submission than shoot them, and he believed that most of them, if given a chance, would show that they were at heart loyal to the King. In a parley with commissioners from Congress he offered the alternatives of submission with royal

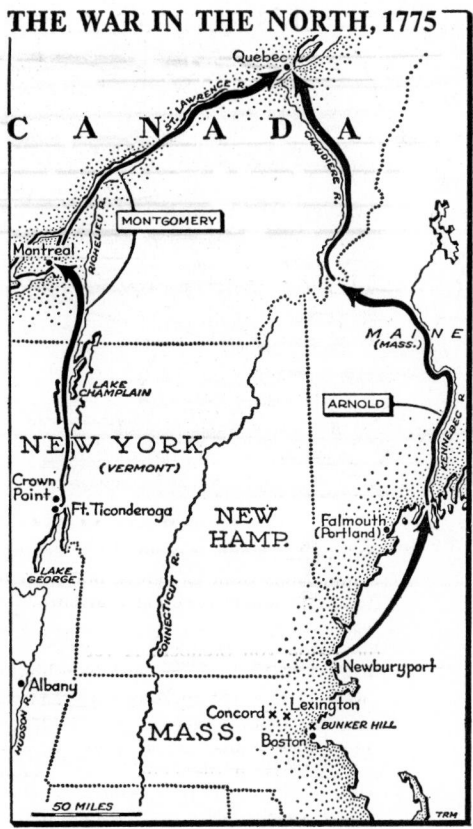

THE WAR IN THE NORTH, 1775

pardon or battle against overwhelming odds. To oppose Howe's awesome array, Washington could muster only about 19,-000 poorly armed and trained soldiers, including both Continentals and state troops, and he had no navy at all. Yet without hesitation the Americans chose continued war, which meant inevitably a succession of defeats. The British pushed the defenders off Long Island, compelled them to abandon Manhattan Island, and drove them in slow retreat over the plains of New Jersey, across the Delaware River, and into Pennsylvania.

Warfare being for eighteenth-century Europeans a seasonal activity, the British settled down for the winter with occupation forces at various points in New Jersey and with an outpost of Hessians at Trenton on the Delaware. But Washington did not content himself with sitting

WASHINGTON'S RETREAT, 1776

still. On Christmas night, 1776, he daringly recrossed the icy river, surprised and scattered the Hessians, and occupied the town. Then he advanced and drove off a force of redcoats at Princeton. Unable to hold either Princeton or Trenton, he finally took refuge for the rest of the winter in the hills around Morristown. As the campaign of 1776 came to an end, the Americans could console themselves with the thought that they had won two minor victories, that their main army was still intact, and that the invaders were really no nearer than ever to the decisive triumph which Howe so confidently had anticipated.

For the campaign of 1777 the British devised a strategy which, if Howe had stuck to it, might have cut the United States in two and prepared the way for final victory by Great Britain. According to this plan, Howe would move from New York up the Hudson to Albany while another force, in a gigantic pincers movement, would come down from Canada to meet him. One of Howe's ambitious younger officers, the dashing John Burgoyne, "Gentleman Johnny," secured command of this northern force and

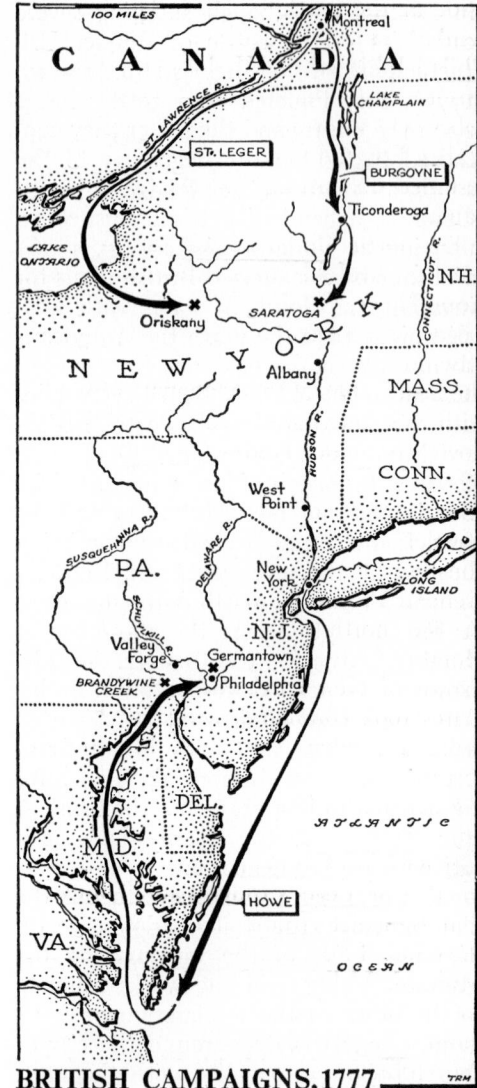

BRITISH CAMPAIGNS, 1777

elaborated upon the plan by preparing for a two-pronged attack along both the Mohawk and the upper Hudson approaches to Albany.

Then, fortunately for the United States, Howe adopted a different plan for himself, intending to dispirit the Patriots and rally the Loyalists by seizing the rebel capital, Philadelphia. Taking the bulk of his forces away from New York by sea, Howe landed at the head of Chesapeake Bay, brushed Washington aside at the battle of Brandywine (September 11), and proceeded to occupy Philadelphia, while Washington, after an unsuccessful attack at Germantown (October 4), went into winter quarters at Valley Forge, and the scattered Congress resumed its sittings in York, Pennsylvania.

Up north, Burgoyne was left to carry out his twofold campaign without aid from Howe. Sending Colonel Barry St. Leger with a fast-moving force up the St. Lawrence River toward Lake Ontario and the headwaters of the Mohawk, Burgoyne with his own army advanced directly down the upper Hudson Valley. He got off to a flying start, easily taking Fort Ticonderoga and an enormous store of powder and supplies, and causing such consternation that Congress removed General Philip Schuyler from command in the north and replaced him with Horatio Gates, in response to the demands of New Englanders. By the time Gates took command, Burgoyne already faced a sudden reversal of his military fortunes in consequence of two staggering defeats. In one of them, at Oriskany, New York (August 6), Nicholas Herkimer with his German farmers checked a force of St. Leger's Indians and Tories, so that Benedict Arnold had time to go to the relief of Fort Stanwix and close off the Mohawk Valley to St. Leger's advance. In the other battle, at Bennington, Vermont (August 16), the Bunker Hill veteran John Stark, with his New England militiamen, severely mauled a detachment that Burgoyne had sent out to seek supplies. Short of materials, with all help cut off, Burgoyne fought a couple of costly engagements and then withdrew to Saratoga, where Gates surrounded him. Burgoyne was through, and he knew it. On October 17, 1777, he ordered what was left of his army, nearly 5,000 men, to lay down their arms.

Not only the United States but also Europe took note of the amazing news from the woods of upstate New York, and France in particular was impressed. The British surrender at Saratoga, a great turning point in the war, led directly to an alliance between the United States and France.

Foreign Friends

Shortly after the fighting had begun, Congress appointed a secret committee with Franklin as chairman for the purpose of corresponding with "our friends" in Great Britain and, more significantly, in "other parts of the world." Later Congress replaced this agency with a Committee for Foreign Affairs and then (1781) with a Department of Foreign Affairs, the immediate ancestor of the State Department. As far as possible, however, Congress as a whole conducted foreign relations, often overruling or bypassing the agencies it created.

Even before the Declaration of Independence, Congress drew up a treaty plan for liberal commercial arrangements with other countries and prepared to send representatives to the capitals of Europe for negotiating treaties—which necessarily would mean European recognition of the United States as one of the sovereign nations of the world. "Militia diplomats" John Adams called the early American representatives abroad, and unlike the diplomatic regulars of Europe they knew little of the formal art and etiquette of Old World diplomacy. Yet most of them were well acquainted with certain fundamentals, for they had gained much diplomatic experience through their dealings with one another in intercolonial affairs, with the Indian tribes in war and peace, and with the British government as colonial agents in London. Since overseas communication was slow and uncertain (it took from one to three months to cross the Atlantic) these representatives abroad sometimes had to interpret the instructions of Congress very freely and make crucial decisions entirely on their own.

Of all the possible foreign friends of the United States, the most promising and most powerful was France, who still resented her defeat at the hands of Great Britain in 1763. France, under King Louis XVI, who came to the throne in 1774, had an astute and determined foreign minister in the Count de Vergennes, an expert practitioner of Machiavellian principles, thoroughly trained in the cutthroat diplomacy of eighteenth-century Europe. Vergennes soon saw that France had a vital interest in the outcome of the American war. If the colonies should assert and maintain their independence, the power of Great Britain would be seriously weakened by the loss of a good part of her empire, and the power of France would be correspondingly increased. But Vergennes was too shrewd to talk to Americans about the interests of France. As he once had said regarding French relations with the Turks, "Let us enlighten them as to their true interests; let us appear to be occupied only with what concerns them, without reference to ourselves."

From the start of the troubles between England and her colonies, the French had maintained observers in America to report the course of events, and after the shooting began both Americans and Frenchmen put out diplomatic feelers. In London the Massachusetts colonial agent Arthur Lee met the French musical composer and political genius Caron de Beaumarchais, and the two discussed the possibilities of secret assistance to the colonies. Beaumarchais reported to Vergennes, and Vergennes dispatched an army officer to America to encourage the rebellion, urge independence, and promise supplies. After several meetings with Vergennes' spokesman, Franklin's committee of secret correspondence sent Silas Deane to France as a "merchant" to make "commercial" arrangements. In consequence of these arrangements Beaumarchais shipped large quantities of munitions to America through a fictitious trading firm which he had rigged up to disguise the fact that most of the shipments were financed by the King of France and the King of Spain. Whether this sort of lend-lease was a gift or a loan became later a question of bitter dispute between Congress and Beaumarchais.

After the Declaration of Independence Franklin himself went to France to get further aid and outright recognition of the United States. A natural diplomat, the equal if not the superior of the world's best at that time, Franklin immediately captivated Frenchmen of all classes—and Frenchwomen too. But Vergennes hesitated. At the first news of the American Declaration, he was inclined to make a treaty recognizing United States independence, but he did not wish to act without Spain, and when reports came of Washington's defeat on Long Island he decided to wait and watch the military developments in America. If and when the Americans should show that they had a real chance of winning, then France would intervene. Meanwhile Vergennes was willing to go on financing the American war. He initiated a series of subsidies which in time amounted to nearly $2 million and a series of loans which totaled over $6 million.

The news that Vergennes and Franklin were waiting for—the news from Saratoga —arrived in London on December 2 and in Paris on December 4, 1777. In London the knowledge of Burgoyne's surrender caused Lord North to decide in favor of a peace offensive, an offer of complete home rule within the Empire for Americans if they would quit the war. In Paris, learning of Lord North's intentions from a British spy, Franklin let the word get out for Vergennes to hear. Vergennes worried. If the Americans should accept the British offer, his opportunity to weaken France's traditional enemy would be gone, and if they could not get what they wanted from France, they might accept. Without waiting for Spain to go along with France, Vergennes on Feb-

TREATY OF ALLIANCE WITH FRANCE

1778

1. If war should break out between France and Great Britain, France and the United States will make "common cause" against Great Britain.

2. The aim of this alliance is to maintain the independence of the United States.

3. France "renounces forever" all claim to Canada or other one-time British possessions in North America.

4. "Neither of the two parties shall conclude either truce or peace with Great Britain without the formal consent of the other first obtained."

5. The two parties guarantee "forever against all other powers" the possessions of one another in the Western Hemisphere.

ruary 6, 1778, signed two treaties with Franklin and Deane, one a treaty of commerce and amity, and the other, which was supposed to be secret, a treaty of conditional and defensive alliance, to take effect if Great Britain should go to war with France. Congress and the King quickly ratified the treaties, and Congress received and banqueted a minister from France while the King welcomed Franklin as minister from the United States.

France soon drifted into war with Great Britain, and in 1779 Spain with objectives of her own declared war as an ally of France though not of the United States; Spain refused even to receive officially the American representative in Madrid, John Jay. A year later The Netherlands, persisting in its profitable trade with both the French and the Americans, found itself also at war with Britain and agreed to a treaty with the United States. The League of Armed Neutrals—Russia, Denmark, Sweden—assumed a defiant attitude toward Britain, but refrained from considering war and refused to have any official dealings with the upstart nation in America.

Indirectly all the countries arrayed in hostility to Britain contributed to the ultimate success of the United States by complicating the task of the latter's foe. Directly, The Netherlands provided loans to the Americans but was powerless to give military or naval support, and Spain gave unofficial subsidies but confined her military and naval activities to strictly Spanish objects. France (for her own reasons, of course) was the true friend in need of the Americans. Not only did she furnish them most of their money and munitions, but she also provided a navy and an expeditionary force that, with Washington's army, made possible the decisive victory at Yorktown.

Victory at Yorktown

During the first two years of the war the important campaigns and battles had taken place in the North, but after Saratoga the fighting in that part of the country developed into a stalemate. Replacing General Howe, Sir Henry Clinton withdrew from Philadelphia and took what had been Howe's army back to New York. Washington used most of his army to keep watch around New York while (1778–1779) sending part of it to chastise the Indians along the frontier for their horrible massacres in the Cherry Valley (New York) and the Wyoming Valley

(Pennsylvania). During that same winter George Rogers Clark, with orders from the state of Virginia and not from Washington or Congress, led a heroic expedition over the mountains and redeemed the settlements of the Illinois country from the British and their Indian allies. In 1779 the treason of Benedict Arnold shocked Washington and Patriots everywhere but did little military damage except for the transfer of Arnold's services to the British, since his scheme for betraying the Hudson River stronghold of West Point was frustrated in the nick of time. During the final two years of fight-

coast with ease, that the difficulties of overland travel would make American counteraction ineffectual, and that Loyalists would rise en masse to welcome and assist the redcoats as liberators. With the conquered South as a base, Clinton and Cornwallis thought they could dispose of the rest of the country at their leisure. While it was true that in Georgia and the Carolinas there were numerous Tories, some of them disgruntled veterans of the Regulator movement, it was also true that in Virginia as in Massachusetts the mass of the people were fiercely patriotic and that even in the lower South the Loyalist

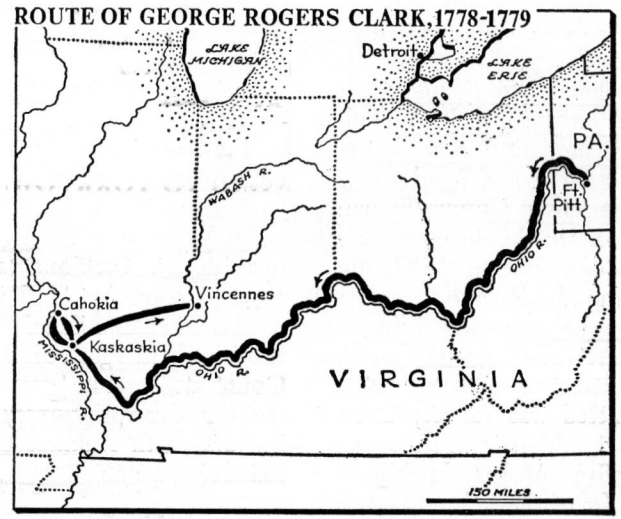

ROUTE OF GEORGE ROGERS CLARK, 1778-1779

ing, all the significant action occurred in the South.

Sir Henry Clinton, a rather timid strategist, planned a Southern offensive that was supposed to end the American will to resist, but he put the command of the operation in the hands of Lord Cornwallis, an able general but one as rash as Clinton himself was cautious, and capable of changing plans and disobeying orders in mid-campaign. Clinton and Cornwallis based their strategy on assumption which was not to prove fact. They assumed that seapower would enable them to move their troops from point to point along the

strength was grossly overestimated. Actually, having the support of most of the countryside, the Patriot forces were to be better off than the British in matters of logistics and supply. And the French, while far from able to maintain consistent control of the coastal waters, were finally to have a fleet in the right place at the right time.

The British succeeded in taking Savannah (December 29, 1778) and Charleston (May 20, 1779), inspiring many Loyalists to take up arms, and advancing far into the interior. At every turn they were harassed, however, by Patriot guerillas led by such resourceful fighters as Thomas Sumter, Andrew Pickens, and Francis Marion, the "Swamp Fox." Penetrating to Camden, well up the Wateree River in South Carolina, Cornwallis met and crushed (August 16, 1780) a combined force of militiamen and Continentals under Horatio Gates, who did not quite deserve his fame as the hero of Saratoga. Congress recalled Gates, and Washington gave the southern command to Nathanael Greene, an erstwhile Quaker blacksmith of Rhode Island and probably the ablest of all the American generals of the time, next to Washington himself.

Before Greene arrived in the war theater along the North and South Carolina line, the tide of battle already had begun to turn against Cornwallis. At King's Mountain (October 7, 1780) a band of Patriot riflemen from the backwoods killed, wounded, or captured an entire force of 1,100 New York and South Carolina Tories, upon whom Cornwallis had depended as auxiliaries. Once arrived, Greene confused and exasperated Cornwallis by dividing the American forces into fast-moving contingents while refraining from a showdown in open battle. One of the contingents inflicted what Cornwallis admitted was "a very unexpected and severe blow" at Cowpens (January 17, 1781). At last, having received the reinforcements he awaited, Greene combined all his forces and arranged to meet the British on ground of his own choosing at Guilford Court House, North Carolina. After a hard-fought battle (March 15, 1781) Greene was driven from the field, but Cornwallis lost so many men that he decided at last to abandon the Carolina campaign.

For a while Cornwallis thought of joining with the forces of Benedict Arnold, now in command of British raiders in Virginia, and undertaking the conquest of that state. In Virginia he set out new raiding parties, drove off a Patriot army under Lafayette, and then—despite the expostulations of his superior officer, Gen-

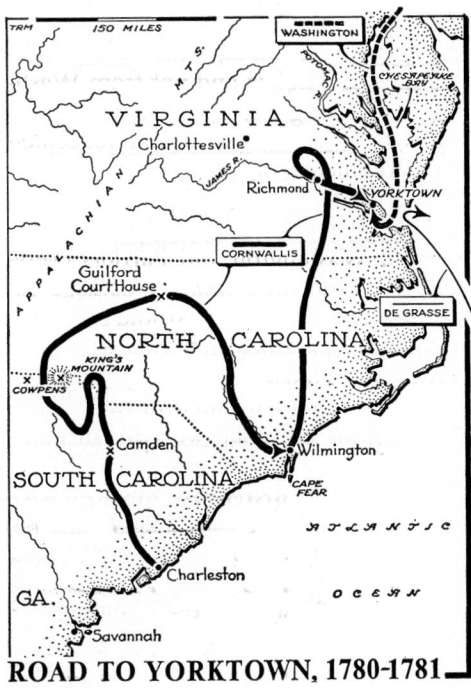

ROAD TO YORKTOWN, 1780-1781

eral Clinton—retreated to the peninsula between the York and James rivers and began to build fortifications at Yorktown. While Clinton worried about Cornwallis' moves, Washington made plans with the Count de Rochambeau, commander of the French expeditionary force in America, and with Admiral de Grasse, commander of a French fleet in American waters, for trapping Cornwallis. Washington and Rochambeau marched a Franco-American army from the New York vicinity to join Lafayette in Virginia while Grasse sailed with additional troops for Chesapeake Bay and the York River. These joint operations, perfectly timed and executed, caught Cornwallis between land and sea. After a few shows of resistance, he asked for terms on October 17, 1781, four years to the day after the capitulation of Burgoyne, and two days later he surrendered his whole army of more than 7,000.

The fighting was over, but the war was not quite won. The United States continued to be something of an occupied country, with British forces holding the seaports of Savannah, Charleston, Wilmington, and New York. Before long a British fleet met and defeated Admiral de Grasse's fleet in the West Indies, ending Washington's hopes for further seapower assistance. So far as the naval and military situation was concerned, the British still held the upper hand in America. And peace was yet to be made.

Winning the Peace

Until Yorktown, peace had been for Americans an illusory and at times a dangerous proposition, and the prospects even after that victory, though improved, were not ideal. The trouble was with Spain. She entered the war solely to recover lost territories in America and Europe, above all the island of Gibraltar, and she had an alliance binding France to make no separate peace. The United States had promised in its treaty of alliance to conclude no peace without France. Now, if Spain should fight on till she won Gibraltar back, and if France should stick by Spain, and the United States by France, the Americans might be at war forever. That, however, was not the real danger to American interests. The danger was that Spain, to get Gibraltar or American territory, might enter into a deal with Great Britain at the expense of the United States, and that France might feel compelled to go along with Spain. In making peace, the United States had as much to fear from its ally as from its enemy.

When, in 1779, Spain in the role of mediator proposed a peace conference, Congress promptly named John Adams as the American delegate and sent him instructions to enter into no negotiations unless Great Britain first recognized the United States as "sovereign, free, and independent." Adams, already abroad as a militia diplomat, proceeded to Paris and remained there waiting for new peace opportunities after the Spanish proposal had

been forgotten. The blustery Adams did not get along with Vergennes as well as the soft-spoken Franklin did. Vergennes sent to America a new minister, La Luzerne, to do something about the Adams nuisance. Lobbying with congressmen and playing up to the Secretary for Foreign Affairs, La Luzerne secured the replacement of the single delegate with a whole delegation, including Franklin and John Jay as well as Adams, and La Luzerne virtually dictated the delegation's instructions. These instructions told the prospective peacemakers to keep in close touch with the French government, tell it everything, follow its advice. Thus the United States was put into the hands of Vergennes by the time (1781) Austria and Russia made their joint mediation offer that led eventually to a general peace settlement.

Then Yorktown, by giving the Americans new bargaining power, rescued them from the worst of their dependence upon Vergennes. In England, Cornwallis' defeat provoked outcries against continuing the war and demands for cultivating American friendship as an asset in international politics. Lord North resigned and Lord Shelburne emerged from the political wreckage as prime minister. British emissaries appeared in France to talk informally with Franklin. He suggested what he called "necessary" terms of peace, including independence and the establishment of the Mississippi as the western boundary of the United States, and "desirable" terms including the cession of Canada for the purpose of "reconciliation," a "sweet word," as he said. But John Jay, recently arrived from his fruitless mission to Spain, where he had acquired reason to be suspicious of Spaniards and all Europeans, objected to continuing the negotiations on the grounds that the Americans were addressed not as plenipotentiaries of a sovereign nation but as "persons" from "colonies or plantations." The negotiations were delayed until Jay was satisfied.

All along Franklin and Jay and Adams had kept Vergennes informed of their conversations with British agents, in accordance with the instructions from Congress. Then, one day, Jay learned that Vergennes' private secretary was off on a secret mission to England. Jay feared that Vergennes was going to leave the United States in the lurch and make a makers and which might have proved disadvantageous to the United States. From that day on, Franklin and Jay and Adams ceased to inform Vergennes of their diplomacy but went ahead on their own and soon drew up a preliminary treaty with Great Britain. In doing so, they may have violated the spirit but they did not violate the letter of the Franco-American

---

TREATY OF PARIS

1783

1. "His Britannic Majesty acknowledges the said United States . . . to be free, sovereign and independent States."

2. Boundaries shall run, as described in some detail, from Nova Scotia to and through the Great Lakes and the Lake of the Woods, "thence on a due west course to the river Mississippi," down the Mississippi to the thirty-first parallel, and then east to the Atlantic Ocean.

3. The people of the United States shall have fishing rights and liberties in the waters of British North America.

4. Creditors on either side "shall meet with no lawful impediment to the recovery of the full value, in sterling money, of all *bona fide* debts heretofore contracted."

5. Congress "shall earnestly recommend to the legislatures of the respective States" that they make restitution for confiscated Loyalist property.

6. There shall be no future confiscations or prosecutions on account of the part that anyone may have taken in the war.

7. Hostilities shall cease, and "His Britannic Majesty shall, with all convenient speed, and without causing any destruction, or carrying away any negroes or other property of the American inhabitants, withdraw all his armies, garrisons and fleets from the said United States, and from every post, place and harbour within the same."

---

separate peace by which Great Britain and Spain would divide between themselves the territory west of the Alleghenies and east of the Mississippi. Such a deal, as Franklin exclaimed, would have "cooped us up within the Allegheny Mountains." Though Jay was mistaken as to the details of the secret mission, he was right in thinking that Vergennes was suggesting separate negotiations which were to be kept from the American peace- alliance, since they were not making a separate final peace. Of course, they disregarded their instructions from Congress, but those instructions had come originally from Vergennes himself.

After the preliminary articles were signed (November 30, 1782), Jay and Adams left to Franklin the delicate task of telling Vergennes what had been done. Franklin admitted to Vergennes that the Americans perhaps had violated etiquette in failing to keep the French informed, but he trusted that the incident would cause no rift in the Franco-American alliance. Cleverly Franklin observed: "The English, I just now learn, flatter themselves they have already divided us. I hope this little misunderstanding will therefore be kept a secret, and that they will find themselves totally mistaken." Vergennes, dealing with a fellow master of diplomacy, could not say much and was doubtless glad to have an excuse for ending the war regardless of the wishes of his Spanish ally. Franklin coolly asked for another loan from France—and got it!

The preliminary treaty became effective on January 20, 1783, when Spain as well as France agreed to end hostilities. It included a number of provisions that Franklin and Jay and Adams had opposed, and some of these were to lead to serious friction with Great Britain and with Spain

in the years ahead. Yet it also included essentially the "necessary" terms which Franklin originally had indicated, though not his "desirable" ones such as the cession of Canada. On the whole the peace was remarkably favorable to the United States in granting a clear-cut recognition of independence and a generous, though ambiguous, delimitation of territory—from the southern boundary of Canada to the northern boundary of Florida and from the Atlantic to the Mississippi. Indeed, by playing off the powers of Europe against one another, Franklin and his colleagues had achieved the greatest diplomatic success in the history of the United States. With good reason the American people celebrated as the last of the British occupation forces embarked from New York and General Washington at the head of his troops rode triumphantly in.

BIBLIOGRAPHY

An up-to-date synthesis is J. R. Alden's The American Revolution, 1775–1783 (1954), which is especially good on military events. A popularly written survey is J. C. Miller's Triumph of Freedom, 1775–1783 (1949). E. B. Greene, The Revolutionary Generation, 1763–1790 (1943), emphasizes social changes. These changes, resulting from the "stream of revolution," are also stressed—and perhaps overstressed—in J. F. Jameson's influential interpretive essay, The American Revolution Considered as a Social Movement (1926).

For wartime as well as prewar development of political ideas, see C. L. Becker's The Declaration of Independence (1922) and R. G. Adams's The Political Ideas of the American Revolution (1922). Both of these authors see a progression of ideas culminating in the concept of a federated empire and finally of a separate and sovereign nation. See also the more recent study by Edward Dumbauld, The Declaration of Independence and What It Means Today (1950). Americans who opposed the idea of independence are sympathetically treated

by C. H. Van Tyne in The Loyalists in the American Revolution (1905).

Government during the Revolution is the subject of E. C. Burnett's The Continental Congress (1941) and Lynn Montross's The Reluctant Rebels: The Story of the Continental Congress, 1774–1789 (1950). In The Articles of Confederation (1948) Merrill Jensen interprets the Articles as a democratic and workable constitution. For state governments, see the thorough study by Allan Nevins, The American States during and after the Revolution (1924), and Douglass, Rebels and Democrats.

For campaigns and battles, the most complete modern account is Christopher Ward, The War of the Revolution (2 vols., 1952). W. M. Wallace, Appeal to Arms (1951) is briefer but also contains precise military details. Lynn Montross, Rag, Tag, and Bobtail (1952) is a readable story of the Continental army. G. F. Scheer and H. F. Rankin, Rebels and Redcoats (1957) fights the battles mainly in the words of the officers and soldiers themselves.

The central figure of the period is fully

portrayed in Freeman's *George Washington.* C. P. Nettels, *George Washington and American Independence* (1951), reveals the forces leading Washington to favor a break with Great Britain. See also Bernard Knollenberg, *Washington and the Revolution* (1940). Louis Gottschalk does justice to the Marquis de Lafayette in three excellent volumes: *Lafayette Comes to America* (1935), *Lafayette Joins the American Army* (1937), and *Lafayette and the Close of the American Revolution* (1942). C. L. Ver Steeg's *Robert Morris, Revolutionary Financier* (1954) is a fresh, scholarly appraisal that clarifies Morris's career. Aspects of Benjamin Franklin's wartime career are well treated in A. O. Aldridge's *Franklin and His French Contemporaries* (1957), a judicious study of Franco-American political and cultural relations, and in W. B. Clark's *Ben Franklin's Privateers* (1956), which reads like fiction though solidly grounded on fact. Gerald Stourzh, *Benjamin Franklin and American Foreign Policy* (1954), analyzes the diplomatic thinking of America's greatest diplomat.

On foreign relations, S. F. Bemis, *The Diplomacy of the American Revolution* (1935), is indispensable.

6

A MORE PERFECT UNION

As usually happens at the end of a long and hard-fought war, peace in 1783 brought to the American people tasks almost as trying as those of the war itself. Congress, with the inadequate powers granted to it in the Articles of Confederation, did not quite succeed in solving the problems of the time. Historians used to refer to the 1780's as the "Critical Period" of American history—a period supposedly of impending chaos and collapse from which the nation was rescued only by the timely adoption of a new Constitution. Actually the 1780's were years of hopeful striving rather than black despair, of economic recovery and not merely depression, of governmental progress under the Articles of Confederation despite temporary failures. Nevertheless, the new Constitution created a "more perfect union" than was otherwise possible at that time, and it provided a fundamental law capable of growth and adaptation to meet the needs of the nation for centuries to come.

Failures in Foreign Affairs

The peace treaty of 1783 recognized the independence of the United States and granted the new nation a vast domain —on paper—but Americans found it hard to exercise their full sovereignty in fact. At once they ran into serious conflict with both Great Britain and Spain, yet they could not count upon the support of France even though France remained technically America's ally.

Despite the treaty provisions calling upon the British to evacuate American soil, British forces continued to occupy a string of frontier posts along the Great Lakes within the United States. Secret orders to hold these forts went from the Colonial Office in London to the Governor-General of Canada on April 8, 1784, just one day before King George III proclaimed the peace treaty as being in final effect and called upon all his subjects to obey its terms! The real reason for the secret orders was the Canadian and British desire to maintain points of contact with Indian tribes in the Northwest for the conduct of the fur trade and the continuance of defensive alliances with them. The avowed reason, which was an afterthought, was the alleged failure of the United States to carry out its treaty obligations, particularly in regard to private debts.

These debts, dating from pre-Revolutionary days, were owed by American citizens, mostly Southern planters, to merchants and other creditors in England. The American debtors had no intention of paying—many of them had supported the Revolution in order to gain independence and thus throw off their old obligations. The treaty provided only that the United States should place no obstacle in the way of the collection of the debts, and the United States did place no obstacle in the way. True, the individual states interfered with debt collections, through the passage of debtor stay laws, the issuance of paper money as legal tender, and the rulings of courts sympathetic with local debtors.

According to the ill-founded British complaints, the United States was violating not only the article regarding private debts but also the one regarding Loyalist property. On this point the treaty said merely that Congress should recommend to the various states that they make restitution to certain categories of Loyalists whose possessions had been confiscated during the war. Congress did recommend, but the states did not respond. The British had not really expected them to. The article was put into the treaty as a gesture of the King's concern for the fate of his faithful subjects. Anticipating that the states would do little or nothing for Loyalist refugees, Parliament itself appropriated money for their relief. Thus the British complaints were insincere.

To British allegations of bad faith, Americans countered with the charge that Great Britain, besides refusing to abandon the frontier posts, was disregarding the treaty provision which obligated her to compensate American slaveowners whose slaves had been carried off by the British armies at the end of the war. And the two countries disputed the meaning and application of still another article, the one defining the northeastern boundary of the United States. Over part of its course the boundary was supposed to follow the St. Croix River, but unfortunately the river had two major branches, and the treaty did not specify which of the two was meant.

The peace arrangements led also to a boundary dispute between the United States and Spain. In her settlement with Spain, Great Britain gave back Florida (which had been British from 1763 to 1783) with the Atlantic and the Mississippi specified as its eastern and western limits but with no precise definition of its northern border. In the preliminary treaty with the United States, however, Great Britain had agreed secretly that, if she herself were to keep Florida, its boundary would be set at latitude 32° 28' and that, if she ceded it to Spain, its boundary would be located farther south, at the thirty-first parallel. Afterwards the United States insisted upon the more southerly of these lines, but Spain demanded the additional northern strip as rightfully a part of Florida. Spain also claimed extensive territory even north of that, as belonging to her by virtue of her (rather small-scale) military operations in the American West during the Revolutionary War.

There was another conflict between Anglo-American arrangements and the claims of Spain. In their treaty of peace Great Britain and the United States recognized the right of subjects and citizens of both countries to navigate the Mississippi River to its mouth. But Spain, possessing Louisiana as well as Florida and thus occupying both banks of the lower Mississippi, denied that Great Britain had any rights there to grant to the United States. In 1784 Spain exercised her lawful power over her territorial waters by closing the lower Mississippi to American navigation.

Thus several provisions of the peace with Great Britain failed to give Americans the benefits they desired and expected, and the treaty omitted entirely still other provisions they had hoped for. Above all, American shippers and traders wanted commercial arrangements that would give them privileges of trading and

shipping on equal terms with British subjects in all parts of the British Empire.
No longer colonists, these businessmen, it
is true, now had opportunities for exploiting world-wide routes of trade which,
before the war, had been legally closed
to them. Congress proceeded to make
satisfactory commercial treaties with the
nations of Europe—with France (1778),
The Netherlands (1782), Sweden
(1783), and Prussia (1785). Congress
also agreed to pay protection money to
the Sultan of Morocco (1786) so that
American merchantmen in the Mediterranean would be free from the depredations of at least some of the Barbary pirates. Without benefit of treaty, American
enterprisers opened fabulously profitable
trade routes to the Orient, beginning
with the voyage of the *Empress of China*
in 1784–5. Yet, though commerce flourished in new directions, most American
trade persisted as much as possible in the
old, prewar patterns. In the United
States the bulk of imports continued to
come from British sources, for Americans
were used to British goods, and British
merchants knew and catered to American
tastes, offered attractive prices, and extended long and easy credit. To earn the
British funds needed to pay for these imports, Americans desired free access to
more British markets than were open to
them after the war.

In 1784 Congress sent John Adams as
minister to London with instructions to
get a commercial treaty and speed up the
evacuation of the frontier posts. Taunted
by the query whether he represented one
nation or thirteen, Minister Adams made
no headway in England, partly because
Congress had no power to retaliate against
the kind of commercial warfare which
Great Britain was pursuing against the
United States. Throughout the 1780's the
British government refused even to return
the courtesy of sending a minister to the
American capital.

The Spanish government, by contrast,
was willing to negotiate its differences
with the United States, and in 1785 its
representative, Don Diego de Gardoqui,
arrived in New York (whither Congress
had moved from Philadelphia) to deal
with the Secretary for Foreign Affairs,
John Jay. After months of the most
friendly conversations, Jay and Gardoqui
initialed a treaty (1786). By its terms, the
Spanish government would have granted
Americans the right to trade with Spain
but not with her colonies; would have
conceded the American interpretation of
the Florida boundary; and (in a secret
article) would have joined in an alliance
to protect American soil from British encroachments. The United States, besides
guaranteeing Spanish possessions in
America, would have agreed to "forbear"
the navigation of the Mississippi for
twenty years, though not to abandon the
right of navigation. Jay found it hopeless,
however, to secure the necessary nine
state votes for the ratification of his treaty
by Congress, since the delegates from the
five Southern states objected bitterly and
correctly that the interests of Southerners
in Mississippi navigation were being sacrificed to the interests of Northerners in
Spanish trade.

Planning for the West

Into the areas of postwar border conflict
with Great Britain and Spain moved an
unprecedented horde of American settlers
during and after the Revolution. When
the war began, only a few thousand lived
west of the Appalachian divide; by 1790
their numbers had increased to 120,000.
Most of the migrants made the mountain
crossing under the auspices of able and
far-seeing land promoters. James Robert-
son and John Sevier led pioneers from
North Carolina to the Watauga settlements (1770) and later to the Cumberland Valley (1779), thus laying the foundations for the future state of Tennessee.
Richard Henderson, promoter of the
Transylvania Company and employer of
Daniel Boone, stimulated the growth of

Kentucky by selling lands, organizing a provisional government (1776), and having the Wilderness Road hewn out. The managers of the Vandalia Company encouraged migration to what eventually became West Virginia. And the Allen brothers—Ethan, Ira, and Levi—attracted purchasers for their regal holdings of real estate in the Green Mountains of Vermont. Upon such speculators the frontiersman usually had to depend for his land title and for other favors, yet he was characteristically an individualist determined to make a future for himself. He and his family, together with the thousands of others like him, comprised what was potentially the strongest single factor for redeeming the West for the United States.

But the United States could realize this potentiality only if the government were able to meet the needs of the frontier settler and keep him loyal to its distant authority. The settler needed protection from the Indians, access to outside markets for his surplus crops, and courts with orderly processes of law. In dealing with the West, Congress inherited responsibilities which formerly had baffled King and Parliament.

At first Congress lacked clear-cut jurisdiction over the trans-Appalachian region, and for several years conflicts of authority persisted among Congress, the states, and the frontier settlements themselves. Of course, with Virginia's cession in 1781, the landed states had begun to yield their Western claims to the Confederation. But Virginia had ceded her territory on the condition that private grants within it be canceled, and for a few years the grantees lobbied successfully to keep Congress from accepting the territory with that stipulation. North Carolina temporarily took back its ceded land, other states postponed their cessions, and not till 1802 did the last of them, Georgia, give up its claim. Meanwhile these states transferred the actual ownership of most of the land south of the Ohio River to private indi-

LAND SURVEY UNDER THE ORDINANCE OF 1785

A TOWNSHIP

A TOWNSHIP IS 6 MILES SQUARE AND CONTAINS 36 SQUARE MILES OR SECTIONS. ONE SECTION EQUALS 640 ACRES.

36	30	24	18	12	6
35	29	23	17	11	5
34	28	22	16	10	4
33	27	21	15	9	3
32	26	20	14	8	2
31	25	19	13	7	1

viduals and companies, and impatient settlers proceeded to set up their own state governments for Frankland or Franklin (Tennessee) and for Kentucky, while North Carolina attempted to incorporate the one and Virginia the other as mere counties.

In 1784, having persuaded Virginia to make a new cession without specific restrictions, Congress accepted Virginia's Western lands and began to make policy for the national domain. The most momentous decision, already resolved upon, was that settlements in the territory should not be held in permanent subjection as colonies but should be transformed ultimately into states equal with the original thirteen. In the Ordinance of 1784 Congress temporarily adopted Thomas Jefferson's very democratic plan for the transition to statehood of the territory between the Ohio River and the Great Lakes. This territory was to have been divided into ten districts, each to be self-governing from the start, to be represented by a delegate in Congress as soon as its population reached 20,000, and to be admitted as a state when its population equalled the number of free inhabitants of the smallest existing state.

Having thus prepared a scheme of territorial government, Congress in the Ordinance of 1785 provided a system of land survey and sale. The land to the north of the Ohio was to be surveyed and marked off in a rectangular pattern before any of it was sold. Sections were to be sold at auction for not less than a dollar an acre. Since there were 640 acres in a section, the prospective buyer of government land had to have at least $640 in ready cash or in United States certificates of indebtedness.

These terms favored the large speculators too much and the ordinary frontiersmen too little to suit Jefferson, who believed that the West ought to belong to actual settlers on the ground. But the large speculators desired still further advantages, and Congress, in a hurry to realize returns from its domain, soon gave in to lobbying groups composed of some of its own members and various former army officers. To the Ohio and Scioto companies and the associates of John Cleves Symmes, Congress disposed of several million acres at only a few cents an acre. Millions of acres besides had been reserved at the time of cession by Virginia and Connecticut as bounty lands for their Revolutionary soldiers. Thus, before the government surveys had been well started,

most of the choicest land north of the Ohio River was already spoken for (as was all the land south of the Ohio, to which the ordinances of Congress did not apply).

To protect their interests in the Northwest, the directors of the Ohio and Scioto companies demanded a territorial government that would give less influence to the inhabitants than would the one outlined in Jefferson's Ordinance of 1784, and the companies' skilful lobbyist Manasseh Cutler carried their case to Congress. Some of the congressmen themselves disliked Jefferson's idea of creating as many as ten new states north of the Ohio, since these states in time might gain political ascendancy. Soon Congress replaced the original law—which had never gone into actual effect—with the Ordinance of 1787. This famous "Northwest Ordinance" established one Northwest Territory for the time being, provided for its subsequent division into several territories, not fewer than three nor more than five, and laid out three stages for the evolution of each territory into a state. In the first stage, Congress-appointed officials would govern the territory, in the second an elected legislature would share power with them, and in the third, when the people numbered 60,000 or more, they might frame a constitution and apply for statehood. The Northwest Ordinance, embodying as it did the views of conservative Easterners, failed to satisfy the restless inhabitants of the Ohio country.

The Indian policy of Congress fell short of the requirements of land speculators as well as of frontier settlers. In 1785 and 1786 congressional commissioners made treaties with representatives of the Iroquois and other tribes, who thereby surrendered their claims to a stretch of land north of the Ohio in return for comparatively worthless trinkets. Repudiating the treaties, many of the tribesmen went on the warpath. Congress vainly instructed Colonel Josiah Harmar, commanding the federal troops in the Ohio country, to

THE NORTHWEST ORDINANCE

1787

1. Congress shall appoint a governor, a secretary, and three judges for the Northwest Territory. These officials shall adopt suitable laws from the original states. When the territory has "five thousand free male inhabitants of full age," they shall be allowed to elect representatives. These, together with the governor and a legislative council of five, shall form a general assembly to make laws for the territory.

2. The inhabitants shall be entitled to the benefits of trial by jury and other judicial proceedings according to the common law.

3. "Religion, morality, and knowledge being necessary to good government and the happiness of mankind, schools and the means of education shall forever be encouraged."

4. "There shall be formed in the said territory not less than three nor more than five States. . . . And, whenever any of the said States shall have sixty thousand free inhabitants therein, such State shall be admitted, by its delegates, into the Congress of the United States, on an equal footing with the original States."

5. "There shall be neither slavery nor involuntary servitude in the said territory, otherwise than in the punishment of crimes whereof the party shall have been duly convicted."

---

drive the Indians back, then in desperation called upon the aging hero George Rogers Clark to save the frontier. While the campaign against the Indians in the Northwest faltered, a new threat arose in the Southwest, where the Creeks under the half-breed Alexander McGillivray not only repudiated their treaties ceding land but also formed an alliance with the Spaniards to resist the advance of American frontiersmen.

Some of the frontier leaders in the Southwest, instead of fighting the Spaniards, turned to collaborating with them. These leaders and their followers thought for a time that they saw advantages for themselves in the possible creation of a Southwestern confederacy under Spanish tutelage. They might thus get what the United States seemed unable to give them—protection from the Indians, cheap or free land, and an outlet to Eastern and foreign markets through the navigation of the Mississippi. After the collapse of the Jay-Gardoqui negotiations, the "Spanish Conspiracy" began to hum, attracting not only unscrupulous adventurers like General James Wilkinson but also prominent politicians such as William Blount of Kentucky and John Sevier of Tennessee. At the same time another underground separatist movement was afoot on the far northern frontier. The aspirations of Vermont for statehood having been frustrated by the rival claims of New York and New Hampshire to its soil, the Allen brothers intrigued with British agents for returning the Green Mountain country to the British Empire.

Debts, Taxes, and Daniel Shays

At the end of the war foreign ships crowded into American seaports with cargoes of all kinds, and the American people bought extravagantly with cash or credit. In consequence the wartime accumulations of specie were drained out of the country, consumer indebtedness to importing merchants was multiplied, and a postwar depression lasting from 1784 to 1787 was made worse than it might otherwise have been. The depression, with its money scarcity, bore heavily upon debtors both public and private, complicating the financial problems of many citizens and of the Confederation and state governments.

The Confederation government had canceled most of its war debt to Americans by repudiating hundreds of millions of dollars in Continental currency. Yet it still owed a domestic debt estimated at about $34 million in 1783, and through continued borrowings from abroad, mostly from The Netherlands, its foreign debt increased to more than $10 million by 1788. During the 1780's Congress received a sizeable annual income, though a fluctuating and inadequate one, chiefly from the proceeds of foreign loans and from requisitions upon the states. Promptly making interest payments on these loans, Congress maintained an excellent credit rating with Dutch and other foreign bankers, but could not keep up with its domestic obligations and lost credit at home. At a fraction of the face value, shrewd speculators bought up Confederation certificates of indebtedness from former Revolutionary soldiers and others who despaired of payment from Congress and who needed ready cash.

The states, too, came out of the war with large debts, and one by one they added to their obligations by taking over parts of the Confederation debt owed to their respective citizens. Taxable resources varied a good deal from state to state. The chief reliance everywhere was upon the direct tax on land and its improvements, income taxes then being unthought of. The states supplemented their revenues by means of customs duties and harbor fees,

though these tariff and navigation laws served also to protect the states' manufacturers and shippers from foreign competition. To some extent the tariffs interfered with trade between states, but with a few exceptions they were designed to limit importations of foreign and not American goods. Actually there were fewer barriers to interstate trade in the 1780's than there are today.

Suffering seriously from the postwar deflation and from the tax burden upon their land, the debtor farmers of the country demanded relief in the form of paper money, and seven of the states responded by issuing such currency. Of these seven, Rhode Island went to the greatest extremes, not only designating its paper as legal tender but compelling creditors to accept it or lose the right to collect their debts. While creditors fled from debtors eager to pay in Rhode Island currency, the highest court of the state, in the case of *Trevett* v. *Weeden* (1786), held that the monetary legislation was unconstitutional, and the legislature summoned the judges before it and censured them for their action.

The other six states refused to yield to the advocates of inflation and pursued policies of unrelieved taxation to support their public debts. To the state creditors —that is, the bondholders—all this was sound and honest public finance. But it seemed like robbery and tyranny to many of the poverty-stricken farmers, especially in New England, who felt that money was being extorted from them to swell the riches of the wealthy bondholders in Boston and other towns. At a time when cash was not to be had, these farmers were called upon to pay in specie not only state tax collectors but also mortgage holders and other private creditors. When debtors failed to pay they found their mortgages foreclosed and their property seized, and sometimes they found themselves in jail.

Mobs of distressed farmers rioted in various parts of New England but caused the most serious trouble in Massachusetts. There the malcontents of the Connecticut Valley and the Berkshire Hills, many of them Revolutionary veterans, found a leader in Daniel Shays, himself a former captain in the Continental Army. Organizing and drilling his followers, Shays put forth a program of demands including paper money, tax relief, a moratorium on debts, the removal of the state capital from Boston to the interior, and the abolition of imprisonment for debt. During the summer of 1786 the Shaysites concentrated upon the immediate task of preventing the collection of debts, private or public, and went in armed bands from place to place to break up court sittings and sheriff's sales. In Boston, members of the legislature, including Samuel Adams, denounced Shays and his men as rebels and traitors. When winter came these rebels, instead of laying down their arms, advanced upon Springfield to get more of them from the arsenal there. From Boston approached an army of state militiamen financed by a loan from wealthy merchants who feared a new revolution. In January, 1787, this army met the ragged troops of Shays, killed several of them, captured many more, and scattered the rest to the hills in a blinding snowstorm.

As a military enterprise, Shays's Rebellion was a fiasco, yet it had important consequences for the future of the United States. In Massachusetts it resulted in a few immediate gains for the discontented groups. Shays and his lieutenants, at first sentenced to death, were soon pardoned, and some concessions to his earlier demands were granted in the way of tax relief and the postponement of debt payments. Far more significant, the rebellion also affected the country as a whole by giving added urgency to the movement for a new Constitution.

A New Government Needed?

Before 1787 the Confederation government, for all its unfinished business, was already a going and a growing concern. Though it did not rest directly upon the people, it supported and was supported by a bureaucracy of reasonably faithful employees. Though it lacked sufficient immediate revenues, it possessed a resource in the public lands, which, once sales were well under way, could be expected to provide a plentiful independent income. Though it had no judicial system of its own, the state courts served well enough for most purposes, and the states settled disputes among themselves either through arbitration under the auspices of Congress or through the deliberations of interstate commissioners. Though it had no single, separately elected executive, the Confederation administered its laws through departments with secretaries responsible to Congress. If the procedures had been left to go on developing, with only a few amendments, most likely the secretaries in time would have formed a cabinet with one of their number functioning as a sort of prime minister—so that today the United States would have a modified parliamentary system of government.

True, the government under the Articles of Confederation was "weak," and deliberately so. Having just fought a war to avert the danger of remote and tyrannical authority, many Americans desired to keep the centers of political power close to the people in the thirteen states. Others, however, either disliked the Confederation plan from the outset or came eventually to desire something different. Disgruntled at the refusal of Congress to grant them half pay for life, some of the military men through their exclusive and hereditary Society of the Cincinnati hoped to control and to invigorate the government, some of them even aspiring to a kind of army dictatorship. Artisans or "mechanics," the manufacturers of the time, preferred a uniformly high national tariff to the varying state tariffs. Merchants and shippers preferred a single and effective commercial policy to thirteen

different and ineffective ones. Land speculators wished to see the Indian menace
finally removed from their Western tracts,
and creditors desired to stop the state issues of paper money. Investors in Confederation securities hoped to have the
Confederation debt made good and the
value of their securities enhanced. Large
property owners in general looked for a
reliable means of safety from the threat of
mobs.

So, during the 1780's, the country was
divided between the proponents of a new,
more highly centralized government and
the friends of the existing loose Confederation. Some of these state-rights men
were opposed to change because they did
not wish to lose the authority and prestige
they enjoyed in the existing state governments. Such men preferred local and individual liberties to centralization. On the
other hand, the advocates of a new central government valued national freedom
and efficiency more than individual or
local liberties.

The issue was not whether the Confederation should be changed but how drastic
the changes should be. Even its defenders
came reluctantly to agree that the government needed strengthening at its weakest
point, its lack of power to tax. To save the
Articles of Confederation, its friends
backed the impost amendment of 1783,
which would have authorized Congress to
levy customs duties, and all the states ratified the amendment except Rhode Island,
whose single veto was of course enough to
kill it. Later the state-rights advocates
proposed that the states make to Congress
a temporary and qualified grant of taxing
authority (not an amendment to the Articles), but most of the centralizers had
begun to lose interest in such remedies.
These critics no longer wanted the Confederation to succeed: they hoped it
would fail, so that they could get the
country behind them in seeking a thorough change.

The most resourceful of them was the
political genius, New York lawyer, one-

time military aide to General Washington, and illegitimate son of a Scottish
merchant in the West Indies—Alexander
Hamilton. From the beginning he had
been dissatisfied with the Articles of Confederation, had seen little to be gained by
piecemeal amendments, and had urged
the holding of a national convention to
overhaul the entire document. To achieve
his aim he took advantage of a movement
for interstate cooperation which began in
1785 when a group of Marylanders and
Virginians met in Alexandria to settle differences between their two states over the
use of the Potomac River and the Chesapeake Bay. As the owner of thousands of
acres beyond the mountains, Washington
was much interested in the development
of the upper Potomac as a waterway, and
he invited the conferees to his home at
Mount Vernon. There they decided to invite the other states to send delegates to a
larger conference on commercial questions to meet at Annapolis in 1786. Hamilton was present at the Annapolis meeting as a delegate from New York, and he
found the turnout disappointing, for only
five of the states were represented. Yet he
took satisfaction in seeing the conference
adopt his report and send copies to the
state legislatures and to Congress. His report forcefully criticized the Articles of
Confederation and recommended that
Congress call a convention of special
delegates from all the states to foregather
in Philadelphia the next year and consider ways to "render the constitution of
the federal government adequate to the
exigencies of the union."

At the moment, in 1786, there seemed
little possibility that the Philadelphia convention would be any better attended or
would accomplish any more than the previous meeting at Annapolis. The leadership of Washington would be essential for
success, and Washington appeared to be
well satisfied with the condition of the
country as it was. He wrote privately that,
despite the states' refusal to grant Congress the power to tax, the "internal

governments" were "daily acquiring strength," the laws were well enforced and crime was rare, the people were more industrious than ever, the "ravages of war" were already repaired, and the "foundations of a great empire" were firmly laid. One of the wealthiest men in the country, but temporarily short of cash, Washington doubted whether he would undertake the trouble and expense of a trip to Philadelphia.

Then, early in 1787, the news of commotion and bloodshed in Massachusetts spread throughout the country and the world, news which seemed to foretell other and more dangerous insurrections than that of Shays. In Paris the American minister, Thomas Jefferson, was not alarmed. "I hold," he confided in a letter to his Virginia friend James Madison, "that a little rebellion, now and then, is a good thing, and as necessary in the political world as storms in the physical." At Mount Vernon, however, Washington did not take the news so calmly. "There are combustibles in every State which a spark might set fire to," he exclaimed. "I feel infinitely more than I can express for the disorders which have arisen. Good God!" Washington refused to listen to renewed suggestions that he make himself a military dictator, but after Congress had issued its call for a constitutional convention he borrowed money for the journey and, in May, left Mount Vernon for Philadelphia.

The Constitutional Convention

Fifty-five men, representing all the states except Rhode Island, attended one or more sessions of the convention which from May to September, 1787, sat in the Philadelphia State House. Never before or since has there been a more distinguished gathering in America. These "Founding Fathers," instead of being graybearded ancients as the term implies, were on the whole relatively young men, many of them in their twenties and thir-

ties and only one (Benjamin Franklin) extremely old; his 81 years raised the average age from 43 to 44. Despite their comparative youth, the delegates were men of vast practical experience in business, plantation management, and politics, and they were well educated for their time, more than a third of them being college graduates. Practically all of them represented, both directly and indirectly, the great property interests of the country. Most of the delegates desired a strong government and feared what one of them called the "turbulence and follies" of democracy. Certain of the Revolutionary leaders—for example, Patrick Henry, Thomas Paine, and Thomas Jefferson— were conspicuously absent from the constitutional convention.

At the outset the nationalist or strong-government majority, better prepared than the state-rights minority, took the initiative. One of the majority members nominated Washington to preside and easily secured his election. Another introduced and carried a motion that the proceedings be absolutely secret. And Edmund Randolph, of the Virginia delegation, proposed a resolution, passed by the convention, that "a *national* government ought to be established, consisting of a *supreme* Legislative, Executive and Judiciary." Then Randolph submitted a plan for such a government, a plan the Virginians already had worked out. To proceed along this line would be to abandon the Articles of Confederation and build the government anew.

But the call of Congress and the commissions from the states to their "deputies" in Philadelphia had authorized only a *revision* of the Articles, and some delegates now raised doubts whether the convention properly could entertain such proposals as were embodied in the Virginia plan. A debate went on for weeks, with the state-rights men compelled to take the negative, since they had not been ready with a plan of their own. Finally William Paterson of New Jersey introduced an al-

THE PHILADELPHIA STATE HOUSE (INDEPENDENCE HALL). Here, in the building at the right, the Second Continental Congress held its meetings, and here the Declaration of Independence was signed. Here also the constitutional convention met, in 1787. This view, from an engraving made in the 1790's, shows the Chestnut Street approach. Construction of the State House was begun in 1732. The near-by building, with the cupola, is the City Hall, which was built between 1789 and 1792. This building housed the United States Supreme Court during the 1790's, while Philadelphia was the national capital. Note the stone-paved street and sidewalk and the pump (between the sidewalk and the State House).

ternative scheme which left "the United States in Congress" as the nucleus of the government.

Along with other nationalists, Hamilton denounced Paterson's plan, but unlike most of them he was not satisfied with Randolph's either. He explained that, personally, he would like to see the state governments "extinguished" entirely, or at least reduced to the status of mere administrative units, and a single "General Government" substituted for them, with a lifetime "elective monarch" and Senators who also would hold office for life. Hamilton's suggestions did not affect the actual shaping of the Constitution, nor did they help to break the deadlock which, after a month of bickering, had arisen in the convention.

By the end of June the convention seemed in danger of dissolving, with nothing accomplished. If this should happen, the men at Philadelphia would "become a reproach and by-word down to future ages," said the venerable Franklin, the voice of calmness and conciliation throughout the summer. "And what is worse, mankind may hereafter, from this unfortunate instance, despair of establishing governments by human wisdom, and leave it to chance, war and conquest." Franklin moved that the convention thereafter open its daily sessions with prayer, and though Hamilton objected, the motion was carried without a vote.

Through the calming influence of Franklin and others, especially Oliver Ellsworth of Connecticut, the delegates managed to compromise the most serious of their differences and go on with their work. To the men from the small states, the worst feature of the Virginia plan was its system of representation in the proposed two-house legislature. In the lower house, which was to be popularly elected, the states were to be represented in proportion to their population, and thus the largest would have several times as many representatives as the smallest. In the upper house, which was to be elected by the lower, some of the smaller states at any given time might have no representatives at all! To the small-state delegates the Congress of the Articles of Confederation, as well as the Congress of the New Jersey plan, at least had the merit of equal

representation for all the states, regardless of size. These delegates were appeased when Ellsworth proposed and the convention accepted the "Connecticut Compromise" or "Great Compromise," by which the states were to be represented in the House of Representatives proportionately to their populations and in the Senate (to be elected by the state legislatures) equally, with two senators apiece.

After the settlement of the issue between large and small states, there remained troublesome differences between the North and the South. Northerners thought the new Congress should have power to impose tariffs and regulate trade. They also thought that slaves, most numerous of course in the Southern states, should be counted in determining a state's share of direct taxes (to be levied on the state in proportion to its population) but not in determining its representation in the House. Southerners, on the other hand, believed that slaves should be included in computing representation but not direct taxation. Southerners also

---

THE VIRGINIA (OR RANDOLPH) PLAN

1787

The following branches of government were recommended in the Virginia Plan:

1. A "National Legislature," with the states represented in proportion either to their "quotas of contribution" or to "the number of free inhabitants." Two branches, the members of the first to be elected by the people, the members of the second to be nominated by the state legislatures and elected by the first. Powers: to "legislate in all cases to which the separate states are incompetent," to "negative all laws passed by the several states, contravening in the opinion of the National Legislature the articles of Union," and to use force against recalcitrant states.

2. A single "National Executive" to be chosen by the National Legislature.

3. A "National Judiciary" to be chosen by the National Legislature.

4. A "Council of Revision," consisting of the National Executive and part of the National Judiciary, with power to "examine" and reject state and national laws before they went into effect.

THE NEW JERSEY (OR PATERSON) PLAN

1787

The main features of the New Jersey Plan were:

1. The continuance of the existing one-house Congress, with one vote for each state, but with the following additional powers: to raise a revenue from import duties, stamp taxes, and postage; to regulate interstate and foreign commerce; and to provide for the collection of taxes within any state failing to pay its share of the requisitions upon the states.

2. A plural "Federal Executive" to be elected by Congress.

3. A "Federal Judiciary" to be appointed by the Executive.

4. The establishment of acts of Congress and federal treaties as the "supreme law" of the states, and the authorization of the Federal Executive to "call forth the power of the Confederated States . . . to enforce and compel an obedience."

feared that Congress might impose export duties on their crops, interfere with the slave trade, and agree to commercial treaties (like the one recently signed between Jay and Gardoqui) which would sacrifice the interests of the South to those of the North.

Eventually the sectional differences were adjusted by means of several constitutional provisions. According to an arbitrary but satisfying formula, three fifths of the slaves were to be counted in the apportionment of both representatives and direct taxes among the states. By other provisions Congress was permitted to regulate commerce but not to levy export duties nor, for twenty years, to prohibit the importation of slaves. And the executive was allowed to make treaties, including treaties of commerce, but these were to require the approval of a two-thirds majority rather than a simple majority of the Senate, and hence the South could exercise a veto over them.

The Constitution as it finally took form at the end of summer in 1787, with James Madison responsible for most of the actual drafting, was an outgrowth of the Virginia plan, though incorporating a few significant features from the New Jersey plan and the Articles of Confederation. The Constitution outlined an original and ingenious form of government, derived from diverse forms ancient and contemporary but copying none of them. Though both federal and national, the proposed government was to be more national than federal. The Constitution and all laws and treaties made under it were to be the "supreme law" of the land, regardless of anything in the constitution or laws of any state to the contrary. Broad powers were granted to the central government, including the congressional powers of taxation, regulation of commerce, control of money, and the passage of laws "necessary and proper" for carrying out its specific powers. Within the allotted sphere of its powers, the new government was authorized to act directly upon the people of the United States. At the same time the individual states were deprived of a number of the powers—such as the issuance of money and the passage of laws "impairing the obligations of contracts," that is, debtor stay laws and the like— which the states had been free to exercise under the Articles of Confederation. And nowhere in the Constitution as written in 1787 were the former claims of the states to individual sovereignty recognized.

The Constitution was designed to prevent any single group from gaining absolute and unchecked power. This was the purpose of the separation of powers and the checks and balances set up among the legislative, executive, and judicial branches of the new government. The government was deliberately divided against itself so as to frustrate tyranny from whatever source.

None of the delegates was quite satisfied with the completed Constitution, such a patchwork of compromises had it become, and several including Randolph himself refused to sign it, while Hamilton and thirty-eight others signed. Since the delegates had exceeded their instructions from Congress and the states, they had reason to doubt whether the Constitution would ever be ratified if they followed the procedures laid down in the Articles of Confederation, which required the state *legislatures,* and *all* of them, to approve alterations in the form of the government. So the convention changed the rules, specifying in the Constitution that the new government should go into effect among the ratifying states when only *nine* of the thirteen had ratified, and recommending to Congress that the Constitution be submitted to specially called state *conventions* rather than to the legislatures of the states.

"Federalists" v. "Antifederalists"

The Congress in New York, completely overshadowed by the convention in Philadelphia, accepted the latter's work and submitted it to the states for their approval or disapproval. The state legislatures, again with the exception of Rhode Island, arranged for the election of delegates to ratifying conventions, and sooner or later each of these conventions got down to business. Meanwhile, from the fall of 1787 to the summer of 1788,

the merits and demerits of the new Constitution were debated in the legislatures, in mass meetings, and in the columns of newspapers, as well as in the convention halls. For the most part the struggle, though intense, was peaceful and deliberative, yet the opposing factions sometimes came to blows, and death and injury resulted in at least one place (Albany, New York).

Despite the reference of its preamble to "We the people," the Constitution was not in literal fact ordained and established by the whole people of the United States. As is shown by the elections for the state conventions, something like three fourths of the adult white males in the country as a whole failed to vote for delegates, mainly because of indifference, and therefore exercised no real influence upon the outcome. Of those who did vote, a large majority favored ratification. The voters, however, did not have a clear-cut choice between a "federal" and a "national" government. The issues were confused by the terminology which was employed. Since the idea of a strongly national government was thought to be unpopular, the advocates of the new Constitution (which was strongly national as written in 1787) chose to call themselves "Federalists" and to call their opponents "Antifederalists." These misnomers stuck, despite the insistence of opponents of ratification that they were "Federal Republicans," the true federalists of the time.

In the contest over ratification the so-called Federalists who favored the Constitution had a number of advantages. They possessed a positive program and an appealing name, while the so-called Antifederalists by that very word were made to stand for nothing constructive, for chaos itself. The Federalists were the better organized group and had the weight of fame and superior leadership on their side. They could point to the support of the two most eminent men in America, Franklin and Washington. And

Washington himself declared that the choice lay between the Constitution and disunion. The Federalists included also some of the most profound political philosophers of any period or place in Hamilton, Madison, and Jay, who under the joint pseudonym "Publius" wrote a long series of newspaper essays expounding the meaning and virtues of the Constitution. Afterwards published in book form as *The Federalist*, these papers have been considered as the most authoritative of all constitutional commentaries and, indeed, as one of the greatest of all treatises on political science.

The opponents of ratification produced no comparable set of Antifederalist papers, yet these men too were able and sincere and they made a vigorous case for themselves in their own speeches and newspaper propaganda. Among the outstanding Antifederalists were George Clinton, governor of New York and bitter foe of Hamilton; Luther Martin of Maryland, one of the most powerful as well as wordy lawyers in the entire country; and the redoubtable and eloquent Patrick Henry. In the nature of the case the Antifederalists necessarily resorted mainly to negative argument. The Constitution, they protested, was illegal—as indeed it was if judged by the Articles of Confederation, the existing fundamental law. The new government would increase taxes, obliterate the states, wield dictatorial powers, favor the "well born" over the common people, and put an end to individual liberty, the Antifederalists added. Of all their specific criticisms the most compelling was this: the Constitution lacked a bill of rights.

For all the efforts of the Antifederalists, ratification proceeded apace during the winter of 1787–8. Delaware, the first to act, did so unanimously as also did two others of the smallest states, New Jersey and Georgia. In the large states of Pennsylvania and Massachusetts the Antifederalists put up a determined struggle but lost in the final vote. By June of 1788,

when the New Hampshire convention at last made up its mind, nine of the states had ratified and thus had made it possible for the Constitution to go into effect among themselves. A new government could hardly hope to succeed, however, without the participation of Virginia and New York, whose conventions remained closely divided. Before the end of the month Virginia and then New York consented to the Constitution by rather narrow votes. The New York convention yielded to expediency, even some of the most staunchly Antifederalist delegates fearing that the state's commercial interests would suffer if, once the other states had got together under the "New Roof," New York were to remain outside. Massachusetts, Virginia, and New York all ratified on the assumption, though not on the express condition, that certain desired amendments would be added to the Constitution, above all a bill of rights. Deciding to wait and see what became of these hopes for amendment, the North Carolina convention adjourned without taking action. Rhode Island, for the time being, did not even call a convention to consider ratification.

Elaborating upon the Constitution

When the first elections under the Constitution were held, in the early months of 1789, the results showed that the new government was to be in the hands of its friends. Few if any of the newly elected congressmen and senators had been extreme Antifederalists; almost all had favored ratification, and many had served as delegates to the Philadelphia convention. The President-elect, George Washington, had presided at the convention; many who had favored ratification did so because they expected him to preside over the new government also. He received the votes of all the presidential electors whom the states, either by legislative action or by popular election, had named. John Adams, a firm Federalist though not

FEDERAL HALL, NEW YORK. Here George Washington was inaugurated as President on April 30, 1789, taking his oath of office on the balcony that overlooks Wall Street. The building was originally constructed as the City Hall in 1699–1700. It was extensively remodeled and enlarged after the Revolution, and was renamed Federal Hall when it served as the temporary Capitol of the United States, in 1789–1790. At the end of Wall Street is the Gothic-styled Trinity Church (Anglican). It was built in 1688, destroyed in a great fire following the British occupation of the city in 1776, and rebuilt in 1788. Behind the church was a meadow sloping down to the Hudson River.

a member of the convention, received the next highest number of electoral votes and hence was to be Vice President.

For the time being the seat of government was to continue to be the city of New York, and thus the sensibilities of the geographical sections were neatly balanced, the President being from the South, the Vice President from New England, and the capital in the Middle States. Congressmen were so slow to reach New York that not until April was a quorum on hand to make an official count of the electoral vote and send a messenger to notify General Washington of his election. After a journey from Mount Vernon marked by elaborate celebrations along the way, Washington was inaugurated on April 30.

The responsibilities facing the first President and the first Congress were in some ways greater than those facing any President or Congress to follow. Though these men of 1789 had the Constitution as a guide, that document provided only a general plan which had yet to be applied to specific situations as they arose. It left many questions unanswered. What, for example, should be the rules of the two houses for the conduct of their business? What code of etiquette should govern the relations between the President on the one hand and Congress and the people on the other? Should he have

WASHINGTON'S FIRST INAUGURATION

1789

The temporary capitol of the new government was the City Hall in New York. Here George Washington was inaugurated as President on April 30, 1789. William Maclay, a diary-keeping senator from Pennsylvania, recorded the ceremonies thus:

"The President was conducted out of the middle window into the gallery [overlooking Wall Street], and the oath was administered by the Chancellor [the highest judicial officer of the state of New York]. Notice that the business [was] done was communicated to the crowd by proclamation, etc., who gave three cheers, and repeated it on the President's bowing to them.

"As the company returned into the Senate chamber, the President took the chair and the Senators and Representatives their seats. He rose, and all arose also, and [he] addressed them. This great man was agitated and embarrassed more than ever he was by the leveled cannon or pointed musket. He trembled, and several times could scarce make out to read, though it must be supposed he had often read it before. . . . When he came to the words *all the world*, he made a flourish with his right hand, which left rather an ungainly impression. I sincerely, for my part, wished all set ceremony in the hands of the dancing-masters, and that this first of men had read off his address in the plainest manner, without ever taking his eyes from the paper, for I felt hurt that he was not first in everything. He was dressed in deep brown, with metal buttons, with an eagle on them, white stockings, a bag [for his back hair], and sword."

some high-sounding title, such as "His Highness the President of the United States and Protector of Their Liberties"? (John Adams, who would have been horrified at the thought of a later Vice President being called "The Veep," thought both he and the President ought to have dignified forms of address.) What was the true meaning of various ambiguous phrases in the Constitution? In answering these and other questions, Washington and his colleagues knew they were setting precedents that, in many cases, would give lasting direction to the development of the Constitution in actual practice.

By filling certain gaps in the Constitution, the first Congress served almost as a continuation of the constitutional convention itself. The work of the convention had been incomplete in various respects, especially in that it had omitted a bill of rights. Dozens of amendments, intended to make good this lack, had been proposed in the state ratifying conventions, and Congress now undertook the task of sorting these, reducing them to a manageable number, and sending them to the states for ratification. Of the twelve sent out, ten were ratified, and these took effect in 1791. The first nine of them were intended to guarantee to the people certain basic rights, such as freedom of religion, of speech, and of the press, immunity from arbitrary arrest, and trial by jury. The tenth amendment, reserving to the states all powers except those specifically withheld from them or delegated to the federal government, bolstered state rights and changed the emphasis of the Constitution from nationalism to federalism.

In regard to the structure of the federal courts, the Constitution had only this to say: "The judicial power of the United States shall be vested in one Supreme Court, and in such inferior courts as the Congress may from time to time ordain and establish." Thus the convention had left up to Congress the number of Supreme Court judges to be appointed and the kinds of lower courts to be organized. In the Judiciary Act of 1789 Congress provided for a Supreme Court of six members, one chief justice and five associate justices, for thirteen district courts with one judge apiece, and for three circuit courts, each to consist of one of the district judges sitting with two of the Supreme Court justices. In the same act Congress gave the Supreme Court the power to make the final decision in cases involving the constitutionality of state laws. If the Constitution was in fact to be the "supreme law of the land," the various state courts could not be left to decide for themselves whether the state legislatures were violating that supreme law.

As for executive departments, the Constitution referred indirectly to them but did not specify what or how many they should be. The first Congress created three such departments—State, Treasury, and War—and also the offices of Attorney General and Postmaster General.

In appointing department heads and other high officials, President Washington determined to select men who were qualified by character and experience, who were well disposed toward the Constitution (no Antifederalists need apply), and who as a group would provide a balanced representation of the different sections of the country. To the office of Secretary of the Treasury he appointed Alexander Hamilton, of New York, who had taken the lead in the calling of the constitutional convention and who, though only thirty-two, was an expert in public finance. For Secretary of War he chose the Massachusetts Federalist, General Henry Knox. As Attorney General he named Edmund Randolph, of Virginia, author of the plan upon which the Constitution had been based. He picked as his Secretary of State another Virginian, Thomas Jefferson, who had not opposed the Constitution though he had had nothing to do with its framing or adoption, having been away from the country as minister to France.

From time to time Washington called upon these four men for advice, usually as individuals. They did not form a cabinet in the sense of a group of presidential counselors holding regular meetings (the cabinet in this sense began to develop during the Presidency of Jefferson). When Washington took office he supposed, as did many others, that the Senate would act for certain purposes as an advisory council, since according to the Constitution the Senate was to give its advice and consent for the appointment of high officials and for the ratification of treaties. With only 22 members in the beginning, the Senate was small enough so that Washington could expect to consult personally with it. He changed his mind, however, after taking a treaty draft to the Senators for their advice. They demanded that he leave the document for them to inspect and change at their leisure, and he refused, resolving never again to submit a treaty to the senators until it had been completed and signed. Thus he set a precedent in treaty-making which for the most part his successors have followed.

BIBLIOGRAPHY

Charles A. Beard, *An Economic Interpretation of the Constitution of the United States* (1913; new ed., 1935), maintains that the Constitution was the work of a minority who had selfish as well as idealistic motives. R. L. Schuyler, *The Constitution*

of the United States (1923), has a thesis
similar to Beard's, and so does Merrill Jensen, *The New Nation: A History of the
United States during the Confederation,
1781–1789* (1950). Critical of the Beard
thesis are Charles Warren, *The Making of
the Constitution* (1928); R. E. Brown,
Charles Beard and the Constitution
(1956); and Forrest McDonald, *We the
People: The Economic Origins of the Constitution* (1958).

Leading Federalists and Antifederalists
are treated in the following: E. M. Burns,
*James Madison, Philosopher of the Consti-
tution* (1938); Irving Brant, *James Madison: The Nationalist, 1780–1787* (1948),
and *James Madison: Father of the Constitution, 1787–1800* (1950); Nathan Schachner, *Alexander Hamilton* (1946); Broadus
Mitchell, *Alexander Hamilton: Youth to
Maturity, 1755–1788* (1957); C. P. Smith,
James Wilson: Founding Father, 1742–
1798 (1956); E. W. Spaulding, *His Ex-
cellency George Clinton, Critic of the Constitution* (1939); and Helen Hill, *George
Mason, Constitutionalist* (1938).

The inside story of the constitutional convention was little known until the publication of Madison's notes in 1840; these are
now available in *James Madison's Journal of
the Federal Convention* (1893), edited by
E. H. Scott. A comprehensive edition of
Madison's notes and other original sources
is *Records of the Federal Constitution* (4
vols., 1911–37), edited by Max Farrand.

The following deal with phases of history
in the 1780's: R. A. East, *Business Enterprise in the American Revolutionary Era*
(1938); B. W. Bond, Jr., *The Civilization
of the Old Northwest* (1938); A. P. Whitaker, *The Spanish-American Frontier, 1783–
1795* (1927); and M. L. Starkey, *A Little
Rebellion* (1955), which brings Daniel
Shays and his followers convincingly to life.

7

THE FEDERALISTS
IN POWER

For the first dozen years under the Constitution, while the Federalists controlled the Presidency, they accomplished much. Under President Washington they infused vigor into the government (the *national* government, as he always called it) and set the nation upon a path of neutrality and diplomatic independence. Under his successor, John Adams, they maintained the rights and the self-respect of the republic in international affairs, and though in consequence they brought on hostilities with France and thus departed from neutrality, the President steered away from all-out war and finally made a satisfactory peace. In their grasp for power, however, the Federalists overreached themselves. They faced the dilemma of all rulers in a government that depends upon the will of the people—that is, the dilemma of choosing between governmental strength and individual freedom—and they made their choice in favor of strong government at the expense of popular liberty and popular support. The Federalists never won another presidential election after 1796, yet their main

achievements endured and, in one form or another, still endure.

Hamilton's Economic Planning

As President, Washington thought it his duty to see that the laws of Congress, if constitutional, were faithfully carried out. A man of strong will, he was the master of his own administration, but he did not conceive of himself as a popular leader (as did, for example, Andrew Jackson and Franklin D. Roosevelt in after years) who should find out the will of the people and then see that Congress enacted it into law. One of his department heads, Secretary of the Treasury Hamilton, undertook to provide the legislative leadership which Washington himself did not. According to the act creating the Treasury Department, its head was to report directly to Congress. Hence Hamilton concluded that his position gave him a special relationship with the law-making body, that his position made him, indeed, a kind of prime minister. Though his conception of the Treasury Secretary's role

ALEXANDER HAMILTON. Hamilton was not a big man physically. He stood about five feet, six inches. Yet he had an imposing and commanding presence. His dignity was enhanced by his handsome, clean-cut features and his piercing look. Something of his energy, will, and personal force is suggested in John Trumbull's portrait of him. Trumbull, born in Connecticut, served as a soldier in the Revolutionary War, studied under Benjamin West in London, and (in 1804) opened a studio in New York. His father, Jonathan Trumbull, governor of Connecticut during the Revolution, had been a friend and adviser of General Washington. The general called him "Brother Jonathan," and this became a nickname for New Englanders and then for the American people as a whole. Not till about 1850 did "Uncle Sam" replace "Brother Jonathan" as the popular symbol of the United States. (COURTESY, MUSEUM OF FINE ARTS, BOSTON)

did not establish an enduring precedent, Hamilton exerted a greater positive influence than anyone else upon both domestic and foreign policies during Washington's Presidency, continuing to be influential even after his resignation in 1794.

Of all the leading men of his time, Hamilton was one of the most aristocratic in his personal tastes and in his political philosophy. He distrusted the common people. An admirer of the British political system, with its rule by King and upper

classes, he wished to adapt its principles as closely as he could to government in the United States. What the country most needed, he thought, was order and stability; the people already had enough liberty, indeed too much of it. He thought the new government could be strengthened and made to succeed if the support of the wealthy men of the country could be brought to it. And, believing that all men were motivated by self-interest, he assumed that the way to gain the support of the wealthy was to give them a stake in the success of the new government. He therefore planned a program of financial legislation which, among other things, was intended to cause the propertied classes to look to the federal government for profitable investments and for the protection and promotion of their property interests.

If men of means were to have faith in the government, then it must keep faith with them by making good its debts and establishing its credit on a sound basis. So, first of all, Hamilton proposed that the existing public debt be "funded," or in other words that the miscellaneous, uncertain, depreciated certificates of indebtedness, which the old Congress had issued during and since the Revolution, be called in and exchanged for uniform, interest-bearing bonds, payable at definite dates. Next he recommended that the Revolutionary state debts be "assumed" or taken over by the United States, his object being to cause the state as well as the federal bondholders to look to the central government for eventual payment. His plan was not to pay off and thus eliminate the debt, either state or federal, but just the opposite: to create a large and permanent public debt, new bonds being issued as old ones were paid off.

Hamilton also planned the establishment of a national bank. At the time, there were only a few banks in the country, located in Boston, Philadelphia, and New York. A new, national bank would serve several purposes. It would aid business by providing loans and also currency —in the form of banknotes, which in those days were used instead of checks. It would aid the government by making available a safe place for the deposit of federal funds, by facilitating the collection of taxes and the disbursement of the government's expenditures, and by keeping up the price of government bonds through judicious bond purchases. The kind of institution that Hamilton had in mind was to be "national" in the sense that it was to be chartered by the federal government, was to have a monopoly of the government's own banking business, and was to be government-controlled to some degree, one fifth of the directors being appointed by the government.

The funding and assumption of the debts, together with the payment of regular interest on them, would cost a great deal of money, and so Hamilton had to find adequate sources of revenue. He thought the government should depend mainly upon two kinds of taxes (in addition to the receipts to be anticipated from the sales of public land). One of these was an excise to be paid by distillers of alcoholic liquors. This tax would hit most heavily the whiskey distillers of the back country, especially in Pennsylvania, Virginia, and North Carolina. These were small farmers who converted part of their corn and rye crop into whiskey, so as to have a concentrated and valuable product that they could conveniently take to market by horseback or muleback over poor mountain roads.

The other tax upon which Hamilton relied was the tax on imports, that is, the tariff. Such a tax would serve not only to raise a revenue, but also to protect and encourage American manufactures by raising the price of competing manufactured goods brought in from abroad. In the old Articles of Confederation, according to its defenders as well as its critics, the worst defect had been Congress's lack of power to levy customs duties. One of the first acts of the new Congress, in 1789, was the passage of a tariff law designed to foster industries while raising a revenue, but the average level of duties under this law was extremely low. Hamilton advocated a higher and more decidedly protective tariff. In his Report on Manufactures he glowingly set forth the advantages, as he saw them, of stimulating the growth of industry in the United States. Factories, he said, would make the nation more nearly self-sufficient in wartime, would increase prosperity by creating a home market for the produce of the farms, and would make possible the fuller utilization of all kinds of labor, including the labor of women and children, even those (to quote Hamilton himself) of "tender years."

Between 1789 and 1792 Hamilton succeeded in persuading Congress to pass the necessary laws for erecting his financial system—but only after a bitter struggle with a rising opposition group.

As for the funding of the public debt, very few of the congressmen objected to the plan itself, for they agreed with Hamilton that the government must make its credit good. Many of them disagreed, however, with his proposal to fund the debt *at par*, that is, to exchange new bonds for old certificates of indebtedness on a dollar-for-dollar basis. These old certificates, as has been seen, originally had been issued to merchants and farmers in payment for war supplies during the Revolution, or to officers and soldiers of the Revolutionary army in payment for their services. Many of these original holders had been forced to sell at a sacrifice during the hard times of the 1780's, to speculators who bought up the securities at a fraction of their face value. Admitting that the government should arrange to pay every cent it owed, to *whom* should it arrange to pay? Many congressmen believed that the original holders deserved some consideration, and James Madison, now a representative from Virginia, argued for a plan by which the new bonds would be divided between the orig-inal holders and the later purchasers. But the friends of Hamilton insisted that such a plan was impracticable and that the honor of the government required a literal fulfillment of its earlier promises to pay. Congress finally passed the funding bill in the form that Hamilton desired.

His assumption bill ran into even greater difficulty. Its opponents had a

sumption bill. Finally the bill got the sup-port of some of them and so managed to pass, but only because of a logrolling deal. The Virginians wanted the national capi-tal to be permanently located near them in the South. Hamilton having appealed to Jefferson, shortly after the latter's re-turn from France, Jefferson held a dinner at which arrangements were made to bar-ter Virginia votes for the assumption bill

CONSTITUTIONALITY OF THE BANK: JEFFERSON

"The incorporation of a bank, and the powers assumed by this bill, have not, in my opinion, been delegated to the United States by the Constitu-tion.

"I. They are not among the powers specially enumerated. . . .

"II. Nor are they within either of the general phrases, which are the two following:—

"1. 'To lay taxes to provide for the general welfare of the United States.' . . . They [Congress] are not *to do anything they please*, to pro-vide for the general welfare, but only *to lay taxes* for that purpose. . . . It was intended to lace them up straitly within the enumerated powers, and those without which, as means, these powers could not be carried into effect. . . .

"2. The second general phrase is, 'to make all laws *necessary* and proper for carrying into execution the enumerated powers.' But they can all be carried into execution without a bank. A bank, therefore, is not *necessary*, and consequently not authorized by this phrase.

"It has been much urged that a bank will give great facility or conven-ience in the collection of taxes. Suppose this were true; yet the Constitu-tion allows only the means which are 'necessary,' not those which are merely 'convenient,' for effecting the enumerated powers."

very good case, for if the federal govern-ment took over the state debts, the people of one state would have to pay federal taxes for servicing the debts of other states, and some of these debts, such as that of Massachusetts, were much larger than others, such as that of Virginia. Naturally, Virginians did not think it fair for them to have to pay a share of the large Massachusetts debt, and their rep-resentatives in Congress balked at the as-

in return for Northern votes for a South-ern location of the capital. In 1790 the capital was changed back to Philadelphia for a ten-year period, and after that a new capital city was to be built on the banks of the Potomac River, on land to be se-lected by Washington himself.

When Hamilton's bank bill was intro-duced into Congress, Madison and others opposed it on the grounds that it was un-constitutional, and though a majority voted for it, President Washington himself had his doubts. He therefore asked his official advisers for written opinions on the subject. In Hamilton's opinion the establishment of a bank was a fitting exercise of the powers of Congress, though the Constitution nowhere gave Congress the right in so many words. But Jefferson, with the support of his fellow Virginian, Randolph, argued that the Constitution should be construed in a strict sense and

heavily on the smaller distillers. He did not succeed in getting from Congress a tariff as highly protective as he had hoped for, yet the tariff law of 1792 did raise the rates somewhat.

Once enacted, Hamilton's program worked as he had intended. The public credit quickly was restored; the bonds of the United States were soon selling at home and abroad at prices even above their par value. The national prosperity

CONSTITUTIONALITY OF THE BANK: HAMILTON

"It is conceded that *implied powers* are to be considered as delegated equally with *express ones*. Then it follows, that as a power of erecting a corporation may as well be *implied* as any other thing, it may as well be employed as an *instrument* or *mean* of carrying into execution any of the specified powers, as any other *instrument* or *mean* whatever. . . .

"It is objected that none but necessary and proper means are to be employed; and the Secretary of State maintains that no means are to be considered as *necessary* but those without which the grant of the power would be *nugatory*. . . .

"It is certain that neither the grammatical nor popular sense of the term requires that construction. According to both, *necessary* often means no more than *needful, requisite, incidental, useful,* or *conducive to.* . . .

"If the *end* be clearly comprehended within any of the specified powers, and if the measure have an obvious relation to that *end,* and is not forbidden by any particular provision of the Constitution, it may safely be deemed to come within the compass of the national authority. . . .

"A bank has a natural relation to the power of collecting taxes—to that of regulating trade—to that of providing for the common defence. . . . [Therefore] the incorporation of a bank is a constitutional measure. . . ."

that Congress should be allowed no powers not clearly given to it. Washington found Hamilton's case the more convincing, and he signed the bank bill when it came to him. The Bank of the United States began operations in 1791, under a charter which granted it the right to continue in business for twenty years.

Hamilton also had his way with the excise tax, though after its passage the law was altered somewhat, in response to protests from farmers, so as to bear less

rose to new heights. The future of the national government was made secure.

At the same time, speculators got rich and corruption was rife. Not that Hamilton himself profited by his program: he was careful to protect his reputation for public honesty. But some of Hamilton's associates, including his Assistant Secretary William Duer, who eventually landed in jail, did take advantage of their inside knowledge for improper speculation schemes. Moreover, many congressmen

THE FIRST BANK OF THE UNITED STATES. The headquarters of the Bank of the United States, which was founded through Alexander Hamilton's efforts, were in Philadelphia. The Bank building on Third Street was completed in 1795. It is a good example of Early Republican architecture, with its rather box-like shape, its balustrade along the roof edge, its quoins at the angle of the walls, and its Roman pediment and columns in front. From a drawing and engraving by W. Birch & Son of Philadelphia, published in 1799.

had bought up large amounts of the old certificates of indebtedness, and these men profited by their own legislation in funding the debt at par. Directly or indirectly, properly or improperly, thousands of wealthy merchants in the seaports also gained from the Hamilton program.

The mass of the people, the farmers scattered over the countryside, profited much less. While these people shared some of the benefit of national strength and prosperity, they bore most of the burden of paying for it. The financial program required taxes, and these came mostly from the farmers, who had to pay

not only land taxes to their state governments but also the excise and, indirectly, the tariff to the federal government. The feeling grew that the Washington administration was not treating all the people fairly, and out of this feeling an organized political opposition arose.

Rise of Political Parties

The Constitution made no reference to political parties, and the Founding Fathers, George Washington in particular, believed that such organizations were evil and should be avoided. Yet parties soon arose from a division between the followers of Hamilton and those of Madison and Jefferson.

Jefferson and Madison were such close collaborators that it is sometimes difficult to separate the contributions of the two. To describe the political philosophy of one is, in the main, to describe the political philosophy of both. Jefferson, himself a farmer, believed that farmers were God's chosen people and that an ideal republic would consist of sturdy citizens each tilling his own soil. Though an aristocrat by birth, his mother belonging to one of the first families of Virginia, the Randolphs, he had faith in the good intentions of such farmer-citizens and thought that, if properly educated, they could be trusted to govern themselves through the election of able and qualified men. But, in the 1790's, he feared city mobs as "sores upon the body politic." He then opposed the development of extensive manufactures because they would lead to the growth of cities packed with propertyless workers. While Hamilton emphasized the need for order and stability, Jefferson stressed the importance of individual freedom.

As a member of President Washington's official circle, Jefferson differed so strongly with his colleague Hamilton on particular issues such as the Bank that he soon offered to resign. But Washington preferred to keep both men in office so as to preserve national unity if possible. His became a coalition government, though he himself agreed more often with Hamilton than with Jefferson. The two Secretaries continued to work against each other, and each began to organize a following in Congress and in the country at large. Hamilton's followers came to be known as Federalists, Jefferson's as Republicans.

The Federalists of the 1790's were not entirely the same men as the Federalists of 1787–8 who had campaigned for the ratification of the Constitution, nor were the Republicans exactly the same men as the old Antifederalists. There were nu-

merous exceptions, the most noteworthy being Madison, who had played a leading role at the constitutional convention and in the ratification effort, then had broken with Hamilton on the questions of funding and the Bank, and had become one of the founders of the Republican party. Both of the parties contained members in all sections of the country, but the Federalists were most numerous in the commercial centers of the Northeast, though also strong in such Southern seaports as Charleston, while the Republicans were most numerous in the rural areas of the South and the West.

Unlike the old Antifederalists, the new Republicans did not denounce the Constitution. On the contrary, they professed to be its special friends and accused their opponents of violating it.

Republicans and Federalists differed in their social philosophies as well as in their economic interests and their constitutional views. Their differences in social outlook are seen in their reactions to the progress of the revolution in France. When that revolution first began, as a rather mild movement in favor of constitutional monarchy and the rights of man, practically all Americans hailed it as a step in the right direction. But when the revolution went to radical extremes, with attacks on organized religion, the overthrow of the monarchy, and eventually the guillotining of the King and Queen, Americans adopted different views about the events in France, the Federalists denouncing and the Republicans applauding them. Indeed, many of the Republicans imitated the French radicals (the Jacobins) by cutting their hair short, wearing pantaloons, and addressing one another as "Citizen" Smith or "Citizeness" Jones. Thus, for a time, it was possible to tell a man's party by his manners and appearance, for the Federalists kept the old-fashioned long hair or powdered wig, knee breeches, and traditional etiquette of the gentleman. Republicans accused the Federalists of being aristocratic and even "monarchical." Federalists referred to the Republicans, in horrified tones, as "Jacobins" and as "Jacobinical rabble"—terms which then had much the same implication as the word "Communist" many years later was to have.

The two parties had quite different leanings in foreign affairs. Both were pro-American, but Jefferson and the Republicans believed that American interests would best be served by maintaining close relations with France, while Hamilton and the Federalists believed that friendship with Great Britain was essential for the success of the United States.

When the time came for the election of 1792, the Republicans had no candidate to put up against Washington. Jefferson as well as Hamilton urged him to run for a second term, and the President consented for the good of the country, though he would have preferred to retire to Mount Vernon.

Problems of the Frontier

While, during the early 1790's the American people began to be divided between two political parties, they became more strongly united than ever in their loyalty to the government itself. Previously, during the 1780's, the old Congress had been powerless to tie the outlying parts of the country firmly to the United States, as farmers in western Massachusetts rose in revolt and settlers in Vermont, Kentucky, and Tennessee toyed with the idea of separating these territories from the Union. Now, however, the Washington administration made the power of the federal government felt even on the farthest reaches of the frontier.

The federal authority was challenged when, in 1794, the farmers of western Pennsylvania refused to pay the whiskey excise and terrorized the would-be tax collectors, much as the colonists had done throughout America at the time of the

Stamp Act. The so-called Whiskey Rebellion was not left to the authorities of Pennsylvania as Shays's Rebellion had been left to the authorities of Massachusetts. Urged on by Hamilton, Washington took drastic steps. Calling out the militia of three states, he raised an army of nearly 15,000, a larger force than he had commanded against the British during most of the Revolution, and he personally accompanied this army as far as the town of Bedford. At the approach of the militiamen, the farmers around Pittsburgh, where the rebellion centered, either ran for cover or stayed home and professed to be law-abiding citizens. The rebellion quickly collapsed.

While the whiskey rebels were intimidated into obedience, other frontiersmen were made loyal to the government by its acceptance of new states as members of the Union. First to be admitted were two of the original thirteen, North Carolina (1789) and Rhode Island (1790), both of which had ratified the Constitution when they found that a bill of rights was definitely to be added and that they could not conveniently go on as independent commonwealths. Then Vermont, which had had its own state government since the Revolution, was accepted as the fourteenth state (1791) after New York and New Hampshire finally agreed to give up their claims to sovereignty over the Green Mountain country. Next came Kentucky (1792) with the consent of Virginia, which previously had governed the Kentucky counties as its own. After North Carolina finally ceded its Western lands to the Union, these were given a territorial government similar to that of the Northwest Territory and after six years became the state of Tennessee (1796). With the admission of these frontier states, the schemes for separating Vermont, Kentucky, and Tennessee from the Union soon came to an end.

In the more remote areas of the North

west and the Southwest, meanwhile, the government had to contend with the Indians and their foreign allies, British and Spanish, in order to get a firm grasp upon all the territory belonging to the United States. The Indians of the Southwest— Cherokees, Creeks, Choctaws, and Chickasaws—were led by the colorful and vengeful Alexander McGillivray, a half-breed Creek chieftain who had fought as a Tory during the Revolution and who continued to hate Americans. In his efforts to resist the advance of American frontiersmen into the lower Mississippi Valley, McGillivray received the support and encouragement of Spain. In 1790 President Washington tried to buy peace with the Southwestern Indians by inviting McGillivray to New York and agreeing to pay him $100,000. Despite McGillivray's treaty with the United States, the Indians continued to accept subsidies from the Spaniards and to raid American settlements along the border. At last, in 1793–1794, the Tennesseans went on the warpath themselves, their militia invading the Indian country and chastising several of the tribes. Thus the Southwestern frontier was made safe for the time being.

In the Northwest the government pursued a policy of force against the Indians, even at some risk of becoming involved in hostilities with their protector and ally, Great Britain. Two expeditions failed before a third one finally succeeded in the conquest of the Ohio country. Washington gave the frontier command to General Wayne, who, despite his nickname "Mad Anthony," was a careful planner as well as a dashing soldier. With over 4,000 men, including a large contingent of Kentucky sharpshooters, Wayne moved cautiously toward the Maumee River, building forts as he went. The British officials in Canada, who were providing the Indians with supplies, themselves ordered the construction of a fort about twenty miles from the mouth of the river,

well within the boundary of the United States. Near the British fort, at a place where trees had been blown over by a windstorm, Wayne in the summer of 1794 met and decisively defeated the Indians in the Battle of Fallen Timbers, the British garrison prudently keeping out of the fight. Next summer the Indians agreed in the Treaty of Greenville to abandon to the white men most of what afterwards became the state of Ohio.

Before the government could be sure of its hold upon the border areas, it had to bring to terms the foreign powers which persisted in exerting influence there—Great Britain and Spain. In its diplomacy the Washington administration, by taking advantage of the opportunities that arose from the accidents of international politics, managed to reassert American independence and redeem the West.

Neutrality and Jay's Treaty

When Washington became President, Great Britain had not yet deigned to send a minister to the United States, though all the other powers of Europe (except Russia) had entered into normal diplomatic relations with the young republic. In Congress Madison and the Republicans argued that Great Britain, in refusing to make a commercial treaty with the United States, was waging a kind of economic warfare against this country, and that the United States should retaliate by imposing special customs duties and harbor dues, in excess of the regular rates, upon her goods and ships. Though this legislation did not pass, the threat of it induced the British government finally, in 1791, to dispatch a regular minister to America—the young and supercilious George Hammond, who soon began to court a Philadelphia girl.

Hammond had instructions to forestall hostile economic legislation by pretending to discuss American grievances, without actually conceding anything. The worst of these grievances, besides the lack of a commercial treaty, was the continued British occupation of frontier posts upon American soil.

A new crisis in foreign affairs faced the Washington administration when the French revolutionary government, after guillotining King Louis XVI, went to war in 1793 with Great Britain and her allies. Should the United States recognize the radical government of France by accepting a diplomatic representative from it? Was the United States obligated by the alliance of 1778 to go to war on the side of France? These questions Washington put to his official advisers, and both Hamilton and Jefferson recommended a policy of neutrality, though they presented quite different arguments for it. Washington decided to recognize the French government and to issue a proclamation announcing the determination of the United States to remain at peace. The proclamation (1793), though it did not mention the word "neutrality," was generally interpreted as a neutrality statement, which it actually was. Next year Congress passed a Neutrality Act, forbidding American citizens to participate in the war and prohibiting the use of American soil as a base of operations for either side.

The first challenge to American neutrality came from France. Not that the French revolutionaries asked for a declaration of war: they did not, for they supposed that the United States would be of more use to them as a nonbelligerent. Their purposes became apparent when their first minister to this country arrived. Instead of landing at Philadelphia and presenting himself immediately to the President, the youthful and brash Citizen Edmond Genêt disembarked at Charleston. There he made plans for using American ports to outfit French warships, issued letters of marque and reprisal authorizing American shipowners to serve as French privateers, and commissioned the aging George Rogers Clark to undertake an overland expedition against the possessions of Spain, which at the moment was an ally of Great Britain and an enemy of France. In all these steps, Genêt brazenly disregarded Washington's proclamation and flagrantly violated the Neutrality Act. When he finally reached Philadelphia, after being acclaimed by pro-French crowds on a tour through the interior, he got a stony reception from the President. He then assumed that the people were behind him, and he repeatedly appealed to them over the President's head. His conduct not only infuriated Washington and the Federalists but also embarrassed all except the most ardent Francophiles among the Republicans. At last Washington demanded that the French government recall him, but by that time Genêt's party, the Girondins, were out of power in France and the still more extreme Jacobins in control, so it would not have been safe for him to return. Generously the President granted him political asylum in the United States, and he settled down to live to a ripe old age with his American wife on a Long Island farm. Meanwhile the neutrality policy had survived its first great test.

The second challenge, an even greater one, came from Great Britain. Early in 1794 the Royal Navy suddenly seized hundreds of American ships engaged in trade in the French West Indies. The pretext for these seizures was a British interpretation of international law—known as the Rule of 1756—which held that a trade prohibited in peacetime (as American trade between France and the French overseas possessions had been) could not be legally opened in time of war. At the news of the seizures, the prevalent opinion in the United States became as strongly anti-British as it had recently been anti-French, and the anti-British feeling rose still higher at the report that the Governor-General of Canada had delivered a rousing and warlike speech to the Indians on the northwestern frontier.

With peace thus endangered, Hamilton grew concerned, for war would mean an end to imports from England, and most of the revenue for maintaining his financial system came from duties on those imports.

To him and to other Federalists it seemed that this was no time for ordinary diplomacy. Jefferson had resigned in

spoliations, withdrawal of British forces from the frontier posts, and a satisfactory commercial treaty, without violating the terms of the existing treaty of amity and commerce with France, signed at the time of the alliance in 1778.

The treaty that Jay negotiated (1794) was a long and complex document, dealing with frontier posts, boundaries, debts,

---

JAY'S TREATY

1794

Frontier Posts. "His Majesty will withdraw all his troops and garrisons from all posts and places within the boundary lines assigned by the treaty of peace to the United States."

Boundaries. Joint surveys will be made to locate the U.S.-Canadian boundary west of the Lake of the Woods and at the northeast, between Maine and New Brunswick.

Debts. The United States "will make full and complete compensation" for uncollectible debts owed by Americans to British creditors.

Commerce. There shall be freedom of commerce and navigation between the United States and Great Britain and the British East Indies. (Article XII, permitting the United States to trade with the British West Indies also, but only in ships too small to cross the ocean, was stricken out before ratification.)

Ship Seizures. The British government will compensate Americans for ships and cargoes illegally captured in the past, the amount of payment to be determined by arbitration.

Neutral Rights. American ships carrying enemy (French) property, when captured by the British, shall be taken to British ports and the enemy property removed. (This was inconsistent with the usual American principle that "free ships make free goods.")

1793 to devote himself to organizing a political opposition, and the State Department was now in the hands of an even more ardently pro-French Virginian, Edmund Randolph. Bypassing the State Department, Washington named as a special commissioner to England the staunch New York Federalist, former Secretary for Foreign Affairs under the old Confederation, and current Chief Justice of the Supreme Court, John Jay. Jay was instructed to secure damages for the recent

commerce, ship seizures, and neutral rights. It yielded more to Great Britain and obtained less for the United States than Jay had been authorized to give or instructed to get. When the terms were published in the United States, the treaty was denounced as no treaty before or since, and Jay himself was burned in effigy in various parts of the country. The Republicans were unanimous in decrying it; they said it was a departure from neutrality, favoring Great Britain and unfair to France. Even some of the Federalists were outraged by its terms, those in the South objecting to the payment of the pre-Revolutionary debts. Opponents of the treaty went to extraordinary lengths to defeat it in the Senate, and French agents aided them and cheered them on. The American minister to France, James Monroe, and even the Secretary of State, Edmund Randolph, cooperated closely with the French in a desperate attempt to prevent ratification. Nevertheless, after amending the treaty a bit, the Senate gave its consent.

There was much to be said for Jay's Treaty, despite its very real shortcomings. By means of it the United States gained valuable time for continued peaceful development, obtained undisputed sovereignty over all the Northwest, and secured a reasonably satisfactory commercial agreement with the nation whose trade was most important. More than that, the treaty led immediately to a settlement of the worst of the outstanding differences with Spain.

In Madrid the Spanish foreign minister feared that the understanding between Great Britain and the United States might prove a prelude to joint operations between those two countries against Spain's possessions in North America. Spain was about to change sides in the European war, abandoning Great Britain for France, and it was therefore to Spain's interest to appease the United States. The relentless pressure of American frontiersmen advancing toward the Southwest made it doubtful whether Spain could long hold her borderlands in any event. And so, when Thomas Pinckney arrived in Spain as a special negotiator, he had no difficulty in gaining practically everything that the United States had sought from the Spaniards for over a decade. Pinckney's Treaty (1795) recognized the right of Americans to navigate the Mississippi to its mouth and to deposit goods at New Orleans for reloading on ocean-going ships; fixed the northern

boundary of Florida where Americans always had insisted it should be, along the thirty-first parallel; and bound the Spanish authorities to prevent the Indians in Florida from raiding across the border.

Thus, before Washington had completed his second term in office, the United States had freed itself from the encroachments of both Great Britain and Spain.

Election of 1796

As the time approached for the election of 1796, some of the party friends of Washington urged him to run again. Already twice elected without a single vote cast against him in the electoral college, he could be counted upon to hold the Federalist party together and carry it to a third great victory. But Washington, weary of the burdens of the presidential office, disgusted with the partisan abuse which was being heaped upon him, longed to retire to his beloved home, Mount Vernon. Though he did not object to a third term in principle, he did not desire one for himself. To make his determination clear, he composed, with Hamilton's assistance, a long letter to the American people and had it published in a Philadelphia newspaper.

When Washington in this "Farewell Address" referred to the "insidious wiles of foreign influence," he was not writing merely for rhetorical effect. He had certain real and definite evils in mind. Lately he had dismissed the Secretary of State, Edmund Randolph, and had recalled the minister to France, James Monroe, for working hand in hand with the French to defeat Jay's Treaty. The French were still interfering in American politics with the hope of defeating the Federalists in the forthcoming presidential election.

There was no doubt that Jefferson would be the candidate of the Republicans, and he chose as his running mate the New York Republican leader, Aaron Burr. With Washington out of the running, there was some question as to who the Federalist candidate would be. Hamilton, the very personification of Federalism, was not "available" because he had aroused too many enemies with his forthright views. John Jay was too closely identified with his unpopular treaty, and Thomas Pinckney, though *his* treaty had been enthusiastically received, had the

preferred Pinckney, as did many other Federalists, especially in the South. New Englanders, on the other hand, had no particular liking for Pinckney and feared a plot to make him President instead of Adams. The result was a near disaster for the Federalists. They elected a majority of their presidential electors, despite the electioneering tactics of the French gov-

---

WASHINGTON'S FAREWELL ADDRESS

1796

"Against the insidious wiles of foreign influence (I conjure you to believe me, fellow-citizens) the jealousy of a free people ought to be *constantly* awake, since history and experience prove that foreign influence is one of the most baneful foes of republican government. But that jealousy, to be useful, must be impartial, else it becomes the instrument of the very influence to be avoided, instead of a defense against it. Excessive partiality for one foreign nation and excessive dislike of another cause those whom they actuate to see danger only on one side, and serve to veil and even second the arts of influence on the other. . . .

"The great rule of conduct for us in regard to foreign nations is, in extending our commercial relations, to have with them as little *political* connection as possible. . . .

"It is our true policy to steer clear of permanent alliances with any portion of the foreign world, so far, I mean, as we are now at liberty to do it; for let me not be understood as capable of patronizing infidelity to existing engagements. . . .

"Taking care always to keep ourselves by suitable establishments on a respectable defensive posture, we may safely trust to temporary alliances for extraordinary emergencies."

---

handicap of being a South Carolinian at a time when party leaders thought the next candidate should be a Northerner. John Adams, who as Vice President was directly associated with none of the Federalist measures, finally got the nomination for President at a caucus of the Federalists in Congress, and Pinckney the nomination for Vice President.

With Washington stepping aside, the Federalist party lost much of its coherence and became torn by fierce factional rivalries. Hamilton disliked Adams and

ernment, whose efforts may have boomeranged and helped the Federalists. But when the electors balloted in the various states, some of the Pinckney men declined to vote for Adams, and a still larger number of the Adams men declined to vote for Pinckney. So Pinckney received fewer votes than Jefferson, and Adams only three more than Jefferson. The next President was to be a Federalist, but the Vice President was to be a Republican!

By virtue of his diplomatic services during the Revolution, his writings as a con-

JOHN ADAMS. When elected to the Presidency, Adams was almost thirty years younger than the man depicted in this portrait, painted when he was past eighty. The artist was Samuel F. B. Morse. Afterwards best known as the inventor of the magnetic telegraph, Morse did not give up painting for invention until he was in his forties. He was born in Massachusetts, the son of Jedidiah Morse, who was America's foremost geographer of the late eighteenth and early nineteenth century. The younger Morse graduated from Yale, studied art under Benjamin West and Washington Allston in England, and in 1823 opened a studio in New York. He helped to found and was the first president of the National Academy of Design. (IN THE BROOKLYN MUSEUM COLLECTION)

servative political philosopher, and his devotion to the public weal as he saw it, "Honest John" Adams ranks as one of the greatest of American statesmen. He had his human failings, however. Like most prominent members of the illustrious Adams family afterwards, he lacked the politician's touch which is essential for successful leadership in a republican society. Even Washington, remote and austere as he sometimes seems to have been, was fairly adept at conciliating factions and maintaining party harmony.

As President, Adams was in a position requiring unusual political skill. Not only was his administration divided between a President of one party and a Vice President of another; it was also divided between the followers of Hamilton and those of Adams. Unwisely, the new President chose to continue Washington's department heads in office. Most of them were friends of Hamilton, and they looked to him for advice, though he held no official post. Many of the Congressmen also looked to Hamilton rather than the President. With the government as well as the people badly divided, Adams faced foreign problems as trying as those with which Washington had had to contend.

X. Y. Z. and Hostilities with France

As American relations with Great Britain and Spain improved in consequence of Jay's and Pinckney's treaties, relations with France, now under the government of the Directory, went from bad to worse. Despite the victory of the Federalists in the election of 1796, the leaders of the Directory assumed that France had the sympathy and support of the mass of the American people and could undermine the Adams administration by frustrating it in foreign affairs. Therefore the French, asserting that they were applying the same principles of neutral rights as the United States and Great Britain had adopted in Jay's Treaty, continued to capture American ships on the high seas and, in many cases, to imprison the crews. When Minister Monroe left France after his recall, the French went out of their way to show their affection for him and for the Republican party. When the South Carolina Federalist Charles Cotesworth Pinckney, a brother of Thomas Pinckney, arrived in France to replace Monroe, the Directory considered him *persona non grata* and refused to receive him as the official representative of the United States.

War seemed likely unless the Adams administration could settle the difficulties with France. Some of the President's advisers, in particular his Secretary of State, the stiff-backed New England Francophobe Timothy Pickering, favored war. Others urged a special effort for peace, and even Alexander Hamilton approved the idea of appointing commissioners to approach the Directory. Adams, himself a peace man, appointed a bipartisan commission of three: C. C. Pinckney, the recently rejected minister; John Marshall, a Virginia Federalist, afterwards famous as the great Chief Justice of the Supreme Court; and Elbridge Gerry, a Massachusetts Republican but a personal friend of the President's. In France, in 1797, the three Americans were met by three agents of the Directory's foreign minister, Prince Talleyrand, who had a reputation as the wizard of European diplomacy but who did not understand the psychology of Americans, even though he had lived for a time in the United States. Talleyrand's agents demanded a loan for France and a bribe for French officials before they would deal with Adams' commissioners. According to legend, one of the Americans replied: "Millions for defense but not one cent for tribute!" Actually, the response of the commissioners was summed up in Pinckney's laconic words: "No! No! Not a sixpence!"

When Adams received the commissioners' report, he sent a message to Congress in which he urged readiness for war, denounced the French for their insulting treatment of the United States, and vowed he would not appoint another minister to France until he knew the minister would be "received, respected and honored as the representative of a great, free, powerful and independent nation." The Republicans, doubting the President's charge that the United States had been insulted, asked for proof. Adams then turned the commissioners' report over to Congress, after deleting the names of the three Frenchmen and designating them only as Messrs. X., Y., and Z. When the report was published, the "X. Y. Z. Affair" provoked even more of a reaction than Adams had bargained for. It aroused the martial spirit of most Americans, made the Federalists more popular than ever as the party of patriotism, and led to a limited and undeclared war with France, 1798–1800.

With the cooperation of Congress, which quickly passed the necessary laws, Adams cut off all trade with France, abrogated the treaties of 1778, and authorized public and private vessels of the United States to capture French armed ships on the high seas. Congress set up a Department of the Navy (1798) and appropriated money for the construction of warships to supplement the hundreds of privateers and the small number of government vessels already built for the protection of American shipping in the Mediterranean against the Barbary pirates. The new United States Navy soon gave a good account of itself. Its warships won a number of duels with French vessels of their own class, the most spectacular performance being that of the *Constellation*, which under the command of Thomas Truxtun defeated the *Insurgente* and then the *Vengeance*. In the space of about three years American men-of-war captured a total of eighty-five prizes, including armed merchantmen as well as vessels of the French navy.

Having abandoned neutrality, the United States now was cooperating so closely with Great Britain as to be virtually a cobelligerent, though technically at peace. When the British offered to lend a part of their fleet to the United States, President Adams declined to borrow, since he preferred to build up a navy of his own. Nevertheless, the British provided shot and shell to make up the deficient American supplies, furnished offi-

BUILDING THE NAVY. After the Revolutionary War the United States abandoned the warships it had accumulated, and from 1783 to 1798 there was no American navy. Then, with the outbreak of undeclared hostilities with France, the Navy Department was established and a naval building program begun. In that age of wooden sailing ships, there were three main categories of war vessels: (1) ships of the line, or line-of-battle ships, which were the largest and most heavily armed (roughly corresponding to twentieth-century battleships or dreadnoughts); (2) frigates, which were smaller and faster and had fewer guns (comparable to modern cruisers); (3) corvettes, sloops of war, and other relatively small craft (somewhat like the light cruisers, destroyers, and gunboats of the present). At the outset the United States navy eschewed line-of-battle ships and placed its chief reliance on specially designed frigates which were faster, more maneuverable, and more heavily gunned than their European counterparts. In 1798 the frigates *United States, Constitution,* and *Constellation,* already partly built, were completed, and the *Philadelphia* and several others were started. The illustration shows work in progress on the *Philadelphia* in a Philadelphia shipyard. This frigate was not finished in time to be used against the French, but it saw plenty of action later (1803) in the war with Tripoli. Tripolitan pirates captured the ship, and Americans in a daring raid destroyed her to prevent the enemy's using her against them. (THE HISTORICAL SOCIETY OF PENNSYLVANIA)

cers to help with the training and direction of American crews, and exchanged signaling information so that British and American ships could communicate readily with one another. Thus the United States was involved in the world war as a kind of associate member of the coalition against France.

The French foreign minister, Talley-rand, finally began to see the wisdom of an accommodation with the Americans. He took notice of the rapprochement between the United States and Great Britain, the successes of the American Navy, and the failure of the American people to show the expected enthusiasm for the cause of France. He was enlightened in regard to American public opinion by

George Logan, a Philadelphia Quaker who, with no official authorization but with a letter of introduction from Vice President Jefferson, visited France to work for peace in the midst of the undeclared war. After Logan returned, President Adams gave him a sympathetic hearing, though the Federalists in Congress passed a law, the so-called Logan Act, to prohibit citizens from engaging in private

The Americans agreed to a new treaty which canceled the old ones, arranged for reciprocity in commerce, and ignored the question of damages. When Adams submitted this treaty to the Senate, the extreme Federalists raised so many objections that its final ratification was delayed until after he had left office. Nevertheless, the "quasi-war" had come to an honorable end, and the United States at

---

ALIEN AND SEDITION ACTS

1798

Naturalization Act. No alien shall be admitted to citizenship unless he has resided within the United States for at least fourteen years. No native, citizen, subject, or resident of a country with which the United States is at war shall be admitted to citizenship.

Alien Act. The President may "order all such aliens as he shall judge dangerous to the peace and safety of the United States" to depart.

Alien Enemies Act. When war is declared or invasion threatened, "all natives, citizens, denizens, or subjects of the hostile nation or government, being males of the age of fourteen years and upwards, who shall be within the United States, and not actually naturalized, shall be liable to be apprehended, restrained, secured and removed, as alien enemies."

Sedition Act. Any persons combining or conspiring "with intent to oppose any measure or measures of the government of the United States" shall be liable to fines up to $5,000 and imprisonment up to five years. Any person writing, uttering, or publishing "any false, scandalous and malicious writing or writings" against the government, the Congress, or the President shall be liable to a fine up to $2,000 and imprisonment up to two years.

---

and unofficial diplomacy with foreign governments in the future.

When, in 1800, Adams' new three-man commission arrived in France, Napoleon Bonaparte was in power as First Consul. The Americans requested that France terminate the treaties of 1778 and pay damages for seizures of American ships. Napoleon replied that, if the United States had any claim to damages, the claim must rest upon the treaties, and if the treaties were ended, the claim must be abandoned. Napoleon had his way.

last had freed itself from the entanglements and embarrassments of the "perpetual" alliance with France.

Repression and Protest

The outbreak of hostilities in 1798 had given the Federalists an advantage over the political opposition, and in the congressional elections of that year they increased their majorities in both houses. Meanwhile their new-found power went to their heads. Some of them schemed to go on winning elections by passing laws to weaken and to silence the opposition. They had as an excuse the necessity or the supposed necessity of protecting the nation from dangerous foreign influence in the midst of the undeclared war. By persecuting their critics, the Federalists produced a crop of Republican martyrs, gave rise to protests against their disregard of the Constitution, and provoked a reac-

Alien Act nor deport any aliens, but this law together with the Naturalization Act doubtless had some effect in discouraging immigration and encouraging many foreigners already here to leave. The administration did enforce the Sedition Act, arresting about two dozen men and convicting ten of them. Most of these were Republican newspaper editors whose writings, while tending to bring the Fed-

---

KENTUCKY RESOLUTIONS

1798

"*Resolved*, that the several States composing the United States of America are not united on the principle of unlimited submission to their general government; but that by compact under the style and title of a Constitution for the United States and of amendments thereto, they constituted a general government for special purposes, delegating to that government certain definite powers, reserving each State to itself the residuary mass of rights to their own self-government; and that whensoever the general government assumes undelegated powers, its acts are unauthoritative, void, and of no force: That to this compact each State acceded as a State, and is an integral party, its co-States forming, as to itself, the other party: That the government created by this compact was not made the exclusive or final judge of the extent of the powers delegated to itself; since that would have made its discretion, and not the Constitution, the measure of its powers; but that as in all other cases of compact among parties having no common Judge, *each party has an equal right to judge for itself, as well of infractions as of the mode and measure of redress.*"

---

tion which helped to bring their party to defeat.

Since many Republican critics of the administration were foreigners by birth, especially Irish or French, the Federalists in Congress thought it desirable to limit the political rights of aliens and make it more difficult for them to become citizens of the United States. The Federalists struck at the civil liberties of both native Americans and the foreign-born in a series of laws commonly known as the Alien and Sedition Acts.

President Adams did not invoke the

eralists into disrepute, were not truly seditious at all. One of the editors merely had expressed the wish that, when a salute was fired in honor of the President, the wadding of the cannon had "struck him in the rear bulge of the breeches."

The Republicans had no reason to look to the Supreme Court for relief. Indeed, the Court never yet had declared an act of Congress unconstitutional, and the Republicans denied that it had the power to do so. They believed, however, that the recent Federalist legislation, particularly the Sedition Act, was unconstitutional, for the First Amendment stated that Congress should pass no law abridging freedom of speech or of the press.

What agency of government should decide the question of constitutionality? The Republican leaders Jefferson and Madison concluded that the state legislatures should decide, and they ably expressed their view in two sets of resolutions, one written (anonymously) by Jefferson and adopted by the Kentucky legislature (1798, 1799), and the other drafted by Madison and approved by the Virginia legislature (1798). These Kentucky and Virginia resolutions asserted the following doctrines. The federal government had been formed by a "compact" or contract among the states. It was a limited government, possessing only certain delegated powers. Whenever it exercised any additional and undelegated powers, its acts were "unauthoritative, void, and of no force." The parties to the contract, the states, must decide for themselves when and whether the central government exceeded its powers. And "nullification" by the states was the "rightful remedy" whenever the general government went too far. The resolutions urged all the states to join in declaring the Alien and Sedition Acts null and void and in requesting their repeal at the next session of Congress, but none of the others went along with Virginia and Kentucky.

Election of 1800

In the election of 1800 Jefferson and Burr, representing the alliance of Virginia and New York, were again the Republican candidates. Adams was running for re-election on the Federalist ticket, and his running mate was C. C. Pinckney, brother of the Thomas Pinckney who had been the Federalist vice-presidential candidate in 1796.

During the nearly twelve years of Federalist rule, the party had created numerous political enemies in consequence of Hamilton's financial program, the sup-

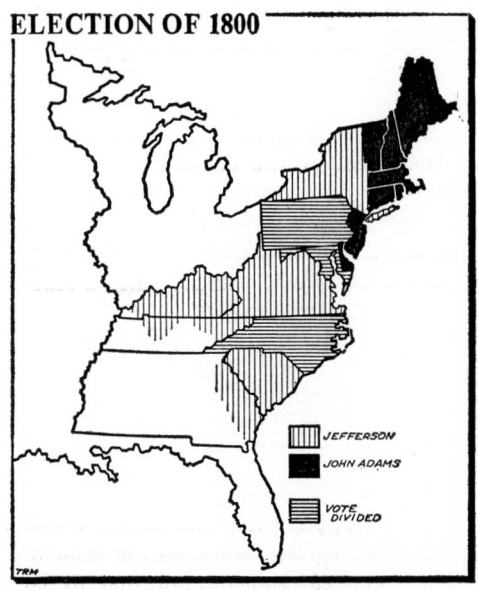

ELECTION OF 1800

JEFFERSON
JOHN ADAMS
VOTE DIVIDED

pression of the Whiskey Rebellion, Jay's Treaty, and the Alien and Sedition Acts. Denouncing these measures, and especially the last of them, the Republicans made state rights and constitutional liberties the main issues of their campaign in 1800. They pictured Adams as a tyrant and a man who wanted to be King. The Federalists, on the other hand, described Jefferson as a dangerous radical and his followers as wild men who, if they got into power, would bring on a reign of terror comparable to that of the French Revolution at its worst.

The contest was close, and the outcome in the electoral college depended upon the voting in one state, New York. In New York City the vice-presidential candidate, Burr, was the organizer of Republican victory. The Revolutionary veterans of the city had formed the Tammany Society to maintain their wartime fellowship and to combat the pretensions of the Society of the Cincinnati, the exclusive and aristocratic organization of Revolutionary officers. Though not himself a member of Tammany, Burr converted it into a political machine and, with its aid, carried the city for the Republicans by such a large majority as to carry the state also. The Republicans gained control of the legislature, and since New York was one of the states in which the legislature cast the electoral vote, the Republicans could count upon that vote in the presidential election.

When the electors of the several states cast their votes, Adams received a total of 65 and Pinckney 64. Jefferson got 73, and so did Burr. To avoid such a tie, Republican leaders had meant for at least one of their electors to refrain from giving Burr his vote. But through a misunderstanding—some said that Burr himself was secretly responsible—the plan went awry. And so the election was not yet over: in accordance with the Constitution the decision between the two highest, between Burr and Jefferson, was up to the House of Representatives, with the delegation from each state casting a single vote.

Since the Federalists controlled a majority of the states' votes in the existing Congress, they had the privilege of deciding which of their opponents was to be the next President, though the Republicans, in making their nominations, had clearly intended for Jefferson to have the first place on their ticket. Some of the more extreme of the Federalists now hoped to postpone or to prevent any breaking of the tie and, instead, to make new arrangements for the presidential succession so that the highest office in the land would yet fall to a Federalist. Others, fearing chaos and possible civil war if no election were made, thought it would be better to come to an understanding with Burr and elect him. Hamilton disapproved both proposals. Though he had a low opinion of Jefferson, he had a still lower one of Burr, his bitter rival in law and politics in New York. Hamilton considered Burr an unprincipled and untrustworthy schemer. Burr himself remained strangely silent, neither electioneering openly for himself nor refusing publicly

to accept office at the hands of the Federalists.

During the winter of 1800–1 the House balloted again and again without mustering a majority for either candidate. Finally, only a few weeks before inauguration day, some of the Federalist die-hards gave in, the tie was broken, and Jefferson was named as President. Afterwards one of the Federalists claimed that he had given in because Jefferson's friends had assured him that Jefferson, if elected, would appoint him to a government job and would preserve the main Federalist policies with respect to commerce, the navy, and the public debt, while making no wholesale removals of Federalists from the lower offices of the government.

Packing the Courts

In addition to a majority of the presidential electors in 1800, the Republicans also won a majority of the seats in both houses of the next Congress. The only branch of the government left in Federalist hands was the judiciary, and Adams and his fellow partisans during his last months in office took steps to make their hold upon the courts secure.

By the Judiciary Act of 1801 the Federalists succeeded in reducing the number of Supreme Court justiceships by one but at the same time greatly increasing the number of federal judgeships as a whole. The act created a separate system of circuit courts of appeal, between the federal district courts and the Supreme Court. Formerly (in accordance with the Judiciary Act of 1789) a district judge had sat with two Supreme Court justices to hear appeals on the circuit. The new law also provided for ten additional district judgeships.

To these newly created positions Adams proceeded to appoint deserving Federalists. It was said that he stayed up until midnight on his last day in office, March 3, 1801, in order to complete the signing of the judge's commissions, and so these officeholders were known as his "midnight appointments." Since federal judges held office for life—that is, with good behavior—Jefferson as the incoming President would be powerless to remove Adams' appointees. Or so the Federalists assumed.

BIBLIOGRAPHY

For an intimate glimpse of the first President and the first Congress, see the *Journal of William Maclay, United States Senator from Pennsylvania, 1789–1791* (1890; new ed., 1928). Senator Maclay was a staunch republican who admired George Washington but feared the "monarchical" tendencies of the time. How well grounded the Senator's fears were, L. B. Dunbar shows in *A Study of the "Monarchical" Tendencies in the United States from 1776 to 1801* (1923). A sound, brief introduction to the men and measures of the first administration is H. J. Ford's *Washington and His Colleagues* (1921). The administrative organization and policies are more thoroughly discussed by L. D. White in *The Federalists* (1948). See also L. K. Caldwell, *The Administrative Theories of Hamilton and Jefferson* (1944).

The origin of political parties—like the origin of the Constitution—was given an economic interpretation by Charles A. Beard. His *Economic Origins of Jeffersonian Democracy* (1915; new ed., 1949) has had an influence second only to that of his *Economic Interpretation of the Constitution*. In *The Origins of the American Party System* (1956) Joseph Charles analyzes afresh the views and actions of Hamilton, Jefferson, Washington, and John Adams. C. G. Bowers, *Jefferson and Hamilton* (1925), is vivid, dramatic, and partial to Jefferson.

L. M. Hacker more than redresses the balance in Hamilton's faver in *Alexander Hamilton in the American Tradition* (1957), which praises Hamilton as a "real conservative" and fully elaborates his economic ideas. Adrienne Koch, *The Philosophy of Thomas Jefferson* (1943), is a lucid analysis. The growth of parties in one commonwealth is expertly told in H. M. Tinkcom's *The Republicans and Federalists in Pennsylvania, 1790–1801* (1950).

On foreign affairs, two standard references, both by S. F. Bemis, are *Jay's Treaty* (1923) and *Pinckney's Treaty* (1926). Bemis emphasizes the European situation —"Europe's distresses"—as the factor making possible American diplomatic successes in the 1790's. A. P. Whitaker, in *The Spanish-American Frontier, 1783–1795* and a sequel, *The Mississippi Question, 1795–1803* (1934), gives more weight to conditions on the American continent, especially the growing strength of the United States along its borders with Spanish territory. See also Frank Monaghan, *John Jay* (1935). An important new study is Alexander De Conde, *Entangling Alliance: Politics and Diplomacy under George Washington* (1958).

The Whiskey Rebellion is interestingly and authoritatively described in L. D. Baldwin's *Whiskey Rebels: The Story of a Frontier Uprising* (1939).

8

LIFE IN

THE YOUNG REPUBLIC

The American people won political independence in the Revolutionary War, and they were to win commercial independence in the War of 1812. Meanwhile they aspired to a kind of cultural independence also. They looked forward to a time when the United States would be uniquely great in science, art, and technology as well as government. This "happy land" was to be the "seat of empire" and the "final stage" of civilization, with "glorious works of high invention and of wond'rous art." So Philip Freneau and Hugh H. Brackenridge proclaimed in their *Poem on the Rising Glory of America* (1772). Later Freneau became an ardent Jeffersonian in politics, but his Federalist contemporaries sang the same theme. Joel Barlow, in his *Vision of Columbus* (1787), saw America as "the last and greatest theatre for the improvement of mankind."

By the early 1800's the United States had not yet fulfilled the promise of its poets, but beginnings had been made which suggested that the promise, or much of it, might eventually be fulfilled.

Education and the Professions

In certain respects the War of the Revolution temporarily handicapped American intellectual life. Some learned men turned from science and scholarship to military or political service. The noted astronomer David Rittenhouse, for example, left his telescopes and devoted himself to a Revolutionary committee, the Pennsylvania Council of Safety, while advising his countrymen to abandon schools and concentrate on defense. Many schools did close, especially in rural areas, and most of the colleges were disrupted. Harvard buildings were used as American army barracks; Nassau Hall at Princeton was damaged during Washington's New Jersey campaign; and the William and Mary campus became the military headquarters of Cornwallis before the Battle of Yorktown.

But the Revolution also stimulated intellectual activity and brought forth ideas that were to have lasting consequences. Through military service thousands of young men got better acquainted with their own country, and by reading patriotic pamphlets, or at least hearing them discussed, these soldiers received something of a political education. With the French alliance there came from France not only troops and supplies but also ideas—the skeptical, experimental, scientific notions of the Enlightenment. And, with independence as a war aim and finally as an accomplished fact, it seemed to thoughtful Americans that widespread literacy and learning were absolutely essential to the success of the new republic. Thomas Jefferson, for one, called for a "crusade against ignorance."

The friends of learning advocated not merely education as such but a special kind of education, one that would fill the minds of youth with patriotic, republican thoughts. The Massachusetts geographer Jedidiah Morse, author of *Geography Made Easy* (1784), said the country must have its own textbooks so that the people would not be infected with the monarchical and aristocratic ideas of England. The Connecticut schoolmaster and lawyer Noah Webster likewise contended that the American schoolboy should be educated as a patriot. "As soon as he opens his lips," Webster wrote, "he should rehearse the history of his own country; he should lisp the praise of liberty, and of those illustrious heroes and statesmen who have wrought a revolution in her favor."

To foster a distinctive culture and unify the nation, Webster insisted upon a simplified and Americanized spelling—*honor* instead of *honour*, for example. His *American Spelling Book* (1783), commonly known as the "blue-backed speller," eventually sold over 100 million copies, to become the best-selling book (except for the Bible) in the entire history of American publishing. Webster also wrote grammars and other schoolbooks. His school dictionary (1806) was republished in many editions and eventually was much enlarged to form *An Ameri-*

can Dictionary of the English Language (1828). By means of his speller and his dictionary he succeeded in establishing a national standard of words and usages for the United States.

In their first constitutions, several of the states endorsed the principle of public education, but none actually required the establishment of free schools. A Massachusetts law of 1789 reaffirmed the colonial laws providing for the support of schools by the various towns. Jedidiah Morse observed later that the enforcement of the law was lax in many places. Even in Boston only seven public schools existed in 1790, and most of these were poorly housed; more than twice as many private schools were in operation. In Virginia, Jefferson as wartime governor proposed a plan by which the elements of reading and writing should be provided for all children, and secondary and higher education for the gifted, with state scholarships for the needy. The plan was not enacted into law. As late as 1815 none of the states (not even Massachusetts) had in actual operation a comprehensive public school system.

Outside of New England, schooling continued to be viewed as the responsibility of the family and the church rather than the state. In the Middle Atlantic region and the South, most schools were run by religious groups, by proprietary schoolmasters, or by philanthropic societies. Though requiring tuition from parents who could afford it, many schools accepted the poor without pay. In the cities, special organizations were formed for the education of the poor. One of these, the New York Free School Society, introduced from England (1806) the Lancastrian method, to economize on instruction costs: the teacher taught a lesson to several superior pupils, and then these "monitors" drilled groups of their fellow pupils.

During and after the Revolution private academies sprang up in increasing

A School in Session About 1800. In such a one-room school, children of practically all ages were brought together. While one group recited, the rest learned their lessons—or were supposed to. Paper and ink were scarce; a slate and a slate pencil were commonly used instead. There was little in the way of furnishings except for backless benches and a few desks, usually placed under the windows, where the light was best. The teacher had to look out for the fire and perform the other chores of a janitor. Often the teacher was a college student, earning money during the long winter vacation from his own studies, or he was a recent college graduate supporting himself while he prepared for the law and politics. Daniel Webster and Thaddeus Stevens once taught school, and so did many another young man who afterwards became prominent in public life. (LIBRARY OF CONGRESS)

numbers. Many were patterned after the academies founded by the Phillips family at Andover, Massachusetts (1778), and at Exeter, New Hampshire (1781). By 1815 there were 30 private secondary schools in Massachusetts, 37 in New York, and more than 100 in the country as a whole. Most of these admitted only boys, but a few academies or seminaries were provided for girls. Salem Female Academy, established in 1772 by North Carolina Moravians, was one of the earliest.

At the outbreak of the Revolution there had been a total of nine colleges in all the colonies; in 1800 there were twenty-two in the various states, and the number continued steadily to increase thereafter. Whereas all but two of the colonial colleges were sectarian in origin and spirit, a majority of those founded during the first three decades of independence were nondenominational. Especially significant, in foreshadowing the future pattern of higher education, was the fact that five were state institutions: the universities of Georgia (1785), North Carolina (1789), Vermont (1791), Ohio (1804), and South Carolina (1805). For the time being, none of these was either quite public or a university in the modern sense. Their offerings were limited, and their financial support was derived mainly from private endowments, gifts, and tuition fees rather than appropriations of the rather niggardly legislatures.

All together, more than twenty colleges, public and private, were in operation during the first decade of the nineteenth century. The largest of them had an enrollment of no more than a few hundred students, and the total endowment of all the institutions amounted to little more than $500,000. Equipment was poor and libraries small—the Harvard library, with 15,000 volumes in 1812, was exceptional. Standards generally were low, and complaints were often heard that serious scholars were not being produced. As of 1775, only about one in a thousand men (and no women at all) had the benefit of such college education as was available; by 1815, the proportion had not risen a great deal.

Jefferson, John Adams, and a few other statesmen nourished the ideal of a true university, providing the best of training in the professions as well as the liberal arts. Nothing came of Jefferson's hope that a national university might be established. As wartime governor of Virginia, he managed to expand the work of William and Mary by adding professorships of law, medicine, and modern languages. George Wythe, the first law professor at the college, taught a remarkable number of youths who afterwards became distinguished lawyers and statesmen. Before 1800 the University of Pennsylvania and Columbia College instituted law courses, and Judge Tapping Reeve opened a private law school in Litchfield, Connecticut. As a rule, lawyers got their training, as in colonial times, by "reading law" in the office of a practicing attorney.

Most physicians likewise still studied medicine and gained experience by working with an established practitioner, but several medical schools were in existence by the early 1800's. The oldest of these, at the University of Pennsylvania, was founded in 1765. Its most distinguished professor, and the outstanding physician

in America, was Benjamin Rush, who had received his medical degree at Edinburgh. As an army surgeon during the Revolutionary War, Dr. Rush protested against improper sanitation and medical care, which caused many more soldiers to die of camp diseases than of battle wounds. Afterwards he interested himself in the effects of diet and drink upon health, and he also made pioneering studies of psychosomatic and psychiatric disorders. As educators, Rush and other physicians had to struggle against age-old superstitions and against popular hostility to the dissection of corpses. In 1788 a riot was provoked when a human limb was hung out of a New York hospital window to dry, and from time to time medical students got into trouble for body-snatching, since cadavers seldom were available by legal means.

The science of public as well as private health remained in its infancy. In the summer of 1793 an epidemic of yellow fever raged unchecked in Philadelphia, bringing death to a tenth of the population in one of the worst disasters ever to befall an American city. The physicians were helpless, though Dr. Rush came near to guessing the cause of the epidemic when he explained it as being due to the miasma arising from decomposed matter. The Philadelphia experience stimulated programs for improving sanitation and making cities cleaner, and thus unwittingly the number of breeding places for the mosquito that transmits yellow fever were reduced. In many cases the prevailing medical practices hastened death instead of prolonging life. George Washington need not have died from a throat infection in 1799, but his physicians, doing their best according to their lights, bled and purged him so thoroughly as to impair his resistance to the disease.

As in colonial America, so also in the young republic scientific investigation (except in medical science) was largely the work of amateurs. But it was becoming more and more specialized, and scien-

1776.   EVENING DRESS.   1780.   1780.   1785.

EVENING DRESS.   1795.   EVENING DRESS.   1797.   1800.   1805.

1805.   1812.   1812.   1812.

tists were growing increasingly conscious of their common professional interests. In 1780 the American Academy of Arts and Sciences was formed in Boston, its announced object being "to cultivate every art and science which may tend to advance the interest, honor, dignity, and happiness of a free, independent, and virtuous people." At meetings of the Academy the members read papers on scientific subjects, and eventually these began to be published in a regular series. The founding of this Academy in the midst of the Revolution indicates that the war did not completely distract Americans from scientific effort. Throughout the war years and afterward the noted botanist William Bartram persisted in collecting specimens and observing the plants and wild life of the South and West. His *Travels* (1791), translated into French, German, and other languages, was acclaimed abroad as well as at home.

On the whole, the republican atmosphere of America was favorable to scientific inquiry. To this country came Dr. Joseph Priestley in 1794, as a refugee from the reactionary spirit then prevailing in England. Already famous as the discoverer of oxygen, Priestley continued his researches in Pennsylvania, discovering carbon monoxide and the possibility of liberating air from water. He stimulated interest in chemistry, though some Americans disagreed with him when he main-

tained that fire consisted of a material substance, known as "phlogiston."

Painting had become a busy profession, and the young republic produced several artists of unusual talent. The first of the notable American-born painters, Benjamin West, did not make his career in the United States. After studying in Rome, West settled in England (1763) and rose to prominence in artistic circles there. His ideal, in art, was the "noble simplicity and quiet grandeur" of republican Rome, rather than strict realism on the one hand or baroque elaborateness on the other. West left his influence upon a whole generation of American artists— John Singleton Copley, Gilbert Stuart, Charles Willson Peale, and many others —who went to England to study under him. Most of them (Copley was a notable exception) returned to their native country and set up studios, to make a living from commissions to paint historical scenes and portraits of wealthy and notable Americans. Peale (1806) founded the Pennsylvania Academy of Fine Arts as a center for the encouragement of American painting, but aspiring artists continued to seek their training abroad, especially in England.

Despite the high hopes and the best efforts of the advocates of republican learning and cultural independence, American arts and sciences remained essentially derivative and provincial for a

FASHIONS IN DRESS, 1776–1812. [OPPOSITE] Before the Revolutionary War, American clothing styles were borrowed from England; afterwards, from France. In 1776 the American gentleman, when dressed up, wore a three-cornered cocked hat, a wig with a queue, a ruffled shirt, a waistcoat, a brightly colored outer coat, knee breeches, stockings, and low buckled shoes. In 1800, wigless, he had a round hat with a low crown and wore tight-fitting pantaloons tucked inside high boots; in 1812 his hat had a higher crown. Loose-fitting trousers did not become fashionable until after the War of 1812. As for the well-dressed woman, in the 1780's she had a high-piled hair-do, a high-necked and low-waisted gown with a tight bodice and a full skirt, which was supported by numerous undergarments and sometimes by hoops or stays. She wore shoes with extremely high heels. During the 1790's and early 1800's her headdress, her neckline, and her heels became lower and her waist much higher, sometimes reaching as high as her bosom, which was now accentuated. Her skirt grew narrower and sometimes rather tight— becoming almost a hobble-skirt. She discarded most of her underclothes (this seemed shocking to later generations in the nineteenth century, when piles of underclothing again were decreed by fashion, as well as by Victorian modesty).

long time after political independence had become a fact. The same was true of American literature.

Letters, Drama, and Music

During the first forty years of independence, the most widely read of American writings—and some of the greatest ones (such as *The Federalist*)—were polemical and political, not belletristic. In pamphlet and newspaper the literate American followed the arguments about British colonial policy, the aims of the Revolution, the question of a new Constitution, and the party contests of the young republic. He became a "newspaper reading animal," as an English visitor observed. This preoccupation with the news of the day drew attention away from literature of a more artistic and permanent kind. Thus, in one way, the newspapers handicapped literary development. Yet, in another way, the newspapers helped it, for they created a reading public and produced a potential market for literary works.

There was a more serious handicap to the rise of American authorship. An aspiring author found it hard to get his manuscript published, or to get it sold after it was in print. Until well into the nineteenth century, there were in America no book publishers in the modern sense, no firms that would bear the cost and take the risk of publishing. The author himself had to pay all or at least the larger part of the expenses. He could find few printers willing to share the burden with him, for they could reprint the works of popular English authors without paying a royalty. No author in the young republic could support himself by means of his writing alone. The first to try it was the novelist Charles Brockden Brown. He produced a series of well-written horror stories but had to take a job as magazine editor in order to eke out his income.

The American author, if he looked to periodicals or the theater for a market, did little if any better than with books. In the late eighteenth century, several magazines were published in the United States, the most important being the *Columbian*, the *American Museum*, the *Massachusetts Magazine*, and the *New-York Magazine*. All of these filled their pages chiefly by clipping material from English publications. Meanwhile the theater had grown into an accepted, permanent institution in American cities, with substantial buildings and regular schedules of performances. George Washington himself attended plays, and opposition to the theater as "the house of the devil" declined, though it by no means disappeared. But the American dramatist, like the writer of books and the contributor to magazines, had to compete with English authors, who did not have to be paid royalties.

Under the circumstances, it is surprising that the young republic contained so many able and active poets, essayists, novelists, and playwrights as it did. Among the most active poets and essayists were the "Hartford Wits," a group of Connecticut writers who met together for sociability and mutual encouragement. The leaders were Joel Barlow, Timothy Dwight, and John Trumbull (not to be confused with the contemporary painter of the same name). These men wrote epics on American greatness and satires on American foibles—as seen from a solid, Federalist, New England point of view. Barlow eventually went over to the Jeffersonian side, but the ablest and most thoroughgoing Jeffersonian poet, a hardy foe of the Hartford Wits, was Philip Freneau of New Jersey.

Novels became the rage in England during the last half of the eighteenth century, and their popularity spread to the United States, where the latest English successes were promptly imported and reprinted, and eagerly read. The most fashionable themes were sex and sentimentality, satire, and terror. When novelists finally appeared in America, they hoped to produce a native, original kind of fiction, but they had to appeal to the prevailing taste. They used essentially the same themes as the English novelists, though substituting American scenes and situations for English ones. The first American novel, William Hill Brown's *The Power of Sympathy* (1789), was intended, the author said, "to expose the fatal consequences" of immorality; it is a story (based on fact) of seduction, incestuous love, rape, and suicide. Hugh Henry Brackenridge's *Modern Chivalry*, an interminable tale published in installments (1792–1815), satirizes certain excesses and errors of democracy. Charles Brockden Brown's *Wieland* (1798), the best work of the greatest of the early American novelists, gives a terrifying account of a man who goes crazy and kills his wife and children.

The first play to be written and professionally performed in America, Thomas Godfrey's *The Prince of Parthia*, was produced in 1767 at the New Theater in Philadelphia. This melodrama of passion and violence in ancient Parthia, though borrowing some elements from Shakespeare and other English playwrights, demonstrated that an American could make original and interesting use of inherited dramatic traditions. So did the first comedy to be written and performed in this country—Royall Tyler's *The Contrast*. An excellent acting-play, on the theme of city versus country manners, *The Contrast* began a long and highly successful run in 1787, at the John Street Theater in New York. During the next twenty years and more, a number of other popular plays came from the pen of Tyler, the ablest native playwright of his time. A more versatile figure, the most influential in the early development of the American drama, was William Dunlap, who not only wrote and adapted plays but also produced them, designed and managed theaters, and made himself the defender and finally the historian of the American stage. No crusader for uniquely

American productions, Dunlap questioned "how far we ought to wish for a national drama, distinct from that of our English forefathers." He presented what the public wanted—Shakespearian and other English plays, translations and adaptations of the latest European hits, and the works of Americans, including himself.

Most of the songs popular during and after the Revolution consisted of new and patriotic words set to familiar English tunes. "Yankee Doodle" was written, during the French and Indian War, by a British army surgeon with the intention of poking fun at the ragged colonial troops. It became a favorite with the Yankees themselves, and during the Revolution they added many variations, some of them unsuitable for polite company. Other popular music was written by Francis Hopkinson, the first notable American composer and a man of amazing versatility. The first student to be graduated from the College of Philadelphia, Hopkinson practiced law, served in the first Continental Congress and signed the Declaration of Independence, wrote verse, essays, and Revolutionary pamphlets, painted, gave public performances on the harpsichord, and sat as a judge in Pennsylvania and federal courts, besides composing music. A collection of his best work was published under the title of *Seven Songs* (1788). His son, the eminent lawyer Joseph Hopkinson, wrote the words for "Hail, Columbia" during the undeclared war with France (1798); for many years, this stirring song remained the nearest equivalent to a national anthem.

The Churches and Religion

Americans of the young republic might have been patriotic enough but, from the point of view of many a religious leader, they were insufficiently pious. The religious exictement of the Great Awakening had passed, and sermons of the Revolu-

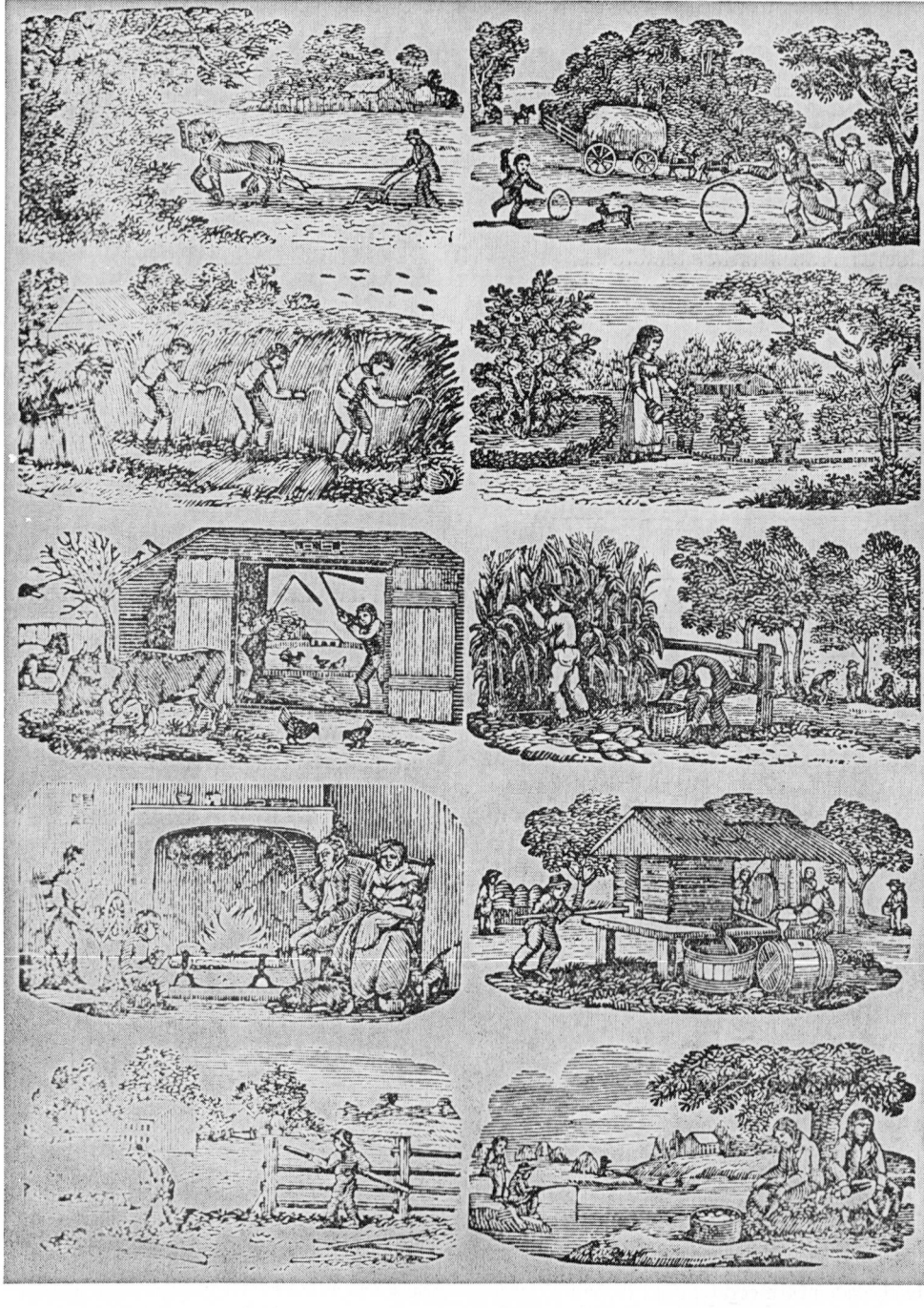

tionary era lamented the "decay of vital piety," the "degeneracy of manners," and the luxurious growth of "vice."

Certainly large numbers of the people were turning away from familiar faiths. Many interested themselves in Deism, the rational religion of Enlightenment philosophers, especially those in France. The Deists believed in God but considered Him a rather remote being who had created the universe, not an intimate presence who was concerned with human individuals and their sins. Franklin, Jefferson, and others among the Founding Fathers held Deistic views. Such views, at first confined to the well-educated, finally spread among the people at large. By 1800, books and articles attacking religious "superstitions" found eager readers all over the country. The most influential of such writings, Thomas Paine's *The Age of Reason* (1794-6), was discussed in homes, colleges, taverns, stagecoaches, everywhere. Paine once declared that Christianity was the "strangest religion ever set up," for "it committed a murder upon Jesus in order to redeem mankind from the sin of eating an apple." No wonder the preachers regularly denounced Paine and Deism and called for a new revival of religious faith.

While resisting the spread of free thought, the churches also had to deal with other problems. After the Declaration of Independence the groups with foreign ties had to reconsider their position, and even those without such ties faced the task of reorganizing on a national basis. As population moved westward, the churches had to follow the frontier if they were to grow with the country's growth. In responding to the challenges of the time—revitalization, reorganization, and

expansion—some denominations succeeded much better than others. Old sects developed faster than ever, or they lagged behind as never before. New sects arose. The grim doctrines of Calvinism gave way to more optimistic faiths, and the religious pattern of the young republic became even more variegated than that of colonial America had been.

The Congregationalists, who led in numbers and influence at the close of the colonial period, soon lost their preeminence. They continued to be tax-supported in Massachusetts, Connecticut, and New Hampshire even after those colonies were transformed into states. But the Congregationalists lacked the missionary zeal, appealing theology, and strong, centralized organization that were essential for winning and holding converts.

In New England, its home ground, the Congregational church was weakened by the growing popularity of universalist and unitarian doctrines. Many of its members rejected not only the idea of predestination but also the idea of the Trinity. They believed that salvation was available to all, and that God was one (not three), Jesus being only a great religious teacher and not the son of God. The Universalist church came into existence (1779) when believers in universal salvation began to hold meetings in Gloucester, Massachusetts. A little later (1782) the Unitarian church was founded in Boston. The Universalists appealed to the poor and the Unitarians to the well-to-do, but both groups held essentially the same beliefs. The Universalists, it has been said, thought God was too good to damn man, while the Unitarians thought man was too good to be damned by God.

FARM LIFE ABOUT 1800. [OPPOSITE] The seasonal round of farm activities is illustrated in a contemporary engraving, which incidentally reveals the rather crude state of the engravers' art in the United States. The scenes at the left, from top to bottom, show plowing, harvesting (with sickles), threshing (with flails), spinning and knitting, and fence-mending. The scenes at the right show haying, flower-watering, corn-picking, cider-making, and sheep-shearing. Young boys enjoyed such recreations as hoop-rolling (top right) and fishing (bottom right).

In the West the Congregationalists lost ground to the Presbyterians after agreeing to the Plan of Union of 1801. By this plan, members of the two denominations combined and chose either a Congregational or a Presbyterian minister in newly settled areas where neither group was numerous enough to justify a separate church. Eventually most of the united "Presbygational" congregations became Presbyterian.

American Presbyterians had adopted a constitution (1789) by which the whole country was divided into sixteen presbyteries and four synods, with a general assembly that served as the highest ecclesiastical court. Already well entrenched on the frontier, where so many of the Scotch-Irish had settled before the Revolution, the church expanded with the expanding nation. Indeed, it grew too fast for the maintenance of internal harmony. Bickering reappeared between Old and New Lights, between traditional Calvinists and believers in salvation for all. New sects splintered off, as did the followers of Thomas and Alexander Campbell, who in the early 1800's rejected the Calvinist dogma of limited election. Later the Campbellites formed a separate church known as the Disciples of Christ.

Among the Baptists, as among the Presbyterians, there were disputes about the question of predestination or free will, but theological differences did not prevent the Baptists from growing more rapidly than any other denomination except one (the Methodist) during the late eighteenth and early nineteenth century. Scattered over the whole country, they were especially numerous in Virginia and the Carolinas. Long the most militant advocates of the separation of church and state, they ceased to impress others as dangerous radicals after this principle was adopted in the Virginia statute of religious liberty and in the federal Bill of Rights. Like the Congregationalists, the Baptists had a loose organization, but unlike the Congregationalists they did not rely on an educated and salaried ministry. They depended on zealous but unlearned farmer-preachers who carried the gospel to the common people in language that the common people could understand.

More than the Baptists or any other religious group, the Roman Catholics gained in prestige (though not in numbers) as a consequence of the Revolution. On the advice of Charles Carroll of Carrollton, Maryland statesman and Catholic lay leader, most of the Catholics in America supported the Patriot cause during the war. The French alliance brought Catholic troops and chaplains to this country. In such times as these, Catholic Americans no longer seemed, as in colonial days, like agents of the devil. After the war the Vatican provided for the United States a church government separate from that of England. In 1784 Father John Carroll was appointed head of Catholic missions in this country, and with the elaboration of the American hierarchy he was made the first American bishop (1789) and finally Archbishop of Baltimore (1808).

The Anglicans suffered more than any other religious group as a result of the Revolution. They were badly divided on the issues of the war, the clergy being mostly Loyalist in the states where Anglicans were few, and partly Loyalist in Virginia and Maryland. In these two states the Anglican church had benefited from tax support, which was lost when the church was disestablished. In other states the church had depended upon aid from the mother country, and that aid was withdrawn. By the end of the war a large proportion of the parishes lacked clergymen, for there were few recruits to take the places of those who had died or had left the country as Loyalist refugees. Since there never had been an American bishop or an intercolonial organization of the church, postwar Anglican leaders had to start from scratch in setting up an independent, national hierarchy. By 1789 they had succeeded in organizing the Protestant Episcopal church. Till after the War of 1812 the church remained weak,

A CAMP MEETING. Originating in 1800, the camp meeting soon became a popular American religious institution in rural areas, especially in the South and West.
By 1820, about 1,000 meetings a year were held. The painting reproduced here
was made in the 1830's. A typical camp meeting (in Maryland, in 1806) was
described by a participant who wrote of the tents, the wagons, the plank seats,
the covered stand for the preacher, and the daily schedule. "At day break the
trumpets were blown round the camp for the people to rise 20 minutes afterward
for family prayer at the door of every tent—if fair weather—at sunrise they blew
at the stand for public prayer, and then breakfasted. At 10 oclock they blew for
preaching—by 2 ocl. dinner was to be over in every tent. At 3 ocl. preaching again,
and again at night." After several days of this, "hundreds were prostrate upon the
earth before the Lord. . . . Will I ever see anything more like the day of Judgment on this side of eternity—to see the people running, yes, running, from every
direction to the stand, weeping, shouting, and shouting for joy. Prayer was then
made—and every Brother fell upon the neck of his Brother, and the Sisters did
likewise. Then we parted. O! glorious day they went home singing and shouting."
(COURTESY OF THE NEW-YORK HISTORICAL SOCIETY, NEW YORK CITY)

gaining few members, and losing many
with the departure of the Methodists.

John Wesley, the founder of Methodism, did not set up a new church in England, nor did he intend to do so in America. In 1776, ten years after his lay ministers had begun to organize Methodist
"classes" in the colonies, American Methodists insisted that they were not "common dissenters" but "a religious society in
communion with the Church of Eng-

land." But the war changed their attitude.
When peace came, the greatest of Wesley's agents in America, Francis Asbury,
concluded that American conditions required the formation of a separate body.
In 1784, Asbury called a meeting of
Methodist preachers, at Baltimore, and
launched the Methodist Protestant
church, with himself as the first bishop.

The Methodists had a unique and effective organization. It was authoritarian,

with power concentrated at the top, in the hands of the bishops. The preachers were itinerants: each of them had charge of several widely scattered congregations and rode the rounds from one to another. Every year the preachers met in a conference (by 1796 there were six annual conferences in different parts of the country) where a bishop conferred with them, ordained new ministers, and assigned all the riders to their circuits, making frequent changes. This system was well adapted to a growing, moving, frontier society. As the historian W. W. Sweet has said, the Presbyterian minister in the West "was called by the people," the Baptist farmer-preacher "came with the people," and the Methodist circuit-rider "was sent to the people." The circuit-rider brought a message of individual responsibility for eternal happiness. It was a welcome message. The Methodist Protestant church, within sixty years after its foundation, became the largest in the United States.

Along with the Baptists and the Presbyterians, the Methodists gained many converts in the Second Awakening, a new wave of revivalism that swept the country at the turn of the century. This revivalism had two distinct phases. It began among the Presbyterians in certain colleges of the East and South, reaching its height at Yale under the leadership of President Timothy Dwight (1797–1817). Then, with zealous graduates carrying the evangelical spirit to the West, it went to even greater extremes on the frontier. In 1800, in Kentucky, the Presbyterians held their first camp meeting, an outdoor revival that lasted several days. The Methodists soon took up the camp-meeting technique, and the circuit-rider Peter Cartwright won fame as the most effective soul-saver of all backwoods revivalists. The camp meeting was a Methodist "harvest time," as Bishop Asbury said. It became increasingly popular, the bishop noting with satisfaction in 1811 that 400 camp meetings were to be held that year.

Crowds of sinners as well as salvation seekers attended these open-air get-togethers, and the atmosphere sometimes was far from church-like. Many Presbyterians, especially Campbellites, came to frown on the camp meeting. Even Cartwright deplored the worst outbreaks of frenzy, when men and women had fits, rolled in the dust, and lay twitching with the "holy jerks."

After 1800 the devil and the Deists were on the run. Freethinkers by no means disappeared (the young Abraham Lincoln took up free thought in frontier Illinois), but they were put upon the defensive. The great majority of Americans subscribed to some variant of revealed Christianity, though it usually was not quite the same as the predominant faith of their forefathers. The churches in the nineteenth century placed more emphasis on the New Testament and the saving grace of Jesus—and less emphasis on the Old Testament and the stern decrees of Jehovah—than those of the seventeenth or even the eighteenth century had done.

Technology and Industry

While religious patterns were changing, so were industrial techniques, even more fundamentally. A new technology was developing, which was to have profound effects upon the future of the United States.

In part, the new technology came from England, where the Industrial Revolution was beginning at the time the American Revolution occurred. The essence of the Industrial Revolution was simply this: more rapidly and extensively than ever before, power-driven machines were taking the place of hand-operated tools. To tend the machines, workers were brought together in factories or mills located at the sources of power. New factory towns arose, with a new class of dependent laborers and another of mill-owners or industrial capitalists. The factory system was adapted most readily to the manufacture of cotton thread and cloth. In textile making, invention called forth invention. Improvements in weaving made necessary improvements in spinning, so that the spinners could keep up with the weavers, and these improvements required new devices for carding, that is, combing and straightening the fibers for the spinner. Water, wind, and animal power continued to be used but began to be supplemented and replaced by steam. Especially was this true after the appearance of James Watt's steam engine (patented in 1769), which, though cumbersome and inefficient, was a great improvement upon Thomas Newcomen's earlier "atmospheric" engine.

Though Americans copied all they could from England, the Industrial Revolution in the United States was largely an indigenous growth, with roots extending far back into the colonial period. In colonial America, though no factories existed, there were countless homes and workshops where craftsmen developed mechanical skills. Along many a creek stood water-power mills for grinding grain, sawing wood, and fulling cloth, and even for manufacturing iron, with triphammers and rolling and slitting machinery. Before 1776 America was well supplied with mechanics and inventors who could, and did, adapt their knowledge eventually to the production and operation of machines that became more and more complex.

When English imports were cut off by the prewar boycott and then by the Revolutionary War, desperate efforts were made to stimulate the manufacture of certain necessities in America. Homespun became both patriotic and fashionable, and to speed up the output of linens and woolens a few of the states gave loans or bounties for the making of wire for card teeth. Several of the states offered loans or bounties for the production of cannon, gunpowder, camp kettles, and other war material. Public efforts to encourage industry continued after the war, and to these a bit of tariff protection was added after the adoption of the Constitution. Private companies were formed, and one of these with Alexander Hamilton as a sponsor founded (1791) the town of Paterson, New Jersey, to exploit the available water power for manufacturing.

Still, the American textile industry lagged behind that of England. Capital was scarce in the United States, even after certain American shipowners began to invest some of their shipping profits in textile mills. For years prospects of profit were dim because of the abundance of cheap English imports, and the machinery available remained inferior to the steadily progressing English inventions. To protect England's superior position as a manufacturing nation, the British government tried to prevent the export of textile machinery and the emigration of skilled mechanics. Nevertheless, a number of mechanics and millwrights made their way to the United States, the most important of them being Samuel Slater. In 1790, with the aid of American mechanics, Slater built a spinning mill for the Quaker merchant Moses Brown at Pawtucket, Rhode Island. Though a few inferior spinning mills already were in operation, Slater's work is generally considered as the beginning of the factory system in America.

Despite the success of the Slater mill, the American textile industry grew rather slowly until English imports were checked by Jefferson's Embargo of 1807 and then by the War of 1812. The first census of manufacturing, in 1810, counted 269 cotton and 24 woolen mills in the country. From 1807 to 1815 the total number of cotton spindles increased from 8,000 to 130,000. Most of the factories were located in New England. Until 1814 they produced only yarn and thread: the weaving of cloth was left to families operating hand looms at home. Then the Boston merchant Francis C. Lowell, after examining textile machinery in England, perfected a power loom that was an improvement on its English counterpart. Lowell organized the Boston Manufacturing Company and founded at Waltham, Massachusetts, the first mill in America to carry on the processes of spinning and weaving under a single roof.

In textiles and in some other manufactured goods the young republic did not measure up to England. Americans generally produced the coarser kinds of yarn and cloth, and though they supplied their own needs in common metalware, they still imported the finer grades of cutlery and other metal products. Yet in certain respects American industry was neither imitative nor inferior, and some American inventors and engineers were equal to the greatest in the world. They were especially advanced in certain new techniques of mass production.

One of the most ingenious mechanics of his time was Oliver Evans, a Delaware farmer's son. Evans invented a card-making machine, constructed an automatic flour mill, improved upon the steam engine, and combined theory and practice in America's first textbook of mechanical engineering, The Young Mill-Wright's and Miller's Guide (1795). He put his flour mill into operation the same year the constitutional convention met, in 1787. Before that time, in the typical flour mill, men had to carry bags of wheat to an upper loft where a "hopper boy" emptied them. The grain fell down through the turning millstones to be cracked and ground. Then the men carried the meal back upstairs in tubs, raked it out to dry, and finally sifted it by hand. In Evans' mill, all this work was done by a variety of machines geared to the same water wheel. Vertical conveyors—endless belts with buckets attached—lifted the grain and later the meal, which was raked and sifted by machinery. Horizontal conveyors—large screws turning within tubes—moved material back and forth. Only two workers were needed. At one end of the mill a man emptied bags of wheat, and at the other end a man closed and rolled away barrels full of flour. Here was probably history's first continuous automatic production line, the beginning of automation.

Another pioneer in mass production was the Massachusetts-born, Yale-educated Eli Whitney. He is best known for the cotton gin, but he is even more important for the revolution he accomplished in the manufacture of guns.

The rise of the textile industry in England and America had created a tremendous demand for the cotton which planters had begun to grow in the American South. But the planters were faced with the problem of separating the seeds from the cotton fast enough to meet the demand. There was a variety of cotton with smooth black seeds and long fibers that were easily cleaned, but this "long-staple" or "sea-island" variety could be grown successfully only along the coast or on the offshore islands of Georgia and South Carolina. There was also a short-staple cotton which could be raised almost anywhere in the South, but its sticky green seeds were very difficult to remove, a skilled slave being able to clean no more than a few pounds a day by hand. The planters were casting about for a machine or "gin" (that is, an engine) to clean the short-staple cotton when Whitney, then serving as a tutor on the Georgia plantation of General Nathanael Greene's widow, made his famous invention in 1793.

The gin was quite simple. A toothed roller caught the fibers of the cotton boll and pulled them between the wires of a grating, which held back the seeds, and a revolving brush removed the lint from the roller's teeth. But the gin had momentous consequences. With it, one slave could clean cotton as fast as several could by hand. Soon cotton growing spread into the upland South, and within a decade the total crop increased eightfold. Slavery, which with the decline of tobacco produc-

WHITNEY'S GUN FACTORY. The factory, construction of which began in 1798, was well located at Mill River and on the new turnpike from New Haven to Hartford, in Connecticut. At the right of the picture is a covered wooden truss bridge by which the turnpike crossed the river. At the left of the bridge are two large buildings (with a flume for water power) which housed the machine shops. Farther to the left, on the opposite side of the road, is a row of stone dwellings for the workmen. In the right foreground are the forging shop and a group of storehouses. From a painting made about 1825 by William Giles Munson, a resident of New Haven. (COURTESY OF YALE UNIVERSITY ART GALLERY)

tion had become a dying institution, was now revived, expanded, and firmly fixed upon the South.

During the undeclared war with France (1798–1800) all-out war was expected, and so the army needed many thousands of muskets in a hurry. Muskets then were made one at a time, and no two of them exactly alike, by skilled gunsmiths. There were not enough gunsmiths, and there was not enough time, to meet the army's anticipated need. But Whitney had a plan. He made a contract with the govern-

ment for the delivery of 10,000 muskets within two years. Months passed, and not a single gun appeared. When government officials began to worry, Whitney reassured them with a demonstration such as they never had seen before. From piles of assorted pieces he put together a complete and well-made weapon. He had been waiting while he "tooled up" his Connecticut factory. He had designed a machine to make each of the parts exactly according to a pattern. Then all he had to do was to assemble the guns.

This was the beginning of standardized quantity production through the manufacture of interchangeable parts. Before long, the same system was used for making clocks, and eventually it was applied to sewing machines and many other complicated products.

By fastening cotton and slavery upon the South, Whitney's gin contributed to the coming of the Civil War. His techniques of mass production, by building up the industrial strength of the North, helped the Union to win the war that the gin did so much to bring on. Such were some of the aftereffects of the industrial developments in the period of the young republic. There were also other political and social consequences of the changes then just getting under way. In America as in England, though somewhat more slowly, the Industrial Revolution created new classes and class conflicts, hastened the growth of crowded manufacturing towns, and gave rise to troublesome political issues, such as the perennial issue of the protective tariff.

Transportation and Trade

Before the full potential of the Industrial Revolution could be realized in the United States, transportation had to be improved. What was needed was a system of roads and waterways which would connect all parts of the country and create a market extensive enough to justify production on a reasonably large scale. In the late eighteenth and early nineteenth century goods still moved far more cheaply by water than by land. For the Atlantic seaports, ocean commerce with other continents was more easily carried on than overland trade with American settlements west of the Appalachian range. As Charles and Mary Beard have written, "the streets of London, the quays of Lisbon, and the Hong of Canton were more familiar sights to the merchants of the coast than were the somber forests and stump-studded clearings of Western America."

Temporarily, the Revolutionary War unsettled merchant shipping, as the British navy drove American merchantmen and fishing vessels from the seas. But, before the war was over, Americans learned to evade the enemy with light, fast, maneuverable ships. Indeed, the Yankees began to prey upon British commerce with hundreds of privateers. For many a shipowner, privateering proved to be more profitable than ordinary peacetime trade.

After the war the most important routes of the old colonial commerce were legally closed. The British government imposed severe restrictions on American trade and shipping to the West Indies and to the British Isles themselves. Before long, American shippers nevertheless managed to develop a prosperous business, partly by getting around the restrictions on the old routes and partly by working out new patterns of commerce. Especially important was the opening of the China trade. In 1784 the *Empress of China* sailed from New York to Canton and, the next year, brought back a cargo of silk and tea, which yielded a fabulous profit. Within five years Yankee ships were trading regularly with the Far East. Generally these ships carried various manufactured goods to the Pacific coast, exchanged them for hides and furs, and with these proceeded on across the Pacific, to barter them in China.

Not only in China but also in Europe and the Near East enterprising Yankees from Salem and other ports sought out every possible opportunity for commerce. These Yankees were aided by two acts of the new Congress (1789) giving preference in tariff rates and port duties to home-owned ships. American shipping was greatly stimulated (despite the loss of ships and cargoes seized by the belligerents) by the outbreak of European war in the 1790's. Yankee vessels took over most of the carrying trade between Europe and the European colonies in the Western Hemisphere. Eventually (as will be seen) this profitable business was brought to an end by the shipping laws of the American government and by the War of 1812.

Meanwhile, as early as 1793, the young republic had come to possess a merchant marine and a foreign trade larger than those of any other country except Eng-

American ships increased from 30 to 90, and imports from 17.5 to 93. As these figures indicate, ocean transportation thrived.

Transportation and trade within the United States labored under handicaps,

---

FULTON'S FAMOUS VOYAGE

1807

In August 1807 Robert Fulton wrote this letter to his friend Joel Barlow, a diplomat and poet, one of the group of authors known as the "Hartford Wits":

"My steamboat voyage to Albany and back has turned out rather more favourable than I had calculated. The distance from New York to Albany is 150 miles; I ran it up in thirty-two hours, and down in thirty hours; the latter is just five miles an hour. I had a light breeze against me the whole way going and coming, so that no use was made of my sails, and the voyage has been performed wholly by the power of the steam engine. I overtook many sloops and schooners beating to windward, and passed them as if they had been at anchor.

"The power of propelling boats by steam is now fully proved. The morning I left New York, there were not perhaps thirty persons in the city who believed that the boat would ever move one mile an hour, or be of the least utility; and while we were putting off from the wharf, which was crowded with spectators, I heard a number of sarcastic remarks. This is the way, you know, in which ignorant men compliment what they call philosophers and projectors.

"Having employed much time, and money and zeal, in accomplishing this work, it gives me, as it will you, great pleasure to see it so fully answer my expectations. It will give a cheap and quick conveyance to merchandise on the Mississippi and Missouri, and other great rivers, which are now laying open their treasures to the enterprise of our countrymen. And although the prospect of personal emolument has been some inducement to me, yet I feel infinitely more pleasure in reflecting with you on the immense advantage that my country will derive from the invention."

---

land. In proportion to its population, the United States had more ships and commerce than any other nation in the world. And the shipping business was growing fast. Between 1789 and 1810 the total tonnage of American vessels engaged in overseas traffic rose from less than 125,000 to nearly 1,000,000. The percentage of the country's exports carried in

but improvements were steadily being made. Difficulties were presented by the natural features of the country. Along the Atlantic seaboard the rivers, most of them running in a southeasterly direction, carried traffic from the back country to the sea, but there was no easy way of going overland from Maine southwestward to Georgia and Louisiana, though to some extent coastwise shipping made up for this lack. At the west of the mountains, the Mississippi River and its tributaries furnished a fairly good water route southward to New Orleans, but of course there existed no such natural route eastward to the Atlantic ports. The transportation problem was intensified with the movement of population into the Mississippi Valley, and this problem could not be fully solved until, somehow, the mountain barrier was overcome.

taking 30 hours to go 150 miles. In 1811 a partner of Livingston's, Nicholas J. Roosevelt, introduced the steamboat to the West by sending the *New Orleans* from Pittsburgh down the Ohio and Mississippi. The next year this vessel entered upon a profitable career of fairly regular service between New Orleans and Natchez. Then the coming of the War of 1812 delayed the extension of steamboat lines on both eastern and western waters. Not till 1816 did a river steamer, the

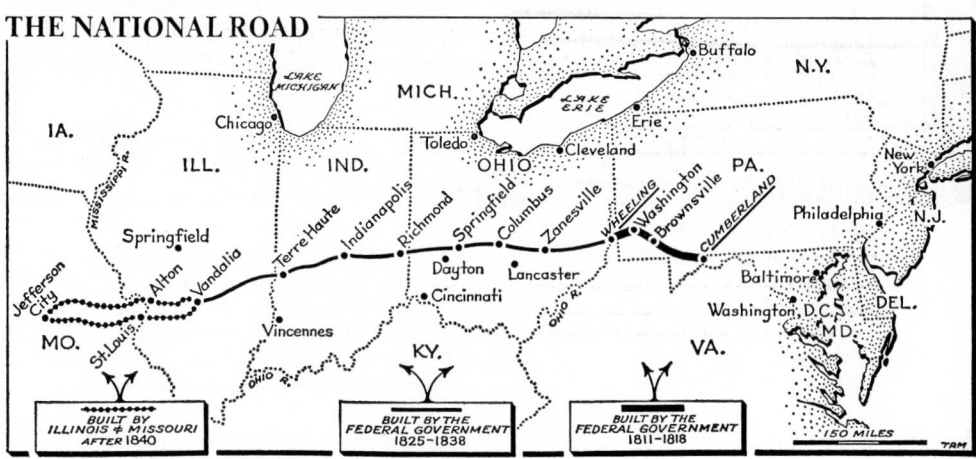

THE NATIONAL ROAD

In river transportation a new era began with the development of the steamboat. Oliver Evans' high-pressure engine, lighter and more efficient than James Watt's, made steam more feasible than before for powering boats as well as mill machinery and eventually the locomotive. Even before the high-pressure engine was available, a number of inventors experimented with steam-powered craft, and John Fitch exhibited to some of the delegates at the constitutional convention a 45-foot vessel with paddles operated by steam. The perfecting of the steamboat was chiefly the work of the inventor Robert Fulton and the promoter Robert R. Livingston. Their *Clermont*, equipped with paddle wheels and an English-built engine, voyaged up the Hudson in the summer of 1807, demonstrating the practicability of steam navigation even though

Washington, make a successful voyage upstream as far as Louisville, at the falls of the Ohio. Within a few years steamboats were carrying far more cargo on the Mississippi than all the flatboats, barges, and other primitive craft combined.

Though the steamboat made navigable rivers more useful, it of course did nothing to change the basic pattern of inland water transportation. The difficulty of getting over the mountains remained. Before 1800, when canals began to crisscross England, these appealed to forward-looking Americans as a means of improving transportation in the United States, though in this country the rugged terrain complicated canal-building. George Washington interested himself in a project for canalizing the upper Potomac, so as to make a water connection with the West. This work was left unfinished,

ON THE NATIONAL ROAD. A scene at Fairview Inn, near the eastern terminus of
the road, in Maryland. From its opening, in 1818, the road was heavily traveled
by stage coaches, Conestoga wagons, and other vehicles, besides droves of cattle,
sheep, and hogs. Note, at the left, the zigzag rail fence (known as a "worm" or
"snake" fence) which was common in the early nineteenth century. The workmen,
at the side of the highway, are crushing stones for repairing the road's surface.
From a painting (1889) by Thomas Ruckle. (MARYLAND HISTORICAL SOCIETY)

though short canals in Connecticut, Massachusetts, and the Carolinas were completed and in operation during the early 1800's. The canal age was yet to come to the United States.

Meanwhile the turnpike era began. In 1792 a corporation constructed a toll road the sixty miles from Philadelphia to Lancaster, with a hard-packed surface of crushed rock. This venture proved so successful that similar turnpikes (so named from the kind of tollgate frequently used) were laid out from other cities to neighboring towns. The invention of the wooden truss bridge made it possible for these roads to cross streams which previously had to be forded or else spanned by an expensive stone bridge. Since the turnpikes were built and operated for private profit, construction costs had to be low enough and the prospective traffic heavy enough to assure an early and ample return. So these roads, radiating from Eastern cities, ran for comparatively short distances and through rather thickly settled areas. If similar highways were to be extended over the mountains, the state governments or the federal government would have to finance the construction, at least in part.

When Ohio was admitted as a state (1803) the federal government agreed that part of the proceeds from the sale of public lands there should be used for building roads. In 1807 Jefferson's Secretary of the Treasury, Albert Gallatin, proposed that a national road, financed partly by Ohio land sales, be built from the Potomac to the Ohio, and both Congress and the President approved. The next year Gallatin presented a comprehensive plan of internal improvements, requiring an appropriation of $20 million, but Jefferson doubted the constitutionality of such an expenditure, and the plan was shelved. Finally, in 1811, construction of the national road began, at Cumberland, Maryland, on the Potomac. By 1818 this highway, with a crushed stone surface and massive stone bridges, was completed to Wheeling, Virginia, on the Ohio. Meanwhile the state of Pennsylvania contributed $100,000 to a private company which extended the Lancaster pike westward to Pittsburgh.

Over both of these roads, once they had been opened, there rolled a heavy traffic of stagecoaches, Conestoga wagons, private carriages, and other vehicles, as well as droves of cattle. Despite the high tolls, freight rates across the mountains now were lower than ever before. They were not low enough to permit the long-distance hauling of bulky loads like wheat or flour. But commodities with a high value in proportion to their weight, especially manufactures, moved from the Atlantic seaboard to the Ohio Valley in unprecedented quantities.

City and Country

The young republic was a land of remarkable diversity—in learning, in literary tastes, in religion, and in economic and social development. Much of the country remained a wilderness, yet its leading cities ranked in size and urban sophistication with the largest of England and Europe, except for such national capitals as London and Paris. The United States had no comparable capital of politics, science, literature, and art. The total population, by the second census (1800), was nearly five and a half million. Only three people in a hundred lived in towns of more than 8,000. Ten in a hundred lived at the west of the Appalachian mountains. Though Virginia was the most populous of the states, it contained none of the largest cities. Philadelphia (70,000) ranked first; New York (60,000) was close behind; and next in order were Baltimore (26,000), Boston (24,000), and Charleston (20,000). Washington City, the newly founded national capital, was only a raw and straggling village, the entire District of Columbia containing no more than 3,200 people. With its broad but unpaved avenues radiating from the uncompleted Capitol and the President's House, in accordance with the elaborate plan of the French architect P. C. L'Enfant, this small town nevertheless provided a new focus for the growing nationalism of Americans, and it symbolized their grand hopes for the future of their country. Hither President Adams and his wife Abigail, sacrificing the comforts and attractions of Philadelphia, moved in 1800. And here President-elect Jefferson was inaugurated the following year.

BIBLIOGRAPHY

A survey of economic, social, and cultural developments in the late eighteenth and early nineteenth century is provided by J. A. Krout and D. R. Fox in The Completion of Independence, 1790–1830 (1944). For the American scene in 1800, see the brilliant opening chapter in Henry Adams's History of the United States (9 vols., 1889–1891). The cultural nationalism of the time and the career of its leading exponent are revealed in Harry Warfel's Noah Webster: Schoolmaster to America (1936) and in E. C. Shoemaker's Noah Webster (1936).

Aspects of religion in the young republic are treated by the following: G. A. Koch, Republican Religion: The American Revolution and the Cult of Reason (1933); H. E. Luccock and Paul Hutchinson, The Story of Methodism (1926); W. W. Sweet (ed.), Religion on the American Frontier: The Presbyterians, 1783–1840 (1936); R. G. Torbet, A History of the Baptists (1950); Conrad Wright, The Beginnings of Unitarianism in America (1955); J. T. Ellis, American Catholicism (1956), which compresses the story of more than 300 years into fewer than 300 pages; and A. M. Melville,

John Carroll of Baltimore (1955), a biography of the founder of the American Catholic hierarchy.

Medical progress is shown in N. G. Goodman's biography of the leading physician of the young republic, *Benjamin Rush* (1934), who had his theories about the cause of yellow fever. A fine essay by R. H. Shryock on the yellow-fever epidemic of 1793 in Philadelphia is contained in *America in Crisis* (1952), edited by Daniel Aaron. See also R. H. Shryock, *Medicine and Society in America, 1660–1860* (1960).

Jeannette Mirsky and Allan Nevins, *The World of Eli Whitney* (1952), tells the story of Whitney's inventions largely in his own words. A brief, readable, and valuable supplement is C. M. Green, *Eli Whitney and the Birth of American Technology* (1956). C. F. Ware, *The Early New Eng-* *land Cotton Manufacture* (1931), is excellent on the beginnings of the American textile industry.

A. B. Hulbert, *Paths of Inland Commerce* (1920), gives a short and readable account of transportation developments. Phases of land travel in the late eighteenth and early nineteenth century form the subjects of the following: P. D. Jordan, *The National Road* (1948); J. A. Durrenburger, *Turnpikes: A Study of the Toll Road Movement in the Middle Atlantic States and Maryland* (1931); and F. J. Wood, *Turnpikes of New England* (1919). River travel is treated by Thomas Boyd, *Poor John Fitch: Inventor of the Steamboat* (1935); T. J. Flexner, *Steamboats Come True* (1944); L. D. Baldwin, *The Keelboat on Western Waters* (1941); and L. C. Hunter, *Steamboats on the Western Rivers* (1949).

9

JEFFERSONIAN PRINCIPLES

IN PRACTICE

Jefferson and the Republicans, while out of power, had championed the rights of the states against the powers of the federal government. They had denounced the Federalists for stretching those powers too far and interpreting the Constitution too loosely. But, once they were themselves in control of the government, the new President and his party followers went even further, in some respects, than the Federalists had gone in the exercise of federal authority. If Jefferson seemed inconsistent, so did many of his opponents, for they now adopted the theory of state rights and used his own earlier arguments against him. Thus it was to be throughout American history: one party and then the other (usually the one out of power) claimed to be the special protector of the Constitution and of the rights of the states. But the idea of state rights was not the essence of the Jeffersonian political philosophy. Jefferson stood primarily for the interests of the majority as he conceived them. As President, he did much to advance those interests, his greatest accomplishment being to double the territory of the United States.

President and Party Leader

Long afterwards Jefferson referred to his party's victory as "the revolution of 1800," but in his inaugural address of 1801, trying to sweeten the bitterness of the recent campaign, he emphasized the common principles of the two parties while restating the principles of his own. Noting that the country was separated by a wide ocean from the "devastating havoc" of the European war, he recommended a foreign policy of "peace, commerce, and honest friendship with all nations, entangling alliances with none" —much as George Washington had done in the Farewell Address. With respect to domestic affairs, Jefferson proposed a "wise and frugal government" such as would leave men free to "regulate their own pursuits of industry." Yet he also favored the "encouragement of agriculture and of commerce as its handmaid."

From the outset Jefferson acted in a

spirit of democratic simplicity, which was quite in keeping with the frontier-like character of the raw city of Washington, but which was very different from the ceremonial splendor of former Federalist administrations in the metropolis of Philadelphia. He walked like an ordinary citizen to and from his inauguration at the Capitol, instead of riding in a coach at the head of a procession. In the presidential mansion he disregarded the

Even at his best, the tall, freckle-faced, sandy-haired Jefferson did not make a very impressive appearance, what with his shyness, his awkward posture, and his shambling gait. Yet, though a rather ineffective public speaker, he charmed his guests in conversation and he wrote with greater literary skill than any President before or since, with the possible exceptions of Abraham Lincoln and Woodrow Wilson. More than that, he was a genius

---

JEFFERSON'S FIRST INAUGURAL

1801

"We are all Republicans, we are all Federalists. If there be any among us who would wish to dissolve this Union or to change its republican form, let them stand undisturbed as monuments of the safety with which error of opinion may be tolerated where reason is left free to combat it. I know, indeed, that some honest men fear that a republican government can not be strong, that this Government is not strong enough; but would the honest patriot, in the full tide of successful experiment, abandon a government which has so far kept us free and firm on the theoretic and visionary fear that this Government, the world's best hope, may by possibility want energy to preserve itself? I trust not. I believe this, on the contrary, the strongest Government on earth. I believe it the only one where every man, at the call of the law, would fly to the standard of the law, and would meet invasions of the public order as his own personal concern. Sometimes it is said that man can not be trusted with the government of himself. Can he, then, be trusted with the government of others? Or have we found angels in the forms of kings to govern him? Let history answer this question."

---

courtly etiquette of his predecessors, widower that he was, without a First Lady to take charge of social affairs. At state dinners, adopting the "rule of pell-mell," he let his guests scramble for places at the table. He did not always bother to dress up, and the fastidious minister from Great Britain complained of being received by the President in slippers which were down at the heels and coat and pantaloons which were "indicative of utter slovenliness and indifference to appearances."

with a wider diversity of talents than any other President, without exception. Besides being a politician and a diplomat, he was an architect, educator, inventor, scientific farmer, and philosopher-scientist, who in the presidential mansion diverted himself with such pastimes as sorting the bones of prehistoric animals. As a shrewd and practical politician, he was excelled by no other President, though he was equalled by Lincoln and by Franklin D. Roosevelt.

Jefferson was a strong executive, but

THOMAS JEFFERSON. Jefferson was 62 years old when this portrait was painted, in 1805, at the President's mansion in Washington, by Rembrandt Peale, son of Charles Willson Peale. (COURTESY OF THE NEW-YORK HISTORICAL SOCIETY, NEW YORK CITY)

neither his principles nor his nature inclined him to dictate to Congress. To avoid even the semblance of dictation, and to indulge his distaste for public speaking, he decided not to deliver his messages to Congress in person as Presidents Washington and Adams had done. Instead, he submitted his messages in writing, thus setting a precedent which was followed for more than a century, until President Wilson revived the practice of addressing Congress in person. Yet Jefferson, as party leader, gave direction to his fellow partisans among the senators and representatives, by quiet and sometimes by rather devious means.

To his cabinet he appointed a group of Republicans who were like-minded with him but were more than mere yes-men. Two of the ablest were the Secretary of State, James Madison, and the Secretary of the Treasury, Albert Gallatin. Madison, Jefferson's long-time neighbor and friend, continued to be so close a collaborator that, throughout Jefferson's Presidency, it is hard to tell how much of the impetus to policy came from the President himself and how much from the Secretary of State, particularly in foreign affairs. Gallatin, born in Switzerland, his speech marked by a French accent, was as able a public financier as the great Hamilton had been and was in addition a thoroughgoing democrat, who at the time of the Whiskey Rebellion had used his talents as a lawyer to defend the oppressed farmers of the Pennsylvania frontier.

Jefferson used the patronage as a political weapon. Like Washington before him, he believed that federal offices should be filled with men loyal to the principles and policies of the administration. True, he did not attempt a sudden and drastic removal of Federalist officeholders, possibly because of assurances to the contrary which had been given in his name when Federalist votes in Congress were needed to break the tie with Burr. Yet, at every convenient opportunity, he replaced the holdovers from the Adams administration with his own trusted followers. By the end of his first term about half the government jobs, and by the end of his second term practically all of them, were held by good Republicans. The President punished Burr and the Burrites by withholding patronage from them; he never forgave the man whom he believed guilty of plotting to frustrate the intentions of the party and the ambitions of its rightful candidate.

A tie vote between the presidential and vice-presidential candidates of the same party could not occur again. The Twelfth Amendment, added to the Constitution in 1804 before the election of that year, by implication recognized the function of political parties; it stipulated that the electors should vote for President and Vice President as separate and distinct candidates. Burr had no chance to run on the ticket with Jefferson a second time. In place of Burr, the congressional caucus of Republicans nominated his New York factional foe, George Clinton. The Federalist nominee, C. C. Pinckney, made a poor showing against the popular Jefferson, who carried even the New England states except Connecticut and was reelected by the overwhelming electoral majority of 162 to 14, while the Republican membership of both houses of Congress was increased.

During his second term Jefferson lost some of his popularity, and he had to deal with a revolt within the party ranks. His brilliant but erratic relative John Randolph of Roanoke, the House leader, turned against him, accused him of acting like a Federalist instead of a state-rights Republican, and mustered a handful of anti-Jefferson factionalists who called themselves "Quids." Randolph became a fanatic on the subject of the Yazoo land claims. These arose from the action of the Georgia legislature, which, before ceding its territorial rights to the federal government, had made and then canceled a grant of millions of acres along the Mis-

JOHN RANDOLPH OF ROANOKE. Randolph added "of Roanoke" (his plantation) to his name so as to distinguish himself from relatives of the same name whom he disliked. A distant cousin of Jefferson's, he began his political career as a Jeffersonian, then disagreed with Jefferson and became a critic of both Republicans and Federalists. As a Virginia Congressman (off and on from 1799 to 1829) he made himself an extreme defender of Southern rights. Often he filibustered with interminable, rambling speeches, which were lit with occasional flashes of brilliance. A master of invective, he once referred to an opposing politician as "this being, so brilliant yet so corrupt, which, like a rotten mackerel by moonlight, shined and stunk." Randolph had a freakish appearance—he was tall and skinny, with a small head and a wrinkled, parchment-like skin. When in his forties and fifties, he looked boyish from a distance but incredibly aged from close up. From a rotogravure after a painting by Chester Harding.

sissippi to the Yazoo Land Companies. Jefferson favored a compromise settlement which would have satisfied both the state of Georgia and the Yazoo investors, many of whom were Northern Republicans whose support he needed. But Randolph, insisting that the claims were fraudulent, charged the President and the President's friends with complicity in cor-

ruption. A number of Randolph's colleagues in Congress were investors in the land companies or supporters of their claims, and time and again the tall, skinny Virginian would point his bony finger at one or another of these men and shriek "Yazoo!" He prevented the government from making any settlement of the question until after both he and Jefferson were out of office.

Randolph had a special antipathy toward Madison, whom he considered as one of the worst of the Yazoo men. He did all he could, which was not enough, to prevent Madison's nomination for the Presidency in 1808. Jefferson refused to consider a third term for himself, for he was opposed to it in principle, unlike Washington, who had declined to run again in 1796 only because he was weary of public office. Jefferson's refusal established a tradition against a third term for any President, a tradition which remained unbroken until Franklin D. Roosevelt was elected for a third time in 1940 (and then for a fourth time in 1944). Though unwilling himself to be a candidate in 1808, Jefferson was determined that his *alter ego*, Madison, should succeed him and carry on his policies without a break.

The Jeffersonians and the Judges

The Federalists had used the courts as a means of strengthening their party and persecuting the opposition, or so it seemed to the Republicans, and soon after Jefferson's first inauguration his followers in Congress launched a counterattack against the Federalist-dominated judiciary. They repealed the Naturalization Act, changing the residence period for citizenship of foreigners from fourteen to five years, and they allowed the hated Alien and Sedition Acts to expire. Then they repealed the Judiciary Act of 1801, abolishing the new Circuit Courts and arranging for each of the Supreme Court justices to sit with a district judge on circuit duty. As President, Jefferson did not have the power to remove Adams' "midnight" appointees from their newly created jobs, but Congress achieved the same object by pulling their benches out from under them, despite Federalist protests that the repeal violated the constitutional provision that judges should hold office during good behavior, that is, for life.

In the debate on the question of the Judiciary Act of 1801 the Federalists maintained that the Supreme Court had the power of reviewing acts of Congress

William Marbury, one of President Adams' "midnight appointments," had been named as a justice of the peace in the District of Columbia, but his commission, though duly signed and sealed, had not been delivered to him at the time Adams left the Presidency. Madison, as Jefferson's Secretary of State, refused to hand over the commission, and so Marbury applied to the Supreme Court for an order (writ of mandamus) directing Madison to perform his official duty. In

---

MARBURY v. MADISON

1803

Chief Justice Marshall: "It is emphatically the province and duty of the judicial department to say what the law is. Those who apply the rule to particular cases must of necessity expound and interpret that rule. If two laws conflict with each other, the courts must decide on the operation of each.

"So if a law be in opposition to the constitution; if both the law and the constitution apply to a particular case, so that the court must either decide that case conformably to the law, disregarding the constitution, or conformably to the constitution, disregarding the law, the court must determine which of these conflicting rules governs the case. This is of the very essence of judicial duty.

"If, then, the courts are to regard the constitution, and the constitution is superior to any ordinary act of the legislature, the constitution, and not such ordinary act, must govern the case to which they both apply."

---

and disallowing those that conflicted with the Constitution. The Constitution itself said nothing about such a power of judicial review, but Hamilton in one of the *Federalist* papers had argued that the Supreme Court should have the power, and the Court actually had exercised it as early as 1796, though upholding the law of Congress then in question. In 1803, in the case of *Marbury* v. *Madison*, the Court for the first time declared a congressional act, or part of one, unconstitutional. (Not for more than half a century, in the Dred Scott case of 1857, did the Court do so a second time.)

the case of *Marbury* v. *Madison*, Chief Justice John Marshall, who had been appointed by President Adams, decided that Marbury had a right to the commission but that the Court had no power to issue the order. True, the original Judiciary Act of 1789 had conferred such a power upon the Court, but, said Marshall, the powers of the Court had been defined in the Constitution itself, and Congress could not rightfully enlarge them. Marshall did not claim, however, that only the federal judges could decide what the Constitution meant; he implied that each of the three branches of the federal government could decide for itself. In delivering his opinion, he went out of his way to discredit the Jefferson administration, yet shrewdly avoided an open conflict. Since he decided the immediate question (whether Madison should be ordered to deliver Marbury's commission) in Madison's favor, the administration had no opportunity to defy the decision by disobeying it.

While the case of *Marbury v. Madison* was still pending, President Jefferson prepared for a renewed assault upon that Federalist stronghold, the judiciary. If he could not remove the most obnoxious of the judges directly, perhaps he could do so indirectly through the process of impeachment. According to the Constitution, the House of Representatives was empowered to bring impeachment charges against any civil officer for "high crimes and misdemeanors," and the Senate sitting as a court was authorized to try the officer on the charges. Jefferson sent evidence to the House to show that one of the district judges, John Pickering of New Hampshire, was unfit for his position. The House accordingly impeached him, and the Senate, despite his obvious insanity, found him guilty of high crimes and misdemeanors. He was removed.

Later the Republicans went after bigger game, after one of the justices of the Supreme Court itself. Justice Samuel Chase, a rabidly partisan Federalist, had applied the Sedition Act with seeming brutality and had delivered political speeches from the bench, insulting President Jefferson and denouncing the Jeffersonian doctrine of equal liberty and equal rights. In doing so, Chase of course was guilty of no high crime or misdemeanor in the constitutional sense, and he was only saying what thousands of Federalists believed. Some of the Republicans came to the conclusion, however, that impeachment should not be viewed merely as a criminal proceeding, and that a judge could properly be impeached for political reasons—for

obstructing the other branches of the government and disregarding the will of the people. As for Justice Chase, he could easily be shown to be out of step with Congress, the President, and public opinion, especially after the overwhelming victory of the Republicans in the election of 1804.

At Jefferson's own suggestion, the House of Representatives set up a committee to investigate Chase's conduct. Impeached on the basis of the committee's findings, the justice was brought to trial before the Senate early in 1805. Jefferson did his best, or his worst, to secure a conviction, even temporarily cultivating the friendship of Aaron Burr, who as Vice President presided over the trial. But Burr performed his duties with aloof impartiality, and John Randolph as the impeachment manager bungled the prosecution for the House of Representatives. A majority of the Senators finally voted for conviction, but not the necessary two-thirds majority. Chase was acquitted.

From the Republican point of view, the Pickering and Chase impeachments, though only half successful, did considerable good, for they caused the federal judges as a whole to be more discreet and less partisan in statements from the bench. If the Republicans had succeeded in getting rid of Chase, they might have been emboldened to take action against the Chief Justice himself. As things stood, Marshall remained secure in his position, and the political duel between the Chief Justice and the President continued.

Dollars and Ships

According to the Republicans, the administrations of Washington and Adams had been extravagant. Yearly expenditures had risen so much that by 1800 they were almost three times as high as they had been in 1793, and the public debt also had grown, though not so fast, since revenues had increased considerably. A part of these revenues came from internal taxation, including the hated whiskey excise. In 1802 the Republicans in Congress abolished the whole system of internal taxes, leaving customs duties and land sales as practically the only sources of revenue. Despite the tax cut, the new administration was determined to reduce the public debt by economizing on federal expenses. Secretary of the Treasury Gallatin proceeded to carry out a drastic retrenchment plan, scrimping as much as possible on expenditures for the ordinary operations of the government and effecting what Jefferson called a "chaste reformation" in the army and the navy. The tiny army of 4,000 men was reduced to only 2,500. The navy was pared down from twenty-five ships in commission to seven, and the number of officers and men was cut accordingly.

These reductions in the armed forces reflected other Jeffersonian principles as well as the desire for government economy. Jefferson feared that anything except the smallest of standing armies might become a menace to civil liberties and to civilian control of government. He believed that the navy, while no such threat to the principle of civilian supremacy, was likely to be misused as a means of forcing the expansion of overseas commerce, which he thought should be kept subordinate to agriculture. Yet, though he once said "peace is our passion," Jefferson was far from a pacifist fanatic. He desired an efficient if small military force, and his administration deserves credit for founding the United States Military Academy at West Point (1802). He also contributed to the efficiency of the navy, even while reducing the size of it, for most of the decommissioned ships were outmoded, and many of the discharged officers were deadwood. And, in spite of himself, he was compelled to reverse his small-navy policy and build up the fleet because of trouble with pirates in the Mediterranean.

For years the Barbary states of North Africa—Morocco, Algiers, Tunis, and Tripoli—had made piracy a national enterprise. They demanded protection money from all nations whose ships sailed the Mediterranean, and even the mistress of the seas, Great Britain, gave regular contributions (she did not particularly desire to eliminate the racket, since it hurt her naval rivals and maritime competitors more seriously than it did her). During the 1780's and 1790's the United States agreed to treaties providing for annual tribute to Morocco and the rest, and from time to time the Adams administration ransomed American sailors who had been captured by the corsairs and were being held as slaves. Jefferson doubted the wisdom of continuing the appeasement policy. "Tribute or war is the usual alternative of these Barbary pirates," he said. "Why not build a navy and decide on war?"

The decision was not left to Jefferson. In 1801 the Pasha of Tripoli, dissatisfied by the American response to his extortionate demands, had the flagpole of the American consulate chopped down, that being his way of declaring war on the United States. Jefferson concluded that, as President, he had a constitutional right to defend the United States without a war declaration by Congress, and he sent a squadron to the relief of the ships already at the scene. Not till 1803, however, was the fleet in the Mediterranean strong enough to take effective action, under Commodores Edward Preble and Samuel Barron. In 1805 the Pasha, by threatening to kill captive Americans, compelled Barron to agree to a peace which ended the payment of tribute but exacted a large ransom ($60,000) for the release of the prisoners. This was hardly a resounding victory for the United States. While the navy, as a whole, had not acquitted itself very well, certain individual officers such as Lieutenant Stephen Decatur gained fame for their heroic exploits, and several of "Preble's boys" acquired experience and spirit which were to be of inestimable value later, during the War of 1812. Meanwhile, in 1807, the fleet was brought home because of a crisis with Great Britain, leaving unfinished the task of wiping out piracy in the Mediterranean.

Though the Tripolitan war cost money, Secretary Gallatin pressed on with his plan for diminishing the public debt. He was aided by an unexpected increase in tariff revenues. By the time Jefferson left office, the debt had been cut almost in half (from $83 million to $45 million), despite the expenditure of $15 million to buy Louisiana from Napoleon Bonaparte.

Jefferson and Napoleon

In the year that Jefferson was elected President of the United States, Napoleon made himself dictator of France with the title of First Consul, and in the year that Jefferson was re-elected, Napoleon assumed the name and authority of Emperor. These two men, the democrat and the dictator, had little in common except that both were revolutionary leaders. Yet they were good friends in international politics until Napoleon's ambitions leaped from Europe to America and brought about an estrangement.

Napoleon failed in a grandiose plan to seize the British Empire in India, though he succeeded in the conquest of Italy. Then he was reminded that France at one time had possessed a vast empire of her own in North America. In 1763 her possessions east of the Mississippi had gone to Great Britain, and those west of it to Spain. The former were lost for good, but the latter might be recovered. In 1800 (on the very day after the signing of the peace settlement with the United States) Napoleon arranged for Spain to cede these possessions to him in the secret treaty of San Ildefonso. Thus he got title to Louisiana, which included roughly the whole of the Mississippi Valley to the west of the river, plus New Orleans to the east of the river near its mouth. He in-

tended Louisiana to form the continental heartland of his proposed empire.

Other essential parts of his empire-to-be were the sugar-rich and strategically valuable West Indian islands which still belonged to France—Guadeloupe, Martinique, and above all Santo Domingo. Unfortunately for his plans, the slaves on Santo Domingo had been inspired by the French revolution to rise in revolt and create a republic of their own, under the leadership of the remarkable Negro, Toussaint L'Ouverture. Taking advantage of a truce in his war with England, Napoleon sent to the West Indies an army under his brother-in-law, Charles Leclerc, to put down the insurrection and restore French authority.

Meanwhile, unaware of Napoleon's ultimate aim, Jefferson pursued the kind of foreign policy that was to be expected of such a well-known friend of France. He appointed as the American minister to Paris the ardently pro-French Robert R. Livingston. Continuing and hastening the peace policy of Adams, he carried through the ratification of the Franco-American settlement of 1800 and put it into effect even before it was ratified. With respect to Santo Domingo, however, he did not continue the policy of Adams, who had cooperated with the British in recognizing and supporting the rebel regime of Toussaint. Jefferson assured the French minister in Washington that the American people, especially those of the slaveholding states, did not approve of the Negro revolutionary who was setting a bad example for their own slaves. He even gave the French minister to believe that the United States would join with France in putting down the rebellion.

But Jefferson began to reappraise the whole subject of American relations with France when he heard rumors of the secret retrocession of Louisiana. "It completely reverses all the political relations of the U.S.," he wrote to Minister Livingston (April 18, 1802). Always before, we had looked to France as our "natural friend." But there was on the earth "one single spot" the possessor of which was "our natural and habitual enemy." That spot was New Orleans, the outlet through which the produce of the fast-growing West was shipped to the markets of the world. If France should actually take and hold New Orleans, Jefferson said, then "we must marry ourselves to the British fleet and nation."

Jefferson was even more alarmed when, in the fall of 1802, he learned the news that the Spanish intendant in charge at New Orleans had prohibited Americans from continuing to deposit their goods at that port, for transshipment from river craft to ocean-going vessels. By the Pinckney Treaty (of 1795) Spain had guaranteed to Americans the right of deposit either at New Orleans or at some other suitable place; without such a right of deposit, the use of the lower Mississippi was of little value to the United States. With the Mississippi thus practically closed off, the men of the "Western waters" (there were already a quarter of a million people in Kentucky alone) faced economic ruin, for there was no feasible route by which they could carry their crops directly over the mountains to the ports and markets of the East. These frontiersmen suspected, as did Jefferson himself, that Napoleon had procured the closing of the river for sinister purposes of his own. They demanded that something be done to reopen the river, and some of the more extreme among them clamored for war with France, the supposed source of all their troubles. The Federalists of the Northeast, though they had no real concern for the welfare of the West, played upon the discontent of the frontiersmen and encouraged the war cry for political reasons. The more the Federalists could arouse the West, the more they could embarrass the Jefferson administration. The President faced a dilemma. If he

yielded to the frontier clamor and sought satisfaction through force, he would run the risk of war with France. If, on the other hand, he disregarded the clamor, he would stand to lose the political support of the West.

There was possibly a way out of the dilemma, and that was to purchase from Napoleon the port so indispensable to the United States. Or, assuming that the First Consul should prove unwilling to sell New Orleans, and assuming also that he had acquired East and West Florida along with Louisiana in the secret treaty with Spain, it might be possible to obtain from him all or part of the Floridas, or at least the rights of navigation and deposit on some river flowing into the Gulf of Mexico to the east of New Orleans. Jefferson did not think of trying to buy any part of Louisiana to the west of the Mississippi; he was content, for the time being, to let that river form the boundary between the French empire and the United States. Soon, after hearing rumors of the Louisiana retrocession, he instructed Livingston in Paris to negotiate for the purchase of New Orleans, and Livingston on his own authority proceeded to suggest to the French that they might be glad to be rid of the upper part of Louisiana as well.

Jefferson also induced Congress to provide an army and a river fleet, and he allowed the impression to get out that American forces, despite his own desire for peace, might soon descend upon New Orleans. Then he sent a special envoy to work with Livingston in persuading the French to sell. For this extraordinary mission he chose an ideally suited man, James Monroe, who was well remembered in France and who, at the same time, had the confidence of the American frontiersmen; his appointment would reassure them that the President was looking after their interests. Jefferson told Monroe that if he and Livingston could not obtain even the minimum needs of the United

States—even the use of the Mississippi or some other river emptying into the Gulf —they were to cross the channel to England and there discuss some kind of understanding with the British government. Whether Jefferson, in his hints at an attack on New Orleans and an alliance with Great Britain, merely meant to bluff the French, he had no chance to show. While Monroe's coach was still rumbling on its way to Paris, Napoleon suddenly made up his mind to dispose of the entire Louisiana territory.

Startling though this decision seemed to some of his advisers, Napoleon had good reasons for it. His plans for an American empire had gone awry partly because of certain mischances, which might be summarized in two words—*mosquitoes* and *ice.* The mosquitoes brought yellow fever and death to General Leclerc and to thousands of the soldiers whom Napoleon had sent to reconquer Santo Domingo. The ice, forming earlier than expected in a Dutch harbor as winter came in 1802, delayed the departure of an expeditionary force that Napoleon was readying to reinforce Leclerc's army and also to take possession of Louisiana. By the spring of 1803 it was too late. Napoleon then was expecting a renewal of the European war, and he feared that he would not be able to hold Louisiana if the British, with their superior naval power, should attempt to take it. He realized also that, quite apart from the British danger, there was danger also from the United States: he could not prevent the Americans, who were pushing steadily into the Mississippi Valley, from sooner or later overrunning Louisiana.

The Louisiana Purchase

Napoleon left the negotiations over Louisiana to his finance minister, Barbé-Marbois, rather than his foreign minister, Talleyrand, since Talleyrand was remembered for the X. Y. Z. Affair and was distrusted by Americans, while Barbé-

Marbois had their respect, having lived for some time in the United States and having married an American girl. Livingston and Monroe, after the latter's arrival in Paris, had to decide first of all whether they should even consider making a treaty for the purchase of the entire Louisiana territory, since they had not been authorized by their government to do so. They dared not wait until they could get new instructions from home, for Napoleon in the meantime might change his mind as suddenly as he had made it up. They decided to go ahead, realizing that Jefferson could reject their treaty if he disapproved what they had done. After a little haggling over the price that Barbé-Marbois asked—and he asked and got somewhat more than Napoleon's minimum—Livingston and Monroe put their signatures to the treaty, on April 30, 1803.

By the terms of the purchase arrangement, the United States was to pay 60 million francs directly to the French government and up to 20 million more to American citizens who held claims against France for ship seizures in the past—or a total of approximately $15 million. The United States was also to give France certain commercial privileges in the port of New Orleans, privileges not extended to other countries. Moreover, the United States was to incorporate the people of Louisiana into the Union and grant them as soon as possible the same rights and privileges as other citizens. This seemed to imply that the Louisiana inhabitants were to have the benefits of statehood in the near future. The boundaries were not defined, Louisiana being transferred to the United States simply with the "same extent" as when owned by France and earlier by Spain. When Livingston and Monroe appealed to Talleyrand for his opinion about the boundary, he merely replied: "You have made a noble bargain for yourselves, and I suppose you will make the most of it."

In Washington, the President was both pleased and embarrassed when he re-

LOUISIANA PURCHASE AND EXPLORATIONS

ceived the treaty. He was glad to get such a "noble bargain," but, according to his oft-repeated views on the Constitution, the United States lacked the constitutional power to accept the bargain. In the past he had always insisted that the federal government could rightfully exercise only those powers assigned to it in so many words, and nowhere did the Constitution say anything about the acquisition of new territory. Now he thought, at first, that an amendment should be adopted so as to give the government the specific right to buy additional land; he even went so far as to draft a suitable amendment. But his advisers cautioned him that ratification might be long delayed or possibly defeated, and they assured him that he already possessed all the constitutional power he needed: the President with the consent of the Senate obviously could make treaties, and the treaty-making power would justify the purchase of Louisiana. Years afterward (in 1828) the Supreme Court upheld this view, but Jefferson—strict constructionist that he had been—continued to have doubts about it. Finally he gave in, trusting, as he said, "that the good sense of our country will correct the evil of loose construction when it shall produce ill effects." Thus, by implication, he left the question of constitutional interpretation to public opinion, and he cut the ground from under his doctrine of state rights.

When Jefferson called Congress into special session, a few of the die-hard Federalists of New England raised constitutional and other objections to the treaty, but the Senate promptly gave its consent and the House soon passed the necessary appropriation bill. The Spanish minister in Washington protested to Secretary Madison that the transaction was illegal, since Napoleon when acquiring Louisiana had promised never to part with it and also had agreed to provide an Italian kingdom for the son of the Spanish king but had never done so. Madison easily disposed of the protest by reminding the Spanish minister that the latter once had advised the United States to apply to France, not Spain, in response to a query whether Spain would be willing to sell a part of Louisiana.

Though Madison and Jefferson had a good case for the American title to Louisiana itself, they had considerably less justification when, taking advantage of the vagueness of the boundaries, they also claimed part of West Florida as American by virtue of the treaty with France. The Spaniards denied that any of Florida was included in Louisiana, and indeed the two provinces had had separate histories and had been separately administered. To persuade the Spaniards to give up Florida, Jefferson tried both promises of money and threats of force. Despite John Randolph's outraged opposition, he obtained from Congress an appropriation for secret uses, one of which was to bribe France to bring pressure upon Spain. It was no use. All of Florida remained in Spanish hands until after Jefferson left the Presidency.

When the United States concluded the purchase treaty with France, Spain was still administering Louisiana, the French never having taken actual possession. They did not take possession until late in 1803, and then only to turn the territory over to General James Wilkinson, the commissioner of the United States and the commander of a small occupation force. In New Orleans, beneath a bright December sun, the recently raised French tricolor was brought down and the Stars and Stripes was run up. For the time being, Louisiana territory was given a semi-military government with officials appointed by the President; later it was organized on the general pattern of the Northwest Territory, with the assumption that it would be divided into states. The first of these was admitted to the Union as the state of Louisiana in 1812.

Meanwhile the geography of the far-flung territory was revealed by a series of explorations. Even before he became President, Jefferson as a scientist had been interested in finding out all he could about the nature and extent of the North American continent, and he had encouraged explorers interested in the Far West. After becoming President he renewed his efforts. In 1803, before Napoleon's offer to sell Louisiana, Jefferson planned an expedition which was to cross all the way to the Pacific Ocean and gather not only geographical facts but also information about the prospects for Indian trade. Congress having secretly provided the necessary funds, Jefferson named as leader of the expedition his private secretary and Virginia neighbor, the thirty-two-year-old Meriwether Lewis, who as a veteran of Indian wars was skilled in wilderness ways. Lewis chose as his colleague the twenty-eight-year-old William Clark, who like his older brother George Rogers Clark and like Lewis himself was an experienced frontiersman and Indian fighter.

Lewis and Clark, with a picked company of four dozen hardy men, set up winter quarters in St. Louis at about the time the United States took formal possession of Louisiana. In the spring of 1804 they started up the Missouri River, and with the Shoshoni squaw Sacajawea as their guide, her papoose on her back, they eventually crossed the Rocky Mountains, descended the Snake and the Columbia rivers, and in the late autumn of 1805 encamped on the Pacific coast. In September, 1806, they were back again in St. Louis, bringing with them carefully kept records of what they had observed along the way. No longer was the Far West a completely unknown country.

While Lewis and Clark were on their epic journey, Jefferson sent out other explorers to fill in the picture of the Louisiana Territory. The most important of these was Lieutenant Zebulon Montgomery Pike. In the fall of 1805, then only 26, Pike led an expedition from St. Louis up

THE LEWIS AND CLARK EXPEDITION, 1804–1806. Patrick Cass, one of the men who accompanied Lewis and Clark, wrote *A Journal of the Voyages and Travels of a Corps of Discovery* (1811), which was the first account of the expedition to be published. This book was illustrated with crude drawings. The one here reproduced was captioned "Captain Lewis & Clark holding a Council with the Indians."

the Mississippi River in search of its source, and though he did not find it he learned a good deal about the upper Mississippi Valley. In the summer of 1806 Pike was sent out again, this time by Wilkinson instead of Jefferson, to proceed up the valley of the Arkansas. He discovered, but failed in his attempt to climb, the peak that now bears his name. Then he turned southward into Mexico and ran into a Spanish army; he was compelled to surrender his maps and papers and return to the United States. His account of his Western travels left the impression that the land between the Missouri and the Rockies was a desert which American farmers could never cultivate and which ought to be left forever to the nomadic Indian tribes.

The Burr Conspiracy

In the long run the Louisiana Purchase prepared the way for the growth of the United States as a great continental power. Immediately, however, the Purchase provoked reactions which threatened or seemed to threaten the very existence of the Union. From both the Northeast and the Southwest there soon arose rumors of secession plots.

Most of the American people heartily approved the acquisition of the new territory, as they indicated by their presidential votes in 1804, but some of the New England Federalists raged against it. Their feelings are understandable enough. Both their party and their section stood to lose in importance with the growth of the West. From their point of view the existence of the Northwest Territory was bad enough, for they would soon be outnumbered in national politics with the creation of new states, the first of which in that area was admitted to the Union as the state of Ohio in 1803. The addition of Louisiana Territory, with its potential for still more new states, only

AARON BURR. For many years the name of Aaron Burr was bracketed with that of Benedict Arnold as a synonym for traitor. Yet Burr never was proved guilty of treason, and historians still differ about his guilt. Among his contemporaries he was loved and admired by those who knew him best, especially by his daughter Theodosia, whom he raised to be one of the best educated women of her time. "I had rather not live than not be the daughter of such a man," she once wrote. She married Joseph Alston, a prominent politician and riceplanter of South Carolina. In 1812, with her young son, she embarked from South Carolina for a visit with Burr in New York. She never arrived: her ship disappeared without a trace. Of all the blows that fate dealt Burr, the loss of his beloved daughter grieved him the most. From a contemporary sketch by James Sharples. (LIBRARY OF CONGRESS)

made the evil worse in the minds of New England Federalists. A group of the most extreme of these men, known as the Essex Junto, concluded that the only recourse for New England was to secede from the Union and form a separate "Northern Confederacy." They justified such action by means of state-rights arguments similar to those Jefferson had used only about five years earlier in opposition to the Alien and Sedition Acts.

If a Northern Confederacy was to have any hope for lasting success as a separate nation, it would have to include New York as well as New England, or so the prospective seceders believed. But the prominent New York Federalist Alexander Hamilton had no sympathy with the secessionist scheme. He wrote: "Dismemberment of our empire will be a clear sacrifice of great positive advantages without any counterbalancing good, administering no relief to our real disease, which is *democracy*." He feared that disorders like those of the French Revolution were about to sweep over the United States. Then, he thought, the country would need a military dictator, a sort of American Napoleon, to bring order out of chaos, and he imagined that he himself would emerge as the man of the hour. He had no future so far as ordinary politics was concerned.

His New York Republican rival, Aaron Burr, was another politician without prospects, at least within the party of the vengeful Jefferson. When some of the Federalists approached Burr, he agreed to run with their support for governor in 1804. Rumor had it that he was implicated in the disunion plot and that, if elected, he would lead the state into secession along with New England, but the rumor lacked proof and the plot itself was fantastic, an impossible dream. Nevertheless, Hamilton accused Burr of plotting treason and cast slurs upon his personal character. Burr lost the election, then challenged Hamilton to a duel. Hamilton dared not refuse; if he did, he would sacrifice his reputation for honor and manliness, a reputation that would be indispensable to the career supposedly awaiting him as the savior of his country. And so the two men with their seconds met at Weehawken, New Jersey, across the Hudson River from New York City, on a July morning in 1804. Hamilton was mortally wounded, and died the next day.

Burr, indicted for murder in both New Jersey and New York, presided over the United States Senate the following winter and then, at the end of his term as Vice President, faced a political outlook more hopeless than ever. He was ambitious and resourceful, with almost magical powers of attracting men (and women) to him. What could he do? During the next year he busied himself with mysterious goings and comings in the Southwest. He talked and corresponded with prominent men of the region, especially with General James Wilkinson, now governor of Louisiana Territory. Burr was up to something, and Wilkinson was his partner in it, but no one except Burr and Wilkinson themselves knew just what it was, and Burr told different stories. Some people believed (and some historians still believe) that he intended to separate the Southwest from the Union and rule it as an empire of his own. Very likely he did have imperial notions, for such notions were much in the air: Bonaparte had just become the Emperor Napoleon I of France, and Burr doubtless envisaged himself as the Emperor Aaron I —of Mexico. His ultimate aim most probably was the conquest of Spanish territory beyond the boundaries of Louisiana and not the division of the United States.

In the fall of 1806 the armed followers of Burr, with Blennerhassett's Island as their rendezvous, started by boat down the Ohio River, Burr himself joining them after they were well under way. Wilkinson, suddenly turning against Burr, sent a messenger to tell Jefferson that treason was afoot and that an attack upon New Orleans was expected. So Jefferson issued a proclamation calling for the arrest of Burr and his men as traitors. Eventually Burr was captured and brought to Richmond for trial.

The Burr trial (1807–8) was one of the most dramatic in all American history, with its horrendous charge of treason and its colorful cast of characters: Burr himself, as charming as always; a galaxy of brilliant lawyers on both sides; the eccentric John Randolph as foreman of the grand jury; the stern Chief Justice, John Marshall, presiding over the trial on circuit duty; and the President of the United States, Thomas Jefferson, not present in Richmond but managing the prosecution by remote control, from Washington. Jefferson was determined to convict his one-time running mate, and the prosecution relied hopefully upon its star witness, General Wilkinson, though Wilkinson was a despicable character who accepted pay as a spy for the Spaniards and who demanded extra money from them on the grounds that, in heading off the Burr expedition, he had saved their territory from attack! Marshall, on the other hand, for political as well as judicial reasons, was determined that Burr should have a fair trial. As the presiding judge, Marshall applied quite literally the clause of the Constitution which provides that no one shall be convicted of treason except upon the testimony of at least two witnesses to the same "overt act." He excluded all evidence not bearing directly upon such an act, and so the jury had little choice but to acquit Burr, since not even one witness had actually seen him waging war against the United States or giving aid and comfort to its enemies.

Though freed, Burr gained lasting notoriety as a traitor; after exiling himself abroad for a few years, he returned and lived long enough to hail the Texas revolution (1836) as the fruition of much the same sort movement as he had hoped to start. The trial had given the Chief Justice another chance to frustrate the President. It had set a precedent which made it almost impossible to convict anyone of treason against the United States. And the loyalty of the Southwestern frontiersmen had been proved beyond a doubt by their patriotic reaction to the cry of treason in their midst.

BIBLIOGRAPHY

A work of historical genius is Henry Adams's *History of the United States during the Administrations of Jefferson and Madison* (9 vols., 1889–91). This work is also available in a two-volume abridgment edited by Herbert Agar (1947). Henry Adams had one serious weakness as a historian: he was maliciously biased against his two leading characters, the one-time political foes of his great-grandfather. C. G. Bowers, without Adams's genius but with a flair for colorful writing, is violently prejudiced in Jefferson's favor in *Jefferson in Power* (1936). Irving Brant, *James Madison: Secretary of State, 1800–1809* (1953), with careful research corrects some of Adams's errors and portrays Jefferson as a great man and Madison as a man equally great. Adrienne Koch, *Jefferson and Madison: The Great Collaboration* (1950), in a more graceful style also depicts Madison as much more than a yes-man to Jefferson. L. D. White, *The Jeffersonians: A Study in Administrative History, 1801–1829* (1951), continues the high standards set in his *The Federalists*. A work of enduring value is Edward Channing's *The Jeffersonian System* (1906). Allen Johnson presents a brief and readable survey in *Jefferson and His Colleagues* (1920). One of the important and often neglected colleagues is presented in Raymond Walters, *Albert Gallatin: Jeffersonian Financier and Diplomat* (1957). D. J. Boorstin, *The Lost World of Thomas Jefferson* (1948), recaptures the intellectual atmosphere of Jefferson's time.

On the Louisiana Purchase, see E. W. Lyon's *Louisiana in French Diplomacy, 1789–1804* (1934) and *The Man Who Sold Louisiana: The Life of François Barbé-Marbois* (1942). Oscar Handlin, *Chance or Destiny: Turning Points in American History* (1955), has an interesting chapter on the accidents that led up to the Purchase. On Jefferson's troubles with Mediterranean pirates, see G. W. Allen's *Our Navy and the Barbary Corsairs* (1905). See also Fletcher Pratt, *The Navy: A History* (1938), an impressionistic account.

Henry Adams did not like John Randolph any better than he did Jefferson or Madison, and Adams's *John Randolph* (1882) is brilliant but unfair. More superficial but also more sympathetic is G. W. Johnson's *Randolph of Roanoke: A Political Fantastic* (1929). Randolph's ideas form the subject of Russell Kirk, *Randolph of Roanoke: A Study in Conservative Thought* (1951).

Historians generally have condemned Aaron Burr, while most of his many biographers have sided with him. W. F. McCaleb acquits him of treason in *The Aaron Burr Conspiracy* (1903), and so does Nathan Schachner in *Aaron Burr: A Biography* (1937). But T. P. Abernethy, *The Burr Conspiracy* (1954), is convinced of Burr's guilt.

On the Far West explorations, see John Bakeless, *Lewis and Clark: Partners in Discovery* (1947); Bernard De Voto (ed.), *The Journals of Lewis and Clark* (1953), a highly readable edition; and S. H. Hart and A. B. Hulbert (eds.), *Zebulon Pike's Arkansas Journal* (1937).

10

THE WAR OF 1812

The European war, renewed in 1803, was both a blessing and a curse for the United States. The continual conflict abroad enabled Americans to develop a profitable trade with the belligerents on both sides and at times to play them off against each other to the diplomatic advantage of this country, as in the cases of the Pinckney Treaty with Spain and the Louisiana treaty with France. Yet the war in Europe jeopardized the policy proclaimed by Washington and endorsed by Jefferson—the policy of neutrality and peace. Twice the United States became involved in the European struggle, the first time (1798) in opposition to France, the second time (1812) in opposition to Great Britain.

Neutral Rights and Impressment

In the early 1800's the warring nations of Europe found it impossible to take care of their own shipping needs. The merchant ships of France and Spain seldom ventured far upon the ocean, dominated as it was by the sea power of Great Britain, and the merchant marine of Britain herself was too busy in the waters of Europe and Asia to devote much attention to those of America. To some degree or other, all the belligerents had to depend upon the neutrals of the world for cargoes essential to effective war-making, and in the size and activity of its merchant marine the United States was much the most important of the neutrals. American shipowners prospered as, year after year, they engrossed a larger and larger proportion of the carrying trade between Europe and the West Indies. Farmers shared in the prosperity, for exports from the United States to the West Indies and Europe also increased prodigiously.

In the battle of Trafalgar (1805) a British fleet practically destroyed what was left of the French navy. Thereafter the supremacy of Great Britain upon the seas was unchallenged, while Napoleon proceeded to extend his domination over the continent of Europe. Powerless to invade the British Isles, Napoleon devised a scheme, known as the Continental System, which he hoped would bring the enemy to terms. The British, he reasoned, were a nation of shopkeepers who depended for their existence upon buying and selling in the rest of the world, especially in Europe. If he could close the continent to their trade, he thought, they ultimately would have to give in. So, in a series of decrees beginning with those of

Berlin (1806) and Milan (1807), he proclaimed that British ships and neutral ships touching at British ports were not to land their cargoes at any European port controlled by France or her allies.

The British government replied to Napoleon's decrees with a succession of orders-in-council. These announced an unusual kind of blockade of the European coast. The blockade was intended not to keep goods out of Napoleon's Europe but only to see that the goods were carried either in British vessels or in neutral vessels stopping at a British port and paying for a special license. Thus, while frustrating the Continental System, Britain would compel the neutrals to contribute toward financing her war effort, and she would limit the growth of her maritime rivals, above all the United States.

Caught between Napoleon's decrees and Britain's orders, American vessels clearing directly for Europe took the chance of capture by the British, and those going by way of a British port ran the risk of seizure by the French. Both of the warring powers disregarded American rights and sensibilities, yet to most Americans the British seemed like the worse offender of the two. Possessing effective sea power, they pounced upon Yankee merchantmen all over the wide ocean; the French could do so only in European ports. True, Napoleon's officials sometimes imprisoned and brutally mistreated the crews of confiscated ships, but the British navy far more often infringed upon personal liberty and national sovereignty, stopping American ships on the high seas and taking sailors off the decks as victims of impressment.

The British navy—with its floggings, its low pay, and its dirty and dangerous conditions on shipboard—was a "floating hell" to its sailors. They had to be impressed (forced) into the service and at every good opportunity they deserted, many of them joining the merchant marine of the United States and even its navy. To check this loss of vital man-

power, the British claimed the right to stop and search American merchantmen, though not naval vessels, and reimpress deserters. They did not claim the right to take native-born Americans, but they did seize naturalized Americans born on British soil, for according to the laws of England a true-born subject could never give up his allegiance to the King: once an Englishman, always an Englishman. In actual practice the British often impressed native as well as naturalized Americans, and thousands upon thousands of sailors claiming the protection of the Stars and Stripes were thus kidnapped. To these hapless men, impressment was little better than slavery. To their shipowning employers it was at least a serious nuisance. And to millions of proud and patriotic Americans, even those living far from the ocean, it was an intolerable affront to the national honor.

In the summer of 1807, in the Chesapeake-Leopard incident, the British went to more outrageous extremes than ever. The Chesapeake was a public and not a private vessel, a frigate of the United States navy and not an ordinary merchantman. Sailing from Norfolk, with several alleged deserters from the British navy among the crew, the Chesapeake was hailed by His Majesty's ship Leopard, which had been lying in wait off Cape Henry, at the entrance to Chesapeake Bay. Commodore James Barron refused to allow the Chesapeake to be searched, and so the Leopard opened fire and compelled him, unprepared for action as he was, to strike his colors. A boarding party from the Leopard dragged four men off the American frigate.

This was an attack upon the United States! When news of the outrage got around the country, most of the people cried for a way of revenge. Not since the days of Lexington and Concord had Americans been so strongly aroused; never again were they to be so solidly united in opposition to Great Britain. Even the "most temperate people and those most attached to England," the British minister reported home, "say that they are bound as a people and that they must assert their honor on the first attack upon it." If Congress had been in session, or if President Jefferson had called a special session, as he was urged to do, the country might have stampeded into war. But, as the French minister in Washington informed Talleyrand, "the President does not want war," and "Mr. Madison dreads it now still more."

Instead of assembling Congress and demanding a war declaration, Jefferson made a determined effort to maintain the national honor with peace. First, he issued an order expelling all British warships from American waters, so as to lessen the likelihood of future incidents. Then he sent to his minister in England, James Monroe, instructions to get satisfaction from the British government and to insist again upon the complete renunciation of impressment. On the whole the British government was conciliatory enough. It disavowed the action of Admiral Berkeley, the officer primarily responsible for the *Chesapeake-Leopard* affair, recalled him, and offered to indemnify the wounded and the families of the killed and to return the captured sailors (only three were left; one had been hanged). But the British cabinet refused to concede anything to Jefferson's main point; instead, the cabinet issued a proclamation reasserting the right of search to recover deserting seamen.

Thus the impressment issue stood between the British and American governments and prevented a compromise that might have led away from war. Though by 1812 the British had made a money settlement, the *Chesapeake* outrage meanwhile remained an open sore in Anglo-American relations. This incident, together with the impressment issue involved in it, was probably the most important single cause of the War of 1812, even though its final effect was delayed for five years.

"Peaceable Coercion"

Even at the height of the excitement over the *Chesapeake*, Jefferson made no preparations for a possible war. He and Madison believed that, if worst came to worst, the United States could bring Great Britain to terms, and France as well, through the use of economic pressure instead of military or naval force. Dependent as both nations were upon the Yankee carrying trade, they presumably would mend their ways if they were completely deprived of it.

So, when Congress met for its regular session, Jefferson hastily drafted an embargo bill, Madison revised it, and both the House and the Senate promptly enacted it into law. The embargo prohibited American ships from leaving this country for any port in the world; if it had specified only British and French ports it could have been evaded by means of false clearance papers. Congress also passed a force act to make the embargo effective.

Though the law was nevertheless evaded in various ways, it was effective enough to be felt in France, much more in Great Britain, and still more in the United States itself. Throughout the United States—except in the frontier areas of Vermont and New York, which soon doubled their overland exports to Canada—the embargo brought on a serious depression. The planters of the South and the farmers of the West, though deprived of foreign markets for their crops, were willing to suffer in comparative silence, devoted Jeffersonian Republicans that most of them were. But the Federalist merchants and shipowners of the Northeast, still harder hit by the depression, made no sercet of their rabid discontent.

Though the Northeastern merchants disliked impressment, the orders-in-council, and Napoleon's decrees, they hated Jefferson's embargo much more. Previously, in spite of risks, they had kept up their business with excellent and even

JAMES MADISON. Madison was rather small of stature, reserved, and shy. His Federalist opponents pictured him as a weak President who yielded to the "war hawks" in Congress and came out for war in 1812 in order to gain their support for his renomination. For many years, historians accepted this view, but recent studies show Madison to have been a fairly strong President, the dominant figure in the making of foreign policy during his two terms. He insisted that American rights be respected by both Great Britain and France and early decided that the United States should go to war, if necessary, to preserve these rights. He chose war with Great Britain because he concluded that her offenses were more serious than Napoleon's, since her policies were deliberately designed to limit the independence and the commercial growth of the United States. The portrait reproduced here was painted by Asher B. Durand from an original by Gilbert Stuart. Stuart's painting was done in 1804 when Madison—then Secretary of State—was 53 years old. (COURTESY OF THE NEW-YORK HISTORICAL SOCIETY, NEW YORK CITY)

fabulous returns; now they lost money every day their ships idled at the wharves. Again, as at the time of the Louisiana Purchase, they concluded that Jefferson had violated the Constitution (as indeed he had—if judged by the principles he

had advocated before becoming President).

In the midst of the embargo-induced depression came the election of 1808. The Federalists, with C. C. Pinckney again their candidate, made the most of the embargo's unpopularity and won a far larger proportion of the popular and electoral votes than in 1804, yet Madison was safely elected as Jefferson's successor. The Federalists also gained a number of seats in the House and the Senate, though the Republicans continued to hold a majority in both houses. To Jefferson and Madison the returns indicated plainly enough that the embargo was a great and growing liability in politics. A few days before going out of office, Jefferson approved a bill terminating his and Madison's first experiment with what he called "peaceable coercion." But Jefferson's succession by Madison meant no basic change in policy, and other experiments with measures short of war were soon to be tried.

By the time he entered upon his presidential duties, James Madison already had behind him a career that would assure him immortality in history books. He was not only well experienced in affairs of government; he was also a more profound and original thinker than he was credited with being by his contemporaries and by later generations who have assumed that he was merely Jefferson's echo. Unfortunately for his reputation, he was not an impressive figure of a man, but was small and wizened, with a scholarly frown. Nor was he equipped with the personal charm or politician's skill needed for strong presidential leadership. What he lacked in personality, his wife more than supplied. Dolley Madison, North Carolina born, was as gay and gracious a First Lady as ever adorned the White House.

Soon after Madison's inauguration, Congress passed and he signed a modified embargo bill known as the Nonintercourse Act. The Nonintercourse Act was soon replaced (1810) by another expedient commonly called Macon's Bill No. 2. This freed commercial relations with the whole world, including Great Britain and France, but authorized the President to prohibit intercourse with either belligerent if it should continue its violations after the other had stopped. The freeing of American trade was more to the advantage of the British than the French, since it fitted in with the efforts of the former to pierce and weaken the Continental System. Napoleon had every incentive to induce the United States to reimpose the embargo against his enemy. He succeeded in doing so by means of a trick, the Cadore letter, which pretended to revoke the Berlin and Milan decrees as far as they interfered with American commerce. Madison accepted the Cadore letter as evidence of Napoleon's change of policy, even though the French continued to confiscate American ships. He announced that early in 1811, an embargo against Great Britain alone would automatically go into effect, in accordance with Macon's Bill, unless Britain meanwhile rescinded her orders-in-council.

In time the new embargo, though less well enforced than the earlier, all-inclusive one had been, hurt the economy of England enough to cause influential Englishmen to petition their government for repeal of the orders-in-council. Eventually the orders were repealed—too late to prevent war, even if they had been the only grievance giving rise to the martial spirit in the United States. But they were not the only grievance. There was also impressment, and there was, besides, a border conflict between the British Empire and the expanding American frontier.

Red Men and Redcoats

Ever since the days of the Revolution the Indians generally had looked to their old "white father," the King of England, for protection against the relentlessly advancing Americans. And the British in Canada had relied upon Indian friendship to keep up their fur trade, even within the territory of the United States, and to maintain potentially useful allies. At one time, in 1794, this country nearly went to war with Great Britain because of her Indian policy, but Wayne's victory over the tribes at Fallen Timbers and the conclusion of Jay's Treaty dispelled the war danger and brought on a period of comparative peace. Then, in 1807, the border quiet was disturbed by an event occurring far away—the British assault upon the *Chesapeake*. The ensuing war crisis had repercussions that, as will be seen, terribly aggravated the frontier troubles already brewing in consequence of the growing conflict between tribesmen and settlers. Much of this conflict of red men and white was personified in the two opposing leaders, Tecumseh and William Henry Harrison.

The Virginia-born Harrison, already a veteran Indian fighter at 26, went to Washington as the congressional delegate from the Northwest Territory in 1799. He was largely responsible for the passage (1800) of the Harrison Land Law, which enabled settlers to acquire farms from the public domain on much easier terms than before. Land in the Northwest Territory soon was selling fast. The growth of population led to a division of the area into the state of Ohio and the territories of Indiana, Michigan, and Illinois. By 1812 Ohio contained 250,000 people and was beginning to look like an eastern state, as paths widened into roads, villages sprang up and in some cases grew into cities, and the forests receded before the spreading cornfields. By 1812 Michigan had few settlers, but Illinois contained a scattered population of about 13,000 and Indiana 25,000.

Receiving from Jefferson an appointment as governor of Indiana Territory, Harrison devoted himself to carrying out Jefferson's policy of Indian removal. According to the Jeffersonian program, the

Indians must give up their claims to tribal lands and either convert themselves into settled farmers or migrate to the west of the Mississippi. Playing off one tribe against another, and using whatever tactics suited the occasion—threats, bribes, trickery—Harrison made treaty after treaty with the separate tribes of the Northwest. By 1807 the United States claimed treaty rights to eastern Michigan, southern Indiana, and most of Illinois. Meanwhile, in the Southwest, millions of acres were taken from other tribes in the states of Georgia and Tennessee and in Mississippi Territory. Having been forced off their traditional hunting grounds, the Indians throughout the Mississippi Valley seethed with discontent. But the separate tribes, helpless by themselves against the power of the United States, probably would have quieted down and accepted their fate if two complicating factors had not arisen.

One complication was the policy of the British authorities in Canada. For years they had neglected their Indian friends across the border to the south. Then came the *Chesapeake* incident and the surge of anti-British feeling throughout the United States. Now the Canadian authorities, expecting war and an attempted invasion of Canada, began to take desperate measures for their own defense. "Are the Indians to be employed in case of a rupture with the United States?" asked the lieutenant governor of Upper Canada (December 1, 1807). And Sir James Craig, the governor general of the entire province, replied: "If we do not employ them, there cannot exist a moment's doubt that they will be employed against us." Craig at once took steps to renew friendship with the savages and provide them with increased supplies. Thus the trouble on the sea, over the question of impressment, intensified the border conflict hundreds of miles inland.

The second factor intensifying this conflict was the rise of a remarkable na-

tive leader, one of the most admirable and heroic in Indian history. Tecumseh, "The Shooting Star," chief of the Shawnees, aimed to unite all the tribes of the Mississippi Valley, resist the advance of white settlement, and recover the whole of the Northwest, making the Ohio River the boundary between the United States and the Indian country. He maintained that Harrison and others, by negotiating with individual tribes, had obtained no real title to land in the various treaties, since the land belonged to all the tribes and none of them could rightfully cede any of it without the consent of the rest. "The Great Spirit gave this great island to his red children. He placed the whites on the other side of the big water." So Tecumseh eloquently told Harrison. "They were not contented with their own, but came to take ours from us. They have driven us from the sea to the lakes—we can go no farther."

In his plans for a united front, Tecumseh was aided by his brother, a one-eyed, epileptic medicine-man known as the Prophet. The Prophet, visiting the Great Spirit from time to time in trances, inspired a religious revival which spread through numerous tribes and helped bring them together. Few savages doubted his supernatural powers after, having secretly learned from Canadian traders of a forthcoming eclipse, he commanded the sun to be dark on the appointed day. The Prophet's town, at the confluence of Tippecanoe Creek and the Wabash River, became the sacred place of the new religion as well as the headquarters of Tecumseh's confederacy. Leaving his brother there after instructing him to avoid war for the time being, Tecumseh journeyed the Mississippi in 1811 to bring the Indians of the South into his alliance. At that time a great earthquake occurred centering at New Madrid, Missouri, and rumbling up and down the Mississippi Valley, causing much of the river to change its course. To many of the Indians, this seemed another awesome sign that a new era was at hand for them.

During Tecumseh's absence, Governor Harrison saw a chance to destroy the growing influence of the two Indian leaders. With 1,000 soldiers he camped near the Prophet's town, provoked an attack (November 7, 1811), and though suffering losses as heavy as those of the enemy, succeeded in driving off the Indians and burning the town. This, the Battle of Tippecanoe, disillusioned many of the Prophet's followers, for they had been led to believe that his magic would protect them from the white man's bullets. Tecumseh returned to find his confederacy shattered, yet there were still plenty of warriors eager for the warpath, and by the spring of 1812 they were busy with hatchet and scalping knife all along the frontier, from Michigan to Mississippi.

Westerners blamed Great Britain for the bloodshed along the border. Her agents in Canada encouraged Tecumseh, used the Prophet as a "vile instrument," as Harrison put it, and provided the guns and supplies that enabled the savages to attack. To Harrison and to most of the frontiersmen, there seemed only one way to make the West safe for Americans. That was to drive the British out of Canada and annex that province to the United States.

While frontiersmen in the North demanded the conquest of Canada, those in the South looked to the acquisition of Florida. In Spanish hands, that territory was a perpetual nuisance, with slaves escaping across the line in one direction and Indians raiding across it in the other. Through Florida ran rivers like the Alabama, the Apalachicola, and others which in American possession would give access to the Gulf of Mexico and the markets of the world. In 1810 American settlers in West Florida took matters into their own hands, fell upon the Spanish fort at Baton Rouge, and requested that the territory be annexed to the United States. Presi-

BATTLE OF TIPPECANOE, 1811

dent Madison unhesitatingly proclaimed its annexation, then schemed to get the rest of Florida too. With Madison's connivance, the one-time Georgia governor George Mathews attempted (1811) to foment a revolt in East Florida. Spain protested, and Madison backed down, but the desire of Southern frontiersmen for all of Florida did not abate. Spain was Britain's ally, and a war with Britain would give these frontiersmen an excuse for taking Spanish territory as well as British.

Thus the war fever was raging on both the Northern and the Southern frontiers by 1812. The denizens of these outlying regions were not numerous as compared with the population of the country as a whole, and for the most part they were not directly represented in Congress, except by a few territorial delegates. Nevertheless, they had able and determined spokesmen at the national capital after the arrival there of a group of young congressmen who, with good reason, soon gained the name of "war hawks."

The War Hawks

Three days before the Battle of Tippecanoe a new Congress met in Washington for the session of 1811–12. In the congressional elections of 1810, most of the voters had indicated their disgust with such expedients as Macon's Bill No. 2 by turning out of office large numbers of Republican advocates of measures short of war, as well as Federalist advocates of continued peace. Of the newly elected congressmen and senators, the great majority were warlike Republicans, and after the news of Tippecanoe they became more eager than ever for a showdown with the power which seemed to threaten both the security of the frontier and the freedom of the seas.

A new generation had arrived upon the political scene, a group of daring young men of whom the most influential came from the new states in the West or from the back country of the old states in the South. Two of the natural leaders were Henry Clay and John C. Calhoun, whose careers were to provide much of the drama of American politics for the next four decades. The tall, magnetic Clay, barely 34, was a Virginian by birth but had made Kentucky his home. Already, while still under the legal age for a senator, he had appeared briefly in the United States Senate. As handsome as Clay though less appealing, the 29-year-old Calhoun was the son of Scotch-Irish pioneers in the South Carolina hills.

When Congress organized in 1811, the war faction of young Republicans got control of both the House and the Senate. As Speaker of the House, Clay held a position of influence then second only to that of the President himself. Clay filled the committees with the friends of force, appointing Calhoun to the crucial Committee on Foreign Affairs, and launched a drive toward war for the con-

quest of Canada. This would bring Great Britain to terms and avenge the wrongs which Clay recited eloquently and at length. Or at least he supposed it would, and he imagined further that the conquest would be quick and easy.

The Federalists in Congress, representing the commercial interests of the Northeast, deprecated the clamor for Canada and war. But they were powerless to stem the drive toward hostilities, even with the aid of dissident Republicans like the eccentric "Quid," John Randolph of Roanoke. Dubbing the Clay men "war hawks," Randolph ridiculed their cry as being like that of the whippoorwill, "one eternal monotonous tone—Canada! Canada! Canada!"

While Congress debated, President Madison moved reluctantly toward the conclusion that war was necessary. In May the war faction took the lead in the caucus of Republican congressmen who renominated him for the presidency, and on June 1 he sent his war message to Congress.

In his message the President maintained that Great Britain—by impressing American citizens, interfering with American trade, and inciting the Indians along the frontier—was already waging war against the United States. He recommended that Congress declare war in return. Congress responded with a declaration of hostilities on June 18, two days after a new ministry had announced in Parliament that the orders-in-council were to be suspended, but before the news could reach Washington. The close vote on the declaration, 19 to 13 in the Senate and 79 to 49 in the House, showed how badly the American people were divided.

The division of public opinion was again revealed in the election of 1812. Opposing Madison and the war, a peace faction of the Republicans nominated a rival candidate, De Witt Clinton of New York, and the Federalists gave their support to him. Most of the electors in the

Northeast voted for Clinton and peace, but all of those in the South and the West sustained Madison and the war, the President being re-elected by 128 to 89.

With the people thus divided, the country as a whole was not psychologically prepared for war, nor was it financially or militarily prepared. Congress had adjourned without increasing the army and navy, voting war taxes, or renewing the charter of the government's indispensable financial agency, the Bank of the United States, which expired in 1811. The war hawks, however, were not worried. On to Canada!

The Course of Battle

At first Great Britain, preoccupied with her mighty struggle against Napoleon, paid little attention to the American war, a mere annoyance to her. Then, in the fall of 1812, Napoleon launched the Russian campaign which, before the winter was over, was to bring him disaster and prepare the way for his ultimate defeat. As the months passed, Great Britain was able to divert more and more of her military and naval power to America. Only for about a year did the United States undertake the offensive; thereafter this country was forced to fight a defensive war, a war to protect its own territory.

The conquest of Canada, supposedly a "mere matter of marching," as Jefferson himself put it, soon proved to be an exercise in frustration. A three-pronged invasion was planned to strike into Canada by way of Detroit, the Niagara River, and Lake Champlain, with the greatest concentration of force at Detroit. At Detroit, however, after marching into Canada, the elderly General William Hull, Governor of Michigan Territory, retreated and surrendered the fort (August, 1812). The other invasion efforts also failed, and Fort Dearborn (Chicago) fell before an Indian attack.

During the year of disaster and defeat on land, the Madison administration

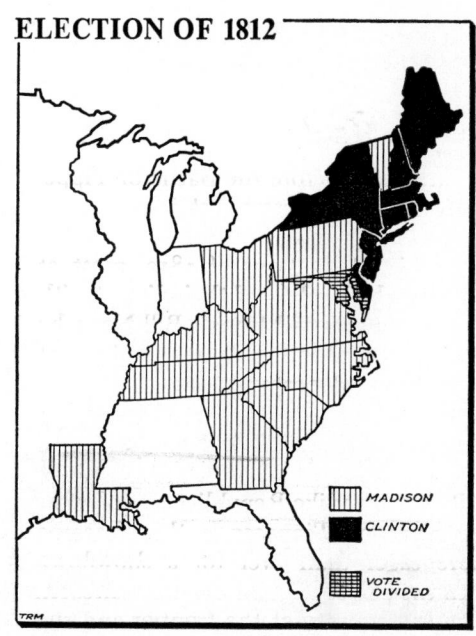

ELECTION OF 1812

MADISON

CLINTON

VOTE DIVIDED

and its supporters took what consolation they could in the news of successes on the sea. American frigates engaged British warships in a series of duels and won some spectacular victories, one of the most renowned being the victory of the *Constitution* over the *Guerrière*. American privateers destroyed or captured one British merchant ship after another, occasionally braving the coastal waters of the British Isles and burning vessels within sight of the shore. After that first year, however, the score was evened by the British navy, which not only drove the American frigates to cover but also instituted a close blockade of the United States and harried the coastal settlements from Virginia to Maine.

While British seapower dominated the ocean, American fleets arose to control the Great Lakes. First, the Americans took command of Lake Ontario, enabling troops to cross over to York (Toronto), the capital of Canada. At York (April 27, 1813) the invaders ran upon a cunningly contrived land mine, the explosion of which killed more than fifty, including General Zebulon M. Pike. Some of the

VICTORY AT SEA. As of 1812, in the Napoleonic War, the British navy had fought 200 battles and won 200 victories, in engagements between single ships or whole fleets. Great Britain seemed invincible on the ocean. Then, on August 19, 1812, in the North Atlantic, the U.S. frigate *Constitution* boldly challenged and decisively defeated His Majesty's Ship *Guerrière*. On October 25, 1812, off the Canary Islands, the frigate *United States* met and destroyed H. M. S. *Macedonian*. This engagement is pictured in the painting by Thomas Birch, reproduced here. Commanding the *United States* was Stephen Decatur, a hero of the naval wars with Tripoli (1803) and Algiers (1815) as well as the War of 1812. Afterwards Decatur made the famous toast: "Our country! In her intercourse with foreign nations may she always be in the right; but our country, right or wrong." In 1812 the score, in naval duels on the high seas, was five American and three British victories; by the end of the war the score was approximately even. (COURTESY OF THE NEW-YORK HISTORICAL SOCIETY, NEW YORK CITY)

enraged survivors, without authorization, set fire to the capital's public buildings, which burned to the ground. After destroying also some ships and military stores, the Americans returned across the lake.

Next, Lake Erie was redeemed for American use, mainly through the work of the youthful Oliver Hazard Perry. Having constructed a fleet at Presqu' Isle (Erie, Pennsylvania), Perry took up a position at Put-in-Bay, near a group of islands off the mouth of the Maumee River. With the banner "Don't Give Up the Ship" flying on his flagship, he awaited the British fleet, whose intentions he had learned from a spy. He smashed the fleet upon its arrival (September 10, 1813) and established American control of the lake.

This made possible, at last, an invasion of Canada by way of Detroit. The post had been hard to reach overland, for supply wagons either had to struggle through

THE WAR OF 1812

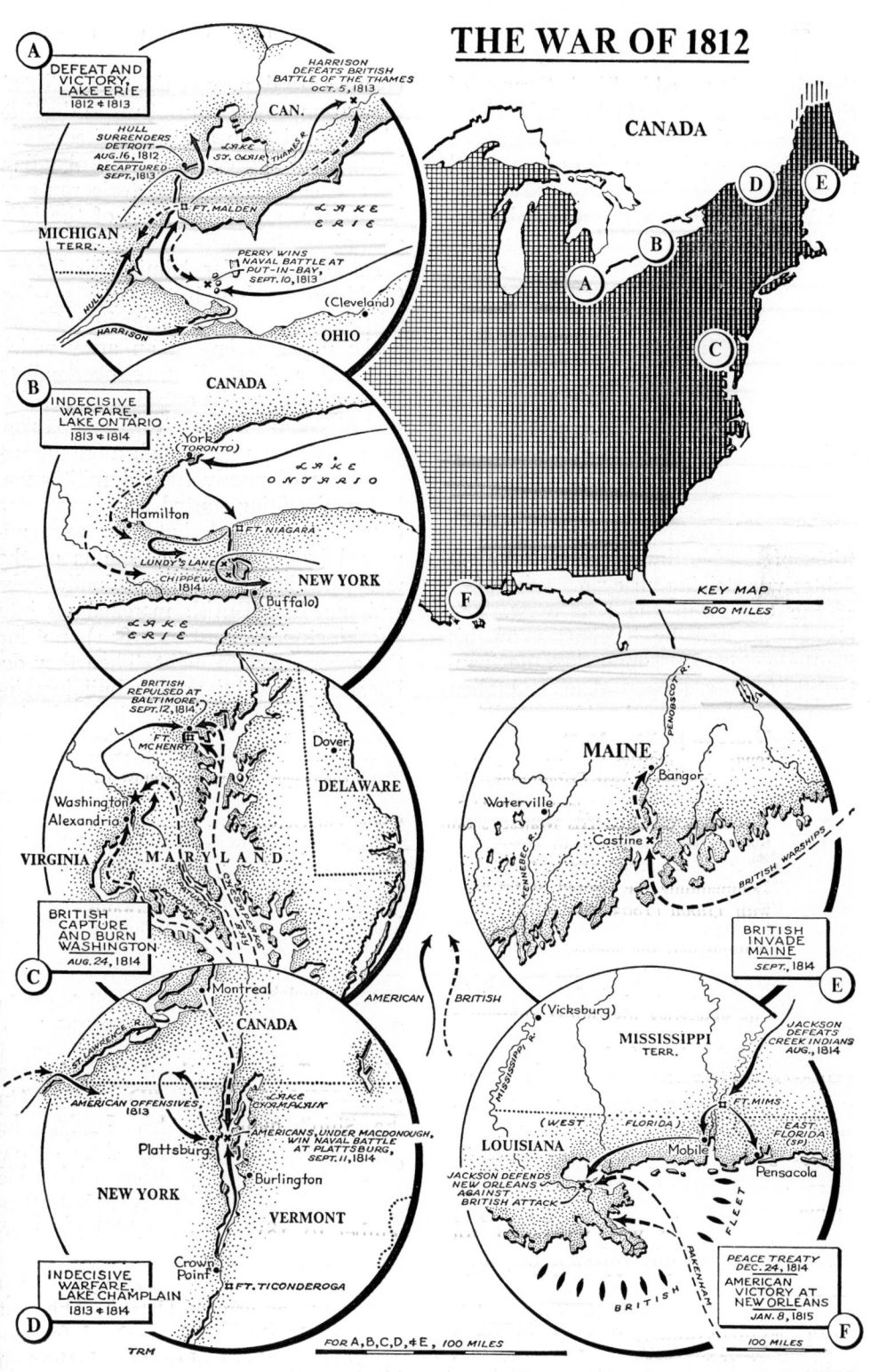

A DEFEAT AND VICTORY, LAKE ERIE 1812 & 1813

HARRISON DEFEATS BRITISH BATTLE OF THE THAMES OCT. 5, 1813

CAN.

HULL SURRENDERS DETROIT AUG. 16, 1812 RECAPTURED SEPT., 1813

LAKE ST. CLAIR THAMES R.

FT. MALDEN

MICHIGAN TERR.

LAKE ERIE

HULL

HARRISON

PERRY WINS NAVAL BATTLE AT PUT-IN-BAY, SEPT. 10, 1813

(Cleveland)

OHIO

B INDECISIVE WARFARE, LAKE ONTARIO 1813 & 1814

CANADA

York (TORONTO)

LAKE ONTARIO

Hamilton

FT. NIAGARA

LUNDY'S LANE
CHIPPEWA 1814

NEW YORK

(Buffalo)

LAKE ERIE

CANADA

BRITISH REPULSED AT BALTIMORE, SEPT. 12, 1814

FT. McHENRY

Dover

DELAWARE

Washington
Alexandria

VIRGINIA   MARYLAND

C BRITISH CAPTURE AND BURN WASHINGTON AUG. 24, 1814

Montreal

CANADA

AMERICAN OFFENSIVES, 1813

LAKE CHAMPLAIN

AMERICANS, UNDER MACDONOUGH, WIN NAVAL BATTLE AT PLATTSBURG, SEPT. 11, 1814

Plattsburg

Burlington

NEW YORK

VERMONT

Crown Point

FT. TICONDEROGA

D INDECISIVE WARFARE, LAKE CHAMPLAIN 1813 & 1814

TRM

CANADA

D

E

B

A

C

F

KEY MAP
500 MILES

MAINE

Bangor

Waterville

Castine

BRITISH WARSHIPS

PENOBSCOT R.

KENNEBEC R.

E BRITISH INVADE MAINE SEPT., 1814

AMERICAN   BRITISH

(Vicksburg)

MISSISSIPPI TERR.

JACKSON DEFEATS CREEK INDIANS AUG., 1814

MISSISSIPPI R.

FT. MIMS

(WEST FLORIDA)

EAST FLORIDA (SP.)

LOUISIANA   Mobile

Pensacola

JACKSON DEFENDS NEW ORLEANS AGAINST BRITISH ATTACK

FLEET

PAKENHAM

BRITISH

F PEACE TREATY DEC. 24, 1814 AMERICAN VICTORY AT NEW ORLEANS JAN. 8, 1815

FOR A, B, C, D, & E, 100 MILES

100 MILES

the almost impassable Black Swamp of the Maumee Valley or had to make a long detour around it. After Perry's victory at Put-in-Bay, supplies as well as men could be quickly and easily transported by water. William Henry Harrison, who had replaced Hull in the Western command, now pushed up the River Thames into Upper Canada and won a victory (October 5, 1813) notable for the death of Tecumseh, who had been commissioned a brigadier general in the British army. The Battle of the Thames resulted in no lasting occupation of Canadian soil, but it disheartened the Indians of the Northwest and eliminated the worst of the danger they had offered to the frontier.

While Harrison was chastising the tribes of the Northwest, another Indian fighter was striking an even harder blow at the Creeks in the Southwest. The Creeks, aroused by Tecumseh on his Southern visit, were supplied by the Spaniards in Florida. These Indians had fallen upon Fort Mims, on the Alabama River just north of the Florida border, and had massacred the frontier families taking shelter within its stockade. Andrew Jackson, Tennessee planter and militia general, turning from his plans for invading Florida, tracked down the Creeks. In the Battle of Horseshoe Bend (March 27, 1814) Jackson's men took frightful vengeance, slaughtering squaws and children along with warriors. Then Jackson went into Florida and seized the Spanish fort at Pensacola.

After the Battles of the Thames and Horseshoe Bend, the Indians were of little use to the British. But, with the surrender of Napoleon in Europe, the British could send their veterans of the Euro-

pean war to dispose of the "dirty shirts," the unkempt Americans. In 1814 the British prepared to invade the United States by three approaches—Chesapeake Bay, Lake Champlain (the historic route of Burgoyne), and the mouth of the Mississippi.

An armada under Admiral Sir George Cockburn, a hard-bitten old sea-dog, sailed up the Patuxent River from Chesapeake Bay and landed an army which marched a short distance overland to Bladensburg, on the outskirts of the District of Columbia. Hastily drawn up to oppose this army was a much more numerous force of poorly trained militiamen. When the firing started they gave more than they received, but they were unnerved by the repeated assaults of the well-disciplined redcoats and finally broke and ran. The British marched on into Washington (August 24, 1814), putting the government to flight. Then they deliberately burned the public buildings, including the White House, in retaliation for the earlier unauthorized incendiarism at York. The sack of Washington marked the low point of American fortunes in the war; better days were coming.

Leaving Washington in partial ruins, the invading army re-embarked and proceeded up the bay, toward Baltimore. But Baltimore, guarded by Fort McHenry, was ready. To block the river approach, the garrison had stretched a chain across the Patapsco and had sunk several boats in the river. From a distance the British bombarded the fort (September 13, 1814) while through the night an American, Francis Scott Key, watched from one of the enemy ships where he had gone to secure the release of a prisoner. At the

THE BATTLE OF NEW ORLEANS, January 8, 1815. [OPPOSITE] This sketch, drawn on the field of battle by H. Laclotte, one of Jackson's men, shows Sir Edward Pakenham's army advancing in open formation against Jackson's well-protected militia (left of center) on Chalmette Plain, on the east bank of the Mississippi River about five miles below New Orleans. In the left foreground may be seen some of Jackson's heavy guns in action, as well as hand-to-hand combat between the guns' defenders and the attacking redcoats. (COURTESY OF THE NEW-YORK HISTORICAL SOCIETY, NEW YORK CITY)

"dawn's early light," as Key wrote the next day, the flag on the fort was still flying "o'er the land of the free and the home of the brave." The British withdrew, and Key's words, set to the tune of an old drinking song, quickly became popular.

Meanwhile another invasion force was descending upon northern New York. On Lake Champlain the British mustered a fleet about the size of the American fleet drawn up to oppose it, and near by they had an army three times as large as the mixed force of regulars and militia facing it. Yet, in the Battle of Plattsburg (September 11, 1814), the defenders destroyed the invading fleet, and the invading army then retreated to Canada. The northern border was safe.

Far to the south the most serious threat of all soon materialized. In December, 1814, a formidable array of battle-hardened veterans, fresh from the Duke of Wellington's Peninsular campaign against the French in Spain, landed below New Orleans. On Christmas, Wellington's brother-in-law Sir Edward Pakenham arrived to take command. Neither he nor anyone else in America knew that, the day before, a treaty of peace between the British and American governments had been signed in faraway Belgium. Awaiting Pakenham's advance up the Mississippi was Andrew Jackson with a motley collection of Tennesseans, Kentuckians, creoles, Negroes, and pirates drawn up behind breastworks. For all their drill and bravery, the redcoats advancing through the open (January 8, 1815) were no match for Jackson's well-protected men. Making good use of artillery as well as rifles, the Americans held their fire as each wave of attackers approached, then sent out deadly volleys at close range. Finally the British retreated while an American band struck up "Hail Columbia!" Left behind were 700 dead, including Pakenham himself, 1,400 wounded, and 500 other prisoners. Jackson's losses: 8 killed, 13 wounded.

New England Objections

With notable exceptions, such as the battle of New Orleans, the military operations of the United States, 1812–15, were rather badly bungled. This should cause little surprise. What is surprising is the fact that American arms succeeded as well as they did. After all, the government was woefully unprepared for the war at the outset and faced increasing popular opposition as the contest dragged on. The opposition centered in New England, and it went to remarkable extremes. Some of the Federalists there celebrated British victories, sabotaged their own country's war effort, and even plotted disunion and a separate peace.

The blockade, until 1814, did not extend north of Newport, Rhode Island, the British government deliberately cultivating the New England trade. Goods carried in Yankee ships helped to feed British troops in Canada as well as Spain, and for a time many a ship owner grew rich by trading with the enemy while denouncing Madison and the war, though eventually the business of the shipowners as a whole fell far below the level of the prosperous prewar years.

Though most of the money in the nation was concentrated in New England, only a small part of the government's war bonds could be sold there. One of the Treasury loans, desperately needed to keep soldiers in the field, almost fell through because of the refusal of the New England banks to lend. Secretary of the Treasury Gallatin had to turn to his friend John Jacob Astor of New York and two foreign-born bankers of Philadelphia for the necessary funds. On several occasions the governors of New England states refused to allow the state militia to take orders from the President or to fight outside the country.

In Congress the Republicans had continual trouble with the Federalist opposition. The leadership of the administration party fell to Calhoun, who devoted himself to justifying the war and raising men and money with which to fight it. At every step he ran against the obstructionists, foremost among them the young congressman from New Hampshire, Daniel Webster. Introducing resolution after enlistments. In its extremity the administration decided to draft men into the regular army from the state militia. Helping to defeat the conscription bill, Webster warned that no such law could be enforced in his part of the country.

THE HARTFORD CONVENTION

1815

New England opponents of the war, meeting at Hartford, Connecticut, late in 1814, demanded the following amendments to the Federal Constitution in their report, published early in the following year:

1. "Representatives and direct taxes shall be apportioned among the several states . . . according to their respective numbers of free persons. . . ."

2. "No new state shall be admitted into the Union by Congress . . . without the concurrence of two thirds of both houses."

3. "Congress shall not have power to lay any embargo . . . for more than sixty days."

4. "Congress shall not have power, without the concurrence of two thirds of both houses, to interdict the commercial intercourse between the United States and any foreign nation. . . ."

5. "Congress shall not make or declare war, or authorize acts of hostility against any foreign nation, without the concurrence of two thirds of both houses, except such acts of hostility be in defence of the territories of the United States when actually invaded."

6. "No person who shall hereafter be naturalized, shall be eligible as a member of the senate or house of representatives of the United States, nor capable of holding any civil office under the authority of the United States."

7. "The same person shall not be elected president of the United States a second time; nor shall the president be elected from the same state two terms in succession."

resolution to embarrass the administration, Webster demanded reasons for the war and intimated that Napoleon had tricked the President into antagonizing England, as in fact Napoleon had. Every measure to finance the fighting—by loans, taxes, tariffs, or a national bank—Webster and his Federalist allies vehemently denounced. At a time when volunteering lagged and the army was seriously undermanned, he opposed a bill to encourage

As new states in the South and West, strongly Republican, were added to the Union, the Federalists had become more and more hopelessly a minority party in the country as a whole. But they were the majority in New England. If that section were to become a separate confederacy, they could control its destinies and escape the dictation of slaveholders and backwoodsmen. The talk of secession, heard before at the time of the Louisiana purchase and again at the time of Jefferson's embargo, was revived during the war and reached a climax in the winter of 1814–15, when the Republic appeared to be on the verge of ruin.

On December 15, 1814, while the British were beginning their invasion by way of New Orleans, delegates from the New England states met in Hartford, Connecticut, to consider the grievances of their section against the Madison administration. The would-be seceders were overruled by the comparatively moderate men who were in the overwhelming majority at the Hartford convention. The convention's report reasserted the right of nullification but only hinted at secession, observing that "the severance of the Union by one or more States, against the will of the rest, and especially in time of war, can be justified only by absolute necessity." But the report proposed seven essential amendments to the Constitution, presumably as the condition of New England's remaining in the Union. These amendments were intended to protect New England from the growing influence of the South and the West.

The Federalists, apparently in a strong bargaining position, assumed that the Republicans would have to give in to the Hartford convention terms, since the government was in such dire extremity. Soon after the convention adjourned, however, the news of Jackson's smashing victory at New Orleans reached the cities of the Northeast. While most Americans rejoiced, the Federalists were plunged into gloom. A day or two later came tidings from abroad concerning the conclusion of a treaty of peace. Of course, the treaty had been signed before the Battle of New Orleans, but the people heard of the battle first. They got the impression that the United States had won the war. "Peace is signed in the arms of victory!" *Niles's Register* exclaimed. The Hartford Convention and the Federalist party were discredited as not only treasonable but also futile.

The Peace Settlement

During the War of 1812 peace talks began before the battles did. President Madison, reluctant to ask for a declaration of war and "regretting the necessity which produced it," looked hopefully toward an early end to hostilities. Soon after the declaration the British government, wishing to liquidate a minor war and concentrate upon the major one, against Napoleon, sent an admiral to Washington with armistice proposals, but negotiations failed to develop because of Madison's continued insistence upon the renunciation of impressment. Britain's ally Russia, eager to get supplies from America as well as unhampered military aid from England, twice offered to mediate, the first time on the day before Napoleon's invading forces entered Moscow (September 13, 1812). The British politely declined both of the Czar's offers but finally agreed to meet the Americans in direct negotiations on neutral ground. After prolonged delays the peacemakers got together in Ghent, Belgium, on August 8, 1814.

The American peace delegation at Ghent happened to be composed of men of exceptional ability, men who were more than a match for their opposite numbers around the peace table. The delegation included men of both parties and all sections. At the head of it was John Quincy Adams, a one-time Federalist who had broken with his party to support Jefferson's embargo, and a diplomat of varied experience who recently had been minister to Russia. One of his colleagues was Henry Clay, once a war hawk, now a peace dove. Another was the Secretary of the Treasury in both Jefferson's and Madison's administrations, Albert Gallatin. A natural diplomat, Gallatin held the delegation together by moderating the disputes of Adams and Clay.

At Ghent the two sets of peacemakers at first presented fantastically extreme demands, then gradually backed down and finally agreed to a compromise. The Americans, in accordance with their instructions, originally demanded the renunciation of impressment as a necessary condition to peace, and they also asked for all or part of Canada and for British aid in acquiring Florida from Spain. The Englishmen, contrary to their instructions, presented an ultimatum requiring the United States to cede territory in the Northwest for the formation of an Indian buffer state. Then, when their home government refused to sustain them in the ultimatum, they withdrew it and proposed that peace be made on the principle of *uti possidetis*. This meant that each of the belligerents should keep the territory it actually held whenever the fighting stopped. Expecting large territorial gains from the invasion of America, the Englishmen at Ghent tried to delay negotiations so as to maximize the gains. But the government in London, becoming more and more alarmed by developments in Europe, decided to hasten the settlement with the United States and recommended peace on the basis of the *status quo ante bellum*, which meant a return to things as they had been before the war began. Already President Madison had advised his delegation that they need no longer make an issue of impressment. A treaty providing for the *status quo*, hastily drawn up, was signed on Christmas Eve, 1814.

According to the Treaty of Ghent, the war was to end not immediately, but when the document had been ratified and proclaimed on both sides (hence it is not exactly true, as is sometimes said, that the battle of New Orleans was fought after the war was over). Each of the belligerents was to restore its wartime conquests to the other. Four commissions with both American and British members were to be appointed to agree upon disputed or undetermined segments of the boundary between Canada and the United States.

The Treaty of Ghent was followed by other settlements which contributed to the improvement of Anglo-American relations. A separate commercial treaty (1815) gave Americans the right to trade freely with England and the British Empire except for the West Indies. A fisheries convention (1818) renewed the privileges of Americans to catch and dry fish at specified places along the shores of British North America. The Rush-Bagot agreement (1817) provided for mutual disarmament on the Great Lakes. Gradually disarmament was extended to the land, and eventually (though not till 1872) the Canadian-American boundary became the longest "unguarded frontier" in the world.

Though the British had not renounced impressment in principle, they ceased to apply it in practice after 1815. With the final end of the Napoleonic wars after the battle of Waterloo, the nations of Europe entered upon a century of comparative peace, broken only by wars of limited scale. So the British no longer had occasion to violate American sovereignty on the high seas, and the government and people of the United States could afford to devote their energies primarily to affairs at home.

The War of 1812 was at best a draw, and the United States was lucky to avoid surrendering some of its own territory. Yet the war had important consequences. It broke the Indian barriers that had stood in the way of the northwestward and southwestward expansion of settlement. It gave rise to a spirit of nationalism which discredited the antiwar party and helped to overcome the divisive forces of postwar sectionalism. Perhaps most important of all, it stimulated the growth of manufactures, thus accelerating the progress of the nation toward industrial greatness.

The year the war ended, 1815, marks a turning point in the relations of the United States with the rest of the world. Previously, this country had become involved again and again in the broils of

Europe, and much of the time the requirements of diplomacy had dictated domestic policies. Afterwards, for most of a century, domestic politics held a clear priority over foreign affairs as the country entered upon a period of comparative "isolation."

Free Seas Again

No sooner had peace come in 1815 than Congress declared war again, this time against Algiers, which had taken advantage of the War of 1812 to loose its pirates once more against American shipping in the Mediterranean. Two American squadrons now proceeded to North African waters. One of the two, under the command of Stephen Decatur, a naval hero of the late war with England, captured a number of corsair ships, blockaded the coast of Algiers, and forced the Dey to accept a treaty which not only ended the payment of tribute by the United States but required the Dey to pay reparations to this country. Going on to Tunis and Tripoli, Decatur collected additional indemnities in both of those places. This naval action in the Mediterranean brought a more clear-cut victory for the freedom of the seas than had the War of 1812 itself. Of course, the victory was made possible by the growth in naval strength and national spirit which the war with England had occasioned. After 1816, when the Dey of Algiers began to make trouble again, only to have his entire fleet destroyed by combined British and Dutch forces, the United States had no further difficulties with the Barbary pirates.

Postwar Economic Issues

The War of 1812 led to chaos in shipping and banking, as well as stimulating the growth of manufactures, and exposed dramatically the inadequacy of the existing transportation system. Hence arose the postwar issues of re-establishing the Bank of the United States, protecting the new industries, and providing a nationwide network of roads and waterways. On these issues the former war hawks Clay and Calhoun became the leading advocates of the national as opposed to the local or sectional point of view. The party of Jefferson now sponsored measures of a kind once championed by the party of Hamilton. In regard to the bank and the tariff the new nationalists were completely successful; in regard to internal improvements, only partly so.

The wartime experience seemed to make necessary another national bank. After the first Bank's charter expired (1811), a large number of state banks sprang up. These issued vast quantities of banknotes (promises to pay, which then served much the same purpose as bank checks were later to do) and did not always bother to keep a large enough reserve of gold or silver to redeem the notes on demand. The notes passed from hand to hand more or less as money, but their actual value depended upon the reputation of the bank that issued them, and the variety of issues was so confusing as to make honest business difficult and counterfeiting easy. This bank money was not legal tender, and it was not issued directly by the state governments, yet its issuance hardly conformed with the clause of the Constitution giving Congress the exclusive power to regulate the currency and forbidding the states to emit bills of credit.

Congress struck at the currency evil not by prohibiting state banknotes but by chartering a second Bank of the United States, in 1816. Except that it was allowed a larger capital, this institution was essentially the same as the one founded under Hamilton's leadership in 1791. In return for the charter, the bank had to pay a "bonus" of $1,500,000 to the government. Though its potentialities were not fully realized during the first few years of its existence, this national bank possessed the power of controlling the state banks by presenting their notes from time to time and demanding payment either in cash or in its own notes, which were as good as gold. Once the Bank of the United States began to exercise its power, the state banks had to stay on a specie-paying basis or risk being forced out of business.

The war had a disastrous effect upon American shipping, especially after the British blockade was extended to include the New England coast. Between 1811 and 1814 exports dropped from $61,000,-000 to $7,000,000 and imports from $53,000,000 to $13,000,000. The total tonnage of American vessels engaged in foreign trade declined from about 950,-000 to less than 60,000 tons. Some ships managed to escape the blockade but others were caught and confiscated, altogether about 1,300 of them.

Farmers, unable to get their produce out to the markets of the world, suffered from the ruin of the carrying trade, but manufacturers prospered as foreign competition almost disappeared in consequence of the embargoes and the blockade. Much of the capital and labor formerly employed in commerce and shipbuilding was diverted to manufacturing. Goods were so scarce that, even with comparatively unskilled labor and poor management, new factories could be started with an assurance of quick profits.

As the war came to an end, the manufacturing prospects of the United States were suddenly dimmed. British ships swarmed alongside American wharves and began to unload their cargoes of manufactured goods at cut prices, even selling below cost. As Lord Brougham explained to Parliament, it was "well worth while to incur a loss upon the first exportation, in order, by the glut, to stifle in the cradle those rising manufactures in the United States, which war had forced into existence, contrary to the natural course of things." Thus, though the war was over, Great Britain persisted in a kind of economic warfare against the United States.

The "infant industries" needed protection if they were to survive and grow strong enough to stand upon their own feet against foreign competition. So the friends of industry maintained, reviving the old arguments of Hamilton. In 1816 the protectionists brought about the passage of a tariff law with rates high enough to be definitely protective, especially on cotton cloth.

Despite the progress being made with steamboats and turnpikes, there remained serious gaps in the transportation network of the country, as experience during the War of 1812 had shown. Once the coastwise shipping had been cut off by the British blockade, the coastal roads became choked by the unaccustomed volume of north-south traffic. At the river ferries, long lines of wagons waited for a chance to cross. Oxcarts, pressed into emergency service, took six or seven weeks to go from Philadelphia to Charleston. In various localities there appeared serious shortages of goods normally carried by sea, and prices rose to new heights, rice costing three times as much in New York as in Charleston, flour three times as much in Boston as in Richmond. On the northern and western frontiers the military campaigns of the United States were partly frustrated by the absence of good roads.

With this wartime experience in mind, President Madison in 1815 called the attention of Congress to the "great importance of establishing throughout our country the roads and canals which can be best executed under the national authority," and he suggested that a constitutional amendment would resolve any doubts about the authority of Congress to provide for the construction of canals and roads. Representative Calhoun promptly espoused a bill by which the moneys due the government from the Bank of the United States—both the "bonus" and the government's share of the annual profits—would be devoted to internal improvements. "Let us, then, bind the republic together with a perfect system of roads and canals," Calhoun urged. "Let us conquer space."

Congress passed the bonus bill, but President Madison, on his last day in office (March 3, 1817), returned it with his veto. While he approved its purpose, he still believed that a constitutional amendment was necessary. And so, with some exceptions, the tremendous task of internal improvements was left to the state governments and to private enterprise.

BIBLIOGRAPHY

On the origins of the War of 1812, the long-standing view was that the freedom of the seas was all-important. J. W. Pratt challenges this view in his *Expansionists of 1812* (1925). Pratt concludes that border considerations—the desire of Northwestern frontiersmen to get Canada, and of Southwestern frontiersmen to get Florida, so as to eliminate the Indian menace—were also highly significant. This interpretation is attacked by A. L. Burt in *The United States, Great Britain, and British North America from the Revolution to the Peace after the War of 1812* (1940). Burt denies that the frontier conflict was a prime cause of war and insists that maritime difficulties, particularly impressment, were as important as they have appeared to be in the traditional view.

Special studies include J. F. Zimmerman, *Impressment of American Seamen* (1925); and L. M. Sears, *Jefferson and the Embargo* (1927).

Important biographical accounts are Glenn Tucker, *Tecumseh: Vision of Glory* (1956); D. B. Goebel, *William Henry Harrison* (1926); Freeman Cleaves, *Old Tippecanoe* (1939); Bernard Mayo, *Henry Clay: Spokesman of the New West* (1937); Clement Eaton, *Henry Clay and the Art of American Politics* (1957); C. M. Wiltse, *John C. Calhoun: Nationalist, 1782–1828* (1944); and Irving Brant, *James Madison: The President, 1809–1812* (1956). The workings of the Hartford convention are revealed in *The Life and Letters of Harrison Gray Otis* (2 vols., 1913), edited by S. E. Morison.

An up-to-date general account is F. F. Beirne, *The War of 1812* (1949). The chapters on the war from Henry Adams's 9-volume history have been republished as *The War of 1812* (1944). The enemy's side is presented in C. P. Lucas, *The Canadian War of 1812* (1906), and in William Wood's *The War with the United States* (1915). Marquis James, *Andrew Jackson: The Border Captain* (1933), recounts Jackson's campaigns. C. F. Adams, *Studies Military and Diplomatic, 1775–1865* (1911), includes an essay analyzing the Battle of New Orleans. A. T. Mahan, *Sea Power in Its Relation to the War of 1812* (2 vols., 1919), is a classic by the influential big-navy advocate.

The state of military preparedness at the start of the war can be seen in J. R. Jacobs's *The Beginning of the United States Army, 1783–1812* (1947). C. C. Alden and Allan Westcott, *The United States Navy: A History* (1943), gives a summary of the navy's role both in the War of 1812 and in the fighting with the Mediterranean pirates. A more extensive account of the Barbary War is provided by Fletcher Pratt in *Preble's Boys: Commodore Preble and the Birth of American Sea Power* (1950).

II

THE ERA
OF GOOD FEELINGS

Sectionalism—the rivalry of one part of the country against another—had roots that went deep in American history. Even in colonial times there were three well-recognized sections (New England, the Middle Colonies, and the South), and occasionally the inhabitants of one expressed their dislike for those of another. Sectional feeling was evident on several occasions thereafter; it was clearly seen, for example, in New England's opposition to the War of 1812. After the war the Northeast and the South began to contend for influence over the rising West. This struggle threatened eventual disunion, but for the time being there fortunately were countervailing forces of nationalism. On the whole the sense of nationhood was strengthened during the presidency of James Monroe (1817–25).

President Monroe

After 1800 the presidency seemed to have become the special possession of Virginians, who passed it from one to another in unvarying sequence. After two terms in office Jefferson named his Secretary of State, James Madison, to succeed him, and after two more terms Madison secured the nomination of *his* Secretary of State, James Monroe. Against this succession of Virginians, the so-called "Virginia Dynasty," many in the North already were muttering, yet the Republicans had no difficulty in electing their candidate in the remarkably listless campaign of 1816. Monroe received 183 ballots in the electoral college; his opponent, Rufus King of New York, only 34, from the states of Massachusetts, Connecticut, and Delaware.

At the time he became President, Monroe was 61 years old. Tall and dignified, he wore the old-fashioned garb of his youthful days, including knee-length pantaloons and white-topped boots. He had reached the peak of a long and varied career as Revolutionary soldier, diplomat, and cabinet officer. Although when young he had been regarded as impulsive and changeable, he now was noted for his caution and patience. He was neither so subtle nor so original as his

JAMES MONROE. When Monroe was governor of
Virginia (1799–1802) an acquaintance said of
him: "To be plain, there is often in his manner
an inartificial and even an awkward simplicity,
which, while it provokes the smile of a more polished person, forces him to the opinion that Mr.
Monroe is a man of most sincere and artless soul."
In 1825, when Monroe was in his last year as
President, a Virginia lady gave her impression of
him after attending a New Year's reception at the
White House: "From the frank, honest expression of his eye . . . I think he well deserves the
encomium passed upon him by the great Jefferson,
who said, 'Monroe is so honest that if you turned
his soul inside out there would not be a spot on
it.' " The portrait here reproduced was done by
Gilbert Stuart, who painted portraits of all the
men who served as Presidents during his lifetime
—Washington, Adams, Jefferson, Madison, Monroe, and John Quincy Adams. (THE PENNSYL-
VANIA ACADEMY OF THE FINE ARTS)

gifted predecessors from Virginia, Jefferson and Madison, yet he was more able
than posterity generally has considered
him. He had a mind of his own, and he
was the master of his administration, even
though he picked a group of exceptionally
strong men for his advisers.

In choosing his cabinet, Monroe intended to recognize and harmonize the
major interests of the country. For the
first and most important position, that of
Secretary of State, he selected the New
Englander and one-time Federalist, John
Quincy Adams. This choice was significant in view of the well-established custom which made the State Department a
stepping stone to the Presidency: Monroe
appeared to be announcing that he would
be the last of the Virginia Dynasty and
that the next President (after a second
term for Monroe) would be a Massachusetts man. For Secretary of War,
Monroe chose the forceful South Carolinian, John C. Calhoun, after Henry Clay
had declined the office, preferring to
continue as speaker of the House.

Soon after his inauguration Monroe
did what no other President since Washington had done: he made a goodwill
tour through the country, eastward to
New England, westward as far as Detroit.
In New England, so recently the scene of
rabid Federalist discontent, he was greeted
everywhere with enthusiastic demonstrations. The *Colombian Centinel*, a Federalist newspaper of Boston, commenting
on the "Presidential Jubilee" in that city,
observed that an "era of good feelings"
had arrived. This phrase soon became
popular; it spread throughout the country, and eventually it came to be almost
synonymous with the Presidency of Monroe.

There was a good deal of hidden irony
in this phrase of 1817, for the "good feelings" did not last long, and the period
over which Monroe presided turned into
one of very bad feelings indeed. Yet he
was re-elected in 1820 with the nearest
thing to a unanimous electoral vote that
any presidential candidate, with the exception of George Washington, has ever
had. Indeed, all but one of the electors
cast their ballots for Monroe. The lone
dissenter, a strong-minded Yankee from
New Hampshire who thought Monroe
unfit for the Presidency, voted for John
Quincy Adams. The Federalists had not
even bothered to put up an opposing
candidate.

Florida and the Far West

The first big problem facing John Quincy Adams as Secretary of State was that of Florida. Already the United States had annexed West Florida, but Spain still claimed the whole of the province, East and West, and actually held most of it, though with a grasp too feeble to stop the abuses against which Americans long had complained—the escape of slaves across the border in one direction, the marauding of Indians across it in the other. In 1817 Adams began negotiations with the Spanish minister, Don Luis de Onís, for acquiring all of Florida (or rather for acquiring that part of it which the United States did not already claim). Talks between the cantankerous puritan and the wily don progressed haltingly, then were broken off when the hot-tempered Andrew Jackson took matters forcefully into his own hands.

Jackson, in command of American troops along the Florida frontier, had orders from Secretary of War Calhoun to "adopt the necessary measures" to end the border troubles. Jackson also had an unofficial hint—or so he afterwards claimed—that the administration would not mind if he undertook a punitive expedition into Spanish territory. At any rate he invaded Florida, seized the Spanish forts at St. Marks and Pensacola, and ordered the hanging of two British subjects on the charge of supplying the Indians and inciting them to hostilities. News of these events provoked a sharp discussion behind the scenes in Monroe's cabinet. Calhoun and others insisted that the general should be punished or at least reprimanded for exceeding his authority, but Adams defended Jackson so ably as to prevent any action against him.

Instead of blaming Jackson or disavowing the raid, Adams wished the government to assume complete responsibility for it, for he saw in it a chance to further his Florida diplomacy. Rejecting a Spanish protest, he demanded reparations from Spain to pay the cost of the expedition, though he did not press this demand. He pointed out that Spain had promised in Pinckney's Treaty to restrain the Indians in her territory but had failed to live up to her treaty obligations. The United States, he argued, was justified by international law in taking drastic measures for self-defense. He implied that this country would be justified in going even farther than it had done.

Jackson's raid demonstrated that the United States, if it tried, could easily take Florida by force, unless Spain could get aid from some other power. The only power to which she could look was Great Britain.

Unable to obtain British support, Spain had little choice but to come to terms with the United States, though the resourceful Onís made the most of a bad situation for his country. In the treaty of 1819 it was agreed that the King of Spain should cede "all the territories which belong to him situated to the eastward of the Mississippi and known by the name of East and West Florida." This ambiguous wording was used so as to evade the troublesome question whether Spain was ceding both East and West Florida or whether West Florida already belonged to the United States. In return the United States assumed the claims of its citizens against the Spanish government to the amount of $5,000,000. This money was to be paid to American citizens, not to the Spanish government: we did not "purchase" Florida, as is sometimes said. The United States also gave up its claims to Texas, and Spain her claims to territory north of the forty-second parallel from the Rockies to the Pacific. Thus a line was drawn from the Gulf of Mexico northwestward across the continent delimiting the Spanish empire and transferring to the United States the Spanish title to the West Coast north of California. Adams and Onís had concluded something more than a Florida agreement: it was a "transcontinental treaty."

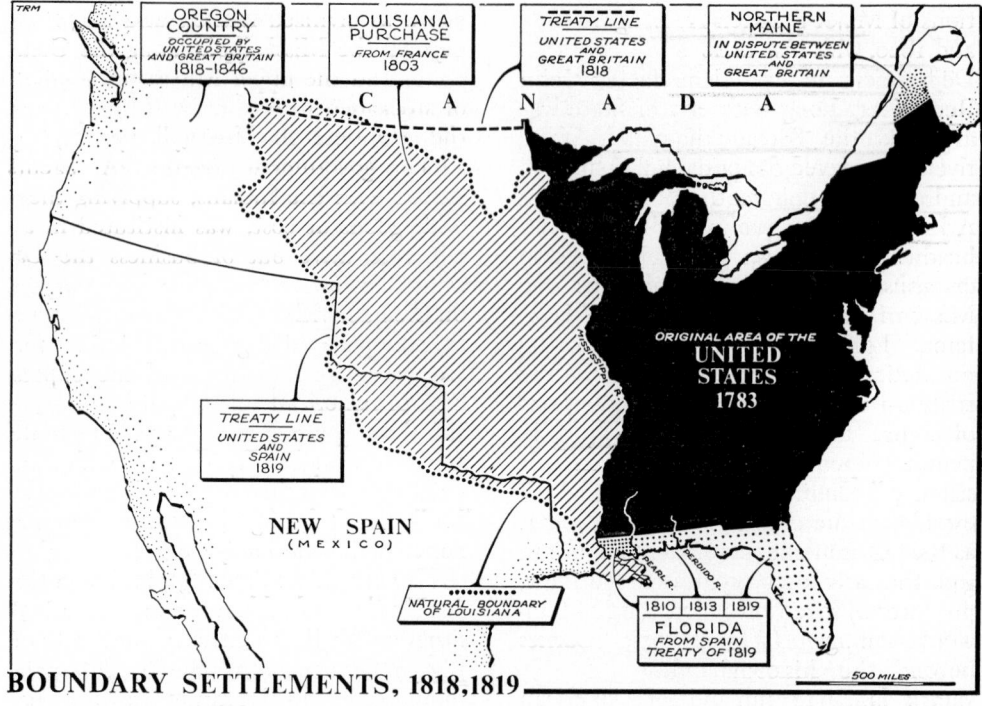

OREGON
COUNTRY
OCCUPIED BY
UNITED STATES
AND GREAT BRITAIN
1818-1846

LOUISIANA
PURCHASE
FROM FRANCE
1803

TREATY LINE
UNITED STATES
AND
GREAT BRITAIN
1818

NORTHERN
MAINE
IN DISPUTE BETWEEN
UNITED STATES
AND
GREAT BRITAIN

C A N A D A

ORIGINAL AREA OF THE
UNITED
STATES
1783

TREATY LINE
UNITED STATES
AND
SPAIN
1819

NEW SPAIN
(MEXICO)

NATURAL BOUNDARY
OF LOUISIANA

PEARL R. PERDIDO R.

1810 | 1813 | 1819
FLORIDA
FROM SPAIN
TREATY OF 1819

500 MILES

BOUNDARY SETTLEMENTS, 1818,1819

President Monroe, with the approval of the Senate, promptly ratified the treaty, but the coming of a revolution delayed ratification by Spain. The treaty finally went into effect in 1821. Thereafter the whole of Florida was, without question, territory belonging to the United States. And for the first time the area of the Louisiana Purchase had a definite southwestern boundary.

At the time of his negotiations with Onís, Adams showed much more interest in the Far West than did most of his fellow countrymen. Few Americans were familiar with the Oregon coast except for New Englanders engaged in Pacific whaling or in the China trade. Only the fur traders and trappers knew intimately any of the land between the Missouri and the Pacific. Before the War of 1812 John Jacob Astor's American Fur Company had established Astoria as a trading post at the mouth of the Columbia River, but when war came Astor sold his interests to the Northwestern Fur Company, a

British concern operating from Canada, and after the war he centered his own operations in the Great Lakes area, from which he eventually extended them westward to the Rockies. Manuel Lisa's Missouri Fur Company, founded in 1809, with headquarters in St. Louis, sent traders and supplies up the Missouri and its tributaries and brought back peltries obtained from the Indians. The Rocky Mountain Fur Company, which Andrew Henry and William Henry Ashley organized in 1822, pushed the trade farther north and west and revolutionized the business by sending out white trappers who procured their furs directly and brought them to an annual "rendezvous" in the mountains to be sold to the company's agents.

The trappers or "mountain men," notably Jedediah S. Smith, explored the Far West and gained an intimate knowledge of it, but they did not write books. General information about the region was increased in consequence of the explorations of Major Stephen H. Long. In 1819 and 1820, with instructions from the War Department to find the sources of the Red River, Long with nineteen soldiers ascended the Platte and South Platte rivers, discovered the peak named for him, and returned eastward by way of the Arkansas River, but failed to find the headwaters of the Red. "In regard to this extensive section of country between the Missouri River and the Rocky Mountains," Long said in his report, "we do not hesitate in giving the opinion that it is almost wholly unfit for cultivation, and of course uninhabitable by a people depending upon agriculture for their subsistence." On the published map of his expedition the Great Plains were marked as the "Great American Desert." Thus he gave increased currency to the idea earlier put forth by Pike that the farming frontier would run against a great natural barrier beyond the Missouri. Meanwhile the vacant lands to the east, between the Appalachians and the Mississippi, were rapidly being converted into plantations and farms.

The Great Migration

One of the central themes of American history, for nearly three centuries after the founding of Jamestown, was the movement of population from the Atlantic coast to the interior and ultimately across the continent. This was no steady march, uniform along a broad front. It proceeded in irregular waves, following the lines of greatest attraction and least resistance, and accelerating in times of prosperity and peace. A sudden surge, greater than any preceding it, swept westward during the boom years which followed the War of 1812.

Weakened though it had been, the Indian threat still had to be taken into account. In a series of treaties forced upon the tribes after 1815, the federal government resumed the policy of compelling the redmen to choose between settling down as civilized farmers and migrating beyond the Mississippi. Along the Great Lakes and the upper Mississippi a chain of stockaded forts was erected to protect the frontier. A "factory" system, by which government factors or agents traded with the Indians, supplying them with goods at cost, was instituted in an effort to drive out of business the Canadian traders who persisted in carrying on their activities on American soil. After several years the government factories were abandoned because of the opposition of American fur companies who objected to government competition with private enterprise. By that time the Canadian traders had retreated across the border, and foreign influence over the American tribes finally came to an end.

The land abandoned by the Indians in the Northwest had been richly favored by nature, though its qualities were not entirely understood by the early pioneers. Over most of the Northwest extended the great primeval forest, but in central Illinois the forest gave way to a grand prairie billowing with wild grass as tall as six feet. The first settlers avoided this treeless stretch, for they saw unfamiliar problems in its tough sod and scarcity of wood, and they little knew the productivity of its black loam.

"Old America seems to be breaking up and moving westward," remarked an Englishman who joined the throng. Some were Kentucky and Tennessee frontiersmen, restless spirits who had begun to feel crowded as their states became increasingly populous. Others were small farmers from the back country of Virginia and the Carolinas who fled the encroachment of slavery and the plantation system. Still others came from the middle states, New England, and foreign countries, but the great majority were Southerners. Whatever the starting point, the Ohio River was for most of the migrants the main route, the "grand track," until the completion of the Erie Canal in 1825. They took the turnpike to Pittsburgh or the national road to Wheeling and thus reached the river, or they took one of its tributaries such as the Kanawha, the Cumberland, or the Tennessee. Downstream they floated on flatboats bearing all their worldly goods. Then, leaving the Ohio at Cincinnati or at some place farther down, they pressed on overland with wagons, handcarts, packhorses, cattle, hogs.

Once having arrived at his destination, preferably in the spring or early summer, the settler built a lean-to or cabin for his family, then hewed a clearing out of the forest and put in a crop of corn to supplement the wild game he caught and the domestic animals he had brought with him.

These frontier folk knew loneliness and poverty and dirt, suffered much from the forest fevers and from malnutrition, commonly had a lean and sallow look. Yet they were on the whole remarkably proud, bold, and independent. They were "half wild and wholly free."

To the Southwest moved people from Kentucky, from Tennessee, and from as far away as New England. Most numerous among the settlers on the Southern frontier, however, were farmers and planters from the South Atlantic states, especially from the piedmont of Georgia and the Carolinas. Their motive for migrating was, in a word, cotton. With the spread of cotton cultivation throughout the uplands of the older South, the soil there lost much of its natural fertility from repeated croppings, or washed away as torrential rains gullied the hillsides. Seeking fresh soil with a climate suitable for cotton, the planters naturally looked to the Southwest, around the end of the Appalachian range, where there stretched a broad zone within which cotton could thrive. Included in this zone was the Black Belt of central Alabama and Mississippi, a prairie with a fabulously productive soil of rotted limestone.

The advance of the Southern frontier meant the spread of cotton and slavery. Usually the first arrivals were ordinary frontiersmen like those farther north, small farmers who made rough clearings in the forest. Then came planters who bought up the cleared or partially cleared land, while the original settlers moved on west and started over again. As a rule the planters made the westward journey in a style quite different from that of the other pioneers. Over the alternately dusty and muddy roads came great caravans consisting of herds of livestock, wagonloads of household goods, long lines of slaves, and, bringing up the rear, the planter and his family riding in carriages. Soon the clearings expanded into vast fields white with cotton, and the cabins of the pioneers gave way to more sumptuous log dwellings and ultimately to imposing mansions which demonstrated the rise of a class of the newly rich.

Though by 1819 settlers already were pushing beyond the Mississippi, much of the area to the east of the river, around the Great Lakes and along the Gulf of Mexico, was yet to be occupied. Despite the gaps in settlement, the population of the Mississippi Valley had increased far more rapidly than that of the nation as a whole. The census of 1810 indicated that only one American in seven lived to the west of the Appalachian mountains; the census of 1820, almost one in four. During the immediate postwar years four new states were erected in this region—Indiana (1816), Mississippi (1817), Illinois (1818), and Alabama (1819). Meanwhile Missouri had grown populous enough for statehood, and the struggle over her admission indicated how important, politically and otherwise, the West was becoming in the eyes of the rest of the nation. For the time being, however, the westward movement was slowed down by the onset of the depression following the Panic of 1819.

In part the Panic of 1819 was a delayed reaction to the War of 1812 and to the preceding years of warfare in Europe. Since 1793 the continual fighting had drawn manpower from European fields, disrupted business as well as agriculture, and created an abnormal demand for the produce of American plantations and farms. The whole period was one of exceptionally high prices for American producers, and though some prices fell with the decline of trade in 1814, they recovered with the resumption of exports to Europe after the war.

office auctions, bidding became so spirited that much of the public land sold for prices far above the minimum of $2 an acre, some in the Black Belt of Alabama and Mississippi going for $100 and more. Still higher prices sometimes were paid by optimistic real-estate promoters who laid out town sites, even in swamps, and expected to make fortunes through the sale

---

PUBLIC LANDS: TERMS OF SALE

1785–1820

Ordinance of 1785. Allowed a minimum purchase of 640 acres and set a minimum price of $1 an acre. Made no provision for credit.

Act of 1796. Raised the minimum price to $2 an acre but allowed a year's credit on half of the amount due.

Act of 1800. Reduced the minimum purchase from 640 to 320 acres and extended credit to four years, with a down payment of one fourth of the whole amount and three later installments.

Act of 1804. Further reduced the minimum purchase to 160 acres. (Now a man with as little as $80 on hand could obtain a farm from the government, although he would still owe $240 to be paid within four years.)

Act of 1820. Reduced the minimum purchase still further, to 80 acres, and the minimum price to $1.25 an acre, but abolished the credit system.

Note: Under each of these laws, the land was first offered for sale at auction, and much of it sold for more than the minimum price.

Rising prices for farm products stimulated a land boom in the United States, particularly in the West. After the war the government land offices did a bigger business than ever before; not for twenty years were they to do as good a business again. In 1815 sales totaled about a million acres and in 1819 more than five million. Many settlers bought on credit: under the land laws of 1800 and 1804 they could pay as little as $80 down, and they hoped to raise the remaining three installments within four years from the proceeds of their farming. Speculators bought large tracts of choice land, hoping to resell it at a profit to incoming settlers. At the land-

of city lots. Until 1817 neither the settlers nor the speculators needed hard cash to buy government land: they could borrow from the state banks and pay the government with banknotes.

Even after the founding of the Bank of the United States in 1817, wildcat banks continued to provide easy credit for a couple of years. Indeed, the U.S. Bank itself at first offered easy loans. Then in 1819, under new management, it suddenly began to tighten up. It called in loans and foreclosed mortgages, acquiring thousands of acres of mortgaged land in the West. It gathered up state banknotes and presented them to the state banks for payment in cash. Having little money on hand, many of these banks closed their doors. Most of the rest soon had to follow suit, for they were beset by depositors with notes to be cashed. The panic was on.

Six years of depression followed. Prices rapidly fell. With the prices of farm products so low, those settlers buying land on credit could not hope to keep up their payments. Some stood to lose everything —their land, their improvements on it, their homes. They demanded relief from their congressmen, and Congress responded with the land law of 1820 and the relief act of 1821. By the new land law the credit system was abolished but the minimum price was lowered from $2.00 to $1.25 and the minimum tract from 160 to 80 acres. Hereafter a purchaser would have to buy his farm outright, but he could get one for as little as $100. The relief act allowed a previous buyer to pay off his debt at the reduced price, to accept the reduced acreage and apply the payments to it, and to have an extension of time in meeting his installments.

The Missouri Compromise

When Missouri applied for admission as a state, slavery already was well established there. The French and Spanish inhabitants of the Louisiana country (including what became Missouri) had owned slaves, and in the Louisiana Purchase treaty of 1803 the American government promised to maintain and protect the inhabitants in the free enjoyment of their property as well as their liberty and religion. By 1819 approximately 60,000 people resided in Missouri Territory, of whom about 10,000 were slaves. In that year, while Missouri's application for statehood was being considered in Congress, Representative James Tallmadge, Jr., of New York, moved to amend the enabling bill so as to prohibit the further introduction of slaves into Missouri and to provide for the gradual emancipation of

those already there. This Tallmadge amendment provoked a controversy that was to rage for the next two years.

Though the issue arose suddenly, waking and terrifying Thomas Jefferson like "a fire bell in the night," as he said, sectional jealousies that produced it had been accumulating for a long time. Already the concept of a balance of power between the Northern and Southern states was well developed. From the beginning, partly by chance and partly by design, new states had come into the Union more or less in pairs, one from the North, another from the South. With the admission of Alabama in 1819, the Union contained an equal number of free and slave states, eleven of each. Thus the free and slave states were evenly balanced in the Senate, though the free states with their more rapidly growing population had a majority in the House. If Missouri should be admitted as a slave state, not only would the existing sectional balance be upset but also a precedent would be established which, in the future, would still further increase the political power of the South.

In the North the most active antislavery people were well-to-do philanthropists and reformers who generally supported the Federalist party. They opposed the extension of slavery on both humanitarian and political grounds. On the eve of the dispute over Missouri the Manumission Society of New York was busy with attempts to rescue runaway slaves, and the Quakers were conducting a campaign to strengthen the laws against the African slave trade and to protect free Negroes from kidnappers who sold them into slavery. In the South there were still a large number of critics of slavery and its abuses, but here the humanitarian impulse was not reinforced by political interest as it was in the North. Northerners, in particular the Federalists, never tired in their denunciations of the Virginia Dynasty and the three-fifths clause which, they charged, gave the Southern states

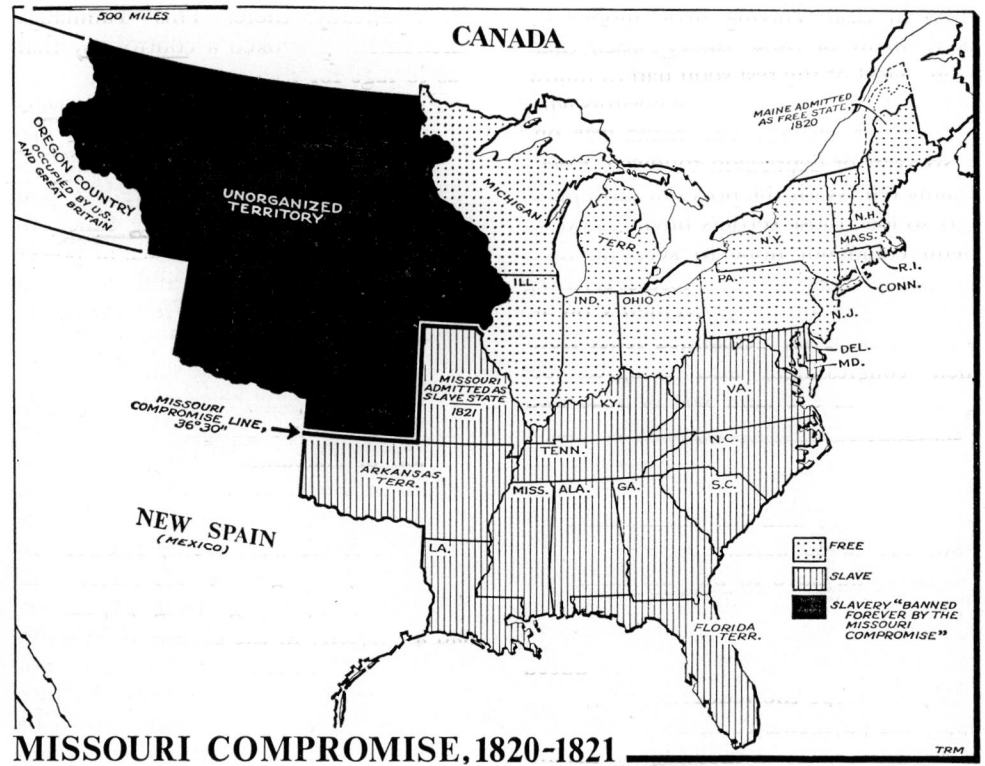

MISSOURI COMPROMISE, 1820-1821

a disproportionate weight in national politics.

Once the Missouri controversy had arisen, it provided the opportunity, which Federalist leaders such as Rufus King had awaited, to attempt a revival and reinvigoration of their party. By appealing to the Northern people on the issue of slavery extension, the Federalists could hope to win many of the Northern Republicans away from their allegiance to the Republican party's Southern leadership. In New York the De Witt Clinton faction of the Republicans, who had joined with the Federalists in opposition to the War of 1812, and who were outspoken in their hostility to "Virginia influence" and "Southern rule," were more than willing to cooperate with the Federalists again. The cry against slavery in Missouri, Thomas Jefferson wrote, was "a mere party trick." He explained: "King is ready

to risk the union for any chance of restoring his party to power and wriggling himself to the head of it, nor is Clinton without his hopes nor scrupulous as to the means of fulfilling them." Though Jefferson himself took a biased, partisan view of the subject, there seems little reason to doubt that some of the Federalists desired to use the Missouri controversy for creating a new, sectional alignment of parties, the North against the South.

The Missouri question soon was complicated by the application of Maine for admission as a state. Massachusetts had consented to the separation of the northern part of the Commonwealth but only on the condition that Maine be granted statehood before March 4, 1820. The speaker of the House, Henry Clay, informed Northerners that if they refused to consent to Missouri's becoming a slave state Southerners would deny the application of Maine. In the House the Northern majority nevertheless insisted on the principle of the Tallmadge amendment, but in the Senate a few of the Northerners sided with the Southerners and prevented its passage.

A way out of the impasse opened when the Senate combined the Maine and Missouri bills, without prohibiting slavery in Missouri. Then, to make the package more acceptable to the House, Senator Jesse B. Thomas of Illinois proposed an amendment prohibiting slavery in all the rest of the Louisiana Purchase territory north of the southern boundary of Missouri (latitude 36° 30'). The Senate adopted the Thomas amendment, and Speaker Clay undertook to guide the amended Maine-Missouri bill through the House. Eventually, after the measure had been broken up into three separate bills, he succeeded. A group of Northern Republicans, some of them suspecting the political designs of the Federalists, voted with the Southerners to make the compromise possible.

The first Missouri Compromise (1820) did not end the dispute; a second compromise was necessary. In 1820 Maine was actually admitted as a state, but Missouri was only authorized to form a constitution and a government. When the Missouri constitution was completed, it contained a clause forbidding free Negroes or mulattoes to enter the state. Several of the existing states, denying the right of citizenship to free persons of color, already had laws against their immigration. Other states, among them New York, recognized colored persons as citizens. According to the federal Constitution, "The citizens of each State shall be entitled to all privileges and immunities of citizens in the several States." This meant that a citizen of such a state as New York, whether he was white or black, was entitled to all the privileges of a citizen of Missouri, including of course the privilege of traveling or residing in the state. The anti-Negro clause was clearly unconstitutional, and a majority in the

House of Representatives threatened to exclude Missouri until it was eliminated. Finally Clay offered a resolution that Missouri should be admitted to the Union on the condition that the clause should never be construed in such a way as to deny to any citizen of any state the privileges and immunities to which he was entitled under the Constitution of the United States. In the circumstances, this resolution was meaningless, yet Clay secured its passage and enhanced his reputation as the "Great Pacificator," a reputation he was again and again to confirm during his long career. Clay's resolution made possible the admission of Missouri as a state, in 1821.

Though the Missouri controversy did not unite the North, as some of the Federalists hoped it would, it made at least a beginning toward the creation of a solid South. At that time the most disaffected of the Southern states was Virginia and not, as later on, South Carolina. The Carolinian Calhoun hailed the compromise as a means of preserving the Union. The Virginian Jefferson looked to the fateful day when the South might have to defend itself in a civil war. In this perspective the subject of education, always one of his chief concerns, became even more crucial. He was afraid that Southern youths attending Northern colleges might be indoctrinated with "lessons of anti-Missourianism." Already the University of Virginia, the favorite project of his old age, was under construction. He hoped that this university, devoting itself to sound Southern doctines, would attract from Virginia and other Southern states a large number of students who otherwise would have pursued their studies in the North. For him, education once had been a means of liberating the human mind; now it became also a means of enabling slaveholders to protect their interests. Henceforth, in the South, the liberal and equalitarian philosophy which we think of as Jeffersonian declined in popularity and respect. Jefferson himself,

THE UNIVERSITY OF VIRGINIA. The campus and its buildings, at Charlottesville, were designed by Thomas Jefferson. From his hilltop home, "Monticello" (right of center, in the distance), he watched with a telescope the construction of the university, 1819–1825. The large building, the "Rotunda," contained the library and classrooms. On both sides of the "Lawn," fronting the Rotunda, are rows of dwellings for professors and students. In planning a curriculum for the university, Jefferson was concerned lest the "poison" of improper political doctrines be diffused among the students. He undertook to prevent this, not by proscribing books and ideas he disliked, but by prescribing certain works that he considered basic to an understanding of American government—essays on government by the Englishmen John Locke and Algernon Sidney; and the Declaration of Independence, *The Federalist*, the Virginia Resolutions of 1799, and George Washington's Farewell Address. (COURTESY OF HENRY SHAW NEWMAN, THE OLD PRINT SHOP, NEW YORK)

in response to the Missouri controversy, had done much toward launching the new conservative trend.

Marshall and the Court

While the divisive spirit of sectionalism came to a head in the Missouri controversy, the national pride inspired by Andrew Jackson's glorious victory at the close of the War of 1812 did not entirely disappear. The ideals of nationalism were not dead, and they were vigorously reasserted by the Supreme Court under the Federalist John Marshall, himself a Virginian.

Marshall remained as Chief Justice for almost thirty-five years, from 1801 to 1835. During these years Republican Presidents filled vacancies with Republican justices, one after another, and yet Marshall continued to carry a majority with him in most of the Court's decisions. He was a man of practical and penetrating mind, of persuasive and winning personality, and of strong will. The members of the Court boarded together, without their families, during the winter months when

JOHN MARSHALL. "Marshall is of a tall, slender figure, not graceful or imposing, but erect and steady. . . . I love his laugh, it is too hearty for an intriguer; and his good temper and unwearied patience are equally agreeable on the bench and in the study." Thus, about 1810, wrote the young lawyer Joseph Story, who later was to be an associate justice of the Supreme Court, the author of *Commentaries on the Constitution of the United States* (3 volumes, 1833), and an outstanding American authority on jurisprudence. In his appraisal of Marshall, the young Story added: "He examines the intricacies of a subject with calm and persevering circumspection and unravels its mysteries with irresistible acuteness." The portrait was done by Chester Harding, who began as a self-taught, itinerant painter and rose to become one of the most successful American artists of the first half of the nineteenth century. (BOSTON ATHENAEUM)

the Court was in session, and Marshall had abundant opportunity to bring his talents to bear upon his younger associates. He not only influenced their ways of thinking; he also molded the development of the Constitution itself. The net effect of the hundreds of opinions delivered by the Marshall Court was to strengthen the judicial branch at the ex-

pense of the other two branches of the government; increase the power of the United States and lessen that of the states themselves; and advance the interests of the propertied classes, especially those engaged in commerce.

No state, the Constitution says, shall pass any law "impairing the obligation of contracts." The first Supreme Court case involving this provision was that of *Fletcher v. Peck* (1810), which arose out of the notorious Yazoo land frauds. The Court had to decide the question whether the Georgia legislature of 1796 could rightfully repeal the act of the previous legislature granting lands under shady circumstances to the Yazoo Land Companies. In the decision, which was unanimous, Marshall held that a land grant was a contract and therefore, regardless of any corruption involved, the repeal was invalid. This was the first time the Supreme Court had voided a state law on the ground that it conflicted with a provision of the United States Constitution, though the Court previously had declared state laws unconstitutional because they were inconsistent with federal laws or treaties.

Dartmouth College v. Woodward (1819) was an even more famous case concerning the contract clause. The case had originated in a quarrel between the trustees and the president of the college, and it became a hot political issue in New Hampshire when the Republicans championed the president, and the Federalists took the side of the trustees. Getting control of the state government, the Republicans undertook to revise Dartmouth's charter (granted by King George III in 1769) so as to convert the private college into a state university. Webster, himself a Dartmouth graduate, represented the trustees when the case came before the Supreme Court in Washington. The Court, he reminded the judges, had decided in *Fletcher v. Peck* that "a *grant* is a contract." The Dartmouth charter, he went on, "is embraced within the very terms of that decision," since "a grant of corporate powers and privileges is as much a *contract* as a grant of land." Then, according to a later story, he brought tears to the eyes of the justices with an irrelevant peroration concluding: "It is, sir, as I have said, a small college. And yet there are those who love it—" After delaying a year, while some of the justices made up their minds, the Court gave its decision in favor of Webster and the trustees. While the importance of the case often has been exaggerated, it had a significant bearing upon the development of business corporations. It proclaimed the principle that corporation charters were contracts and contracts were inviolable; thereafter the states had to contend against this doctrine in their efforts to control corporate activity.

Did the Supreme Court rightfully have the power to hear appeals from the state courts, as in the Dartmouth College case? The Judiciary Act of 1789 provided that whenever the highest state court decided against a person claiming rights under the federal Constitution, laws, or treaties, the judgment could be reviewed and possibly reversed by the Supreme Court. But Virginia state-rightists denied the constitutionality of the Judiciary Act. They insisted that the federal government, of which the Supreme Court was a branch, could not be the final judge of its own powers, for, they said, it would then be a consolidated government instead of a true federal one such as the Constitution had intended. In the case of *Cohens* v. *Virginia* (1821) Marshall gave the Court's reply to the dissident Virginians. A Virginia court had convicted the Cohens of selling lottery tickets in violation of a state law, and the Cohens had appealed their case under the disputed provision of the Judiciary Act. Though Marshall decided against the Cohens, he did not satisfy the state of Virginia. He affirmed the constitutionality of the Judiciary Act, explaining that the states no longer were sovereign in all respects, since they had given up part of their sovereignty in ratifying the Constitution. The state courts, he insisted, must submit to federal jurisdiction; otherwise the government would be prostrated "at the feet of every state in the Union."

Meanwhile, in *McCulloch* v. *Maryland* (1819), Marshall had confirmed the "implied powers" of Congress by upholding the constitutionality of the Bank of the United States. The Bank, with headquarters in Philadelphia and branches in various cities throughout the country, became so unpopular in the South and the West that several of the states tried to drive the branches out of business by outright prohibition or by prohibitory taxes. Maryland, for one, laid a heavy tax on the Baltimore branch of the Bank. This case presented two constitutional questions to the Supreme Court: could Congress charter a bank and, if so, could one of the states thus tax it? As one of the Bank's attorneys, Webster first repeated the arguments used originally by Hamilton to prove that the establishment of such an institution came well within the "necessary and proper" clause. Then, to dispose of the tax issue, Webster added an ingenious argument of his own. The power to tax, he said, involved a "power to destroy," and if the states could tax the bank at all, they could tax it to death. But the Bank with its branches was an agency of the federal government: no state could take an action tending to destroy the United States itself. Marshall adopted Webster's words in deciding for the Bank.

The case of *Gibbons* v. *Ogden* (1824) brought up the question of the powers of Congress, as against the powers of the states, in regulating interstate commerce. The state of New York had granted Robert Fulton's and Robert Livingston's steamboat company the exclusive right to carry passengers on the Hudson River to New York City. From this monopoly Aaron Ogden obtained the business of navigation across the river between New York and New Jersey. Thomas Gibbons, with a license granted under an act of Congress, went into competition with Ogden, who brought suit against him and was sustained by the New York courts. When Gibbons appealed to the Supreme Court, the justices faced the twofold question whether "commerce" included navigation and whether Congress alone or Congress and the states together could

was the first conspicuous one in which the Marshall court appeared to be on the popular side. Most people, then as always, hated monopolies and he had declared a monopoly unconstitutional! The lasting significance of *Gibbons* v. *Ogden* was that it freed internal transportation from restraints by the states, and thus prepared the way for the unfettered economic

---

MCCULLOCH *v.* MARYLAND

1819

Chief Justice Marshall used the following argument in his decision that a state, such as Maryland, could not constitutionally tax a branch of the United States Bank:

"That the power to tax involves the power to destroy; that the power to destroy may defeat and render useless the power to create; that there is a plain repugnance in conferring on one government a power to control the constitutional measures of another, which other, with respect to those very measures, is declared to be supreme over that which exerts the control, are propositions not to be denied. . . .

"If the States may tax one instrument, employed by the [federal] government in the execution of its powers, they may tax any and every other instrument. They may tax the mail; they may tax the mint; they may tax patent rights; they may tax the papers of the customhouse; they may tax judicial processes; they may tax all the means employed by the government, to an excess which would defeat all the ends of government. This was not intended by the American people. They did not design to make their government dependent on the States."

---

regulate interstate commerce. Marshall replied that "commerce" was a broad term embracing navigation as well as the buying and selling of goods. Though he did not exactly say that the states had no authority whatever regarding interstate commerce, he asserted that the power of Congress in regard thereto was "complete in itself" and might be "exercised to its utmost extent." He concluded that the state-granted monopoly was void.

Here was a grant which neither Marshall nor Webster, Gibbons' attorney, considered as sacred. The decision, the last of Marshall's great pronouncements,

development of the nation. More immediately, it had the effect of helping to head off a movement which was under way for hamstringing the Supreme Court.

For some time Virginia Republicans like Thomas Jefferson, Spencer Roane, and John Taylor of Caroline (a Virginia county) had protested against the views of their fellow Virginian John Marshall. In *Construction Construed and Constitutions Vindicated* (1820) Taylor argued that Marshall and his colleagues were not merely interpreting but were actually changing the nature of the Constitution, which should properly be changed only by the amending process, requiring the approval of three fourths of the states. In Congress some critics of the Court, mostly from the South and the West, proposed various means of curbing what they called judicial tyranny. A Kentucky senator suggested making the Senate, not the Court, the agency to decide the constitutionality of state laws and to settle interstate disputes. Other senators and congressmen introduced bills to increase the membership of the Court (from seven to ten) and to require more than a mere majority to declare a state law unconstitutional. The Court reformers did not succeed, however, in passing any of their various panaceas, and after the *Gibbons* v. *Ogden* decision the hostility to the judicial branch of the government gradually died down, to be revived in later years.

Latin American Independence

To most people in the United States, South and Central America had been "dark continents" before the War of 1812. Suddenly they emerged into the light, and Americans looking southward beheld a gigantic spectacle: the Spanish empire struggling in its death throes, a whole continent and more in revolt, new nations in the making with a future no man could foresee.

Already a profitable trade had developed between the ports of the United States and those of the Río de la Plata in South America, of Chile, and above all of Cuba, with flour and other staples being exported in return for sugar and specie. This trade was small in comparison with that of Great Britain, whose exports to Latin America were several times as large as those of the United States, but the trade was growing steadily and during the depression after 1819 it held up better than business in general did. Presumably the trade would increase much faster once the United States had established regular diplomatic and commercial relations with the countries in revolt.

In 1815 the United States proclaimed its neutrality in the wars then raging between Spain and her rebellious colonies. This neutrality in itself was advantageous to the rebels, since it implied a recognition of them as belligerents, as nations for the purposes of waging war, though not as nations for all purposes. It meant, for example, that their warships would be treated as bona-fide belligerent vessels, not as pirate ships. Moreover, even though the neutrality law was revised and strengthened in 1817 and 1818, it still permitted the revolutionists to obtain unarmed ships and supplies in the United States. It prohibited the purchase of arms or armed vessels and the enlistment of men in this country, but these prohibitions could be evaded and often were. In short, the United States was not a strict and impartial neutral but a nonbelligerent whose policy, though cautious, was intended to help the insurgents and actually did so.

Secretary Adams and President Monroe hesitated to take the risky step of recognition unless Great Britain would agree to do so at the same time. In 1818 and 1819 the United States made two bids for British cooperation, and both were rejected. Finally, in 1822, President Monroe informed Congress that five nations—La Plata (Argentina), Chile, Peru, Colombia, and Mexico—were ready for recognition, and he requested an appropriation for sending ministers to them. This was a bold stroke: the United States was going ahead alone as the first country to recognize the new governments, in defiance of the rest of the world.

Origin of the Monroe Doctrine

In 1823 President Monroe stood forth as an even bolder champion of America against Europe. Presenting to Congress his annual message on the state of the Union, he announced a policy which afterwards—though not for thirty years— was to be known as the "Monroe Doctrine." One phase of this policy had to do with the relationship of Europe to America. "The American continents," Monroe declared, ". . . are henceforth not to be considered as subjects for future colonization by any European powers." Furthermore, "we should consider any attempt on their part to extend their system to any portion of this hemisphere as dangerous to our peace and safety." And we should consider any "interposition" against the sovereignty of existing American nations as an unfriendly act. A second aspect of the President's pronouncement had to do with the relationship of the United States to Europe. "Our policy in regard to Europe," said Monroe, ". . . is not to interfere in the internal concerns of any of its powers."

How did the President happen to make these statements at the time he did? What specific dangers, if any, did he have in mind? Against what powers in particular was his warning directed? To answer these questions, it may be well to consider first the relations of the United States with the European powers as of 1823, and then the main steps in the decision of the Monroe administration to make an announcement to Congress and the world.

After Napoleon's defeat the powers of Europe combined in a "concert" to uphold the principle of "legitimacy" in government and prevent the overthrow of existing regimes from within or without. When Great Britain withdrew from the concert, it became a quadruple alliance with Russia and France as the strongest of its four members. Tsar Alexander I of Russia also sponsored the "Holy Alliance," which eventually was joined by all the European sovereigns except the pope and the King of England, and which was supposed to put into practice the Tsar's rather fuzzy ideal of peace and justice based upon Christian principles. Though the quadruple alliance and the Holy Alliance were separate, most Americans made no distinction between them, commonly referring to the European concert

as the "Holy Alliance." In 1823, after assisting in the suppression of other revolts in Europe, the European allies authorized France to intervene in Spain to restore the Bourbon dynasty that revolutionists had overthrown. Some observers in England and the Americas wondered whether the allies next would back France in an attempt to retake by force the lost Spanish empire in America.

Actually, France was still a relatively weak power, not yet recovered from the long and exhausting Napoleonic wars. Though France disliked Latin American independence, she was willing to accept it as one of the realities of the world, especially if it should result in the creation of monarchies instead of republics. France endeavored to bring about the establishment of pro-French kingdoms in Latin America by means of intrigue, but dared not challenge British seapower with an expedition to subvert the new governments by force.

Russia, the great land power of Europe, lacked naval strength. She desired the friendship of the United States because of her world-wide conflicts with Great Britain. When the Tsar expressed his wish that the United States become a member of the Holy Alliance, Secretary Adams politely let him know that this country could best serve the exalted purpose of the alliance by remaining apart from it. While American pacifists admired the Tsar as a friend of brotherhood and peace, Adams grew sarcastic about the supposedly peace-loving Tsar who sold warships to Spain to assist her war against her revolting colonies. Besides the vague threat Russia offered to Latin American independence, there were other causes of friction between her and the United States. Russia owned Alaska, and Russian fur traders ranged as far south as California. In 1821 the Tsar issued a ukase (imperial order) requiring foreign ships to keep approximately 100 miles from the Northwest coast above the fifty-first parallel. This order perturbed Adams not only because it interfered with the activities of American traders and whalers in the North Pacific but also because it implied a Russian territorial claim which would enlarge the area of Russian America. Adams protested strongly to the Russians. Instead of taking offense, they agreed to negotiate regarding the southern boundary of their possessions. The settlement was not completed until 1824, when the Russians abandoned their claims south of 54° 40', but already in 1823 the negotiations were under way and Russian-American relations were reasonably good.

In the minds of most Americans, certainly in the mind of their Secretary of State, Great Britain at that time seemed a serious threat to American interests. Adams was much concerned about supposed British designs upon Cuba. Like Jefferson and others before him, Adams opposed the transfer of Cuba from a weak power like Spain, its owner, to a strong power like Great Britain. He thought Cuba eventually should belong to the United States, for the "Pearl of the Antilles" had great economic and strategic value and, because of its location, was virtually a part of the American coastline. Adams did not desire to seize the island; he wanted only to keep it in Spanish hands until, by a kind of political gravitation, it should fall naturally to the United States. Despite his worries over the supposed British threat to Cuba, he and other American leaders were pleased to see the rift between Great Britain and the concert of Europe. He was willing to cooperate with her, but only to the extent that her policies and his own coincided in regard to this hemisphere.

These policies did not exactly coincide, however, as was shown by Castlereagh's rejection of the American overtures for joint recognition of Latin American independence in 1818 and 1819, and as was shown again by the American reaction to a British proposal for a joint statement in 1823. That summer, Castlereagh's rival and successor, George Canning, suggested to the American minister in London, Richard Rush, that Great Britain and the United States should combine in announcing to the world their opposition to any European movement against Latin America. Though Rush lacked instructions to act, he was ready to go ahead with Canning on one condition—that Great Britian agree to recognize the Latin American nations as the United States already had done. When Canning declined to promise recognition, Rush wrote home for instructions. During the summer Canning remained eager for Rush's cooperation, but in the fall, having been assured by the French minister that France had no intention of "acting against the colonies by force of arms," Canning suddenly lost interest in his idea of a joint statement with the United States.

Meanwhile the Monroe administration was considering the proposal that Canning earlier had made. Monroe sent the Rush correspondence to former Presidents Madison and Jefferson for their advice, and both of them recommended that Rush be authorized to sign a joint statement with Canning. Adams objected. For one thing, he did not like the statement that Canning had proposed: it included a pledge by Great Britain and the United States that neither of the two would seek further territory in this hemisphere, and Adams did not wish to estop this country from future territorial acquisitions. For another thing, he believed it would be more honorable for the American government to speak out on its own instead of following along like a "cockboat in the wake of the British man-of-war." Actually, when the time arrived for Monroe's message to Congress, the President no longer faced a question of acting with Great Britain or alone. He had the choice of acting alone or not at all, since Canning had changed his mind about cooperation with the United States.

Though Canning's overture led to Monroe's announcement, the message

FOURTH OF JULY, 1819. This public celebration, in Center Square, Philadelphia, was typical of celebrations held annually throughout the country on Independence Day. The painting by J. L. Krimmel shows gaily clad militiamen parading, small boys firing off toy guns, women preparing picnic lunches, and some of the men getting drunk. Over the tent at the left is a portrait of George Washington and a print of the engagement between the *Chesapeake* and the *Shannon* in the War of 1812, with the famous words of the *Chesapeake's* captain, James Lawrence: "Don't give up the ship." (THE HISTORICAL SOCIETY OF PENNSYLVANIA)

was directed against all the powers of Europe, including Great Britain, which seemed at least as likely as Russia to undertake further colonizing ventures in America. The message was intended to head off the threat of European schemes against Latin American independence, but the most serious threat was one of undermining that independence by subtle influences rather than overt military action. The message aimed to rally the people of Latin America to look to their own security. It also aimed to stir the people of the United States. In issuing his challenge to Europe, Monroe had in mind the domestic situation as well as the international scene. At home the people were bogged down in a business depression, were divided by sectional politics, were

apathetic toward the rather lackluster administration of Monroe. In the rumors of European aggression against this hemisphere lay an opportunity for him to arouse and unite the people with an appeal to national pride.

The Heritage of Patriotism

Like the Declaration of Independence, the Constitution of the United States, and the national flag, the Monroe Doctrine has become one of the symbols that unify and inspirit the American people. In Monroe's own time the Fourth of July, another of the symbols of American patriotism, was a far more important holiday than it has since become, and a much stronger bond of union than was his doctrine. Annually recalled with fife and drum and flamboyant speeches, the American Revolution gave the nation a common heritage of heroic memories. The War of 1812 was too recent for the unpatriotic factionalism it had engendered to be entirely forgotten, but the earlier war with Great Britain, as it receded into the past, was more and more surrounded by a haze of heroic legend.

cial guest, and Congress voted him $200,000 and a whole township of public lands. The honors done the distinguished visitor, as Jefferson observed, seemed for the moment to overshadow all questions of politics.

The Revolutionary heritage was most dramatically brought home to the American people by news of the deaths of Thomas Jefferson and John Adams. Jeffer-

---

JEFFERSON AND ADAMS DESCRIBE EACH OTHER

In 1787 Jefferson wrote to James Madison about John Adams, one of God's stewards on earth: "He is vain, irritable, and a bad calculator of the force and probable effects of the motives which govern men. This is all the ill which can possibly be said of him. He is as disinterested as the being who made him: he is profound in his views; and accurate in his judgment, except where knowledge of the world is necessary to form a judgment." Adams was in turn inclined to be rather patronizing toward Jefferson, eight years his junior. In 1809, after the vigorous disputes about policy between the Yankee and the Virginian, Adams wrote to Benjamin Rush: "There has never been the smallest interruption of the personal friendship between me and Mr. Jefferson that I know of. You should remember that Jefferson was but a boy to me. . . . I am bold to say I was his preceptor in politicks and taught him everything that has been good and solid in his whole political conduct."

When General Lafayette revisited the United States in 1824–5, the glorious past was revived as never before. Not only was Lafayette a hero of the Revolution; he was also a leading European liberal and a foe of the Holy Alliance, and recently had congratulated Monroe and Adams for causing the United States to stand forth boldly "as the protecting genius of America." The beloved general toured the East, the South, and the West. Everywhere, without distinction of faction or party, crowds cheered him in frenzied celebrations. He appeared in Congress as an offi-

son, the author of the Declaration of Independence, and Adams, "its ablest advocate and defender" (as Jefferson said), who at one time were bitter political rivals, had become friendly correspondents in their old age. They died on the same day, and that day was July 4, 1826, exactly half a century after the signing of the Declaration of Independence. To some, this appeared to be more than a coincidence, perhaps a sign from God instructing the American people to cherish the nationality their ancestors had so dearly won.

BIBLIOGRAPHY

General accounts are George Dangerfield, *The Era of Good Feelings* (1952); W. P. Cresson, *James Monroe* (1946); and F. J.

Turner, *Rise of the New West* (1906), a classic treatment of the whole period from 1819 to 1829.

On the early Middle West, see L. K. Mathews, *The Expansion of New England* (1909); L. D. Stilwell, *Migration from Vermont, 1776–1860* (1937); A. L. Kohlmeier, *The Old Northwest as the Keystone of the Arch of the American Federal Union* (1938); S. J. Buck, *Illinois in 1818* (1917); T. C. Pease, *The Frontier State, 1818–1848* (1918), dealing with Illinois; J. D. Barnhart, *Valley of Democracy* (1953); and R. C. Buley, *The Old Northwest: Pioneer Period, 1815–1840* (2 vols., 1950).

On the Far West: Cardinal Goodwin, *The Trans-Mississippi West, 1803–1853.* On the Southern frontier: S. W. Martin, *Florida in the Territorial Days* (1944), and Everett Dick, *The Dixie Frontier* (1948). Protection against the Indians is the subject of E. B. Wesley, *Guarding the Frontier: A Study of Frontier Defense from 1818 to 1825* (1935), and H. P. Beers, *The Western Military Frontier, 1815–1846* (1935).

The question of slavery expansion is treated in Glover Moore, *The Missouri Controversy, 1819–1821* (1953); F. C. Shoemaker, *Missouri's Struggle for Statehood* (1916); and A. D. Adams, *The Neglected Period of Anti-Slavery in America, 1808–1831* (1908).

Important studies of diplomacy are S. F. Bemis, *John Quincy Adams and the Foundations of American Foreign Policy* (1949); P. C. Brooks, *Diplomacy and the Borderlands: The Adams-Onís Treaty of 1819* (1939); Dexter Perkins, *The Monroe Doctrine, 1823–1826* (1927); E. H. Tatum, *The United States and Europe, 1815–1823* (1936); C. C. Griffin, *The United States and the Disruption of the Spanish Empire* (1937); A. P. Whitaker, *The United States and the Independence of Latin America, 1800–1830* (1941); and J. H. Powell, *Richard Rush: Republican Diplomat, 1780–1859* (1942).

Constitutional issues are discussed in A. J. Beveridge, *The Life of John Marshall* (4 vols., 1916–19); E. S. Corwin, *John Marshall and the Constitution* (1919); A. C. McLaughlin, *A Constitutional History of the United States* (1935); and E. T. Mudge, *The Social Philosophy of John Taylor of Caroline: A Study in Jeffersonian Democracy* (1939).

For the development of patriotism, see Merle Curti, *The Roots of American Loyalty* (1946); W. E. Davies, *Patriotism on Parade: The Story of Veterans' and Hereditary Organizations in America, 1783–1900* (1955); and W. F. Craven, *The Legend of the Founding Fathers* (1956).

12

THE TRIUMPHS
OF ANDREW JACKSON

Andrew Jackson dominated American politics for a time. Like a powerful magnet, he attracted some (the majority) of the voters to him, and he polarized the others into a pattern of opposition. Thus, after a brief period of one-party politics, there arose a new alignment of parties— Jacksonians against anti-Jacksonians or, as they were eventually known, Democrats against Whigs. Viewing himself as the true representative of the people, Jackson as President took a decisive part in the major controversies that arose. These concerned the role of the common man in government, the rights of the states and the rights of the Indians, the nullification threat from South Carolina, and the alleged danger to democracy arising from a great financial monopoly, the Bank of the United States.

"Corrupt Bargain!"

From 1796 to 1816, presidential candidates had been nominated by caucuses of the members of each of the two parties in Congress. In 1820, when the Federalists declined to oppose his candidacy, Monroe ran as the Republican nominee without the necessity of a caucus nomination. If the caucus system should be revived and followed in 1824, it would mean that the nominee of the Republicans in Congress would run unopposed, as Monroe had done, for the Federalist party had ceased to exist as a national organization. Several men aspired to the Presidency, however, and they and their followers were unwilling to let a small group of congressmen and senators decide the question.

In 1824 "King Caucus" was overthrown. Fewer than a third of the Republicans in Congress bothered to attend the gathering which went through the motions of nominating a candidate (William H. Crawford) and he found the caucus nomination as much a handicap as a help in the campaign. The rest of the candidates received nominations from state legislatures and endorsements from irregular mass meetings throughout the country.

John Quincy Adams, Secretary of State for two terms, had made a distinguished

ELECTION OF 1824

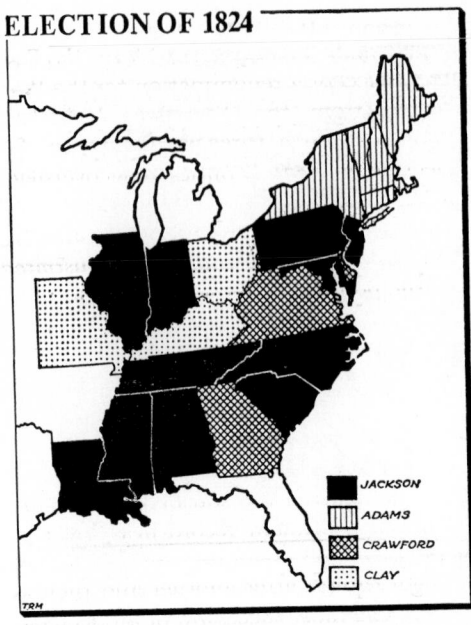

JACKSON
ADAMS
CRAWFORD
CLAY

record in the conduct of foreign affairs, and he held the office that had become traditionally the stepping stone to the Presidency. But, as he himself ruefully realized, he was a man of cold and forbidding manners: he was not a candidate with strong popular appeal. Contending against Adams was the Secretary of the Treasury, William H. Crawford of Georgia, an impressive giant of a man who seemed to have a promising future in national politics. The caucus candidate, Crawford had the backing of the extreme state-rights faction of the Republican party. In mid-campaign, however, he was stricken by a paralyzing illness.

Challenging the cabinet contenders was Henry Clay, the speaker of the House. This tall, black-haired Kentuckian, with his broad smile and his ready handshake, had a personality that gained him a devoted following. He also stood for a definite and coherent program, which he called the "American System." His plan, a familiar one but attractive to citizens just recovering from a business depression, was to create a great home market for factory and farm producers by means of rais-

ing the tariff to stimulate industry, maintaining the national bank to facilitate credit and exchange, and spending federal funds on internal improvements to provide transportation between the cities and the farms.

Andrew Jackson offered no such clear-cut program as did "Harry of the West." Though Jackson had served briefly as a representative in Congress and was a member of the United States Senate, he had no legislative record to run on. Nevertheless, he had the inestimable advantages of a military hero's reputation and a campaign shrewdly managed by the Tennessee politician friends who had put him forward as a candidate. To some of his contemporaries he seemed a crude, hot-tempered frontiersman and Indian-fighter. Actually, though arising from humble backgrounds as an orphan in the Carolinas, he had become a well-to-do planter who lived in an elegant mansion ("The Hermitage") near Nashville and was, at least by his own lights and the standards of the West, a gentleman.

Once the returns were counted, there was no doubt that the next Vice President was to be Calhoun, who ran on both the Adams and the Jackson tickets. But there was considerable doubt as to who the next President would be. In those states where the people chose the presidential electors, Jackson led all the rest at the polls. In the electoral college also he came out ahead, with 99 votes to Adams's 84, Crawford's 41, and Clay's 37. He lacked the necessary majority, however. So, in accordance with the Twelfth Amendment, the final decision was left to the House of Representatives, which was to choose among the three candidates with the highest electoral vote. Clay, for all his charm, was out of the running.

If Clay, in 1825, could not be President he could at least be President-maker, and perhaps he could lay the ground for his own election later on. As speaker, he was in a strategic position for influencing the decision of the House of Representatives.

n deciding among the three leading candidates, the House was to vote by states,
he delegation from each state casting one
ote. Clay, as the winner of the recent
election in Kentucky, Ohio, and Missouri,
could swing the congressional delegations
of those three states at least.

Before Congress got around to making
he decision, the friends of Jackson, Craw-
ord, and Adams approached Clay in behalf of their respective candidates. To
which of the three should he give his support? Jackson's followers insisted that
ackson, with his popular and electoral
pluralities, was really the people's choice
nd that Congress had no rightful alterna-
ive but to ratify the people's will. But
ackson was Clay's most dangerous rival
or the political affections of the West,
nd he could not be depended upon to
champion Clay's legislative program.
Crawford was out of the question, for he
was now a paralytic, incapable of discharg-
ng the duties of the Presidency. Only
Adams was left. Personally, he was no
riend of Clay and had clashed with him
repeatedly, when both were peace delegates at Ghent, and afterward. Politically,
however, Adams was similar to Clay in
cherishing nationalistic principles such as
hose of the "American System." Finally
Clay gave his support to Adams, and the
House elected him.

The Jacksonians were angry enough at
his, but they became far angrier when the
new President made known his appointments. Clay was to be the Secretary of
State! The State Department being the
well established route to the Presidency,
Adams thus appeared to be naming Clay
as his own successor. The two must have
greed to make each other President—
Adams now, Clay next—or so the Jackso-
ians exclaimed, and they pretended to
be horrified by this "corrupt bargain."
Very likely there had been some sort of
understanding, and though there was
nothing improper in it, it proved to be
politically unwise for both Adams and
Clay.

Soon after Adams's inauguration as
President, Jackson resigned from the Senate to accept a renomination for the Presidency from the Tennessee legislature
and to begin a three-year campaign for
election in 1828. Politics now overshadowed everything else. Throughout his
term in the White House, Adams and his
policies were to be thoroughly frustrated
by the political bitterness arising from the
"corrupt bargain."

The Second President Adams

The career of John Quincy Adams di-
vides naturally into three parts. In the first
part, as befitted the son of John Adams,
he made a brilliant record in diplomacy,
serving as the American minister in one
foreign capital after another and then as
one of the most successful of all Secretaries of State. In the second phase of his career, as President (1825–9), he endured
four ineffectual years which amounted to
a mere interlude between the periods of
his greatness. In the third, as a congressman from Massachusetts, he served his
constituents and the nation with high distinction, gaining fame as "Old Man Eloquent," the foremost congressional champion of free speech. His frustration in the
White House shows that the Presidency
demands more than exceptional ability
and high-mindedness, for John Quincy
Adams possessed both. The Presidency
also requires political skill and political
luck, and these he did not have.

In his inaugural address and in his first
message to Congress he boldly stated a
broad conception of the powers and duties of the federal government. He recommended "laws promoting the improvement of agriculture, commerce, and manufactures, the cultivation of the mechanic
and of the elegant arts, the advancement
of literature, and the progress of the
sciences, ornamental and profound." He
had no chance of getting an appropriation from Congress to improve the minds
of his countrymen. The most he could

JOHN QUINCY ADAMS. Adams was a handsome youth of about twenty-eight when John Singleton Copley painted this portrait of him, in 1795. By the time he became President, Adams was a balding, watery-eyed, rather unprepossessing though highly intelligent man of nearly sixty. A hard, conscientious worker, he rose at four in the morn- and built a fire before the White House servants were up. Then he made a long entry in his diary for the previous day. He wrote so much that he suffered from paralyzing writer's cramps; finally he taught himself to use his left hand so as to relieve his right. Occasionally, in the early morning, he swam, nude, in the Potomac River. Once his boat overturned with his clothes, and he hid in the shrubbery along the bank while his servant fetched a dry outfit. (COURTESY, MUSEUM OF FINE ARTS, BOSTON)

get was a few million dollars for improving rivers and harbors and for extending the National Road westward from Wheeling. This amount was more than Congress had appropriated for internal improvements under all his predecessors together, but it was far less than he hoped for.

Even in the field of diplomacy, where Adams had more experience than any other President before or since, he failed in the major efforts of his administration. Yielding to Secretary of State Clay's wish for cooperation with the Latin American

governments, Adams appointed two dele gates to attend an international confe ence which the Venezuelan liberator, S mon Bolívar, had called to meet at Par ama in 1826. Objections arose in Congre for two reasons. One was that Southerne hated to think of white Americans min gling in Panama with colored delegate from Haiti, the independence of whic the United States refused to recogniz The other reason for obstruction was sim ply politics—the determination of Jackso nians to discredit the administration They charged that Adams aimed to sacr fice American interests and involve th nation in an entangling alliance. Whi the Jacksonians filibustered, Congress d layed the Panama mission so long that became futile. One of the American dele gates died on the way to the conferenc and the other arrived after it was ove The United States had accomplishe nothing to offset British influence, whic prevailed in Latin America.

Adams was worsted also in a contes with the state of Georgia. That state at tempted to remove the remaining Cree and Cherokee Indians so as to gain add tional soil for cotton planters. The Creek however, had a treaty with the Unite States (1791) which guaranteed them th possession of the land they occupied. new treaty (1825) ceded the land to th state, but Adams refused to enforce th treaty, believing that it had been obtaine by fraud. The Georgia governor defie the President of the United States an went ahead with plans for Indian re moval. At last (1827) the Creeks agree to still another treaty in which the yielded their claims. Adams's stand ha been honorable but unpopular. South erners condemned him for encroachin upon state rights, and Westerners as we as Southerners disapproved of his interfe ing with efforts to get rid of the Indian

Southerners again denounced the ad ministration and its supporters on accoun of the tariff of 1828. This measure orig nated in the demands of Massachuset

nd Rhode Island woolen manufacturers,
who complained that the British were
dumping woolens on the American mar-
et at prices with which the domestic mill-
wners could not compete. Petitioning
Congress, the distressed mill-owners ex-
ected relief from the Woolens Bill of
827. It passed the House but was de-
ated in the Senate when Vice Presi-
ent Calhoun cast his negative vote to
reak a tie. Thus frustrated, the protec-
onists of New England combined with
ose of the Middle and Western states to
ring further pressure upon Congress,
ter getting together in a grand tariff
onvention at Harrisburg, Pennsylvania.
The bill of 1828 contained high duties
ot only on woolens but also on a number
f other items, such as flax, hemp, iron,
ad, molasses, and raw wool. Thus it dis-
leased New England manufacturers, for
would raise the cost of their raw materi-
s as well as the price of their manufac-
red goods A story arose that the bill had
ken its shape from a Jacksonian plot to
nbarrass New Englanders and discredit
dams. The bill related to "manufactures
f no sort or kind but the manufacture of
President of the United States," John
andolph said. Supposedly it was in-
nded to put Adams in a dilemma that
ould lose him friends whether he signed
vetoed it. While some politicians did
e the measure as an electioneering de-
ce, others intended it seriously as a
eans of benefiting the farmers and man-
facturers of the Middle States and the
est.

When the bill was considered item by
em, Southerners voted against reduc-
ons in the hope that some of its outra-
ous duties would so antagonize New
nglanders that they would help defeat it.
ut when it came to a final test, Daniel
ebster voted for it despite its duties on
w materials, and he carried with him
ough New England votes to enable it
pass. Adams signed it. The Southerners,
hose tactics had backfired, cursed it as
e "tariff of abominations."

Jackson Vindicated

By 1828, the Republican party having
split completely, there were again two parties in the campaign—the Adamsites, who
called themselves National Republicans,
and the Jacksonians, who took the name
of Democratic Republicans. Adams himself once had been a Federalist, and most
of the old Federalists joined his party,
though some became followers of Jackson.

Issues figured little in the campaign of
1828, though much was said about the
"corrupt bargain" and something was said
about the West Indian trade and the "tariff of abominations." Regarding the tariff,
Adams was on record, having signed the
abominations bill, but nobody knew exactly where Jackson stood. Again, as in
1824, more was made of personalities than
of policies, and this time there was far
worse mudslinging than ever before. Indeed, one would have thought that two
criminals were running for the highest office in the land.

As for Adams, the Jacksonians charged
that as President he had been guilty of
gross waste and extravagance, using public
funds to buy gambling devices (a chess set
and a billiard table) for the White House.
But that was not the worst of Adams's alleged crimes. Once, as minister to Russia,
he had tried to procure a beautiful American girl for the sinful pleasures of the Tsar,
or so the Jacksonians said. Of course, these
charges were wholly false. Indeed, they
were fantastic things to say about a man
as conscientious and puritanical as John
Quincy Adams.

As for Jackson, the Adamsites had accusations even worse. He was a murderer
and an adulterer, according to the
speeches, handbills, and pamphlets of his
party foes. A "coffin handbill" listed
within coffin-shaped outlines the names
of militiamen whom Jackson was said to
have shot in cold blood during the War of
1812. Actually, these men had been deserters who were executed after due sentence by a court martial. It was also ru-

ELECTION OF 1828

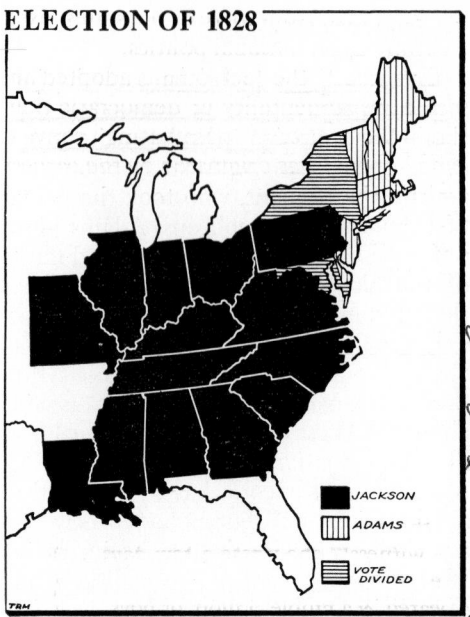

JACKSON

ADAMS

VOTE DIVIDED

TBM

"It was a proud day for the people," one of the Jacksonians, Amos Kendall, reported to his newspaper in Kentucky, "General Jackson is *their own* president." But most old Federalists and all lovers of political decorum were horrified. John Marshall's friend and colleague Justice Joseph Story disgustedly remarked: "The reign of King 'Mob' seemed triumphant." Though the new President was no democratic philosopher like Jefferson, he nevertheless held certain democratic convictions, notably the conviction that government should offer "equal protection and equal benefits" to all the people. His enemies denied that he ever really championed the people's cause, but they could not well deny that he became a living symbol of democracy or that, far more than any of his predecessors, he gave a sense of participation in government to the common man.

mored that Jackson knowingly had lived in sin with the wife of another man. Actually, he had married the woman, his beloved Rachel, at a time when the pair honestly though mistakenly supposed her first husband had divorced her.

Though the majority voted for Jackson, a large minority (44 per cent) favored Adams, who received all but one of the electoral votes from New England, all from New Jersey and Delaware, and some from New York and Maryland. These totaled only 83, however, as compared with 178 for Jackson, who carried the rest of the country. His victory was decisive enough, even though not quite so sweeping as it seemed. In the eyes of his followers, he—and they—were vindicated in their claim that he had been wrongfully deprived of the Presidency in 1825.

On March 4, 1829, unprecedented thousands of Americans attended the inaugural ceremonies at the Capitol, and then the noisy crowd followed their hero to the White House, where at a public reception they trampled one another and even the elegantly upholstered sofas and chairs in their eagerness to shake his hand.

As President, Jackson promptly set about to "reform" the personnel procedures of the federal government. For a generation, ever since the downfall of the Federalists in 1800, there had been no complete party turnover in Washington. Officeholders accordingly stayed on year after year and election after election, many of them growing gray and some of them growing corrupt in office. "Office is considered as a species of property," Jackson told Congress, "and government rather as a means of promoting individual interests than as an instrument created solely for the service of the people." He believed that official duties could be made "so plain and simple that men of intelligence may readily qualify themselves for their performance." According to him, offices belonged to the people, not to the entrenched officeholders. Or, as one of his henchmen, William L. Marcy of New York, more cynically put it, "To the victors belong the spoils."

A corollary to the spoils system was the doctrine of rotation in office. Since ordinary men ("of intelligence") presumably were fit or could easily be fitted for gov rnment service, and since loyal members of the victorious party deserved government jobs, a particular position should not be held too long by any one person but should be passed around, or rotated, among several deserving applicants.

In actual practice, Jackson did not make such drastic removals as his partisan critics

spoils system from some of the states, fixed it firmly upon national politics.

Eventually the Jacksonians adopted another instrumentality of democratic politics—the national nominating convention—which was originated by the earliest of the third parties in American history, the Anti-Masonic party. This party was a

---

JACKSON'S INAUGURAL RECEPTION

1829

Andrew Jackson's inauguration impressed a Washington society woman, Mrs. Samuel H. Smith, as a solemn and sublime event. Afterwards Mrs. Smith went with a party of friends to the inaugural reception at the White House. "But what a scene did we witness!" she wrote a few days later, in a letter to an out-of-town relative.

"The *Majesty of the People* had disappeared, & a rabble, a mob, of boys, negros, women, children, scrambling, fighting, romping. What a pity, what a pity! No arrangements had been made, no police officers placed on duty & the whole house had been inundated by the rabble mob. We came too late. The President, after having been *literally* nearly pressed to death & almost suffocated & torn to pieces by the people in their eagerness to shake hands with Old Hickory, had retreated through the back way or south front & had escaped to his lodgings at Gadsby's. Cut glass & china to the amount of several thousand dollars had been broken in the struggle to get the refreshments, punch & other articles had been carried out in tubs & buckets, but had it been in hogsheads it would have been insufficient, ice-cream, & cake & lemonade, for 20,000 people, for it is said that number were there, tho' I think the estimate exaggerated. Ladies fainted, men were seen with bloody noses & such a scene of confusion took place as is impossible to describe,—those who got in could not get out by the door again, but had to scramble out of windows."

---

hen and afterward asserted. During the entire eight years of his Presidency he removed a total of no more than one fifth of the federal officeholders, and many of these he removed for cause, such as misuse of government funds. Proportionally, Jackson dismissed no more of the jobholders than Jefferson had done. Nor did he appoint illiterate coon-hunters or the like to positions requiring special training or skill. The fact remains, nevertheless, that the Jackson administration, adapting the

response to widespread resentment against the secret and exclusive, hence supposedly undemocratic, Society of Freemasons. Feeling rose to new heights when, in 1826, a man named William Morgan mysteriously disappeared from his home in Batavia, New York. Since Morgan had been about to publish a book purporting to expose the secrets of Freemasonry, his friends believed that vengeful Masons had done away with him. The excitement spread, and politicians in New York,

ANDREW JACKSON. Albert Gallatin once described Jackson as "a tall, lank, uncouth-looking personage, with long locks of hair hanging over his face, and a cue down his back tied in an eel-skin; his dress singular, his manners and deportment that of a rough backwoodsman." Yet Daniel Webster considered him very "presidential" in appearance, and many others testified that he could be gentlemanly, distinguished, and even elegant in bearing, though he sometimes pretended to be a half-savage boor in order to get rid of unwelcome visitors. The portrait by Ralph Earl captures Jackson's finer qualities. (COURTESY OF THE MABEL BRADY GARVAN COLLECTION, YALE UNIVERSITY ART GALLERY)

Pennsylvania, and several other states seized upon it to organize a party with popular appeal. The party was anti-Jackson as well as Anti-Mason, Jackson being a high-ranking member of the lodge. In 1831 the Anti-Masons held a national convention in Harrisburg, Pennsylvania, to nominate a candidate for the next year's presidential campaign.

President Jackson took office with no clearly announced program to carry out. His followers—who soon began to call themselves simply Democrats—had interests so diverse that a statement of definite aims would have alienated many of the party at the outset. This is not to say that Jackson himself was wishy-washy or lacking in convictions. Far from it. Besides believing in government by and for the common man, he stood for strong presidential leadership and, while respecting what he considered the legitimate rights of the states, he was devoted to the national Union. He did not hesitate to assert his principles when South Carolina tried to put into effect the nullification (or interposition) theory of John C. Calhoun.

Calhoun: His Theory

At the age of forty-six (in 1828) Calhoun had a promising future as well as a distinguished past. A congressional leader during the War of 1812, afterwards head of the War Department for eight years (making a record that entitles him to rank as one of the few truly great Secretaries of War), then Vice President in John Quincy Adams's administration, he now was running as the vice-presidential candidate on the Jackson ticket, and he could look forward to the Presidency itself after a term or two for Jackson—if all went well.

But the tariff question placed Calhoun in a dilemma. Once he had been a forthright protectionist, coming out strongly for the tariff of 1816, but since that time many South Carolinians had changed their minds on the subject, and so had he.

Carolina cotton planters were disturbed because their plantations did not pay, or at least were less profitable than it seemed they should have been. The whole state appeared to be stagnating, its population remaining almost stationary, its countryside showing signs of ruin and decay. One reason was the exhaustion of the South Carolina soil, which could not well compete with the newly opened, fertile lands of the Southwest. But the Carolinians blamed their trouble on quite another cause—the tariff, in particular the "tariff of abominations," the law of 1828. They reasoned that protective duties raised the prices of the things they had to buy, whether they bought them at home or from abroad, and lowered the price of the cotton they sold, most of which was exported. They had a point: in order to export, a nation has to import, and to the extent that the tariff kept foreign goods out of the United States it also reduced the foreign market for American cotton. Some exasperated Carolinians were ready to seek escape from the hated law through revolution—that is, through secession. Here was a challenge Calhoun had to meet in order to maintain his leadership in the state and make a future for himself in national politics.

Quietly he worked out a theory to justify state action in resisting the tariff law. He intended for this action, if and when it became necessary, to be strictly legal and constitutional, not revolutionary. So he had to find a basis for his plan in the Constitution itself. In his earlier career, as a nationalist, he had said the Constitution was not a thing for logicians to exercise their ingenuity upon, but should be construed with plain good sense. Now he himself resorted to subtle and ingenious logic, discovering implications in the Constitution that were not obvious to everybody —not even to the "father of the Constitution," James Madison, who denounced the Calhoun theory when he heard of it. Calhoun believed, however, that he was following the lines laid down by Madison and Jefferson in their Virginia and Kentucky Resolutions of 1798–9. Indeed, his reasoning was quite similar to theirs, but he carried it farther than they had done, and he provided a definite procedure for state action, which they had not.

Calhoun started his reasoning with the assumption that sovereignty, the ultimate source of power, lay in the states considered as separate political communities. He went on to assume that these separate peoples had created the federal government, through their conventions that ratified the Constitution after it had been drawn up. Putting this in legal terminology, he described the states (meaning their peoples, not their governments) as the "principals," the federal government as their "agent," and the Constitution as a "compact" containing instructions within which the agent was to operate.

From these assumptions the rest of his theory followed logically enough. The Supreme Court was not competent to judge whether acts of Congress were constitutional, since the Court, like the Congress, was only a branch of an agency created by the states. No, Calhoun reasoned, the principals must decide, each for itself, whether their instructions were violated. If Congress enacted a law of doubtful constitutionality—say, a protective tariff—a state could "interpose" to frustrate the law. The people of the state could hold a convention, and if (through their elected delegates) they decided that Congress had gone too far, they could declare the federal law null and void within their state. In that state the law would remain inoperative until three fourths of the whole number of states should ratify an amendment to the Constitution specifically assigning Congress the power in question. And if the other states should ever get around to doing this, the nullifying state would then submit—or it could secede.

The legislature of South Carolina published Calhoun's first statement of his theory, anonymously, in a document entitled *The South Carolina Exposition and Protest* (1828). This condemned the recent tariff as unconstitutional, unfair, and unendurable—a law fit to be nullified. Calhoun had good reason for not wishing to be identified publicly as the author of the document. It was bound to arouse a certain amount of opposition in parts of the country, and of course he hoped to be reelected Vice President and later to be elected President.

After the Jackson-Calhoun ticket had won its victory at the polls, Calhoun was no more eager than before to see nullification put into effect. He waited, hoping that Jackson as President would persuade Congress to make drastic reductions in tariff rates and thus mollify the outraged Carolina planters. It remained to be seen what chance Calhoun would have for the Presidency as Jackson's friend and successor. As soon as the major appointments had been made, he gained an inkling of his importance, or unimportance, in the new administration. He then realized he had a powerful rival for Jackson's favor in the person of Martin Van Buren.

Van Buren to the Fore

Van Buren, about the same age as Calhoun and equally ambitious, was quite different in background and personality. Born of Dutch ancestry in the village of Kinderhook near Albany, New York, he advanced himself through skillful maneuvering to the position of United States Senator (1820–8). He also made himself the party boss of his state by organizing and leading the Albany Regency, the Democratic machine of New York. Though he supported Crawford for President in 1824, he afterwards became one of the most ardent of Jacksonians, doing much to carry his state for Jackson in 1828 while getting himself elected as governor. By this time he had a reputation as something of a political wizard. Short and slight, with reddish gold sideburns and a quiet manner, he gained a variety of revealing nicknames, such as "the Sage of

Kinderhook," "the Little Magician," and "the Red Fox." Never giving or taking offense, he was in temperament just the opposite of the choleric Jackson, yet the two were about to become the closest of friends. Van Buren promptly resigned the governorship and went to Washington when Jackson called him to head the new cabinet as Secretary of State.

Except for Van Buren, this cabinet contained no one of more than ordinary talent. It was intended (as cabinets usually are) to represent and harmonize the sectional and factional interests within the party. No Virginian was included: for the first time since 1789 Virginia provided neither the President nor any of the Secretaries. Friends of both Van Buren and Calhoun were given places. This cabinet was not intended to form a council of advisers: Jackson did not even call cabinet meetings.

Instead, he relied on an unofficial circle of political cronies who came to be known as the "Kitchen Cabinet." Noteworthy in this group were several newspaper editors, among them Isaac Hill, a hunchbacked master of invective from New Hampshire, and Amos Kendall and Francis P. Blair from Kentucky. Blair edited (after 1830) the administration's official organ, the Washington *Globe*. The close-mouthed, asthmatic, "invisible" Kendall was said to be the genius who, behind the scenes, really ran the administration. While doubtless influential, he was no more so than several others, especially Jackson's old Tennessee friend and political manager William B. Lewis, who roomed at the White House and had ready access to the President. Soon to be the most important of all was Van Buren, a member of both the official and the unofficial cabinet.

Vice President Calhoun, to his dismay, saw signs of Van Buren's growing influence when he viewed the division of the spoils. Not only did Van Buren get cabinet places for himself and his friends: he also secured the appointment of his followers to most of the lesser offices. Al-

MARTIN VAN BUREN. As a younger man, Van Buren had the same shrewd, kindly expression as in this picture, taken when he was an aging, retired politician, living as a country gentleman at "Lindenwald," his estate near Albany, New York. The photographer was Matthew B. Brady. As a boy in 1839, when daguerreotypes were first introduced into the United States from France, Brady became interested in the new art, and later he rose to be the foremost American photographer of the nineteenth century. A daguerreotype was made by exposing a silver plate to light and then treating it chemically. In 1855 Brady began using the wet-plate process—glass plates were coated with silver salts and had to be exposed and developed while wet. Though an improvement on daguerreotypy, the wet-plate process required long exposures and cumbersome equipment. Van Buren's picture was taken by this process.

ready, beneath the surface, there was the beginning of a rift between the Vice President and the President. Then Calhoun and Jackson were further estranged, and at the same time Jackson and Van Buren were brought closer together, in consequence of a curious quarrel over a woman and etiquette.

Peggy O'Neil, the bright-eyed, vivacious daughter of a Washington tavernkeeper, was the kind of woman whom men admire and women dislike. Andrew Jackson thought highly of Peggy when, as Senator from Tennessee, he lived at her father's inn, the Franklin House. Jackson's Tennessee colleague and fellow boarder, Senator John H. Eaton, grew extremely fond of her. While still a girl she married a man named Timberlake, who was away most of the time attending to his duties as a purser in the navy. During her husband's absences Senator Eaton squired her about, and after Timberlake's death at sea he took the young widow as his wife, with Jackson's blessing. Washington gossips told and retold scandalous stories about her relationship with Eaton while her former husband had been still alive. All the talk would have amounted to little if Jackson had not appointed Eaton as his Secretary of War and thus made Mrs. Eaton a cabinet wife.

In those days the administration wives considered themselves the elite of Washington society. For this select circle the War Secretary's wife was morally unfit, or so most of the others maintained. Led by Mrs. Calhoun, they snubbed Mrs. Eaton at official balls, refused to call on her, declined to invite her to their homes. Jackson was furious. While his nephew's wife, the mistress of the White House, sided with the offended wives, the President chivalrously took up Mrs. Eaton's cause. His own wife, the dead Rachel, had been slandered by his political enemies, and he was confident that Peggy too was virtuous, an innocent victim of dirty politics. He not only defended her virtue: he demanded that his secretaries and associates concede it and treat her with respect. Even if they had been willing, they had their wives to contend with, and these ladies would not yield. Calhoun, for one, had no choice but to take sides against Mrs. Eaton, which meant taking sides against her champion, Jackson.

With Van Buren the case was different. A widower, without daughters, he had no womenfolk to worry about. From the out-

set he cultivated the Eatons, staged receptions for them, and showed them every courtesy he could. Thus he more and more ingratiated himself with the President.

The Eaton affair dragged on, and finally (1831) Jackson decided to get rid of his uncooperative Secretaries and reorganize his cabinet. Van Buren resigned and so did two of his friends; the others took the hint and submitted their resignations too. Jackson appointed a new cabinet which on the whole was considerably stronger than the first one. Thereafter he relied more on his official advisers, less on the Kitchen Cabinet. As for Van Buren, he was sent to England as American minister, the appointment being made while the Senate was not in session. When the Senate met, there was a tie vote on the question of confirming the appointment, and Calhoun as the presiding officer broke the tie by casting his own ballot against Van Buren. This brought Van Buren home but gave no advantage to Calhoun.

Already Jackson had picked Van Buren for the presidential succession and had marked Calhoun as no friend but the worst of foes. The final break came when Jackson learned the inside story of a Monroe cabinet meeting years earlier. At the time of Jackson's Florida raid (1817) and for a long time afterward he supposed that Calhoun, as Monroe's Secretary of War, had stood up for him when others in the administration proposed to punish him for his action. The truth, as Calhoun's enemies at last convinced Jackson, was quite otherwise.

If there had been only personal differences between the two men, their parting would have been less significant than it actually was. But there were also differences of principle. At the height of the Eaton affair the opposing views of Jackson and Calhoun were dramatically revealed in consequence of a great debate on the nature of the Constitution.

The Webster-Hayne debate, in January 1830, grew out of a Senate discussion of public lands, a discussion provoked when

WEBSTER REPLYING TO HAYNE. Hayne is sitting in the front center, with his hands together. Calhoun, presiding as Vice President, leans intently on his desk, in the shadow at the extreme left. Note the bonneted ladies in the gallery and the page-boy in the left foreground. From G. P. A. Healy's painting, which hangs in Faneuil Hall, Boston. (FRICK ART REFERENCE LIBRARY)

a senator from Connecticut suggested that all land sales and surveys be discontinued for the time being. This suggestion immediately aroused Senator Thomas Hart Benton of Missouri, once Jackson's antagonist in a wild frontier brawl, now the Jacksonian leader in the Senate and a sturdy defender of the West. Always suspicious of New England, he charged that the proposal to stop land sales was intended to keep New England workers from going West and thus to choke off the growth and prosperity of the frontier.

A young, debonair senator from South Carolina, Robert Y. Hayne, took up the argument after Benton. Hayne and other Southerners hoped to get Western support for their drive to lower the tariff, and at the moment they were willing to grant abundant and cheap lands to the Westerners in exchange for such support. He hinted that the South and the West might well combine in self-defense against the Northeast.

Daniel Webster, now a senator from Massachusetts, once had been a state-rights and antitariff man but, like Calhoun, only in reverse, he had changed his position with the changing interests of his section. The day after Hayne's speech he took the floor in an effort to head off the threatened rapprochement of the West and the South and thus to protect the interests of New England, including the tariff interest. Ignoring Benton, he directed his remarks to Hayne and, through him, to Calhoun in the Vice President's chair. He reviewed much of the history of the republic, with occasional disregard for historical facts, to prove that New England always had been the friend of the West. Referring to the tariff of 1816 he said that New England was not responsible for beginning the protectionist policy but had accepted it after other sections had fixed it upon the nation. Then, changing the subject, he spoke gravely of disunionists and disunionism in South Carolina.

Thus he challenged Hayne to meet

him, not on the original grounds of the public lands and the tariff, but on the issue of state rights versus national power, an issue that could be made to seem one of treason versus patriotism. And in due time Hayne, coached by Calhoun, came back with a flashing defense of the nullification theory. It took Webster two afternoons to deliver what schoolboys were afterward to know as the second reply to Hayne. "I go for the Constitution as it is, and for the Union as it is," he declaimed, as he turned to an exposition of the "true principles" of the Constitution. "It is, Sir, the people's Constitution, the people's government, made for the people, made by the people, and answerable to the people." And he meant one people, the whole nation. He concluded with the ringing appeal: "Liberty *and* Union, now and for ever, one and inseparable!"

Calhoun's followers were sure that Hayne had the better of the argument. The important question at the moment, however, was what President Jackson thought, what side if any he would take.

An answer soon was given at a Democratic banquet which was supposed to honor Thomas Jefferson as the founder of the party. At the banquet the friends of Calhoun hoped to build up the alliance of South and West and strengthen his presidential prospects by identifying his principles with those of Jefferson. As was customary at such affairs, the guests settled down after dinner to an evening of drinking toasts. The President, forewarned by Van Buren, was ready with a toast of his own, which he had written down, underscoring certain words. When his turn came, he stood up and proclaimed: "Our *Federal* Union—*It must be preserved.*" While he spoke he looked sternly at Calhoun. Van Buren, who stood on his chair the better to see from the far end of the table, thought he saw Calhoun's hand shake and a trickle of wine run down the outside of his glass. Calhoun responded to Jackson's toast with his own: "The Union—next to our

liberty most dear. May we always remember that it can only be preserved by distributing evenly the benefits and the burthens of the Union."

The Veto, the Indians, and Georgia

Jackson's pro-Union and antinullification feelings, as expressed in his Jefferson's Birthday toast, did not mean that he was opposed to state rights as such. On the contrary, as he had declared in his inaugural address, he believed in none but "constitutional" undertakings by the federal government. During his administration he readily vetoed laws that he thought exceeded the powers originally granted to Congress by the states; in fact, he used the veto more freely than any President before him. And he stood up for state rights when Georgia defied the Supreme Court in dealing with the Indians within its borders.

The Maysville Road Bill (1830) brought on the most significant of Jackson's vetoes. This bill, by authorizing the government to buy stock in a private company, would have given a federal subsidy for the construction of a turnpike from Maysville to Lexington, within the state of Kentucky. The Maysville pike was a segment of a projected highway which was to form a great Southwestern branch of the National Road. Nevertheless, since the pike itself was an intrastate and not an interstate project, Jackson doubted whether Congress constitutionally could give aid to it. Earlier (in 1822) President Monroe, vetoing the Cumberland Road Bill, had declared that the federal government should support only those improvements which were of general rather than local importance, and Jackson then had agreed with Monroe. Now, with Van Buren's assistance, Jackson prepared a veto message based on similar grounds. He also urged economy, denounced the selfish "scramble for appropriations," and stressed the desirability of paying off the national debt.

Though Jackson also refused to sign other appropriation bills, he did not object to every proposal for federal spending to build roads or improve rivers and harbors. During his two terms such expenditures continued to mount, far exceeding those of even the John Quincy Adams administration.

The Maysville veto was not popular in the West, where better transportation was a never-ending demand, but Jackson's Indian policy was wholeheartedly approved in both the West and the South. As an old Indian fighter, Jackson was no lover of the red man, and he desired to continue and expedite the program, which Jefferson had begun, of removing all the tribes to the west of the Mississippi. The land between the Missouri and the Rockies, according to such explorers as Lewis and Clark and Stephen H. Long, was supposed to be a vast desert, unfit for white habitation. Why not leave that land for the Indians? By the Indian Removal Act of 1830 Congress proposed to exchange tribal lands within the states for new homes in the West, and by the Indian Intercourse Act of 1834 Congress marked off an Indian country and provided for a string of forts to keep the Indians inside it and the whites outside. Meanwhile the President saw that treaties, nearly a hundred in all, were negotiated with the various tribes and that reluctant tribesmen along with their women and children were moved west, with the prodding of the army.

In the process of Indian removal there was much tragedy and a certain amount of violence. When (1832) Chief Black Hawk with a thousand of his hungry Sac and Fox followers—men, women, and children—recrossed the Mississippi into Illinois to grow corn, the frontiersmen feared an invasion. Militiamen and regular troops soon drove the unfortunate Indians into Wisconsin and then slaughtered most of them as they tried to escape down the Wisconsin River. Such was the Black Hawk War, in which Abraham Lin-

coln was a captain of militia (he saw no action) and Jefferson Davis a lieutenant in the regular army. More serious was the Seminole War. It began when Chief Osceola led an uprising of his tribesmen (including runaway Negroes), who refused to move west in accordance with a treaty of 1833, and the fighting lasted off and on for several years. Jackson sent troops to Florida, but the Seminoles with their Negro associates were masters of guerilla warfare in the jungly Everglades. Even after Osceola had been treacherously captured under a flag of truce and had died in prison, the red and black rebels continued to resist.

Unlike the Sacs and Foxes or the Seminoles, the Cherokees in Georgia were a civilized people, with a written language of their own (invented by the half-breed Sequoyah in 1821) and with a settled way of life as farmers. Yet the state of Georgia, after getting rid of the Creeks, was eager to remove the Cherokees also and open their millions of acres to white occupation. In 1827 these Indians adopted a constitution and declared their independence as the Cherokee Nation. Promptly the Georgia legislature extended its laws over them and directed the seizure of their territory. Hiring a prominent lawyer, the Cherokees appealed to the Supreme Court. In the case of *Cherokee Nation* v. *Georgia* (1831) Chief Justice Marshall gave the majority opinion that the Indians were "domestic dependent nations" and had a right to the land they occupied until they voluntarily ceded it to the United States. In another case, *Worcester* v. *Georgia* (1832), Marshall and the Court held that the Cherokee Nation was a definite political community with territory over which the laws of Georgia had no force and into which Georgians could not enter without permission.

President Jackson did not sympathize with the Cherokees as President Adams had done with the Creeks. Vigorously supporting Georgia's position, Jackson did nothing to aid the Indians or to see that the rulings of the Supreme Court were carried out. The Chief Justice had implied that it was the President's duty to uphold the rights of the Indians. Jackson's attitude is well expressed in the comment attributed to him: "John Marshall has made his decision; now let him enforce it." The decision was never enforced. After a few years the Cherokees signed a treaty and most of them migrated, some at the point of a bayonet, to what afterwards became Oklahoma. About a thousand fled across the state line to North Carolina, where eventually the federal government provided a reservation for them.

In a sense Georgia nullified federal authority when, proclaiming state rights, she flouted the rulings of the highest court of the United States. In doing so, nevertheless, the state had the backing of the President. But when, in the midst of the Georgia controversy, another state attempted out-and-out nullification of an act of Congress, Jackson reacted quite differently.

South Carolina Interposes

After waiting four years for Congress to undo the "tariff of abominations," the South Carolina followers of Calhoun had little patience left, and they lost that little when Congress denied them any real relief in the tariff of 1832. Though making certain changes in individual rates, the new law did not significantly lower the tariff as a whole.

Some of the South Carolinians now were ready for revolt, and had it not been for Calhoun's program and leadership, they might have taken even more drastic action than they did. Having ceased to be Jackson's friend and prospective successor, Calhoun had come out openly for nullification, elaborated the doctrine further, and induced the extremists to adopt it as their remedy. To nullify or not to nullify —that was the question in the state elec-

tion of 1832. The nullifiers proved to be the majority, but their opponents (who called themselves Unionists) made up a large minority, the vote being approximately 23,000 to 17,000. Without delay the newly elected legislature called for the election of delegates to a state convention. The convention adopted an ordinance of nullification, which declared null and void the tariffs of 1828 and 1832 and forbade the collection of duties within the state. The legislature then passed laws to enforce the ordinance and make preparations for military defense. Needing a strong man to take command at home, and another to present the South Carolina case ably in Washington, the nullifiers arranged for Hayne to become governor and for Calhoun to replace Hayne as Senator. So Calhoun resigned as Vice President.

While the nullifiers prepared for war they hoped for peace. According to the Calhoun theory the federal government had no rightful recourse, and the rest of the states could do nothing except to amend the Constitution. When the theory was put to the test, however, not a single state came to South Carolina's support.

Unofficially the President threatened to hang Calhoun. Officially he proclaimed that nullification was treason and its adherents traitors. Jackson did not confine himself to mere words. Cooperating closely with the Unionists of South Carolina, he also took steps to strengthen the federal forts in the state, ordering General Winfield Scott and a warship and several revenue cutters to Charleston.

When Congress met, the President asked for specific authority with which to handle the crisis. His followers introduced a "force bill" authorizing him to use the army and navy to see that acts of Congress were obeyed. The force bill, like Jackson's proclamation, further antagonized the South Carolina extremists. Violence seemed a real possibility early in 1833, as Calhoun took his place in the

Senate to defend his theory and its practice. He introduced a set of resolutions on the "constitutional compact," then made a speech against the force bill.

Webster's reply to Calhoun (February 16, 1833), if less colorful than his reply to Hayne three years earlier, dwelt more fully and more cogently upon the constitu-

must govern." They pretended to be concerned about minority rights, but did they practice what they preached? "Look to South Carolina, at the present moment. How far are the rights of minorities there respected?" Obviously the nullificationist majority was proceeding with a "relentless disregard" for the rights of the Un-

---

JACKSON'S PROCLAMATION

1832

"Our present Constitution was formed . . . in vain if this fatal doctrine [nullification] prevails. It was formed for important objects that are announced in the preamble, made in the name and by the authority of the people of the United States, whose delegates framed and whose conventions approved it. The most important among these objects—that which is placed first in rank, on which all the others rest—is 'to form a more perfect union.' Now, it is possible that even if there were no express provision giving supremacy to the Constitution and laws of the United States over those of the States, can it be conceived that an instrument made for the purpose of 'forming a more perfect union' than that of the Confederation could be so constructed by the assembled wisdom of our country as to substitute for that Confederation a form of government dependent for its existence on the local interest, the party spirit, of a State? Every man of plain, unsophisticated understanding who hears the question will give such an answer as will preserve the Union. Metaphysical subtlety, in pursuit of an impracticable theory, could alone have devised one that is calculated to destroy it. . . .

"The laws of the United States must be executed. I have no discretionary power on the subject; my duty is emphatically pronounced in the Constitution."

---

tional issues at stake. The Constitution, Webster argued, was no mere compact among sovereign states that might secede at will. It was an "executed contract," an agreement to set up a permanent government, supreme within its allotted sphere and acting directly upon the people as a whole. Webster dismissed secession as a revolutionary but not a constitutional right, then denounced nullification as no right at all. The nullifiers, he said, rejected "the first great principle of all republican liberty; that is, that the majority

ionist minority—"a minority embracing, as the gentleman himself will admit, a large portion of the worth and respectability of the state."

At the moment Calhoun was in something of a predicament. South Carolina, standing alone, itself divided, could not hope to prevail if a showdown with the federal government should come. If the nullifiers meekly yielded, however, they would lose face and their leader would be politically ruined. Calhoun was saved by the timely intervention of the Great Pacificator, Henry Clay. Newly elected to the Senate, Clay in consultation with Calhoun devised a compromise scheme by which the tariff would be lowered year after year, reaching in 1842 approximately the same level as in 1816. Finally Clay's compromise was carried. So was the force bill, on the same day (March 1, 1833). Webster consistently opposed any concessions to the nullifiers, but Jackson was satisfied: he signed the new tariff measure as well as the force bill.

In South Carolina the Convention reassembled and repealed its ordinance of nullification as applied to the tariffs of 1828 and 1832. Then, as if to have the last word, the convention adopted a new ordinance nullifying the force act. This proceeding meant little, since the force act would not go into effect anyhow, the original ordinance (against which it was directed) having been withdrawn. The second nullification was intended to reinforce the impression that Calhoun's program was a success and was still to be reckoned with. Though Calhoun and his followers, having brought about tariff reduction, claimed a victory for nullification, the system had not worked out in the way its sponsors had intended. Calhoun had learned a lesson: no state could assert and maintain its rights by independent action. Thereafter, while continuing to talk of state rights and nullification, he devoted himself to building up a sense of Southern solidarity so that, when another trial should come, the whole section might be prepared to act as a unit in resisting federal authority.

The Bank War

The Bank of the United States, it will be recalled, was a private corporation with a charter from the federal government, which owned one fifth of the stock. It was a monopoly, having an exclusive right to hold the government's deposits. With its headquarters in Philadelphia and its branches in twenty-nine other cities, it

also did a tremendous business in general banking, totaling about $70 million a year. Its services were important to the national economy because of the credit it provided for profit-making enterprises, because of its banknotes which circulated throughout the country as a dependable medium of exchange, and because of the restraining effect which its policies had upon the less well-managed banks chartered by the various states.

Nicholas Biddle, president of the Bank from 1823 on, had done much to put the company on a sound and prosperous basis. A member of an aristocratic Philadelphia family, Biddle was educated at the University of Pennsylvania and thereafter devoted himself to a number of intellectual interests, including poetry. He personally owned a large proportion of the Bank's stock, so much of it that together with two other large stockholders he controlled the Bank. He could and did choose the officials of the branches, decide what loans were to be made, and set the interest rates. For several years after he took charge he made these decisions according, as a rule, to financial considerations. A banker, not a politician, he had no desire to mix in politics. But he finally concluded it was necessary to do so in self-defense when, with the encouragement of Jackson, popular opposition to the Bank rose to a threatening pitch.

Opposition came from two very different groups, the "soft-money" and the "hard-money" men. The former, consisting largely of state bankers and their friends, objected to the Bank of the United States because it restrained the state banks from issuing notes as freely as some of them would have liked, through its policy of collecting such notes and presenting them for payment in cash. These critics of the Bank desired more paper money (that is, banknotes circulating as money), not less. The other set of critics, the hard-money people, had the opposite complaint. Believing in coin as the only safe currency, these people condemned

THE SECOND BANK OF THE UNITED STATES. Architecturally, the home office building of the Bank, in Philadelphia, was an excellent example of the Greek Revival style. In 1818 architects were invited to submit competitive plans for "a chaste imitation of Grecian architecture." William Strickland won the competition with a design modeled on that of the Parthenon of ancient Athens. Benjamin H. Latrobe, who had submitted a similar plan, charged that Strickland had stolen the Latrobe design. After the expiration of the Bank's charter, the building became the Philadelphia Custom House.

all banks of issue—all banks issuing banknotes—whether chartered by the states as all but one of them were, or by the federal government as the Bank alone was.

Jackson himself was a hard-money man. At one time in his life he had dealt in grandiose land and mercantile speculations based on paper credit. Then a financial panic (1797) ruined his business and put him deeply into debt. Thereafter he was suspicious of all banks. After he became President he raised the question, in his inaugural address and in other statements, whether the charter of the Bank of the United States should be renewed. Unless renewed, it would expire in 1836.

To preserve the institution, Biddle began to grant banking favors to influential men in the hope of winning them to his side. At first he sought to cultivate Jackson's friends, with some success in a few instances. Then he turned more and more to Jackson's opponents. He extended loans on easy terms to several prominent newspaper editors, to a number of important state politicians, and to more than fifty Congressmen and Senators. In particular, he relied upon Senators Clay and Webster, the latter of whom was connected with the Bank in various ways—as legal counsel, director of the Boston branch, frequent and heavy borrower, and Biddle's personal friend.

Clay, Webster, and other advisers persuaded Biddle to apply to Congress for a recharter bill in 1832, four years ahead of the expiration date. After investigating

NICHOLAS BIDDLE. Before becoming president of the Bank of the United States, Biddle edited a literary magazine. After failing to get the Bank's federal charter renewed, he secured a state charter from Pennsylvania, but his new bank collapsed during the depression following the Panic of 1837. Biddle died penniless and disgraced in 1844. Without doubt he was a man of unusual ability as a banker, but in his "war" with Jackson he seems to have been misguided, though he has strong defenders among experts in American economic history. This portrait is from a rotogravure after a painting by Thomas Sully, a Philadelphia artist who is best known for his historical canvas, "Washington Crossing the Delaware."

the Bank and its business, Congress passed the recharter bill. At once Jackson vetoed it, sending it back to Congress with a stirring message in which he denounced the Bank as unconstitutional, undemocratic, and un-American. The veto stood, for the Bank's friends in Congress failed to obtain the two-thirds majority necessary for overriding it. And so the Bank question emerged as the paramount issue of the coming election, just as Clay had fondly hoped it would.

In 1832 Clay ran as the unanimous choice of the National Republicans, who had held a nominating convention in Baltimore late the previous year. Jackson,

with Van Buren as his running mate, sought re-election as the candidate of the Democratic Republicans, or Democrats. Still another candidate was in the field, representing a third party for the first time in American history. He was William Wirt, a prominent Baltimore lawyer and man of letters, the nominee of the Anti-Masonic party. Though he preferred Clay to Jackson, Wirt drew more votes away from the former than from the latter, though he did not draw a great many from any source, carrying only the state of Vermont. The legislature of South Carolina gave that state's electoral vote in protest to a man who was not even a candidate, John Floyd, one of Calhoun's Virginia followers. Of the remaining electoral votes, Jackson received more than five times as many as Clay.

Jackson took his decisive re-election as a sign that the people endorsed his views on the Bank of the United States. As soon as the nullification crisis had been disposed of, he determined to strike a blow at this banking "monster," this dangerous money power, as he saw it. He could not put an end to the Bank before the expiration of its charter, but at least he could lessen its power by seeing to the removal of the government's deposits. By the law establishing the Bank, the Secretary of the Treasury had to give the actual order for removing them. When the incumbent Secretary refused to give the order, Jackson appointed a new one, and when this man procrastinated Jackson named a third, Roger B. Taney, previously the Attorney General and a member of the Kitchen Cabinet. Taney was more than willing to cooperate.

With Taney at the head of the Treasury Department, the process of removing the government's deposits was immediately begun. The government stopped putting new funds in the Bank but continued paying its bills by drawing on its existing deposits, which steadily dwindled. Meanwhile the government opened accounts with a number of state banks, depositing its incoming receipts with them. These banks, including one in Baltimore with which Taney himself was associated, were chosen presumably on the basis of their financial soundness but not always without consideration of their political leanings. Jackson's enemies called them his "pet banks." By 1836 there were 89 of them.

The proud and poetic Biddle, "Czar Nicholas" to Jacksonians, was not the man to give in without a fight. "This worthy President," he wrote sarcastically, "thinks that because he has scalped Indians and imprisoned Judges, he is to have his way with the Bank. He is mistaken." Biddle struck back when the Jackson administration began to transfer funds directly from the U.S. Bank to the pet banks. He felt that the loss of government deposits, amounting to several millions, made it necessary for him to call in loans and raise interest rates, since the government deposits had served as the basis for much of the Bank's credit. He realized that, by making borrowing more difficult, he was bound to hurt business and cause unemployment, but he consoled himself with the belief that a short depression would help to bring about a recharter of the Bank. "Nothing but the evidence of suffering," he told the head of the Boston branch, would "produce any effect in Congress."

During the winter of 1833–4, with in-terest high and money scarce, there was suffering indeed, as many businessmen failed and thousands of workers lost their jobs. All over the country, friends of the Bank organized meetings to adopt petitions begging for relief from Congress, petitions which delegates then brought in person to Washington, and which pro-Bank senators or representatives introduced with appropriately lugubrious speeches. But Jackson and the Jacksonians denied responsibility. When distressed citizens appealed to the President he answered, "Go to Biddle."

The banker finally carried his contraction of credit too far to suit his own friends among the anti-Jackson businessmen of the Northeast, and some of them did go to Biddle, a group of New York and Boston merchants protesting (as one of them reported) that the business community "ought not and would not sustain him in further pressure, which he very well knew was not necessary for the safety of the bank, and in which his whole object was to coerce a charter." To appease the business community he at last reversed himself and began to grant credit in abundance and on reasonable terms.

The "Bank War" was over, and Jackson had won it. But, with the passing of the Bank of the United States (in 1836), the country lost an indispensable financial institution. Economic troubles lay ahead.

BIBLIOGRAPHY

S. F. Bemis's *John Quincy Adams and the Union* (1956) continues and completes the biography begun with *John Quincy Adams and the Foundations of American Foreign Policy*. The Adams personality is revealed in *The Memoirs of John Quincy Adams* (12 vols., 1874–1877), edited by C. F. Adams. A one-volume selection from these memoirs is available under the title *The Diary of John Quincy Adams*, edited by Allan Nevins.

Jackson and his times form the subject of many books, among the most important of which are the following: G. G. Van Deusen, *The Jacksonian Era, 1828–1848* (1959); Marvin Meyers, *The Jacksonian Persuasion: Politics and Belief* (1957); C. G. Sellers, Jr., *James K. Polk: Jacksonian, 1795–1843* (1957); J. W. Ward, *Andrew Jackson: Symbol for an Age* (1955); H. C. Syrett, *Andrew Jackson: His Contribution to the American Tradition* (1953); A. M. Schlesinger, Jr., *The Age of Jackson* (1945); Marquis James, *Andrew Jackson: Portrait of a President* (1937); T. P. Abernethy, *From Frontier to Plantation in Tennessee* (1932);

and C. G. Bowers, *The Party Battles of the Jackson Period* (1922).

Other relevant biographical works are *The Autobiography of Peggy Eaton* (1932); Queena Pollock, *Peggy Eaton: Democracy's Mistress* (1931); J. A. Garraty, *Silas Wright* (1949); W. B. Hatcher, *Edward Livingston: Jeffersonian Republican and Jacksonian Democrat* (1940); W. N. Chambers, *Old Bullion Benton: Senator from the New West* (1956); and E. B. Smith, *Magnificent Missourian: The Life of Thomas Hart Benton* (1958).

Sections, sectional issues, and sectional leaders are discussed by a master in F. J. Turner's *The United States, 1830–1850: The Nation and Its Sections* (1935). See also C. S. Sydnor, *The Development of Southern Sectionalism, 1819–1848* (1948); and A. G. Smith, Jr., *Economic Readjustment of an Old Cotton State: South Carolina, 1820–1860* (1958) .

On nullification, consult C. M. Wiltse, *John C. Calhoun: Nullifier, 1829–1839* (1949); Richard Hofstadter, *The American Political Tradition* (1948), the chapter on Calhoun; C. S. Boucher, *The Nullification Controversy in South Carolina* (1916); and Frederic Bancroft, *Calhoun and the South Carolina Nullification Movement* (1928).

Aspects of the Indian problem are treated in H. T. Malone, *Cherokees of the Old South* (1956); A. H. Abel, *The History of Events Resulting in Indian Consolidation West of the Mississippi* (1908); Grant Foreman, *Indian Removal: The Emigration of the Five Civilized Tribes* (1932); U. B. Phillips, *Georgia and State Rights* (1902); and *Black Hawk: An Autobiography* (1955), edited by Donald Jackson.

On the bank question, the most extensive work is Bray Hammond, *Banks and Politics in America from the Revolution to the Civil War* (1957). See also R. C. H. Catterall, *The Second Bank of the United States* (1903); R. C. McGrane (ed.), *The Correspondence of Nicholas Biddle Dealing with National Affairs, 1807–1844* (1919); S. R. Gammon, *The Presidential Campaign of 1832* (1922); W. B. Smith, *Economic Aspects of the Second Bank of the United States* (1953); and T. P. Govan, *Nicholas Biddle: Nationalist and Public Banker, 1786–1844* (1959).

13

DEMOCRACY AND
WHIGGISM

Jackson's admirers (both in his time and afterwards) thought that his presidency signified a rather sudden arrival of democracy in the United States. This was not the case, since essential elements of democracy had long been present. Yet certain extensions of democratic thought and practice preceded, accompanied, and followed Jackson's rise to power, and the Jacksonians generally endorsed and aided these changes. The Jacksonians also made a strenuous effort to arouse and organize the citizens and bring them out to vote. Then, stealing the Jacksonians' thunder, the Whigs in 1840 came into office by stirring up the electorate as not even Jackson had been able to do. This, rather than 1828, was the year of a "mighty democratic uprising." Politicians now developed new techniques of mass manipulation, and politics took on a modern look.

Coming of Mass Politics

When Ohio and other new states in the West joined the Union, they adopted constitutions which gave the vote to all adult white males and allowed all voters the right to hold public office. Thus the new states set an example for the older ones. These older states became concerned about the loss of their population to the West, and they began slowly and haltingly to grant additional political rights to their people so as to encourage them to stay at home. Even before the War of 1812 a few of the Eastern states permitted white men to vote whether or not they owned property or paid a tax. After 1815 the states began to revise their constitutions by calling conventions that served as grand committees of the people to draw up new documents and submit them for public approval. Eventually all the states (some of them not till after the Civil War) changed their constitutions in the direction of increased democracy.

Change was resisted, and at times the democratic trend was stopped short of the aims of the more radical reformers, as, for example, when Massachusetts held its convention in 1820. The reform-minded delegates complained that in the Massachusetts government the rich were better represented than the poor, both because

of the restrictions on voting and officeholding and because of the peculiar system of property representation in the
state senate. The number of senators from
each district of the state depended not

and that "property as such should have
its weight and influence in political arrangement." Webster and the rest of the
conservatives could not prevent the reform of senate representation, nor could

---

AN ARGUMENT AGAINST UNIVERSAL SUFFRAGE

1821

According to the original constitution of New York, the state senate was
elected by owners of land worth at least $250, and the assembly by owners
of land worth at least $50. At the constitutional convention of 1821 the
radicals proposed to abolish all property qualifications for voting. A conservative delegate, James Kent, objected. Then chancellor of the state
chancery court, Kent was one of the nation's foremost legal authorities.
Later he wrote a classic four-volume work entitled *Commentaries on
American Law* (1826–1830). In 1821 he was willing to abolish the property qualification for assembly elections, but he wished to "preserve our
Senate as the representative of the landed interest." He told his fellow
delegates:

"By the report before us, we propose to annihilate, at one stroke, all
those property distinctions and to bow before the idol of universal suffrage.
That extreme democratic principle, when applied to the legislative and
executive departments of the government, has been regarded with terror,
by the wise men of every age, because in every European republic, ancient
and modern, in which it has been tried, it has terminated disastrously,
and been productive of corruption, injustice, violence, and tyranny. . . .

"The apprehended danger from the experiment of universal suffrage applied to the whole legislative department, is no dream of the imagination.
It is too mighty an excitement for the moral constitution of men to endure. The tendency of universal suffrage is to jeopardize the rights of
property and the principles of liberty. There is a constant tendency . . .
in the poor to covet a share in the plunder of the rich; in the debtor to relax or avoid the obligation of contracts; in the majority to tyrannize over
the minority, and trample down their rights; in the indolent and profligate
to cast the whole burthens of society upon the industrious and the virtuous; and *there is a tendency in ambitious and wicked men to inflame these
combustible materials*."

---

upon the number of people in the district
but upon the amount of its taxable
wealth. The reformers urged an amendment apportioning senators according to
population alone. Daniel Webster, one of
the conservative delegates, opposed the
change on the grounds that "power *naturally* and *necessarily* follows property"

they prevent elimination of the property
requirement for voting. But, to the disgust of the radicals, the new constitution
required that every voter be a taxpayer
and that the governor be the owner of
considerable real estate.

In the New York convention of 1821
the conservatives, led by Chancellor

James Kent, insisted that a taxpaying requirement for the suffrage was not enough and that, at least in the election of state senators, the property qualification should be retained. Kent argued that society "is an association for the protection of property as well as of life" and that "the individual who contributes only one cent to the common stock ought not to have the same power and influence in directing the property concerns of the partnership as he who contributes his thousands." The reformers, appealing to the Declaration of Independence, maintained that life, liberty, and the pursuit of happiness, not property, were the main concerns of society and government. The property qualification was abolished in New York.

Other states proceeded more slowly in the broadening of democracy, none of them going to radical extremes. Progress was peaceful, except in Rhode Island. There the constitution was the old colonial charter, little changed, and it disqualified as voters more than half of the adult males of the state. Thomas L. Dorr and his suffragist followers, despairing of reform by legal processes, held a convention of their own, drew up a new constitution, and tried to set up an administration with Dorr as governor. When the existing state government began to imprison his followers he led a band of his men in an attack upon the Providence arsenal (1842). The Dorr Rebellion quickly was put down, yet it hastened the reforms which afterward came in Rhode Island.

In the South reformers criticized the overrepresentation of the tidewater areas and the underrepresentation of the back country in the legislatures. When the Virginia constitutional convention met, in 1829, the delegates from the western counties gained some slight concessions but not enough to satisfy them. Elsewhere in the Southeast the planters and politicians of the older counties continued to dominate the state govern-

ments. In South Carolina there was no popular vote for President until after the Civil War, the legislature keeping to itself the choice of presidential electors. With few exceptions, free Negroes could not vote anywhere in the South.

Nor could Negroes vote in most of the Northern states. Pennsylvania at one time allowed Negro suffrage but eventually (1837) amended the constitution so as to prohibit it. In North and South, women continued to be denied the vote, regardless of the amount of property they might own. Everywhere the ballot was open, not secret, and often it was cast as a spoken vote rather than a written one. The lack of secrecy meant that voters could be, and sometimes were, bribed or intimidated.

Despite the persisting limitations, the number of voters increased far more rapidly than did the population as a whole. In the presidential election of 1824 fewer than 27 in 100 of adult white males voted (though previously, in some of the states, more than 50 had done so). In the election of 1828, the proportion rose to about 55 in 100—more than twice the figure for 1824—and in the elections of 1832 and 1836 the proportion remained approximately the same as in 1828. Then, in 1840, people flocked to the polls as never before, 78 in 100 white men casting their ballots. The multiplication of voters was due only in part to the widening of the electorate. It was due in greater measure to a heightening of interest in politics and a strengthening of party organization. Citizens now were aroused and brought out to vote who in former times had seldom bothered with elections.

Not only did the number of voters increase: so did the number of elective offices in the states. The very first state constitutions had provided for the appointment of high state officials by the governor or by the legislature. The newer constitutions put the election of these officials, including judges in some cases,

ELECTION DAY. Neither sobriety nor secrecy was required at nineteenth-century polling places. Here one citizen takes a drink, while another staggers drunkenly. A voter, sitting on the steps, marks his ballot while another looks over his shoulder. Other voters hand their ballots—which were furnished by the political parties—to a polling official on the porch. From the painting, "The County Election," by George Caleb Bingham. After studying at the Pennsylvania Academy of the Fine Arts and in Germany, Bingham began his career in Missouri, setting up a studio in Jefferson City, then in St. Louis, and finally in Kansas City. His paintings of real-life scenes are noted for their honesty and humor. (COURTESY OF THE CITY ART MUSEUM, ST. LOUIS)

into the hands of the people. Supposedly the people thus were to have increased control over government. Actually, with authority so divided and diffused, it was harder than ever for the people to locate and hold to account the officials responsible for particular policies.

Political parties became more important as both the electorate and the elections grew in number and complexity. Parties were necessary for bringing together voters of diverse interests and providing common goals so that the will of the people could express itself in a united and meaningful way. Parties were necessary also to give central direction to governments made up of independently elected officials. Hence, as the states became more democratic, political organizations within them became more tightly knit. Political machines and party bosses appeared in states which, like New York and Pennsylvania, had large and heterogeneous electorates with a variety of conflicting interests. In New York and Pennsylvania the spoils system was introduced before it was transplanted to the federal government. State jobs were awarded to loyal workers of the victorious party, and job-seeking came to be the motive which held together and inspirited the core of the party membership.

Whigs and Democrats

During the bank war the opponents of Jackson not only formally censured him in the Senate but also denounced him throughout the country for his allegedly high-handed and arbitrary actions. His opponents often referred to him as a tyrant, "King Andrew I," and they began to call themselves "Whigs," after the party which in England stood traditionally for limiting the power of the King.

The Whig party, organized in time for the congressional elections of 1834 and the presidential election of 1836, was a congeries of dissimilar groups. It included the National Republicans who had opposed Jackson in 1828 (some of these were old Federalists, others former Jeffersonian Republicans), and it included also many people who had supported Jackson in 1828 but had turned against him afterward because of his stand on internal improvements, nullification, or the Bank. Some of the Whigs, as in Virginia, were really state-rights Democrats who had broken with the President when he threatened to use force against a sister state, South Carolina. On the whole the new party was strongest among the merchants and manufacturers of the Northeast, the wealthier planters of the South, and the farmers most eager for internal improvements in the West. But the party as a rule did not appeal very strongly to the mass of voters. Throughout its existence of twenty years or so the party was able to win only two presidential elections (1840 and 1848), both of them with military heroes as its candidates.

In Jackson the Democrats had a military hero and popular leader whom no Whig could match. True, each of the two foremost Whigs, Clay and Webster, had a devoted following. The glamorous Clay, "Harry of the West," won friends throughout the country—but not enough friends ever to elect him President, though he was a candidate three times. The eloquent Webster gained fame and respect for his speeches expounding the Constitution and upholding the Union, and some of his businessman admirers thought him a greater man than any President. But his close connection with the unpopular Bank of the United States and his dependence on rich men for his financial support disqualified him in the minds of many voters. He and Clay were bitter rivals, and their rivalry weakened the party, though at times they cooperated in politics. Sometimes associated with them and sometimes opposing them was Calhoun, the third member of what came to be known as the Great Triumvirate. Calhoun did not consider himself a Whig: after his break with Jackson he thought of himself as a no-party man. Nevertheless he joined with Webster and Clay on the Bank issue. One thing the three men and all Whigs had in common: they opposed Jackson and most of what he stood for.

Jackson and his party, in the course of his two presidential terms, developed a fairly definite and coherent political philosophy. The Jacksonians believed in laissez faire. That is, they believed that the government should let economic activities pretty much alone. They proposed the elimination of governmental favors to private enterprise, the destruction of government-granted monopolies and other corporate privileges. Then in theory the people through free and fair competition would be able to take care of themselves, each prospering in accordance with his own labor and skill. The worst of poverty and of social inequality would thus be done away with when the government ceased to help the rich and hinder the poor. While the Democrats did not advocate social revolution, the more radical of them (known as "Loco Focos") maintained that revolutionary violence might unfortunately appear unless economic inequalities were removed.

Calhoun agreed with the Loco Focos that the dangers of class struggle were very real, and he explored the nature and prospects of the struggle more thoroughly than anyone else of his time. Long before Karl Marx and Friedrich Engels published their *Communist Manifesto* (1848) he elaborated a similar view, though he hoped to prevent revolution whereas they intended to hasten it. In his *South Carolina Exposition and Protest* (1828) and in later writings he predicted that capitalist society would tend to divide into only two classes, "capitalists" and "operatives," that the former would expropriate and impoverish the latter, and that a revolutionary crisis would eventuate. "There is and always has been in an advanced stage of wealth and civilization," he insisted (1837), "a conflict between labor and capital." He hoped that the revolutionary danger would cause Northern businessmen to join with Southern planters in self-defense.

Webster, the leading Whig philosopher, stoutly denied the contentions of Calhoun and the radical Democrats. "In the old countries of Europe there is a clear and well-defined line between capital and labor," Webster conceded, but he declared there was no line so "broad, marked, and visible" in the United States. If there was any revolutionary discontent among the American people, he charged, it was due to the policies of the Jackson administration and the clamor of Democratic agitators. He maintained that the people had common interests rather than conflicting ones, at least so long as the government pursued the correct policies. He believed that a wise and active federal government, by stimulating and regulating economic activity through a national banking system, a protective tariff, and expenditures for internal improvements, could assure the economic well-being of all the people and thereby harmonize the interests of every section and class.

Thus both parties thought of themselves as representing the best interests of the whole country, though they differed in their notions of the appropriate means of achieving the general welfare. For the time being the Democrats were in power and so their policies prevailed.

Party feeling affected opinions on foreign as well as domestic affairs. The Whigs opposed Jackson on an issue of foreign policy when he became involved in a dispute with France. A number of American citizens held claims against the French government on account of ships seized or destroyed under Napoleon's decrees before the War of 1812. In 1831 the French government agreed to pay 25 million francs in partial satisfaction of these so-called spoliation claims. The French Chamber of Deputies, however, failed to appropriate money for making the payment. Demanding that France make good its acknowledged debt, Jackson recommended to Congress the confiscation of French property in this country. The French took this as an insult to their national honor and insisted upon an apology. Though he refused to apologize, Jackson explained that he had meant no insult. As if expecting war he asked Congress (1835) for appropriations to build up the navy and the fortifications along the coast. The Whigs, denouncing him as a warmonger, voted against such appropriations. Despite political opposition at home he won a diplomatic victory when the Chamber of Deputies at last provided funds and the debt was paid.

At stake in the party contests of the time were not only issues of foreign and domestic policy but also questions of federal jobholding and other prerequisites of political power. The Democrats had the power and the jobs; the Whigs wanted them. As the presidential election of 1836 approached, the Democrats had the advantages of patronage, Jackson's prestige, and a superior party organization. Jackson, not desiring a third term for himself, was able to choose the President to succeed him. The Democratic convention readily nominated his favorite, Van Buren.

The Whigs in 1836 could boast no such unity and discipline. Indeed, they could not even agree upon a single candidate. Their strategy, master-minded by Biddle, was to run several candidates, each of them supposedly strong in part of the country. Webster was the man for New England, and Hugh Lawson White of Tennessee was to seek the votes of the South. The third and strongest of all the Whig contenders, the one-time Indian fighter and hero of the War of 1812 from Ohio, William Henry Harrison, was counted upon in the Middle States and the West. As Biddle advised: "This disease is to be treated as a local disorder—apply local remedies—if General Harrison will run better than anybody else in Pennsylvania, by all means unite upon him." None of the three candidates could expect to get a majority in the electoral college, but separately they might draw enough votes from Van Buren to prevent his getting a majority. The election would then devolve, as in 1824–1825, upon the House of Representatives, where conceivably the Whigs might be able to elect one of their men.

The three Whigs proved to be no match for the one Democrat. When the returns were in, Van Buren had 170 electoral votes to 124 for all his opponents. Again the South Carolina legislature gave that state's 11 electoral votes to a man who was not a regular candidate—Willie P. Mangum, of North Carolina. One of the Whig leaders of New York, William H. Seward, explained the victory of Van Buren thus: "The people are for him. Not so much for him as for the principle they suppose he represents. That principle is Democracy."

The Panic of 1837

At the time of the election of 1836 a nationwide boom was reaching its height. Canal enterprisers and railroad builders

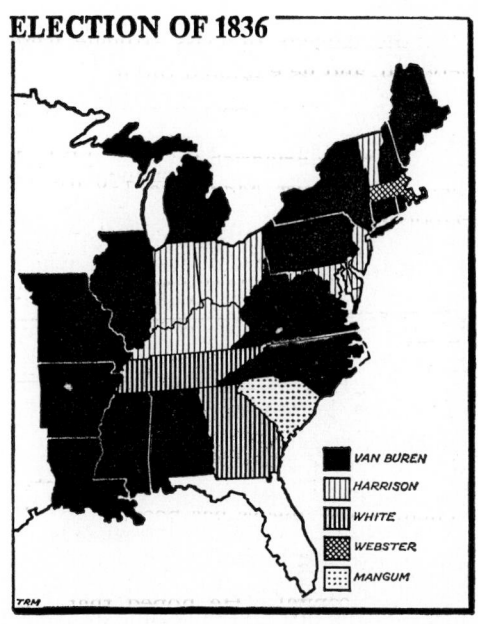

ELECTION OF 1836

VAN BUREN
HARRISON
WHITE
WEBSTER
MANGUM

were busy digging ditches and laying tracks here, there, and everywhere. Prices were high and going higher, as people indulged in an orgy of spending and speculating. Money was plentiful. Much of it came from abroad, English investors buying large amounts of American corporation securities and state bonds. Most of it was manufactured by the banks, which multiplied their loans and notes with little regard to their reserves of cash, until by 1837 bank loans outstanding amounted to five times as much as in 1830. Never had the nation seemed so prosperous.

Land as usual was a favorite speculation, especially the land sold by the federal government. After the act of 1821 had abolished installment buying and set the minimum price at $1.25 an acre, sales of public lands reached an average of 300,000 to 400,000 acres a year in the late 1820's and early 1830's. Then the business suddenly boomed. Between 1835 and 1837 nearly 40 million acres were disposed of, and the expression "doing a land-office business" came into use to describe fast selling of any kind. Nearly three fourths of the land being sold went to speculators—men acquiring large tracts in the hope of reselling at a profit—and only about a fourth of it to actual settlers. Speculators generally borrowed from the banks to make payment at the land offices.

For the time being the government profited. Receipts from land sales, which had averaged less than $2.4 million annually for the ten years preceding 1835, rose to more than $24 million in 1836. This was the government's largest source of revenue, but customs duties under the compromise tariff of 1833 added considerably to total income. The government received more money than it paid out. Steadily the national debt was reduced, as Jackson insisted it should be, and finally from 1835 to 1837 the government for the first and only time in its history was out of debt. Not only that: there was also a large and growing surplus in the federal treasury.

The question for Congress and the administration was how to get rid of the treasury surplus. Tampering with the tariff was not to be considered, since the recent compromise had put to rest that touchy subject and few wanted to reopen it.

Why not give the federal surplus to the states? This would be an effective way of getting rid of it, and the idea appealed to Congress, though the congressmen preferred to think of the distribution as a loan rather than a gift. In 1836 Congress passed and Jackson signed a distribution act providing that the surplus accumulated by the end of the year (estimated at $40 million) be paid to the states in four quarterly instalments as a loan without security or interest, each state getting a share proportional to its representation in Congress. No one seriously expected the "loan" to be repaid. As the states began to receive their shares they promptly spent the money, mainly to encourage the construction of highways, railroads, and canals. The distribution of the surplus thus gave further stimulus to the speculative boom. At the same time the withdrawal of federal funds strained the "pet banks," for they had to call in a large part of their own loans in order to be able to make the transfer of funds to the state governments.

Congress did nothing to check the speculative fever, with which many congressmen themselves were badly infected, Webster for one buying up thousands of acres in the West. But the President was much concerned. Though money continued to pour into the treasury from the land offices, most of it was money of dubious value. The government was selling good land and was receiving in return a miscellaneous collection of state banknotes, none of them worth any more than the credit of the issuing bank. Jackson finally decided to act. He issued his Specie Circular (1836) announcing that in the future only hard money or the notes of specie-paying banks would be accepted in payment for public lands. This was but one sign of trouble ahead for prosperity-crazed Americans. There were also other signs, for those who cared to see them.

As Jackson reached the end of his second term the nation was still seemingly prosperous. On his last full day in office, March 3, 1837, he recognized the independence of Texas (this subject will be treated in a later chapter) and on the following day he saw his hand-picked successor, Van Buren, inaugurated as President. Soon Jackson, justifiably proud of the success of his two administrations, left for the peace and quiet of his beloved home.

Van Buren had been in office less than three months when the panic broke. The banks of New York, followed by those of the rest of the country, suddenly suspended specie payments (that is, they stopped paying cash on demand for their banknotes and other obligations). During the next few years hundreds of banks failed, and so did hundreds of other business firms. As unemployment grew, bread riots occurred in some of the larger cities. Prices fell, especially the price of land, which now became a burden to the recently optimistic speculators, Webster being only one of a great many who all at once found themselves "land-poor." Many railroad and canal schemes were abandoned; several of the debt-burdened state governments ceased to pay interest on their bonds and a few repudiated their debts, at least temporarily. The depression, the worst the American people ever had experienced, lasted for about five years.

The Whigs blamed Jackson for the depression. It had come, they said, because of his destruction of the national bank and his mismanagement of public finance. But they were also in part to blame. The distribution of the treasury surplus was a Whig measure, though Jackson signed it (with the onset of the panic, the distribution was halted before the entire surplus had been transferred to the states). This step, by weakening the pet banks, helped to bring on the crash. So did Jackson's Specie Circular, which started a general run on the banks as land buyers rushed to get cash in return for banknotes to make land office payments. Distribution of the surplus and the Specie Circular only precipitated the depression, however; they did not cause it.

While the Bank of the United States, if continued, could have lessened the overexpansion of credit, a period of financial stringency doubtless would have come anyhow, sooner or later. For the depression was international, affecting England and Western Europe as well as the United States. As English investors faced a financial crisis at home, they began to withdraw funds from America, thus accounting for part of the strain on American banks. A succession of crop failures on American farms not only reduced the purchasing power of farmers but also necessitated imports of foodstuffs; to pay for these imports, additional money was drawn out of the country.

Besides its economic consequences, the Panic of 1837 had other significant results. Hard times increased social, sectional, and economic tensions. Want in the cities heightened the feeling that there existed even in America a real and dangerous class conflict—a struggle between the poor and the rich. Heavy losses suffered by Southern planters confirmed them in their conviction that national policies worked to their disadvantage, while the decline of business profits in the North intensified the belief of manufacturers that the compromise of 1833 must be undone and the tariff raised. Defaults on interest payments and outright repudiation of state bonds, many of them held by Englishmen, added to difficulties in the relations between the United States and Great Britain. Distress among the people was turned into dissatisfaction with the administration, so that the predominance of the Democrats was brought temporarily to an end after Van Buren had served but a single term.

The Van Buren Program

The modern concept that government can successfully fight the onset of depression, and has an obligation to do so, simply did not exist in President Van Buren's time. Nor were there any agencies in the government as it was then organized that could have acted to combat depression conditions. The only tradition of government intervention in economic matters was the Federalist–National Republican– Whig program of aid to business, to which Democrats were fiercely opposed. Consequently Van Buren recommended but few direct antidepression measures. He contented himself with advising Congress to authorize the borrowing of $10 million to meet expenses during the emergency, which advice the legislators agreed to, and he urged that the government should accept only specie for taxes and other due payments, which was hardly a measure calculated to raise either prices or confidence.

In formulating a program of permanent legislation, the administration clearly reflected the wishes of the dominant farmer-labor segment of the party. The President urged Congress to reduce the price of public lands, and he recommended passage of a general pre-emption bill giving settlers the right to buy 160 acres at a set minimum price before land in any particular area was opened for public sale. A bill graduating land prices downward passed the Senate three times but was blocked in the House. A similar fate befell a pre-emption bill. His program of agrarian reform foiled by legislative opposition, Van Buren had to resort to executive action to please his urban followers. By presidential order he established a ten-hour work day on all federal works. For the first time in the nation's history the government had taken direct action to aid the rising labor class.

The most important measure in the President's program, and the most controversial, was his proposal for a new fiscal system. With the Bank of the United States destroyed and with Jackson's expedient of "pet banks" discredited, some kind of new system was urgently needed. Van Buren's fiscal ideas attest both his mental ingenuity and his sincere devotion to Democratic principles. The plan he suggested, known as the "Independent Treasury" or "Subtreasury" system, was simplicity itself. Government funds would be placed in an independent treasury at Washington and in subtreasuries in specified cities throughout the country. Whenever the government had to pay out money, its own agents would handle the funds. No bank or banks would have the government's money or name to use as a basis for speculation. The connec-

tion between the government and the banking community would be broken permanently.

Van Buren placed the Independent Treasury proposal before Congress in a special session called in 1837. It encountered the immediate and bitter opposition of most Whigs and of many conservative Democrats. Twice a bill to establish an independent treasury passed the Senate only to fail in the House. Not until 1840, the last year of Van Buren's Presidency, did the administration succeed in driving the measure through both houses of Congress.

The Log Cabin Campaign

As the campaign year of 1840 approached, the Whigs scented victory. The effects of the depression still gripped the country, and the Democrats, the party in power, could be blamed for the depression. So reasoned the Whigs, who now realized that a party representing the upper income groups must, if it expected to win, pose as a party of the people.

The Whigs also realized that they would have to achieve more unity and a stronger organization than they had demonstrated in 1836; in particular, they would have to settle on one candidate who could appeal to all segments of the party and to all sections of the country. Obviously the easiest way to coordinate the party was through the new mechanism of the national nominating convention, already used by the Democrats. Accordingly the Whigs held their first convention in Harrisburg, Pennsylvania, in December, 1839. Their veteran leader, Henry Clay, "Mr. Whig," expected the nomination, but the party bosses decided otherwise. Clay had too definite a record; he had been defeated too many times; he had too many enemies. Passing him over, the convention nominated William Henry Harrison of Ohio, and for Vice President, John Tyler of Virginia.

William Henry Harrison was a descendant of the Virginia aristocracy, but all of his adult life had been spent in the North-west, where he first went as a young army officer in General Wayne's campaign against the Indians. His governmental experience might have been limited and his military abilities might be questioned, but he was undeniably a renowned Indian fighter (like Jackson) and a popular national figure.

The Democrats, meeting in national convention at Baltimore, nominated Van Buren, pointed proudly to their record, especially the Independent Treasury, and condemned all the works of Whigs, especially the Bank of the United States. Demonstrating that their party was, in some respects, no more united than the Whigs, the Democrats failed to nominate a vice-presidential candidate, declaring vaguely that they would leave the choice of that office to the wisdom of the voters.

The campaign of 1840 set a new pattern in American politics. It inaugurated the circus-carnival atmosphere that would mark presidential elections for years in the future and that would awe or amuse European beholders—vast meetings, shouting parades, party badges and other insignia, and campaign songs.

Throughout the campaign the eager Whigs were on the offensive. They depicted themselves as the party of the people and the party that could save the nation from depression. They said Van Buren was an aristocrat who used cologne, drank champagne, and engaged in other undemocratic and un-American practices. A Democratic newspaper unwisely sneered that Harrison was a simple soul who would be glad to retire to a log cabin if provided with a pension and plenty of hard cider. In a country where many people lived or had lived in log cabins, this was almost handing the election to the Whigs, and they took the cue fast. Yes, their candidate was a simple man of the people, they proclaimed, and he loved log cabins and cider (actually he was a man of substance and lived in a large and well-appointed house).

WILLIAM HENRY HARRISON. At his inauguration Harrison was 68—the oldest man to become President. Although he was an extensive land-owner, he had slipped into debt, and at the time of his election was supporting his family on his income as county recorder. (LIBRARY OF CONGRESS)

Thereafter the log cabin was an established symbol at every Whig meeting, and hard cider an established beverage. Hundreds of Whig orators bragged that they had been born in log cabins or apologized for having been brought into the world in more sumptuous edifices. Thousands of Whig auditors listened to these effusions and happily chanted the songs that turned every Whig gathering into a frenzy of enthusiasm: "Tippecanoe and Tyler too" and "Van, Van is a used-up man." Against such techniques and the lingering effects of the depression the Democrats could not avail. When the votes were counted in November, Harrison had 234 electoral votes to 60 for Van Buren. The Whig victory was not as sweeping as it seemed; of the popular vote, Harrison had 1,275,000 to Van Buren's 1,129,000, a majority of less than 150,000.

Harrison was never to have a chance to demonstrate what sort of President he would have made. Though he seemed to be in good health, he was sixty-eight years old in 1841, and the strain of the campaign and the inauguration and the pressing demands of his office-seeking supporters were apparently too much for him. He contracted a cold which turned into pneumonia, and he died on April 4, 1841, exactly one month after he had been inaugurated—the first President to die in office. In his brief presidential tenure he had looked for advice to the accepted leaders of the party, particularly to Clay and Webster. Webster became Secretary of State, and four of Clay's friends went into the Cabinet. Clay and Webster had expected to guide the old soldier through the political jungle, but now "Tippecanoe" was dead. "Tyler too," a practising politician and a Southern Whig, was in the White House.

Tyler Too

John Tyler was the first Vice President to succeed to the office of chief executive. Though some contended that he was merely the second officer acting as the first, he assumed the title as well as the powers of the Presidency. A member of an aristocratic Virginia family, Tyler had been in politics since he was twenty-one. He had served in both houses of the Virginia legislature, in both houses of Congress, and as governor of his state. In every phase of his long political career he had cast himself in the role of representative of the conservative planter class. He went to Congress as a Democrat, but he left that party in protest at what he considered Jackson's overly equalitarian program and imperious methods. One reason the Whigs put him on the ticket with Harrison was the hope that he would attract the votes of similar conservative former Democrats.

Nevertheless, Clay apparently had the impression that the new President would throw the support of the administration behind a new bank and other Whig projects. But soon Tyler broke with Clay and fought the latter's program, which was also the program of the majority of Northern and Southern Whigs.

At first all seemed to be harmony. Tyler retained Harrison's cabinet, and

---

THE SINGING WHIGS

In the campaign of 1840 the Whigs introduced several political techniques that became standard instruments of democracy—mass meetings, stump speakers, popular newspapers, campaign songs. Harrison was the first presidential candidate to stump the country. A favorite song at Whig rallies ran as follows:

What has caused the great commotion, motion, motion,
  Our country through?
  It is the ball a rolling on.
For Tippecanoe and Tyler too—Tippecanoe and Tyler too,
And with them we'll beat little Van, Van, Van,
Van is a used up man,
And with them we'll beat little Van.

continued the late President's policy of discharging Democrats from government jobs and putting Whigs in their places. In the Senate Clay offered a set of resolutions which he intended as a kind of platform for the party—a program which, if adopted, would keep the party in power. These resolutions declared for (1) repeal of the Independent Treasury Act, (2) the creation of a new Bank of the United States, (3) an increase in the tariff rates, and (4) the distribution of the proceeds of public land sales among the states.

A part of Clay's proposed platform was enacted without causing serious division in the party. With near unanimity the Whigs passed a measure, which Tyler signed, abolishing the Independent Treasury system. Clay's distribution bill, which was more of a personal matter with him than an article of party faith, aroused some opposition. In order to get his pet measure accepted, Clay had to agree to an amendment that distribution would stop whenever it became necessary to raise tariff rates above the 20 per cent level set by the tariff of 1833. Clay hoped that later he could persuade Congress to repeal the amendment; but in this he failed, and his failure hurt him when he took up the tariff issue. Twice he carried the party in Congress with him on bills raising tariffs above the 1833 maximum rates and at the same time retaining distribution. But Tyler refused to accept any combination of distribution and higher duties; he vetoed both bills. He was demanding, in effect, that the party decide for one or the other. Faced by a choice, the Whigs took the tariff. They agreed on a bill, the tariff of 1842, which set the rates at approximately the same level as in the tariff of 1832; since the new rates were higher than those of 1833, distribution was out. Tyler accepted the act but with no great show of enthusiasm.

The Whig legislative program made a bid for the approval of Western settlers and farmers. Between 1836 and 1845 the

JOHN TYLER. Tall, slender, charming in manner, Tyler impressed people in personal intercourse. But in his political dealings he made a host of enemies. Henry Clay in his own time called him a "traitor" to Whiggery, and Theodore Roosevelt in a later age referred to him as "a politician of monumental littleness." His defenders have pointed out that he was a skilled administrator and diplomat. (LIBRARY OF CONGRESS)

West continued its steady expansion. Arkansas became a state in 1836, Michigan in 1837, and Florida in 1845. The greatest rush of settlers was into the future states of Wisconsin, Iowa, and Minnesota. To attract Western voters the Whig leadership put through Congress the Pre-emption Act of 1841, which made it possible for a man to claim 160 acres of land before they were offered publicly for sale and to pay for them later at $1.25 an acre. Sometimes called the "log cabin bill," this measure was hailed by the Whigs as a relief measure for sufferers from the depression and as a proof of their party's devotion to the welfare of the common man.

Though the Whigs enacted a positive program, the results of their success were largely nullified and the unity of their organization seriously threatened by an ugly fight in the party on the big issue of the period: the bank question.

The Whig leadership was committed to restoring a financial system similar to the Bank of the United States. Tyler desired a kind of "state-rights national bank," one that would confine its operations to the District of Columbia and establish branches in the states only with their consent. Apparently sensing that Tyler did not like the idea of a national bank, the leaders framed a measure creating such an institution but tried to disguise it by calling it a "Fiscal Bank." Not deceived, the President vetoed the bill. Thinking they could meet his objections by playing with words, Clay and his colleagues secured the passage of another act creating what they called a "Fiscal Corporation." Again Tyler interposed a veto.

Lacking a sufficient majority to override the veto, the Whig majority knew that their plan of restoring the Bank was dead. They fumed with rage at the President, who added to their anger by vetoing a number of internal improvement bills. In an unprecedented action for a political party, a conference of congressional Whigs, attended by most of the Northern members and a majority of the Southern members, read Tyler, the titular leader of the party, out of the organization. All the cabinet members resigned except Webster, who had some diplomatic business with Great Britain that he wished to settle. To fill their places, the President appointed five men of his own stripe—former Democrats.

A portentous new political alignment was taking shape. Tyler and the small band of conservative Southern Whigs who followed him were getting ready to rejoin the Democrats. When the office of Secretary of State became vacant in 1843, Tyler appointed Calhoun—who had been a Democrat, had left the party in the 1830's, and had become a Democrat again. Into the common man's party of Jackson and Van Buren was about to enter a group of men who had aristocratic ideas about government, who thought that government had an obligation to protect and even expand the institution of slavery, and who believed in state rights with a single-minded, almost fanatical devotion. As the movement of planters into the Democratic party would continue in the years ahead, the character of that party would change; it would become less equalitarian, more conservative, more Southern. Correspondingly, the Whig party would change too, becoming less agrarian and more industrial, less Southern and more Northern. The Tyler administration saw the start of an ominous trend that would result in both parties becoming less national and more sectional.

Webster's Diplomacy

Starting in the late 1830's a series of incidents unfolded that brought Great Britain and the United States into diplomatic controversy and close to actual war. In 1837 rebellion broke out in the eastern provinces of Canada. Many Americans, especially on the northeastern border adjoining Canada, applauded the rebels and furnished them with material aid. Were not the Canadians doing what the Americans had done in 1776? And if they won their independence, might they not wish to join the United States? The rebel leaders retired to Buffalo, New York, where they recruited Americans to their cause and organized raiding parties to cross the Niagara River. To supply their forces over the river they chartered a small American steamship, the Caroline. One night while the ship was moored at a wharf on the American side the Canadian authorities sent over a picked party which forcibly took possession of the Caroline and burned her; in the mêlée one American was killed.

Instantly excitement flared on both sides of the border. President Van Buren issued a proclamation asking Americans to abide by the neutrality laws, and he sent

General Winfield Scott to the border to act as a pacificator. At the same time the President was resolved to uphold American rights. He believed that the attack on the *Caroline* was an utterly indefensible act and a violation of American sovereignty. Through the State Department a protest was delivered to Britain along with a demand for an apology and reparations. The English government, although not upholding the attack, did not disavow it; nor did the British offer to pay the compensation the American government had asked.

While the *Caroline* affair simmered, other troublesome issues arose. One was the question of the Maine boundary. As defined by the Treaty of 1783, this line was impossible to locate. Previous attempts to fix it by mutual agreement and by arbitration had failed. In 1838 Americans and Canadians, mostly lumberjacks, began to move into the Aroostook River region in the disputed area. A head-smashing brawl between the two parties, dignified by the title of the Aroostook War, threatened more trouble between England and America. It was averted when Van Buren sent General Scott to the "war" zone with instructions to stop the fighting. Scott persuaded the Maine and Canadian authorities to withdraw their forces until the boundary could be set by diplomatic negotiation.

Another inflammatory episode involved a Canadian named Alexander McLeod, who was suspected of being a member of the party that had boarded the *Caroline*. Being imprudent enough to enter New York, he was arrested by the state authorities and charged with murder and arson. Immediately the British government reacted with majestic rage. Admitting that the boarding party had been an official one, England contended that McLeod could not be accused of murder because he had acted under orders. The Foreign Secretary, the bellicose Lord Palmerston, demanded McLeod's release and threatened that his execution would bring "immediate and frightful" war. McLeod came to trial in the Tyler administration, when Webster was Secretary of State. Although Webster did not think McLeod was worth a war, he could do nothing to effect his freedom. The prisoner was under New York jurisdiction and had to be tried in the state courts, a peculiarity of American jurisprudence which the British did not seem to understand. Fortunately for the cause of peace —and for himself—McLeod was able to establish an alibi, and was acquitted.

There still remained festering points of disagreement that might produce war, especially with a man like Palmerston in power. England, the leading antislavery nation and hence the leader in the attempt to stamp out the African slave trade, was asking for the right to search American merchant ships suspected of carrying black cargoes. Although the slave trade between Africa and the United States had been closed since 1809, Americans could engage in traffic between Africa and other countries. Moreover, slavers of other nations frequently sought to avoid capture by hoisting the American flag. The British had sought this right for years; always the American government, particularly sensitive on the matter of search of its vessels by England, had refused it. Complicating the situation was a practice in the domestic slave trade in the United States whereby slaves were carried by sea from port to port. Sometimes the ships in this trade were blown off their course to the British West Indies, where the authorities, acting under English law, freed the slaves. In 1841 an unusual incident occurred that aroused widespread anger in the United States, especially in the South. An American brig, the *Creole*, sailed from Virginia for New Orleans with over a hundred slaves aboard. En route the slaves mutinied, took possession of the ship, and took her to the Bahamas. Here British officials declared the bondsmen free. Although Webster protested strongly that the *Creole* had entered the port under compulsion and that hence she was under American law, England refused to return the slaves.

At this critical juncture a new government came to power in Great Britain, one that was more disposed to conciliate the United States and to settle the outstanding differences between the two coun-

lomats had disagreed and to reach a decision through the medium of informal discussions. The result of their deliberations was the Webster-Ashburton Treaty of August 9, 1842.

The most important issue settled by the treaty was the Maine boundary, which was fixed at its present location. By the terms of this arrangement, the United

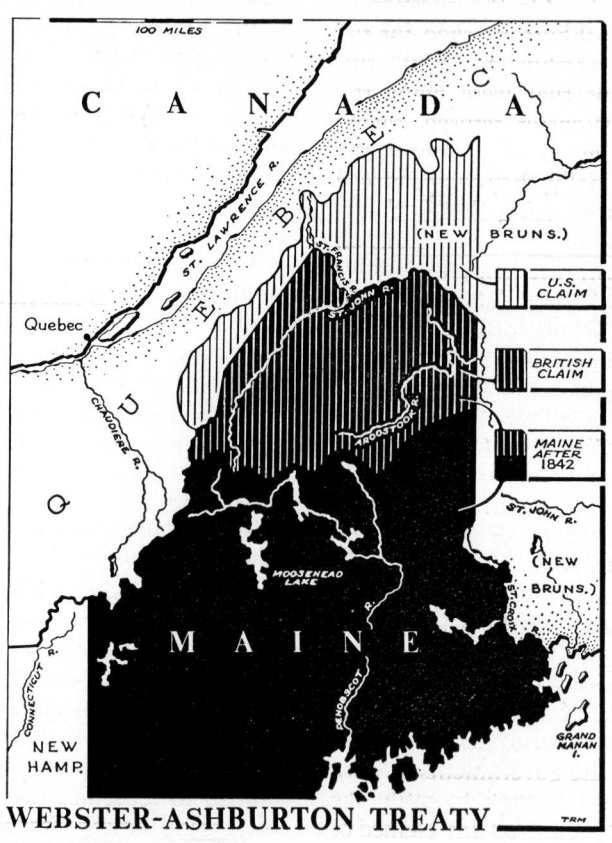

WEBSTER-ASHBURTON TREATY

tries. One of the first acts of the new ministry was to send an emissary, Lord Ashburton, to America to negotiate an agreement on the Maine boundary and other matters. Ashburton liked Americans, and Webster admired the English. Both men sincerely wished to avoid war, and to gain this objective both were willing to compromise. Soon after they met, they agreed to discard most of the documents and data over which previous dip-

States received about seven twelfths of the disputed area, which was about as much as it could expect. Minor rectifications in the boundary were made in the Lake Champlain area and from Lake Superior to the Lake of the Woods. These changes were based upon more recent and accurate geographical information, and were fair to the United States. As a result of Webster and Ashburton's work, the boundary was now established as far west as the Rocky Mountains; only the Oregon country was still in dispute. The negotiators showed no disposition to deal with the knotty Oregon question.

Other issues disposed of by the treaty were the extradition of criminals and the slave trade. One section listed seven crimes for which the United States and Canada would extradite accused citizens of the other country. On the question of the slave trade, Ashburton asked for the right of British warships to "visit" suspected slave ships that were flying the American flag. Webster refused, saying that the right of visit was the same as the right of search. Finally, they compromised the difference by agreeing that both nations would maintain naval squadrons off the African coast, the American ships being charged with the duty of chasing slavers using the American flag.

Through exchanges of notes that were not technically part of the treaty, Webster and Ashburton also eased the memories of the *Caroline* and *Creole* affairs. Ashburton expressed "regret" for the raid on the *Caroline*; he also pledged that in the future there would be no "officious interference" with American ships forced by "violence or accident" to enter British ports—presumably meaning there would be no repetition of the *Creole* episode.

The Webster-Ashburton agreements were the product of reasonable compromise. Although neither country was completely satisfied, the governments of both felt they had won enough to ratify the treaty. The treaty removed any chance of immediate war and eased the way for further agreements in the future.

During the Tyler administration the United States established diplomatic relations with China. The possibilities of the China trade had long attracted the interest of England, whose government resented the restrictions which the weak Chinese government imposed on the economic activities of foreigners. In 1842 Britain forced China to open certain ports to foreign trade. Eager to share the new privileges, American mercantile interests persuaded Tyler and Congress to send a commissioner to China to negotiate a trade treaty. The choice of the first commissioner to China was a fortunate one: Caleb Cushing turned out to be a brilliant diplomat. In the Treaty of Wanghia, concluded in 1844, he secured all the economic concessions which American interests desired. He also persuaded the Chinese to grant Americans the right of extraterritoriality—the right, if accused of crimes, to be tried by American officials rather than by Chinese judges. In the next ten years American trade with China steadily increased.

The Taney Court

Though the Democrats had lost control of the executive branch of the government and were generally a minority in Congress, they had an iron grasp on the Supreme Court. Jackson had been able to appoint seven new justices; thus, of the nine members, seven were agrarian Democrats. And the Chief Justice after 1835, Roger B. Taney, was a Jacksonian of the Jacksonians.

Between the Marshall-dominated Court and the Taney-dominated Court there was no sharp break in constitutional interpretation. But there was a marked change in emphasis. Taney and the majority of his colleagues were moderate agrarian liberals. In general they tended to recognize the right of popular majorities, acting through state legislatures, to regulate private property rights and the activities of corporations. In general, without adhering at all to the doctrines of Calhoun, they were inclined to modify the nationalism of the Marshall Court.

The attitude of the Court was revealed in the case of *Charles River Bridge v. Warren Bridge* (1837). In briefest essence, the background of this case was as follows: one company had a charter from Massachusetts to operate a toll-bridge for

JACKSONIAN JURIST. "The Constitution is gone," wailed Daniel Webster when Roger B. Taney became Chief Justice of the Supreme Court in 1835. Conservatives professed to fear that Taney would plunge the judiciary into radical excesses. Actually, during his twenty-eight years on the Court, the tall, slender Marylander would demonstrate both liberal and conservative qualities. The descendant of an indentured servant who had become a planter, Taney was devoted to the ideals of an agrarian society and a limited national government. But he also believed that the states should act to control the segments of economic power represented by business. (NATIONAL ARCHIVES)

a specified period of years; the legislature authorized another corporation to erect a bridge that would be toll-free; the first company contended that the state's action was invalid because it was a breach of contract. It was the old question— Could a state alter an agreement with a corporation?—which in the Dartmouth College case Marshall had decided against the state. But now Taney, speaking for the Democratic majority, supported Massachusetts. Though he advanced legal precedents to justify the decision, Taney based his position broadly on Jacksonian social doctrine. The object

of government, he said, was to promote happiness, and this purpose was superior to property rights; a state had power to regulate corporations if such action was necessary to achieve the well-being of the community. Although the decision opened the way to increased state control and was wildly denounced by conservatives, it really aided the development of business. Industry was not going to grow if older corporations could maintain monopolies and choke off the competition of newer companies.

Another Taney decision which enlarged state powers was *Bank of Augusta v. Earle* (1839). The question here was whether a corporation chartered in one state could do business in another which wished to exclude it. The Court held that under interstate comity a corporation had a general right to operate in other states, but that a state could, if it wished, exclude a foreign corporation or establish regulations for its entrance. This decision led many states to enact regulatory laws for corporations from other states. In the absence of any federal regulation of interstate commerce, these measures were the only restrictions on companies engaged in business on a regional or on a national scale.

The question of interstate commerce and who was to control it involved issues that bothered Southerners: the domestic slave trade and the rendition of fugitive slaves. A federal law of 1793 placed the responsibility for the return of runaway slaves upon national and state courts and required state officials to help enforce the national law. But as the antislavery movement waxed in strength, some Northern states passed "personal liberty laws" which made it difficult if not impossible to catch fugitives and banned state officers from assisting in their capture. In 1842 the constitutionality of these measures was challenged before the Court in the case of *Prigg v. Pennsylvania*. The court held that the Pennsylvania law was void; no state law could impede the right of an owner to get his property back. But because the enforcement of the fugitive slave clause in the

Constitution was exclusively a federal power, state authorities were not required to aid in the rendition of fugitives.

BIBLIOGRAPHY

Important studies of political and governmental developments include the following: M. Ostrogorski, *Democracy and the Organization of Political Parties* (2 vols., 1902); C. R. Fish, *The Civil Service and the Patronage* (1905); D. G. Fowler, *The Cabinet Politician: The Postmasters General, 1829–1909* (1943); L. D. White, *The Jacksonians: A Study in Administrative History, 1829–1861* (1954); K. H. Porter, *A History of the Suffrage in the United States* (1918); J. T. Horton, *James Kent: A Study in Conservatism, 1763–1847* (1939); Louis Hartz, *The Liberal Tradition in America* (1955); D. R. Fox, *The Decline of Aristocracy in the Politics of New York* (1919); A. B. Darling, *Political Changes in Massachusetts, 1824–1848* (1925); Charles McCarthy, *The Anti-Masonic Party* (1903); R. G. Gunderson, *The Log-Cabin Campaign* (1957); A. C. Cole, *The Whig Party in the South* (1913); E. M. Carroll, *Origins of the Whig Party* (1925); and O. D. Lambert, *Presidential Politics in the United States, 1841–1844* (1936).

Among the relevant biographies, in addition to those cited at the end of the previous chapter, are Holmes Alexander, *The American Talleyrand* (1935), on Van Buren; J. C. Fitzpatrick (ed.), *The Autobiography of* *Martin Van Buren* (1920); C. B. Swisher, *Roger B. Taney* (1935); C. M. Fuess, *Daniel Webster* (2 vols., 1930); R. N. Current, *Daniel Webster and the Rise of National Conservatism* (1955); G. R. Poage, *Henry Clay and the Whig Party* (1936); G. G. Van Deusen, *The Life of Henry Clay* (1937); J. A. Shackford, *David Crockett: The Man and the Legend* (1956); Freeman Cleaves, *Old Tippecanoe* (1939); J. A. Green, *William Henry Harrison* (1941); and O. P. Chitwood, *John Tyler* (1939).

On the boom and the depression, see R. C. McGrane, *The Panic of 1837* (1924); and W. B. Smith and A. H. Cole, *Fluctuations in American Business, 1790–1860* (1935). See also D. R. Dewey, *State Banking before the Civil War* (1910); R. G. Wellington, *The Political and National Influence of the Public Lands, 1826–1842*; and B. H. Hibbard, *A History of the Public Land Policies* (1924).

Foreign relations are treated in J. S. Reeves, *American Diplomacy under Tyler and Polk* (1907); A. B. Corey, *The Crisis of 1830–1842 in Canadian-American Relations* (1941); J. B. Brebner, *North Atlantic Triangle* (1945); Tyler Dennett, *Americans in Eastern Asia* (1922); and F. R. Dulles, *China and America* (1946).

14

THE BROADENING

OF BUSINESS

Americans between the War of 1812 and the Civil War acquired a strong material basis for national unity. Engineers and laborers advanced toward a solution of the transportation problem by building canals and eventually railroads to link the coastal cities with the interior, the East with the West, the North with the South. Merchants widened the scope of their activities till business came to be conducted on a scale more nearly nationwide than ever before. With the continued growth of industry, some workers began to show at least faint signs of self-consciousness as members of a distinct class, with common interests transcending those of their separate localities. The people as a whole, benefiting from the new developments in transportation and production, were able to raise their living standards while steadily increasing in numbers. Material progress prepared the way for their ultimate unification, politically as well as economically (though, as late as 1860, this unifying process had not gone far enough to overcome the divisive forces within the nation).

The People, 1815–60

During the early nineteenth century, as during the whole of American history, three trends of population were fairly obvious: rapid increase, migration to the West, and movement to towns and cities.

Americans continued to multiply almost as fast as in the colonial period, the population still doubling every twenty-five years or so. The total figure, lower than 4 million in 1790, approached 10 by 1820 and rose to nearly 13 in 1830 and to about 17 million in 1840. Between 1850 and 1860 the number increased from approximately 23 million to over 31 million. The United States was growing much more rapidly than the British Isles or Europe; by 1860 it had gone ahead of the United Kingdom and had nearly overtaken Germany and France.

The Negro population increased more slowly than the white. After 1808, when the importation of slaves was made illegal, the proportion of Negroes to whites in the nation as a whole steadily declined. In 1820 there was one colored person to every four whites; in 1840, one to every five. The slower increase of Negroes was due to their comparatively high death rate, not to a low birth rate. Slave mothers had large families, but life was shorter for both slaves and free Negroes than for whites.

The mortality rate for whites slowly declined. Public health improved a little, though epidemics continued to take their periodic toll, among them a cholera epidemic which swept the country in 1832. On the average, people lived somewhat

lation of nearly 13 million in 1830, the foreign-born numbered less than half a million, mostly naturalized citizens. Soon immigration began to grow to new heights, reaching a total of 60,000 for 1832 and nearly 80,000 for 1837. Then, after a decline due to economic depression, the annual numbers rose still higher, an unprecedented flood of foreigners arriving in the 1840's and 1850's.

Since the United States exported more goods than it imported, returning ships often had vacant space and filled it with

LIFE EXPECTANCY

	At Birth		At Age 20	
	Massachusetts			
	Male	Female	Male	Female
1789	34.5	36.5	54.2	54.3
1850	38.3	40.5	60.1	60.2
	U.S. (White)			
1945	64.4	69.5	68.6	72.9

Note: Figures for the United States as a whole are not available for the earlier years. The U.S. figures for 1945 are given for purposes of comparison. The much geater rise in life expectancy at birth than at age twenty reflects the fact that infant mortality was reduced much more than the death rate for those who survived infancy.

longer than in earlier generations. The population increase, however, was due less to lengthened life than to the maintenance of a high birth rate, which more than offset the death rate.

Immigration accounted for little of the population growth before the 1840's. The long years of war in Europe, from 1793 to 1815, had kept the number of newcomers to America down to not more than a few thousand a year, and then the Panic of 1819 checked the immigrant tide which had risen after Waterloo. During the 1820's arrivals from abroad averaged about 14,000 annually. Of the total popu-

immigrants as ballast, so to speak. Competition among shipping lines reduced fares so that, by the 1830's, the immigrant could get passage across the Atlantic for as little as $20 or $30. No longer did he need to sell his services to a temporary master in America in order to pay for the voyage. And so the system of indentured servitude, which had dwindled steadily after the Revolution, disappeared entirely after the Panic of 1819.

From 1840 to 1850 over 1,500,000 Europeans moved to America; in the last years of the decade the average number arriving yearly was almost 300,000. Of the

23,000,000 people in the United States in 1850, 2,210,000 were foreign-born; of these almost a million were Irish and over half a million were Germans. Special reasons explained the prevalence of immigrants from Ireland and Germany: widespread poverty caused by the economic dislocations of the Industrial Revolution; famines resulting from the failure of the potato and other crops; dislike of English rule by the Irish; and the collapse of the liberal revolutions of 1848 in Germany. The great majority of the Irish settled in the Eastern cities where they swelled the ranks of unskilled labor. Not until after 1850, however, when the tide of immigration reached even greater heights, would foreigners outnumber native-born in the labor population. Most of the Germans, having a little more money than the Irish, who had practically none, moved on to the Northwest, where they became farmers or went into business in the Western towns.

The number who came in the fifties exceeded even that of the previous decade, reaching an estimated aggregate of over two and a half million. As before, the overwhelming majority of the newcomers hailed from Ireland and Germany. By 1860 more than a million and a half Irish had migrated to the United States, and approximately a million Germans.

Generally the newcomers, the Irish as well as others, were welcomed in the United States. They were needed to provide labor for building canals and railroads, manning ships and docks, and performing other heavy work essential to the expanding economic system. But the Irish, as Roman Catholics, excited Protestant prejudices in some communities. In 1834 an anti-Catholic mob set fire to a convent in Charlestown, Massachusetts, and the next year Samuel F. B. Morse (who is better remembered as a portrait painter and as the inventor of the telegraph) published his *Foreign Conspiracy*, which served thereafter as a textbook for nativists crusading against what they imagined was a popish plot to gain control of the United States.

Out of these tensions and prejudices there emerged a number of secret societies to combat the "alien menace." Originating in the East and later spreading to the West and South, these groups combined in 1850 to form the Supreme Order of the Star-Spangled Banner. Included in the official beliefs of the order were opposition to Catholics or aliens holding public office and support of stricter naturalization laws and literacy tests for voting. When members were asked to define their platform, they replied, because of the secrecy rule, "I know nothing," and hence were popularly called "Know-Nothings." Soon the leaders decided to seek their objectives by political methods, and formed the American party. In the East the new organization scored an immediate and astonishing success, casting in the elections of 1854 a large vote in Pennsylvania and New York and win-

SOURCES OF IMMIGRATION, 1821–1870

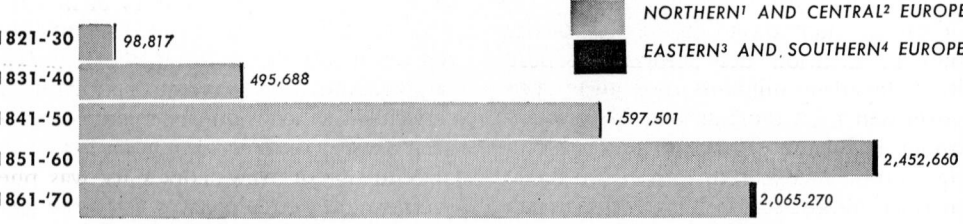

| | NORTHERN[1] AND CENTRAL[2] EUROPE |
| | EASTERN[3] AND SOUTHERN[4] EUROPE |

1821-'30	98,817
1831-'40	495,688
1841-'50	1,597,501
1851-'60	2,452,660
1861-'70	2,065,270

[1] Great Britain, Ireland, Scandinavia, Netherlands, Belgium, France, Switzerland
[2] Germany, Poland, Austria-Hungary

[3] Russia and Baltic States, Rumania, Bulgaria, Turkey
[4] Italy, Spain, Portugal, Greece

ning control of the state government in Massachusetts.

Still, despite the nativist movement, the federal government did nothing to check immigration, and shipowners, employers, and some of the states took measures to encourage it.

The West (including both Northwest and Southwest) continued to grow much more rapidly than the rest of the country. By 1830 more than a fourth of the Amer-

barns left to rot, as its people scattered over the country in search of an easier life than the granite hills afforded.

Not all the migrating villagers and farmers sought the unsettled frontier: some moved instead to increasingly crowded population centers. Cities (considered as communities of 8,000 or more) grew faster than the nation as a whole. In 1820 there were more than twice as many cities, and in 1840 more than seven times

---

URBAN GROWTH

1840–1860

In 1840 the largest cities in the country were in the Northeast and the South. But in the next two decades, as the East became increasingly industrialized, cities there shot ahead of their Southern rivals. The following figures show the comparative rates of growth:

	1840	1850	1860
New York	312,000	515,000	805,000 (1,200,000 counting Brooklyn)
Philadelphia	220,000	340,000	565,000
Boston	93,000	136,000	177,000
Baltimore	102,000	169,000	212,000
New Orleans	100,000	116,000	165,000

The most spectacular population gains were scored by the new Western cities. From 40,000 in the 1830's, Cincinnati climbed to 161,000 in 1860. In the same period St. Louis went from 10,000 to 160,000, and Chicago, astonishing everybody but itself, from 3,000 to 109,000.

---

ican people lived to the west of the Appalachians; by 1850, nearly a half. Some of the seaboard states suffered serious losses of manpower and womanpower, not to mention the personal property that departing migrants took away. Year after year the Carolinas gave up nearly as much in human resources as they gained by natural increase; their populations remained almost stationary. The same was true of Vermont and New Hampshire. Many a village in these two states was completely depopulated, its houses and

as many, as there had been in 1790. While the vast majority of Americans continued to reside in the open country or in small towns, the number of city dwellers increased remarkably. In 1790 one person in thirty lived in a community of 8,000 or more; in 1820, one in twenty; and in 1840, one in twelve.

The rise of New York City was phenomenal. By 1810 it had surpassed Philadelphia, which earlier had replaced Boston as the largest city in America. New York steadily increased its lead in both

NEW YORK PORT, 1828. A view of South Street, from the intersection with Maiden Lane, which got its name from the fact that Dutch washer-maidens in New Amsterdam used to come here to do their laundry in a brook outside of town. The East River docks lined South Street; there were other docks along the Hudson River on the opposite side of Manhattan Island. Below Maiden Lane, the city by 1828 was almost solidly built up. Above the Lane, there were gardens around the houses, and there were vacant lots which in some cases ran out into open fields. Nude boys swam in the East River in summers. The population of the city was approaching 150,000. Note the cobblestone pavement. From a contemporary print. (COURTESY OF THE NEW YORK PUBLIC LIBRARY, STOKES COLLECTION)

population and trade. Its growth was based on the possession of a superior natural harbor and on several historical developments after the War of 1812. After the war the British chose New York as the chief place to "dump" their manufactured goods, and thus helped make it an import center. State laws, which were liberal with regard to auction sales, encouraged inland merchants to do their buying in New York. The first packet line, with regularly scheduled monthly sailings between England and the United States, made New York its American terminus (1816) and hence a more important center of overseas commerce than

ever. And the Erie Canal (completed in 1825) gave the city unrivalled access to the interior.

New Waterways

Despite the road improvements of the turnpike era (1790's–1820's) Americans continued as in colonial times to depend wherever possible on water routes for travel and transportation. The larger rivers, especially the Mississippi and the Ohio, became increasingly useful as steamboats grew in number and improved in design.

A special kind of steamboat evolved to

meet the problems of navigation on the Mississippi and its tributaries. These waters were shallow, with strong and tricky currents, shifting bars of sand and mud, and submerged logs and trees. So the boat had to have a flat bottom, paddle wheels rather than screw propellers, and a powerful, high-pressure engine, which meant a dangerously explosive one. To accommodate as much cargo and as many passengers as possible, the boat was triple-decked, its superstructure rising high in the air. Such a "floating palace" at its best was an impressive sight, elaborately ornamented with gilt and "gingerbread." More and more steamboats plied the western waters every year, a couple of hundred in 1830, three times as many in 1850. They grew in size until they averaged about 500 tons. So keen was competition that passenger fares and freight rates were steadily lowered and schedules speeded up. Races were common, and so were accidents.

River boats carried to New Orleans the corn and other crops of Northwestern farmers, the cotton and tobacco of Southwestern planters. From New Orleans ships took the cargoes on to Eastern ports. Neither the farmers of the West nor the merchants of the East were completely satisfied with this pattern of trade. Farmers could get better prices for their crops if the alternative existed of sending them directly eastward to market, and merchants could sell larger quantities of their manufactured goods if these could be transported more directly and more economically to the West.

True, the highways across the mountains, such as the Philadelphia-Pittsburgh turnpike and the National Road, provided a partial solution to the problem. But the costs of hauling goods overland were too high for anything except the most compact and valuable merchandise. Waterways were needed rather than highways. It was calculated that four horses could pull a wagon weight of one ton 12 miles a day over an ordinary road and

one and a half tons 18 miles a day over a turnpike. On the other hand, four horses could draw a boatland of a hundred tons 24 miles a day on a canal.

Sectional jealousies and constitutional scruples stood in the way of action by the federal government, and the necessary expenditures were too great for private enterprise. If extensive canals were to be dug, the job would be up to the various states.

New York was the first to act. It had the natural advantage of a comparatively level route between the Hudson River and Lake Erie, through the only break in the entire Appalachian chain. Yet the engineering tasks were imposing. The distance was more than 350 miles, several times as long as any of the existing canals in America, and there were ridges to cross and a wilderness of woods and swamps to penetrate. For many years New Yorkers debated whether the scheme was practical. The canal advocates finally won the debate after De Witt Clinton, a late but ardent convert to the cause, was elected governor. Digging began on the Fourth of July, 1817.

This, the Erie Canal, was by far the greatest construction job that Americans ever had undertaken, and it was the work of self-made engineers. Though one of them made a careful study of English canals, he and his associates did more than merely copy what he saw abroad. They devised ingenious arrangements of cables, pulleys, and gears for bringing down trees and uprooting stumps. Instead of the usual shovel and wheelbarrow, they used specially designed plows and scrapers for moving earth. To make watertight locks they produced an ideal cement from native limestone. The canal itself was simply a big ditch, forty feet wide and four feet deep, with towpaths along the banks for the horses or mules which were to draw the canal boats. (Steamboats were not to be used: the churning of a paddle wheel or propeller would cave in the earthen banks.) Cuts and fills, some of them enormous, enabled the canal to pass through hills and over valleys; stone aqueducts carried it across streams; and 88 locks, of heavy masonry, with great wooden gates, took care of the necessary ascents and descents.

Not only was the Erie Canal an engineering triumph; it quickly proved a financial success as well. It was opened for through traffic in October, 1825, with fitting ceremonies. Governor Clinton at the head of a parade of canal boats made the trip from Buffalo to the Hudson and then downriver to New York City, where he emptied a keg of Erie water into the Atlantic to symbolize the wedding of the lake and the ocean. Soon traffic was so heavy that, within about seven years, the tolls brought in enough to repay the whole construction cost. The prosperity

of the Erie encouraged the state to enlarge its canal system by building several branches. An important part of the system was the Champlain (or Northern) Canal, begun at about the same time as the Erie and completed in 1822, which connected Lake Champlain with the Hudson River. Though some of the branches did not pay for themselves, they provided useful water connections between New York City and the larger towns of the state. The main line, giving access to Lake Erie as it did, led beyond the state's borders, to the West.

The range of the New York canal system was still further extended when the states of Ohio and Indiana, inspired by the success of the Erie Canal, provided water connections between Lake Erie and the Ohio River. In 1825 Ohio began

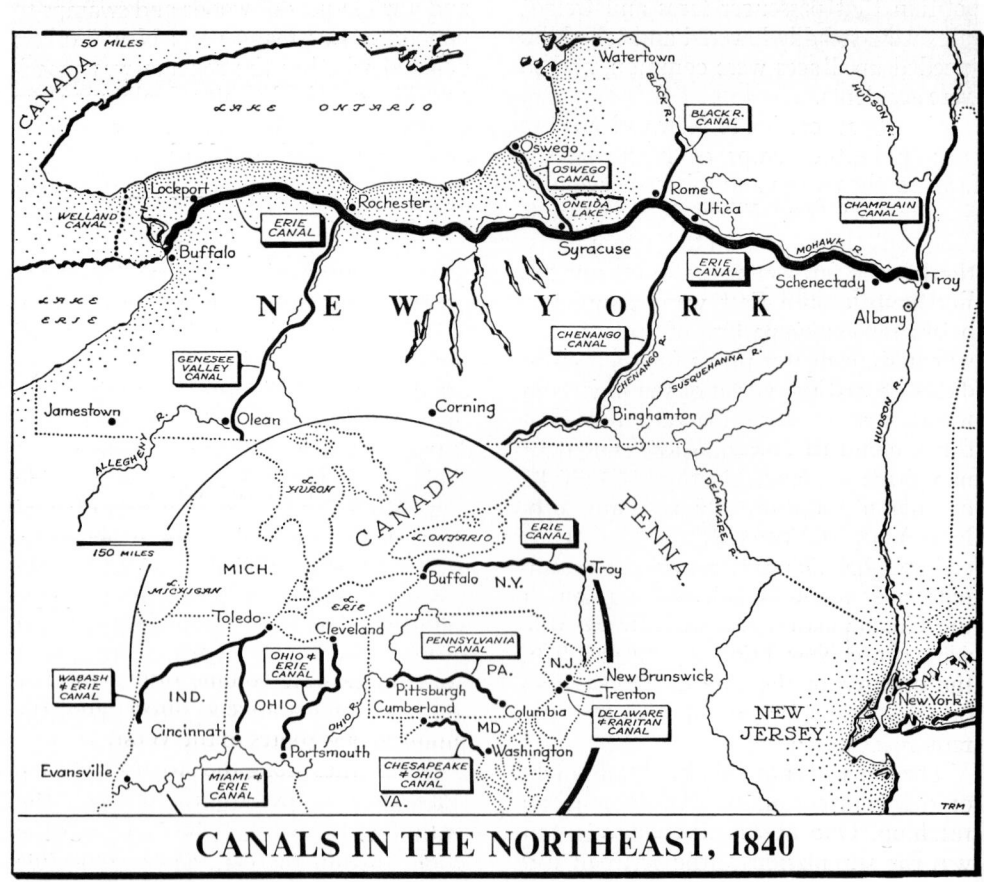

CANALS IN THE NORTHEAST, 1840

THE ERIE CANAL. The junction of the Erie and the Northern canals, near the eastern terminus of the Erie, north of Albany. Note the double set of locks and, at the right, the tandem team of horses on the towpath. From an aquatint by John Hill. (COURTESY OF THE NEW-YORK HISTORICAL SOCIETY, NEW YORK CITY)

the building of two canals, one between Portsmouth and Cleveland and the other between Cincinnati and Toledo, both of which were in use by 1833. In 1832 Indiana started the construction of a canal which was to connect Evansville with the Cincinnati-Toledo route. These canals made it possible to ship or to travel by inland waterways all the way from New York to New Orleans, though several changes between canal, lake, and river craft would be necessary. By way of the Great Lakes it was possible to go by water from New York to Chicago. After the opening of the Erie Canal, shipping on the Great Lakes by sail and by steam rapidly increased.

The consequences of the development of this transportation network were far-reaching. One of the immediate results was the stimulation of the settlement of the Northwest, not only because it had become easier for migrants to make the westward journey but also, and more important, because it had become easier for them, after taking up their farms, to ship their produce to markets. Towns boomed along the Erie and other canals, New York City benefiting the most of all. Though much of the Western produce, especially corn, continued to go down-river to New Orleans, an increasing proportion of it and most of the wheat of the Northwest went in the direction of New York. And manufactured goods now went in growing volume from New York by the comparatively direct and economical new routes to the West.

Rival cities along the Atlantic seaboard took alarm at the prospect of New York's acquiring so vast a hinterland, largely at their expense. If they were to hold their own, they too must find ways of tapping the Western market. Boston, remote from the West, her way to the Hudson River impeded by the Berkshire Hills, seemed out of the running, at least so far as a canal was concerned. Philadelphia and Baltimore, though they had the still more formidable Allegheny Mountains to contend with, did not give up without an effort at canal building. Beginning in 1834, the commonwealth of Pennsylvania invested in a complicated and costly system of waterways and railways—with an arrangement of "inclined planes," stationary engines, and cable cars to take canal boats over the mountains—intending thus to connect Philadelphia with Pittsburgh. This "Pennsylvania system" proved a failure, financially and otherwise. From Baltimore a canal was projected to ascend the Potomac Valley and tunnel through the mountains, thus achieving essentially the same object as George Washington once had hoped to accomplish. This grandly conceived Chesapeake and Ohio Canal began to be dug in 1828, but it never got farther west than Cumberland. In the South, Richmond and Charleston also aspired to reach the Ohio Valley; Richmond, planning at first to join the James and the Kanawha, eventually saw a canal built as far as Lynchburg.

For none of these rivals of New York did canals provide a satisfactory way to the West. Some cities, however, saw their opportunity in a different and newer means of transportation. Before the canal age had reached its height, the era of the railroad already was beginning.

Development of Railroads

It is hard to date the beginning of railroads, since they resulted from a combination of different elements, each of which had a separate history. One of these was the use of rails, wooden or iron, laid on a prepared roadbed to make a fairly straight and level track. Another was the employment of steam-powered locomotives, and a third was the operation of trains as public carriers of passengers and freight. For nearly two hundred years before the nineteenth century opened, railways with cars pulled by men (and women) or by animals had been used to haul coal from English mines, and in the early 1800's similar railways appeared in the United States. By 1804 both English and American inventors had experimented with steam engines for propelling land vehicles as well as boats. In 1820 John Stevens ran a locomotive and cars around a circular track on his New Jersey estate. Finally, in 1825, the Stockton and Darlington railroad in England began to operate with steam power over a short length of track and to carry general traffic.

This news quickly aroused the interest of American businessmen, especially in those seaboard cities that sought better communications with the West. First to organize a railroad company was a group of New Yorkers, who in 1826 obtained a charter for the Mohawk and Hudson and five years later began running trains the 16 miles between Schenectady and Albany. First to begin actual operations was the Baltimore and Ohio; the only living signer of the Declaration of Independence, Charles Carroll of Carrollton, dug a spadeful of earth in ceremonies to start the work on July 4, 1828, and a 13-mile stretch opened for business in 1830. In that same year the Charleston and Hamburg ran trains over a segment of its track in South Carolina; when this line was completed, in 1833, it was the longest in the world (136 miles). The next year the commonwealth of Pennsylvania finished its line from Philadelphia to the Susquehanna River as part of the "Pennsylvania system" of rail and waterways. Meanwhile, in Massachusetts, three companies received charters for routes radiating out from Boston, the most important of these being the Western Railroad which reached Worcester in 1836.

An Early Locomotive. Built in 1834, the "Mississippi" was first regularly operated between Natchez and Hamburg, Mississippi, a distance of about 19 miles. Early locomotives were individually named—like ships. The "Mississippi" was rather advanced in design for its time. It had a horizontal boiler, a front smoke-stack, and four drive-wheels. In these respects it was more like later locomotives than were most of its contemporaries. Like its contemporaries, however, it had no pilot wheels and no cow-catcher. (ILLINOIS CENTRAL RAILROAD)

Not only the seaboard but also the Mississippi Valley became the scene of railroad building. By 1836 a total of more than 1,000 miles of track had been laid in eleven states.

There did not yet exist what could be called a railroad system. Even the longest of the lines was comparatively short, and most of them served mainly to connect water routes and supplement water transportation. But there was no lack of railroad enthusiasts and grandiose railroad plans, some of which were eventually to be realized. Charleston was never to get its direct, through route over the mountains to the Ohio Valley. Boston, however, was reaching westward to tap the

trade of the Erie Canal. The Mohawk and Hudson (nucleus of the New York Central), the Baltimore and Ohio, and the Pennsylvania were ultimately to become through lines from New York to St. Louis and Chicago. With a few exceptions, as in Pennsylvania, these early railroads were built and operated by private corporations (the commonwealth of Pennsylvania soon sold its railroad interests to the Pennsylvania Railroad, a private company).

During the 1830's the railroad underwent a rapid technological development. At first the track consisted of strap-iron rails laid on wooden stringers which were anchored to granite blocks set in the ground, but this kind of track proved too rigid to absorb the shocks of actual use and was soon replaced by heavier iron rails on wooden ties ballasted with crushed rock. The tracks of different companies varied in width, so that when two different lines connected, the cars and engines of the one might not fit on the

burg's *Best Friend of Charleston* were put into use, and before long only American locomotives were used on American roads; some were even exported. Since railroads in this country were built with sharper curves and steeper grades, the locomotives had to be both more flexible and more powerful than in England. Pas-

RAILROADS IN THE 1850's. As railroads extended their lines and enlarged their business, they also sought to develop greater locomotive power and to improve their cars and service. By the 1850's locomotives had become standardized to what was known as the "American type." A locomotive of this type is shown above. Note that it has a four-wheel leading truck and two pair of driving wheels, coupled. The blunderbuss shape of the smokestack was for the purpose of catching sparks thrown by the wood-burning stoves used on all trains. The average speed of such a locomotive in passenger traffic was thirty miles an hour. To accommodate passengers on long journeys, the railroads introduced sleeping cars. They were three-decker affairs, and separate cars were provided for men and women. Pullman sleepers convertible to day use were introduced in 1857 but did not become popular until after the Civil War. (ASSOCIATION OF AMERICAN RAILROADS)

tracks of the other. In the early years experiments were made with various forms of motive power—horses, sails, and stationary steam engines with windlasses and cables (for steep grades), as well as steam locomotives. The very first locomotives were imported from England, but as early as 1830 engines of American manufacture like the Charleston and Ham-

senger cars, originally mere stage coaches adapted to rails, took the form of a large elongated wooden box with two rows of reversible seats and a center aisle soon after 1840. Schedules were erratic and wrecks frequent, most of the roadbeds and bridges being hastily and poorly constructed.

From the outset railroads and canals

were bitter competitors. For a time the Chesapeake and Ohio Canal Company blocked the advance of the Baltimore and Ohio Railroad through the narrow gorge of the upper Potomac, and the state of New York prohibited railroads from hauling freight in competition with the Erie Canal and its branches. Canal partisans and railroad advocates furiously debated the relative merits of the two methods of transportation. Where free competition existed, railroads took most of the passenger traffic and the light freight. The future, in fact, belonged to the towns and cities along the path of

The railroads also obtained assistance from the federal government in the shape of public land grants. In 1850 Senator Stephen A. Douglas and other railroad-minded politicians persuaded Congress to grant lands to the state of Illinois to aid the Illinois Central, then planning to build toward the Gulf of Mexico; Illinois was to transfer the land to the Central as it carried its construction forward. Other states and their railroad promoters demanded the same privileges, and by 1860 Congress had allotted over 30 million acres to eleven states.

The railroads revolutionized transpor-

SPEED BY WATER AND BY RAIL

1850's

The following table indicates the rapidity of rail as compared with water travel and transportation between New York City and Western cities:

From New York to:	Mile Distance	Time by Water	Time by Rail
Cleveland	700	9 days	3 days
Detroit	825	10 days	4 days
Chicago	1,500	14½ days	6½ days

---

the "iron horse," not to those that continued to depend exclusively upon waterways.

An outburst of rail construction without previous parallel occurred in the 1850's. The amount of trackage tripled, going from 9,021 miles in 1850 to 30,626 in 1860. Capital to finance this railroad boom came from various sources. Some of it was provided by American investors, and large sums were borrowed abroad. Substantial aid was provided by local governmental units—states, cities, towns, counties—eager to have a road to serve their needs. This support took the form of loans, stock subscriptions, subsidies, and donations of land for rights of way.

tation. At the opening of the century the average freight rate by wagon was 33¢ per ton mile; the average passenger rate was 6¢ per mile. In the stagecoach era of the 1830's a trip from Boston to New York consumed forty-one hours; from New York to St. Louis, a distance of 1,600 miles, over three weeks were required. The average coach fare for 300 miles was $15. The principal result of the advent of water transportation was to reduce freight charges. According to one estimate, the cost of traffic on the various means of transportation in 1840 were as follows: roads, 10–20¢ per mile; canals, 1½¢; lake steamers, 2–4¢; river steamers, 1½¢; railroads, 2½¢. Water transport continued

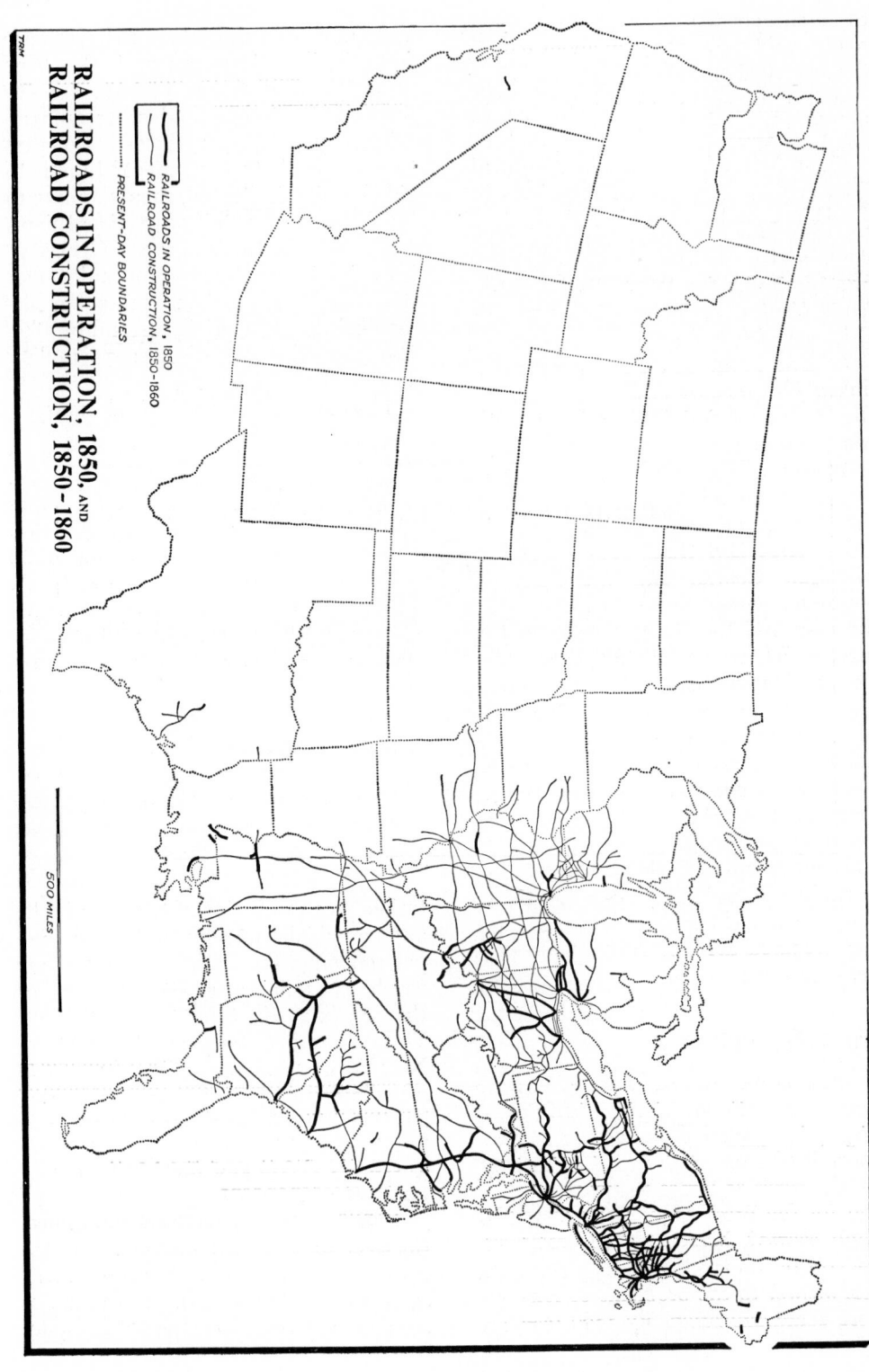

RAILROADS IN OPERATION, 1850, AND
RAILROAD CONSTRUCTION, 1850-1860

RAILROADS IN OPERATION, 1850
RAILROAD CONSTRUCTION, 1850-1860
PRESENT-DAY BOUNDARIES

500 MILES

to be cheaper than railroad, but the railroads could move goods in about half the time required on water.

A new feature of railroad development in the 1850s—and one that profoundly affected the nature of sectional alignments—was the trend toward the consolidation of short lines into trunk lines. By 1853 four roads had surmounted the Appalachian barrier to connect the Northeast wth the West. Two, the New York Central and the New York and Erie, gave New York City access to the Lake Erie ports. The Pennsylvania road linked Philadelphia and Pittsburgh, and the Baltimore and Ohio connected the Maryland metropolis with the Ohio River at Wheeling. From the terminals of these lines other roads into the interior touched the Mississippi River at eight points. Other important trunk routes were the Michigan Central and the Michigan Southern, which entered Chicago from the east, and the Rock Island and Chicago, which connected the Great Lakes and the Mississippi. Chicago became the rail center of the West, served by fifteen lines and over a hundred daily trains. The great trunk lines increasingly diverted traffic from the water routes, the Erie Canal and the Mississippi River. By lessening the dependence of the West upon the Mississippi, the railroads helped to weaken West-South economic ties; by binding more closely the East and West, they prepared the way for a coalition of those sections.

The Telegraph

Culminating several years of experimentation with an electric (magnetic) telegraph, Samuel F. B. Morse in 1844 transmitted from Baltimore to Washington the news of James K. Polk's nomination for the Presidency. The Morse telegraph seemed, because of the relatively low cost of constructing wire systems, the ideal answer to the problems of long-distance communication. By 1860 over 50,-

000 miles of wire connected all parts of the country, and a year later the Pacific telegraph, with 3,595 miles of wire, was open between New York and San Francisco. Nearly all of the independent lines had been absorbed into one organization, the Western Union Telegraph Company. American enthusiasm for wire communication was not limited to the confines of the nation. Cyrus W. Field, a New York businessman, conceived the project of laying an Atlantic cable between Newfoundland and Ireland. With financial aid from associates and encouragement from the British and American governments, he completed a cable in 1858. Messages between Great Britain and the United States were exchanged, and man seemed to have accomplished another conquest of distance. But within a few weeks the cable went dead, nor could Field, who continued to believe in his idea, get it to working again. (After the Civil War, Field returned to his labors, and in 1866 succeeded in laying a permanent cable.)

Yankee Enterprise

Developments in transportation and communication steadily broadened the scope of business enterprise while bringing about a greater degree of geographical specialization in economic activity. More than ever, a particular locality could concentrate upon the production of a certain kind of goods, since it could depend on other parts of the country to buy its surplus and supply its needs. While such specialization intensified differences of economic interest and thus accounted for much of the growing sectionalism in politics, it also made the East and the West, the North and the South, increasingly interdependent.

While mills and factories multiplied, the household and the workshop declined but slowly as producers of manufactured goods. In the textile industry the use of machinery and the dependence on water power (occasionally steam power) made it necessary to bring operations together under a single roof. Yet a good deal of spinning and weaving continued to be done in the home, either for sale or for home use. Though shoes were still made by hand and not by machines, shoe manufacture was increasingly the work of men and women who, in a careful division of labor, specialized in one or another of the various tasks. Mass-produced shoes, in ungraded sizes and without distinction as to rights or lefts, came chiefly from eastern Massachusetts and were bought mostly by frontier emigrants, sailors, and Southern planters who used them for their slaves. Other people still made their own shoes or had them made to order by a cobbler. Iron came largely from Pennsylvania, where it was produced in furnaces using local sources of ore, limestone, and charcoal. Other furnaces were scattered over the country, however, and finished iron products were wrought in thousands of local blacksmith shops. Sizeable wagon and carriage factories appeared in cities like New York, but smaller towns almost everywhere had their own wheelwrights and carriagemakers, though some of these were beginning merely to assemble vehicles from spokes, felloes, and other parts which came ready-made from the big-city manufacturers.

Between 1840 and 1860 American industry experienced a steady and in some fields a spectacular growth. In 1840 the total value of manufactured goods produced in the United States was $483,-278,000; ten years later the figure had climbed to $1,055,500,000; and in 1860 it stood at $1,885,861,000. For the first time the value of manufactured goods was approximately equal to that of agricultural products ($994,000,000 in 1850 and $1,910,000,000 in 1860). Technological advances and improved methods of manufacturing were expanding the productivity of American factories, but as yet American industry, which exported very little, was unable to satisfy fully the wants of American consumers.

Technology and industrial ingenuity were, however, preparing the way for future American industrial supremacy. The machine tools used in the factories of the Northeast, such as the turret lathe, the grinding machine, and the universal milling machine, were better than those in European factories. The principle of interchangeable parts, applied earlier in gun factories by Eli Whitney and Simeon North, was being introduced into other lines of manufacturing. Coal was replacing wood as an industrial fuel, particularly in the smelting of iron. Coal was also being used in increasing amounts to generate power in the steam engines beginning in some areas of industry to replace the water power that earlier had driven most of the factory machinery in the Northeast. The production of coal, most of it mined in western Pennsylvania in the Pittsburgh area, leaped from 50,000 tons in 1820 to 14,000,000 tons in 1860.

The great technical advances in American industry owed much to American inventors; indeed, these advances could not have occurred without the contributions of the ingenious men who discovered new inventions or devised improvements on existing models. The patent records reveal the searching curiosity of American inventors and technicians in the decades before the Civil War. In 1830 the number of inventions patented was 544; in 1850 the figure rose to 993; and in 1860 it stood at 4,778. Charles Goodyear, a New England hardware merchant, discovered in 1839 a method of vulcanizing rubber; his process had been put to 500 uses by 1860, and the rubber industry was firmly established. In 1846 Elias Howe of Massachusetts constructed a sewing machine, upon which improvements were shortly made by Isaac Singer. The Howe-Singer machine was soon employed in manufacturing ready-to-wear clothing and shoes; a little later, in the Civil War, it would contribute mightily to supplying the Northern armies and would be one reason for Northern victory. Goodyear, Howe, and Singer, and many another inventor and technologist were laying the foundations for the system of mass production that after 1865 would make the United States the marvel of the industrial world.

The expansion of business was not simply a more or less automatic result of

whales from the Atlantic, voyaged far into the Pacific in their hazardous tracking of the source of spermaceti for candles, whale oil for lamps, and whalebone for corset stays and other uses. Another example of Yankee enterprise was the ice industry. Though for years Northeastern farmers had harvested winter ice from ponds and stored it for the summer, the large-scale transportation and sale of ice

THE ICE INDUSTRY. Harvesting natural ice became a big business in New York State as well as New England. This lithograph of 1845 pictures the cutting and storing of ice at Rockland Lake in New York. (COURTESY OF THE NEW-YORK HISTORICAL SOCIETY, NEW YORK CITY)

transportation improvements or other technological changes. It was also the result of daring and imagination on the part of businessmen and their employees. Two industries, one old and one new, illustrate the capacities of Yankee enterprise. One was the whaling industry, which was reaching its heyday in the 1830's. From New Bedford and other New England ports, bold skippers and their crews, having driven most of the

as a commodity began in the 1830's. The New England ice harvest then found a ready market in Northern cities, on Southern plantations, and around the world in India, whither it was carried in fast sailing ships; a voyage was considered highly successful if no more than half the cargo melted on the way.

American ships and shipping entered upon a golden age. With their advantages in natural resources and with two centuries of experience behind them, Yankee shipbuilders produced vessels unmatched for economy, speed, and beauty of design. Many of these ships were sold abroad; most remained in American hands, though their crews were increasingly made up of foreigners of every seagoing nationality. So efficient were the ships and crews, and so enterprising the shipowners and captains, that eventually vessels flying the Stars and Stripes carried nine tenths of this country's exports and imports and much of the business of other nations besides (by law they had a monopoly of American coastal shipping). The American merchant marine was on the way to becoming, for a time, the largest in the world.

Overseas commerce thrived. True, with the rise of the home market, exports and imports (though increasing) became a smaller and smaller part of the nation's total business. Yet, for the prosperity of Americans in general and some of them in particular, foreign trade was extremely important. Most of the cotton crop and a large part of the wheat crop, for example, were sold abroad. So was much of the output of American textile mills—coarse and cheap fabrics, for which there was more demand in China than in the United States. On the other hand, finer clothes were regularly imported, as were countless other items, necessities as well as luxuries. Exports annually exceeded imports in value, so that the United States had what the old mercantilists had considered a "favorable" balance of trade, the difference being made up largely by the shipment of specie to this country.

During the 1840's and 1850's many of the ships in the overseas trade were the famous clippers, the most beautiful and the fastest sailing ships afloat. In their heyday in the late forties and early fifties, the clippers were capable of averaging 300 miles a day, which compared favorably with the best time then being made by steamships. Although the value of American exports, almost entirely agricul-

tural in nature, increased from $123,609,000 in 1840 to $333,576,000 in 1860, American merchants saw in the 1850's much of their carrying trade fall into the hands of British competitors, who enjoyed the advantages of steam-driven iron ships and government subsidies.

The distribution of goods, whether of foreign or of domestic origin, continued to be rather haphazard by present-day standards, though it was becoming more and more systematic. Stores specializing in groceries, dry goods, hardware, or other lines appeared in the larger cities, but smaller towns and villages depended on the general store, like the one where Abraham Lincoln once clerked in New Salem, Illinois. The typical general store was crammed with a bewildering variety of merchandise. The storekeeper did much of his business by barter, taking country eggs and other produce in exchange for such things as pins and needles, sugar, and coffee. Many customers, living remote from any store, welcomed the occasional visits of the peddler, who came afoot or by horse, with his pack or with his peddler's wagon equipped with sloping sides which opened to reveal his racks of wares. A special variety of peddler, the Connecticut Yankee, toured the West and the South as a factory agent to sell clocks, at one time made of wood (including the works) but in the 1830's and after usually made of brass.

The organization of business was undergoing a gradual change. Most of it was, and continued to be, operated by individuals or partnerships operating on a small scale. The dominating figure was the great merchant capitalist, who owned and directed much of the big business of the time. He owned his own ships, and he organized certain industries, as for example that of shoe manufacturing, on the putting-out system, according to which he provided the materials, directed the work, and sold the finished product. In the larger enterprises, however, the individual merchant capitalist was giving way before the advance of the corporation. Corporations had the advantage of combining the resources of a large number of shareholders, but their development was long held back by handicapping laws. A corporation had to have a charter, granted by the state, and at first a special act of the legislature was required. By the 1830's the states were beginning to pass general incorporation laws according to which any group meeting certain requirements could secure a charter merely by paying a fee. Moreover, the laws began to grant the privilege of limited liability, which meant that the individual stockholder was liable only to the extent of losing the value of his stock if the corporation should fail.

Corporations made possible the accumulation of larger and larger amounts of capital for manufacturing enterprises as well as for banks, turnpikes, and railroad companies. Some of this capital came from the profits of wealthy merchants who turned from shipping to newer ventures, some from the savings of men of only moderate means, and some from tax collections, since state governments often bought shares in turnpike, canal, and railroad companies. A considerable part was supplied by foreign, especially English, investors. From all these sources too little was derived to meet the demands of promoters with ambitious schemes of personal profit or community improvement. Hence the banks, which should have confined their long-term lending to the limit of their savings deposits, often were induced to issue excessive amounts of banknotes as a means of providing capital for expanding business ventures. As a result of this practice, bank failures were more frequent and bank deposits less secure than they might otherwise have been.

Workers and Unions

The growth of industry required labor as well as capital. From the colonial beginnings, labor had been scarce in America. At the opening of the nineteenth century nearly 90 of every 100 Americans still lived and worked on the land: they were farmers. City workers were comparatively few, and many of them were skilled artisans who owned and managed their shops: they were small businessmen, not employees. There were also some unskilled laborers—longshoremen and the like—but there was no sizeable reservoir of manpower for new industries to draw upon. In response to the needs of industry a considerable class of wage-earners finally began to form. Its members came mostly from the marginal farms of the East (those farms least able to compete with the fertile fields of the West) and somewhat later from the British Isles and Europe.

In the textile mills two different methods of labor recruitment were used. One of these, which prevailed in the Middle States and parts of New England, brought whole families to the mill. Father, mother, and children, even those no more than four or five years old, worked together in tending the looms. The second, the Waltham or Lowell system, which was common in Massachusetts, enlisted young women in their late teens and early twenties. These unmarried girls went from farms to factories to work for only a few years and then returned with their savings, to settle down as housewives. They did not form a permanent working class.

Labor conditions in American mills seemed very good in comparison with conditions in English factories and mines. Child labor, indispensable for eking out the manpower supply, entailed fewer evils in the United States, where the working children remained under the control of their parents, than in England, where asylum authorities hired out orphans to factory employers. The lot of the working woman in mills like those of Lowell appeared idyllic in contrast with the plight of contemporary women who worked in British mines. A parliamentary investigation revealed that some of these unfortunates, naked and filthy, crawled on their hands and knees to pull coal carts through narrow tunnels. No wonder that English visitors considered Lowell a female paradise. The Lowell girls lived in pleasant boardinghouses (much like college residence halls) where their morals were carefully supervised. They were well paid by the standards of the period. They found time to write and publish a monthly magazine, the *Lowell Offering*, even though working hours were long—from sunup to sundown six days a week. In the early days of the factory these hours seemed natural enough to people who were used to the day-long labor of the farm.

Much worse off were the construction gangs who performed the heavy, unskilled work on turnpikes, railroads, and canals. A large and growing number of these men were Irish immigrants. They received low pay and, since their work was seasonal and uncertain, did not make enough in a year to maintain a family at what was generally considered a decent living standard; many of them lived in the most unhealthful of shanties. After about 1840 Irish men and women began to be employed in textile mills. As these newcomers replaced the native farm girls, the earlier paternalistic system broke down and working conditions deteriorated somewhat. Piece rates were paid instead of a daily wage; these and other devices were used to speed up production and exploit the labor force more efficiently.

Neither ditch-diggers nor millhands, however, were the first to organize and act collectively to improve the conditions of their work. Skilled artisans formed the earliest labor unions and arranged the first strikes (shortly before 1800). From the 1790's on, the printers and cordwainers took the lead. The cordwainers —makers of high-quality boots and shoes, each man fashioning his entire product—

suffered from the competition of merchant capitalists who put out work to be performed in separate tasks. These artisans sensed a loss of security and status with the development of mass-production methods, and so did members of other skilled trades, such as carpenters, joiners, masons, plasterers, hatters, and shipbuilders. In cities like Philadelphia, Baltimore, Boston, and New York, the skilled workers of each craft formed societies for mutual aid. During the 1820's and 1830's the craft societies began to combine on a city-wide basis and set up central organizations known as trade unions. Since, with the widening of the market, workers of one city competed with those at a distance, the next step was to federate the trade unions or to establish craft unions of national scope. In 1834 delegates from six cities founded the National Trades' Union, and in 1836 the printers and the cordwainers set up their own national craft unions.

This labor movement soon collapsed. Labor leaders struggled against the handicap of hostile laws and hostile courts. By the common law, as interpreted by judges in the industrial states, a combination among workers was viewed as, in itself, an illegal conspiracy. But adverse court decisions did not halt, though they handicapped, the rising unions. The death blow came from the Panic of 1837 and the ensuing depression.

Thereafter, during the 1840's and 1850's, conditions of labor were on the whole somewhat worse than they had been earlier. Most mill towns were cheerless, ugly places in which to live, and most factories were unsanitary, unhealthful buildings in which to work. The average work day was 12 to 15 hours. The wages of skilled workers ranged from $4 to $10 a week; unskilled workers and women and children received $1 to $6 per week.

Labor was not strong enough to do much toward bettering working conditions. The unions attempted, with little success, to persuade state legislatures to

THE BIG STRIKE IN PHILADELPHIA

1835

John Ferral, a leader of the Philadelphia General Trades' Union, told a "brother" labor leader in Boston how "the workies" of Philadelphia had won the ten-hour day by a general strike in the summer of 1835:

"Fortunately, at this crisis, the Cordwainers [shoemakers] of the Ladies' Branch struck for wages; the Handloom Weavers had already declared their intentions, and the Laborers on the wharves of Schuylkill were out on strike several days previous. The Cordwainers, with that sympathy of feeling which prevades all intelligent working men, marched out to meet the laborers. Addresses were then delivered, calling upon all day workmen to strike for the hours; and nobly the call was responded to. Bricklayers, plasterers, house carpenters, stone masons, laborers, &c., vied with each other in this generous rivalry of action. . . .

"The recognition and adoption of the ten hour system by the public servants of Philadelphia city and county could not with safety have been longer deferred; each day added thousands to our ranks. We marched to the public works, and the workmen joined in with us; when the procession passed, employment ceased, business was at a stand still, shirt sleeves were rolled up, aprons on, working tools in hand were the orders of the day. Had the cannon of an invading enemy belched forth its challenge on our soil, the freemen of Philadelphia could not have shown a greater ardor for the contest; the blood-sucking aristocracy, they alone stood aghast; terror-stricken, they thought the day of retribution was come, but no vengeance was sought or inflicted by the people for the wrongs they had suffered from their enemies."

pass laws setting a maximum work day. New Hampshire, in 1847, enacted a statute providing that no person be required to work more than ten hours in one day unless he agreed to an "express contract" calling for greater time; in the following year Pennsylvania adopted a similar law for the textile and paper industries. These measures were largely inoperative because many employers forced prospective employees to sign agreements for longer hours. Three states— Massachusetts, New Hampshire, and Pennsylvania—passed laws regulating child labor, but the statutes merely forbade the employment of minors for more than ten hours in a day without the consent of their parents. Probably the greatest legal victory achieved by labor was in a judicial case in Massachusetts. The supreme court of that state, in *Commonwealth* v. *Hunt* (1842), declared that unions were lawful organizations and that the strike was a lawful weapon. Other state courts gradually accepted the principles of the Massachusetts decision.

Farming, East and West

Life and labor on the farm became somewhat easier with the introduction of new tools, though not all such advantages were readily accepted. The spring wagon (1825) seemed to some a useless luxury, and the cast-iron plow (1819) gained acceptance slowly among farmers who, believing that iron poisoned the soil, preferred the older wooden plow.

First Demonstration of the McCormick Reaper. In 1831 Cyrus H. Mc-
Cormick demonstrated the first successful reaper near the town of Steele's Tavern,
Virginia. The amazed onlookers saw the machine cut grain much faster than men
with cradle scythes could do. Two men were required to operate this reaper, one to
ride the horse and one to rake the platform. Other workers followed to bind the
grain. In the picture McCormick is anxiously walking behind his invention. He
and his father, a substantial landowner, were profoundly interested in machines
that would lighten farm labor. After improving his reaper, McCormick, with great
foresight, built a manufacturing plant in Chicago, the obvious market center for
farm machinery, and came to dominate the industry. He introduced many modern
techniques, including a guarantee for his product, installment buying, and advertising. A favorite slogan was "Westward the course of empire takes its way—
with McCormick reapers in the van." (STATE HISTORICAL SOCIETY OF WISCONSIN
AND INTERNATIONAL HARVESTER COMPANY)

But by 1830 iron plows were in such great demand that they were mass produced, two factories in Pittsburgh alone turning out nearly 35,000 a year. Before long, steel plows came into use, especially in the prairie country, where the sod was too tough for cast-iron implements, to say nothing of wooden ones. An even better implement appeared in 1847 when John Deere established at Moline, Illinois, a factory to manufacture plows with steel moldboards, which were more durable than those made of iron and were also self-scouring. Harvesting was traditionally backbreaking work, though the addition of the cradle to the scythe had made it possible to cut and shock a field of grain faster than before. As early as 1831 Cyrus Hall McCormick demonstrated his horse-drawn mechanical reaper on a Virginia wheatfield. The reaper enabled a crew of six or seven men to harvest in a day as much wheat (or any other small grain) as could fifteen using the older methods. McCormick, who patented his device in 1834, established in 1847 a factory at Chicago in the heart of the grain belt. By 1850 he was turning out 3,000 reapers a year; by 1860, 20,000; and in the latter year over 100,000 reapers were in use on Western farms. After 1840 horse-powered mowers, reapers, hay-rakes, and other such farm machinery began to come into fairly general use.

By 1850 the growing Western population had settled the prairie regions east of the Mississippi, and was pushing beyond the river. Stimulated to greater production by rising prices and conscious of the richness of his soil, the average Western farmer engaged in wasteful, exploitative methods of farming that often resulted in rapid soil exhaustion.

Some improvements in farming methods did, however, find their way into use. New varieties of seed, notably Mediterranean wheat, which was hardier than the native type, were introduced in some areas; better breeds of animals, such as hogs and sheep from England and Spain, were imported to take the place of native stock. In nearly every case these and similar innovations were first tried out on Eastern farms, and later won whole or partial acceptance in the West.

Areas of agricultural activity in which the centers of production shifted from East to West were wheat, corn, vineyards, and the raising of cattle, sheep, and hogs. In 1840, when the total national wheat crop was 84,823,000 bushels, the leading wheat growing states were New York, Pennsylvania, Ohio, and Virginia; in 1860, with the national output standing

at 183,105,000 bushels, the bulk of the crop was produced in Illinois, Indiana, Wisconsin, Ohio, and Michigan. The same pattern was true of corn, with Illinois, Ohio, and Missouri supplanting New York, Pennsylvania, and Virginia as the centers of production. In the growing of the minor grains, oats, rye, and barley, the East maintained a slight edge, although the West was forging up to a position of equality. In 1840 the most important cattle-raising areas in the country were in New York, Pennsylvania, and New England, but by the 1850's the leading cattle states were Illinois, Indiana, Ohio, and Iowa, in the West, and Texas, in the South. In similar fashion, the centers of sheep and hog production moved from East to West. Ohio replaced New York as the chief wool-producing state, and Chicago and Cincinnati became the great markets for the sale of hogs as well as cattle.

In some fields of farm production the Northeast held its own or even surpassed the West. As the urban centers of the section increased in population, many farmers turned profitably to the task of supplying foods to the city masses, engaging in truck gardening (vegetables) or fruit raising. New York led all other states in apple production. Other lucrative fruit crops of the section were melons, berries, and peaches. New Jersey was a center of peach production, as were also Delaware and Maryland on the Southern border. Also stimulated by the rise of cities was dairy farming: the profits to be derived from supplying milk, butter, and cheese to local markets attracted many farmers in central New York, southeastern Pennsylvania, and various parts of New England. Approximately half of the dairy products of the country were produced in the East; the other half came from the West, with Ohio being the dairy center of that section. Partly because of the expansion of the dairy industry, the Northeast led other sections in the production of hay. New York was the leading hay state in the nation, and large crops were grown in Pennsylvania and New England. The Northeast also exceeded other areas in producing potatoes, but in the 1840's the crop was hit by a blight from which it never fully recovered.

Increasing Comfort

While during hard times countryfolk were less likely to experience downright want than were the unemployed in towns and cities, many urbanites were beginning to enjoy conveniences unknown to the farm. By the 1820's New York and Philadelphia had municipal waterworks, and some houses even had water piped indoors. Though in summer this water was tepid and tasteless in comparison with that from a rural well or a spring, it could be improved by the addition of ice, regularly supplied to householders for their iceboxes. Streets began to be lighted by gas, the New York Gas Company being chartered in 1823, and other cities acquiring gasworks in subsequent years. Urban sanitation still left much to be desired—scavenging pigs rooted in New York streets as late as the 1830's—yet on the whole cities were taking on a cleaner and more civilized appearance.

No longer did the well-to-do have their houses built in the Classical or Early Republican style, which had succeeded the colonial Georgian. New fashions were appearing in the 1820's and 1830's. Greek Revival architecture called for dwellings that resembled or at least were reminiscent of the temples of ancient Athens. The Gothic style was inspired by visions of medieval castles, and the Italian was supposed to recall the villas of Florentine merchant princes. The wealthier the home-owner, the more stylishly elaborate his house, particularly if it was located in the city. New styles were slow to reach rural areas and small towns, and, as applied by carpenters serving buyers of modest means, these styles became simpler and more chaste. Altogether, the range in housing was extreme—from the city mansion or the plantation house to the slum hovel and the frontier lean-to.

As yet, central heating in residences was rare. Hot-air furnaces had been installed here and there for some time, but not till 1840 did improvements make such furnaces practical and safe. Meanwhile stoves for heating and ranges for cooking were becoming common. The Franklin stove, invented by the great scientist, prepared the way, though it burned only wood and was not very efficient except in comparison with the fireplace. Numerous inventors turned their talents to designing better and better coal stoves after 1820. The fireplace, though vastly more charming in retrospect, grew unfashionable in the eyes of up-and-coming families; often it was blocked off and one of the modern heaters placed in front of it. Lighting the fire was easier after the phosphorus match (first American patent, 1836) made it unnecessary to use flint, steel, and tinder or to hoard coals from bedtime to morning.

Though kerosene was not yet available, continual improvements were made in lamps burning whale oil or camphene, the latter a rather hazardous combustible. A majority of families, though a steadily declining majority, continued to burn candles which they dipped or molded at home.

The list of new household conveniences could be lengthened, but such a dry recital would give a wholly inadequate notion of what material progress meant to Americans of the time. To most of them it was almost a religion. As invention followed invention they were confirmed in the faith that they lived in a wondrous age of infinitely increasing ease and plenty. Some assumed that progress in material things led automatically to progress in society and government as well. Others came to the conclusion that active effort would be needed if they were to keep social and political improvement abreast of technological advance.

BIBLIOGRAPHY

Improvements in the material conditions of
life are treated in C. R. Fish, *The Rise of
the Common Man, 1830–1850* (1927);
A. A. Ekirch, *The Idea of Progress in America, 1815–1860* (1944); and E. W. Martin,
*The Standard of Living in the United States
in 1860* (1942).

The story of American technological invention is told in Roger Burlingame, *March
of the Iron Men* (1938); J. A. Kouwen-
hoven, *Made in America* (1948); and J. W.
Oliver, *History of American Technology*
(1956). See also W. Kaempffert (ed.), *A
Popular History of American Invention* (2
vols., 1924); Holland Thompson, *The Age
of Invention* (1921); and Mitchell Wilson,
American Science and Invention (1954), a
pictorial record.

On industrial and business developments,
see V. S. Clark, *History of Manufactures in
the United States* (3 vols., 1929); L. M.
Hacker, *The Triumph of American Capitalism* (1940); and T. C. Cochran and William Miller, *The Age of Enterprise* (1942).
Specific industries are studied in Ware, *The
Early New England Cotton Manufacture*,
previously cited; A. H. Cole, *The American
Wool Manufacture* (2 vols., 1926); and Allan Nevins, *Abram S. Hewitt, with Some
Account of Peter Cooper* (1935), good on
the iron industry.

G. R. Taylor, *The Transportation Revolution, 1815–1860* (1951), is an important
general account of the subject. See also Seymour Dunbar, *A History of Travel in America* (4 vols., 1915; one-vol. ed., 1937),
which is well illustrated. On railroads:
Slason Thompson, *A Short History of American Railways* (1925); J. A. Miller, *Fares,
Please!* (1941), on street railways; A. D.
Turnbull, *John Stevens* (1928); Edward
Hungerford, *The Story of the Baltimore and
Ohio Railroad, 1827–1927* (2 vols., 1928);
F. W. Stevens, *The Beginnings of the New
York Central Railroad* (1926); S. M. Der-
rick, *Centennial History of the South Caro-
lina Railroad* (1930); and P. W. Gates,
*The Illinois Central Railroad and Its Col-
onization Work* (1934).

On Canals: M. S. Waggoner, *The Long
Haul West: The Great Canal Era, 1817–
1850* (1958); A. F. Harlow, *Old Towpaths:
The Story of the American Canal Era*

(1926); and W. S. Sanderlin, *The Great
National Project* (1947), a history of the
Chesapeake and Ohio Canal.

On overseas commerce and shipping:
S. E. Morison, *The Maritime History of
Massachusetts, 1783–1860* (1921); F. R.
Dulles, *The Old China Trade* (1930);
R. G. Albion, *Square-Riggers on Schedule*
(1938); E. P. Holman, *The American
Whalemen* (1928); A. H. Clark, *The Clip-
per Ship Era, 1843–1869* (1910); C. C.
Cutler, *The Story of the American Clipper*
(1930); and E. R. Johnson and others, *His-
tory of the Domestic and Foreign Com-
merce of the United States* (2 vols., 1915).

On the telegraph: Carleton Mabee, *The
American Leonardo: A Life of Samuel F. B
Morse* (1943); and R. L. Thompson, *Wiring a Continent: The History of the Telegraph Industry in the United States, 1832–
1866* (1947).

Urban histories include R. G. Albion,
The Rise of New York Port, 1815–1860
(1939); Ralph Weld, *Brooklyn Village,
1816–1834* (1938); Blake McKelvey, *Rochester, The Water-Power City, 1812–1854*
(1945); L. D. Baldwin, *Pittsburgh: The
Story of a City* (1938); N. M. Blake, *Water
for the Cities* (1956); and J. W. Livingood,
*The Philadelphia–Baltimore Trade Rivalry,
1780–1860* (1947).

A standard account of labor history is
J. R. Commons and others, *History of Labour in the United States* (4 vols., 1918–
35). See also Norman Ware, *The Industrial
Worker, 1840–1860* (1924). Immigration
may be studied in M. L. Hansen, *The Atlantic Migration, 1607–1860* (1940);
G. W. Stephenson, *History of American Immigration* (1926); and Carl Wittke, *We
Who Built America* (1939).

The economic structure of a region is
presented in H. C. Hubbart, *The Older
Middle West, 1840–1860* (1936). On agricultural developments, see P. W. Bidwell
and J. I. Falconer, *History of Agriculture in
the Northern United States, 1620–1860*
(1925), and A. H. Sanford, *The Story of
Agriculture in the United States* (1916).
On the introduction of farm technology:
W. T. Hutchinson, *Cyrus Hall McCormick*
(2 vols., 1930–5).

15

A SEARCH
FOR HEAVEN ON EARTH

America, the scene of Thomas More's sixteenth-century *Utopia*, still seemed in the nineteenth century a land of utopian possibilities, at least to a great many Americans. They believed that their country led the rest of the world in moral as well as material progress (except for the embarrassing persistence of slavery in the South). They leaped to the defense whenever foreigners criticized American ways, as foreigners often did. Yet these progress-minded Americans themselves readily found fault with conditions in their own country when these conditions seemed to hinder the perfection of society and man. There resulted a tumultuous and variegated movement for intellectual awakening and social reform, which gained headway soon after the War of 1812, picked up momentum in the 1830's, then concentrated most of its force on a single reform—the elimination of slavery. The reform spirit, this "freedom's ferment," never had stirred the South so much as it had the North, and with the development of an antislavery crusade Southerners resisted more strongly than ever the "isms" of the day

as they rallied to a defense of their "peculiar institution." Thus the nation began increasingly to divide on moral as well as economic and political grounds.

Democracy and Civilization

"In the four quarters of the globe, who reads an American book? or goes to an American play? or looks at an American picture or statue?" So asked the English wit Sydney Smith in the *Edinburgh Review* (1820), and he assumed that the answer was obvious—nobody. Like him, many cultivated Europeans believed that the American democracy was a cultural vacuum.

On the whole, British travelers in the United States confirmed this impression. Occasionally these book-writing tourists had a kind word about the American and his habits. One of the most sympathetic, Harriet Martineau, author of *Society in America* (1837), admitted that the American people already had realized many ideals for which the rest of the world still strove. Though Americans had their faults, she added, they could not be discouraged by them, for they "are in possession of the glorious certainty that time and exertion will infallibly secure all wisely desired objects." Even when the British were complimentary, however, they were inclined to be condescending, and much of the time they were highly critical. To them the typical Yankee seemed filthy, rude, ignorant, quarrelsome, boastful, and greedy, as well as sickly and sallow. The Southerner seemed even worse, tyrannical and brutal, a beater of slaves. North, South, and West, the American male according to the British visitors was an inveterate tobacco chewer and spitter, with an aim that was none too good.

Quite different was the attitude of the young French visitor, Alexis de Tocqueville, whose two volumes on *Democracy in America* (1835–40) still stand as the most perceptive analysis of American ways ever penned by a foreigner. Believing that political equality was the way of the future, Tocqueville toured this country to learn democracy's good and bad, its essential and nonessential elements, so that France might be better prepared for the inevitable transition to democracy. Even though he disapproved of much that he saw, he sought to understand American behavior, not to denounce it. Like the British observers, he concluded that Americans were backward in respect to science, literature, and the arts, but he did not blame their backwardness upon democracy. He wrote: "Their strictly Puritanical origin—their exclusively commercial habits—even the country they inhabit, which seems to divert their minds from the pursuit of science, literature and the arts—the proximity of Europe, which allows them to neglect these pursuits without relapsing into barbarism—a thousand special causes, of which I have only been able to point out the most important—have singularly concurred to fix the mind of the American upon purely practical objects."

Colonial attitudes persisted in America

so far as things of the mind were concerned. Seldom was an American author appreciated at home until he had been praised by critics abroad, and sometimes not even then. In 1830, it has been estimated, 70 per cent of the books sold in America were published in England. By 1840 this percentage had been drastically reduced, to only about 30. In the space of one decade the American book industry had grown tremendously, though most of the books had to be subsidized or else produced for advance orders secured by subscriptions. Despite the rise of book publishing in several American cities, especially in New York, the great majority of books published and sold were written, as before, by English authors.

American writers had other outlets for their wares besides publication in books, however. Hundreds of magazines appeared and disappeared, their average life being about two years, but at any given time a large number were being published, approximately 600 in 1850. Some were successful and long-lasting, such as the *Southern Literary Messenger* (founded 1834), *Godey's Lady's Book* (1837), *Harper's New Monthly Magazine* (1850), and the *Atlantic Monthly* (1857), besides the venerable *North American Review* (1815). In these magazines some of the greatest of native authors found a market for their works. In many other magazines, however, neither the writers nor their stories were great by any standard except popular appeal. The taste of most readers, especially women, was little different from that of their descendants who a century later were to listen to soap operas on radio or television. Sentimental and sirupy tales of struggling womanhood were favorites a hundred years ago as now.

Newspapers provided an occasional vehicle for fiction as well as journalism. Nevertheless, the main attraction of newspapers continued to lie in their news and editorial opinion. They grew rapidly in number, size, and circulation, as the United States became increasingly a nation of newspaper readers. Something new was the penny daily, the first being the New York *Sun* (1833), which soon was followed by James Gordon Bennett's New York *Herald* and Horace Greeley's New York *Tribune*. The *Sun* and the *Herald* specialized in scandal and crime, the *Tribune* in self-improvement and social uplift. With a separate weekly edition, the *Tribune* came to be a national or at least a sectional newspaper, having mail subscribers scattered throughout the North and West. The early nineteenth century was an age of personal journalism, with editors like Bennett and Greeley and lesser men over the country impressing their personalities upon their papers. In 1846 occurred two events that vastly facilitated the collection and distribution of news: the introduction of the Hoe cylinder rotary printing machine and the organization of the Associated Press. The latter was a response to the spread of the telegraph, following the first practical demonstration of Samuel F. B. Morse's invention (1844).

As in the Revolutionary era, so also in the period following the War of 1812 the question of literary independence drew much discussion from American writers. Ralph Waldo Emerson, in his notable Phi Beta Kappa address at Harvard (1837), urged scholars, philosophers, and men of letters to do all they could toward developing a self-reliant nationhood. But there were also arguments on the other side. Confessing that American literature was largely derivative, James Russell Lowell said (1849), "There is no degradation in such indebtedness"; and he suggested, "It may not be our destiny to produce a great literature."

Literature: A Golden Age

Foreign critics were too severe and native commentators too modest in their appraisals of American letters. In retrospect the period from the 1820's to the 1850's has seemed, indeed, a kind of golden age of literature in the United States. It was the time of Washington Irving, James Fenimore Cooper, Herman Melville, and Walt Whitman (all New Yorkers); Edgar Allan Poe (a Southerner by affirmation though not by birth); and Ralph Waldo Emerson, Henry David Thoreau, and Nathaniel Hawthorne (New Englanders). All these writers contributed to world literature: sooner or later they won lasting renown abroad as well as at home. Besides them, a number of others gained the esteem at least of their own countrymen and their own generation.

Irving, author of the earliest American literary "classics," was the first to achieve foreign recognition. His *History of New York* (1809) aimed, in his words, "to embody the traditions of the city in an amusing form," and did so in the stories of an imaginary historian of Dutch descent, Diedrich Knickerbocker. Irving's most famous work, *The Sketch Book* (1819–20), containing "Rip Van Winkle" and "The Legend of Sleepy Hollow," made further use of the Dutch folklore of New York. Afterwards Irving lived for a number of years in Spain and found story materials there, and still later he wrote historical works about the American West. A conservative in politics, he avoided contemporary political and social problems as literary themes.

Cooper, a less polished but more prolific writer, turned out more then thirty novels in thirty years (1820–50). Growing up on the New York frontier, then serving for several years in the navy, Cooper knew the forest and the sea, the settings of his adventure stories. Among the most successful were *The Spy* (1821), a novel of the Revolutionary War, and several "Leatherstocking" tales, including *The Last of the Mohicans* (1826) and *The Deerslayer* (1841). Over and over Cooper used the same formula of heroic action, breathless pursuit, and narrow escape. A

"THE SPY" ON THE STAGE. In the 1820's James Fenimore Cooper's popular novel of the Revolutionary War, *The Spy*, was adapted as a play. This painting was done by William Dunlap, a versatile dramatist and producer who has been called the father of the American theater. (COURTESY OF THE NEW YORK STATE HISTORICAL ASSOCIATION, COOPERSTOWN, NEW YORK)

born storyteller, he held his readers' attention despite the stilted dialogue of his stylized characters—the noble red man, the resourceful pioneer, the virtuous maid, and the enemy villain. He created an enduring character in the frontiersman Natty Bumppo ("Leatherstocking"). In his novels Cooper refrained from social criticism, but he also wrote essays in which, as a Democrat with aristocratic ideals, he condemned the pushing, go-getting spirit of his fellow Americans.

Melville, once a sailor and a resident of the South Seas, had a background even more adventurous than Cooper's, and he too wrote novels of adventure. But Melville was vastly more subtle and sophisticated in his writing, and he filled his stories with discursive philosophizing and with puzzling symbolism. In the best-known of his novels, *Moby Dick* (1851), Captain Ahab vengefully pursues the great white whale which has bitten his leg off; the captain catches the whale and is killed by him. Presumably the whale stands for evil, and the point of the story is that for a human being to attempt to destroy the evil in the universe is hopeless but heroic. For all the vividness of his scenes, the depth and complexity of his characters, and the richness of his style,

Melville's plots moved too slowly and his meaning was too obscure for the reading public of his time. A century later he was recognized as one of the greatest novelists ever to write in the English language.

Whitman, the self-proclaimed poet of American democracy, likewise was more widely appreciated by posterity than by his contemporaries, though some of them hailed him as the most original and authentic voice of the United States. The son of a Long Island carpenter, Whitman roamed the country and supported himself by odd jobs while composing his first poems. When he hired a printer to put out a thin volume of his work, *Leaves of Grass* (1855), he could find few buyers or readers, and he scandalized most of them. His verse, unconfined by rhyme, sang exuberantly of the flesh as well as the spirit. Whitman identified himself with the American people. He wrote:

I celebrate myself, and sing myself,
And what I assume you shall assume,
For every atom belonging to me
*   as good belongs to you.*

Five more editions of *Leaves of Grass*, with added poems, appeared before Whitman's death (1892), and so did other volumes of poetry and essays. His work eventually was translated into many languages.

Poe, in a short and unhappy life which ended in 1849, made himself an even more controversial figure than Whitman. After briefly attending the University of Virginia and the United States Military Academy, Poe made a living as best he could by editing literary magazines and selling an occasional bit of writing. He devised a theory of esthetics—supposedly based on music and mathematics—which he put into practice in his haunting onomatopoetic verse, his macabre tales (he invented the detective story), and his sharp literary criticisms. His first book, *Tamerlane and Other Poems* (1827), published anonymously, brought him little money and no fame, but he gained a

national reputation with "The Raven" when it appeared in a newspaper, in 1845. Some critics were contemptuous of his musical effects, and Emerson referred to him sneeringly as the "jingle man." In England, however, Alfred Lord Tennyson hailed Poe as a true, original poet, and in France Charles Baudelaire took him as an inspiration and a model. Indeed, Poe's writings influenced European literature far more than did those of any other nineteenth-century American.

New York, where Poe spent his last years, had become the literary capital of the nation after 1820. Then during the 1840's and 1850's New York, as a center of authorship, was largely eclipsed by New England, if not by the one village of Concord, Massachusetts.

Emerson, leader of the Concord literary circle, began his career as a Unitarian minister, then resigned (1833) and devoted himself to the exposition of a "transcendental" philosophy. He derived his ideas from wide reading in the works of Plato, Plotinus, seventeenth-century Neoplatonists, and writers of China, Persia, and India. He was inspired also by European travel and by conversation with English romantic authors such as Samuel Taylor Coleridge and Thomas Carlyle. From various sources Emerson put together a distinctively American philosophy of optimism, which saw reality as essentially good, and individualism, which stressed the capability of self-reliant man. Though he also wrote poetry and other works, Emerson was most noted for his platform lectures, some of which were condensed and revised for publication under the title *Essays* (1841-44). Through both the printed and the spoken word, he reached and influenced a wide audience, though he did not convince all who read or heard him, not even all his friends. One admirer, Melville, thought him full of "oracular gibberish" at times.

Thoreau, a friend and disciple of Emerson's, built a shack in the woods on Emerson's property and lived there, beside Walden Pond, for two years. Afterwards he explained: "I went to the woods because I wished to live deliberately, to front only the essential facts of life, and see if I could not learn what it had to teach, and not, when I came to die, discover that I had not lived." He was delayed five years in finding a publisher for his account of the experience, which finally appeared as *Walden* (1854). A man of ruggedly honest principles as well as ruggedly honest prose, Thoreau meanwhile spent a night in jail for refusing to pay taxes for the support of what he considered an unjust government (the United States then being at war with Mexico). He justified his stand in *Resistance to Civil Government* (1849), an essay on "passive resistance" that afterwards influenced a number of revolutionaries abroad, among them Mahatma Gandhi in India.

Hawthorne, at different times a friend and neighbor of Emerson's and of Melville's, had an outlook more like Melville's than Emerson's. A latter-day Puritan, Hawthorne dwelt upon somber themes from the Puritan past, with a conviction that evil was a grim reality. In a series of magazine stories, collected in *Twice-Told Tales* (1837), he probed the psychology of sin, much as Jonathan Edwards might have done if Edwards had written fiction instead of theological treatises. Hawthorne's first great success was *The Scarlet Letter* (1850), which is still regarded as one of the most nearly perfect of American novels. Treating the familiar "triangle" in an unfamiliar way, this psychological novel tells of the beautiful Hester Prynne, her husband, and her lover, and their very different responses to the evil in their lives.

Besides Emerson, Thoreau, and Hawthorne there were other New England authors who, in their own time, enjoyed reputations as high or higher than any of those three. William Cullen Bryant, as a young man in the Berkshire Hills, wrote "Thanatopsis" and other poems which brought him a reputation as America's foremost poet by 1832, after he had moved to New York to edit a newspaper, the *Evening Post*. Henry Wadsworth Longfellow, a sedate Harvard professor, appealed to popular tastes with his short poems on familiar subjects, like the village blacksmith, and his long poems elaborating historic traditions, such as *Evangeline* (1847), *The Song of Hiawatha* (1855), and *The Courtship of Miles Standish* (1858). His books sold well— a total of 300,000 copies by 1857. Oliver Wendell Holmes, another Harvard professor, a physician who taught in the Medical School, had time to write light verse and witty essays. James Russell Lowell, the first editor of the *Atlantic Monthly*, was a leading critic, essayist, and versifier. John Greenleaf Whittier, the "Quaker Poet," composed gentle, homespun verse about rural life in New England—and not so gentle verse attacking slavery in the South.

Art and Sciences

In the arts of the drama, painting, sculpture, and music, and in the sciences, Americans produced much less of originality and lasting value than in literature. Yet, even in these fields, Americans were not always wholly imitative during the four decades from 1820 to 1860.

The theater became increasingly popular, though not entirely respectable, despite its efforts to appear on the side of morality through the presentation of temperance dramas like *The Drunkard* and *Ten Nights in a Bar-room*. Regular stock companies, English and American, toured the cities and larger towns. The companies depended on their stars to attract audiences. Fanny Kemble and William Charles Macready, both English, were outstanding attractions. So were the Americans Joseph Jefferson, who played the role of Rip Van Winkle before countless applauding audiences after 1859, and

FANNY KEMBLE. The most famous leading lady of her time, Frances Anna Kemble came to the United States in 1832 with her father, a prominent English actor. She married an American, Pierce Butler, and after fourteen years divorced him. She gave Skakespearean readings and performed in plays in this country and abroad. In 1833, during her first season in America, Chief Justice John Marshall and Associate Justice Joseph Story attended a couple of her performances in Washington, D.C. "We have seen Miss Kemble as Julia in 'The Hunchback,' and as Mrs. Haller in 'The Stranger,'" Story wrote. "I have never seen any female acting at all comparable to hers. She is so graceful that you forget that she is not very handsome. In [as] Mrs. Haller she threw the whole audience into tears. The chief justice shed them in common with younger eyes." Painting by Henry Inman. (IN THE BROOKLYN MUSEUM COLLECTION)

Edwin Forrest, famous for Shakespearean parts. Intense rivalries developed between celebrities and between their respective fans. In 1849 a mob of Forrest's admirers marched upon a New York theater where Macready was playing, and in the ensuing riot 22 persons were killed and many more injured. The legitimate stage often resorted to cheap showmanship so as to compete with such spectacles as circuses, minstrel shows, and "museums," containing freaks and oddities like the midget

Tom Thumb. In the 1840's P. T. Barnum rose to become the leading promoter of these kinds of mass amusement.

Painters generally conformed to the sentimental taste of their customers, who demanded soft landscapes, flattering portraits, and storytelling pictures. Among the better artists, Asher B. Durand and others of the "Hudson River School" concentrated upon natural scenery, William Sidney Mount portrayed his fellow Long Islanders at work and play, and George Caleb Bingham recorded everyday scenes of life in Missouri. The most successful sculptor was Hiram Powers, whose statue of a naked woman, entitled "The Greek Slave," attracted attention and provoked controversy on moral rather than esthetic grounds.

By the 1840's New York, Philadelphia, and Boston possessed orchestras of their own, and Americans flocked to the performances of foreign celebrities such as the Norwegian violinist Ole Bull and the "Swedish Nightingale" Jenny Lind. But American composers were rare, the most successful (judged by their enduring popularity) being John Howard Payne, Lowell Mason, and Stephen C. Foster. Payne, an actor and playwright, wrote "Home, Sweet Home" for an opera (1823). Mason, a Boston music teacher, composed the tunes for "Nearer, My God, to Thee," "From Greenland's Icy Mountains," and other stately hymns. Foster wrote "Oh! Susanna," "Old Black Joe," and more than 200 other melodies, most of them to accompany his own verse. Many of these songs, written for black-face ministrel bands, convey a sense of genuine nostalgia for the plantation, though Foster was born in Pittsburgh and spent his brief and tragic life in the Northeast.

Americans were more noted for applied science than for scientific theory. Nevertheless, from observation and experiment, some of them made significant contributions to scientific knowledge. John J. Audubon, pioneer ornithologist, published his exquisite sketches in *Birds of America* (1827–38). Joseph Henry, the most original American scientist since Benjamin Franklin, made important discoveries in electromagnetism (thus preparing the way for Morse's invention of the telegraph). A Georgia physician, Crawford W. Long, demonstrated the practicability of ether as an anesthetic (1842).

The federal government sponsored some kinds of scientific work, though not as generously as it might have done, had Congressmen not opposed expenditures on grounds of thrift and state rights. Geographical knowledge was increased by the United States Coast Survey, begun in 1832, and by the United States Exploring Expedition, which between 1838 and 1842 surveyed extensive areas of the Pacific Ocean, under the leadership of Lieutenant Charles Wilkes. The great oceanographer, Matthew Fontaine Maury, was appointed director of the United States Naval Observatory and Hydrographic Office in 1841, and his work was thus supported by the government. In 1846 the Smithsonian Institution was founded in Washington, after an Englishman had willed his fortune of $500,000 to the United States "for the increase and diffusion of knowledge." Appropriately the noted physicist Joseph Henry became the first head of the institution.

The leading colleges, Yale and Harvard, also served as important patrons of science. At Yale Benjamin Silliman taught chemistry and mineralogy for a half century after his appointment in 1802, and for many years he edited the *American Journal of Science and Art*, after founding it in 1818. Though not a notable researcher, Silliman was an outstanding teacher who kept American students and scholars informed of scientific developments throughout the world. At Harvard the zoologist and geologist Louis Agassiz and the botanist Asa Gray not only taught but also carried on important researches in their respective fields. Through his studies of plant distribution Gray assisted the English scholar Charles Darwin in formulating the theory of evolution. When Darwin's epoch-making book *On the Origin of Species* appeared (1859), Gray endorsed and Agassiz rejected the idea that plants and animals, instead of remaining unchanged since God created them, had developed through a process of natural selection.

Spirit of Social Reform

"In no country in the world has the principle of association been more successfully used, or more unsparingly applied to a multitude of different objects, than in America," Tocqueville observed. "Societies are formed to resist enemies which are exclusively of a moral nature, and to diminish the vice of intemperance: in the United States associations are established to promote public order, commerce, industry, morality, and religion; for there is no end which the human will, seconded by the collective exertions of individuals, despairs of attaining."

Indeed, Americans organized reform societies of all kinds, not only for temperance but also for education, world peace, the care of the poor and the handicapped, the improvement of prisons, women's rights, the abolition of slavery, and dozens of other idealistic purposes.

This reform spirit derived from a variety of sources, religious and rational, domestic and foreign. The Christian doctrine of human worth, the Revolutionary philosophy of the equality of man—these were part of the general background. More immediately, the rise of industrialism in the British Isles and Western Europe as well as the United States produced social dislocations and suffering but at the same time gave promise of a more abundant life for all. No doubt, with some people, a determination to improve human welfare was stimulated by the contrast between what actually was and what apparently might be. Certainly the humanitarian stirrings of the time were to be found in many lands at once, and most conspicuously in those countries that were being most rapidly industrialized.

Emerson's philosophy of "transcendentalism" contributed to the reform spirit in America. Emerson evolved the doctrine of the Oversoul or spiritual essence from which all things derived, including the soul of man. Since all humanity shared in this essential Being, this all-in-all, there existed a very real brotherhood of mankind. And since the Oversoul was good there could be no such thing, in the last analysis, as evil. (The later teachings of Mary Baker G. Eddy, founded of Christian Science, were in some respects similar to those of Emerson.) This philosophy, for all its obscurities and inconsistencies, had practical consequences for its believers. It made them optimistic. It taught them that they were potentially divine and could increase their divinity by identifying themselves more and more fully with the Oversoul, with Being, with Truth. It led them to believe in the perfectability of man.

Still more important as a call to reform were the preachings of the revivalist, Charles G. Finney, who was at first a Presbyterian and later a Congregationalist. In upstate New York and in Ohio, beginning in the 1820's, Finney delivered many a memorable sermon on the dangers of damnation and the possibilities of salvation—through good works as well as faith. "The church," he maintained, "must take right ground on the subject of Temperance, and Moral Reform, and all the subjects of practical morality which come up for decision from time to time." Not all the churches did so, and some reformers (known as "come-outers") left the fold and even turned against organized religion, denouncing it as a bulwark to the status quo.

Reform leaders implied by their activities that they believed in a sort of earthly millennium as well as a heavenly one.

Going a step farther, one religious prophet together with his thousands of followers expected and awaited the actual second coming of Christ. From his studies of the Bible and from other signs and calculations William Miller of Low Hampton, New York, predicted that on a certain day in 1843 Christ would appear and all true believers would ascend bodily to heaven. After new predictions and repeated disappointments he made the date indefinite. His followers formed a lasting sect, the Seventh-Day Adventists.

Miller and other prophets of the time, such as Finney and also Joseph Smith, the founder of Mormonism, were New Englanders by birth and residents of upstate New York at some stage in their careers. So, too, the great majority of reform leaders were New England born, and a large number of them lived at least temporarily in New York state. Most reform leaders disbelieved in unions, opposed strikes, and were indifferent to the plight of the unemployed. William Lloyd Garrison, the abolitionist, denounced labor agitators for trying "to inflame the minds of our working classes against the more opulent, and to persuade men that they are contemned and oppressed by a wealthy aristocracy." A few of the "more opulent," such as the merchants Arthur and Lewis Tappan of New York and Amos and Abbott Lawrence of Boston, contributed vast sums to finance various reforms, especially abolition. This is not to say, however, that big business in general was favorable to social reform. More often than not, reform was resisted by both the laborer and the capitalist. It was essentially a middle-class movement, receiving its greatest support from the reasonably well-to-do farmers, shopkeepers, and professional people of the North and the West.

Toward Universal Education

As of 1830 no state could yet boast a general system of free public education in the modern sense, with full tax support, compulsory attendance, and enforced maintenance of schools, though Massachusetts, as in earlier times, came fairly close to it. A very high proportion of American children had the benefit of the three R's, but most of them still got their learning from church schools, proprietary institutions, private tutors, or members of their own families. Then, during the 1830's, a widespread demand for state-supported primary education arose. This demand came from reformers

reformers made considerable headway in several of the states. The greatest of these leaders was Horace Mann, the first secretary of the Massachusetts board of education, which was established in 1837. He reorganized the state's school system, lengthened the school year (to six months), doubled teacher's salaries, enriched the curriculum, and improved teacher training and teaching methods. Henry Barnard led the way to better schools in Connecticut and Rhode Island. In Pennsylvania a school law was passed

---

HORACE MANN ON EDUCATION

1848

"Now surely nothing but universal education can counterwork this tendency to the domination of capital and the servility of labor. If one class possesses all the wealth and the education, while the residue of society is ignorant and poor, it matters not by what name the relation between them may be called: the latter, in fact and in truth, will be the servile dependents and subjects to the former. But, if education be equally diffused, it will draw property after it by the strongest of attractions; for such a thing never did happen, and never can happen, as that an intelligent and practical body of men should be permanently poor. Property and labor in different classes are essentially antagonistic; but property and labor in the same class are essentially fraternal."

---

who feared the consequences of allowing every man to vote, including in many cases even the newly arrived immigrant, without making public provision for his literacy at least. The demand came also from workingmen who hoped that book learning would enable their children to rise in the world. Opposition was forthcoming, however, from taxpayers (especially childless ones) who objected to paying for the education of other people's families, and from Lutherans, Roman Catholics, and other religious groups who already supported their own church schools and did not wish to be taxed for public education besides.

Against such opposition, educational

in 1835, making state funds available for the education of all children and not merely the children of paupers, as formerly; but only the exertions of Thaddeus Stevens in the legislature saved the law from an early repeal. In New York, after William H. Seward became governor in 1839, the upstate system of school districts supporting their own schools was extended to the metropolis. This step aroused much opposition, since it gave control of some new districts to the local Roman Catholic majorities.

By the 1850's the principle of tax-supported elementary schools was accepted in all the states, and all of them were making at least a start toward putting the principle into practice. Still, there were vast differences in the quantity and quality of public schools from place to place, the poorest performances and the lowest literacy rates being found in the newly settled areas of the West and in the more sparsely populated parts of the South. Taking the country as a whole, only a small proportion of children of school age were actually going to school, one white child out of every seven in the South and one out of every six elsewhere (1860).

Most teachers were poorly paid and poorly prepared, many of them being themselves scarcely able to read, write, and cipher. In rural district schools, containing husky youths along with tender tots, what the schoolmaster needed was a strong arm rather than a well-stocked mind. If he could not thrash the most obstreperous of his pupils, he could get nowhere with his lessons. Reformers like Mann and Barnard, believing that human nature was essentially good, advocated gentleness and understanding as practised by progressive educators in Switzerland (notably Johann Pestalozzi). Most teachers—and parents too—subscribed to the old Calvinist doctrine of inborn wickedness: they did not wish to spare the rod. Under the circumstances the majority of teaching positions continued to be filled by men, even in the elementary schools. Seldom did these men look upon teaching as a career; often they were aspiring lawyers or preachers who worked their way through college by doubling as schoolmasters in vacation periods. Nevertheless, teaching was beginning to be looked upon as a profession, and an increasing number of young women were going into it. With Mann taking the lead, Massachusetts in 1839 established the first American state-supported teacher-training or "normal" school, at Lexington. In 1845 he brought about the formation of a state association of teachers.

Since so many teachers were poorly

prepared, both they and their pupils had to rely heavily upon textbooks. Noah Webster's spellers and grammars continued to be widely used. Supplementing them and rivaling them in popularity were the six graded *Eclectic Readers* (1835–57) prepared by William Holmes McGuffey, who was an Ohio professor and college president and then for many years a professor at the University of Virginia. The McGuffey readers were filled with moral lessons, patriotic declamations, sentimental verse, and fascinating facts. A favorite recitation piece was the following:

> *Woodman, spare that tree;*
> *Touch not a single bough.*
> *In youth it sheltered me,*
> *And I'll protect it now.*

Eventually adopted in 37 states, the McGuffey books gave thousands of schoolchildren a shared background of popular culture and helped to mold the literary tastes of the reading public.

The principle of state support was applied later to secondary than to elementary schools. By 1860 there were 22 tax-supported "free academies" in New York, more than 100 public high schools in Massachusetts, and a total of about 300 such institutions in the nation as a whole. At the same time there were approximately 6,000 private academies. Most of them were open to boys only, a few were coeducational, and a growing number were "female seminaries."

While the private academies were multiplying, so were the private colleges, though at a slower rate, about 80 being founded between 1830 and 1850. Almost all of these were denominational colleges, with close church connections, and their chief though not their only purpose was to prepare a learned clergy. These institutions became too numerous for their own good. Their enrollments were small, in many cases fewer than 100 in the 1850's (even Harvard and Yale had only 400 or 500 students apiece, though the College of William and Mary had nearly 1,000). Generally endowments were scanty, facilities poor, salaries low, and professors unscholarly, though self-sacrificing and sincere. None of these institutions admitted women until, in 1837, Oberlin accepted four girls as regular students and thus became the first coeducational college. Some outsiders feared that coeducation was a rash experiment which approximated free love, but the Oberlin authorities were confident that "the mutual influence of the sexes upon each other is decidedly happy in the cultivation of both mind & manners." Only a few other institutions copied Oberlin's example before the Civil War. Some of the young ladies' seminaries—notably Mount Holyoke, which the most famous of all women educators, Mary Lyon, founded in Massachusetts in 1837—eventually became full-fledged women's colleges.

The idea of state support for higher education had to contend against the prevailing concept of private, denominational control. Besides the older states with public universities (Vermont, North Carolina, Georgia, Ohio, Virginia) many of the newer states of the Northwest and Southwest committed themselves to the support of higher learning. State universities were established in Indiana, Michigan, Kentucky, Missouri, Mississippi, Iowa, Wisconsin, Minnesota, and Louisiana before the Civil War. None of these, whether old or new, was a true university in the European sense of an institution devoted to high-level, graduate training.

The standard curriculum, whether in the private college or the state university, still emphasized the old-fashioned liberal arts. A young man who desired training for a professional career (other than the ministry) had few institutions to choose from. He could study engineering at the United States Military Academy, Rensselaer Polytechnic Institute (1824), or at Yale or Harvard, which set up engineering schools in 1846 and 1847. He could study law or medicine at one of several institutions, but no American medical school compared with the best ones abroad. In most cases, as in earlier times, he apprenticed himself to a practising physician, learned engineering on the job (the Erie Canal was a most productive "school" for engineers), or "read law" in the office of some successful lawyer.

Adult education was furthered by the founding of numerous libraries, study clubs, and self-improvement societies of various kinds. Noteworthy was the Lyceum, which was started by Josiah Holbrook in Massachusetts (1826) and spread rapidly throughout the North. "The first step to form a Lyceum," Holbrook explained, "is for a few neighbors or citizens to agree to hold meetings for their mutual improvement." Next, they could acquire books, scientific apparatus, specimens of rocks and plants, and the like. Then they could conduct experiments, carry on discussions among themselves, and sponsor public lectures. The sponsorship of lectures soon became their principal activity. Through the Lyceum many thousands of Americans were able to hear scientists like Agassiz, foreign authors like Dickens, exemplars of self-culture like the "learned Blacksmith" Elihu Burritt, popular philosophers like Emerson, and social reformers like the abolitionist Garrison or the repentant drunkard John B. Gough.

Perfecting Society and Man

While many reformers hoped to make possible a better life by creating opportunities through education or by eliminating specific social evils, some of the more advanced thinkers aspired to start afresh and remake society by founding ideal, cooperative communities. America still seemed a spacious and unencumbered country where models of a perfect society could be set up with a good chance to succeed. Presumably success would lead to imitation, until communities free of crime, poverty, and other evils would cover the land. A number of religious groups, notably the Shakers, practiced a kind of communism as a means of realizing what they considered a truly Christian life. But the impetus to communism (or communitarianism) as a way of perfecting earthly society came chiefly from nonreligious, rationalistic thinkers.

Among the communitarian philosophers, three of the most influential were Robert Owen, Charles Fourier, and John Humphrey Noyes. Owen, famous for his humanitarian policies as owner of prosperous textile mills in Scotland, reached the conclusion that faulty environment was to blame for human failings, and hence that poverty and crime would not appear in a rationally planned society. In 1825 he put his principles into practice at New Harmony, on the banks of the Wabash in Indiana. Within a few years New Harmony failed as an economic enterprise, though in other respects it was a success. Fourier, a mere commercial employee in France, never visited the United States but influenced many Americans through the writings of Albert Brisbane, whose *Social Destiny of Man* (1840) explained the principles of Fourierism with its self-sufficient associations, or "phalanxes." One or more of these phalanxes was organized in every Northern state, the most famous of them being Brook Farm, a community of intellectuals including Hawthorne, near Boston. Noyes, a native Vermonter and a one-time Yale divinity student, founded the most bizarre and most enduring of all the utopian colonies, the Oneida Community in upstate New York (1848), were his followers carried out his unorthodox sexual theories, old men mating with young women and *vice versa*, all changing partners at his direction, supposedly in the interest of scientific breeding. Needless to say, none of these experiments set a pattern for American life.

Less thoroughgoing reforms, however, did much to alleviate the ills of society as it actually was. No evil was more glaring than the treatment of social offenders and unfortunates. Criminals of all kinds, debtors unable to pay their debts, senile paupers, and the mentally ill were crowded indiscriminately into prisons and jails which in many cases were literally holes, one jail in Connecticut being an abandoned mine shaft. From the 1820's on, the states one by one abolished imprisonment for debt, and some of them greatly improved their handling of the criminal and the insane. New York, with the erection of its new prison at Auburn (1821), introduced a system of solitary confinement by night and group work with absolute silence by day; Pennsylvania tried solitary confinement for both day and night. Though both of these systems now seem harsh, they were then hailed as progressive steps, since they gave each prisoner an opportunity to meditate upon his wrongdoing and also checked the tendency for old convicts to corrupt the young. Public hangings, supposedly a deterrent to crime, used to attract spectators by the thousands, including thieves and pickpockets busily plying their trade. In the 1830's several states began to hold executions within the privacy of prison walls, and a few states did away with capital punishment entirely. While there already existed a few mental hospitals, the insane (unless cared for at home) generally were kept in jail and treated brutally. The Boston schoolmistress Dorothea Dix, shocked by her chance visit to the Cambridge jail (1841), devoted her life to securing the establishment of insane asylums in Massachusetts and other states.

In looking for causes of insanity, pauperism, and crime, many reformers concluded that these evils could be traced largely to strong drink. Americans of earlier generations had been an alcoholically convivial people, with a remarkable per capita consumption of whiskey, hard cider, and rum. The Puritans had been hard drinkers, many respectable preachers

THE "COLD WATER" PLEDGE. Members of the Washington Temperance Society
—themselves reformed drunkards—urged drinkers to join them in signing a pledge
of total abstinence. This lithograph of 1846, which associates poverty with drink,
is dedicated to "the Washingtonians of the United States" and is "commemorative
of their Declaration of Independence from the dominion of King Alcohol."
(LIBRARY OF CONGRESS)

continued to resort to stimulants, and few Americans supposed that a birth, a wedding, or a funeral could be properly observed without plenty of liquor—the story is told of drunken pallbearers who lost their way to the grave. From colonial times on, however, a few men like Cotton Mather and Dr. Benjamin Rush had spoken out against intemperance. In the early 1800's an organized temperance movement began with the formation of local societies in New England, and in 1826 the American Society for the Promotion of Temperance appeared as a coordinating agency for the various groups. The movement gained in sensationalism when (1840) six reformed drunkards of Baltimore organized the Washington Temperance Society and began to draw crowds to hear their intriguing confessions. As the temperance forces grew and spread over the country, the crusaders diverged, some advocating total abstinence and others seeing no harm in wine or beer, some favoring prohibition laws and others relying on the individual conscience. Massachusetts and other states experimented with legislation for local option, allowing communities to regulate or prohibit liquor sales,

THE BLOOMER COSTUME. An enterprising Philadelphia music publisher, taking advantage of a timely topic, brought out "The New Costume Polka" and dedicated it to Mrs. Amelia Bloomer. The cover of the sheet music was adorned with this picture of a demure yet stylish young lady wearing the clothes that Mrs. Bloomer recommended. (LIBRARY OF CONGRESS)

and Maine (1851) passed a statewide prohibition law. Prohibitionists in a few other states gained similar victories, but the laws were unpopular and soon were repealed except in Maine.

To some it seemed that not only alcoholic beverages but also tobacco, coffee, and improper foods hindered the full realization of man's perfectionist possibilities. A leading health faddist, Dr. Sylvester Graham, believed that one way to social happiness was through the eating of coarse, whole wheat bread (the "Graham cracker" is a faint reminder of him). Other health reformers relied on hydropathy with its regimen of bathing and water-drinking; spas like the Hot Springs in Virginia became fashionable places for taking the "water cure." Orson Fowler, the foremost exponent of phrenology (a "science" based on the notion that char-

acter and personality are revealed in the contour of the cranium), expected to bring about a "renovating of mankind" through the self-understanding that was supposed to result from the examination of bumps on the head. This science gained such popularity that practically everyone turned into an amateur phrenologist.

Whatever the social handicaps that beset man as man, those that a woman had to face were considerably worse. In America she enjoyed a freer life and greater respect than in England or Europe, yet in this country too she was legally an inferior. According to the Anglo-American common law a husband had almost absolute authority over the person and property of his wife: what was his was his, and what was hers was his also. In case of divorce he was far more likely than she to get custody of the children. Though women worked in household and mill, they could not look forward to careers in medicine, the ministry, politics, or law. By custom they were forbidden to speak in public to a mixed audience, lest they "unsex" themselves and lose their feminine charm.

Though women were active in the reform movements, especially temperance and abolition, male reformers usually compelled them to take a back seat. This discrimination against them intensified an already growing demand for women's rights. In 1848 Lucretia Mott and Elizabeth Cady Stanton called a convention of women; it met in Seneca Falls, New York, and adopted resolutions (patterned on the Declaration of Independence) to the effect that all men *and women* are created equal and endowed with certain inalienable rights. While the feminists failed to obtain the right to vote or hold office, they made noticeable gains before the Civil War. As early as 1839, Mississippi had recognized the right of married women to control their own property; during the next two decades several other states did the same. At least one woman,

Dr. Elizabeth Blackwell, gained acceptance and fame as a physician; several women, prominent among them Lucy Stone (who with her husband's approval retained her maiden name), became successful lecturers; a still larger number, including Emma Willard and Catherine Beecher, made great contributions to progressive education, especially for women. Some of the feminists, apparently thinking equality with men meant similarity to them, cut their hair short and wore more or less mannish clothes. Mrs. Amelia Bloomer, for example, attempted to popularize the skirt-and-pantalettes costume which was named for her.

Recalling the Napoleonic Wars and the War of 1812, many reformers agreed with the Quakers that one of the worst ills of the world was war. By 1819 more than a dozen local peace societies had sprung up in various parts of the United States, and in 1828 the Maine merchant William Ladd undertook to coordinate the movement by founding the American Peace Society with headquarters in New York. Later (1840) Ladd devised a peace plan embracing a Congress of Nations and a Court of Nations whose decisions were to be enforced by public opinion rather than economic or military sanctions. Meanwhile the pacifists disagreed, some approving defensive but not offensive wars, others taking a pledge of complete nonresistance. To most of the peace workers in New England, the Mexican War (1846-8) seemed an act of proslavery aggression on the part of the United States, and they took their stand against it, Henry David Thoreau refusing to pay taxes for its support, and James Russell Lowell writing in the *Biglow Papers*: "Ez fer war, I call it murder,—there you hev it plain an' flat." But the Civil War put the pacifists in a dilemma, at least momentarily, since most of them were also abolitionists. Finally the antislavery cause took precedence over the antiwar cause, as it already had taken precedence over the rest of the reform crusades.

The Antislavery Movement

After the Missouri excitement of 1819–21, Americans involved in the antislavery movement calmed down somewhat, though they continued their work and gradually increased the number of antislavery societies and members. For the next decade their program continued to be mild and gradualistic, and they were most numerous in the South, particularly in the border slave states. The most active national organization was the American Colonization Society (established in 1817), which had adherents in both the North and the South. It aimed to "colonize" freed Negroes in their homeland, and under its auspices the black republic of Liberia was founded on the African coast. The society received private contributions and appropriations from the legislatures of Virginia and Maryland to carry on the work, but in ten years it succeeded in transporting to Africa fewer Negroes than were being born in America each month. Northern members began to suspect that their Southern associates were more interested in strengthening slavery, by getting rid of Negroes already free, than in hastening the end of the institution by encouraging slaveowners to manumit their slaves. During the 1820's the most active crusader against slavery itself was the New Jersey Quaker Benjamin Lundy, who published the leading antislavery newspaper of the time, the *Genius of Universal Emancipation*, in Baltimore.

In 1831 Lundy's helper, the young Massachusetts-born printer William Lloyd Garrison, sounded a new and strident note with the first issue of his own paper, *The Liberator*, in Boston. From the outset Garrison condemned the thought of gradual, compensated emancipation and demanded immediate abolition, without reimbursement for

"THE LIBERATOR": FIRST ISSUE

1831

William Lloyd Garrison made clear his fiery spirit and his uncompromising aim in the very first number of his abolitionist newspaper, *The Liberator*. He told his readers:

"I am aware that many object to the severity of my language; but is there not cause for severity? I *will* be as harsh as truth, and as uncompromising as justice. On this subject, I do not wish to think, or speak, or write with moderation. No! No! Tell a man whose house is on fire, to give a moderate alarm; tell him to moderately rescue his wife from the hands of the ravisher; tell the mother to gradually extricate her babe from the fire into which it has fallen;—but urge me not to use moderation in a cause like the present. I am in earnest—I will not equivocate—I will not excuse—I will not retreat a single inch—*AND I WILL BE HEARD*."

---

slaveowners. Under his leadership the New England Anti-Slavery Society was founded in 1832 and the American Anti-Slavery Society the following year. But he shocked many friends of freedom by the extremes to which he went. He opposed the government, characterizing the Constitution as "a covenant with death and an agreement with hell," and he opposed the churches on the grounds that they were bulwarks of slavery. In 1840 he split the American Anti-Slavery Society by insisting upon the right of women to participate fully in its activities, even to speak before audiences that included men as well as women.

By that time there were in existence nearly 2,000 local societies with a total of almost 200,000 members. These societies remained alive, active, and growing after the disruption of the national organization. The movement as a whole was far bigger than Garrison. His influence was confined mainly to New England, and even in that part of the country he was but one of many important leaders, a few of the others being William E. Channing, Theodore Parker, and Wendell Phillips. In New York and the Middle West the most influential was Theodore Weld, who was far more sane and sensible than Garrison and equally devoted to the cause. Converted to reform by Finney's preaching, Weld worked within the churches, especially the Presbyterian and Congregational. Through the labors of men like Weld, thousands came to disapprove slavery who never joined an anti-slavery society. Thus it is hard to say how many antislavery people there were at any given time, especially since "antislavery" was a term so broad as to include all kinds and degrees of opposition to slavery.

Most of the active members of organized societies were "abolitionists" in the sense that they favored immediate abolition. But this did not mean precisely what it seemed to mean. The abolitionists aimed at what they called "immediate abolition gradually accomplished." That is, they hoped to bring about a sudden and not a gradual end to slavery, but they did not expect to achieve this for some time. At first, they counted on "moral suasion": they were going to appeal to the conscience of the slaveholder and convince him that slaveholding was a sin.

Later they turned more and more to political action, seeking to induce the Northern states and the federal government to aid the cause where possible. Employing propaganda of the deed as well as the word, they helped runaway slaves find refuge in the North or in Canada, though in doing so they did not set up any such highly organized system as the term "Underground Railroad" implies. After the Supreme Court (in *Prigg v. Pennsylvania*, 1842) held that the states need not aid in enforcing the federal fugitive-slave law of 1793, abolitionists secured the passage of "personal liberty laws" in several of the Northern states; these laws forbade state officials to assist in the capture and return of runaways. Above all, the anti-slavery societies petitioned Congress to abolish slavery in places where the federal government had jurisdiction—in the territories and the District of Columbia—and to prohibit the interstate slave trade. Not even the most ardent abolitionists supposed that Congress constitutionally could interfere with a "domestic" institution like slavery within the Southern states themselves.

While the abolitionists engaged in pressure politics, they never formed a political party with an abolition platform. In 1840 the Liberty party was launched, with the Kentucky antislavery leader James G. Birney as its presidential candidate, but this party and its successors did not campaign for outright abolition: they stood for "free soil," that is, for keeping slavery out of the territories. Some free soilers were friends of the slave; others were Negrophobes who cared nothing about slavery but desired to make the West a white man's country. Garrison said free-soil-ism was really "white-man-ism."

In the North, where there was widespread anti-Negro if not proslavery feeling, the antislavery movement provoked much hostility during the 1830's. When Prudence Crandall undertook to admit Negro children to her private school in Connecticut, she aroused the opposition of the community, and the state supreme court decided against her in a lawsuit arising from the controversy. A mob attacked Garrison on the streets of Boston, and another (1837) killed the antislavery editor Elijah Lovejoy in Alton, Illinois. Throughout the North antislavery lecturers, risking their health if not their lives, time and again were attacked with rotten eggs or stones.

In the South the reaction was far stronger, and if no abolitionists were killed, it was only because (from the 1830's on) they dared not even venture into that part of the country.

BIBLIOGRAPHY

An introduction to Englishmen's comment on American ways may be obtained from *American Social History as Recorded by British Travellers*, edited by Allan Nevins (1923; new ed., 1931), and from Max Berger's *The British Traveller in America, 1836–1860* (1943). Alexis de Tocqueville, *Democracy in America* (4 vols., 1835–40), is available in a number of editions.

Important interpretations of the literary productivity of the time may be found in Van Wyck Brooks, *The Flowering of New England, 1815–1865* (1936); F. O. Matthiessen, *American Renaissance* (1941); and Lewis Mumford, *The Golden Day* (1926). A biography of a foremost literary figure is R. L. Rusk, *The Life of Ralph Waldo Emerson* (1949). See also Carl Bode, *The Anatomy of American Popular Culture, 1840–1861* (1959).

The best survey of the reform movements as a whole is A. F. Tyler, *Freedom's Ferment: Phases of American Social History to 1860* (1944). R. E. Riegel's *Young America, 1830–1840* (1949) contains a good deal on reform agitation during that decade. R. S. Fletcher, *A History of Oberlin College from Its Foundation through the*

Civil War (2 vols., 1943), amounts to vastly more than a mere college chronicle, since it treats Oberlin as the important reform center it was. A. M. Schlesinger, in *The American as Reformer* (1950), provides a brief, thoughtful introduction to the reform spirit. The relations between religion and reformism form the themes of C. C. Cole, Jr., *The Social Ideals of the Northern Evangelists, 1826–1860* (1954), and T. L. Smith, *Revivalism and Social Reform in Mid-Nineteenth-Century America* (1957), which emphasizes the ideas of the common man rather than those of the "crackpot fringe." C. A. Johnson, *The Frontier Camp Meeting* (1955), covers the subject of revivalism in the Mississippi Valley during the first four decades of the nineteenth century.

On individual reformers and reforms, see Arthur Bestor, *Backwoods Utopias: The Sectarian and Owenite Phases of Communitarian Socialism in America: 1663–1829* (1950); Everett Webber, *Escape to Utopia: The Communal Movement in America* (1959); H. E. Marshall, *Dorothea Dix,*

Forgotten Samaritan (1937); H. S. Commager, *Theodore Parker* (1936); J. D. Davies, *Phrenology: Fad and Science* (1955); N. K. Teeters and J. D. Shearer, *The Prison at Philadelphia* (1957), a study of the rise and decline of Pennsylvania's system of solitary confinement; Carl Bode, *The American Lyceum* (1956); and Paul Monroe, *The Founding of the American Public School System* (1940).

Betty Fladeland, *James Gillespie Birney: Slaveholder to Abolitionist* (1955), shows that not all abolitionists were "Northern fanatics." R. B. Nye, *William Lloyd Garrison and the Humanitarian Reformers* (1955), succinctly recounts the career of the most famous abolitionist and places him in the context of the reform movement as a whole. See also Nye's *Fettered Freedom: Civil Liberties and the Slavery Controversy, 1830–1860* (1949). G. H. Barnes, *The Anti-Slavery Impulse, 1833–1844* (1933), makes a case for Theodore Weld as the most important of the abolitionists.

16

SECTIONALISM AND
THE SOUTH

Beginning in the 1840's and increasing in intensity during the next decade, sectionalism—in a much more extreme shape than in earlier years—appeared as a potent force in American life. Sectional dissimilarities seemed to characterize American society, and sectional controversies threatened to dominate American politics. At times sectionalism seemed to endanger the very existence of the Federal Union. Significantly, these divisive factors came into play at a time when other forces—economic, cultural, geographic—were combining their influence to strengthen the bonds of national unity and to exalt the mood and the concept of nationalism. The angry brawls of these troubled years were the growing pains of a young nation which was approaching, with some reluctance, an inexorable homogeneity. The aggressive attitude assumed by one section, the South, was partly the result of a determination not to be pressed into a national norm that some Southerners felt was inevitable —unless the South could in some way check the political agent of centralism: the federal government.

The Character of Sectionalism

At the risk of some oversimplification, it is possible to say that in the 1840's and 1850's the United States, in a political-geographic sense, consisted of three sections: the Northeast, the West, and the South. The Northeast was made up of the New England states and New York, Pennsylvania, and New Jersey. The West, sometimes called the Northwest, included Ohio, Indiana, Illinois, Michigan, Wisconsin, Iowa, and Minnesota; today we call this area the Middle West. The South, embracing every state where slavery existed, stretched from Maryland to Texas, from Missouri to Mississippi. In a previous period some of the states in this section (Arkansas or Mississippi, for example) had exhibited characteristics that justified classifying them as Western states, but during the time of the sectional controversy any state that practiced slavery has to be considered as being, at least in a political meaning, in the Southern system.

It should be noted that the boundaries of sectional division were not quite as neat or definite as the preceding paragraph might indicate. Within each section were subregions, like the Upper and Lower South, that might exhibit marked cultural differences. And there were geographic subregions, like the Ohio River Valley, that cut over sectional lines and had their own peculiar form of entity. Particularly at the edges of the sectional divisions the lines of demarcation sometimes tended to become blurred. Parts of Ohio, such as the Western Reserve district in the northeastern area of the state, developed an economy similar to that of the neighboring Northeast and a culture similar to that of New England, from which most of its inhabitants had originally come. Missouri, a Southern state, contained many people who had emigrated from the Northern States or from Europe; its economy was partly Southern in nature and partly Western. As a result Missouri acted sometimes like a Southern state and on other occasions like a Western one.

Despite the qualifications that must be made, the fact remains that three sections existed in the United States. As the sectional controversy developed and the Northeast and West acted together on many issues, people spoke of the country as being comprised of two sections, the North (the East and West) and the South. Had it not been for the appearance of the slavery issue, it is possible that the dividing line might have run from north to south and divided the nation into an East and a West. On one side would have been the older states from Maine to Florida and on the other the newer states of the West from Wisconsin to Louisiana. If proof of the awful potency of the slavery issue is required, the evidence is apparent in slavery's power to split the natural entity of the Mississippi Valley and array the states of that area in opposite political camps.

Any analysis of the sectional controversy must emphasize the differing economic systems of the three sections, not only because many of the political issues were economic in origin, but also because the economy of each section had much to do with determining the general form of its culture. The economic systems of the sections contained within themselves a number of variations, and yet the system of each manifested a peculiar unity. Thus, in the Northeast, which had a predominantly industrial economy, there were manufacturers, bankers, merchants (in foreign and domestic trade), laborers, and farmers. In the agricultural West were farmers and, in smaller numbers and of less importance than in the East, manufacturers, bankers, and laborers. In the South, which was even more agricultural than the West, were planters, farmers, some merchants and bankers, and a few manufacturers and laborers.

The all-important fact to be grasped concerning sectional economics is that in each section a particular economic activity dominated the life of the region, and hence a particular class, the one that managed the dominant activity, tended to control the wealth of the region and to lead the other classes in politics. In the Northeast the most lucrative activity was industry, and here the leadership was generally held by the manufacturrer-banker group. In the South, the great staple-producing area, the planters, sometimes working in alliance with the merchants, exercised a controlling influence. The regnant factions in both the East and South, it should be noted, were minorities. In the West, on the other hand, not only were the farmers the most numerous element in the population, but they controlled most of the wealth of the region as well; no powerful minority group comparable to the planters of the South appeared in the West to offer leadership to the farmers.

The above generalizations require several qualifications. For one thing, they do not mean that members of the same class always felt enough group identity to work together; farmers in one part of a Western state, for example, might oppose the desires of their fellows in another part. Nor do they mean that the planters of the South or the magnates of the East led other people around by their noses or had everything their own way or even wielded consistent power. In these sections there were often bitter internal divisions and struggles, and sometimes the lower economic groups were able to win control of state governments or to force the upper groups to agree to a division of power. In both sections the dominant classes, aware of the limitations placed on them by the democratic myth and themselves influenced by its precepts, strove to cajole and please the masses. This was particularly true in the South, where the planters often managed the farmers, who were the most numerous segment of the population, by giving them what they wanted or telling them what they wanted to hear. Leaders in the Northeast and South, and also in the West, were frequently able to unite their masses by convincing them that a particular program in national politics would benefit all groups in the region.

But even after taking necessary qualifications into account, it is broadly accurate to say that the salient feature of American economy before 1860 was the concentration of different economic interests in different geographic sections instead of a diffusion of these interests throughout the nation. And this was a fact of momentous and ominous significance for the peace and durability of the Federal Union. It meant that the normal class differences always present in a democracy were intensified and exacerbated because they became also sectional differences. A clash between business and agriculture, for example, was more than a contention between two classes. It was capable of developing into a controversy between the Northeast and the South. It excited two sets of opinions and emotions, and was, therefore, harder to compromise, more difficult to settle. Even without the ap-

pearance of the moral question of slavery, the political-economic issues at stake in the sectional controversy would have strained the ablest statesmanship the nation had to offer.

Elements of Southernism

Of the three great sections of the country, the South was the one that possessed the highest degree of cultural unity, the one that presented the strongest appearance of sectional solidarity to the outside world. The South was an entity, even though within its vast expanse it exhibited immense differences in climate, soil, and people—more perhaps than were to be found in any other region. In addition to coherence, the South had uniqueness. While the social systems of all three sections contained many common cultural features, they also manifested certain striking variations. But no section deviated as much from the central pattern or displayed as many differences from other areas as did the South. In the story of the sectional controversy, the culture complex of the South is of privotal importance.

The qualities that gave the South its peculiar flavor are not easy to define. The South was, and is, the hottest part of the country. Throughout most of the section the climate is warm and mild; in one part, the lower Gulf coast, it is subtropical. The growing seasons are longer than in the North, varying from six months in the Upper South to nine months in the Gulf states. The South's economy was predominantly agrarian, and was characterized by the presence of the large plantation as well as the small farm. Southern farming was largely commercial in nature, concentrating on producing certain staple crops—cotton, tobacco, sugar, and rice—for sale to outside areas. Unlike the West, the South disposed of the bulk of its products in England and Europe instead of in the domestic market; it felt closer economic ties with England than with the Northeast. The South was a rural land, with fewer cities, towns, and villages than there were in the Northern states, and its population was more diffused than that of the North (about 13 persons per square mile in 1860 as compared with 20 in the North). The great majority of the Southern white people were Anglo-Saxon in origin and in their cultural ideals, and in preponderant numbers they were Protestant in religion.

Some observers have seen the South primarily as the expression of a state of mind or a way of life. According to this concept, the essence of Southernism is to be found in the section's rural character, in its people's love of the land, and in their devotion to English cultural standards. The rural South was stable and conservative, satisfied with things as they were and little given to change. "Soil, scenery, all the color and animation of the external world, tempted a convivial race to an endless festival of the seasons," wrote the twentieth-century Virginia novelist, Ellen Glasgow. "In the midst of a changing world all immaterial aspects were condensed for the Southern planter into an incomparable heartiness and relish for life. What distinguished the Southerner . . . from his severer neighbors to the north was his ineradicable belief that pleasure is worth more than toil, that it is even worth more than profit."

The eminent historian of the plantation system, U. B. Phillips, found the "central theme" of Southern history in the presence of the Negro slaves. The South was the only area in the United States (indeed in all Western civilization with the exceptions of Brazil and Cuba), where slavery existed. It was the only section that contained vast numbers of a race of another color than white. Southerners might differ among themselves on political and economic questions, but on the issue of race they closed ranks with iron resolution. They were determined to keep the South a white man's country,

and they viewed slavery as the best means to their end. Slavery, according to this formula, was more than a labor supply system. It was also a white supremacy device, and as such it enlisted the support of the Southern white masses, including the great majority who did not own slaves. Race consciousness, then, and the compulsion felt by white Southerners to establish a system of race relations that would enable them to control the blacks were the factors that account for the oneness of the South.

Both rural conservatism and race consciousness were essential elements in Southern culture and compelling determinants of Southernism. The two concepts are in reality interconnected and hard to separate. Would the ideal of a conservative agrarian society have developed without the presence of a plantation aristocracy? And could there have been such an aristocracy without slavery?

From the 1820's on, slavery was subjected to an ever mounting and almost constant condemnation, emanating not only from the Northern states, but also from the Latin American countries where it had been declared illegal, and from Great Britain, whose government (1833) abolished it throughout the British Empire. The South, then, was an area of Western civilization, not a nation but a section of a nation (and in point of population a minority section), that cherished an institution at violent variance with the culture of the civilization of which it was a part. Where slavery was concerned, the South seemed to defy the opinions of its world, and that world let the South know it disapproved.

It has been surmised that the South secretly and uneasily recognized the rightness of world opinion, which is like saying that the section labored under the weight of a huge guilt complex. Probably the great majority of Southerners would have preferred to live lives similar to those of other peoples in Western civilization and to be approved instead of criticized. Undoubtedly they were sometimes nagged by misgivings about their position when they faced the moral scorn of all Western culture. But they could conceive of no escape. The only way out was to abolish slavery, an impossible course of action because they could think of nothing to put in its place to maintain white supremacy. It has been said that the South was like a man who had a wolf by the ears and did not know how to let it go.

Thoughtful Southerners realized that

Social Organization

Only a minority of Southern whites owned slaves. In 1850, when the total white population of the South was over 6,000,000, the number of slaveholders was 347,525. In 1860, when the white population was just above 8,000,000 (the slave population was 3,950,513), the number of slaveholders had risen to only 383,637. These figures, taken in themselves, give a somewhat misleading impression. Each

PROGRESS OF THE SOUTH TOWARD A MINORITY STATUS

	Percentage of total population of United States	Percentage of white population of United States	Percentage of House of Representatives	Percentage of electoral college
1790	49.9	40.1	44	45
1820	46.7	35.8	42	42
1840	42.8	32.5	39	39
1860	39.1	29.9	35	35

Note: Seven of the original thirteen states were Northern. In the 1790's the number of Northern and Southern states became equal and remained so until 1850. Then the North took the lead. In 1860 there were eighteen Northern and fifteen Southern states, giving the North thirty-six votes in the Senate to the South's thirty.

slavery isolated their region from Western society. Said William Harper of South Carolina: "The judgment is made up. We can have no hearing before the tribunal of the civilized world. Yet, on this very account, it is more important that we, the inhabitants of the slaveholding States, insulated as we are by this institution, and cut off, in some degree, from the communion and sympathies of the world by which we are surrounded, . . . and exposed continually to their animadversions and attacks, should thoroughly understand this subject, and our strength and weakness in relation to it."

slaveholder was normally the head of a family averaging five members. To arrive at the number of whites having a proprietary interest in slavery, it is necessary to multiply by five the number of slaveholders. This formula shows 1,737,625 whites connected with slave ownership in 1850, and 1,937,625 in 1860. Broadly speaking, one family in four owned slaves.

Of the minority of whites holding slaves only a small part, another minority, owned substantial numbers. The census figures of 1850 afford a convenient point of departure from which to analyze the distribution of slave ownership.

Half of the total number of slaveholders owned four slaves or fewer; five sevenths owned nine or fewer. The holders of 50 or more numbered less than 8,000, and the holders of 100 or more less than 1,800. Only a negligible few owned more than 500.

	Holders of	
1 *slave each*		68,820
2–4 *slaves each*		105,683
5–9	" "	80,765
10–19	" "	54,595
20–49	" "	29,733
50–99	" "	6,196
100–199	" "	1,479
200–299	" "	187
300–499	" "	56
500 or more		11
Total Number Slaveholders		347,525

The foregoing data provide a helpful, if a partial, basis from which to study the social organization of the slaveholding states. Eight important social groups comprised the free population of the South. These groups were the major planters, the medium and small planters, the farmers, the manufacturers and merchants, the professional classes, the highlanders of the mountain areas, the poor whites, and the free Negroes.

At the apex of the Southern system stood the major planters—the lords of the manor, the aristocrats of the South, the cotton magnates, and the sugar, rice, and tobacco nabobs. A convenient and reasonably accurate standard of measurement for a major planter would seem to be that he had to own at least forty or fifty slaves and 800 or more acres. He would require a labor force of that size to clear his land and place a considerable part of it under cultivation, to specialize in producing one of the staple crops, and, what was most important, to maintain a credit rating with the domestic or foreign merchant who marketed his produce

and handled the purchases of his finished goods. By this formula, there were in 1850 something over 8,000 major planters. (Some scholars say that ownership of twenty or more slaves is sufficient to make a major planter, which would place the figure at 37,662.) Holders of from ten slaves to a figure in the forties can be classified as small and medium planters; over 80,000 owners fall into this category. The approximately 255,000 individuals who held from one to nine slaves are ranked as farmers, although they possessed greater economic substance and higher social prestige than the many thousands of other farmers who owned no slaves.

The total number of planters—large, medium, and small—then, was 92,257 in 1850. The major planters represented the social ideal of the South. Enriched by vast annual incomes, dwelling in palatial homes, surrounded by broad acres and many slaves, they were the class to which all Southerners paid a certain deference and to which every ambitious Southerner aspired. Enabled by their wealth to practice the leisured arts, they cultivated gracious living, good manners, learning, and politics. Their social pattern determined to a considerable degree the tone of all Southern society. The medium and small planters aped the behavior of the major magnates; they lived in much the same manner, but less lavishly.

The planter class constituted the closest approach to an aristocracy to be found in America. In comparison with the factory masters of the Northeast, the social position of the planters was higher, their political power stronger, and their leadership more unhesitatingly accepted.

Class distinctions were more sharply drawn in the South than in other sections. Southern society approximated in some respects a caste system, and some Southerners spoke scornfully of the democratic faith and voiced their criticisms more openly than leaders in other regions would have dared. But, particu-

larly in the newer states, class arrangements were fairly fluid and an ambitious person could move from one class to another. Farmers nursed the hope of becoming small slaveholders, and small planters aimed to become large ones. Many achieved their goal. In fact, the great majority of the cotton lords of the Mississippi Valley states had come from the ranks of the obscure and the ordinary. Furthermore, in most areas of the South, and again the statement applies especially in the newer states, most of the essentials of the democratic myth were accepted, or at least were widely preached, and therefore must have had some influence. Planters who wished to exercise political influence or hold political office had to take account of this reality. Whether or not they believed in majority rule, they had to affect democratic manners and to mouth principles that would please the multitudes.

Fundamentally, it would seem that the planters exercised a dominating leadership because the great majority of whites desired them to execute such a function. As the planters were the models of social

aspiration in the section, so they also appeared to the masses as the natural leaders of Southern life.

The farmers, those who owned a few slaves and the greater number who owned none, constituted the majority of the white population. They were the middle class of the South. In general, they lived lives of rude plenty, devoting more attention to subsistence farming than the planters. Most of them owned their land. In fact, in the 1850's the number of non-slaveholding landowners increased at a much faster rate than the number of slaveholding owners. Although there was a tendency in some states for the planters to crowd the farmers out of the most fertile areas, it is probable that about 80 per cent of the farmers owned their holdings. Very definitely, the farmers felt that they had a stake in Southern society. Because they cherished hopes of rising to the planter group and because they were intensely race conscious, they were militant defenders of slavery, being often more aggressive in their attitudes than the planters themselves.

Usually neglected or ignored in delineations of Southern society are the business classes—the manufacturers and merchants. And yet they were a social group of some numbers and of considerable importance. Flour milling and textile and iron manufacturing were the principal Southern industries, with the principal mill areas being located in Virginia, the Carolinas, and Georgia. The Tredegar Iron Works in Richmond compared favorably with the best iron mills in the East; the value of Southern textile goods increased from $1,500,000 in 1840 to $4,500,000 in 1860. But despite some promising beginnings, Southern industry before 1860 remained largely in a formative stage. Most Southerners showed a kind of distaste for industrialism, and most Southerners with surplus capital to invest preferred to put it in slaves and land.

More important than the budding manufacturers were the merchants, particularly the brokers or factors who marketed the planters' crops. These individuals, in towns like New Orleans, Charleston, Mobile, and Savannah, acted as selling agents for the planters, for which service they charged a commission, and sometimes also as purchasing agents, for which they exacted an additional fee. Frequently the broker became a banker to the planter, furnishing money or goods on credit; in such cases the planter might be in hock to his factor for a long period during which time he would have to consign his entire crop to the broker. It is evident that the merchant, dominating as he did the credit facilities of the rural South, was in a position to exert great economic pressure on the planter.

Closely linked economically with the planters were the professional classes—lawyers, editors, doctors, and others. Because their well-being largely depended on planter prosperity, the professional groups usually agreed with and voiced the ideals of the dominant class.

In the Southern mountains—the Appalachian ranges east of the Mississippi and the Ozarks west of the river—lived the Southern highlanders, the white group set most apart from the mainstream of Southern life. The culture pattern of the mountain people differed drastically from that of the inhabitants of the rest of the section and indeed from the rest of the country. It was not just that the mountaineers practiced a crude kind of subsistence agriculture or lived in what outsiders considered primitive conditions; nor was it that hardly any slaves were in the mountain areas. Rather, the difference was in the physical isolation of the highlanders and in their own proud sense of seclusion from the outside world. They held to old ways and old ideals, which included a somewhat emotional devotion to the concept of nationalism, and they refused to worship the new political gods of state rights that the South adopted after 1850. The mountain region was the only part of the South that defied the trend toward sectional conformity. In the Civil War, areas like western Virginia and eastern Tennessee would be centers of resistance to Southern independence.

Occupying the lowest position in Southern white society was that tragic and degraded class known as the poor whites, who in 1850 comprised perhaps half a million of the section's population. Not to be confused with poor white people, the poor whites were distinct from the lowliest farmers and the highlanders, and ranked just a little above the slaves. Their distinguishing traits were laziness, ignorance, and lack of ambition. Found in almost every state and known variously by such uncomplimentary names as "crackers," "sand hillers," "white trash," and others, they occupied the infertile lands of the pine barrens, the red hills, and the swamps. Here they lived in miserable cabins surrounded by almost unbelievable squalor, subsisting on a poorly balanced diet which the men provided by hunting and fishing and which was sometimes supplemented by a few home-raised vegetables. The origins of this submerged class are obscure. One theory is that they were the weaker and less competent members of the frontier population who permitted themselves to be pushed back into the poorer lands by more enterprising individuals. A more likely explanation is that their degradation was the result of dietary deficiencies and disease. Afflicted by pellagra, hookworm, and malaria, the poor whites resorted to such degenerative activities as eating clay, a practice which in itself indicated a serious shortcoming in their diets. After 1900 modern medicine would correct their food and health habits. The diseases then practically disappeared, and so did the class known as poor whites.

Perhaps the strangest social group in Southern society was the free Negroes. In many respects, they were a displaced group. Though they were not slaves, they were, because of their color, not completely free. They did not have the assured status which other groups, even the poor whites, possessed. They were former slaves or descendants of former slaves who, for personal or humanitarian reasons, had been freed by their masters. Manumission was usually accomplished by will or deed, although a few bondsmen seem to have purchased their freedom. In 1860 there were some 250,000 free Negroes in the slaveholding states, of whom over half lived in Virginia and Maryland. Although a few free Negroes attained wealth and prominence (and also the ownership of slaves), most of them lived in poverty. Many avenues of economic advancement were closed to them by law or custom; the white South did not want free colored men to rise in the economic scale. Their very presence seemed to endanger the institution of slavery. State laws denied citizenship to them, forbade them to assemble without white supervision or to migrate from one area to another, and placed numerous other restraints upon them. Of course, not all the laws were enforced, and the lot of the freemen was not as somber as the statutes might indicate. Some free Negroes absorbed the tenets of Southernism, and offered their support to the Southern cause when the Civil War started.

Southern Agriculture

The Southern agricultural system was organized around the production of the great staples: tobacco, rice, sugar, and cotton. These were the section's money crops, but they did not constitute by any means its only forms of agricultural effort. What might be termed general, or diversified, farming was carried on in many areas, notably in the Shenandoah Valley of Virginia and the Bluegrass region in central Kentucky. Most planters aimed to produce on the plantation the foodstuffs needed by the family and the slaves. On some large units, more acres were planted in corn than in cotton, and in 1850 half the corn crop of the country was raised in the South. The section produced 87 per cent of the nation's hemp supply (in Kentucky and Missouri) and 80 per cent of its peas and beans. Other important products of Southern husbandry were apples, peaches, peanuts, sweet potatoes, hogs, and mules. Despite the planters' efforts to achieve self-sufficiency, they could not supply all the needs of their slaves, and large amounts of corn and pork had to be imported annually from the Northwest.

But the staples dominated the economic life of the section and absorbed the attention of the majority of the people. Climatic and geographical conditions dictated the areas where each was produced. Tobacco, which needed but a fairly short growing season (six months), was grown in tidewater Maryland west of the Chesapeake, in piedmont Virginia and adjacent North Carolina, in northern and western Kentucky, in northwestern Tennessee, and in the Missouri River Valley of Missouri. Rice demanded a growing season of nine months and irri-

A Plantation Home of the Old South. This Louisiana plantation house, "Richland," illustrates the lavish way of life of the planter class of the Old South and one of the architectural styles prevailing in the antebellum period. Clearly in the tradition of the Greek Revival, with its Doric columns supporting a Grecian pediment, Richland was built in 1826. (LOUISIANA DEPARTMENT OF COMMERCE AND INDUSTRY)

gation, and hence was restricted to the coastal region of South Carolina and Georgia. Sugar, with a similar period necessary for maturation, was concentrated in south Louisiana and a small area in east Texas (around Galveston). Cotton, which required a growing season of seven to nine months and could be produced in a variety of soil formations, occupied the largest zone of production. The Cotton Kingdom stretched from North Carolina to Texas.

From the sale of the great staples the South derived its chief sources of revenue. Into the markets of the world in the 1850's the section poured annually over 400,000 pounds of tobacco, over 360,000 hogsheads of sugar, and over 240,000 pounds of rice. But the big money crop was cotton. From 1,000,000 bales in 1830,

Southern production of cotton steadily increased until it reached 4,000,000 bales in 1860. In that year Southern cotton brought $191,000,000 in the European markets and constituted almost two thirds of the total export trade of the United States. (By way of contrast, the annual value of the rice crop was $2,000,000.) No wonder that Southerners said smugly, "Cotton is King."

As cotton culture expanded, the centers of production moved westward into the fresher lands of Alabama, Mississippi, Arkansas, Louisiana, and Texas. The extension of the Cotton Kingdom into this area bore certain resemblances to the rush of gold seekers into a new frontier. The prospect of tremendous profits drew settlers quickly by the thousands. Some who came were wealthy planters from the older states who transferred their assets and slaves to a cotton plantation. Most were small slaveholders or slaveless farmers who intended to become planters.

A similar shift occurred in slave population. The number of slaves in Alabama leaped from 41,000 in 1820 to 435,000 in 1860, and in Mississippi from 32,000 to 436,000. In the same period in Virginia, the increase was only from 425,000 to 490,000. It has been estimated that between 1840 and 1860, 410,000 slaves were moved from the Upper South to the cotton states. The transfer of slaves from one part of the South to another (when the slaves were not carried by their migrating owners) was accomplished through the medium of professional slave traders. In long-distance traffic the slaves were moved on trains or on river or ocean steamers. Sometimes they were moved afoot; in coffles of several hundreds they would be marched along Southern highways to their destination. Eventually all the slaves in the domestic trade arrived at some central market like Natchez, New Orleans, Mobile, or Galveston, where purchasers collected to bid for their ownership. From 1840 to 1860 the price for a good field hand varied from $500 to $1,700, the wide range resulting largely from falling or rising cotton prices; the average figure was probably $800. Inevitably the slave trade generated a degree of brutality in the men connected with it and in the system itself. Southern leaders condoned the trade but eased their consciences by assigning a low social position to the traders, except those who invested their profits in plantations.

Like the farmers of the West, those of the South employed farming methods that exhausted the soil. Little attention was devoted to crop rotation, the use of fertilizers, or deep plowing. Like other Americans, Southerners considered it easier to migrate to new lands than to restore old ones. Still, there were agricultural societies and journals in the South, as in the other sections, and there were dedicated individuals who labored to improve farm techniques. Such a man was the famous Edmund Ruffin of Virginia, advocate of fertilization, rotation, and deep plowing. The author of a work on calcareous manures and the founder of the excellent *Farmers' Register*, Ruffin was one of the best informed men in the country on agricultural questions. Through his efforts and those of others, some progress in checking soil depletion was made in the older states.

The "Peculiar Institution"

Slavery was an institution established by law and regulated in detail by law. The slave codes of the Southern states forbade a slave to hold property, to leave his master's premises without permission, to be out after dark, to congregate with other slaves except at church, to carry firearms, to strike a white man even in self-defense. The codes prohibited teaching a slave to read or write, and denied the right of a slave to testify in court against a white person. They contained no provisions to legalize slave marriages or divorces. Any person showing a strain of Negro ancestry was presumed to be a slave unless he could prove otherwise. If an owner killed a slave while punishing him, the act was not considered a crime. These and dozens of other restrictions and impositions would seem to indicate that the slaves lived under a harsh and dismal regime, which would have been the case had the laws been drastically enforced. Actually they were applied so unevenly that it is difficult to say what their effect was. Sometimes slaves did acquire property, were taught to read and write, and assembled with other slaves, the laws to the contrary notwithstanding. Most slave offenses were tried by the master, who might inflict punishments ranging from some mild disciplinary action to flogging or branding. Major offenses, including crimes, were generally referred to the courts.

SLAVE SCENES. The picture of the cotton pickers is of a post-Civil War date, but the harvesting techniques were the same as those used in slavery times. The other picture shows slave huts on a plantation near Savannah, Georgia. These brick dwellings were superior to the usual wooden slave dwellings. (BROWN BROTHERS)

The routine of plantation life was governed by a system of rules created by custom and the planters. A small planter directly supervised the work on his place. A medium or major planter hired an overseer and perhaps an assistant overseer to represent him. The "head driver," a trusted and responsible slave, acted under the overseer as a kind of foreman. Under him might be several subdrivers. Two methods or systems of assigning slave labor were employed. One was the task system, most widely used in rice culture. Here a slave was allotted a particular task in the morning, say to hoe one acre; when he completed his job he was free for the rest of the day. The other was the gang system, employed on the cotton, sugar, and tobacco plantations. Under this method, the slaves were simply divided into groups, each of which was directed by a driver, and were worked for as many hours as the overseer considered a reasonable work day.

As far as physical conditions of life were concerned, the slaves were about as well off as most members of the world's laboring population. They were furnished with an adequate if rough diet, consisting mainly of corn meal, salt pork, and molasses; they were encouraged to raise gardens for their own use, and were issued fresh meats on special occasions. They received issues of cheap clothes and shoes. They lived in cabins, the slave quarters, generally constructed of wood. Medical care was provided by the plantation mistress or a doctor retained by the owner. Although the slave worked hard, beginning with light tasks as a child, his work day was no longer than that of the Northern farmer or laborer. He was given time off to hunt and fish, and he attended the church and some of the social festivities of his white family

Slaves were subjected to the severest penalties for two offenses: resisting or killing a white man, and exciting and participating in revolt. Hard punishment was also meted out to slaves who attempted to run away to the free states or to Canada. The exact number of fugitives who tried to escape or who succeeded is not known. It was undoubtedly small; but the problem of runaways caused real concern in the South, and some of the penalties inflicted on those caught approached the barbarous. As for brutality occurring in the routine of the plantation, there was enough to give color to some of the charges of the abolitionists. But, as a rule, the master treated his charges with mildness and even leniency, as indeed he had every economic motive for doing.

Was slavery profitable? On the whole, the planters themselves believed they were making very satisfactory profits, which is the important thing. At the same time there can be no doubt that the slave system, or rather the economic system of which slavery was a part, retarded Southern development and posed some grave problems for the section. Because of the concentration on agriculture, the South had to purchase its finished goods from the outside. Thoughtful Southerners realized the economic subordination of their region. "From the rattle with which the nurse tickles the ear of the child born in the South to the shroud that covers the cold form of the dead, everything comes to us from the North," exclaimed Albert Pike. Said a writer in De Bow's Review: "I think it would be safe to estimate the amount which is lost to us annually by our vassalage to the North at $100,000,000. Great God!" The antebellum South had a colonial economy.

The Mind of the South

Southern culture, in the literary and aesthetic sense, also was colonial. Most Southerners took their literary cues from English or New York sources and bought only books recommended by authorities in those places. Although the planter class bought books in large numbers, they usually purchased the works of English and

Northern writers, almost ignoring the authors of their own section. They showed the same lack of appreciation for Southern magazines. Of the one hundred magazines founded in the South, only nine survived for any length of time. And of the nine, but three attained much vogue: the excellent literary journals, *The Southern Literary Messenger* (Richmond, 1834–64) and *The Southern Quarterly Review* (New Orleans and Charleston, 1842–57), and the magazine of Southern commercial and agricultural expansion, *De Bow's Review* (New Orleans, 1846–80). Even these periodicals had to take second place to Northern productions. In that hotbed of Southern sentiment, Charleston, *De Bow's Review* sold an average of 173 copies, while *Harper's Magazine* was regularly purchased by 1,500 Carolinians.

Considering the bleak reception accorded local authors, it is surprising that the section contained as many fine writers as it did. In the 1830's most of the outstanding authors had been from the Virginia-Maryland area: Nathaniel Beverly Tucker (*The Partisan Leader*), William Alexander Caruthers (*The Cavaliers of Virginia*), and John Pendleton Kennedy (*Swallow Barn* and *Horseshoe Robinson*). They were novelists who wrote historical romances or romantic eulogies of the plantation system in the Upper South. After 1840 the Southern literary capital shifted to Charleston. Here lived and wrote the antebellum South's most distinguished man of letters, William Gilmore Simms. Primarily a novelist, although he composed some tolerable poetry, Simms wrote over thirty works of fiction, some of them novels glorifying Charleston and South Carolina, others historical romances of the Revolution. Although *The Yemassee* is his most widely known book, his best volumes are the ones dealing with the Revolution (*The Partisan, The Forayers, Woodcraft*). Simms had a rare talent for earthy description of common folk, and his better work compares favorably with that of Cooper. Also at Charleston were Hugh Swinton Legaré, perhaps the best linguist in America and an authority on the history of law, and the young poets Henry Timrod and Paul Hamilton Hayne, who would achieve their chief renown after the Civil War.

Just as significant as the genteel-plantation authors and producing works that were more distinctively American were the writers of the Southern frontier. These men depicted the society of the backwoods rural areas; they described ordinary people and poor whites instead of aristocratic cavaliers; they were deliberately and sometimes painfully realistic; and they seasoned their sketches with a robust, vulgar humor that was something new in American literature. The leading light among the frontier writers was Augustus B. Longstreet of Georgia (*Georgia Scenes*). Others who wrote in the same vein were Joseph G. Baldwin (*Flush Times of Alabama and Mississippi*) and Johnson J. Hooper (*Some Adventures of Captain Simon Suggs*). Although the Southern realists were few and composed but few books, they have an important place in Southern and American literature. In departing from the standards of delicate romance that characterized their times, they were originals. And in their humor they established a tradition that was uniquely American and that ultimately found a supreme exponent in Mark Twain.

It has been said (by H. C. Nixon) that in the South there were more people who could read Latin and fewer who could read English than in any part of the country. The educational system of the section reflected the aristocratic ideals of the plantation regime. In 1860 there were 260 Southern colleges and universities, public and private, with 25,000 students enrolled in them, or more than half the total number of students in the United States. The South had twice as many students per one thousand of white population in college as any other section. The Lower South had 11,000 students in its institutions of higher learning, while New England, with approximately the same population, could boast of only 3,748. Below the college level, the schools of the South were inferior to those of the East, about as good as those of the West. There were 3,000 private academies, with 200,-000 students. The public school system, which developed mainly after 1840, numbered 18,000 schools and 600,000 students. One child in every seven attended a public school; the average for the rest of the country was one in six. Institutions like libraries where an enterprising individual might educate himself were fewer in the South than in the North. In Louisiana there were only 100 books to each 1,218 white people, while in Massachusetts there were 100 to each 118 persons. The South had over 500,000 white illiterates, or more than half of the country's total.

In the fields of belles-lettres and science, the South was primarily a section of consumers rather than producers. Although Southern contributions to the nation's cultural life were greater than is sometimes supposed, the fact remains that the section did not produce a literature or a body of scientific findings to compare with those of the Northeast. Among the reasons for the relative backwardness of the South is the rural character of the region. There were few cities, and not one like New York or Boston that could act as a focal point of culture, and there were few publishing facilities. The high illiteracy rate among white adults decreased the potential reading audience. In the simple nature of Southern society there were few complexities to intrigue the writer and impel him to find an explanation. The planters, the class that might have patronized a Southern literature, viewed writers with good-natured scorn; they considered oratory and statesmanship to be much more significant activities than literature. At a time when writing

was becoming a recognized and respected profession in the North, Southern authors, as so many of them bitterly testified, were regarded as amusing fellows who had little to offer their society. Furthermore, after 1830 much of the creative energy of the South was channeled into the defense of slavery. Under attacks from the outside, the section felt a compulsion to glorify its image of itself and to enforce conformity to that image. Freedom of thought, which was largely accepted in the North and which Jefferson and other former Southern leaders had said was necessary in a good society, was seriously stifled in the South.

The Proslavery Reaction

Southern slaveholders expressed horror at the teachings of William Lloyd Garrison; they identified the whole antislavery movement with him and gave him far more notoriety than his importance justified. The attitude of slaveowners was a response to developments in the South as well as the North. Even if Garrison never had existed, the slaveholders would have been prompted to strengthen the defenses of slavery, for the institution was threatened by Southern slaveless farmers and by the slaves themselves. Between 1830 and 1832 a Virginia constitutional convention and then the state legislature, responding to demands from the western part of the state, considered ending slavery through compensated emancipation but were discouraged by the tremendous expense it would have required. Meanwhile, in 1831, the Negro preacher Nat Turner led a slave insurrection in Southampton County, Virginia, and several dozen whites were slain before Turner and his followers could be captured and put to death. While slave conspiracies were common in the South, Turner's was the only one that actually culminated in rebellion. Always uneasy, always mindful of the horrors of the slave uprising in Santo Domingo (in the 1790's), Southerners now were terrified. They blamed the Turner insurrection on Garrison and his newspaper, the *Liberator*.

While the Southern states strengthened their slave codes, controlling the movements of slaves and prohibiting their being taught to read, Southern leaders proceeded to elaborate an intellectual defense of slavery. In 1832 Professor Thomas R. Dew of the College of William and Mary published a pamphlet outlining the slavery case; in subsequent

more secure—than the Northern factory worker. It was good for Southern society because it was the only way two races so different as the black and the white could live together in peace. It was good for the nation as a whole because the entire Southern economy depended on it, and the prosperity of the nation depended on the prosperity of the South. It was good in itself because the Bible sanctioned it—did not the Hebrews of the Old Testament own bondsmen, and did

---

CALHOUN ON SLAVERY

1837

"I hold that in the present state of civilization, where two races of different origin, and distinguished by color, and other physical differences, as well as intellectual, are brought together, the relation now existing in the slave-holding States between the two is, instead of an evil, a good—a positive good. I feel myself called upon to speak freely upon the subject where the honor and interests of those I represent are involved. I hold then, that there never has yet existed a wealthy and civilized society in which one portion of the community did not, in point of fact, live on the labor of the other. . . . I may say with truth that in few countries so much is left to the share of the laborer, and so little exacted from him, or where there is more kind attention paid to him in sickness or infirmities of age. Compare his condition with the tenants of the poor houses in the more civilized portions of Europe—look at the sick and the old and infirm slave, on one hand, in the midst of his family and friends, under the kind superintending care of his master and mistress, and compare it with the forlorn and wretched condition of the pauper in the poor house."

---

years many others added their contributions to the cause, and in 1852 the defense was summed up in an anthology, *The Pro-Slavery Argument*. As early as 1835 John C. Calhoun boasted that Southerners had ceased to apologize for slavery as a necessary evil and had been convinced that it was "a good—a positive good." According to the proslavery argument it was good for the slave because he was an inferior creature who needed the master's guidance and who was better off —better fed, clothed, and housed, and

not the New Testament apostle Paul advise, "Servants, obey your masters"? These and other arguments convinced most Southerners, even those (the great majority) who owned no slaves and had no direct interest in the peculiar institution. Some proslavery propagandists concluded that slavery was such a good thing it should be extended to include white workers in the North as well as black laborers in the South. In *Sociology for the South, or the Failure of Free Society* (1854) George Fitzhugh praised slavery as the only workable form of socialism and urged the whole world to adopt it, at once, as the sole cure for class conflict and the other ills of competitive society.

While spreading proslavery propaganda, Southern leaders tried to silence the advocates of freedom. Southern critics of slavery found it healthful to leave home, among them Hinton Rowan Helper of North Carolina, whose *Impending Crisis of the South* (1857) contended that slavery hurt the welfare of the non-slaveholder and made the whole region backward. In 1835 a mob destroyed sacks containing abolition literature in the Charleston post office, and thereafter Southern postmasters generally refused to deliver antislavery mail. Southern state legislatures passed resolutions demanding that Northern states suppress the "incendiary" agitation of the abolitionists. In Congress, Southern representatives with the cooperation of Northerners secured the adoption of the "gag rule" (1836) according to which antislavery petitions were automatically laid on the table without being read.

As a champion of freedom of speech and petition, John Quincy Adams led a struggle against the gag rule, finally (1844) securing its repeal. Throughout the North many people who were not abolitionists began to feel that civil liberties were endangered in the entire country, not just the South. These people were inclined to sympathize with the abolitionist as a martyr for freedom in the broadest sense. They came to suspect that there really existed, as the abolitionist claimed, a kind of "Slave Power Conspiracy" to destroy the liberties of the country as a whole. They began to wonder, as Abraham Lincoln did, whether the nation could long continue to be half slave and half free—whether the nation might not become all slave. Thus the majority of Northerners, though not necessarily for love of the Negro, eventually came to sympathize in varying degrees with the antislavery cause, while an even larger and more determined majority of Southerners rallied to the defense of the peculiar institution, thereby laying the foundation for a "solid South."

BIBLIOGRAPHY

All aspects of the social structure of the antebellum South are discussed with different emphases in three textbooks: W. B. Hesseltine, *The South in American History* (1943); Clement Eaton, *A History of the Old South* (1949); and F. B. Simkins, *A History of the South* (1953). More specialized studies are W. E. Dodd, *The Cotton Kingdom* (1919), brief but stimulating; R. S. Cotterill, *The Old South* (1939), unusually good; and U. B. Phillips, *Life and Labor in the Old South* (1929), a mellow description of the plantation system. A penetrating analysis of Southern political thought is J. T. Carpenter, *The South as a Conscious Minority, 1789–1861* (1930). In *The Mind of the South* (1941), W. J. Cash maintains that certain thought patterns have existed throughout Southern history. The student is again referred to Sydnor's fine study, *Development of Southern Sec-*

tionalism, 1819–1848. The classic description of the South by a Northern traveler is F. L. Olmsted, *The Cotton Kingdom* (1953 edition, edited by A. M. Schlesinger).

There are two histories of slavery, each with a different viewpoint: U. B. Phillips, *American Negro Slavery* (1918), and K. M. Stampp, *The Peculiar Institution* (1956). Phillips saw many positive features in slavery. Stampp is more critical of the institution. See also Frederic Bancroft, *Slave-Trading in the Old South* (1931); J. H. Franklin, *From Slavery to Freedom* (1947); and S. M. Elkins, *Slavery* (1959).

Southern economic life is treated in E. Q. Hawk, *Economic History of the South* (1934). The basic work on agriculture is L. C. Gray, *History of Agriculture in the Southern United States to 1860* (2 vols., 1933). A. O. Craven, *Edmund Ruffin, Southerner* (1932), describes the career of a pioneer in scientific farming. Broadus Mitchell, *William Gregg* (1928), is a study of a pioneer Southern industrialist. Monographs that explore phases of the Southern economy and society are Dick, *The Dixie Frontier;* L. E. Atherton, *The Southern Country Store, 1800–1860* (1949); F. L. Owsley, *Plain Folk of the Old South* (1949); and R. R. Russel, *Economic Aspects of Southern Sectionalism, 1840–1861* (1924).

On Southern intellectual life, a basic work is Clement Eaton, *Freedom of Thought in the Old South* (1940). In *The Southern Plantation* (1924), F. P. Gaines has critically examined the plantation tradition and its influence on Southern thought.

J. H. Franklin describes a thread of violence in Southern history in *The Militant South* (1956). Dominant intellectual infleunces on Southern thinking are treated in R. G. Osterweis, *Romanticism and Nationalism in the Old South* (1949). The best work on literature is J. B. Hubbell, *The South in American Literature, 1607–1900* (1954). A biography of one of the South's most important intellectual figures is Frank Freidel's *Francis Lieber* (1947).

On the proslavery argument see W. S. Jenkins, *Pro-Slavery Thought in the Old South* (1935), and Harvey Wish, *George Fitzhugh: Propagandist of the Old South* (1943).

17

WESTWARD TO THE
PACIFIC

During the James K. Polk administration, over one million square miles of new territory came under American control, and the western boundaries of the United States advanced from the Louisiana Purchase line to the Pacific Ocean. Well might the ordinary-looking little man from Tennessee feel proud of his work. No other President except Jefferson had acquired so much for his country.

When the westward thrust of the 1840's was finished, the United States was a larger, richer, and more powerful nation. The new western empire and its immense resources opened possibilities of national development almost beyond calculation. The ultimate effect, then, of expansion would be to strengthen nationalism. But the immediate result was to weaken it; outward expansion provoked internal conflict.

Manifest Destiny

Those four years, 1845–9, were a period of tremendous territorial expansion. The tide of emigration continued to roll into the upper Mississippi Valley, increasing the population of the states in that area and bringing two new states, Iowa (1846) and Wisconsin (1848), into the Union. The settled frontier had now moved to a line halfway across the continent.

The expansive energies of the American people were not, however, confined to the territorial limits of the United States, even though huge regions in the trans-Mississippi West were still unsettled. Americans looked longingly toward lands not clearly owned by their government—the Oregon country—and to lands owned by another government—Mexico—as places where they would like to live and which they would like to possess.

A contemporary editor who approvingly observed the expansionist spirit of the 1840's called it "Manifest Destiny," and his apt phrase has been adopted by historians to characterize both the mood and the process of expansion. The editor meant that it was the destiny or fate of the American people to advance into and to take possession of certain regions. Although Manifest Destiny had the virtue of elasticity and could, if necessary, be stretched to cover any coveted area, its

AN IMPERIALIST VIEW OF OREGON

Although most Americans justified the acquisition of Oregon and California with the simple formula of Manifest Destiny, the leading advocates of expansion foresaw more immediate commercial goals: possession of the Pacific ports would enable the United States to dominate the Pacific and Oriental trade. A principal exponent of this view was Senator Thomas Hart Benton of Missouri. In a speech in 1848 he painted a glowing picture of Oregon and its value as a trade base: "Agricultural capabilities to sustain a great population, and to furnish the elements of commerce and manufactures—a vast and rich commerce and navigation at its hands—a peaceable sea to navigate—gentle and profitable people to trade with them —a climate of supreme and almost miraculous salubrity—a natural frontier of mountain ramparts—a triple barrier of mountains—to give her a military impregnability. . . . I now come to another advantage, common to all North America, and long since the cherished vision of my young imagination. A Russian Empress said of the Crimea: Here lies the road to Byzantium. I say to my fellow-citizens: Through the valley of the Columbia, lies the North American road to India."

advocates commonly gave it defined limits: the United States was preordained to control all of North America. Furthermore, the United States was charged with a mission to demonstrate to all the Western world the virtues and the glory of democracy. The lesson might be taught, the goal achieved, by the power of example, with other nations voluntarily adopting American ideals. But those ideals could be spread more easily and immediately by forcing them, if necessary, on peoples in regions adjacent to the United States.

The campaign of 1844 illustrates the truth that professional politicians sometimes mistake the popular will. Many of the professionals, particularly those of the conservative Whig party, who were more removed from the masses than the Democrats, did not seem to sense the expansionist mood of the country. Clay expected to be the Whig candidate, and Van Buren the Democratic nominee. Both wanted to avoid taking a stand on the annexation of Texas, because a stand, no matter on which side, was certain to

lose some votes. Consequently, they issued separate statements, so similar in tone as to indicate previous consultation between the authors, opposing annexation without the consent of Mexico.

Clay's action did not harm his candidacy. The Whig convention nominated him unanimously, although the platform discreetly omitted any reference to Texas. But Van Buren had destroyed his chances with the Democrats, particularly with those from the South, who were enraged by his opposition to annexation. The Democratic convention threw him aside, and nominated James K. Polk, a champion of expansion. The platform caught fairly the prevailing mood in its key resolution: "That our title to the whole of the Territory of Oregon is clear and unquestionable; that no portion of the same ought to be ceded to England or any other power, and that the re-occupation of Oregon and the re-annexation of Texas at the earliest practicable period are great American measures, which this Convention recommends to the cordial support of the Democracy of the Union."

The "re-'s" in the resolution were clever attempts to make the proposed acquisitions seem entirely legal: Oregon had always belonged to the United States and Texas was originally a part of the Louisiana Purchase. Cleverness marked every aspect of the Democratic platform and every phase of Democratic planning for the campaign. By combining Oregon and Texas, the Democrats separated Texas from the slavery question. One territory would eventually add to the strength of the free states, the other to the slave states. Nobody could accuse the Democrats of sectionalism; rather, they stood forward as the champions of *national* expansion.

A third party appeared in the campaign, one that had been organized four years earlier. This was the Liberty party, made up mostly of Western abolitionists who demanded the abolition of slavery in the territories and in the District of Columbia. In 1840 their candidate, James G. Birney, had polled some 7,000 votes. Now Birney was running again and hoping to do better. The Liberty party was a cloud on the horizon, one that showed some Americans were sufficiently excited about the slavery issue to inject it into politics.

Throughout the campaign the Democrats, like the Whigs four years earlier, took the offensive. Too late Clay realized that he had muffed the expansion issue, and announced that under certain circumstances he might be for the acquisition of Texas. His tardy straddling probably cost him more votes than it gained. Polk carried the election by 170 electoral votes to 105, although his popular lead was less than 40,000. Significantly, the Democrats secured a majority in both houses of Congress. If the votes meant anything, they were a mandate for expansion. Of another kind of significance was the popular vote of the Liberty party, which increased to 62,000.

James K. Polk has been called the first "dark horse" presidential candidate,

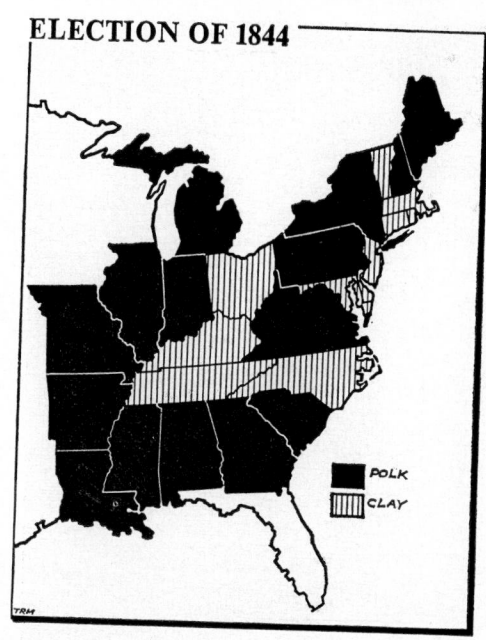

ELECTION OF 1844

POLK
CLAY

meaning one who suddenly emerges from relative obscurity to win the race. He was not quite as obscure in 1844 as some people, particularly the Whigs, affected to believe. Born in frontier North Carolina, he emigrated, when in his mid-twenties, to Tennessee, thus following the pattern of the man who became his political mentor, Andrew Jackson. In Tennessee Polk practiced law and politics, soon becoming recognized as one of the state's Democratic leaders. Elected to the national House of Representatives he held his seat for fourteen consecutive years, serving for four of them as speaker.

Nobody ever accused Polk of possessing personal glamor. In appearance he was thin, worn, even grim, and his public manners comported with his looks. But he had a good mind, he worked hard at his job, and above all he had an iron, implacable will. Probably no other President entered office with so clearly defined a program and accomplished so much of it as Polk. He settled the Oregon question (though he did not get the whole of the Oregon country), he completed the annexation of Texas (which his predecessor

JAMES K. POLK. Slight of stature and unimpressive in appearance, Polk was a man of iron determination. In his daily schedule he arose at six o'clock in the morning and worked far into the night. Always frail in health, he drove himself too hard in the Presidency and left the office physically broken. Three months after his retirement he was dead. (LIBRARY OF CONGRESS)

Tyler already had begun), and through the Mexican War he acquired California and New Mexico. Besides, he brought about a reduction of the tariff and a re-establishment of the Independent Treasury.

The Partitioning of Oregon

The ownership of Oregon was long in dispute, but its boundaries were clearly defined—on the north the latitude line of 54° 40', on the east the crest of the Rocky Mountains, on the south the forty-second parallel, and on the west the Pacific Ocean. Included in its half-million square miles were the present states of Oregon, Washington, and Idaho, parts of Mon-

tana and Wyoming, and half of British Columbia.

At various times in the past the Oregon country had been claimed by Spain, Russia, France, England, and the United States. By the 1820's only the last two nations remained in contention. The others had withdrawn and surrendered their rights to Britain or to the United States or to both. The American and British claims were equally valid—or invalid. Both countries could assert title on the basis of the activities of their explorers, maritime traders, and fur traders. The English had one solid advantage: they were in actual possession of a part of the area. In 1821 the powerful British fur trading organization, the Hudson's Bay Company, under the leadership of its factor, John McLoughlin, established a post at Fort Vancouver, north of the Columbia River.

Several times the English government proposed the Columbia as a suitable line of division. The United States, also showing a desire to compromise, countered by suggesting the forty-ninth parallel. This difference in official views prevented a settlement of the Oregon question in the treaty of 1818. Unable to agree on a demarcation line, the diplomats of the two powers negotiated a compact whereby the citizens of each were to have equal access to Oregon for ten years. This arrangement, called joint occupation, was renewed in 1827 for an indefinite period, with either nation empowered to end it on a year's notice.

The first real American interest in Oregon came as a result of the activities of missionaries. Ministers like Jason Lee, Marcus Whitman, and Father Pierre Jean de Smet made the long journey to Oregon to establish missions. All of the missionaries located their posts south of the Columbia River; the Protestants tended to concentrate in the fertile Willamette Valley, where, being married men with families to support, they engaged in agriculture. The missionaries described their work in reports and letters that were published in influential religious journals and widely reprinted in secular newspapers. These reports dwelt quite as much on the rich soil and lovely climate of Oregon as on the spiritual condition of the Indians. Suddenly, vast numbers of Americans seemed to be aware of Oregon. Just as suddenly, beginning in 1841, thousands of pioneers took the trail to the Far West. Amazed observers remarked upon the "Oregon fever." Two thousand miles in length, the Oregon Trail penetrated into Indian country, and it crossed mountains and semidesert regions. To the emigrants, traveling in caravans of covered wagons and accompanied by huge herds of cattle, it presented enormous problems in transportation. The average period required for the journey was from May to November. Some never lived to complete it. But the great majority got through. By 1845, 5,000 Americans were living south of the Columbia—and demanding that their government take possession of Oregon.

When Polk assumed office, though in his inaugural address he seemed to reassert American title to all of Oregon, he was in reality willing to compromise—to effect a division on the line of the forty-ninth parallel. The British minister in Washington rejected Polk's offer without referring it to London.

Abruptly Polk took a more militant attitude. Saying America should look John Bull "straight in the eye" and hinting at war, he asserted claim to all of Oregon. In his annual message to Congress, in December, 1845, he asked that body to give notice to England that joint occupation would end in a year. The United States, he said, would not permit a European colony to be established in North America by force or by diplomatic action. This last was a restatement of the Monroe Doctrine, largely forgotten since 1823. Congress, with some Whigs dissenting, complied with the President's request.

Although there was some loose talk of war on both sides of the Atlantic, neither

AMERICAN EXPANSION IN OREGON

nation really wished to resort to force. The British government now offered to divide Oregon at latitude forty-nine—that is, to accept Polk's original proposal. The President affected to believe the offer should be rejected, but he was easily persuaded by his cabinet to submit it to the Senate for advice. Probably he was relieved to shift the responsibility for making a decision to the Senators. They accepted the proposed agreement, and on June 15, 1846, a treaty was signed fixing the boundary at the forty-ninth parallel. The United States had secured the greater and better part of the Oregon country and certainly all that it could have legitimately expected to get.

The Annexation of Texas

Southwest of the international boundary of the United States stretched the northern provinces of Mexico—Texas, New Mexico, and Upper California—

once parts of Spain's colonial empire in North America but since 1822 states in the independent "Republic of Mexico." Under Spanish rule the provinces had been subject to only the lightest supervision from the government of the viceroyalty in Mexico, and only a few thousand white men had settled in them. The same conditions prevailed under the Republic, which lacked the power and the population to govern and settle such distant areas. At one time the United States had advanced a claim to Texas as a part of the Louisiana Purchase, but had renounced the claim in 1819. Twice thereafter, however, in the presidencies of J. Q. Adams and Jackson, the United States had offered to buy Texas, only to meet with indignant Mexican refusals.

The Mexican government invited the inevitable in Texas. In the early 1820's it encouraged American immigration by offering land grants to men like Stephen Austin who would promise to colonize the land. Probably the motive of the government was to build up the economy of Texas, and hence it tax revenues, by increasing the population with foreigners, but the experiment was to result in the loss of Texas to the United States. Thousands of Americans, attracted by reports of the rich soil in Texas, took advantage of Mexico's welcome. Most of them settled in the coastal plain area; the great majority, by the very fact of geography, came from the Southern states, sometimes bringing with them slaves, although slavery was forbidden in Mexico after 1829. By 1835 approximately 35,000 Americans were living in Texas.

Almost from the beginning there was friction between the settlers and both the Mexicans and the Mexican government. The virile, pushing Anglo-Saxon culture of the United States came into natural conflict with the older, more leisurely Latin civilization of Mexico. Finally the Mexican government, realizing that its power to control Texas was in effect being challenged by the settlers, moved to exert control. A series of restrictive measures was followed by an act abolishing the powers of the various states of the Republic, a measure that the Texans took to be aimed specifically at them. In the best American tradition they resolved to uphold their rights by rebelling. In 1836 Texas proclaimed its independence.

The Mexican dictator, Santa Anna, advanced into Texas with a large army that should have been able to defeat the Texans, who even with the aid of volunteers, money, and supplies from private groups in the United States were having difficulty in organizing a resistance. Indeed, for a time it seemed that Santa Anna would crush the rebellion. A Texas garrison at the Alamo mission in San Antonio was exterminated; another at Goliad suffered substantially the same fate when the Mexicans murdered most of the force after it surrendered. But General Sam Houston, emerging as the national hero of Texas, kept a small army together, and at the battle of San Jacinto (April 21, 1836, near present-day Houston) he defeated the Mexican army and took Santa Anna prisoner. Although the Mexican government refused to recognize the captured dictator's vague promises to withdraw Mexican authority from Texas, it made no further attempts to subdue the province. Texas had won its independence.

The new Republic did not wish, however, to remain independent. It desired to become a possession of the United States, and through its president, Sam Houston, Texas asked for recognition, to be followed by annexation. Although President Andrew Jackson, then in his second administration, favored annexation, he proceeded cautiously. Sentiment for adding Texas to the United States was strong in all sections but particularly so in the South, where it was believed that the huge area would open new borders for cotton cultivation and, when it entered the Union as one or several states, enlarge the political influence of the South.

But there were signs of opposition, too. Abolitionism was beginning to make its influence felt in politics. Many Northerners expressed a conviction that it would be immoral to extend the dominion of slavery; others, not quite so idealistic or frank about their motives, were opposed to incorporating a region that would add to Southern votes in Congress and in the electoral college. To Jackson it seemed that annexation would cause an ugly

in Europe. Her leaders talked about creating a vast southwestern nation, stretching to the Pacific, which would be a rival to the United States; some of them probably believed what they were saying, although it is more probable that they were trying to put additional pressure on the government in Washington. Whatever their motives, it was the kind of talk that Europe, particularly England, was charmed to hear. An independent Texas

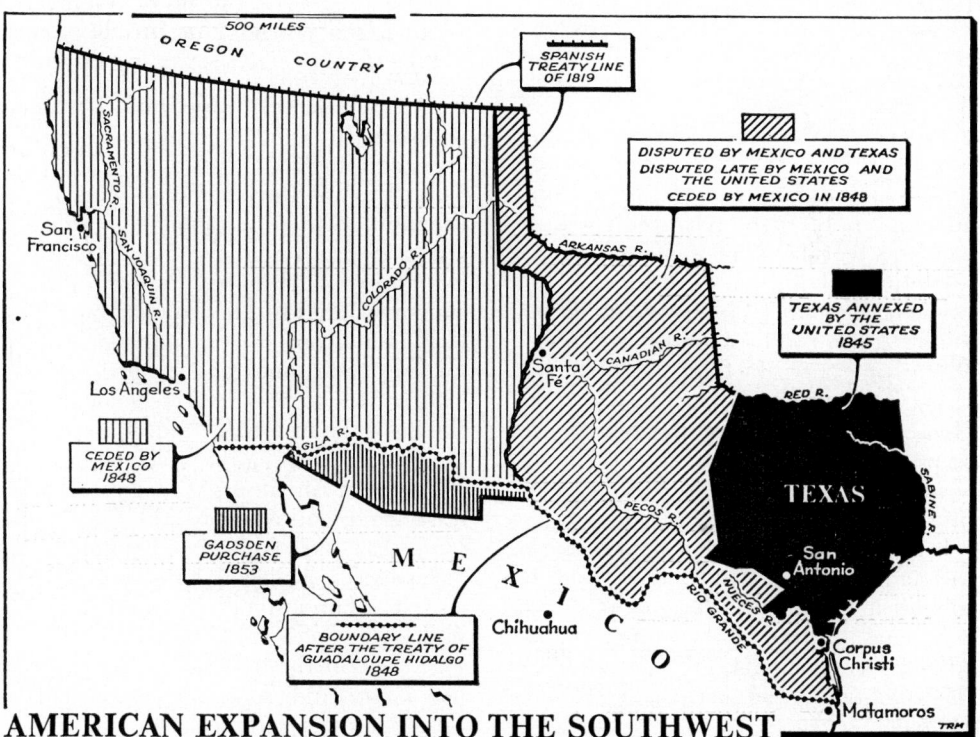

AMERICAN EXPANSION INTO THE SOUTHWEST

sectional controversy and disrupt the Democratic party in an election year (1836). Furthermore, it was almost certain to bring on a war with Mexico. He did not, therefore, propose annexation to Congress, and did not even extend recognition to Texas until just before he left office in 1837. His successor, Van Buren, also forebore, for similar reasons, to press the issue.

Refused by the United States, Texas sought recognition, support, and money

would be a counterbalance to the United States and a barrier to further American expansion; it would supply cotton for European industry and provide a market for European exports. England and France jumped to recognize Texas and to conclude trade treaties with her. The English government played with the idea of guaranteeing the independence and boundaries of the new nation.

News of Britain's interest in Texas reached the United States in 1843-4, when Manifest Destiny was beginning to seize the imagination of large segments of the American people. The result was another attempt to annexation. President Tyler, eager to increase Southern power, persuaded Texas, not so eager to receive another possible snubbing, to apply again, and Secretary of State Calhoun submitted an annexation treaty to the Senate in April, 1844. Unfortunately for Texas, Calhoun presented annexation as if its only purpose was to extend slavery. Put forward on a sectional basis and backed by an unpopular President, the treaty had no chance, and was soundly defeated.

President Tyler, who remained in office until March, 1845, viewed the election returns of 1844 as a mandate to carry annexation through. He proposed to Congress that Texas be annexed by joint resolution of both houses, a device which would get around the necessity of obtaining a two-thirds majority in the Senate for annexation by treaty. In February, 1845, Congress voted (120 to 98 in the House and 27 to 25 in the Senate) to admit Texas to the Union. Conditions were affixed: Texas could be subdivided into not more than four additional states; it had to pay its own public debts but was to retain its public lands; and it had to submit any boundary disputes in which it became involved to the United States. After Polk's inauguration Texas accepted the conditions, and became a state in December, 1845.

Promptly, the Mexican government broke off diplomatic relations with the United States. To further embitter the situation, a dispute over Texas's boundary with Mexico now developed. Texas claimed that the Rio Grande River, from source to mouth, constituted her western and southern border, an assertion which would place much of what is now New Mexico in Texas. Mexico, while not formally conceding the loss of Texas, replied that the southern border of Texas had always been the Nueces River. Polk recog-

nized the Texas claim, and in the summer of 1845 sent a small army force under General Zachary Taylor to the Nueces line—to protect Texas, he said, against the Mexicans. The President was undoubtedly sincere in thinking he had to support the Texans, now Americans, but to Mexico his course smacked of aggression. The United States had Texas, and now it seemed to be reaching out for New Mexico.

New Mexico and California

New Mexico, the second of Mexico's frontier provinces, supported a scanty population on a semiprimitive economy. Its small metropolis and trade center, Santa Fe, was three hundred miles from the most northern settlements in Mexico. Under Spanish rule the New Mexicans had to export their few products over a thousand miles to Mexico City and Vera Cruz and from these economic centers import their meager finished goods. When Mexico became independent, she let it be known that traders from the United States would be welcome in New Mexico. An American, William Becknell, wagoned a load of merchandise to Santa Fe in 1821 and sold it at a high profit. Out of his success, widely reported in the East, arose the famous and colorful "Santa Fe trade."

Every year the traders, who were small merchants and sometimes even enterprising farmers, gathered a stock of simple manufactured goods to be moved to Santa Fe in wagons. They collected at some central point, usually Independence, Missouri, and after reaching Council Grove traveled in an organized caravan over what soon became known as the Santa Fe Trail. Over 800 miles in length, the trail crossed the Kansas plains to the bend of the Arkansas, and followed that river upstream a short distance before dipping into New Mexico. Usually the lumbering covered wagons of the traders required six weeks to complete the trip.

On the return journey, the merchants carried gold, silver, furs, and mules.

The real significance of the Santa Fe trade was in its influence upon American concepts of expansion. It focused attention on a new area, opened up still another route to the West, and pointed another direction for Manifest Destiny.

More distant from the homeland than New Mexico and even freer from Mexican supervision, if that was possible, was the third of the northern provinces, Cali-

good example of the merchant adventurer is Thomas O. Larkin, who set up business in Monterey in 1832 and soon attained the status of a leading citizen. Although Larkin maintained close and friendly relations with the Mexican authorities, he secretly longed for the day when California would become an American possession. In 1844-5 he accepted an appointment as United States consul, with instructions to arouse sentiment among the Californians for annexation.

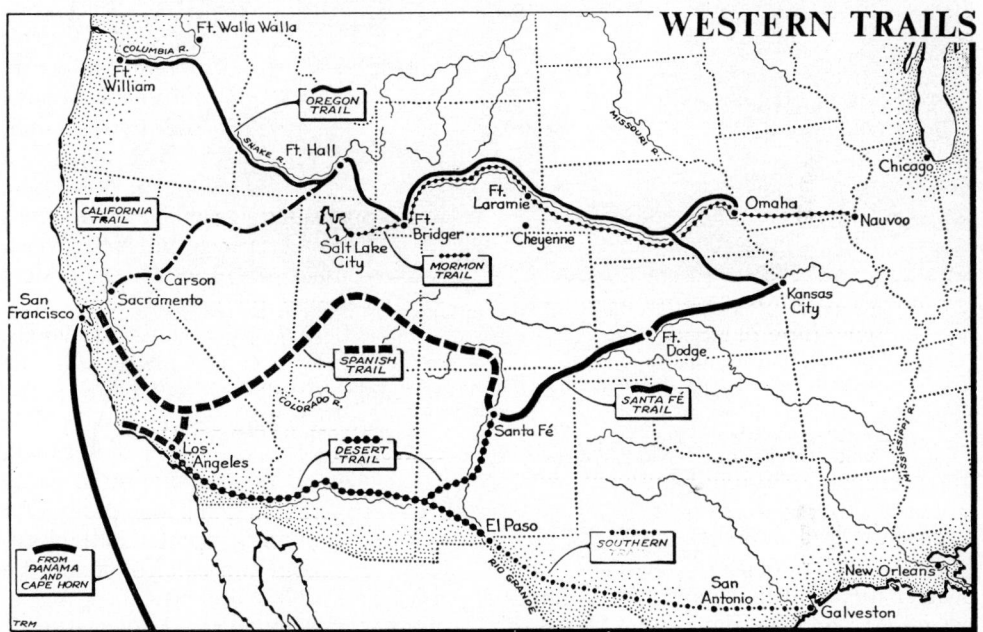

WESTERN TRAILS

fornia. In this vast, rich region lived perhaps 7,000 Mexicans, descendants of Spanish colonists, who engaged in agricultural pursuits, chiefly ranching, lived lives of primitive plenty, and carried on a skimpy trade with the outside world.

The first Americans to enter California were maritime traders and captains of the Pacific whaling ships, who put in to California harbors to barter goods or acquire supplies. Following them came merchants, who established stores, imported merchandise, and conducted a profitable trade with the Mexicans and Indians. A

Nearly all of the first settlers had come to California by sea, but as reports spread of its rich soil and mild climate, immigrants began to enter from the east by land. These were pioneering farmers, men of the type who were penetrating Texas and Oregon in search of greener pastures. Indeed, some of the first agricultural migrants were people who had started for Oregon and changed their destination to California. By 1845 there were 700 Americans in California, most of them concentrated in the valley of the Sacramento River. The overlord of this region, and in

MIGRANTS CROSSING THE PLAINS. Migrants on the Western trails traveled in canvas-covered wagons. Some of the heaviest wagons weighed from 3,000 to 7,000 pounds, and required the pulling service of ten or twelve horses or oxen. Smaller wagons of the type shown in the print weighed about 2,500 pounds. A wagon train of migrants operated under the direction of a captain who assigned each wagon a position. An average day's trip for a train was from fifteen to twenty miles. (LIBRARY OF CONGRESS)

a sense the leader of the Americans, was John A. Sutter, once of Germany and Switzerland, who had moved to California in 1839 and had become a Mexican citizen. His headquarters at Sutter's Fort was the center of a magnificent domain where the owner ranched thousands of cattle and horses and maintained a network of small manufacturing shops to supply his armed retainers.

The United States government had shown an interest in California even before many Americans had moved there. Jackson had toyed with the idea of buying a part of the area, and so had Tyler. As with Oregon and Texas, the United States feared that Great Britain wanted to acquire or dominate California, a suspicion that was given credence by the activities of British diplomatic agents in the province.

President Polk's dreams of expansion went beyond the Democratic platform. He entered office determined to acquire for his country New Mexico and California and possibly other parts of northern Mexico as well. He hoped to acquire them by Pacific methods: through the use of diplomacy and money. But if he could not get them peaceably he was ready to resort to war.

At the same time that he sent Taylor to the Nueces, Polk also sent secret instructions to the commander of the Pacific naval squadron to seize the California ports if he heard that Mexico had declared war. A little later Consul Larkin was informed that while the government had no aggressive designs on California, if the people wanted to revolt and join the United States they would be received as brethren. The hint was not lost on Larkin, who immediately began to stir up sentiment for annexation. Still later an exploring expedition led by Captain John C. Frémont, of the army's corps of topographical engineers, entered California. The Mexican authorities, alarmed by the

would assume the damage claims, amounting to several millions, which Americans held against Mexico. If she would cede New Mexico, the United States would pay $5,000,000. And for California, the United States would pay up to $25,000,000. Slidell arrived in Mexico at a time when the government was about to be changed by the customary method of revolution. The government that was

---

EMIGRANTS ON THE OREGON TRAIL

In 1846 Francis Parkman, cultured young Easterner and future historian, traveled through the West. He described what he saw in *The Oregon Trail* (1849), a classic account of the West: "We were late in breaking up our camp on the following morning, and scarcely had we ridden a mile when we saw, far in advance of us, drawn against the horizon, a line of objects stretching at regular intervals along the level edge of the prairie. An intervening swell soon hid them from sight, until, ascending it a quarter of an hour after, we saw close before us the emigrant caravan, with its heavy white wagons creeping on in slow procession, and a large drove of cattle following behind. Half a dozen yellow-visaged Missourians, mounted on horseback, were cursing and shouting among them, their lank angular proportions enveloped in brown homespun, evidently cut and adjusted by the hands of a domestic female tailor. As we approached, they called out to us: 'How are ye, boys? Are ye for Oregon or California?' As we pushed rapidly by the wagons, children's faces were thrust out from the white coverings to look at us; while the care-worn, thin-featured matron, or the buxom girl, seated in front, suspended the knitting on which most of them were engaged to stare at us with wondering curiosity. By the side of each wagon stalked the proprietor, urging on his patient oxen, who shouldered heavily along, inch by inch, on their interminable journey."

---

size of the party and its military aspects, ordered Frémont to leave. He complied, but moved only over the Oregon border.

After preparing measures that looked like war, Polk resolved on a last effort to achieve his objectives by diplomacy. He dispatched to Mexico a special minister, John Slidell, a Louisiana politician, with instructions to settle all the questions in dispute between the two nations—to settle them with American money. If Mexico would acknowledge the Rio Grande boundary for Texas, the United States

going down did not dare to negotiate with him, and the one that took over, having risen to power partly by denouncing the American offer and blustering about war, did not dare even to receive him. Accordingly, Slidell notified his government that his mission had failed. Immediately after receiving Slidell's information, on January 13, 1846, Polk ordered Taylor's army to move across the Nueces to the Rio Grande.

If Polk was hoping for trouble, he was disappointed for months. Taylor's army encamped on the north bank of the river near its mouth, while across the stream Mexican forces contented themselves with observing the Americans. Finally in May after Slidell had returned to Washington, Polk decided to ask Congress to declare war on the grounds that Mexico had refused to honor its financial obligations and had insulted the United States by rejecting the Slidell mission. While Polk was working on a war message, the electrifying news arrived from Taylor that Mexican troops had crossed the Rio Grande and attacked a unit of American soldiers. Immediately Polk revised his message. Instead of asking for war to redress past grievances he demanded force to defend the nation against present invasion. Ignoring some salient facts in the situation, he declared that "Mexico has passed the boundary of the United States . . . and shed American blood upon the American soil" and that "war exists by the act of Mexico herself." Congress accepted Polk's interpretation of events, and on May 13, 1846, declared war by votes of 40 to 2 in the Senate and 174 to 14 in the House. Manifest Destiny had come to its great climax.

Although the country accepted war with apparent enthusiasm and near-unanimity, there was more opposition than appeared on the surface. The war was most popular in the Mississippi Valley states, which furnished most of the volunteer troops to fight it. In the Northeast, it was received with coolness if not disapproval, particularly by Whigs and antislavery groups. Even in the older Southern states there was a feeling that expansion was going too far, that the acquisition of too much territory would provoke sectional controversy. Opposition increased and intensified as the war continued and costs and casualties came home to the people. The Whigs in Congress supported the war appropriation bills, but they became ever bolder and more bitter in denouncing "Mr. Polk's war" as agressive in origin and objectives.

The Mexican War

During the war the United States raised a total armed force of a little over 100,000 troops. Of these about 60,000 were volunteers, most of whom had enlisted for a twelve-months term and consequently saw little or nothing of the war. Despite the seemingly large size of the American forces, the largest single army in the field did not number more than 14,000 men. Of the army commanders, only one, Winfield Scott, possessed outstanding ability. If the level of the general officers was ordinary, that of the lower-ranking commissioned officers was unusually high. By 1846 West Point had graduated 1,000 students, many of whom served in the war. For the first time American armies contained large numbers of professionally trained officers. The young West Pointers were the future generals of the Civil War. In the Mexican war they had their only important military experience before 1861. It was their "rehearsal for conflict."

In the opening phases of the war President Polk assumed the planning of grand strategy, a practice which he continued almost to the end of the war. His basic idea was to seize key areas on the Mexican frontier and then force the Mexicans to make peace on American terms. Accordingly, he ordered Taylor to cross the Rio Grande and occupy northeastern Mexico, taking as his first objective the city of Monterrey. Polk seems to have had a vague idea that from Monterrey Taylor could advance southward, if necessary, and menace Mexico City, the enemy capital. Taylor, "Old Rough and Ready," beloved by his soldiers for his courage and easy informality but ignorant of many technical aspects of war, attacked Monterrey in September, 1846; after a hard fight he captured it, but at the price of agreeing to let the garrison evacuate without pursuit. Although the country hailed Taylor as a hero, Polk was disgusted with the general, and concluded

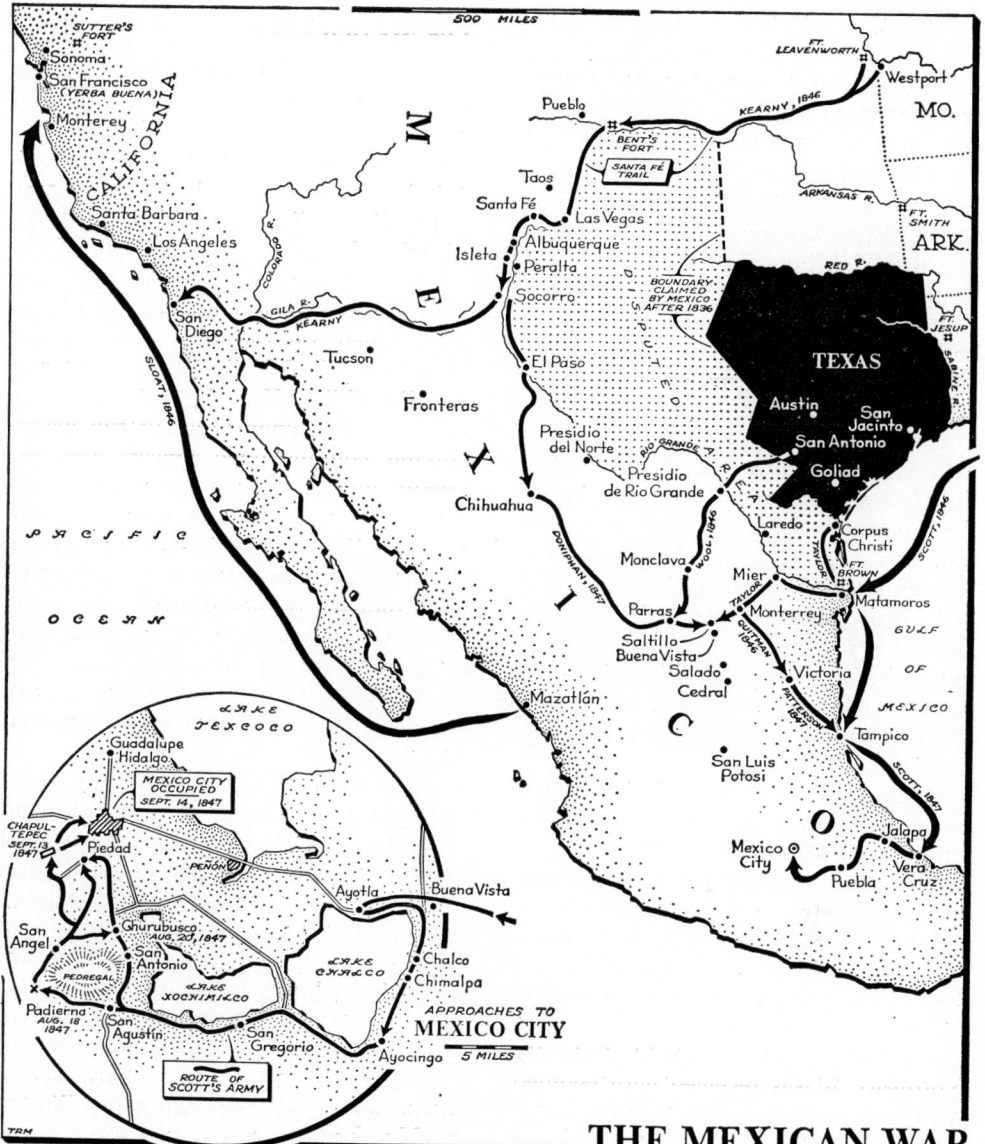

THE MEXICAN WAR

that he did not possess the ability to lead an offensive against Mexico City. Also, Polk began to realize that an advance south through the mountains would involve impossible problems of supply.

Two other offensives planned by Polk were aimed at New Mexico and California. In the summer of 1846 a small army under Colonel Stephen W. Kearny made the long march to Santa Fe and occupied the town with no opposition. Kearny sent part of his army (Missouri volunteers under Colonel A. W. Doniphan) south to join Taylor, and disposed other parts to garrison the province. Then, acting under instructions from Polk, Kearny proceeded with a few hundred troopers to California to take charge of operations there. In California a combined revolt and war was being staged by the settlers,

Frémont's exploring party, and the American navy. The settlers had proclaimed California an independent state (in the "Bear Flag Revolution"); Frémont had returned from Oregon to lead the rebels; and the navy had landed forces and annexed California to the United States. When Kearny arrived, the Americans were fighting under the direction of Commodore R. F. Stockton of the navy. Not without some difficulty, Kearny brought the disparate American elements under his command, and by the autumn of 1846 completed the conquest of California.

In addition to northeastern Mexico, the United States now had possession of the two provinces for which it had gone to war. In a sense, the objectives of the war had been achieved. The only trouble was that Mexico refused to recognize realities; she would not agree to a peace and cede the desired territory. At this point Polk turned to General Scott, the commanding general of the army and its finest soldier, for help.

Together Polk and Scott devised a plan to force the Mexicans to accept peace by capturing their capital. Scott would assemble at Tampico an army to be made up partly of troops from Taylor's army and partly of forces from other areas. The navy would transport this army down the coast to Vera Cruz, which would be seized and made into a base. From Vera Cruz, Scott would move west along the National Highway to Mexico City. Late in 1846 Scott went to Mexico to organize his forces. Taylor, who lost about half of his army to Scott and thus was left with less than 5,000 men, was instructed to stand on the defensive.

While Scott was assembling his army off the coast, General Santa Anna, the Mexican dictator, decided to take advantage of the division of American forces by marching northward and crushing Taylor and then returning to deal with Scott. With an army much larger than Taylor's, Santa Anna attacked the Americans at Buena Vista (February, 1847), where "Old Rough and Ready," angered at being subordinated to Scott, had placed his army in a dangerously exposed position. Although Santa Anna handled Taylor roughly, he could not break the American line, and had to retire from the field and return to defend Mexico City without his expected victory.

In the meantime Scott had taken Vera Cruz by siege and was moving inland. His campaign is one of the most brilliant in American military annals. With an army that never numbered more than 14,000 and that at times sank to 9,000, he advanced 260 miles into enemy territory, conserved the lives of his soldiers by using flanking movements instead of frontal assaults, and finally achieved his objective without losing a battle. After leaving Vera Cruz, Scott first encountered Santa Anna at Cerro Gordo, in the mountains, and inflicted a smashing reverse on the Mexicans. Scott met no further resistance until he was within a few miles of Mexico City. Before the capital, Santa Anna made a desperate stand, but Scott defeated him badly at Contreras and Churubusco (August, 1847), and drove on the city. After capturing the fortress of Chapultepec in a hard fight, the Americans occupied, on September 14, the enemy capital. A new Mexican government came into power, one that recognized the fact of defeat and that was willing to make a peace treaty.

By a strange circumstance, a peace commissioner was present with Scott's army. Polk, in his growing anxiety to get the war finished, had sent with the invading army a presidential agent who was authorized to negotiate an agreement, on terms similar to those Polk had proposed in the Slidell mission, whenever the Mexicans seemed disposed to treat for peace. The man selected for this post was Nicholas P. Trist, chief clerk of the State Department. After the fall of Mexico City, Polk became disgusted with Trist's failure to accomplish anything, and recalled his

ENTRANCE OF SCOTT'S ARMY INTO MEXICO CITY. This print of the American army taking possession of the Mexican capital appeared in a history of the war written by George W. Kendall of the New Orleans *Picayune*, who was one of the first war correspondents to accompany an army. (LIBRARY OF CONGRESS)

envoy. At that moment, Trist was about to enter into negotiations with the Mexican authorities, so he disregarded the President's orders and stayed on. On February 2, 1848, he concluded the treaty of Guadalupe Hidalgo, which embodied the essence of Polk's original instructions. Mexico agreed to cede California and New Mexico and to acknowledge the Rio Grande boundary of Texas. In return, the United States contracted to assume the claims of its citizens against Mexico and to pay $15 million to Mexico.

Polk, despite his irritation with Trist, decided to submit the treaty to the Senate. After all, it secured what the United States had gone to war to get, and it was probably the only agreement Mexico would consent to. Besides, new factors were intruding in the situation and threatening ominous complications that the President wanted to avoid. Some of the expansionists in both sections were de-

manding that the United States hold out for the annexation of *all* Mexico, and this permitted the antislavery leaders to charge that Southern slaveholders were running the government for their own ends. (Actually, some antislavery men, convinced that slavery could never thrive in Mexico, favored taking the whole country.) Acceptance of the treaty, Polk thought, would silence the extremists on both sides. Accordingly, he submitted it to the Senate with a recommendation for ratification. By a vote of 38 to 14, with a majority of both Democrats and Whigs supporting it, the treaty was approved.

New Settlers in the Far West

When the war ended, a portion of the territory acquired from Mexico was already settled by Americans who, oddly enough, had left their country because they were unhappy there. These people were adherents of a religious sect formally known as the "Church of Jesus Christ of Latter Day Saints," the members of which were known as Mormons. The Mormon faith had originated in western New York; it was one of the numerous new religions that flowered in America in the 1820's and 1830's. Like some others of the new sects, the Mormons believed in a tightly knit and disciplined community life directed by the church elders, and they practiced a communal form of economic life. Seeking a more congenial environment, the Mormons, under the leadership of their prophet, Joseph Smith, moved to Ohio, then to Missouri, and finally to Nauvoo, Illinois. Everywhere they met with resentment, largely caused by their economic and community organization. At Nauvoo they particularly outraged the opinions of their neighbors by introducing polygamy. Their troubles came to a climax when a mob lynched Smith.

Brigham Young, who succeeded Smith, and the elders now decided that if the Mormons were to escape further persecution they would have to move outside the United States. In 1846 almost the entire Mormon community, 12,000 emigrants, left Nauvoo for the Council Bluffs (in the vicinity of present Omaha), where they stayed until their leaders could determine upon a final destination. The place picked out by Young was the Great Salt Lake basin in Utah, distant and isolated from the authority of any government and so arid that no other people would have the courage to live there. In 1847–8 several thousand Mormons made the long, hard trip to their new home, and by 1850 over 11,000 people were settled in and around the Mormon metropolis of Salt Lake City. It was one of the epic mass migrations of American history. Under the driving leadership of Young, the Mormons prospered. With the aid of irrigation they successfully engaged in agriculture, they established thriving home industries, and they built up a profitable trade with emigrants on the way to California.

Although the Mormons were disillusioned to find themselves once again in the United States, they soon realized that federal control over them could be only nominal. In fact, the national government made little actual effort to govern the area. Utah was organized as a territory in 1850, but Brigham Young was appointed territorial governor. The Mormon community was almost autonomous until after the Civil War.

In January, 1848, gold was accidentally discovered in the Sacramento Valley in California. As word of the strike spread, inhabitants of California and the whole Far West, fired by hopes of becoming immediate millionaires, stampeded to the area to stake out claims. By the end of summer the news had reached the eastern states and Europe. Then the gold rush really started. From the United States and, so it seemed, all the world, thousands of people, the "Forty-Niners," poured into California. Those who left from the older states could choose between three routes of travel: overland by covered wagon, inexpensive but involving a long journey over the Great Plains and across the Rockies: by ship around Cape Horn, quicker but more expensive; or the dangerous, difficult shortcut across the Isthmus of Panama. By all three routes, disdaining starvation, thirst, disease, and even death, the seekers after gold came —more than 80,000 of them in 1849. By the end of that year, California had a population of approximately 100,000, more than enough to entitle her to statehood.

Wartime and Postwar Politics

In domestic politics President Polk was as aggressive—and successful—as he was in foreign policy. At his insistence Congress re-established the Independent Treasury system, thus pleasing all sections of the Democratic party and redeeming one of its platform promises. Again at Polk's demand, Congress fulfilled another platform pledge by lowering the tariff. The Walker Tariff, framed by the able Secretary of the Treasury, Robert J. Walker, reduced the average tariff rates to a level of 26.5 per cent. It delighted the South, which had at last succeeded in its long fight to get the tariff down, but it could not have been passed without the votes of Western Democrats. Naturally, the Westerners expected something in return, and specifically they expected Southern support for internal im-

Outraged that the United States had gotten only part of Oregon, they were bitterly convinced that the President had betrayed the party's platform and sacrificed the interests of the West. There had been no compromise on Texas, they pointed out.

Before Polk left office, a much more dangerous issue emerged. In August, 1846, while the war was in progress, Polk had asked Congress to provide him with $2 million that he could use to purchase territory from Mexico. When the appropriation was introduced in the House,

---

NORTHWESTERN RESENTMENT AT POLK

1846

When Polk vetoed an internal-improvements bill, leaders in the Old Northwest charged that Southern influence was blocking the development of their section. Cried a Chicago newspaper: "The North can and will be no longer hoodwinked. If no measures for protection and improvement of anything Northern or Western are to be suffered by our Southern masters, . . . a signal revolution will inevitably ensue. . . . The North and West will look to and take care of their own interests henceforth. . . . They will see that the power to oppress shall not again be entrusted to men who have shown themselves to be slaveholders, but not Americans. The fiat has gone forth—Southern rule is at an end."

---

provements. Although the Democratic platform had declared against a "general" program of internal improvements, Western Democrats did not think this restriction applied to their section. Two internal improvements bills passed Congress, but Polk, who sincerely believed that the national government had no legal power to finance such projects, vetoed both of them. The Westerners were disappointed and angered; as in the case of Oregon, they thought that Polk was sacrificing their interests to those of the South.

Most of the votes against the Oregon treaty came from Senators of Polk's own party, Democrats from the Northwest.

David Wilmot of Pennsylvania, an antislavery Democrat from a high-tariff state, moved an amendment that slavery should be prohibited in any territory secured from Mexico. The so-called Wilmot Proviso passed the House, but failed in the Senate. It would be called up again and be debated and voted on for years.

Diametrically opposed to the Wilmot Proviso was the formula of the Southern extremists. They contended that the states jointly owned the territories and therefore that the citizens of each and every state possessed equal rights in the territories, including the right to move to them with their property, meaning particularly slave property. According to this view, Congress, which was only the agent for the joint owners, had no power to prohibit the movement of slavery into the public domain or to regulate it in any way except by extending protection; neither could a territorial legislature, which was a creature of Congress, take any action to ban slavery.

For the consideration of moderate men in both sections, two compromise plans were presented. One, which numbered President Polk among its advocates, proposed to run the Missouri Compromise line of 36° 30′ through the new territories to the Pacific coast, banning slavery north of the line and permitting it south. The other, first prominently espoused by Lewis Cass, Democratic Senator from Michigan, was originally called "squatter sovereignty"; later, when taken up by Stephen A. Douglas, an Illinois Senator of the same party, it was given the more dignified title of "popular sovereignty." According to this formula, the question of slavery in each territory should be left to the people there, acting through the medium of their territorial legislature.

Congress and the country debated the various formulas, but at the end of Polk's administration a decision had still not been reached. No territorial government had been provided for California and New Mexico (New Mexico included most of present New Mexico and Arizona, all of Utah and Nevada, and parts of Colorado and Wyoming). Even the organization of Oregon, so far north that obviously slavery would never enter it, was held up by the controversy. Southern members of Congress, hoping to gain some advantage in the regions farther south, blocked a terriorial bill for Oregon until August, 1848, when a free-soil government was finally authorized.

The debate was partially stilled by the election of 1848. Neither of the major parties wished to make either expansion or exclusion of slavery a major issue. To do so was a sure way of losing votes in one section or another; in addition, many leaders in both parties sincerely believed that a continuation of the bitter argument would intensify sectional divisions and possibly lead to disunion. In their official pronouncements, therefore, the Democrats and the Whigs tried to avoid definite and provocative references to the slavery question.

The Democrats nominated as their candidate Lewis Cass of Michigan, an elderly, honest, dull wheel-horse of the party. Although the Democratic platform was purposely vague in its references to slavery, it was capable of being interpreted as an endorsement of squatter sovereignty. The Whigs adopted no platform and presented as their candidate a military hero with no political record—General Zachary Taylor of Louisiana.

Ardent abolitionists and even moderates who merely opposed the expansion of slavery found it difficult to swallow either Cass or Taylor. The situation was ripe for the appearance of a third party—if the various dissatisfied elements could be brought together. The potential sources for a new party were the existing Liberty party and the antislavery members of the old organizations. Late in the campaign (August, 1848), the third-party promoters called for a national convention. The convention adopted a platform endorsing the principle of the Wilmot Proviso and declaring for free homesteads and a higher tariff. Former President Van Buren was nominated for the Presidency. Because the platform emphasized "Free Soil, Free Labor, Free Speech, and Free Men," the new party became known as the Free-Soil party.

In comparison with the two preceding elections, the campaign was quiet and even apathetic. When the votes were counted, it was found that Taylor had won a narrow victory. He received 1,360,000 popular votes to 1,220,000 for Cass—a plurality of only 140,000—and 163 electoral votes to Cass's 127—a majority of 36. Although Van Buren did not carry a single state, he polled an impressive 291,-000 votes, and the Free-Soilers elected ten members to Congress. It is probable that Van Buren pulled enough Democratic votes away from Cass, particularly in New York, to throw the election to Taylor.

Taylor and the Territories

Zachary Taylor was the first man to be elected President with no previous political training or experience. He was also the first professional soldier to sit in the White House. Although he came from the South and was a slaveholder, Taylor was a Southerner only in a technical sense. From his long years in the army he had acquired a national outlook and an attachment to the concept of nationalism.

Because of the failure of Congress to provide civil government for the area annexed from Mexico, those regions were being administered by military officials who were responsible to the President. The situation was unsatisfactory to everybody concerned with it: to the national government, which was unable to establish efficient agencies of administration, and to the people of the new lands, who desired the benefits of civil government.

To President Taylor, assuming office in March, 1849, statehood seemed to be the solution to California's problem. More important, statehood appealed to the old soldier as the perfect solution for the controversy over slavery in the territories. All sides conceded that a territory, as it became a state, could do whatever it wanted about slavery. With his penchant for seeking simple answers, Taylor reasoned thus: California and also New Mexico should be encouraged to frame state constitutions and apply for admission to the Union. Nobody could deny their right to dispose of slavery as they wished; they would become states, and two areas of potential sectional conflict would be removed. That both territories contained but a few Southerners and

ZACHARY TAYLOR. Of medium height and rather heavy build, Taylor was informal in his dress to the point of carelessness. In the Mexican War some of his soldiers commented that he looked more like a farmer than a general. Easy and cordial in manner, he was pre-eminently the general of the enlisted men, who admiringly called him "Old Rough and Ready." (LIBRARY OF CONGRESS)

hence were certain to exclude slavery did not bother the President at all; his only thought, and it became almost an obsession, was to settle the slavery issue by getting the new acquisitions into the Union. He urged California and New Mexico to frame constitutions, and directed military officials in the territories to expedite statehood movements.

California needed no prodding; by October she had prepared and ratified a constitution in which slavery was prohibited. In their haste, the Californians, without waiting for congressional approval of their work, as required by law, elected a state government and representatives to Congress. New Mexico, with a smaller population and less pressing governmental problems, moved more slowly, but nevertheless by May, 1850, she too had adopted a constitution banning slavery. When Congress assembled in December, 1849, Taylor rather proudly described his efforts, and recommended that California be admitted as a free state and that New Mexico, when she was ready, be permitted to come in with complete freedom to decide the status of slavery as she wished.

Immediately it was apparent that Congress was not going to accept the President's program. For one reason, the legislative branch felt a natural jealousy of the power of the executive, a feeling that had been increasing since Jackson's time; many legislators believed Taylor should have consulted Congress before acting.

Complicating the situation was the emergence of side issues generated by the conflict over slavery in the territories. One such issue concerned slavery in the District of Columbia. The antislavery people, charging that human servitude in the capital was a national disgrace, were demanding that it be abolished there; to this charge Southerners angrily replied that the institution could not be touched without the consent of Maryland, which had originally donated the land, and that to abolish it would place a stigma on the entire South. Another disturbing question involved the rendition of fugitive slaves. Since the *Prigg* v. *Pennsylvania* case, a number of Northern states had passed "personal liberty laws," forbidding their courts and police officers to assist in the return of runaways. Southern extremists, taking the position that these statutes were designed to prevent slaveholders from recovering their property, were calling for the passage of a stringent *national* fugitive slave law. A third issue related to the boundary between Texas and New Mexico. Texas claimed the portion of New Mexico east of the Rio Grande, although the national government during the Mexican War had as-

signed this region to New Mexico. To Texans it seemed that Washington was trying to steal part of their territory; they also resented the government's refusal to assume the Texas war debt. Southern extremists supported the pretensions of Texas, while their fellows in the North, eager to cut down the size of a slave state, upheld New Mexico.

But the biggest obstacle in the way of the President's program was the South—angered and frightened by the possibility that two new free states would be added to the Northern majority. With its social system under constant attack from the North and from most centers of opinion in Western culture, the South had developed a strong sense of insecurity. Only in the Senate did the South still maintain equality. The number of free and slave states was equal in 1849; there were fifteen of each. But now the admission of California would upset the balance and deprive the South of its last constitutional protection—and New Mexico, Oregon, and Utah were yet to come!

Responsible Southern leaders stated that if California was admitted and if slavery was prohibited in the territories, the time had come for the South to secede from the Union. At the suggestion of Mississippi, a call went out for a Southern-rights convention to meet in June, 1850, at Nashville, Tennessee, to consider whether the South should resort to the ultimate act of secession. In the North excitement ran equally high. Every Northern state legislature but one adopted resolutions demanding that slavery be barred from the territories; public meetings all through the free states called for the Wilmot Proviso and the abolition of slavery in the District of Columbia. Such was the situation that confronted Congress and the country as the tense year of 1850 opened.

BIBLIOGRAPHY

The expansion of the Western frontier is reated in several general works, notably in Billington, *The Far Western Frontier, 1830–1860* and *Westward Expansion* (1949); L. R. Hafen and C. C. Rister, *Western America* (1950); and Cardinal Goodwin, *The Trans-Mississippi West, 1803–1853* (1922). Other studies dealing with broad aspects of Western developments are H. N. Smith, *Virgin Land* (1950); Everett Dick, *Vanguards of the Frontier* (1941); G. P. Garrison, *Westward Extension* (1906); and Bernard De Voto, *The Year of Decision, 1846* (1943). The relationship between territorial expansion and politics is discussed in W. E. Dodd, *Expansion and Conflict* (1915), and more recently and challengingly in N. A. Graebner, *Empire on the Pacific* (1955). A. K. Weinberg analyzes the philosophy of expansionism in *Manifest Destiny* (1935). The classic work on the fur trade is H. M. Chittenden, *The American Fur Trade of the Far West* (3 vols., 1902).

For the Oregon country, see the general treatment by O. O. Winther, *The Great Northwest* (1947); C. L. Skinner, *Adventurers of Oregon* (1921); M. C. Jacobs, *Winning Oregon* (1938); K. W. Porter, *John Jacob Astor* (2 vols., 1931); C. M. Drury, *Marcus Whitman* (1937); and Francis Parkman's superb source account, *The Oregon Trail* (1849 and later editions). For California, consult John Caughey, *California* (1953); R. G. Cleland, *From Wilderness to Empire* (1944); and A. B. Hulbert's collection of documents, *The Forty-Niners* (1931). For Texas, see E. C. Barker, *Mexico and Texas, 1821–1835* (1928) and

Stephen F. Austin (1925); R. N. Richardson, *Texas, the Lone Star State* (1943); W. R. Hogan, *The Texas Republic* (1946); W. C. Binkley, *The Texas Revolution* (1952); and Marquis James, *The Raven* (1929), a biography of Sam Houston. For Utah, see W. A. Linn, *Story of the Mormons* (1902); Nels Anderson, *Desert Saints* (1942); M. R. Werner, *Brigham Young* (1925); and F. M. Brodie, *No Man Knows My History* (1945), a biography of Joseph Smith. For New Mexico, go to R. L. Duffus, *The Santa Fe Trail* (1930), and the vivid source work by Josiah Gregg, *Commerce of the Prairies* (1954 edition, edited by M. L. Moorhead).

Ample treatment of the background of the Mexican War is found in J. S. Reeves, *American Diplomacy under Tyler and Polk* (1907) and G. L. Rives, *The United States and Mexico, 1821–1848* (2 vols., 1913). The standard work on the war is Justin H. Smith, *The War with Mexico* (2 vols., 1919), but the best one-volume study is R. S. Henry, *Story of the Mexican War* (1950). Shorter but good accounts are N. W. Stephenson, *Texas and the Mexican War* (1921), and A. H. Bill, *Rehearsal for Conflict* (1947). Relevant biographies are E. I. McCormac, *James K. Polk* (1922); Allan Nevins (ed.), *Polk: The Diary of a President* (1952); Allan Nevins, *Fremont, Pathmarker of the West* (1955); C. W. Elliott, *Winfield Scott* (1937); Holman Hamilton, *Zachary Taylor, Soldier of the Republic* (1946) and *Zachary Taylor, Soldier in the White House* (1951); Brainerd Dyer, *Zachary Taylor* (1946); and F. B. Woodford, *Lewis Cass* (1950).

18

THE ROAD TO DISUNION

Bonds of union began to break. Once Northerners and Southerners had belonged to the same national churches. Then, in the 1840's, the Methodists and Baptists divided, because of the slavery question, into separate Northern and Southern organizations, and thereafter other churches were torn by sectional quarrels. Political parties, organized on a national scale, remained one of the strongest ties holding the sections together. But during the 1850's the Whig party disintegrated, and the Democratic party, essentially an alliance of South and West, was weakened by the strains of conflicting Southern and Western interests. A new Republican party arose, to draw the West into an alliance with the East.

Long before, George Washington had warned that political parties formed on a geographical basis would endanger the Union. By 1859 the time of danger was at hand. No longer could North and South achieve a Union-saving compromise as they had done in 1820–1, in 1833, and again in 1850.

The Compromise of 1850

Faced by the threat of a national crisis, moderate men and lovers of the Union naturally turned their thoughts to the framing of a great congressional compromise that would satisfy both sections and restore sectional tranquility. Just as naturally, the promoters of compromise turned for a leader to the venerable statesman from Kentucky, Henry Clay. Quite ready to head the forces of conciliation, Clay believed that Taylor's California statehood formula was inadequate to deal with the crisis. To Clay's way of thinking, no compromise would have any significant or lasting effects unless it settled all the issues in dispute between the sections. Accordingly, he took a number of separate measures which had been proposed by various members of both parties from the North and the South, and combined them into one set of resolutions which on January 29, 1850, he presented to the Senate. His proposals were as follows:

a. California was to be admitted as a free state.

b. Territorial governments were to be established in the rest of the Mexican cession region with no restrictions upon slavery and no mention of its status.

c. Texas was to relinquish her claim to New Mexico in return for the national government's assuming her public debt.

d. Slavery in the District of Columbia was never to be abolished unless its residents and those of Maryland consented and compensation was paid.

e. The slave trade in the District was to be abolished.

f. Congress was to enact a more drastic and effective fugitive slave law.

g. Congress was to declare that it had no power to regulate the interstate slave trade.

and the only subject—the minority South —and he asked more for his section than could be given. Because of Northern aggressions, the cords that bound the Union were snapping, he said. What would save the Union? The North must admit that the South possessed equal rights in the territories, must agree to observe the laws concerning fugitive slaves, must cease attacking slavery, and must accept an amendment to the Constitution guaranteeing a balance of power between the sections. The amendment he

---

WHITTIER'S DENUNCIATION OF WEBSTER

The New England abolitionists were outraged by Webster's speech supporting the Compromise of 1850 and the Fugitive Slave Act, and they denounced him in bitter terms. Emerson said: "All the drops of his blood have eyes that look downward." Whittier expressed his feelings about Webster's speech in a poem, "Ichabod":

> All else is gone; from those great eyes
>   The soul has fled:
> When faith is lost, when honor dies,
>   The man is dead!
>
> Then, pay the reverence of old days
>   To his dead fame;
> Walk backward, with averted gaze,
>   And hide the shame!

These resolutions inaugurated a debate in the Senate, and in the House and throughout the country, that lasted until September. Clay, who had but two years to live, started the oratorical tournament with a defense of his measures and a plea to North and South to be mutually conciliatory and forebearing.

Early in March, Calhoun, who would die within the month, presented the views of the Southern extremists. Too ill and weak to speak, he sat grimly in his seat while a colleague read his speech. Almost ignoring Clay's proposals, he devoted his argument to what to him was the larger

had in mind provided for the election of dual Presidents, one from the North and one from the South, each possessing a veto power. In short, nothing would satisfy Calhoun except abject surrender by the North.

After Calhoun came the third of the elder statesmen, Webster, who, like Clay, had but two years of life left. The address he delivered, "the Seventh of March speech," was probably the greatest forensic effort of his long oratorical career. Although he still nourished White House ambitions, Webster now sought to calm angry passions and to rally Northern

MILLARD FILLMORE. Few Presidents have exemplified the American success story as completely as Fillmore. Born in a log cabin and raised in poverty, by sheer industry he made himself into a successful lawyer and wealthy man. His support of the Compromise of 1850 alienated many Whig leaders and cost him the party's nomination in 1852. He was the last Whig President. (LIBRARY OF CONGRESS)

moderates to support of compromise, even at the risk of alienating the strong antislavery sentiment of his native New England.

Other speakers, important and insignificant, moderate and extremist, entered the debate. Some recommended popular sovereignty; others advocated extending the Missouri Compromise line. Of particular import were the views of the Northern extremists, voiced by the New York Whig William H. Seward, who maintained extremely cordial personal relations with President Taylor, and Ohio's Salmon P.

Chase, who had been sent to the Senate by a combination of Democratic and Free-Soil votes. There was a higher law than the Constitution, Seward proclaimed, the law of God, and slavery contravened divine law.

After most of the speeches had been made, Clay's resolutions were referred to a special committee, headed by Clay, which was to frame them into acceptable laws and report back to the Senate. When the bills were introduced, popular sentiment in all sections was slowly swinging in favor of some kind of compromise. The country was entering upon a period of prosperity—the result of an expanding foreign trade, the flow of gold from California, and a boom in railroad construction—reminiscent of the flush days of the 1830's. Conservative economic interests everywhere wanted to terminate the sectional dispute and concentrate the attention of the nation upon internal expansion. Even in the South excitement seemed to be abating. The Nashville convention met in June, and after adopting some tame resolutions adjourned to await final action by Congress.

For a time, however, it seemed that Congress was not going to act. One reason was the opposition of Taylor. The President persisted in his stand that the admission of California, and possibly New Mexico, must come first and alone; after that, it might be possible to discuss other measures. In the meantime, if the South wanted to try anything like secession, "Old Zack" was ready to use force against his native section and to lead the armed forces in person.

On July 9, President Taylor suddenly died, the victim of a violent stomach disorder following an attack of heat prostration. He was succeeded by the Vice President, Millard Fillmore of New York. The new chief executive was a handsome, dignified man of no great abilities; but he was also a practical professional politician who understood the importance of compromise in statecraft. At once he

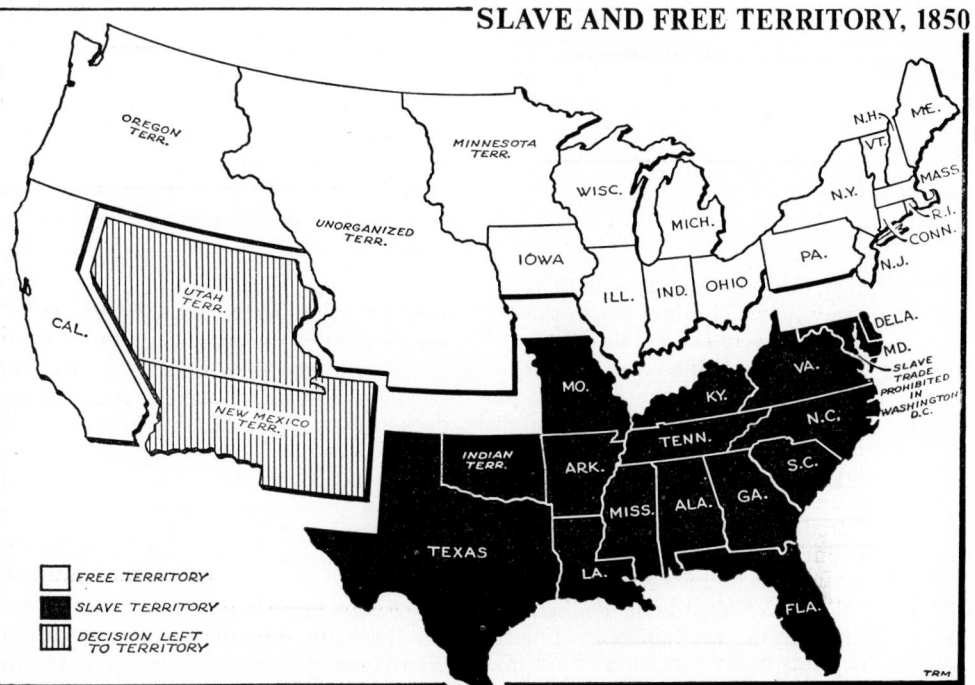

FREE TERRITORY

SLAVE TERRITORY

DECISION LEFT TO TERRITORY

ranged himself on the side of the advocates of adjustment, using his powers of persuasion and patronage to swing Northern Whigs into line. At about the same time, Clay, exhausted by his labors, temporarily left Congress, and Stephen A. Douglas took over the leadership of the compromise forces. Discarding the Kentuckian's all-or-nothing strategy, Douglas broke up the various measures reported by Clay's committee, and presented them one by one.

By mid-September the series of measures had been enacted by both houses of Congress and signed by the President. This Compromise of 1850 consisted of five laws, which may be summarized as follows:

a. California was admitted as a free state.

b. New Mexico was organized as a territory, and Texas was to relinquish her claim to New Mexico territory in return for a payment of $10,000,000 from the national government.

c. Utah was organized as a territory.

d. The slave trade was abolished in the District of Columbia.

e. A new and more severe Fugitive Slave Act placed the enforcement agencies of the national government at the disposal of slaveholders.

The ambiguous phrases in the acts concerning slavery in New Mexico and Utah did not specifically ban or authorize slavery in either territory. They were intended to invest the territorial legislatures with power to prohibit or exclude slavery in the territorial stage, and thus to extend a limited recognition to popular sovereignty.

It was one thing to pass the Compromise through Congress and another to persuade the country to accept it. In the North the task of winning popular acceptance was easier than in the South. The only provision that really gagged Northern opinion was the Fugitive Slave Act. By this measure, a Negro accused of being a runaway was denied trial by jury and the right to testify in his own behalf.

Georgia accepted the Compromise of 1850 but listed possible acts by the North that would lead her to reconsider her decision. These conditions may be taken as minimum Southern demands for sectional peace:

"Fourth. That the State of Georgia, in the judgment of this Convention, will and ought to resist, even (as a last resort) to a disruption of every tie which binds her to the Union, any future Act of Congress abolishing Slavery in the District of Columbia, without the consent and petition of the slave-holders thereof, or any Act abolishing Slavery in places within the slave-holding States, purchased by the United States for the erection of forts, magazines, arsenals, dock-yards, navy-yards, and other like purposes; or in any Act suppressing the slave-trade between slave-holding States; or in any refusal to admit as a State any Territory applying because of the existence of Slavery therein; or in any Act prohibiting the introduction of slaves into the Territories of Utah and New Mexico; or in any Act repealing or materially modifying the laws now in force for the recovery of fugitive slaves.

"Fifth. That it is the deliberate opinion of this Convention, that upon the faithful execution of the Fugitive Slave Bill by the proper authorities, depends the preservation of our much loved Union."

His status was to be decided by a federal judge or by a special commissioner appointed by the federal circuit courts. He could be remanded to slavery on the bare evidence of an affidavit presented by the man who claimed to be his owner.

The advocates of the Compromise in the South had to fight hard to carry the day. The adjourned session of the Nashville convention met in November, 1850 (with only about a third of the original delegates present), and condemned the Compromise. Eventually, the South brought itself to accept the Compromise, but only after much agonizing, and then only conditionally. Epitomizing the feelings of its people were the resolutions of the "Georgia Platform." They declared that Georgia would acquiesce in the Compromise—but if the North disregarded the Fugitive Slave Law, or attempted to abolish slavery in the District of Columbia, or denied admission to a state because it wished to have slavery, then

Georgia would consider the compact broken and would protect its rights even to the length of seceding.

The Compromise was a truce, and it proved to be of short and uneasy duration.

Election of 1852 and After

At their national convention in 1852 the Democrats adopted a platform pledging their unswerving devotion to the Compromise of 1850 and their united opposition to all attempts in any "shape or color" to renew the agitation of the slavery question. Not so unanimous when it came to choosing a candidate, they wrangled through forty-nine ballots, with no one of the leading contenders—Cass, Douglas, or James Buchanan of Pennsylvania—being able to secure a two-thirds majority. Finally, the prize went to one of the more obscure aspirants, another "dark horse," Franklin Pierce of New

Hampshire. The Whigs likewise endorsed the Compromise but in much milder terms and over the opposition of many Conscience Whigs. Instead of nominating a man connected with and committed to the Compromise, they named, after fifty-three ballots, General Winfield Scott, whose views were unknown and whose support by Northern delegates made him suspect to Southerners. He would be the last Whig candidate. The only party to repudiate the Compromise was the Free-Soilers, who offered, as their candidate, John P. Hale of New Hampshire.

Probably because they had taken a stronger stand for the Compromise, the Democrats won the election. Pierce carried twenty-seven states and Scott four, and the Democrats had 254 electoral votes to the Whig's 42, the largest majority that any candidate had attained since Monroe's victory in 1820. In the popular vote, however, Pierce's triumph was much narrower, 1,601,000 to 1,386,000, or a majority of only about 215,000. The Free-Soilers lost almost half the number of votes they had polled in 1848. If their votes are reckoned as part of the opposition to the Democrats, Pierce's majority was a mere 60,000.

When Franklin Pierce was inaugurated in 1853, he was, at the age of forty-nine, the youngest man up to that time to become President. He was also generally considered to be the handsomest chief executive the country had ever had. Amiable and charming, he had been selected as the Democratic nominee largely for reasons of party harmony. In his short political career he had upheld few opinions and had made few enemies. As President, he was dominated by the strong men of his cabinet, namely Secretary of State William L. Marcy of New York, Secretary of War Jefferson Davis of Mississippi, and Attorney General Caleb Cushing of Massachusetts.

The Compromise did not dissolve the abolitionist organizations or step their

FRANKLIN PIERCE. Handsome and slender, Pierce looked almost boyish at the time of his inauguration. Although he had an appealing personality, he lacked firmness of character and was easily dominated by stronger men in his cabinet and in Congress. (LIBRARY OF CONGRESS)

crusade to convince the Northern masses that slavery was a sin. In the 1850's the abolitionists intensified their efforts, and partly because recent events had focused attention on slavery, they found a larger audience. They also found new allies and new and more effective media of expression. The Free-Soil upsurge had placed several members of that group in Congress, and these men—such as Charles Sumner of Massachusetts in the Senate, and Joshua R. Giddings of Ohio in the House—could denounce slavery from the vantage point of the national forum. Furthermore, they could use their congressional mailing privileges to send their speeches free to people all over the Northern states.

The most powerful, the most telling document in the abolitionist propaganda attack was a novel, Uncle Tom's Cabin, by Harriet Beecher Stowe, published in

AN ABOLITIONIST VIEW OF THE FUGITIVE SLAVE ACT. In this abolitionist broad-side a party of "slave catchers" has run down some escaping slaves and is about to murder them. The Fugitive Slave Act was bitterly resented in the North, and abolitionist depictions of its enforcements were readily believed. (LIBRARY OF CONGRESS)

1852. Mrs. Stowe, "Crusader in Crino-line," was a member of a famous New England ministerial family (her father and her seven brothers were preachers), and she married a minister. It has been said that she was raised and smothered in orthodox New England Calvinism. For several years she had lived in Cincinnati, and from there had made several forays into Kentucky to view slavery and planta-tion life. These excursions were her only direct contact with the South. Her novel, written after she and her husband had left Cincinnati for Maine, was an indict-ment of slavery although not of the slave-holders; her purpose was to show that the slave system was inherently brutal and had a brutalizing effect on all who were connected with it.

This moving tale of poor, persecuted Uncle Tom had a terrific impact on the Northern mind. Other abolitionists had attacked slavery in the abstract or as an evil institution, but Mrs. Stowe assailed it in terms of human personalities. In such a form, her message appealed to emotions and sympathies that no pre-vious attack had touched, and inspired other similar novels to follow. The book sold over 300,000 copies in its year of publication. Dramatized into a play which was presented by countless professional and amateur companies all over the North, it reached other thousands who may not have read its pages.

Another explosive force in national so-ciety was the Fugitive Slave Act of the Compromise. Many people in the North, including some who were not abolition-ists, were hostile to the law from the moment it was passed, believing that it violated various procedural guarantees of the Constitution and the basic concepts of English-American law. This hostility was intensified and increased when Southerners appeared in the Northern states to pursue fugitives or to claim as former slaves Negroes who had been living for years in Northern communities. Mobs or organized groups attempted to impede enforcement of the act. In 1851 a crowd in Boston took a runaway named Shadrach away from a federal marshal and sent him on his way to Canada. Later in the same year at Syracuse, New York, there was a similar rescue of a slave named Jerry McHenry. In 1854 in Boston a mob led by respectable and prominent men tried unsuccessfully to take one Anthony Burns from the custody of federal officers.

These displays of violence alarmed the South, but making an even stronger impact were the new personal-liberty laws passed by several Northern legislatures. The frank purpose of the statutes was to render the Fugitive Slave Act a nullity. They interposed state power between the accused fugitive and the federal authority. Wisconsin and Massachusetts instructed state courts to issue writs of habeas corpus against any person detaining a fugitive, and granted the fugitive a judicial hearing in which the burden of proof was placed on the pursuer. The supreme court of one state, Wisconsin, in the case of *Ableman v. Booth* (1857), declared the national law void; and when the Supreme Court of the nation in reviewing the case decided against the state, the Wisconsin court ignored the decision. Viewing the legal and judicial barriers being thrown in the way of the one provision of the Compromise which the South considered a positive victory, Southerners were deeply angered. The North, they felt, was showing that it did not intend to observe the compact of 1850. Talk of secession began to revive.

Foreign Affairs in the 1850's

As a result of the acquisition of California and Oregon, the United States had become a Pacific power. The rapid settlement of California following the discovery of gold and the sustained movement of migrants to Oregon indicated that a new center of American population was about to come into being in the Far West. And yet communication with this area, by horse and wagon over the plains and mountains or by water around Cape Horn, was distressingly slow and dangerous. There was an imperative need to bind the Pacific coast communities more tightly to the rest of the country, and obviously this need could be met most immediately by improved water transportation. In this situation interested Americans turned their thoughts to a project which had long intrigued men's minds —the construction of a canal across Central America that would link the Atlantic and Pacific oceans.

If the United States undertook to build a canal, it would have to deal with Great Britain, which had colonies and important commercial interests in Central America. Neither nation wanted to go to the length of war to defend its interests. Both preferred to negotiate the difficulty. England sent to America an able minister, Henry Lytton Bulwer, to treat with Taylor's Secretary of State, John M. Clayton. The result of their deliberations was the Clayton-Bulwer Treaty (April 19, 1850), a characteristic Anglo-American compromise. As neither nation would consent to let the other have sole control of a canal, they agreed to join in promoting a waterway, with the understanding that neither should ever fortify or exercise exclusive control over the project.

When Fillmore became President, he appointed Webster Secretary of State. At that moment the great democratic and nationalist revolutions of 1848 in Europe were running their course, some succeeding, others petering out in failure. A vision of a republican Europe, with governments based, of course, on the model of the United States, stirred the American imagination. In the Democratic party a "Young America" movement started, with the idea of aiding oppressed peoples over the seas. Politicians in both parties, particularly those who had minority groups like the Irish and Germans in their districts, contributed to the excitement by denouncing the decayed monarchies of the Old World.

Webster and other moderates sensed in the situation an opportunity to make the people forget the recent sectional fight by directing their attention to events abroad. When the government of Austria officially protested against the apparent readiness of the United States to recognize the Hungarians, who were in revolt against Austria, Webster resolved to write a reply that would touch the national pride of Americans in all sections and that would awaken Europe to the greatness of America. He declared that in comparison with the extent of the United States, the possessions of Austria were "but as a patch on the earth's surface."

After the Hungarian uprising collapsed, the magnetic national hero of Hungary, Louis Kossuth, came to America to seek aid for his people. He was wined and dined and lionized, and Webster spoke at a banquet in his honor; but Kossuth could secure no pledge from the government to intervene in Europe on Hungary's behalf. He departed after learning that American interest in persecuted nationality groups was confined mainly to talk.

In another area of foreign relations, Webster proceeded with less bombast and more prudence. Lying at the mouth of the Gulf of Mexico and controlling the Caribbean communications of the United States was the rich Spanish colony of Cuba. American statesmen had long been aware of the island's importance to their country, and previous administrations probably would have acted to take it if a strong foreign power had sought to oust decrepit Spain. President Polk had tried, without success, to induce Spain to sell. After the Mexican War, American interest in Cuba mounted, partly as a result of

the continued influence of Manifest Destiny but mainly because of the slavery question. Observant Southerners recognized that the territories acquired from Mexico were unfit for slave labor and that the South could hope for no new slave states within the present national limits. Only to the south—to the Caribbean and Central America—could the South look for lands where slavery would be profitable, and in this region the richest prize was Cuba. Southern expansionists talked of organizing filibustering expeditions to seize the island for the United States, and New Orleans became a center where plans for Cuban conquest were hatched.

Coincidentally a filibustering leader appeared, one General Narciso López, a Venezuelan adventurer, who proposed to invade Cuba with a force of volunteer Americans, eject the Spanish, and present the island to the United States. In 1849 he prepared an expedition, but Federal officials in New Orleans and New York broke up his plans. In the following year he succeeded in reaching Cuba but had to flee to the United States when the Spanish dispersed his small force. Encouraged by Southern supporters, López made plans in 1851 for a third try. He landed in Cuba with over 400 men, mostly Americans, and almost immediately suffered a decisive defeat, he and part of his army being captured. The Spanish authorities executed him and more than fifty of his followers. When news of his fate reached the United States, popular indignation was widespread and intense, especially in the South. In New Orleans a mob wrecked the Spanish consulate and a Spanish newspaper office. Now it was Spain's turn to be indignant; her government demanded reparation and an apology. Webster did not want a war. In a conciliatory note, he admitted the wrong committed by the mob and extended satisfactory amends.

His action did not mean his government was abandoning interest in Cuba.

England and France, alarmed by the filibustering movements, proposed to Washington a tripartite agreement guaranteeing Spain's sovereignty in Cuba. The United States rejected the idea. Edward Everett, who succeeded Webster, explained to England and France the strategic importance of Cuba, commanding the sea approaches to the United States and dominating the Caribbean and Isthmian water routes. The American government, said Everett, could make no pledge never to acquire Cuba. Indeed, "Under certain contingencies it might be almost essential to our safety."

In Cuba and in other areas the Pierce administration was more aggressive and expansionist than either the Taylor or the Fillmore administrations had been. New trouble with Great Britain arose from the activities of the most famous of all American filibusters, William Walker. This tiny (he weighed just 100 pounds), dynamic, and dangerous man appeared in Nicaragua in 1855 with a band of American adventurers, and succeeded in establishing himself as dictator. He seems to have had a vision of becoming the head of a federation of Central American states. The British government (and antislavery Americans) suspected that he was acting as an agent for Pierce and preparing the way for American annexation; this suspicion, although without foundation, was strengthened when the President extended recognition to Walker's government.

Walker might eventually have caused real trouble between England and the United States, but his too-ambitious plans miscarried. Forced to leave Nicaragua by military pressure exerted by neighboring republics, he attempted to return in 1860. He landed in Honduras but was arrested by British naval officials. They turned him over to the Honduran authorities, who promptly had him executed by a firing squad.

Meanwhile, Anglo-American relations were troubled on another front. Ameri-can fishermen complained to Washington that Canadian authorities were restricting their rights, as guaranteed by the Convention of 1818, to ply their trade off the Newfoundland and Labrador coasts. Pierce responded by dispatching a naval force to the area to protect American interests. The situation was complicated by Canada's grave economic difficulties. As a result of England's free trade program and the United States' tariff policy, the colony had lost a substantial portion of its export trade. Some Canadians contended that Canada's position would be improved by union with the United States, but the majority thought that the colony should merely seek closer trade relations with her southern neighbor. The Canadian legislature asked the home government to negotiate a treaty based on reciprocal principles.

Great Britain, beset by troubles in Europe, decided to conciliate the United States on the fisheries question and at the same time to appease Canadian economic grievances. She sent to Washington a special mission headed by Lord Elgin. The result of his discussions with Secretary of State Marcy was the Canadian Reciprocity Treaty of 1854, the first agreement of its kind ever made by the American government. By its terms American fishermen were granted enlarged privileges in Canadian waters. Of more importance, a number of commodities, most of them agricultural, were to be admitted to both countries without tariff duties. Canada was being drawn into the American economic orbit.

The Pierce administration also applied its vigorous foreign policy in the middle Pacific and in Asia. Talk began, in the press and out, of annexing Hawaii or seizing it by a filibuster. Secretary Marcy tried to take advantage of the new expansion boom by negotiating a treaty of annexation with the Hawaiian government, but the pact proved unacceptable to the Senate. Nevertheless, it was clear that the United States intended to maintain its influence in the middle Pacific, and observers could have predicted that some day the Hawaiian Islands would go the way of Texas.

The administration's most notable Asiatic success was in opening trade relations with Japan. For over two centuries this island kingdom had followed a policy of seclusion from the outside world; only the Dutch among Occidental peoples were allowed trade privileges, and these at only one port. As America's Oriental trade grew in volume, there were demands from shippers and businessmen that the government take steps to open Japan to American commerce. In 1852 President Fillmore sent out a naval expedition commanded by Commodore Matthew C. Perry, who was instructed to sound out the Japanese on a trade agreement. Perry reached Japan the following year, and, conducting himself with great firmness and tact, delivered his message. Realizing that the island people would require time to reach a decision involving a break with their past, he did not attempt to conclude a treaty, but left after stating that he would return the next year with a stronger force.

In 1854, acting now under the sponsorship of the Pierce administration, Perry returned to Japan. He found the Japanese ready to negotiate a pact, partly because they had been impressed by Perry's display of American naval might but mainly because the more progressive Japanese leaders had decided that relations with the outside world were desirable. Perry secured a treaty which opened two ports to American trade and provided for the residence in one of them of an American consul general. To this post Pierce named a brilliant diplomat, Townsend Harris, and gave him instructions to conclude a more comprehensive treaty. After years of patient work, Harris persuaded the Japanese to accept an agreement (in 1858) that gave the United States a more favored position than any other nation.

Pierce's foreign policy with respect to Canada, Hawaii, and Japan had been marked by a kind of eager aggressiveness, yet it had been a national policy: it had sought objectives which could be said to benefit the national interest. In dealing with Cuba (as with Walker's Nicaragua), however, Pierce and his advisers adopted a program which, whatever their motives, seemed specifically designed to profit the South. The result was to precipitate a minor controversy in domestic politics and to place the South in the position of seeming to conspire to violate the Compromise of 1850.

Pierce's reference in his inaugural to the possibility that the United States might have to acquire certain new possessions was commonly taken to mean Cuba. This impression was strengthened when he appointed Pierre Soulé of Louisiana as minister to Spain. Soulé, an enthusiastic expansionist, seemed to think that the purpose of his mission was to provoke war.

In 1854 Marcy instructed Soulé to offer Spain up to $130 million for Cuba. If Spain refused to sell, Soulé was to try to "detach" Cuba from Spanish rule, that is, to start a movement for Cuban independence. After independence, it was hoped, the island would join the United States. Before Soulé could act, Marcy instructed Soulé to meet with James Buchanan, minister to England, and John Y. Mason, minister to France, and determine ways and means of acquiring Cuba. The three men embodied their recommendations in a diplomatic dispatch which shortly found its way into the newspapers and became known as the Ostend Manifesto. This remarkable document stated that the United States should endeavor to purchase Cuba for a reasonable price. If Spain should reject an offer, the United States would be justified in "wresting" the island from Spain.

Publication of the essence of the dispatch in the American press caused a terrific uproar. In the North it was charged that the administration, acting as the tool of the South, was endeavoring to add a new slave state to the Union even at the risk of war.

The Kansas-Nebraska Act

By the 1850's the line of frontier settlement had reached the great bend of the Missouri. Beyond the western boundaries of Minnesota, Iowa, and Missouri stretched the vast expanse of prairie land earlier called the Great American Desert and designated as an Indian reserve. Now it was known that large sections of this region were suited to farming, and in the Northwest people were saying that the national government should open the area to settlement, provide it with territorial government, and remove the Indians. The problem of communication between the older states and the trans-Mississippi West became more urgent.

The idea of a transcontinental railroad had been discussed in Congress and out for years. Disagreement entered the picture—and disagreement of an ominous character—when people talked about the eastern terminus of the road and its specific route. Several cities pressed their claims, but the leading contenders were Chicago, St. Louis, Memphis, and New Orleans. The transcontinental railroad, like nearly everything else in the fifties, became entangled in sectionalism. It became a prize that the North and South would struggle to secure and try to deny to each other.

One argument against a southern route had been removed through the foresight of Secretary of War Davis, one of the leading promoters of a southern railroad. Surveys had indicated that a road from a southern terminus would probably have to pass through an area south of the Gila River, in Mexican territory. At Davis' suggestion, Pierce appointed James Gadsden, a Southern railroad builder, to negotiate with Mexico for the sale of this region. Gadsden persuaded the Mexican government to dispose of a strip of land that today comprises the southern portion of Arizona and part of southern New Mexico, the so-called Gadsden Purchase (1853), which cost the United States $10 million.

One man who was interested in a transcontinental railroad was Senator Stephen A. Douglas, and his interest influenced him to introduce in Congress a fateful legislative act, one that accomplished the final destruction of the truce of 1850. As a Senator from Illinois and a resident of Chicago and, above all, as the acknowledged leader of the Northwestern Democrats, Douglas naturally wanted the transcontinental railroad for his own city and section. He realized too the potency of the principal argument urged against the northern route: that west of the Mississippi it would run largely through unsettled Indian country. In January, 1854, as chairman of the Committee on Territories, he acted to forestall this argument. He introduced a bill to organize a huge new territory, to be known as Nebraska, west of Iowa and Missouri.

Douglas seemed to realize that his bill would encounter the opposition of the South, partly because it would prepare the way for a new free state, the proposed territory being in the Louisiana Purchase area north of the 36° 30' line of the Missouri Compromise and hence closed to slavery. In an effort to make the measure acceptable to Southerners, Douglas inserted a provision that the status of slavery in the territory would be determined by the territorial legislature, that is, according to the doctrines of popular sovereignty. Theoretically at least, this would open the region to slavery. This concession was not enough to satisfy extreme Southern Democrats, particularly those from Missouri who were fearful that their state would be surrounded by free territory. They demanded more, and Douglas had to give more to get their support. He agreed to a clause specifically repealing the territorial section of the Missouri

Compromise and to a provision creating two territories, Nebraska and Kansas, instead of one. Presumably the latter, because of its more southern location, would become a slave state. In its final form the measure was known as the Kansas-Nebraska Act.

Douglas induced President Pierce to endorse his bill, and so it became an official Democratic measure. But even with the backing of the administration, it encountered stiff opposition and did not become a law until May, 1854. Nearly all the Southern members of Congress, whether Whigs or Democrats, supported the bill, and nearly all the Northern Whigs opposed it. The Northern Democrats split, with half of their votes in the House going for the act and half against it.

Of greater importance than the opposition to the Kansas-Nebraska Act in Congress was the reaction against it in the Northern states. The whole North seemed to blaze with fury at this latest demonstration of the power of the slavocracy, and much of the fury was directed at Douglas, who, to the eyes of many Northerners, had acted as a cat's-paw for the slaveholders. No other piece of legislation in congressional history produced as many immediate, sweeping, and ominous changes as the Kansas-Nebraska Act. It destroyed the Whig party in the South except in the border states. At the same time, as many Southern Whigs became Democrats, it increased Southern influence in the Democratic party. It destroyed the popular basis of Whiggery in the North, with the result that by 1856 the national Whig party had disappeared and a conservative influence in American politics had been removed. It divided the Northern Democrats and drove many of them from the party. Most important of all, it called into being a new party that was frankly sectional in composition and creed.

Men in both the major parties who opposed Douglas's bill took to calling themselves Anti-Nebraska Democrats and Anti-Nebraska Whigs. In their anger at the South, in their fear that the slavocracy meant to push its institution into the Western territories, they were in a mood to defend their opinions by forming a new party. And in 1854 their party took shape, and it took a name—the Republican party. Originating in a series of spontaneous popular meetings throughout the Northwest, the Republican movement soon spread to the East. The new party showed an immediate strength that was sensational. In the elections of 1854, the Republicans, often acting in concert with the Know-Nothings, elected a majority to the House and won control of a number of Northern state governments. For the moment the Republican party was a one-idea organization: its only platform was opposition to the expansion of slavery into the territories. Composed mainly of former Whigs and Free-Soilers but including also a substantial segment of former Democrats, it represented in large part the democratic idealism of the North. But it contained, in addition, Northern power groups who felt that the South—the champion of a low tariff, the enemy of homesteads and internal improvements—was blocking their legitimate economic aspirations.

The pulsing popular excitement aroused in the North by the Kansas-Nebraska Act was sustained by events occurring during the next two years in Kansas. Almost immediately immigrants in substantial numbers moved into this territory.

Many people had come to make homes and not to be contenders in an ideological contest. But there were some who came for the specific purpose of engaging in a struggle of ideologies. They were dedicated men who were determined to make Kansas free—or slave. Those who came from the North were encouraged by press and pulpit and the powerful organs of abolitionist propaganda; often they received financial help from organizations like the New England Emigrant Aid Company, which had been created to render such assistance. Those who came from the South were stimulated by similar influences of a Southern nature; often they received financial contributions from the communities they had left.

In the spring of 1855 elections were held for a territorial legislature. Thousands of Missourians, some traveling in armed bands, moved into Kansas and voted. Although there were probably only some 1,500 legal votes in the territory, over 6,000 votes were counted. With such conditions prevailing, the proslavery forces elected a majority to the legislature, which proceeded immediately to enact a series of laws legalizing slavery. The outraged free-staters, convinced that they could not get a fair deal from the Pierce administration, resolved on extralegal action. Without asking permission from Congress or the territorial governor, they elected delegates to a constitutional convention which met at Topeka and adopted a constitution excluding slavery. They then chose a governor and legislature, and petitioned Congress for statehood. Pierce stigmatized their movement as unlawful and akin to treason. The full weight of the government, he announced, would be thrown behind the proslavery territorial legislature.

A few months later a proslavery federal marshal assembled a huge posse, consisting mostly of Missourians, to arrest the free-state leaders in Lawrence. The posse not only made the arrests but sacked the town. Retribution came immediately. Among the more extreme antislavery men was a fierce, fanatical old man named John Brown who considered himself as an instrument of God's will to destroy slavery. Estimating that five antislavery men had been murdered, he decided that it was his sacred duty to exact vengeance —a life for a life. He gathered six followers, and in one bloody night murdered five proslavery settlers (the "Pottawatomie massacre"). The result was to touch off civil war in Kansas—irregular, guerrilla war conducted by armed bands, some of them more interested in land claims or loot than in ideologies.

People in the North and the South believed (and whether or not their beliefs were completely correct is historically unimportant) that the aggressive designs of the other section were epitomized by what was happening in Kansas. Thus "Bleeding Kansas" became a symbol of the sectional controversy.

In May, 1856, Charles Sumner of Massachusetts arose in the Senate to discuss affairs in the strife-torn territory. He entitled his speech "The Crime against Kansas." Handsome, humorless, sincere, doctrinaire, Sumner embodied the extreme element of the political antislavery movement. In his address he fiercely denounced the Pierce administration, the South, and slavery; and he singled out for particular attention as a champion of slavery Senator Andrew P. Butler of South Carolina. It was an age when orators were wont to indulge freely in personal invective, but in his allusions to Butler and others, Sumner went farther than most.

Particularly enraged by the attack was Butler's nephew, Preston Brooks, a member of the House from South Carolina. He resolved to punish Sumner by a method approved by the Southern code— by publicly and physically chastizing the Senator. Approaching Sumner at his desk when the Senate was not in session, he proceeded to beat his kinsman's traducer with a cane until Sumner fell to the floor in bloody unconsciousness. The injured Senator stayed out of the Senate four years, and during his absence his state refused to elect a successor. Brooks, censured by the House, resigned and stood for re-election. He was returned by an almost unanimous vote.

The violence in Congress, like that in Kansas, was a symbol. It showed that Americans were becoming so agitated by their differences that they could not settle them by the normal political processes of debate and the ballot.

Election of Buchanan

The presidential campaign of 1856 got under way with the country convulsed by the Brooks assault and the continuing violence in Kansas. The Democrats adopted a platform that endorsed the Kansas-Nebraska Act and defended popular sovereignty as the safest solution of the slavery issue. Logically the party should have nominated one of the outstanding advocates of popular sovereignty, Pierce or perhaps Douglas. But political parties cannot always be logical in elections. The leaders wanted a man who had not made many enemies and who was not closely associated with the explosive question of "Bleeding Kansas." As a result, the nomination went to James Buchanan of Pennsylvania, a reliable party stalwart who had been minister to England and hence had been safely out of the country during the recent troubles.

The Republicans, engaging in their first presidential contest, faced the campaign with a confidence born of party youth and their spectacular success in the elections of 1854. Still primarily a one-idea party, they filled their platform with denunciations of the Kansas-Nebraska Act and the expansion of slavery into the territories. They did, however, approve a program of internal improvements, an indication that their leaders were beginning to grasp the advantage of combining the idealism of anti-slavery with the economic aspirations of the North. Just as eager as the Democrats to present a safe candidate, the Republicans nominated John C. Frémont, who, working first for the United States army and later for private interests, had made a national reputation as an explorer of the Far West. Although he was a sincere Republican, the glamorous "Pathfinder" was selected because he was a famous

figure who had no political record and hence was highly available.

The American or Know-Nothing party entered the campaign with its strength seriously sapped. It was beginning to break apart on the inevitable rock of sectionalism. At its convention, many Northern delegates had withdrawn because the platform was not sufficiently firm in opposing the expansion of slavery. The remnant that was left nominated Millard Fillmore. The candidacy of the former President was endorsed by the sad remnant of another party, the few remaining Whigs who could not bring themselves to support either Buchanan or Frémont.

The campaign was the most exciting since 1840. Its frenzied enthusiasm was due largely to the Republicans. They featured huge mass meetings, lavish circulation of political literature, and wholesale employment of party symbols and slogans. They shouted for "Free Soil, Free Speech, and Frémont," depicted "Bleeding Kansas" as a sacrifice to the evil ambitions of the slavocracy, and charged that the South, using Northern dupes like Buchanan as its tools, was plotting to extend slavery into every part of the country.

The results of the election seemed to indicate that the prevailing mood of the country was conservative. Buchanan, the winning candidate, polled 174 electoral votes, Frémont 114, and Fillmore 8. The Democrats also secured majorities in both houses of Congress. Buchanan carried all the slave states except Maryland (whose eight votes went to Fillmore) and five Northern states (Illinois, Indiana, New Jersey, Pennsylvania, and California). Frémont won the other eleven Northern states, and he received a large minority vote in the five states carried by Buchanan. The popular vote was 1,838,000 for Buchanan, 1,341,000 for Frémont, and 874,000 for Fillmore. A slight shift of popular votes in Pennsylvania and Illinois would have thrown those states into the Republican column and elected Frémont.

James Buchanan had been in politics and in public office almost continuously since he was twenty-three years old. At the time of his inauguration he was nearly sixty-six, the oldest President, with the exception of Harrison, that the country has had. Undoubtedly his age and general physical infirmity had something to do with the indecision he often displayed. He seemed to be obsessed by one idea—to meet every crisis by giving the South what it wanted.

In the year Buchanan took office, a financial panic struck the country, to be followed by several years of stringent depression. Europe had contributed to the causes of the depression by its unusual demand for American food, particularly during the Crimean War (1854–6). When that conflict ceased, the demand fell off, with the result that agricultural prices were seriously depressed.

The depression, instead of drawing the nation closer together in a sense of common misfortune, sharpened sectional differences. The South was not hit as hard as the North. The result was to confirm the opinion of Southern leaders that their economic system was superior to that of the free states; and, smarting under previous Northern criticisms of Southern society, they loudly boasted to the North of their superiority.

In the North the impact of the depression had the effect of strengthening the sectional Republican party and weakening the Democrats. Distressed economic groups—manufacturers and farmers—came to believe that the depression had been caused by unsound policies forced upon the government by Southern-controlled Democratic administrations. They thought that prosperity could be restored by a program embracing such items as a high tariff (the tariff was lowered again in 1857), a homestead act, and internal improvements—all measures to which the South was opposed. In short, the frustrated economic interests of the North

JAMES BUCHANAN. Buchanan came to the presidency with a rich background of education and political experience. But he proved to be a weak President, largely because, like his predecessor Pierce, he had an indecisive character. In his youth Buchanan was engaged to a lady, but the engagement was broken by a quarrel. Soon afterward the girl died. Buchanan never married and became the only bachelor President. (LIBRARY OF CONGRESS)

were, by the force of circumstances, being pushed into an alliance with the antislavery impulse as represented by the Republican party. Northern resentment at what seemed to be Southern restraint of the nation's economic future was one important reason why the Democrats lost their majority in the House in the elections of 1858.

Proslavery Principles and Policies

The Supreme Court of the United States projected itself into the sectional controversy with its decision in the case of *Dred Scott v. Sanford,* handed down two days after Buchanan was inaugurated.

Dred Scott was a Missouri slave, once the property of an army surgeon, who on his military pilgrimages had carried Scott with him Illinois, a free state, and to Minnesota Territory, where slavery was forbidden by the Missouri Compromise. Eventually both the owner and the slave returned to Missouri, where the surgeon died. Scott was persuaded by some abolitionists to bring suit in the Missouri courts for his freedom on the ground that residence in a free territory made him a free man. The state supreme court de-

crats (five of them being from the South), one was a Whig, and one was a Republican. Chief Justice Taney, in the majority opinion, announced two important principles. First, the Chief Justice declared that Scott was not a citizen of Missouri and hence could not bring a suit in the federal courts. The second principle was concerned with the question of whether Scott's residence in territory north of the Missouri Compromise line had made him free. Taney met the issue squarely: Scott's sojourn in Minnesota had not affected his status as a slave. Slaves were property, said

REPUBLICAN COMMENT ON THE SUPREME COURT

Republican anger at the Dred Scott decision was intense. Party leaders denounced the Court's reasoning and proclaimed that when the party came to power it would take action to have the decision reversed. Presumably they meant to "pack" the Court and bring a new case. A typical Republican reaction came from the Chicago *Tribune*: "That bench full of Southern lawyers which gentlemen of a political temperament call 'august tribunal' is that last entrenchment behind which despotism is sheltered; and until a national convention amends the Constitution so as to defend it against the usurpations of that body, or until the Court itself is reconstructed by the dropping off of a few of its members and the appointment of better men in their places, we have little to hope for by congressional action in the way of restricting slavery."

cided against him, but in the meantime the officer's widow had married an abolitionist. Ownership of Scott was now technically transferred to a New Yorker, J. F. A. Sanford. The purpose of this arrangement was to enable Scott to get his case into the federal courts with the claim that the suit lay between citizens of different states. Regardless of the decision, Scott would be freed, as his abolitionist owners would not keep him a slave. The case was intended to secure a federal decision on the status of slavery in the territories.

Of the nine justices, seven were Demo-

Taney, and the Fifth Amendment prohibited Congress from taking property without "due process of law." Consequently, Congress possessed no authority to pass a law depriving persons of their slave property in the territories. The Missouri Compromise, therefore, had always been null and void.

Few judicial opinions have stirred as much popular excitement as the decision involving this obscure Missouri Negro. The South, naturally, was elated: the highest tribunal in the land had invested with legal sanction the extreme Southern argument. In Republican circles the decision was denounced. It had been conceived in a partisan spirit by a partisan body, cried the Republicans, and deserved as much consideration as any pronouncement by a group of political hacks. As for settling the status of slavery in the territories, that section of the opinion was an *obiter dictum* and had no legal justification. Boldly the Republicans announced that when they secured control of the national government they would reverse the decision—by altering the personnel of the Court; that is, by "packing" it with new members.

President Buchanan, who had known in advance the nature of the Dred Scott decision (having been tipped off by two of the Justices), had said in his inaugural address that he hoped the forthcoming opinion would end the agitation over slavery in the territories. With equal blindness, he decided that the best solution for the Kansas troubles was to force the admission of that territory as a slave state.

The existing proslavery territorial legislature called an election for delegates to a constitutional convention. The free-state people refused to participate. As a result, the proslavery forces won control of the convention, which met in 1857 at Lecompton and framed a constitution establishing slavery. The antislavery groups, when an election for a new territorial legislature was called, turned out to vote. They won a majority. Promptly the legislature moved to submit the Lecompton constitution to the voters. The document was rejected by more than 10,000 votes.

Although both sides had resorted to fraud and although both still on occasion indulged in violence, the picture in Kansas was clear enough. The majority of the people did not want to see slavery established. Unfortunately Buchanan could not see, or did not want to see, the true picture. He urged Congress to admit Kansas under the Lecompton constitution, and threw the full weight of the administration into a move to force the party to back his proposal. But Douglas and other Western Democrats refused to accept this perversion of popular sovereignty. Openly breaking with the administration and angering Southern Democrats, Douglas denounced the Lecompton proposition. And although Buchanan's plan passed the Senate, Western Democrats helped to block it in the House. Partly to avert further division in the party, a compromise measure, the English bill, was now offered (1858) and passed. It provided that the Lecompton constitution should be submitted to the people of Kansas for the third time. If the document was approved, Kansas was to be admitted and given a federal land grant; if it was disapproved, statehood would be postponed until the population reached 93,600, the legal ratio for a representative in Congress. Again, and for the last time, the Kansas voters decisively rejected the Lecompton constitution. Not until the closing months of Buchanan's administration, in 1861, when a number of Southern states had withdrawn from the Union, would Kansas enter the Union—as a free state.

Lincoln, Douglas—and Brown

The congressional elections of 1858 were of greater interest and importance than is usually true of such mid-term contests. Not only did they have an immediate and powerful influence on the course of the sectional controversy, but they projected into the national spotlight the man who would be the dominating figure in the tragic years just ahead when sectional strife would deepen into civil war, the man who by giving up his life in that conflict would become the great folk hero of the American democratic tradition.

For various reasons, the contest that excited the widest public attention was the senatorial election in Illinois. There Stephen A. Douglas, the most prominent Northern Democrat, was a candidate for re-election, and he was fighting for his political life. Since Douglas, or his successor, would be chosen by a legislature which was yet to be elected, the control of that body became a matter of paramount importance. To complicate the situation, the Buchanan administration, in order to punish Douglas for his opposition to the Lecompton constitution, entered opposition Democratic candidates against him in many legislative districts. But Douglas's greatest worry was that in the Republican candidate, Abraham Lincoln, he faced the ablest campaigner in the opposition party.

Lincoln had been the leading Whig in Illinois. After the passage of the Kansas-Nebraska Act he had, after some hesitation, joined the new party, and he was now the leading Republican in his state. He was hardly a national figure—his reputation could not compare with that of the famous Douglas. Lincoln challenged the Senator to a series of seven joint debates. Douglas accepted, and the two candidates argued their cases before huge crowds in every congressional district in the state. The Lincoln-Douglas debates, as the oratorical jousts came to be known, were widely reported by the nation's press, and before their termination the Republican who had dared to challenge the "Little Giant" of the Democracy was a man of national prominence.

Douglas devoted his principal efforts to defending popular sovereignty and attacking the Republicans. He accused them, and Lincoln, of promoting a war of sections, of wishing to interfere with slavery in the South, and of advocating social equality of the races. Lincoln, denying that these charges were true (and they were not), flung his own accusations. He accused the Democrats, and Douglas, of being in a conspiracy to extend slavery into the territories and possibly, by means of another Supreme Court decision, into the free states as well (a charge which was not true either). Lincoln was particularly effective in making it appear that Douglas did not regard slavery as morally wrong. He quoted Douglas as saying that he did

not care whether slavery was "voted down, or voted up."

Lincoln was opposed to slavery—on moral, political, and economic grounds. He believed that a vigorous and expanding system of slavery gave the lie to the American ideal of democracy. He thought that slavery and the aristocratic philosophy of its advocates threatened to subvert the great principle of American society: equality of opportunity. Let the idea be established that Negroes were not created with an equal right to earn their bread, he said, and the next step would be to deny the right to certain groups of whites, probably laborers. His solicitude for the economic well-being of the white masses impelled Lincoln to oppose the introduction of slavery into the territories. He maintained that the national lands should be preserved as places for poor white people to go to to better their condition. But these lands would not be a refuge for such people if slavery was planted in them, because free labor could not compete with slave labor.

And yet Lincoln was opposed to the abolitionists. The physical fact of slavery, he believed, must be taken into account by its opponents. "Because we think it wrong, we propose a course of policy that shall deal with it as a wrong," he said. But "We have a due regard to the actual presence of it amongst us and the difficulties of getting rid of it in any satisfactory way and all the constitutional obligations thrown about it." What policy did Lincoln propose for dealing with slavery? He and his party would "arrest the further spread of it," that is, prevent its expansion into the territories, and thus place it in a state of "ultimate extinction." His plan, then, was to pen up slavery in the South, where it would eventually die a natural death, he hoped.

In the debate at Freeport, Lincoln asked Douglas a question which made this meeting historically the most significant of all the debates. His query was: Can the people of a territory exclude slav-

LINCOLN AND DOUGLAS IN DEBATE. This is a depiction by a later artist, R. M. Root, of the debate between Lincoln and Douglas at Charleston, Illinois. Lincoln, who was beardless until 1861, is speaking, and Douglas sits at his right. Various dignitaries of both parties are on the platform. The man behind Lincoln and to the left taking notes is probably a reporter. In the 1850's speeches were frequently recorded by men known as "stenographic reporters." They used a system of shorthand devised by Isaac Pitman and described by him in a book published in 1837, *Stenographic Sound Hand*. (ILLINOIS STATE HISTORICAL LIBRARY)

ery from its limits prior to the formation of a state constitution? Or in other words, is popular sovereignty still a legal formula despite the Dred Scott decision? The question was a deadly trap, because no matter how Douglas answered it, he would lose something. If he disavowed popular sovereignty, he would undoubtedly be defeated for re-election and his political career would be ended. But if he reaffirmed his formula, Southern Democrats would be offended, the party split deepened, and his chances of securing the Democratic nomination in 1860 damaged if not destroyed.

Boldly Douglas met the issue. The people of a territory, he said, could, by lawful means, shut out slavery prior to the formation of a state constitution. Slavery could not exist a day without the support of "local police regulations": that is, without territorial laws recognizing the right of slave ownership. The mere failure of a legislature to enact such laws would have the practical effect of keeping slaveholders out. Thus, despite the Dred Scott deci-

sion, a territory could exclude slavery. Douglas's reply became known as the Freeport Doctrine or, in the South, as the Freeport Heresy. It satisfied his followers sufficiently to win him a return to the Senate, but throughout the North it aroused little enthusiasm.

The elections went heavily against the Democrats, who lost ground in almost every Northern state. The administration retained control of the Senate but lost its majority in the House, where the Republicans gained a plurality. In the hold-over or short session of 1858–1859, in which the Democrats were in the majority, and in the regular session of 1859 (elected in 1858), every demand of the Republicans and Northern Democrats was blocked by Southern votes or by presidential vetoes; these defeated measures included a tariff increase, a homestead bill, a Pacific railroad, and federal lands grants to states for the endowment of agricultural colleges. The 1859 session was also marked by an uproarious hassle over the election of a speaker of the House.

Alarming to the South was another event occurring in 1859. John Brown, the grim fanatic of the Pottawatomie killings, now made a spectacular appearance on the national scene. Still convinced that he was God's instrument to destroy slavery, he decided to transfer his activities from Kansas to the South itself. With encouragement and financial aid from certain Eastern abolitionists, some of whom were aware of his purpose, he devised a wild scheme to liberate the slaves. His plan was to seize a mountain fortress in Virginia to the scene by the national government. With ten of his men killed, Brown had to surrender. He was promptly tried in a Virginia court for treason against the state, found guilty, and sentenced to death by hanging. Six of his followers met a similar fate.

Probably no single event had as much influence as the Brown raid in convincing southerners that the welfare of their section was unsafe in the Union. Despite all the eulogies of slavery they penned, one great fear always secretly gnawed at their

---

THOREAU ON JOHN BROWN

After the Harpers Ferry raid, many abolitionists proclaimed Brown to be a martyr for freedom. Henry D. Thoreau announced his views at a church meeting in Concord: "I am here to plead his cause with you. I plead not for his life, but for his character,—his immortal life; and so it becomes your cause wholly, and is not his in the least. Some eighteen hundred years ago Christ was crucified; this morning, perchance, Captain Brown was hung. These are the two ends of a chain which is not without its links. He is not Old Brown any longer; he is an angel of light. I see now that it was necessary that the bravest and humanest man in all the country should be hung. Perhaps he saw it himself. I *almost fear* that I may yet hear of his deliverance, doubting if a prolonged life, if *any* life, can do as much good as his death."

---

from which he could make raids to free slaves; he would organize his freedmen, whom he intended to arm, into a Negro state within the South, and eventually he would force the South to concede emancipation. In short, he was out to incite a violent slave insurrection. Because he needed guns, Brown fixed on Harpers Ferry, where a United States arsenal was located, as his base of operations. In October, at the head of eighteen followers, he descended on the town and captured the arsenal. Almost immediately he was attacked by citizens and local militia companies, who were shortly reinforced by a detachment of United States marines sent hearts: the possibility of a general slave insurrection. Southerners now jumped to the conclusion that the Republicans were responsible for Brown. This was, of course, untrue; prominent Republicans like Lincoln and Seward condemned Brown as a criminal. But Southerners were more impressed by the words of such abolitionists as Wendell Phillips and Ralph Waldo Emerson, who glorified Brown as a new saint. Undoubtedly his execution made him a martyr to thousands of Northerners. The State of Virginia would have been better advised to declare him insane and confine him in an asylum.

BIBLIOGRAPHY

General accounts of prewar sectionalism include A. C. Cole, *The Irrepressible Conflict, 1850–1865* (1934); R. F. Nichols, *The Disruption of American Democracy* (1948); U. B. Phillips, *The Course of the South to Secession* (1939); H. H. Simms, *A Decade of Sectional Controversy* (1942); T. C. Smith, *Parties and Slavery* (1906); and D. L. Dumond, *Anti-Slavery Origins of the Civil War* (1939). A. O. Craven interprets the backgrounds of the Civil War in four books: *The Repressible Conflict, 1830–1861* (1939); *The Coming of the Civil War* (1942; rev. ed., 1957); *The Growth of Southern Nationalism, 1848–1861* (1953); and *Civil War in the Making, 1815–1860* (1959). The most comprehensive treatment of the prewar period is Allan Nevins, *The Emergence of Lincoln* (2 vols., 1950).

Important biographies are C. M. Wiltse, *John C. Calhoun: Sectionalist, 1840–1850* (1951); G. F. Milton, *Eve of Conflict: Stephen A. Douglas and the Needless War* (1934); G. M. Capers, *Stephen A. Douglas, Defender of the Union* (1959); R. J. Bartlett, *John C. Frémont and the Republican Party* (1930); R. J. Rayback, *Millard Fillmore* (1959); J. A. Isely, *Horace Greeley and the Republican Party* (1947); G. G. Van Deusen, *Horace Greeley* (1953); A. J. Beveridge, *Abraham Lincoln, 1809–1858* (2 vols., 1928); I. D. Spencer, *The Victor and the Spoils: A Life of William L. Marcy* (1959); R. F. Nichols, *Franklin Pierce* (1931); Frederic Bancroft, *William H. Seward* (2 vols., 1900); and G. G. Van Deusen, *Thurlow Weed* (1947). See also the previously cited books on Clay, Frémont, Taylor, and Webster.

Special studies include G. W. Van Vleck,

The Panic of 1857 (1943); Vincent Hopkins, *Dred Scott's Case* (1951); P. S. Foner, *Business and Slavery* (1941); R. A. Billington, *The Protestant Crusade, 1800–1860* (1938); and W. D. Overdyke, *The Know-Nothing Party in the South* (1950). P. O. Ray, *Repeal of the Missouri Compromise* (1909), should be read in the light of an article by R. F. Nichols in the *Mississippi Valley Historical Review*, XLIII (1956). On Kansas and John Brown, which are highly controversial subjects, see G. R. Gaedert, *The Birth of Kansas* (1940); Jay Monaghan, *Civil War on the Western Border* (1955); O. G. Villard, *John Brown* (1910; new ed., 1943); and J. C. Malin, *John Brown and the Legend of Fifty-Six* (1942), and *The Nebraska Question* (1953). An excellent state study is R. H. Shryock, *Georgia and the Union in 1850* (1926).

On foreign affairs in the 1850's, see M. W. Williams, *Anglo-American Isthmian Diplomacy, 1815–1915* (1916); Basil Rauch, *American Interests in Cuba, 1848–1955* (1948); L. B. Shippee, *Canadian-American Relations, 1849–1874* (1939); P. J. Treat, *The Diplomatic Relations between the United States and Japan, 1853–1895* (1932); Dexter Perkins, *The Monroe Doctrine, 1826–1867* (1933); A. A. Ettinger, *The Mission to Spain of Pierre Soulé* (1932); W. O. Scroggs, *Filibusters and Financiers* (1916); and E. S. Wallace, *Destiny and Glory* (1957).

Paul M. Angle has prepared a new and complete edition of the Lincoln-Douglas debates under the title *Created Equal?* (1958); and H. V. Jaffa interprets the issues of the debates in *Crisis of the House Divided* (1959).

19

THE NATION DIVIDED

During the 1850's the nation had seemed at first to drift and then to rush toward disunion. The fateful goal was reached during the winter of 1860–1. Thereafter, for more than four years, Americans were divided into what, in effect, amounted to two separate and hostile countries.

The Great Decision of 1860

The election of 1860, judged by its consequences, was the most momentous in our history. The issues were so important that the losing side felt it could not abide by the result and attempted to withdraw from the society of which it was a part.

As the Democrats gathered in convention at Charleston, South Carolina, in April, most of the Southern delegates came with the determination to compel the party to adopt a platform providing for federal protection of slavery in the territories: that is, an official endorsement of the principles of the Dred Scott decision. The Western Democrats, arriving with bitter recollections of how Southern influence had blocked their legislative demands in the recent Congress, were angered at the rule-or-ruin attitude of the Southerners. They hoped, however, to negotiate a face-saving statement on slavery

that would hold the party together. They vaguely endorsed popular sovereignty and proposed that all questions involving slavery in the territories be left up to the Supreme Court. When the convention adopted the Western platform, the delegations from eight Lower South states withdrew from the hall. The remaining delegates then proceeded to the selection of a candidate. Stephen A. Douglas led on every ballot, but he could not muster the two-thirds majority (of the original number of delegates) required by party rules. Finally the managers adjourned the convention to meet again in Baltimore in June. At the Baltimore session, most of the Southerners reappeared, only to walk out again. The rest of the Southerners had assembled at Richmond. The rump convention at Baltimore nominated Douglas. The Southern bolters at Baltimore and the men in Richmond nominated John C. Breckinridge of Kentucky. Sectionalism had at last divided the historic Democratic party. There were now two Democratic candidates in the field, and, although Douglas had supporters in the South and Breckinridge in the North, one was the nominee of the Northern Democrats and the other of the Southern Democrats.

The Republicans held their convention

in Chicago in May. Although the divisions developing in the Democratic ranks seemed to spell a Republican triumph, the party managers were taking no chances on a slip-up. They were determined that the party, both in its platform and its candidate, should appear to the voters as representing conservatism, stability, and moderation; above all, they wanted to erase any possible impression that Republicans were radical idealists. No longer was the Republican party a one-idea or-

publicans affirmed the right of each state to control its own institutions, which was their way of saying that they did not intend to interfere with slavery in the South. But they also denied the authority of Congress or of a territorial legislature to legalize slavery in the territories, which was equivalent to saying that they still would oppose the expansion of slavery.

The leading contender for the nomination was William H. Seward, who faced the competition of a number of favorite-

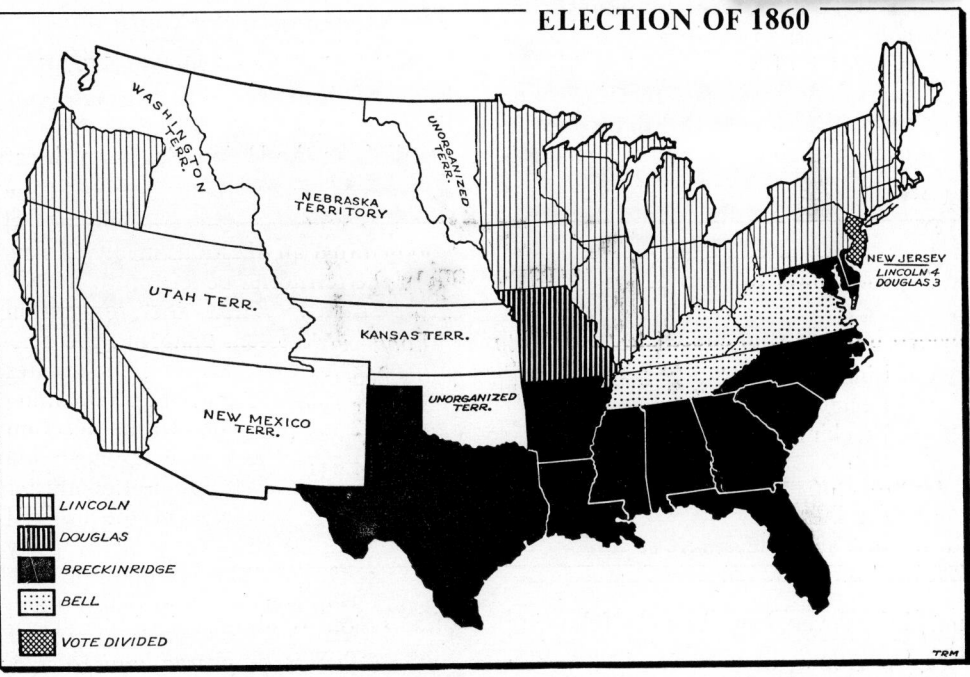

ELECTION OF 1860

NEW JERSEY
LINCOLN 4
DOUGLAS 3

WASHINGTON TERR.

UNORGANIZED TERR.

NEBRASKA TERRITORY

UTAH TERR.

KANSAS TERR.

UNORGANIZED TERR.

NEW MEXICO TERR.

LINCOLN
DOUGLAS
BRECKINRIDGE
BELL
VOTE DIVIDED

ganization composed of grim crusaders against slavery. It now embraced, or hoped to embrace, every major interest group in the North which believed that the South, the champion of slavery, was blocking its legitimate economic aspirations.

The platform reflected the new orientation of the party. It endorsed such measures as a high tariff, internal improvements, a homestead bill, and a Pacific railroad to be built with federal financial assistance. On the slavery issue, the Re-

son candidates. His very prominence and his long political record damaged his chances. Passing him and other aspirants over, the convention nominated on the third ballot Abraham Lincoln—who was prominent enough to be respectable but obscure enough to have few foes, and who was radical enough to please the antislavery faction in the party but conservative enough to satisfy the ex-Whigs. To complete the strategy of availability, the vice-presidential nomination went to Hannibal Hamlin of Maine, a former Democrat.

As if three parties were not enough, a fourth entered the lists—the Constitutional Union party. Although posing as a new organization, it was really the last surviving remnant of the oldest conservative tradition in the country; its leaders were elder statesmen and most of its members were former Whigs. Meeting in Baltimore in May, the party nominated John Bell of Tennessee and Edward Everett of Massachusetts. The platform declared for the Constitution, the Union, and enforcement of the laws.

In the North the Republicans conducted a campaign reminiscent of the exciting contest of 1840, replete with parades, symbols, and mass meetings. For the most part, they stressed the economic promises in their platform, and subordi-

In the November election Lincoln won a majority of the electoral votes and the Presidency. The combined popular vote of Lincoln's opponents was almost a million more than his total. But even if all the opposition strength had been concentrated upon one candidate, the result would have been essentially the same. As it was, the Republicans had elected a President, but they had failed to secure a majority in Congress; and of course they did not have the Supreme Court.

The Secession of the South

During the campaign various Southern leaders had threatened that if the Republicans won the election the South would secede from the Union. Southern threats

ELECTION OF 1860

	Electoral Vote	Popular Vote	Per Cent of Popular Vote
Lincoln	180	1,866,452	40
Douglas	12	1,375,157	29
Breckinridge	72	847,953	18
Bell	39	590,631	13
Total	303	4,680,193	

nated the slavery issue. Lincoln, following the customary practice of candidates, made no speeches, leaving this work to lesser party luminaries. Unlike previous candidates, he refused to issue any written statements of his views, claiming that anything he said would be seized on by Southerners and misrepresented. The two Democratic factions seemed more interested in attacking each other than in defeating the Republicans. Douglas, breaking with precedent, embarked on a speaking tour that carried him into the South. He denounced Breckinridge's supporters as disunionists and warned the South that the Union could not be broken up.

of secession had been voiced at intervals since 1850, without any action following, and Northerners had come to believe they were intended as bluffs. This time, however, the South meant them.

The concept of secession was rooted in the political philosophy which the South had developed to protect its minority status. According to this doctrine, the Union was an association of sovereign states. The individual states had once joined the Union; they could, whenever they wished, dissolve their connections with it and resume their status as separate sovereignties. For a state to leave the Union was a momentous act but a lawful one. Southerners, therefore, had devised a process—one that they considered dignified and legitimate—to accomplish secession. The governor and the legislature would take steps to call an election for a special state convention. This body, while in session, represented the sovereign power of the state; it exercised the supreme powers of government. By a majority vote it could pass an ordinance of secession. Because the convention had been chosen by the people and invested with specific authority, it did not have to submit its decision to popular ratification.

South Carolina, long the hotbed of Southern separatism, led off the secession parade, its convention taking the state out of the Union on December 20, 1860, by a unanimous vote. Before Lincoln ever assumed the Presidency, seven Southern states had left the Union. Not only that, but in February, 1861, representatives of the seceded states met at Montgomery, Alabama, and formed a new, Southern nation—the Confederate States of America.

Something of the indecision in Northern attitudes was reflected in the thinking of President Buchanan. In his message to Congress of December, 1860, he denied the right of a state to secede; but he added that he did not think the federal government possessed the power to coerce a state back into the Union. He intended to avoid a collision of arms and to maintain the symbolic authority of the national government until his successor could take office.

As the various states seceded, they took possession of federal property within their boundaries, but they lacked the strength to seize certain offshore forts, notably Fort Sumter in the harbor of Charleston, South Carolina, and Fort Pickens in the harbor of Pensacola, Florida. South Carolina understood Buchanan's position to mean acquiescence in its independence, and the state sent commissioners to Washington to ask for the surrender of Sumter, garrisoned by a small force under Major Rob-

ert Anderson. Buchanan, fearful though he was of provoking a clash, refused to yield the fort. In January, 1861, he decided to succor Anderson. By his direction an unarmed merchant ship, the *Star of the West*, proceeded to Fort Sumter with troops and supplies. When the vessel attempted to enter the harbor, it encountered the fire of shore batteries and returned to the North.

Meanwhile Buchanan recommended to Congress that it frame compromise measures to hold the Union together. The Senate and the House appointed committees to study plans of adjustment. The Senate committee concentrated on a proposal submitted by Senator John J. Crittenden of Kentucky. The Crittenden Compromise called for a series of constitutional amendments: one would have guaranteed the permanence of slavery in the states; others were designed to satisfy Southern demands on such matters as fugitive slaves and slavery in the District of Columbia. But the heart of Crittenden's plan dealt with slavery in the territories. He proposed to re-establish the Missouri Compromise line of 36° 30′ in all the territory of the United States then held or *thereafter acquired*. North of the line slavery was to be prohibited, south of it slavery was to be recognized. The Southern members of the committee indicated they would accept this territorial division if the Republicans, who were not averse to Crittenden's other points, would agree to it. The Republicans, after sounding out President-elect Lincoln in Illinois, voted against the proposal. Lincoln took the position that the restoration of the Missouri Compromise line would encourage the South to embark on imperialist adventures in Latin America.

One notable attempt to effect a compromise was made outside Congress. The legislature of Virginia invited the other states to send delegates to a peace conference at Washington. Representatives from twenty-one states assembled early in February, and spent most of the month

LINCOLN ARRIVING IN WASHINGTON, 1861. On his way to Washington to be inaugurated, Lincoln was told that detectives had discovered a plot to assassinate him when he passed through Baltimore. Although skeptical of the information, he consented to abandon his published schedule and travel secretly to the capital. On arrival he was met by Congressman Elihu B. Washburn, at his left, one of the few who knew of the change. Behind Lincoln are Ward H. Lamon, a self-appointed guard, and Allan Pinkerton, head of the detective agency of that name. The painting is by H. D. Stitt. (EWING GALLOWAY)

framing compromise proposals. The plan of the Peace Convention, as that body was called, followed closely the Crittenden scheme. The principal difference was that the Convention proposal tried to meet the Republican objection to the 36° 30′ line of division by providing that no new territory should be acquired without the consent of a majority of the Senators from both the free and the slave states. The sponsors of the Convention submitted their plan to the Senate, but it received almost no support.

And so nothing had been resolved when Abraham Lincoln was inaugurated President on March 4, 1861. Lincoln came to Washington with a policy to meet the crisis. In his inaugural address he laid down the following basic principles: the Union was older than the Con-

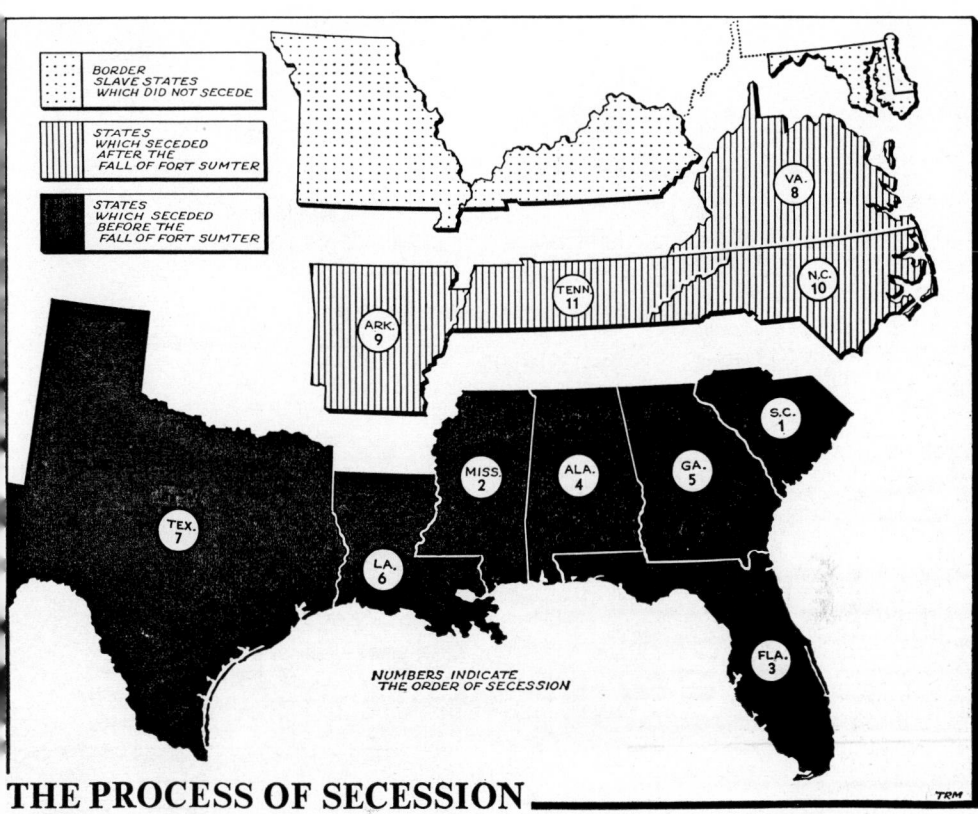

BORDER SLAVE STATES WHICH DID NOT SECEDE

STATES WHICH SECEDED AFTER THE FALL OF FORT SUMTER

STATES WHICH SECEDED BEFORE THE FALL OF FORT SUMTER

VA. 8

TENN. 11

N.C. 10

ARK. 9

S.C. 1

MISS. 2

ALA. 4

GA. 5

TEX. 7

LA. 6

FLA. 3

NUMBERS INDICATE THE ORDER OF SECESSION

THE PROCESS OF SECESSION

stitution, no state could of its own volition leave the Union, the ordinances of secession were illegal, and acts of violence to support secession were insurrectionary or revolutionary. As to the specific situation created by secession, he declared that he meant to execute the laws in all the states and to maintain possession of federal property in the seceded states (Forts Sumter and Pickens).

Lincoln soon found an opportunity to apply his policy in the case of Fort Sumter. Major Anderson was running short of supplies; unless he received fresh provisions the fort would have to be evacuated. If Lincoln permitted the loss of Sumter, the South, and perhaps the North as well, would never believe that he meant to sustain the Union. After much deliberation he decided to dispatch to the fort a naval relief expedition. Carefully he informed

the South Carolina authorities, who, of course, would have to notify the Confederate government, that ships were on the way to bring supplies but not to land troops or munitions unless resistance was offered. His move placed the Confederates in a dilemma. If they permitted the expedition to land, they would be bowing tamely to federal authority; their people would not believe that they meant to sustain secession. But the only alternative was to reduce the fort before the ships arrived—in short, to invoke war. After hours of anguished discussion, the government decided on the latter choice. General P. G. T. Beauregard, in charge of Confederate forces at Charleston, was ordered to demand the surrender of Sumter, and, if the demand was refused, to reduce the fort. Beauregard served his summons, and Anderson rejected it. The Confederates

THE BEGINNING OF THE CIVIL WAR. The war began on April 12, 1861, when Confederate forces in Charleston under General Beauregard opened fire on Fort Sumter. During the attack hundreds of excited Charlestonians crowded the rooftops to observe the spectacle. This contemporary print depicts the scene with essential accuracy. The fort, with its barracks afire, is in the center of the harbor. Off the entrance are the ships of the relief expedition, which made no attempt to enter. (FROM Harper's Weekly, 1861)

then bombarded the fort for two days, April 12–13, 1861. On April 14, Anderson surrendered.

War had come. Lincoln moved to increase the army and called on the states to furnish troops to restore the Union. Now four more slave states seceded and joined the Confederacy: Virginia (April 17); Ar-kansas (May 6); Tennessee (May 7); and North Carolina (May 20). Forty-six mountain counties in northwestern Virginia refused to accept the decision of their state, established their own "loyal" government, and in 1863 secured admission to the Union as the new state of West Virginia. The four remaining slave states, Maryland, Delaware, Kentucky, and Missouri, cast their lot with the Union. Lincoln kept a keen watch on their actions, and in two, Maryland and Missouri, helped to ensure their decision by employing military force. The Confederacy, then, did not represent a solid block of slave states as the embattled hosts of North and South faced each other.

War Potential, North and South

A comparison of the combatants on the eve of war reveals that all the great material factors were on the side of the North. And these advantages became more significant as the conflict continued and the superior economy of the North became geared for war production. The North had a larger manpower reservoir from which to draw its armed forces. In the North, or the United States, were twenty-three states with a population of approximately 22,000,000. In the South, or the Confederate States, were eleven states with a population of some 9,000,000. Of these, approximately 3,500,000 were slaves, leaving a white population of something under 6,000,000.

The North's greater economic potential was most fully and formidably apparent in industrial production. Almost any set of comparative figures can be chosen to illustrate the overwhelming nature of Northern superiority. These statistics, translated into material terms, meant that the Northern armies, once the economic system had been converted to war production, would have more of everything than the Southern forces. This was not true, of course, in the first year of the war, when both sides purchased large amounts of supplies, particularly arms, from Europe. After 1862 the North was able to manufacture practically all of its war materials; its dependence on Europe ceased. The South, on the other hand, had to rely on Europe all during the war, running what goods it could through the Northern naval block-

ade. It also tried desperately to expand its own industrial facilities. The brilliant Confederate chief of ordnance, Josiah Gorgas, accomplished wonders in building arsenals and in supplying the armies with weapons and munitions. Nevertheless, both the quantity and the quality of Confederate firearms was inferior, and the firepower of a Confederate army was rarely equal to that of its enemy. Equally important, the Southern economic system was unable to provide its soldiers, and its civilian society, with the other matériel of modern war: clothes, boots, blankets, stockings, medical supplies, and the like. Its failure in this respect was one reason why Southern morale dropped badly after 1863.

In every respect the transportation system of the North was superior to that of the South. The North had more and better inland water transport (steamboats, barges), more surfaced roads, and more wagons and animals. The North had approximately 20,000 miles of railroads, while the South, containing at least as large a land area, had only 10,000 miles. The trackage figures, however, do not tell the whole story of Southern inferiority. There were important gaps between key points in the South, which meant that supplies had to be detoured long distances or carried between railheads by wagons. As the war wore on, the Confederate railroad system steadily deteriorated, and by the last year and a half of the struggle it had almost collapsed.

The great weapon of sea power was in the hands of the North. Northern sea power served two important strategic functions. First, the federal government proclaimed, when the war started, a blockade of the Southern coast. The mission of sealing off the long coastal line of the Confederacy was an impossible one for the federal navy in the beginning. Even as the navy grew in size and after it reached its maximum, it was unable to establish a completely effective blockade. Blockade runners continued to operate in

COMPARISON OF NORTH AND SOUTH,
1860

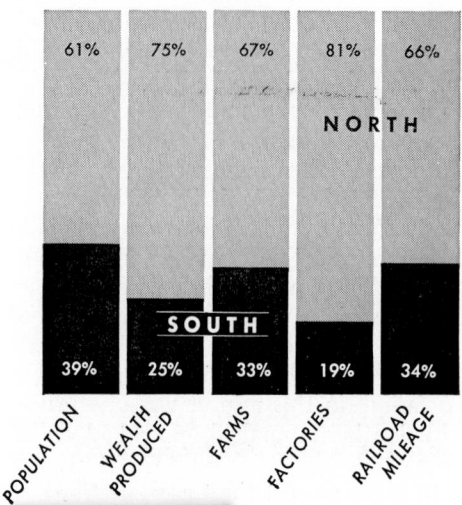

61%	75%	67%	81%	66%

NORTH

SOUTH

39%	25%	33%	19%	34%

POPULATION   WEALTH PRODUCED   FARMS   FACTORIES   RAILROAD MILEAGE

and out of such ports as Wilmington, Charleston, and Mobile. Nevertheless, the blockade did hurt the South. The second function of sea power was in aiding the federal land forces to invade and subjugate the vast Western theater: the region between the Appalachian Mountains and the Mississippi River. In this area the larger rivers were navigable to transport boats and small ships of war. The navy carried supplies for the armies, and joined with them in attacking Confederate strong points.

When the material factors are analyzed and weighed, the impression emerges that the South had absolutely no chance to win the war. Actually, the material odds were not as great as at first glance they appear. The South might have won a decision on the battlefield up to 1863. Southern inferiority in manpower and materials was partially offset by other factors. The South, for the most part, fought on the defensive in its own country and commanded interior lines. The Northern invaders had to maintain long lines of communication, to supply themselves in areas where transportation was defective, and to garrison occupied regions. Furthermore, the North had to do more than capture

the enemy capital or defeat enemy armies. It had to convince the Southern civilian population that the war was hopeless by seizing and holding most of the Confederacy. The South was fighting for something very concrete, very easy for its people to understand. It simply wanted to be independent, to be let alone; it had no aggressive designs on the North. If the South could have convinced the North that it could not be conquered or that the result would not be worth the sacrifices, it might, even after 1863, have won its independence.

When the war started, people in both South and North were gaily confident. One big battle would end it all, men said, and it would be over by the time the cotton crop—or the corn—was in. In large part these cocksure attitudes were the product of a conviction that the other side was of inferior stock and could not fight. A sense of superiority was perhaps more prevalent in the swashbuckling society of the South, where the martial tradition was stronger than in the North. Trumpeted one Southern newspaper: "They may raise plenty of men, men who prefer enlisting to starvation, scurvy fellows from the back slums of cities. . . . But these recruits are not soldiers, least of all the soldiers to meet the hot-blooded, thoroughbred, impetuous men of the South."

Thoughtful Southerners did not indulge in this kind of gasconade. But, they thought, even if the Southern human resources could not make up for Northern material advantages, there was still an almost certain guarantee of Confederate victory: Europe would intervene in the war on the side of the South. England and France had to have Southern cotton, and they would force the North to recognize the Confederacy.

Northern Economic Measures

For the North the wartime years were a period of prosperity and expansion. Both industry and agriculture increased their productive facilities, and at the end of the war were turning out more products than at its beginning.

A powerful stimulant to the expanding economy was provided by the economic legislation enacted by the Republican party during the war. The Republicans represented Northern industry and agriculture, and, now that the war had removed Southern opposition, they proceeded to put into effect the kind of program their supporters expected.

The Homestead Act (1862) and the Morrill Land Grant Act (1862) were measures which the West had long sought. The first provided that any citizen, or any alien who had declared his intention to become a citizen, could register claim to a quarter section of public land (160 acres), and, after giving proof that he had lived on it for five years, receive title on payment of a small fee. Although some Western migration occurred during the war, no great use was made of the act until the years immediately after its close. The Morrill Law was an answer to Western demands for federal aid for the promotion of agricultural education. By its terms each state was to receive 30,000 acres of public land for each of its congressional representatives, the proceeds from the donation to be used for education in agriculture, engineering, and military science. The measure provided the basis for the development of the so-called "land-grant" colleges and universities.

Industry scored its first gain a few days before President Buchanan left office. Congress passed the Morrill Tariff Act, which provided a moderate increase in duties, bringing the rates up to approximately what they had been before 1846. Later measures enacted in 1862 and 1864 were frankly protective. By the end of the war the average of duties was 47 per cent, the highest in the nation's history, and more than double the prewar rate.

Other legislative victories for business were achieved in connection with railroad and immigration. With Southern opposition to a Northern transcontinental railroad now absent, the promoters of that project successfully revived their plans. Two laws (1862, 1864) created two Federal corporations: the Union Pacific Railroad Company, which was to build westward from Omaha, and the Central Pacific, which was to build eastward from California. The government would aid the companies by donating them public lands and advancing government loans. Although actual construction would have to wait until after the war, these measures represented internal improvements on a scale never dreamed of by the Federalists or the Whigs. Immigration from Europe fell off in the first years of the war, partly because of the unsettled conditions. The decrease, coupled with the military demands for manpower, threatened to cause a labor shortage, and President Lincoln and business leaders asked Congress for governmental encouragement of immigration. In 1864 Congress passed a contract labor law by which business was authorized to import laborers, paying the costs of their transportation, with the future wages and homesteads of the migrants being mortgaged to repay the costs. Over 700,000 immigrants entered the country during the war years, some coming in under the new law and others responding to the normal attractions of America.

Perhaps the most important measure affecting the business-financial community was the National Bank Act, enacted in 1863 and amended in 1864. Conceived partly as a long-range reform of the banking system and partly as a solution to the immediate financial needs of the government, the act created the National Banking System, which lasted without serious modification until 1913. Its architects, including Secretary of the Treasury Salmon P. Chase, thought of it as a law that would restore control over the currency to the national government. They argued that both for the military present and the economic future the country needed a uniform and standard banknote currency;

at the outbreak of the war 1,500 banks chartered by twenty-nine states were empowered to issue notes. Furthermore, claimed Chase and his supporters, national supervision of the banking system would enable the government to market its bonds more economically, thus aiding the financing of the war.

The act spelled out a process by which a "banking association" (an existing state bank or a newly formed corporation) could secure a federal charter of incorporation and become a National Bank. Each association was required to possess a minimum amount of capital and to invest one third of its capital in government securities. Upon depositing the securities with the national treasury, it would receive, and could issue as banknotes, United States Treasury notes up to 90 per cent of the current value of the bonds. Various clauses in the law provided for federal supervision and inspection of the banks. When many of the state banks, disliking the regulatory features, held aloof from the new system, Congress (in 1865) placed a tax on all state banknotes. This action forced state notes out of existence and induced many state banks to seek federal charters. By the end of the war the system numbered 11,582 National Banks that were circulating notes amounting to over $200,000,000.

The North financed the war from three principal sources: taxation, loans, and paper money issues. From taxes, including the tariff, the government received approximately $667,000,000; loans, including treasury notes, accounted for $2,600,-000,000; and $450,000,000 of paper currency ("greenbacks") was issued.

Not until 1862, when mounting war expenses forced the country to face realities, did Congress pass an adequate war tax bill. Then it enacted the Internal Revenue Act, which placed duties on practically all goods and most occupations. Embraced in its provisions were manufacturers' taxes, sales taxes, income taxes, stamp duties, and occupational licenses. For the first time in the nation's history, the government levied (in 1861) an income tax, a duty of 3 per cent on incomes above $800. Later (in 1862 and 1865) the rates were increased to 5 per cent on incomes between $600 and $5,000, and to 10 per cent on incomes above the latter figure. Through the medium of the various war taxes, the hand of the government was coming to rest upon most individuals in the country. The United States was in the process of acquiring a national internal revenue system—in fact, a national tax system—one of the many nationalizing effects of the war.

In America's previous wars, bonds had been sold only to banks and to a few wealthy investors. Through the agency of Jay Cooke, a Philadelphia banker, the Treasury launched a campaign to persuade the ordinary man (and woman) to buy a bond. By high-pressure propaganda techniques, Cooke disposed of $400,000,-000 of bonds—the first example of mass financing of a war in our history.

As they bore no interest, were not supported by a specie reserve, and depended for redemption on the good faith of the government (and its ability to win the war), the greenbacks fluctuated in value. In 1864 a greenback dollar, in relation to a gold dollar, was worth only 39¢, and even at the close of the war its value had advanced to but 67¢.

Raising the Union Armies

When hostilities started, the regular army numbered only about 16,000 troops, and many of its units were scattered throughout the West. President Lincoln, in his first call for troops to repress what the government called the "rebellion," summoned 75,000 militia for three months, the usual period of service set for state troops by existing militia law. Lincoln realized that the war would be of longer duration. Confronted by a crisis, he met it with bold decision, even to the point of stretching his powers as commander in chief. Without constitutional sanction, he called for 42,000 volunteers for national service for three years and authorized an increase of 23,000 in the regular army. When Congress met in July, 1861, it legalized the President's acts, and, at his recommendation, provided for enlisting 500,000 volunteers to serve for three years. All in all, the government of the North, despite some minor bungling, adopted a sound military policy from the beginning. It acted to raise a large force (numbers were on the side of the North), and it avoided the mistake of short-term enlistments.

For a time the volunteering system served to bring out enough men to fill the armies. But after the first flush of enthusiasm had worn off, men came forward to enlist in diminishing numbers. Even the generous cash bounties held out to prospective volunteers by the Federal government and by the states were insufficient lures. Finally, in March, 1863, Congress enacted the first national draft law in American history (the South had employed conscription almost a year earlier). Few exemptions were permitted: only high national and state officials, preachers, and men who were the sole support of a dependant family. But a drafted man could escape service by hiring a substitute to go in his place or by paying the government a fee of $300. Eventually this cash commutation was repealed.

The purpose of the draft law was to spur enlistments by threatening to invoke conscription. Each state was divided into enrollment districts, and at announced intervals was assigned a quota of men to be raised. If a state, by bounties or other means, could fill the quota, it escaped the draft completely; if certain districts failed to meet their quota, a sufficient number of men were drafted to make up the difference. Some states and many districts never experienced conscription. Although the draft directly inducted only 46,000 men, it stimulated enlistments enormously. The Federal armies increased steadily in size,

U.S. CASUALTIES IN THE CIVIL WAR AND OTHER WARS

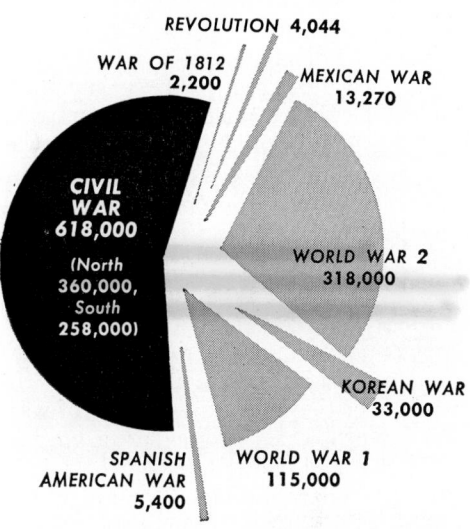

REVOLUTION 4,044

WAR OF 1812 2,200

MEXICAN WAR 13,270

CIVIL WAR 618,000 (North 360,000, South 258,000)

WORLD WAR 2 318,000

KOREAN WAR 33,000

SPANISH AMERICAN WAR 5,400

WORLD WAR 1 115,000

reaching a maximum number in 1865. The vague statistics compiled during the war do not permit an accurate statement of the total number of men serving in the armed forces. The number of enlistments was 2,900,000, but this figure includes many who enlisted several times or served short terms. A reasonably accurate estimate is that 1,500,000 served for three years (as contrasted with 900,000 in the Confederate forces).

The casualty rate was tremendous. This was due to two factors, one military and the other medical. Most military men did not understand that the weapons employed in the war—rifles and artillery with a faster rate of fire and a longer range than those used in previous wars—demanded a change in tactical thinking. With the increased firepower which armies now possessed, frontal assaults made in rigid tactical formation were becoming obsolete. Yet the generals continued to make them, with deadly results. In many battles the proportion of men killed and wounded ranged from 20 to 32 per cent. Medical knowledge and practice had improved greatly by 1861, and further progress would be registered during the war. But much remained to be discovered, particularly about the care of wounds, sanitation, and diet. Not until World War I would military medicine reach a point where fewer men died from sickness than from bullets. Doubtless the death rate in camp and hospital would have been even greater but for the work of a number of private relief organizations, the largest being the United States Sanitary Commission, which provided medical care, medical supplies, and food to the armed forces. These societies were the first instance on a large scale of organized civilian participation in a nation's war effort; they were symbols of the increasing totality of war.

To a people accustomed to a government that had hardly touched their daily lives, conscription seemed a strange and ominous thing. Opposition to the law was widespread, particularly from laborers, immigrants, and Peace Democrats. In places it erupted into violence. Demonstrators against the draft rioted in New York City for four days in 1863, killed several hundred people, and held the town in their grip until subdued by troops. Some Democratic governors who supported the war (like Horatio Seymour of New York) contended that the national government had no constitutional power to conscript, and openly challenged the Lincoln administration on the issue. The government continued, however, to force men into the army—a national army. The whole concept of state rights was being weakened by the war, in the North as well as in the South.

Lincoln and Politics

Lincoln possessed in ample quantity the five qualities that the historian Allan Nevins calls the conditions of statesmanship: intellectual power, moral strength, an instinct for the spirit and needs of the time, an instinctive understanding of the masses, and, in order to mold public opinion, some kind of passion—in Lincoln's case, a passion for democracy.

Because he had the qualities of statesmanship, and the will to employ them, Lincoln was able to fulfill his great task—to preserve a nation. It was a more difficult task than any other American leader before or since has been called upon to meet. He had to bring the seceded states back into the Union, to conduct a bloody civil war, and to achieve a basic unity of purpose among his own divided people.

When Lincoln first came to Washington, he was almost universally considered a small-time prairie politician, unfit for his job. He strengthened this impression by his unpretentious air. Actually, he was well aware of his great abilities and of his superiority over other Northern leaders. His supreme confidence in himself was demonstrated by his choice of a cabinet. Representing every faction of the Republican party and every segment of Northern opinion, it was an extraordinary assemblage of advisers and a difficult set of prima donnas to manage. Three of the secretaries, Seward, Chase, and Stanton, were first-rate men. Seward and Chase thought that they were abler than Lincoln and should be in his place. At the very beginning of the administration, Seward made an attempt to dominate Lincoln, failed, and became his loyal supporter. Chase never learned that the President was a bigger man than he.

Lincoln's confidence in his inner strength was revealed by his bold exercise of the war powers of his office. In order to accomplish his purposes, he was ready to violate parts of the Constitution, explaining that he would not lose the whole by being afraid to disregard a part. In this spirit he issued his proclamation of insurrection calling for troops to repress the rebellion (an act which was equivalent to a declaration of war), illegally increased the size of the regular army, and proclaimed a naval blockade of the South. It is a curious and significant fact that Lincoln and other Northern leaders, heading an established government, exhibited much more revolutionary zeal and even ruthlessness than

LINCOLN AND HIS CABINET READING THE EMANCIPATION PROCLAMATION. From left to right, sitting: Edwin M. Stanton, Secretary of War; Lincoln; Gideon Welles, Secretary of the Navy; William H. Seward, Secretary of State; Edward Bates, Attorney General. Standing: Salmon P. Chase, Secretary of the Treasury; Caleb B. Smith, Secretary of the Interior; Montgomery Blair, Postmaster General. (LIBRARY OF CONGRESS)

did the new and revolutionary government they were opposing.

Opposition to the war came from two sources: from Southern sympathizers in the Union slave states, and from the peace wing of the Democratic party. War Democrats, were willing to support the war and even to accept offices from the administration. Peace Democrats or, as their enemies called them, "Copperheads," feared that agriculture and the West were being subordinated to industry and the East and that state rights were going down before nationalism. Simply stated, their war policy was as follows: to call a truce in the fighting, invite the South to attend a national convention, and amend the Constitution to preserve state rights. On the whole, the Peace Democrats were unionists, in that they did not favor a division of the country. But some of them advocated

the formation of a Western confederacy, and some formed secret societies (Knights of the Golden Circle, Sons of Liberty) which allegedly engaged in treasonable activities and constituted, to use a modern phrase, a fifth column.

To deal with opponents of the war, Lincoln used the weapon of military arrests. He suspended the right of habeas corpus, so that an alleged offender could be arrested and held without trial or, if tried, had to appear before a military court. At first Lincoln denied the civil process only in specified areas, but in 1862 he proclaimed that all persons who discouraged enlistments or engaged in disloyal practices would come under martial law. In all, over 13,000 persons were arrested and imprisoned for varying periods. Among those placed in custody was a Maryland secessionist leader whom Lincoln refused to release, even under a writ from Chief Justice Taney (*Ex parte Merryman*). The most prominent Copperhead in the country, Clement L. Vallandigham of Ohio, was seized by military authorities, although not at Lincoln's instigation, and later exiled to the Confederacy. (After the war, in 1866, the Supreme Court held, in *Ex parte Milligan*, that military trials in areas where the civil courts were capable of functioning were illegal.) Although the arbitrary arrests shocked many believers

servatives was President Lincoln. The Radicals wanted to seize the opportunity of the war to strike slavery down—abolish it suddenly and violently. The Conservatives, who were also antislavery, wanted to accomplish the same result in a different way—easily and gradually. Lincoln made several notable although unsuccessful attempts to persuade the loyal slave states to agree to a program of compensated gradual emancipation. He feared, at first, that the introduction of abolition as a war aim

---

LINCOLN ON UNION AND EMANCIPATION

In a public letter in 1862 to Horace Greeley of the New York *Tribune*, who had demanded an emancipation policy, Lincoln explained his subordination of the slavery issue to the larger question of the Union: "I would save the Union. I would save it the shortest way under the Constitution. . . . My paramount object in this struggle *is* to save the Union, and is *not* either to save or to destroy slavery. If I could save the Union without freeing *any* slave I would do it; and if I could save it by freeing *all* the slaves I would do it; and if I could save it by freeing some and leaving others alone I would also do that. What I do about slavery, and the colored race, I do because I believe it helps to save the Union; and what I forbear, I forbear because I do *not* believe it would help to save the Union. I shall do *less* whenever I shall believe what I am doing hurts the cause, and I shall do *more* whenever I shall believe doing more will help the cause. . . . I have here stated my purpose according to my view of *official* duty; and I intend no modification of my oft-expressed *personal* wish that all men every where could be free."

---

m civil liberty, they were essentially a part of the trend toward enforced unity that total war demands.

There were factions too in the dominant Republican party—the Radicals and the Conservatives. On most questions, including economic matters, they were in fundamental agreement, but they differed, and violently, on the disposition to be made of slavery. Representative leaders of the Radicals were Thaddeus Stevens of Pennsylvania, master of the party machine in the House, and Senators Charles Sumner of Massachusetts and Benjamin F. Wade of Ohio. Heading the Con-

would divide Northern opinion and alienate the border slave states.

A Confiscation Act, passed in August, 1861, declared free all slaves used for "insurrectionary" purposes. But within a year the war began to affect men's thinking about slavery, and the Radicals, gaining an ever increasing ascendancy in the party, started to whittle away at the appendages of the institution. Congress abolished slavery in the District of Columbia, with compensation to owners (April, 1862), and in the national territories (June, 1862). In the summer of 1862 the Radicals decided that Northern opinion had reached a point where they could move against slavery in the states. In July they pushed through Congress the second Confiscation Act, which was in essence a bold attempt to accomplish emancipation by legislative action. The principal provisions were as follows: It declared the property of persons supporting the "rebellion" subject to forfeiture to the United States government; it declared free the slaves of persons aiding and supporting the insurrection; and it authorized the President to employ Negroes, including freed slaves, as soldiers. Although the measure was a "paper" edict so far as immediate concrete results were concerned, it marked a turning point in the war. It meant that the Republican party was coming under Radical control and that the country had come to accept emancipation as an aim of the war.

The signs were not lost on the astute master of politics in the White House. Lincoln saw that in order to achieve his larger purpose of saving the Union he would have to yield his lesser goal of preventing the sudden destruction of slavery. To preserve the nation he had to have the support of his own party and particularly of the Radicals, who were the last-ditch Unionists, the men who would never give up the war. And if a majority of the Northern people wanted slavery destroyed, as seemed the case, he could not afford to divide popular opinion by opposing their will. In July, 1862, he decided to take the leadership of the antislavery impulse away from the Radicals by putting himself at the head of it.

On September 22, 1862, after the battle of Antietam, the President issued his preliminary Emancipation Proclamation, and on the first day of 1863 his final Emancipation Proclamation. This document, which is probably the most misunderstood measure in American history, declared forever free the slaves in designated areas of the Confederacy. Excepted from the edict was the whole state of Tennessee, most of which was under Union control, and western Virginia and southern Louisiana, which were occupied by Federal troops. Presumably these areas were omitted because they were not enemy territory and hence were not subject to the President's war powers. For a similar reason the Proclamation did not apply to the border slave states.

The Proclamation freed immediately but few slaves. Like the Confiscation Act, it would be a paper edict until it could be enforced. But its issuance announced that the war had assumed a new meaning; henceforth it was to be a war for emancipation as well as for the Union. Eventually, as Federal armies occupied large areas of the South, the proclamation became a practical reality, and hundreds of thousands of slaves were freed by its operation. Equally important in the process of emancipation was the induction of many former slaves into the armed forces: some 186,000 served as soldiers, sailors, and laborers, thereby making a substantial contribution to the freeing of their race. Furthermore, the impulse to abolition which the Proclamation symbolized increased in intensity throughout the country, affecting even the border states. Before the end of the war slavery had been abolished in two Union slave states, Maryland and Missouri, and in three "reconstructed" or occupied Confederate states, Tennessee, Arkansas, and Louisiana. The final and inevitable action was taken early in 1865 when Congress approved the Thirteenth Amendment (ratified by the required number of states several months after the war closed), which freed all slaves everywhere and abolished slavery as an institution.

Early in the war, and particularly after the election of 1862, in which the Republicans suffered heavy losses, the party leaders proceeded to form a broad coalition of all groups who supported the war, trying particularly to attract the War Democrats. The new organization, which was composed of a Republican core with a fringe of War Democrats, was known as the Union party. It encountered its major political test in the presidential election of 1864, which was the first national contest held in the midst of a great war.

When the Union convention met in June, it nominated Lincoln, with the chilly assent of the Radicals, and, for Vice President, Andrew Johnson of Tennessee, a War Democrat who had refused to follow his state into secession. In August the Democratic convention nominated George B. McClellan, former Union general and an object of hatred to all good Radicals. The peace faction got a plank into the platform denouncing the war as a failure and calling for a truce to be followed by an invitation to the South to enter a national convention. Although McClellan repudiated the plank, the Democrats stood before the country as the peace party. At the same time several Northern military victories, particularly the capture of Atlanta, Georgia, early in September, rejuvenated Northern morale and gave promise of Republican success in November.

The outcome of the election was a smashing electoral triumph for Lincoln, who had 212 votes to McClellan's 21 and who carried every state except Kentucky, New Jersey, and Delaware. Lincoln's popular majority, however, was uncomfortably small, 2,213,000 to 1,805,000 or an advantage of only 400,000. A slight shift of popular votes in some of the more populous states would have changed the result. But even if McClellan had won and had decided to comply with the peace plank (an unlikely possibility), the war would still have turned out as it did. He would not have taken office until March, 1865, and by that time the Union armies had pounded the Confederacy to defeat.

The Confederate Government

Although the first seven Southern states to secede had left the Union as individual sovereignties, they had no intention of maintaining separate political existences. It was understood from the first that they would come together in a common confederation to which, they hoped, the states of the Upper South would eventually adhere. Accordingly, representatives of the seceded states assembled at Montgomery, Alabama, early in February, 1861, to create a Southern nation. Montgomery, "the cradle of the Confederacy," was the capital of the new nation until after Virginia seceded. Then the government moved to Richmond, partly out of deference to Virginia, partly because Richmond was one of the few Southern cities large enough to house the government.

There was significance in the name of the Southern government: it was a confederation of sovereign states, not a federation of united ones. State sovereignty was expressly recognized in the constitution. Interestingly enough, proposals to insert the right of a state to secede failed of adoption; the right was implied but never mentioned. In structure, the Confederate government was an almost exact duplicate of the model which Southerners had just discarded.

As President the Montgomery convention elected Jefferson Davis of Mississippi, and as Vice President, Alexander H. Stephens of Georgia. Davis had been a firm but not extreme advocate of Southern rights in the former Union; he was a moderate but not an extreme secessionist. Stephens had been the chief among those who had contended that secession was unnecessary.

Jefferson Davis embodied the spirit of the nation he had been called to lead. His family, which was of Southern yeoman stock, had moved from Kentucky, where he was born, to the new lush cotton lands of Mississippi, where they became rich planters almost overnight. Davis was a first-generation aristocrat. So also were most of the members of his government. The Confederacy was run by the cotton nabobs of the newer "Western" South, not by the old aristocracy of the seaboard states. Whereas Lincoln's task was to preserve a nation, Davis's was to make one. Lincoln succeeded; Davis failed. He failed partly because he lacked some of the qualities of statesmanship. He possessed integrity and a fine intelligence. Indeed, his mind was his greatest pride; he was sensitively proud of the correctness of his opinions and would support even a wrong decision to the last.

nent organization that could fight a war in the normal fashion of older countries. Whereas the situation demanded that the South act with ruthless efficiency, Davis assumed that it should observe every constitutional punctilio. Lincoln, without clear constitutional sanction, suspended habeas corpus; Davis asked his Congress to let him suspend and received only partial permission. Watching the workings of the government, one shrewd official (R. G. H.

AN ENGLISH VIEW OF JEFFERSON DAVIS

William Howard Russell, war correspondent for the *Times* of London, visited the Confederate President at Montgomery, Alabama, in 1861. Although the Britisher had some reservations about Davis, he was favorably impressed with his freedom from the almost universal American habit of chewing tobacco: "I had an opportunity of observing the President very closely: he did not impress me as favorably as I had expected, though he is certainly a very different looking man from Mr. Lincoln. He is like a gentleman—has a slight, light figure, little exceeding middle height, and holds himself erect and straight. He was dressed in a rustic suit of slate-colored stuff, with a black silk handkerchief round his neck; his manner is plain, and rather reserved and drastic; his head is well formed, with a fine full forehead, square and high, covered with innumerable fine lines and wrinkles, features regular, though the cheekbones are too high, and the jaws too hollow to be handsome; the lips are thin, flexible, and curved, the chin square, well defined; the nose very regular, with wide nostrils; and the eyes deep-set, large and full—one seems nearly blind, and is partly covered with a film, owing to excruciating attacks of neuralgia and tic. Wonderful to relate, he does not chew, and is neat and clean-looking, with hair trimmed, and boots brushed."

Davis failed primarily because he did not realize in two important respects what his task was. First, he spent too much time on routine items, on what one observer called "little trash." He was a good administrator who loved to administer; he was his own Secretary of War but he rarely rose above the secretarial level. Second, Davis failed to grasp the all-important fact that the Confederacy was not an established, recognized nation but a revolution. He proceeded on the basis that the Confederacy was a legal and permanent

Kean) wrote: "All the revolutionary vigor is with the enemy. . . . With us timidity —hair splitting. . . ."

The Confederate cabinet was a body of shifting personnel displaying, at best, only average ability. Davis selected the first incumbents almost entirely on a geographical basis: he wanted to include a representative from each state except his own Mississippi. This practice resulted, in some cases, in a man's being named to one post when he was better fitted for another that had to be allotted to an in-

JEFFERSON DAVIS AND HIS CABINET. From left to right, sitting: Stephen R. Mallory, Secretary of the Navy; Judah P. Benjamin, Attorney General; Davis; John H. Reagan, Postmaster General; Christopher G. Memminger, Secretary of the Treasury. Standing: Leroy P. Walker, Secretary of War; General Lee; Vice-President Stephens; Robert Toombs, Secretary of State. (LIBRARY OF CONGRESS)

dividual whose state had to have a member.

The personnel of the cabinet changed rapidly and frequently. There were three Secretaries of State, two Secretaries of the Treasury, four Attorney Generals, and five Secretaries of War. Not a man in the cabinet ever dared to oppose the will of the President.

Southern Money and Men

The men seeking to devise measures for financing the Confederacy's war effort, Treasury Secretary Christopher G. Memminger and the Congressional leaders, had to reckon with a number of hard facts. A national revenue system had to be created to collect money from a people unaccustomed to bearing large tax burdens. Southern banking houses, except in New Orleans, were fewer and smaller

than those of the North. Because excess capital in the South was usually invested in slaves and land, the sum of liquid assets on deposit in banks or in individual hands was relatively small. The only specie possessed by the government was that seized in United States mints located in the South (amounting to about $1,000,000). In an attempt to secure more specie, the government dispatched an army column into New Mexico, but this force, after some initial success, was expelled.

The Confederate Congress, like its counterpart in the North, showed some reluctance to enact rigorous wartime taxes. In 1861 the legislators provided for a direct tax on property to be levied through the medium of the states. If a state preferred, it could meet its quota by paying as a state. Most of the states, instead of taxing their people, assumed the tax, which they paid by issuing bonds or their own notes. In short, the first tax measure failed to really tax, and it produced a disappointing return of only $18 million. Moving more boldly in 1863, Congress passed an internal revenue tax bill which included license levies and an income tax. A unique feature of the act was a provision bearing on agriculture alone: "the tax in kind." Every farmer and planter had to contribute one tenth of his produce to the government. Although Congress later raised the rates in the internal revenue measure and enacted other taxes, the revenue realized from taxation was relatively small. It has been estimated the Confederacy raised only about 1 per cent of its total income in taxes.

products—"the loan in kind." The loan was subscribed, partly in paper currency and mostly in produce or pledges of produce. But many of the pledges were not redeemed or the promised products were destroyed by the enemy. The Confederacy also attempted to borrow money in Europe by pledging cotton stored in the South for future delivery. Its most notable venture in foreign finance was the famous Erlanger loan, which was sup-

---

HARD TIMES IN RICHMOND

J. B. Jones, a clerk in the Confederate War Department, kept a diary that is one of the primary Confederate sources: A *Rebel War Clerk's Diary* (1866). In this entry for 1863 he details the privations of people on fixed incomes who could not afford the inflated wartime prices:

"February 11th.—Some idea may be formed of the scarcity of food in this city from the fact that, while my youngest daughter was in the kitchen today, a young rat came out of its hole and seemed to beg for something to eat; she held out some bread, which it ate from her hand, and seemed grateful. Several others soon appeared and were as tame as kittens. Perhaps we shall have to eat them!

"18th.—One or two of the regiments of General Lee's army were in the city last night. The men were pale and haggard. They have but a quarter of a pound of meat per day. But meat has been ordered from Atlanta. I hope it is abundant there. All the necessaries of life in the city are still going up higher in price. Butter, three dollars per pound; beef, one dollar; bacon, a dollar and a quarter; sausage meat, one dollar; and even liver is selling at fifty cents per pound."

The bond record of the Confederacy was little better than its tax program. Eventually the government issued bonds in such large amounts that the people suspected its ability to redeem them. Congress authorized a $100-million loan to be paid in specie, paper money, or produce. The expectation was that the bulk of the proceeds would be in the form of

posed to net the Confederacy $15 million. Actually, Erlanger, a French financier, was interested in conducting a huge cotton speculation. The Confederate government received only $2.5 million from the loan.

Partly because ready revenue was needed and partly because it seemed the easiest way to finance the war, the government resorted in 1861 to the issuance of paper money and treasury notes. Once it started, it could not stop. By 1864 the staggering total of one billion dollars had been issued. In addition, states and cities issued their own notes. The inevitable result of this process was to depreciate the value of the money. Federal greenbacks, brought into the South by the invading armies, circulated at a higher premium than Confederate notes: one greenback was worth four Confederate dollars. Prices skyrocketed to astronomical heights. Some sample figures for 1863–1864 are as follows: flour, $300 a barrel; broadcloth, $125 a yard; chickens, $35 a pair; beef, $5 a pound; men's shoes, $125 a pair. Many people, particularly those who lived in towns or who had fixed incomes, could not pay these prices. They did without, and lost some of their will to victory.

Like the United States, the Confederate States first raised armies by calling for volunteers. By the latter part of 1861 volunteering had dropped off badly. As the year 1862 opened, the Confederacy was threatened by a manpower crisis.

The government met the situation boldly. At Davis's recommendation, Congress in April enacted the First Conscription Act, which declared that all able-bodied white males between the ages of 18 and 35 were liable to military service for three years. A man who was drafted could escape his summons if he furnished a substitute to go in his place. The prices for substitutes eventually went up to as high as $10,000 in Confederate currency. The purpose of this provision was to exempt men in charge of agricultural and industrial production, but to people who could not afford substitutes it seemed like special privilege to the rich. It was repealed late in 1863 after arousing bitter class discontent.

The first draft act and later measures provided for other exemptions, mostly on an occupational basis. The government realized that conscription had to be selective, that some men had to be left on the home front to perform the functions of production. It erred in excusing men who were not doing any vital services and in permitting too many group exemptions. The provision most bitterly criticized was that exempting one white man on each plantation with twenty or more slaves. Angrily denounced as the "twenty-nigger law," it caused ordinary men to say, "It's a rich man's war but a poor man's fight."

In September, 1862, Congress adopted a second conscription measure, which raised the upper age limit to 45. At the end of the year, an estimated 500,000 soldiers were in the Confederate armies. Thereafter conscription provided fewer and fewer men, and the armed forces steadily decreased in size. Federal armies seized large areas in the South, depriving the Confederacy of the manpower in the occupied regions. Military reverses in the summer of 1863 convinced many Southerners that the war was lost, causing a kind of passive resistance to the draft as men sought to avoid it by hiding in the hills and woods; desertions began to increase.

As 1864 opened, the situation was critical. In a desperate move, Congress lowered the age limits for drafted men to 17 and raised them to 50, reaching out, it was said, toward the cradle and the grave. Few men were obtained. War weariness and the certainty of defeat were making their influence felt. In 1864–1865 there were 100,000 desertions. An observant Confederate diarist (Mrs. Mary B. Chesnut) wrote in her journal in March, 1865: "I am sure our army is silently dispersing. Men are moving the wrong way, all the time. They slip by with no songs and no shouts now. They have given the thing up." On the army rolls, 200,000 names were carried, but at the end probably only 100,000 were actually in service. In a frantic final attempt to raise men, Congress in 1865 authorized the drafting of 300,000 slaves. The war ended before this incongruous experiment could be tried out.

Confederate Politics

In overwhelming numbers the Southern people were ready to support the war for Southern independence. The only important organized opposition to the war came from the inhabitants of the mountain areas, whose population was less than 10 per cent of the Southern total. Here supporters of the national cause carried on a kind of guerrilla warfare against the occupying Confederate forces until liberated by the Federals late in 1863.

Southerners were united in their desire to sustain the war, but they were bitterly divided on how it should be conducted. The differences that emerged did not take the form of party issues: the Con-

party. They had one simple, basic idea. They believed first in state sovereignty and then in the Confederacy. They wanted the Confederacy to win its independence, but they would not agree to sacrificing one iota of state sovereignty to achieve that goal. If victory had to be gained at the expense of state rights, they preferred defeat.

The state-righters, standing for independence for its own sake, fought every attempt of the government to impose centralized controls, the same kind of

---

THE HATREDS OF WAR

Inevitably the war aroused resentment and even hatred. These emotions were particularly strong in the South, which experienced more directly than the North the impact of war, and were particularly expressed by Southern women, who had to fight the war at home. A Georgia girl wrote in her journal: "If all the words of hatred in every language under heaven were lumped together into one huge epithet of detestation, they could not tell how I hate Yankees. . . . Now that they have invaded our country and killed so many of our men and desecrated so many homes, I can't believe that when Christ said, 'Love your enemies,' He meant Yankees. Of course I don't want their souls to be lost, for that would be wicked, but as they are not being punished in this world, I don't see how else they are going to get their deserts."

---

federacy did not last long enough for distinct parties to develop.

The great dividing force, the creator of explosive dissent, was, ironically enough, the principle of state rights—the foundation stone of Southern political philosophy—for whose conservation and consecration the South had left the old Union. State rights had become a cult with Southerners, to the point that they reacted against any sort of central control, even to controls necessary to win the war. If there was an organized faction of opposition to the government, it was that group of quixotic men who counted Vice President Stephens as their leader and who are usually known as the state-rights

controls to which the Northern people, with some exceptions, were submitting in order to win the war. They concentrated their fire against two powers that the central government sought to exercise: the suspension of habeas corpus, and conscription. In addition, they charged that the Davis administration was neglecting or refusing opportunities to conclude a negotiated peace with the North.

Recalcitrant governors, like Joseph Brown of Georgia and Zebulon M. Vance of North Carolina, contending that the central government had no right to draft troops, tried in every way to obstruct the enforcement of conscription. Their chief weapon was certifying state militia troops

as exempt. In the spring of 1862 an estimated 100,000 men throughout the South
were held in state service. In Georgia in
1864 more men between 18 and 45 were
at home than had gone into the army
since 1861.

The idea of a negotiated peace fascinated the state-righters, especially Vice
President Stephens. They never made it
clear whether they were thinking of a
settlement based on the return of the
South to the Union or on independence.
As early as 1863 they were urging the
central government to seek a peace based
on recognition of state sovereignty and
the right of each state to control its domestic institutions—which implied a restored Union. At other times they proposed negotiations based on the independence of the Confederacy.

The Diplomacy of South and North

The diplomatic policies of both sides
might be summarized by saying that the
objectives of the South were positive and
those of the North negative. The South
hoped to secure foreign recognition and
to persuade England and France to break
the blockade and force the United States
to mediate. The North, believing that it
could handle the South if unhampered
by outside interference, labored to prevent recognition and intervention.
Judah P. Benjamin, who occupied the
Confederate foreign office for the greater
part of the war, was a clever and intelligent man, but he lacked strong convictions and confined most of his energy to
administrative routine. Seward, on the
other hand, after some initial blunders,
learned his job well and went on to become one of the outstanding American
Secretaries of State. In the key diplomatic
post at London, the North was represented by a distinguished minister,
Charles Francis Adams, who seemed to
have inherited the diplomatic abilities of
his father (John Quincy Adams) and
grandfather (John Adams). He easily

outshone the bucolic Confederate
James M. Mason. Perhaps the ablest
Southern diplomat abroad was John Slidell, the wily czar of Louisiana politics
who as minister to France was familiarly
at home in the corrupt court of the Emperor Napoleon III. In general, the Confederate diplomats in Europe were afflicted with a parochial viewpoint resulting from the South's cultural isolation.
They seemed to have little appreciation
of the magnitude of the antislavery sentiment in European society.

In the story of the relationship of Europe to the Civil War, the key nations are
Great Britain and France. These two had
acted together against Russia in the Crimean War and were united by an *en-
tente*, one of the understandings of
which was that questions concerning the
United States fell within the sphere of
British influence. Napoleon III, therefore,
would not act in American affairs without
the concurrence of Britain. The third
power of Europe, Russia, was, like the
United States, an up-and-coming nation
which thought that its aspirations were
being blocked by England. Feeling a
community of interest with democratic
America, autocratic Russia openly expressed sympathy for the Northern cause.
In 1863, when war threatened to break
out between Russia and England over
Poland, Russia, in order to get her navy
into position to attack British commerce,
dispatched two fleets to American waters. One turned up at New York and the
other at San Francisco, thereby creating a
legend that they had come to support
the United States if England and France
should attempt to break the blockade.

At the beginning of the war the sympathies of the ruling classes of England
and France were with the Confederacy.
But English and French opinion was not
unanimously in favor of the South. English liberals of a certain type, men like
John Bright and Richard Cobden—usually manufacturers who were closely associated with the laboring masses—sensed

that the war would have to become one to destroy slavery. They saw it as a struggle between free and slave labor, and they presented it in these terms to their followers. It was an argument that appealed to the politically conscious but unenfranchised workers, particularly those in Britain. They expressed their sympathy for the Northern cause frequently and unmistakably—in mass meetings, in resolutions, and, through the medium of Bright and other leaders, in Parliament itself. After the issuance of the Emancipation Proclamation, they intensified their activities, feeling that Lincoln had justified their faith in his purposes.

In the minds of Southern leaders, cotton was their ace diplomatic weapon. Their analysis was as follows: the textile industry was basic to the economies of England and France, who depended on the South for the bulk of their cotton supply; deprived of Southern cotton, these countries would face economic collapse. Therefore they would have to intervene on the side of the Confederacy.

But this diplomacy based on King Cotton never worked as its champions envisioned. In 1861 English manufacturers had a surplus supply of cotton on hand (in the previous year 2,580,700 bales had been imported from the United States). The immediate effect of the blockade was to enable the textile operators to dispose of their remaining finished goods at high prices. Thereafter the supply became increasingly short (only 72,000 bales were imported from America in 1862), and many mills were forced to close. Both England and France, however, managed to avoid a complete shutdown of their textile industries by importing supplies from new sources, notably Egypt and India. Most important of all, the workers, who were among the people most directly affected by the shortage, did not clamor to have the blockade broken. Even the 500,000 English textile workers thrown out of jobs continued to support the North.

No European nation extended diplomatic recognition to the Confederacy. Nor did England and France, although several times they considered offering mediation to the American contestants, ever move to intervene in the war. Neither could afford to intervene unless the Confederacy seemed on the point of winning; otherwise they would have to reckon with the possibility of war with the North. But the South was never able to develop a prospect of certain victory. The most auspicious period for Southern hopes was in the last half of 1862, when military triumph seemed assured. But Union successes at the battles of Antietam and Stone's River checked any possibility of intervention.

Immediately after the outbreak of hostilities, Great Britain issued a proclamation of neutrality attributing to the Confederacy the status of a belligerent. France and other nations followed suit. Although the Northern government, which officially insisted that the war was not a war but a domestic insurrection, furiously resented England's action, the British government had proceeded in conformity with accepted rules of neutrality and in accordance with the realities of the situation. The United States was fighting a *war*, a fact which Lincoln himself had recognized in his proclamation establishing a blockade. Nevertheless, the North was convinced that Britain did not intend to be truly neutral and that recognition of belligerency would be followed by recognition of Confederate independence. Thereafter during the course of the war, three areas of friction between England and the United States developed, creating three crises or near-crises, any one of which could have resulted in war between the two countries.

The first crisis, and the most dangerous one—the so-called Trent affair—occurred late in 1861. The Confederate commissioners to England and France, Mason and Slidell, had slipped through the then ineffective blockade to Havana, Cuba, where they boarded an English steamer, the *Trent*, for England. Hovering in Cuban waters was an American frigate, the *San Jacinto*, commanded by Captain Charles Wilkes, an impetuous officer who knew that the Southern diplomats were on the *Trent*. Acting without authorization from his government, Wilkes stopped the British vessel, arrested the commissioners, and bore them off in triumph to Boston. The British government drafted a demand for the release of the prisoners, reparation, and an apology. Lincoln and Seward, well aware that war with England would be suicidal, spun out the negotiations until American opinion had cooled off, then returned the commissioners with an indirect apology.

The second episode—the case of the Confederate commerce destroyers—generated much friction but did not assume the proportions of a crisis. In a move to weaken the blockade, the Confederate government decided to build or buy fast ships of war to prey on Northern ocean commerce. The hope was that the North would detach ships from the blockade to hunt the destroyers. (Instead, the North took the loss of its merchant marine and maintained the blockade.) Lacking the resources to construct the vessels, the Confederacy contracted to have them built and equipped in English shipyards. Six destroyers, of which the most famous were the *Alabama*, the *Florida*, and the *Shenandoah*, were built or purchased in England, and sailed from English ports to harry Northern commerce. The British government knew what was going on, being regularly and indignantly informed by Minister Adams, but winked at the practice. Before 1863 the United States, not daring to press England too hard, had to limit its protests to charges that construction of the raiders was in violation of the laws of neutrality. These protests formed the basis, after the war, for damage claims which the United States served on Great Britain.

The third incident—the affair of the Laird rams—could have developed into a crisis, but did not because the English government suddenly decided to mend its ways. In 1863 the Confederacy placed an order with the Laird shipyards for two powerful ironclads, not commerce raiders, but formidable fighting warships with which the Confederacy meant to destroy the blockade. The loss of its ocean trade the North could absorb, but the blockade was another matter. In addition, with the course of the war definitely turning against the South, the United States could now speak with a more imperious voice. Adams was instructed to inform the English government that if the rams, or any other ships destined for the Confederacy, left port—then there would be danger of war. Adams delivered his message, but even before it was received the government had acted to detain the rams and to prevent the Confederacy from obtaining any other ships.

If Napoleon III had had his way, France and England would have intervened in the American war at an early date. Unable to persuade Britain to act, he had to content himself with expressing sympathy for the Southern cause and permitting the Confederates to order commerce destroyers from French shipyards. The Emperor's primary motive for desiring an independent South was his ambition to establish French colonial power in the Western hemisphere: a divided America could not block his plans. He seized the opportunity of the war to set up a French-dominated empire in Mexico.

Napoleon's Mexican venture was a clear violation of the Monroe Doctrine, perhaps the greatest one that has ever occurred. The United States viewed it in such a light, but for fear of provoking France into recognizing the Confederacy, it could do no more than register a protest. Only after the Civil War was ended did the United States feel strong enough to put pressure on France to get out of Mexico.

BIBLIOGRAPHY

Civil War literature is so voluminous that only a highly selective listing is possible here. The best general treatment of the whole subject is J. G. Randall, *The Civil War and Reconstruction* (1937). B. P. Thomas, *Abraham Lincoln* (1952), is the most satisfactory one-volume life. Outstanding multi-volume biographies are Carl Sandburg, *Abraham Lincoln: The War Years* (4 vols., 1939); and J. G. Randall, *Lincoln the President* (4 vols., 1945–55). Noteworthy special studies are W. E. Baringer, *Lincoln's Rise to Power* (1937); R. S. Harper, *Lincoln and the Press* (1951); and R. V. Bruce, *Lincoln and the Tools of War* (1956). Issues and interpretations are discussed in David Donald, *Lincoln Reconsidered* (1956); and in R. N. Current, *The Lincoln Nobody Knows* (1958).

The following deal with the crisis of 1860–61: R. H. Luthin, *The First Lincoln Campaign* (1944); Ollinger Crenshaw, *The Slave States in the Presidential Election of 1860* (1945); D. L. Dumond, *The Secession Movement* (1931); D. M. Potter, *Lincoln and His Party in the Secession Crisis* (1942); K. M. Stampp, *And the War Came* (1950); and P. G. Auchampaugh, *James Buchanan and His Cabinet on the Eve of Secession* (1926).

Northern politics is treated in T. H. Williams, *Lincoln and the Radicals* (1941); W. B. Hesseltine, *Lincoln and the War Governors* (1948); H. J. Carman and R. J. Luthin, *Lincoln and the Patronage* (1943); Wood Gray, *The Hidden Civil War* (1942); E. C. Kirkland, *Peacemakers of 1864* (1927); W. F. Zornow, *Lincoln and the Party Divided* (1954); and F. L. Klement, *Copperheads in the Middle West* (1960). See also T. G. and M. R. Belden, *So Fell the Angels* (1956), on Chase; David Donald (ed.), *Inside Lincoln's Cabinet* (1954); R. S. West, Jr., *Gideon Welles* (1943); and H. K. Beale (ed.), *The Diary of Gideon Welles* (3 vols., 1960).

Aspects of the war and wartime life in the North are explored in B. I. Wiley, *The Life of Billy Yank* (1952); F. A. Shannon, *Organization and Administration of the Union Army* (2 vols., 1928); G. W. Adams, *Doctors in Blue* (1952); W. Q. Maxwell,

Lincoln's Fifth Wheel (1956), on the U.S. Sanitary Commission; E. P. Oberholtzer, *Jay Cooke: Financier of the Civil War* (2 vols., 1907); D. C. Barrett, *The Greenbacks and the Resumption of Specie Payments, 1862–1879* (1931); G. E. Turner, *Victory Rode the Rails* (1953); Thomas Weber, *The Northern Railroads in the Civil War* (1952); B. A. Weisberger, *Reporters for the Union* (1953); Benjamin Quarles, *The Negro in the Civil War* (1953); and D. T. Cornish, *The Sable Arm* (1956), on Negro troops.

On the South in war time, see R. S. Henry, *The Story of the Confederacy* (1957); E. M. Coulter, *The Confederate States of America* (1950); and Clement Eaton, *A History of the Southern Confederacy* (1954). In *The Road to Appomattox* (1956) B. I. Wiley analyzes the causes of Confederate defeat.

Confederate leadership is appraised in B. J. Hendrick, *Statesmen of the Lost Cause* (1939); R. W. Patrick, *Jefferson Davis and His Cabinet* (1944); and Frank Vandiver, *Rebel Brass* (1956). There are biographies of Davis written by W. E. Dodd (1907), R. M. McElroy (2 vols., 1937), and Hudson Strode (2 vols., 1955–9). Important lives of other Confederate leaders are R. D. Meade, *Judah P. Benjamin* (1943); and J. T. Durkin, *Stephen R. Mallory* (1954).

Weaknesses of the Confederacy may be seen in F. L. Owsley, *State Rights in the Confederacy* (1925); L. B. Hill, *Joseph E. Brown* (1939); C. W. Ramsdell, *Behind the Lines in the Southern Confederacy* (1944); C. H. Wesley, *Collapse of the Confederacy* (1922); A. B. Moore, *Conscription and Conflict in the Confederacy* (1924); and G. L. Tatum, *Disloyalty in the Confederacy* (1934).

Other aspects of the wartime South are treated in R. C. Todd, *Confederate Finance* (1954); R. C. Black, *The Railroads of the Confederacy* (1952); Frank Vandiver, *Ploughshares into Swords* (1952); B. I. Wiley, *The Life of Johnny Reb* (1943), *The Plain People of the Confederacy* (1943), and *Southern Negroes, 1861–1865* (1938); F. B. Simkins and J. W. Patton, *Women of the Confederacy* (1936); and

H. H. Cunningham, *Doctors in Gray* (1958).

On diplomacy, see E. D. Adams, *Great Britain and the American Civil War* (2 vols., 1925; reprint, 1957); D. Jordan and E. J. Pratt, *Europe and the American Civil War* (1931); Jay Monaghan, *Diplomat in Carpet Slippers* (1945); and F. L. Owsley, *King Cotton Diplomacy* (1931; new ed., 1959).

20

FIGHTING THE CIVIL WAR

The Civil War was the first great military experience of the American people. Compared to it, the earlier struggles—the Revolution, the War of 1812, the Mexican War—were minor and episodic. In the perspective of world history, the Civil War is the first of the modern wars: it was a war of matériel as well as of men. It witnessed the employment of mass armies, railroads, the telegraph, armored ships, railroad artillery, balloons, the Gatling gun (the precursor of the machine gun), repeating rifles, trenches, and wire entanglements. Modern war is total in its impact and its effects. It compels a nation to mobilize and direct its whole resources for the end of victory. If the Civil War was not quite total, it marked a transition from the older type of warfare to the new. Unlike the leisurely, limited-objective wars of the eighteenth century, it was a rough, ruthless, all-out fight.

Strategy and Command

The supreme director of the Union military organization was the President, the commander in chief of all the armed forces of the nation. Lincoln had been a civilian all his life; he had had no military education and no military experience except for a brief militia interlude. Yet he became a great war President, a great commander in chief. As a war director he was superior to Jefferson Davis, who was a trained soldier. Lincoln illustrates the truth of the dictum that an acquaintance with military affairs is not the principal qualification for a director of war but that a superior mind and strength of character are better qualifications. By the power of his mind, Lincoln became a fine strategist, often showing keener strategic insight than his generals. He recognized that numbers and matériel were on his side, and immediately he moved to mobilize the maximum strength of Northern resources. He urged his generals to keep up a constant pressure on the whole strategic line of the Confederacy until a weak spot was found—and a breakthrough could be made. At an early date he realized that the proper objective of his armies was the destruction of the Confederate armies and not the occupation of Southern territory.

During the first three years of the war, Lincoln performed many of the functions that in a modern command system would be done by the chief of the general staff or the joint chiefs of staff. He formulated policy, devised strategic plans, and even

directed tactical movements. Some of his decisions were wise, some were wrong. But the general effect of his so-called "interfering" with the military machine was fortunate for the North. Both he and Davis have been criticized for interfering with army movements, as they had every constitutional right to do. Most of Lin-

sea and from the line of the Mississippi River, isolating her from the outside world and gradually squeezing her into submission by economic and psychological pressure: the so-called "anaconda plan." Lincoln rejected the proposal because it would take too long to execute and because it was based on the one-idea

---

CIVIL WAR WEAPONS AND TACTICS

Although breech-loading and repeating rifles were introduced in the war, they were not employed in large numbers. The basic infantry weapon was the Springfield rifle, a muzzle-loading, one-shot gun. Capable of killing at half a mile and most effective at 250 yards, it had a greater range and accuracy than any gun used in previous wars. A good soldier could fire two shots a minute. The basic artillery weapon was the brass "Napoleon," also a muzzle-loading, one-shot piece. With a maximum range of a mile, it was most effective at half that distance. At shorter ranges it had the deadly effect of a huge sawed-off shotgun. These weapons meant that armies packed more fire-power than ever before. A force holding a strong position could stop almost any frontal assault. The traditional tactical formation of attacking in regular lines was in the process of becoming obsolete. Faced by concentrated fire-power, the attackers had to advance in irregular rushes or move around the flank of the enemy. But many generals refused to realize the impact of technology upon tactics and continued to send their troops on suicidal assaults over open ground.

---

coln's interferences were designed to make his generals execute a sound offensive strategy. Davis should not be criticized for interfering but for interfering to make a faulty defensive strategy more defensive.

At the beginning, Lincoln was inclined to take the advice of General Winfield Scott. The old general, however, was unable to adjust his thinking to the requirements of mass war. Asked to present a plan of over-all strategy, he came up with a scheme to blockade the South from the

principle of strategy. Scott retired from service on November 1, 1861, and to his place as general in chief Lincoln moved young George B. McClellan, who was also the commander of the Federal field army in the East, the Army of the Potomac. McClellan, who would demonstrate fatal shortcomings as a field general, did not possess the abilities to formulate strategy for all theaters of the war. The one grand strategic design he submitted was defective because it envisioned operations in only one theater, his

THE NORTH'S GREATEST GENERAL. [OPPOSITE] One wartime observer of Ulysses S. Grant said: "He habitually wears an expression as if he had determined to drive his head through a brick wall, and was about to do it." Of average height and small stature, slouchy in dress and manner, Grant did not look like a great general, but he was, as C. F. Adams, Jr., noted, the kind of man that all would instinctively turn to in a moment of crisis. (LIBRARY OF CONGRESS)

own, and because it made places instead of enemy armies his objective. When McClellan took the field in March, 1862, Lincoln removed him as general in chief, and did not appoint another officer to the post until July. During the interim, Lincoln, advised by Secretary of War Stanton and the Army Board (made up of the heads of the War Department bureaus), acted as his own general in chief. In July Lincoln designated General Henry W. Halleck to direct the armies. Halleck was the foremost American student of the art of war, and he had won in the West an undeserved reputation as a successful general. Lincoln intended that Halleck should be a real general in chief, that he should actually control operations. But Halleck, after a promising start, refused to take responsibility. He cast himself in the role of an adviser instead of a maker of decisions. Again Lincoln was forced to take up the function of forming and directing strategy, a task which he performed until March, 1864, when finally the nation achieved a modern command system.

In the system arrived at in 1864, Ulysses S. Grant, who had emerged as the North's greatest general, was named general in chief. Charged with directing the movements of all Union armies, Grant, because he disliked the political atmosphere of Washington, established his headquarters with the Army of the Potomac but did not technically become commander of that army. As director of the armies, Grant proved to be the man for whom Lincoln had been searching. He possessed in superb degree the ability to think of the war in overall terms and to devise strategy for the war as a whole. Because Lincoln trusted Grant, he gave the general a relatively free hand. Grant,

however, always submitted the broad outlines of his plans to the President for approval before putting them in motion. Under the new arrangement, Halleck became "chief of staff," a post in which he acted as a channel of communication between Lincoln and Grant and between Grant and the departmental commanders. For Halleck, the ideal office soldier, this was the ideal assignment. He read and briefed reports and orders for the President and for Grant, and lifted an immense administrative burden from both. The 1864 system, with a commander in chief to form the general strategy, a general in chief to give it specific shape, and a chief of staff to coordinate information, gave the United States a modern command arrangement. With the possible exception of the Prussian General Staff, it was the most efficient system then in existence.

Lincoln's active command role underlines one of the most important changes occurring in modern warfare: the emergence of the civilian in strategic planning. As war became more technological and total, strategy became a problem of directing the whole resources of a nation. It was too vast a problem for any one set of leaders, especially for the military, and civilian participation in the direction of war began and, once begun, inevitably became greater. As one example, the Northern government, in order to organize its military railroad system, had to call on the services of civilian experts. The most dramatic example of civilian intervention in military affairs in the Civil War was the Committee on the Conduct of the War, a joint investigative committee of both houses of Congress and the most powerful agency which the legislative branch has ever created to secure for

THE SOUTH'S GREATEST GENERAL. [OPPOSITE] Robert E. Lee was a magnificent physical figure. Five feet eleven inches tall and 175 pounds in weight, he seemed larger than he was because of his massive head and wide shoulders. He was grave and reserved in manner like George Washington, his hero and model. And like Washington, he lived by a self-imposed code of high conduct. "Duty is the sublimest word in our language," he once wrote. (LIBRARY OF CONGRESS)

itself a voice in formulating war policies. Established in December, 1861, under the chairmanship of Senator Benjamin F. Wade of Ohio and dominated by the Radical Republicans, it became the spearhead of the Radical attack on Lincoln's war program.

Although its ostensible purpose was to inquire into the causes of past defeats, the Committee devoted its major energies to efforts to control the military machine, trying particularly to force Lincoln to give the important commands to generals having Radical political ideas. The Radicals sensed that many of the Northern generals were not animated by a driving, ruthless desire for victory. They were right but for the wrong reasons. The generals in the first years of the war were influenced by the eighteenth-century concept of war as a kind of game—as chessboard maneuvers conducted in leisurely fashion and without heavy casualties. The Radicals ascribed their hesitancy to a secret sympathy for slavery, which the professionals were supposed to have imbibed at West Point. The generals favored by the Committee—most of them incompetent amateurs—would have been no improvement, but the spirit represented by the Committee helped to infuse a hard, relentless impulse into the conduct of the war. Henceforth in war, no general could assume, as McClellan did, that he could prosecute his operations as a purely military exercise with no relation to political realities.

It would be possible to summarize Southern command arrangements by saying that they consisted mainly of President Davis and that the Confederacy failed to achieve a modern command system. Early in 1862 Davis assigned General Robert E. Lee to duty at Richmond, where, "under the direction of the President," he was "charged" with the conduct of the Confederate armies. Despite the fine words, this meant only that Lee, who had a brilliant military mind, was to act as Davis's adviser, furnishing counsel

when called on by the President. Aft serving a few months, Lee went to tl field, and Davis did not appoint anoth adviser until February, 1864. Then he s lected Braxton Bragg, whom he had bee forced to remove from field command al er Bragg was defeated in the West. Brag had real strategic ability, but he unde stood his position and restricted his fun tion to providing technical advice. I February, 1865, the Confederate Co gress, in a move directed at Davis, creat the position of general in chief, which wa intended for Lee. Davis, who realize the animus behind the act, named Lee t the post but took care to announce th legally he was still commander in chie Lee accepted the job on the basis offere by the President: as a loyal subordinat instead of as the dictator some peop wanted him to be. The war ended b fore the new command experiment coul be fully tested. It is doubtful wheth Lee, burdened with the command of field army, could have formulated and d rected strategy for other armies in othe theaters. Preoccupied as he was with th war in his native Virginia, he might n have been able to adjust his strateg thinking to the problems of "globa strategy.

The Opening Battles: 1861

The year 1861 witnessed several sma battles that accomplished large resul and one big battle that had no importar outcome. The small engagements o curred in Missouri and in western Vi ginia, the mountainous region tha shortly would become the state of We Virginia.

In Missouri the contending forces wei headed on the one hand by Governc Claiborne Jackson and other state off cials, who wanted to take the state ou of the Union, and on the other by Cap tain (later General) Nathaniel Lyor commanding a small regular army forc at St. Louis. Lyon led his column int southern Missouri, where he was defeated, and killed, by a superior Confederate force at the battle of Wilson's Creek (August 10). He had, however, seriously blunted the striking power of the Confederates, and Union forces were able to hold most of the state.

Into western Virginia came a federal force which had been assembled in Ohio under the command of George B. McClellan. Crossing the Ohio River, the invaders succeeded by the end of the year in "liberating" the mountain people. Although possession of the region placed the Federals on the flank of Virginia, they could not, because of the transportation obstacles presented by the mountains, use it as a base from which to move eastward. The occupation of western Virginia was, however, an important propaganda victory for the North: a Union-sympathizing area in the Confederacy had been wrenched from Southern control.

The one big battle of the year was fought in Virginia in the area between the two capitals. On the Virginia front the Federals occupied three positions. A small force held Fort Monroe on the coast between the York and James rivers. Just south of Washington was an army of over 30,000 under the command of General Irvin McDowell. In the northern end of the Shenandoah Valley were 14,000 Federals commanded by General Robert Patterson, a venerable veteran of the War of 1812 and the Mexican War. Confronting the semicircle of Union armies were three Confederate armies: a small force opposite Fort Monroe; an army of over 20,000 under P. G. T. Beauregard based at Manassas in northern Virginia about thirty miles southwest of Washington; and 9,000 troops in the Valley, commanded by Joseph E. Johnston.

The Federals had larger forces in Virginia than the Confederates, and if McDowell's army could knock out Beauregard's (the principal Confederate force), the war might be ended immediately.

The problem was to prevent other Confederate forces from coming to Beauregard's aid. The plan, as worked out, called for Patterson to contain Johnston so that McDowell could deal with Beauregard alone. But Patterson failed.

In mid-July McDowell marched his green troops toward Manassas, his movement well advertised to the Confederates by Northern newspapers and Southern spies. Beauregard retired behind Bull Run, a small stream north of Manassas, and called on the government to order Johnston to join him. Most of Johnston's army reached Beauregard the day before the battle, making the Northern and Southern armies approximately equal in size: each numbered something over 30,000.

The battle of Bull Run, or Manassas (July 21), might be summarized by saying that Beauregard never got his offensive into motion and that McDowell's attack almost succeeded. The Confederates stopped a last strong Union assault. Beauregard then ordered a counterattack. As the Confederates slashed forward, a sudden wave of panic struck through the Union troops, wearied after hours of hot, hard fighting and demoralized by the abrupt change of events. They gave way and crossed Bull Run in a rout. Unable to get them in hand north of the stream, McDowell had to order a retreat to Washington.

The Confederates, as disorganized by victory as the Federals were by defeat, and lacking supplies and transport, were in no condition to undertake a forward movement. Lincoln called to Washington, to replace McDowell, the victor of the fighting in western Virginia, General McClellan, and took measures to increase the army. Both sides girded themselves for real war.

War in the West: 1862

The first decisive operations in 1862 were in the Western theater. Here the

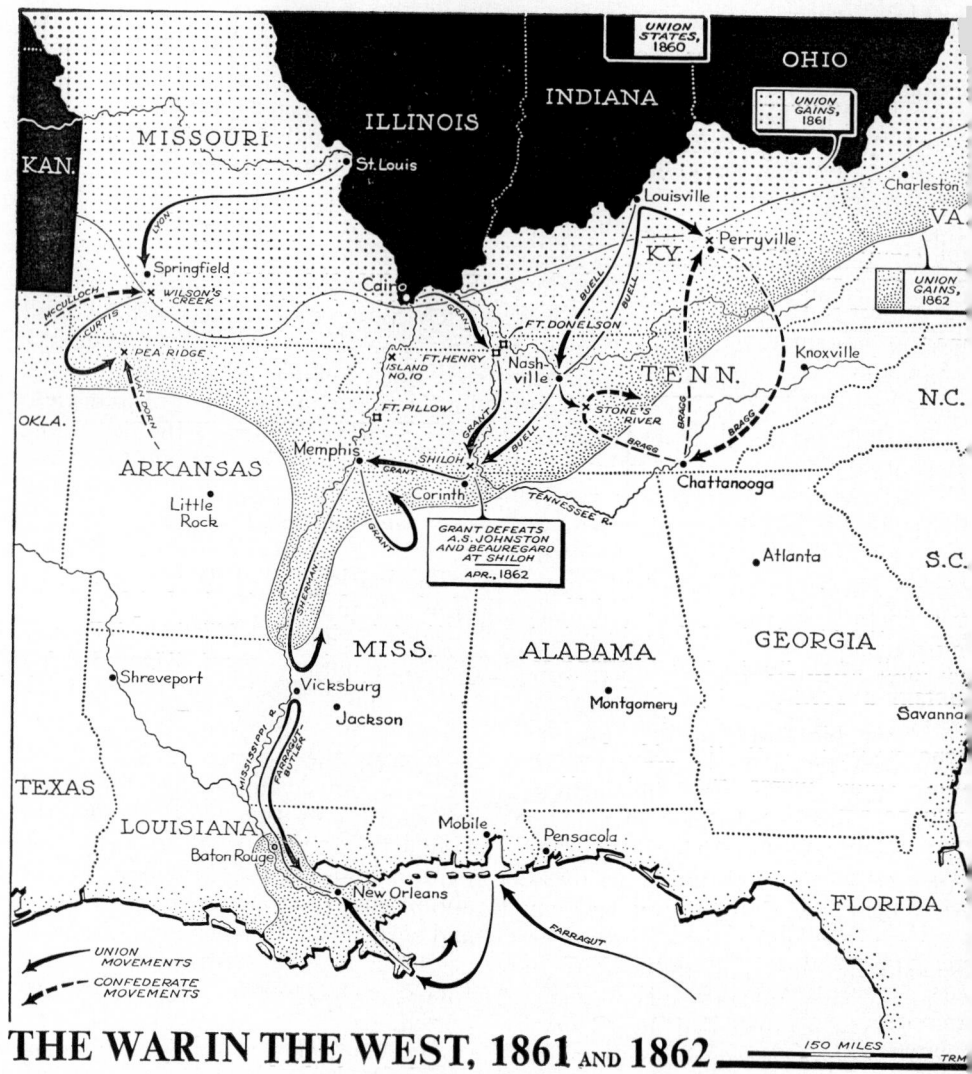

UNION STATES, 1860

UNION GAINS, 1861

UNION GAINS, 1862

THE WAR IN THE WEST, 1861 AND 1862

150 MILES

UNION MOVEMENTS
CONFEDERATE MOVEMENTS

Federals were trying to secure control of the Mississippi line, by moving on the river itself or parallel to it. Most of their offensives were combined land and naval affairs. To achieve their objective, the Federals advanced on the Mississippi from the north and south, moving down from Kentucky and up from the Gulf of Mexico against New Orleans.

In April a Union squadron of ironclads and wooden vessels commanded by David G. Farragut, destined to be the first American admiral, appeared in the Gulf. Smashing by the weak forts near the mouth of the river, Farragut ran up to New Orleans, defenceless because the Confederate high command had expected the attack to come from above, and forced the civil authorities to surrender the city (April 28–May 1). For the rest of the war the Federals held New Orleans and the southern part of Louisiana. They had closed off the mouth of the great river to Confederate trade, they had grasped the South's largest city and greatest banking center, and they had secured a possible base for future operations.

Federal land forces in the West, meanwhile, were under the direction of two departmental commanders. One army, with its base at Louisville, was led by General Don Carlos Buell. West of the Mississippi, Henry W. Halleck, with headquarters in St. Louis, was in command. An army subject to Halleck's control was stationed in western Kentucky under Ulysses S. Grant. All Confederate troops in the West were under the command of one general, Albert Sidney Johnston. A fatal weakness marked the Confederate line in Kentucky. The center, through which flowed the Tennessee and Cumberland rivers, was thrown back (southward) from the flanks, and was defended by two forts, Henry on the Tennessee and Donelson on the Cumberland. The forts had been built when Kentucky was trying to maintain a position of neutrality, and were located just over the Tennessee line. If the Federals, with the aid of naval power, could pierce the center, they would be between the two Confederate flanks and in position to destroy either.

This was exactly what the Federals did in February. Grant secured permission from Halleck to attack Fort Henry, whose defenders, awed by the ironclad river boats accompanying the Union army, surrendered with almost no resistance (February 6). Grant then marched to Donelson while his naval auxiliary moved to the Cumberland River. At Donelson the Confederates put up a scrap, but eventually the garrison of 20,000 had to capitulate (February 16). Grant, by the simple process of cracking the Confederate center and placing himself astride the river communications, had inflicted a near-disaster on the Confederacy. As a result of his movement, the Confederates were forced out of Kentucky and had to yield half of Tennessee.

Halleck now ordered Grant, with about 40,000 troops, to proceed up the Tennessee (southward), and directed Buell, who had occupied Nashville, to march to join Grant. The immediate objective was to destroy Confederate railroad communications in the Corinth, Mississippi, area. Grant debarked his army at Pittsburg Landing, about thirty miles from Corinth. At the latter place, Johnston and Beauregard decided that their only chance to retrieve the recent reverses was to smash Grant before he was joined by Buell. Early in April they moved, 40,000 strong, toward Pittsburg Landing to attack the Federals, who were encamped between two streams flowing into the Tennessee. The battle that ensued (April 6–7) is usually known as Shiloh. The Confederates caught Grant by surprise, and by the end of the first day's fighting drove him back to the river, but here the attack was halted. At the height of the battle Johnston was killed, and Beauregard assumed command. The next day Grant, reinforced by 25,000 of Buell's troops, went over to the offensive, and regained his original lines. Beauregard then disengaged, and withdrew to Corinth. In the tactical sense, Shiloh was an extremely narrow Union victory. The most important result was strategic in nature: the Confederates had failed to prevent a concentration of the federal armies.

After Shiloh, Halleck, bringing reinforcements with him, came to Pittsburg Landing to direct personally the advance on Corinth. Moving with excessive caution, he took the better part of a month to reach the town and to place his army in position to take it by siege. Beauregard, rather than risk the certain entrapment of his forces, wisely evacuated his lines. The Federals now had Corinth and the railroads of which it was the hub. Furthermore, by seizing areas parallel to the Mississippi, they flanked the Confederates out of their positions on the river. By early June the Federals had occupied the river line down as far as Memphis.

At this point Halleck was called to Washington to become general in chief.

Before he left, he had assigned missions to Grant and Buell, who again became departmental commanders. To Grant, the best fighting Union general yet to appear, he gave the relatively unimportant task of guarding communications in western Tennessee and northern Mississippi. To Buell, who had done practically no fighting, he assigned the vital objective of seizing Chattanooga on the Tennessee line. For the next few months Grant did little except to repel a Confederate attempt to recover Corinth. Buell took his army to Nashville to prepare his offensive. The Confederate field army in Mississippi, now commanded by Braxton Bragg (Davis had relieved Beauregard after the loss of Corinth), moved to Chattanooga, where it would be in position to undertake an offensive.

The Confederates held approximately the eastern half of Tennessee. Bragg's problem was to recover the rest of the state and, if possible, return the war to Kentucky. He was a brilliant strategist with a fatal weakness—he lacked the iron resolution to complete his plans. He now conceived a brilliant scheme. Instead of risking battle with Buell between Chattanooga and Nashville, he would rapidly invade Kentucky, forcing Buell to follow and drawing him out of Tennessee. If he could reach Kentucky first, he could place himself between Buell and Louisville and force the Federals to fight on grounds of his own choosing. With Buell smashed, lustrous success would be at hand—with Kentucky redeemed and the Western states open to invasion. Bragg did get to Kentucky first, he did stand between Buell and Louisville. But instead of fighting he withdrew. Buell went into the city, and, reinforced, came out looking for Bragg. The two armies met at the indecisive battle of Perryville (October 8), after which Bragg retired to Tennessee. Buell followed cautiously, and shortly the President relieved him. His successor was William S. Rosecrans. Toward the end of the year Bragg and Rosecrans, moving

forward in simultaneous advances, cam together in the hard-fought battle of Mu freesboro or Stone's River (December 3 January 2). Again Bragg had to retire.

The Virginia Front: 1862

In the fighting in 1862 the Unic navy played an important role off t Southern coast as well as on the rivers the Western theater. During the wint of 1861–2, the navy seized various islan off the Georgia-Carolinas coast (Po Royal, Roanoke Island, Fort Pulaski From these bases Union ships cou blockade Southern harbors and depri the Confederacy of the use of its ow ports. In a bold attempt to seize the nav initiative, the Confederates introduced new weapon—an ironclad warship.

The Confederates constructed the ship by plating with iron a former Unite States frigate, the *Merrimac*, which t Yankees had scuttled in Norfolk harb when Virginia seceded. She was rename the *Virginia*, but is known by her orig nal name. On March 8, 1862, the *M rimac* came out from Norfolk to atta the blockading squadron of wooden shi in Hampton Roads. Easily she destroye two of the federal ships and scattered tl others. Jubilation reigned in Richmon and consternation in Washington. B the federal government had placed c ders for the construction of several iro clads. One of these, the *Monitor*, arrive at Hampton Roads on the night of Marc 8. When the *Merrimac* emerged on tl following day to hunt for more victim she was met by the *Monitor*. There th followed the first battle between ironcla ships. Neither vessel was able to damaξ seriously the other's armor, but the *Moι tor* prevented her foe from destroyiι the blockading squadron. Even if tl *Merrimac* had won, the effect would ha been indecisive. Technical defects in h construction would have caused her founder if she had sought ocean wate she could operate only as a harbor-defen

First Battle of Ironclads. This print depicts, with some exaggeration, the fight between the *Monitor* and the *Merrimac*. The two contestants, in foreground, are represented with reasonable accuracy, but the damaged Union ships were not in the battle. The picture was made for public circulation by the McCormick farm machinery company, which thoughtfully included sketches of its own products in the scene. (LIBRARY OF CONGRESS)

vessel. And with the North alive to the value of ironclads and possessing superior facilities to build them, the South had lost the initiative with the new weapon.

In the Eastern theater in 1862 Union operations were directed by young George B. McClellan, commander of the Army of the Potomac and the most controversial general of the war. McClellan was a superb trainer of men but lacked the fighting instinct, necessary in a great captain, to commit his men to decisive battle.

During the winter of 1861–2 McClellan had remained inactive, training his army of 150,000 men near Washington. He finally settled on a plan of operations for the spring campaign. Instead of striking for Richmond by moving southward from Washington, he would have the navy transport his army to Fort Monroe on the Virginia coast in the region between the York and James rivers known as the Peninsula. Late in March McClellan started putting his troops on transports to begin his Peninsula campaign. After the general himself had departed for Virginia, Lincoln decided, on the basis of good evidence, that McClellan had not complied with the directive to leave enough men to protect Washington. Accordingly, he ordered McDowell's corps of over 30,000 men, about to embark to join McClellan, to remain south of Washington.

McClellan was thus deprived of a substantial part of his army, leaving him with something over 100,000. He had, nevertheless, a decisive numerical superiority over the Confederates when he landed at Fort Monroe. By mid-May he was within

A Civil War Balloon. Signal balloons were given their first practical use in the Civil War. In this picture Professor T. C. Lowe in his hydrogen-inflated balloon is ascending behind the Union lines at Fair Oaks to view the Confederate positions. Although balloons were usually anchored to the ground, they were sometimes cut loose and allowed to drift over the enemy lines. By releasing his ballast, the pilot could ascend higher and catch a contrary wind current that would waft him back to safety. (LIBRARY OF CONGRESS)

20 miles of Richmond, and by the latter part of the month he was approaching the gates of the city. Always he pressed Lincoln to send McDowell to him, and finally the President agreed.

The Confederate high command (Davis and Lee) had misgivings about General Joseph E. Johnston's strategy of drawing McClellan closer to Richmond before fighting and they were worried by the possibility that reinforcements particularly McDowell's corps, might join McClellan. To prevent this, Lee devised a scheme which Davis approved. The commander of the Confederate forces in the Shenandoah Valley, Thomas J. ("Stonewall") Jackson, was directed to move northward, giving the impression that he meant to cross the Potomac. In the brilliant Valley campaign (May 4–June 9) Jackson attacked and defeated two separate federal armies, then drove toward the northern end of the Valley. Partly to defend the approaches to Washington and partly to trap Jackson, Lincoln rushed forces to the Valley, including McDowell's corps. Jackson slipped back to safety before the various Union forces could converge on him. McDowell's troops were so used up by their long march that their movement to McClellan had to be suspended.

While these events were unfolding in the Valley, Johnston at last attacked McClellan at Fair Oaks or Seven Pines (May 31–June 1). The attack failed to budge McClellan, and Johnston was so seriously wounded that he had to relinquish the command. To his place Davis named the man who would lead the Army of Northern Virginia for the rest of the war, Robert E. Lee.

Lee, a brilliant field commander, realized that the Confederacy could not win its independence merely by repelling offensives. It would have to destroy a Union army, and to achieve this purpose Lee was ready to take chances, to risk something. Informed by his cavalry leader, J. E. B. Stuart, that one third of McClellan's army was north of the Chickahominy and two thirds south, Lee devised a daring plan. He would call Jackson from the Valley, bringing his army up to 85,000 (as compared to McClellan's 100,000), mass his forces north of the Chickahominy, and fall on the exposed Union right and chew it to pieces. Lee's thought was that then McClellan would retreat to the York and that he could follow and smash him before he reached his base. The risk in the plan was that McClellan would discover he confronted only a small enemy force on his left and would move into Richmond.

The operation that followed, which involved several engagements, is known as the Battle of the Seven Days (June 25–July 1). It did not go off as Lee expected. He drove back the Union right wing but was unable to destroy it. Then McClellan, instead of retiring to the York, abandoned his base there and headed southward for the James, where he had asked the navy to set up a new base. Lee followed, trying desperately to destroy the Federals, but McClellan extricated his army, even inflicting a bloody repulse on Lee at Malvern Hill. He reached Harrison's Landing on the James, where with naval support, he was safe from any attack Lee could launch.

At Harrison's Landing the federal army was only 25 miles from Richmond, and it had a secure line of water communications. But Lincoln, instead of replacing McClellan with a more aggressive commander, decided to evacuate the army to northern Virginia where it would be combined with a smaller force under John Pope—in short, to begin a new operation on the Washington-to-Richmond "overland" route.

As the Army of the Potomac left the Peninsula by water, Lee, understanding what was happening, moved his army northward with the purpose of striking Pope before he was joined by McClellan. As Lee approached, Pope retired north of the Rappahannock River. Some units of McClellan's army had reached him, and, as it developed that he might be forced into a battle, others were sent on as soon as they arrived. By a brilliant stratagem, Lee passed part of his army to Pope's rear, drawing the Federals north, and then followed with the remainder of his force. Pope, who was rash where McClellan was timid, was under the delusion he faced only Jackson's corps. Although not all of McClellan's troops had joined him, he attacked the Confederates near

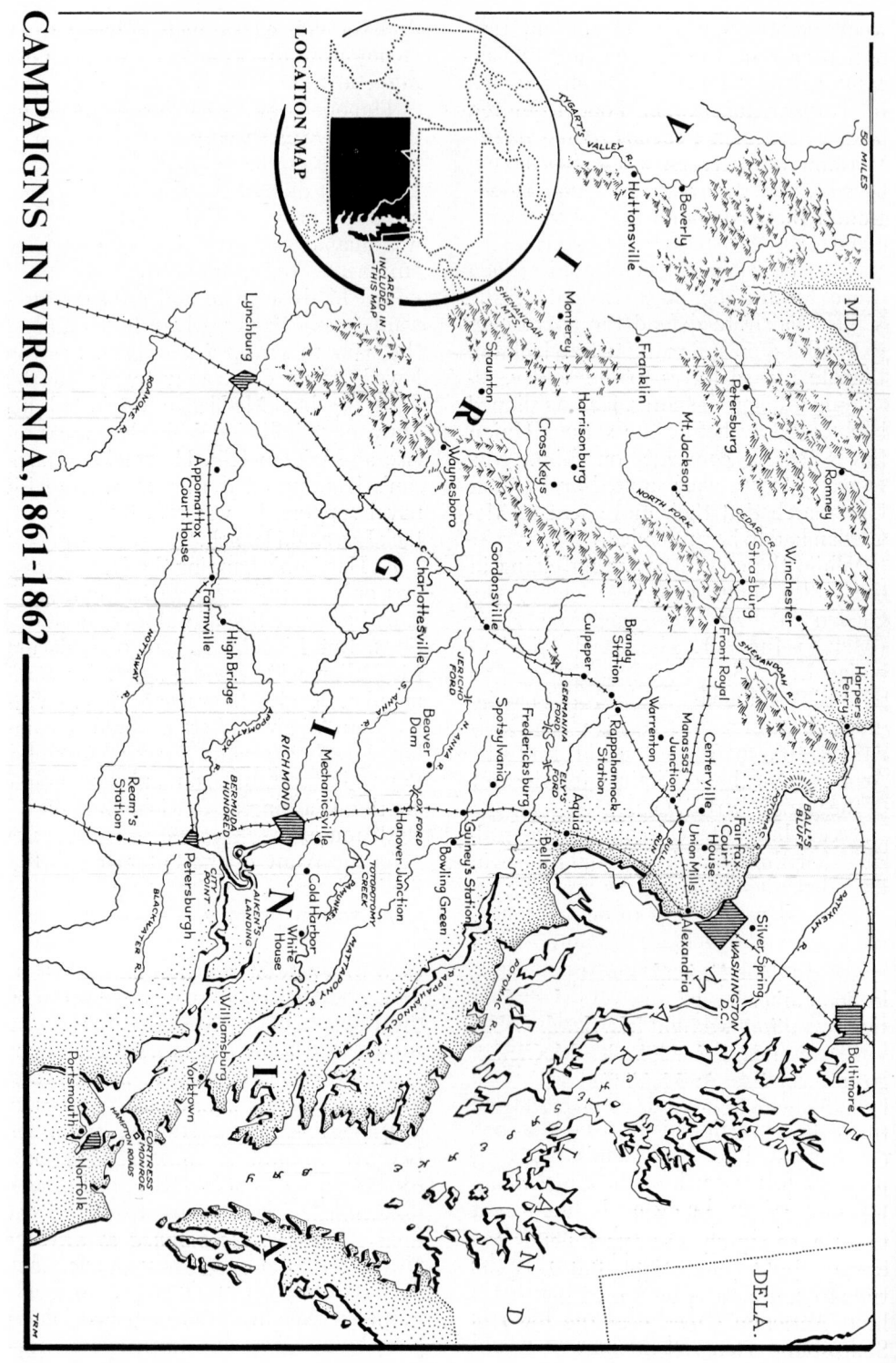

LOCATION MAP

AREA INCLUDED IN THIS MAP

50 MILES

MD.

DELA.

W. VA.

V I R G I N I A

M A R Y L A N D

Huttonsville

Beverly

Monterey

Franklin

Petersburg

Romney

Winchester

Strasburg

Front Royal

Mt. Jackson

Cross Keys

Harrisonburg

Staunton

Waynesboro

Lynchburg

Appomattox Court House

Farmville

High Bridge

Ream's Station

Charlottesville

Gordonsville

Brandy Station

Culpeper

Rappahannock Station

Warrenton

Manassas Junction

Centerville

Fairfax Court House

Union Mills

Alexandria

WASHINGTON D.C.

Silver Spring

Baltimore

Harpers Ferry

BALL'S BLUFF

Spotsylvania

Fredericksburg

Aquia

Belle

Guiney's Station

Bowling Green

Hanover Junction

Beaver Dam

Mechanicsville

RICHMOND

BERMUDA HUNDRED

CITY POINT

AIKEN'S LANDING

Petersburgh

Cold Harbor

White House

Williamsburg

Yorktown

Portsmouth

Norfolk

FORTRESS MONROE

HAMPTON ROADS

TRM

Manassas: the Battle of Second Manassas or Second Bull Run (August 29–30). Lee easily halted the assault, and in a powerful counterstroke swept Pope from the field. The beaten Federals retired to the Washington defenses, where Lincoln relieved Pope and placed all the troops around the city under McClellan's command.

Clellan, with 87,000 men, threw a series of powerful attacks at Lee's 50,000. Late in the day it seemed that the Confederate line would break, but at this moment the rest of Jackson's troops arrived from Harpers Ferry to plug the hole. Even then McClellan might have won with one more assault. But his caution asserted itself, and he called off the battle. Lee re-

CONFEDERATE DEAD IN THE BLOODY LANE AT ANTIETAM. (LIBRARY OF CONGRESS)

Lee gave the Federals no respite. Early in September he went over to the offensive, invading western Maryland. With some misgivings, Lincoln let McClellan go to meet Lee. As McClellan advanced, he had a wonderful piece of luck. He captured an order by Lee showing that the Confederate army was divided, a part of it under Jackson having gone to capture Harpers Ferry. McClellan's move was to advance rapidly and attack before the enemy could concentrate. But Lee had time to pull most of his army together behind Antietam Creek near the town of Sharpsburg. Here (September 17) Mc-

tired to Virginia, and after an interval of reorganization McClellan followed. Lincoln, disgusted by McClellan's failure to exploit his victory, removed him from command in November. It was McClellan's last military appearance in the war.

As McClellan's successor Lincoln appointed Ambrose E. Burnside, a modest mediocrity. Burnside thought that the government desired him to fight, and fight he would. He planned to drive at Richmond by crossing the Rappahannock at Fredericksburg, the strongest defensive point on that river. On December 13 he flung his army at Lee's defenses in a hope-

THE SOUTH'S GOOD SOLDIER. At the first battle of Manassas, Thomas J. Jackson received the name by which he is always known, "Stonewall." Another officer, rallying his troops, cried that Jackson was standing like a stone wall. Deeply religious, Jackson conceived of the South's struggle for independence as a holy war. He became Lee's most trusted subordinate, and his death after Chancellorsville was a sad blow to Confederate hopes. (NATIONAL ARCHIVES)

less, bloody attack. At the end of a day of bitter failure and after suffering 12,000 casualties, he withdrew to the north side of the Rappahannock. Shortly he was relieved at his own request.

The Year of Decision: 1863

As 1863 opened, the Union army in the East was commanded by Burnside's successor, Joseph Hooker—"Fighting Joe," as the newspapers called him. His army, which numbered 120,000, lay north of the Rappahannock opposite Fredericksburg. Hooker maneuvered opposite the town to hold Lee's attention, and crossed part of his army far up the Rap-

pahannock. This flanking force came down on the south side, threatening turn Lee's left. To complete his brillia movement Hooker had only to push to the open country around Frederick burg—and he would have Lee in a vic But Hooker lost his nerve. Now he hes tated, and fell back to a defensive pos tion at Chancellorsville in the desola area of scrub trees and brush known Virginia as the Wilderness. Here Le came up to attack him.

The battle of Chancellorsville (May 5) was one of Lee's most brilliant e ploits. With an army of only 60,000 (pa of his force had been detached for oth service), he took great but justified risk Leaving a small force at Fredericksbu to contain the Federals at that point, I moved to confront Hooker. He divided h army and sent Jackson to hit the Unic right, which was exposed, while he struc from in front. Finally Hooker, aided by diversion from his troops at Frederick burg, extricated his forces to the nort side of the river. Again Lee had won, b not the decisive victory he had hop for. And he had lost his ablest lieutenan Jackson, wounded in the fighting, di soon afterward.

While the Federals were failing in tl East, a different story was unfolding the West, one that would influence f ture operations in the Eastern theate U. S. Grant was driving at Vicksbur the strongest Confederate fortified poi on the Mississippi River. Coming dow the river with naval support, he debarke his army on the Louisiana side above tl city. From here he crossed to the ea bank, and struck at the Confederate d fenses, which were commanded l John C. Pemberton. He struck sever blows, and each one failed. The terrain I was operating in north of Vicksburg wa low, marshy, and laced by numerou streams and bayous, and it baffled eve attempt of the army and navy to traver it. Grant had little confidence that ar of his moves would succeed; he was kee ing his forces busy until the spring, when he intended to try another route to the city.

In May he unveiled his plan. The navy ran transports past the river batteries to a point below Vicksburg. The army marched down the west side, where it was met by the navy and transported to the east side. Now Grant was south of Vicksburg on relatively high and dry ground. Moving rapidly, he defeated enemy forces barring his way at Cham-

At last the Federals had achieved one of their principal strategic aims; they had got control of the Mississippi line. The Confederacy was split into two parts, and the Trans-Mississippi area was isolated from the main section. A great turning point in the war had been reached.

When the siege of Vicksburg began, the Confederate high command in Richmond was dismayed at the prospect of losing the great river fortress. Various plans to relieve the city were discussed,

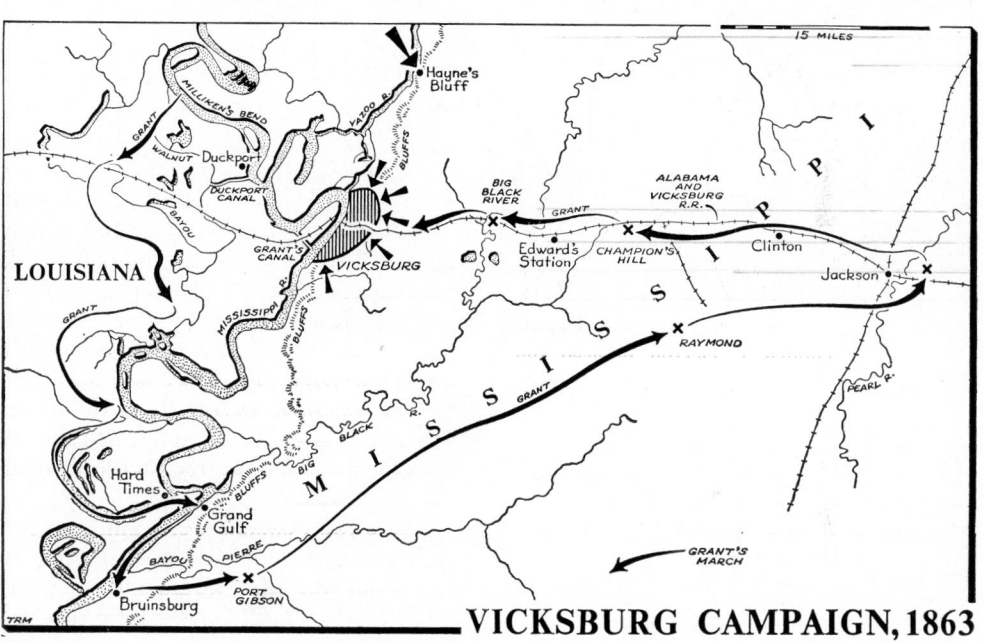

VICKSBURG CAMPAIGN, 1863

pion's Hill and the Big Black River, and closed in on Vicksburg itself. After failing to storm the strong works, he settled down to a siege, which endured for six weeks. Pemberton, realizing that his government could not break Grant's hold and that his garrison of 30,000 was exhausted by constant fighting, surrendered on July 4. Immediately thereafter the other Confederate strong point on the river, Port Hudson (Louisiana) surrendered to a Federal force which had come up from New Orleans under N. P. Banks.

the principal one being a proposal to send part of Lee's army to Tennessee, possibly with Lee himself in command, to launch an offensive. But Lee demurred; he did not want to leave Virginia. He put forward a counter-scheme: he would invade Pennsylvania. If he could win a victory on Northern soil, he said, great results would follow. The North might abandon the war, England and France might intervene, the pressure on Vicksburg and other fronts would be broken. The government assented, and in June Lee started his movement, swinging his

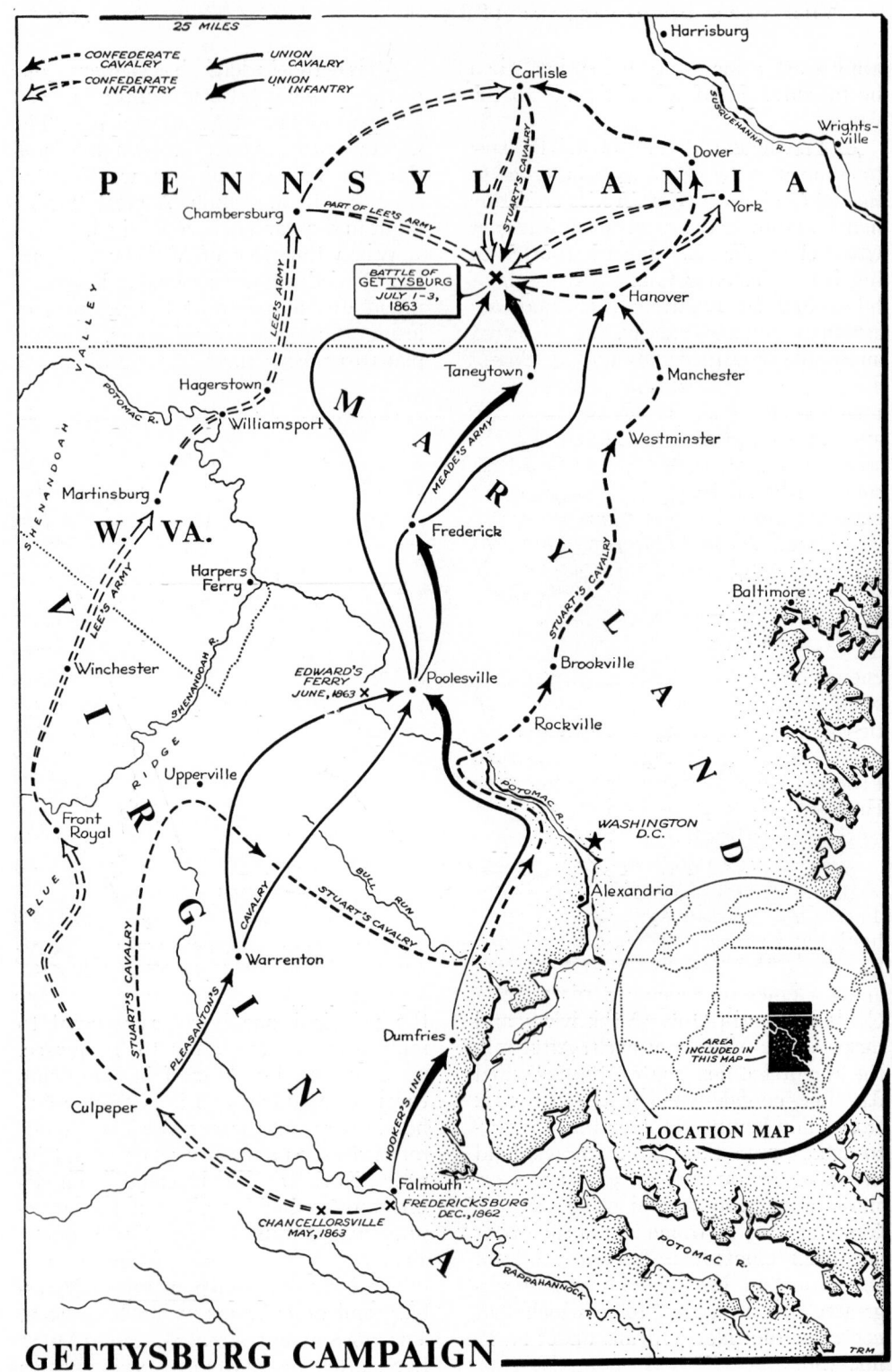

25 MILES

CONFEDERATE CAVALRY
UNION CAVALRY
CONFEDERATE INFANTRY
UNION INFANTRY

• Harrisburg

P E N N S Y L V A N I A

• Carlisle

• Dover

Wrights-ville

SUSQUEHANNA R.

Chambersburg • ·······PART OF LEE'S ARMY·······

STUART'S CAVALRY

• York

BATTLE OF
GETTYSBURG
JULY 1-3,
1863
✕

• Hanover

SHENANDOAH VALLEY

POTOMAC R.

Hagerstown •

M A R Y L A N D

• Taneytown

• Manchester

Williamsport •

• Westminster

Martinsburg •

W. VA.

Frederick •

MEADE'S ARMY

Baltimore •

LEE'S ARMY

Harpers
Ferry •

STUART'S CAVALRY

SHENANDOAH R.

Winchester •

V I R G I N I A

EDWARD'S
FERRY
JUNE, 1863 ✕

Poolesville •

• Brookville

Upperville •

BLUE RIDGE

• Rockville

POTOMAC R.

WASHINGTON
D.C. ★

Front
Royal •

BULL RUN

CAVALRY

PLEASANTON'S

STUART'S CAVALRY

• Alexandria

• Warrenton

LOCATION MAP

AREA
INCLUDED IN
THIS MAP

• Dumfries

HOOKER'S INF.

Culpeper •

CHANCELLORSVILLE
MAY, 1863 ✕

Falmouth •
✕ FREDERICKSBURG
DEC., 1862

POTOMAC R.

RAPPAHANNOCK R.

GETTYSBURG CAMPAIGN

TRM

army west toward the Valley and then north through Maryland into Pennsylvania.

As Lee advanced, Hooker moved back to confront him, marching parallel to the line of Lee's route. But Hooker evidently had been unnerved by his experience at Chancellorsville. He seemed to be looking for a chance to escape his responsibility, and he soon found an excuse to ask to be relieved. To his place Lincoln appointed a corps commander in the army, George G. Meade, a solid if unimaginative soldier. Meade followed Lee, and approached what might be called the strategic rear of the Confederate army in southern Pennsylvania. Lee, who had not expected the Federals to move so rapidly, was astounded when he learned of their nearness. With his army marching in three columns, he was in a dangerous position; hurriedly he had to concentrate his forces. Meade, realizing that Lee in enemy country had to attack or retreat, selected a strong defensive site at the little town of Gettysburg, a road hub in the region, and Lee, seeking contact with the Federals, moved toward the same spot. Here on July 1–3 was fought the most celebrated battle of the war.

The federal army occupied a formidable position on heights south of the town. Their line resembled an inverted fishhook, the right resting on Culp's Hill and Cemetery Hill and the front stretching along Cemetery Ridge for three miles. On the first day (July 1) the two armies jockeyed for position around Gettysburg; the tough fighting started the following day. Lee, confident of the prowess of his troops and combative by nature, decided to attack even though he was outnumbered 90,000 to 75,000. On July 2 he threw an assault at the Union left on Cemetery Ridge which crumpled up an advanced federal corps but failed to reach the main line. On July 3 he mounted a greater effort: 15,000 men were to hit the center of the ridge and crack the federal line wide open. The attacking force advanced over almost a mile of open space swept by enemy fire (the famous Pickett's charge). It was a gorgeous display of the older mode of warfare—frontal attacks by lines of infantry—which modern technology and improved weapons were making obsolete, and it was almost hopeless. Only about 5,000 men reached the ridge, and these had to surrender or retreat. After a day of sullen waiting by both armies, Lee withdrew his shattered forces to Virginia. Meade, who had little aggressive instinct, made but a feeble pursuit. Although Meade had thrown away an opportunity to end the war, Gettysburg was another turning point. The total Confederate losses in the campaign were close to 25,000. Never again would Lee feel strong enough to fight offensively.

A third turning point against the Confederacy was reached in Tennessee. In the autumn Rosecrans moved toward Chattanooga. Bragg, in order to secure room to maneuver, evacuated the town, which was occupied by the Federals on September 9. Rosecrans, forgetting that he had not defeated Bragg, rashly plunged over the Georgia line in pursuit, where Bragg, reinforced by troops from Lee's army, was lying in wait to attack. Rosecrans barely got his scattered forces in hand before Bragg delivered his assault at Chickamauga (September 19–20). This was one of the few battles in which the Confederates enjoyed a numerical superiority (70,000 to 56,000). On the second day Bragg smashed the Union right wide open. Rosecrans and his corps generals on that flank fled to Chattanooga even though his left continued to fight under the command of George H. Thomas, who here won the sobriquet of "the Rock of Chickamauga." Shortly Thomas too had to retire, and the beaten army fell back into the Chattanooga defenses.

Bragg did not move rapidly to exploit his victory, partly because of his heavy casualties (17,000), but eventually he advanced and occupied the heights south of

Chattanooga. Mounting batteries on these points, he commanded the roads leading into the city and virtually shut off its supplies. The Union high command, however, had ample resources to break the siege. Grant was named departmental commander of the West. Immediately he replaced Rosecrans with Thomas, and came with part of his own army to Chattanooga. The reinforced federal army numbered 60,000, while Bragg's army was weakened by the detachment of a force for a fruitless operation against Knoxville. At the battle of Chattanooga (November 23–25) the Federals hurled Bragg from his lines on Missionary Ridge and Lookout Mountain and back into northern Georgia. They then proceeded to occupy most of East Tennessee.

A second objective of Northern strategy had been achieved: possession of the Tennessee River line. From the Chattanooga base the Federals were in position to split the Confederacy again—what was left of it. Chattanooga deserves to be ranked with Vicksburg and Gettysburg. After 1863 the Confederacy had no chance on any front to win its independence by a military decision. Now it could hope to triumph only by exhausting the Northern will to fight.

The End: 1864–65

Grant's plans for 1864 called for two great offensives. The Army of the Potomac, commanded by Meade but accompanied and directed by Grant, was to seek to bring Lee to decisive battle in northern Virginia. From near Chattanooga the Western army, commanded by William T. Sherman, was to advance into northern Georgia, destroy the Confederate army, now commanded by Joseph E. Johnston, and wreck the economic resources of Atlanta.

The two offensives jumped off in May. From its position in northern Virginia the Army of the Potomac, 115,000 strong, crossed the Rappahannock and

Rapidan rivers, and plunged into the Wilderness area. Grant's plan was to envelop Lee's right and force him to a showdown battle. Lee, whose army numbered about 75,000 at the beginning of the campaign, was determined to avoid a showdown unless he saw a chance to deal a decisive blow. In the Battle of the Wilderness (May 5–6) each commander struck savagely at the other. Demonstrating superb defensive skill, Lee prevented Grant from turning his right. But the federal commander, instead of retiring to reorganize as his predecessors had done after a reverse, slid off to his left and to the southeast. He turned up at Spotsylvania Court House, where Lee moved to meet him. Here another bloody, indecisive engagement was fought (May 8–12). Again Grant sidled to his left, and again Lee slid with him. In this manner, without fighting another major clash, the two armies moved until they reached Cold Harbor, a few miles north of Richmond. At this point Grant made a last attempt to destroy Lee north of Richmond (June 1–3), and was bloodily repulsed. In a month of fighting Grant had lost in total casualties 55,000 men, and Lee, 31,000.

Now Grant had to alter his strategy. If he remained where he was, Lee would retire into the Richmond defenses to stand a siege, something Grant wanted to avoid. Masking his movements from his adversary, Grant moved southward across the James heading for Petersburg, directly south of Richmond. Petersburg was the hub of all the railroads feeding into the capital; if Grant could secure it he could force Lee to come into the open to fight for his communications. He almost succeeded. Petersburg was defended only by a small force under Beauregard, who managed, however, to hold Grant off until Lee's army could arrive. Grant now realized that he would have to resort to siege operations. He dug in, and so did Lee. The trench lines of the two armies stretched for miles above and below Petersburg. Always Grant strove to ex-

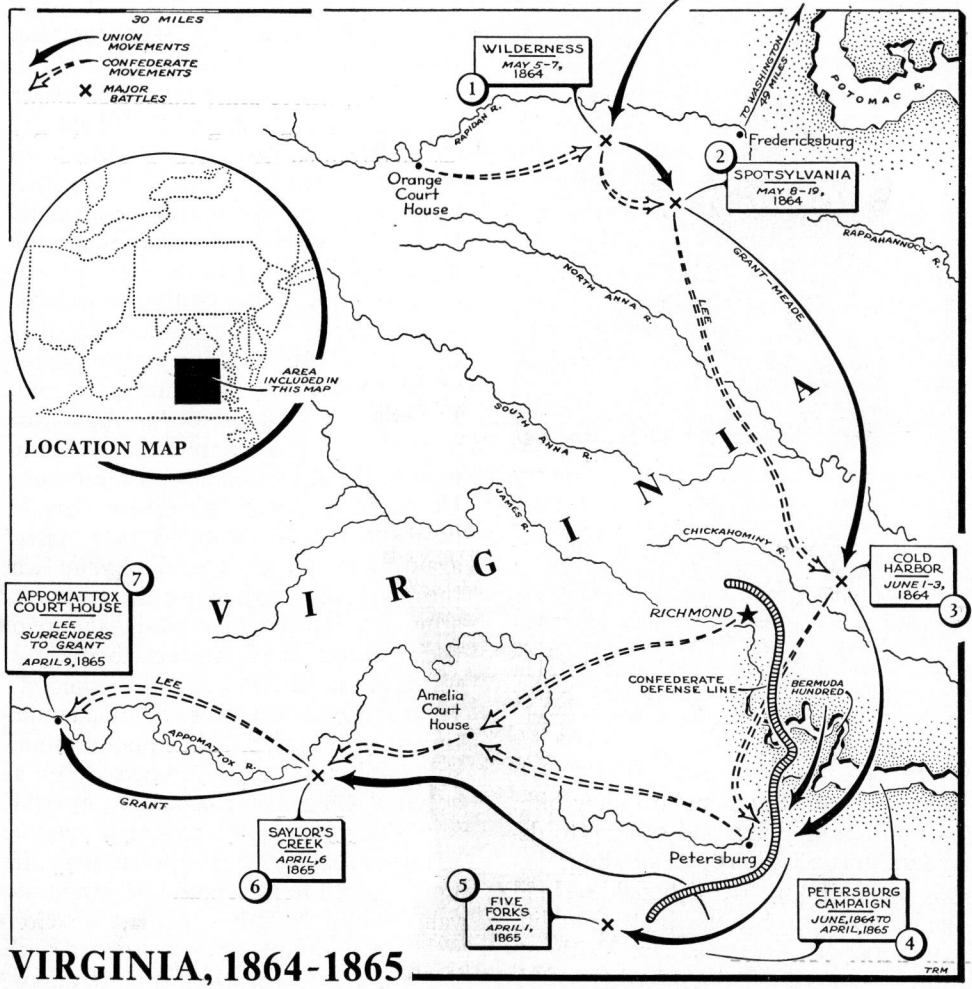

WILDERNESS
MAY 5-7, 1864
①

SPOTSYLVANIA
MAY 8-19, 1864
②

COLD HARBOR
JUNE 1-3, 1864
③

APPOMATTOX COURT HOUSE
LEE SURRENDERS TO GRANT
APRIL 9, 1865
⑦

SAYLOR'S CREEK
APRIL, 6 1865
⑥

FIVE FORKS
APRIL 1, 1865
⑤

PETERSBURG CAMPAIGN
JUNE, 1864 TO APRIL, 1865
④

LOCATION MAP

AREA INCLUDED IN THIS MAP

POTOMAC R.
Fredericksburg
RAPIDAN R.
Orange Court House
NORTH ANNA R.
GRANT-MEADE
RAPPAHANNOCK R.
SOUTH ANNA R.
JAMES R.
CHICKAHOMINY R.
RICHMOND
CONFEDERATE DEFENSE LINE
BERMUDA HUNDRED
Amelia Court House
APPOMATTOX R.
GRANT
LEE
Petersburg

V I R G I N I A

VIRGINIA, 1864-1865

tend his left around Lee's right so as to get on the railroads that were the lifeline of the Southern army. It would be nine months until he reached his objective.

In May, Sherman, with an army of over 90,000, moved against Atlanta and Johnston's army, which numbered 60,000 at the beginning. Johnston's plan was to delay Sherman, to fight for time, and not to commit his forces unless the conditions were exceptionally favorable. The Atlanta campaign developed primarily into a game of maneuver in which Sherman tried to trap his rival, who avoided being caught. The two armies skirmished

and fought almost constantly, but the only set battle was at Kennesaw Mountain (June 27). As Sherman was approaching Atlanta, President Davis replaced Johnston with John B. Hood. Combative by nature, Hood threw two successive attacks at Sherman, both of which failed. The Union army occupied Atlanta on September 2.

Sherman had not destroyed the enemy army. Eager to strike deeper into Georgia, he sent 30,000 of his army to Tennessee under Thomas, and prepared to move for Savannah on the coast. At the same time Hood decided to invade Tennessee,

THE APOSTLE OF MODERN WAR. More than any American general of his time, William T. Sherman understood the nature of modern war— total warfare against the civilian population, as well as the armies, of the enemy. And no general in the Civil War did as much to inaugurate the new kind of war as did Sherman in his march through Georgia and the Carolinas. Although the spare, redheaded Sherman made himself hated in the South, he liked Southerners and after the war opposed a harsh Reconstruction policy. (LIBRARY OF CONGRESS)

hoping to force Sherman to follow him.

Confronting Hood, and seeking to delay him, was a Union force of about 30,-000 under John M. Schofield. Hood caught up with Schofield at Franklin, Tennessee, on November 30. With no artillery support, Hood resolved to attack across two miles of open space, though the Federals were entrenched in a strong position. In six fruitless charges he lost 6,000 men; eleven of his generals were killed or wounded. After that he might as well have gone back to Georgia. But he moved forward and took up a position south of Nashville. In the city Thomas was gathering an army that would eventually number over 60,000. When he was ready, he came out looking for Hood. At the Battle of Nashville (December 15-16 he smashed Hood from the field. As the Confederates retreated toward Mississippi, they were harried by the most merciless cavalry pursuit of the war. Only

a few units reached Mississippi intac The Confederate Army of Tennessee ha in effect, ceased to exist.

In the meantime Sherman was marc ing almost unopposed across Georgia, i augurating a new kind of warfare. H was the prophet of modern total war— war against the civilian population of th enemy, war intended to break the enem people's will to resist. His army marche on a sixty-mile front, destroying proper and supplies that might be used I the Confederate forces—and committi many individual depredations as we But the greatest result of Shermar march was psychological rather than ec nomic. What Southerner that heard of Union army moving at will through th heart of the South could ever belie again that the Confederacy could w the war? In Virginia soldiers in Lee army deserted to go home to take care their families. By December 20 Shermar was at Savannah.

Into South Carolina Sherman the turned, still facing slight opposition ar still ripping up enemy property. He w accomplishing two objectives: destro ing both Confederate resources and t railroads that brought supplies from t Lower South to Lee's army. When he a vanced into North Carolina, the Co federate government got together army of 30,000 under Johnston to oppo him, but this small force could do litt more than delay his march. Nor cou Lee move against him, for he was pinne down at Petersburg by Grant.

In April, 1865, Grant finally passed part of his army around Lee's right the vital railroads. The Confederat evacuated Petersburg and Richmond, ar Lee moved his army, now shrunk to abo 25,000, westward. His one forlorn hop was to reach a rail line to North Caroli and unite with Johnston. But the pu suing federal army barred his escape rout At last he realized that further fighti was hopeless, and on April 9 he m Grant at Appomattox and surrender

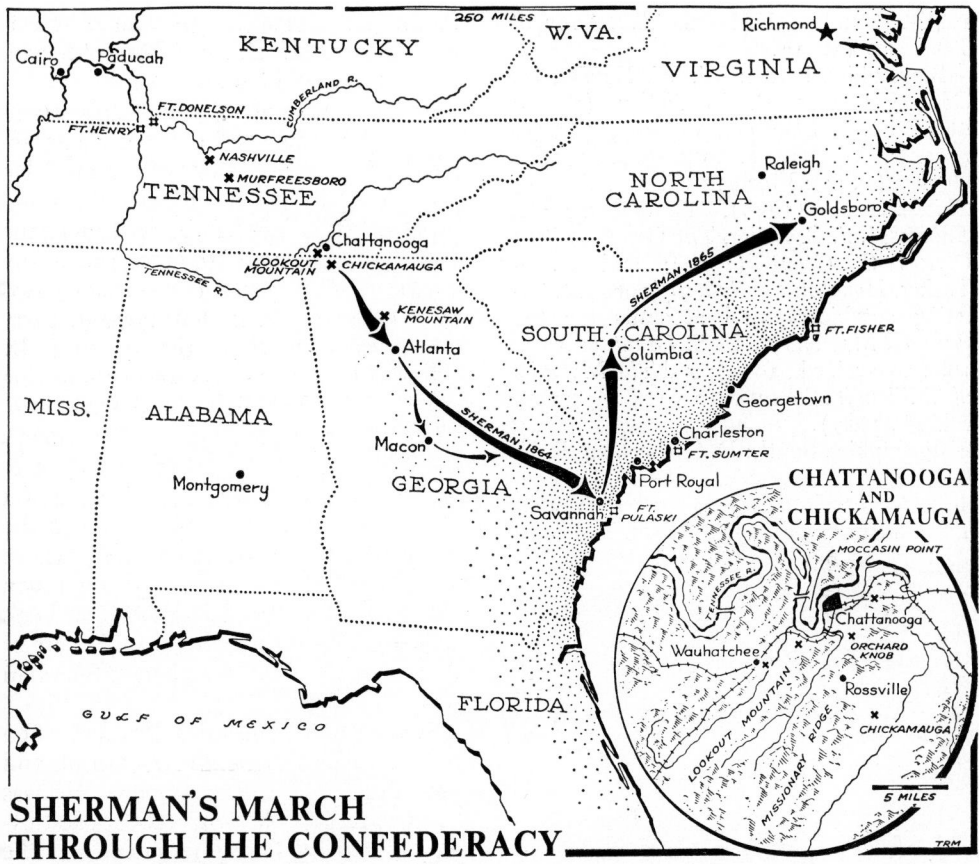

**SHERMAN'S MARCH
THROUGH THE CONFEDERACY**

the Army of Northern Virginia. In North Carolina Joe Johnston reached the same conclusion, and on April 26 he surrendered to Sherman near Durham. Jefferson Davis, defiant to the last and unable to recognize defeat, fled southward, and was captured in Georgia. The war was soon over.

BIBLIOGRAPHY

Collections of first-hand battle accounts are H. S. Commager (ed.), *The Blue and the Gray* (2 vols., 1950); and O. Eisenschiml, R. Newman, and E. B. Long (eds.), *The Civil War: The American Iliad* (2 vols., 1956). David Donald (ed.), *Divided We Fought* (1953), is a pictorial presentation. From the great account by participants, *Battles and Leaders of the Civil War* (4 vols., 1887; new ed., 1956), Ned Bradford has put together a one-volume edition (1956).

Top-level command problems are discussed in C. R. Ballard, *The Military Gen-*ius of Abraham Lincoln (1952); Sir Frederick Maurice, *Statesmen and Soldiers of the Civil War* (1925); and T. H. Williams, *Lincoln and His Generals* (1952). See also J. F. C. Fuller, *Grant and Lee* (1933; new ed., 1957). Among military histories, the following are especially to be recommended: J. B. Mitchell, *Decisive Battles of the Civil War* (1955); K. P. Williams, *Lincoln Finds a General* (5 vols., 1949–59); Bruce Catton, *Mr. Lincoln's Army* (1951), *Glory Road* (1952), *A Stillness at Appomattox* (1954), and *Grant Moves South* (1960); D. S. Freeman, *Lee's Lieutenants* (3 vols.,

1942–4); and S. F. Horn, *The Army of Tennessee* (1941).

Biographies, North: W. W. Hassler, Jr., *General George B. McClellan* (1957); Lloyd Lewis, *Sherman, Fighting Prophet* (1932); W. H. Hebert, *Fighting Joe Hooker* (1944); Freeman Cleaves, *Rock of Chickamauga* (1948), on George H. Thomas; J. F. C. Fuller, *The Generalship of Ulysses S. Grant* (1929); and Glenn Tucker, *Hancock the Superb* (1960). Interesting autobiographical accounts are the *Personal Memoirs of U. S. Grant* (2 vols., 1885; one-vol. ed., 1952); and *The Memoirs of William T. Sherman* (2 vols., 1875; one-vol. ed., 1957).

Biographies, South: D. S. Freeman, *R. E. Lee* (4 vols., 1934–5), a classic; F. Vandiver, *Mighty Stonewall* (1957); J. P. Dyer, *The Gallant Hood* (1950); T. H. Williams,

Beauregard, Napoleon in Gray (1955 R. S. Henry, *"First with the Most" Forre* (1944); Burke Davis, *Gray Fox* (1956 on Lee; J. W. Thomason, Jr., *Jeb Stua* (1930); G. Govan and J. W. Livingood, *Different Valor* (1956), on Joseph Johnston; and D. B. Sanger and T. R. Ha *James Longstreet* (1952).

On naval operations, see A. T. Maha *The Gulf and Inland Waters* (1883); J. Scharf, *History of the Confederate Stat Navy* (1887); J. P. Baxter, *Introduction the Ironclad Warship* (1933); and J. Hill, *Sea Dogs of the Sixties* (1935). Tw studies that approach the most famous n val battle of the war from different vie points are T. C. and Ruth White, *Tin Ca on a Shingle* (1957); and R. W. Daly, *Ho the Merrimac Won* (1957).

21

RECONSTRUCTING
THE SOUTH

The Civil War had decided many things. It determined that the United States would remain one nation, unified as never before. It placed that nation on the road to becoming a great world power. By destroying slavery and demonstrating that a popular government could preserve political liberties during an internal conflict, the war vitalized and vindicated democracy at home and everywhere in the world. But these results would not be completely realized until long years had passed. Meanwhile, in the immediate aftermath of war, a number of immediate problems emerged to test the statesmanship of the victors.

The most urgent of these problems concerned the South. Not only were the South's farmlands and cities ravaged—its entire social organization had been disrupted. By what was perhaps the most gigantic act of confiscation in history, four million slaves had been seized from their owners and made freedmen. What would their status be and who would determine that status: the white people of the Southern states or the national government? Upon what terms and by what process would the states of the defeated Confederacy be restored to the Union?

Lincoln's and Johnson's Plans

The normal pattern of politics in the postwar years was immensely complicated by the problem of Reconstruction. As the men of the period employed the term, Reconstruction had a strictly political connotation. It referred to the process by which the defeated states of the late Confederacy would be governed and to the conditions on which they would be restored.

Dominated by the Radical faction of the party, the Republicans advocated a program of Reconstruction that would impose stringent penalties on the South, enforce a position of political equality for the former slaves, and recast Southern society in the image of the rest of the country. Although some Republicans were animated by idealistic or democratic motives, most Republican politicians approached Reconstruction in terms of political realities. They favored a program that would serve the needs of the party. These needs dictated that the Republicans remain in office and that the legislative gains won during the war by the Northern economic groups composing the party—the protective tariff, the National Bank system, subsidies to railroads, and others—be maintained and expanded. The Democrats, as the opposition party, opposed, whether or not it was shrewd to do so, everything that the Republicans proposed.

whether the defeated states were in or out of the Union he dismissed as a useless abstraction. They were merely out of their proper relationship to the Union, he said, and they should be restored to their former relation in the shortest possible time.

Specifically Lincoln's plan, which he announced to the public in a proclamation of December, 1863, offered a general amnesty to all who would take an oath pledging future loyalty to the govern-

---

THE RUINS OF COLUMBIA, SOUTH CAROLINA

The Southern cities suffering the greatest devastation were Columbia, Atlanta, and Charleston. Sidney Andrews, a Northern reporter, described Columbia in *The South After the War* (1866): "It is now a wilderness of ruins. Its heart is but a mass of blackened chimneys and crumbling walls. Two thirds of the buildings in the place were burned, including, without exception, everything in the business portion. Not a store, office, or shop escaped; and for a distance of three fourths of a mile on each of twelve streets there was not a building left. Every public building was destroyed, except the new and unfinished Statehouse. This is situated on the summit of tableland whereon the city is built, and commands an extensive view of the surrounding country, and must have been the first building seen by the victorious and on-marching Union army. From the summit of the ridge, on the opposite side of the river, a mile and a half away a few shells were thrown at it, apparently by way of reminder, three or four of which struck it, without doing any particular damage."

The process of Reconstruction was first put into motion during the Civil War, and the first plan of Reconstruction was presented by President Lincoln. Without much consideration for the effects of Reconstruction upon the future of his party, Lincoln was almost exclusively concerned with the principle that always dominated his thinking: the inviolability of the Union. He wanted to restore as soon as possible the American experiment in democracy. Consequently Lincoln proposed an "easy" process of Reconstruction. He would subordinate to his larger goal such questions as punishment of the defeated side or determination of the status of the freedmen. The issue of

ment. Temporarily excluded from the right to swear the oath were high civil and military officials of the Confederacy. Whenever in any state 10 per cent of the number of voters in 1860 took the oath, they could proceed to set up a state government that Lincoln promised to recognize. The oath required acceptance of the wartime acts and proclamations of Congress and the President concerning slavery—this was the only provision in the plan that imposed a condition for readmission on the South and the only part of the plan that dealt with national supervision of race relations. In three Southern states—Louisiana, Arkansas, and Tennessee—loyal governments reconstructed under the Lincoln formula were established in 1864.

The Radical Republicans were angered and astonished at the mildness of Lincoln's program, and they were able to induce Congress to repudiate his governments. Representatives from the Lincoln states were not admitted to Congress, and the electoral vote of those states was not counted in the election of 1864. In defeating Lincoln's plan, the Radicals were aided by a number of moderate Republicans who thought that the President's scheme did not provide adequate protection for the freedmen. The Radicals could not stop, however, with a rejection of Lincoln's plan. The requirements of politics dictated that they produce a plan of their own. But at the moment the Radicals had not thought the Reconstruction problem through. They were not agreed as to how "hard" a peace they should enforce on the South, and they were not certain that Northern opinion would support the ideas of their more extreme leaders.

Under pressure, they prepared and passed (in July, 1864) the Wade-Davis Bill, which may be considered the first Radical plan of Reconstruction. By its provisions, the President was to appoint for each conquered state a provisional governor who would take a census of all adult white males. If a majority of those enrolled—instead of Lincoln's 10 per cent—swore an oath of allegiance, the governor was to call an election for a state constitutional convention. The privilege of voting for delegates to this meeting was limited to those who could swear that they had never borne arms against the United States, the so-called "iron-clad oath." The convention was required to put into the new constitution provisions abolishing slavery, disfranchising Confederate civil and military leaders, and repudiating the Confederate and state war debts. After these conditions had been met, Congress would readmit the state to the Union. The Wade-Davis Bill

was more drastic in almost every respect than the Lincoln plan. But although it assumed that the seceded states were out of the Union and hence under the dictation of Congress, the act did not, any more than the President's proposal, attempt to establish national control over race relations.

The Wade-Davis Bill was passed a few days before Congress adjourned, which enabled Lincoln to dispose of it with a pocket veto. His action enraged the authors of the measure, Benjamin F. Wade and Henry Winter Davis; they issued a blistering denunciation of the veto, the Wade-Davis Manifesto, warning the President not to interfere with the powers of Congress to control Reconstruction. The bitterness and the strength of the Radical opposition gave Lincoln pause. Practical as always, he realized that he would have to accept some of the objections of the Radicals. He began to move toward a new approach to Reconstruction, possibly one that included greater national supervision of the freedmen. What plan he would have come up with cannot be exactly stated. On April 14, 1865, a crazed actor, John Wilkes Booth, under the delusion he was helping the South, shot the President in a Washington theater. Lincoln died early the following morning, and because of the circumstances of his death—the heroic leader, the Great Emancipator struck down in the hour of victory by an assassin —he achieved immediate martyrdom. In the wild excitement of the hour, it was widely assumed that Booth had been instigated to his mad act by men in the South, and the Radicals played on this theme with reckless charges implicating high Confederates. Ironically, Lincoln's death helped to kill his policy of a generous peace.

The conservative leadership in the controversy over Reconstruction fell upon Lincoln's successor, Andrew Johnson. Of all the men who accidentally inherited the presidency, Johnson was undoubtedly

ANDREW JOHNSON. Johnson, who was a tailor before going into politics, was of medium height and size. He had a dark complexion and boring black eyes. A powerful orator on the stump, he easily lost his temper when heckled and used crude and intemperate language. Sincerely devoted to his principles, he was sometimes too theoretical in upholding them. (LIBRARY OF CONGRESS)

the most unfortunate. A Southerner and former slaveholder, he became President as a bloody war against the South was drawing to a close. A Democrat before he had been placed on the Union ticket with Lincoln in 1864, he became the head of a Republican administration at a time when partisan passions, held in some restraint during the war, were about to rule the government. As if these handicaps of background were not enough, Johnson was intemperate in language and tactless in manner, and he lacked Lincoln's skill in handling people. Unlike Lincoln, he was theoretical rather than practical, dogmatic rather than pragmatic. In dealing with Reconstruction, he stood righteously on the Constitution, even though that document obviously did not

envision the unprecedented constitutional situation that existed after the war.

Johnson revealed his plan of Reconstruction soon after he took office, and proceeded to execute it during the summer of 1865 when Congress was not in session. It was applied to the eight states of the late Confederacy that had not come under the Lincoln plan; Johnson recognized as legal organizations the Lincoln governments in Louisiana, Arkansas, and Tennessee. In some ways his scheme resembled Lincoln's, in others it was similar to the Wade-Davis Bill. Like his predecessor, Johnson assumed that the seceded states were still in the Union, and, also like Lincoln, he announced his design in a proclamation of amnesty which extended pardon for past conduct to all who would take an oath of allegiance. Denied the privilege of taking the oath until they received individual pardons from the President were high-ranking Confederate officials; Johnson excluded a larger number of leaders than Lincoln had. For each state the President appointed a provisional governor who was to invite the qualified voters to elect delegates to a constitutional convention. Johnson did not specify that a minimum number of voters had to take the oath, as had the Lincoln and Wade-Davis proposals, but the implication was plain that he would require a majority. As conditions of readmittance, the state convention had to abolish slavery and repudiate the Confederate and state war debts, or the same stipulations that had been laid down in the Wade-Davis Bill. The final procedure before restoration was for a state to elect a state government and send representatives to Congress.

By the end of 1865 the states affected by Johnson's plan had complied with its requirements. Indeed, if the Lincoln governments are included, all of the seceded states had been reconstructed and were ready to resume their places in the Union —if Congress chose to recognize them when it met in December, 1865. Recog nition of the Johnson governments was exactly what the Radicals were determined to prevent. And many people in the North agreed with them that Reconstruction was being rushed too fast and was being accomplished too easily. Northern opinion was particularly aroused by the passage by the Lincoln-Johnson

between the races and to invest the Negroes with a legal although subordinate status. The acts conferred certain civil rights upon colored people, but they also placed special restrictions on Negroes that did not apply to whites. To the South, the Black Codes were a realistic approach to a great social problem. To

---

THE BLACK CODE OF LOUISIANA

The sections in the Black Codes regulating Negro labor angered Northern opinion and turned many people in favor of Radical Reconstruction. The Louisiana Code had this to say:

"Sec. 1. Be it enacted by the Senate and House of Representatives of the State of Louisiana in general assembly convened, That all persons employed as laborers in agricultural pursuits shall be required, during the first ten days of the month of January of each year, to make contracts for labor for the then ensuing year, or for the year next ensuing the termination of their present contracts. All contracts for labor for agricultural purposes shall be made in writing, signed by the employer, and shall be made in the presence of a Justice of the Peace and two disinterested witnesses, in whose presence the contract shall be read to the laborer, and when assented to and signed by the latter, shall be considered as binding for the time prescribed. . . .

"Sec. 2. Every laborer shall have full and perfect liberty to choose his employer, but, when once chosen, he shall not be allowed to leave his place of employment until the fulfillment of his contract . . . and if they do so leave, without cause or permission, they shall forfeit all wages earned to the time of abandonment. . . ."

---

legislatures of the so-called Black Codes. These measures were the South's solution for the problem of the free Negro laborer, and they were also the South's substitute for slavery as a white-supremacy device. Economically, the codes were intended to regulate the labor of a race that, in the opinion of the whites, would not work except under some kind of compulsion. Although the economic provisions varied in stringency from state to state, they all authorized local officials to apprehend unemployed Negroes, fine them for vagrancy, and hire them out to private employers to satisfy the fine. Socially, the codes were designed to govern relations

the North, they seemed to herald a return to slavery.

Radical Reconstruction

When Congress convened in December, 1865, one of the first acts of the Radical machine was to deny admission to representatives from the reconstructed states. These men should not be recognized, explained Radical leaders, until Congress knew more about conditions in the South and until it was determined that Southerners loyally accepted the results of the war. Accordingly, a joint committee of fifteen—the Committee on Re-

ARCHITECT OF RECONSTRUCTION. Thaddeus Stevens represented the Lancaster district of Pennsylvania in the House of Representatives. Bald since a sickness in youth, he wore a wig that often fell out of place in debate. Bitter and sarcastic in speech, he ruled the Republican majority with a sure hand and drove to passage the Radical Reconstruction program. He advocated the confiscation of planter estates and the division of the land among the freedmen. He maintained that the defeated states were "conquered provinces" and that Congress in dealing with them was not limited by the Constitution but only by the rules of international law as these affected the relationship of victor and vanquished after a war. (NATIONAL ARCHIVES)

construction—was created to investigate the temper of Southern opinion and to advise Congress in framing a Reconstruction policy. In little more than a year the Radicals had moved beyond the Wade-Davis Bill to a harder peace plan.

The first move of the Radicals was to strike at the Black Codes. They put through Congress the Civil Rights Bill, which forbade states to discriminate against citizens on account of race. Promptly Johnson vetoed the measure,

and just as promptly the veto was over ridden. Emboldened by their evident sup port in Congress, the Radicals struc again and harder. The Committee o Reconstruction submitted to Congress i April, 1866, a proposed amendment t the Constitution, the Fourteenth, whicl constituted the second Radical plan o Reconstruction.

The Fourteenth Amendment, whicl was adopted by Congress and sent to th states for approval in the early summe is so important, both in its immediat bearing upon Reconstruction and in it future influence upon federal-state r lationships, as to deserve particular analy sis. Section 1 declared that all person born or naturalized in the United State were citizens of the United States and o the state of their residence. This claus which set up for the first time a nationa definition of citizenship, was followed b a statement that no state could abridg the rights of citizens of the United State or deprive any person of life, liberty, o property without due process of law o deny to any person within its jurisdictio the equal protection of the laws. In th light of later judicial developments, th provision was the most important part o the amendment; its meaning and inten would later become matters of disput Undoubtedly the framers intended t guarantee to Negroes the rights of citizen ship. They may also have intended to e tend the restrictions of the Bill of Right and particularly of the Fifth Amendmen which applied only to Congress, to th states. A few men on the committe may have foreseen that the word "person could mean a "legal person"—a corpora tion—and that the amendment could b utilized, as it would be before the turn o the century, to protect business organiza tions from state regulation.

Section 2 provided that if a state denie the suffrage to any of its adult male in habitants, its representation in the Hous of Representatives and the Electora College should suffer a proportionate r duction. This clause was intended to be a corrective to the curious effect of emancipation upon the basis of representation. By the "three-fifths compromise" of the Constitution, five slaves were counted as equal to three whites in determining a state's representation; now there were no slaves, and with representation based on total population every Southern state stood to increase its influence in the national government. Section 3 disqualified from any national state office all persons

fourths of the states and was defeated—but only temporarily. When the time was more propitious, the Radicals would bring it up again. Meanwhile, its rejection by the South strengthened the Radical cause. To many people in the North, the amendment had seemed to be a reasonable and moderate proposal.

Public acceptance of the Radical program was strikingly manifested in the elections of 1866. The voters returned to Congress an overwhelming majority of

---

THADDEUS STEVENS ON RECONSTRUCTION

Stevens of Pennsylvania was the Radical Republican leader in the House. Bitterly frank in speech, he announced his purposes in Reconstruction in a speech delivered in 1865: "The whole fabric of southern society *must* be changed and never can it be done if this opportunity is lost. Without this, this Government can never be, as it never has been, a true republic. Heretofore, it had more the features of aristocracy than of democracy.—The Southern States have been despotisms, not governments of the people. It is impossible that any practical equality of rights can exist where a few thousand men monopolize the whole landed property. The larger the number of small proprietors the more safe and stable the government. If the South is ever to be made a safe republic let her lands be cultivated by the toil of the owners or the free labor of intelligent citizens. This must be done though it drive her nobility into exile. If they go, all the better."

---

who had previously taken an oath to support the Constitution and later had aided the Confederacy until Congress by a two-thirds vote of each house should remove their disability.

The Southern legislatures knew that if they ratified the amendment their states would be readmitted and Reconstruction probably would be ended. But they could not bring themselves to approve the measure because of Section 3, which put a stigma on their late leaders. Only Tennessee, of the former Confederate states, ratified the amendment, winning readmittance as a reward; the other ten, joined by Kentucky and Delaware, voted it down. The amendment thus failed to receive the required approval of three

Republicans, most of them of the Radical variety. In the Senate the line-up of the parties was 42 Republicans to 11 Democrats; in the House, 143 Republicans to 49 Democrats. Now the Radicals could enact any kind of Reconstruction plan they desired. Confidently they looked forward to the struggle with Johnson that would ensue when Congress assembled in December, 1866—and to their final victory over the President.

Moving rapidly, the Radicals formulated their third and final plan of Reconstruction in three bills that passed Congress in the early months of 1867. All three were vetoed by Johnson and repassed. As these bills, which for convenient classification may be termed the

CHARLES SUMNER. The Massachusetts Senator, sometimes called "the scholar in politics," was one of the most idealistic Republican leaders in the postwar period. One of the most dogmatic and uncompromising of all politicians, he was especially noted as an early and insistent advocate of Negro suffrage. He argued that the late Confederate states had committed political suicide by seceding and were subject to whatever form of government the national government wished to impose. (PHOTO BY U.S. ARMY SIGNAL CORPS)

Reconstruction Acts of 1867, were really parts of one piece, their provisions may be studied as a unit. The final Radical plan was based squarely on the principle that the seceded states had lost their political identity. The Lincoln-Johnson governments were declared to have no legal standing, and the ten seceded states (Tennessee was now out of the Reconstruction process) were combined into five military districts. In charge of each district was a military commander, supported by troops, who was to prepare his provinces for readmission as states. To this end, he was to have made a registra-

tion of voters, which was to include all adult Negro males and white males who were not disqualified for participation in rebellion. The whites who were excluded were those coming under the disability of the Fourteenth Amendment; but each voter had to swear a complicated loyalty oath, and the registrars were empowered to reject white men on suspicion they were not acting in good faith. After the registration was completed in each province, the commanding general was to call on the voters to elect a convention to prepare a new state constitution that had to provide for Negro suffrage. If this document was ratified by the voters, elections for a state government could be held. Finally, if Congress approved the constitution, if the state legislature ratified the Fourteenth Amendment, and if the amendment was adopted by the required number of states and became a part of the Constitution—then the state was to be restored to the Union.

In imposing Negro suffrage upon the former Confederate states, the Radicals had laid themselves open to an inevitable question from the more idealistic elements among the Republicans. If it was right for Negroes to vote in the seceded states, asked the idealists, was it not equally right that they should have the privilege everywhere in the nation? The Radicals had set in motion one of those great historical changes that once started could not be recalled. The movement for national Negro suffrage became too strong to resist. Nor did the Radicals wish to resist it. It suited their strategy to enshrine Negro suffrage, the basis of Republican strength in the South, in the Constitution, where it would be beyond the reach of repeal. Accordingly, the Radicals prepared the Fifteenth Amendment, which forbade states to deny the suffrage to any citizen because of race or color. This measure, going into effect in 1870, was the last perfecting touch to the final Radical plan.

The remorseless manner in which the Radicals drove through their program indicated a revolutionary spirit that would stop at nothing to attain its ends. And the Radicals thought of themselves as architects of a revolution. They were prepared, if necessary, to curb the power of the other branches of the government and to establish a kind of congressional dictatorship.

Their resentment was directed principally at the Presidency, because that office was held by an enemy. In 1867 they put through Congress the Tenure of Office Act, which forbade the President to remove civil officials, including members of his cabinet, without the consent of the Senate. The chief purpose of the measure was to prevent Johnson from discharging Secretary of War Edwin M. Stanton, who was cooperating with the Radicals. Johnson believed the act to be unconstitutional, and he decided to deliberately violate it in order to secure a court test case. He suspended Stanton and named General Ulysses S. Grant, commanding general of the army, as his successor. But when the Senate refused to concur in the suspension, Grant relinquished the office to Stanton, thus foiling Johnson's plan to get a test case. The President then dismissed Stanton, but the Secretary, pointing to the action of the Senate, refused to give up the office.

Johnson's action delighted the Radicals. They had long hoped to bring impeachment charges against him, and for months they had vainly searched for evidence that he had committed crimes and misdemeanors in office, the only legal grounds for removal by impeachment. Hastily the Radical machine in the House framed and presented to the Senate eleven charges against Johnson. The first nine accusations dealt with the President's violation of the Tenure of Office Act; the tenth and eleventh charged Johnson with making speeches calculated to bring Congress into disrespect and of impeding the enforcement of the various Reconstruction acts. In the trial before the Senate, which lasted from March 25 to May 26, 1868, Johnson's lawyers emphasized that he was justified in technically violating the Tenure of Office Act. The House managers of the impeachment, while giving some attention to the removal of Stanton, harped on the theme that Johnson had opposed the will of the majority in Congress, implying that in so doing he had been guilty of crimes and misdemeanors. Terrific pressure was brought upon all the Republican Senators to vote for conviction, but seven Republicans joined the Democrats to support acquittal. On three of the charges the vote fell one short of the two-thirds majority required for removal of the President. Thereupon the Radicals called off the proceedings.

The Southern States, 1867–77

By 1868 six of the former Confederate states—Arkansas, North Carolina, South Carolina, Louisiana, Alabama, and Florida—had complied with the process of restoration outlined in the Reconstruction Acts and were readmitted to the Union; delaying tactics by the whites held up the return of Mississippi, Virginia, Georgia, and Texas until 1870. In all ten states, the Republicans constituted a majority and controlled the machinery of government. The Republican party in each Southern state rested on a basis of Negro voters who gratefully supported the party that had given them the suffrage and who were organized by white leaders: Northerners who had come South, the "carpetbaggers"; and Southern planters and businessmen, the "scalawags."

With the passage of the Reconstruction Acts of 1867, Negro suffrage and political influence became a reality. The common whites continued to oppose enlarged rights for the freedmen. But the upper-income whites, many of whom were former large slaveholders and were accustomed to dealing with Negroes, attempted at first to cooperate with the new voters and to direct their political action along lines favorable to the white minority.

All attempts of the rich whites to dominate the Negro vote failed, and finally the promoters joined the general white opposition to Radical Reconstruction. The

sired to reduce state services and keep taxes down to a minimum.

The financial and social record of the Reconstruction governments is a many sided story. As many of the leaders in the conventions that framed the new state constitutions were Northerners, they put into those documents some of the most advanced provisions in the organic char

THE RECONSTRUCTION PROCESS

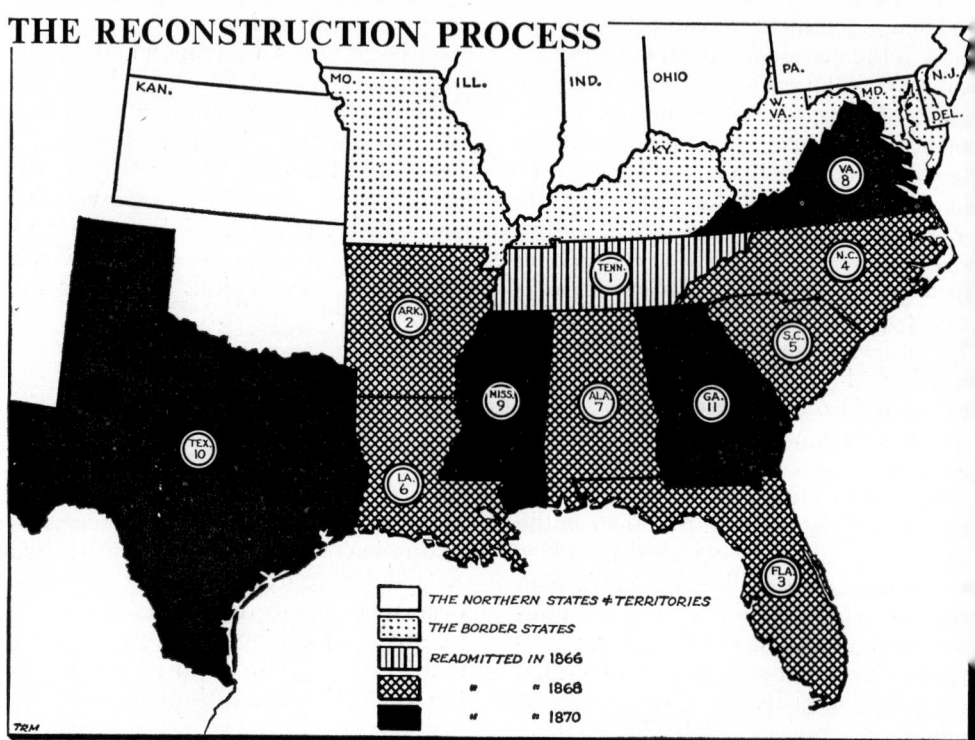

THE NORTHERN STATES + TERRITORIES
THE BORDER STATES
READMITTED IN 1866
"   "   1868
"   "   1870

attempts failed for several reasons: the reluctance of the whites, no matter how far they went in other directions, to concede social equality, and the competing leadership of the carpetbaggers who were always ready to outbid the scalawags. But fundamentally these experiments in white-colored collaboration collapsed because the contrasting parties had differing economic aspirations. The Negroes, being poor people, wanted a program of social services financed by the state, which meant high taxes. The Southern whites, representing a propertied minority, de-

ters of the most progressive Northern states: provisions embodying the latest revisions in local government, judicial organization, public finance, and poor relief. These changes had the effect of modernizing Southern state government, of placing it in step with governmental trends in the rest of the country, but some of the provisions, which looked excellent on paper, were not suited to the peculiar environment of the rural South.

The financial program of the Republican governments was a compound of blatant corruption and well-designed, if sometimes impractical, social legislation. The corruption and extravagance are familiar aspects of the Reconstruction story. State budgets expanded to hitherto unknown totals, and state debts soared to previously undreamed-of heights. In South Carolina, for example, the public debt increased from $7 million to $29 million in eight years.

In large measure, the corruption in the South was a phase of a national phenomenon, with the same social force—an expanding capitalism eager to secure quick results—acting as the corrupting agent. Included in the spending programs of the Reconstruction governments were subsidies for railroads and other internal improvements, some of which materialized and some of which did not—because the promoters and the politicians pocketed the subsidies. That much of the alleged corruption was a product of deep forces in contemporary society is demonstrated by the continuance of peculation in state government after Republican rule was overthrown.

The swollen state expenditures of the Reconstruction years seem huge only in comparison with the niggardly budgets of the conservative governments of the pre-war era; they do not appear large when measured against the sums appropriated by later legislatures. A clearer understanding of Reconstruction emerges if one remembers that the Southern state governments represented poor people, the Negroes, and that these people had a concept, albeit a vague one, of what today would be called the welfare state. They demanded public education, public-works programs, poor relief, and other services that cost money. By the side of the thieving and the foolish spending there should be set some positive and permanent accomplishments, particularly in education. One example is offered by South Carolina, which in 1860 had only 20,000 children in public scools; by 1873 some 50,000 white and 70,000 Negro students were enrolled in the school system.

The period of Republican control in the South varied from state to state. In some states it was overthrown by the whites almost before it began; in others it endured for years. The dates of Democratic (or Conservative) recovery of power in each state are as follows: Virginia, North Carolina, Georgia (1870); Texas (1873); Alabama, Arkansas (1874); Mississippi (1875); Louisiana, South Carolina, Florida (1877).

Republican power in the South rested upon three bases: the Negro vote, Republican control of the national government and particularly of the Presidency, and the presence of federal troops in the South. Should any of these be shattered or weakened, the structure of Republican rule would topple. Between 1867 and 1877 the Republicans controlled Congress for the greater part of the period, and between 1869 and 1877 a Republican President sat in the White House. For a time, whenever in a Southern state the results of an election were disputed by Republicans and Democrats, or whenever Southern whites threatened to oust the Republicans by force, the national administration intervened to save the local Republicans. The military commander in the state concerned would be directed to install the Republican governor and legislature in office or to prevent the whites from driving them out of office. Without this support from Washington, Republican dominance in the South would have been destroyed long before it was. As the 1870's wore on, however, a rising conservative opinion in the North criticized the government for deciding elections with troops, and Republican leaders became increasingly aware that the propped-up reconstructed governments of the South were becoming a political liability.

In the states where the whites constituted a majority—the Upper South states —overthrow of Republican control was a relatively simple matter. The whites had only to organize and win the elections

THE KU KLUX KLAN: A SOUTHERN VIEW. This Klan broadside depicts the organization as most Southerners saw it. The figure with the flag and sword epitomizes white culture and has over-thrown the Negro enemy. Note the incendiary torch in the hand of the Negro and the broken chains symbolizing his former slave status. (RUTH-ERFORD B. HAYES LIBRARY)

Their success was facilitated by the early restoration of the suffrage to those whites who had been deprived of it by national or state action. Presidential and congressional pardons returned the privilege to numerous individuals, and in 1872 Congress, responding to public demands to forgive the penalties of the war, enacted the Amnesty Act, which restored political rights to 150,000 ex-Confederates and left only 500 excluded from political life.

In other states, where the Negroes were in the majority or the population difference between the races was small, the whites resorted to intimidation and violence. Frankly terroristic were the secret societies that appeared in many parts of the South—the Ku Klux Klan, the Knights of the White Camellia, and others—which attempted to frighten or physically prevent Negroes from voting. Although the societies were effective, their influence has been exaggerated by writers intrigued by their romantic hooded and robed apparel and their elaborate ritual. The national government moved quickly to stamp out these societies, Congress passing two Force Acts (1870–1) and the Ku Klux Klan Act (1871) which authorized the President to use military force and martial law in areas where the orders were active. Finally, the leaders of the organizations, discovering that individual members were taking advantage of the secrecy arrangements to commit private crimes, ordered them disbanded.

More potent than the secret orders were the open semimilitary organizations that operated under such names as Rifle clubs, Red Shirts, and White Leagues. The first such society was founded in Mississippi, whence the idea spread to other states, and the procedure employed by the clubs was called the Mississippi Plan. Briefly stated, the plan called for the whites in each community to organize and arm, and to be prepared, if necessary, to resort to force to win elections. But the heart of the scheme was in the phrase "drawing the color line." By one method or another, legal or illegal, every white man was to be forced to join the Democratic party or leave the community. By similar methods, every Negro male was to be excluded from political action; in a few states he was permitted to vote—if he voted Democratic.

Perhaps an even stronger influence than the techniques practiced by the armed bands was the simple and unromantic weapon of economic pressure. The war had freed the Negro, but he was still a laborer—a hired worker or a tenant—dependent upon the whites for his livelihood. The whites readily discovered that this dependence placed the Negro in their power. Planters refused to rent land to

THE KU KLUX KLAN: A NORTHERN VIEW. This drawing in a Northern Illustrated paper shows a group of Klansmen about to murder a carpetbagger whom they have abducted. (LIBRARY OF CONGRESS)

Republican Negroes, storekeepers refused to extend them credit, employers refused to give them work. Economic pressure was a force which the Negro could not fight. If the Radicals, in bringing the Negro to political power, had accomplished a revolution, it was a superficial one. They failed to provide the Negro with economic power, as they might have done by giving him possession of confiscated land. Hence, his political rights had no lasting basis.

White Supremacy

By 1876 the whites had recovered control in every Southern state except Louisiana, South Carolina, and Florida. But in each "redeemed state" a Republican party still existed; and as long as the Republicans controlled the national government and federal troops remained in the South, Reconstruction was still a reality. The three remaining states might stay under Republican rule, white victory in the others might be undone. In 1876 there occurred the famous disputed presidential election (to be described in the next chapter), in which both the Republicans and the Democrats claimed to have elected their candidate. After months of tense suspense, the issue was decided by a complicated compromise which allowed the Republicans to retain the Presidency. One result of the election was that the new chief executive, Rutherford B. Hayes, withdrew federal troops from the South in 1877. Immediately the Republican governments in Louisiana, South Carolina, and Florida fell, and white supremacy was restored in the ten states that the Radicals just a few years before had reduced to the status of conquered provinces.

The withdrawal of the troops was a symbol that the national government was giving up its attempt to control Southern politics and to determine the place of the Negro in Southern society. The surrender, it is to be noted, was made by the Republicans. They could yield with good grace because after 1877 they had no

tions. That is, railroads, hotels, theaters and the like could legally practice segregation. Eventually the Court validated state legislation which discriminated against Negroes. In *Plessy* v. *Ferguson* (1896), a case involving a law that required separate seating arrangements for the races on railroads, the Court held that separate accommodations did not deprive the Negro of equal rights if the accommodations were equal. And in *Cumming* v *County Board of Education* (1899) the

---

A CARPETBAG ANALYSIS OF RECONSTRUCTION

Albion W. Tourgee was an Ohio-born carpetbagger who became prominent in Reconstruction politics in North Carolina. He wrote A *Fool's Errand* (1879), probably the first novel dealing with Reconstruction. In the following passage the "Fool," the central character and a carpetbagger (undoubtedly expressing Tourgee's own ideas), explains why he thinks Reconstruction collapsed. It reveals the sense of failure and frustration felt by men like Tourgee after 1877: "We tried to superimpose the civilization, the idea of the North, upon the South at a moment's warning. We presumed, that, by the suppression of rebellion, the Southern white man had become identical with the Caucasian of the North in thought and sentiment; and that the slave, by emancipation, had become a saint and a Solomon at once. So we tried to build up communities there which should be identical in thought, sentiment, growth, and development, with those of the North. It was A Fool's Errand."

---

particular need for the support of the reconstructed South. The economic legislation of the war and postwar years was safe from repeal; industry was securely entrenched in the national economy; and Republican dominance could be maintained without Southern votes.

Another symbol of retreat was furnished by the Supreme Court, which in a series of decisions emasculated the Fourteenth and Fifteenth amendments of much of their significance. In the Civil Rights Cases (1883) the Court took the position that the Fourteenth Amendment prohibited states from discriminating against people on account of color but did not restrict private individuals or organiza-

Court held that laws establishing separate schools for whites and Negroes were valid if the facilities were equal for both.

The men who came to power in the South after 1877 were not in the old agrarian, planter tradition. Known as Bourbons or Redeemers, they were industrialists or would-be industrialists. They preached the industrialization of the South through the importation of Northern capital, a policy of low taxes to attract business, and a political alliance with the Northeast instead of with the South's traditional ally, the West. Controlling state governments through the medium of the Democratic party, which as a result of Reconstruction was the only party in the section, they practiced a program marked by economy in government, reduced taxes, and few social services. They did not attempt to abolish Negro suffrage but instead used the Negro vote, as men of their class had tried to use it during Reconstruction, to maintain their power. Negroes continued to vote after the return of white supremacy, but in reduced numbers. In some states they were prevented from voting by an implied threat of force; in others, their influence was nullified by tricky devices—tissue ballots and a complicated arrangement of ballot boxes—that disqualified their votes. But in many areas the colored vote was a purchased and directed vote, paid for by the Bourbons and used by them to beat down attempts of the farmers to take over control of the Democratic party.

Not until the 1890's did the Southern states pass laws to disfranchise the Negroes, and the impetus for the attempt when it came was furnished by the white farmers. The farmers demanded disfranchisement because they were opposed for racial reasons to Negro voting and because they objected to the Negro vote being employed against them. The rich whites acquiesced, partly out of a desire to placate the white masses and partly because in the agrarian unrest that characterized the nineties the farmers in some states had sought to vote the Negroes on their side. The threat of competition for the Negro vote frightened all whites, and there was a general feeling that the time had come to close ranks if white supremacy was to be maintained.

In devising laws to disfranchise the Negroes, the Southern states had to take care to evade the intent of the Fifteenth Amendment. That measure did not confer suffrage upon the Negroes, but merely prohibited states from denying it because of color. The Southern problem, then, was to exclude Negroes from the franchise without seeming to base the exclusion on race. Two devices were widely employed before 1900. One was the poll tax or some

form of property qualification. The other was the literacy and understanding test, which required a voter to demonstrate an ability to read and to interpret the Constitution. The reasoning behind the latter law was that local registrars could administer an impossible reading test to Negroes or rule that their interpretation of the Constitution was inadequate. Both of these devices could be used, and were used, to deny the franchise to poor white men, who protested against tests being applied to them. So, many states passed so-called "grandfather laws," which permitted men who could not meet the literacy and property qualifications to be admitted to the suffrage if their ancestors had voted before 1867 or some date before Reconstruction began.

The Supreme Court proved as compliant in ruling on the disfranchising laws as it was in dealing with the civil rights cases. Although the Court eventually voided the grandfather laws, it validated the literacy tests (*Williams* v. *Mississippi*, 1898), and manifested a general willingness to let the Southern states define suffrage standards—provided the evasions of the Fifteenth Amendment were not too glaring. As the turn of the century approached, the South seemed to have won a complete victory over the outside influences that had sought to disturb its way of life, and Reconstruction seemed to the white South like a bad dream receding in the past. But the deep and turbulent forces generated in the years between 1865 and 1877 were only temporarily exhausted. They would appear again in American life as Americans continued to search for solutions to all the problems created by the Civil War and its troubled aftermath.

Economic Changes

With relative rapidity, the South recovered from the effects of war and restored its economic life. Since it was an agricultural society, its productive powers rested on the basis of land, and the land had survived the war. The chief problem was to get the plantations and farms under cultivation again. Work began at once (crops were made in 1865), and progress was steady. By 1879 the cotton crop exceeded that of 1860, part of the increase resulting from the opening of new growing areas west of the Mississippi, in Texas and Arkansas.

The rehabilitation of the South's agrarian economy was accomplished with relatively few changes in the nature of Southern agriculture. There was something of a shift in the distribution of land ownership, in the direction of an increase in the number of small holders. In the economic travail following the war, many planters were unable to hold on to their property and were forced to offer their land for sale at low prices. In many cases the purchasers were white yeomen. According to the census, the number of farms in Mississippi increased from 43,-000 in 1860 to 68,000 by 1870, in South Carolina from 33,000 to 52,000, in Louisiana from 17,000 to 28,000. Actually, these figures are somewhat deceptive, because some of the farms listed were under 10 or 20 acres in area and were really units in a plantation, worked by tenants who were sometimes white but usually colored. The plantation system was modified, but it did not disappear. In the ownership of the system, however, an important change took place. The old planter (or the old type of planter who lived on the plantation) tended to disappear. More and more, the large land units were owned and administered by merchants, banks, corporations—or by planters who lived in towns or cities where they could devote themselves to business as well as agricultural pursuits.

During the Reconstruction period, perhaps a third or more of the farmers in the South were tenants; by 1900 the figure had increased to 70 per cent. Several factors accounted for the trend toward tenancy. The Negroes, when they became freedmen, had, of course, no property. They were forced, as a simple matter of survival, to become laborers or tenants and most of them were unable to accumulate enough resources to rise above this status. As late as 1890 there were only 121,000 Negro landowners in the South. Probably the strongest influence promoting tenancy among both races was the lack of an adequate credit system, with a resulting scarcity of money. The National Bank System was slow to establish itself in the Southern states, and state banks were slow to recover from the effects of the war. Landlords did not have enough cash to hire laborers to work their land and laborers could not secure loans to buy land or even raise sufficient currency to rent land on a cash basis.

Out of this situation developed an economic arrangement peculiar to the South, the share-crop and crop-lien system, in which produce and labor took the place of money. There were share tenants and sharecroppers, and there was a difference between the two groups. The share tenants, most of whom were whites, worked strips of land on a large unit, and paid as rent to the landlord one fourth to one third of their crop; they provided their own tools, seed, stock, and other supplies. The sharecroppers, most of whom were Negroes, provided nothing but their own labor. For the average cropper, the landlord would furnish all the above materials, and a horse or mule and a house as well. In addition, until the crop was harvested, he would arrange credit facilities for the cropper and his family at a local country store owned by himself or a merchant. The cropper, for his part, agreed to consign from one third to one half of his crop to the landlord. Moreover, the storekeeper, the source of credit, protected his interest by taking a mortgage or lien on the tenant's share of the crop. (As time passed, the landlord and the merchant tended to become one person, and the planter-storekeeper became a major figure in the Southern credit complex.)

The lien system was a necessary credit device in the postwar years; but when continued and expanded after that period, it had a hurtful influence upon Southern agriculture. The merchant or landlord pressed the cropper to produce a single money crop, cotton, to the neglect of diversified farming and scientific farming methods. More serious were the social results of the system. The typical share-cropper was an unlettered person who did not know how to handle his own money carefully and who did not understand the mechanics of credit. Frequently, after harvesting his crop, he found himself owing money to the storekeeper and hence forced to pledge his labor to the same source for another year. Not only did the lien system prevent tenants from rising to the owning class; it also operated to bind them to particular pieces of land, to create a state of peonage. The Negro sharecropper was not a slave, but he was not completely free.

The Reconstruction period witnessed a restoration of Southern industrial facilities damaged or destroyed during the war as well as some promising beginnings in new industrial activities. Most of the rehabilitation and expansion was financed with Southern capital, with capital that often was really "local," being subscribed by the people of a town who wanted to improve their community by locating a factory in it. The only Southern enter-prise that attracted Northern and European investors was the railroads. With outside aid, the war-weakened rail system was soon put in running order again, and by 1873 over 4,000 miles of new track had been constructed. Modest but noteworthy progress was recorded in tobacco manufacturing, in the lumber industry, and in iron making; in 1880 the South produced 212,000 tons of iron. The most substantial growth occurred in textiles, which had a prewar basis to build on. Southern leaders during Reconstruction preached the economic advantage of building cotton mills where the raw material was produced, and the Southern people took this logic to heart. Practically all the mills that began to appear in Southern towns were financed by local investors. By 1880 the South could boast of 161 textile factories housing 524,000 spindles and employing 16,000 workers. But the great industrial development of the South, the development that created the "New South," would not come until later. And even that forward economic surge would not greatly change the nature of Southern life, would not make the South very "new." As late as 1910 only 15 per cent of all the people in the region were connected with manufacturing. For many years the South would remain, as it was in the Reconstruction era, a rural and a traditional land.

BIBLIOGRAPHY

For an introduction to the issues of reconstruction history, see the articles by H. K. Beale in the *American Historical Review*, XLV (1940), F. B. Simkins in the *Journal of Southern History*, V (1939), and T. H. Williams in the same journal, vol. XII (1946).

An interpretation favorable to Democrats and Southern whites is given in W. A. Dunning, *Reconstruction, Political and Economic* (1907); W. L. Fleming, *The Sequel of Appomattox* (1919); C. G. Bowers, *The Tragic Era* (1929); G. F. Milton, *The Age of Hate* (1930); R. S. Henry, *The Story of Reconstruction* (1938); E. M. Coulter, *The South During Reconstruction* (1947); and Hodding Carter, *The Angry Scar* (1959). For the various states, there are separate studies, most of them written by students of Dunning. In a class by itself is F. B. Simkins and R. H. Woody, *South Carolina During Reconstruction* (1932).

A general account of the nation as a whole is Allan Nevins, *The Emergence of Modern America, 1865–1878* (1927). Special studies, many of them reinterpretations, include the following: H. K. Beale, *The Critical Year* (1930), on the elections of 1866; F. W. Klingberg, *The Southern Claims Commission* (1955); G. R. Bentley, *A History of the Freedmen's Bureau* (1955); J. B. James, *The Framing of the Fourteenth Amendment* (1956); and S. F. Horn, *The Invisible Empire* (1939), on the Ku Klux Klan. The postwar role of leading Southerners is discussed in W. B. Hesseltine, *Confederate Leaders in the New South* (1950), and N. K. Burger and J. K. Bettersworth, *South of Appomattox* (1959).

President Johnson is defended in R. W. Winston, *Andrew Johnson, Plebeian and Patriot* (1928); and L. P. Stryker, *Andrew Johnson: A Study in Courage* (1929). He is treated as a small-minded, vindictive man in E. L. McKitrick, *Andrew Johnson and Reconstruction* (1960). Quite different impressions of a leading Radical are given by the following two books: R. N. Current, *Old Thad Stevens: A Story of Ambition* (1942); and F. M. Brodie, *Thaddeus Stevens: Scourge of the South* (1959).

The role of the Negro is studied in W. E. B. DuBois, *Black Reconstruction* (1935); O. A. Singletary, *The Negro Mili-tia and Reconstruction* (1957); R. W. Logan, *The Negro in American Life and Thought* (1954); S. R. Spencer, Jr., *Booker T. Washington and the Negro's Place in American Life* (1955); Booker T. Washington, *Up from Slavery* (1901); V. L. Wharton, *The Negro in Mississippi, 1865–1900* (1947); G. B. Tindall, *South Carolina Negroes, 1877–1900* (1952); Paul Lewinson, *Race, Class, and Party* (1932); C. V. Woodward, *The Strange Career of Jim Crow* (1953; paperback ed., 1957); and R. F. Durden, *James Shepherd Pike: Republicanism and the American Negro, 1850–1882* (1957). Tensions in Southern society are discussed in Roger Shugg, *Origins of Class Struggle in Louisiana* (1939).

The emergence of the New South receives attention in P. A. Bruce, *The Rise of the New South* (1905); Holland Thompson, *The New South* (1919); and M. B. Hammond, *The Cotton Industry* (1897); but the standard work is C. V. Woodward, *Origins of the New South, 1877–1913* (1951). In *The Road to Reunion, 1865–1900* (1937), P. H. Buck traces the influences that tended to heal the psychological wounds of war.

22

THE POLITICS
OF COMPLACENCY

In the two decades after Appomattox the politicians and the parties reflected the mood and standards of the nation. Politics, like American life, was flamboyant, crudely virile, and slightly unreal. James Bryce, observing the American scene through sedate British eyes in the 1880's, could see no essential difference between the Republican and Democratic parties. "Tenets and policies, points of political doctrine and points of political practice, have all but vanished," he wrote. "All has been lost, except office or the hope of it."

Republicans and Democrats

Republicanism was almost a religion in the North. The Republican party, the Grand Old Party of Abraham Lincoln and the boys in blue, had saved the Union and freed the slaves. In election after election Republican campaigners recalled the war record of their own party and attacked the opposition as the party of treason and slavery. One stump speaker cried: "Every man that shot Union soldiers was a Democrat. Every man that starved Union prisoners . . . was a Democrat.

The man that assassinated Abraham Lincoln was a Democrat." This technique of reviving wartime emotions to win postwar elections came to be known, among the Democrats, as "waving the bloody shirt." Related to this was the practice, every four years (except in 1884), of nominating as the Republican presidential candidate an officer veteran of the Union army.

Flights of campaign oratory masked but thinly the economic composition and goals of the dominant party. Even more powerful in the party's councils than in the prewar era was the business faction, composed of manufacturers, bankers, investors, and government bondholders—more powerful because business was forging ahead of agriculture in the indices of national wealth and because industry was reaching out into every area and raising up champions in the West and South, which had been solidly agricultural. But still influential in the party was the farming wing, particularly because the farmers had more votes than businessmen. Other important elements of the party were the veterans of the Union armies, numbering perhaps a million and organized in potent pressure groups such as the Grand Army of the Republic, which found the Republicans cordial to the idea of soldier pensions, and the Negroes, the great majority of them Southern freedmen emancipated by Republican action, who cast a thankful and regular Republican vote of perhaps 450,000 (until disfranchised).

There were substantial reasons for the minority status of the Democrats. Their war record, or rather the version of that record pinned on them by their opponents, undoubtedly damaged their cause. Moreover, the defeat of the South in the war and the imposition of Reconstruction on that section tore from the Democrats for years one of their greatest areas of voting strength. Before 1860 the South had provided most of the party's national leadership. That leadership was shut off during Reconstruction, and the Southerners never recovered their influence.

In its economic composition the Democratic organization was, much as it had been in Jackson's time, a party of farmers and laborers—of small property holders. But it was a party without clear direction or goals, and here probably is the principal reason for its minority condition. The important Eastern wing, representing importing interests, was willing to accept the traditional Democratic low-tariff policy, but on other issues, and particularly on the question of a "sound" currency, it was as conservative as the Republicans. Any Democratic move to challenge the Republicans on economic issues was certain to scare off the Easterners. Even on the tariff, the Democrats failed to demonstrate unity or take a firm position. As industry moved into the West and South, islands of protection appeared in these once free-trade regions to divide a once cohesive public opinion. In many elections the Democrats, responding to local tariff pressures or bidding for business support, adopted an ambiguous tariff plank that hardly differed from that of their opponents, causing wags to quip

that the party of Jefferson and Jackson stood for "a protective tariff for revenue only." In short, the party failed to devise a program that distinguished it from the Republicans, failed to offer a set of issues to those groups who were alarmed by the rise of big business, failed, above all, to be a party of opposition. It was a "me too" party asking for votes on the grounds that it could do what the Republicans were doing—only better and with less corruption.

The voters did not think that they were avoiding issues or problems, and certainly the preponderant majority of the politicians had no sense of fighting sham battles. Most people did not believe there were any economic issues or problems of sufficient importance to merit political attention or governmental action. The economy was expanding and seemed soundly based, and the country recovered with relative rapidity from economic setbacks and depressions. In overwhelming numbers Americans accepted the principles of laissez faire and rejected the idea of government regulation as an invasion of individual liberty.

All this is not to say that there were no vital problems in American society. There were—the currency and tariff questions, farm prices and agrarian indebtedness, the rise of labor and its relations with capital, the emergence of big business and monopoly—but these issues largely developed under the surface until the 1890's when they erupted into politics with a violence that shook existing modes of thought and patterns of political behavior.

One reason for the absence of economic issues in national campaigns was the amorphous nature of the two major parties. Although the Republicans in a general sense represented the upper and middle income groups and the Democrats the average and lower groups, neither spoke for a precise economic interest. Both included people from all economic levels, and both embraced business and agrarian elements, conservatives and liberals, high and low tariff advocates, and hard and soft money supporters. If a party took a firm stand on an economic question, it was certain to alienate some of its followers, and the leaders preferred to ignore such distracting issues that did not seem too important anyway. When economic legislation was considered in Congress, the votes usually followed sectional rather than party lines; Western Republicans and Southern Democrats, for example, were likely to unite behind a measure of benefit to the agricultural interests.

Although the Republicans usually dominated the Presidency, they did not always control Congress. The Democrats, with the Solid South behind them and with the support of highly organized machines in Northern cities and states, sometimes managed to secure a majority in one or both houses of the legislative branch and thereby block Republican programs. When a Democrat sat in the White House, the converse was often true: the Republicans ruled at least one house and voted down Democratic measures. The failure of either party to control consistently all branches of the government is, of course, another reason for the absence of firm issues and the relative paucity of positive legislation.

Of the three branches of government, Congress was predominant. Retaining most of the powers and prerogatives it had seized in the struggle with Andrew Johnson, it easily overshadowed the Presidency and the judiciary. Nor did it encounter any serious challenge from its traditional rival, the executive arm. None of the Presidents elected between 1868 and 1888, with the possible exception of Grover Cleveland, was a strong and colorful leader. Rarely if ever in our history has politics been as completely professional as it was in these years. In part, this was the product of the general conformity of opinion in the country and the consequent absence of real issues between the parties. The politicians were thus able

to practice their trade apart from the requirements of society, as it were, and to conduct it as a sort of game that had little impact upon society. Another reason for the professionalization of politics was the ever-swelling patronage at the disposal of the parties. With the national, state, and city governments increasing their civil personnel, there were more jobs available for the party that could gain power, and hence more incentive to win.

In cities and states powerful machines dominated by a single boss arose to control government. Matt Quay in Pennsylvania and Roscoe Conkling and Tom Platt in New York were outstanding examples of the boss type. Of Platt one observer said: ". . . Mr. Platt ruled the state; for nigh upon twenty years he ruled it. It was not the governor; it was not the legislature; it was not any elected officers; it was Mr. Platt. And the capital was not here [Albany]; it was at 49 Broadway; with Mr. Platt and his lieutenants." Tall, handsome, flamboyant Roscoe Conkling ruled the Republican party in New York and swayed its councils in the United States Senate. To him politics was a game for professionals and not for amateur "carpet knights," and it was a rough game: "Parties are not built by deportment, or by ladies magazines, or gush."

When Benjamin Harrison won the Presidency in 1888, he ascribed his victory to Providence. Matt Quay knew better. "Providence hadn't a damn thing to do with it," he announced, and wondered if the candidate knew how many men had approached the gates of the penitentiary to make him President. Harrison soon found out the facts of political life. "When I came into power," he said later, "I found that the party managers had taken it all to themselves. I could not name my own Cabinet. They had sold out every place to pay the election expenses." The machines sustained their position by various techniques: making alliances with business interests and securing campaign contributions and other subsidies, assessing officeholders a share of their salaries, and employing gangs of vote "repeaters" or "floaters" or using other fraudulent methods to carry elections.

Election of 1868 and U. S. Grant

There were no political polls in 1868, but any reasonably competent observer could have predicted that the Republicans would nominate the lustrous Northern war hero, General Ulysses S. Grant. In fact, at the end of the war both parties had angled to make Grant their candidate in 1868, and the general could have had whichever nomination he desired. Although he had no rigid political principles, he, like other professional soldiers, naïvely believed that Congress, more than any other branch of the government, represented the supreme popular will; and as he watched the Congressional Radicals triumph over President Johnson, he concluded that the Radical Reconstruction policy expressed the real wishes of the people. When the Radical leaders approached him with offers of the Republican nomination, Grant, who had developed understandable presidential ambitions, was highly receptive. His availability put every other aspirant out of the running.

The Republicans placed candidate Grant on an ambiguous platform. They endorsed Radical Reconstruction and Negro suffrage for the south, but, demonstrating that the Republican viewpoint of Reconstruction was not completely idealistic, declared that in the loyal North the question of Negro voting should be determined by each state. Reflecting the influence of business, the platform called for the payment of the national debt in "the spirit of the laws" under which it had been contracted, which meant in gold instead of greenbacks; on the tariff issue, the platform was discreetly silent. Obviously, the Republicans meant to make Reconstruction the big issue while subordinating economic questions that might divide the party.

Unwisely the Democrats decided to meet the Republican challenge. Their platform also emphasized Reconstruction, denouncing in extravagant terms the Radical program and demanding restoration of home rule in the South. Thus the Democrats chose to fight the campaign on an issue that was related to the war and its emotions and that enabled their opponents to associate them with rebellion. They did, however, attempt to inject a new question of an economic nature into the contest. In 1868 approximately $356 million of the Civil War greenbacks were in circulation, and Middle Western Democrats, led by George Pendleton of Ohio, wanted to keep the paper currency and use it when legally possible to pay off the national debt. Behind this so-called "Ohio idea" was the larger question of retaining the greenbacks as a permanent part of the money supply, a proposal that appealed to the debtor classes of the agrarian regions and which shortly would become a flaming issue in politics. The Westerners succeeded in writing the Ohio idea into the platform, but in selecting a candidate the party passed over men like Pendleton and Andrew Johnson, who would have supported it, and nominated Horatio Seymour of New York, a gold or "sound money" man, who repudiated the currency plank.

After a bitter campaign revolving around Reconstruction and Seymour's war record as governor of New York (he was accused of being a Peace Democrat), Grant carried twenty-six states with an electoral vote of 214, and Seymour took eight (only three, New York, New Jersey, and Oregon, in the North) with 80 electoral votes. The popular vote belied the apparent crushing Republican triumph. Grant had 3,012,000 votes to Seymour's 2,703,000, or a majority of only 310,000.

Ulysses S. Grant was the second professional soldier to be elected to the Presidency (Zachary Taylor having been the first), and the last to be chosen until Dwight D. Eisenhower was selected in

1952. After graduating from West Point with no particular distinction, Grant entered the regular army, from which after years of service he resigned under something of a cloud. In civilian life he undertook several dismal ventures that barely yielded him a living. His career before 1861 could be characterized as a failure. Then came the Civil War, and Grant found at last the one setting, the one vocation for which he was supremely equipped —war.

The people looked trustingly to the great soldier to guide the nation through the troubled postwar years. Grant assumed the executive office in a terribly difficult period in our history and under conditions that would have taxed the abilities of a master of statecraft. Only a superb politician with profound spiritual qualities— some rare leader like Lincoln—could have held the Presidency and escaped with an undamaged reputation. Grant never had a chance.

His political naïvete was displayed in many of his appointments. For the important office of Secretary of State he chose an old friend, the former Illinois Congressman Elihu B. Washburne, who by agreement was to hold the position only a week before resigning to become minister to France; the only purpose of this strange arrangement was to enable Washburne to brag in Paris that he had headed the foreign office. After offering the appointment to another individual who declined it on the grounds of expense, Grant named Hamilton Fish of New York, who turned out to be an extremely able secretary. Like other Americans of the Gilded Age, Grant inordinately admired millionaires, and he appointed A. T. Stewart, a wealthy merchant, Secretary of the Treasury. Stewart, however, was ineligible because of a law barring from the office any person in "trade or commerce."

In choosing his official family, Grant proceeded on the basis that he was creating a military staff. He sent several appointments to the Senate for confirmation without asking the recipients if they would serve; they first heard the news in the papers. Fish, who had been out of politics for twenty years, wired Grant that he could not accept, but his name was already being acted on in the Senate and he was persuaded to let it go through. During his two administrations, Grant named in all twenty-five men to the cabinet. Most of his later appointments went to men who were, at the best, average, and some to individuals who were incompetent or corrupt, or both. Increasingly, in dispensing cabinet and executive patronage, Grant came to rely on the machine leaders in the party, on the men and factions most ardently devoted to the spoils system.

The General in the White House

During Grant's eight years in the Presidency, a number of important issues emerged in domestic politics, most of which dealt with in his first administration, and a series of scandals rocked the government, most of which occurred in his second term. For convenience, the domestic problems may be listed under three headings: (1) economic issues, (2) reconstruction, and (3) civil service.

Foremost among the economic problems were the payment of the interest and principal of the national debt and the permanent place of the greenbacks in the national currency. On the first, supporters of the Ohio idea, representing debtor interests, argued that the bonds had been purchased in greenbacks of depreciated value and should, unless stipulated otherwise by law, be redeemed in the same currency. The President favored payment in gold, and the Republican Congress moved speedily to promise redemption in "coin or its equivalent" and to enact a refunding act providing for long-term refinancing of the debt (1869–70).

Behind the skirmish over payment of the bonds was the more fundamental question of the status of the greenbacks. Approximately $450 million of these notes had been issued during the Civil War, and $400 million of them were still in circulation at the end of the conflict. In the Johnson administration, Congress had authorized the Treasury to reduce their quantity, but the protests of farmers and some business groups had halted further action. When Grant entered the White House, the greenback circulation was some $356 million, and the gold value of a greenback dollar was 73¢.

Before Congress could make any disposition of the problem, the Supreme Court intervened with a decision concerning the legality of the greenbacks as legal tender. In *Hepburn* v. *Griswold* (1870) Chief Justice Salmon P. Chase, who had been appointed by Lincoln in 1864, speaking for a divided four-to-three Court, declared that greenbacks were not legal tender for debts contracted prior to their issuance. This pronouncement angered the agrarian areas and alarmed those business interests who had incurred obligations before the war that would now have to be retired in a more valuable dollar. Obviously the decision, coming before the status of the greenbacks had been settled, threatened to confuse wide areas of the economic community, and demands for a reversal were insistent. It so happened that Congress was about to increase the number of justices (previously fixed at seven to prevent Johnson from making any appointments) to nine, and Grant appointed two men who were known to oppose the decision. It was charged that he had ascertained their opinions and was in effect packing the Court, but no proof of this exists. The government did, however, move immediately for a rehearing, and in *Knox* v. *Lee* (1871) the Court by a five-to-four vote reversed the previous decision.

With the legality of greenbacks established, the Treasury, as a relief measure in the panic of 1873, increased the amount in circulation. For the same reason Congress, in the following year, voted to raise the total to $400 million. Grant, respond-

ing to pressures from the financial interests, vetoed the measure. In 1875 the Republican Congress enacted the Resumption Act, providing that after January 1, 1879, the government would exchange gold dollars for greenbacks and directing the government to acquire a gold reserve for redemption purposes. The law had its intended result: with the specie value of greenbacks assured, they were equal in worth to gold. The interests of the creditor classes were adequately protected, but at the same time, the debtor groups could take some comfort in the retention of the greenbacks (subsequently, in 1878, Congress decided that some $346 million of greenbacks should form a permanent part of the money supply). Not all the agrarian-debtor groups accepted resumption as a satisfactory conclusion. Some dissident elements created the National Greenback party in 1875, which was active in the next three presidential elections. It failed, however, to attract wide support. After 1879 those interests favoring inflation would turn to forms of currency other than paper.

During Grant's administrations the final radical plan of Reconstruction was applied with full vigor to the South, ran its course, and by the time Grant left the White House had been largely undone by Southern opposition. Before becoming President, Grant had manifested a vaguely conservative position on Reconstruction, but after assuming office he gave general support to the Radical program.

Civil service was not such a popular issue as the greenbacks or the tariff, but it enlisted the support of some Republican leaders and most of the party's intellectual elite: politicians of the order of Jacob D. Cox, Carl Schurz, and Charles Sumner, who were better educated and more theoretical than most of their calling, and scholarly journalists like E. L. Godkin of the *Nation* and George William Curtis of *Harper's Weekly*. These men argued that with the government expanding its services and personnel it was necessary to base appointments on the fitness of applicants as determined by competitive examinations, a practice already employed in England. Although the civil-service reformers were a small group, they were exceedingly vocal, and they forced a hearing for their ideas. At Grant's request, Congress authorized in 1871 a Civil Service Commission to devise an appointments system based on merit. This agency, headed by Curtis, submitted a set of proposed rules that seemed to win Grant's approval. But actually the President was not greatly interested in civil service, and even if he had been he could not have persuaded his followers to accept a system that seemed to threaten the very basis of party organization. Congress neglected to renew the commission's appropriation, thereby ending its existence, and the reform upsurge temporarily lost its impetus.

Revolt of the Liberals

Midway through Grant's first administration, serious factional differences emerged in the Republican ranks, and by the election year of 1872 the rift had reached such formidable proportions that a substantial segment bolted the party. The bolters, who were opposed to Grant's renomination, called themselves Liberal Republicans, and proceeded to set up their own organization preparatory to naming candidates for the Presidency and Vice Presidency.

Behind this split was a set of diverse motives and discordant men. Many Liberals objected to Grant and the Republican leadership because of Reconstruction; they denounced the use of troops to uphold the carpetbag governments and contended the time had come to soften or even end the party's Southern policy. Others were disgusted by Grant's hesitant course on civil service and his association with the most ruthless machine politicians in the party. Some, for varying reasons, dissented

from the administration's high tariff or "sound" currency program. Here, where economic issues were concerned, was the greatest weakness of the Liberal movement: its lack of unity and coherence.

The confusion of the Liberals was cruelly revealed at their national convention. They were able to settle on a platform ratifying the legislative fabric of Reconstruction but calling for universal amnesty and the withdrawal of troops from the South; they approved civil service and resumption of specie payments on the greenbacks; they opposed further land grants to railroads. But when it came to the tariff, the convention split into irreconcilable camps, and finally compromised on a two-faced plank referring the issue to the people and Congress. This action augured ill for the Liberals' hopes of securing Democratic endorsement of their candidate and of evoking Southern support. They compounded their blunder in choosing a nominee. Passing over Charles Francis Adams and other able and available men, they named Horace Greeley, veteran editor and publisher of the New York *Tribune*.

Greeley over a course of thirty years had stated his position on practically every issue before the country. He had been a Whig and a Republican, a proponent of antislavery and a high tariff, an economic and political nationalist. Impulsive and erratic, he had crusaded for most of the fads that had at one time or another intrigued popular attention—spiritualism, vegetarianism, and others—and he cultivated an idiosyncratic dress and manner. With his record and personality, he was hardly the strongest candidate the Liberals could have put forward to attract the Democratic, Southern, and independent vote. The Democratic convention, seeing in his candidacy the only chance to unseat the Republicans, endorsed him with no great enthusiasm. Although his recent attacks on Radical Reconstruction appealed to the South, many Southerners, remembering Greeley's past, prepared to stay at

HORACE GREELEY. Founder of the New York *Tribune*, Greeley was perhaps the greatest American editor. Through his editorials and lectures he was known to millions of his countrymen. But many, including those who admired him, viewed him as a somewhat ridiculous figure. His odd appearance—throat-whiskers framing a pink face; white overcoat and socks—his peculiar mannerisms, his advocacy of queer causes gave him the reputation, fatal in politics, of being an eccentric. The object of cruel abuse in the campaign of 1872, he wondered whether he was running for the Presidency or the penitentiary. (NATIONAL ARCHIVES)

home on election day. The Republicans, with Grant as their standard-bearer and a platform justifying Reconstruction and calling for a high tariff, moved into the campaign with confidence.

To everybody's surprise, Greeley turned out to be a vigorous and hard-hitting campaigner. Breaking with precedent, he stumped the country advocating the Liberal cause. But the factors surrounding his candidacy made the odds against him impossible. In November Grant polled 286 electoral votes and 3,597,000 popular votes to Greeley's 62 and 2,834,000. The optimistic editor carried only two Southern and four border states. Three weeks later Greeley, apparently crushed by his defeat, died.

During the election of 1872 a political

scandal broke upon the country. Although the wrongdoing had occurred before Grant took office, it involved his party and the onus for it fell on his administration. This scandal originated with the Crédit Mobilier construction company that helped build the Union Pacific Railroad. In reality, the Crédit Mobilier was controlled by a few Union Pacific stockholders who awarded huge and fraudulent contracts to the construction company, thus milking the Union Pacific, a company of which they owned a minor share, of money which in part came from government subsidies. To avert a congressional inquiry into the deal, the directors, using Oakes Ames, a Massachusetts Representative, as their agent, sold at a discount (in effect gave) Crédit Mobilier stock to key members of Congress. A congressional investigation was held, and it revealed that some high-placed Republicans, including Schuyler Colfax, now Grant's Vice President had accepted stock.

One dreary episode followed another in Grant's second term. Benjamin H. Bristow, Grant's third Secretary of the Treasury, discovered that some of his officials and a group of distillers operating as a "Whiskey Ring" were cheating the government out of taxes by means of false reports. Among the prominent Republicans involved was the President's private secretary Orville E. Babcock. Grant defended Babcock, appointed him to another office, and eased Bristow out of the Cabinet. A House investigation revealed that William W. Belknap, Secretary of War, had accepted bribes to retain an Indian posttrader in office. Belknap resigned with Grant's blessing before the Senate could act on impeachment charges brought by the House. Lesser scandals involved the Navy Department, which was suspected of selling business to contractors, and the Treasury, where John D. Sanborn, a special agent appointed to handle overdue taxes, collected $427,000 and retained, for himself and the Republican bigwigs who had placed him in the job, a commission of 50 per cent. Not to be left out of the picture, Congress passed an act doubling the annual salary of the President (from $25,000 to $50,000, the first increase since George Washington's time) and raising the salaries of members of Congress from $5,000 to $7,500 a year. The increases were justifiable, but the country was enraged to learn that its representatives had also voted themselves

ments to the opposition party, and fearful of the third-term issue, they searched for a candidate who was not associated with the scandals of the last eight years and who could entice the Liberals back into the fold and unite the party until after the election. Senator James G. Blaine of Maine offered himself, but he had recently been involved in an allegedly crooked railroad deal. In a remarkable dis-

---

INGERSOLL'S SPEECH NOMINATING BLAINE

At the Republican convention in 1876 Robert G. Ingersoll nominated Blaine in a speech typical of the extravagant rhetoric of the Gilded Age. Like all Republican orators, Ingersoll seized the opportunity to recall the emotions of the Civil War and to equate Democrats with traitors. After this speech Blaine was known to his admirers as "the plumed knight": "This is a grand year—a year filled with recollections of the Revolution; filled with the proud and tender memories of the past; with sacred legends of liberty; a year in which the sons of freedom will drink from the fountains of enthusiasm; a year in which the people call for a man who has preserved in Congress what our soldiers won upon the field; a year in which they call for the man who has torn from the throat of treason the tongue of slander—for the man who has snatched the mask of Democracy from the hideous face of rebellion; for this man who, like an intellectual athlete, has stood in the arena of debate and challenged all comers, and who is still a total stranger to defeat. Like an armed warrior, like a plumed knight, James G. Blaine marched down the halls of the American Congress and threw his shining lance full and fair against the brazen foreheads of the defamers of his country and the maligners of her honor."

---

two years of back pay. Bowing before a storm of denunciation, the next Congress hastened to repeal the so-called "Salary Grab."

The Hayes-Tilden Dispute

U. S. Grant was eager to run for another term in 1876, and Conkling and other bosses tried to secure the nomination for him. But the majority of the Republican leaders ruled Grant out. Impressed by the recent upsurge of Democratic strength, which had delivered the House of Representatives and a number of state govern-

play of oratory and effrontery, Blaine defended himself against the charge of corruption by reading to Congress some private letters that were supposed to incriminate him. Actually, he had carefully selected innocent portions of the correspondence, and many people were unconvinced. The so-called "Mulligan letters" hurt his chances in 1876 and would dog his career in the future. The Republican convention passed over Blaine and other hopefuls and named as the standard-bearer Rutherford B. Hayes, three times governor of Ohio and a champion of civil service. The platform included the usual endorsements of Reconstruction and Republican economic legislation.

No personal rivalries divided the Democrats. Only one aspirant commanded serious attention, and with him as their candidate the Democrats were confident of returning to power. The bearer of the party's hopes was Governor Samuel J. Tilden of New York, whose name had become synonymous with governmental reform. A corporation lawyer and a millionaire, Tilden had long been a power in the Democratic organization of his state, but he had not hesitated to turn against Tammany's corrupt Tweed Ring and aid in its overthrow. His fight against Tweed brought him national fame and the governorship, in which position he increased his reputation for honest administration. The Democratic platform contained some general references to the tariff and currency problems, but its emphasis was upon reform in government. It called for an end to Reconstruction and the establishment of civil service, and declared that the primary issue of the campaign was the ejection of rascals from government and the installation in their place of "honest men."

Despite the fury of the charges flung at each other by the parties in the canvass, there were almost no differences of principle between the candidates. Hayes was on record as favoring withdrawal of troops from the South, he advocated civil service, and his record for probity was equal to Tilden's. Although the New York governor, reflecting Eastern importing interests, was amenable to some kind of tariff reduction, on other economic issues he was at least as conservative as his rival. He was a gold or "sound-money" man, and he believed that government had no business interfering with economic processes. Indeed, in the second half of the nineteenth century and in a modern industrial society, Tilden looked on himself as a counterpart of Thomas Jefferson.

The November election revealed an ap-

parent Democratic victory. In addition to the South, Tilden carried several large Northern states, and his popular vote was 4,300,000 to 4,036,000 for Hayes. But the situation was complicated by disputed returns from three Southern states, Louisiana, South Carolina, and Florida, whose total electoral vote was nineteen. Both parties claimed to have won these states, and double sets of returns were presented to Congress. Adding to the confusion was a contested vote in Oregon, where one of the three successful Republican electors was declared ineligible because he held a federal office. The Democrats contended that the place should go to the highest Democratic elector, but the Republicans insisted that according to state law the remaining electors were to fill the vacancy. The dual and disputed returns threw the outcome of the election into doubt. As tension and excitement gripped the country, two clear facts emerged from the welter of conflicting claims. Tilden had for certain 184 electoral votes, only one short of a majority. The twenty votes in controversy would determine who would be President, and Hayes would need all of them to secure the prize.

With surprise and consternation, the public now learned that no measure or method existed to determine the validity of disputed returns. The Constitution stated: "The President of the Senate shall, in the presence of the Senate and House of Representatives, open all the certificates and the votes shall then be counted." The question was how and by whom? The Senate was Republican and so, of course, was its president, and the House was Democratic. Constitutional ambiguity and Congressional division rendered a fair and satisfactory solution of the crisis impossible. If the president of the Senate counted the votes, Hayes would be the victor. If the Senate and House judged the returns separately, they would reach opposite decisions and checkmate each other. And if the houses voted jointly, the Democrats, with a numerical majority, would decide the result. Resort to any one of these lines of action promised to divide the country and possibly result in chaos.

Not until the last days of January, 1877, did Congress act to break the deadlock. Then it created a special Electoral Commission to pass on all the disputed votes. The Commission was to be composed of five Senators, five Representatives, and five Justices of the Supreme Court. Because of the party lineup, the Congressional delegation would consist of five Republicans and five Democrats. The creating law named four of the judicial commissioners, two Republicans and two Democrats. The four were to select their fifth colleague, and it was understood that they would choose David Davis, an independent Republican, thus ensuring that the deciding vote would be wielded by a relatively unbiased judge. But at this stage Davis was elected to the Senate from Illinois and suddenly resigned his seat. His place on the Commission fell to Joseph P. Bradley, a Republican. Sitting throughout February, the Commission by a partisan vote of eight to seven decided every disputed vote for Hayes. Congress accepted the final verdict of the agency on March 2, only two days before the inauguration of the new President.

Ratification of the Commission's findings was not accomplished, however, without some complicated compromising among the politicians. Behind the dealing, and partially directing it, were certain powerful economic forces with a stake in the outcome. A decision by the Commission was not final until approved by Congress, and the Democrats could have prevented action by filibustering. The success of a filibuster, however, depended on concert between Northern and Southern Democrats, and this the Republicans disrupted by offering the Southerners sufficient inducement to accept the Commission's findings. According to the traditional account, certain Republicans and Southern Democrats met at Washington's

A DAMAGING VICTORY. In this cartoon Thomas Nast depicted the effects of the disputed election of 1876 on the Republican party. The triumphant but battered elephant sits at the grave of the Democrats saying: "Another such victory, and I am undone." Nast created the elephant as the symbol of the Republican party and the donkey as the symbol of the Democratic party. (FROM Harper's Weekly, 1877)

Wormley Hotel, and the Republicans pledged that if the South would not impede the Commission's work, Hayes, after becoming President, would withdraw the troops from the South. As withdrawal would mean the downfall of the last carpetbag governments, the Southerners, convinced they were getting as much from Hayes as they could from Tilden, abandoned the filibuster.

Actually, the story behind the "Compromise of 1877" is somewhat more complex. Hayes was on record before the election as favoring withdrawal of the troops, and in any event the Democrats in the House could have forced withdrawal simply by cutting out appropriations for the army in the Reconstruction process. The real agreement, the one that brought the

RUTHERFORD B. HAYES. At the age of nineteen Hayes wrote: "I am determined to acquire a character distinguished for energy, firmness, and perseverance." This early seriousness of purpose marked his entire life and handicapped him as a politician. Sincere and high-minded, he irritated many Republican leaders, who were glad to see him retire from the Presidency. (RUTHERFORD B. HAYES LIBRARY)

Southern Democrats over, was reached before the Wormley meeting. As the price for their cooperation the Southerners exacted from the Republicans the following pledges: the appointment of at least one Southerner to the Hayes cabinet, control of federal patronage in their sections, generous internal improvements, national aid for the Texas and Pacific Railroad, and, finally, withdrawal of the troops. The Conservatives who were running the redeemed Southern states were primarily interested in economics—in industrializing the South—and they believed that the Republican program of Federal aid to business would be more beneficial for their region

than the archaic state-rights policy of the Democrats.

The Hayes Administration

Like most of the prominent political figures in the years after 1865, Rutherford B. Hayes had been a volunteer officer in the Union army, attaining the rank of major general. After a brief service in Congress, he was three times elected governor of Ohio. He was a sincere, capable, and high-minded man, but his administration was only partially successful and was largely in the negative pattern of the era.

Before the end of Hayes's administration two groups—the Stalwarts, led by Conkling of New York, and the Half-Breeds, captained by James G. Blaine of Maine—were competing for control of the party, and threatening to split it. Only a subtle difference separated the Republican factions. The Stalwarts, comprised of state bosses like Conkling and Oliver P. Morton of Indiana and Zachariah Chandler of Michigan, stood for machine politics and the allocation of political and material spoils to the victor. They were professional operators who believed in politics for its own sake. The Half-Breeds had practically the same concept of the functions of parties, but circumstances—specifically, the fact that the Stalwarts at first were stronger—forced them to adopt a more circumspect and sanctimonious role. They rendered lip service to such issues as civil service and governmental efficiency, although most of them were no more interested in reform than the Stalwarts.

Although Hayes awarded some offices to the machine elements of his party, he consistently held up merit as the primary standard of appointment. His cabinet, headed by William M. Evarts as Secretary of State, John Sherman as Secretary of the Treasury, and Carl Schurz as Secretary of the Interior, was an exceptionally able one; but four of the members had bolted the party in the Liberal defection of 1872 and one was a Southern Democrat. Hayes's patronage policy horrified the Stalwarts and hardly pleased the Half-Breeds; at the same time, it was sufficiently political to raise doubts among the civil-service reformers. The President yielded up much of his power to influence any faction of his party when he announced early in his administration that he would not be a candidate for reelection. To complete Hayes's handicaps, the Democrats controlled the House when he entered office, and two years later they captured the Senate too.

In his inaugural address Hayes stressed the Southern problem. While he took care to say that the rights of the Negroes must be preserved, he announced that the most pressing need of the South was the restoration of "wise, honest, and peaceful local self-government"—which meant that he was going to withdraw the troops and let the whites take over control of the state governments. Hayes laid down this policy knowing that his action would lend color to current charges that he was paying off the South for acquiescing in his election and would strengthen those critics who referred to him as "His Fraudulency."

The President hoped to build up a "new Republican" party in the South composed of whatever conservative white groups could be weaned away from the Democrats and committed to some acceptance of Negro rights. But his efforts, which included a tour of Southern cities, failed to produce any positive results. Although many Southern leaders sympathized with the economic credo of the Republicans, they could not advise their people to support the party that had imposed Reconstruction. Nor were Southerners pleased by Hayes's bestowal of offices on carpetbaggers who now had to leave the section or by his vetoes of Democratic attempts to repeal the Force Acts. The "Solid South" had come into existence, and there was nothing Hayes or any Republican could do to crack it.

THE "PLUMED KNIGHT" OF THE REPUBLICANS. James G. Blaine was speaker of the House of Representatives, United States Senator from Maine, and twice Secretary of State. Like Henry Clay in an earlier period, he was widely loved, but he just missed the Presidency. He inspired devotion, but not always respect. (NATIONAL ARCHIVES)

After settling the Reconstruction issue to his satisfaction, Hayes turned to the problem of governmental reform. Long an advocate of civil service, he instructed his executive deputies that he wished appointments awarded on the basis of merit, that assessments of salaries of employees for political purposes must stop, and that the party activities of officials should be limited. Schurz placed the Interior Department on a merit basis, and Treasury Secretary Sherman and a few other department heads also made some effort to comply with their chief's wishes. Others ignored or evaded them. The strength of the spoils system was so great that Hayes

THE STALWART BOSS OF THE REPUBLICANS. Handsome Roscoe Conkling, Senator from New York, led the Stalwart faction of the Republicans. Blaine, who despised him, described Conkling as having a "majestic, supereminent, overpowering, turkey-gobbler strut." In this cartoon Conkling is casting covetous eyes at the Republican presidential nomination for 1880, represented by the eagle. The smaller bird looking doubtfully at the boss is the independent vote. Another Nast cartoon. (FROM Harper's Weekly, 1879)

could not force the executive branch to accept his policy. He had even less luck with Congress. Despite repeated appeals by the President, the legislators refused to appropriate money to renew the civil service commission created under Grant.

Hayes's persistent advocacy of civil service precipitated his biggest fight with Congress. As part of his campaign to reform the spoils-ridden Treasury bureaucracy, he removed from office two prominent officials in the New York custom house, Chester A. Arthur and Alonzo B. Cornell. Both men were leaders on Roscoe Conkling's organization, and the Senator interpreted their removal as an attempt to undermine his machine. Striking back with the arrogance of a great state boss, he persuaded the Senate to deny confirmation of the men Hayes had named to replace Arthur and Cornell. Stubbornly the President refused to retreat, and kept on transmitting new appointments until finally the Senate ratified his choices. Hayes was the first President since 1865 to resist successfully the constant attempts of Congress to encroach on executive prerogatives.

Garfield and Arthur

Fortunately for the faction-rent Republicans, prosperity had returned by the time of the election of 1880. An increased export trade and an upward spurt in industrial and agricultural production signalled the end of the depression and the beginning of another boom period. But the Republican leaders knew that not even prosperity could guarantee victory: they had to patch up their dissensions and settle on a nominee who could unite the party for another contest. Grant, backed by Conkling and the Stalwarts, was again a candidate, while the Half-Breeds divided between Blaine and Sherman. At the Republican convention Grant led for thirty-five ballots but could not reach a majority. Then the anti-Grant forces united to nominate a "dark horse," James A. Garfield, a

JAMES A. GARFIELD. In Garfield the American success story had a shining example. Born in a log cabin, as a boy he worked a short period on the Ohio Canal. He was almost completely a self-educated and self-made man. He was successively teacher, preacher, lawyer, and politician. The first elevator in the White House was installed in his Presidency. (LIBRARY OF CONGRESS)

veteran member of the House of Representatives from Ohio. As Garfield was known as a Half-Breed, the convention, to conciliate the Stalwarts, gave the second place on the ticket to Chester A. Arthur, the Conkling henchman just dismissed from office by Hayes.

With the ancient and ill Tilden unavailable, the Democrats were without a leader. They acted as though they were also without hope of victory. As their candidate, they selected General Winfield Scott Hancock, who had won some fame as a corps commander in the Union army but was hardly a commanding national figure. Their apparent purpose was to refute the usual Republican charges of Democratic disloyalty in the Civil War. Also, having witnessed the success of the Republicans in running generals, they wanted to try their luck with a Democratic officer against Garfield, who had been a volunteer general. Although the platform called for a revenue tariff, it emphasized the "great fraud" of the election of 1876 as the paramount issue. As usual, the Democrats were harking back to the past instead of looking to the future. During the bitter campaign, which revolved around such questions as Garfield's complicity in the Crédit Mobilier scandal and alleged errors committed by Hancock in the war, the Democratic candidate was pressed for a statement on the tariff. He replied that it was entirely a "local issue." As a description of how tariff schedules were arrived at in Congress, his phrase was reasonably accurate, but it constituted a virtual repudiation of the platform and removed the tariff as a campaign issue. In November Garfield piled up a decisive electoral majority of 214 to 155. But his popular vote was only about ten thousand more than his rival's: 4,454,000 to 4,444,000. The Republicans also captured both houses of Congress.

Up to the time of his accession to the Presidency, the career of James A. Garfield had been a perfect example of the American success legend. Born in humble Ohio surroundings, in fact, in a log cabin, he worked from boyhood up, once laboring as a mule-driver on the Ohio Canal— "from canal boy to the White House" was a theme the Republicans emphasized in the 1880 election. He worked his way through college, became a teacher, studied law and was admitted to the bar. In 1863 he was elected to the House of Representatives, where he served with increasing distinction until he became the Republican standard-bearer.

No one can say with certainty what kind of President he would have made. Four months after his inauguration he was shot by a frustrated and deranged office

seeker. For over two months more he lingered in pain before dying.

During his brief tenure of office, Garfield gave evidence that he intended to conduct a moderate Half-Breed administration. He appointed Blaine as Secretary of State, and as Postmaster-General (the cabinet official having the most to do with patronage) Thomas L. James, a civil-service champion. Almost immediately James exposed a scandal in his department—the so-called "star-route" frauds. In many areas of the West mail was carried by stages or riders and assigned to contractors; on the postal list these routes were designated by stars. If a contractor could demonstrate that his costs had increased, his compensation could be raised without reopening the agreement. Investigation disclosed that collusive contracts had been awarded to certain Republican politicians, who then had secured increased payments for their services. Despite protests from some leading Republicans, Garfield backed up James in his inquiry. In dispensing patronage, Garfield gave the important jobs to Half-Breeds. He provoked a fight with Conkling by naming his own followers to federal positions in New York. When the President appointed a bitter Conkling foe to a juicy post in the port of New York, the Senator tried to prevent Senate confirmation. Failing this, he and his colleague, Platt, resigned and asked the legislature to reelect them. Their purpose was to awe Garfield into submission, but the legislators, in a fine display of perversity, selected two other men.

As Garfield's assassin stood over his fallen victim, he shouted that he was a Stalwart and that now Arthur would be President. This announcement of succession was not calculated to cheer those Americans who were disturbed by the menace of machine politics. Even some Republicans echoed the sentiment of the man who groaned: "Chet Arthur President of the United States! Good God!" For all of his political lifetime Chester A.

Arthur had been a devoted, skilled, and open spoilsman. Before the assassination of Garfield, he had gone to Albany to lobby for the re-election of his benefactor and mentor, Conkling. But on becoming President, he completely reversed his past political credo. He pursued an independent course between the Republican factions, affiliating with neither and being dominated by neither, and he worked zealously and with partial success for the cause of reform. Undoubtedly he was shocked by the killing of Garfield and the grisly circumstances that brought him to the Presidency. It may be that he realized he now stood in the spotlight of history, and guided his actions accordingly.

The revelation of the "new" Arthur dismayed most of the party bosses. Although the President reorganized the cabinet, he left the majority of Garfield's appointees in office. He pushed vigorously the prosecution of the star-route Republicans, who managed, however, to escape punishment. He vetoed a huge river and harbors bill on the grounds it was "pork-barrel" legislation, but Congress overrode him. In his first message to Congress he recommended a civil-service law, and he kept prodding the legislators to act. Although the spectacle of the great spoilsman championing reform seemed incongruous, Arthur was undoubtedly sincere, and his course was smart politics. With the public shocked by Garfield's assassination and disgusted by the postal frauds, sentiment for civil service was running high, and some kind of legislation would have been enacted whether Arthur had intervened or not.

Responding to popular as well as presidential pressure, Congress passed in 1883 the first national civil service measure, the Pendleton Act. By its terms a limited number of federal jobs were to be "classified": applicants for them were to be chosen on the basis of competitive written examinations. The law also forbade assessment of office-holders for political purposes. To administer the act, a bipartisan

CHESTER A. ARTHUR. Before becoming Vice President, Arthur had not been interested in holding elective office. He preferred a position where he controlled patronage jobs—like collector of the port of New York. Personally honest, he was a frank exponent of the spoils system. But deeply shocked by Garfield's death, as President he opposed the same men and interests with whom he had previously worked. Six feet two inches in height, handsome and dignified, he looked like a President. (LIBRARY OF CONGRESS)

Civil Service Commission, headed by reformer Dorman B. Eaton, was established. At first only about 14,000 of some 100,000 offices were placed on the classified list. But the act provided that future Presidents might by executive order enlarge the number of positions subject to civil service. Every chief executive thereafter extended the list, primarily to "blanket" his appointees into office and prevent their removal by his successor. By this piecemeal and partisan process, the government finally achieved by the 1940's a system in which the majority of the people working for it were under civil service.

Return of the Democrats

The election of 1884, with its absence of issues and its emphasis on the personal qualities of the candidates, epitomized the politics of the era of conformity. Arthur would have accepted the Republican nomination, but his independent course had pleased neither Half-Breeds nor Stalwarts. Ignoring him and other aspirants, the Republican convention nominated its most popular man and most vulnerable candidate, James G. Blaine, known to his adoring admirers as "the plumed knight" but to thousands of other Americans as "Old Mulligan Letters." His selection split the party badly. To the Stalwarts he was anathema; Conkling, asked if he intended to campaign for Blaine, snapped that he did not engage in criminal practice. The independent reform faction, now called the Mugwumps, announced they were prepared to bolt the party and support an honest Democrat. Rising to the bait, the Democrats nominated Grover Cleveland, the reform governor of New York. The platforms of the two parties were almost identical. Both endorsed revision of the tariff without endangering domestic industries, both approved and claimed credit for civil service, and both, taking account of popular rumblings against big business, spoke vaguely about subjecting corporations to some kind of national regulation.

With no real issues between the parties, the election was essentially a struggle for office, and the campaign developed into a mud-slinging contest involving the personal fitness, or more accurately, unfitness of the candidates. Happily the Democrats went to work on the plumed knight's not too savory past record, reprinting the Mulligan correspondence without Blaine's expurgations and uncovering new damning letters. One of these ended with an exhortation from the candidate: "Burn this letter." Singing characterized the mass rallies of the campaign, and one rousing Democratic song dedicated to the proposition that Blaine of Maine was "a continental liar" concluded with an exuberant "Burn this letter." Frantically the Republicans researched Cleveland's brief political career as mayor of Buffalo and governor of New York for evidence of corruption—a politician had to be corrupt, they seemed to assume—but found nothing. They did discover, however, a juicy sexual item. As a young man Cleveland had been accused of being the father of an illegitimate child, and whether he was or not, he had agreed to support the infant. He did not specifically deny the imputation when the Republicans brought it into the campaign. Thereafter at their rallies the Republicans roared out:

Ma! Ma! where's my Pa?
Gone to the White House. Ha! Ha! Ha!

In addition to sex, the canvass featured the bloody shirt, waved vigorously by Blaine, freedom for Ireland from the British rule, held out to the Irish voters by Republican orators, and religion, a last-minute issue that may have decided the election. In the closing days of the campaign a delegation of Protestant ministers called on Blaine in New York City; their spokesman, Dr. Samuel Burchard, in the course of his remarks referred to the Democrats as the party of "Rum, Romanism, and Rebellion." Apparently Blaine, whose mother was a Catholic, did not catch the statement or notice its linking of elements. Soon the Democrats were spreading the news through New York and other Eastern cities that Blaine had countenanced a slander on the Catholic church, and his denial came too late to counteract the charge. The so-called Burchard incident may have swung New York state to the Democrats, and New York was the pivotal state in what turned out to be an extremely close election. Cleveland had 219 electoral votes to Blaine's 182; the popular vote showed 4,875,000 for Cleveland and 4,852,000 for Blaine, a Democratic plurality of only 23,000.

Grover Cleveland was the first Demo-

GROVER CLEVELAND. Cleveland was the first Democrat to be elected President since the Civil War. Honest, courageous, and stubborn, he was extremely conservative and unable to understand some of the new economic problems emerging in his administration. A bachelor when elected, he married while in the White House. He weighed 250 pounds. (LIBRARY OF CONGRESS)

crat to be elected President since James Buchanan in 1856. Cleveland also was the ablest President between Lincoln and Theodore Roosevelt. Short and corpulent (he weighed over 200 pounds), brusque in manner, boldly beardless in a hirsute age, he was far from being an impressive figure. Nor were his mental attainments, although respectable, of the first order. He did possess, however, certain qualities that were rare in his era, at least in combination: character, courage, and integrity. In his brief career in prominent offices—he had been elected mayor of Buffalo in 1881 and governor of New York in 1882—he had fought politicians, grafters, pressure groups, and Tammany Hall. He had become famous as the "veto mayor" and the "veto governor," as an official who was not afraid to say "No." This ability to be honestly negative was the most positive feature of his political personality; it was at once his greatest strength and his most distressing weakness as a political leader. It enabled him to withstand pressure from any quarter, to oppose the spoilsmen, and to uphold high standards of official probity. It also rendered him tragically incapable of understanding the problems of an industrial society or the role of government in a changing economic order.

Cleveland's First Term

When Cleveland became President, he was absorbed with plans to improve the administrative machinery of the government, to install business standards in its operations, and to purify its processes. Issues such as the currency and the tariff did not greatly interest him, nor was he concerned with the problems of the farmer and the laborer. His knowledge of economics was slender and his economic philosophy almost primitively simple. He was sincerely opposed to a paternalistic and positive government that extended special favors to any group. Let all stand equal, the giant corporation and the worker, he proclaimed, never comprehending that there were vital power-differences between contesting economic interests. He summed up his faith in a veto of an appropriation of $10,000 for drought-stricken farmers. The lesson must never be forgotten, he moralized, that "though the people support the Government, the Government should not support the people."

Although Cleveland was known as a civil-service supporter, in dealing with patronage he had to proceed with due partisan caution. After years of wandering in the political wilderness, the Democrats were hungry for offices, and they expected the President to throw the Republican "rascals" out—immediately and in wholesale lots. Instead, the President compromised in a manner that did not satisfy completely either his own party or his Mugwump followers. He added approximately 12,000 offices to the classified list, but of the jobs not under civil service he removed two thirds of the incumbents and replaced them with deserving Democrats. Determined to check extravagance and congressional raids on the surplus, Cleveland vetoed a river and harbors bill, and attempted to introduce principles of economy and honesty into the awarding of soldier pensions.

On the pension issue, he stirred up a hornet's nest. For years real or alleged veterans of the Union army had had no difficulty in getting Congress to enact private pension bills for their benefit. Many of the claims were fraudulent but nobody ever examined them. Cleveland actually took the trouble to read them, and, outraged by what he found, vetoed over 200 such measures. When Congress, responding to pressure from the powerful Grand Army of the Republic, passed a Dependent Pension Bill to grant pensions to all veterans suffering from disabilities, no matter when or how contracted, he killed it with a veto. In reality, Cleveland was sympathetic to the claims of genuine veterans, and the total appropriation for pensions increased during his administration. But his vetoes enabled Republican and G.A.R. orators to remind the voters of the peril of placing a Southern-dominated Democrat in the White House.

On another front of battle against corruption, Cleveland instructed his Secretary of the Interior to inspect past grants of public lands in the West to railroad, lumber, and cattle interests, and where the lands had been obtained on fraudulent or false grounds to institute suits to recover them. Eventually some 81 million acres were restored to the government. Although businessmen bellowed that the President was acting like a radical, he was only being consistently conservative: no special favors to any group.

Cleveland himself precipitated one economic issue into the political arena. Always mildly dubious of the high tariff, he concluded after thorough study that the existing rates were responsible for the annual surplus that tempted Congress to reckless legislation. Once convinced, he acted with sudden and startling vigor. In December, 1887, he devoted almost all of his annual message to the lawmakers to discussing the tariff and demanding its downward revision. Although he spoke bitingly of the great fortunes that had been built on protective duties and of the inflated living costs of the poor, he rested his case on immediate and practical considerations: the tariff was bringing in an unneeded surplus and the piling up of this surplus would eventually depress the economy. In a phrase that intrigued the public, he said: "It is a *condition* that confronts us, not a theory." Characteristically, he assured Congress that reductions could be made without endangering the interests of American manufacturers.

Immediately, the Southern and Western Democrats, who had been moving rapidly to a low-tariff position, responded to the President's leadership. They pushed through the House the Mills Bill, incorporating Cleveland's recommendations and providing for moderate reduc-

tions. Only four Democrats voted against it, and doubtless some of the Easterners went along in the knowledge that the Republican Senate would kill the measure. In the upper chamber the Republican chieftains, believing that they could sell the tariff to the voters, met the issue head-on. As an alternative to the Mills Bill they enacted a protective measure. Action was deadlocked for the moment, and the tariff was squarely before the people as an issue in the election of 1888.

As the tariff fight swirled to a climax, the Democrats again named Cleveland as their standard-bearer, although some machine bosses and some Easterners, disgusted by his stand on civil service and lower duties, would have preferred another candidate. The platform emphasized the tariff question and pledged support to the President's policy of moderate revision. The Republicans had in protection what they were certain was a winning issue, but they were hard put to find an acceptable and available nominee. They finally decided on Benjamin Harrison of Indiana, who was relatively obscure and formidably respectable, and in their platform endorsed protection for American producers and generous pensions for Union veterans.

The campaign of 1888 was the first since the Civil War that was fought out on a definite issue, the first that involved a question of economic difference between the parties. It was also one of the most corrupt campaigns in American political history. Both parties employed the usual fraudulent methods of the day, but the Republicans, with a campaign fund contributed by apprehensive business interests and amounting to several million dollars, were the worst offenders.

When the votes were counted after the great referendum, it was obvious that the people had not registered a clear decision or authorized a definite mandate. Harrison had an electoral majority of 233 to 168, but Cleveland's popular vote exceeded Harrison's, 5,540,000 to 5,440,000.

BIBLIOGRAPHY

General accounts include L. D. White, *The Republican Era, 1869–1901: A Study in Administrative History* (1958); M. Josephson, *The Politicos, 1865–1896* (1938); James Bryce, *The American Commonwealth* (3 vols., 1888; rev. ed., 2 vols., 1931–3), a classic by a distinguished English observer; and W. E. Binkley, *American Political Parties* (rev. ed., 1958).

Political biographies of Republican leaders: G. F. Howe, *Chester A. Arthur* (1934); D. S. Muzzey, *James G. Blaine* (1934); J. A. Barnes, *John G. Carlisle* (1931); L. B. Richardson, *William E. Chandler, Republican* (1940); D. B. Chidsey, *The Gentleman from New York: A Life of Roscoe Conkling* (1935); R. G. Caldwell, *James A. Garfield* (1931); W. B. Hesseltine, *U. S. Grant, Politician* (1935); W. H. Hale, *Horace Greeley* (1950); Harry Barnard, *Rutherford B. Hayes and His America* (1954); H. J. Eckenrode, *Rutherford B. Hayes* (1930); H. G. Gosnell, *Boss Platt and His New York Machine* (1924); R. N. Current, *Pine Logs and Politics: A Life of Philetus Sawyer, 1816–1900* (1950); and C. F. Fuess, *Carl Schurz* (1932).

On Democratic leaders: W. V. Byars, *An American Commoner* (1900), a life of Richard P. Bland; Allan Nevins, *Grover Cleveland* (1932); H. S. Merrill, *Bourbon Leader: Grover Cleveland and the Democratic Party* (1957); Brainerd Dyer, *The Public Career of William M. Evarts* (1933); C. L. Barrows, *William M. Evarts* (1941);

W. A. Cate, *L. Q. C. Lamar* (1935); Stewart Mitchell, *Horatio Seymour* (1938); and A. C. Flick, *Samuel Jones Tilden* (1939).

Phases of political history are studied in C. H. Coleman, *The Election of 1868* (1933); E. D. Ross, *The Liberal Republican Movement* (1919); E. F. Goldman, *Rendezvous with Destiny* (1951; paperback ed., 1956), a brillant interpretation of reform movements from the Grant era on; M. R. Dearing, *Veterans in Politics* (1952); C. V. Woodward, *Reunion and Reaction: The Compromise of 1877 and the End of Reconstruction* (1951), an invaluable contribution; V. P. De Santis, *Republicans Face the Southern Question: The New Departure Years, 1877–1897* (1959); P. P. Van Riper, *History of the United States Civil Service* (1958); A. B. Sageser, *The First Two Decades of the Pendleton Act* (1935); and H. S. Merrill, *The Bourbon Democracy of the Middle West* (1953).

On economic issues, see A. D. Noyes, *Forty Years of American Finance* (1909); W. J. Schultz and M. B. Caine, *Financial Development, the United States* (1937); Edward Stanwood, *American Tariff Controversies in the Nineteenth Century* (2 vols., 1903); and F. W. Taussig, *The Tariff History of the United States* (1931). On the pension question: J. W. Oliver, *History of the Civil War Military Pensions* (1917); and W. H. Glasson, *Federal Military Pensions in the United States* (1918).

23

FILLING IN THE WEST

Between the presidencies of Andrew Johnson and Grover Cleveland a tremendous and dramatic transformation of the American scene was occurring west of the Mississippi River. There, in the vast area stretching from the middle valley to the far western highlands, a great movement of population overran the last unsettled space within the national continental limits. In a span of little more than a generation this westward surge swept over plains, mountains, and deserts, broke the power of the Indian tribes in its path, and established civilized institutions in what had been a wilderness. By the turn of the century practically every part of the region had been organized into states or territories.

The Last West

In 1860 the frontier line, the western rim of settlement, conformed roughly to the western boundaries of the tier of states immediately beyond the Mississippi —Minnesota, Iowa, Missouri, Arkansas —jutting outward to include the eastern parts of Nebraska and Kansas and cutting across central Texas. West of this line was a huge expanse inhabited by Indians and wild animals and peopled only thinly by whites until the settled districts of California and Oregon on the Pacific coast were reached. Within the confines of this vast West were three distinct natural, or physiographic, regions: the Great or High Plains, the Rocky Mountains, and the Basin and Plateau region hugged on the east by the Rockies and on the west by the Sierra Nevada–Cascade mountain system.

When the westward-pushing pioneers entered upon the Great Plains, they saw a strange and even alien environment, utterly different from the fertile prairie lands behind them or the wooded areas of the Ohio Valley and the East. The physical features that in combination distinguished the Great Plains from previous frontiers were a level surface, a dearth of timber, and a deficiency in rainfall. Early explorers had dubbed this region "the Great American Desert," and in the 1840's settlers had hastened through it on their way to California and Oregon. Its forbidding reputation was largely responsible for the curious fact that the frontier, after crossing the Mississippi, had jumped 1,500 miles to the Pacific coast.

Historians often speak of the Great Plains as beginning at the ninety-eighth meridian and extending west to the foot-

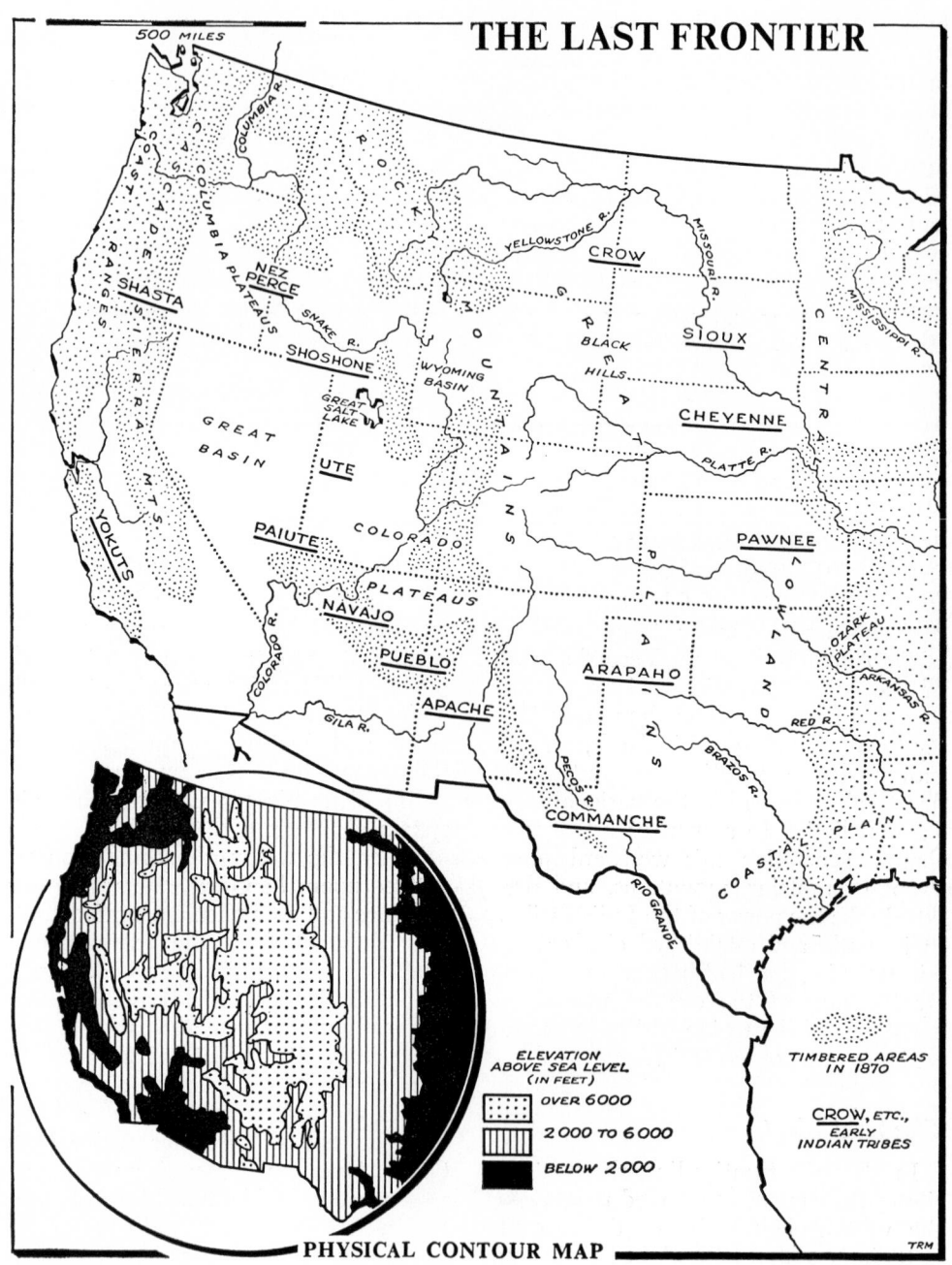

THE LAST FRONTIER

500 MILES

COAST RANGES
CASCADE RANGES
COLUMBIA R.
ROCKY
COLUMBIA PLATEAUS
NEZ PERCE
SHASTA
SHOSHONE
SNAKE R.
WYOMING BASIN
SIERRA NEVADA MTS.
GREAT BASIN
GREAT SALT LAKE
UTE
COLORADO
YOKUTS
PAIUTE
PLATEAUS
NAVAJO
PUEBLO
COLORADO R.
APACHE
GILA R.
YELLOWSTONE R.
CROW
MISSOURI R.
BLACK HILLS
SIOUX
MOUNTAINS
CHEYENNE
PLATTE R.
GREAT
PLAINS
ARAPAHO
PECOS R.
COMMANCHE
RIO GRANDE
BRAZOS R.
RED R.
CENTRAL
MISSISSIPPI R.
LOWLAND
PAWNEE
OZARK PLATEAU
ARKANSAS R.
COASTAL PLAIN

ELEVATION
ABOVE SEA LEVEL
(IN FEET)

OVER 6000

2000 TO 6000

BELOW 2000

TIMBERED AREAS
IN 1870

CROW, ETC.,
EARLY
INDIAN TRIBES

PHYSICAL CONTOUR MAP

TRM

hills of the Rockies. Geographers prefer to set a more irregular eastern border marked by the line of 20 inches average annual rainfall; west of this line the annual precipitation decreased to 10 or 12 inches and in some areas was often less. The climate featured extremes and violent vagaries of nature: hot summers and cold winters, burning winds and howling blizzards, high winds, "Northers," and tornadoes. The light brown soil was covered with short, tough grass; trees were present only along the streams.

Beyond the Great Plains loomed the barrier of the Rocky Mountains. Interspersed between peaks towering 12,000 to 14,000 feet above sea level were basins, plateaus, and valleys suitable for ranching and irrigated farming. In most parts of the region the rainfall was deficient, and the growing season was short, averaging from ninety to a hundred days. If climate and lack of arable land precluded an extensive agricultural life, the varied mineral resources of the Rockies provided the basis for another activity. Gold, silver, copper, lead, and zinc were amply and widely distributed throughout the ranges.

Between the Rockies and the Sierra Nevada and Cascade mountains stretched the third segment of the last West, the immense Basin and Plateau area, extending from the Mexican border almost to Canada. It was a region of high plateaus, basins, deserts, and highlands, most of its surface marked by huge tilted blocks of rock. The average annual rainfall was only 5 to 10 inches, making it the driest section in the United States, and the average growing season was a hundred days. Because of its topography, climate, and deficiency of moisture, this region was less suited for agriculture than any other part of the country; even in the modern era of irrigation only 3 per cent of it is under cultivation. It was, however, rich in mineral resources, like the Rockies.

Settlers were pushing into the plains and mountains on the eve of the Civil War, and even during the war years migra-

tion continued. In 1864 an estimated 75,-000 persons passed through Omaha, gateway to the Great Plains. During the decade of the sixties, the population of the last frontier increased 160 per cent, and its later growth was equally spectacular.

Political organization followed on the heels of settlement. After the admission of Kansas as a state in 1861, the remaining territories of Washington, New Mexico, Utah, and Nebraska were divided into smaller and more convenient units. By the close of the sixties territorial governments were in operation in the new provinces of Nevada, Colorado, Dakota, Arizona, Idaho, Montana, and Wyoming. Statehood rapidly followed. Nevada became a state in 1864, Nebraska in 1867, and Colorado, attracting attention as the centennial state, in 1876. In 1889 the "omnibus states," North and South Dakota, Montana, and Washington, won admission; Wyoming and Idaho entered the next year. Utah was denied statehood until its Mormom leaders convinced the government in 1896 that polygamy had been abandoned. At the turn of the century only three territories remained outside the fold: Arizona and New Mexico, excluded because of their scanty population and wrong politics (they were usually Democratic) and their refusal to accept admission as a single state, and Oklahoma, opened to white settlement and granted territorial status in 1889–90.

Three major factors stimulated the headlong settlement of the last West. One was the great transcontinental railroad lines (whose construction will be described in the next chapter). These roads and their feeders moved settlers and supplies into the vast interior spaces and furnished access to outside markets; they provided what the region could not have had without them, the basis for a permanent population and a durable economy. In addition, they directly excited migration by disposing of their lands to settlers. All told, in national and state land grants, the railroads owned over 183 million acres. Although some companies attempted to reserve their lands or sell them at fancy prices, most of the lines realized that an increased population meant larger freight and passenger revenues. Consequently, they offered land for as little as $2.50 an acre, advertised the glories of the West in the East and in Europe, and transported prospective buyers at reduced rates.

A second factor was the readiness of the national government to police and subdue the Indians who resisted the white advance. A third was the land policy of the government. The influence of this factor, however, has been exaggerated. On occasion the land laws slowed rather than speeded settlement. At the close of the Civil War two statutes determined land policy. Most important was the Homestead Act of 1862 providing that for a small fee a settler could obtain a plot of 160 acres if he occupied and improved it for five years. A similar acreage could be secured, ordinarily for $1.25 per acre, by the terms of the Preemption Act of 1841. A good deal of idealism had gone into the framing of the Homestead Act. It was represented and intended to be a democratic measure, the bestowal of a free farm on any American who needed one, a form of government relief to raise the living standards of the masses. But in practice the act proved a distressing disappointment. Prior to 1890 the government awarded title to only 48,225,000 acres of homesteaded land. Some 400,000 registrants proved their claims, but many more abandoned the attempt to stake out a farm on the windswept plains.

On several counts the Homestead Act was defective. Its loose provisions invited fraud and evasion. Its assumption that mere possession of land was enough to sustain farm life ignored the increasing mechanization of agriculture and the rising costs of operation. But fundamentally the measure fell short because it was based on eastern agricultural experiences that were inapplicable to the region west of the Mississippi. A unit of 160 acres was too small for the grazing and grain farming that came to be carried on in the Great Plains. Responding to Western pressures, Congress acted to increase allotments. The Timber Culture Act (1873) permitted a homesteader to receive a grant of 160 additional acres if he planted on it forty acres of trees. The Desert Land Act (1877) provided that a claimant could buy 640 acres at $1.25 an acre provided he irrigated part of his holding within three years. The Timber and Stone Act (1878), presumably applying to nonarable land, authorized sales of quarter-sections at $2.50 an acre. Through the operation of the various laws, it was possible for an individual to acquire at little cost 1,280 acres or two full sections. Some enterprising persons got much more. Fraud ran rampant in the administration of the acts. Lumber, mining, and cattle companies, by employing "dummy" registrants and using other tricky devices, grasped millions of acres of the public domain.

The Mining Frontier

The first colonists of the last frontier were miners, and the first part of the area to be settled was the mineral-rich region of mountains and plateaus. The life span of the mining frontier was brief. It burst into being around 1860, flourished brilliantly until 1880, and then abruptly declined. But in its ephemeral era of glory, the mineral empire of the Far West played a large role in the development of the nation and influenced significantly the course of national history. It drew the attention of the entire nation to the resources and problems of the West. It prepared the way for permanent settlement of the region. Through its outpourings of millions of dollars of gold and silver, it increased national wealth, contributed to the vitality of domestic and foreign trade, and magnified the currency issue in politics. And with its romance and color and overwhelming cast of dynamic characters, it would enrich beyond calculation the future archives of escapist literature, the moving pictures, and television.

Gold and silver were the minerals that brought the mining frontier into sudden, pulsing existence. News of a strike in an area would start a stampede reminiscent of the California gold rush of 1849. Settlement usually followed a pattern of successive stages: (1) individual prospectors exploited the first ores with pan and placer mining; (2) after the shallower deposits were depleted, corporations moved in to engage in lode, or quartz, mining; (3) commercial mining either disappeared eventually or continued on a restricted basis, and ranchers and farmers appeared on the scene to establish a more permanent economy.

The first great strikes occurred just before the Civil War. In 1858 gold was discovered in the Pike's Peak district of what would soon be the territory of Colorado, and the following year a mob of 50,000 prospectors stormed in from California and the Mississippi Valley and the East. Denver and other mining camps blossomed into "cities" overnight. Almost as rapidly as it developed, the boom ended. Eventually corporations, notably the Guggenheim interests, revived some of the glories and profits of the gold boom, and the discovery of silver near Leadville supplied a new source of mineral wealth.

While the Colorado rush of 1859 was in progress, news of another strike drew miners to Nevada, then a part of Utah Territory. Gold had been found in the Washoe district of western Nevada, but further exploration demonstrated that the most valuable ore in the great Comstock Lode and other veins was silver. The first prospectors to reach the Washoe fields came from California (here the frontier movement was from west to east), and from the beginning Californians dominated the settlement and development of Nevada. Stuck off in a desert and devoid of railroad transportation, the territory produced no supplies of its own, and everything, from food and machinery to whiskey and prostitutes, had to be freighted in from California to Virginia City, Carson City, and other roaring camp towns. When the placer deposits ran out, California capital bought the claims of the pioneer prospectors and installed quartz mining. For a brief span the outside owners reaped tremendous profits; from 1860 to 1880 the Nevada lodes yielded bullion worth $306 million.

After the great strikes of the Civil War period, no new discoveries agitated the mining frontier until 1874, when gold was found in the Black Hills of southwestern Dakota Territory. The last rush followed the usual pattern of settlement. From all parts of the West thousands of prospectors swarmed into the area, then and for years later served only by stagecoach transportation. Deadwood burst into life as a center of supplies and sin for other camps. For a short time the boom flared, and then came the inevitable fading of resources. Corporations took over from the miners, and one gigantic company, the Homestake, came to dominate the fields. The population declined, and the Dakotas, like other boom areas of the mineral empire, waited for the approach of the agricultural frontier.

Life in the camp towns of the mineral empire had a hectic tempo and a gaudy flavor not to be found in any other part of the last frontier. A speculative spirit, a mood of incredible optimism, a get-rich-quick philosophy gripped every individual and dominated every phase of community activity. Mark Twain, who came to the Far West during its flamboyant heyday, described it unforgettably in *Roughing It*.

Settlement of the region preceded the railroads, and even when the transcontinentals reached it they did not penetrate its inner recesses. For years all transportation was in conveyances drawn by animals—horses, mules, or oxen. At the beginning of the Civil War the dominant figure in the transportation business of the plains and mountains was John Butterfield, who operated a fleet of Concord stagecoaches and conveyed government mails to California. Presently Ben Holladay displaced Butterfield. He controlled 5,000 miles of stagelines and built up a fabulous reputation. When one of Mark

staging; in a boom year the freight bill of the mining area might be $31 million. To serve the camp towns, Wells, Fargo, which eventually monopolized the whole transportation field, maintained 6,000 wagons and 75,000 oxen.

The mining frontier was settled so rapidly that institutions of government and

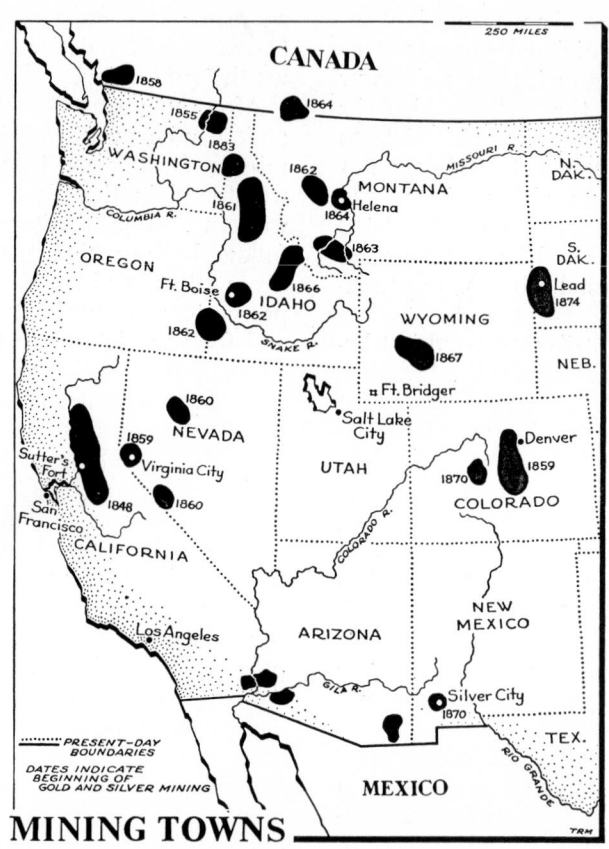

MINING TOWNS

Twain's American tourists in *Innocents Abroad* was told of the wanderings of the Israelites in the wilderness, he exclaimed scornfully that Ben Holladay would have had them out right away! In 1866 Holladay sold his interests to Wells, Fargo, and Company. People and mail were generally carried in coaches, while supplies were handled by ponderous freight wagons pulled by slow-gaited ox teams. Freighting was more remunerative than

law were not established until after the boom or rush culminated in crime and disorder. The very conditions of mine life—the presence of precious minerals, the vagueness of claim boundaries, the cargoes of gold being shipped out—tempted outlaws and "bad men," operating as individuals or gangs, to ply their trade. When the situation became intolerable in a community, those members interested in order set up their own law

THE OVERLAND MAIL. Congress authorized the establishment of an overland mail line to California in 1857, providing for the payment of an annual subsidy to the carrier. John Butterfield secured the contract and organized the famous Overland Mail. On the Butterfield line, coaches of the Concord type operated between San Francisco and St. Louis or to a rail terminal west of St. Louis. They followed an indirect southern route over 2700 miles in length. The average time for a trip was twenty-five days. In addition to letters, the coaches carried passengers, who paid $100 for a rough, jolting journey. The coach in the picture is about to take off from San Francisco on the first leg of the run eastward. (FROM Harper's Weekly, 1858)

and enforced it through a vigilance committee, an agency used earlier in California. It was indicative of the fluidity of legal evolution that sometimes criminals secured control of the committee and that sometimes the vigilantes appeared after the creation of regular governments.

The frontier of the mines and plains added to the American scene a choice collection of magnificently unrestrained individuals. Some were on the right side of the law, some on the wrong side, and some on both sides. Prominent in the cast were Buffalo Bill (William F.) Cody, scout, hunter, and guide, who earned his name by slaughtering 4,280 buffalo in eighteen months; Wild Bill (James B.) Hickok, "the prince of pistoleers," stagecoach superintendent, gunslinger, and marshal, who enjoyed the most lethal reputation in the West before he was shot in the back at Deadwood; Wyatt Earp, marshal of Dodge City and Tombstone, who upheld the law in such deadly fashion that lawful citizens felt uncomfortable; Calamity Jane (Martha Jane Canary), a large and lewd bullwhacker on the freight wagons, able to swear, chew, drink, and love with any man, who fixed her place in folklore by claiming an unlikely romance with Wild Bill; Billy the Kid (William H. Bonney), a cherubic juvenile desperado, who boasted that he had killed twenty-one men not counting Indians and Mexicans; and a host of lesser but equally florid characters—outlaws Sam Bass and Henry Plummer, and the fantastic Judge Roy Bean, "the law west of the Pecos." They were a varied and vivid lot, and their departure was another symbol of the passing of the frontier.

The Cattle Kingdom

Shortly after the gold and silver seekers surged into the mineral empire, another great economic province began to take shape in the last frontier. The cattle kingdom was born on the Great Plains, its imperial boundaries stretching from the ninety-eighth meridian to the Rockies, from Texas to Canada. Like the mining domain, it had a brief and brilliant existence, from approximately 1865 to 1885, but during that period it influenced materially the course of national development and added another colorful chapter to the record of the last West.

Various factors enabled the cattle industry to spread over the West—the suppression of the Indians, the elimination of the buffalo, the laxity of the land laws —but the most important were the open range and the railroads. The open range, that is, the unclaimed grasslands of the public domain, provided a huge area where cattlemen could graze their herds free of charge and unrestricted by the boundaries which would have existed in a farming economy. The railroads gave the cattle kingdom access to markets and thus brought it into being; then they destroyed it by bringing the farmers' frontier to the plains.

In ancestry the cattle industry was Mexican and Texan. Long before the Americans invaded the Southwest, Mexican ranchers and vaqueros had developed the techniques and tools employed later by the cattlemen and cowboys of the Great Plains: branding (a device known in all frontier areas where stock was common), roundups, roping, and the equipment of the herder—his lariat, saddle, leather chaps, and spurs. All these things and others were taken over by the Americans in Texas and by them transmitted to the northernmost ranges of the

cattle kingdom. Also in Texas were found the largest herds of cattle in the country, the animals descended from imported Spanish stock and allowed to run wild or semiwild, the famous wiry, hardy longhorns; here too were the horses that enabled the caretakers of the herds to control them, the small, muscular broncos or mustangs, sprung from blooded progenitors brought in by the Spanish and ideally adapted to the requirements of the cow country

The practice of driving cattle herds to market centers or from old to new ranges had been known before the Civil War and had been attempted on a limited scale in many parts of the country. But the concept of moving huge numbers of animals over long distances on a regular schedule was born in the postwar period, and its origin was directly related to the advance of the railroads across the plains. At the end of the war an estimated 5,000,000 cattle roamed the Texas ranges, and Northern markets were offering fat prices for steers in any condition. Early in 1866 some Texas cattlemen started their combined herds, some 260,000 head, north for Sedalia, Missouri, on the Missouri Pacific Railroad. Traveling over rough country and beset by outlaws, Indians, and property-conscious farmers, the caravan suffered heavy losses, and only a fraction of the animals were delivered to the railroad. But a great experiment had been successfully tested—cattle could be driven to distant markets and pastured along the trail and would gain weight during the journey. The first of the "long drives" prepared the way for the cattle kingdom.

With the precedent established, the next step was to find an easier route leading through more accessible country. Special market facilities were provided at Abilene, Kansas, on the Kansas Pacific Railroad, and for years this town reigned as the railhead of the cattle kingdom. Between 1867 and 1871, 1,460,000 cattle were moved up the Chisholm Trail to Abilene, a town that, filled with rampaging cowboys at the end of a drive, rivaled the mining towns in robust wickedness. But as the farming frontier pushed farther west in Kansas and as the supply of animals increased, the cattlemen had to develop other market outlets specified place to round up the stock of the owners from the open range. As the cattle were driven in, the calves were branded with the marks of their mothers. Stray calves with no identifying symbols, "mavericks," were divided on a pro-rata

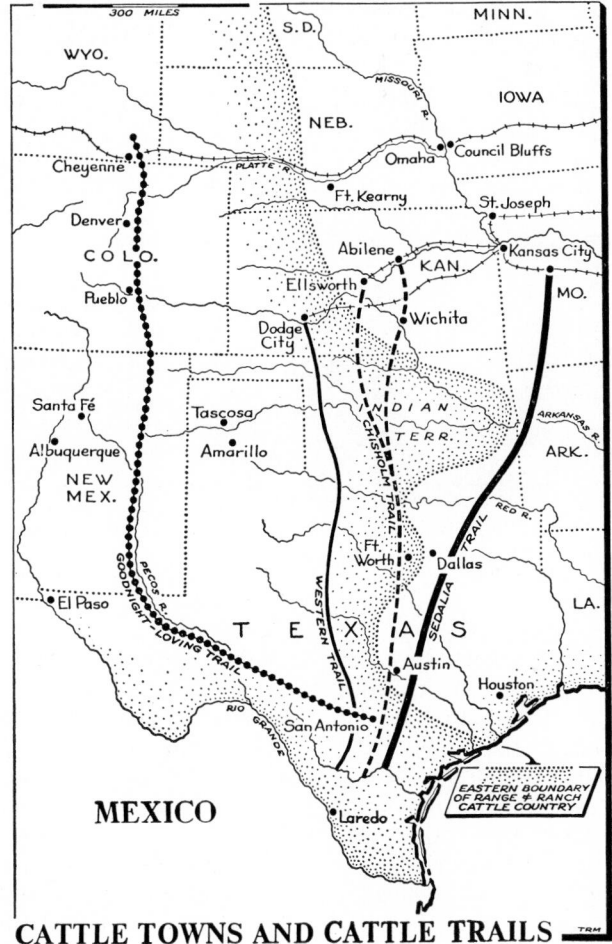

CATTLE TOWNS AND CATTLE TRAILS

and trails. Railroad towns that flourished after Abilene were Dodge City and Wichita in Kansas, Ogallala and Sidney in Nebraska, Cheyenne and Laramie in Wyoming, and Miles City and Glendive in Montana.

From first to last, a long drive was a spectacular episode. It began with the spring, or calf, roundup. The ranchers of a district collected with their cowboys at a basis. Then the cows and calves were turned loose to pasture, while the yearling steers were readied for the drive to the north. The combined herds, usually numbering from 2,000 to 5,000 head, moved out, attended by the cowboys of each outfit. In addition to the individual brand of its owner, each animal bore a "road brand" to indicate it belonged to this particular assemblage. By all odds,

BRANDING CALVES. This typical scene of the cattle kingdom shows several steps in the branding process: catching the calves, "Wrassling" them to the ground, and branding them. The man at the left is about to place an iron on a calf, and in the foreground other irons are heating. (CHARLES J. BELDEN PHOTOGRAPH)

the most important person on a drive was the cowboy or "cowpuncher," replete with forty-pound saddle, twenty-foot lariat, "six-shooter" revolver, chaps, and sombrero. Whether riding the range with his charges, stopping a stampede, or singing to himself or the steers under the stars, he seemed an incredibly romantic figure. Actually, he was a highly skilled technician engaged in work that was mostly dull and dangerous, and he could have had no comprehension of the stature he would later assume in American folklore.

For a period the cattle kingdom boomed with prosperity—and with swollen profits for the cattlemen. These magnates moved their stock over the open range, and the range was free. They asserted, nevertheless, claims to land, claims that were peculiar to the cow country, where large units were essential, and that

could be characterized as occupancy rather than ownership. The big operators or companies leased acres by the millions from the Indians, appropriated huge areas along waterways, and obtained other blocks by manipulating loopholes in the land laws. Sometimes they threw barbed wire fences around their domains, but mostly they merely proclaimed grazing rights on a particular section and maintained their position by consent or physical power. Some cattle kings claimed rights to ranges 100 or 150 miles long and 50 miles wide.

All cattlemen, however, had to have a permanent base from which to operate, and so the ranch emerged. The Texans had always moved from fixed abodes, and as the northern ranges filled up with cattle the cowmen found it desirable to develop ranches. A ranch consisted of a dwelling, quarters for employees, and a tract of grazing land. It might be fenced in or open, owned or leased or held by some quasi-legal claim, but it was definite and durable. Possession of a ranch meant solid benefits to the owner. He could secure unquestioned access to precious water, and, perhaps most important, he had a place where he could hold his herd until the market price was satisfactory. As farmers and sheepmen encroached on the open plains, the ranch came to replace the range.

There had always been an element of risk and speculation in the open-range cattle business. At any time the "Texas fever," transmitted by a parasite carried by ticks, might decimate a herd. Rustlers and Indians frequently drove off large numbers of animals. Sheepmen from California and Oregon brought their flocks onto the range to compete for grass and force cattle out (cattle will not graze after sheep); bitter "wars" followed between ranchers and sheepers in which men and stock were killed and equipment destroyed. Farmers, "nesters," threw fences around their claims, blocking trails and breaking up the open range, and more wars, bringing losses to both sides, were fought.

In the early eighties, as the country entered on another period of expansion after the depression of 1873, Eastern and European demands for meat boomed the price of steers to as high as $50 a head. Producers hastened to increase the supply, even importing animals from the Middle West and East. Accounts of the lofty profits to be made in the cattle business—it was said that an investment of $5,000 would return $45,000 in four years—tempted Eastern, English, and Scottish capital to the plains. Increasingly the structure of the cattle economy became corporate in form; in one year twenty corporations with a combined capital of $12 million were chartered in Wyoming. The inevitable result of this frenzied extension was that the ranges, already sev-

ered and shrunk by the railroads and the farmers, were overstocked. There was not enough grass to support the crowding herds or sustain the long drives. Overstocking tumbled prices downward, and then nature intervened with a destructive finishing blow. Two severe winters, in 1885-6 and 1886-7, with a searing summer between them, stung and scorched the plains. Hundreds of thousands of cattle died, streams and grass dried up, princely ranches and costly investments disappeared in a season. The cattle kingdom never recovered. Cattlemen turned to more modest endeavors, fencing in their tracts, raising hay for winter feed, becoming settled ranchers. Another phase of the frontier had receded forever into the American past.

The Taming of the Tribes

When the miners and cowmen sifted into the last frontier, they came face to face with its Indian inhabitants, and they had to advance against more determined and sustained resistance than whites had met anywhere else in the sweep across the continent. In the end the invaders triumphed. The Indian tribes were broken and their members were forced to adapt themselves to an approximation of the white man's culture.

On the rolling, semiarid, treeless plains, the Indians followed a nomadic life. Riding their small but powerful horses, which were descendants of Spanish stock, the tribes roamed the spacious expanses of the grasslands. Permanent abodes were rare; when a band halted, tepees carried on the journey were quickly pitched as temporary dwellings. The magnet that drew the wanderers and guided their routes was the buffalo, or bison. This huge grazing animal provided the economic basis for the plains Indians' way of life. Its flesh was their principal source of food, and the skin supplied materials for clothing, shoes, tepees, blankets, robes, and utensils. To the Indians, the buffalo was, as someone has said, "a galloping department store." They trailed the herds, estimated to number at least 15,000,000 head in 1865, all over the plains. The plains Indians were almost uniformly martial, proud, and aggressive. Mounted on their horses, they were a formidable foe, whether armed with bow, spear, or rifle. They possessed a mobility enjoyed by no previous Indians, and students of war have ranked them among the best light cavalry in military history.

It was the traditional policy of the federal government to regard the tribes as independent nations (but also as wards of the Great White Father in Washington) and to negotiate agreements with them in the shape of treaties that were solemnly ratified by the Senate. This concept of Indian sovereignty was responsible for the attempt of the government before 1860 to erect a permanent frontier between whites and red men, to reserve the region west of the bend of the Missouri as permanent Indian country. But by the sixties the related principles of tribal independence and a perpetual line of division were breaking down before harsh realities. Administration of Indian matters was divided between the Bureau of Indian Affairs, located in the Department of the Interior, and the army. The Bureau was vested with general powers to supervise the disposition of Indian lands, disburse annuities, and, through its agents in Western posts, distribute needed supplies. From top to bottom, the personnel was shot through with the spoils system. Although some agents were conscientious and able men, more were dishonest and incompetent.

The army came into the picture only when trouble developed—when bands of Indians attacked homes or stagecoach lines or when a tribe went on the warpath. In short, its principal function was to punish, not to police. The army of the frontier was an effective fighting body, and it was led by some able officers. Still, in its "wars" with the Indians the army

frequently experienced rugged going. The mobile plains tribesmen were fully a match for cavalrymen armed with carbines. But soon the superior technology of the whites shifted the balance. The Colt repeating revolver gave the army increased firepower, the railroads facilitated quick troop concentrations, and the telegraph reported immediately the movements of hostile bands. Even so, the business of suppressing Indians was frightfully expensive. Three wars in the sixties cost the government $100,000,000, and one official estimated that the cost per Indian killed was $1,000,000.

The subjection of the fierce plains Indians was accomplished by economic as well as orthodox warfare—by the slaughter of the buffalo herds that supported their way of life. After the Civil War the demand for buffalo hides became a national phenomenon. It was partly based on economics: a commercial demand for the hides developing in the East; and it was partly a fad: suddenly every one east of the Missouri seemed to require a buffalo robe from the romantic West. Gangs of professional hunters swarmed over the plains to shoot the huge animals, divided by the Union Pacific Railroad into southern and northern herds. Some hunters killed merely for the sport of the chase, though the lumbering victims did not present much of a challenge. The southern herd was virtually exterminated by 1875, and within a few years the smaller northern herd met the same fate. Less than a thousand of the magnificent beasts survived. The army and the Indian agents condoned and even encouraged the killing. With the buffalo went the Indians' source of food and supplies and their will and ability to resist the white advance.

There was almost incessant Indian fighting on the frontier from the sixties to the eighties. During the Civil War the eastern Sioux in Minnesota, cramped on an inadequate reserve and exploited by agents, suddenly took to the warpath.

Led by Little Crow, they killed over 700 whites before being subdued by a force of regulars and militia. Thirty-eight of the Indians were hanged, and the tribe was exiled to the Dakotas. At the same time trouble flared in Colorado, where the Arapaho and Cheyenne had been restricted to the Sand Creek reserve. Bands of braves attacked stagecoach lines and settlements, provoking a concentration of territorial militia and threats from the army. The governor urged all friendly Indians to congregate at army posts before retribution fell on the hostiles. One Arapaho and Cheyenne band under Black Kettle came in to Fort Lyon on Sand Creek and encamped nearby. Although some braves just off the warpath were undoubtedly members of the party, Black Kettle understood he was under official protection. Nevertheless, Colonel J. M. Chivington, apparently encouraged by the army commander of the district, led a militia force to the unsuspecting camp and massacred a disputed (but large) number of men, women, and children. The government then forced the Arapaho and Cheyenne to accept an even less desirable reservation, but the Senate neglected to ratify the treaty.

At the end of the war against the Confederates, wars against Indians flared up on several frontier fronts. The most serious and sustained conflict was in Montana, where the army attempted to build a road, the Bozeman Trail, from Fort Laramie, Wyoming, to the mining centers. The western Sioux resented this intrusion into the heart of their buffalo range, and led by one of their great chiefs, Red Cloud, they so harried the soldiers and the construction party that the road could not be completed. Meanwhile, Congress, shocked by the Chivington massacre and the continued hostilities, appointed a committee to investigate the situation on the scene, and after studying its report created an Indian Peace Commission, composed of soldiers and civilians, to recommend a permanent Indian

SIOUX MEDICINE MAN. Sitting Bull was a somewhat controversial figure, even among his own people. He was not a war chief but a medicine man—in reality, a sort of Indian political boss. Always hostile to the whites, he used his great influence to stir the Sioux to war. But at the Little Bighorn he spent his time "making medicine" and did no fighting. (LIBRARY OF CONGRESS)

policy. The commission called the southern tribes to council at Medicine Lodge Creek in 1867, and the following year it met with the northern tribes at Fort Laramie. At Medicine Lodge the Arapaho and Cheyenne and other tribes agreed to accept reserves in the Indian Territory. At Laramie the Sioux accepted a reserve in southwestern Dakota, with rights to hunt as far as the Big Horn Mountains in Wyoming; they insisted, however, that the government abandon the Bozeman road, marking probably the only instance in which whites formally yielded to Indians.

The minor plains tribes and the mountain tribes consented to smaller reserves. For its part, the government pledged annuity payments and regular supplies. Some of the Arapaho and Cheyenne had another bad experience before being finally settled on their reserve. Black Kettle, who had escaped the Chivington massacre, and his Cheyennes, some of whom had taken the warpath, were caught on the Washita River, near the Texas border, by Colonel George A. Custer, and the chief was killed and his people slaughtered.

After 1870 the broad outlines of a new Indian policy began to take shape. The tribes were now concentrated in two large reserves, one in Dakota and one in the Indian Territory. So restricted, they found their powers to wage war severely limited. An advisory civilian Board of Indian Commissioners counseled the government to continue the reservation program and to break down the tribal structure with a view to assimilating the Indians to white culture. Congress responded in 1871 by abolishing the practice of treating the tribes as sovereignties, a step calculated to undermine the collective nature of Indian life.

But Indian resistance was far from ended. A source of potential conflict smouldered on the northern plains, where the Sioux roamed from Dakota to Wyoming. It burst into flame in 1875 when many of the tribesmen, angered by the dealings of crooked agents and alarmed by the entrance of miners into the Black Hills, suddenly left the reserve. Commanded to return, they gathered in Montana under Crazy Horse, probably the greatest leader of the plains Indians, and Sitting Bull. Three army columns, commanded by Generals George Crook, Alfred Terry, and John Gibbon, were sent to round them up. With the expedition as colonel of the famous Seventh Cavalry was the colorful and controversial George A. Custer, golden-haired romantic and alleged glory-seeker. At the battle of the Little Bighorn (1876) the Indians surprised Custer with part of his regiment and killed every man. Custer has been accused of rashness, but he seems to have ridden into something that no white man would have believed possible. On this occasion the chiefs had concentrated at least 2,500 warriors, perhaps 4,000, the largest Indian army ever assembled at one time in the United States. But the Indians did not have the political organization or the commissary to keep their troops united. Soon they drifted off in bands to elude pursuit or search for food, and the army ran them down singly and returned them to Dakota. The power of the Sioux was now broken. The proud

---

CHIEF JOSEPH'S LAST SPEECH

At the end of his great retreat Joseph, realizing that resistance to the army was hopeless, advised his chiefs to surrender. His speech is one of the gems of Indian rhetoric: "I am tired of fighting. Our chiefs are killed. The old men are all dead. It is the young men who say yes or no. He who led the young men is dead. It is cold and we have no blankets. The little children are freezing to death. My people, some of them, have run away to the hills and have no blankets, no food. No one knows where they are—perhaps freezing to death. I want to have time to look for my children and see how many of them I can find. Maybe I shall find them among the dead. Hear me, my chiefs. I am tired. My heart is sick and sad. From where the sun now stands I will fight no more forever."

leaders, Crazy Horse and Sitting Bull, accepted defeat and the monotony of
agency existence, and both were later
killed by reservation police after being
tricked or taunted into a last pathetic
show of resistance.

In 1877 one of the most dramatic episodes in Indian history occurred in Idaho.
Here the Nez Percé, a small and relatively
pacific and civilized tribe, refused to accept a smaller reservation and were, in
effect, forced into resistance. When
troops converged on them, their able
leader, Chief Joseph, attempted to conduct the band to Canada. A remarkable
chase ensued. Joseph moved with 200
warriors and 350 women, children, and
old people. Pursued by four columns, he
covered 1,321 miles in seventy-five days,
but was caught just short of the Canadian
border. Like so many other crushed tribes,
the Nez Percés were shipped to the Indian Territory.

The last Indians to maintain organized
resistance against the whites were the
Apaches, who fought intermittently from
the sixties to the late eighties. The two
ablest chiefs of this fierce tribe were
Mangas Colorados and Cochise. Mangas
was murdered during the Civil War, and
in 1872 Cochise agreed to peace and a
reservation for his followers. But one
leader, Geronimo, continued to lead a
war faction. When he was finally captured in 1886, formal warfare between
Indians and whites may be said to have
ended.

A final, tragic encounter in 1890 was
hardly a battle. As the Indians saw their
culture and their glories fading, they
turned to an emotional religion which
emphasized the coming of a Messiah and
featured "ghost dances," trances, and visions. Agents on the Sioux reservation,
fearing the frenzy might turn into an outbreak, called for troops, and some of the
Indians fled to the Badlands. They were
pursued and slaughtered at a creek called,
with an unmeditated but curiously fitting
symbolism, Wounded Knee.

APACHE WARRIOR. Although Geronimo was not
a chief, he assumed the leadership of one of the
Apache tribes and fought the whites fiercely until
he was captured in Mexico in 1886. General
N. A. Miles, who fought him, said that he was
one of the cruelest Indians he had met in his frontier experience. (LIBRARY OF CONGRESS)

In 1887 Congress finally moved to destroy the tribal structure that was the cor-
nerstone of Indian culture. Although the
motivation was partially a humanitarian
impulse to help the Indian, the action
was frankly designed to force him to become a landowner and farmer, to abandon his collective society and culture, to
become, in short, a white man. The
Dawes Severalty Act provided for the
gradual abrogation of tribal ownership of
land and the allotment of tracts to individual owners: 160 acres to the head of
a family, 80 acres to a single adult or orphan, 40 acres to each dependent child.
Adult owners were accorded the status of

A Sod House on the Plains. Settlers on the treeless Great Plains frequently lived their first years in sod houses. A sod house was constructed by plowing up long strips of the tough turf and cutting these into smaller pieces in the shape of bricks. The pieces were then laid on top of each other to make a wall. The roof consisted of a support of poles or canvas covered by earth. Damp, dark, and poorly ventilated, the sod house was used until its owner could import enough wood to build a frame house. (THE KANSAS STATE HISTORICAL SOCIETY, TOPEKA)

citizenship but, unlike other citizens, they could not alienate their property for twenty-five years. The act was hardly a success. The Indians were not ready for a wrenching change from a collective society to individualism. Congress attempted to facilitate the transition with the Burke Act of 1906. Citizenship was deferred until after the completion of the twenty-five year period contemplated in the Dawes Act, but Indians who proved their adaptability could secure both citizenship and land ownership in a shorter period. Full rights of citizenship were conferred on all Indians in 1924. Even then many resisted white ways, and in the 1930's the government would make a notable attempt to restore some of the institutions of tribal culture.

The Farming Frontier

Some farmers had drifted into the West during its first stages of development, following the miners and cattlemen, but the great rush of settlement came in the late seventies. In the next decade the relentless advance of the farming frontier would gradually convert the plains country to an agricultural economy. The surge of migration came at a time when for years in succession the rainfall was well above the average. People scoffed at the tradition of the Great American Desert and looked forward to an indefinite era of prosperity. They scoffed too at the old cowmen who warned that the light soil of the plains should not be deprived of its protecting turf by cultivation.

But even under the most favorable conditions, farming on the plains presented problems not encountered in any previous region. First and most critical was the problem of fencing. The farmer had to enclose his land, if for no other reason than to protect it from the herds of the ranchers. But the traditional wood or stone fences were impossible on the plains. The cost of importing the material was prohibitive, and besides, such barriers were ineffective against range cattle. In the mid-seventies two Illinois farmers,

Joseph H. Glidden and I. L. Ellwood, solved this problem by developing and putting on the market barbed wire. Produced in mass quantities—40,000 tons a year—it sold cheaply, became standard equipment on the plains, and revolutionized fencing practices all over the country.

The second problem, present even when the rainfall was above average, was

to them in the Carey Act (1894) several million acres of public land to be reclaimed. The states made little progress, largely because the problems of reclamation cut over state boundaries. In the Newlands, or Reclamation, Act (1902) the national government finally accepted the responsibility for an irrigation program.

Farming on the plains was always an

A GRASSHOPPER PLAGUE ON THE PLAINS

Among the many visitations of nature that might wipe out a plains farmer were the grasshoppers. Stuart Henry describes a raid in *Conquering Our Great American Plains* (New York: E. P. Dutton, 1930): "In 1874 came a gigantic calamity in the form of a raid of grasshoppers which ate up every bit of green vegetation from the Rocky Mountains to and beyond the Missouri River. I recall that when coming home late one afternoon for supper I stepped back surprised to see what became known as Rocky Mountain locusts covering the side of the house. Already inside, they feasted on the curtains. Clouds of them promptly settled down on the whole country—everywhere, unavoidable. People set about killing them to save gardens, but this soon proved ridiculous. Specially contrived machines, pushed by horses, scooped up the hoppers in grain fields by the barrelful to burn them. This, too, was then nonsensical. Vast hordes, myriads. In a week grain fields, gardens, shrubs, vines, had been eaten down to the ground or to the bark. Nothing could be done. You sat by and saw everything go."

---

water. It became particularly acute after 1887, when a series of dry seasons began. One expedient resorted to was the use of deep wells and steel windmills, which assured a steady water supply for stock. Another was dry farming, a system of tillage designed to conserve moisture in the soil by covering it with a dust blanket and emphasizing utilization of drought-enduring crops. It was evident that in many areas of the plains, agriculture could not exist without irrigation. It was also evident that large-scale irrigation, the only practicable kind, would have to be planned and supported by the government. The national government tried to hand the issue to the states, turning over

expensive and often a risky proposition. The uncertainty of rainfall and the danger of such caprices of nature as grasshopper plagues and tornadoes made every farm year a speculative experiment. Costs of operation ran high, partly because so many supplies had to be imported into the region from distant points, but mainly because of the nature of plains farming. In all the farm areas of the country, machines were playing a larger part in the agricultural process, and they were especially vital on the plains, where grain farming was conducted on large land units.

The last West was not, as has so often been claimed, a refuge for the urban poor or a safety valve for proletarian unrest. The men who settled this area were mostly farmers, and they came from farms in the Middle West, the East, or Europe. In the booming eighties, with land values rising, credit was easy, and the farmers confidently expected to retire their obligations. With the advent of the arid years of the late eighties, the prospect changed with grim suddenness.

In 1890 the census report noted that the unsettled area of the country had been so broken up by bodies of settlement that a frontier line no longer could be drawn. Three years later a young professor from the University of Wisconsin, Frederick Jackson Turner, startled the American Historical Association with an epochal paper, "The Significance of the Frontier in American History." The roots of the national character lay not in the European or colonial background, he asserted, but in the recurring frontiers that had formed the fabric of American history; the frontier environment, with its corollary of cheap or free land, had promoted nationalism, democracy, and individualism. With a touch of foreboding, he concluded: "Now, four centuries from the discovery of America, at the end of a hundred years of life under the Constitution, the frontier has gone, and with its going has closed the first period of American history."

The foreboding voiced by Professor Turner and other commentators were exaggerated. There was still plenty of available land; in fact, in the forty years after 1890 the government gave away almost four times as much land as it had given away before that year. Turner was right in sensing that an opportunity in American life had disappeared, but it was not so much the opportunity to acquire land cheaply as the opportunity to farm at a low cost of operation. And while a great source of abundance had disappeared when cheap land was occupied, an even greater source was emerging with the creation of an industrial economy. Long before 1890 migrations to the city were becoming the typical American folk movement.

BIBLIOGRAPHY

Basic for the West of this period is W. P. Webb, *The Great Plains* (1931). Other important general works are L. R. Hafen and C. C. Rister, *Western America* (1950); J. C. Malin, *The Grasslands of North America* (1948); Everett Dick, *The Sod-House Frontier* (1937); O. O. Winther, *The Great Northwest* (1947); H. E. Briggs, *Frontiers of the Northwest* (1940); and C. C. Rister, *The Southwestern Frontier, 1865–1890* (1947). A perceptive brief survey is F. L. Paxson, *The Last American Frontier* (1910).

Standard for its subject is E. S. Pomeroy, *The Territories and the United States, 1864–1890* (1947). On land policies, see R. M. Robbins, *Our Landed Heritage* (1942). On transportation: L. R. Hafen, *The Overland Mail, 1849–1869* (1926); Arthur Chapman, *The Pony Express* (1932); J. V. Frederick, *Ben Holliday*

(1940); and R. C. Overton, *Burlington West: A Colonization History of the Burlington Railroad* (1941).

On the mining frontier: T. A. Rickard, *A History of American Mining* (1932); W. J. Trimble, *The Mining Advance into the Inland Empire* (1914); G. C. Quiett, *Pay Dirt: A Panorama of American Gold Rushes* (1936); C. B. Glasscock, *The Big Bonanza* (1931); G. D. Lyman, *The Saga of the Comstock Lode* (1934); N. P. Langford, *Vigilante Days and Ways* (1912); C. H. Shinn, *Mining Camps* (1885; reprint 1948); Stanley Vestal, *Mountain Men* (1937); and Mark Twain, *Roughing It* (2 vols., 1872).

On the cattle kingdom: E. S. Osgood, *The Day of the Cattleman* (1929); E. E. Dale, *The Range Cattle Industry* (1930); Louis Pelzer, *The Cattlemen's Frontier* (1936); Andy Adams, *Log of a Cowboy*

(1903); P. A. Rollins, *The Cowboy* (1922); and J. B. Frantz and J. E. Choate, Jr., *The American Cowboy* (1955). On the coming of the sheepherders and farmers: C. W. Towne and E. N. Wentworth, *Shepherd's Empire* (1945); and F. A. Shannon, *The Farmer's Last Frontier* (1945). Other aspects of the story: E. D. Branch, *The Hunting of the Buffalo* (1929); W. M. Raine, *Famous Sheriffs and Western Outlaws* (1929); Wayne Gard, *Frontier Justice* (1949); and F. H. Harrington, *Hanging Judge* (1951).

On the Indians: Ruth Underhill, *Red Man's America* (1953); Paul Radin, *The Story of the American Indian* (1927); Clark Wissler, *Indians of the United States* (1954); W. C. MacLeod, *The American Indian Frontier* (1928); L. B. Priest, *Uncle Sam's Stepchildren* (1942); Paul Wellman, *Death on Horseback* (1947); Stanley Vestal, *Warpath and Council Fire* (1948), and *Sitting Bull* (1957); and C. A. Fee, *Chief Joseph* (1936). The Indian-fighting general George A. Custer is unsympathetically portrayed by F. F. Van de Water in *Glory Hunter* (1934). A more balanced treatment is Jay Monaghan's *Custer* (1959).

24

TRIUMPHANT

INDUSTRIALISM

In the years between 1865 and 1900 the American nation gained remarkably in productive facilities; the increase of material goods was without parallel in the modern world. The impact upon American society in all its parts, especially upon the forms of social and economic organization, was so tremendous as to deserve the title of "economic revolution." Although the economic revolution caught up in its vortex every segment of the economy—agriculture, labor, finance—it was primarily an industrial transmutation, and it was in industry that its immense transforming effects were most vividly apparent.

More Production, Fewer Firms

Statistics tell part of the story. In 1860 approximately a billion dollars was invested in manufacturing plants; the annual value of manufactured products was $1,885,000,000; and 1,300,000 workers were employed in American factories. Before the turn of the century, the amount of capital invested had risen to more than $12 billion, the yearly value of products to

over $11 billion, and the number of workers to 5,500,000. But as the historians of American civilization (Charles A. and Mary R. Beard) remark, statistics but dimly shadow the progress of the era: "With a stride that astonished statisticians, the conquering hosts of business enterprise swept over the continent; twenty-five years after the death of Lincoln, America had become in the quantity and value of her products, the first manufacturing nation of the world. What England had once accomplished in a hundred years, the United States had achieved in half the time."

Four factors exercised a potent influence upon industrial productivity. First, Americans continued to exhibit the same technological skills that had characterized their productive activities since the 1830's, as well as the same ingenuity in devising new industrial and agricultural machines or adapting old ones to new uses that seemed to be a hallmark of the national character. Also, they continued to demonstrate their already proven abilities to organize production: to create corporations, recruit a managerial class, subdivide and specialize labor, and advertise their products to a national market. In short, Americans, more than any other people, understood the modern techniques of mass production. Second, American investors and producers had ready to hand a seemingly inexhaustible supply of raw materials: coal, iron ore, timber, oil, water power, and almost every form of

years after Lee's surrender witnessed a laissez-faire Utopia. Lastly, and perhaps most important, American producers functioned in a great domestic or interior market which was guarded against outside competition by tariff walls and connected in all its parts by rail and water transportation. Moreover, it was a market which constantly expanded in size and

---

THE STOCK EXCHANGE

The New York Stock Exchange became an important barometer of the nation's industrial economy in the years after the Civil War. Its origins stretched back into the eighteenth century. In the 1790's a group of merchants and auctioneers decided to meet daily to buy and sell government securities and stock in banks and insurance companies. At first they gathered under a buttonwood tree on Wall Street, but later they moved to an indoor location at the Tontine Coffee House at Wall and William streets. As the economy expanded after 1800, more companies came to list their stock with this unofficial exchange, and in 1817 the brokers decided to organize themselves with a formal constitution and name: the New York Stock and Exchange Board. At this time stocks were sold only on "call" —the president at a specified hour called the names of stocks on the list, and brokers made their offers. Not until 1871 did the call market give way to a continuous market. Other important dates in stock market history are as follows: 1863, the name "New York Stock Exchange" adopted; 1867, first stock tickers installed; 1868, memberships made salable; 1879, first telephones used on the Exchange; and 1886, first time that a day's volume exceeded 1,000,000 shares. After operating in several locations, the Exchange moved to its present site, 18 Broad Street, in 1903.

---

metal. The American economy was young, profuse, opulent—and waiting to be exploited. Third, many of these resources were owned by a friendly and receptive national government that was willing to hand them over to private interests for exploitation and eager to aid business expansion with such measures as protective tariffs, a favorable financial policy, and subsidies of land and money. Furthermore, private enterprise operated in a sympathetic political climate. It seldom had to worry that the national government would inquire into its practices or attempt to regulate its activities. The

consequently enlarged its demands with population growth.

The industrial beginnings of the United States stretched back to the 1790's, and industry had experienced a steady although deliberate development up to the time when the agrarian South seceded from the Union. What the Civil War did was to stimulate and accelerate—with enormous impulsive power—a growth already well under way.

And yet there is a difference in the eras before and after the war. In the earlier period, we see the institutions that seem to characterize an older and mellower America: rural folkways, small towns, and small economic and social organizations. The old American ways would continue after 1865, but gradually they would be supplanted by new social forms. In the later period, we see taking shape the institutions that distinguish modern America: urban mores, the huge metropolis, and large-scale organization in almost every phase of national life. Of the new forces that were making a new America, the most important by far was

concentration were powerful propulsive forces. As industry expanded and opportunities for undreamed-of profits unfolded, competition for the rewards became more intense and unrestrained. Combination would limit or eliminate competition, permit economies in the manufacturing process, and facilitate the accumulation of capital reserves. In the simple language of business, the curbing of competition would result in large profits for the curbers.

SOURCES OF ENERGY IN THE UNITED STATES, 1860–1950

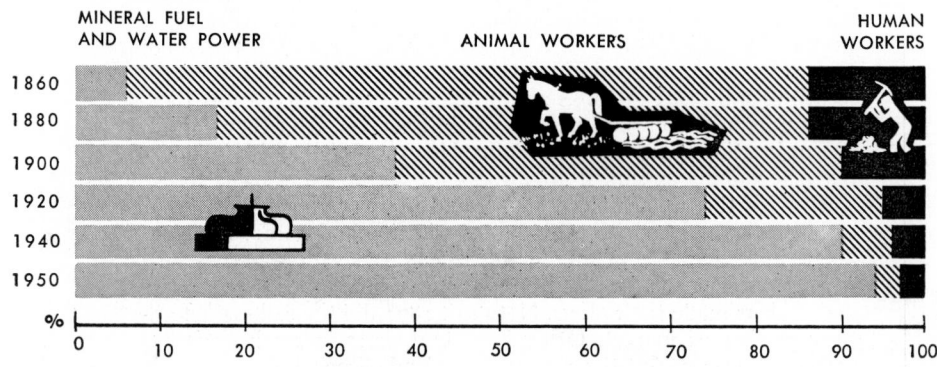

the change that occurred in the forms of business organization. In the postwar epoch bigness became a ruling principle in business organization—and big business reached out to rule the national economy.

Before the Civil War business concerns in the United States had employed a variety of organizational patterns: the single proprietorship, the partnership, and the corporation. After the war the corporate arrangement came into increasing and widespread use. Small companies often were merged to form large ones. The corporation was not, however, the biggest form of organization that appeared in the postwar years. Looming above it were even vaster combinations—pools, trusts, and holding companies.

Behind the movement toward business

Thus American business moved in the direction of monopoly. Fewer and fewer companies produced more and more of the nation's goods. In industry after industry between 1865 and 1900 the number of firms decreased, and yet the annual value of the products turned out increased ten, twelve, and fifteen times. The various combinations, regardless of their specific form, were known to the public as "trusts." As the twentieth century opened, there were in the country 318 of these "trusts"; they had a total capitalization of over $7 billion and represented mergers of nearly 5,300 separate plants. Less than 2 per cent of the manufacturing establishments—the hugest organizations—produced almost 50 per cent of all the manufactured goods in the country.

Bigness in the Basic Industries

The economic revolution was accompanied by a flood of inventions and technological innovations. In the entire history of the country up to 1860 only 36,000 patents had been granted, but for the period from 1860 to 1890 the figure was 440,000.

Many of the postwar inventions and discoveries were in the field of communication. In 1866 Cyrus W. Field succeeded in his project of laying a trans-Atlantic cable to Europe. During the next decade Alexander Graham Bell developed the first practicable telephone, and by the 1890's the American Telephone and Telegraph Company, which handled his interests, had installed nearly half a million instruments in American cities. Other inventions that speeded the pace of business organization were the typewriter

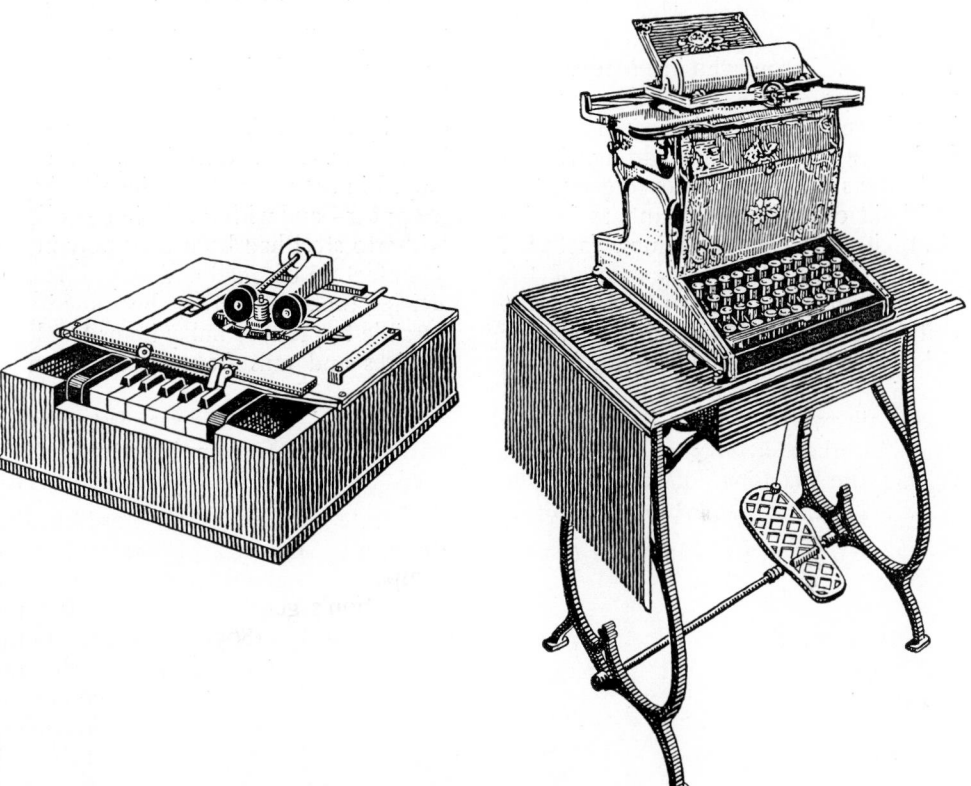

EARLY TYPEWRITERS. The first practical writing machine was developed in Milwaukee, 1867–1873, by Christopher Latham Sholes, James Densmore, and their associates. In 1873 the patent owners made an arrangement with E. Remington & Sons, gun makers of Ilion, N.Y., for the manufacture of typewriters on a commercial scale. Not till the late 1880's did the typewriter become standard equipment in business offices. It then began to have revolutionary effects, making possible truly big business and creating new and respectable job opportunities for women. The illustration shows, on the left, an incomplete model of the first Sholes machine to be patented (1868); and, on the right, the first Remington-made machine (1874), with a treadle for returning the carriage. (F. E. COMPTON & COMPANY)

(by Christopher L. Sholes in 1868), the calculating or adding machine (by William S. Burroughs in 1891), and the cash register (by James Ritty in 1879).

Undoubtedly the technological innovation that had the most revolutionary effect upon industry and upon lives of the urban masses in the industrial centers was the introduction in the 1870's of electricity as a source of light and power. Among the several men who pioneered in developing a commercially practical dynamo were Charles F. Brush, who devised the arc lamp for street illumination, and Thomas A. Edison, who invented, among many other electrical contrivances, the incandescent lamp, which could be used for both street and home lighting. Edison and others designed improved generators and built central power plants to furnish electricity to office buildings, factories, and dwellings. Before the turn of the century, 2,774 power stations were in operation, and some two million electric lights were in use in the country. Already electric power was being employed in street railway systems and in electric elevators in urban skyscrapers, as well as for driving the machines of factories. The electric power industry was dominated by two large corporations: the General Electric Company, which took over the Edison interests, and the Westinghouse Electric and Manufacturing Company.

The Age of Steel began in 1865. A process by which iron could be transformed into steel had been discovered simultaneously in the 1850's by an Englishman, Henry Bessemer, and an American, William Kelly (it consisted of blowing air through the molten iron to burn out the impurities), but it was not put into use until after the Civil War. In 1868 another method of making steel, the open-hearth process, was introduced from Europe by Abram S. Hewitt, a New Jersey ironmaster. Both techniques were employed in the many steel mills that began to appear—and with revolutionary effects. Hitherto steel had been used only in the manufacture of small and very expensive articles, tools and cutlery, but now it was possible to produce bulky items like locomotives and rails from steel instead of iron.

The steel industry was first concentrated where the iron industry had existed, in western Pennsylvania and east-

GROWTH OF BASIC INDUSTRY, 1865–1900

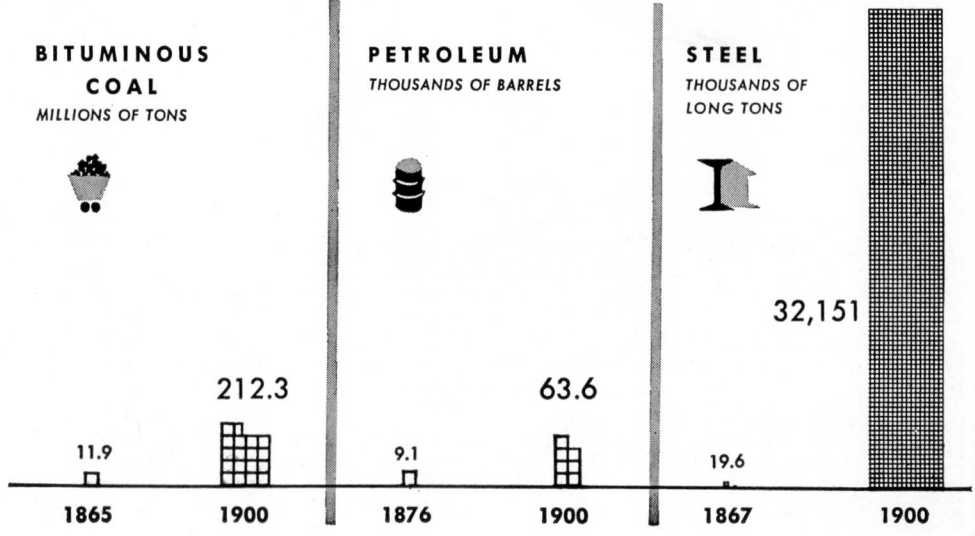

BITUMINOUS COAL MILLIONS OF TONS		PETROLEUM THOUSANDS OF BARRELS		STEEL THOUSANDS OF LONG TONS	
11.9	212.3	9.1	63.6	19.6	32,151
1865	1900	1876	1900	1867	1900

ern Ohio. Here, in a region where iron ore and coal were found in abundance, Pittsburgh reigned as the center of the steel world. But as the industry expanded, new sources of ore had to be tapped, and by the 1870's the mines of the northern Michigan peninsula were furnishing over half of the supply. Then in the 1890's the Eastern steelmasters began to exploit the extensive Mesabi range in Minnesota, which developed into the greatest ore-producing region in the world. Another rich source was discovered around Birmingham, Alabama. Although the Michigan and Minnesota fields were located at a great distance from the Eastern plants, the ore could be transported easily and cheaply by means of railroads and Great Lakes steamers. Eventually new centers of production with ready access to ore and coal arose: Cleveland and Lorain in Ohio, Detroit, Chicago, and Birmingham.

Inevitably the high profits to be made in steel tempted consolidation, and inevitably there appeared in the industry, as

in other areas of business, men who had a genius for organization and a vision of the advantages of concentration. The central figure in the centralization of steel was Andrew Carnegie, a Scottish immigrant boy who worked his way up from economic obscurity to a position of trust

THE STEEL MASTER AND HIS PLANT. Andrew Carnegie and the Homestead works of his company as they appeared about 1890. (UNITED STATES STEEL CORPORATION)

in the railroad world. After 1865 he turned his interests to iron and then to steel manufacturing. Adopting the Bessemer process, he opened in 1873 the J. Edgar Thompson Steel Works in western Pennsylvania, named in honor of his former railroad employer, the head of the Pennsylvania Railroad. Soon Carnegie had built up his company to a place of dominance in the industry.

His methods were those commonly employed by other great consolidationists of the times. He obtained rebates from railroads on his shipments, so that he could cut his costs and hence his prices, and he bought out rival concerns that could not meet his competition. In collaboration with his ablest associate, Henry Clay Frick, he set up a policy of integration designed to control the processing of steel from mine to market. His company operated a fleet of ore ships on the Great Lakes, acquired railroads and coal mines, and leased part of the Mesabi range. Meanwhile other companies were emulating Carnegie's practices, if not always achieving his success.

The machines of the Age of Steel could not run without lubrication, and so another vast enterprise came into being in the postwar era, the petroleum industry. For years before the Civil War the existence of petroleum had been known, particularly in western Pennsylvania where it often seeped to the surface of streams and springs. No one was quite sure what it was or what to do with it. Some enterprising individuals peddled it in bottles as a patent medicine. The first person to glimpse its commercial possibilities as an illuminant was George H. Bissell, who sent a sample of oil to Professor Benjamin Silliman of Yale for analysis. Silliman reported, in 1855, that the substance could be used for lighting purposes, and that it would also yield such products as paraffin, naphtha, and lubricating oil. Bissell then raised enough money to begin drilling operations, and in 1859 Edwin L. Drake, employed by Bissell, put down the first

oil well near Titusville, Pennsylvania. Labeled "Drake's folly" by the skeptical, it was soon producing oil at the rate of 500 barrels a month.

It also started an oil rush, as promoters searched for and found other fields, not only in Pennsylvania but in Ohio and West Virginia as well. By the 1870's nearly forty million barrels of petroleum had been produced, oil had advanced to fourth place among the nation's exports, and the annual production was approaching twenty million barrels. Because relatively little capital was required for a man to make a start in the oil business, either as a producer or a refiner, competition at first ran wild. Refineries, which were even more profitable than wells, dotted the Pennsylvania-Ohio region, with Pittsburgh and Cleveland constituting the two principal refining centers. Then there stepped into the picture to bring order to the industry the greatest consolidationist of the age.

John D. Rockefeller was a successful businessman at an age when most boys of today would be in college. When he was nineteen, he became a partner in a produce commission company in Cleveland that took solid profits selling goods to the government during the Civil War. Farsighted, highly acquisitive, and possessing abundant talents for organization, he decided that his economic future lay with oil. He also concluded that Cleveland, connected by rail and water with the Eastern and Western markets, was destined to surpass Pittsburgh, which had access only to the East through the Pennsylvania Railroad, as the oil-refining center of the country. At the end of the war he and Sidney Andrews, a Cleveland refiner, launched their own business. From the beginning Rockefeller sought to eliminate the competition and the small-scale companies that in his opinion were ruining the petroleum industry. He and Andrews enlarged their operations, took in H. M. Flagler and S. V. Harkness as allies, and proceeded methodically to buy out other refineries. In 1870 the associates formed the Standard Oil Company of Ohio, which in a few years had acquired twenty of the twenty-five refineries in Cleveland, in addition to plants in Pittsburgh, Philadelphia, New York, and Baltimore.

In its rise to dominance the Standard employed the familiar consolidating devices of the period, plus a few which were its own invention. The company emphasized efficient and economic operation, research, and sound financial practices. At Rockefeller's insistence, a large cash reserve was maintained to avoid reliance on banks and to purchase competitors. The company obtained rebates from railroads, and even, for a brief time, forced three of the Eastern roads to pay rebates to it on oil shipped by competing companies. Price wars were inaugurated to drive competitors out of business, and

The Early Oil Industry. These pictures show a typical early Pennsylvania oil field, 1865, and John D. Rockefeller as he appeared in the 1880's. (STANDARD OIL COMPANY, NEW JERSEY)

Standard, always victorious, took over the defeated concerns.

Like Carnegie in steel, Rockefeller set up an integrated system of production. He built his own terminal warehouses and barrel factories and a network of pipelines that gave him control over most of the facilities for transporting petroleum. Standard also owned its own marketing organization, thus escaping having to pay commissions to middlemen. For sales purposes the United States was divided into districts, each of which was administered by a company executive who was assisted by a corps of agents. The salesmen were under orders to sell Standard products by almost any method, and almost always they succeeded. When the Standard Oil Trust was formed in 1882, it was only a formal recognition of the near-monopoly that Rockefeller and his associates had already established.

Three factors emerged to revolutionize the meat-packing business. They were the appearance in Texas and the Great Plains of the range-cattle industry, the extension of railroad lines across the Mississippi into the plains country, and the introduction of the refrigerated freight car. Chicago, situated close to the cattle supply of the trans-Mississippi area and the hog supply of the Middle West, and elaborately connected by railroads with both the producing areas and the urban markets, became the undisputed capital of the meat-packing industry. Imaginative and aggressive leaders, the counterparts of Rockefeller and Carnegie, appeared to form the inevitable combinations: Philip D. Armour, Nelson Morris, and Gustavus F. Swift. It was Swift who pushed the most important technological development in the industry, the refrigerator car cooled by artificial ice.

Like the meat business, flour milling was originally a localized enterprise, carried on in thousands of small mills in all parts of the country. And like meat packing, the milling industry moved west to be nearer the source of the wheat supply,

adopted new technological processes, and originated large-scale organizations which turned out standardized products. By the close of the Civil War the center of wheat production had shifted to the upper Mississippi Valley, and Minneapolis, Minnesota, became the center of the milling industry. The leading millers were Cadwallader C. Washburn, Charles A. Pillsbury, and George M. Christian, the last of whom eventually merged his interests with Washburn. Two manufacturing methods introduced from Europe resulted in a greatly improved product. The first, called the "middlings-purifier" or "gradual-reduction" process, preserved a higher content of gluten in finished flour than previously had been the case. The second was a process of passing wheat slowly through chilled iron rollers to achieve a flour of superior quality and unusual whiteness. By 1880 flour milling had become one of the country's largest businesses, and was supplying its product to European as well as to American markets.

The location of the flour and meat industries in the West illustrates one of the important economic trends of the postwar era: the movement of industry from the Northeast to other sections of the country. With the Middle West boasting of its iron and steel, packing, and milling enterprises, and with the South building up its textile, steel, and tobacco manufactures, it could no longer be said that one section was predominantly industrial and others primarily agrarian or that economic sectionalism sharply divided the nation.

The Railroads and Consolidation

In 1860 the railroads constituted the biggest business and the most important single economic interest in the United States. Their mileage total was approximately 30,000, and in rolling stock they counted 100,000 freight and passenger cars and 1,000 locomotives. Every decade

RAILROADS AFTER THE CIVIL WAR. In the decades after the Civil War the railroads introduced more powerful locomotives for both passenger and freight traffic and provided improved and often lavish services for passengers. The famous locomotive No. 999 established a world speed record in 1893 when it hauled the Empire State Express at 112 miles per hour. This was a startling contrast to the thirty miles per hour speed of railroads in the 1850's. Passengers on the crack trains enjoyed through Pullman service, sleeping and dining cars, and lounges. Electric lights were substituted for gas illumination by 1900. (ASSOCIATION OF AMERICAN RAILROADS)

the trackage figure increased: 52,000 miles in 1870, 93,000 in 1880, 163,000 in 1890, and 193,000 in 1900. The railroads made it possible for industry to secure its raw materials from a national producing area and to distribute its products in a national market.

Accompanying the expansion of railroad facilities was a host of technological improvements that made rail travel and transportation more efficient, convenient, and safe. Among the innovations were steel rails, heavier locomotives and cars, a uniform gauge (4 feet, 8½ inches), and wider roadbeds. Perhaps the most important invention affecting railroads was the Westinghouse air brake, developed by George Westinghouse in 1869. In 1874 interlocking block signals were introduced from England. George Pullman had produced in 1864 the first sleeping car, and within a few years dining, parlor, and drawing-room cars appeared.

The major Eastern railroads were the New York Central, the Pennsylvania, the Erie, and the Baltimore and Ohio. By 1874 all of them had consolidated lesser lines into their systems and established connections with the Western market at Chicago. The creator of the New York Central system was Cornelius Vanderbilt, a salty, colorful character who had previously operated a steamship line and was enduringly known as "Commodore." A ruthless competitor but a sound railroad man, Vanderbilt improved facilities on the Central and bought up smaller roads to complete his empire. Second only to the Central in facilities was the Pennsylvania Railroad, whose original route

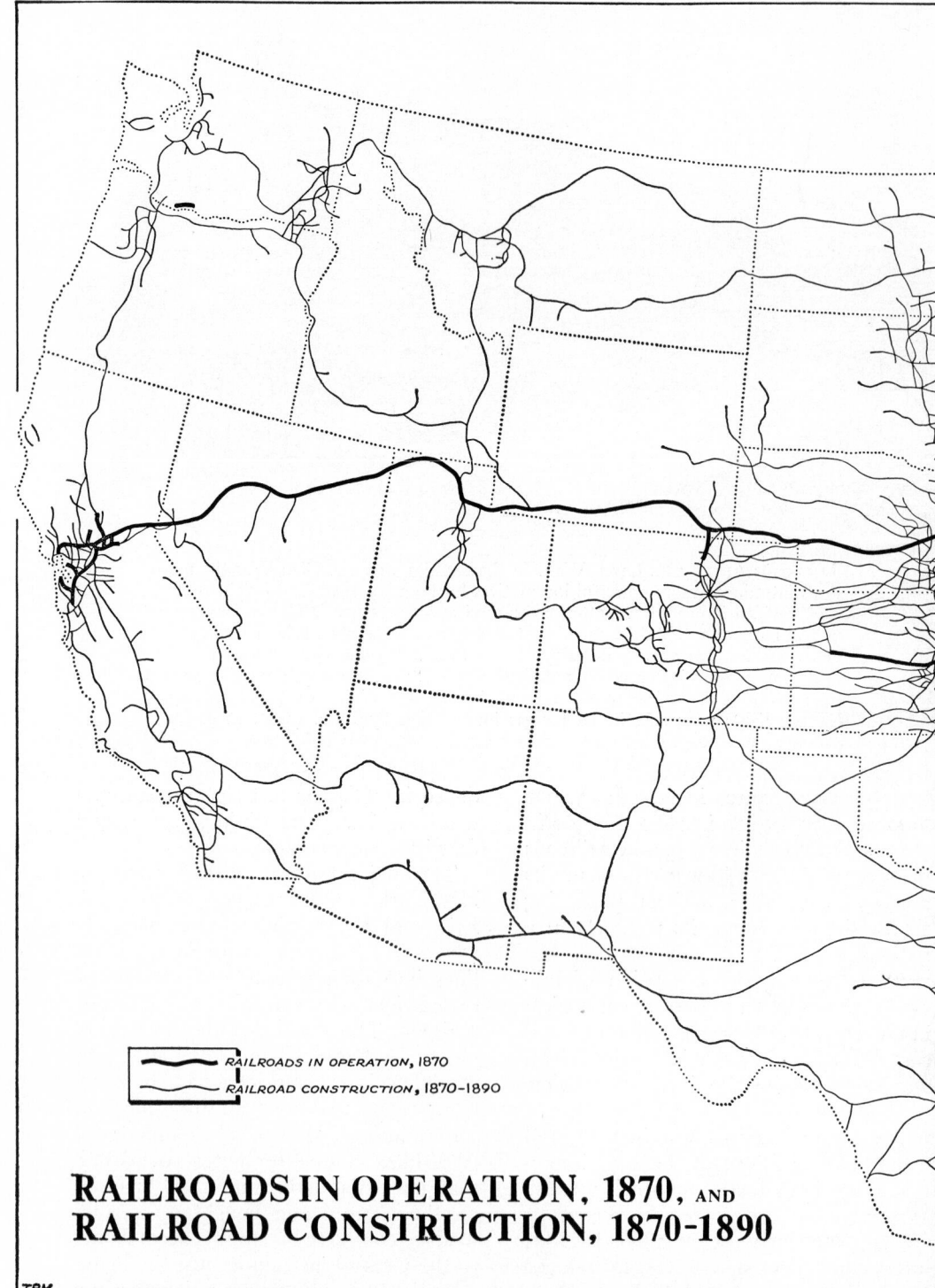

RAILROADS IN OPERATION, 1870
RAILROAD CONSTRUCTION, 1870-1890

RAILROADS IN OPERATION, 1870, AND
RAILROAD CONSTRUCTION, 1870-1890

TRM

500 MILES

ran between Philadelphia and Pittsburgh. Under the leadership of J. Edgar Thompson, the Pennsylvania established connections with Chicago, St. Louis, Baltimore, and Richmond, and in 1899, by tunneling under the Hudson River, entered New York City to compete directly with the Central. The Erie, chartered in the 1850's to link New York City and Lake Erie, in the postwar years stretched its connections to Cleveland, Cincinnati, and St. Louis. Unfortunately for the Erie, it was controlled during the seventies by Daniel Drew, Jay Gould, and James Fisk, three of the most unscrupulous speculators of the era, who were more interested in milking it of profits than in making it into a railroad. The Baltimore and Ohio had built from Baltimore as far as Wheeling on the Ohio River before the Civil War. After the war John W. Garrett, its president, extended its lines to Chicago, Cincinnati, St. Louis, and Philadelphia; it was not able, however, to obtain access to New York.

In the South the first railroad activity in the years immediately after 1865 was the rehabilitation of facilities damaged in the war. Then an outburst of construction, financed by Northern and European capital, got under way, and by 1890 the South had increased its trackage from 9,000 to 50,000 miles. In 1893, the Southern Railway was organized, with lines extending from Washington to New Orleans and connecting with the Middle West at St. Louis and Cincinnati. Chief rival to the Southern was the Atlantic Coast Line Railroad, which consolidated dozens of small roads to monopolize transportation from Richmond to Florida. The third big system in the South, the Illinois Central, was really a Middle Western road with a Southern terminal. Shortly before the Civil War it had built as far as Cairo, Illinois, at the confluence of the Ohio and the Mississippi. In the postwar era the Central achieved its original purpose of reaching the Gulf of Mexico. By gobbling up smaller lines in the South, it

increased its trackage from approximately 1,000 to 9,000 miles, reached New Orleans on the Gulf, and eventually touched the Atlantic at Savannah, Georgia.

From 1865 to 1873 there was more railroad construction in the Mississippi Valley than in any part of the country. The Chicago and Northwestern stretched its lines to Omaha; the Chicago, Burlington and Quincy drove through to Kearney, Nebraska; the Missouri Pacific built from Kansas City to St. Louis; and the Kansas Pacific moved from Kansas City to Denver and then on to Cheyenne in Wyoming Territory.

Of all the stupendous railroad projects of the era between 1865 and 1900, none so gripped the popular imagination as the great "transcontinental" lines. An act of Congress passed in 1862 and amended in 1864 chartered two railroad corporations, the Union Pacific and the Central Pacific. The Union Pacific was to build westward from Omaha, Nebraska, and the Central Pacific eastward from Sacramento, California, until they met.

To provide the financial aid deemed necessary to initiate the roads, Congress donated a right of way across the public domain and offered the companies special benefits: for each mile of track a company laid, it would receive 20 square miles of land in alternate sections along the right of way and a thirty-year loan of $16,000, $32,000, or $48,000, depending on whether the construction was in plains, foothill, or mountain country. In addition, the government accepted a second mortgage on the loans, and permitted the companies to issue first mortgage bonds up to the amount of the official loan. A generous government could hardly have been more liberal. By the terms of the war legislation, the Union Pacific and the Central Pacific stood to receive approximately 20 million acres of land and $60 million in loans.

Because of a scarcity of labor, the Union Pacific resorted to hiring thousands of Irish immigrants, while the Central Pacific imported several thousand Chinese workers. The builders had to cross deserts, penetrate mountain ranges, and fight off Indians, but under the direction of Grenville M. Dodge, chief engineer of the Union Pacific, and Theodore D. Judah, who held a similar post with the Central Pacific, the rails of the two lines steadily pushed closer together. In the spring of 1869 engines of the two lines met at Promontory Point in Utah Territory, and the nation was linked by rail from the Atlantic to the Pacific.

By the end of the century five transcontinental systems were in operation: (1) the Union Pacific-Central Pacific, joining Omaha to Sacramento and San Francisco; (2) the Southern Pacific, extending from San Francisco to St. Louis and New Orleans; (3) the Northern Pacific, linking St. Paul and Minneapolis to Portland, Oregon; (4) the Atchison, Topeka and Santa Fé, running from Atchison, Kansas, to San Diego, California; and (5) the Great Northern, stretching from Duluth and St. Paul to Seattle and Tacoma, Washington. All except the Great Northern were built with some form of assistance from the national government or from state governments.

State governments put up an estimated $228 million to entice promoters into their boundaries, and in addition placed their credit at the disposal of railroads, subscribed to stock, and donated 50 million acres of land. The federal government granted over 130 million acres and provided over $60 million in loans to various Western roads. In a number of cases, the aid supplied by government more than paid the cost of construction. It was small wonder that many people regarded the railroads, although operated by private enterprise, as essentially public projects.

As the network of rails covered the country, it became evident that the railroad industry was being overbuilt and overextended; many railroad corporations, including some of the largest ones, were overexpanded, overcapitalized, and afflicted with impossible debt burdens. Moreover, many roads were looted and wrecked by their own directors or subjected to harassing competition by speculators like Jay Gould. In some areas of the country certain railroads enjoyed monopolies, but wherever competition existed it was savage and sustained. Competing roads fought ferocious rate wars and struggled for business by offering rebates to big shippers. The inevitable effects of overexpansion, fraudulent management, and cutthroat competition were apparent in the depression of the seventies, when 450 roads went into bankruptcy. Twenty years later, in the hard times of the nineties, 318 companies controlling 67,000 miles fell into the hands of receivers.

After the economic crisis of 1893 railroad capitalists moved to curb competition by creating larger systems. Reorganizing the railroads required huge sums of cash and credit, which could be supplied only by the big New York investment banking houses. The investment bankers, led by J. P. Morgan, were eager to finance consolidation in order to stop the railroads, with their wild financing and frenzied speculating, from ruining the investment business. But the bankers, as the price for their aid, insisted on being given a voice in the management of the roads, a condition which the railroad promoters had to accept. By the end of the century a few major railroad systems controlled over half the mileage in the country, and these systems were wholly or partially controlled by two banking houses.

Business Philosophy and Its Critics

The economic revolution raised up in America a new ruling class. The industrialist and the investment banker now sat in the seats of power formerly held by Southern planters and Northeastern merchants, by members of the old aristocracy of inherited wealth and the old middle class, by politicians and statesmen of the antebellum Webster-Clay model. Most of the new business tycoons had begun their careers from comfortable and privileged positions in the economic scale. But some —enough to invest the entire group with the aura of the American success story— had emerged from obscurity to riches. Andrew Carnegie had worked as a bobbin boy in a Pittsburgh cotton mill, James J. Hill had been a frontier clerk, John D. Rockefeller had started out as a clerk in a Cleveland commission house, and E. H. Harriman had begun as a broker's office boy. Regardless of economic background, the new millionaires were—or considered themselves to be—self-made men. They employed, in business and politics, methods that were pushing, pugnacious, and sometimes crude. Unlike the older rich, they had little tradition of culture, education, and public service.

Most tycoons believed that they had attained their wealth by exercising the old American and Protestant virtues of hard work, acquisitiveness, and thrift. They had got where they were because they deserved it; people who were not so fortunate were lazy, unintelligent or profligate. In some way it was all connected with the moral law and with divine will. "God gave me my money," explained John D. Rockefeller.

To some businessmen, the formula of Social Darwinism seemed to explain both their own success and the nature of the society in which they operated. Social Darwinism was Charles Darwin's law of evolution applied to social organization. As expounded by the Englishman Herbert Spencer, it taught that struggle was a normal human activity, especially in economic life. The weak went down, the strong endured and became stronger, and society was benefited because the unfit were eliminated and the fit survived. Men who had risen to dominance by crushing their competitors were intrigued and comforted by a doctrine that justified any method that succeeded and proclaimed that wealth was a reward of competence.

Carnegie, who made himself the leading disciple of Spencer in the United States, contended that the natural law of competition was responsible for the great material growth of the country.

According to Social Darwinism, all attempts by labor to raise its wages by forming unions and all endeavors by government to regulate economic activities would fail, because economic life was controlled by a natural law, the law of competition, which could not be superseded by human restraints. This aspect of Darwinism coincided with another "higher law" which seemed to justify business practices and business dominance: the economic law of supply and demand as defined by Adam Smith and the classical economists. According to the economists, the economic system was like a great and delicate machine functioning by natural and automatic rules. Greatest among these rules was the law of supply and demand which determined all economic values—prices, wages, rents, interest rates—at a level that was just to all concerned. Supply and demand supposedly worked because man was essentially an economic creature who understood the intricacies of the market and because he operated in a free market where competition was open to all. Businessmen mouthed the clichés of classical economics even though the combinations they were creating were undermining the foundations of the free competitive market and modifying, if not destroying, the validity of the law of supply and demand.

These beliefs of businessmen were not shared by all Americans. Many books—a whole literature of protest—questioned or denounced various aspects of the economic system. Henry George's angrily eloquent *Progress and Poverty*, published in 1879, was an immediate success; reprinted in successive editions, it became one of the ten best selling nonfiction works in American publishing history. George addressed himself to the question of why poverty existed amidst the wealth created by modern industry. "This association of poverty with progress is the great enigma of our times," he wrote. "So long as all the increased wealth which modern progress brings goes but to build up great fortunes, to increase luxury and make sharper the contrast between the House of Have and the House of Want, progress is not real and cannot be permanent." He blamed all this on monopoly, and he proposed a remedy, a "single tax" on unimproved land. An increase in the value of such land resulted from the growth of society around it. Thus when land increased in value, George argued, the private owner had not earned the increment, and the community should receive the increase. Such a tax would destroy monopolies, distribute wealth more equally, and eliminate poverty. Single-tax societies sprang up in many cities, and in 1886 George, backed by labor and the Socialists, narrowly missed being elected mayor of New York.

Rivaling George in popularity was Edward Bellamy, whose *Looking Backward*, published in 1888, became a best seller within a few years and eventually topped the million mark. Bellamy's book was a novel, a romance of a socialist Utopia. It described the experiences of a young Bostonian who in 1887 went into a hypnotic sleep from which he awakened in the year 2000. He found a new social order, based on collective ownership of property, where want, politics, and vice were unknown, and where people were incredibly happy. Shortly, over 160 "Nationalist Clubs" sprang up to propagate Bellamy's ideas, and the author devoted the remainder of his life to championing Utopian socialism.

Thirty-eight similar novels appeared in the nineties, though none of them approached Bellamy's in success. It is not to be thought that the hundreds of thousands of Americans who read Bellamy and the other Utopian authors wished to see a socialist system established in the United States. Nor were they merely

seeking in literary fantasies an escape from the real problems of their times. The great majority were intrigued by the descriptions of societies that were prosperous and stable because government played a large role, and in their own troubled society they saw the need, not for a collective state, but for a larger place for government.

More realistic and firmly rooted in the requirements of the American scene was the philosophy in Henry Demarest Lloyd's *Wealth Against Commonwealth*. Published in 1894, this book was a tremendous, although not always accurate, attack on the Standard Oil trust and the methods by which it had risen to dominance. Lloyd was the first major American writer to call attention to the disappearance of absolute free competition in industrial society and the first to advocate regulation as the only solution for the problems created by the emergence of large-scale economic organizations.

Protest against the new economic order and against the laissez-faire attitude of government took various forms and drew increasing support from those members of society who did not fully share in the benefits of industrial productivity—from immigrants and other urban wage-earners and from the poorer farmers.

Immigration and the Urban Scene

From 1860 to 1900 the population of the United States leaped from approximately 31 million to almost 76 million. Immigration accounted for a substantial portion of the increase; in this forty-year period some 14 million aliens entered the country.

Up to 1880 the great majority of the immigrants had originated in the countries of western and northern Europe: England, Ireland, Germany, and the Scandinavian countries. Although there had always been points of friction between these people and "native" Americans and some resistance to their presence, especially to the Irish, they were in culture and outlook essentially similar to those among whom they settled, and they were assimilated without too much difficulty. But in the eighties the immigrant stream began to flow from another source —southern and eastern Europe. Among the new ethnic stocks were Austrians, Hungarians, Bohemians, Poles, Serbs, Italians, Russians, and Jews from Poland and Russia. They came for the reasons that had always brought immigrants to the United States: the desire to escape unfavorable economic and political con-

and their influx called into existence a short-lived nativist organization, the American Protective Association, which was vaguely but bitterly anti-alien and anti-Catholic. Laborers, fighting to raise their incomes and improve their working conditions, were incensed by the willingness of the immigrants to accept lower wages and to take over jobs of strikers.

The later immigrants flocked in preponderant numbers to the industrial cities of the East and became unskilled laborers. They did not have the capital to begin farming operations in the West;

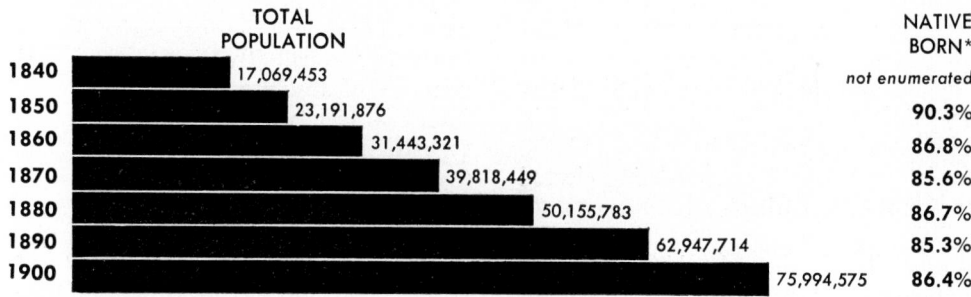

POPULATION TRENDS, 1840–1900

	TOTAL POPULATION		NATIVE BORN*
1840		17,069,453	*not enumerated*
1850		23,191,876	90.3%
1860		31,443,321	86.8%
1870		39,818,449	85.6%
1880		50,155,783	86.7%
1890		62,947,714	85.3%
1900		75,994,575	86.4%

*percentage of total population

ditions at home; the advertising propaganda of railroads, which in their eagerness to dispose of their landholdings painted an alluring picture of America; and the demand for cheap labor by industry, which until 1885 could import workers under the labor contract law.

The later immigrants provoked more fear and resentment among Americans than had the earlier arrivals, most of whom, or their offspring, were now assimilated and thoroughly suspicious of new foreigners. To natives of whatever origin, the newcomers seemed strange indeed. They had different cultural and economic standards and spoke diverse languages (the British and Irish who composed the bulk of the previous immigration had presented no language dissimilarity). They were in overwhelming numbers Catholics in a predominantly Protestant country,

they had to have immediate employment, and this was offered them by the meat packers, railroads, coal producers, and steel manufacturers, hungry for cheap labor; and in a strange land they felt the need of that association with their fellows which only city life could give.

Crowded into miserable slums, exploited economically, patronized by natives, the aliens seemingly offered prime material for the recruiters of reforms. The leaders of the extreme left, the anarchists and socialists, expecting a ready response, directed their appeals squarely to the immigrant masses. Most of the support the anarchists were able to enlist came from aliens, but the great bulk of the newcomers were repelled by its justification of violence. The doctrines of socialism were only slightly more attractive. The Socialist Labor party, founded in the seventies, fell under the leadership of Daniel De Leon, an immigrant from the West Indies; other party chiefs hailed from eastern Europe. Although De Leon aroused something of a following in the industrial cities, the party never succeeded in polling over 82,000 votes.

The newcomers had at first little comprehension of such native ideals, preached but not always practiced, as civic participation and responsibility and efficient and honest government. They were accustomed to being governed instead of governing, they had profoundly

legislation of the nineties enlarged the proscriptive list and increased the tax. These measures reflected rising American fears that continued unlimited immigration would exhaust the resources of the nation and endanger its social institutions. The laws kept out only a small number of aliens, however, and were far from fulfilling the purposes of the extreme exclusionists. The latter group worked for a literacy test, a device intended to exclude immigrants from eastern and southern Europe. Congress passed a literacy law in 1897, but Cleve-

SOURCES OF IMMIGRATION, 1861–1900

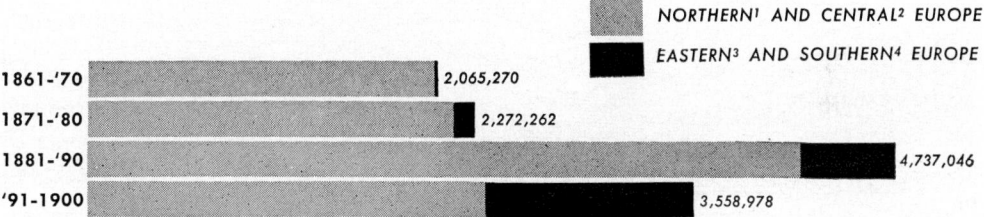

NORTHERN[1] AND CENTRAL[2] EUROPE

EASTERN[3] AND SOUTHERN[4] EUROPE

1861-'70	2,065,270
1871-'80	2,272,262
1881-'90	4,737,046
'91-1900	3,558,978

[1] Great Britain, Ireland, Scandinavia, Netherlands, Belgium, France, Switzerland

[2] Germany, Poland, Austria-Hungary

[3] Russia and Baltic States, Rumania, Bulgaria, Turkey

[4] Italy, Spain, Portugal, Greece

personal notions of political relations, and they wanted jobs, help, and kindness instead of abstract concepts and lectures on Americanism. They turned to the one political agent in the national scene who was ready to gratify their requirements, the urban boss. The boss accepted the immigrant for what he was, got him a job, and provided aid for him and his family in lean times. In return the boss expected and received the political support of the alien after naturalization: it was immigrant votes that furnished the basis for the power of the city machines.

With the mounting of the alien tide, the first demands for immigration restrictions rose in the land. Congress acted in 1882 to exclude the Chinese. In the same year it passed a general immigration law denying entry to certain undesirables—convicts, paupers, idiots—and placed a tax of 50¢ on every person admitted. Later

land, just before leaving office at the end of his second term, vetoed it.

The city was a place of violent contrasts. There could be seen, often in close proximity, the richest and the poorest people in America, the most palatial homes and the worst slums and tenements in Western civilization. Jacob Riis, a Danish immigrant and New York City reporter, crusaded against slum conditions and described them without restraint in *How the Other Half Lives*.

The urban masses had to have a means of rapid and cheap transportation. Before the Civil War some cities had experimented with streetcars drawn by horses, and after 1865 horsecar lines appeared in all the metropolitan centers. Richmond, Virginia, introduced an electric railway system in 1887, and soon other cities followed suit. New York opened its first elevated railway (with steam locomotives)

The Bridge is to cross the river by a single span of 1600 feet to start on the New York side from the City Hall rising by a gradual approach of 2361 feet in length and on the Brooklyn side by an approach of 1901 feet its elevation above the river in the

centre of the bridge will be 130 feet its floor is to be 80 feet wide with tracks for steam-cars, roadway for carriages and walks for foot-passengers, it is to have an elevated promenade commanding a view of extraordinary beauty and extent, and its cost is to be about $8,000,000.

THE GREAT EAST RIVER BRIDGE.
To Connect the Cities of New York & Brooklyn.

BROOKLYN BRIDGE. As a story of presevering courage, the erection of Brooklyn Bridge by John A. and Washington Roebling can match anything in American military history. In 1866, Manhattan Island was connected with Brooklyn and the rest of Long Island only by ferries. When the East River froze, the tie was sundered. A bridge was needed. John Roebling, engineer and manufacturer of wire cables, proposed a suspension bridge with a central span of 1,600 feet—longer than had been built anywhere in the world. Other great engineers said it could not be done. But Roebling's prestige and forcefulness got approval for the idea, and he designed the bridge. Then he unexpectedly died. His son Washington Roebling was stricken by caisson bends. An invalid, he was confined to his bed at Columbia Heights. His wife watched the construction by telescope, and he supervised every detail by letter. In 1883, twelve years after work began, the bridge opened, an object of practical use which also was a thing of beauty. Here was the austere art of the Age of Steel: the massive granite towers were united in tension with the spidery cables of nineteen wire strands, and the tension held the bridge aloft. The father was dead; the son, paralyzed, growing deaf and blind; but they had shown how straightforward statement of fact could unify industrialism with esthetics. (PRINT BY CURRIER & IVES)

in 1870, and in 1897 Boston, putting the streetcars underground, completed the first American subway.

In the dark and dirty slums, where families huddled in single rooms with inadequate toilet and sanitary facilities, thousands died annually of epidemics. From the slums, disease spread into other sections. Most cities took few precautions to guard the purity of their water supply and no satisfactory measures to dispose of their sewage and garbage. The great conflagrations that gutted Chicago and Boston in the seventies revealed the inadequacies of existing fire fighting arrangements, and municipalities hastened to establish better systems. In the larger cities the volunteer fire departments, long a colorful but not always an efficient feature of the urban scene, were scrapped in favor of paid departments. But fire losses continued to mount; the wooden structures of the crowded cities invited destruction.

Humanitarian groups and individuals interested themselves in improving the physical environment and raising the standards of the poor, particularly the immigrant poor. Working in conjunction with city governments or private philanthropists, they secured money to construct parks and playgrounds in the slum areas. Social workers established settlement houses in the foreign colonies to entice the aliens from the saloons and streets and bring them under religious influences. The most famous of the houses were the Henry Street Settlement in New York, founded by Lillian D. Wald, and Hull-House in Chicago, directed by Jane Addams. By 1900 fifty such centers were operating in American cities.

The Organization of Labor

As business became big, consolidated, and national, inevitably labor attempted to create its own organizations that would

NEW YORK'S ELEVATED RAILROAD. With the rise of the city in America there emerged the problem of urban rapid transit—how to transport huge number of people, particularly workers who went to their jobs or left them at the same hours of the day. New York was the first to experiment with an elevated railroad. A short line was opened in 1870, and a longer one, the Sixth Avenue Elevated, shown above, in 1878. Other cities to follow suit were Brooklyn, Kansas City, Chicago, and Boston. Steam locomotives furnished the power on the "L's." Transit on streets in New York, as in many other cities, was provided by horse-drawn cars, also depicted in the print. (LIBRARY OF CONGRESS)

match the power of capital. The economic revolution changed the worker from an artisan who owned his own tools to a factory laborer who operated machines owned by his employer; it placed his wages, his tenure, his working environment at the pleasure of an impersonal corporation too powerful for the individual worker to bargain with. Between 1865 and 1897—a period of falling prices and a consequent decline in the cost of living —real wages increased, except in times of economic fluctuation or depression. Nevertheless, at the turn of the century the income of the average worker was pitifully small: $400–500 a year. Students of the standard of living estimated that, to maintain a decent level of comfort, a yearly income of $600 was the absolute minimum. According to one survey, 10 million Americans lived in poverty. The average work day in 1900 was ten hours, for a six-day week. Because employers paid little attention to safety devices or programs, the accident rate was appalling. One in every 26 railroad workers was injured, one in every 399 killed per year.

Against such conditions, labor fought back by forming unions to bargain collectively with employers. During the Civil War, 20 craft unions were formed, and by 1870 the industrial states counted 30 such organizations, nearly every one of which represented skilled workers. The first attempt to federate separate unions into a single national organization came in 1866, when, under the leadership of William H. Sylvis, the National Labor Union was founded. Claiming a membership of 640,000, it was a polyglot association that included, in addition to a number of unions, a variety of reform groups having little direct relationship with labor. After the panic of 1873 the National Labor Union disintegrated and disappeared.

The trade unions experienced stormy times during the hard years of the 1870's. Their bargaining power weakened by depression conditions, they faced antagonistic employers eager to destroy them, and a hostile public that rejected labor's claim to job security. Several of the disputes with capital were unusually bitter and were marked by violence, some of it labor's fault and some not, but for all of which labor received the blame. Startling to most Americans was the exposure of the activities of the "Molly Maguires" in the anthracite coal region of Pennsylvania. A terrorist group, the "Mollies" operated within the Ancient Order of Hibernians and intimidated the coal operators with such direct methods as murder. But excitement over this was as nothing compared to the near-hysteria that gripped the country during the railroad strikes of 1877. The trouble started when the principal Eastern railroads announced a 10 per cent slash in wages. Immediately railroad workers, whether organized or not, went out on strike. Rail service was disrupted from Baltimore to St. Louis, equipment was destroyed, and rioting mobs roamed the streets of Pittsburgh and other cities.

The strikes were America's first big labor conflict and a flaming illustration of a new reality in the American economic system: with business becoming nationalized, disputes between labor and capital could no longer be localized but would affect the entire nation. State militia were employed against the strikers, and finally, and significantly, federal troops were called on to suppress the disorders. The power of the various railroad unions was seriously sapped by the failure of the strikes, and the prestige of unions in other industries was weakened by similar setbacks.

Meanwhile, another national labor organization appeared on the scene, the Noble Order of the Knights of Labor, founded in 1869 under the leadership of Uriah S. Stephens. Instead of attempting to federate unions, as the National Labor Union had done, the Knights organized their association on the basis of the individual. Membership was open to all who "toiled," and the definition of toilership was extremely liberal: the only excluded groups were lawyers, bankers, liquor dealers, and professional gamblers. The amorphous masses of members were arranged in local "assemblies" that might consist of the workers in a particular trade or a local union or simply all the members of the Knights in a city or district. Presiding laxly over the entire order was an agency known as the General Assembly. Much of the program of the Knights was as vague as the organization. Although they championed an eight-hour day and the abolition of child labor, the leaders were more interested in long-range reform of the economy than in the immediate objectives of wages and hours which appealed to the trade unions.

Under the leadership of Terence V. Powderly, the order entered upon a spectacular period of expansion that culminated in 1886 with the total membership reaching 700,000. Important factors contributing to the increase in numerical strength were a business recession in 1884 which threw many workers out of jobs and a renewal of industrial strife which impelled unorganized laborers as well as some trade unions to affiliate with the Knights. Not only was the membership enlarged, but the order now included many militant elements that could not always be controlled by the moderate leadership. Against Powderly's wishes, local unions or assemblies associated with the Knights proceeded to inaugurate a series of strikes. In 1885 striking railway workers forced the Missouri Pacific, a link in the Gould system, to restore wage cuts and recognize their union. Although this victory redounded to the credit of the Knights, it was an ephemeral triumph. In the following year a strike on another Gould road, the Texas and Pacific, was crushed and the power of the unions in the Gould system was broken. By 1890 the membership of the Knights had shrunk to 100,000, and within a few years the order would be a thing of the past.

Even before the Knights had entered on their period of decline, a rival organization, based on an entirely different organizational concept, had appeared. In 1881 representatives of a number of craft unions formed the Federation of Organized Trade and Labor Unions of the United States and Canada. Five years later this body took the name which it has borne ever since, the American Federation of Labor. Under the direction of its president and guiding spirit, Samuel Gompers, the Federation soon became the most important labor group in the country. As its name implies, it was a federation or association of national trade unions, each of which enjoyed essential autonomy within the larger organization. Rejecting completely the idea of individual membership and the corollary of one big union for everybody, the Federation built on the principle of the organization of skilled workers into craft unions.

The program of the Federation differed as markedly from that of the Knights as did its organizational arrangements. Gompers and his associates accepted the basic concepts of capitalism; their purpose was to secure for labor a greater share of capitalism's material rewards. Repudiating all notions of fundamental alteration of the existing system or long-range reform measures or a separate labor party, the A. F. of L. concentrated on labor's immediate objectives: wages, hours, and working conditions. While it hoped to attain its ends by collective bargaining, the Federation was ready to employ the strike if necessary.

As one of its first objectives, the Federation called for a national eight-hour day, to be attained by May 1, 1886, and to be obtained, if necessary, by a general strike. On the target day, strikes and demonstrations for a shorter workday took place all over the country. Although the national officers of the Knights had refused to cooperate in the movement, some local units joined in the demonstrations. So did a few unions that were dominated by anarchists—European rad-

THE HAYMARKET TRAGEDY. This is a contemporary artist's conception of the bomb exploding among the police. (LIBRARY OF CONGRESS)

icals who wanted to destroy "class government" by terroristic methods—and that were affiliated with the so-called Black International. The most sensational demonstrations occurred in Chicago, which was a labor stronghold and an anarchist center.

At the time, a strike was in progress at the McCormick Harvester Company; and when the police harassed the strikers, labor and anarchist leaders called a protest meeting at the Haymarket Square. During the meeting, the police appeared and commanded those present to disperse. Someone—his identity was never determined—threw a bomb that resulted in the death of seven policemen and injury to sixty-seven others. The police, who on the previous day had killed four strikers, fired into the crowd and killed four more people. The score was about even. News of the Haymarket affair struck cold fear into Chicago and the business commu-

nity of the nation. Blinded by hysteria, conservative, property-conscious Americans demanded a victim or victims—to demonstrate to labor that it must cease its course of violence. Chicago officials finally rounded up eight anarchists and charged them with the murder of the policemen on the grounds that they had incited the individual who hurled the bomb. In one of the most injudicious trials in the record of American juridical history, all were found guilty. One was sentenced to prison and seven to death. Of the seven, one cheated his sentence by committing suicide, four were executed, and two had their penalty commuted to life imprisonment.

Although some of the blame for the Haymarket tragedy was unloaded on the A. F. of L., at least as much fell on the Knights, who had had almost nothing to do with the May demonstrations. But in the public mind the Knights were dominated by anarchists and Socialists. The order was never able to eradicate this conviction, but the Federation managed to escape the stigma of radicalism.

Climax of Industrial Conflict

Some of the most violent strikes in American labor history occurred in the nineties. Two of the strikes, the one at the Homestead plant of the Carnegie Steel Company in Pennsylvania and the one against the Pullman Palace Car Company in the Chicago area, took place in companies controlled by men who prided themselves on being among the most advanced of American employers: Andrew Carnegie, who had written magazine articles defending the rights of labor, and George M. Pullman, who had built a "model town" to house his employees.

The Amalgamated Association of Iron and Steel Workers, which was affiliated with the American Federation of Labor, was the most powerful trade union in the country. It had never been able, however, to organize all the plants of the Carnegie Steel Company, the largest corporation in the industry; of the three major steel mills in the Carnegie system, the union was a force only in one, the Homestead plant. In 1892, when the strike occurred, Carnegie was in Scotland, visiting at a castle that he maintained as a gesture of ancestral pride, and the direction of the company was in the hands of Henry Clay Frick, manager of Homestead and chairman of the Carnegie firm. Carnegie was, nevertheless, responsible for the company's course. Despite his earlier fine words about labor, he had decided with Frick before leaving to operate Homestead on a nonunion basis, even if this meant precipitating a clash with the union.

The trouble began when the management announced a new wage scale that would have meant cuts for a small minority of the workers. Frick abruptly shut down the plant, and asked the Pinkerton Detective Agency to furnish 300 guards to enable the company to resume operations on its own terms. (The Pinkerton Agency was really a strikebreaking concern.)

The hated Pinkertons, whose mere presence was enough to incite the workers to violence, approached the plant on barges in an adjacent river. Warned of their coming, the strikers met them at the docks with guns and dynamite, and a pitched battle ensued on July 6, 1892. After several hours of fighting, which brought death to three guards and ten strikers and severe injuries to many participants on both sides, the Pinkertons surrendered and were escorted roughly out of town. The company and local law officials then asked for militia protection from the Pennsylvania governor, who responded by sending the entire National Guard contingent, some 8,000 troops, to Homestead. Public opinion, at first sympathetic to the strikers, turned abruptly against them when an anarchist made an unsuccessful attempt to assassinate Frick. Slowly workers dritfed back to their jobs.

A dispute of greater magnitude and equal bitterness, although involving less loss of life, was the Pullman strike in 1894, a depression year that saw over 700,000 workers throughout the country out on strike. Near Chicago were the works of the Pullman Palace Car Company, a corporation that leased sleeping and parlor cars to most of the nation's railroads and that manufactured and repaired its own cars and also freight and passenger cars; over 5,000 workers were employed in the various shops and factories of the company. At the instigation of George M. Pullman, inventor of the car that bore his name and president of the firm, the company had built the 600-acre town of Pullman, containing dwellings that were rented to the employees, and churches and schools, parks and playgrounds, a bank and a library—all owned and operated by the company. Pullman liked to exhibit his town as a model solution of the industrial problem and to refer to the workers as his "children"; his attitude was completely feudalistic and patronizing.

Nearly all of the workers were members of a union, a very militant one, the American Railway Union; this association had recently been organized by Eugene V. Debs, a sincere and idealistic labor leader formerly active in the Railroad Brotherhoods. Becoming disgusted with the brotherhoods' lack of interest in the lot of the unskilled workers, he had formed his own union, which soon attained a membership of 150,000, mainly in the Middle West.

The strike at Pullman began when the company during the winter of 1893-4 slashed wages by an average of 25 per cent. With revenues reduced by depression conditions, there was some reason for the company's action, but the cut was drastic, and several workers who served on a committee to protest to the management were discharged. At the same time, Pullman refused to reduce rentals in the model town, even though the charges were 20 to 25 per cent higher than for comparable accommodations in surrounding areas. The strikers appealed to the Railway Union for support, and that organization voted to refuse to handle Pullman cars and equipment.

The General Managers' Association, representing twenty-four Chicago railroads, prepared to fight the boycott. Switchmen who refused to handle Pullman cars were summarily discharged. Whenever this happened, the union instructed its members to quit work. Within a few days thousands of railroad workers in twenty-seven states and territories were on strike, and transportation from Chicago to the Pacific coast was paralyzed.

Ordinarily, state governors responded readily to appeals from strike-threatened business, but the governor of Illinois was different. John P. Altgeld was a courageous and committed liberal and a somewhat visionary champion of lost causes. He had pardoned the Haymarket anarch-

ists remaining in prison. Business was not likely to appeal to such an executive for aid, and Altgeld was not the man to employ militia to smash a strike.

Bypassing Altgeld, the railroad operators besought the national government to send regular army troops to Illinois. At the same time federal postal officials and marshals were bombarding Washington with information that the strike was preventing the movement of mail on the trains. President Cleveland was inclined to gratify the companies, and so was his Attorney General, Richard Olney, a former railroad lawyer and a bitter foe of labor. Cleveland and Olney decided that the government could employ the army to keep the mails moving, and in July, 1894, the President, over Altgeld's strident protest, ordered 2,000 troops to the Chicago area.

Not content with employing troops, the government threw another blow at the union. At Olney's suggestion, government lawyers obtained from a federal court an injunction restraining Debs and other union officials from interfering with the interstate transportation of the mails. The injunction was so broad in scope, a "blanket injunction," that it practically forbade Debs and his associates to continue the strike. They ignored it, and were arrested, tried for contempt of court (without a jury trial), and sentenced to six months in prison. With federal troops protecting the hiring of new workers and with the union leaders in a federal jail, the strike quickly collapsed.

But it left a bitter heritage. Labor was convinced that the government was not a neutral arbiter representing the common interest, but a supporter of one side in a social struggle. Debs emerged from prison a martyr, a convert to socialism, and a dedicated enemy of capital.

Despite all the organizations that were formed and all the strikes and demonstrations that were so hopefully employed, labor accomplished relatively little for its cause in the years between 1865 and 1900.

It could point to a few legislative victories: the abolition by Congress in 1885 of the Contract Labor law of the Civil War; the establishment by Congress in 1868 of an eight-hour day on public works and in 1892 of the same work period for government employees, and a host of state laws governing hours of labor and safety standards, most of which were not enforced. But an overwhelming majority of employers still regarded labor as a force to be disregarded when possible and to be crushed when practicable, and the American public in overwhelming numbers considered unions to be alien and dangerous elements in the national economy. Labor's greatest weakness was that only a small part of its vast strength was organized. The American Federation, with its some half million members, and the Railroad Brotherhoods (engineers, conductors, firemen, trainmen) represented the skilled workers, but the mass of laborers were not enrolled in any union. All told, only 868,500 workers were union members at the turn of the century. Big Business was firmly entrenched; Big Labor awaited the future.

The Farmer's Problems

Americans had always like to talk about the wonderful life of the farmer. According to the popular myth, he was a sturdy yeoman, a simple, honest, happy man who dwelt close to nature and embodied all the virtues. Producing on his own holding most of the things he and his family required, he was uniquely nonpecuniary and noncommercial. Above all, he was independent, subsisting on his own labor, depending not on the market place, and owing no man. The myth may have had some basis in Jefferson's time, but it was losing much relation to reality before the Civil War and became a fiction, though a widely believed one, after that conflict. Its reality was destroyed by one of the great agricultural changes of the nineteenth century, the shift from subsistence, or self-sufficient, farming to commercial farming.

In commercial husbandry, the farmer specialized in a cash crop, sold it in a national or world market, ceased making his household supplies and bought them at the town or village store. This kind of farming, when it was successful, raised the farmer's living standards. But now he was dependent on other people and on impersonal factors he could not control: bankers and interest rates, railroads and freight rates, national and European depressions, world supply and demand. In short, he had become a businessman—but with a difference. Unlike the capitalists of the industrial order, he could not regulate his production or influence the prices of what he sold.

Machines came to the aid of the farmer as to the manufacturer. Before 1860 American inventive genius had developed a multitude of machines—among them the reaper, thresher, mower, iron plow, disc harrow, grain planter, and straddle cultivator—but farmers, innately conservative and overly impressed with the costs of the implements, were slow to accept them. The mechanization of agriculture began in the Civil War when the government called thousands of laborers into military service and forced farmers to employ labor-saving devices. For example, approximately 100,000 reapers were in use at the beginning of the war but 250,000 at its close.

In the years after 1860 a host of new machines—and improved models of old ones —were unveiled. Among these were the chilled steel plow, perfected by James Oliver; the sulky, or riding, plow; the disc and gang plows; various improvements of the reaper, notably the twine binder, introduced by John F. Appleby, which cut and bound grain, the grain drill, the seed planter, the corn binder, the corn lister, the potato planter, the cream separator, and the poultry incubator. The effect of the machines on production and labor was revolutionary.

THRESHING WHEAT ON THE GREAT PLAINS. The first threshers used in the United States were stationary and were powered by men or walking horses. Later steam engines were introduced to power larger and more complex machines. The threshers that came into use after the Civil War were too expensive for the average farmer. In some areas those who could afford them went from farm to farm with a hired crew during the threshing season. The masters of the huge wheat farms of the plains might employ several threshers. This print of a Dakota field shows the magnitude of threshing operations on a large landed unit and gives an idea of the high cost of farming on the plains. (BETTMANN ARCHIVE)

Before 1900 farmers were generally hostile to the theories and teachings of scientific agriculture, to what they scornfully termed "book learning." In 1887 Congress passed the Hatch Act, providing for a system of agricultural experiment stations; this was the only major agricultural legislation passed by Congress between 1865 and 1900. But farmers generally spurned the new information because they felt no need for its aid and could see no benefits for themselves in its lessons. American agriculture before 1900 was, as it always had been, extensive and wasteful.

The period between 1865 and 1900 witnessed a tremendous expansion of agricultural facilities, not only in the United States but all over the world: in Brazil and the Argentine in South America, in Canada, in Australia and New Zealand, and in Russia. World production increased at the same time that modern means of communication and transportation—the telephone, telegraph, cable, steam navigation, railroads—were welding the producing nations into one international market. The American commercial farmer, always augmenting his production, produced more than the domestic market could absorb and disposed of his surplus in the world market. Cotton farmers depended on export sales for 70 per cent of their annual income, and wheat farmers for 30 to 40 per cent; other producers relied on a smaller proportion

—it might be 10 to 25—but it was large enough to make the difference between a year of profit and one of loss.

In the forty years after 1860 huge new areas of land were put under cultivation in America, machines became standard equipment on most farms, land values boomed, and production soared to ever higher levels. But while costs of operation increased, prices dropped after 1870. Meanwhile, although the proportion of people living on farms declined in relation to the total population, farm population increased by absolute standards. From 1860 to 1910 the number of farm families rose from 1,500,000 to over 6,000,000. In 1860 agriculture represented 50 per cent of the total wealth of the country, in the early 1900's only 20 per cent. The farmer received 30 per cent of the national income in 1860 and 18 per cent in 1910. But the most accurate indicator of farm distress was the dramatic increase in indebtedness and tenantry. By the decade of the nineties, 27 per cent of the owned farms in the country were under mortgages, and by 1910 the number stood at 33 per cent. In the latter year farm mortgages totaled over $3 billion. In 1880, 25 per cent of all farms were operated by tenants; in 1910, 37 per cent. The agrarian scene as it presented itself in the 1890's hardly realized Jefferson's dream of a sturdy and independent yeomanry owning the land it tilled.

The farmers were painfully aware that something was wrong. They did not recognize—and it would have been strange if they had—the intricate implications of national and world overproduction. Instead, they concentrated their attention and anger on more immediate and easily understood problems, problems that were in truth real and important to them, such as freight rates, interest charges, and an adequate currency.

The farmers' first and most burning grievance was that against the railroads. In all sections the iron lines that carried farm products to the markets were of vital importance to agriculture, and in the states west of the Mississippi, dependence on the railroads was nothing short of absolute. In many cases the roads discriminated against farmers in fixing carrying charges; that is, they charged higher rates for farm than for other shipments and higher rates in the South and West than in the Northeast. Freight rates sometimes consumed so much of the current price that farmers refused to ship their crops and either let them rot or used them as fuel. Actually, freight rates as a whole declined after 1865, and it would seem that the farmers' plight was more the result of declining prices for his crops than excessive freight charges. Resting on a somewhat firmer basis were farmer complaints against the railroads' control of elevator and warehouse facilities in buying centers, which enabled them to charge arbitrary storage rates and to influence commodity prices by a system of grading or classification of grains, and the often complete and arrogant power that the roads exercised over state governments.

In the farmers' list of villains the sources that controlled credit—banks, loan companies, insurance corporations —ranked second to the railroads. Commercial farming was by its nature expensive, and ambitious producers needed credit to purchase machines or enlarge their holdings. Although the creditor interests were eager to advance loans during the boom period of rising land values, they were in a position to insist, and did insist, on high interest rates. The farmers were in no position to resist, and the West and the South had to submit to charges running from 10 to 25 per cent. Usually the farmer borrowed money when it was cheap, or abundant, and then had to retire his debt when money had become dear, or scarce. According to one estimate, 1,200 bushels of grain would buy a $1000 mortgage in the 1860's; twenty years later it took 2,300 bushels to repay the mortgage. With good reason, the farmers fought for an increase in the volume of currency.

A third grievance of the farmer concerned prices, both the prices he received for his products and the prices he paid for goods he bought. He disposed of his products as an individual in competition with countless other individuals in this and other countries. He possessed little or no advance information on the state of the market and probable price changes; he did not have storage facilities that would enable him to hold his crop for a favorable price; and he was powerless to regulate his production. But instead of changing his marketing procedures, the farmer tended—as was quite natural under the circumstances—to blame his price woes on personal villains, the grain speculators in distant cities, the international bankers, or the regional and local middlemen to whom he often sold his products. These operators, he became convinced (sometimes with justice), were combining to fix prices to their advantage and his hurt.

The farmer was also convinced that there was something of a conspiracy against him in the prices of the goods he purchased. He sold his crops in a competitive market but bought in a domestic market protected by tariffs and dominated by trusts and corporations. According to government reports, over 100 articles purchased by farmers—farm machinery, tools, sewing machines, blankets, staple foods, clothing, plowshares, and others—carried tariff charges; on these necessary items the farmer paid a tax of from 33 to 60 per cent.

Last on the agrarian catalog of grievances was a vague yet tremendous resentment. In part, this was an outgrowth of the isolation of farm life before the days of paved roads, the automobile, the telephone, and the radio. Farm families in some parts of the country, particularly in the prairie and plains region where large farms were scattered over vast areas, were virtually cut off from the outside world and from other human companionship during the winter months or protracted spells of bad weather. This enforced seclusion was only partially alleviated when the national government established rural free delivery of mail in 1896. Increasingly, thoughtful farm leaders realized the drabness and the dullness of farm existence, the lack of adequate educational, recreational, and medical facilities, and the absence of community culture and action. Ample evidence that rural life was becoming unattractive to rural folk was provided in the tremendous migration of young people from the farms to the cities. The farmer, once eulogized as the finest figure in the American myth and the surest support of American democracy, was now ridiculed as a "hayseed" and regarded with amiable condescension. The farmer was losing status, and he knew it. He might recover his position by the power of organization—if he could conquer the rampant individualism that had always marked rural society.

BIBLIOGRAPHY

General accounts are B. J. Hendrick, *The Age of Big Business* (1920); John Moody, *The Masters of Capital* (1921); Matthew Josephson, *The Robber Barons* (1934); I. M. Tarbell, *The Nationalizing of Business, 1878–1898* (1936); William Miller (ed.), *Men in Business* (1952); E. C. Kirkland, *Dream and Thought in the Business Community, 1860–1900* (1956); and

S. P. Hays, *The Response to Industrialism, 1885–1914* (1957).

On invention, in addition to previously cited works, see Roger Burlingame, *Engines of Democracy* (1940); F. L. Dyer and T. C Martin, *Edison: His Life and Inventions* (2 vols., 1929); M. Josephson, *Edison* (1959); and R. N. Current, *The Typewriter and the Men Who Made It* (1954).

For the development of the steel industry, see Herbert Casson, *The Romance of Steel* (1907); B. J. Hendrick, *Andrew Carnegie* (2 vols., 1932), an official biography; J. K. Winkler, *Incredible Carnegie* (1931), a satiric study; Carnegie's *Autobiography* (1920); and Allan Nevins, *Abram S. Hewitt* (1935). For oil: P. H. Giddens, *The Birth of the Oil Industry* (1938); Giddens, *Standard Oil Company (Indiana)* (1956); Allan Nevins, *Study in Power: John D. Rockefeller* (2 vols., 1953); and J. T. Flynn, *God's Gold* (1932), an older study of Rockefeller. For the food industry: R. A. Clemen, *The American Livestock and Meat Industry* (1932), and C. B. Kuhlmann, *The Development of the Flour-Milling Industry in the United States* (1929).

Good introductions to railroad developments are John Moody, *The Railroad Builders* (1919), and Slason Thompson, *A Short History of American Railways* (1925). On a higher level are T. C. Cochran, *Railroad Leaders, 1845–1890* (1953), and G. R. Taylor and I. D. Neu, *The American Railroad Network* (1956). Excellent special works are R. E. Riegel, *The Story of the Western Railroads* (1926); G. C. Quiett, *They Built the West* (1934); Oscar Lewis, *The Big Four* (1938), on the Central Pacific; R. C. Overton, *Burlington West* (1941); and J. F. Stover, *Railroads of the South, 1865–1900* (1955). There are satisfactory biographies of two railroad magnates: W. J. Land, *Commodore Vanderbilt* (1942), and Julius Grodinsky, *Jay Gould* (1957).

A penetrating analysis is Sidney Fine, *Laissez Faire and the Welfare State, 1865–1901* (1956). Other noteworthy studies: Irvin G. Wyllie, *The Self-Made Man in America* (1954); Richard Hofstadter, *Social Darwinism in American Thought* (paperback ed., 1955); Broadus and G. S. Mitchell, *The Industrial Revolution in the South* (1930); Stuart Daggett, *Railroad Reorganization* (1908); E. G. Campbell, *The Reorganization of the American Railroad System 1893–1900* (1938); and Eliot Jones, *The Trust Problem in the United States* (1921).

On labor and strikes: Norman Ware, *The Labor Movement in the United States, 1860–1895* (1929); Herbert Harris, *American Labor* (1939); Samuel Yellen, *American Labor Struggles* (1936); Henry David, *History of the Haymarket Affair* (1936); R. V. Bruce, *1877: Year of Conflict* (1959); L. L. Lorwin, *The American Federation of Labor* (1933); and Philip Taft, *The A. F. of L. in the Time of Gompers* (1957); and A. L. Lindsay, *The Pullman Strike* (1942). Two of the early labor leaders have left interesting autobiographies: Terence V. Powderly, *Thirty Years of Labor* (1889), and Samuel Gompers, *Seventy Years of Life and Labor* (2 vols., 1925).

On the urban background: A. M. Schlesinger, *The Rise of the City, 1878–1898* (1933); Lewis Mumford, *The Culture of Cities* (1938); R. H. Bremner, *From the Depths: The Discovery of Poverty in the United States* (1956); Jacob Riis, *How the Other Half Lives* (1890; paperback ed., 1957); Jane Addams, *Forty Years at Hull-House* (1935); M. L. Hansen, *The Immigrant in American History* (1940); and Oscar Handlin, *The Uprooted* (1951). In *Strangers in the Land* (1955), John Higham emphasizes the reception of the immigrants in America.

25

THE

POLITICS OF PROTEST

A swelling tide of protest struck American politics with full force in the early 1890's. Spearheaded by farmers but embracing other dissatisfied factions whose ranks were increased by depression, it encountered the forces of conservatism and partially recoiled before them, but recovered to reach a roaring climax in the election of 1896. Thereafter the protest movement faded, its strength blunted by the capacity of the economic system to produce new wealth and by the traditional ability of the political system to absorb dissenting third parties into the structure of the major parties. Meanwhile, the protesters had displayed a moral fervor and a class bitterness that appalled and frightened the more secure and sober classes. "It was a fanaticism like the crusades," wrote a Kansas editor.

The Granger Movement

The first farm organization to appear after the Civil War was established in boom times as a social association and was turned into an agency of agrarian protest at the onset of the 1873 depression. On a tour through the South, Oliver H. Kelley, a clerk in the Department of Agriculture at Washington, became impressed with the isolation and drabness of rural life. In 1867 he and other department employees founded the National Grange of the Patrons of Husbandry, to which Kelley devoted years of labor as secretary. Local lodges of the order were called granges, and the organization is commonly known as the Grange. The announced purposes of the Grange were social, cultural, and educational. By bringing farm men and women together in groups, it aimed to diffuse knowledge of scientific agriculture, machines, and markets, to furnish a community concert hitherto absent in rural society, and, as one of Kelley's circulars put it, to keep agriculture in "step with the music of the age." Recognizing that human nature is intrigued by secrecy and ceremony, the founders provided for an elaborate system of initiation and ritual. At first the Grange grew slowly. It filled an obvious rural need, but farmers were not attracted to it in large numbers while times were good. Then the depression of 1873 struck, and suddenly the

A Grange Meeting. Intense and interested, the farmer audience listens as an orator expounds the aims of the Grange. The banners in the crowd call for equal rights and education and denounce corruption in government. (BROWN BROTHERS)

farmers saw benefits to be achieved through organization. By 1875 the Grange could count over 800,000 members and 20,000 local lodges. The order appeared in almost every state, but it was strongest in the staple-producing sections of the Middle West and the South.

As membership increased, the lodges in the Middle West turned to economic issues. They stressed the necessity of collective action by farmers to eliminate the middleman—through the organization of cooperatives—and the urgency of political action to curb the monopolistic practices of the railroads and warehouses. All over the midlands on Independence Day, 1873, the "Farmers' Fourth of July," embittered yeomen assembled to hear Granger orators read "The Farmers' Declaration of Independence." The resolutions proclaimed that the time had come for the agrarians, "suffering from long continued systems of oppression and abuse, to rouse themselves from an apathetic indifference to their own interests," and vowed that the farmers would use "all lawful and peaceful means to free [themselves] from the tyranny of monopoly."

The Grangers launched the first major cooperative movement in the United States, although successful collective societies had existed earlier in England and other countries. The Grangers set up cooperative stores, creameries, elevators, warehouses, insurance companies, and factories that turned out machines, stoves, and other items. Some 400 enterprises were in operation at the height of the movement, but eventually most of them failed, because of the inexperience of the operators, extravagant management, and opposition from middleman interests. Not all business groups fought the cooperatives; some sought their trade, and one corporation was formed specifically in 1872 to meet the wants of the Grangers, Montgomery Ward and Company, which brought a new industry, the mail-order business, into existence.

In the sphere of political action the Grangers labored to elect to state legislatures candidates pledged to their program. Usually they operated through the existing Republican and Democratic parties, only occasionally putting up nominees under such party labels as "Anti-Monopoly" or "Reform." Marshaling their votes in the local lodges, they were able to gain control of the legislatures in most of the Middle Western states. Their purpose, openly and angrily announced, was to subject the railroads to social controls.

Between 1870 and 1874 the legislatures of Illinois, Iowa, Minnesota, and Wisconsin enacted laws to regulate railroads and warehouse and elevator facilities. These "Granger laws" authorized maximum rates for passenger and freight traffic, provided rules and rates for the storing of grain, and prohibited a number of alleged discriminatory practices. They were to be administered and enforced by special state commissions.

The railroads contested the legality of the laws, and eventually fought them from the state courts up to the United States Supreme Court. In 1876 the highest tribunal handed down several decisions concerning the validity of the laws and usually referred to as the "Granger cases." The first decision was *Munn v. Illinois*, involving the right of a state to fix storage rates for warehouses. The others, of which *Peik v. Chicago and Northwestern Railroad Co.* and *Chicago, Burlington, and Quincy Railroad Co. v. Iowa* were the most important, concerned state laws establishing maximum rates for railroads.

Chief Justice Morrison R. Waite spoke for the Court in the Munn case, and his opinion formed the basis for the decisions on the railroad laws. The complainants, the warehouses and railroads, had rested their cause on two points: (1) the laws infringed the power of Congress to regu-

late interstate commerce; and (2) they violated the due-process clause of the Fourteenth Amendment, namely, that a state could not deprive a "person" of property without due process of law. The plaintiffs were contending not only that a corporation was a person within the meaning of the Fourteenth Amendment, but also that expected income was property and that any regulation reducing income was deprivation of property within the meaning of the amendment. The Court rejected their arguments and validated the Granger laws. It held that a state in the exercise of its police power could regulate private property devoted to public use and affecting the general community; it conceded the right of a state to regulate interstate commerce in the absence of national regulation; and it dismissed due process with the observation that it was not intended to restrict the police power.

The railroads continued to contest the validity of the regulatory laws in the courts and eventually succeeded in destroying their effectiveness. The undoing of the statutes came after new justices friendly to an expanded notion of property rights and not averse to striking down state powers ascended to the Supreme Court.

The first step came in 1886 in the so-called Wabash case (*Wabash, St. Louis, and Pacific Railway Co. v. Illinois*). Involved was a statute prohibiting higher rates for a "short haul" than a "long haul" between points in Illinois and New York City. The Court held that the statute attempted to regulate interstate commerce and infringed on the exclusive power of Congress. Interstate rates were thus removed from state control, but within its own limits a state could still regulate railroads if the regulations did not directly affect interstate commerce. This power the roads effectively nullified by persuading the Court to accept the due process clause as a "substantive" restriction on state authority. That is, due process, previously conceived of as guaranteeing the accused certain procedural rights, came to be defined as a limitation on the power of states to regulate private property or vested rights—with the judiciary acting as the guardian of property and reviewing the acts of legislatures. The Court arrived at this position gradually and with some indirection. It affirmed it in essence, although not explicitly, in *Chicago, Milwaukee and St. Paul Railroad* v. *Minnesota* (1890), and thereafter in starkly specific terms. Constant judicial review of state decrees meant, of course, that state regulation had become a mockery.

The only answer to the problem was national regulation. Since the 1870's demands had been voiced in and out of Congress for some kind of supervisory legislation, and revelations of such railroad practices as pooling, rebates, and other discriminatory devices stirred public support for action. Even some railway operators, alarmed by the fierce competition in their industry, were willing to accept regulation. Sentiment became so strong that Congress was finally forced to act. In 1887 it passed the Interstate Commerce Act, a measure described by its sponsor, Senator Shelby M. Cullom, as "conservative legislation."

The Interstate Commerce Act prohibited rebates, pools, long-short haul discriminations, and drawbacks. It required railroads to publish their rate schedules and file them with the government. It provided that all charges in interstate rail transportation should be "reasonable and just," but failed to furnish a standard or method to determine the justness of a rate. To administer the act, a five-man agency, the Interstate Commerce Commission, was created, with powers to hear complaints from shippers, examine witnesses, and inquire into the books and accounts of railroads. The law did not clearly authorize the Commission to fix rates. After investigating a complaint, the Commission could issue a cease-and-desist order to a carrier to lower its charges.

If the road refused, the Commission had to take its case to the courts and justify its decree, a cumbersome procedure that militated against effective regulation.

For almost twenty years after its passage, the Interstate Commerce Act was without practical effect; it did not accomplish widespread rate reduction or eliminate discrimination. No wonder an Attorney General of the United States advised a railroad president not to ask for repeal of the act: "It satisfies the popular clamor for government supervision of the railroads at the same time that that supervision is almost entirely nominal."

The Grange, the original precipitator of state and federal regulation, had lost its position as a major force in the agricultural scene long before the issue was resolved. By 1880 its membership had shrunk to 100,000. The collapse of its cooperative experiments and the ineffectiveness of its railroad laws drove some members away. But above all, it was weakened by a return of prosperity in the late seventies. The embattled farmers, who once had shouted for collective action, soon left the fold and resumed their old and familiar individualistic ways.

Rise of the Populists

In the 1880's the prices of the great staples again declined, hard times returned to the South and the prairie West, and the farmers of those regions, more embittered and frustrated than the Grangers, turned to more militant forms of organization. From the Carolinas to the Dakotas a multitude of farm societies bearing a variety of names mushroomed into existence, but by the end of the decade they had been combined, through absorption or federation, into two major organizations: the National Farmers' Alliance, founded by Milton George and centered in the prairie states west of the Mississippi and usually known as the Northern or Northwestern Alliance, and the Farmers' Alliance and Industrial

HISTORY REPEATS ITSELF.—THE ROBBER BARONS OF THE MIDDLE AGES, AND THE ROBBER BARONS OF TO-DAY.

THE MODERN ROBBER BARONS. In this cartoon the millionaires of business are likened to the "robber barons" of the Middle Ages. As the serfs brought tribute to the feudal lords, so farmers, laborers, and small businessmen had to pay tribute in the form of wages and interest to the masters of the trusts. The term "robber baron" as a descriptive tag for the big businessmen of the period became popular and even passed into historical usage. (FROM Puck, 1889)

Union, founded by Dr. C. W. Macune and largely restricted to the South and known as the Southern Alliance. Loosely affiliated with the Southern order was a Negro branch, the Colored Farmer's Alliance. Of the two alliances, the Southern was the more tightly knit and the larger, numbering over a million members. Although leaders of the alliances sought to weld them into a single organization and although the two groups were able to cooperate politically, differences in aims and methods prevented an organic union.

At their beginning both alliances toyed with the same kind of objectives that had intrigued the Grange: social and educational activities and cooperative enterprises. But almost immediately they shifted their emphasis to politics—and to a program designed to save the farmer by

state and national legislation rather than through improved business techniques. First to plunge into the arena of politics was the Northern Alliance, and it entered boldly and brashly flying third-party colors. At an early date the Northern leaders decided that the farmers could expect nothing from the Democrats or Republicans and would have to create their own political organization. In the elections of 1890 they ran candidates for national and state office under diverse party labels in all the prairie states. The Southern Alliance turned to politics more reluctantly, but by 1890 it too was ready for action, though not in the form of a third party. Fearful that a new party would split the solidity of the one-party South and endanger white supremacy, the Southerners, heeding the counsel of such farm leaders as Benjamin F. Tillman of South Carolina, set their sights on capturing control of the Democratic party from its conservative Bourbon rulers; in 1890 Alliance-backed candidates competed with Bourbon aristocrats in every corner of the former Confederacy.

The farmers startled conservatives and surprised themselves with their success in 1890. The farm forces won partial or complete control of the legislatures in twelve states, eight in the South and four in the West, and elected six governors, three United States Senators, and approximately fifty Congressmen. The magnitude of the agrarian sweep was not, however, as great as it seemed. In the South, where the triumph was most complete, the farmers had stuck fast to the Democratic party. Over forty of the farm Congressmen were Southern Alliance-endorsed Democrats; the one Southern Representative to admit a third-party affiliation was Georgia's Thomas E. Watson.

After the elections of 1890, the leaders of the Northern Alliance were certain that the time was ripe for the formation of a national third party. Some of the Southern leaders—the fiery Watson, consumed with an emotional hatred for monopoly, and Leonidas L. Polk of North Carolina, perhaps the ablest mind in the agrarian movement—were coming to the same conclusion. Reluctantly the Southerners were recognizing that their local successes would have no weight whatsoever in determining the course of the national Democratic party or in influencing Grover Cleveland and Eastern Democrats to adopt the farmers' program. Plans for a third party were laid at meetings in Cincinnati (May, 1891) and in St. Louis (February, 1892), attended by many representatives of the Northern Alliance, some Southerners, and spokesmen of the fading Knights of Labor. Then in July, 1892, 1,300 excited and exultant delegates poured into Omaha, Nebraska, in the heart of the plains country, to proclaim the new party, approve an official set of principles, and nominate candidates for the Presidency and Vice Presidency. By common consent the party already had a name, one first used by the Kansas agrarians—the People's party—from which, by way of Latin, were derived the terms Populist and Populism.

Amidst turbulence not seen in American politics since Andrew Jackson's time and in a spirit of dedicated idealism reminiscent of the antislavery crusade, the delegates at Omaha adopted a platform. To achieve their ends, they were willing to invest government with powers that would horrify business conservatives or liberals of the Grover Cleveland type: "We believe that the power of government—in other words, of the people—should be expanded . . . as rapidly and as far as the good sense of an intelligent people and the teachings of experience shall justify, to the end that oppression, injustice, and poverty shall eventually cease in the land."

Coming down to specific items, the Populist platform called for ownership and operation by the national government of the railroads and the telephone and telegraph systems (a significant advance on the state regulation urged by the Grangers); a flexible national currency issued by the government and not by the banks; the free and unlimited coinage of silver; government-operated postal savings banks; a graduated income tax; the subtreasury plan, an arrangement whereby farmers could deposit nonperishable produce in government warehouses and borrow in United States treasury notes up to 80 per cent of the current value of their commodities (thus enabling farmers to withhold crops from sale until the price was right); prohibition of alien land ownership; and reclamation of lands held by railroads and other corporations "in excess of their actual needs." Bidding for the support of labor, the platform demanded shorter hours for labor and restrictions on immigration, and denounced the employment of private de-

POPULIST LEADER. In his long political career James B. Weaver epitomized the aspirations of nineteenth-century liberalism. He ran the political gamut, always seeking a party that represented the interests of the small property holder. Beginning as a Democrat, he left that party because he thought the slavocracy dominated it. He became a Republican but left that party after the Civil War because he believed the big financiers controlled it. He became a Greenbacker and then a Populist. In 1896 he advocated Populist endorsement of Bryan, and so ended in the party he had begun with, the Democrats. (STATE HISTORICAL SOCIETY OF IOWA)

tective agencies as strikebreakers in labor disputes. There were planks dealing with governmental reform, but they had an economic purpose; they were intended to increase the political power of the producers and curb the power of the corporations. The Populists advocated new political techniques designed to place government more directly under democratic control: the Australian, or secret, ballot; the popular election of United States Senators; the initiative, a device whereby in states legislation could be introduced or enacted by the voters; and the referendum, a method whereby the voters could veto actions of state legislatures.

Not all of the spirit of Populism was in the platform. "It is a struggle," cried one Populist orator, "between the robbers and the robbed." Crush the sinister enemies of the people, the money kings and the business princes, the Populists thought, and miraculously all would be well in America. Many believed that a vast conspiracy existed to destroy the farmer, a conspiracy that had been hatched in New York and London by Jewish and English bankers. Along with the undoubted democratic idealism of Populism went some dark undertones of nativism and prejudice.

Populism was strong in only three geographic centers: the South, the plains and prairie region (but chiefly Kansas, Nebraska, and North and South Dakota), and the Rocky Mountain states. The Populists evoked little response in the old Granger states of the Middle West. In this previous center of protest, diversified techniques, emphasizing dairying and a corn-hog complex, had brought a new prosperity and induced a new agrarian conservatism. Even in the South the hold of Populism was tenuous and temporary. Populist leaders, seeking to unite politically poor white and colored people, encountered the unyielding barriers of race. They could not, except for short periods and in a few states, persuade the white masses that class was paramount to color, and they could not overcome the traditional white loyalty to the Democratic party. Moreover, Democratic leaders, following Ben Tillman's cue in South Carolina, weaned strength from the Populists by taking over some of their demands.

The Populists failed to unite under their standard the forces of urban protest. This was partly because, despite their brave platform talk about the common interests of rural and city workers, they had no real interest in effecting such a combination, and partly because no realistic basis for an alliance between Populist farmers and urban dissenters existed. The Knights of Labor endorsed Populism, but the Knights were a dying organization.

Hardly any of the party leaders were dirt farmers. The great majority were of the rural middle class; they were professional men, editors and lawyers, or professional politicians and agitators. Only a handful had held office or exercised the responsibility of power. James B. Weaver, the party's presidential nominee in 1892, had run the political gamut. He had begun as a Democrat and deserted that party because it was controlled by the slavocracy, had joined the Republicans and left them because they were dominated by the business plutocracy, and had then become successively a Greenbacker and a Populist. Despite his seemingly erratic course, Weaver was a man of balance and ability and a fine sense of justice.

Too many Populist leaders gave an impression of personal failure, of brilliant instability, of brooding communion with mystic forces. The matchless orator, Ignatius Donnelly of Minnesota, wrote one book locating the lost isle of Atlantis, another proving that Bacon wrote Shakespeare's plays, and a novel purporting to describe a Populist Utopia. Georgia's Tom Watson, author of biographies of Jefferson and Napoleon (he referred curiously to the latter as a "great Democratic despot"), once championed political union across racial lines but ended his career baiting Negroes and Jews. Jerry Simpson of Kansas ridiculed a rival candidate for wearing silk socks and won the undying title of "Sockless Jerry, the Socrates of the prairies."

Despite the weaknesses of the People's party, its leaders and adherents looked forward enthusiastically to the election of 1892.

The Trusts and the Tariff

Benjamin Harrison, the victor in the close and corrupt election of 1888, assumed the Presidency the following year in the nation's centennial inauguration. Just forty-eight years before, his grand-

THE KANSAS PYTHONESS. The leading female orator of Populism was Mrs. Mary E. Lease. Although hostile critics said a woman should not be a stump speaker, Mrs. Lease talked frequently and vividly, delivering some 160 speeches in 1890. In one address she recalled that the farmers had been asked to raise a big crop and had done so. What came of their efforts? "Eight-cent corn, ten-cent oats, two-cent beef, and no-price at all for butter and eggs—that's what came of it." On another occasion she advised Kansas farmers to "raise less corn and more hell." (THE KANSAS STATE HISTORICAL SOCIETY, TOPEKA)

father, William Henry Harrison, had entered the same office and died almost immediately, leaving no trace of his influence on the Presidency, Benjamin Harrison would serve his term, but he too would have little impact on the course of history and he would leave behind a record of negative accomplishment. Intelligent and honest, he was colorless in personality, cold in manner, and singularly aloof—from people, from the new currents of social change, and from the more sordid realities of politics. In White House annals his administration is notable for the wiring of the executive mansion for electricity.

Harrison's Cabinet was like himself, competent but drab. Secretary of State Blaine was the only member who rose above the level of average ability. In dispensing appointments, Harrison was limited by the requirements of his party. He was the first Republican President since Lincoln to succeed a Democrat, and the party faithful were hungry for spoils. Moreover, the bosses had promised, without his knowledge, many of the major offices during the recent campaign. Although he was known as a moderate civil-service supporter, he extended the classified list but slightly, and permitted his Postmaster General, John Wanamaker, a hefty contributor to his campaign fund, to sweep 30,000 postmasters out of office in a year. One of his worst appointments was that of "Corporal" James Tanner as commissioner of pensions. Tanner, announcing that he was going to raise all pensions even though his actions wrung from some people the prayer, "God help the surplus," proceeded to replace Cleveland's policy of careful examination with a reckless generosity that delighted politicians and veterans alike.

Like other Presidents of the Conservative era, Harrison exerted little effort to influence legislation. Lawmaking he was content to leave to the party leaders in Congress. With slender majorities in both houses, the Republicans could carry through a program only by submitting to rigid leadership and acting as a disciplined unit. The leadership came from Maine's Thomas B. Reed, Speaker of the House and a master of parliamentary law and savage wit. Some fruits of his control were a Dependent Pensions Act that almost doubled the number of pensioners and even stunned the G. A. R., and a flood of appropriations bills for internal improvements, subsidies to steamship lines, and naval expansion.

Public opinion forced the Reed Congress to consider legislation affecting broad areas of the economy, and in 1890 important measures dealing with big business and the tariff were enacted. Some fifteen Western and Southern states had adopted laws prohibiting combinations that restrained competition. But corporations found it easy to escape limitations by incorporating in states that offered special privileges (New Jersey and Delaware were notorious examples). Acceptance by the Supreme Court of the argument that a corporation was a "person" before the law and entitled to the protection of the due-process clause of the Fourteenth Amendment in *Santa Clara County* v. *Southern Pacific Railroad* (1886) meant that any form of state control was subject to judicial negation. If antitrust legislation was to be effective, it would obviously have to come from the national government. In 1888 both parties promised to curb the monopolies.

With little debate and by almost unanimous votes in both houses of Congress, the Sherman Antitrust Act became law in July, 1890. Its provisions and phraseology were determined by the fact that the only basis for national action against trust derived from the power of Congress to regulate interstate commerce. The heart of the measure was in the first two sections: (1) "Every contract, combination in the form of trust or otherwise, or conspiracy, in restraint of trade or commerce among the several States, or with foreign nations, is hereby declared to be illegal"; (2) "Every person who shall monopolize, or attempt to monopolize . . . any part of the trade or commerce among the several States, or with foreign nations, shall be deemed guilty of a misdemeanor. . . ."

For over a decade after its passage there was little attempt to enforce the Sherman Act. Before 1901 the Justice Department instituted only fourteen suits under the law against business combinations, and failed to obtain convictions in almost every one. The courts, uniformly hostile to the law, proceeded to emasculate it. The crowning decision came in *United States*

v. *E. C. Knight Co.* (1895), a case in which the government charged that the defendants controlled 98 per cent of the manufacture of refined sugar in the country. Chief Justice Melville W. Fuller, speaking for the Supreme Court, threw out the government's case with a curious distinction between manufacturing and commerce. He admitted that the present combination was a trust to monopolize the refining of sugar but denied that it was therefore illegal: the trust was not in interstate commerce but in manufacturing. The Knight decision created a "twilight zone" between state and national powers, an area of economic life outside the authority of any agency of government.

Having made an effort to dispose of the trust question, the Republicans turned with anticipation to the subject that most interested them and their business backers and that had been the paramount issue in the campaign of 1888, the tariff. William McKinley of Ohio, a rising party luminary and chairman of the House Ways and Means Committee, and Senator Nelson W. Aldrich of Rhode Island framed, with the assistance of the tariff lobbies, the highest protective measure yet offered to a Congress. As the McKinley Tariff Act it became law in October, 1890.

Seldom in American political history has a party in power suffered such a stunning reverse as befell the Republicans in the mid-term elections of 1890. Their majority in the Senate was slashed to eight, and in the House they could count only 88 seats to 235 for the Democrats and 9 for the Alliance-Populists. Popular revulsion against the McKinley duties, pictured by the Democrats as raising the living costs of the masses, was an undoubted factor in causing the Republican debacle; McKinley himself was among those going down to defeat. But the elections registered more than condemnation of a tariff. They reflected the deep anxieties of millions of Americans who were beginning to question the economic order.

BENJAMIN HARRISON. Only five feet six inches tall, Harrison was known as "Little Ben." But the Republicans said that he was big enough to wear his grandfather's hat, referring to his forebear in the White House, William Henry Harrison. Serious and sincere, Harrison was dignified and even aloof in manner, and was popular with neither the people nor the politicians. One Republican leader always advised callers on the President to wear overcoats—so they would not catch cold. (NATIONAL ARCHIVES)

In the presidential election of 1892 Benjamin Harrison was again the Republican nominee and Grover Cleveland the Democratic. Once more the platforms of the two parties were almost identical except for the tariff, with the Republicans upholding protection and the Democrats pledging reduction. Both parties in their official pronouncements ignored the pulsing currents of unrest in the country. Only the Populists, with James B. Weaver as their candidate, advocated economic reform. Cleveland amassed 277 electoral and 5,557,000 popular votes as compared to Harrison's 145 and 5,176,000 votes. For the first time since the Civil War the Democrats won a majority of both houses of Congress. Weaver polled 22 electoral votes from six mountain and plains states and over a million popular votes, and the Populists elected at least a dozen Senators and Congressmen. The showing of the new party was impressive, but it had demonstrated practical strength in only a few thinly populated states. Weaver won the electoral votes of Kansas (10), Colorado (4), Idaho (3), Nevada (3), and picked up single votes in North Dakota and Oregon.

Plainly the election was a repudiation of Republican policies, but it was not plain to the politicians what policies the voters wanted to substitute. Despite Cleveland's past negative record, a large proportion of the people who voted for him expected that the Democrats would devise some original approach to the new problems troubling America. His inaugural address rudely disillusioned them, as he reaffirmed his devotion to laissez faire: "The lessons of paternalism ought to be unlearned and the better lesson taught that while the people should . . . support their Government its functions do not include the support of the people."

Cleveland called on his party to redeem its pledge to lower the existing tariff rates. In the House William L. Wilson of West Virginia introduced a bill in 1894 designed to accomplish moderate downward revision and yet provide adequate protection for domestic producers. In a bid for Populist support and to compensate for an anticipated loss in revenues, the bill contained an income tax provision providing for a 2-per-cent levy on incomes over $4,000. When the Wilson bill reached the Senate, the customary lobbying and log-rolling began. Eastern Democrats, directed by Maryland's Arthur P. Gorman and abetted by Republicans, added 634 amendments, most of them altering Wilson's duties upward. Strong pressure from the Democratic leadership induced the House to accept the Senate version. Cleveland denounced it as a violation of the party's platform but allowed it to become law without his signature. The Wilson-Gorman Tariff reduced the

general scale of duties only 10 per cent, and its duties on raw and refined sugar and other items afforded ample protection to the Sugar Trust and every other trust. Far from the kind of tariff the Democrats had promised the country, the act seemed to confirm the Populist contention that tariff-making was a sham battle between the major parties.

Even the one crust thrown to the agrarian interests, the income tax, was shortly snatched away by the courts. In a case testing the right of the government to levy an income tax (*Pollack* v. *The Farmer's Loan and Trust Co.*, 1895), the Supreme Court declared in a five-four decision that a tax on incomes was a "direct" tax and hence had to be apportioned among the states according to population. Since an income tax, by its very nature, would be effective only if applied on a basis of individual wealth and would have no reality if reckoned on the distribution of population, the Court had made it impossible to levy such a tax.

The Money Question

The Cleveland administration was hardly settled in office when the panic of 1893 struck the country. There followed one of the most severe depressions up to that time, its grim hold on the economy not being loosened until shortly before the turn of the century. The causes of the panic were various and complicated. The eighties had been a typical boom period, featuring overexpansion and overinvestment in railroads and industrial combinations. Depressed prices in agriculture since 1887 had weakened the purchasing power of a substantial section of the population. Depression conditions that had begun earlier in Europe were resulting in a loss of American markets abroad, a decline in the export trade, and a withdrawal by foreign investors of gold invested in this country. Whatever the causes of the depression, its effects were terrifying and embraced all segments of the economy. Over 8,000 business concerns failed in a period of six months, 156 railroads went into receivership, and 400 banks suspended operations. Agricultural prices tumbled to new lows, and perhaps as many as a million workers, 20 per cent of the laboring force, were thrown out of jobs.

Jacob S. Coxey, a Massillon, Ohio, businessman and Populist, proposed two lines of action: (1) Congress should issue $500 million in legal-tender notes to be used in the construction of roads throughout the country; and (2) local governments wishing to undertake public improvements should be authorized to issue noninterest-bearing bonds which could be exchanged at the federal Treasury for legal-tender notes. Coxey's ideas were hooted at in conservative circles. (But the notion of creating jobs by a building program would appeal to a later generation afflicted by depression. At the onset of the next great depression in the 1930's the government would inaugurate a public works program. Coxey, who lived until 1951, thus saw his scheme finally put into effect.)

Seeking to dramatize his program, Coxey organized a march of the unemployed on Washington to present a petition for work relief to Congress. Only 500 of "Coxey's army" were able to make their way to Washington, and they were barred from the Capitol by armed police. Coxey was arrested on a trumped-up charge of walking on the grass, and the marchers were herded into camps because their presence supposedly endangered public health.

The panic deranged the government's monetary system, and in the minds of people like Cleveland the silver policy became the primary cause of the depression. This money question had a long history.

Since the beginning of the republic the country had been on a bimetallic standard: the government purchased and coined all the gold and silver offered to it for sale. At first the relative value of the two metals had been set by commercial demand for them, but eventually the government fixed a legal ratio. Back in Andrew Jackson's period the ratio had been placed at sixteen to one, meaning that the silver dollar had sixteen times as much silver as the gold dollar did gold. For sound economic reasons, hardly any silver dollars were coined. Because of the relative scarcity of silver bullion, the price of gold in the open market was almost never sixteen times the price of silver, so that what silver was mined was sold for commercial purposes. Nobody objected when in 1873 Congress enacted a measure that, while keeping existing silver money in circulation, removed the silver dollar from the coinage list. Soon the inflationists, charging a banker conspiracy, would be calling this act the "Crime of '73."

Almost immediately there occurred a drastic change in the supply of silver. The discovery of huge new deposits of the metal in the Far West, notably in Nevada, increased the amount in the domestic market; at the same time, several European countries went on the gold standard, melting their silver coins and swelling the world supply. The inevitable result was that the price of silver plunged downward and fell far below the legal ratio. Silver-mine owners, pinched by the dropping price, joined the agrarian elements in demanding that the government return to the bimetallic system, that it purchase all the silver brought to the mint— "the free and unlimited coinage of silver."

In 1878 the inflationists, a coalition of Democrats and Republicans from the Middle West, South, and Far West, attempted to pass a free-silver measure through Congress. They were forced, however, to accept a compromise, the Bland-Allison Act, which provided that each month the government must purchase not less than $2 million and not more than $4 million worth of silver and convert it into dollars at the ratio of sixteen to one. The inflation forces had won only a partial victory.

Later, in 1890, the Sherman Silver Purchase Act directed the Treasury to buy each month 4,500,000 ounces of silver, an amount estimated to be the maximum domestic production, and to pay for the purchased bullion in treasury notes. These notes were to be, at the discretion of the Secretary of the Treasury, redeemable in gold or silver coin. Many Democrats and the uncompromising free-silver men, pointing out that the purchased silver was not to be coined, opposed the act as an empty gesture, and subsequent events seemed to confirm their position. The Treasury adopted the practice of redeeming the silver notes in gold, the amount of money in circulation did not increase materially, and the price of silver continued to drop. The Sherman Act did not quiet either side in the currency controversy. The creditors and the conservatives argued for the adoption of a single metallic standard; the debtors and inflationists agitated for the unlimited coinage of silver at the rate of sixteen to one.

The Populists at first did not emphasize silver. But as the party developed strength, the money question came to overshadow all other issues. Currency reform was the simple and single kind of cure-all that appealed to the Populist and agrarian mind. It had the great virtue of being easily explained and easily comprehended. Moreover, it was already a popular issue with debtor farmers, who with some reason believed that inflation would ameliorate their ills. The Populists desperately needed money to finance their campaigns, and the only source of help was the silver-mine owners, who insisted on an elevation of the money plank and the subordination of other proposals.

The influence of silver on the thinking of Populists, agrarian Democrats, and farmers was graphically illustrated by the enormous popularity of a small and not particularly profound book, *Coin's Financial School*, written by William H. Harvey and published in 1894. "Professor Coin" ran a school, an imaginary institution specializing in finance, and the book reproduced his lectures and his dialogues with his students. The professor clearly indicated the marvelous restorative qualities of free silver: "It means the reopening of closed factories, the relighting of fires in darkened furnaces; it means hope instead of despair; comfort in place of suffering; life instead of death."

Ever since the Resumption Act of 1875 the Treasury had aimed to maintain a minimum gold reserve of $100 million to redeem its paper and silver dollars. During the prosperous eighties the reserve increased, and it reached the figure of $190 million by 1890. But in the last two years of the Harrison administration, because of the financial legislation of the Republicans, it fell off sharply. The prohibitive duties of the McKinley Tariff reduced imports and hence revenue; the pension and internal improvements appropriations ate up the surplus; and the Sherman Silver Purchase Act forced the government to buy increased amounts of silver and issue new treasury notes that the Treasury insisted on redeeming in gold. Holders of greenbacks and silver certificates, jittery at rumors the government might be swept off the gold standard, demanded gold, and when Cleveland assumed office in 1893, the reserve had shrunk to a little over $100 million.

The panic intensified the rush for gold, and soon the reserve sank below the minimum deemed necessary to sustain the gold standard. Cleveland had always disliked the Sherman Silver Purchase Act, and now he was convinced that it was the chief factor draining gold from the Treasury and that it would, if allowed to stand, force the country off the gold standard and impair the government's financial honor. In one of his rare moods of leadership, the President summoned Congress into special session and demanded the repeal of the Sherman Act. He worked his will, but only by swinging the patronage lash hard on recalcitrant Democrats and enlisting the support of Eastern Republicans. Western and Southern Democrats fought repeal to the last, and in defeat were incredibly bitter. A historic party split was in the making.

The President had his victory, but the financial crisis deepened. In 1895, Cleveland approached the big New York bankers for help. A banking syndicate headed by J. P. Morgan agreed to take up a $65 million bond issue, securing the bonds at a price below their market value, and pledged to obtain half the gold abroad, not to withdraw any of it from the Treasury, and to use the influence of the financial community to check the flow of gold to Europe. As a result of this unique arrangement, public faith that the government would maintain the gold standard was strengthened. The stampede to redeem notes eased, and a little later the government was able to float a popular loan with no difficulty. But to agrarian Democrats and Populists it seemed that Cleveland had sold out to Wall Street and concluded a crooked deal with the money lenders. There had been no deal and no corruption, though the bankers undoubtedly turned an excessive profit.

The Cleveland administration ended amidst flaming portents of social unrest. The Democratic party was bitterly divided. The President's sabotage of silver and the tariff debacle had aligned the Southern and Western Democrats in a solid phalanx against him and his Eastern followers.

The Farm Uprising, 1896

As the election of 1896 approached, Republicans were confident of victory.

Marcus A. Hanna, boss of the Ohio machine and soon to be national boss of the party, was a wealthy industrialist who aspired to be a President-maker; he represented a new type in politics, the businessman who held office and actively manipulated parties instead of remaining in the background and paying out money for services rendered. Hanna was determined that the Republicans would ride to power with the right candidate, and he had picked out his man and had been grooming him carefully since 1890. The man was William McKinley, also of Ohio, author of the tariff act of 1890 and presently governor of his state. Hanna's support of McKinley included providing him with generous campaign contributions, bailing him out of a threatened bankruptcy, and advertising his availability to Republican bosses in other states.

By the time the convention met, Hanna had lined up enough Middle Western and Southern delegations to nominate McKinley. Everywhere and on every occasion he presented his candidate as "Bill McKinley, the advance agent of prosperity" and the champion of protection for American producers.

The platform as finally framed endorsed the protective tariff, ignored completely such questions as the income tax, railroad and trust abuses, and labor injunctions, and opposed the free coinage of silver except by international agreement with the leading commercial nations. As other countries, and particularly Great Britain, were unlikely to abandon the gold standard, the Republicans were making a safe gesture; they were supporting gold but in a way that was a little difficult for silverites to criticize. Thirty-four delegates from the mountain and plains states walked out when the currency plank was adopted. Their obvious destination was the Democratic party.

The Democrats met amidst scenes of drama seldom equalled in American politics. The Southern and Western delegates came to the convention determined to seize control of the party from the Easterners. Alarmed by the rise of Populist strength in their sections, they intended to write free silver and other planks of the third party into the platform and to nominate a silver candidate.

The resolutions committee presented to the convention two reports. The majority platform demanded tariff reduction,

THE ORATOR OF THE SILVER CRUSADE. America has produced many orators who could sway crowds with the magic of their voices, but it is generally agreed that in power and persuasiveness William Jennings Bryan was without an equal. This picture shows him at a later date than 1896. Although no longer the Boy Orator of the silver campaign, he was still a young man, in the political sense, and at the height of his career. (BROWN BROTHERS)

endorsed the principle of the income tax, denounced the issue of currency notes by the national banks, condemned the use of injunctions in industrial disputes, pledged a "stricter control" of trusts and railroads, and—this was the issue that headlined the platform—called for free silver: "We demand the free and unlimited coinage of both silver and gold at the present legal ratio of 16 to 1, without waiting for the aid or consent of any other nation." The minority resolution opposed the free coinage of silver except by international agreement, a stand identical to that of the Re-

publicans and tantamount to endorsing the gold standard.

Six speakers appeared to debate the resolution, three for gold and three for silver. The defenders of gold had the better of the oratorical tournament—up to the final address. Then from the Nebraska delegation a strikingly handsome young man walked to the platform to close the debate. He was William Jennings Bryan, 36 years of age. His political experience was limited to two terms in the House of Representatives, but he was widely known in the plains country as a magnetic orator and he was a conscious although a minor aspirant for the presidential nomination. Through the farthest reaches of the vast hall now rang his magnificent organ-like voice.

He ended with a peroration that brought the delegates and the spectators to their feet in a frenzied tumult of passion and that was declaimed by later generations of schoolboys all over rural America: "If they dare to come out in the open and defend the gold standard as a good thing, we will fight them to the uttermost. Having behind us the producing masses of this nation and the world, supported by the commercial interests, the laboring interests and the toilers everywhere, we will answer their demand for a gold standard by saying to them: 'You shall not press down upon the brow of labor this crown of thorns; you shall not crucify mankind upon a cross of gold.' "

The majority platform was adopted. The agrarians had found their leader, and the following day Bryan was nominated on the fifth ballot. It is doubtful if he understood the technical implications of the money problem that he discussed so eloquently before the convention. It is even more dubious if he realized the full import of the protest movement or the Populist program. He seized on one Populist plank, free silver, the most superficial of the various protest proposals, and erected it into a personal and political obsession.

One Republican (Joseph Foraker), when asked if he thought Bryan's title, the Boy Orator of the Platte, was an accurate phrase, replied that it was, because the Platte River was six inches deep and six miles wide at the mouth. More descriptive was another designation applied to Bryan: the Great Commoner. Born in Illinois of typical middle-class stock, he had attended a small sectarian college, had practiced law with only average success, and then, repeating a normal American pattern, had moved to Nebraska, a frontier area, to try his fortunes. Almost completely he represented the feelings and emotions of rural, middle-class America.

The choice of Bryan and the nature of the Democratic platform placed the Populists in a cruel quandary. They had anticipated that both the major parties would adopt conservative programs and nominate conservative candidates, leaving the Populists to represent the growing forces of protest. But now the Democrats had stolen much of the Populists' platform thunder. The Populists faced the choice of naming their own candidate and splitting the protest vote, or endorsing Bryan and losing their identity as a party. When the party assembled, the convention voted to approve Bryan but nominated its own vice-presidential candidate, Tom Watson, whom the Democrats were expected to adopt but whom they ignored.

There has never been a campaign quite like the one of 1896. It had unequalled drama, intense excitement, a clean-cut issue, and a David and Goliath theme: the boy orator Bryan contending against the powerful boss Hanna. The boss had the great advantage of ample funds to spend on organization. The business and financial community, frightened beyond reason at the prospect of Bryan's sitting in the White House and taking advice from John P. Altgeld and Ignatius Donnelly, pressed contributions upon Hanna. Just how much money Hanna had to dispense has been disputed, but the lowest estimate is $3,500,000 and the highest is $7,000,000. The Democrats, by contrast, reported expenditures of only $300,000, a sum only slightly larger than the contribution of one firm, Standard Oil, to the Republican war chest. With his almost inexhaustible resources, Hanna organized the most lavish propaganda machine yet to operate in American politics.

Shrewdly, Hanna kept McKinley off the hustings, knowing better than to pit his solemn candidate against the matchless Bryan. From his home at Canton, Ohio, McKinley conducted a dignified "front-porch" campaign. To Canton

came pilgrimages of the Republican faithful, organized and paid for by Hanna, to
offer tribute to the standard-bearer. They
came every day but McKinley always had
a speech ready for them, and always he
stressed one theme: the Republican party
was the only agency that could bring prosperity to the country.

No such decorous restraint marked the
campaigning of the young and vital
Bryan. Joyously bearing the brunt of the

lutionaries were about to seize the government. The shrillness of the denunciations of Bryan betrayed the fright of those
who uttered them. The Boy Orator, who
was strictly orthodox in morals and religion and who would end his life fighting
the teaching of evolution in the schools,
was described as "an apostle of atheism,
repudiation, and anarchy."

Employers told their workers not to report for work in case of a Democratic vic-

---

A CONSERVATIVE VIEW OF BRYAN

The terror which the Bryan movement inspired in many conservative
Americans is illustrated by the comment of the New York Tribune after
the election of 1896:

"There are some movements so base, some causes so depraved, that
neither victory can justify them nor defeat entitle them to commiseration.
The wicked rattle-pated boy, posing in vapid vanity and mouthing re-
sounding rottenness, was not the real leader of that league of Hell. He was
only a puppet in the blood-imbrued hands of Altgeld the anarchist and
Debs the revolutionist. But he was a willing puppet, Bryan was, willing
and eager. None of his masters was more apt than he at lies and forgeries
and blasphemies and all the nameless iniquities of that campaign against
the Ten Commandments."

---

battle for his party, he inaugurated techniques never before witnessed in American political contests. Previous candidates
had addressed audiences in campaigns
and had even toured the country to speak
at a few selected points. But Bryan was
the first to stump systematically every section, to appear in villages and hamlets,
the first, really, to say frankly to the voters
that he wanted to be President. He traveled 18,000 miles, speaking several times
a day, and addressed an estimated 5,000,-
000 people.

As Bryan's campaign mounted in intensity, cold fear gripped the East, and by
late summer many Republicans were conceding his election. The reactions of people in conservative circles bordered on
hysteria. Sensible men acted as if red revo-

tory: industry would have to close down
in anticipation of being taken over by the
government. Some employers threatened
to dismiss workers who voted for Bryan.
The banks let it be known that farmers
supporting the Democratic candidate
probably would have their mortgages foreclosed or at least not renewed.

Everything broke right for the Republicans in the closing weeks of the election.
Crop failures abroad brought an increased
demand for American products, and on
the eve of the election the price of wheat
almost doubled.

On election day, McKinley polled 271
electoral votes to Bryan's 176. The popular vote was 7,105,000 to 6,503,000. Bryan
won the Confederate South plus Missouri, swept the plains and mountain

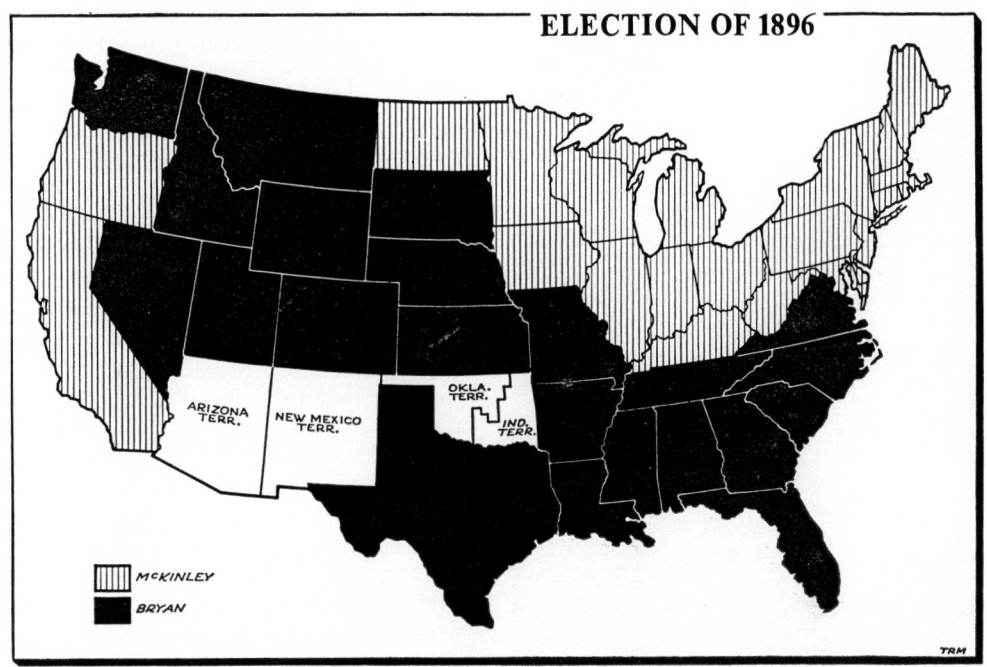

MCKINLEY

BRYAN

states with the exception of North Dakota, but lost California and Oregon on the Pacific coast. In short, he carried only the mining regions and the areas where staple farming was predominant and agricultural prices were lowest. He went down to defeat in all the Granger states in the Middle West. The Democratic program, like that of the Populists, had been designed to serve the needs of one segment of one class, the most depressed fraction of agriculture, and this was too narrow an appeal to win a national election or grasp control of the government.

McKinley and Prosperity

William McKinley, a shrewd political operator, was the last of a long list (beginning with Grant) of Northern officer veterans to sit in the White House. Friendly, kindly, and lovable, he was inclined to defer to stronger characters like Hanna and to act in harmony with his party's leaders. He and they realized the dangers inherent in the currency issue. Silver had many ad-

herents, as evidenced by Bryan's huge popular vote, and the Republican party numbered many silverites in its Western wing. Impulsive action might divide the party in its hour of victory.

Postponing action on the money problem until a more propitious time, the administration turned to an issue on which Republicans were agreed, the necessity for higher tariff rates. Immediately after assuming office, McKinley summoned Congress into special session to consider tariff revision. With record brevity the Republican majority whipped into shape and passed the Dingley Tariff, raising the duties to an average of 57 per cent, the highest in history.

On the currency question the administration proceeded with cool caution and in accordance with the party's platform pronouncement that bimetallism could not be established except by international action. McKinley sent a commission to Europe to explore the possibility of a silver agreement with Great Britain and France. As he and everyone else antici-

WILLIAM McKINLEY. Cheerful, friendly, and gracious, McKinley lived up to the role in which the Republicans cast him in 1896: "the advance agent of prosperity." Short and stocky, he carried himself in an erect and somewhat pompous posture. Critics said that he was trying to look like Napoleon. He customarily wore a white linen vest and sported a red carnation in the buttonhole of his coat. (LIBRARY OF CONGRESS)

pated, Britain refused to modify her gold standard system, thus effectively ending any hopes for international bimetallism. The administration could now argue that if the United States embarked on a silver program alone it would be economically

isolated from the rest of the world, and the argument was hard to refute. Believing that their position was unassailable, the Republicans finally moved to enact currency legislation. The Currency, or Gold Standard, Act of 1900 legalized the gold standard and enlarged the redemption fund, which was to be maintained as a separate and special charge to protect it from depletion.

And so the "battle of the standards" ended in victory for the forces of conservatism. Economic developments seemed to prove that the conservatives had been right in the struggle. In 1898 prosperity returned to America. Foreign crop failures enlarged the farmers' market and sent farm prices surging upwards. At the same time business entered another cycle of booming expansion. Prosperity and gold had come hand in hand—the lesson seemed obvious.

But it was not quite that simple. Bryan and the silverites and the agrarians had a point in demanding currency inflation. They were essentially right. In the quarter century before 1900 the countries of Western civilization had experienced a spectacular augmentation of productive facilities and population. Yet the supply of money had not kept pace with economic progress, because the supply was tied to gold and the amount of gold remained practically constant. A committee of the British House of Lords, hardly a radical agency, reported after a careful investigation that the world's economy required a larger money supply.

It so happened that the supply was vastly increased soon after the Republicans took over the government in 1897. A new technique for extracting gold from low-content ores, the cyanide process, made it possible to work mines previously considered marginal or unprofitable. At the same time huge new gold deposits were discovered in Alaska, South Africa, and Australia. In 1898 two and a half times as much gold was produced as in 1890, and the currency supply had been inflated far beyond anything proposed by Bryan. The price level, which had been declining since 1865, started on an upward swing.

With McKinley, then, there came a tariff increase, the gold standard, and prosperity. There also came a new departure in foreign policy, as the nation entered upon the path of overseas imperialism and took its place among the "great powers" of the world.

BIBLIOGRAPHY

Several good books deal with the urban protest movement: Daniel Aaron, *Men of Good Hope* (1951); Arthur Mann, *Yankee Reformers in the Urban Age* (1954); C. W. Patton, *The Battle for Municipal Reform* (1940); T. H. Greer, *American Social Reform Movements* (1949); and H. H. Quint, *The Forging of American Socialism* (1953). For the agricultural protest: C. C. Taylor, *The Farmers' Movement, 1620–1920* (1953); C. M. Destler, *American Radicalism, 1865–1901* (1946); S. J. Buck, *The Granger Movement* (1913) and *The Agrarian Crusade* (1920); and C. V. Woodward, *Tom Watson, Agrarian Radical* (1938).

See also Richard Hofstadter, *The Age of Reform* (1955); J. D. Hicks, *The Populist Revolt* (1931; new ed., 1955); R. B. Nye, *Midwestern Progressive Politics* (1951); G. H. Knoles, *The Presidential Campaign and Election of 1892* (1942); F. P. Weberg, *The Background of the Panic of 1893* (1929); and Nathan Fine, *Labor and Farmer Parties in the United States, 1828–1928* (1928). Populism on the state level is discussed in A. M. Arnett, *The Populist Movement in Georgia* (1922); R. C. Martin, *The People's Party in Texas* (1933); and W. D. Sheldon, *Populism in the Old Dominion* (1935).

For details of the political story the student should go to biographies: W. A. Robinson, *Thomas B. Reed* (1930); Elmer Ellis, *Henry More Teller* (1941); N. W. Stephenson, *Nelson W. Aldrich* (1930); M. D. Hirsch, *William C. Whitney* (1948); J. L. Lambert, Jr., *Arthur Pue Gorman* (1953); F. B. Simkins, *Pitchfork Ben Tillman* (1944); F. H. Haynes, *James Baird*

Weaver (1919); Stuart Noblin, *Leonidas Lafayette Polk* (1949); C. A. Barker, *Henry George* (1955); F. L. Allen, *The Great Pierpont Morgan* (1949); Harry Barnard, *"Eagle Forgotten"* (1938), on Altgeld the liberal Democrat; and Ray Ginger, *The Bending Cross* (1949), on Debs the Socialist.

There are several biographies of Bryan, all adequate but no one of them quite catching the man: J. C. Long, *Bryan, the Great Commoner* (1926); M. R. Werner, *Bryan* (1929); and Paxton Hibben, *Peerless Leader* (1929). No good study of McKinley exists, but his career and program can be traced in C. S. Olcott, *The Life of William McKinley* (2 vols., 1916). Material on the McKinley administration can be found in A. W. Dunn, *From Harrison to Harding* (2 vols., 1922), and H. H. Kohlsaat, *From McKinley to Harding* (1923). Shrewd and vivid sketches of McKinley and other leaders appear in W. A. White, *Masks in a Pageant* (1928). The best treatment of the McKinley period as a whole is Margaret Leech, *In the Days of McKinley* (1959). See also Herbert Croly, *Marcus Alonzo Hanna* (1912), and Thomas Beer, *Hanna* (1929).

For the literature of protest, see Lewis Mumford, *The Story of Utopias* (1922), and A. E. Morgan, *Edward Bellamy* (1944). The protest of the unemployed is developed in D. L. McMurry, *Coxey's Army* (1929). A descriptive account of the 1890's is H. U. Faulkner, *Politics, Reform, and Expansion, 1890–1900* (1959). An interpretive account is Ray Ginger, *Altgeld's America* (1958).

26

EMERGENCE

OF A WORLD POWER

The United States, by 1900 an empire with overseas possessions, pursued three general and long-standing foreign policies—one for each of three broad areas of the world. With respect to Europe, the aim was to promote commerce while avoiding diplomatic involvements. With respect to the Americas, the purpose was expressed in the Monroe Doctrine, as supplemented by the idea of Pan Americanism. With respect to Asia, the slogan came to be the Open Door, signifying opportunity for American commercial interests in China. The Monroe Doctrine and the Open Door were reaffirmed and strengthened by events after 1865. The policy of "isolation" began to be questioned, however, on the grounds that it was inconsistent with imperial obligations, with the responsibilities of "world leadership," and with the spirit of Anglo-American friendship which, by the end of the century, was about to prevail.

The Work of Seward and Fish

Some of the diplomatic developments of the later nineteenth century were fore-

shadowed, soon after the Civil War, by the aims and accomplishments of two outstanding Secretaries of State: William H. Seward (1861-9) and Hamilton Fish (1869-77).

An ardent expansionist and advocate of a vigorous foreign policy, Seward acted with as much daring as the demands of Reconstruction politics and the Republican hatred of President Johnson would permit. By exercising firm but patient pressure, he persuaded Napoleon III of France to abandon his Mexican empire, established during the war when the United States was in no position to protest. Napoleon withdrew his troops in 1867, his puppet Emperor Maximilian was executed by the Mexicans, and the validity of the Monroe Doctrine was strikingly reaffirmed.

When Russia let it be known that she would like to sell Alaska to the United States, the two nations long having been on friendly terms, Seward readily agreed to pay the asking price of $7,200,000. Only by strenuous efforts was he able to induce the Senate to ratify the treaty and the House to appropriate the money

(1867–8). Critics jeered that the Secretary had bought a useless frozen wasteland—"Seward's Icebox" and "Walrussia" were some of the terms employed to describe it—but Alaska, a center for the fishing industry in the North Pacific and potentially rich in such resources as gold, was a distinct bargain. Seward was not content with expansion in continental North America. In 1867 he engineered the annexation of the tiny Midway Islands west of Hawaii.

In contrast with its sometimes shambling course in domestic politics, the performance of the Grant administration in the area of foreign affairs was generally decisive and firm, yet showing a wise moderation. For this, Secretary Fish, to whom President Grant gave almost a free hand, deserves the major credit. A number of delicate and potentially dangerous situations confronted Fish from the beginning, but by all odds the most serious one arose out of our strained relations with Great Britain.

Against England the United States had a burning grievance which had originated during the Civil War. At that time the British government, according to the American interpretation, had violated the laws of neutrality by permitting Confederate cruisers, the *Alabama* and others, to be built and armed in English shipyards to prey on Northern commerce. American demands that England pay for the damages committed by these vessels became known as the "Alabama claims." Although the British government realized its diplomatic error in condoning construction of the cruisers—in a future war American-built *Alabamas* might operate against Britain—it at first hesitated to submit the issue to arbitration.

Other differences clouded Anglo-American relations. England contended that the United States should compensate British subjects who had suffered property losses in the shape of cotton and ships during the war. The ancient controversy of the North Atlantic fisheries and Amer-

HAMILTON FISH. Fish, a member of a distinguished New York family, had been out of politics for years when Grant offered him the position of Secretary of State. Accepting it reluctantly, he served for both of Grant's terms, and left a record of solid accomplishments. Fish represented the older tradition of cultivated gentlemen in politics. (NATIONAL ARCHIVES)

ican rights off Canadian shores had flared up again. Another dispute involved the location of the boundary between the United States and British Columbia in Puget Sound. And finally there were the Fenians—the Irish-American crusaders who thought they could free Ireland of British rule by conquering Canada. Several times during the Johnson-Grant period Fenian "armies" harassed the Canadian border. Although the American government tried to restrain these outbreaks, it refused British suggestions that it should pay for the damages committed by the Fenians.

Seward tried earnestly to settle the Alabama claims before leaving office. The American minister to England, Reverdy

Johnson, negotiated an agreement, the Johnson-Clarendon Convention (1869), providing that all claims on both sides since 1853 be submitted to arbitration. The pact was distasteful to Americans because it embraced so many issues and contained no expression of British regret for the escape of the *Alabama*. Coming before the Senate immediately after Grant took office, it was rejected 54 to 1. The debate featured a speech by Charles Sumner, chairman of the Committee on Foreign Relations, denouncing Britain for her course in the Civil War and arguing that her conduct had prolonged the war by two years. Therefore, said Sumner, England owed the United States for "direct damages" committed by the cruisers and "indirect damages" for the cost of the war for two years—which would have reached the staggering total of some $2 billion. Americans who supported Sumner's position, and they were undoubtedly a majority, professed themselves willing to accept the cession of Canada as a substitute for a cash payment.

England naturally would have nothing to do with any arrangement involving indirect claims, and settlement of the problem was temporarily stalled. Secretary Fish, however, continued to work for a solution, and finally in 1871 the two countries agreed to the Treaty of Washington, one of the great landmarks in international pacification, providing for arbitration of the cruiser issue and other pending controversies. The Alabama claims were to be laid before a five-member tribunal appointed by the governments of the United States, England, Italy, Switzerland, and Brazil. In the covenant Britain expressed regret for the escape of the *Alabama* and agreed to a set of rules governing neutral obligations that virtually gave the British case away. In effect, this meant that the tribunal would have only to fix the sum to be paid by Britain. Convening at Geneva in Switzerland, the arbitrators awarded $15,500,000 to the United States.

Just as pacifically, the other disputes covered by the treaty were compromised. The question of the Puget Sound boundary was submitted to the German Emperor, who ruled in favor of the United States title to the contested San Juan Islands. An arbitration commission awarded nearly $2 million to England for damages suffered by her citizens during the Civil War. Because the treaty had extended American fishing privileges, England claimed a payment for the concessions, and a special commission, after some wrangling, decided in 1877 that the United States should compensate Britain with $5,500,000. If the value of the arbitrations were computed in money, which of course it really could not be, the United States thus netted approximately $8 million from the awards. The real and enduring significance of the procedure was that again the two countries—as they had been doing since 1818—adjusted serious differences without resorting to force.

The New Manifest Destiny

In the two decades after 1870 the American people seemed to have forgotten the expansionist impulse of the prewar years. They were occupied with things closer to home—reconstructing the South, settling the last frontier, building a network of railroads, and expanding their great industrial system.

By the 1890's they were ready—indeed, eager—to try imperialism, to resume the course of Manifest Destiny that had impelled their forebears to wrest an empire from Mexico in the expansionist forties. Like the 1840's, the nineties were years of augmentation of American territory and power. Great social and economic forces were responsible for altering national psychology so drastically in such a short period. Settlement of the frontier had entered its last phase, industry had essentially completed its productive plant and was organizing in new and bigger forms, American exports were climbing to record figures, and political dissent was convulsing society. All these developments subtly played a part in shifting the attention of Americans from their own country to lands across the seas.

Adding to the sense of insecurity created by the passing of the frontier was the bitter class protest that marked the nineties: the Populist movement, the free-silver crusade, the bloody labor disputes. Many Americans honestly believed that the nation was threatened with internal collapse. In such a situation, some people looked to overseas expansion as a relief from domestic troubles, and some politicians advocated a more aggressive foreign policy to divert the popular mind from dissensions at home.

The swelling volume of American exports to other countries altered the nature of our trade relations and directed the attention of political leaders to the importance of foreign markets—and to the possible necessity of securing foreign colonies. The value of American exports in 1870 was approximately $392,000,000; in 1890 the figure was $857,000,000, and by 1900 it had leaped to $1,394,000,000. By the late seventies the United States was exporting more than it imported, and every decade thereafter the balance of trade shifted more markedly in its favor. Senator Albert J. Beveridge of Indiana, arguing for the acquisition of colonial possessions, cried (1899): "But today, we are raising more than we can consume. Today, we are making more than we can use. Therefore, we must find new markets for our produce, new occupation for our capital, new work for our labor. . . ."

In the century's closing years the powers of Europe partitioned most of Africa between themselves and then turned eager eyes on the Far East and the feeble Chinese Empire. Imperialism was in the air, and a leading American expansionist, Senator Henry Cabot Lodge of Massachusetts, who wanted his country to acquire extensive holdings in the Pacific and the Atlantic, warned that the United States "must not fall out of the line of march."

Politicians like Lodge, Beveridge, and young Theodore Roosevelt of New York furnished vocal support for imperialism, but the philosophic justification for expansionism was provided by historians, professors, clergymen, and other intellectuals. These literary advocates found a basis for imperialism in Charles Darwin's theories. The struggle for existence applied to nations as well as to biological forms, they contended, and the strongest nations or the ablest races were destined to survive. If in the process the strong suppressed or subordinated weaker competitors, they were only executing the law of nature and progress. From this principle it was easy to proceed to the conclusion that one or two races, by reasons of their natural superiority, were fated to exercise imperial power: the Anglo-Saxon (Americans and British) and possibly the Teutonic (Germans).

One of the first writers to argue this proposition was the Darwinian historian and popularizer, John Fiske, who predicted in an article in *Harper's Magazine* in 1885 that the English-speaking races would eventually control every land in the world that was not already the seat of an established civilization. Support for Fiske's position came in the same year from Josiah Strong, a Congregational clergyman and champion of overseas missionary work. In a book entitled *Our Country: Its Possible Future and Its Present Crisis*, Strong declared that the Anglo-Saxon race, and especially its American branch, represented the great ideas of civil liberty and pure Christianity and was "divinely commissioned" to spread its institutions over the earth. Five years later John W. Burgess, founder of Columbia University's School of Political Science, gave the stamp of scholarly approval to imperialism. In his *Political Science and Comparative Law*, he flatly stated that the Anglo-Saxon and Teutonic nations, possessing the highest political talents, were destined to world dominion. It was the duty of these nations, he said, to uplift less fortunate peoples, even to force superior institutions upon them if necessary: "There is no human right to the status of barbarism."

The ablest and probably the most effective apostle of imperialism was Alfred Thayer Mahan, an officer in the navy, a close student of naval theory, and a really distinguished military historian. Mahan presented his philosophy in three major works: *The Influence of Sea Power upon History, 1660–1783* (1890); *The Influence of Sea Power upon the French Revolution and Empire, 1793–1812* (1892); and *The Interest of America in Sea Power* (1897). His thesis may be briefly stated. The sea-power nations were the great nations of history, and the United States, a huge island, had to build its greatness on sea power. The essential links in sea power were a productive domestic economy, foreign commerce, a merchant marine to monopolize national trade, a navy to defend the trade routes and national interests, and colonies to provide raw materials and markets and to serve as bases for the navy. Specifically, Mahan advocated that the United States construct a canal across the isthmus of Central America to join the oceans, acquire defensive bases on both sides of the canal in the Caribbean and the Pacific, and take possession of Hawaii and other Pacific islands. "Whether they will or no," he proclaimed, "Americans must now begin to look outward."

Mahan doubted that the United States would achieve its destiny, because its navy was not large enough to play the role he envisioned for it. But he did not accurately gauge the progress of the naval construction program launched in the Garfield-Arthur administration and continued by every succeeding administration. By 1898 the United States had advanced to fifth among the world's naval powers, by 1900 to third. When the nation decided to embark on the path of imperialism, it would have the force to back up its choice.

Hemisphere Hegemony

The most ardent practitioner of the new, assertive diplomacy was Harrison's Secretary of State James G. Blaine, who in 1889 was beginning his second tour of duty in the foreign office. Not as zealous an expansionist as he had been in his younger days, Blaine still had large ideas about America's place in the world. He believed that his country was destined to dominate the Caribbean and the Pacific, and that Cuba, Puerto Rico, and Hawaii were parts of the American system, to be controlled if not annexed outright. He thought that the United States had an essential interest in an Isthmian canal, and as Secretary of State under Garfield he had belligerently attempted to persuade Great Britain to abandon the canal rights in Central America guaranteed to her by the Clayton-Bulwer Treaty. Blaine's expansionist policy was based largely on his conviction that the United States had to find enlarged foreign markets for its surplus goods. The most likely foreign outlet, he believed, was Latin America, with whose countries he wanted friendly commercial relations.

During his first term of office (1881), Blaine had invited the Latin nations to a Pan-American conference at Washington to discuss trade matters and arbitration of disputes. But after Garfield's death Blaine left office, and his cautious successor, fearing political repercussions to such a departure from isolation, withdrew the invitations. Blaine's idea won increasing public favor, however, and shortly before the Harrison administration took office Congress authorized the convoking of a conference, and the State Department issued the invitations. With delegates from nineteen American nations in attendance, the first Pan-American Congress, as the meeting came to be known, assembled in 1889. Blaine made a notable attempt to persuade the conference to endorse his two principal objectives: (1) to draw the United States and Latin America into a customs union and (2) to create machinery to arbitrate controversies between the hemispheric nations. The Latin delegates rejected both proposals. They preferred to buy in the cheaper European market, and they feared the dominance of the United States in arbitration. Still the meeting was not a failure. Out of it arose the Pan-American Union, an agency housed in Washington that became a clearing house for distributing information to the member nations, and other congresses would meet in the future to discuss common hemispheric matters.

When, after the election of 1892, the Democrats took over, the change in personnel meant no break in the new self-assertive diplomacy. Indeed, in 1895 President Cleveland and his Secretary of State, Richard Olney, in a dispute with Great Britain over the boundary of Venezuela carried the country close to the brink of war. For years England and Venezuela had argued about the boundary between Venezuela and British Guiana, the dispute assuming new importance when gold was discovered in the disputed area. Both Cleveland and Olney, as well as the American public, were disposed to sympathize with Venezuela as the little, underdog country confronting the great power. The President and Congress publicly expressed hopes that Britain would see fit to arbitrate the matter. When the English government took no action, Olney drafted a note to Lord Salisbury of the Foreign Office protesting that Britain was violating the Monroe Doctrine. Any European interference with hemispheric affairs—and a boundary dispute constituted interference —came within the scope of the famous doctrine, said the Secretary. In bellicose language designed to make England sit up and listen, he declared: "Today the United States is practically sovereign on this continent, and its fiat is law upon the subjects to which it confines its interposition."

After months of delay Salisbury replied to Olney. With firm finality and a touch of condescension, he informed the Secretary that the Monroe Doctrine did not apply to boundary disputes or the present situation and was not recognized as international law anyway. Britain was not going to arbitrate. Cleveland was enraged. In December, 1895, he sent a special message to Congress reviewing the controversy. He asked for authority to create a special commission to determine the boundary line, and declared that if Britain resisted the commission's decision the United States should fight.

Enthusiastically Congress voted support for Cleveland's plan, and war talk flamed all over the country. The American reaction astounded and dismayed the English. Belatedly the British government realized that it had stumbled into a genuine diplomatic crisis. The last thing in the world that England wanted or could afford was a war with the United States—especially over an issue involving no vital national interest. In fact, Britain, confronted by the rising menace of German imperialism, needed the friendship of the great Western republic. Suddenly stung into an awareness of the realities, the British, with proper diplomatic deliberation, proceeded to back down. Britain and Venezuela signed a treaty providing for the submission of the dispute to an arbitral agency. The British did insist on excepting from the settlement territory held by either side for fifty years, thus ensuring that they would retain the greater part of the disputed area.

The swaggering, spread-eagle diplomacy of Cleveland and Olney has inspired many conjectures as to its motivation. Perhaps the two men were primarily influenced by the requirements of domestic politics—were trying to create a favorable issue for their party. But it is more likely that they were expressing the attitude toward Europe then held by most Americans. In common with their countrymen, they were determined to make the great nations of Europe recognize that the United States was also and at last a great power. And however clumsy the Cleveland-Olney techniques had been, they had gotten the desired results. The prestige of the United States was enhanced, the Monroe Doctrine was vitalized, and the bonds of friendship between the two great English-speaking nations were strengthened by strain.

Hawaii and Samoa

The first area into which the United States directed its expansionist impulse after the Civil War was the vast Pacific Ocean region.

The islands of Hawaii in the mid-Pacific had been an important stopover station for American ships in the China trade since the early 1800's. The first American settlers to reach Hawaii were New England missionaries, who, like their fellows in Oregon at approximately the same time, advertised the economic possibilities of the islands in the religious press. Soon other Americans arrived to become sugar planters and to found a profitable new industry. Eventually, officers of the growing navy looked longingly on the magnificent natural base of Pearl Harbor on the island of Oahu.

The American residents of Hawaii came to dominate the economic life of the islands and also the political policies of the native ruler. Commercial relations were inexorably pushing Hawaii into the American orbit and making it, as Blaine accurately contended, a part of the American system. Indicative of the intimate bonds between the United States and its Pacific outpost was a reciprocity treaty signed in 1875 permitting Hawaiian sugar to enter the United States duty-free and binding Hawaii to make no territorial or economic concessions to other powers. The reciprocity feature tied the islands

into the American economy, and the political clauses meant that, in effect, the United States was guaranteeing Hawaii's independence. In 1887 a new treaty renewed the existing arrangements and granted the United States exclusive use of Pearl Harbor as a naval station. The course of events was rendering outright political union almost inevitable.

Spurred by the favorable provisions of the treaties, sugar production in Hawaii boomed, and prosperity burgeoned for the American planters. Then the McKinley Tariff of 1890 dealt the planters a bad blow; by removing the duty on foreign raw sugar and giving domestic producers a bounty, it deprived Hawaii of its privileged position in the American sugar market. Annexation seemed the only alternative to economic strangulation. At the same time there ascended to the throne a new ruler, Queen Liliuokalani, who was determined to eliminate American influence in the government.

The American element decided to act at once. They started a revolution (1893) and called on the United States for protection. At a critical moment the American minister, John L. Stevens, an ardent annexationist and friend of Blaine, ordered 160 marines from a warship in Honolulu harbor to go ashore to aid the rebels. The Queen yielded her authority, and a delegation representing the triumphant provisional government set out for Washington to negotiate a treaty of annexation. They found President Harrison highly receptive, but before the resulting treaty could be acted on by the Senate he was succeeded by Cleveland.

However disposed Cleveland was to upholding American rights under the Monroe Doctrine, he had old-fashioned ideas about taking other people's property. Suspicious of what had happened in Hawaii, he withdrew the treaty for examination and sent a special representative to the islands to investigate the situation. When this agent reported that the American element and Stevens had engineered the revolution, Cleveland endeavored to restore the Queen to her throne. But the Americans were in control of the kingdom and refused to budge. Reluctantly the President had to accord recognition to their government as representing the "republic" of Hawaii. Cleveland, actuated by honorable motives but opposing the course of history, had only delayed the inevitable. In 1898, with the Republicans again in power and with the United States, as we shall see, constructing a colonial empire in both oceans, Hawaii was annexed by joint resolution of both houses of Congress.

Three thousand miles to the south of Hawaii, the Samoan Islands dominated the sea lanes of the south Pacific and had long served as a way station for American ships in the Pacific trade. As American commerce with Asia increased after the completion of the first transcontinental railroad in 1869 and the extension of a steamship line from San Francisco to New Zealand, certain business groups regarded Samoa with new interest, and the navy eyed the harbor of Pago Pago on the island of Tutuila. In 1872 a naval officer visited the islands and negotiated a treaty granting the United States the use of Pago Pago. President Grant, always eager to expand national interests, submitted the treaty for ratification, but the Senate rejected it. The President, however, dispatched a special representative to Samoa to encourage American trading and business interests. The familiar chain of events leading to involvement was being set in motion. In 1878 a native prince was brought to Washington, where he signed a treaty, which was approved by the Senate, providing for an American naval station at Pago Pago and binding the United States to employ its "good offices" to adjust any differences between a foreign power and Samoa. This was not a protectorate but it clearly indicated that this country meant to have a voice in anything happening in Samoa.

The opportunity for expression soon came. Great Britain and Germany were also interested in the islands, and they hastened to secure treaty rights from the native princes. For the next ten years the three powers scrambled and intrigued for dominance in Samoa, playing off one ruler against another and coming dangerously close to war. In 1889 warships of the contending nations appeared in one Samoan harbor, and a clash seemed imminent. But a tropical hurricane dispersed the vessels, and the German government, not wishing to antagonize the United States, suggested a conference of the interested powers in Berlin to settle the dispute. Germany and Britain would have preferred a division of the islands, but Secretary Blaine insisted on preserving native Samoan rule. The result was that the conferees agreed on a tripartite protectorate over Samoa, with the native chiefs exercising only nominal authority.

The tripartite arrangement proved thoroughly unsatisfactory, failing altogether to halt the intrigues and rivalries of the signatory members. It was abrogated in 1899 when the United States and Germany divided the islands between them, with Britain being compensated elsewhere in the Pacific. Germany obtained the two largest islands, but the United States retained Tutuila with its incomparable harbor. Everyone was satisfied—with the possible exception of the Samoans.

War with Spain: The Background

The immediate background of the Spanish-American War lay in the Caribbean island of Cuba, which with nearby Puerto Rico comprised nearly all that was left of Spain's once extensive Latin American empire. The Cubans had long resented Spanish rule, and they had engaged in a notable attempt to overthrow it between 1868 and 1878 (the Ten Years' War). During that revolution the American people had been strongly sympathetic to the Cuban cause, but their feelings had not gone beyond expressions of support. The government had maintained a position of strict neutrality, despite the provocation offered by Spain in the *Virginius* affair. In 1873 the Spanish captured a Cuban-owned, arms-running ship, the *Virginius*, and executed fifty-three of her crew. Because the vessel had flown an American flag and some of her seamen were Americans, popular indignation was intense. But Secretary Fish avoided a crisis by inducing the Spanish Government to return the *Virginius* and pay an indemnity to the families of the executed men.

In 1895 another revolution broke out in Cuba, brought on partly by the continuing corruption in Spanish administration and, by an odd twist of fate, partly by American tariff policy. Cuba's principal export was sugar, and the bulk of the crop went to the United States. The Wilson-Gorman Tariff of 1894, with its high duties on raw sugar, shut off the island's chief source of wealth, prostrated its economy, and created conditions of misery that prepared the way for revolt.

From the beginning the struggle in Cuba took on aspects of ferocity that horrified Americans. The Cubans, determined to win this revolution, deliberately devastated the island to force the Spaniards to leave. Just as determined to repress the insurrection, the Spanish resorted to extreme methods of coercion. General Valeriano Weyler—or "Butcher" Weyler, as he soon came to be known in the American press—in an effort to stamp out the Cuban guerrilla forces ordered the entire civilian population in certain areas confined to hastily prepared concentration camps, where, not surprisingly, they died by the thousands, victims of disease and malnutrition.

Many of the same savage techniques

had been employed earlier in the Ten Years' War without shocking American sensibilities. But when they were used in the nineties, a white-hot wave of anger gripped the American public. Why were Americans aroused now by events that had not excited them before? A partial explanation is that the revolution of 1895 was reported more fully and floridly by the American press than the former outbreak—and so reported as to give the public the impression that all the cruelties were being perpetrated by the Spanish.

The Cuban revolt came when Joseph Pulitzer with his New York *World* and William Randolph Hearst with his New York *Journal* were revolutionizing American journalism. This new "yellow press" specialized in lurid and sensational news; when such news did not exist, editors were not above creating it. To Hearst and Pulitzer, engaged in a ruthless circulation war, the struggle in Cuba was a journalist's dream. It had, or could be made to have, violence, murder on a monumental scale, and sex. Both papers sent batteries of reporters and illustrators to Cuba with orders to provide lavish accounts of Spanish atrocities—without being too careful to check their accuracy. "You furnish the pictures," Hearst supposedly told a too scrupulous artist, "and I'll furnish the war." The newsmen obliged with stories of Cubans massacred and tortured, of noncombatants starved in the concentration camps, and of young native women subjected to sexual indignities. A few of the tales were true, many were exaggerated, and some were pure fabrications. But the yellow press splashed them over the front pages as gospel, and most of the newspapers of the country followed their lead.

THE YELLOW KID OF JOURNALISM. [OPPOSITE] Pulitzer's principal competitor was William Randolph Hearst, whose New York *Journal* on occasion outdid the *World* in sensationalism. This hostile cartoon attacks Hearst's methods and accuses him of bringing on the War with Spain and of making an alliance with "Boss" Croker of Tammany Hall, whom he had formerly opposed. (FROM The Bee, 1898)

The mounting storm of indignation against Spain left President Cleveland unmoved. Convinced that both sides in Cuba were guilty of atrocities and that the United States had no interests justifying involvement in the struggle, he issued a proclamation of neutrality and attempted to arrest the numerous filibustering expeditions being organized by a "junto" of Cuban refugees in New York City. When Congress, in a great state of excitement, passed a concurrent resolution favoring recognition of Cuban belligerency, he ignored its action. His only concession to the demands for intervention was to offer America's good offices to mediate the conflict, a proposition which Spain declined.

When McKinley took over the Presidency in 1897, he too was disposed to move cautiously. He renewed the American mediation offer, which was again refused, but, taking a stronger line than his predecessor, protested to Spain against its "uncivilized and inhuman" conduct of operations. The Spanish government, alarmed that McKinley's course might forebode American intervention in Cuba, recalled Weyler, modified the concentration policy, and took steps to grant the island a qualified autonomy. At the end of 1897, with the insurrection losing ground, it seemed that war might be averted.

If there was any chance of a peaceful settlement, it was extinguished by two dramatic incidents in February, 1898.

A Cuban agent in Havana stole a private letter written by Dupuy de Lôme, the Spanish minister in Washington, and thoughtfully turned it over to the American press. First published in Hearst's New York *Journal*, the minister's letter described McKinley as a weak man and "a bidder for the admiration of the crowd." This was no more than many Americans, including some Republicans, were saying about their President—Theodore Roosevelt described McKinley as having "no more backbone than a chocolate éclair"

—but when a foreigner made such a remark it was a national insult. Popular anger was intense, and Dupuy de Lôme resigned before the outraged McKinley could demand his recall.

While the excitement was still at fever pitch, even more sensational news hit the front pages: the battleship *Maine* had been blown up in Havana harbor with a loss of over 260 lives. This vessel had been ordered to Cuban waters in January on a "friendly" visit, but the real reason for its presence was to protect American lives and property against possible attacks by Spanish loyalists. Many Americans jumped to the conclusion that the Spanish had sunk the ship—"an act of dirty treachery," Theodore Roosevelt announced—and the imperialists and the jingoists screamed for war. This opinion seemed confirmed when a naval court of inquiry reported that an external explosion by a submarine mine had caused the disaster. As war hysteria swept the country, Congress unanimously appropriated $50 million for military preparations. "Remember the Maine" became a national chant for revenge. (Later historical opinion discounts the easy American assurance of 1898 that Spanish officials instigated the destruction of the *Maine*. The Spanish government was bending every effort to prevent American intervention and was hardly stupid enough to countenance an act almost certain to invite war.)

After the *Maine* episode there was little chance that the government could keep the people from war. Possibly a strong President might have headed off the rush to war by openly denouncing the clamor for intervention, but McKinley was not a strong executive. He did not wish to resort to force, and he did for a period withstand terrific pressures, some from within his own party. In March, 1898, the United States asked Spain to agree to an armistice, with negotiations for a permanent peace through the President to follow, along with an immediate and

WRECK OF THE MAINE. (NATIONAL ARCHIVES)

complete ending of the concentration system. After a slight delay, Spain essentially accepted the American demands on April 9. Two days later McKinley asked Congress for authority to use military force to end the hostilities in Cuba—in short, for a declaration of war. After reviewing the reasons that impelled him to recommend war ("in the name of humanity, in the name of civilization, in behalf of endangered American interests") he mentioned only casually, at the end of the message, that Spain had capitulated to his requests.

It is doubtful whether any emphasis he might have given Spain's submission would have influenced Congress. That body, reflecting the people's will, was not going to be cheated out of a war by anything Spain might yield at the last minute. By huge majorities Congress passed a joint resolution declaring Cuba free and authorizing the President to employ force to expel the Spanish from the island. Added to the resolution, which was really a declaration of war, was the Teller Amendment, disclaiming any intention on the part of the United States to annex Cuba.

The "Splendid Little War"

The Spanish-American War was, in the words of Roosevelt's friend John Hay, "a splendid little war." Indeed, to all Americans, with the possible exception of the enlisted men who fought it, it was almost an ideal war. It was the last small, short, individualistic war before the huge, protracted, impersonal struggles of the twentieth century. Declared in April, it was over by August. Newspaper readers easily and eagerly followed the campaigns and the heroic exploits of American soldiers and sailors. Only 460 Americans were killed in battle or died of wounds, but some 5,200 perished of disease: malaria, dysentery, typhoid, and other ills.

Blithely and confidently the United States embarked on a war it was not prepared to fight. The regular army, numbering only 28,000 troops and officers scattered around the country at various posts, was a tough little force, skilled at quelling Indian outbreaks, but with no experience in anything resembling large-scale war. Hastily Congress directed the President to increase the army to 62,000 and to call for 125,000 volunteers. It was expected that the National Guard, the state militia, would furnish the bulk of the volunteers, and in addition the President was authorized to accept directly into the national service three volunteer cavalry regiments. By far the most colorful of the latter units was the Rough Riders, nominally commanded by Leonard Wood but actually by Theodore Roosevelt, who was about to burst onto the front pages as a war hero. The services of supply, manned by elderly bureaucratic officers, proved incapable of meeting the modest wants of the forces raised during the war. On hand were enough Krag-Jorgensen repeating rifles, using smokeless powder, for the regulars, but the volunteers were equipped with the old black-powder, single-shot Springfields. American soldiers campaigning in tropical regions were clothed in the traditional heavy blue uniforms and fed horrible canned rations that they derisively called "embalmed beef."

The Spanish army numbered almost 130,000 troops, of whom 80,000 were already in Cuba at the beginning of the war. Despite its imposing size, it was not an efficient army; its commanders seemed to be paralyzed by a conviction of certain defeat. The American navy, fifth largest in the world, was superior to the Spanish in ships, gunnery, and personnel, possessing a marked edge in the number of battleships.

The greatest weakness in the American military system was that no agency in it, either in the army or the navy, was charged with strategic planning. Only the navy prior to the war had worked out an objective, and its objective had nothing to do with freeing Cuba.

The Assistant Secretary of the Navy in the McKinley administration was Theodore Roosevelt, ardent imperialist and proponent of war. In consultations (unknown to his superior) with naval officers, Roosevelt prepared to seize Spain's Philippine Islands in the far Pacific. He strengthened the Asiatic Squadron and secretly instructed its commander, Commodore George Dewey, in event of war to attack the Philippines. Immediately after war was declared, Dewey left the China coast and headed for Manila, where a venerable Spanish fleet was stationed. On May 1 he steamed into Manila Bay, and as his ships prepared to pass down the line of anchored enemy vessels he uttered the first slogan of the war: "You may fire when ready, Gridley." When the firing was finished, the Spanish fleet was completely destroyed, one American sailor was dead—of a heat stroke—and George Dewey, immediately promoted to admiral, became the first hero of the war. The hero was, however, in something of a precarious position. The Spanish held Manila city, and Dewey had no force to attack them. While Dewey waited nervously, the government assembled an expeditionary force to relieve him and take the city. Not until August 13 did the Americans receive the surrender of Manila.

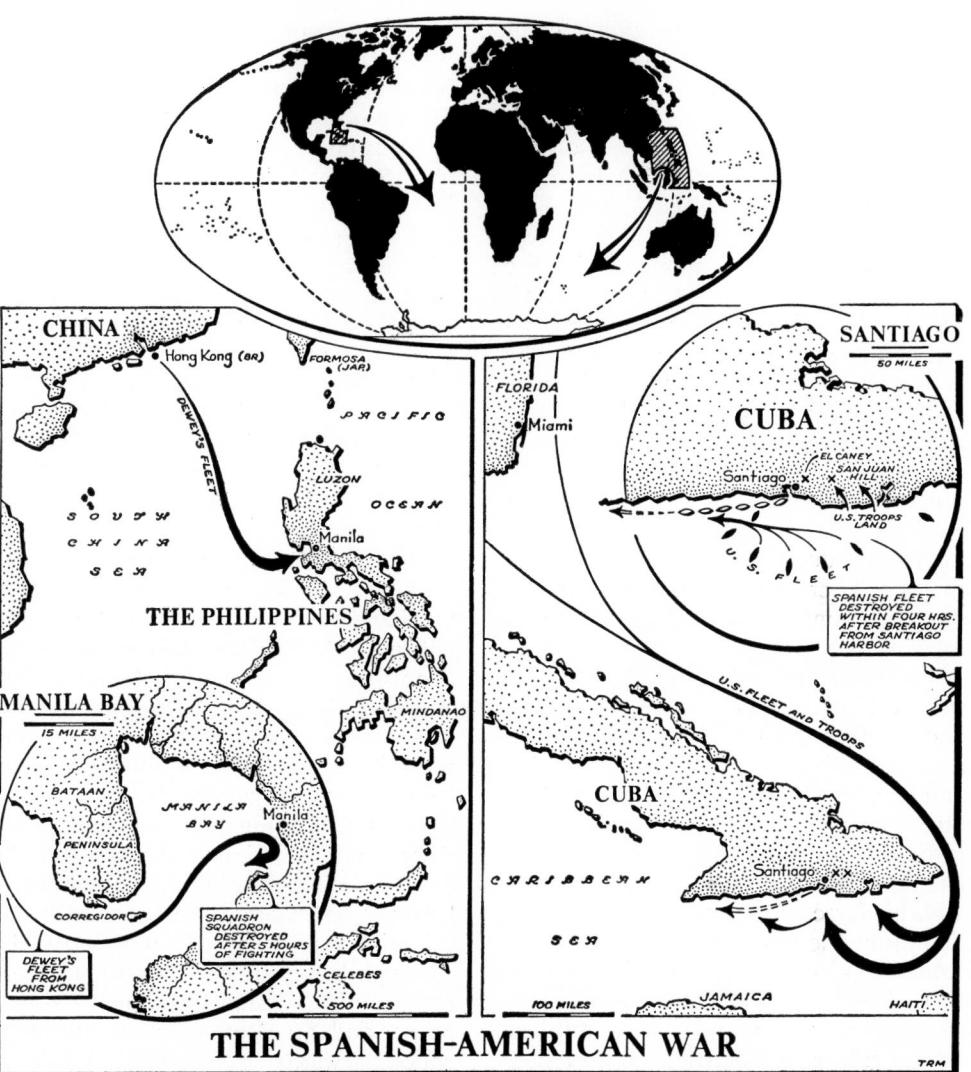

THE SPANISH-AMERICAN WAR

In the rejoicing over Dewey's victory, few Americans paused to note that the character of the war was being subtly altered. What had begun as a war to free Cuba was becoming a war to acquire colonies.

But Cuba was not to be left out of the war picture. Late in April it was known in the United States that a Spanish fleet under Admiral Pascual Cervera had sailed for the west, presumably for a Cuban harbor. Cervera's antique armada, lacking a single battleship was no match for the powerful American Atlantic Squadron, as the Spanish government well knew. It was dispatched as a gesture to Spanish opinion and a sacrifice to national honor. The Atlantic Squadron, commanded by Admiral William T. Sampson, with Commodore W. S. Schley second in command, was expected to intercept and destroy Cervera before he reached his destination. (The squadron was "as strong as Sampson and as Schley as a fox," newspapers happily assured their readers.) But the Spaniard turned out to be the fox. Easily eluding his pursuers, he slipped into Santiago harbor on the southern coast of Cuba, where he was not discovered by the Americans until ten days after his arrival. Immediately the Atlantic fleet moved to bottle him up.

While the navy was monopolizing the first phases of the war, the War Department was coming apart at the seams trying to mobilize and train an army. The volunteer and National Guard units were collected near Chattanooga, Tennessee, while the regulars, plus the Rough Riders, were assembled at Tampa, Florida, under the command of General William R. Shafter. The entire mobilization process was conducted with remarkable inefficiency. There were appalling shortages of arms, ammunition, food, clothing, and medical supplies.

The army's commanding general, Nelson A. Miles, veteran of the Civil War, had planned to train the troops until autumn, then to occupy Puerto Rico and in conjunction with the Cuban rebels attack Havana. But with a Spanish naval force at Santiago, plans were hastily changed. It was decided to send Shafter with his force of 17,000 to take Santiago. So in June the expedition left Tampa, the Rough Riders, for want of transport space, having to leave their horses behind. The embarkation was accomplished amidst scenes of fantastic incompetence, but it was efficiency itself compared to the landing. Five days were required to put the army ashore, and this with the enemy offering no opposition.

Once landed, Shafter moved his army toward Santiago, planning to surround and capture it. On the way he fought and defeated the Spaniards at two battles, El

Caney and San Juan Hill. In both engagements the Rough Riders were in the middle of the fighting and on the front pages of the newspapers, and Colonel Roosevelt was rapidly emerging as a hero of the war. Shafter was now before Santiago, but his army was so decimated by sickness that he feared he might have to abandon his position. When he besought Sampson to unite with him in a joint attack on the city, the admiral answered that mines in the harbor made it too dangerous to take his big ships in.

At this point disaster seemingly confronted the Americans, but unknown to them the Spanish government had decided that Santiago was lost. On July 3 Cervera, acting under orders from home, broke from the harbor to attempt an escape that he knew was hopeless. The waiting American squadron destroyed his entire fleet. Shafter then pressed the Spanish army commander to surrender, and that official, after bargaining Shafter into generous terms, including free transportation back to Spain for his troops, turned over Santiago on July 16. While the Santiago campaign was in its last stages, an American army landed in Puerto Rico and occupied it against virtually no opposition.

Spain was whipped and knew it. Through the medium of the French ambassador in Washington she asked for peace, and on August 12 an armistice ended the war.

The Colonial Empire

In agreeing to a preliminary peace, the United States had laid down terms on which a permanent settlement must be based: Spain was to relinquish Cuba, cede Puerto Rico to the United States,

THE VICTORS OF SAN JUAN HILL. [OPPOSITE] Colonel Theodore Roosevelt, center with glasses, and the Rough Riders stand on San Juan Hill. Roosevelt and his men received more newspaper publicity than any unit in the army, and to some readers it must have seemed that T. R. was winning the war single-handed. When Roosevelt announced that he was going to write a book about his war experiences, Mr. Dooley suggested as a title "Alone in Cuba." (LIBRARY OF CONGRESS)

cede also to the victor an island in the Ladrones, midway between Hawaii and the Philippines (this turned out to be Guam), and permit the Americans to hold Manila pending the final disposition of the Philippines. The last clause reflected the confusion in the McKinley administration as to what to do about the islands where its forces had won a foothold. The demands for Puerto Rico and Guam showed how quickly the war to free Cuba had assumed an imperialist character. Aroused by the excitement of military victory and a heady sense of mastery, the American government and people were disposed to keep what American arms had won.

In October, 1898, commissioners from the United States and Spain met at Paris, France, to determine a permanent peace. With little protest Spain agreed to recognize Cuba's independence, to assume the Cuban debt, and to cede Puerto Rico and Guam to the victor. Then the American commissioners, acting under instruction from McKinley, startled the conference by demanding the cession of all the Philippines. The President later said that he had arrived at his decision as a result of divine guidance. Probably such mundane factors as the swelling sentiment for annexation in the country and the pressure of the imperialist leaders of his party influenced his thinking more. Stubbornly the Spanish resisted the American demand, although they realized they could retain the islands only by resuming the war. They yielded to the inevitable when the United States offered a money payment of $20 million. The Treaty of Paris was signed on December 10, 1898, and sent to the United States for ratification by the Senate.

When the treaty was submitted to the Senate, it encountered immediate and fierce criticism and occasioned in that body and throughout the country one of those "great debates" that frequently precede a departure in American foreign policy. The chief point at issue was the acquisition of the Philippines, denounced by many, including prominent Republicans, as a repudiation of America's high moral position in the war and a shameful occupation of a land that wanted to be free. Favoring ratification were the imperialists, the big navy lobby, the Protestant clergy, who saw in a colonial empire enlarged fields for missionary enterprise, and most Republicans. Business, which had opposed the war, swung over to support the treaty, converted by the notion that possession of the Philippines would enable American interests to dominate the Oriental trade. In the forces opposing the treaty were old-fashioned Americans who objected to their country's annexing other people against their will, traditionalists who feared that a colonial empire would necessitate large armaments and foreign alliances, a majority of the intellectuals, economic interests like the sugar growers who foresaw colonial competition, and most Democrats.

After weeks of bitter wrangling, the treaty was ratified, February 6, 1899, but only because it received an unexpected assist from William Jennings Bryan. The Commoner, who expected to be his party's candidate in the election of 1900, persuaded a number of Democratic Senators to vote for ratification. It has been charged that he was looking for a campaign issue, and in his defense it has been said that he thought the question of the Philippines should be decided by a national referendum: if the Democrats won in 1900 they would free the islands. Whatever his reasoning, it was faulty. The Philippines, once grasped, would not be easily loosed, no matter who carried the election.

Bryan was the Democratic standard-bearer in 1900, running against McKinley again, the principal issue was imperialism, and Bryan went down to a crushing defeat. McKinley's electoral vote was 292 and his popular vote 7,208,000 to Bryan's 155 and 6,358,000. Although the

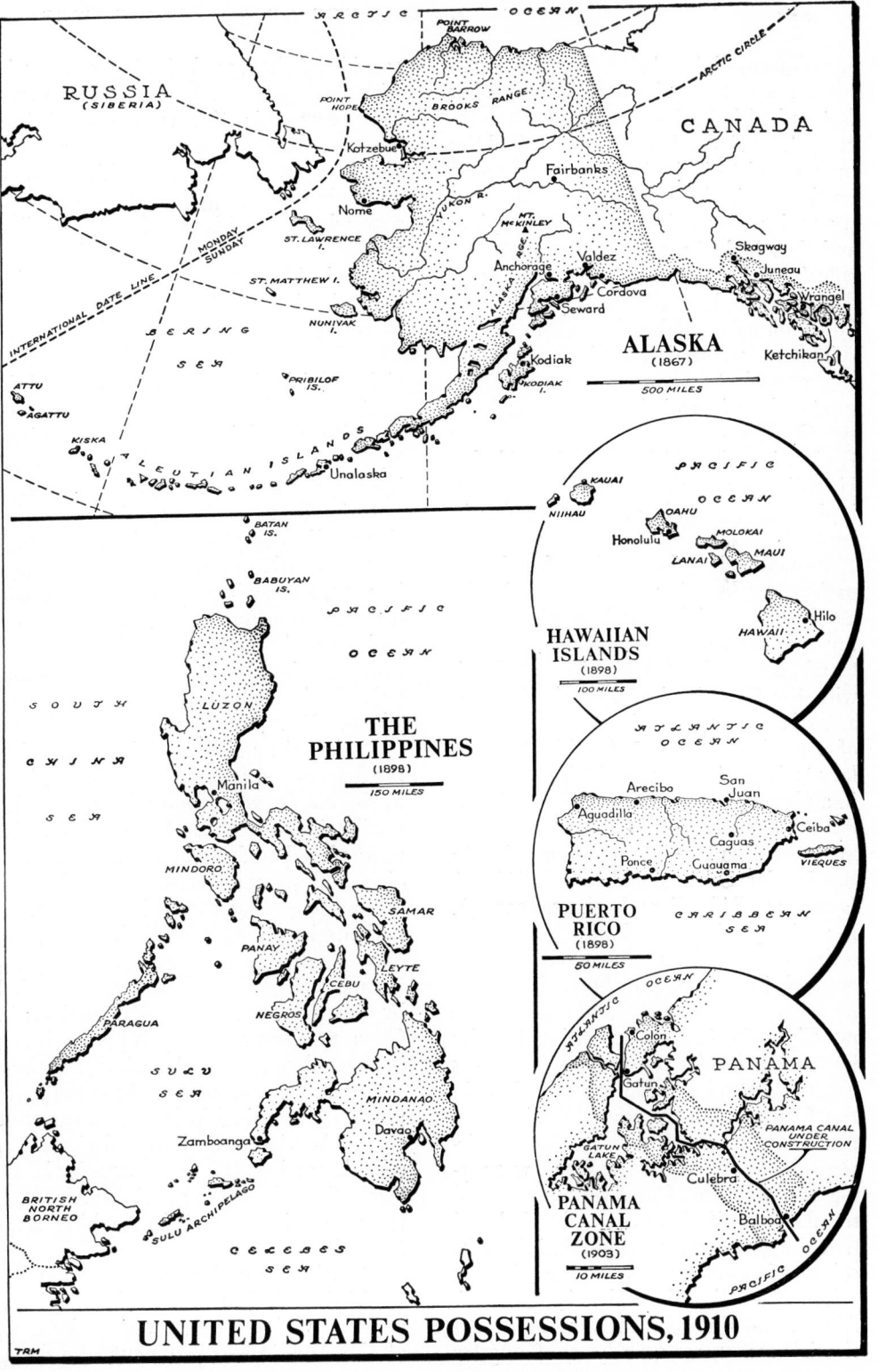

UNITED STATES POSSESSIONS, 1910

Republicans claimed that the results constituted a mandate for imperialism, other factors had helped to determine the outcome. The victors had again exploited the money and tariff issues; they had harped on the continuing prosperity in the country under a Republican administration; and they had displayed to the voters the colorful personality of their vice presidential candidate, the hero of San Juan Hill, Colonel Theodore Roosevelt.

The new colonial empire was extensive enough to warm the heart of the most ardent imperialist. Stretching from the Caribbean to the far reaches of the Pacific, it embraced Puerto Rico, Alaska, Hawaii, a part of Samoa, Guam, the Philippines, and a chain of minor Pacific islands.

Immediately, the nation faced the problem of how it was to govern its dependencies, and here a host of perplexing questions arose. Did Congress have to administer the colonies in accordance with the Constitution? Did the inhabitants of the new possessions have the rights of American citizens? Could Congress levy tariff duties on colonial imports? Or, in a phrase that pleased the public fancy, did the Constitution follow the flag? The Supreme Court pointed to a solution in the Insular Cases (*De Lima* v. *Bidwell*, *Downes* v. *Bidwell*, and others, 1900–4), involving duties on colonial trade. In a series of decisions the Court distinguished, in extremely technical language, between "incorporated" and "unincorporated" territories. In legislating for the latter—the insular possessions—Congress was not bound by all the limitations in the Constitution applicable to incorporated territories, although some restrictions did apply. What the Court was saying was that the Constitution followed the flag only if Congress so decided and that the government could administer its colonies in almost any way it saw fit.

Three of the dependencies, Hawaii, Alaska, and Puerto Rico, were given territorial status as quickly as Congress

considered them ready for it. For Hawaii, with its large American population and close economic ties with the United States, a basis for government was provided by an act of 1900. This measure granted American citizenship to all persons who were citizens of the Hawaiian republic, authorized an elective two-house legislature, and vested executive authority in a governor appointed from Washington. By the terms of an act of 1884 Alaska was governed by appointed civil officials. The discovery of gold in 1896 caused the first substantial influx of Americans, and in 1912 Alaska received territorial status and a legislature, and its inhabitants were given the rights of citizenship. Because Puerto Rico's population readily accepted American rule, military occupation of the island was ended in 1900, and civil government was established by the Foraker Act. The governor and upper house of the legislature were to be appointed from Washington, while only the lower house was to be elected. The act did not declare the Puerto Ricans to be American citizens, this privilege being deferred until 1917. Lesser possessions in the empire were dealt with more arbitrarily. Such places as Guam and Tutuila were placed under control of naval officials, and many of the small islands, containing only a handful of inhabitants, experienced no form of American Government at all.

American military forces, commanded by General Leonard Wood, remained in Cuba until 1902, the occupation being protracted to enable American administrators to prepare the island for the independence promised in the peace treaty of 1898. The vigorous occupiers built roads, schools, and hospitals, reorganized the legal, financial, and administrative systems, and introduced far-reaching sanitary reforms.

At Wood's urging a convention assembled to draft a constitution for independent Cuba. To the disappointment of the American government, the docu-

McKINLEY MEASURES UNCLE SAM FOR A NEW SUIT. Tailor McKinley is
fitting Uncle Sam with a new suit—one to go with his new imperialist proportions. Anti-expansionist Carl Schurz offers some reducing medicine, but Sam scornfully says that he has never taken any of the stuff and does not intend to begin.
(FROM Puck, 1900)

ment contained no provisions concerning
relations with the nation responsible for
Cuba's freedom. The United States was
quite willing to relinquish Cuba, but,
with its expanding interests in the Caribbean, it expected to exercise some kind of
control over the island republic. The nature of this control was spelled out by
Congress in 1901 in the Platt Amendment, a rider to an army appropriation
bill, which Cuba was pressured into incorporating in her constitution. The principal provisions of the Platt Amendment
stated that Cuba should never impair her
independence by treaty with a foreign
power (this was equivalent to giving the
United State a veto over Cuba's diplomatic policy), that the United States had
the right to intervene in Cuba to preserve
its independence and life and property,
and that Cuba must sell or lease to the

United States lands for naval stations.
The amendment left Cuba only nominally independent. With American capital taking over the island's economy—investments jumped from $50 million in
1898 to $220 million by 1914—Cuba was
in fact, if not in name, an American ap-
pendage.

Alone among the possessions in the imperial system, the Philippines offered resistance to American rule. The Filipinos,
rebellious against Spain before 1898, had
hailed Dewey and the expeditionary force
sent to Manila as their deliverers from tyranny, but they soon realized that American altruism for a free Cuba did not include them. When the hard fact sank in
that the Americans had come to stay, the
Filipinos resolved to expel the new invaders. In 1899 they resorted to war (by
the American definition, rebellion) and,

ably led by Emilio Aguinaldo, they fought the army of occupation from island to island until 1901. In the end the Americans repressed the uprising, but only after employing methods unpleasantly reminiscent of Weyler's tenure in Cuba, including the use of concentration camps, and at a cost of $170 million and 4,300 American lives. Civil government began taking over from the military in 1901, and the Filipinos, with great adaptability, began the process of adjusting to American culture. Thus they started on the long road that would lead, in 1946, to the independence they so ardently desired.

The Open Door

The acquisition of the Philippines made the United States an Asian power. American interest in the Far East, already aroused by our growing trade with China, reached a new intensity immediately after 1898. Other nations older in the ways of empire were casting covetous eyes on China, ancient and enfeebled and seemingly open to exploitation by stronger countries. By the turn of the century the great European imperialistic powers—England, France, Germany and Russia—and one Asian power, Japan, were beginning to partition China into "spheres of influence." One nation would force the Chinese government to grant it "concessions" to develop a particular area; another would use pressure to secure a long-term lease to a region. In some cases the outside powers even asserted ownership to territory. The process, if continued, threatened to destroy American trade with China. More ominous still, if one of the powers came to dominate China, American possession of the Philippines might be endangered.

The situation posed a delicate problem for the men directing American foreign policy. Knowing that public opinion would not support any use of force, they had to find a way to protect American

interests in China without risking war. McKinley's Secretary of State, John Hay, attempted an audacious solution. In September, 1899, he addressed identical notes to England, Germany and Russia, and later to France, Japan, and Italy, asking them to approve a formula that became known as the "Open Door." It embodied three principles: (1) each nation with a sphere of influence was to respect the rights and privileges of other nations in its sphere; (2) Chinese officials were to continue to collect tariff duties in all spheres (the existing tariff favored the United States); and (3) each nation with a sphere was not to discriminate against other nations in levying port dues and railroad rates.

Hay could hardly have expected an enthusiastic response to his notes, and he got none. Russia declined to approve the Open Door, and the remaining powers gave evasive replies. Each one stated in effect that it approved Hay's ideas in principle but could make no commitment until the others had acted. Apparently the United States had met a humiliating rebuff, but Hay surmounted the situation by announcing that since all the powers had accepted the principle of the Open Door, his government considered their assent to be "final and definitive." Although the American public applauded Hay's diplomacy, Hay had won little more than a theoretical victory. The United States could not prevent any nation that wanted to violate the Open Door from doing so—unless it was willing to resort to war.

Almost immediately after the diplomatic maneuvering over the Open Door ended, a secret Chinese society known as the Boxers instigated an uprising against foreigners in China. The movement came to a blazing climax when the Boxers and their supporters besieged the entire foreign diplomatic corps in the British embassy in Peking. At this point the powers with interests in China decided to send an international expeditionary force to rescue the diplomats. The situation seemed to offer a perfect excuse to those nations with amitions to dismember China.

The United States contributed 2,500 troops to the rescue force, which in August, 1900, fought its way into Peking and broke the siege. McKinley and Hay had decided on American participation in order to secure a voice in the settlement of the uprising and to prevent the partition of China. Again Hay sent a note to the powers. This time he asked for support of the Open Door not only in the spheres of influence but in "all parts of the Chinese Empire." Moreover, he said that the United States wanted a solution that would maintain China's territorial integrity. He persuaded England and Germany to approve his views, and then with their support he induced the participating powers to accept a money indemnity as satisfaction. The sum allotted to the United States amounted to almost $25 million, which greatly exceeded damages, and later the American government reduced the obligation and even remitted an unpaid balance. China gratefully used part of the remission to educate Chinese students in the United States.

The New Military System

The war with Spain had revealed glaring deficiencies in the military system. The greatest weaknesses had appeared in the army, but there had been an absence of coordination in the entire military organization that might have resulted in disaster had the United States been fighting a first-rate power. The army, now being called upon to police the new colonial possessions, obviously needed a thorough overhauling. To do the job McKinley in 1899 appointed as Secretary of War an extremely able administrator, Elihu Root.

Between 1900 and 1903 Root put into effect, by congressional authorization or by executive order, a series of reforms that gave the United States what amounted to a new military system.

The Root reforms may be conveniently listed in summary form:

1. An enlarged regular army, with a maximum size of 100,000.
2. Federal supervision of the National Guard, provided by the Dick Act of 1903.
3. The creation of a system of officer-training schools, crowned by the Army Staff College (later the Command and General Staff School) at Fort Leavenworth, Kansas, and the Army War College at Washington.
4. The establishment in 1903 of a General Staff headed by a Chief of Staff, who would replace the former commanding general of the army and act as military adviser to the Secretary of War.

While Root was intent on improving the professional quality and the efficiency of all segments of the army, his primary concern was to provide it with a central planning agency modeled on the example of European staffs. The General Staff was charged with many functions (it was to "supervise" and "coordinate" the entire army establishment) but one of its branches, supposedly the most important, was to devote its whole work to planning for possible wars. To ensure interservice strategic cooperation, an Army and Navy Board, representing both services, was created.

Whatever the shortcomings of the Root reforms, they invested the army with a new and needed competence. The United States entered the twentieth century with something resembling a modern military system.

BIBLIOGRAPHY

For the Johnson and Grant periods, see Allan Nevins, *Hamilton Fish* (1936); J. P. Nichols, *Alaska* (1930); B. P. Thomas, *Russo-American Relations, 1815–1867* (1930); Sumner Welles, *Naboth's Vineyard* (2 vols., 1928), on Santo Domingo; C. L. Jones, *Caribbean Interests of the United States* (1916); and Goldwin Smith, *The Treaty of Washington, 1871* (1941).

Special studies include A. F. Tyler, *The Foreign Policy of James G. Blaine* (1927); M. R. Coolidge, *Chinese Immigration* (1909); A. K. Weinberg, *Manifest Destiny* (1935); W. D. Puleston, *Mahan* (1939); Dexter Perkins, *The Monroe Doctrine, 1867–1907* (1937); G. R. Dulebohn, *Principles of Foreign Policy under the Cleveland Administration* (1941); L. M. Gelber, *The Rise of Anglo-American Friendship* (1938); and C. S. Campbell, Jr., *Special Business Interests and the Open Door Policy* (1951).

Good discussions of the background of the war with Spain appear in J. W. Pratt, *Expansionists of 1898* (1936); Walter Millis, *The Martial Spirit* (1931); Orestes Ferrara, *The Last Spanish War* (1937); and F. E. Chadwick, *The Relations of the United States and Spain: Diplomacy* (1909). The influence of the press in exciting popular feeling is described in M. M. Wilkerson, *Public Opinion and the Spanish-American War* (1932), and J. E. Wisan, *The Cuban Crisis as Reflected in the New York Press* (1934). For American pre-war diplomacy, see Tyler Dennett, *John Hay* (1933).

The most exhaustive treatment of the war is F. E. Chadwick, *The Relations of the United States and Spain: The Spanish-American War* (2 vols., 1911). More recent are Millis, *Martial Spirit*, and Frank Freidel, *The Splendid Little War* (1958). For naval operations, R. S. West, Jr., *Admirals of the American Empire* (1948), is good. J. H. Blount, *The American Occupation of the Philippines* (1912), is only adequate. A colorful but subjective source work is Theodore Roosevelt, *The Rough Riders* (1899).

Two general works deal with the colonial empire: W. H. Haas (ed.), *The American Empire* (1940), and J. W. Pratt, *America's Colonial Experiment* (1950). There are numerous studies of specific areas: H. W. Bradley, *The American Frontier in Hawaii* (1942), carrying the story up to 1843; S. K. Stevens, *American Expansion in Hawaii, 1842–1898* (1945); and R. S. Kuykendall and A. G. Day, *Hawaii* (1948); G. H. Ryden, *Foreign Policy of the United States in Relation to Samoa* (1933); G. A. Grunder and W. E. Livezey, *The Philippines and the United States* (1951); L. H. Jenks, *Our Cuban Colony* (1928), and J. F. Guggenheim, *The United States and Cuba* (1934); V. S. Clark and others, *Puerto Rico and Its Problems* (1930); and B. W. and J. W. Diffie, *Puerto Rico* (1931).

For the military reorganization after the war, see P. C. Jessup, *Elihu Root* (2 vols., 1938), and J. D. Hittle, *The Military Staff* (1949).

27

CULTURE IN
THE GILDED AGE

Materialism, corruption, and an indifference to many of the old American values seemed to characterize the late nineteenth century. Mark Twain, who savagely satirized the manners of the era, called it by a name that has stuck, "the Gilded Age." And E. L. Godkin of the influential and intellectual weekly, the *Nation*, who was appalled by the excesses of America's industrial culture, although he approved the acquisitive practices which had produced it, said that the United States had a "Chromo Civilization." Both critics were partially right, yet American society in the Gilded Age was not all that it seemed on the surface. Under the tawdry exterior, forces were at work that ultimately would reinvigorate the enduring values of American life.

Currents in American Thought

In the half century from 1860 to 1910 the rural population almost doubled, but the urban population increased seven times. In 1860 approximately one sixth of the people lived in towns of 8,000 or more population; by 1900 one third lived in such centers. Cities with more than 50,000 inhabitants increased from 16 in 1860 to 109 by 1910. The population of the New York urban area jumped from almost a million in 1860 to over three million by 1900. Chicago numbered 100,000 inhabitants in 1860 and over a million at the end of the century. Rates of increase almost as great were recorded in cities and towns in all sections of the country. And this vast industrial-urban complex that was taking shape was linked in all its parts by rapid railroad transportation and instantaneous telegraphic communication.

The impact of the new economic and social order upon the inherited social thought of an older and rural America was shattering. American thought before the Civil War, much of which was embodied in the philosophy of transcendentalism, was essentially romantic, optimistic, and supernatural. Drawing much of its inspiration from the ideals of the eighteenth century, it was admirably suited to the individualistic society that long existed in America. The basic tenets of this philosophy, which were accepted by many intellectuals and the great mass of the people, may be presented in summary form. God, the supernatural force, ruled the universe and often intervened directly in the affairs of men. Moreover, He had created a divine or fundamental law, of which men were aware and to which they should seek to approximate their human laws. George Bancroft, one of the leading historians of the antebellum period, expressed this belief in divine control when he wrote that God had largely determined the course of American history, and Abraham Lincoln affirmed his agreement with it when he said that God rather than human beings like himself was responsible for emancipation.

Although divine will governed society, men presumably possessed a large measure of freedom of choice and action, and could, within the divine framework, determine their own destinies. This was possible because of the nature of man. He was not just another form of animal life, not just a biological organism—he was something special. He had a higher nature; he could reason and distinguish between right and wrong; he had within him, as Americans liked to say, a spark of the divine. Therefore he could know and practice God's will; he could, at least in God-favored America, achieve a good or even a perfect society. In short, Americans of the prewar era lived in a cheerful and comforting world.

Suddenly this simple and genial philosophy was subjected to the realities of the new and frightening industrial order, for which, obviously, many of its beliefs had no value. Now Americans had to face up to new problems or to old problems cast in new forms. They had to consider whether social change, as they were witnessing it, was a progressive movement guided by supernatural force toward always higher goals or was a haphazard and uncontrolled process tending to no particular end. Confronted by class differences and strifes to which they were unaccustomed, they had to decide whether society was an interdependent organism directed by some central guiding authority or a complexity that would be destroyed by its differences. In the light of the discoveries of science, they had to determine if truth was as constant and evident as it had seemed and if man was as superior a being as had been thought. Above all loomed the problem of whether America was still a land of boundless opportunity where the enterprising individual could make of himself what he wished.

Accompanying the economic revolution and helping to usher in what would be a revolution in thought was the doctrine of evolution, which was propounded by the English scientist Charles Darwin in his *Origin of Species* (1859). Darwin offered the thesis that all living animals and plants had evolved from earlier forms and that species were the result of natural selection: that is, in all areas of life there was constant struggle to survive, and the fittest species, those best adapted to the environment, those that developed helpful variations which were passed on to their offspring, managed to exist.

Here in evolution, which was a part of the thrust of science into social thought, was a doctrine that challenged almost every tenet of the American faith. If Darwin and the scientists were right, man was not endowed with a higher nature, but was only a biological organism, another form of animal life—the highest form, it was true, but still like the other animals that had had their day in past ages. Instead of history's being the result of divine design, it was a random process dominated by the fiercest or luckiest competitors.

In the United States Darwinism became a subject of popular interest and an issue of debate. By 1900 the evolutionists had carried the day, except in the South and parts of the rural Midwest. Many Protestant ministers, especially those in urban centers, had managed a reconciliation between religion and science; a substantial portion of the population, particularly in the cities and larger towns, accepted the basic principles of evolution; and science was enshrined in the university and college curriculums.

It was, perhaps, characteristic of optimistic America to combine the Darwinian method with the older idea of

thought. They also departed from former notions in insisting that change was evolutionary instead of revolutionary and that American development was a phase of a larger European or world scheme and not a unique experiment in a specially favored land.

The sometimes divergent impact that Darwinism had on American scholars and

CHRISTIAN SCIENCE

Of the various faiths that have arisen in the United States, the most distinctive are Mormonism and Christian Science. The latter was founded by a woman, Mary Baker G. Eddy, who gave an authoritative statement of her religious views in her book *Science and Health* (1875). The first Church of Christ, Scientist, was founded in 1879. Mrs. Eddy once put the essence of her belief as follows:

"The Scriptures name God as good, and the Saxon term for God is also good. From this premise comes the logical conclusion that God is naturally and divinely infinite good. How, then, can this conclusion change, or be changed, to mean that good is evil, or the creator of evil? What can there be besides infinity? Nothing! Therefore the Science of good calls evil *nothing*. In divine Science the terms God and good, as Spirit, are synonymous. That God, good, creates evil, or aught that can result in evil,—or that Spirit creates its opposite, named matter,—are conclusions that destroy their premise and prove themselves invalid. Here is where Christian Science sticks to its text, and other systems of religion abandon their own logic. Here also is found the pith of the basal statement, the cardinal point in Christian Science, that matter and evil (including all inharmony, sin, disease, death) are *unreal*."

progress and come up with a hopeful prognostication. Such an analysis was attempted by Lewis H. Morgan, a pioneer anthropologist, in his *Ancient Society* (1878), in which he traced human development from its first simple beginnings to the complex but beneficent industrial order of the nineteenth century. The works of men like Morgan stressed that change was gradual and cumulative in character and that present society was safely linked with the past. Although they foresaw a hopeful future, they rejected the concept of unlimited progress which had marked earlier American

the opposing directions often taken by American Darwinians is illustrated by the writings of two men who were pioneers in sociology: William Graham Sumner and Lester F. Ward.

Sumner, a rough and rugged academic personality, possessed of a tough mind and a sharp tongue, elaborated his theories in lectures at Yale, in magazine articles, and finally in a famous book, *Folkways* (1906). He was primarily interested in why groups or classes behaved as they did. In contradiction to earlier thinkers, who held that man was a free agent actuated by rational powers, Sumner contended that the human mind was molded by situations and circumstances beyond its control and that men's activities consisted of routine behavior determined by mechanistic forces. In short, man had no innate ideas and no power to reform his environment. His freedom was limited to certain narrow areas in which tradition permitted him to operate. But within these areas, Sumner insisted, man must have absolute freedom to struggle, to compete, to gratify his instinct for self-interest. The struggle for survival should be allowed to work itself out, should not be delimited by laws or the state. Sumner's devotion to the principle of the survival of the fittest caused him to be known as the foremost champion of social Darwinism, and his insistence on the freedom to compete, which included opposition to a protective tariff, caused him to be labeled a conservative. Essentially, he was trying to preserve the older America of free enterprise by employing the new techniques of Darwinism.

Standing in direct opposition to Sumner was Lester Ward, just as much a Darwinian as the Yale sage; he expressed his concepts in a number of notable books, *Dynamic Sociology* (1883), *Pure Sociology* (1903), and *Applied Sociology* (1906). Ward argued that various factors or forces took shape in the course of evolution and altered the Darwinian process when applied to complex societies. In simple societies brute desire dominated the struggle for survival, Ward conceded, but in more complex organizations desire became subordinated to and controlled by intelligence. Mind thus became the master of nature, and man became capable of devising instruments to direct and improve his evolutionary future. The chief goal of modern society, Ward said, was the greatest good of all its members, and the best instrument to attain the goal was government. In contrast to Sumner, who believed that state intervention to remodel the environment was futile, Ward thought that a positive, planning government was man's only hope.

There came to be almost unanimous acceptance of the principle that institutions should conform to social needs and achieve social ends, that they should, as the phrase went, be "functional." Even in the churches there was an effort to accommodate functional concepts. Noted ministers and theologians like Washington Gladden, Walter Rauschenbusch, and Shailer Mathews proclaimed that religion had to concern itself with the material conditions in which Christ's children lived, and these men advocated such causes as industrial peace, better working conditions, slum clearance, and temperance.

Out of the ferment created by the controversy over Darwinism arose finally a new set of philosophic concepts, a new philosophy that was peculiarly American and peculiarly suited to America's changing material civilization. The name of the philosophy was pragmatism, and its principal formulators were Charles Peirce and William James in the period before 1900, and, later, John Dewey.

Pragmatism is difficult to define, partly because its advocates, notably Peirce and James, differed as to its meaning, but mainly because it avoided absolutes and dealt with relative standards. According to the pragmatists, who accepted the idea of organic evolution, the validity of human institutions and actions should be determined by their consequences; if the ends of an institution or the techniques of a group did not satisfy social needs, then a change was in order. In blunt terms, the pragmatists applied their one standard: Does it work? They employed the same test to truth. There were no final truths or answers, they contended, but a series of truths for each generation and each society. Truth, like institutions, had to be validated by consequences. Said James: "The ultimate test for us of what a truth means is the conduct it dictates or inspires." And Oliver Wendell

Holmes, who is sometimes linked with the pragmatists, defined truth as that which he could not help believing. Pragmatism was a uniquely American philosophy. It fitted in with the utilitarian spirit which had always characterized the nation, and it harmonized with the American genius for constant, gradual, experimental change.

Upon the business and financial community the impact of Darwinism, social and scientific, was almost as varied as in intellectual circles. Tempering the principle of the survival of the fittest was what came to be known as the gospel of wealth. If rich men held the reins of economic power, they also had grave responsibilities to exercise their power with Christian magnanimity; if God gave the tycoons their money, as John D. Rockefeller believed, it behooved them to use the money for social purposes. So began the belief that millionaires should contribute generously to churches, schools, and private charities, thus demonstrating that capitalism was aware of the moral code of Christianity. Perhaps the most vociferous advocate of the gospel of wealth was Russell H. Conwell, a Baptist minister, who delivered one lecture on the subject, *Acres of Diamonds*, over 6,000 times. "We ought to get rich if we can by honorable and Christian methods," cried Conwell (who got rich by lecturing), "and those are the only methods that sweep us quickly toward the goal of riches."

Conwell was a champion of another concept that was becoming a part of the American myth: the success story, the notion that any poor boy who was industrious and thrifty could succeed in business. Most of the millionaires in the country, claimed Conwell, had begun on the lowest rung of the economic ladder. Another practitioner of the success story was Horatio Alger, a New York minister who wrote over a hundred novels whose sales totaled 20 million copies. These books rejoiced in such titles as *Andy Grant's Pluck, Tom the Bootblack, Sink or Swim*, and other similar designations, but they never varied in theme. In every volume a poor boy from a small town went to New York to seek his fortune, and by hard work, by perseverance, and by getting his hands on some capital became rich.

Free Schools

Mary Antin, a Russian girl who came as an immigrant to the United States, had heard that in America everything was free. Best of all: "Education was free. That subject my father had written about repeatedly, as comprising his chief hope for us children, the essence of American opportunity, the treasure that no thief could touch, not even misfortune or poverty." Education in America after the Civil War was indeed free or in the process of becoming so—free, public, and almost universal.

In 1860 there were only 100 public high schools in the country, but by 1900 the number had reached 6,000; their total enrollment, however, was not more than 200,000. The most spectacular expansion occurred in the elementary or grade school area, where the great majority of pupils were concentrated. Below the elementary level appeared the kindergartens, the first of which was established in St. Louis in 1873; by 1900 there were approximately 3,000 of these schools in existence. By 1900 compulsory school attendance laws were in effect, although not always enforced, in 31 states and territories.

In the expansion of school facilities, the Northeast led, followed by the Middle West, with the South trailing substantially behind. That the last section should lag is not surprising when one considers the effects of the Civil War on its economy and the dislocating impact of Reconstruction on its social system.

Most of the elementary schools in all sections, and many of the high schools, were, by modern standards, small, inadequate, and unattractive. Dominating the curriculum were the traditional "three R's"—reading, writing, and arithmetic—with history and a few other subjects holding a secondary place. Also traditional were the textbooks used, the Webster Spellers, the McGuffey Readers, the Barnes Histories.

Most public school teachers were women: in 1900 they comprised probably 70 per cent of the teaching force. Although then as always teaching attracted a number of dedicated individuals, most teachers took it up as a temporary expedient, young men to get enough cash to go into farming or business, young girls to support themselves until they were married. As late as 1910, more than half of the teachers were under 25 years of age and nearly a fourth under 21; the average term of service for teachers was only four years.

In short, teaching was not yet regarded as a profession. Perhaps the pay had something to with the failure of education to hold its teachers; in 1900 the average annual salary was a mere $325, or below the average wage of unskilled workers. Thousands of teachers had no

more than a high school or elementary education, and knew little more than their pupils. Nevertheless, real progress was achieved in establishing the idea that teaching was a profession and education a science. In 1865 there were only twelve teacher-training institutions, or normal schools, as they were called, in the country. By 1900 every state supported at least one such school, and in some of the leading universities, Chicago, Harvard, Columbia, Stanford, and others, schools of education had been set up. The states created boards or commissions of education to raise standards, and in 1867 the national government manifested its interest in education by establishing the office of Commissioner of Education to collect and disseminate educational information. By the turn of the century one in every five of the elementary teachers was a graduate of a professional school.

In the 1880's a number of innovations in educational methods began to make their influence felt. Various new textbooks were introduced, and the curriculum was expanded to include more science and practical or vocational courses. At the same time German educational doctrines, stressing the necessity of arous-

EDUCATIONAL PROGRESS

1870–1910

	1870	1910
Number of pupils enrolled in public schools of all types	6,871,520	17,813,850
Total expenditures on education	$63,000,000	$214,000,000
Annual per-capita expenditure for education	$1.64	$4.64
Average number of days in school session	132	157
Average per person years of education	4	6
Rate of literacy	80%	94%

CHANGES IN EDUCATION. By 1900 there was a trend, in the larger towns and cities, toward the kind of education represented by the high-school botany class pictured below. Many country schools, however, were still quite similar to those that had existed a century earlier. In these institutions pupils of all ages and grades studied and recited together under the direction of a single teacher. The rural schoolground generally lacked play equipment. Recreations were simple and unsupervised, as shown in Winslow Homer's 1872 painting, "Snap the Whip" (above). As a rule, Homer chose his subjects from the world of nature rather than the world of man. He excelled at watercolors and paintings of the sea and the woods, which were popular with his middle-class contemporaries. (THE METRO-POLITAN MUSEUM OF ART; INDIANA HISTORICAL SOCIETY LIBRARY)

ing the student's desire to learn, stirred the attention of American educators. Among those impressed by the German theories was John Dewey, one of the pragmatic philosophers and a member of the faculty of the school of education of the University of Chicago. In lectures and essays in the 1890's, Dewey proposed that education should be considered as a part of the social process, that its purpose should be to prepare students to live in modern society, and that pupils should learn by doing instead of by the traditional rote or drill method. Although his program, later to be known as progressive education, found wide favor, it would not have its greatest impact until after 1900.

Paralleling the rise of the public school system and constituting a perhaps even more significant educational development was the expansion of facilities at the university and college level, a growth in which both public and private institutions participated. In the field of higher learning the American devotion to education and the American faith that education was a talisman to the good life were particularly and sometimes pathetically manifested. It is little exaggeration to say that placing a college education at the disposal of every boy—and eventually of every girl—became a national ideal.

Colleges and Universities

Powerfully stimulating the expansion of higher learning were the huge new financial resources made available to colleges and universities by the national government and private benefactors. The national government stepped into the financial picture through the medium of the Morrill Land Grant Act of the Civil War period, which donated land to states for the establishment of colleges to teach, among other subjects, agriculture and mechanical arts. After 1865, particularly in the West and the South, states began to exploit the possibilities of the act, in some cases using their grant to found a single state university with an agricultural and mechanical division and in others creating a separate college for the practical arts. In all, 69 "land grant" institutions came into existence, among them Wisconsin, California, Minnesota, Iowa State, and Illinois. As acceptance of a grant placed a financial responsibility on a state to keep its institution going, the Morrill Act can be said to be the ancestor of the modern state university. It frankly recognized the principle that every citizen who wished it was entitled to receive educational aid from the government.

Supplementing the resources of the government were the millions of dollars contributed to education by the business and financial tycoons of the Gilded Age, who generally gave their money to endow existing private institutions or to found new schools bearing their names. The motives of the magnates were various: they were influenced by the gospel of wealth; they thought that education would blunt class differences; they realized that the demands of an industrial society called for specialized knowledge— or they were simply vain. In many cases, men like Rockefeller and Carnegie gave generously to the endowments of such schools as Harvard, Chicago, Northwestern, Syracuse, Yale, Columbia, and many others. Other philanthropists preferred to endow new universities named for them. Among this group were Cornelius Vanderbilt, Johns Hopkins, Ezra Cornell, Paul Tulane, and Leland Stanford.

Fortunately for higher education during this period of expansion, a number of outstanding presidents presided over the principal institutions, furnishing a sound leadership to the entire university community. Chief among these by universal opinion was Charles Eliot of Harvard. Other noted presidents were Frederick A. P. Barnard of Columbia, Daniel Coit Gilman of Johns Hopkins, William

Rainey Harper of Chicago, Andrew D. White of Cornell, and James B. Angell of Michigan.

Eliot, taking over at Harvard in 1869 at the age of 35, pioneered a break with the traditional curriculum. The usual course of studies at American universities emphasized classical and humanistic courses: classical languages, mathematics, ethics, and rhetoric; and each institution prescribed a rigid program of required courses. Under Eliot's leadership, Harvard dropped most of its required courses in favor of an elective system and increased its course offerings to stress the physical and social sciences, the fine arts, and modern languages. Soon other institutions in all sections of the country were following Harvard's lead. Eliot was also influential in bringing about important reforms in professional education. He renovated the Harvard medical and law schools, raising the requirements and lengthening the residence period, and again the Harvard model affected other schools. Improved technical training in other professions accompanied the advances in medicine and law. Both state and private universities hastened to establish schools of architecture, engineering, education, journalism, and business. Although Harvard was one of the first universities to found a graduate school, the recognized center for graduate study, based on the German system with the Ph.D. degree as its highest award, was Johns Hopkins. In 1875 there were only 399 graduate students in the United States, but by 1900 the number had risen to over 5,000. All in all, specialized knowledge and specialized skills were coming into their own in American education.

The expansion of higher education was more than a mere physical phenomenon. As the universities became wealthier, as library and research facilities improved, American scholarship matured. Not all the men who rose to eminence in the scholarly world were associated with in-

BOOKER T. WASHINGTON. (NATIONAL ARCHIVES)

stitutions, but the work of the few who were not was still a part of the educational renaissance sweeping the country. Here we can only list the names of some who ornamented the rolls of American learning: J. Willard Gibbs, in physics; Clarence King and J. W. Powell, in geology (successive heads of the United States Geological Survey); Edward Pickering, in astronomy; O. C. March, in pioneer paleontology; G. Stanley Hall and William James, in psychology; James Ford Rhodes, J. B. McMaster, Henry Adams, and Frederick Jackson Turner, in history; Thorstein Veblen and John R. Commons, in economics; and Peirce, James, and Dewey, in philosophy. Many of these scholars could stand comparison with the best European ones.

Two groups in American society—women and Negroes—did not receive the full benefits of higher education. Before the Civil War, girls had been generally admitted on an equal basis to elementary and secondary schools, but the doors of most colleges were closed to them. A few private colleges for women had been founded, and a very few schools (three, to be exact) admitted girls to study with boys. After the war a number of additional women's colleges came into existence, generally as the result of donations from philanthropists: Vassar, Wellesley, Smith, Bryn Mawr, and Goucher. In addition, some of the largest private universities established on their campuses separate colleges for women. But the greatest educational opportunities for women

by Northern philanthropy: Howard University, in Washington; Fisk University, in Nashville; Straight University, in New Orleans; or Shaw University, in Raleigh. Some Negro leaders were disturbed by the tendency of their people to seek a "classical" education that did not fit them for the economic position they occupied in the South. For the transitional period after emancipation, these leaders believed, an industrial education, stress-

---

BOOKER T. WASHINGTON ON NEGRO EDUCATION

Washington rose from slavery to the leadership of his people. Founding Tuskegee Institute in Alabama, he advocated that the Negro improve his economic status before reaching for political rights. To that end Washington, in a speech in 1895, advocated a vocational type of education, which prompted some Negroes to accuse him of subordinating the race's struggle for equal rights. "Our greatest danger," he said, "is that in the great leap from slavery to freedom we may overlook the fact that the masses of us are to live by the productions of our hands, and fail to keep in mind that we shall prosper in proportion as we learn to dignify and glorify common labour and put brains and skill into the common occupations of life; shall prosper in proportion as we learn to draw the line between the superficial and the substantial, the ornamental gewgaws of life and the useful. No race can prosper till it learns that there is as much dignity in tilling a field as in writing a poem. It is at the bottom of life we must begin, and not at the top. Nor should we permit our grievances to overshadow our opportunities."

---

opened in the Middle West, where the state universities began to admit women along with men. With a few exceptions, the West was the only section that accepted coeducation before 1900.

Of all the social groups in the country, the Negroes reaped the fewest advantages from the educational renaissance. In the South, and also in most parts of the North, they attended segregated elementary and secondary schools that were nearly always poorer than the white schools. Negroes desiring a higher education were almost universally barred from white institutions and had to attend one of the colleges established for their race

ing vocational training and the dignity of labor, was preferable. The result of their thinking was the establishment, with aid from private sources, of the Hampton Normal and Industrial Institute in Virginia and the Tuskegee Institute in Alabama, the latter presided over by Booker T. Washington, the greatest Negro leader of his times.

Not all the education of a people is embodied in its schools. Many Americans, some of whom had attended lower-level schools and some of whom had received little formal training, sought their own learning through other devices than the schools, through processes that today would be called adult education. Thousands flocked to the Chautauqua Institution in western New York in the summer to hear lectures on a variety of subjects. Chautauqua was a concentrated short course for adults and teachers; for its clients it also provided extension courses and a four-year home reading program. Other communities organized similar institutions, and in addition "Chautauqua" companies toured rural America bringing music and lectures to people who received no other exposure to culture. Some individuals slaked their desire for education in the public libraries that appeared in increasing numbers, especially in the cities and larger towns. Andrew Carnegie gave $45 million of his steel fortune for the construction of public libraries, wisely stipulating that communities taking his money had to maintain the libraries. Because of the benefactions of men like Carnegie and because of public support, over 9,000 free libraries had come into being by 1900.

Directions in Literature

The broad trends in literature after 1870 reflected the social changes that were altering the nature of American society. Writers, like other Americans, had to face up to the realities of the economic revolution—or seek in their writings an escape for themselves and their readers.

The number of people who could read was greater than ever before, but this did not mean that a larger audience existed for serious writers. Many Americans in the hurly-burly of the industrial revolution were too busy making money to take time out for books, and many of those who made the most money, the great tycoons, lacked a cultural tradition that placed a high value on things of the mind. Philip D. Armour, the meat-packing king, spoke for many of his class when he said: "I do not love the money. What I do love is the getting of it. . . . What other interest can you suggest to me? I do not read. I do not take any part in politics. What can I do?"

Publishing became a business, and, in line with the trend in industry, a big business. The corporation replaced the individual publisher, and publishing became more impersonal and increasingly commercial. For approximately twenty years after the war most publishing houses, of whom the American Publishing Company of Hartford, Connecticut, was a leading example, sold books only by subscription. But gradually this type of organization was supplanted by the large firm that sold its products to book stores and reached the public through advertising techniques. By 1900 most of the big publishing houses were centered in New York City, the recognized publishing capital of the country and also the largest literary market. The passage by Congress in 1891 of an International Copyright Law prevented American publishers from pirating foreign books without payment (and also prevented foreign pirating of American books); the result was to force publishers to rely more on American books and to pay the authors decently. For the first time native writers had an opportunity to achieve a livelihood through their novels and plays.

Although New York was the focal publishing point, the production of literature —the actual writing—shifted to other areas than the East. A literary renaissance began in the West and the South. Writers in these sections celebrated their areas in the so-called local-color story, and found a national market for their wares.

Writers of the local-color school thought of themselves as realists. Rebelling against the sentimentality of the tear-jerking popular novelists like Mrs. E. D. E. N. Southworth and Mary Jane Holmes (the latter's thirty-nine novels sold more than 2,000,000 copies), they insisted on careful reporting, real people and real plots, and an honest rendition of such things as dialect, dress, food, and manners. Usually, however, they were content with an accurate surface description that did not come to grips with fundamental problems, and on occasion some of them, like Bret Harte in his short stories about the Far West ("The Luck of Roaring Camp" and "The Outcasts of Poker Flat") were capable of descending to sheer sentimentality. A few local colorists hewed rigidly to the realistic line, notably Edward Eggleston in *The Hoosier Schoolmaster* (1871). In the South, George Washington Cable described Louisiana life so grimly that he had to leave his section and settle in the North.

Every region had its local-color writers. In New England, Sarah Orne Jewett and Mary E. Wilkins Freeman portrayed the disappearing social order of their section: its rural scenes and ways, its isolated farms, and its decaying seaport towns. Of the two, Miss Jewett was the finer artist; her *The Country of the Pointed Firs* (1896) was several cuts above the reportorial surface level of the average local-color author. Southern writers exploited the rich and varied cultural scenes of their section: Cable described Creole life in Louisiana; Thomas Nelson Page, the old Virginia aristocracy; and Mary N. Murphree, the Southern mountaineers. Most famous of the Southern writers was Joel Chandler Harris, who recorded Georgia folk tales and Negro life in *Uncle Remus, His Songs and Sayings* (1880). Invariably Southern literature was Confederate in sympathy, and almost always the Southern position was accepted in the North. One critic declared that a foreigner studying American literature would conclude that the South was the seat of intellectual empire in the country and the Negro the chief romantic element in the population.

But the principal source of local-color literature was the West—the Middle West of the Mississippi Valley and the Far West of the Rocky Mountains and the Pacific coast. Writers working the Western vein first attracted the attention of the East with humorous short stories

and poems exploiting the romance of the frontier. Among the pioneer writers of the Far West were the poet, Joaquin Miller, who dedicated himself to celebrating the glories of the West, and the short story writers, Bret Harte and Mark Twain. Twain, who burst into national prominence with a humorous sketch, "The Celebrated Jumping Frog of Calaveras County," also described the passing frontier in a book, *Roughing It* (1872). Local colorists who developed Middle Western themes, besides Eggleston, were Constance Fenimore Woolson, who portrayed the Great Lakes region, and John Hay and James Whitcomb Riley, who specialized in folksy rural poetry.

Mark Twain (born Samuel Clemens) began his career on a newspaper, and he long considered himself to be a journalist. Because his first writings dealt with Western humor and local color, the public long insisted on regarding him as a funny man. But he was probably the greatest American novelist in the era between 1865 and 1900. His first important success, *The Innocents Abroad* (1869), a tale of American tourists in Europe, was a loud and scornful laugh at Old World decay and hypocrisy—and also at American worship of European institutions. In *The Gilded Age* (1873), written in collaboration with Charles Dudley Warner, he satirized the men and manners of industrial society and gave an enduring name to an epoch. His literary fame, however, rests primarily on *The Adventures of Tom Sawyer* (1876) and *The Adventures of Huckleberry Finn* (1885), sensitive and sympathetic accounts of life in rural mid-America which have become classics of our national literature. Twain's career and writings and literary rank have long troubled critics. He criticized savagely the morals of business but hobnobbed with the biggest tycoons. He had a huge national audience, and made more money than any of the earlier writers. He has been called unique, the Lincoln of literature, a mountebank, a gen-

MARK TWAIN. William Dean Howells called Twain "the Lincoln of our Litera-ture." Other critics have said that he was primarily a story-teller who failed to become a great artist. He made more money from his books than any of the earlier writers, but he spent heavily, invested unwisely, and ended up in debt. After paying off his obligations, he entrusted his financial affairs to a friend, H. H. Rogers of the Standard Oil Company. In his later years he always wore a white suit. (LIBRARY OF CONGRESS)

ius that never found himself, a comic and a pessimist, the supreme artist of the West and of nationalism.

Not all the writers of the postwar years were concerned with depicting departing cultures. Some viewed with misgiving the culture of their own times, and de-

resentment of their group at being dethroned. No novelist of stature voiced the aspirations of labor, although Stephen Crane in *Maggie: A Girl of the Streets* (1893) described slum conditions and urban poverty with somber realism. For rural America and its small towns, Hamlin

---

THE AMERICAN THEATER

1877–1900

The urbanization of American life and the increased leisure of city dwellers stimulated a new popular interest in the theater. Before the Civil War many cities possessed resident stock companies which regularly presented plays. After the war railroad transportation destroyed these organizations and brought in their place the traveling road company featuring a "star" actor. The appetite of the public for dramatic productions was so great that between 1880 and 1900 the number of actors increased from 5,000 to 15,000.

Usually the road companies presented Shakespearean plays, and American audiences saw some of the most distinguished actors of the stage in great dramatic roles: Edwin Booth, Lawrence Barrett, Mary Anderson, and Louisa Lane Drew. But theatergoers demanded plays portraying their image of the American scene or of American conditions. Essentially they wanted what the reading public desired in fiction—a somewhat romanticized version of life. Producers and playwrights hastened to gratify the tastes of the market. Perhaps the most representative playwright of that period was Bronson Howard (1842–1908). Among his more successful plays were *The Banker's Daughter* (first entitled *Lillian's Last Love*), *One of Our Girls*, and *The Young Mrs. Winthrop*. His themes were life and love and family complications among upper-income groups. Although he was regarded as the foremost native dramatist of his times, his plays have not survived except as indexes to the culture of the age; they lacked realism and substance and did not conform to standards of serious dramatic literature.

---

plored its materialism and economic inequalities. Gradually there developed a literature of protest, expressed chiefly in the medium of the problem novel. The dissenters attacked their targets from many and varied angles. A few, like Henry Adams in *Democracy* (1880) and John Hay in *The Breadwinners* (1884), spoke for the old aristocracy, the former ruling class; in criticizing the crassness of the new rich, they merely expressed the

Garland and Edgar W. Howe performed grimly a similar descriptive job. Garland, smashing the traditional idyllic picture of pastoral culture, portrayed in *Main-Travelled Roads* (1891) the ugliness, isolation, and drudgery of farm life, and Howe in *The Story of the Country Town* (1883) painted starkly the narrow, provincial nature of the American village.

A few literary critics of the American scene retreated from its vigor and materialism and found refuge in Europe. Preeminent among them was Henry James, who studied and described his country from England. In such novels as *The American* (1876), *An International Episode* (1878), and *Daisy Miller* (1879), he detailed the impact of Europe's ancient culture upon visiting Americans. In his coldly realistic volumes, the Americans are usually frustrated or defeated by Europe, but nearly always they appear more virile than the civilization they cannot understand. During his later years, James confessed he wished he had remained in America.

Writers like Crane and Garland regarded themselves as realists, or, to use Garland's term, "veritists." They were intent on recording all aspects of life, even, or one might say especially, the commonplace. Toward the end of the century, realism of this type began to give way to what was called "naturalism," a literary philosophy whose influence was strongest in France and Russia and which itself was strongly influenced by the teachings of science. Realism was concerned with the typical and the commonplace. In contrast, naturalism often seemed to say that the abnormal was the commonplace. Its practitioners, fascinated with the scientific method, indulged in almost clinical studies of human activities, especially those involving sex. They tended to believe that man was a creature living in a world controlled by great hostile and impersonal forces that would ultimately destroy him.

The greatest realistic novelist of the period, ranking second only to Twain in the hierarchy of letters, was William Dean Howells. His realism was confined to the common and the average; shunning the abnormal, he was the most painstaking literary historian of what was normal in the America of his age. In *The Rise of Silas Lapham* (1884), he portrayed shrewdly and in not completely flattering terms the psychology of the self-made businessman. His later novels, writ-

ten during the social upheaval and labor strife of the nineties, dealt with social problems and social injustices. In the so-called "Hazard trilogy"—*A Hazard of New Fortunes* (1890), *The Quality of Mercy* (1892) and *The World of Chance* (1893)—he explored the impact of the industrial revolution upon social classes. By the turn of the century younger writers, more naturalistic than realistic, more interested in exposing than in describing the currents in national life, were coming to the front. Frank Norris in *The Octopus* (1901) and *The Pit* (1903) depicted the destructive influence of society and nature on the individual and revealed fully his belief that men were puppets at the mercy of a hostile environment; and Theodore Dreiser in *Sister Carrie* (1900) began a vigorous career that would stretch into the coming century.

Newspapers and Magazines

Observers of national life noted that Americans seemed to be little interested in the past but were fascinated by the contemporaneous. This absorption with the present was hardly surprising in a people living in a rapidly changing society, and it reflected itself in an almost passionate attention to literary institutions concerned with day-to-day affairs. The newspapers and some of the magazines constituted the literature read by most Americans. The number of daily newspapers in the country increased from 574 in 1870 to 1,611 by 1900, and in another ten years the total stood at 2,600. During the same period the circulation of daily newspapers rose from 2,800,000 to 24,-200,000. The number of newspapers of all types increased from approximately 7,000 to over 12,000.

Meanwhile, journalism changed in various ways: (1) Newspapers became predominantly news organs, and editorial opinion and the editorial page declined in importance. (2) The nature of news changed. Politics received less attention, and there was an increasing emphasis on what was called the "human-interest" story. (3) Journalism became a recognized and respected profession. Salaries of reporters doubled. Able and educated men were attracted to the profession, and schools of journalism were begun on university campuses. (4) With the passing of personal journalism, newspapers became corporations, impersonal business organizations similar to those emerging in industry, their worth often reckoned in millions of dollars. At the same time, they tended to become standardized. The press services furnished the same news to all their subscribing papers, and syndicates came into existence to provide their customers with identical features, columns, editorials, and pictures. By the turn of the century there were several newspapers chains, harbingers of a development that would become stronger in the future. Thus the newspapers conformed to the trend toward uniformity that characterized American society as a whole. (5) There was a distinct improvement in the physical appearance of newspapers. The traditional pages of poorly and closely printed columns, each with its own headlines, disappeared; in their place came something resembling the modern paper, complete with varied make-up, pictures, cartoons, and imaginative advertising.

For almost twenty years after the Civil War, the principal magazines in the country were monthlies and weeklies that reached only a limited audience of readers. Essentially, they were literary journals run by literary men; they were always genteel and in good (but often dull) taste; they sold for 35¢ a copy (a high price for those times); and the circulation of the largest did not exceed 130,000. The leading monthlies were *Harper's Magazine* and the *Atlantic Monthly*, both of which antedated the war, *Scribner's Monthly*, which was founded in 1870 and became the *Century* in 1881, and *Scribner's Magazine*, established in

1887. All these organs had common characteristics. They were handsomely illustrated with drawings and woodcuts by such artists as Frederic Remington, Howard Pyle, Charles Dana Gibson, and Joseph Pennell; they were attractively printed on fine paper and decked out in artistic covers, all of which added to their expense and cost; and they published some of the best fiction and poetry being produced by American writers, attempting to reach a national audience by securing authors from all sections. But they avoided issues and subjects that were controversial or not respectable, they imposed rigid standards of taste on contributors (even expurgating Mark Twain), and they failed utterly to interest readers below the level of the upper-middle class. Most of the buyers and readers of the magazines were women who demanded, as they did with books, a sugared-up picture of life.

Similar in nature, although more democratic in content, were the weeklies: the *Nation*, the *Independent*, and *Harper's Weekly*, all published in New York. The *Nation*, brilliantly edited by E. L. Godkin, was a journal of political opinion which profoundly influenced the upper and middle classes. Although Godkin criticized corruption wherever he found it, in politics or business, he was fundamentally a conservative with no understanding of the urban and rural masses and no sympathy for their aspirations. The *Independent* also dealt with opinion, but its emphasis was upon religious thought. *Harper's Weekly*, edited by George William Curtis, printed articles and short stories to entertain the average family; it was also a picture magazine, its pages richly laden with drawings and cartoons, many of them by Thomas Nast, perhaps the most gifted political cartoon-artist of the period.

During the decade of the eighties, a new type of magazine appeared—the popular magazine, designed to appeal to the masses and to achieve a mass circulation. One of the important pioneers of the popular journal was Edward W. Bok, who took over the *Ladies' Home Journal* in 1889 and, by employing writers who produced material to appeal to female prices, and lavish advertising—to make *Munsey's Magazine* one of the most widely read organs in the country. In 1893 Samuel S. McClure established *McClure's Magazine*, which specialized in

---

AMERICAN MUSIC

1877–1900

The decade of the 1880's witnessed the first craze of popular music in the United States. Among the reasons for this new phenomenon on the national scene was Edison's phonograph, greatly improved in operation and tone reproduction since its introduction in the 1870's. In 1900 over 150,-000 phonographs and 3,000,000 records were bought by the public. The typical popular songs had a brief but brilliant career, then died only to be succeeded by others. Invariably they were sentimental and moral, like the fiction and the drama of the period. Some of the more popular pieces, their content indicated by their titles, were "The Picture That Is Turned to the Wall," "The Fatal Wedding," "She May Have Seen Better Days," and "After the Ball."

> Many a heart is aching,
> If you could read them all;
> Many the hopes that here vanish'd
> After the ball.

At the same time interest in serious music grew, as evidenced by the establishment of the New England Conservatory (1867), the Cincinnati College of Music (1878), the New York Symphony Orchestra (1878), the New York Metropolitan Opera House (1883), and the Chicago Orchestra (1891). American composers appeared, some of them attaining international recognition. By far the greatest was Edward A. McDowell (1861–1908), whose concertos, sonatas, and other orchestral works were performed in Europe as well as in the United States. Although he received most of his training in Europe, he was intensely American in his emotions and attachments. But he did not completely understand American culture; nor did his countrymen, who admired his reputation, completely understand his aspirations as an artist. Despite the increasing interest in good music, most Americans still regarded it as a "frill." McDowell accepted a professorship of music at Columbia University; but was unhappy in the position, probably because many of his students were not prepared for his kind of instruction and no academic credit was awarded for music courses, and eventually he resigned.

---

readers, built the circulation of the magazine to over 700,000. Following Bok was Frank A. Munsey, the greatest of the popular publishers, who utilized the techniques of mass production and technology—cheap but attractive printing, low articles exposing political and business abuses. Other similar magazines were *Everybody's*, *Cosmopolitan*, and *Collier's*. The older *Saturday Evening Post* adopted many of the new methods and, by catering to the standards of the middle class, it led all other journals in circulation. Men like Munsey and McClure applied the techniques of industry to publishing. They were convinced that people would buy good fiction and solid articles if they were packaged attractively and priced low. They sold their magazines for 10 or 15¢ and saw their products attain circulation totals of between 500,-000 and 1,000,000.

The Arts and Architecture

American attitudes toward the arts in the Gilded Age paralleled those manifested toward literature. Popular tastes, largely determined by the middle class, admired paintings that told a conventional story, pointed a moral, or photographically reproduced familiar people and scenes. The artists whose works were most widely viewed were the illustrators for the popular magazines and the weeklies. It would be a mistake, however, to suppose that national taste was completely static in this period. The newly rich business magnates set out with vigorous determination to patronize art and artists and to acquire, as part of their process of acquiring culture, the finest collections their money would buy. They purchased, regardless of cost, many of the art treasures of Europe, which possessed, their agents taught them, the only art worthy of the name, and installed them in their palace homes. Sometimes they did more—they established public art galleries or museums of fine arts, and eventually nearly all of the private collections found their way into public depositories. At the close of the Civil War not a single American city could boast of a good art gallery, but by 1900 there was a gallery or museum of at least adequate status in every metropolitan center. Thousands of Americans could and did see the best paintings and sculpture of Europe's past.

In the years after the Civil War most American painters received their training in Europe, the majority studying in the French schools at Paris or Barbizon and a smaller number in Germany at Munich and Dusseldorf. The teaching of the Barbizon school, which stressed the use of color and the creation of an impression or a mood, influenced many American artists: it was strikingly apparent in the works of George Inness, our first great landscape painter. One group of American painters, led by James McNeill Whistler and John Singer Sargent, repeating the experience of the writer Henry James, expatriated themselves from the American scene and settled in Europe. Whistler, who is often ranked as the greatest genius in the history of American art, was a versatile and industrious artist who was equally proficient in several media—oil, watercolor, etching—and with several themes—portraits and his so-called "nocturnes," impressionistic sketches of moonlight on water and other scenes. He was one of the first to appreciate the beauty of Japanese color prints and to introduce Oriental concepts into Western art. Equally versatile but not as talented was Sargent, who built his international reputation on his portraits.

Breaking away from European influences was a small group of artists, of whom the ablest were John La Farge, Winslow Homer, and Thomas Eakins. La Farge was an exceptionally talented and versatile craftsman. Although he was too independent to belong to any school, his experiments with light and color anticipated the Impressionists. He worked with both landscapes and portraits, was our first important muralist, and probably is still America's most distinguished stained-glass artist. Homer, who began as a magazine illustrator, was vigorously and almost blatantly American. All of his powerful and rugged paintings dealt with native scenes and people; his best pictures were of the sea and maritime life on the New England coast. Perhaps the most talented of the artists depicting the American scene was Eakins. He abhorred "respectability" and "prettiness" in art and introduced into American painting a hard and sometimes grim spirit hitherto lacking.

American sculpture in the years immediately following the Civil War was dominated by Italian influences and the neoclassical tradition. When American sculptors made statues of American leaders, they produced figures that resembled Roman senators, and indeed the subjects were often clothed in flowing robes or togas. But gradually France supplanted Italy as an influence, and American sculptors, many of whom were trained in Paris, began to work out an art form distinctively American. One of the first to break from the Italian tradition was John Quincy Adams Ward with his statues of Indians and Negroes. Another was Daniel Chester French, who produced a number of realistic statues of great Americans, the most famous being the imposing Lincoln in the Lincoln Memorial at Washington. Incomparably the greatest American sculptor of the period was Augustus Saint-Gaudens, an Irish shoemaker's son who did more than any native artist to free American sculpture from its European bonds. His statues of General Grant and Sherman and of Admiral Farragut and, above all, his Lincoln in Lincoln Park, Chicago, were authentically American and impressively beautiful.

Before the Civil War the dominant influence in American architecture was the Greek classic. Public buildings and dwellings throughout the country copied the lines of ancient Greek edifices. By 1860, however, the so-called Greek revival had spent its force, and another style, also a revival, had appeared. It became the rage of the Gilded Age. This was Gothic or, more accurately, an American version of the Gothic, with generous borrowings from other styles and some original native techniques added. Often called Victorian Gothic, it was applied to public buildings, notably churches and railroad

SELF-PORTRAIT, BY THOMAS EAKINS. A student of human anatomy, of human and animal motion, a craftsman who modeled many of his subjects in clay before painting them, Eakins was the most profound and creative American painter of his time. He sought his subjects in the everyday world: a doctor performing an operation, an oarsman in his scull, a boxing match. His portraits showed precision of observation and deep sympathy with the subject. But his frankness in painting the human body was offensive to the genteel tastes that ruled in artistic circles, causing him to lose a teaching job in 1886, and he was so neglected during his lifetime that at his death only three museums owned paintings he had done. Later there was wide recognition of the truth of the judgment expressed by the poet Walt Whitman, a fellow resident in Philadelphia and himself the subject of a famous Eakins portrait. "I never knew of but one artist, and that's Tom Eakins," said Whitman, "who could resist the temptation to see what they thought ought to be rather than what is." (PERMANENT COLLECTION, NATIONAL ACADEMY OF DESIGN)

stations, but primarily to houses.

One of the first Americans to break with the Gothic tradition was Richard Morris Hunt, who designed dozens of homes for the business tycoons and became known as the architect of fashionable society. Although his houses were as large and elaborate as the Gothic edifices, they sprang from a different influence

CHATEAU ON FIFTH AVENUE. Right after the Civil War most New York millionaires lived in relatively simple brownstone houses. Then Richard Morris Hunt (1827–1895), the favorite architect of the Gilded Age, wrought a revolution. He first made a reputation with the French Renaissance house he designed for William K. Vanderbilt on the corner of Fifth Avenue and Fifty-second Street. Built of gray limestone and topped with a slate roof, the house supposedly cost $3,000,-000. The banquet hall across the rear was two stories high. Hunt's contemporaries considered the Vanderbilt house to be his loveliest creation, and businessmen all over the country hastened to acquire similar homes. But Louis Sullivan, a greater architect, ridiculed the idea of a French chateau set down in the heart of a city. (BETTMANN ARCHIVE)

and reproduced a different mood—the light and lavish spirit of the French Renaissance. French chateaux and townhouses by Hunt dotted the rural resort areas of the East and its cities. Another rebel against the Gothic was Henry Hobson Richardson, the best-known architect of the period, who attempted to adapt the Romanesque form of France and Spain to the American scene. His public buildings, of which his churches are the most famous, and his houses were marked by solid but often graceful arches, heavy, short pillars, and simple carving; in their low-lying strength they resembled nothing so much as forts. Still another dissenting note was sounded by C. F. McKim, of the New York firm of McKim, Mead, and White, who endeavored to revive the classical style by fitting it to American needs.

These men, however large their talents, were essentially imitative and derivative. They copied and adapted European forms, and their designs had little relevance to the facts of American life and little utility for the needs of the American scene, especially for the growing urban centers. Both the virtues and the faults of American architecture were demonstrated at the Chicago World's Fair of 1893. Most of the buildings shown were in the classical style; although they possessed a certain stately beauty, they revealed fully the unimaginative character of American architecture and the strength of the European bonds holding it. But there also emerged from the Fair an authentic genius, the first great original American architect—Louis Sullivan. Sullivan, who designed the Transportation Building for the Fair, denounced the work done there by most of his colleagues as mere copies rather than creations, "a naked exhibition of charlatanry . . . conjoined with expert salesmanship of the materials of decay."

New Uses of Leisure

Many Americans, especially those of the urban middle and professional classes, found that they had more leisure at their command, and they had incomes sufficient to gratify their demands for pleasure. Even the workers had more free time, and they too sought satisfactory forms of recreation. The late nineteenth century witnessed the rise of organized spectator sports in national life, the presentation of athletic events as entertainment for large audiences, and the organization of sports as a business.

Most popular of all the organized sports and well on its way to becoming the national game was baseball. Its origins stretched back to before the Civil War, probably to 1839 when Abner Doubleday, a civil engineering student, laid out a diamond-shaped field at Cooperstown, New York, and attempted to standardize the rules governing the playing of such games as town ball and four old cat, the ancestors of baseball. By the end of the Civil War, interest in the game had grown rapidly. Over 200 teams or clubs existed, some of which toured the country playing rivals; they belonged to a national association of "Baseball Players" that had proclaimed a set of standard rules. These teams were amateurs in the sense that the players received no direct compensation; they were, perhaps, by modern standards semiprofessional organizations. But as the game waxed in popularity, it was obvious that it offered opportunities for profit, and the first professional team, the Cincinnati Red Stockings, appeared in 1869. Other cities soon fielded professional teams, and in 1876 the present National League was organized, chiefly by Albert Spalding. Soon a rival league appeared, the American Association; competition between the two was intense, and in 1883 they played a postseason contest, the first "world's series." The American Association eventually folded, but in 1900 the American League was organized by Ban Johnson.

Baseball had developed as a professional sport, but the second most popular game, football, arose in the colleges and universities. At first football had been played by rival student groups at the same school. Then in 1869 occurred the first intercollegiate game in this country, between Princeton and Rutgers, with twenty-five men on each side. Soon other Eastern schools fielded teams, organized a conference, the American Intercollegiate Football Association, and attempted to standardize the rules. To aid them in the latter endeavor, they called on the services of Walter Camp, former Yale star and the "father of American football." Camp persuaded the rulemakers to reduce the number of players to eleven, to permit the offensive team

to put the ball in play from scrimmage (eliminating "scrum," in which the ball was placed on the ground for the players to scramble for), and to require a team to advance the ball five yards in three plays or lose it (the origin of the present ten-yards-in-four-downs rule). Camp was also instrumental in introducing the position of quarterback and in eliminating the excessive roughness and brutality that at first characterized the game, and he picked the first All-American team.

As football grew in popularity, it spread to other sections, notably to the Middle Western state universities, soon destined to overthrow the Eastern schools as the powers of the game. It also began to exhibit those taints of professionalism that have marked it ever since. Some schools employed as players "ringers," tramp athletes who were not even registered as students. In an effort to eliminate such abuses, Amos A. Stagg, athletic director and coach at the University of Chicago, led in forming the Western Conference, or Big Ten, in 1896. A game that would eventually become one of the great spectator sports, basketball, was invented in 1891 at Springfield, Massachusetts, by Dr. James A. Naismith. It is the only major sport that is completely American in origin.

Boxing did not become a respectable sport until the 1880's. Before that time prize fights were illegal in practically every state, and bouts had to be conducted in isolated places beyond the reach of law officials. The existing rules were few and encouraged brutality. Contestants fought without gloves, a round ended when one man was knocked down, and a fight continued until one of the participants was badly beaten. In the 1870's the Marquis-of-Queensberry rules were introduced in England and later in the United States. By these regulations, fighters were required to wear padded gloves, a round was limited to three minutes, and certain rough practices and types of blows were ruled out. The first American boxer to adopt the new rules was John L. Sullivan, who had become heavyweight champion of the world in 1882. Although Sullivan occasionally returned to bare-knuckle fighting, he invested the sport with a respectability it had never known. It was raised to a higher plane by James J. Corbett, who dethroned Sullivan in 1892; it was significant that Corbett, a fighter, was widely known as "Gentleman Jim." Five years later Corbett dropped the title to Bob Fitzsimmons, who in turn was knocked out by James J. Jeffries in 1899.

WAINWRIGHT BUILDING, ST. LOUIS. [OPPOSITE] Tall buildings were made possible by the invention of the elevator in the 1850's and its improvement in the 1870's. They were made desirable by the growing value of urban real estate which resulted from the growing size of cities. But the weight of the building was still carried by thick stone walls; in the superb Monadnock Building in Chicago, designed by John Wellborn Root, the sixteen stories required walls that were fifteen feet thick at the base. This impeded use of the first-floor windows by stores for display purposes, and wasted valuable space. Invention of structural steel had already created a new possibility—tall buildings in which the exteriors were thin sheathings hung from the hidden steel skeletons. But technical possibilities are not realities: individual men must find the engineering and architectural forms that take advantage of new materials. A great pioneer was Louis Sullivan, designer for the Chicago firm of Adler and Sullivan. In the Wainwright Building, begun in 1890, the first two floors were a sweeping horizontal of large windows. This band was broken by corner piers that soared unbroken from sidewalk to cornice. The vertical pillars were tied together by horizontal panels and the topmost frieze, all in terra cotta and decorated with Sullivan's free-flowing designs. Here was an integrated shell of red granite, brick, and sandstone which was worthy of the light but strong steel framework of the building. (MISSOURI HISTORICAL SOCIETY)

Before 1900 golf and tennis were almost completely participant rather than spectator sports. The first modern golf course in the United States was laid out at Yonkers, New York, in 1888, and the first golf tournament in the country was played at Newport, Rhode Island, six years later. Because the only courses were at exclusive private clubs, golf was until after 1900 a game restricted to the rich. Much the same was true of tennis, first played at eastern resorts frequented by the wealthy. The United States Lawn Tennis Association was organized in 1881 to standardize the rules and encourage the game, and in 1897 American tennis players engaged an English team in the first international match.

In the small towns and villages of rural America recreation continued to follow more traditional patterns. People came together for entertainment at county fairs, political rallies, and court sessions. Always a big event in a rural community was the arrival of a Chautauqua company with its tent and array of lecturers, musicians, and other luminaries. A featured performer on the circuit was William Jennings Bryan, who tried to keep cool by speaking with one hand on a cake of ice; he always finished as the cake melted. Even more colorful than the Chautauqua was the circus with its display of exotic wonders, so amazing to rural people who had never traveled far from their birthplace. To tour a circus across the country was an expensive proposition, and many smaller companies could not stand the cost. By 1900 the circus industry was dominated by two large firms, Barnum and Bailey, and Ringling Brothers.

The nineties saw the birth of the bicycle craze. Bicycling was both a participant sport and, for many people in urban areas, a convenient method of transportation. Use of the bicycle was stimulated by the development in 1884 of a new model vastly superior to the existing awk-

AN EARLY BASEBALL GAME, 1866. (LIBRARY OF CONGRESS)

AN EARLY FOOTBALL GAME, CORNELL V. ROCHESTER, 1889. (LIBRARY OF CONGRESS)

ward machines: the low, "safety" bicycle, equipped with two wheels of equal size and pneumatic tires. By 1900 an estimated ten million Americans were riding bicycles. While it lasted, the mania had some influence on American life. It brought into being a new industry, the manufacturing of the vehicles, which survived the fad. The cyclists, organized in the League of American Wheelmen, spurred local governments to improve highways. And finally, bicycles, ridden by both sexes, helped to bring about an important change in the dress of women— shorter and skimpier skirts.

The bicycle remained important until the early 1900's and then was superseded by a machine developed in the nineties —the automobile.

BIBLIOGRAPHY

H. S. Commager, *The American Mind* (1950), stresses the period after 1890. Perry Miller (ed.), *American Thought: Civil War to World War I* (1954), gives selections from representative thinkers. Merle Curti, *Social Ideas of American Educators* (1935), is broader in scope than the title indicates. On philosophy, see Philip Wiener, *Evolution and the Founders of Pragmatism* (1949).

Biographies of some leading thinkers: S. Chugeman, *Lester F. Ward* (1939); R. B. Perry, *The Thought and Character of William James* (2 vols., 1935); F. O. Mathiessen, *The James Family* (1947); Sidney Hook, *John Dewey* (1939); Max Lerner, *The Mind and Faith of Justice Holmes* (1943); Elizabeth Stevenson, *Henry Adams* (1955); and *The Education of Henry Adams* (1918), a classic autobiography.

Van Wyck Brooks provides a mellow introduction to literary developments in *New*

England: Indian Summer (1940), and *The Confident Years, 1885–1915* (1952). Illuminating the whole literary scene are several special studies: Bernard De Voto, *Mark Twain's America* (1932); Dixon Wecter, *Sam Clemens of Hannibal* (1952); and Everett Carter, *Howells and the Age of Realism* (1954). Hamlin Garland relates movingly his struggle to become a writer in *A Daughter of the Middle Border* (1921). For an analysis of mass tastes in books, J. D. Hart, *The Popular Book* (1950), is invaluable. The career of one of the most popular writers is described in H. R. Mayes, *Alger: A Biography Without a Hero* (1928).

On education and religion, see C. F. Thwing, *A History of Higher Education in America* (1906); E. W. Knight, *Education in the United States* (1951); Thomas Woody, *History of Woman's Education in the United States* (2 vols., 1929); H. M. Bond, *The Education of the Negro in the American Social Order* (1934); E. D. Ross, *Democracy's College* (1942), on the land-grant institutions; Sidney Warren, *American Freethought, 1860–1914* (1943); E. A. White, *Science and Religion in American Thought* (1952); and H. F. May, *The Protestant Churches and Industrial America* (1949).

On the arts: Suzanne La Follette, *Art in America* (1929); Lewis Mumford, *Sticks and Stones* (1924); W. A. Starrett, *Skyscrapers and the Men Who Built Them* (1928); and John Szarkowski, *The Idea of Louis Sullivan* (1957). On newspapers and periodicals: F. L. Mott, *American Journalism* (1950); D. C. Seitz, *Joseph Pulitzer* (1924); J. K. Winkler, *W. R. Hearst* (1928); F. L. Mott, *A History of American Magazines* Vol. III: *1865–1885* (1938) and Vol. IV: *1885–1905* (1957); and A. B. Paine, *Thomas Nast: His Period and His Pictures* (1904).

On manners and mores: Andrew Tully, *The Era of Elegance* (1947); V. and R. O. Case, *We Called It Culture* (1948); and the following biographies which mirror much social history: D. T. Lynch, *"Boss" Tweed* (1927); R. H. Fuller, *Jubilee Jim* (1928); and Paxton Hibben, *Henry Ward Beecher* (1942). On uses of leisure: F. R. Dulles, *America Learns to Play* (1940); J. A. Krout, *Annals of American Sport* (1940); A. G. Spalding, *America's National Game* (1911), on baseball; A. M. Weyland, *American Football* (1926); and Alexander Johnson, *Ten and Out* (1927), on boxing.

28

PROGRESSIVE AMERICA

Progressivism was a great middle-class movement in the opening years of the twentieth century; its aim was to make the American dream of a modern Utopia come true. As the United States advanced technically with ever-increasing rapidity and became more and more involved in global affairs, the progressives tried to adjust the new industrial America, the potential world power, to the fulfillment of their old aspirations. They held that the nation should provide for its citizens, and so far as possible it should export to other countries, a revitalized political and economic democracy.

The New Technology

Middle-class Americans, as they self-consciously greeted the twentieth century, congratulated themselves upon the enormous technical achievements that had advanced the United States to a position of pre-eminence in the world. The steel furnaces of Pittsburgh outproduced those of England and Germany, and functioned with such efficiency and low cost that Carnegie could have sold steel rails at a profit in Birmingham, England. New manufacturing marvels of every sort had been invented and were already in pro-

duction. These were giving Americans the highest standard of living in the world's history; there was every indication that twentieth-century technology would soon bring them an even higher living standard.

In the factories, the new era meant acceleration of the introduction of labor-saving machinery. There was, for example, a bottle-making machine patented in 1903 that virtually eliminated the hand blowing of glass bottles, and another that ended manual production of window glass. The invention of a rotating kiln in 1899 made possible the cheap, standardized production of Portland cement at about the time a demand was gaining momentum for paved highways. A shift toward electric power was already well advanced. The first 5,000-horsepower alternating-current generator had been installed at Niagara Falls in 1895; within a few years steam generators of 100,000 horsepower were commonplace. Electricity was entering the home, but even more important, it was becoming a great new source of efficient industrial motive power. In 1899 it ran only 5 per cent of the machinery; by 1919, 55 per cent; by 1925, 73 per cent. Large-scale electric power also made possible electrolytic

THE DURYEA CAR. J. Frank Duryea sits at the tiller of his automobile after winning the first motor vehicle race in America in 1895. With him is one of the umpires. (AUTOMOBILE MANUFACTURERS ASSOCIATION)

processes in the rapidly developing heavy chemical industry.

A communications revolution, essential to the more efficient conduct of business, was already under way. The Bell system operated 677,000 telephones at the turn of the century; by 1915 the number was nearly 6,000,000, and coast-to-coast lines were in operation. Radio was in its infancy. In 1901 the Italian inventor, Guglielmo Marconi, flying a kite aerial in Newfoundland, caught signals from Cornwall, England. The next year the Marconi Wireless Telegraph Company of America was established, and by 1910 all large ships were equipped with radios.

A new transportation revolution also was beginning. Since the introduction of railroads, men had been intrigued with the idea of installing some kind of engine in carriages or cars that would run on roads. Throughout the nineteenth century, inventors had experimented with engines driven by steam or electric power, but the vehicles thus propelled all demonstrated impossible mechanical drawbacks. In the 1870's designers in France, Germany, and Austria began to develop the internal-combustion engine using the expanding power of burning gas to drive pistons, and the gasoline engine soon supplanted all other types. France seized the lead in the early automotive industry; from French dominance come such terms as "garage," "chassis," and the word "automobile" itself.

Meanwhile, in the United States inventors were busily designing their own models—the Duryea brothers, Charles E. and J. Frank, Elwood Haynes, Ransom Olds, and Henry Ford. In 1893 the Duryeas built and operated the first gasoline-driven motor vehicle in the United States. Three years later Ford produced the first of the famous cars that would bear his name, a two-cylinder, four-horsepower affair. Other "first" followed in rapid succession. In 1898 the first auto-

lumber. In 1900 the several automobile companies turned out over 4,000 cars, but the big development of the industry had to wait until the first decade of the new century.

A number of factors held back production. For one thing, the country's roads were not adequate for automobile transportation. Only 150,000 miles, 7 per cent of the total mileage, were improved with gravel, oil, shell, or other forms of surfacing; by contrast, there were over 2,000,000 miles of dirt roads. The greatest deterring force was the expense involved in

MOTOR VEHICLES, AND HORSES ON FARMS, 1900–1956

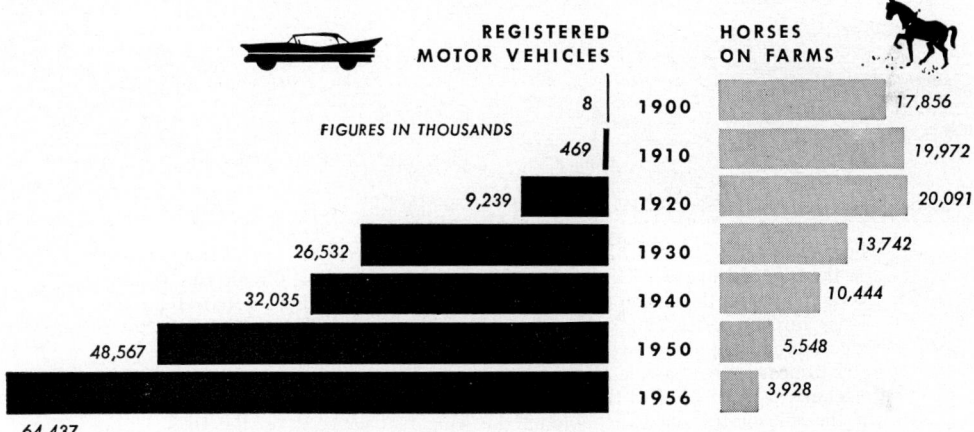

mobile ad in the country appeared in the *Scientific American*; its headline read: "Dispense with a horse." The first automobile salesroom was opened in New York in 1899, and the next year the first automobile show was held at Madison Square Garden. In 1901 Ransom Olds built 1,500 curved-dash Oldsmobiles, thus becoming the first mass-producer of automobiles.

The first automobiles were built in various Eastern cities, but gradually production came to center at Detroit, Michigan. Detroit offered several attractions: it had an established carriage industry that could construct automobile bodies, and it was close to supplies of iron ore and

the manufacturing process, which resulted in a car priced too high for the mass market. The first builders had to order their parts from many sources, including sewing-machine and bicycle companies, and then begin the job of assembling. The day of the automobile—and the airplane—was at hand.

There had been only four automobiles on the American highways in 1895; by 1917 there were nearly five million, and the automobile was beginning to remake American life. Automobiles then had become commonplace among upper-middle-class families, just as telephones were almost essential in middle-class homes.

In 1903 the Wright Brothers made

THE WRIGHT BROTHERS MAKING THEIR FIRST FLIGHT. On December 17, 1903, on the side of Kill Devil Hill at Kitty Hawk, North Carolina, Orville and Wilbur Wright became the first men to fly in a motor-driven machine heavier than air. Their airplane had a wing span of forty feet; its two propellers were driven by an engine producing about twelve horsepower. "After running the motor a few minutes to heat it up," Orville Wright later wrote, "I released the wire that held the machine to the track, and the machine started forward into the wind. Wilbur ran at the side of the machine, holding the wing to balance it on the track. . . . Wilbur was able to stay with it till it lifted from the track after a forty-foot run. One of the Life Saving men snapped the camera for us, taking a picture just as the machine had reached the end of the track and had risen to a height of about two feet." It traveled a little over 120 feet. Later Wilbur Wright stayed aloft 59 seconds and flew 852 feet. Only three papers bothered to print the news the next morning. (OFFICIAL U.S. AIR FORCE PHOTO)

their first flight at Kitty Hawk, North Carolina. It lasted only twelve seconds and was for a distance less than the wing span of the largest airplanes of fifty years later.

In the automobile industry the new principles of scientific management of production found their most spectacular application. Scientific management began with the work of an engineer, Frederick Winslow Taylor, who helped revolutionize the machine-tool industry with carbon steel high-speed cutting edges. As soon as Taylor learned how to manufacture tools which could cut efficiently while running white hot, he began to insist that machinists operate their lathes at correspondingly fast speeds. What in effect Taylor was doing was to apply the same sort of scientific techniques to management as to machinery. At first he looked upon workmen much as he did at machines, integrating them into a more efficient industrial system. Fewer men could perform simpler tasks at infinitely greater speed; if not, Taylor would discard them as unhesitatingly as he had the poorer cutting steel.

The whole new industrial system sometimes referred to as Taylorism, based as it was on specialization of men and machines, meant less need for skills among workmen and more monotonous tasks for them. At first organized labor rebelled, and won at least a minor victory when it persuaded Congress in 1915 to forbid the introduction of efficiency systems into government arsenals or navy yards.

Taylor and his followers regarded themselves as scientific seekers after higher production, and thus after a higher living standard. At first Taylor had taken a rather ruthless view. Only one pig-iron handler in eight could make good under his system, but Taylor had felt only the fittest should survive. "All employees should bear in mind," he had written, "that each shop exists, first, last, and all the time for the purpose of paying dividends to its owners. They should have patience and never lose sight of this fact." Later, Taylor talked in more persuasive terms of the greatest good for the entire populace, including even the workers. Indeed, if Taylorism were used to eliminate the intolerable inefficiencies in many industries, it could mean not only lower prices for consumers but also higher wages for workers. By the 1920's some unions recognized this and were cooperative. As staunch a progressive as Louis D. Brandeis, in arguing against a rise in freight rates, asserted that through efficiency systems the railroads could save a million dollars a day.

American industrialists, usually ready to try new techniques, increasingly undertook Taylor "scientific management" studies of workers' motions. They also brought scientists and engineers into their plants to engage in research for new tools and products. A few years earlier any industrialist who established a laboratory would have been looked upon as a crackpot. Now laboratories became accepted, partly due to the urging of engineers, partly because of the phenomenal success of some of the pioneering ones. There was, as every schoolboy could proudly cite, the industrial laboratory of Thomas A. Edison at Menlo Park, New Jersey, out of which came the incandescent lamp, the phonograph, the motion picture, and scores of other devices. By 1913 Bell Telephone, Du Pont, General Electric, Eastman Kodak, and about fifty other companies had established laboratories with budgets totaling hundreds of thousands of dollars per year.

Out of these new methods and machines came mass production. It required the technology, large supply of raw materials, excellent transportation, and huge markets that the United States could supply in the twentieth century. Specialized precision manufacturing made possible interchangeability of parts even in assembling a machine as complicated as an automobile. Ford began with stationary assembly, earlier used in manufacturing guns, clocks and the like, then gradually changed by 1914 to subdivision of the work and the use of the assembly line. This revolutionary technique cut the time for assembling a Ford chassis from twelve and a half hours to an hour and a half. Mass production had come to the automobile industry. While Ford raised the wages and lowered the hours of his workers, he cut the base price of his Model T from $950 to $290. Other industrialists, following his example, soon took over the assembly line and mass production for their plants also.

By 1914 American manufacturers were producing 76 per cent more goods than in 1899. They were doing so with only 36 per cent more workers, and 13 per cent more establishments. The greater output of goods reflected the rising living standards and the growth of population at home and increased markets abroad. The slower increase in workers demonstrated the greater efficiency of the new technical age; the very slow increase in establish-

THE FORD ASSEMBLY LINE. In August, 1913, at the main Ford plant in the Detroit suburb of Highland Park, it took 12½ man-hours of labor to assemble every Model T chassis. Then the world's first moving assembly line for automobiles was installed; instead of the workers moving to the stationary work, the moving work came to the workers. Within six months, each chassis was being assembled in only 1 hour 33 minutes. This picture, taken in 1914, shows a portion of the final assembly line where the radiator and the wheels were placed on the Model T chassis. At this time the company employed about 12,000 men making cars, and another 1,000 men in making better tools to use in making cars—a fact that shows how the technical revolution in modern industry has been institutionalized and made continuous. (FORD MOTOR COMPANY)

ments pointed to the rapid growth of industrial concentration.

Social and Cultural Advances

In other ways, too, the United States took giant strides into the twentieth century. Medical advances helped bring about marked improvement in public health. The Caribbean adventures of the United States led to great discoveries in tropical medicine. In 1900 Dr. Walter Reed and his associates proved conclusively the hypothesis of a Cuban doctor that a striped variety of mosquito transmitted yellow fever. During the digging of the Panama Canal (1904–14),

Major William C. Gorgas applied the new knowledge so thoroughly that not one case of yellow fever originated there, and malaria was virtually eradicated. In Puerto Rico, Major Bailey K. Ashford discovered that the cause of the widespread anemia was hookworm, and developed an inexpensive cure.

All this knowledge was valuable in the southern United States. In 1909 Rockefeller gave a million dollars for the eradication of hookworm in the South, where almost 60 per cent of the school children had some infestation. With chemicals and vaccines, some of which were important European developments, the nation made encouraging progress in combating venereal diseases, typhus, typhoid, and diphtheria. Sanitariums and a national association successfully combated tuberculosis. Campaigns against mosquitoes and flies, improved sanitation, milk inspection, and, beginning in 1908, the chlorination of water supplies reflected the new vigor of the state and municipal boards of health. To cap the entire program, the old marine hospital service expanded in 1902, and in 1912 became the United States Public Health Service. The death rate dropped from 17 per thousand in 1900 to 13.2 in 1920; life expectancy increased from 49 years in 1901 to 56 in 1920.

These medical advances and comparable scientific gains had come about through observations and experiments, the testing of hypotheses against practical results. Expressed philosophically, this mode of thought was what William James was expounding at Harvard as pragmatism.

The number of public high schools nearly doubled between 1900 and 1914; the number of students increased two and a half times. In higher education, enrollment more than doubled (to 216,493), while professional and graduate schools were greatly strengthened. In many fields, American universities at last rivaled those of Europe. Nevertheless, much remained to be accomplished in education. In 1900 the average child in elementary school attended a one-room school about half the time during a 143-day year, to be taught by rote by an untrained young woman who received $38 per month. By 1914, he might attend 86 days out of 158, and be taught rather better by a woman receiving $66. American children went to school an average of only 6.16 years.

Americans were far from well educated, but at least were largely literate. In increasing numbers they purchased the new popular newspapers, sending their circulation soaring, making them also big business. Several newspaper chains developed; the most powerful, that of Hearst, by 1914 already numbered nine newspapers and two magazines. Most of the papers used their new wealth for greatly improved reporting, sprightly features and cartoons, and increased pictures. As papers drew more of their news from the Associated Press and the new United Press, founded in 1907, they tended to become more standardized. Before 1898 few American novels had sold 100,000 copies; by 1901 a number were doing so. Edwin Wescott's homespun *David Harum* sold 520,000 copies, and two historical novels of the American Winston Churchill, *Richard Carvel* and *The Crisis*, 420,000 and 320,000 respectively. By 1904 the craze for historical fiction gave way to a vogue for the hairy-chested stories of Jack London and Rex Beach, the sentimentalism of Kate Douglas Wiggin and Alice Hegan Rice, and the shrewd limning of American life, whether middle-class or genteel, of Booth Tarkington and Edith Wharton. Popular fiction was for the most part American in theme, and some of it became progressive in overtone. London lost much of his audience when he turned from adventure to socialism, but Churchill kept his when he attacked the railroads in *Mr. Crewe's Career* (1908). Tarkington's first bestseller, *The Gentlemen from Indiana* (1899) had portrayed an idealistic small-town editor, almost the progressive prototype.

The literary pioneers of the period, the so-called naturalists, drew for inspiration upon the French writer Emile Zola and European literary movements, but presented American realities harshly, in the spirit of rural and urban revolt. Hamlin Garland ripped the agrarian dream with his sketches of the bleakness of farm life; Stephen Crane indicted the slum environment in *Maggie: A Girl of the Streets* (1892). Theodore Dreiser's blunt, powerful *Sister Carrie* (1900) dealt so frankly with sex that it was suppressed by its publisher; it was not until 1911 when the public attitude had changed that his next

THE ARMORY SHOW, NEW YORK CITY, 1913. "American art," wrote one of the promoters of the show, "needs the shock that the work of some of these men will give." Many of the 1,600 pictures and sculptures, including works by a number of well-known nineteenth-century artists, gave no shock. But the French postimpressionists jolted the classicists. An outraged Academician, Kenyon Cox, asserted that Cézanne was "absolutely without talent and absolutely cut off from tradition" and Van Gogh "too unskilled to give quality to an evenly laid coat of pigment." As for Matisse: "It is not madness that stares at you from his canvases, but leering effrontery." Cubism was worse. Cox complained that in the lines of the nonrepresentational painters (all lumped together by him as cubists) there was "a total destruction of the art of painting." The public was less outraged by such pictures as Marcel Duchamp's arrangement of lines intended to convey movement and entitled "Nude Descending a Staircase." The wisecrack spread that it should have been called, "Explosion in a Shingle-Factory." Theodore Roosevelt, who saw better cubism in his Navaho rug than at the show, nevertheless expressed his pleasure over an exhibit so far from ordinary and containing so much of striking merit. The Metropolitan Museum purchased a Cézanne that had been on exhibit —and became the first public museum to acquire one. Despite the continued warnings of the American Academy of Arts and Letters, much of the work that seemed so intolerable to Cox and other conservative critics was on its way toward familiarity and respectability. (MUSEUM OF MODERN ART)

novel appeared. Then in *The Financier* (1912) and *The Titan* (1914) he portrayed an acquisitive traction baron with such frank vigor that his publishers again became frightened.

The new poets either extolled the common man or wrote about him with realism. Carl Sandburg in free verse applied the themes of Whitman to Chicago; Vachel Lindsay wrote chants like *The Congo*, full of mysticism and rhythm. In Chicago, Harriet Monroe founded *Poetry* magazine in 1912. In New England, Edward Arlington Robinson seemed to represent a fading afterglow of Puritanism and transcendentalism; his verses in the *Outlook* received the praises of President Roosevelt. Robert Frost, writing in a quiet, almost vernacular way about the rural folk and nature of New England, failed at first to find an audience. In 1915 he returned from England, where he had published two books, to take his place as an accepted poet. Closer to European movements than American, Ezra Pound, an expatriate from Idaho, proclaimed the techniques of the Imagists. Among them were Amy Lowell of Boston and later T. S. Eliot of St. Louis, who in 1914 moved permanently to London. The Imagists discarded rhyme from their work as an obstacle in the way of creating a pure image of everyday life.

A similar ferment stirred other branches

FRANK LLOYD WRIGHT'S TALIESIN EAST, 1911. Wright, born in Wisconsin in 1869, began designing houses in 1888. Until 1893, he worked in the office of Louis Sullivan; Sullivan specialized in commercial structures, while Wright worked on domestic architecture. In 1900, Wright built the first of the "prairie houses," thus achieving, according to H. R. Hitchcock, an expert on modern architecture, "something of as much consequence in the history of dwelling as the architects of the fifteenth century who turned the defensive castle into the residential mansion." For his own home and studio, Wright built "Taliesin" (in Welsh, "shining brow") around a Wisconsin hillcrest. Wright has written of it: "The buildings became a brow for the hill itself. . . . Taliesin was to be an abstract combination of stone and wood as they naturally met in the aspect of the hills around about. And the lines of the hills were the lines of the roofs, the slopes of the hills their slopes, the plastered surfaces of the light wood-walls, set back into shade beneath broad eaves, were like the flat stretches of sand in the river below and the same in color, for that is where the material that covered them came from."

In designing public buildings and factories as well as homes, Wright tried to make his architecture fit the surroundings, both physically and in keeping with the historic spirit. At the same time he used modern materials and engineering techniques. Thus the Imperial Hotel in Tokyo, designed in 1915–1922, harmonized with Japanese traditions yet was such a triumph of engineering that it withstood the devastating 1923 earthquake. "After the industrial revolution . . . had driven architecture to take refuge in applied decoration," wrote Bruno Zevi, Wright "effected a completed artistic synthesis."

ON THE EDISON STUDIO SET, 1914. "It is difficult to realise the proportions which these American studio-stages have attained, or the work they can carry out. . . . The present Edison studio, which cost something like $100,000 . . . to build, is a huge glass building measuring 100 feet in length, by 60 feet in width, and has a height of 45 feet. The stage has a proscenium opening of 30 feet and an area of 2,400 feet. In addition there is a huge water-tank with a capacity of 130,000 gallons, which is used for aquatic spectacles. . . . As the average output is three films per week—the Edison establishment produces four or five subjects in that time—the scene painters are kept busily engaged from morning to night. . . . The Edison establishment is but one of many. In Brooklyn the Vitagraph Company has a huge building, the Lubin films are produced in spacious studios in Philadelphia, while Chicago boasts the famous Essanay and Selig plants."—Frederick A. Talbot, *Moving Pictures* (Philadelphia: J. B. Lippincott, 1912). (MUSEUM OF MODERN ART)

of the arts. A group of eight young American painters rebelling in 1908 against conventional academicians—the group included John Sloan, George Luks, and George W. Bellows—painted the urban life as Crane and Dreiser wrote about it. Conservatives dismissed these realists as the "Ash-Can School," but were even more shocked by the Armory Show of 1913 which exhibited the American moderns and brought French postimpressionism to America. Modernistic architecture began with the low-lying "prairie houses" of Frank Lloyd Wright, whose designs until the late 1920's influenced Europe more than the United States. While Americans did not accept Wright, they did revert to graceful colonial styles for their homes.

The expanding theatrical business was dominated by a syndicate which nationally booked romantic plays and popular vaudeville. It was the heyday of the matinee idol. Experimental realism began, but only in the realm of little-theater groups like the Provincetown Players and in the "47 Workshop" of Professor George P. Baker of Harvard. These could hardly appeal to wide audiences. The real threat to the great theatrical producers like David Belasco and the mediocre playwrights who served them came from the motion picture. At first the idea of movies competing with the stage was ludicrous. The first film telling a continuous story was a melodrama, *The Great Train Robbery*, produced in 1903. Stores by 1905 were being converted into "nickelodeons," which still seemed no threat to the stage, but by 1915 the lengthy, impressive feature film had arrived with *The Birth of a Nation*. It was as significant in marking the coming of age of a new art form as it was deplorable in its glorification of the Ku Klux Klan. A motion-picture monopoly movement had begun in 1909 and had been smashed by the government in 1914, but motion pictures had become a multimillion dollar industry and were moving into large and impressive theaters.

Thus in many ways the first years of the twentieth century swept Americans far beyond the old nineteenth-century patterns of life.

High Noon of Monopoly

Progressive Americans were well aware of the assets and liabilities of twentieth-century industrialism. Monopolies could lead to higher prices and higher profits, which were often the basic reasons for the creation of combinations. (Their promoters argued the reverse, that they led to greater efficiency, lower prices, and a higher living standard.) Furthermore, the monopolists could use their great economic strength to wield proportionately great political power. This also the progressives feared.

Despite all the agitation against "trusts," American industry moved toward greater consolidation and monopoly. From 1887 to 1897 there had been only 86 industrial combinations, and the capitalization of all of these combined had been less than a billion and a half dollars. By 1904 John Moody tabulated 318 so-called trusts with a capitalization of over seven billion dollars. These combinations included basic industries like copper, oil, and steel, and industries directly affecting the consumer like sugar and tobacco. Six financial groups controlled 95 per cent of the nation's railway mileage. In the highly competitive steel industry, twenty-one significant mergers between 1898 and 1901 prepared the way for a large-scale struggle between Carnegie and Morgan. When Carnegie announced plans for plants that might be ruinous to Morgan and his associates, they chose to buy him out at his own inflated figure of $447,-000,000, and they then established the nation's first billion-dollar corporation, United States Steel. Through a "base-point" system it was able to set standard prices for steel everywhere in the United States—prices from which none of the smaller steel companies dared to deviate.

Whatever pride Americans might have felt over the emergence of these industrial giants was mingled with serious misgivings. It was all too apparent that regardless of the efficiences these combinations might effect, often they did not lead to important savings for the consumers. The United States Industrial Commission reported in 1902, "In most cases the combination has exerted an appreciable power over prices, and in practically all cases it has increased the margin between raw materials and finished products. Since there is reason to believe that the cost of production over a period of years has lessened, the conclusion is inevitable that the combinations have been able to increase their profits." Whether or not monopolies were to blame, prices were rising so rapidly between 1897 and 1913 that altogether the cost of living went up about 35 per cent.

The Need for Reform

Populists, socialists, and the relative few who had followed reform theoreticians like the single-taxer Henry George and the utopian Bellamy no longer were alone in proclaiming that the American economic system was in need of reform. Even the thoroughly conservative Judge Peter S. Grosscup, who had issued the injunction to help break the Pullman strike, proclaimed in 1905 that the modern corporation was destroying the opportunity for the individual to participate in the proprietorship of the country. This was the recurring complaint of the middle

fortable or even rich, four fifths lived precariously. A careful estimate in 1904 indicated that about one eighth of the people, or a total of ten million, lived in poverty.

What this could mean was that at the top Carnegie had earned an estimated $23 million from his steel company alone in the one year 1900. It had paid him an average of $10 million a year during the previous five years. On none of this did

---

MIDDLE-CLASS LIVING STANDARDS

When Professor Woodrow Wilson was trying to persuade Frederick Jackson Turner of the University of Wisconsin to come to Princeton in 1896, Mrs. Wilson set up a sample budget for a professor on a $3,500-a-year salary:

"MONTHLY STATEMENT

"Food and lights 75.00
servants 29.00
rent 42.00
coal 12.00
water 4.00
                                     $162.00

"These items with the exception of the *first* are exactly what we pay ourselves. Our 'food and lights' cost cost about $100.00 a month; but our family, including the two servants, averages ten persons, *two* of them being very large and hearty college boys! As a matter of fact when our family was the size of yours, I was able to keep that item down to $65.00."

---

class: that the industrial behemoths had seized political and economic power, and were smothering individual opportunity.

For men like Judge Grosscup this may have been no more than a moral abstraction; for millions of Americans the economic system meant personal poverty and misery. There was a disparity between the incomes of the wealthy few and the poor multitudes which seemed almost incredible a half century later. One per cent of the American families owned nearly seven eighths of the wealth; seven eighths of the families owned only one eighth. While a fifth of the families were com-

he have to pay a cent of income tax. Biographers have pointed out that Carnegie lived comparatively modestly and devoted his millions to worthy causes, but many of the very rich created sensational headlines through their ostentatious living. The Vanderbilts, like a clan of feudal barons, maintained, in addition to their many country estates, seven mansions in seven blocks on Fifth Avenue.

These wealthy few often spent incredible sums on parties, accounts of which fascinated, but also angered, readers of yellow journals. The most notorious was the ball upon which Mrs. Martin Bradley spent $250,000; it created such a furore that she and her husband fled to exile in England. A less exceptional dinner, served on gold plates at the old Waldorf-Astoria in 1899, cost $10,000 for forty people, or $250 apiece. At this time, $250 was six months' wages for the average working-man. In part the millionaires were able to earn their huge incomes because of the low cost of labor in their factories, and to afford their huge estates and townhouses through the low cost of servants. The middle class too benefited from cheap labor. While they did not enjoy the great variety of household appliances of later generations, they were able with the aid of servants to maintain large homes.

Although servants were paid almost incredibly low wages, at least they were entitled to meals and garret rooms. Working girls could not count upon even these. One woman in five worked, and often for wages as low as $6 or $8 per week. Unless a girl lived at home, it was almost impossible for her to exist upon these wages. O. Henry was reflecting the widespread indignation of progressive America when he described in his short stories how strong the temptation was for these nearly starving girls to succumb to predatory men. Late in the progressive era, advocates of a minimum wage law to protect women created a sensation in Chicago by bringing several women to a hearing to testify that low pay and poverty had driven them to prostitution. Nevertheless, the Illinois legislature failed to enact a law.

Child labor, which had always existed in the United States, was becoming an increasingly serious problem by the early 1900's. At least 1,700,000 children under 16 were employed in factories and fields. Ten per cent of the girls between 10 and 15, and twenty per cent of the boys, were gainfully employed. At least 38 states had laws to protect children, but these typically applied only to children employed in factories, and set a minimum age of 12 years and a maximum

workday of ten hours. Sixty per cent of the child workers were employed in agriculture, which could mean a twelve-hour day picking or hoeing in the fields. In the cotton mills of the South, children working at the looms all night were kept awake by having cold water thrown in their faces. In canneries, little girls cut fruits or vegetables sixteen hours a day. Some children worked at dangerous machines without safety devices. As these young workers became exhausted at the end of a long day, or night, they might become careless as they leaned over a loom to retie broken threads, have their hair caught in machinery, and be scalped as it suddenly started up again.

Industrial accidents were commonplace. For most laborers, whether children, women, or men, working conditions were far from ideal. Many women labored in dark, cold, dirty factories or sweatshops without restrooms or fire escapes. For men, working conditions were even worse. As early as 1877 Massachusetts had required safety devices upon elevators and machinery; some states also required mine inspection. But there was little effective enforcement of the laws, if indeed personnel for enforcement existed. In American factories and mines, and on the railroads, the accident rate was higher than in any other industrial nation in the world. As late as 1907 an average of twelve railroad men a week were killed. In factories, little had been done to prevent occupational diseases such as phosphorus and lead poisoning.

Nor was there economic incentive for employers to improve working conditions. Under the common law, if an accident was due, even in part, to the negligence of an employee himself or a fellow employee, the employer bore no responsibility. Even if the employer were liable under the common law, the courts were slow, and often too expensive for the maimed worker or his widow. Until 1911 there were almost no state workmen's compensation laws.

Cheap labor was one of the reasons for high profits; unrestricted immigration seemed one of the reasons for cheap labor. At the same time that the big industrialists fought against a lowering of the tariff bars, they welcomed in, or even recruited, the low-paid workers of Europe. While the flow of the "old immigrants" from northern and western Europe continued, a new flood, comprising about 72 per cent of the total between 1900 and 1910, poured in from southern and eastern Europe. For the most part they were Italians, Slavs, and Jews. In the single year 1905, over 1,250,000 arrived. In most big cities of the North, immigrants and their children outnumbered the native-born. Bewildered at being thrust into an alien culture, living under conditions far below the level of native Americans (except Negroes), they filled most of the backbreaking unskilled jobs in the new

CHILD AT SPINDLES IN A CAROLINA TEXTILE MILL, 1909. According to the 1900 census, one out of three of the employees in Southern cotton mills was a child under 16. Under strong pressure from within, Southern states gradually passed laws prohibiting the worst of the abuses. In North Carolina, manufacturers drafted a law passed in 1907 prohibiting children under 16 from working more than sixty-six hours per week, banning children under 14 from night work, and allowing children of 12 to work only as apprentices. As a means of obtaining graphic evidence of violations of even this lenient law, the Secretary of the National Child Labor Committee brought Hine, a documentary photographer of city slums, into some of the worst of the mills. Hine's pictures, of which this one is representative, were instrumental in arousing public indignation against child-labor abuses. (PHOTOGRAPH BY LEWIS HINE, GEORGE EASTMAN HOUSE MEMORIAL COLLECTION)

"THE STEERAGE," BY ALFRED STIEGLITZ. When Stieglitz (1864–1946), crossing the Atlantic in 1907, caught this unposed photograph of immigrants crowded in the cheapest quarters, his intent was not documentary, nor was his object to publicize the misery of these passengers. Rather, he was trying to utilize photography as a form of creative expression—an art in itself, not an imitation of other arts.

Stieglitz demonstrated the way in which an art form could take advantage of technical advances (in this instance, photographic emulsions) by taking unparalleled night photographs and capturing the feeling of rainstorms and snow. He also helped change American taste in painting. Between 1905 and 1917 at his New York gallery he displayed, in addition to photographic art, the work of French painters then unknown in the United States, from Cézanne through Picasso. He became associated with an equally advanced group of American artists, including John Marin, Max Weber—and Georgia O'Keeffe, whom he married. (COURTESY MISS GEORGIA O'KEEFFE FOR THE ALFRED STIEGLITZ ESTATE; COLLECTION MUSEUM OF MODERN ART)

CHICAGO'S "GHETTO": JEFFERSON AND 12TH STREETS, 1906. Typical of the residents in this area were a Russian man and his wife who earned two dollars a day finishing coats. Their household was thus described in 1892: "Three small children and the grandmother constitute the family, the latter dying of a cancer without medical attendance or nursing. Man has been 18 years in this country and owns a populous frame tenement house. He also owns the wretched rear cottage, on the second floor of which his family lives. His work room contains a bed, an upright piano, dining table, sewing machine and the couch on which his mother lies dying. The filth and smell are intolerable. He does only the finest custom work and was making a valuable coat. Most of the year he has been making police uniforms." *Seventh Biennial Report of the Bureau of Labor Statistics of Illinois* (Springfield, Ill., 1892). (COURTESY CHICAGO HISTORICAL SOCIETY)

heavy industries, on the railroads, and around the cities. The Jews, many of whom brought their skill with the needle, went into the garment trade, but under just as wretched circumstances.

The American Federation of Labor (whose president, Samuel Gompers, was himself an immigrant) fought to cut off this flood of cheap, unskilled foreign labor, which was said to keep wages down and hamper unionization. Many Americans, both conservative and progressive, were susceptible to the popular dogma of Anglo-Saxon superiority, and joined in

the anti-immigration movement. They feared the high birthrate among immigrants as compared with the low birthrate among natives in the higher-income groups; Theodore Roosevelt warned darkly against "race suicide." They blamed the squalor of the slums and the power of the political bosses largely upon the immigrants, and felt that through restriction could come improvement. In 1907 they succeeded in stopping the immigration of Japanese to the agricultural lands of the Pacific Coast through the "gentleman's agreement" that Roosevelt negotiated with the Japanese government. A series of restrictive laws prohibited various undesirables, ranging from ex-convicts to alcoholics, from entering the United States. In 1917, over the veto of President Wilson, Congress passed a law setting up a literacy test as a means of reducing the number of immigrants.

For all those, immigrant or native, crowded into city tenements, life was far from enviable. Jacob Riis, the crusading journalist, thought that by 1900 the worst of the New York slums were gone. In their place were a scattering of parks and playgrounds; in some of the worst remaining areas there were privately financed settlement houses to aid the poor. Nevertheless, for millions of city dwellers, housing was barely tolerable. In New York City, two thirds of the city's three and a half millions lived in tenement houses. Most of them were by no means slum dwellings but were nevertheless of the "dumbbell" type, which provided direct light and air for only four rooms of the fourteen on each floor.

Origins of Progressivism

It was the goal of progressives to right the various wrongs. Where from among the American people could there come a movement forceful and persistent enough to overcome the entrenched economic power which maintained these conditions? Populists had vented their indignation against many of the same evils and had proposed some concrete remedies. But Populism had been a protest movement limited largely to the distressed farmers of the West and South. Now, the farmers were enjoying a renewed prosperity.

Progressive leaders were chiefly from the urban middle class, to a remarkable extent college-educated self-employed professional men or small businessmen, of native-born Protestant background. For the most part they were about forty years old, financially secure civic leaders who

had earlier been McKinley Republicans.

Following these leaders was a middle class, like them still clinging to the traditional agrarian values, but caught up in the social whirlpool of the new industrial age. The older segment of the middle class, the independent professional and business men from which such a high proportion of progressive leaders came, somewhat more than doubled between 1870 and 1910. This meant it grew as rapidly as the population as a whole, which increased about two and a third times. The working class (including farm laborers) trebled; farmers and farm tenants doubled. But there was another group, a new middle class of white-collar workers—the clerks, sales people, and technicians who worked for corporations or service enterprises. It increased almost eight times, from 756,000 to 5,609,000 people, thus reaching a number almost double the size of the older middle class.

While members of this new white-collar class did not provide leadership for the progressive movement, to a considerable extent they did provide it with voting strength. Political action was their only outlet for economic protest, since they did not belong to unions or trade associations. Often it was they, on their fixed salaries, who were worst caught by rising prices. And basically, like the older middle class, they were urbanites who still expressed the emotions of their rural roots. These two groups, the white-collar class and the older middle class, combined to form the respectable element of the towns and cities who, along with many of the more successful farmers and some of the laborers, were ready to accept the new progressive creed.

Urban political bosses frightened the middle classes, not only because of their corrupt ties with the industrial moguls but also because of their hold over the ignorant laboring masses (often largely immigrants) of the cities. Also, these middle-class people had some fear of the new rising labor unions. Populist farmers had shared these urban middle-class suspicions of the moguls and the masses. One of the Populist papers had said the purpose of the party was to serve as a "bulwark against the anarchy of the upper and lower scums of society." Progressives continued the same prejudices.

Theodore Roosevelt in his *Autobiography* has stated clearly the reasoning which led him, a conservative young plutocrat of the upper middle-class gentry, to enter politics. The men Roosevelt knew best, cultivated clubmen, warned him that politics was a cheap affair of saloon keepers and horsecar conductors, which gentlemen should shun. "I answered," Roosevelt wrote, "that if this were so it merely meant that the people I knew did not belong to the governing class, and that the other people did—and that I intended to be one of the governing class."

If Roosevelt and others like him, of high intellect and social position, were to win a wide following, they would have to modify their conservatism. And so they did. They still clung fundamentally to laissez-faire economics as their guiding star, but as a means of returning to laissez faire they came to advocate government intervention of varying sorts and degrees. They were of aristocratic tendencies, and certainly had no love for the masses, but they became the ardent advocates of more popular government. In greater democratization they saw the way back to an old Utopia, which of course had never actually existed.

The Progressive Movements

Various progressives differed in their aims and objectives, for actually progressivism was not a single movement but an aggregate of movements, aiming at widely divergent goals. To one progressive, regulation of trusts might be the great end; to another, clean municipal government; to a third, equal rights for women. Various of the progressive forces would coalesce

for different objectives; occasionally they would even oppose each other. Thus some progressives favored imperialism while others fought it bitterly. Out of all these varying drives there emerged two great streams of progressivism—the movement for social justice, as it was called, and the demand for political reform.

The social-justice movement was already well advanced by the turn of the century. It had its roots in European, especially English, reform movements. Almost every prominent English reformer visited the United States, and conversely almost every American progressive leader fell under the influence of the British. Young Jane Addams had worked at the newly established Toynbee Hall in the Limehouse section of London; in 1889 she returned to the United States to establish Hull-House, a slum relief center, in Chicago. Settlement houses, slum clearance agitation, and a great variety of other English reforms quickly had their counterpart in the United States.

The Salvation Army, which had recently come to the United States from England, by 1900 boasted a corps of 3,000 officers and 20,000 privates. It offered aid as well as religion to the dregs of the cities. So did ministers, priests, and rabbis who by the nineties were working in the slums; these men were united in their determination to improve the existence of the miserable people around them in addition to saving their souls. "One could hear human virtue cracking and crushing all around," Walter Rauschenbusch wrote of Hell's Kitchen in New York City. To him the way of salvation for these human souls seemed to be a Christian reform of the social and economic system. "Translate the evolutionary themes into religious faith," he asserted, "and you have the doctrine of the Kingdom of God." Thus many an American Protestant minister arrived at the social gospel. Catholics like Father John Augustine Ryan joined in the fight for social justice under the authority they found in Pope Leo XIII's encyclical *Rerum Novarum*. It declared that "a small number of very rich men have been able to lay upon the masses of the poor a yoke little better than slavery itself. . . . No practical solution of this question will ever be found without the assistance of religion and the church."

Close behind the ministry were middle-class and upper-class women. In the 1890's many of them had seemed restless and discontented, reading more widely than their husbands or brothers, joining literary circles and women's clubs. By the early 1900's these clubs were beginning to display a remarkable growth; the General Federation of Women's Clubs, from a membership of 50,000 in 1898, grew to over 1,000,000 by 1914. In the new era, the members of the clubs were quick to take up the fight for the ballot and legal equality for themselves, and for a wide array of reforms on behalf of children and working women.

Another small but mighty social-justice group consisted of those who gathered careful data and statistics on the need for reform. They were often social-welfare workers who prepared articles for *Survey* magazine. Or they were frustrated crusaders working for federal or state agencies. In many a state before 1900 there were bureaus of labor which could and did, as in the case of Illinois, compile great quantities of data on deplorable working and living conditions. But research alone could not gather a great force of public opinion behind the progressive movement. That was the task of the muckrakers and the politicians.

The muckrakers were the many journalists who dramatized the need for reform by writing exposures of the unsavory in business and government. They began to attract attention toward the end of 1902 and were at their peak of popularity in 1906. There long had been a literature of exposure, from the *Harper's Weekly* crusade against the Tweed Ring through Lloyd's denunciation of Standard Oil

in *Wealth against Commonwealth* (1894). What was new was the scale of the revelations and the rapid attraction of a wide audience. It began almost by accident in about ten of the new popular magazines, selling for 10 or 15¢, which were then building mass circulation. *McClure's*, already a magazine of broad appeal, began publishing Ida Tarbell's series on Standard Oil. The publisher, S. S. McClure, sent a new editor, Lincoln Steffens, out to see the country first-hand; this experience led Steffens to begin a series on municipal corruption. At the same time, Ray Stannard Baker contributed an article belaboring a union for wrongdoing during a coal strike.

At the height of the muckraking movement, ten journals with a combined circulation of about three million were devoting considerable space to the literature of exposure. In addition some books like Upton Sinclair's *Jungle* (1906), an exposure of the meat-packing industry, sold over 100,000 copies. Many newspapers, most notably the New York *World* and the Kansas City *Star*, printed articles by muckrakers. It was exciting for a while, but by 1912 it was over. This was due partly to the hostility of business, which at times withheld credit and advertising from the muckraking magazines, but probably it was more because the public became fatigued.

Grassroots Reform—in the Cities

The Shame of the Cities was the title Lincoln Steffens gave to his notable series of exposures which first appeared in *McClure's*, and shame was what civic-minded progressives felt. They tried to wrest control of their city governments away from the machines, reorganize the governments scientifically, and use them as instruments of economic and social reform.

Arrayed in the opposition were the bosses, and behind them those interests so abhorrent to the progressives, the saloons and brothels, and various businesses which could gain more from the bosses than from clean government. Allied with the bosses were some newspapers that ridiculed the progressives as either killjoys or scoundrels. Finally, there was the great constituency of city working people, mostly of immigrant origins. To them the bosses were friends who could be counted upon to help them when they ran afoul of the law in some minor way, or were in need of jobs or food. The bosses, to an extent which sometimes surpassed the progressives, did keep in close touch with the common man; their records were not merely ones of unmitigated evil. Progressives, on the other hand, seemed to be do-gooders who were trying to take away the saloon, the poor man's club, and to deprive him of his amusements from prize-fighting to Sunday baseball. What could be more logical than his readiness to deliver his vote to the boss?

Many progressives, finding it difficult to grasp the relationship between the bosses and their constituents, saw the problem in simple moral and legal terms. Bad government, they thought, came from bad charters. They should seize the municipal governments and, by remaking the charters, usher in the urban millennium. For a time they seemed remarkably successful.

The beginning grew out of tragedy in Galveston, Texas, where the old, ineffective government broke down in the wake of a tidal wave. The citizens replaced it with a commission of five, whose members by 1908 were jointly enacting ordinances and were singly running the main city departments. In 1907 Des Moines adopted the commission plan with modifications to make it more democratic, and other cities followed. Another variation was the city-manager plan which placed a trained expert, similar to the manager of a business, in charge of the city, and made him responsible to the commission or the mayor and council. Staunton, Virginia, hired a city manager in 1908; the new device attracted national attention when Dayton, Ohio, adopted it in 1913 to speed rehabilitation from a serious flood. By the end of the progressive era some 400 cities were operating under commissions, and another 45 under city managers.

Whether through old or new city machinery, progressives fought to destroy economic privilege on the municipal level. During these years it meant primarily trying to prevent the sale of streetcar franchises, or to force exorbitantly high fares downward. The most notable of the reform mayors was Tom Johnson of Cleveland, who had invented the streetcar fare box. He was a traction magnate converted to the ideas of Henry George. As mayor, Johnson fought to raise the ridiculously low assessments upon railroad and utility property, introduce city planning, and above all, lower streetcar fares to 3¢. After his defeat and death, his brilliant aide, Newton D. Baker, was elected mayor, and helped maintain Cleveland's position as the best governed American city.

Many of the urban gains of progressivism were permanent, but in some cities, as soon as progressives relaxed, the old forces recaptured the city hall. Cities seemed to require periodic cleanups. In other municipalities, state control over city government made reform almost impossible. Cities derived all of their powers from the state, and many a state legislature granted new charters only reluctantly, or controlled a large city within the state through special legislation. In the state of New York, which functioned this way, the reform mayor of Schenectady complained, "Whenever we try to do anything, we run up against the charter. It is an oak charter, fixed and immovable." Consequently, a municipal home-rule movement spread, to try to obtain state laws allowing cities to write their own charters. Much of the difficulty with state legislatures was even more serious. Many a reformer, like Johnson in Cleveland, or Joseph W. Folk in St. Louis, found himself helpless in the cities because the trail of corruption led back to the legislature.

Progressivism in the Statehouse

Hiram Johnson in California, Folk in Missouri, and other progressives moved on from cities where they had been crusading district attorneys to become progressive governors. It was only by taking this step that Folk, for example, was in a position to break the bosses and control the big corruptions behind them. It was Johnson's avowed purpose as governor of California to end the political hold of the Southern Pacific Railroad upon the state, a hold so firm that earlier at a banquet eighteen months before an election, Edward H. Harriman, president of the railroad, had been able to predict accurately that an obscure congressman would become the next governor.

At the state level, progressives enacted a wide array of legislation to increase the power of crusading governors, give the people more direct control over the government, and decrease, sometimes almost to the point of insignificance, the functions of legislators. It was these ill-paid, relatively inconscpicuous men who were being exposed by muckrakers as the villains in many a state. William Allen White in *McClure's*, December, 1905, described the Missouri legislators:

"The legislature met biennially, and enacted such laws as the corporations paid for, and such others as were necessary to fool the people, and only such laws were enforced as party expediency demanded. . . . Boodling, bribe-giving, public blackmail, legislative hold-ups, corrupt political deals and combinations carrying thousands of dollars with them flourished, and politicians who benefited thereby were accounted shrewd."

This view of the legislatures led progressives to circumscribe and circumvent them in almost every conceivable way. The most important of the devices, the initiative and the referendum, were first enacted in Oregon in 1902 as a result of the quiet but persistent advocacy of the secretary of several voters' organizations, William S. U'Ren. The initiative enabled voters to short-circuit the legislature and vote upon measures at general elections; the referendum forced the return of laws from the legislature to the electorate. By 1918 twenty states had adopted these schemes. A number had limited their state legislatures through prescribing a wide variety of matters upon which the state could act only through constitutional amendments that the voters must approve. From 1900 to 1920 the electorates voted upon a total of about 1,500 constitutional amendments, and approved some 900. In some states, these devices created long ballots crammed with technical measures. Such ballots continued long after the progressive era; a half-century later the crowded California ballot was forcing voters to be what one commentator called "do-it-yourself legislators."

Although progressives threw part of the legislative burden back onto the electorate, they also tried to obtain better officials. They tried to eliminate machine choice of candidates through the direct primary, first instituted in Mississippi in 1902 and adopted in some form by every state by 1915. Unfortunately, if they were not vigilant, machines operated one step further back and dominated the primaries. Another way many progressives hoped to thwart the machines was through giving the vote to women. For decades this had been the keystone of the women's rights movement, since women felt that once they obtained this they could vote in their other rights. As early as 1897 Colorado women obtained the right to vote, at a time when those of Kentucky still could not legally even make wills. By 1914 women could vote in twelve states, all west of the Mississippi; in 1916 Montana elected the first woman to the House of Representatives. During the first World War, Congress finally gave in to the suffragists, and in 1919 the Nineteenth Amendment was added to the Constitution. It seemed to make no spectacular change in voting patterns.

A more controversial and less used device for improving officials was the recall, which made possible their removal at a special election to be called after sufficient numbers of the electorate had signed petitions.

and passed reform legislation. Robert M. La Follette in Wisconsin obtained firm regulation of railroads, compensation for workmen injured in industrial accidents, and graduated taxation of inheritances. Charles Evans Hughes in New York obtained a commission to regulate public utilities. In New Jersey, when Woodrow Wilson, fresh from the presidency of

---

THE SUPREME COURT AND STATE LEGISLATION LIMITING HOURS OF WORK

Lochner v. New York (1905): The court invalidated a New York law limiting hours worked in a bakery to not more than ten a day or sixty a week: "The statute necessarily interferes with the right of contract between the employer and employees. . . . The general right to make a contract in relation to his business is part of the liberty of the individual protected by the Fourteenth Amendment of the Federal Constitution."

Justice Oliver Wendell Holmes, dissenting, declared: "The case is decided upon an economic theory which a large part of the country does not entertain. . . . United States and state statutes and decisions cutting down the liberty to contract by way of combination are familiar to this court. . . . Some of these laws embody convictions or prejudices which judges are likely to share. Some may not. But a constitution is not intended to embody a particular economic theory, whether of paternalism and the organic relation of the citizen to the state or of *laissez faire*. It is made for people of fundamentally differing views, and the accident of our finding certain opinions natural and familiar, or novel, and even shocking, ought not to conclude our judgment upon the question whether statutes embodying them conflict with the Constitution of the United States."

Bunting v. Oregon (1917): The court held valid an Oregon law establishing a ten-hour day in manufacturing establishments.

---

tions. It became a national issue when President Taft vetoed a bill admitting Arizona as a state became its constitution authorized recall of judges. Horrified conservatives approved of the veto, but soon after Arizona entered the union without the offensive provision the state's voters restored it.

Undoubtedly all these devices did bring about a greater degree of democratization. Progressives used them to obtain control of states, and then eradicated corruption

Princeton University, became governor in 1911, he obtained from the legislature a substantial array of measures to transform the state from the backward "mother of trusts" into one of the progressive leaders.

Nevertheless, much social justice legislation came only late and after much struggle. New York failed to enact factory-safety legislation until it was shocked into action by the Triangle Shirtwaist Factory fire in New York City in 1911, in which 148 people, mostly young women, were helplessly trapped and killed in a few minutes. When factory bills were introduced, several of the Tammany legislators, especially Alfred E. Smith and Robert F. Wagner, were active upon their behalf. Boss Charles F. Murphy had found that Tammany had gained many votes by supporting an earlier law limiting women to 54 hours of work a week, and now was ready to put his machine behind welfare legislation on behalf of his working-class constituents.

Throughout the era, progressive legislators ran the risk that the Supreme Court would invalidate their handiwork. The Court made one great, although temporary, shift toward progressivism. This came in 1908 when Louis D. Brandeis argued before it on behalf of an Oregon law to limit women workers to a ten-hour day. He presented a brief in which he devoted only 2 of 104 pages to the legal precedents and the remainder to proofs that Oregon's police power was necessary to protect the health and general welfare of the mothers, and thus of all mankind. The Supreme Court accepted this argument although in effect it was moving toward the "sociological jurisprudence" which Dean Roscoe Pound of the Harvard Law School had been developing. This, Pound explained, was a movement to adjust "principles and doctrines to human conditions they are to govern rather than to assumed first principles."

Progressives engaged in state reforms looked not only to the Supreme Court but also to the Congress and the White House. Here obviously rested the ultimate power for the control of the many problems that crossed state lines. They obtained from the Congress in 1910 several laws to reinforce state legislation. The Webb-Kenyon Act, passed over Taft's veto, prohibited the interstate shipment of liquor into dry areas; the Mann Act outlawed the interstate transportation of "white slaves," and thus helped in the progressive fight to break up prostitution

syndicates, one of the main sources of underworld income.

At the state level progressives fought to liberalize the United States Senate through the direct election of Senators. State legislatures were occasionally open to bribery, and much too often they elected conservatives who did not represent the public choice. David Graham Phillips in his sensational articles, "The Treason of the Senate," scourged the body as a rich men's club; a California Senator replied that there were only ten millionaires in the Senate. Lord Bryce had written in 1888, "Some, an increasing number, are senators because they are rich; a few are rich because they are senators."

By 1902 the House of Representatives had already five times passed resolutions for a constitutional amendment for direct election of Senators; each time the Senate blocked the amendment. Impatient progressives in various states developed techniques for circumventing the Constitution and providing in effect for direct election. By 1912 twenty-nine states had adopted these devices. In 1911 Governor Wilson of New Jersey gained renown by blocking the legislative election of a party boss, while at the same time in New York, Franklin D. Roosevelt, just 29, won his political spurs by leading legislative insurgents against Tammany's hand-picked candidate, a Buffalo traction magnate. That same year, the Senate ousted one of its members, Boss William E. Lorimer of Chicago, for vote-buying. In the wake of the public indignation that followed, the Senate in 1912 passed the Seventeenth Amendment, and by 1913 the requisite number of states had ratified it. The new amendment did not startlingly modify the nature of the Senate, since most progressive states had already elected Senators of a new mettle.

Neither did another progressive reform measure, the preferential presidential primary, have much consequence. This was begun in Oregon in 1910 and had spread to twenty states by 1920, but it by no means eliminated the maneuvering in conventions. Its main effect was to con- duct a series of state-wide popularity contests among leading candidates in the months before the convention.

BIBLIOGRAPHY

A popular comparison of the turn of the century with America at midcentury is F. L. Allen, *The Big Change* (1952). For chapters on the intellectual history of the Progressive era, see Richard Hofstadter, *The Age of Reform* (1955), and E. F. Goldman, *Rendezvous with Destiny* (1951; paperback ed., 1956). Harold U. Faulkner's *The Decline of Laissez-Faire* (1951) and *Quest for Social Justice* (1931) are, respectively, economic and social histories of the era. A popular social history of the years 1900–25, useful for its portrayal of contemporary attitudes, is Mark Sullivan, *Our Times* (6 vols., 1926–35).

A disillusioned view of Progressivism is John Chamberlain's *Farewell to Reform* (1932); an exciting but sometimes misleading political history is Matthew Josephson, *The President Makers* (1940); an account of the journalists is C. C. Regier, *The Era of the Muckrakers* (1932). For biographical sketches of some Progressives, see Louis Filler, *Crusaders for American Liberalism* (1950), chapters 7–8 of Aaron, *Men of Good Hope*; and Mann, *Yankee Reformers in the Urban Age*.

A brief interpretation of business history is Thomas C. Cochran, *The American Business System: A Historical Perspective, 1900–1955* (1957). F. L. Allen, *The Lords of Creation* (1935) is on business leaders; Allan Nevins, F. E. Hill, and others, *Ford* (2 vols., 1954–1957) has much detail on mass production; on changes in industrial technique also see Kendall Birr, *Pioneering in Industrial Research: The Story of the General Electric Research Laboratory* (1957) and Milton J. Nadworny, *Scientific Management and the Unions, 1900–1932* (1955).

On labor, see Philip Taft, *The A.F. of L. in the Time of Gompers* (1957); and the books on labor cited in the general bibli-

ography; on urban poverty, R. H. Bremner, *From the Depths: The Discovery of Poverty in the United States* (1956); on the "new" immigration and the restriction movement, Oscar Handlin, *The Uprooted* (1951); John Higham, *Strangers in the Land* (1955); and Barbara Miller Solomon, *Ancestors and Immigrants* (1956); on patriotic societies, Wallace Davies, *Patriotism on Parade* (1955); on trends in religion, C. H. Hopkins, *The Rise of the Social Gospel in American Protestantism, 1865–1915* (1940; on the South, C. V. Woodward, *Origins of the New South*.

For an account of Progressive politics on the state level, see Mowry, *California Progressives* (1951); A. D. Kirwan, *Revolt of the Rednecks* (1951); and Robert S. Maxwell, *La Follette and the Rise of the Progressives in Wisconsin* (1956); E. A. Fitzpatrick, *McCarthy of Wisconsin* (1944); and D. W. Grantham, Jr., *Hoke Smith and the Politics of the New South* (1958). On the municipal level, see Walton Bean, *Boss Ruef's San Francisco* (1952) and Harold Zink, *City Bosses in the United States* (1930). On Socialism see H. H. Quint, *The Forging of American Socialism* (1953); Ira Kipnis, *The American Socialist Movement, 1897–1912* (1952); David Shannon, *The Socialist Party of America* (1955), and Ray Ginger, *The Bending Cross*.

On literature, see Alfred Kazin, *On Native Grounds* (1942); Van Wyck Brooks, *The Confident Years, 1885–1915* (1952); and K. S. Lynn, *The Dream of Success* (1955). On the arts, see J. I. H. Baur, *Revolution and Tradition in Modern American Art* (1951); F. L. Wright, *Modern Architecture* (1931); C. W. Condit, *The Rise of the Skyscraper* (1951); and Aaron Copland, *Our New Music* (1941). For a reinterpretation of cultural trends, see H. F. May, *The End of American Innocence* (1959).

29

T. R., TAFT, AND WILSON

For progressives the path of reform led from the city hall to the state legislature and then to the national Capitol and the White House. Many conspicuous evils of the time required action by the federal government. So prominent figures of both parties brough progressivism into national politics. Among the leading Republicans were Robert M. La Follette, Theodore Roosevelt, and William Howard Taft; among the Democrats, William Jennings Bryan and Woodrow Wilson. From 1901 to 1916 politics and government largely reflected the opinions and ambitions of these men—especially Roosevelt and Wilson—and their respective followings.

The First Roosevelt

It was Theodore Roosevelt who gave the muckraking movement its name. At a banquet shortly after the appearance of David Graham Phillip's shocking articles on "The Treason of the Senate," Roosevelt arose to liken the writers to the man in *Pilgrim's Progress* who was so busy raking the muck at his feet that he could not see the heavens above. The cynical, conservative Speaker of the House, Uncle Joe Cannon, is supposed to have replied

to Roosevelt's remarks, "Yes, you're the chief muckraker." This was literally true. The great role of the muckraker was to publicize the need for reform. No one succeeded better than Roosevelt in dramatically arousing the indignation of the progressives, and in leading them toward political action on a national scale.

Roosevelt entered the White House by accident; he became President in September, 1901, when an assassin mortally wounded President McKinley. Roosevelt was not yet a progressive, even if Mark Hanna, who regarded him as a wild man, lamented, "Now look, that damned cowboy is President of the United States."

As a rather uncertain fledgling President, only 43 years old in 1901, Roosevelt had little inclination to put a vigorous progressive program into operation. He later admitted, "I cannot say that I entered the presidency with any deliberately planned and far reaching scheme of social betterment." His greatest ambition obviously was to be elected President in his own right.

Even had Roosevelt possessed a detailed plan of legislation, he could have done little to forward it in the fall of 1901. Congress, like most of the governmental machinery in the United States from the

municipalities up, was under the control of old-style politicians. "Uncle Joe" Cannon, as speaker of the House, operated under the autocratic powers "Czar" Reed had seized in 1890. Though genial, he so firmly controlled appointments to committees and debates on legislation, that the few Progressives beginning to appear in the House were obliged either to cooperate or sit as impotent witnesses to Cannon's dictatorship. The Senate was under the domination of an intelligent and competent oligarchy of conservatives. The most commanding of them was tall, austere Nelson Wilmarth Aldrich of Rhode Island, more reserved and less a newspaper personality than Cannon, but even more effective. Aldrich, a wealthy banker, was allied, through his son's marriage, to the Rockefellers.

Roosevelt realized how futile it would be to thrust his spear single-handed against these well-organized congressional phalanxes. For the time being, therefore, he was cautious and conciliatory toward their leaders. As he planned his first annual message to Congress, his strategy obviously was to try to attract a wide following without alienating these powerful men. "Before I write my message," he wrote Aldrich in 1901, "I should like to have a chance to go over certain subjects with you." Similarly, Roosevelt with sound political logic could draft diatribes against corporate plutocracy, then write Senator Chauncey Depew of the New York Central Railroad, "*How* I wish I *wasn't* a reformer, oh, Senator! But I suppose I must live up to my part, like the Negro minstrel who blacked himself all over!"

With equal logic, Roosevelt dispensed patronage throughout the Middle West in a manner calculated to break Hanna's control over the party, although the policies of the two men were in reality basically similar. It made little difference whether these appointments took Roosevelt to the left or right. In Kansas he backed a former Populist against Hanna's G.A.R. supporter; from Wisconsin, to the chagrin of La Follette, he chose Henry Clay Payne of the Old Guard to be Postmaster General. Payne, through his wide distribution of spoils, helped rally northern right-wing Republicans and Southern Gold Democrats behind Roosevelt. Finally, Roosevelt cemented alliances with businessmen in the North and reshuffled the unstable Republican organizations in the South, using as his agent one of President Harrison's spoilsmen, James S. Clarkson. In the South, he reversed Hanna's "lily-white" policy, to appoint some qualified Negroes to office. Indeed, it was to discuss appointments that Roosevelt took the sensational step of inviting Booker T. Washington to the White House in the fall of 1901.

While playing the game of political patronage, Roosevelt markedly improved the quality of officeholders. Gradually he was able to pull into public service a group of distinguished men, both old and young, of a sort that previously had shunned government work. Henry L. Stimson, who had been earning enormous fees as a corporation lawyer, became United States attorney for the New York City area and brought into his office a group of brilliant and idealistic young lawyers, including Felix Frankfurter.

Partly because Roosevelt had attracted into the government progressives of stat-

T. R. SPEAKING IN EVANSTON, ILLINOIS, 1903. [OPPOSITE] On the stump, Theodore Roosevelt, with his jutting jaw and flailing fist, was remarkably effective in stirring progressive enthusiasms. With a deadly earnestness reflected in the faces of his spectators, he repeatedly preached the manly and womanly virtues in time of peace and war, and gradually assumed leadership in the progressive crusade. His audiences overlooked his high-pitched voice and delighted in his mannerisms. The strenuosity he practiced was their ideal, and his exhortations were the creed of progressive America. (UNDERWOOD)

ure, bound to him by strong ties of personal loyalty, and even more because he had won over or neutralized the Republican machines, he was in firm control of the party by 1904. He had not made it progressive, but he had made it answerable to him. Hanna died early in the year; had he lived and felt the inclination, he could have mustered little strength against Roosevelt at the convention.

In 1904 the Democrats abandoned Bryan to nominate Cleveland's former law partner, Alton B. Parker. It was a futile maneuver, for the electorate had no interest in going back to Cleveland, nor would businessmen trust a party which had twice nominated Bryan. When Roosevelt, fearing that Wall Street was putting $5 million behind Parker, allowed his campaign manager to tap the trusts, the money came pouring in. Businessmen might call Roosevelt the "mad messiah," but they were not really afraid of him. Harriman personally contributed $50,000 and Morgan, $150,000; far more came from their associates. The steel, beef, oil, and insurance trusts, and the railroads all aided. Roosevelt was not altogether aware of the source of all the donations, nor did he feel he was putting himself under obligation.

After a dull campaign, he won by a popular majority of two and a half million votes. While businessmen were convinced he was safe, progressives were confident he would lead in reform. In state elections throughout the nation, progressives were generally victorious. As a sidelight, the Socialists under Eugene V. Debs (often regarded as a left-wing offshoot of the progressives), received 400,000 votes, four times as many as in 1900. Their growth gave Roosevelt a convincing argument that sane and slow reform was essential to forestall a violent upheaval.

Policing the Trusts

While Roosevelt was quietly taking over the Republican machinery, he was spectacularly building an excited national following. He launched a series of attacks upon the corporate plutocracy—attacks that were vigorous but at the same time moderate.

In his first annual message to Congress, December 3, 1901, he set forth his basic policy toward trusts: "There is a widespread conviction in the minds of the American people that . . . trusts are in certain of their features and tendencies hurtful to the general welfare. This . . . is based upon sincere conviction that combination and concentration should be, not prohibited, but supervised and within reasonable limits controlled; and in my judgment this conviction is right." Roosevelt's position on trusts was ready-made for burlesque by Finley Peter Dunne's character, Mr. Dooley: "Th' trusts, says he, are heejoous monsthers built up be th' enlightened intherprise iv th' men that have done so much to advance progress in our beloved country, he says. On wan hand I wud stamp thim undher fut; on th' other hand not so fast."

Specifically, Roosevelt asked for legislation to give the government the right to inspect and examine the workings of great corporations, and subsequently to supervise them in a mild fashion, rather similar to the regulation of banks. What he desired first was the power to investigate trusts and publicize their activities; on the basis of these data, Congress could later frame legislation to regulate or tax the trusts. Consequently he requested the establishment of a Department of Commerce and Labor, containing a Bureau of Corporations to carry on investigations. Congress set up such a department in 1903.

The establishment of a great railroad monopoly in the Northwest, after a bitter and spectacular stockmarket battle in 1901, gave Roosevelt an opportunity to begin prosecution under the Sherman Anti-Trust Act. And so he did, even though his avowed purpose had been to regulate, not destroy, and to stamp underfoot only "malefactors of great wealth," while sparing large corporations that were benign. The new Northern Securities Company had emerged out of the struggle for control of the Northern Pacific between E. H. Harriman of the Union Pacific on the one side, and James J. Hill of the Great Northern and J. P. Morgan on the other. In the eyes of

induced to come to an agreement to ruin none." Roosevelt was not set upon ruining Morgan, but to the joy of progressives, he was using his power as President to discipline industry.

When the Supreme Court in 1904 did dissolve the Northern Securities combine, it in no material way injured Harriman, Hill, or Morgan. But it did convince

---

THE SUPREME COURT AND THE SHERMAN ACT

U.S. v. E. C. Knight Co. (1895): In this case involving a monopoly in the manufacture of sugar, Chief Justice Melville W. Fuller declared, "Commerce succeeds to manufacture, and is not a part of it." Since the Sherman Act was based on the constitutional power of Congress to regulate commerce, this narrow interpretation left the sugar trust untouched.

U.S. v. Trans-Missouri Freight Association (1897): The court five-to-four applied the Sherman Act to dissolve a railroad combination. Justice Edward D. White, dissenting, protested the combination was valid because its "contract does not unreasonably restrain trade." The principle on which he based his dissent was known as the "rule of reason."

Addyston Pipe and Steel Co. v. U.S. (1899): The court unanimously decided against a combination of manufacturers of cast-iron pire because it was setting prices in interstate commerce.

Northern Securities Co. v. U.S. (1904): By a five-to-four vote, the Court ordered a railroad holding company dissolved. The dissenters, including Justice Oliver Wendell Holmes, again stated the "rule of reason."

Standard Oil Co. v. U.S. (1911): The court broke the Standard Oil combination, but the majority accepted Chief Justice White's "rule of reason": trusts were not to be dissolved unless they unreasonably restrained trade.

U.S. v. United States Steel (1920): The court refused to dissolve the corporation although it was the largest in its field, holding that it had not engaged in unlawful conduct.

---

progressives, these men were malefactors.

Morgan, feeling his position challenged, hastened to the White House, accompanied by Senators Hanna and Depew. According to Roosevelt, Morgan declared, "If we have done anything wrong, send your man to my man and they can fix it up." Morgan, Roosevelt later remarked, "could not help regarding me as a big rival operator, who either intended to ruin all his interests or else could be

progressives that Roosevelt, however cautious his avowed policies might be, was a heroic trust-buster. To this extent it served to whet the appetite of progressives for reform and to heighten their enthusiasm for Roosevelt. It did also have the intangible but significant effect, as Roosevelt later declared, of establishing "the principle that the government was supreme over the great corporations"—that the government was being injected as a vigorous force in the control of the economy.

Trust-busting was popular and proceeded apace. Roosevelt's attorneys obtained twenty-five indictments altogether and instituted suits against the beef, oil, and tobacco combinations. In these, the government was ultimately successful, but the Supreme Court instituted a "rule of reason," declaring in effect that the Sherman Act prohibited only unreasonable restraints upon trade. Even though President Taft initiated ninety more suits and obtained forty-three additional indictments, the results of trust-busting were disappointing.

Although Roosevelt's followers believed he was leading them into the millennium, the panic of 1907 bluntly illustrated the serious flaws still plaguing the American economic structure—and the President's unwillingness to go too far in trying to remedy them. Speculation and mismanagement during the boom years since the Spanish-American War led to a sharp break in prosperity in 1907. Roosevelt was quick to conciliate Wall Street. Judge Elbert H. Gary and Henry C. Frick called upon him one morning to tell him that unless United States Steel took over shares of the Tennessee Coal and Iron Company from a New York banking house, it would fail, and thus threaten a widespread industrial smashup. They wanted assurance that the government would not consider the purchase a violation of the Sherman Act. Roosevelt tacitly agreed. United States Steel was thus able to buy out a vigorous competitor at a bargain price, further stifle competition, and hold back the development of the iron and steel industry in the South.

Government and Labor Unions

The entrance of the government as a force in the economy could also mean regulation of collective bargaining. This Roosevelt dramatically demonstrated in 1902. Presidential intervention in labor disputes was nothing new—there had been, for example, the Pullman strike—but the government had usually acted as a strikebreaker for the captains of industry. Now Roosevelt was ready instead to make the government an impartial arbiter. Here again, as in dealing with capitalists, he wished the government to be paramount over the conflicting economic forces, and neutral in dealing with them. This became the progressive position. Organized labor, as long as it was well-behaved, did not frighten the progressives nearly as much as did organized capital. The unions were comparatively weak; despite the great upsurge of the American Federation of Labor in the 1890's, by 1900 only about 4 per cent of the working force, even excluding agricultural laborers, was organized.

One of the economic areas in which the union leader was most reasonable and personable, and injustice toward the workers most intolerable, was anthracite coal mining. Eight coal railroads dominated by Morgan held a virtual monopoly over the industry. Wages were substandard, hours long, and the accident rate shockingly high. The workers, under John Mitchell, struck in May, 1902, for an eight-hour day, a 20-per-cent wage increase, and recognition of the union. Mitchell so effectively presented the miners' claims, and George F. Baer, spokesman for the operators, was so truculent, that public sympathy for the first time in a major strike was aligned with the strikers. Baer foolishly asserted the divine right of the operators to deal with miners as they saw best, thus adding blasphemy to stupidity, in the eyes of many observers. He remained adamant when Roosevelt early in October called operators and miners to the White House to ask them to accept arbitration. In contrast, Mitchell had repeatedly offered to arbitrate. Roosevelt, who was in a wheelchair (having been injured in a carriage accident), hinted darkly afterwards that

POWDER MEN IN THE PERRIN COAL MINE, ABOUT 1902. "During the last two generations a slow, stubborn contest has been waged by labor in the anthracite coal fields against the ever-growing power of monopoly and the strike of 1902 was but the culmination of a development lasting through three-fourths of a century. . . . Much of . . . even [the] low wages . . . was never paid in cash to the mineworkers. There were in vogue many systems for cheating the men. . . . The size of the ton increased, so that 2,900 and even 3,190 pounds came to be considered a ton, while the price remained at the same level. . . . Where the coal was paid by the car, the same system was adopted, and the car grew, as the men said, as though it were made of live oak. . . . The miners were obliged to buy their powder from the companies and to pay $2.75 for a keg which was not worth over $1.10. Since it is impossible to blast coal without powder, the powder grievance became an increasingly serious one as the veins of coal grew thinner and harder to mine."—John Mitchell, *Organized Labor* (Philadelphia: American Book and Bible House, 1903). (THEODORE ROOSEVELT COLLECTION, HARVARD UNIVERSITY)

he had been tempted to chuck Baer out of the window. He toyed with schemes to send federal troops to take over the mines, but would not have had a shred of authority to do so. The solution was ironic. He persuaded Morgan to force arbitration upon the operators.

Morgan had good reason to act since

he wished to keep the Republicans in power. With crisp weather coming, voters might have gone from their cold homes to register their protest in the November congressional elections. (Anthracite was the chief fuel used in heating Eastern residences.) Nor did a settlement harm Morgan's monopoly interests, since the increased wages were passed on to consumers in a higher standard price for coal. The miners after their long strike failed to gain union recognition and obtained only a 10-per-cent wage increase.

The coal strike and its settlement were evidence of what has been called "a honeymoon period of capital and labor," stretching from McKinley's inauguration through Roosevelt's first term. Union membership jumped from less than a half million to over two million. Monopolies could well afford to deal liberally with union labor, since they could thus avoid work stoppages in prosperous periods, and pass on increased laobr costs to the consumers. It was altogether fitting that Hanna, the high priest of modern big business, should assume the presidency of the National Civic Federation, which was founded in 1901 to bring about friendly relations between capital and labor, and that Samuel Gompers should become vice president.

This foreshadowed at least dimly an era of monolithic corporations and unions, but it was not the predominant pattern of the early 1900's. Unionism was repugnant to most of the heads of the new trusts, many of whom were utopian capitalists as vehemently antiunion in their principles as was Baer.

Not all laborers were ready to accept the assumption of leaders like Gompers and Mitchell that differences with capitalists could easily be adjusted around a conference table. The Socialist minority within the American Federation of Labor succeeded in capturing unions of machinists and miners; Socialists won municipal elections in Milwaukee, Schenectady, and Berkeley. More radical labor, especially

militant western miners, in 1905 founded the Industrial Workers of the World, which tried to organize the great masses of unskilled workers, mostly immigrants, whom the A.F.L. ignored. In the process the I.W.W. employed violent means against which employers retaliated with equal violence. Two episodes, neither the work of the I.W.W., especially outraged orderly progressives. These were the blowing up of a former governor of Idaho, and the dynamiting of the plant of the Los Angeles *Times*, which was militantly antiunion.

Such episodes prompted many progressives to return to their earlier prejudices, and to listen to the antiunion slogans of the National Association of Manufacturers and kindred organizations. The N.A.M., which proclaimed itself against union recognition in 1903, was predominantly made up of men who ran small plants and were dependent upon low labor costs to survive in highly competitive markets. It called the open shop the "American Plan," and the independent workman (strikebreaker) the "American hero." President Charles W. Eliot of Harvard gave formidable support by asserting that nothing was "more essential to the preservation of individual liberty" than protection of the independent workman.

The manufacturers won much public sympathy. At the same time, what they could not obtain from the President, as they had done in Cleveland's day, they were able to obtain from federal judges, most of whom had been appointed in the earlier era. These judges made the courts the refuge of small business against collective bargaining. The most spectacular court blow against collective bargaining grew out of the Danbury Hatters' strike of 1902. The courts held that the union's efforts to obtain a nation-wide boycott of Loewe hats was a violation of the Sherman Act, and assessed triple damages of $240,000 against the union. Another boycott case, involving the Buck's Stove and

Range Company of St. Louis, was even more painful to labor because a federal court issued a sweeping injunction. It forbade the A.F.L. to carry on the boycott, to include the company in a "We Don't Patronize" list in its newspaper, or even to mention the dispute orally or in writing. When Gompers and other A.F.L. officials defied the injunction by mentioning the dispute, they were sentenced to prison for contempt of court. The case dragged on in the courts so long that the sentences were never carried out, but the principle of the injunction stood. Union officials began a concerted and vigorous campaign to have organized labor exempted from the Anti-Trust Act, and to outlaw antilabor injunctions.

Gompers and his followers wanted simply not to be discriminated against by the government; they were not asking for welfare legislation. President Roosevelt was to a certain degree sympathetic with the aspirations of the union leaders. He denounced the Buck's Stove decision, and inveighed against court abuse of injunctions. But he was more interested in paternalistic legislation for labor, similar to that being proposed in many state legislatures. He asked Congress for legislation to regulate the hours and working conditions of women and children, establish employers' liability for accident compensation, and improve railroad safety measures. For the moment he made no headway.

Indeed, if he had, the courts would have invalidated most of Congress's handiwork, for they were striking down most state laws as rapidly as they were enacted. The Supreme Court held, in the Lochner case in 1905, that a New York law limiting hours of bakers, who pursued an unhealthy occupation, to ten a day or sixty a week was unconstitutional, because it violated the right of the bakers to make contracts as they saw fit, under the Fourteenth Amendment. Justice Oliver Wendell Holmes, who had been appointed to the court by Roosevelt because of his enlightened views on labor, tartly dissented:

"Some of these laws embody convictions or prejudices which judges are likely to share. Some may not. But a constitution is not intended to embody a particular economic theory, whether of paternalism and the organic relation of the citizen to the state or of *laissez faire*."

Railroads, Conservation, Health

Unhesitatingly, Roosevelt accepted his 1904 victory as a mandate for progressive reform. Further, he was free from his earlier preoccupation with being elected, since on the evening of his overwhelming victory he publicly announced he would not seek another term. He continued to operate politically from a center position. He so seriously offended the trusts which had contributed to the campaign that Henry Clay Frick, the steel magnate, complained, "We bought the . . . and he didn't stay bought." He equally offended the advanced progressives of the Middle West with his undisguised disdain for "the La Follette type of fool radicalism." La Follette felt that Roosevelt was betraying progressives with his middle-of-the-road policies.

The problem that faced Roosevelt at the beginning of his second term was whether to try to force through Congress a lower tariff or stricter regulation of railroads. The West was clamoring for both of these. Although La Follette came into the Senate in January, 1905, and numerous progressives were entering the House, it still would be difficult to push a downward tariff revision through Congress.

While leaving the tariff alone, Roosevelt ably exercised his presidential leadership to obtain more effective railroad-rate regulation. The courts had practically nullified the Interstate Commerce Act of 1887. By a series of intricate maneuvers, Roosevelt managed to force a new regulatory law through Congress. At one point he seemed to join La Follette in demands for really drastic regulation of railroads. La Follette wished to give the I.C.C. power to evaluate railroad property as a base for determining rates; when Roosevelt abandoned him, he felt betrayed. But Roosevelt had been intent only upon obtaining a moderate law. Although the Hepburn Act of June, 1906, was in La Follette's eyes only half a loaf, it was at least the beginning of effective railroad regulation. It empowered the I.C.C. to put into effect reasonable rates, subject to later court review; extended its jurisdiction to cover express, sleeping car, and pipeline companies; separated railroad management from other enterprises such as mining; prescribed uniform bookkeeping; and forbade passes and rebates.

It was a large half-loaf, and La Follette and his supporters in Congress soon were able to obtain the remaining part. In 1910 insurgent Republicans and Democrats in Congress passed the Mann-Elkins Act abolishing the "long-and-short-haul" evil, further extending the jurisdiction of the I.C.C., and strengthening other features of the Hepburn Act. The I.C.C. could suspend proposed new rates up to ten months, and could demand proof from the railroad that they would be reasonable. Finally, in 1913 La Follette's long agitation resulted in passage of a law authorizing the I.C.C. to evaluate railroads, and to set rates to give a fair return of profit on their value.

One of the many reasons for the clamor for lower freight rates had been to cut the rising cost of lumber. The best forests of the Great Lakes area were cut over, and the increasing amounts of lumber coming from the Pacific Northwest had to bear the heavy cost of transportation eastward. Furthermore, trees were being felled faster than they were being grown. It was one of many signs that progressives must abandon the profligate ways of pioneering America. At this point sharp conflict developed between Progressives in the West and those in the East. Westerners wanted the government to aid in the rapid development of their resources; the growth of their economy depended upon this. East-

erners were more interested in preserving the remaining wilderness; their concern was more aesthetic and recreational.

Roosevelt, ardent sportsman and naturalist that he was, along with his Chief Forester, Gifford Pinchot, and most Eastern progressives, felt that the United States must develop great national forests like those of the European countries. For years Major John Wesley Powell, explorer of the Grand Canyon, and other experts had been advocating new policies for husbanding the public domain.

A beginning had come with the passage of the Forest Reserve Act of 1891; under its provisions 47,000,000 acres had been set aside as National Forests. Roosevelt, clothing his actions with the terminology of the progressive struggle against the vested interests, rapidly extended the government reserves. In 1907 Western Congressmen succeeded in attaching a rider (unrelated amendment) to an appropriation bill, prohibiting him from withdrawing further lands. Roosevelt could not veto the appropriations bill without calamitous effects. He acted swiftly, first to withdraw practically all remaining forests in the public domain, and then to sign the bill. Altogether he added about 125,-000,000 acres to the National Forests, and reserved 4,700,000 acres of phosphate beds and 68,000,000 acres of coal lands—all the known coal deposits in the public domain.

At the same time Roosevelt prepared the way for a new government policy on electric power by reserving 2,565 water-power sites. These were just the years when expanding private utility companies were interested in obtaining them. Further, he vetoed a bill to permit private exploitation of the power at Muscle Shoals on the Tennessee River, which a generation later became the heart of the T.V.A. This left the way open for government development of huge power projects, a program as popular in the West as the withdrawal of other land was unpopular.

It was not the President, but a Demo-

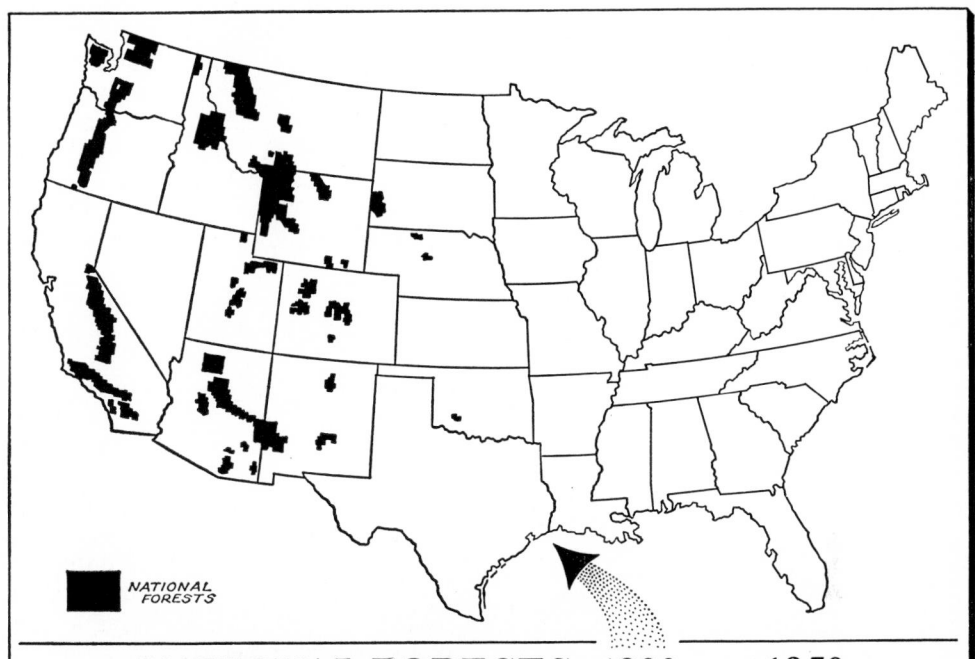

NATIONAL
FORESTS

NATIONAL FORESTS, 1900 AND 1950

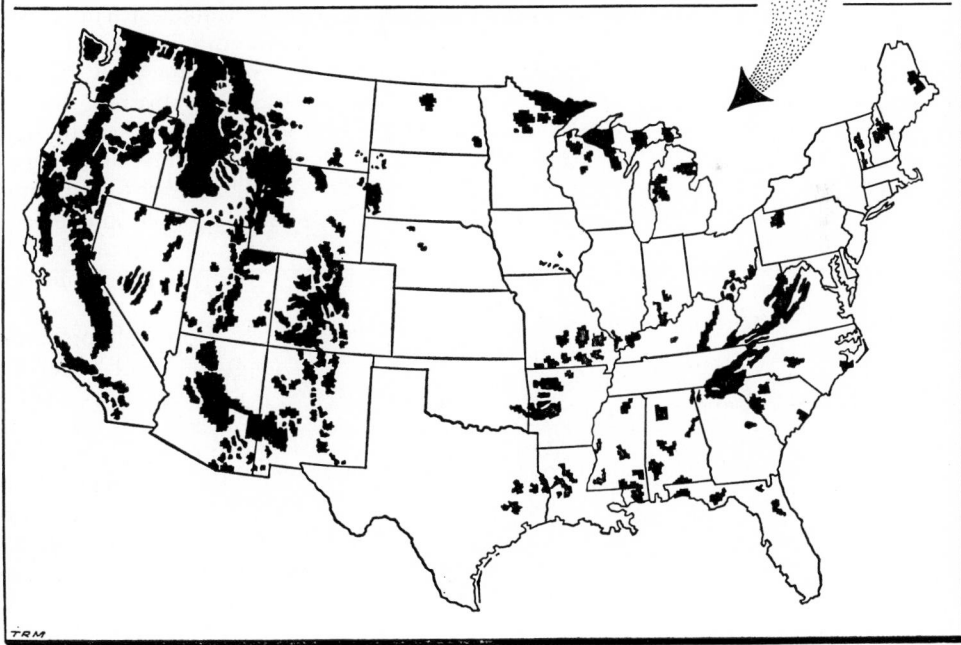

TRM

cratic Senator from Nevada, Francis G. Newlands, who proposed an extensive federal reclamation program for the West. Roosevelt endorsed it, and to a considerable extent was able to win political credit for the Newlands Reclamation Act of 1902. It provided that money from the sale of Western lands should go into a revolving fund to undertake irrigation projects too large for private capital or state resources. Eventually, the government built huge dams for the development of power

ous foods and adulterants. The muckrakers also had made the public shockingly aware of the disgusting and dangerous things they were sometimes eating. None created a more shocked reaction than Upton Sinclair, who wrote a powerful novel of protest against exploitation of immigrant labor in the stockyards, and incidentally included nauseating descriptions of the preparation of meats. When *The Jungle* appeared in 1906, it hit Americans' stomachs as much as their consciences,

THE SAUSAGES

"There was never the least attention paid to what was cut up for sausage; there would come all the way back from Europe old sausage that had been rejected, and that was mouldy and white—it would be doused with borax and glycerine, and dumped into the hoppers, and made over again for home consumption. There would be meat that had tumbled out on the floor, in the dirt and sawdust, where the workers had tramped and spit uncounted billions of [tuberculosis] germs. There would be meat stored in great piles in rooms; and the water from leaky roofs would drip over it, and thousands of rats would race about on it. It was too dark in these storage places to see well, but a man could run his hand over these piles of meat and sweep off handfuls of the dried dung of rats. These rats were nuisances, and the packers would put poisoned bread out for them; they would die, and then rats, bread, and meat would go into the hoppers together."—Upton Sinclair, *The Jungle* (New York: Doubleday, Page & Company, 1906).

and storage of water, and extensive systems of canals to carry the water to arid lands. Already by 1915 the government had invested $80 million in twenty-five projects, of which the largest was the Roosevelt Dam on the Salt River of Arizona. The principle of government aid in irrigation and power development in the West had become firmly established.

In the same fashion that the progressives were trying to regulate natural resources scientifically, they undertook to legislate the nation into better health. Within the Department of Agriculture, Dr. Harvey Wiley had long agitated for the protection of consumers from danger-

even in the White House. "Tiddy was toying with a light breakfast, idly turning over the pages iv the new book," Mr. Dooley declared. "Suddenly he rose from th table, an crying: I'm pizened, began throwin sausages out iv th window."

Roosevelt was indeed horrified, and when a commission verified the descriptions in *The Jungle*, he sought reform. The result was two pieces of legislation passed in June, 1906. One was the Meat Inspection Act, which while fairly ineffective at first, over a period of time did much to bring about eradication of some animal diseases, especially tuberculosis. The other was the Pure Food and Drug

Act, which bore the impressive descriptive title, "An Act for preventing the manufacture, sale, or transportation of adulterated or misbranded or poisonous or deleterious foods, drugs, medicines, and liquors, and for regulating traffic therein, and for other purposes."

Taft and the Tariff

As early as 1904 Roosevelt had tentatively decided that his Secretary of War, Taft, should be his successor, for Taft and Secretary of State Elihu Root, an able, conservative corporation lawyer, were the two men closest to him in the official family.

Taft was known less for his background as a former federal judge than for his notable achievements as one of the first viceroys of the new American empire. Between 1900 and 1908, he traveled over 100,000 miles on assignment to Manila, Rome, Panama, Cuba, and within the United States. His achievements were almost all in the realm of colonial or foreign policy; he had little to do with Roosevelt's domestic policies, although privately he subscribed to almost every one of them. If he were to the right of Roosevelt, it was only by a hairline. The great distinction was that while he regarded Roosevelt's objectives as justifiable, he felt, as he commented in 1910, that Roosevelt "ought more often to have admitted the legal way of reaching the same ends." This typically turgid way of saying things was another marked contrast between Taft and Roosevelt.

In 1908 Roosevelt had no difficulty in securing the nomination of Taft. The well-greased, conservatively run Republican machinery followed Roosevelt's bidding and gathered the votes of the delegates: organization men, officeholders, and Southern Republicans.

Business moguls preferred the gingerly progressive Republican candidate to the more forthright William Jennings Bryan, running forlornly for a third time. Rocke-

CHIEF JUSTICE WILLIAM HOWARD TAFT IN THE 1920's. Taft always had one crowning ambition, not to be President, but to be Chief Justice. The son of a successful Cincinnati politician, he was at 23 an assistant prosecuting attorney, and at 34 a federal judge, dreaming of the Supreme Court; he was a methodical, distinguished legal thinker. As an administrator under McKinley and Roosevelt, he demonstrated equal ability. At the height of his career, Taft weighed about 350 pounds. He suffered from habitual caution and occasional procrastination, but these were primarily a result of his judicial turn of mind. After an unhappy Presidency, in 1921 he achieved his fondest dream and became Chief Justice. (NATIONAL ARCHIVES)

feller wired Taft congratulations on the nomination; Morgan remarked, "Good! good!" Carnegie sent a campaign contribution of $20,000. This did not mean that Taft had capitulated to Wall Street; indeed he was more careful about accepting corporate campaign contributions than Roosevelt had been in 1904.

Taft campaigned as the champion of smaller business interests. In his acceptance address he promised that he would

Democratic governors even though they gave their electoral votes to Taft. Republican progressives, pleased at the outcome, proclaimed, "Roosevelt has cut enough hay; Taft is the man to put it into the barn." Republican conservatives rejoiced that they were rid of the "mad messiah." The merchant John Wanamaker declared, "It will be such a comforting thing to have old times restored again."

Certainly Taft's intention was to load

"Revising the Tariff Downward (?)" (j. n. "ding" darling in the des moines *Register*)

perfect the machinery for restraining lawbreakers and at the same time interfere with legitimate business as little as possible. Most important, he appealed to small-business and middle-class concern over the rising cost of living by firmly promising a reduction in the tariff.

The election result was a foregone conclusion, a sweep for Taft. The electoral vote was 321 to 162, but there were portents of national unrest in the victory. Taft's lead over Bryan was only half the size of Roosevelt's plurality in 1904; several Western states shifted to Bryan, and several others in the Middle West elected

Roosevelt's hay into the barn, but it soon was drenched by violent political storms. Taft seemed incapable of negotiating with the Old Guard as had Roosevelt, without giving the impression that he had joined them. To the progressives this seemed betrayal.

The first of these betrayals in the eyes of progressives was the fiasco that occurred when Taft called Congress into special session to enact a lower tariff. "I believe the people are with me," he had written in January, 1909, "and before I get through I think I will have downed Cannon and Aldrich too." But having proclaimed a tariff crusade, he remained behind while Middle Westerners carried their lances into battle. They were not "free traders" like some Southern Democrats, but they did want to thwart thrusts by exposing them to foreign competition. The way to do this, they thought, was to lower rates substantially—the "Iowa idea," this was called. They thought the President was behind them, but he failed to send Congress a fighting message or to intervene with his patronage powers when Congressmen began to succumb to the blandishments of lobbyists or logrollers.

Over the votes of Midwest Republicans, the Payne-Aldrich tariff passed Congress, and was signed by Taft on August 5, 1909. He said it was not a perfect bill, but that it did represent "a sincere effort on the part of the Republican party to make a downward revision." Also it provided for a Tariff Commission which was to make scientific studies of rates—an appealing approach to some progressives, who felt that the tariff, like most problems, should be determined scientifically and taken out of politics.

Nevertheless, the Payne-Aldrich tariff seemed to favor Senator Aldrich's New England, at the expense of the rest of the rest of the country. On a swing around the country in the fall of 1909, Taft tried to defend the new tariff in a hastily prepared speech delivered in the heart of the area of resentment, Winona, Minnesota. One line from that speech made damaging headlines against the President. He said, "On the whole . . . the Payne bill is the best bill that the Republican party ever passed." The remainder of the trip through the Midwest, wrote a reporter, was "a polar dash through a world of ice."

In 1911 Taft further alienated Middle Westerners over the tariff issue when he took an economically liberal position. He submitted to the Senate a reciprocal trade agreement with Canada which in effect would bring the two countries into an economic union. Many eastern manufac-

turers, seeing larger Canadian markets for their goods, were enthusiastic, but the Middle Westerners, fearing a flood of competing Canadian farm products and raw materials, were bitterly hostile. La Follette proclaimed, "It singles out the farmer and forces free trade upon him, but it confers even greater benefits upon a few of the great combinations sheltered behind the high rates found in the Payne-Aldrich tariff." He and his cohorts formed a strange alliance with die-hard members of the Old Guard, but were defeated by Eastern Republicans and Southern free-trade Democrats. The Senate approved the reciprocity arrangement, 55 to 27. In Canada nationalistic voters, frightened by talk that this was the first step toward annexation by the United States, voted out the Liberal government that had negotiated the agreement, and thus killed reciprocity.

A Rift in Republican Ranks

Long since, the progressive Republicans of the Midwest had cut loose from Taft. They blamed him, unjustly, for their failure to oust Speaker Cannon in 1909. By 1910, without his blessing, they were strong enough to make a fight. Under the leadership of George W. Norris, on March 15, they breached Cannon's formidable parliamentary defences and opened a fierce debate which raged for nearly thirty hours. It ended with Cannon's removal from the Rules Committee, which henceforth was to be elected by the House. He remained as speaker, however, and the conservative Republicans continued to control committees. The immediate change was not great but it gave impetus to the progressive movement. Taft, who was doubtless sympathetic toward Norris, received none of the credit.

Meanwhile, through the sensational Ballinger-Pinchot controversy, Taft lost the sympathy of most of Theodore Roosevelt's following in the urban East and the

Far West. The root of the trouble was that Taft had replaced Roosevelt's Secretary of the Interior with a man who wished to distribute to private interests for development the natural resources in the public domain. The viewpoint of the new Secretary, Richard Ballinger, was dominant among businessmen of the West, who wished themselves to prosper and to see their region grow. But Taft had

ing Ballinger's rebuttal, publicly exonerated him. Immediately Roosevelt progressives throughout the country championed Pinchot as the defender of the national domain against the corrupt onslaught of big business. Pinchot, by going over the President's head directly to Congress, in effect forced Taft to discharge him for insubordination. A Congressional committee investigated, and since the Old Guard

---

THE PROMISE OF AMERICAN LIFE

"The political corruption, the unwise economic organization, and the legal support afforded to certain economic priviliges are all under existing conditions due to the malevolent social influence of individual and incorporated American wealth; and . . . these abuses, and the excessive 'money power' with which they are associated, have originated in the peculiar freedom which the American tradition and organization have granted to the individual. Up to a certain point that freedom has been and still is beneficial. Beyond that point it is not merely harmful; it is by way of being fatal. Efficient regulation there must be; and it must be regulation which will strike, not at the symptoms of the evil, but at its roots. The existing concentration of wealth and financial power in the hands of a few irresponsible men is the inevitable outcome of the chaotic individualism of our political and economic organization, while at the same time it is inimical to democracy, because it tends to erect political abuses and social inequalities into a system. The inference which follows may be disagreeable, but it is not to be escaped. In becoming responsible for the subordination of the individual to the demand of a dominant and constructive national purpose, the American state will in effect be making itself responsible for a morally and socially desirable distribution of wealth."—Herbert Croly, *The Promise of American Life* (New York: The Macmillan Co., 1909).

---

left in charge of the Forestry Service in the Department of Agriculture Roosevelt's ardent admirer, Gifford Pinchot of Pennsylvania, whose zeal, like that of most Eastern nature lovers and sportsmen, was to preserve the public domain unspoiled, as a part of the nation's heritage. A violent clash between these two men was almost inevitable.

The occasion was the spectacular charge that Ballinger was conniving to turn over valuable coal lands in Alaska to a Morgan-Guggenheim syndicate. Taft, accept-

dominated it, reported in favor of Ballinger. To the end, Taft stood by his Secretary of the Interior, whom he correctly considered to be an honorable man. But in refusing to dismiss Ballinger as an anti-conservationist, Taft drove a rift between himself and the Roosevelt following that was as wide and deep as that separating him from the La Follette supporters.

As early as the tariff fiasco in 1909 progressives had begun to looking to the African jungle for their next presidential candidate. In the middle of June, 1910, loaded with trophies from Africa and fresh impressions of reform from Europe, Roosevelt returned. Observers noted that his first hello was to Pinchot, and that he did not accept Taft's invitation to the White House. Indeed, he had already met Pinchot in Europe, bearing messages from progressives, and had come to the conclusion that Taft had "completely twisted around the policies I advocated and acted upon."

Although Roosevelt was furious with Taft for helping bring about the split in the party, he determined to do all he could to reunify it. He told reporters he was seeing all Republicans—"regulars and insurgents, party men and independents." But at Osawatomie, Kansas, on September 1, he delivered a speech which returned him to command of the progressives. At Osawatomie, he proclaimed the doctrines of the New Nationalism, emphasizing that social justice could be attained in the nation only through strengthening the power of the federal government so that the executive could be the "steward of public welfare." Men thinking primarily of property rights and personal profits "must now give way to the advocate of human welfare, who rightly maintains that every man holds his property subject to the general right of the community to regulate its use to whatever degree the public welfare may require it." Beyond these generalizations, in themselves so frightening to the Old Guard, Roosevelt enumerated his "square deal" program: graduated income and inheritance taxes, workmen's accident compensation, regulation of the labor of women and children, tariff revision, and firm regulation of corporations through a more powerful Bureau of Corporations and Interstate Commerce Commission. From the Mississippi westward, progressives were ready to acclaim him as the next presidential candidate, but among his right-wing enemies, Lodge warned him, he was regarded as "little short of a revolutionist."

Progressive Republicans of the Middle West hoped they could wrest the presidential nomination from Taft in 1912. In January, 1911, a group of them formed the National Progressive Republican League to work for the nomination of La Follette. But a great majority of the progressive Republicans continued to hope that Roosevelt could be persuaded to run.

With Roosevelt receptive, many of La Follette's supporters switched to him with indecent haste after La Follette on February 2, 1912, exhausted and worried, delivered a rambling repetitive talk. Roosevelt thus acquired new recruits, but he also won the undying hatred of La Follette and his loyal Middle Western progressive following. Nevertheless, in the primaries Roosevelt demonstrated that he was overwhelmingly the presidential choice of Republican voters.

Some politicians thought Roosevelt would win the nomination at the convention, but it would depend upon the seating of the delegates; more than a third of them were contested. The Republican National Committee, made up almost entirely of loyal Taft supporters, allowed Roosevelt only 19 out of 254 contested seats, and thus in advance counted him out of the nomination.

Roosevelt had come in person to the convention to direct his forces, and the night before it opened, he told a hysterically cheering throng of 5,000 that he would not be bound by the convention if it failed to seat his contested delegates. He concluded thunderously, "We stand at Armageddon, and we battle for the Lord." As good as his word, he bolted, leaving the conservatives in complete command at the Republican convention. With Roosevelt's onetime friend Elihu Root presiding, Warren G. Harding, one of the most regular of the regulars, mellifluously nominated Taft, who was chosen on the first ballot.

It was in a different atmosphere that the Progressive party came into existence. During the Republican convention, Roo-

ROBERT M. LA FOLLETTE CAMPAIGNING IN WISCONSIN. "Battling Bob" La Follette (1855–1925) in the 1880's was a Republican Congressman sufficiently regular to help prepare the McKinley tariff. Although he remained in the party during the 1890's, he began to champion reforms of a populist nature. In 1901, pledged to fight for a direct primary, tax reform, and railroad control, he was elected Governor of Wisconsin. His advice came from experts at the University of Wisconsin, his votes largely from a rural constituency. In 1905 he finally obtained a legislature that would enact his program. Although he had already been elected United States Senator, he remained governor until the end of the year when his proposals had become law. In Washington he advocated a similar national program, especially rigorous regulation of railroads. It brought him into conflict with both the Old Guard and President Roosevelt; he entitled a chapter of his autobiography, "Alone in the Senate." Roosevelt, La Follette wrote, "acted upon the maxim that half a loaf is better than no bread. I believe that half a loaf is fatal whenever it is accepted at the sacrifice of the basic principle sought to be attained." Although nationally La Follette was at times isolated in his advanced agrarian progressive position, in Wisconsin he and his sons commanded so loyal a following that they dominated the state politically for nearly forty years. (STATE HISTORICAL SOCIETY OF WISCONSIN)

sevelt agreed to its formation when Frank Munsey, the newspaper magnate, and George W. Perkins, of United States Steel and International Harvester, promised him financing. Roosevelt, agreeing publicly to run, remarked that he was as fit as a bull moose, giving the party a symbol as well as a name. When the Progressives met at Chicago in August to nominate Roosevelt formally, the conclave was far more symbolic of progressivism than of

ordinary American politics. Missing were La Follette and his following, five of seven governors who had signed a call for Roosevelt in January, and such notable Republican insurgents as Norris of Nebraska and William E. Borah of Idaho.

The convention was more like a camp meeting than the gatherings to which Roosevelt was accustomed. The delegates sang "Onward Christian Soldiers," and closed the convention with the "Doxology." Roosevelt seemed to a newspaper-man to appear bewildered as he acknowledged their almost fanatical, hymn-singing welcome, because "they were crusaders; he was not."

What was distinctive and different about Roosevelt's program was his willingness to accept big business, provided it should be regulated through a national industrial commission. At the same time a Federal Securities Commission would police stocks and bonds. In the program

litical minority, they almost certainly were nominating the next President. Bryan, who long had dominated the party, stood aside while four contenders battled for the nomination. They were Governor Woodrow Wilson of New Jersey, Speaker Champ Clark of Missouri, the right-wing Governor Judson Harmon of Ohio, and Representative Oscar W. Underwood, the champion of Southern conservatives and a low tariff. Wilson's spectacular reform achievements in New Jersey had

---

BACKGROUND OF PROGRESSIVE LEADERS

Alfred D. Chandler, Jr., has made a study of the social, political, and occupational backgrounds of 260 leaders of the Progressive party of 1912 —people who were national committeemen or state chairmen, or who gave time and money. He found 95 businessmen, 75 lawyers, 36 editors, 19 college professors, 7 authors, 6 professional social workers, and a scattering of men in several professions. Only one was a labor-union leader; there was not a single farmer, white-collar worker, or salaried manager for one of the new large-scale corporations. On the whole, Chandler observes, the Progressive leaders had retained an individualism free from the restraints of the new corporate institutionalism, and thus represented, "in spite of their thoroughly urban backgrounds, the ideas of the older, more rural America."—Elting E. Morison, ed., *The Letters of Theodore Roosevelt* (Cambridge: Harvard University Press, 1954), 8:1462–1465.

---

there was much to appeal to the progressives of the cities, whether reformers or businessmen, but little of interest to farmers, and much paternalism but no guarantee of collective bargaining for organized labor. In an effort to win disgruntled Southern businessmen away from the Democratic party, Roosevelt endorsed a lily-white (excluding Negroes) Progressive party for the South.

Woodrow Wilson Wins

Between the Progressive bolt of the Republican convention and their nomination of Roosevelt, the Democratic party met at Baltimore, exultant with the heady knowledge that, although they were a po-

early made him the favorite of Democratic progressives in Eastern cities, and he took a quick lead for the nomination as he crisscrossed the nation to make hundreds of inspiring speeches denouncing special privilege and heralding the new progressive order. Yet, in 1912, he emerged from the primaries and state conventions with only 248 delegates to Clark's 436. Underwood swept most of the South.

It was little short of a miracle that Clark, who had the rural Democrats and most of the bosses behind him, and who obtained more than a majority of the votes on ballot after ballot, nevertheless failed to win the nomination. The main reason for the miracle was that the Wil-

son and Underwood forces stood firm, blocking Clark's nomination while Wilson's managers negotiated deals with the machines and the Underwood following. To some slight extent it may have been due to Bryan, who fought for a progressive keynoter, and received the unequivocal endorsement of only Wilson.

A crusade requires a crusader, and this the Democrats obtained at last on the forty-sixth ballot when they nominated Wilson. This lean, lantern-jawed son of a Southern Presbyterian preacher looked as well as acted the part. His aspiration had always been to become a political leader, but when he had found the road rough as a beginning lawyer in Atlanta, he had taken a Ph.D. degree at Johns Hopkins, had become a Professor of Political Economy, and then served as president of Princeton University.

Both as president of Princeton and as governor of New Jersey, Wilson demonstrated the courageous strength and alarming weaknesses that would characterize his Presidency. Both times he fought through major reform programs, and then, through personality difficulties, lost control. He had the vision to inspire multitudes, but was dogmatic and distant with individuals. He could lecture an opposition in high moral terms, but his sense that he and he alone was absolutely right prevented him from stooping to necessary political negotiations.

Wilson had won the nomination without badly splitting the party. Backed by a progressive platform, he appeared before the electorate in armor at least as shiny as Roosevelt's. The distance between the positions of the Democratic party and the new Progressive party was not as great as campaign oratory made it out to be, just as personality more than principles separated Wilson from Roosevelt. Nevertheless, the differences in platform were significant in the campaign and in Wilson's future program as President.

Wilson's program, called the New Freedom, emerged as the campaign unfolded. His conversion to progressivism had come only two or three years before, and he had continued to cling to the state-rights position that the task of the federal government was the purely negative one of destroying privilege. Thus Wilson hoped to restore the good old days, which in reality had never existed, to re-create full opportunity for the small enterpriser. Roosevelt's New Nationalism, Wilson charged, would mean the federal licensing of the juggernauts of big business to crush the American people. In contrast, Wilson proclaimed his New Freedom as the fight for emancipation of the small businessman, the "man on the make." He proclaimed, "If America is not to have free enterprise, then she can have freedom of no sort whatever."

Wilson's appeal was greatest in the hinterland. He was able during the campaign to win over Bryan's rural and small-town following, with the same religious appeal, with the same excoriation of the Wall Street money trust, that the "Great Commoner" had always used. Some well-edu-

PRESIDENT WOODROW WILSON. [OPPOSITE] Born in the Valley of Virginia, brought up in Confederate Georgia and the South Carolina of Reconstruction, Wilson had matured in an atmosphere of romantic nostalgia for the lost cause, and Calvinistic fervor for what was right and moral. In his emotions he was deeply devoted to his kinfolk and fervently religious. As a professor at Princeton, Wilson's lectures, evoking images of the selfless founding fathers, inspired his students with a respect for an idyllic American past. His graceful writings were also more inspirational than analytical. Wilson drew his own intellectual strength from the Bible, and from the political essays of the English conservatives, especially Edmund Burke and Walter Bagehot. The British parliamentary system was his ideal, and as President he patterned himself more on Gladstone than on Jefferson. (NATIONAL ARCHIVES)

cated people who had always scorned Bryan as a fool came to worship Wilson as a saint.

Thus Wilson was able to hold Democratic progressives, while Roosevelt was able only to pull progressives out of the Republican party. As for Taft, after several sad speeches, so conservative that they might have been written by Aldrich,

sevelt, and only 8 for Taft. In popular votes, Wilson polled 6,293,000; Roosevelt, 4,120,000; and Taft, 3,485,000. Wilson had received less than 42 per cent of the popular vote, fewer votes than Bryan in any of his three campaigns, but, considering the combined Democratic and Bull Moose totals, an overwhelming progressive mandate.

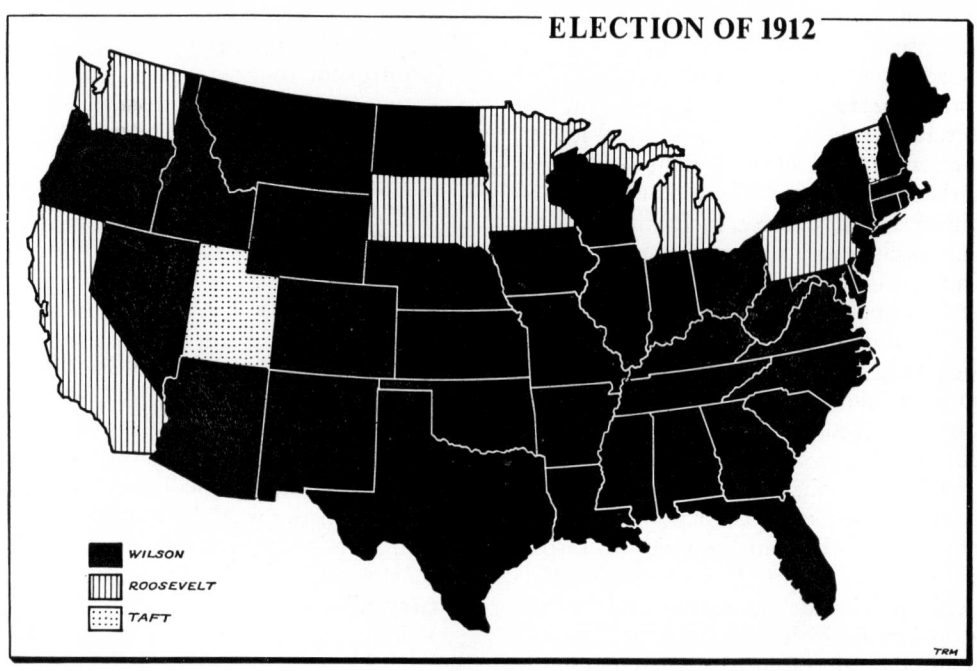

ELECTION OF 1912

WILSON
ROOSEVELT
TAFT

he lapsed into silence. The Socialists, at the peak of their strength that year under Eugene V. Debs, attacked the fundamental acceptance of the established order by all three major candidates. The main effect of the Socialists was to serve as a bugaboo for progressive leaders, who could warn that the only alternative to their safe, moderate programs would be the drastic remedies of Socialism. Even in 1912, their heyday, the Socialists attracted only 901,000 votes, 6 per cent of the total cast.

Because of the three-cornered contest, Wilson carried the electoral college overwhelmingly, with 435 votes to 88 for Roo-

Enacting the New Freedom

Few Presidents have taken more seriously their electoral mandate or worked more effectively to transform it into law than did Wilson. He brought back into the White House a strong belief in firm, positive presidential leadership.

The closest of Wilson's advisers was the shrewd and ubiquitous Colonel Edward M. House, who, through intelligent service and the refusal to accept a cabinet position, virtually shared presidential powers as Wilson's *alter ego* until 1919. He served as agent for Wilson in negotiations first with the men of economic power in America, and later with those of political power in Europe. His discretion and anonymity were so consummate that one contemporary remarked, "He can walk on dead leaves and make no more noise than a tiger."

The cabinet, as was politically necessary, represented the wide range of factions within the Democratic party. Bryan had to be offered the appointment as Secretary of State in recognition of his long leadership of the party. William Gibbs McAdoo, an energetic, ambitious New York entrepreneur from Georgia, became Secretary of the Treasury; Albert S. Burleson, an adroit Texan, as Postmaster General became the political expert in the cabinet. Representative William B. Wilson, earlier Secretary-Treasurer of the United Mine Workers, became the first Secretary of Labor, establishing a twenty-year precedent that the office should be filled by a labor leader. It was the most Southern cabinet since the Civil War; half of its members were Southerners, at least by birth.

Wilson promptly undertook what Roosevelt had avoided and Taft had failed to achieve—a substantial lowering of the tariff. On the day he took office he called a special session of Congress. When it met, he spectacularly broke a precedent in effect since Jefferson's administration and appeared before Congress in person. His short graphic message was aimed less at Congressmen than behind them, at their constituents. It brought to a blaze the sentiment for real tariff reform. With the President's active support, Underwood introduced a bill in the House providing for tariff cuts substantial enough to bring European manufacturers into competition with Americans.

To make up for the loss of revenue under the new tariff, Representative Cordell Hull drafted a section for the bill, providing under the new Sixteenth Amendment for a graduated income tax. Hull cautiously set the rates exceedingly low; to his delight, progressive Republicans and Democrats in the Senate forced upon the conservatives and the administration substantially higher rates. This first modern income tax imposed upon individuals and corporations a tax of 1 per cent on all income over $4,000, and an additional surtax of 1 per cent on income over $20,000, ranging up to a maximum of 6 per cent on income over $500,000. It was the beginning of a great change in the American tax structure. More slowly than England and some other nations, the United States was beginning to place upon those of large income a proportionately greater share of the cost of the government. In so doing, it was beginning to chip away at the enormous disparity in incomes in the United States.

Rather than lose momentum, President Wilson held Congress in session through the sweltering summer, to begin work on banking reform. In 1911 he had declared, "The great monopoly in this country is the money monopoly. So long as that exists, our old variety and freedom and individual energy of development are out of the question." A House investigating committee headed by a Democrat, Arsene Pujo, early in 1913 published frightening statistics to back Wilson's accusation. These figures, to which Louis D. Brandeis gave wide circulation in a series of articles entitled "Other People's Money," indicated that small banks were depositing their surpluses with larger ones, which in turn deposited with a few great investment bankers concentrated on Wall Street. These bankers with their enormous capital, representing the aggregate savings of millions of people, were able to demand control over corporations in return for granting them financing, "the life blood of business." The Morgan-Rockefeller empire held "in all, 341 directorships in 112 corporations having aggregate resources or capitalization of $22,245,000,000." This was in 1913, when the entire national wealth was estimated at less than ten times this figure.

To President Wilson, evidence like this

indicated a need to break the money trust. At the same time, paradoxically, one of the serious ills of the American banking system was its decentralization and independence, except through the loose tie of urban clearing houses. This, and the defective functioning of the national banking system, meant that in time of financial crisis and deflation, it was hard for banks to draw upon their reserves or to expand their currency. After the panic of 1907, Congress passed the Aldrich-Vree-

district. The Federal Reserve bank would rediscount their notes, issue a new type of paper currency, Federal Reserve notes, and fulfill other banking functions for member banks and the government. The Act required National Banks to become members, and encouraged other banks to do so. Although the American Bankers' Association had criticized the legislation, nearly half the nation's banking resources were represented in the system within its first year of operation, and four fifths by

---

THE CREDIT MONOPOLY

"Far more dangerous than all that has happened to us in the past in the way of elimination of competition in industry is the control of credit through the domination of these groups over our banks and industries. . . .

"Whether under a different currency system the resources in our banks would be greater or less is comparatively immaterial if they continued to be controlled by a small group. . . .

"If the arteries of credit now clogged well-nigh to choking by the obstructions created through the control of these groups are opened so that they may be permitted freely to play their important part in the financial system, competition in large enterprises will become possible and business can be conducted on its merits instead of being subject to the tribute and the good will of this handful of self-constituted trustees of the national prosperity."—Report of the Pujo Committee, February 28, 1913.

---

land act as a makeshift to permit greater expansion of the currency in time of economic distress. Aldrich recommended, through the National Monetary Commission in 1912, a broader base for currency and the establishment of a great central bankers' bank under bankers' control. To Wilson and the even more vehemently anti-Wall Street Bryan wing of the Democrats, this seemed to threaten a strengthening of the money trust. But Democrats and Republicans alike agreed that banking reform was needed; both parties had promised it in their platforms.

The Federal Reserve Act (1913) created twelve regional banks. Each was to serve and be owned by the banks of its

the late 1920's. Bankers had no cause to fear the Federal Reserve Board, which governed the system, and to which Wilson appointed conservative, sympathetic men.

The Federal Reserve system was a notable advance in banking regulation, providing as it did for a more elastic currency, essential at harvest time in agricultural areas, and in periods of crisis throughout the nation. It did not destroy the so-called money trust, but it did mark a significant start toward government control of credit in the United States.

There remained the problem of the trusts. As several antitrust bills began to move through Congress in 1914, Wilson followed the lead of Brandeis away from the rather negative court approach earlier envisaged in the New Freedom, toward the regulatory solution of the New Nationalism. He gave his strong support to a bill prohibiting unfair trade practices and establishing a Federal Trade Commission to prohibit unfair methods of competition such as price discrimination or exclusive dealing contracts. The Commission would police business through cease-and-desist orders, engaging in prevention as well as punishment. Thus Wilson intended to stop monopolistic practices at an early stage and protect legitimate business, small as well as large.

Simultaneously, Wilson lost interest in the Clayton Anti-Trust bill. Conservatives in Congress put qualifying clauses around the sections outlawing interlocking directorates or stockholdings and exclusive selling contracts, so that the clauses, as a progressive Republican Senator complained, did not have enough teeth to masticate milk toast. Labor, as the American Anti-Boycott Association reported with satisfaction, gained nothing of practical importance from the bill, which did, however, contain a platitude that labor was not a commodity and declared that unions were not conspiracies in restraint of trade. President Gompers of the A.F.L. chose to hail the Clayton Act as "Labor's Magna Carta," and insist that organized labor was now exempted from antitrust prosecution. This assumption served merely to make bitterness and resentment the greater when courts continued in the twenties to follow their earlier inclinations. The Sherman and Clayton Acts might be impotent against trusts, but they were a stout club for disciplining boycotters and strikers.

The debate over antitrust legislation during the first half of 1914 coincided with a deepening depression. This came because the United States, still a debtor nation easily affected by European money markets, suffered from credit restrictions growing out of European pessimism over the Balkan wars and the likelihood of a bigger war. Within this country, businessmen blamed the depression upon the Underwood Tariff, and the other legislation of the New Freedom. Wilson tried to placate business titans through friendly conferences and mild administration of his new reform legislation. He assured the leaders that he opposed only business that expanded "by methods which unrighteously crushed those who were smaller."

Through 1914 and 1915, to the disappointment of many advanced progressives, Wilson again and again applied the brakes to reforms. With a state-rights answer he turned aside the plea for woman suffrage. He condoned the actions of his Southern cabinet members when they introduced Jim Crow into the administration to an unprecedented degree. Only the angry protests of Northern liberals brought some reversal. He opposed a bill to establish federally backed land banks to ease credit to farmers, declaring it went beyond the proper scope of the government. He gave no aid to a child labor bill because he thought it unconstitutional. It was only with reluctance that he signed the La Follette Seamen's bill of 1915, the work of the eloquent president of the Seamen's Union, Andrew Furuseth, which freed seamen of the fetters of their contracts and improved safety regulations.

Beyond the New Freedom

For Wilson, the New Freedom might be complete, but not for the progressive Democrats in Congress. At times they expressed their sharp dismay, but they did not have to engage in warfare with him as the Republican insurgents had done with Taft. When the election year 1916 opened, two things were apparent. The Progressive party, which had never been much more than a Roosevelt vehicle, was disintegrating. Unless the Democrats, who were normally a minority, presented

STUCK ON THE LINCOLN HIGHWAY IN 1915. Many of the leaders in the movement for better roads could speak from personal experience. Henry B. Joy, president of the Lincoln Highway Association, and A. F. Bement, vice president, wished it made a transcontinental highway. On their way to the Panama-Pacific Exposition at San Francisco in 1915, they became marooned in this mud-hole on the Lincoln Highway in Nebraska. (BUREAU OF PUBLIC ROADS, DEPARTMENT OF COMMERCE)

a new, strong progressive program they would be swamped at the polls by the re-united Republicans. Wilson saw this reasoning and went beyond the New Freedom, allying himself with the progressives, farmers, and laborers, to accept a series of laws which in many respects enacted the Progressive party program of 1912. From a negative policy of restriction he moved to a positive one of vigorous Federal intervention in the economy and society. Strangely, this came at a time when Roosevelt had moved to the far right and no longer supported his 1912 proposals.

In January, 1916, Wilson appointed Brandeis to the Supreme Court, and weathered the conservative uproar to obtain his Senate confirmation. In May, he accepted a farm-loan bank system in the Federal Farm Loan Act. At the urging of progressives, he applied pressure upon the Democratic leaders in the Senate to obtain a workmen's compensation system for federal employees, and the first federal child-labor law. The child-labor law, the Keating-Owen Act of 1916, prohibited the shipment in interstate commerce of products manufactured by underage children. It marked not only a significant reversal on the part of Wilson but also a new assumption of federal control over manufacturing through the commerce clause. When the Supreme Court invalidated it in 1918 by a 5-to-4 decision, Congress passed an act levying a heavy tax on the products of child labor. This too President Wilson signed, and this too the Supreme Court ultimately invalidated, with Taft as Chief Justice writing the decision.

Despite the setback in the realm of child labor, this second wave of legislation of the Wilson administration significantly enlarged once more the regulatory function of the federal government. After Wilson had failed to mediate a dispute between the railroad brotherhoods and the railroads, he signed an emergency measure, the Adamson Act, to prevent a nationwide railroad strike that would have paralyzed commerce. The measure provided for an eight-hour day at the previous ten-hours' pay for all railroad workers.

Other less known pieces of legislation brought about even greater changes. Without attracting much attention, they undermined state rights by granting subsidies on a dollar-matching basis for states to undertake various types of programs. These laws, in combination with the new income tax, took money out of the wealthier northeastern areas and redistrib-ute it in the South and West. The first such law was the Smith-Lever Act of 1914, which provided money for states to establish extension work in agricultural education. This made formal and national the new system of county agents to advise farmers, and facilitated the rise of the powerful American Farm Bureau Federation. It was followed by the Smith-Hughes Act of 1917 which subsidized vocational courses in secondary schools. Most important of all, the Federal Highway Act of 1916 appropriated $75 million to be spent for road building over a period of five years.

Wilson was justified in his boast that the Democrats had come close to carrying out the platform of the Progressive party as well as their own. Like many of the fruits of the progressive spirit, some of the laws were limited and cautious in conception and application. Few people of the next generation would accept the exaggerated view of a New York Congressman who denounced one of the measures (the Adamson Act) as "the first step away from the old democracy of Thomas Jefferson and the federal policy of Alexander Hamilton to the socialism of Karl Marx."

BIBLIOGRAPHY

Henry Pringle's readable, highly critical *Theodore Roosevelt* (1931) has appeared also in a revised paperback edition. J. M. Blum, *The Republican Roosevelt* (1954), briefly and brilliantly revises upward the earlier estimates. Roosevelt himself is highly readable in his *Autobiography* (1913) and in Elting Morison and others (eds.), *The Letters of Theodore Roosevelt* (8 vols., 1951–4). Biographies of other leading political figures are: B. C. and Fola La Follette, *Robert M. La Follette* (2 vols., 1953); La Follette's *Autobiography* (1913); John A. Garraty, *Henry Cabot Lodge* (1953); C. G. Bowers, *Beveridge and the Progressive Era* (1932); P. C. Jessup, *Elihu Root* (2 vols., 1938); and the briefer Richard Leopold, *Elihu Root and the Conservative Tradition* (1954). Two newspapermen wrote especially fascinating autobiographies: *The Autobiography of Lincoln Steffens* (2 vols., 1931), and *The Autobiography of William Allen White* (1946). On trusts, see H. R. Seager and C. A. Gulick, Jr., *Trust and Corporation Problems* (1929), and H. B. Thorelli, *The Federal Antitrust Policy: Origination of an American Tradition*. On a key labor episode, see Robert J. Cornell, *The Anthracite Coal Strike of 1902* (1957). Allen, *The Great Pierpont Morgan* is a personal portrait of the dominant financier; and Elsie Glück, *John Mitchell, Miner* (1929), of a labor leader.

Henry Pringle, *William Howard Taft* (2 vols., 1939) is a full and sympathetic account. The Midwest insurgents are analyzed in Kenneth Hechler, *Insurgency: Personalities and Policies of the Taft Era* (1940), and Russell Nye, *Midwestern Progressive Politics* (1951). On the Ballinger-Pinchot controversy, see Alpheus T. Mason, *Bureaucracy Convicts Itself* (1941), and on the far-ranging activities of Brandeis, Mason's biography of him (1946). On the conservative opponents of the insurgents, see N. W. Stephenson, *Nelson W. Aldrich* (1930); W. R. Gwinn, *Uncle Joe Cannon* (1957); and Blair Bolles's journalistic account of Cannon, *Tyrant from Illinois* (1951). On the incipient Progressive revolt, George Mowry, *Theodore Roosevelt and the Progressive Movement* (1946) is essential.

A. S. Link, *The Road to the White House* (1947), covers Wilson's career to his inauguration, and *The New Freedom* (1956) reinterprets Wilson's domestic program. See also Link's *Woodrow Wilson and the Progressive Era, 1910–1917* (1954);

A. C. Walworth, *Woodrow Wilson* (2 vols., 1958); J. M. Blum, *Woodrow Wilson and the Politics of Morality* (1956); J. A. Garraty, *Wilson* (1956); H. C. F. Bell, *Woodrow Wilson and the People* (1945); William Diamond, *The Economic Thought of Woodrow Wilson* (1943); and J. M. Blum, *Joe Tumulty and the Wilson Era* (1951). Two biographies of Southern Democratic leaders are G. C. Osborn, *John Sharp Williams* (1943), and D. W. Grantham, Jr., *Hoke Smith and the Politics of the New South* (1958).

Contemporary expositions of Progressive ideology are Herbert Croly, *The Promise of American Life* (1909), and L. D. Brandeis, *Other People's Money* (1914).

Recent contributions are G. E. Mowry, *The Era of Theodore Roosevelt, 1900–1912* (1958), and S. P. Hays, *Conservatism and the Gospel of Efficiency: The Progressive Conservation Movement, 1890–1920* (1959).

30

PROGRESSIVISM
BY THE SWORD

While Americans clung to the old idea of keeping out of Europe's quarrels, the nation drifted toward the twentieth-century maelstrom of world conflict. The industrial and technical developments in Western countries had brought, along with increased material abundance, a heightened competition among the great powers for markets, sources of raw materials, places for investment—and sheer national prestige. To the industrial nations came not only social gains but also military ambitions, with an arms race that grew more and more frightening as Europe divided into two hostile alliances. As the foremost of all industrial nations, the United States could scarcely remain long unaffected by world events. Its emergence from the Spanish war with Caribbean and Pacific colonies heightened the risks of involvement. Certain phases of the progressive spirit itself led to unwonted activity in foreign affairs. Finally, the First World War brought the greatest challenge in a hundred years to the time-honored policy of neutrality and diplomatic independence.

T. R. and World Politics

One progressive who could see the risks, as he brought the United States into the dangerous business of power politics, was Theodore Roosevelt. As much as any other progressive, he liked to engage in moralizing about the position of the United States in the world. His most often repeated theme was, as he once put it: "The just war is a war for the integrity of high ideals. The only safe motto for the individual citizen of a democracy fit to play a great part in the world is service—service by work and help in peace, service through the high gallantry of entire indifference to life, if war comes on land."

This kind of talk rallied the support of many progressives, even those who were revolted by Roosevelt's blatant militarism —his equally incessant extolling of the soldierly virtues as "the most valuable of all qualities." Beyond and above all this talk, of infinitely more significance, was Roosevelt's realistic conduct of foreign policy as President. In this realm he was an even stronger President than in the domestic area.

Roosevelt's concept of the role of the United States in world politics emphasized sea power. Now that the United States had colonies, it needed to build a navy powerful enough to keep the sea lanes open to them. It also needed to build an Isthmian canal so that naval units could sail quickly from one ocean to another, and not have to make a lengthy and difficult transit around Cape Horn, as had the *Oregon* during the Spanish-American War. In addition it needed to protect the Caribbean approaches to the canal from encroachment. All this predicated a strong naval policy at a time when the key to strength in the world was a powerful fleet. It meant a navy second only to that of Great Britain.

These were the views of President Roosevelt at the time when Kaiser Wilhelm II was launching Germany upon a gigantic naval race with Great Britain. The German fleet laws of 1898 and 1900 committed Germany too to a navy second only to England's, and set forth plans for one that could even challenge England. As Britain in 1905 picked up the gauntlet by beginning construction on the first dreadnought, both Germany and the United States embarked upon an intense naval race, amidst increasing alarums of war.

Under the strong urging of President Roosevelt, who was himself the most effective of naval lobbyists, Congress between 1902 and 1905 voted for ten battleships and four armored cruisers. These were far stronger than the relatively light vessels of the nineties; they were no longer being built primarily to defend the American coastline. The two battleships authorized in 1905 were equal to the dreadnought in firepower and from 1906 through 1913 Congress authorized either one or two dreadnoughts each year.

Roosevelt liked to quote an African proverb, "Speak softly and carry a big stick." This certainly expressed his course of action in the Far East, as well as in the Caribbean.

He hoped to make the Open Door policy effective against Russian expansion in Manchuria. Although for a moment in 1903 he expressed such indignation over the "treachery" and "mendacity" of Russia that he toyed with the idea of going to "extremes" with her, his practical policy was sympathy toward Japanese efforts to check the Russian drive. When these efforts took the form of a Japanese surprise attack upon the Russian fleet at Port Arthur, Manchuria, in 1904, like most Americans he cheered. He warned the French and Germans against aiding Russia, but he did not wish to see the Japanese totally victorious in the war since this might "possibly mean a struggle between them and us in the future."

Roosevelt pursued this same policy in the peace negotiations. The Japanese, even after winning a series of spectacular victories, faced such serious financial difficulties that they asked Roosevelt to mediate. He agreed, but with a justifiable reluctance, for at Portsmouth in the summer of 1905 he brought down upon the United States the wrath of the Japanese public because he would not back Japanese demands for an enormous indemnity. The end result was ill-feeling in spite of Roosevelt's aid to Japan during the war and his acceptance at the conference of Japan's control over southern Manchuria and Korea, and its annexation from Russia of the southern half of Sakhalin Island.

Shortly before the Portsmouth conference opened, President Roosevelt dispatched Secretary of War Taft from Manila to Tokyo to reach a Far Eastern understanding with the Japanese. In the resulting Taft-Katsura executive agreement of July, 1905, the Japanese acknowledged American sovereignty in the Philippines, and the United States recognized the suzerainty of Japan over Korea.

Roosevelt's role in helping negotiate

THE PORTSMOUTH CONFERENCE. When the Russian and Japanese delegates to the Portsmouth peace conference met aboard the Presidential Yacht *Mayflower*, President Roosevelt was uncomfortably in the middle. So were the American people, whom the Japanese blamed for their failure to obtain a large indemnity from Russia. (UNDERWOOD)

the 1905 Treaty of Portsmouth won for him the Nobel Peace Prize. His actions did indeed contribute to preservation of the peace by retaining the power balance between Russia and Japan on the Asian mainland. But in Asian waters, Japan had risen to a new ascendancy through its destruction of the Russian fleets. It repaired and refloated many of the vessels, and in the following years built new ships rapidly. Japan undoubtedly had become powerful enough to seize the Philippines

(which Roosevelt came to regard as an Achilles heel) because the American fleet would have had trouble fighting effectively over such long distances. Unfortunately at this very time, the people of Japan and the United States became angry with each other.

Within a year after Japan's victory over a great European power, the San Francisco school board, in October, 1906, ordered the segregation of Oriental school children. This was the outcome of Californians' resentment over a trickle of 500 to 1,000 Japanese immigrants coming in each year, and their excitement over lurid "Yellow Peril" articles in the Hearst and other newspapers. Resentment in Japan flared high, and jingos in each country fanned the flames hotter.

Roosevelt worked skillfully to douse the flames. He persuaded San Francisco to desegregate its schools, and in return in 1907 he negotiated a new, more effective "gentlemen's agreement" with Japan to keep out agricultural laborers. Then, lest the Japanese government think he had acted through fear, he launched a spectacular naval demonstration. He sent sixteen battleships of the new navy, "the Great White Fleet," on an unprecedented 45,000-mile voyage around the world. It gave the navy invaluable experience in sailing in formation (and demonstrated a dangerous dependence upon foreign coaling vessels). Most important, the Japanese invited this formidable armada to visit Yokohama, and gave it a clamorous welcome. Thus Roosevelt came to feel that through brandishing the big stick he had helped the cause of peace.

For the moment, the United States had demonstrated sufficient naval strength to restore an unsteady balance in Asian waters. In 1908, before the fleet had returned home, Japan and the United States negotiated the comprehensive Root-Takahira Agreement. Both countries agreed to support the Open Door in China. The United States tacitly seemed to give Japan a free hand in Manchuria (where rivalry with Russia continued) in return for an explicit guarantee of the *status quo* in the Pacific. It was a precarious equilibrium, and might be destroyed by any future upset in the naval ratios.

At the same time that he was directly engaged in balancing the powers in the Pacific, Roosevelt was participating somewhat less directly in trying to maintain a balance in Europe. American relations with Great Britain were increasingly cor-

dial. In 1903, the British agreed to the establishment of an Alaskan boundary commission on terms highly favorable to the United States, and then voted on the tribunal against almost all the Canadian claims. After the settlement, the British pulled almost all of their fleet units out of the Caribbean, allowing it to become virtually an American lake. Toward Germany, Roosevelt was outwardly friendly, but had reservations because of German efforts to expand overseas.

When the European powers quarreled over Morocco, Roosevelt was reluctant to involve the United States. "We have other fish to fry," he told Taft in 1905. Nevertheless, he resolved to try "to keep matters on an even keel in Europe." Consequently he intervened on behalf of the Kaiser to persuade France and England to attend an international conference for establishing the status of Morocco. Germany was protesting because the French were excluding foreign economic interests there. Roosevelt insisted that a conference be held, to forestall the danger of war.

At the conference, which was held at Algeciras, Spain, the United States played a less decisive role, but did vote with the British and the French as they defeated the Germans at the conference table. This alignment boded ill for the next European crisis, but for the moment the United States had helped avert, or at least postpone, a war into which it might ultimately be dragged.

The Iron-Fisted Neighbor

Roosevelt's preoccupation with the American strategy of defense in the Caribbean—especially his almost obsessive fear of German penetration—betrayed him into becoming an iron-fisted neighbor toward small countries to the South. He first impetuously used his might to start work on a canal in Panama.

Even before Roosevelt became President, the McKinley administration was negotiating with England to remove an old obstacle, an 1850 treaty agreeing that the two countries would jointly construct a canal. In 1901 the British, eager to court American friendship, consented in the Hay-Pauncefote treaty to exclusive American construction—and fortification —of a canal.

The next question, over which serious trouble arose, was where to build the canal. There were two possible routes. The shortest canal would be across the Isthmus of Panama, but the rights there were owned by a French company that had taken over the assets of Ferdinand de Lesseps' earlier bankrupt enterprise. The French company wanted $109,000,000 for its franchise, which would make a Panama canal more expensive than a Nicaraguan one. Consequently a commission, Congress, and President Roosevelt all favored the Nicaraguan route. But the French company had expert agents in Philippe Bunau-Varilla, who had been chief engineer under de Lesseps, and William Nelson Cromwell, an attorney who had contributed heavily to the Republican campaign fund in 1900. Hastily they cut the price of their rights to $40,-000,000; unless sold to the United States and sold quickly, the rights would be worthless, for they would expire in 1904. This price cut—and able lobbying— caused Congress and the President to change their minds.

Impatient to begin digging the canal, Roosevelt put pressure upon Colombia, which owned Panama, to conclude a treaty authorizing the United States to dig a canal. In January, 1903, Secretary of State Hay signed one with the Colombian chargé d'affaires Tomás Herrán, which was most unfavorable to Colombia. It authorized the United States to construct a canal in return for a payment of only $10,000,000 and an annual rental of $250,000, as compared with the $40,-000,000 the French company was to receive. The Colombian Senate, as it had every right to do, rejected the treaty.

Roosevelt was too furious to give thought to niceties or to the value of a friendly policy toward Latin America. Fuming that the Colombians were "inefficient bandits," he considered seizing Panama through twisting a technicality in an 1846 treaty with Colombia (then New Granada) guaranteeing the neutrality and free transit of the Isthmus. Roosevelt's intended seizure became unnecessary, because Bunau-Varilla helped organize a Panamanian revolution. There had been many such revolutions, all failures. But at the outset of this one, the United States landed troops from the U.S.S. *Nashville*, and, invoking an old treaty obligation to maintain order, prevented Colombian troops from putting down the revolution. Three days later the United States recognized the new republic of Panama, and within a few days negotiated a treaty paying Panama the sum Colombia had rejected, in return for the grant of a zone ten miles wide. The minister from Panama who arranged the treaty was Bunau-Varilla.

Work on the canal proceeded smoothly and efficiently. The elimination of tropical diseases in the area, the digging of the tremendous cuts, and the installation of huge locks at a total cost of $375,000,-000 filled Americans with patriotic enthusiasm. The achievements demonstrated that the United States like other nations could undertake enormous projects in the tropics, and indeed succeed where the French had failed. The canal opened in 1914.

Amid the general self-laudation in the United States, some Americans were ashamed of Roosevelt's ruthlessness. He righteously asserted that his every action had been "in accordance with the highest, finest, and nicest standards of public and governmental ethics," but in 1911 could not resist boasting, "I took the Canal Zone and let Congress debate; and while the debate goes on the Canal does also."

Meanwhile he had to deal with Germany over the Venezuelan blockade. At the outset the blockade appeared to be typical European demonstration on behalf of bankers to force a dead-beat dictator to pay his country's debts. Such demonstrations always aimed at seizing the custom house in the principal port, since it was almost the sole source of rev-

could lead ultimately to the establishment of a base, took a firm position. He claimed later that he warned the German ambassador that Admiral Dewey had the fleet on maneuvers in the Caribbean, and that the United States would use force if Germany tried to acquire territory anywhere in the area.

THEODORE ROOSEVELT'S LATIN AMERICAN POLICY

"It cannot be too often and too emphatically asserted that the United States has not the slightest desire for territorial aggrandizement at the expense of any of its southern neighbors, and will not treat the Monroe Doctrine as an excuse for such aggrandizement on its part. . . . Moreover . . . we do not intend to permit the Monroe Doctrine to be used by any nation on this Continent as a shield to protect it from the consequences of its own misdeeds against foreign nations. . . . On the one hand, this country would certainly decline to go to war to prevent a foreign government from collecting a just debt; on the other hand, it is very inadvisable to permit any foreign power to take possession, even temporarily, of the custom houses of an American Republic in order to enforce the payment of its obligations; for such temporary occupation might turn into a permanent occupation. The only escape from these alternatives may at any time be that we must ourselves undertake to bring about some arrangement by which so much as possible of a just obligation shall be paid. . . . The justification for the United States taking this burden and incurring this responsibility is to be found in the fact that it is incompatible with international equity for the United States to refuse to allow other powers to take the only means at their disposal of satisfying the claims of their creditors and yet to refuse, itself, to take any such steps."—Annual Message to Congress, December 5, 1905.

---

enue of each of these governments. Roosevelt the year before had written a German friend, "If any South American State misbehaves toward any European country, let the European country spank it." But by January, 1903, the nominally Anglo-German-Italian intervention was overwhelmingly German; Americans were upset over the Germans' bombardment of a Venezuelan port and their apparent unwillingness to accept arbitration. At this point, Roosevelt, fearing that taking over a custom house to collect debts

The Germans wished no incident, and quickly agreed to arbitration. One result was that up into World War I, the Americans were even readier than before to suspect the Germans of plans to acquire a foothold in this or that area to the south. There was, in particular, a persistent fear that the Germans might try to acquire the Danish West Indies. In 1902 the Senate ratified a treaty for their purchase, but the Danish parliament rejected it. Finally in 1917 the United States acquired the poverty-stricken little islands, which were then renamed the Virgin Islands, for an exorbitant $25,000,-000. Their value was negative: the United States wanted to make sure they were not in the possession of any potentially hostile power.

The Venezuela incident led to a new Caribbean policy usually called the "Roosevelt corollary" to the Monroe Doctrine, although it was a broad departure from that historic dogma. The Hague Court declared that the powers that had attacked Venezuela had prior claim on payment of their debts; this increased the likelihood of European intervention in the future in the Western Hemisphere. For Roosevelt, who still believed that small nations must pay their just debts, the only way out seemed a drastic new device. If these little countries could not behave themselves, the United States reluctantly would police them and collect debt payments from them in order to forestall European intervention. In effect, Uncle Sam would act as a bill collector for European bankers. Roosevelt declared to the Congress in 1904 that the United States might be forced "however reluctantly, in flagrant cases of . . . wrongdoing or impotence, to the exercise of an international police power."

The occasion for putting the "Roosevelt corollary" into operation was the defaulting of Santo Domingo on about $22,000,000 of its debt to European nations. France and Italy threatened to intervene. In effect, the United States established a receivership, taking over Dominican customs, paying 45 per cent of the receipts to the Dominican government, and paying the rest to foreign creditors.

As a part of an American strategy of defense, Roosevelt's Caribbean policy was doubtless successful. As a means of securing the support and cooperation of nations to the south, it left much to be desired. Roosevelt's tactics inspired fear rather than friendship.

"HERE NO ONE DARES LAY A HAND BUT MYSELF." This is an Argentinian cartoonist's conception of T. R.'s interpretation of the Monroe Doctrine. (MAYOL IN BUENOS AIRES Caras y Caretas)

Taft and Dollar Diplomacy

President Taft was no readier in foreign affairs than at home to exert strong personal leadership as Roosevelt had done. For the most part he left the State Department to his Secretary of State, a former corporation lawyer, Philander C. Knox. Nor was Taft, despite his years of experience in the Philippines, successful in maintaining Roosevelt's foreign policies. He made no real effort to maintain a balance of power either in Europe or Asia. Rather he and Secretary Knox concentrated upon promoting American banking and business interests overseas during these years when capitalists were keenly interested in foreign expansion.

In Far Eastern relations, this policy brought to the forefront young Willard Straight, an agent of American bankers, formerly consul general at Mukden, Manchuria. He argued that dollar diplomacy was the financial expression of the Open Door policy, that it would make "a guaranty for the preservation, rather than the destruction of China's integrity." Taft, therefore, was ready to ignore Roosevelt's tacit arrangement with Japan, that the United States would stay out of Manchuria, and to support the right of Americans to invest both there and in China. When British, French, and German bankers formed a consortium to finance railroads in China, Secretary Knox insisted that Americans should also participate. In 1911 they were admitted. Next Secretary Knox proposed that an international syndicate purchase the South Manchurian Railroad in order to neutralize it. This led the rivals Russia and Japan to sign a treaty of amity in 1910, and jointly close the Manchurian door in Taft's face.

In the Caribbean there were no other great powers to block the amateurish American operations. As a result, a new pattern emerged there of interventions going far beyond Roosevelt's limited ones, to establish firm military, political, and, above all, economic control over several unstable republics to the South. It could be argued that American investors must be invited in and supported in order to supplant European investors who otherwise might in time bring about European control. This was a logical step beyond the Roosevelt corollary.

The new policy began in 1909 when Knox tried to arrange for American bankers to establish a financial receivership in Honduras; in 1910 he persuaded New York bankers to invest in the National Bank of Haiti. Then, in 1909, he sent marines to Nicaragua to protect revolutionaries, sponsored by an American mining company, who were fighting to overthrow a hostile dictator. Knox negotiated a treaty with the new friendly government giving the United States financial control, but the United States Senate failed to ratify it. American bankers, less reluctant, accepted Knox's invitation to

move in. By 1912 the new pro-American government was so unpopular that revolution against it broke out. Taft sent marines to crush the uprising, but the populace remained so anti-American that the United States continued to occupy the country into the Coolidge administration.

Even more than Roosevelt's policies, those of Taft tended to alienate America's neighbors to the south. The dollars reaped were far surpassed by the harvest of ill will.

Wilsonian Intervention

President Wilson brought to the determination of foreign policy a flair for idealistic pronouncements. He was never unsure of his moral position, but was often uncertain about the way to reach it. He and his Secretaries of State and the Navy, William Jennings Bryan and Josephus Daniels, were all three devoutly religious, war-hating men of goodwill, who profoundly disapproved of the exorbitant money-making sometimes connected with dollar diplomacy. But the temptation to make use of the force at their disposal to uplift their brothers to the south was too great to resist. The need to do so seemed compelling to them, because like their predecessors they felt that they must maintain an American-sponsored stability in the Caribbean as a vital part of national defense.

President Wilson expounded his new policies in a speech at Mobile, Alabama, in the fall of 1913; his remarks were aimed especially at Mexico, but encompassed the small republics as well. He utterly disavowed imperialist intent. "The United States will never again seek one additional foot of territory by conquest," he declared. Rather, he sought "the development of constitutional liberty in the world."

The Wilson administration not only regularized through treaty the continuing occupation of Nicaragua, but also initi-

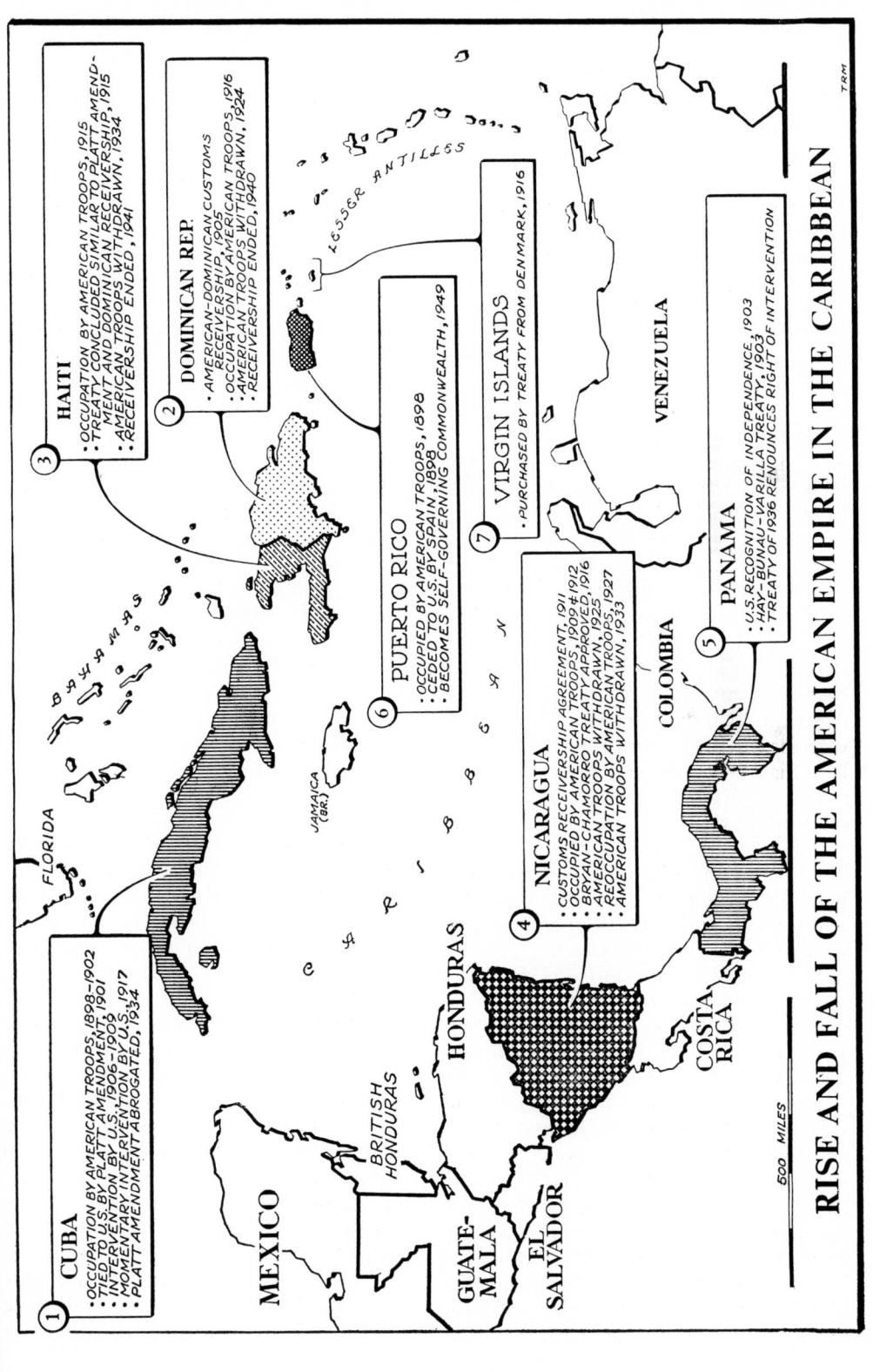

RISE AND FALL OF THE AMERICAN EMPIRE IN THE CARIBBEAN

① CUBA
- OCCUPATION BY AMERICAN TROOPS, 1898–1902
- TIED TO U.S. BY PLATT AMENDMENT, 1901
- INTERVENTION BY U.S., 1906–1909
- MOMENTARY INTERVENTION BY U.S., 1917
- PLATT AMENDMENT ABROGATED, 1934

③ HAITI
- OCCUPATION BY AMERICAN TROOPS, 1915
- TREATY CONCLUDED SIMILAR TO PLATT AMENDMENT AND DOMINICAN RECEIVERSHIP, 1915
- AMERICAN TROOPS WITHDRAWN, 1934
- RECEIVERSHIP ENDED, 1941

② DOMINICAN REP.
- AMERICAN–DOMINICAN CUSTOMS RECEIVERSHIP, 1905
- OCCUPATION BY AMERICAN TROOPS, 1916
- AMERICAN TROOPS WITHDRAWN, 1924
- RECEIVERSHIP ENDED, 1940

⑥ PUERTO RICO
- OCCUPIED BY AMERICAN TROOPS, 1898
- CEDED TO U.S. BY SPAIN, 1898
- BECOMES SELF-GOVERNING COMMONWEALTH, 1949

⑦ VIRGIN ISLANDS
- PURCHASED BY TREATY FROM DENMARK, 1916

④ NICARAGUA
- CUSTOMS RECEIVERSHIP AGREEMENT, 1911
- OCCUPIED BY AMERICAN TROOPS, 1909 & 1912
- BRYAN–CHAMORRO TREATY APPROVED, 1916
- AMERICAN TROOPS WITHDRAWN, 1925
- REOCCUPATION BY AMERICAN TROOPS, 1927
- AMERICAN TROOPS WITHDRAWN, 1933

⑤ PANAMA
- U.S. RECOGNITION OF INDEPENDENCE, 1903
- HAY–BUNAU-VARILLA TREATY, 1903
- TREATY OF 1936 RENOUNCES RIGHT OF INTERVENTION

MEXICO

BRITISH HONDURAS

GUATE-MALA

EL SALVADOR

HONDURAS

COSTA RICA

COLOMBIA

VENEZUELA

FLORIDA

BAHAMAS

JAMAICA (BR.)

LESSER ANTILLES

CARIBBEAN

500 MILES

TRM

ated new interventions into Santo Domingo and Haiti. In spite of American customs control, revolution after revolution had swept through and impoverished Santo Domingo. The United States took over all Dominican finances and the police force, but the Dominicans would not agree to a treaty establishing a virtual protectorate. In 1916 Wilson established a military government. During the eight years that it continued, the United States forcibly maintained order, trained a native constabulary, and promoted education, sanitation, and public works.

On the other end of the island of Hispaniola, the Negro republic of Haiti was even more revolution-wracked, the violence culminating in 1915 when a mob cut an unpopular president into small pieces. Wilson again sent in the marines, established another military government, and began the task of improving living conditions in Haiti. The marines demonstrated their efficiency in 1918 when they supervised an election to ratify a new American-sponsored constitution. The vote for it was 69,377 to 355. Nevertheless, that year they had to put down a serious revolt, in the process killing some hundreds of Haitians.

President Wilson's always idealistic but sometimes ill-informed program for bringing democracy and stability to southern neighbors ran into serious difficulties in Mexico.

American business interests had invested about a billion dollars in Mexico during the regime of a friendly dictator, Porfirio Díaz. They owned over half the oil, two thirds of the railroads, and three fourths of the mines and smelters. Popular though Díaz was in the United States, he came to be hated in Mexico because, while he encouraged foreigners to amass huge profits, he suppressed civil liberties and kept the masses in peonage. For the average Mexican, there was little of the progress toward democracy or economic security that President Wilson desired. In 1910 the aged Díaz was overthrown by

a democratic reform leader, who in turn was murdered by the reactionary Victoriano Huerta just before Wilson took office. Wilson turned a deaf ear to American investors who saw in Huerta an opportunity to return to the "good old days." Rather, he refused to recognize "the government of butchers."

Years of tedious complications followed. Wilson hoped that, by abandoning the traditional policy of the United States government since Jefferson's administration and refusing de facto recognition to Huerta's government, he could bring about its collapse and the development of constitutionalism in Mexico. He offered in June, 1913, to mediate between Huerta and the opposing Constitutionalists of Venustiano Carranza. Both sides refused.

For several months Wilson pursued a policy of "watchful waiting," but when Huerta in October, 1913, established a full military dictatorship, Wilson began to bring increasing pressure against him. First he persuaded the British (who were obtaining most of their naval oil from Mexico) to stop supporting Huerta. Next he offered to send American troops to the aid of Carranza, but again was rebuffed since all Carranza wanted was the right to buy arms in the United States. Wilson granted this in February, 1914, by revoking President Taft's arms embargo, but still the Carranzists did not win.

Wilson was in a difficult dilemma: he might have to choose between recognizing Huerta, stronger than ever, or intervening with armed force, which could mean war against all the Mexican factions. Off the coast of Mexico, the commanders of American fleet units, engaged in watchful waiting, became increasingly restless. The precipitate action of one of them gave Wilson a way out. In April, 1914, one of Huerta's officers arrested several sailors who had gone ashore at Tampico; a superior officer quickly released them and apologized. But the American admiral demanded in addition a twenty-one gun salute to the United States flag. At this Huerta balked. Wilson, deciding to back the admiral, sent all available warships to Mexican waters and asked Congress for authority to take drastic action. Then, anxious to prevent a German ship loaded with munitions from reaching Huerta's forces, Wilson, without waiting for Congress to act, ordered the Navy to seize Vera Cruz. It did so, on April 21 and 22, 1914, but not in the bloodless way that Wilson had anticipated. The Mexicans suffered 126 killed

general of Carranza's, Francisco ("Pancho") Villa, tried to overthrow him. In October, 1915, the United States gave de facto recognition to Carranza's government.

This new friendliness was distasteful to Villa, who was still roaming northern Mexico. He tried to bring about a war between the United States and Mexico by shooting sixteen Americans he seized from a train in January, 1916. When that failed, in March he raided Columbus, New Mexico, just across the border,

THE UNITED STATES IN MEXICO, 1913-1916

and 195 wounded; the Americans, 19 killed and 71 wounded.

At this difficult point, Argentina, Brazil, and Chile offered to mediate. With relief, Wilson accepted, and sent his delegates to confer with Huerta's at Niagara Falls, Canada, from May to July, 1914. As the negotiations went on and on, the Carranzists advanced on Mexico City, bringing finally in mid-July the result Wilson wished, the abdication of Huerta.

The coming into the presidency of Carranza should have ended the Mexican muddle; instead affairs entered a new, more protracted, and more serious phase. By September, 1914, civil war was again devastating Mexico, as a former

killing nineteen more Americans. Wilson retaliated by ordering a punitive expedition under Brigadier General John J. Pershing to hunt down Villa. Wilson tried not to offend Carranza, but as Villa drew the American forces 300 miles into Mexico, two skirmishes occurred with Mexican troops which almost led to war. Again the peace forces outweighed the jingoes in the United States, and again Wilson accepted compromise. Carranza suggested on July 4, 1916, the appointment of a Joint High Commission to consider the problem. It debated into January, 1917, when it broke up without establishing a basis for the withdrawal of American troops. By then the United

States was so close to war with Germany that it withdrew the troops nevertheless, and in March, 1917, gave de jure recognition to Carranza's government.

Nothing but trouble had come out of Wilson's long and muddled intervention in Mexico. His bad tactics had built up hostility among the Mexican people which did not dissipate for years.

In other respects President Wilson and his Secretary of State were slightly more successful in improving relations between the United States and Latin America. During 1913 and 1914 they negotiated a treaty with Colombia expressing "sincere regrets" for the Panama incident and paying an indemnity of $25 million. Roosevelt thundered that it was a "blackmail treaty," and his Republican friends in the Senate blocked it until after his death; finally, in 1921, Congress voted to pay the indemnity but omit the apology.

War in Europe

At the outset of his administration, Wilson was preoccupied with domestic reform. "It would be the irony of fate," he had remarked shortly before his inauguration, "if my administration had to deal chiefly with foreign affairs."

Bryan, before he took office as Secretary of State, suggested to Wilson a scheme for "cooling off" treaties with all the nations of the world. These would provide that disputes should go to permanent commissions for a one-year investigation before either party could strengthen its armaments or go to war. This proposal was in keeping with the progressive theory that war was unthinkable, and that all disputes could be settled through reasonable discussion. Bryan negotiated thirty such treaties with large nations and small.

The problem of the European balance gave Wilson at least slight concern early in 1914 when he authorized Colonel House to sail abroad in May to try to bring an end to the arms race. Within a few months, Europe became Wilson's greatest cause for anxiety, as fate directed his administration toward an overwhelming concern with foreign affairs.

Americans paid little attention to the minor alarms that followed the assassination of the Austrian Archduke in Sarajevo, Bosnia, at the end of June. Balkan crises were familiar and boring news; events in Mexico where Carranza was driving out Huerta seemed more sensational. Even when Austria-Hungary declared war on Serbia on July 28, Americans were not shocked, but the week that followed left them stunned. The declaration of war against Serbia triggered among the alliances a chain reaction of threats and counterthreats, commitments and countercommitments. It detonated an explosion no one seemed really to want, but no one seemed able to avoid. By August 5, England, France, and Russia were at war with Germany and Austria-Hungary. The explosion had blown to bits the comfortable, optimistic Europe that had seemed so safe and stable.

Bewildered Americans congratulated themselves that at least the explosion could not extend to their shores; the New World was still secure. A sizeable number, who were of German ancestry or had been educated in German universities, automatically saw the war as a valiant German struggle against the cruel despotism of Czarist Russia. But the vast majority had greater educational, economic, or sentimental ties with England and France, and were shocked by the German invasion of Belgium in defiance of a treaty. They were pro-Allied without being at all sure what the war was about. None of them in August, 1914, and few of them long thereafter, envisaged American entrance into the war. There was no clear call for an American democratic crusade.

With the outbreak of war in Europe, Wilson feared that Japan would take advantage of the preoccupation of the Western powers to expand in the Orient.

He reverted to a balance-of-power policy to try to stem the Japanese tide as much as possible. Japan declared war upon Germany and seized the German holdings on the Shantung peninsula of China; this the United States could not criticize. Next Japan at the beginning of 1915 tried to impose upon China a treaty embodying twenty-one demands that virtually would have changed it into a protectorate. At this point, the United States, with the aid of the British, brought such strong pressure to bear upon Japan that it abandoned the treaty.

could translate the ambiguous document into strong Chinese; soon they engaged in yet another intervention, into Siberia. The Secretary of State was satisfied because he felt he had protected China for at least the duration of the European war. For both nations, if they held to their policies, there was trouble ahead,

---

THE LANSING-ISHII AGREEMENT

November, 1917

"The Governments of the United States and Japan recognize that territorial propinquity creates special relations between countries, and consequently the Government of the United States recognizes that Japan has special interests in China, particularly in that part to which her possessions are contiguous.

"The territorial sovereignty of China, nevertheless, remains unimpaired, and the Government of the United States has every confidence in the repeated assurances of the Imperial Japanese Government that while geographical position gives Japan such special interests, they have no desire to discriminate against the trade of other nations or to disregard the commercial rights heretofore granted by China in treaties with other powers.

"The Governments of the United States and Japan deny that they have any purpose to infringe in any way the independence or territorial integrity of China, and they declare, furthermore, that they always adhere to the principle of the so-called 'open-door' or equal opportunity for commerce and industry in China.

"Moreover, they mutually declare that they are opposed to the acquisition by any government of any special rights or privileges that would affect the independence or territorial integrity of China, or that would deny to the subjects or citizens of any country the full enjoyment of equal opportunity in the commerce and industry of China."

In the Lansing-Ishii Agreement of November 2, 1917, the United States recognized that Japan had "special interests in China, particularly in the part to which her possessions are contiguous." The Japanese were pleased, because they since an Asian balance was difficult to maintain.

Defense of Neutral Rights

President Wilson distracted by the death of his wife, issued (1914) a conventional proclamation of neutrality and an appeal to the American people to be neutral in thought as well as deed. He too was rather pro-Allied in his thinking, but as late as 1916 referred to the war as "a drunken brawl in a public house."

The immediate problem for Wilson was domestic: to bolster the economy, which was staggering under the impact of war. As European nations sought to liquidate their investments in the United States, Wilson's aim necessitated closing the Stock Exchange to prevent panic, and discouraging loans to belligerents in order to preserve the gold reserve. (Secretary Bryan asserted such loans by banks would be unneutral.) Then war orders began to turn the panic into a boom.

Americans soon learned that the nation in control of the seas would countenance no neutral trade with the enemy. President Wilson acquiesced, though not without protests, as the British developed and tightened their system of control. The United States could have retaliated with an embargo, but this would have created serious economic distress among American farmers and it would have hurt industry. Besides, the basically pro-Allied sympathies of the administration and a great majority of the people made so drastic a step unthinkable. Hence, the United States accepted the British blockade of the Central Powers but was not so ready to accept a German counterblockade.

Blockade warfare became essential to the strategy of both the British and the Germans. The development of rapid-firing cannon and of machine guns made frontal assault prohibitively expensive, so that the war in Europe settled down into an exhausting trench warfare between the combatants. The counterpart on the high seas was the blockade. From the outset, Great Britain made use of her superior navy to wage economic warfare against Germany. Gradually she extended the contraband list and the controls so far that she even seized American vessels carrying foodstuffs to neutral countries, on the grounds that such vessels might release within these countries supplies that could go to Germany. Not only did the control over neutral trade become tight, but at some points Americans complained that the British were using their controls to benefit British firms at the expense of American business.

On the whole, the British blockade was not economically too onerous for the United States, since by early 1915 heavy war orders were arriving which more than filled the trade gap it had created. While trade with the Central Powers almost came to an end, that with the Allies jumped between 1914 and 1916 from $824,000,000 to $3,214,000,000—a staggering figure for that time. In March, 1915, the government relaxed its regulations to allow the Allies to float huge loans in the United States to finance their purchases. In effect the United States, embarking upon the greatest boom in its history, was becoming the great arsenal for the Allies.

This the Germans could not permit. During the first weeks of the war they imposed no blockades, but concentrated upon trying to win a decision in France. The German armies drove deep but were halted short of Paris in the Battle of the Marne in September, 1914. Although on the Russian front great armies continued to move back and forth for several years, in the west the war turned into the grinding attrition of trench combat along lines extending from the North Sea to Switzerland. As a relative stalemate developed along the western front, Germany turned toward the submarine as a possible means of breaking the British blockade. Submarines had the advantage of surprise, but were so vulnerable to attack by an armed ship that they could scarcely follow the accepted rules of international law. These rules called for visit-and-search of enemy merchantmen, and allowed sinking only if provision were made for the safety of passengers and crew. The sinking of merchant vessels without warning seemed to Americans to add a new and frightful dimension to warfare.

Beginning on February 4, 1915, this

THE "LUSITANIA" SAILING FROM NEW YORK CITY. On May 1, 1915, newspapers carried both the Cunard advertisement that the *Lusitania* was sailing that day and an unusual German warning: "Vessels flying the flag of Great Britain, or any of her allies, are liable to destruction . . . and . . . travelers sailing in the war zone on ships of Great Britain or her allies do so at their own risk." Passengers and crew discussed the announcement, but the *Lusitania* sailed on time, and by May 6 was proceeding along the coast of Ireland, much as in peacetime, at a slow pace and not zigzagging. The commander of the German submarine U-20, seeing a large ship, fired a torpedo. Almost immediately the ship listed so sharply that few lifeboats could be launched, then sank. As its bow went high in the air, the U-boat commander for the first time read on the ship the name *Lusitania*. (BROWN BROTHERS)

was what Germany set out to do. She announced that she would sink enemy vessels in a broad zone around the British Isles. This policy, the Germans explained, was in retaliation for the British food blockade, which they claimed would starve women and children in Germany. The United States on February 10 declared it would hold Germany to "strict accountability" for unlawful acts.

A serious crisis came when, on May 7, 1915, a submarine fired a torpedo without warning into the Cunard liner *Lusitania*. It went down in eighteen minutes, drowning 1,198 people, including 128 Americans. "An act of piracy," Theodore Roosevelt called it. A few days earlier, April 22, the Germans had launched against the Allied lines at Ypres a new weapon of frightfulness, poison gas. On

May 13 American newspapers carried lengthy excerpts from an official British report on almost unprintable alleged German atrocities in Belgium. Although it bore the respected name of the former Ambassador to the United States, Lord Bryce, the report contained fabrications. Few Americans questioned its authenticity, for by this time most people were ready to believe almost anything against Germany. Yet even in their revulsion they were not ready to fight.

Nevertheless, Wilson came close to the point of coercion in an exchange of notes with Germany. In his first note he virtually demanded that Germany end its submarine blockade. When the Germans sent an argumentative reply, he drafted a still stronger second note—so strong that the peace-minded Secretary Bryan resigned rather than put his signature on it. Wilson appointed the Counselor of the State Department, Robert Lansing, an expert in international law, to be the new Secretary. Lansing was ready to take an adamant position. Wilson had said, "There is such a thing as a man being too proud to fight," yet he was ready to risk war rather than surrender to Germany what he considered to be American maritime rights.

Office pledged that submarine commanders would observe rules of visit-and-search. The President had won a diplomatic victory, and relations with Germany became less tense during the eight months that followed.

Preparedness—or Pacifism?

With the outbreak of war, generals and admirals, who in peacetime attracted little

---

EXCERPT FROM THE SUSSEX NOTE

"If it is still the purpose of the Imperial Government to prosecute relentless and indiscriminate warfare against vessels of commerce by the use of submarines without regard to what the Government of the United States must consider the sacred and indisputable rules of international law and the universally recognized dictates of humanity, the Government of the United States is at last forced to the conclusion that there is but one course it can pursue. Unless the Imperial Government should now immediately declare and effect an abandonment of its present methods of submarine warfare against passenger and freight-carrying vessels, the Government of the United States can have no choice but to sever diplomatic relations with the German Empire altogether. This action the Government of the United States contemplates with the greatest reluctance but feels constrained to take in behalf of humanity and the rights of neutral nations."—Robert Lansing to Ambassador J. W. Gerard (to deliver to Germany), April 18, 1916.

New trouble developed in the early months of 1916 when the Allies began arming merchantmen and ordering them to attack submarines. On February 10, 1916, Germany gave notice that it would sink them without warning. Wilson reiterated his doctrine of "strict accountability," and on March 24, when the channel steamer *Sussex* was torpedoed, he threatened to break off diplomatic relations if Germany did not abandon its unrestricted submarine campaign. He made the threat at a time when Germany still lacked sufficient submarines to maintain a tight blockade and did not wish to bring the United States into the war. Consequently, on May 4, the German Foreign

attention, began to gather followings as they raised a hue and cry for increased defenses. President Wilson through his pacifist Secretary of the Navy, Daniels, was able rather effectively to muzzle the navy. Its demands for a huge fleet-building program and its warnings of the catastrophe that faced America if the British Grand Fleet collapsed appeared for the most part indirectly through friendly politicians and publicists.

Roosevelt's close friend, Major General Leonard Wood, who had just finished a term as Chief of Staff, was not so easy to silence. The Secretary of War, Lindley M. Garrison, was a zealous advocate of preparedness; several influential civilians like

Roosevelt constantly made the headlines with their warnings. Also, the army was much less ready than the navy to fight a major war. The establishment of the General Staff and other administrative reforms had come into effect in the Roosevelt administration, but the older officers were still antagonistic toward such changes. The quartermaster corps in 1913 was thinking about using trucks, but as yet not seriously testing them. The air force, consisting of seventeen planes, was part of the signal corps; its 1913 appropriation was $125,000. The Army numbered less than 80,000 men, a large part of whom were required to maintain the posts within the United States. The National Guard was somewhat larger, but was scarcely professional.

President Wilson opposed new armaments, and so did public opinion, until the crisis over submarine sinkings frightened the nations into preparedness. In November, 1915, the President proposed a long-range program which by 1925 would give the United States a navy second to none and would increase and reorganize the army to provide the nation with a reserve force of 400,000 men. This proposal touched off a hot debate in Congress and throughout the country. Old progressive-conservative lines in Congress disappeared and re-formed, as large numbers of those who had been agrarian progressives of the West and South rallied behind the House majority leader, Claude Kitchin of North Carolina, to block the army program. Throughout the country, the pleas of Bryan and peace organizations strongly appealed to farmers and workingmen. Wilson took the issue to the country in a series of speeches in January and early February, 1916, but the House would not budge.

Wilson had to compromise. He accepted the resignation of Secretary of War Garrison, and appointed in his place Newton D. Baker, an able Ohio Progressive who only a few weeks earlier had opposed preparedness. Ultimately Congress passed legislation providing for substantial increases in the army, the navy, and merchant shipping. The Merchant Marine Act of 1916 established the United States Shipping Board, which was empowered to own and operate vessels and regulate shipping.

Conservatives wished to finance the defense expenditures through bonds, but the administration proposed new, heavier taxes. Progressives denounced the tax proposals as falling too heavily upon the masses, and in Congress fought through a tax measure frankly aimed at making the wealthy, whom they blamed for preparedness demands, pay the bill. The new income and inheritance taxes of the Revenue Act of 1916 for the first time in American history levied heavily upon the rich.

In 1916 Democrats and Republicans fought the presidential campaign over the issue of foreign policy before a seriously divided people.

At the Democratic convention, the keynoter began citing Wilson's interchanges with Germany, and the crowd whooped with enthusiasm. "What did we do? What did we do?" it would chant, and the keynoter would proclaim, "We didn't go to war, we didn't go to war." Out of the convention came the direction for the campaign, and the slogan (which Wilson himself never used), "He kept us out of war." The Democrats went into the campaign far stronger than had been expected of a minority party battling against the reunited Republicans. Many of the ex-Bull Moosers, Republican farmers in the Midwest, and workers who had once voted for a full dinner pail now favored the Democrats. In part they did so because of Wilson's progressive domestic policy, but still more because of their hope that the President could continue to keep the country out of the war.

As for the Republicans, they persuaded Charles Evans Hughes, who had an impeccable progressive record, to resign from the Supreme Court and accept

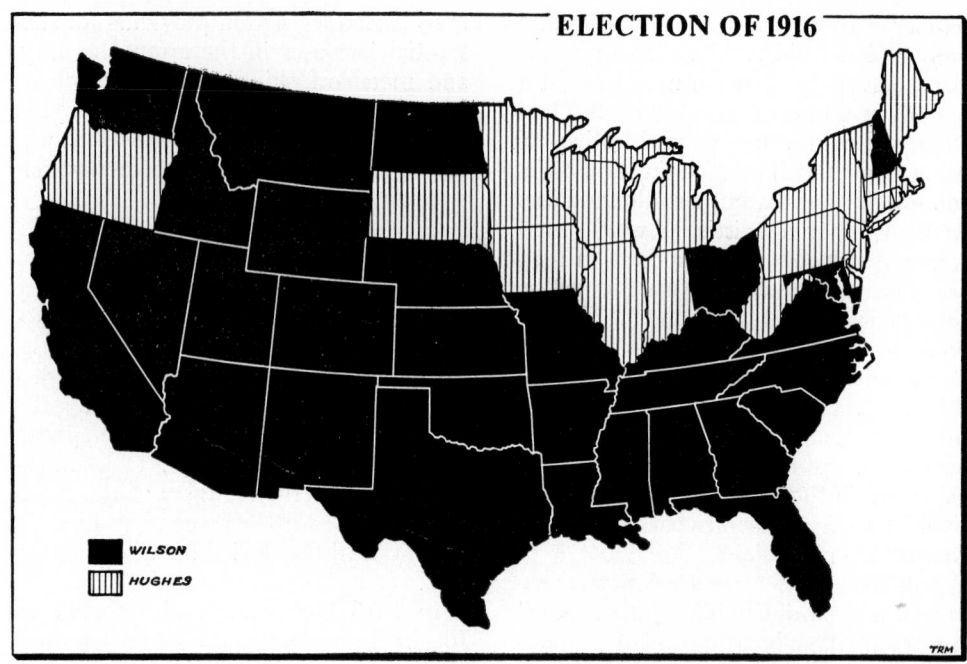

WILSON

HUGHES

the nomination. Primarily because of the whooping of Roosevelt and others on the sidelines, the Republicans gradually began to look like the war party. Hughes, under pressure from militant Republicans, wired Roosevelt congratulations on warlike speeches. This and Hughes's own remarks led voters to believe that he was more likely than Wilson to adopt a militant policy.

Wilson campaigned boldly on the progressive issues, and warned that a Republican victory would mean intervention in Mexico and war in Europe. The lure of progressivism and peace were still so irresistible in 1916 that the Democratic party, though normally a minority, squeezed through to victory. On election night, returns from the East were almost solidly for Hughes; he appeared elected. Then, as returns from the West came in, the picture began to change, though it was not until Friday that Wilson's election was certain. He had received 9,130,-000 votes to 8,538,000 for Hughes—three million more than he had gotten in 1912.

The Socialist vote had dropped 300,000. In the electoral college, Wilson had a majority of 23; the West and the South had re-elected him. The Democrats also retained a precarious control over both houses of Congress.

From Mediation to Intervention

So far as elections can be regarded as national plebiscites, Wilson had received a narrow mandate to continue along the path of progressivism and peace. Undoubtedly he intended to follow such a course.

Even before the war began, he had tried through Colonel House to bring an end to the armaments race. Since the outbreak of the war he had repeatedly sought means to bring the warring nations into a peace conference. But both sides had invested too heavily in the conflict, and were still too hopeful of realizing upon their investment, to feel able to talk of a negotiated peace.

Immediately after the election, in November, 1916, Wilson renewed negotiations looking toward a settlement. Germans, successful on the eastern front, for a while were encouraging. But the top German generals did not want any conference at all. The German attitude doomed Wilson's scheme. Nevertheless, on January 22, 1917, he spread his plan before the Senate, calling for a lasting peace that the American people would help maintain through a league of nations. It would be a peace with freedom of the seas, disarmament, national self-determination for subject peoples, and equality among nations. "Peace among equals"—a lasting peace—could come only through "peace without victory."

On January 9 the military leaders of Germany had decided upon one final cast of the iron dice. They had resolved to return to unrestricted submarine warfare even though it would bring the United States into the war. They hoped that they could crush France on land and starve Britain from the sea before America could make its weight felt. On January 31 the German Ambassador announced that beginning the following day submarines would sink all ships, enemy or neutral, in a broad zone around the British Isles.

President Wilson now faced a dilemma of his own making. He had in effect during the previous eighteen months drawn a narrow line—the right of American citizens and vessels to travel on the high seas in time of war—and threatened Germany with war if she transgressed it. How could Wilson take the United States into a war against Germany for such a limited end, and still bring about the sort of peace he wanted, a just peace among equals, a peace without the victor dictating to the vanquished?

The President found no ready answer in February and even into March. He immediately broke off diplomatic relations with Germany and waited for sinkings, but he still hoped for peace.

Gradually events carried Wilson toward war. On February 25 the British turned over to him an intercepted note from the German Foreign Secretary, Alfred Zimmerman, proposing that in the event of war, Mexico should attack the United States and receive in return her lost provinces north of the border. Americans were infuriated. At about the same time, the Russian revolution eliminated one of the moral problems in Wilson's mind by replacing a despotism among the Allies with a constitutional monarchy. (This government lasted only until November, 1917, when Lenin and the Communists came into power.) It seemed increasingly clear to Wilson—despite the horrors and losses of war, and the way in which it would bring brutality even at home and damage progressive reforms—that American participation would be worthwhile. He believed the German cause to be unrighteous, and had faith that if the United States sat at the conference table, it could bring about a just and lasting peace.

On March 18, 1917, news came that submarines had torpedoed three American ships. On March 20 the Cabinet unanimously advised the President to ask Congress for a declaration of war.

On the evening of April 2, 1917, President Wilson delivered his war message to Congress. He enumerated the German transgressions of American neutral rights, placed a strong emphasis upon these American rights, and declared: "It is a fearful thing to lead this great peaceful people into war, into the most terrible . . . of all wars. . . . But the right is more precious than peace, and we shall fight for the things which we have always carried nearest our hearts—for democracy, . . . for the rights and liberties of small nations, for a universal dominion of right by such a concert of free peoples as shall bring peace and safety to all nations and make the world itself at last free."

Four days later, Congress passed the war declaration and the President signed

SINKING OF THE TANKER "ILLINOIS." On the morning of March 18, 1917, the oil tanker *Illinois*—its name, the initials U.S.A., and a large American flag painted on its side—was steaming down the English channel in ballast, homeward bound for Port Arthur, Texas. A German submarine stopped it, firing a shot at it which destroyed the ship's radio. Six Germans came aboard, took down the American flag, wadded it, and threw it into their boat. They plundered the vessel, leaving little clothing for the crew, then sank it by exploding bombs in the oil compartments. The crew rowed safely in their lifeboats to Alderney Island. When the news arrived in the United States that the *Illinois* and two other ships had been sunk, unofficial government spokesmen asserted that virtually a state of war with Germany existed. "The sinkings were without legal and moral justification," declared the Philadelphia *Public Ledger*. "They were every one acts of war against the United States." (OFFICIAL U.S. NAVY PHOTO)

it. The American people had yet to learn what this would entail, and to realize the broad aims for which they were strug-

gling. No people had ever embarked upon a crusade more reluctantly.

BIBLIOGRAPHY

A readable brief interpretation is G. F. Kennan, *American Diplomacy, 1900–1950* (1951); a short, comprehensive survey is F. R. Dulles, *America's Rise to World Power, 1898–1954* (1954). A penetrating interpretation is H. K. Beale, *Theodore Roosevelt and the Rise of America to World Power* (1956).

On Panama, see Gerstle Mack, *The Land Divided: A History of the Panama Canal and Other Isthmian Canal Projects* (1944), and D. C. Miner, *The Fight for the Panama Route* (1940). On Caribbean policy, see W. H. Callcott, *The Caribbean Policy of the United States, 1890–1920* (1942), and Dexter Perkins, *The United States and the Caribbean* (1947). On Latin America, see S. F. Bemis, *The Latin American Policy of the United States* (1943).

On Great Britain, see C. S. Campbell, *Anglo-American Understanding, 1898–1903* (1957); L. M. Gelber, *The Rise of Anglo-American Friendship: A Study in World Politics, 1898–1906* (1938); and R. H. Heindel, *The American Impact on Great Britain, 1898–1914* (1940). On the Far East, see A. W. Griswold, *The Far Eastern Policy of the United States* (1938); P. J. Treat, *Diplomatic Relations between the United States and Japan, 1895–1905* (1938); T. A. Bailey, *Theodore Roosevelt and the Japanese-American Crises* (1934); E. H. Zabriskie, *American-Russian Rivalry in the Far East, 1895–1914* (1946); J. K. Fairbank, *The United States and China* (1958); and F. H. Harrington, *God, Mammon and the Japanese: Horace N. Allen and Korean-American Relations, 1884–1905* (1944).

On naval policy, see Harold and Margaret Sprout, *The Rise of American Naval Power, 1776–1918* (1942); G. T. Davis, *A Navy Second to None* (1940); Elting Morison, *Admiral Sims and the Modern American Navy* (1942); and William R. Braisted, *The United States Navy in the Pacific, 1897–1909* (1958).

On Wilson's leadership during World War I and his fight for a League of Nations, see A. S. Link, *Wilson the Diplomatist* (1957); E. H. Buehrig (ed.), *Wilson's Foreign Policy in Perspective* (1957); and A. P. Dudden (ed.), *Woodrow Wilson and the World of Today* (1957). On American entrance into World War I, a group of books popular in the 1930's emphasize the isolationist viewpoint: Walter Millis, *Road to War: America, 1914–1917* (1935); C. H. Grattan, *Why We Fought* (1929); E. M. Borchard and W. P. Lage, *Neutrality for the United States* (1937) and C. C. Tansill, *America Goes to War* (1938). A view more favorable to the intervention is Charles Seymour's in *American Diplomacy during the World War* (1934) and *American Neutrality, 1914–1917* (1935). E. R. May, *World War and American Isolation* (1959), also covers the British and Germans.

An interesting discussion of the issues is included in R. E. Osgood, *Ideals and Self-Interest in America's Foreign Relations* (1953). On propaganda, see H. C. Peterson, *Propaganda for War* (1939), and Armin Rappaport, *The British Press and Wilsonian Neutrality* (1950).

31

A RELUCTANT CRUSADE

Having entered the war with hesitation and with little idea of its meaning, the American government proceeded to mobilize economic resources on a grand scale, to launch massive campaigns against German submarines in the Atlantic and German armies in France, and to indoctrinate the American people for winning the war and supporting a durable peace. There was danger that the indoctrination might create conformity rather than understanding and might engender hatred rather than idealism. The outcome of the war would be determined by the course of thought as well as the course of battle.

Organizing for War

In 1917 and 1918 Americans came to accept Wilson's idealistic war aims, and some less idealistic ones of their own, too. Opposition or apathy changed to enthusiasm and even hysteria. The contribution the United States was obliged to make turned out to be a colossal one; clumsily at first, but steadily and impressively, the unprepared nation built a gigantic war machine. In the process it made almost revolutionary changes in the fabric of what had been progressive America.

Theodore Roosevelt, elderly and ill, still seemed to think in terms of the Spanish-American War; backed by a clique of Republican Senators, he fought for permission to take a volunteer division to the Western Front. Speaker Champ Clark was so incensed at the prospect of a draft that he asserted from the floor of the House during debate, "In the estimation of Missourians there is precious little difference between a conscript and a convict." For weeks the debate went on, but in the end Roosevelt was blocked, and the Selective Service Act was passed.

During the debate it had become clear what a large figure in both money and men the President must write into the blank check which Congress (and the American people) had signed. When a distinguished economist suggested that in the first year the nation would spend at least $10,000,000,000, it seemed incredible, for even in the three previous defense years, the government had spent an average of only $718,000,000. In April, British and French missions arrived and made clear for the first time their desperate need for money, men, and ships if they were to stave off imminent defeat. In London, Admiral John Jellicoe revealed to the United States Admiral William S. Sims that the Germans were sinking 900,000 tons of ships per month and would win unless these losses could be stopped, and stopped soon. Before long, army officers arriving in France discovered that the French army, bled almost beyond repair, was groggy and defeatist.

Massive measures were necessary at once if the Germans were not to win their gamble by starving out the British and knocking out the French. Without fully informing the public of the perils facing the Allies, the administration obtained the requisite legislation from Congress, and began moving rapidly. The Navy Department stripped the fleet of destroyers for antisubmarine duty; the War Department worked on plans for an American Expeditionary Force. Congress voted to the Treasury Department the necessary authorization to borrow $7 billion, of which $3 billion were to go as loans to the Allies.

During the preparedness period, in August, 1916, Congress had approved the establishment of a Council of National Defense, consisting of six cabinet members, and an Advisory Commission made up of representatives of industry, transportation, business, and labor. In the spring of 1917 they persuaded the armed forces to establish a Munitions Standard Board, shortly reorganized as the General Munitions Board, to supervise purchasing running into billions of dollars. Since this Board merely proliferated additional weak advisory committees, the Council, on July 8, 1917, established a new, more centralized War Industries Board to coordinate government purchases. It too lacked power at first, and its first two chairmen resigned in despair.

By the winter of 1917–18 the American economic mobilization seemed a failure. Wilson acted boldly by sending Congress

a bill to confer upon him almost unlimited economic power, the Overman Bill, which passed in April, 1918. Before Congress could act, he overhauled the War Industries Board, conferring upon it sweeping powers to coordinate industry, and appointing as chairman a Wall Street broker previously on the Board, Bernard Baruch.

Food was almost as vital as munitions for the Allies. At the suggestion of the Council for National Defense, a Food Administration was set up by the President. It was later authorized by Congress, after vigorous debate, in the Lever Act of August 10, 1917. Its administrator was one of the most spectacular civilian heroes of the war, an American mining engineer, Herbert Hoover, who had supervised the relief feeding of Belgium. His task was to increase food production, cut waste, substitute plentiful for scarce foods, and protect consumers from speculators. Hoover, in keeping with his experience in Belgium, wished to be an administrator, not a dictator, and to run his program as far as possible on a voluntary basis. To a remarkable degree he was able to enlist the patriotic support of the public in conserving food and observing meatless and wheatless days. One of his effective strategies was to distribute posters reading, "Food will win the war."

The shortage of wheat was especially critical because 1916 had been a bad crop year. Hoover encouraged wheat production by guaranteeing the purchase of the entire 1917 crop at $2.20 per bushel, a figure high enough to assure farmers a substantial profit. Wheat acreage jumped from 45 million in 1917 to 75 million in 1919, and the land produced bumper crops.

Hoover opposed retail price-fixing, which he thought would lead to black markets, but he did protect consumers from speculation. Food prices went up gradually.

The Lever Act which established the

Food Administration also authorized a Fuel Administration, which fixed the price of coal high enough to bring sub-marginal coal mines into operation and increase bituminous coal production by about 50 per cent. In spite of this in-crease, the fuel shortage became so acute that the Fuel Administration had to or-der a series of coal holidays for eastern industries in the early months of 1918.

In order to guarantee war production

Board licensed imports and exports in or-der to conserve shipping space, obtain supplies for the United States, and ham-per enemy trade.

Increased production and stringent economy within the United States would be of no avail unless supplies could be delivered to Europe. Into the winter of 1917–18, transportation difficulties plagued the nation. Railroads could not get raw materials to eastern factories or

---

"WAR WORK OF WOMEN IN COLLEGES"

"War courses, economy, the raising of relief funds, and Red Cross work [are] an index to the contribution of the college girl to the war. The pro-gram of war economy in most of the colleges calls for simplicity in social life. Banquets and expensive parties are tabooed. Vassar has abolished Junior Prom and Class Day and has adopted as one of her war mottoes: 'No frills and fripperies.' Half of the usual dances at the University of Colorado have been given up. . . .

"At least a third of the schools have reported not only an observance of the wheatless and meatless days but a willingness for more food saving on the part of the girls. The University of Arizona has six wheatless meals in addition to those on the regular wheatless day. Mount Holyoke girls. . . . voted in the spring to do without butter at dinner in order to devote the money saved to the Red Cross. . . . Grinnell College in Iowa has done away with the selling of sweets on the campus."—Committee on Public Information pamphlet, January, 1918.

---

in German-owned factories in this coun-try, especially those producing chemi-cals, these and all other German assets came under the custody of an Alien Prop-erty Custodian, A. Mitchell Palmer. The Trading-with-the-Enemy Act of October 12, 1917, provided for their seizure and administration. Palmer obtained addi-tional authority to sell German property, which he utilized especially to license dye and chemical patents to American indus-try. This was punitive toward the Ger-mans, immensely profitable for some American businessmen, and helpful for the development of a strong chemical industry in the United States. Under the same piece of legislation, a War Trade

munitions to ports, even through coop-eration with a voluntary Railroad War Board. On December 28, 1917, Wilson put the railroads under a Railroad Ad-ministration headed by Secretary of the Treasury McAdoo. He utilized expert railroad men to run the lines as one uni-fied system. Railroads could draw upon a half-billion dollar revolving fund for im-provements, and received rent equiva-lent to their average earnings in 1914–17. The transportation snarl was so effec-tively untangled that a freight-car short-age of 150,000 in 1917 was transformed into a surplus of 300,000 by the end of 1918.

Shipping was a still greater and more

continuing problem. By the summer of 1917, submarines had sunk nearly a quarter of the British merchant fleet; that of the United States was relatively small, and mainly committed to coastal trade. The Emergency Fleet Corporation under the Shipping Board eventually began to make remarkable progress in building new shipyards to turn out 1,700 ships of steel and 1,000 of wood.

vided five representatives for the board; the two chairmen represented the public. The War Labor Board would not countenance strikes or lockouts, but recognized the right of unions to organize and bargain collectively. It favored the eight-hour day, the establishment in any given area of the wages prevailing in it, the maintenance of a basic living standard for workers, and equal pay for women

---

LIBERTY BONDS

"Why should farmers buy Liberty Bonds?

"1. For Patriotic Reasons:

"Our country is at war with a merciless foe that years ago, before the European War started, wrote in his War Books that America was included in his program of world-wide conquest. To fight this foe requires men, money, and the help of every man, woman and child in the United States. . . .

"2. For Selfish Reasons:

"Your home and property are in danger. Most of your property is of a kind that is easily destroyed by raids. You have absolutely no guarantee against an invasion of America, except our armies. Let the Allied Army break down, and an invasion is a certainty. . . .

"I have $100; shall I buy a bond or shall I buy seed and fertilizer?

"By all means buy the seed and fertilizer, and borrow the money at the bank to buy the bond, paying for it when you harvest your crop. When you buy a bond in this way, you will have to pay a small cash payment down. . . . Then you can leave the bond at the bank and borrow the rest of the money, giving the bond as security."—Fourth Liberty Loan pamphlet.

The Aircraft Production Board failed to produce a promised 22,000 airplanes by July, 1918—a ridiculous figure, since neither side on the Western Front ever had as many as 2,500 planes at one time. The failure to fulfill this over-optimistic promise led to harsh criticism. By the time the armistice was signed, the United States had delivered in France 1,185 De Haviland bombers and 5,460 Liberty motors.

In April, 1918, President Wilson established the National War Labor Board, to serve as a sort of supreme court for labor disputes. Labor and industry each pro-

who did equal work. Like some other war agencies, it had to function through persuasion or use of the President's war powers.

President Gompers of the A.F.L. did much during the war to enhance the prestige of organized labor. He sat with industrialists on the Council of National Defense, and pledged to see that there would be no strikes, in return for recognition of unionism and wage increases. He also cooperated in the government onslaught against labor radicals, which meant the Industrial Workers of the World, who were engaging in sabotage

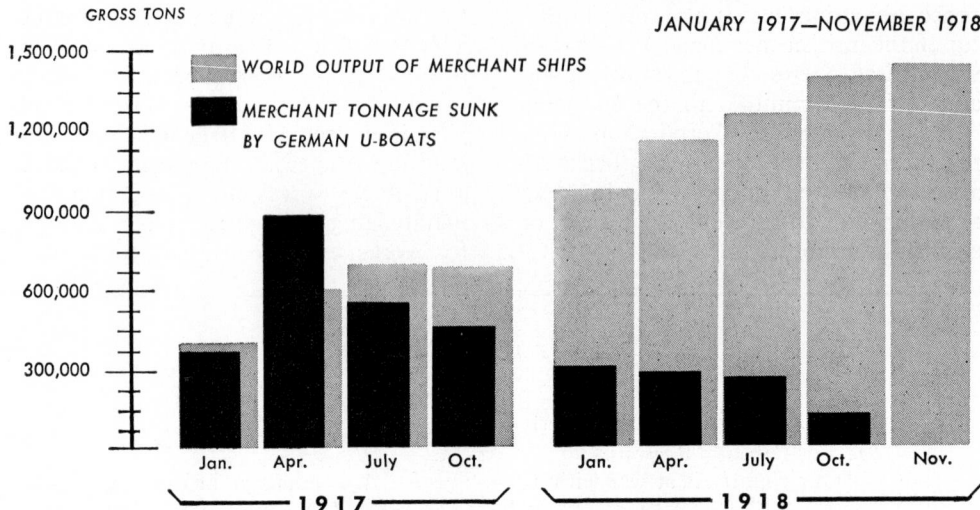

GROSS TONS

JANUARY 1917–NOVEMBER 1918

WORLD OUTPUT OF MERCHANT SHIPS

MERCHANT TONNAGE SUNK
BY GERMAN U-BOATS

1,500,000

1,200,000

900,000

600,000

300,000

Jan.   Apr.   July   Oct.   Jan.   Apr.   July   Oct.   Nov.

1917   1918

in the West. The I.W.W. almost disappeared, while membership in all unions jumped from 2,716,900 in 1914 to 3,104,600 in 1917 and 4,169,100 in 1919. Still, this was no more than one eighth of all wage earners.

One of the greatest of the tasks of the administration, financing the war, was the duty of Secretary of the Treasury William G. McAdoo. He faced firmly the problem of trying to raise as much of the staggering sum as possible through taxes rather than loans. J. P. Morgan wished to limit funds acquired through taxation to 20 per cent of the total to be raised, as in England; the Midwest progressives would have liked to obtain 100 per cent through taxes, in order to make the rich finance the war. McAdoo raised about one third of the $32 billion total through taxes, a ratio he felt was as high as possible without placing a heavy burden on the lower income groups. The War Revenue Act of 1917 imposed a great variety of excise taxes, and raised income taxes to an unprecedented peak, two thirds of a $2 million income. The 1918 law, which did not go into effect until after the war, raised the ceiling to 77 per cent. Altogether, the taxes on individual and corporate incomes, excess profits, and inheritances provided 74 per cent of the war tax revenues. There was one conspicuous loophole: many corporations distributed to their stockholders stock exempt from taxes, rather than giving them dividends.

Through his borrowing policy, McAdoo tried to keep the burden of the war from falling too heavily upon the poorer people. He sought to sell as many Liberty Bonds as possible to them so that they, not richer people, would reap the ultimate profit. The interest rates were lower than ever before, and except for the first series, provided more benefits for small holders. Despite McAdoo's efforts, those with moderate incomes (under $2,000 a year) probably purchased no more than 30 per cent of the $23 billion worth of bonds sold.

Altogether nearly 5,000 war agencies worked in countless areas. They brought an unprecedented degree of economic control and regimentation to American life.

Guarding the Bridge of Ships

For months after April, 1917, it seemed quite possible that the Allies would lose the war. The Germans had provoked American entrance by putting into action their calculated risk that they could knock out the French armies and starve out the British people before the United States could intervene decisively. They came close to making good on this risk.

The solution to the submarine problem came primarily through the establishment of convoys. The British admiralty had opposed such convoys, and kept

substantially. The British provided 70 per cent of the escorting ships and the French 3 per cent, compared with 27 per cent provided by the United States.

The American navy, after a slow start —in keeping with Wilson's policy of neutrality, it had not been on a war footing in April, 1917—grew enormously in size and efficiency. By the time the armis-

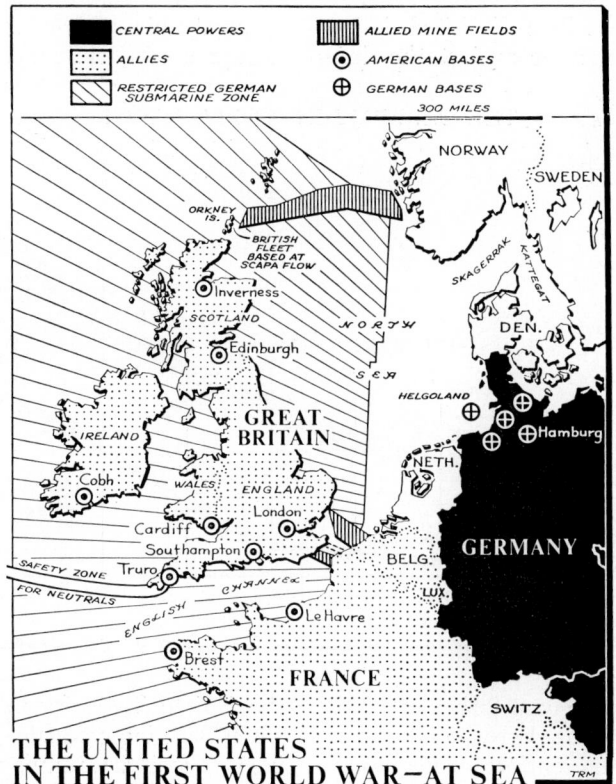

CENTRAL POWERS
ALLIES
RESTRICTED GERMAN SUBMARINE ZONE
ALLIED MINE FIELDS
AMERICAN BASES
GERMAN BASES
300 MILES

THE UNITED STATES IN THE FIRST WORLD WAR—AT SEA

most of its destroyers as a curtain to protect the Grand Fleet and the channel ferries. Eventually, however, United States Admiral William S. Sims broke down the resistance of the admiralty so that a convoying system was well established by August, 1917.

Sinkings, which had totalled nearly 900,000 tons in April, 1917, had dropped to 350,000 tons by December, 1917, and to only 112,000 tons by October, 1918. This was primarily a British achievement, but the United States contributed to it

tice was signed it had 200,000 men and 834 vessels engaged in convoying across the Atlantic or serving in European waters. It had grown in overall size to 533,-000 men and 2,000 ships. It performed great feats in moving men and supplies across the Atlantic.

The Margin of Victory in France

American strategic plans were drawn up after the country entered the war, and essentially these plans were concocted in

France at the headquarters of the commanding general of the American Expeditionary Force, John J. Pershing, a highly intelligent officer and a driving personality.

Pershing's goal was to build an American force in France numbering a million men by June 1, 1918. Many an obstacle stood between him and his objective, as he came to realize after he arrived in Paris on June 14, 1917. The dispirited Allies stood on the defensive against the des-

After a few months the serious need for American troops overweighed these misgivings. In the fall of 1917 the Germans in effect knocked the Russians out of the war; in November, Lenin and his followers in Russia overthrew the constitutional government of Kerensky and opened peace negotiations. With the Austrians, the Germans delivered a near-fatal blow to the Italians at Caporetto. The stunned Allies for the first time organized a Supreme War Council and looked to

THE U.S. ARMY IN WORLD WAR I

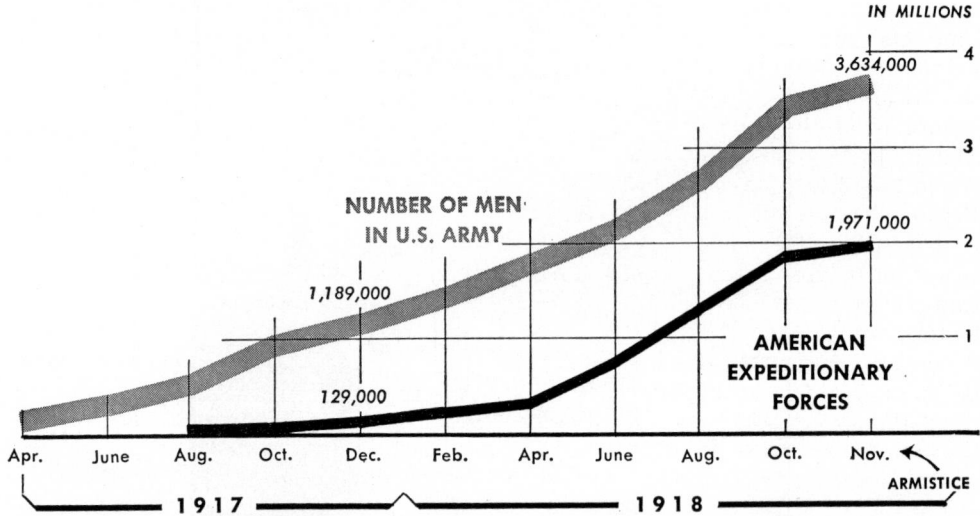

perately aggressive enemy; they wanted fresh American troops, but wanted to use them piecemeal as reinforcements along their own weary lines. They did not like Pershing's insistence that the Americans should operate as a separate army along their own sectors; they had no reason to trust the untried American soldiers or their leadership. In truth, there had been nothing in American military activities during the Spanish-American war and the Mexican intervention to warrant confidence. But General Pershing stood firm, with President Wilson behind him, and consequently the Allies were reluctant to find ships for the A.E.F. and its mountains of supplies.

the United States for manpower. Meanwhile Pershing gradually had been building port facilities, running railroads across France, and constructing training camps and supply dumps. As a trickle of troops began to arrive, he tried to give them three months' training before putting them into combat. While the number was small, he was willing to brigade his units temporarily among the Allies to give them experience and meet emergencies. Thus the First Division went into action with the French in Lorraine in October, 1917, and took over a quiet sector of its own near Toul in January, 1918.

In the early months of 1918 Germany moved troops from the east and slammed them against the Allies in a series of great offensives designed to end the war before the Americans had arrived in numbers. In March, 1918, the Germans smashed through the British and French lines where they met in the Somme, and thus made a gain of thirty miles. They launched a second mighty blow in Flanders in April. The Allies were staggered, but managed to stabilize their lines, and for the first time appointed a Commander in Chief for all their armies, General Ferdinand Foch. They asked the United States to supply as many soldiers as possible in the shortest possible time. Out of fear of defeat, the British found the transports for the troops, and the trickle turned into a flood. At the beginning of the German offensives in March, there were fewer than 300,000 American soldiers in France; by July 1 Pershing had his million. This meant that by late spring, the fresh American manpower for the first time could be a significant factor, since both the Allied and German armies were low on reserves. The Americans distinguished themselves in battle on May 28, 1918, when they captured the strategic town of Cantigny in the Somme sector and held it against several German counterattacks.

The Germans had just mounted a final giant offensive through rough hills, across one river valley, and on to the next, until on May 30 they crossed the Marne River at Château-Thierry and threatened Paris fifty miles away. American and French troops, under French command, fought to blunt the German drive. After a week of bitter attack, the Americans recaptured Belleau Wood, and thus helped stabilize the line. A little further south at Reims, in the great bulge toward Paris, the Germans tried on July 15, the morning after Bastille Day, to crash through the French lines. Some 85,000 American troops helped repel the German thrust. By July 18, the German offensive was over; and the Allies began a counteroffensive, with American divisions partic-

ipating, to liquidate the Marne salient (outward prejection in the battle line). By August 6 it was gone.

In the months that followed, as American troops disembarked at a rate averaging 263,000 per month, the reinvigorated Allies pressed the exhausted Germans from Lorraine to the North Sea. On August 10 Pershing for the first time launched an offensive under his own command. He directed the First Army, consisting of 550,000 American troops, against the St. Mihiel salient protruding south of Verdun. Within 36 hours the drive succeeded. Pershing would have liked to push on through rugged terrain against the vital German fortress of Metz, but Foch wanted the First Army to attack instead north of Verdun in the Meuse-Argonne area.

The American assault along a twenty-four mile front in the Argonne forest began on September 26, 1918, as part of a grand offensive along two hundred miles of the front. The terrain was as difficult as that protecting Metz. The offensive bogged down, had to be reorganized, then continued for a total of forty-seven days. The American troops fought through what Pershing has described as a "vast network of uncut barbwire, the deep ravines, dense woods, myriads of shell craters, and a heavy fog." The Allied high command had not imagined the Americans could make much progress against these obstacles, but after October 4 the regrouped army again advanced. By the end of the month it had overrun almost all of the enemy's fixed positions, was beyond the Argonne forest, and was driving toward vital German communications. On November 7 the Americans established bridgeheads across the Meuse River, planted their guns looking down on the famous fortress of Sedan, and cut the railroad which carried German supplies to the front. It had been the greatest battle in which American troops had ever fought. The 1,200,-000 soldiers had used a greater weight of

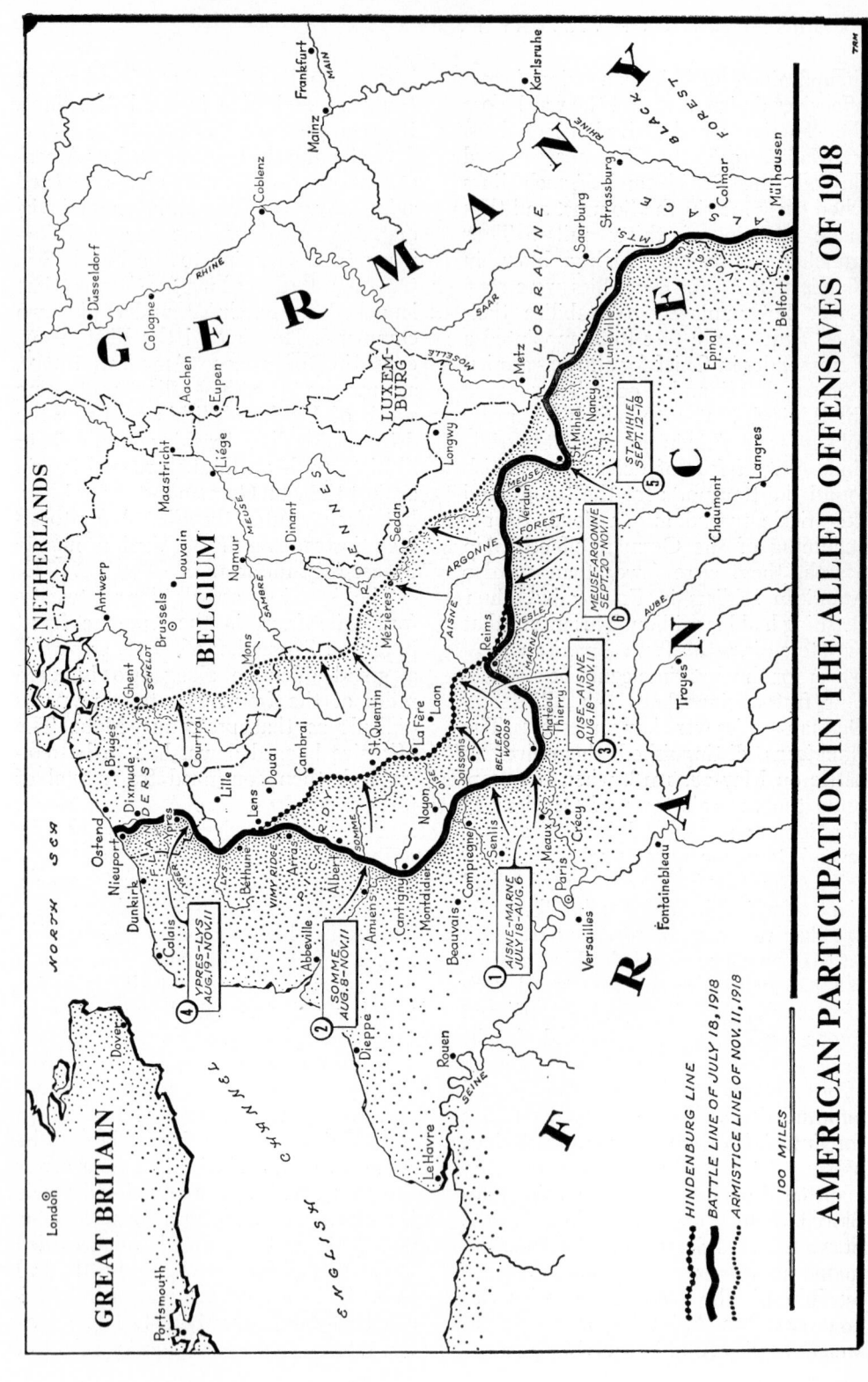

AMERICAN PARTICIPATION IN THE ALLIED OFFENSIVES OF 1918

SOMME,
AUG.8-NOV.11 ②

YPRES-LYS
AUG.19-NOV.11 ④

AISNE-MARNE
JULY 18-AUG.6 ①

OISE-AISNE
AUG.18-NOV.11 ③

ST. MIHIEL
SEPT.12-16 ⑤

MEUSE-ARGONNE
SEPT.20-NOV.11 ⑥

•••••• HINDENBURG LINE
━━━━━ BATTLE LINE OF JULY 18, 1918
••••••• ARMISTICE LINE OF NOV. 11, 1918

100 MILES

GUN CREW OF THE 23RD INFANTRY FIRING A 37MM. GUN DURING AN AD-VANCE AGAINST GERMAN ENTRENCHED POSITIONS. Norman Roberts of Alexandria, Virginia, on September 12, 1918, during the St. Mihiel drive, described an advance in his diary: "Bullets, millions of them, flying like rain drops. Rockets and flares in all directions. Shrapnel bursting the air and sending down its deadly iron. . . . Every minute looking for the next to be gone to the great beyond. A mad dash for 50 feet and then look for cover. A stop for a minute and then the barrage would lift to a farther point and then another mad rush. Always leaving some of your comrades cold in the face of death. . . . The field of dead a terrible sight. Both Americans and German. A day never to be forgotten."—William Matthews and Dixon Wecter, *Our Soldiers Speak, 1776–1918.* (Boston: Little, Brown & Co., 1943). (NATIONAL ARCHIVES)

ammunition than had all of the Union forces through the four years of the Civil War.

Other American divisions had been deployed at the same time on other sectors of the front. Altogether Americans participated in thirteen major operations, of which only two were under Pershing's command. By early November, the weight of American troops was becoming irresistible; two million of them were serving in France.

All along the front, millions of Allied troops had pushed back the Germans. The German reserves were gone, their regiments weakened, and their communications threatened. Invasion of their country, which the Germans could ill repel, was imminent. For weeks they negotiated for an armistice—a temporary ces-

Captain Edward V. Rickenbacker (center) and Other Pilots of the 94th Pursuit Squadron. The "Hat-in-the-Ring" squadron, as it was popularly known, was the first American-trained squadron to engage in combat. It began operations on April 3, 1918. The overall record of the Americans, who engaged for the most part in individual combat against German aviators flying the superior Fokker planes, was not impressive. At the armistice they constituted only 10 per cent of the Allied airpower. Individually they were brave to the point of foolhardiness—they refused to wear parachutes. The exploits of the seventy-one American aces (those who shot down five or more enemy airplanes) were followed eagerly at home by newspaper readers hungry for heroes. Captain Rickenbacker, who shot down at least twenty-six German planes, became more famous than most generals. (NATIONAL ARCHIVES)

sation in the fighting. Pershing was convinced that the Allies should demand surrender instead; he would have liked to push his armies on toward Berlin to make the Germans really feel the war. The day after the Americans reached Sedan, German envoys crossed the lines to meet Foch and receive armistice terms from him—terms so stiff that a resumption of hostilities would be impossible. The Germans accepted, and on November 11, 1918, the armistice went into effect.

Rejoicing Americans were ready to credit their armies with winning the decisive battles, and in subsequent years felt they had won the war for the Allies. Beyond question they had supplied the margin of victory. During the frightful March offensives, the Germans had outmanned the Allies by 300,000 soldiers; by June, arriving Americans troops tipped the balance toward the Allies; by the time of the armistice the Allied lead was a decisive 600,000 men. Further, the raw American troops had made up for their ignorance with their vigor, valor, and quickness to learn. On the other hand, the really crushing burden of the war had not fallen upon them or the American people. They had fought bitterly, but only for a few months. The United States lost 112,000 men from enemy action or disease; 237,000 more were wounded. By comparison 1,385,000 French died, and

900,000 British. Only 7 per cent of the Americans in the services were casualties, compared with 73 per cent of the French, and 36 per cent of those from the British Empire.

Molding Minds for War and Peace

Ever since the hesitant entrance into the war, both official agencies and private publicists and organizations, from President Wilson and the Committee on Public Information to the yellow press, had sought to mold the minds of Americans. In conflicting ways they had tried to explain the significance of the war, encourage Americans in its vigorous pursuit, and prepare them for the peace to follow. As is all too easy in such circumstances, Americans had learned readily to hate the Germans and all those at home whom they might consider German sympathizers, but had prepared themselves less well to assume a commanding role in maintaining a just peace in the postwar world. This in the end was to be the tragedy of President Wilson, of the American people, and consequently of all mankind.

Even before America entered the war, President Wilson had begun his idealistic series of addresses outlining the nature of the postwar world he wished to see emerge. He had talked then of "peace without victory," and about the right of the several submerged nationalities in Europe to organize governments of their own choosing. He had asserted too that the American people would be willing to join a postwar League of Nations. Many Americans of goodwill, like the members of the League to Enforce Peace, had thrilled to Wilson's words. But his speeches had remained merely words, since Wilson had not bound the Allies to his conditions as a basis for American intervention. In fact, until his war message he had not even expounded them to the American people as grounds for American entrance. He had instead placed the entrance of the United States upon the negative basis of German violations of American maritime rights, and he seemed to perpetuate this distinction between the United States and the Allies through the fiction that we were fighting Germany separately as an "associated power."

After American entrance Wilson had discovered that the Allies had made secret treaties among themselves. These were treaties buying the intervention of several nations neutral at the beginning of the war, and agreements designed to avoid postwar friction. Only the Anglo-Japanese agreement affected Germany, the sole power with which the United States was at war. The new Bolshevik government of Russia publicized some of the treaties; their terms seemed to run counter to the idealism for which Wilson was exhorting Americans to fight. Wilson was sure in time he could counteract the treaties and force the British and French to accept a just peace. Meanwhile he unilaterally expounded his own war aims on January 8, 1918, in a speech before a joint session of Congress.

His Fourteen Points, coming when all the belligerent peoples were overwhelmingly weary of the war, met with an enthusiastic response among liberals and working people in the United States, in the Allied nations, and among suppressed people throughout the world. Even many Germans welcomed them and a later clarification of them, "the five particulars," as the promise of a democratic Germany which could assume a position of equality in the community of nations. They were the most stirring and effective piece of propaganda the war produced.

It was not clear that Wilson had the American people behind him, even though his Committee on Public Information had been engaged in a large-scale effort to sell the war. George Creel, a progressive newspaperman who had worked in the 1916 presidential campaign, headed the Committee. He persuaded newspapers to engage in voluntary self-censorship, an idea not entirely palatable to them. The Committee disseminated countless tons of propaganda, and enlisted the services of 150,000 writers, lecturers, actors, and artists. Throughout the country, 75,000 such volunteers arose to

nately, appealed more to fear and hate than to a spirit of altruistic sacrifice. The Committee emphasized the menace of the Germans, and while it balked at dissemination of the worst atrocity stories, private organizations like the National

---

SUMMARY OF THE FOURTEEN POINTS

"I. Open covenants of peace, openly arrived at. . . .

"II. Absolute freedom of navigation upon the seas. . . .

"III. The removal, so far as possible, of all economic barriers, and the establishment of an equality of trade conditions among all the nations consenting to the peace and associating themselves for its maintenance.

"IV. Adequate guarantees given and taken that national armaments will be reduced to the lowest point consistent with domestic safety.

"V. A free, open-minded, and absolutely impartial adjustment of all colonial claims. . . .

"VI. The evacuation of all Russian territory. . . .

"VII. Belgium, the whole world will agree, must be evacuated and restored. . . .

"VIII. All French territory should be freed and the invaded portions . . . and . . . Alsace-Lorraine. . . . [restored].

"IX. A readjustment of the frontiers of Italy should be effected along clearly recognizable lines of nationality.

"X. The peoples of Austria-Hungary . . . should be accorded the freest opportunity of autonomous development.

"XI. Rumania, Serbia, and Montenegro should be evacuated; . . . Serbia accorded free and secure access to the sea. . . .

"XII. The Turkish portions of the present Ottoman Empire should be assured a secure sovereignty, but the other nationalities . . . should be assured . . . autonomous development, and the Dardanelles should be permanently opened. . . .

"XIII. An independent Polish state should be erected . . . which should be assured free and secure access to the sea. . . .

"XIV. A general association of nations must be formed. . . ."

---

speak on almost every conceivable occasion; throughout the United States and the world, 75,000,000 pieces of printed matter carried the American view of the war. Much of what the Creel Committee disseminated was idealistic, in keeping with Wilson's speeches and the Fourteen Points, depicting the war as a great crusade for humanity. Much also, unfortu-

Security League had no such scruples.

Throughout the country spread a hysterical wartime hatred of all that seemed not to conform. Congress passed several stern measures for the protection of the country from disloyal individuals. The Espionage Act of June 15, 1917, provided penalties running up to a $10,000 fine and twenty years' imprisonment, not only for those engaged in espionage, sabotage, and obstruction of the war effort, but even for those who should "willfully cause or attempt to cause insubordination, mutiny, or refusal of duty . . . or . . . willfully obstruct the recruiting or enlistment service." It also empowered the Postmaster General to ban from the mails any matter which in his opinion was seditious. The Trading-with-the-Enemy Act of October 6, 1917, established censorship over international communications and the foreign-language press (in addition to authorizing various types of economic warfare against the Germans). These measures were vigorously, and at times capriciously, enforced, but the administration sought still greater punitive powers to discipline the disloyal.

Congress responded with the Sabotage Act of April 20, 1918, aimed primarily at the I.W.W., and the Sedition Act of May 16, 1918. The Sedition Act, modeled after a Montana statute for supressing the I.W.W., was harsh beyond any previous legislation in American history.

The enforcement of these laws was almost as stern as any lynch mob could desire. Over 1,500 were arrested for seditious utterances, though only 10 were taken into custody for sabotage. The force of the laws continued unabated after the armistice. In the fall of 1918, after a four-day trial, the Socialist leader, Eugene V. Debs, who had been pacifist, not pro-German, was sentenced to ten years in a federal penitentiary under the Espionage Act; in March, 1919, the Supreme Court upheld his conviction. Whatever pacifist or pro-German offenders escaped the Federal net were likely to be caught in the meshes of state sedition laws, or to suffer the wrath of vigilantes. The furore at its mildest was rather ludicrous, as sauerkraut became "liberty cabbage," and hamburger, "liberty sausage." It was a bit less funny to ban all German music, including the compositions of Mendelssohn and Beethoven. It was not funny at all to suspend Bruno Walter,

---

THE SEDITION ACT

"Be it enacted. . . . Whoever, when the United States is at war, shall wilfully make or convey false reports or false statements with intent to interfere with the operation or success of the military or naval forces of the United States . . . or . . . obstruct the sale by the United States of bonds . . . or incite . . . insubordination, disloyalty, mutiny, or refusal of duty in the military or naval forces of the United States, or shall wilfully obstruct . . . the recruiting or enlistment service . . . [or] wilfully utter, print, write, or publish any disloyal, profane, scurrilous, or abusive language about the form of government of the United States, or the Constitution of the United States, or the military or naval forces of the United States, or the flag . . . or the uniform of the Army or Navy of the United States . . . or shall wilfully . . . urge, incite, or advocate any curtailment of production in this country of any thing or things . . . necessary or essential to the prosecution of the war . . . and whoever shall wilfully advocate, teach, defend, or suggest the doing of any of the acts or things . . . enumerated . . . shall be punished by a fine of not more than $10,000 or imprisonment for not more than twenty years, or both. . . ."—May 16, 1918.

the conductor of the Chicago Symphony Orchestra, because he had not become an American citizen; to ban the study of German in some public schools, as in Ohio; or to dump all books in German out of some public libraries, as in Los Angeles. And it was frightening when a vigilance committee in Minnesota, having forbidden a pastor to speak German, caught him praying at the bedside of a dying woman who spoke only German, tarred and feathered him, and rode him out of town on a rail.

A Disgruntled Nation

Although the war raised the living standards of millions of Americans in lower-income brackets, the Wilson administration did not benefit from their votes in the congressional election of 1918. In the East the Democrats lost only two House seats, but they lost 21 in the remainder of the nation. Within his own party Wilson faced dissension throughout the war, as some of his congressional leaders of agrarian progressive background fought drastic war measures, helped impose heavy taxation on the more well-to-do, and hurried through wartime prohibition and a prohibition amendment to the Constitution. City Democrats were particularly unhappy over losing their beer. Southern Democrats prevented a ceiling on the price of cotton in contrast to the pegged price that was placed on wheat; the Midwestern grain belt, as a result, reacted angrily against all Democrats.

Even before the 1918 election, it seemed likely that these factors would influence voters more than the Fourteen Points. Nevertheless, with the war obviously almost over, the President put the election on the basis of high international policy. He succumbed to the pleas of Democratic Congressmen, and on October 24 declared, "The return of a Republican majority to either house of the Congress would . . . be interpreted on

the other side of the water as a repudiation of my leadership." This outraged those Republicans who had supported him in his foreign policy, since he had earlier declared "politics is adjourned" for the duration of the war. The fact that the Republicans captured both houses of Congress in 1918 would itself have had a serious effect on foreign policy; the effect was exaggerated even more by Wilson's ill-considered appeal.

Preludes to Versailles

Sharp partisanship and the semblance of repudiation created a sad atmosphere for Wilson's assumption of peace negotiations. The President, like the nation, was tense and tired, but he was ready to drive ahead; he strove to pull his own country and the reluctant Allies with him in his determination to make the Fourteen Points, and especially the fourteenth,—the League of Nations—become a reality.

The pulling and hauling with the Allies went on through most of October, 1918, during the negotiations which led to the armistice. The Germans sought through Wilson an armistice based on the Fourteen Points and their modifications. The Allies denied even knowing what these points were, for they were by no means ready to give up their claims for reparations and annexations. Only after Wilson had twice threatened to negotiate a separate peace were they willing to present a united facade. The Allies seemed to agree to the Fourteen Points in entirety, except for explicit reservations on reparations and freedom of the seas, and this apparent agreement led the Germans to expect generous treatment. Further misunderstanding developed because, while the Allies laid down military and naval terms that would make it impossible for the Germans to resume warfare, they used the term "armistice," which meant a negotiated pause in hostilities, rather than the word "surrender."

The "Big Four" in Paris. The council of four of the Peace Conference partici-
pants photographed at the Paris home of President Wilson, 11 Place des Etats-
Unis, May 27, 1919. Left to right: David Lloyd George, Prime Minister of Great
Britain; Vittorio E. Orlando, Premier of Italy; Georges Clemenceau, Premier of
France; and President Wilson.

A 35-year-old British economist at the Conference, John Maynard Keynes, described Wilson with a caustic pen: "He had no plan, no scheme, no constructive
idea whatever for clothing with the flesh of life the commandments which he had
thundered from the White House. . . . He not only had no proposals in detail,
but he was in many respects, perhaps inevitably, ill-informed as to European conditions. And not only was he ill-informed—that was true of Mr. Lloyd George also—
but his mind was slow and unadaptable." Keynes concluded, "It was harder to de-
bamboozle this old Presbyterian than to bamboozle him." These stereotypes clung
to Wilson for decades, although the British Foreign Secretary, Arthur Balfour, who
sat at the meetings of the Big Four, declared that Wilson was "firm, modest, restrained, eloquent, well-informed, and convincing." To Balfour's surprise, Wilson
was "as good round a table as he was on paper." General Jan Smuts of South Africa
declared that Wilson was "the noblest figure, perhaps the only noble figure in the
history of the war." (NATIONAL ARCHIVES)

What followed at Versailles was a conclave of victors dictating to a vanquished
country, not a negotiated peace or the
peace without victory that Wilson had
once recommended.

The armistice which went into effect
on November 11, 1918, provided that the
Allies would negotiate peace on the basis
of the Fourteen Points. The Germans
agreed to withdraw their forces from
France and Belgium to a zone well to the
east of the Rhine, and to surrender huge
quantities of matériel. They accepted
what was virtually the unconditional sur-

render of their fleet. Finally, while the peace was being drafted, the Allied blockade continued.

To the Allies as they assembled in Paris, there seemed no need to consult Germany on the nature of the peace. Indeed, the only block between them and the kind of postwar world they had planned in their secret treaties was President Wilson. That was a serious block indeed, for Wilson made the precedent-breaking decision of leaving the United States to attend the peace conference in person. House and other advisers urged him not to go.

Wilson seriously miscalculated in refusing to take with him as one of the Peace Commissioners a leading Republican like Elihu Root or William Howard Taft. He would have done well, too, to have included one of the powerful Republican Senators, since it would take many Republican votes to muster the requisite two-thirds majority for the treaty in the Senate. Nevertheless, Wilson took only a nonpolitical Republican diplomat, Henry White, and relied neither upon him nor upon the other commissioners.

Arriving in Europe in December, 1918, before the other European leaders were ready to confer, Wilson toured France, Italy, and England. Wherever he went, hysterically cheering crowds greeted him; everywhere boulevards and plazas were renamed for him. The cheering millions reinforced his feeling that he was the spokesman for humanity. He was not aware that in each nation these masses looked to him to obtain for them much that ran contrary to the Fourteen Points. A little later, when he fought against some of their national claims, their adulation evaporated into disillusion.

Drafting the Treaty

The sessions at Paris began January 12, 1919, in an atmosphere of idealism tinctured with national aggrandizement, amidst glittering scenes remniscent of the Congress of Vienna; just beyond to the east, however, there was an urgency born of imminent starvation and the threatening spread of Communism. Hoover, trying to get food into central Europe to fend off both threats, declared, "The wolf is at the door of the world." One of the greatest difficulties was that Russia, where Bolsheviks were still fighting White armies, was entirely unrepresented.

At the outset Wilson had to fight to prevent a division of spoils under the secret treaties. He tried to block the Japanese from obtaining permanently the German treaty rights in the Shantung Peninsula of China and the former German islands north of the Equator in the Pacific, which could be Japanese strongholds. He had to give way, however, to the insistence of the British that they honor the treaty promises with which they had lured the Japanese into the war. Wilson with more success persuaded the Allies to hold former German colonies and Turkish territories on a basis of trusteeship responsible to the League of Nations. This was the new and unprecedented "mandate" system. Simultaneously, Wilson worked on the drafting of the League Covenant. He insisted that it form the first part of the treaty, and be inseparable from it, and he labored long and hard fabricating it in meticulous detail. In the League Covenant he saw the one possible way of overriding the vengeful selfishness which seemed dominant among the victorious nations. Whatever imperfections and inequities there were in the Treaty he thought could be rectified through the League: through it and it alone, the world could avoid future wars. In the League he envisaged a potentially powerful (but not armed) international organization through which the nations of the world could share responsibility in maintaining the security of all against any aggressor.

At the end of February, 1919, as Congress prepared to adjourn, Wilson came home to sign bills. He brought with him the League Covenant, determined that he would force the Senate to accept it without compromise. The acclaim with which Bostonians greeted him, the friendliness of editorials in most newspapers, and the energy with which large and influential organizations advocated the League, all encouraged him to think public sentiment overwhelmingly behind him. When Colonel House warned him he must be prepared to compromise with the Senate, he had retorted, "I have found that you get nothing in this world that is worth-while without fighting for it."

A stiff fight was taking form. In the Senate, on March 4, 1919, Henry Cabot Lodge produced a round robin signed by thirty-seven Senators, a number sufficient to block the treaty, announcing they would not accept the Covenant in its existing form. Wilson, about to re-embark for Paris, retorted angrily. But back at the Conference, on the advice of Taft he did obtain some of the reservations for the United States upon which the Senate would obviously insist. These provided that a nation need not accept a mandate against its will, that a member could withdraw with two years' notice, that the League would not regulate immigration and other internal matters, and that it would not infringe upon the Monroe Doctrine. To obtain these, Wilson had to trade concessions with the Allies. He made little progress toward conciliating the Republican Senators. Many of them saw in the struggle over the Covenant a means of embarrassing Wilson, stripping him of some of his glory, and developing a winning issue for the campaign of 1920. There was no good political reason for them to be generous, so despite the concessions they continued to harass him.

While Wilson was obtaining revisions to the Covenant, the Conference was also grappling with the critical problem of Germany and the remaking of the European map. Together with Lloyd George, Wilson resisted the French pro-posal to break up western Germany into buffer states. He did sanction the return to France of Alsace-Lorraine, and the establishment of a strong Poland and Czechoslovakia on Germany's borders, all in keeping with the national self-determination clauses of the Fourteen Points. He also supported German demilitarization, long-term Allied occupation of the west bank of the Rhine, and an Anglo-French-American mutual defense pact. If maintained, these security provisions should have prevented the resurgence of Germany as a military menace to the West. Elsewhere the remapping of Europe proceeded rather fitfully. Italy obtained the Brenner Pass area in which 200,000 Austrians lived, then was outraged at not also receiving Fiume, which Wilson felt must be a port for the new nation of Yugoslavia. In this region and others, the economic needs of nations and the principle of national self-determination of peoples often conflicted. Back in the United States, ethnic groups were ready to clamor for more for their native countries. And the Irish in the United States insisted that Wilson should fight for national self-determination for Ireland, wracked by civil war. Wilson took up the matter privately with Lloyd George but did not make a public stand.

Wilson's most important departure from the Fourteen Points was his acceptance of British and French demands for heavy reparations from the Germans. Even before the armistice, he had partly accepted their demands that Germans must make payment for civilian damages, although such a proposal ran counter to his negotiations with the Germans. At the Conference, he permitted these demands to cover even pensions for veterans; the astronomical sum was to be set later by a reparations commission. Meanwhile, although Wilson himself for years had taken an economic-determinism view of the origins of the war, the other powers insisted that Germany must accept sole responsibility for starting it. The "war guilt" clause and reparations stuck in the craw of Germans. Even in the United States, the harsh peace meted out against Germany disillusioned many liberals and alienated them from Wilson. They regarded the treaty as a "hell's brew" which would ultimately lead to another war.

Defeat in the Senate

Wilson returned to the United States confident that the Senate, despite the difficulties Lodge was stirring up, would ratify the treaty. On July 10, 1919, when he presented it to the Senate, he asked rhetorically, "Dare we reject it and break the heart of the world?"

Through a combination of coercion and compromise he might have brought about ratification. But he was suffering from hardening of the arteries, and in March while in Paris had been so ill that he may have been close to a stroke. His physical condition robbed him of his political suppleness; instead of using patience and tact, he was more likely to shower his opponents with self-righteous anger.

Wilson's opponents in the Senate were not ready to put statesmanship ahead of partisanship. The fourteen "irreconcilables" were men of conscience, of Middle Western or Far Western progressive tradition, like Republicans Johnson of California and La Follette of Wisconsin, and Democrat James Reed of Missouri. They acted out of deep conviction that their nation could best be served by staying out of the League. Other opponents with less conviction were more concerned with constructing a winning issue for the Republicans in the 1920 election than they were with the future of the world. Senator Lodge, applying all his brilliant intellect to his loathing of Wilson, was ready, as chairman of the Senate Foreign Relations Committee, to use every possible tactic to obstruct or delay the treaty. Public sentiment seemed

to favor ratification of the treaty, and Lodge needed time to marshal forces against it. Consequently, he spent the first two weeks after it reached the committee reading aloud every word on its nearly three hundred pages. Next, he held six weeks' of public hearings, listening to the complaints of every disgruntled minority.

From the White House, Wilson did some conferring with Republican Senators. He explained to some of them that he considered the collective-security provision of Article X to be more of a moral obligation upon the United States than a legal one—but to Wilson moral obligations were the more important. The Senators were not impressed; it began to appear that Wilson would have to accept some of Lodge's reservations if he wished to obtain ratification. When one Senator told him this, he retorted, "Never! Never! . . . I'll appeal to the country!"

So Wilson, at the end of his physical resources, against the stern warnings of his physician, undertook a cross-country speaking tour, writing his speeches as he went along, delivering them night after night. In twenty-two days he traveled over 8,000 miles, giving thirty-six speeches averaging an hour in length. At first the halls were not entirely filled nor were his speeches always too polished. As the tour proceeded, he gained larger and more enthusiastic audiences, and grew more eloquent in his moral fervor. Had it been possible to sway the United States Senate through public opinion, the tour might have been a success. But Wilson became more and more frail. Finally after speaking at Pueblo, Colorado, September 25, he suffered such acute headaches that he had to cancel the tour and return to Washington.

Then he suffered an acute stroke which partially paralyzed his left side. For two weeks he was close to death, and for six weeks more so seriously ill that he could attend only to what little business his devoted wife and doctor thought would not unduly upset or fatigue him. When some officials tried to see the President on vital matters, Mrs. Wilson turned them away, saying, "I am not interested in the President of the United States. I am interested in my husband and his health."

At this critical period the Senate Foreign Relations Committee finally reported the treaty, recommending forty-five amendments and three reservations. Lodge managed to marshal the Republican Senators so well that in November he obtained passage of fourteen reservations. By this time Wilson had recovered sufficiently to give stern directions to the Democratic minority: they must vote only for the treaty without any reservations. Although none of the Lodge reservations would have devitalized the League, Wilson preferred no ratification of the treaty to ratification with reserva-

tions. While he was by no means his old self, he was able to exert power enough to maintain discipline over the loyal Democrats. When the vote came, November 19, 1919, 42 Democrats joined with the 13 Republican irreconcilables to vote down the treaty with reservations. Next, the Senate voted on ratification of the treaty without reservations. There were 38 Senators, all but one of them a Democrat, who voted for it; 55 voted against it.

On the day of the final vote, March 19, 1920, when the Senate considered the treaty with fifteen reservations, it came within seven votes of receiving the requisite two-thirds. By this time, President Wilson was ready to look to the campaign of 1920 as the opportunity for a "solemn referendum" on the League issue.

BIBLIOGRAPHY

The most useful survey of the war administration is in F. L. Paxson, *American Democracy and the World War* (3 vols., 1936–48), vol. 2. See also Mark Sullivan, *Our Times*, vol. 5. Some specialized studies are: J. M. Clark, *The Costs of the World War to the American People* (1931); Bernard M. Baruch, *American Industry in War* (1941 edition); W. C. Mullendore, *History of United States Food Administration* (1941); and Herbert Stein, *Government Price Policy during the World War* (1939). A readable account of Baruch's activities is included in Margaret Coit, *Mr. Baruch* (1957); a revealing memoir is Herbert Hoover, *The Ordeal of Woodrow Wilson* (1958).

J. R. Mock and Cedric Larson, *Words That Won the War* (1939) is an account of the Committee on Public Information. Zechariah Chafee, Jr., *Free Speech in the United States* (1941) contains a classic account of wartime restrictions on civil liberties. H. C. Peterson and G. C. Fite, *Opponents of War, 1917–1918* (1957) is an

equally powerful treatise. On military and naval operations, see Paxson, *American Democracy and the World War*, vol. 2, and these specialized accounts and memoirs: T. G. Frothingham, *The Naval History of the World War* (3 vols., 1924–6); Elting Morison, *Admiral Sims and the Modern American Navy* (1942); D. W. Mitchell, *History of the Modern American Navy* (1946); J. J. Pershing, *My Experiences in the World War* (2 vols., 1931); and J. G. Habord, *The American Army in France, 1917–1919* (1936).

On the end of the fighting, see H. R. Rudin, *Armistice, 1918* (1944). On Wilson as a peacemaker, see the previously cited works on Wilson, and T. A. Bailey, *Woodrow Wilson and the Lost Peace* (1944), on the Versailles conference; Bailey, *Woodrow Wilson and the Great Betrayal* (1945), on the Treaty fight in the Senate. On the background of League of Nations sentiment, see R. J. Bartlett, *The League to Enforce Peace* (1944).

32

NORMALCY
AND PROSPERITY

As soon as the great crusade ended, Americans were eager to return to life as it had been—or rather as they dreamed it had been. But they could not return to the "good old days," for both progressivism and the war had brought lasting changes.

The war had raised the living standard of factory workers and built a powerful labor movement; it had created great shifts in population and accompanying tensions. It had given a temporary bonanza to the farmer, stepped up mechanization of agriculture, and brought the plow to tens of thousands of acres of semiarid prairie grasslands. Much of this transformation was painful, and led to further difficult adjustments in the twenties. The war also had changed styles and fashions, and molded consumer demands into new channels. In little ways (such as the introduction of wrist watches for men, shorter skirts for women, and cigarettes for both) and in major ways that involved basic shifts in the economy, it was changing the patterns of life for most Americans.

The Harding Tragedy

In 1920, domestic tensions made impossible a solemn referendum on a League of Nations; only an ill man sequestered from the flow of events, as President Wilson was, could have expected it. A Democratic victory was so improbable that Republican leaders felt no compulsion to put forth any of their strong candidates.

The two leading contenders were Leonard Wood and Frank O. Lowden. General Wood, an ardent conservative nationalist, commanded most of Roosevelt's former following, and collected a campaign chest of startling proportions ($1,773,000), with which he battled Lowden for delegates. Lowden, favorably known as an efficient governor of Illinois, also commanded large campaign funds, totaling $414,000. Progressive Republican charges that both contenders were deeply indebted to big business helped enable party managers to ignore them when the two deadlocked at the convention. A cabal of Senators led by Henry

Cabot Lodge late one night in a smoke-filled hotel room turned to one of the most regular and pliable of their colleagues, Warren G. Harding of Ohio. The convention nominated Harding on the tenth ballot and chose as his running mate the Massachusetts governor, Calvin Coolidge. These two were thoroughly conservative candidates running on a thoroughly conservative platform.

Cox. As a gesture toward the Wilsonians, Assistant Secretary of the Navy Franklin D. Roosevelt was nominated for Vice President.

Cox and Roosevelt campaigned arduously to make the election the referendum on the League that Wilson wished it to be. Harding, following the advice of his managers, made few speeches and took few positions on the issues of the day

---

HARDING CALLS FOR NORMALCY

"America's present need is not heroics, but healing; not nostrums, but normalcy; not revolution, but restoration; not agitation, but adjustment; not surgery, but serenity; not the dramatic, but the dispassionate; not experiment, but equipoise; not submergence in internationality, but sustainment in triumphant nationality. . . .

"The world called for peace, and has its precarious variety. America demands peace, formal as well as actual, and means to have it, regardless of political exigencies and campaign issues. If it must be a campaign issue, we shall have peace and discuss it afterward, because the actuality is imperative, and the theory is only illusive. . . .

"This republic has its ample tasks. If we put an end to false economics which lure humanity to utter chaos, ours will be the commanding example of world leadership today. . . . The world needs to be reminded that all human ills are not curable by legislation, and that quantity of statutory enactment and excess of government offer no substitute for quality of citizenship."—Address, May 14, 1920.

The Democrats assembled at San Francisco rather confused because President Wilson, who could have easily designated a candidate, seemed to be waiting with pathetic coyness to be renominated for a third term. This was patently impossible. For thirty-eight ballots, two of Wilson's cabinet members, his efficient son-in-law McAdoo, and his superpatriotic Attorney General, A. Mitchell Palmer, battled for the nomination. In the end the urban bosses stepped in and secured the nomination of an antiprohibition candidate who might salvage their city tickets for them. This was the former progressive Governor of Ohio, James M.

except to promise a return to what he earlier had called "normalcy." McAdoo joked that Harding's speeches were "an army of pompous phrases moving across the landscape in search of an idea." Certainly Harding displayed an ambivalence that was politically most successful. On the League he at first gave the impression that he favored adherence, then as city resentment against it flared, gave the impression he was against it. Lest Cox's crusade win away Republican votes, thirty-one distinguished Republicans, including Hughes, Stimson, Root, and Hoover, signed a statement declaring that a vote for Harding was a vote for American en-

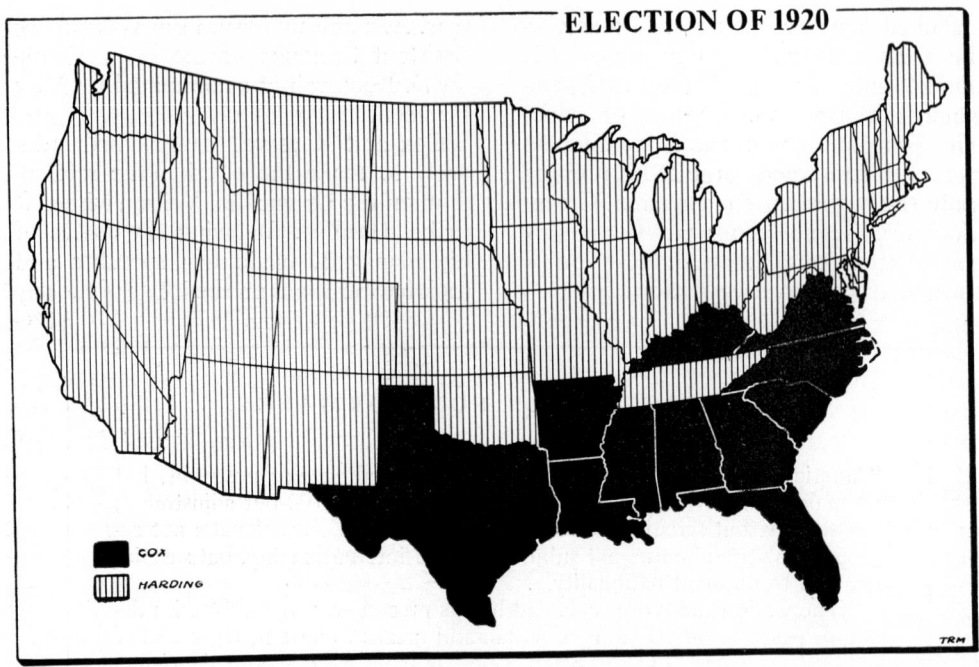

COX

HARDING

TRM

trance into the League with reservations.

The landslide exceeded even the expectations of the Republicans. Harding received 16,152,000 popular votes, 61 per cent of the total, and carried every state outside of the Solid South. He even won Tennessee. Cox received only 9,147,000 popular votes. Debs, running from the Atlanta penitentiary on the Socialist ticket, received 920,000 votes. The sweep brought a Republican majority in the Senate of 22, and in the House of 167.

In voting against Wilsonianism, the electorate brought into power a weak, amiable conservative. Alice Roosevelt Longworth, daughter of a President and wife of the speaker of the House, reared in the genteel tradition of Republican politics, could not forget the sight of a poker session in the President's study. "Harding was not a bad man," she reminisced. "He was just a slob."

He wished to surround himself with the best-qualified men, and in part he succeeded. When he was persuaded that his friend Albert B. Fall was not of a caliber to be Secretary of State, he placed

Fall, a notorious anticonservationist, in charge of the Interior Department. However, he then appointed the brilliant and distinguished Charles Evans Hughes to be Secretary of State. He placed Hoover, the friend of small enterprise and expert on efficiency, in charge of the Commerce Department, and made Henry C. Wallace, spokesman for the Midwest farmers, Secretary of Agriculture. Andrew W. Mellon represented big business as Secretary of the Treasury. These able men, pulling in several directions, together with the congressional leaders developed government policies.

In domestic as in foreign policies, the President seemed to be carrying out his campaign slogan, "Less government in business and more business in government." The Democrats made strong gains in the 1922 elections, reflecting the hard times that followed the war, but the return of prosperity soon afterwards heightened Harding's popularity. He continued to "look like a President," and occasionally was even vigorous in his humanity. He took a step Wilson had curtly declined when on Christmas Day, 1921, he pardoned the Socialist Eugene V. Debs. At the urging of Hoover, he pressured the steel companies into granting an eight-hour day to their workers. The press of the country, overwhelmingly Republican, created the illusion among most of the public that Harding was an exceptionally fine President.

Behind the facade, rot had set in. With singularly bad judgment Harding had placed a number of his poker-playing and drinking companions into positions of trust where they betrayed him and the American people. Probably Harding never knew in detail how shockingly they were looting the government, but he knew enough to be heartsick. One of the "Ohio Gang," Attorney General Harry Daugherty's friend Jesse Smith, had been engaging in large-scale "fixing" in the Department of Justice. After Harding ordered him out of Washington, Smith committed suicide. The Director of the Veterans' Bureau, Charles R. Forbes, engaged in such colossal thievery that the total loss ran to nearly $250 million. When Harding received intimations of the corruption, he allowed Forbes to flee the country and resign. Ultimately Forbes

PRESIDENT HARDING SPEAKING ON HIS WESTERN TRIP. By no means his earlier buoyant self, Harding journeyed to Alaska in the summer of 1923, carrying with him some knowledge of the plundering in Washington. An unsuspecting public greeted him warmly; he returned their cheers with slight enthusiasm. Before his return, which would possibly have been shortly followed by his exposure, he died. Earlier, Harding had enjoyed a happier life. For years he had been editor and publisher of the Marion, Ohio, *Star*, an undistinguished smalltown newspaper. Because of his regularity and his ingratiating ways, he had risen in the Republican party hierarchy until in 1914 he had achieved his life's goal, election to the United States Senate. The ambitions of his wife and of his campaign manager, Harry Daugherty, together with luck, elevated him to the Presidency. Daugherty once explained how he had happened to work for Harding: "He looked like a President." This was Harding's main qualification. (NATIONAL ARCHIVES)

served a two-year penitentiary sentence for defrauding the government.

The most spectacular fraud involved the rich naval oil reserves at Teapot Dome, Wyoming, and Elk Hills, California. Secretary of the Interior Fall persuaded Harding to transfer them to his department, then secretly leased them to Harry F. Sinclair and Edward L. Doheny. Fall, who had been in financial straits, suddenly became affluent. An investigation headed by Senator Thomas J. Walsh of Montana during the fall and winter of 1923 and 1924 uncovered the reason. Sinclair had loaned Fall $308,000 in cash and government bonds and a herd of cattle for his ranch; Doheny had loaned $100,000 more. In 1929 Fall was convicted of bribery, fined $100,000 and sentenced to a year in a federal penitentiary.

In the summer of 1923 Harding journeyed to Alaska. Tired and depressed, he responded wanly to the cheering throngs, who had no inkling of the mess in Washington. He never had to face the coming storm, for upon his return to Seattle he became ill. It was reported that he had been poisoned by seafood, but he had suffered a serious heart attack. He seemed to improve, so he continued to San Francisco. There he had a second attack and suddenly died. In the months that followed, as exposure after exposure crowded the headlines, his reputation collapsed.

Keeping Cool with Coolidge

It was the singular good fortune of Calvin Coolidge to become President of the United States at the only time since the 1890's when his largely negative custodial approach to the Presidency could bring him popularity rather than disaster. He came to be Chief Executive through a curious mixture of luck, political regularity, and Yankee shrewdness. Unlike Harding, he had a clear-cut conservative philosophy; he always cooperated wholeheartedly with the big interests because

he believed in them, and fought unwaveringly for what he believed.

To the older circle in Washington, Coolidge's personality was not especially appealing; Alice Roosevelt Longworth remarked that he had been weaned on a dill pickle. To the American public, however, there was an infinite appeal and security in his folksy virtues, so lavishly detailed and praised in the nation's press. Coolidge reinforced this folksy appeal with little homilies drawn from his Vermont boyhood—exhortations (in which he fervently believed) to thrift, hard work, and respect for business.

Under this comforting moral leadership, the men of power in the United States could take a calm and even incredulous view of the Harding scandals as one by one they came to light in the winter of 1923–1924. Indeed, they and the respectable press showered indignation less upon the corrupt officials than upon those pressing the investigations. The two progressive Democratic Senators Thomas J. Walsh and Burton K. Wheeler appeared to the New York *Times* to be "assassins of character," and to the *Herald-Tribune*, "Montana scandal-mongers." Throughout much of the press, the investigations seemed a "Democratic lynching-bee," a work of "poison-tongued partisanship, pure malice, and twittering hysteria," at bottom the machination of Reds and subversives.

Under Coolidge the Republicans seemed so patently incorruptible that the exposures appeared if anything to backfire against the exposing Democrats. Ultimately Coolidge forced Attorney General Daugherty to resign and helped clean up the scandals. There was no possibility they would be repeated; and, as the election of 1924 approached, they seemed to be doing no appreciable harm to the Republican party. The nation seemed committed in advance to the party's campaign slogan: "Keep cool with Coolidge."

In 1924 the Democratic party was

PRESIDENT COOLIDGE IN VERMONT. President Coolidge had a remarkable knack for obtaining favorable publicity. He had himself photographed on his father's farm haying; in the West, wearing a ten-gallon hat or an Indian bonnet; at the White House, with countless delegations—and always wearing a business suit. He even wore one when he went fishing. Along with his frequent posing for pictures, he said little. The country was full of stories of his taciturnity and frugality. (HARVARD UNIVERSITY)

badly split between its rural and urban wings. Rural Democrats were advancing as their candidate William Gibbs McAdoo, the competent heir to Wilsonianism. Strangely, the Teapot Dome scandal, which did no harm to the Republicans, tarnished McAdoo's reputation because he had served as lawyer to Doheny, the California oil magnate. As for the urban wing of the party, it was advancing the candidacy of the equally competent liberal governor of New York, Alfred E. Smith, who was the son of Irish immigrants and had made his way upward from the lower East Side of New York. Because of his background, and because he was a Catholic and a wet, he was the

idol of many new Americans, and anathema to the Southern and agrarian Democrats.

Finally both contenders withdrew, and on the 103rd ballot at the convention in Madison Square Garden the exhausted delegates nominated a compromise candidate, John W. Davis. Davis, originally a West Virginian, had as Solicitor General under Wilson ably defended the legislation of the New Freedom before the Supreme Court. In the years since, he had become lawyer for J. P. Morgan and some of the great corporations and had amassed a fortune.

While the Democratic convention dragged on, insurgent Republicans and allied representatives of labor had held a third convention to organize a Progressive party, and nominate Robert M. La Follette and Burton K. Wheeler. Their platform reasserted and advanced progressive position, attacking monopoly and promising reforms for the farmers and workingmen. Their support came from agrarians, chiefly on the Great Plains, who had earlier formed the Non-Partisan League and the Farmer-Labor party, and

vote was Coolidge, 382; Davis, 136; and La Follette, 13.

In his inaugural, March 4, 1925, President Coolidge, declaring that the nation had achieved "a state of contentment seldom before seen," pledged himself to the maintenance of things as they were. During the prosperous years of the Coolidge era, as revenues came pouring in, the federal government did not greatly enlarge its services. It spent nothing in such areas

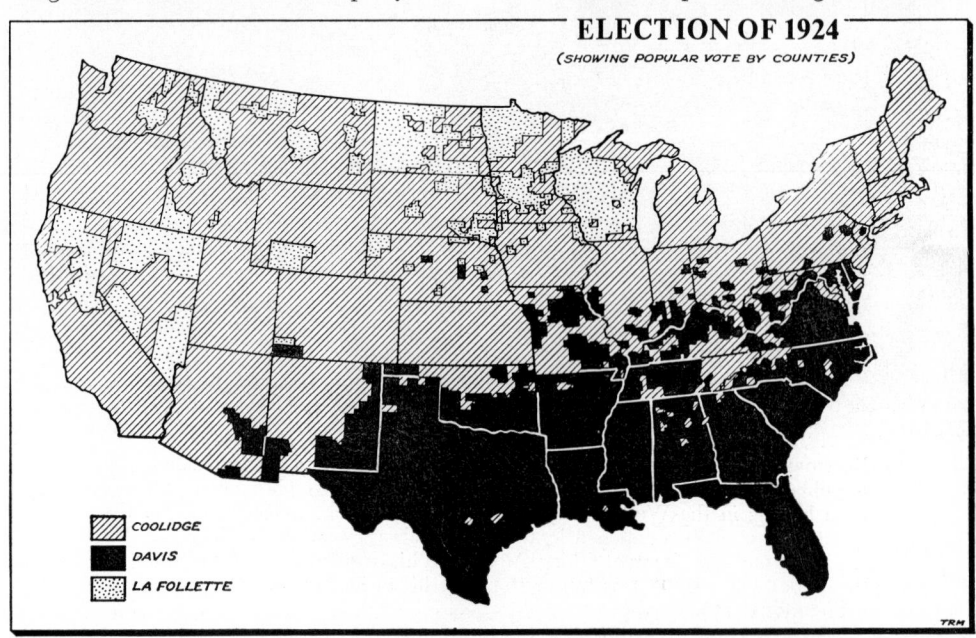

ELECTION OF 1924
(SHOWING POPULAR VOTE BY COUNTIES)

▨ COOLIDGE
■ DAVIS
▦ LA FOLLETTE

from the railroad brotherhoods and the A.F.L. Here, apparently, was a real contrast to the Republican and Democratic tickets, and it served as a made-to-order target for the Republicans. They campaigned to frighten the electorate into choosing Coolidge as the only alternative to the "red radicalism" of La Follette. Before election day, labor became lukewarm toward La Follette; Republican farmers, as crop prices rose, decided to stay within the party. In its last thrust, the old Middlewestern insurgency carried only Wisconsin, and secured 16.5 per cent of the popular vote throughout the country. Coolidge polled 54 per cent, and Davis only 28.8 per cent. The electoral

as public housing, and little for farm relief or public works. Arms expenditures were a relative pittance. Consequently the budget varied little between 1923, when it was $3,250,000,000, and 1929, when it was $3,300,000,000. Meanwhile the national debt dropped by nearly a quarter, from $22,400,000,000 to $17,000,-000,000.

Business as Usual

The wartime production miracles and the clever new writings of American public relations experts and advertising men gave most Americans a new faith in business. The heroes of the twenties were the

THE COOLIDGE PHILOSOPHY

It began with a moral appeal: "If society lacks learning and virtue, it will perish. . . . The classic of all classics is the Bible. . . . The nation with the greatest moral power will win."

Applied to American economy: "What we need is thrift and industry. . . . Let everybody keep at work. . . . We have come to our present high estate through toil and suffering and sacrifice. . . . The man who builds a factory builds a temple. . . . The man who works there worships there. . . . Large profits mean large payrolls."

The role of government: "The law that builds up the people is the law that builds up industry. . . . The Government can do more to remedy the economic ills of the people by a system of rigid economy in public expenditure than can be accomplished through any other action. . . . If the Federal Government should go out of existence, the common run of people would not detect the difference in the affairs of their daily life for a considerable length of time. . . . The business of America is business."

business leaders in the great industries. The bright young men no longer flocked to Washington, nor did they hurry to establish their own small businesses. Rather they aimed for the board room or the industrial laboratory of a large corporation.

Business moguls, for their part, had abandoned their open contempt for the public, and talked the new language of "service." The way they had gone to Washington to serve their country for a dollar a year, while their factories had poured out the munitions to win the war, received wide and respectful attention in the popular press. The former "robber barons" and "malefactors of great wealth" became again "industrial statesmen."

There were some Americans who would have made the twenties quite the reverse of an age of big business, who would have liked to see the continuation of wartime government regulation or even ownership. At the close of the war the government owned most of the nation's commercial radio facilities (used as yet only for sending messages), commanded a vast merchant fleet, and controlled the railroads.

This call for nationalization frightened many Americans, and went beyond the old progressive bounds. Congress was not willing to go so far, but did pass the Esch-Cummins Transportation Act of 1920, establishing over railroad rates and securities federal control as tight as any progressive had ever visualized. Railroads suffered from the new rigorous competition of motor vehicles and other carriers. They were not as a rule able to earn the 6-per-cent return the Interstate Commerce Commission allowed them.

Shipping remained in part under direct government ownership, because private operation had to be heavily subsidized one way or another in order for American companies to compete successfully with those of other countries. These companies were subsidized by low prices and easy terms in buying government-owned ships and by generous mail contracts under the Merchant Marine Act of 1920. Congress refused to allow the navy to continue operating commerical radio communications, and so the navy reluctantly sold its stations to the newly established Radio Corporation of America.

Western progressives obtained two measures to stave off corporate onslaughts in their area. One, the General Leasing Act, was intended to protect the naval oil reserves from oil companies that for some years had been trying to obtain them. It also authorized the leasing of other mineral and oil lands on terms favorable to the government. The other measure, the Water Power Act of 1920, was a first tentative step toward federal regulation of power. It established a Federal Power Commission (consisting of the Secretaries of War, the Interior, and Agriculture) to license the construction and operation of hydroelectric plants on public lands and to regulate rates on power from these plants when it passed across state boundaries.

Soon after the war, Congress helped bring to fruition two other progressive dreams. In June, 1919, it approved the women's suffrage (Nineteenth) amendment, which was ratified by August, 1920. In October, 1919, over the veto of President Wilson it passed the drastic Volstead Act implementing the prohibition (Eighteenth) amendment, submitted by Congress in December, 1917, and ratified by January, 1919. Several states had passed laws outlawing hard liquor but permitting the sale of weak beer, which might have been a successful sop to the millions of urban opponents of prohibition. The Volstead Act prohibited all liquors containing more than ½ of 1 per cent of alcohol. To jubilant members of the Anti-Saloon League and the W.C.T.U., this meant the enforcement of morality; to opponents it meant an unjustifiable infringement upon their personal liberties.

These pieces of legislation seemed to be the last surge of progressivism as the new order emerged.

Through the twenties millions of progressive Americans of both parties ardently shared the dream of Senator George Norris that the government might develop the nation's great water resources to provide cheap electric power. Millions of others accepted the educational program of the utilities companies, which spent $28 million to $35 million per year combating the idea of a national power program. The battle centered around the great dam at Muscles Shoals on the Tennessee River, which had not been finished in time to provide nitrates during the war. Coolidge and the conservatives wished to sell it to Henry Ford for private development; Norris and his cohorts in Congress blocked them. Norris wished to make Muscle Shoals the center of a great regional development on the Tennessee River; Coolidge pocket-vetoed his bill in 1928. In 1931 Hoover as President again vetoed it, and the deadlock continued until the New Deal began.

Big business had a special friend in the government during the 1920's. Andrew Mellon, the Pittsburgh aluminum baron who served as Secretary of the Treasury from Harding's inauguration into the Hoover administration, was widely hailed as the greatest Secretary of the Treasury since Hamilton. His main function seemed to be to preside over tax cuts; cartoonists routinely pictured him slicing tax melons. So far as Mellon could do so, as a matter of principle, he divided these among the wealthy to give them the incentive to earn more money.

Smaller businessmen also had a strong champion in the government, Secretary of Commerce Hoover. In his own spectacular rise as an international mining engineer, Hoover epitomized the self-made businessman. Denouncing both the radicalism and reaction he had seen in Europe, Hoover set forth his own credo in 1922 in a small book entitled *American Individualism*. It extolled the equality of opportunity which enabled Americans to succeed on their own merits, and the "rising vision of service" which led them to develop community responsibility rather than merely to seek "the acquisition and preservation of private prop-

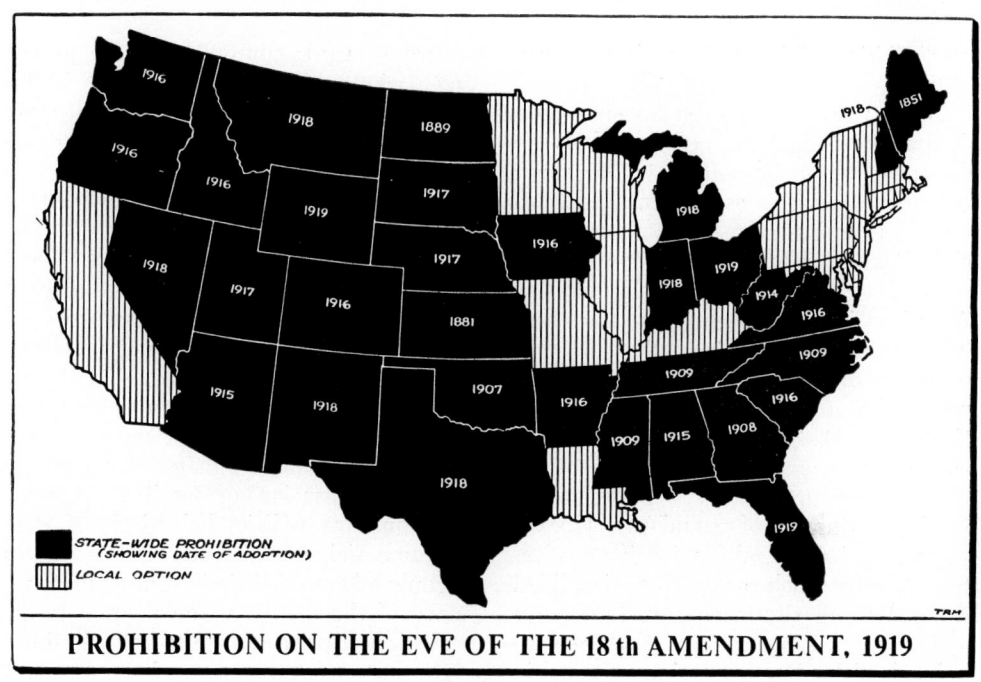

PROHIBITION ON THE EVE OF THE 18th AMENDMENT, 1919

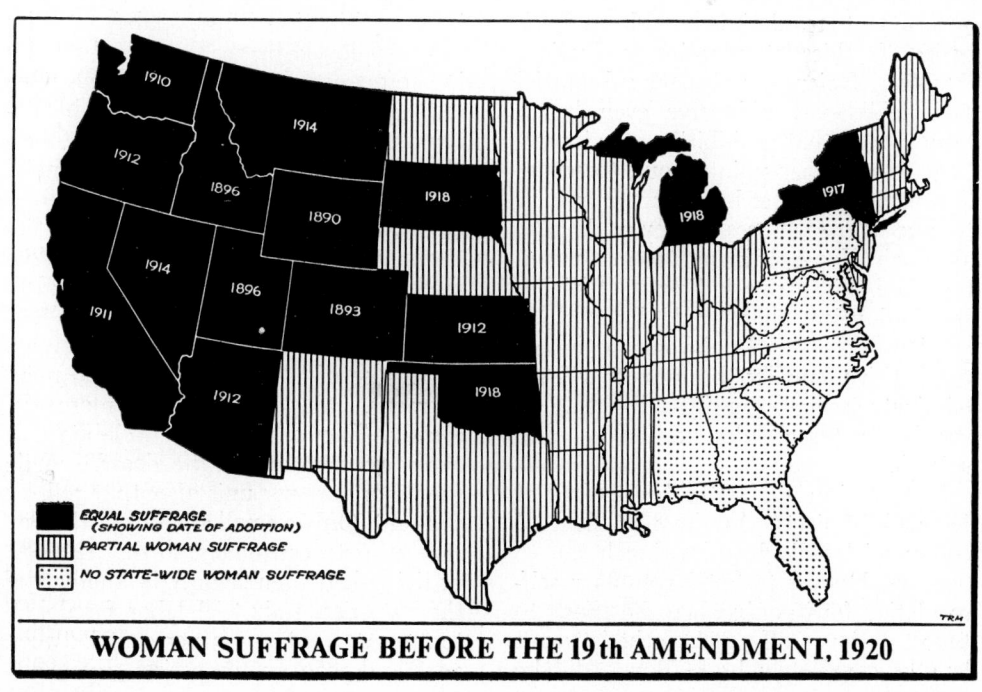

WOMAN SUFFRAGE BEFORE THE 19th AMENDMENT, 1920

erty." This had been Hoover's own way of life.

Hoover to a remarkable extent made Commerce the most spectacular of the departments, as he sought to aid small business to become as efficient and profitable as big business. Through commercial attachés whom he sent to American embassies, he sought foreign orders for American industry at the same time that he favored the tariff to protect it from overseas competition. The Assistant Secretary of State told exporters at a convention in 1928, "Mr. Hoover is your advance agent and [Secretary of State] Kellogg is your attorney." Through the National Bureau of Standards, Hoover performed innumerable scientific services for industry such as setting simplified standards and eliminating waste.

The most significant of the ways to help small business was the sponsorship of voluntary trade associations similar to the committees of the War Industries Board. By 1921 some 2,000 were in operation. These associations, free from government regulation, could establish codes of ethics, standardize production, establish efficiency, and make substantial savings. They could serve even better than government prohibition of evil practices, Hoover has pointed out, to secure "cooperation in the business community to cure its own abuses." They could also, although Hoover did not seem to contemplate this, arrive indirectly at higher standard prices that would bring them good profits. Their real value to highly competitive smaller businesses was to eliminate competition through setting up standardized schedules of quality (and prices).

Voluntarism was at the heart of all of Hoover's projects. As the new field of commercial radio broadcasting began to develop, Hoover fostered voluntary self-regulation for it; only when the efforts to keep stations off each other's wave lengths completely broke down, did he move toward compulsory government regulation through the Federal Radio Commission, established in 1927. In the same way, the Department of Commerce finally took over regulation of commercial aeronautics through the Air Commerce Act in 1926.

On the whole, business thrived from 1923 to 1929. In part, this was due to benign governmental policies: Hoover's laudable efforts to bring about increased standardization and efficiency took the economy further away from free competition and contributed to the increased profits of business and consequently to the concentration of wealth. Secretary Mellon's tax policies helped the rich to become richer, while incomes of poorer people advanced little if at all. The tendency of the courts to frown upon trade-association price schedules helped stimulate mergers. And mergers helped to sustain the trend toward concentration of business which had begun after the Civil War. In the twenties 8,000 mining and manufacturing companies disappeared into combinations; 5,000 public utilities were swallowed by 1928, mostly by holding companies; by 1929 chain stores were selling more than a quarter of the nation's food, apparel, and general merchandise. The 200 largest nonfinancial corporations owned nearly half of all corporate wealth, and 22 per cent of all national wealth. Their combined assets, matching the growth in national wealth, soared from $26 billion in 1909 to $43 billion in 1919, and $81 billion in 1929.

Because of better machinery and management, industry functioned more efficiently. The productivity of labor rose about 50 per cent in the decade, while the labor cost per unit of output fell 9.5 per cent. Only a small amount of the savings went to consumers, so that the cost of living had risen slightly by the end of the twenties. Industrial labor fared better; wages went up 33 per cent between 1922 and 1929. In comparison, white-collar salaries increased 42 per cent; corporate net profits, 76 per cent; and dividends to stockholders, 108 per cent.

Increased productivity did mean a higher living standard for the nation. Consumers purchased 23 per cent more in 1929 than six years earlier, and bought 33 per cent more durable goods like automobiles and furniture. Through their governmental units, they spent three times more for education than before the war. These were some of the substantial rewards of the over-all prosperity of the twenties.

The industrial growth of the decade centered around the automobile and other consumer durable goods. Automobile production jumped from a million and a half cars in 1921 to four and three fourths millions in 1929. By then, automobiles were responsible directly or through countless ramifications for the employment of over three million persons.

Many economists thought it deplorable that Secretary Mellon's policies were leading to such a great concentration of wealth. The 503 persons with the highest incomes received as much money as the total wages of 615,000 automobile workers.

In some respects, business was faring too well in the twenties. It was saving or investing overseas or engaging in speculative enterprises at a greater rate than it was expanding productivity. Nor was it making full use of existing productive capacity, which was about 19 per cent greater than output even in 1929. This may have been even more significant than the failure to put more dollars into workers' pay envelopes.

Radicals and Reactionaries

Union workers tried to preserve their wartime economic gains by striking for higher wages as living costs went upward immediately after the war. A great wave of strikes spread across the country, involving in 1919 some 4,000,000 workers. In many of these strikes, such as those conducted by longshoremen, printers, and laborers in the clothing, textile, telephone, and other industries, the strikers succeeded in raising their living standards. In the process they alienated much of the public, which was quick to accept the industrialists' explanations that higher wages were responsible for higher prices, and that the strike leaders were radicals. Early in 1919 the mayor of Seattle fought a general strike, which had begun in the shipyards, as though he were fending off Bolshevism.

The outbreak of a steel strike in September brought anti-labor feeling to a boil. The grievances of the workers were serious. They were working an average of nearly 69 hours per week for bare subsistence wages and were becoming so discontented that the A.F.L.'s organizing committee made rapid headway among them. United States Steel discharged all union men and refused to negotiate with Gompers or any other union official. Some 343,000 men struck in the Chicago area, and additional workers went on strike in other areas. Despite the workers' valid claims, United States Steel was able to swing public sentiment away from the strikers by claiming that the leaders were Communists. William Z. Foster, the main organizer, had once been a follower of Bryan and was to emerge in 1924 as the presidential candidate of the Communist party. The company brought in Negro strikebreakers. State and federal troops prevented picketing; in rioting at Gary, Indiana, eighteen strikers were killed. Within a few weeks tens of thousands of strikebreakers under armed protection were operating the plants at three-quarters capacity, and by January the workers were starved out.

Public opinion turned even more firmly against organized labor when a police strike broke out in Boston. The policemen were working long hours on pre-war salaries under unpleasant conditions. After their organization, the Boston Social Club, obtained an A.F.L. charter and threatened to strike, a *Mayor's Citizens Committee* prepared to meet their demands except for recognition of their union. The Police Commissioner, responsible only to the Governor, refused and dismissed nineteen leaders. In response, the police struck. As mischief makers and rowdies took over, horrified citizens put on their wartime uniforms and, armed with rifles and shotguns, began patrolling the streets. The mayor mobilized state troops and restored order. The following day Governor Coolidge, who had done nothing to prevent the strike or preserve the peace, suddenly acted. He ordered in troops and backed the decision of the Police Commissioner never to re-employ any of the strikers. When President Gompers of the A.F.L. appealed to Coolidge, the Governor wired back, "There is no right to strike against the public safety, anywhere, anytime." This one telegram made Coolidge a formidable contender for the Republican presidential nomination in 1920.

In Washington Attorney General A. Mitchell Palmer was becoming prominent through his war on both labor and radicals. When the new president of the United Mine Workers, John L. Lewis, took the bituminous coal workers out on strike in November, 1919, Palmer smashed the strike with federal court injunctions.

Palmer attracted even more attention with his crusade against Reds. Throughout the country the violent suppression of pro-German persons during the war had been continued in the persecution of the I.W.W., the Socialists, and all other left wingers. Both Congress and the New York state legislature denied seats to Socialists. By 1920 a third of the states had enacted criminal syndicalist laws to punish radicals. The New York law prohibited "advocating, teaching, or aiding and abetting the commission of crime and sabotage, or unlawful acts of force and violence or unlawful methods of terrorism as a means of accomplishing a change in industrial ownership or control, or affecting any political change."

Bombings and attempted bombings captured the headlines. A bomb damaged the front of Palmer's home in June, 1919; bombs addressed to a number of government leaders were discovered in the mails; a year later an explosion on Wall Street killed 38 people. Four members of the newly founded American Legion were killed in an attack on I.W.W. headquarters in Centralia, Washington, on Armistice Day, 1919. These incidents furnished the material out of which the newspapers, with some aid from Palmer, built a great national panic. Within the country there were numerically very few radicals to undertake a revolution: I.W.W. membership was down to 35,000 and continued to decline; the Socialist party numbered 39,000 and was not revolutionary anyway; the Communist-Labor party (left-wing Socialists) had 10,-000–30,000 members; and the Communist party, organized September 1, 1919, had 30,000–60,000.

Palmer's goal was to ferret out and eliminate the Communists. He proposed a sedition bill so drastic that Congress would not enact it, then he proceeded anyway without it. The Labor Department had already arrested and deported to Finland 249 Russian Communists. Nevertheless, Palmer, without advance notice to the Labor Department, conducted a great Red roundup on January 1, 1920, jailing some 6,000 suspects. Communists who were United States citizens he turned over to states for prosecution. The aliens came under the jurisdiction of the Labor Department, which gave them fair treatment. Only 556 proven Communists were deported.

In Massachusetts, a payroll robbery and murder in April, 1920, led to the trial and conviction of two anarchists, Nicola

VANZETTI AND SACCO BEING TAKEN INTO COURT, 1927. When Sacco and Vanzetti were brought before Judge Webster Thayer on April 9, 1927, they were allowed to speak. Sacco said, "I never knew, never heard, even read in history anything so cruel as this Court. . . . I know the sentence will be between two classes, the oppressed class and the rich class, and there will always be collision between one and the other." Vanzetti said, "I am suffering because I am a radical and indeed I am a radical; I have suffered because I was an Italian, and indeed I am an Italian . . . but I am so convinced to be right that you can only kill me once but if you could execute me two times, and if I could be reborn two other times, I would live again to do what I have done already." Judge Thayer then sentenced them to death.

One of the counsel for the two men who did not "belong even remotely to [their] school of thought," warned after the execution of "minds that are closed by deep prejudice or transient passion." "If," he declared, "the local hostility was inflamed by foolish words of their sympathizers or wicked deeds of their exploiters, this also is a fact to be recollected." The publisher of the conservative Boston *Herald*, which had called for an impartial commission to review the case, asserted: "The momentum of the established order required the execution of Sacco and Vanzetti, and never in your life or mine, has that momentum acquired such tremendous force." (BROWN BROTHERS)

Sacco and Bartolomeo Vanzetti. Many believers in civil liberties felt that the two men were being prosecuted more on the basis of their radicalism than on that of the criminal evidence. Ultimately throughout the country and even in western Europe, outraged liberals and radicals demanded the release of the two men, but in August, 1927, they were executed. The Sacco and Vanzetti case was the *cause célèbre* of the 1920's.

If there had been a blaze of revolution,

which was improbable, it was indeed under control, but the backfire of intolerance swept out of control and began to blacken the country. Not only radicals, but labor organizers, aliens, Catholics, Jews, and Negroes became its victims.

No group suffered more severely than the Negroes. For hundreds of thousands of them, the war had offered an opportunity to break out of the narrow caste structure of the South. Some 400,000 served in the army, half of them in Europe, which drew no color line. Several hundred thousand more moved into the industrial North, where there was less discrimination against them than in the South. Even in the North, however, they suffered from wretched housing, low pay, and the animosity of unskilled white workers who feared their competition. Many Negroes in the North and South alike began to follow the militant leadership of the National Association for the Advancement of Colored People, which demanded larger economic opportunities and greater civil rights for Negroes.

In both North and South Negroes faced explosive resentment against them. In order to intimidate Negroes back into their old subservience, Southerners resorted to the terrorism of the new Ku Klux Klan, founded in 1916, and to lynchings, which increased from 34 in 1917 to more than 70 in 1919. Terrible race riots broke out, beginning in July, 1919, in twenty-six towns and cities, mostly in the North. Hundreds of persons were killed or wounded, and millions of dollars worth of property was destroyed. The worst of the outbursts began on a Chicago bathing beach and continued through thirteen days of pillaging and burning in the Negro district; 23 Negroes and 15 whites were killed, 500 were injured, and 1,000 families, mostly Negro, were left homeless. These terrors led millions of Negroes to follow a persuasive charlatan, Marcus Garvey, founder of the Universal Negro Improvement Association. In return for their contribu-

tions, he promised to take them home to an African empire. In 1923 Garvey was convicted of swindling and sentenced to federal prison, but Negro nationalism nevertheless persisted.

The onslaught against all Americans who did not conform, against any who might disturb the status quo, reacted strongly to the advantage of business leaders, who already basked in the public favor. They were able to establish again in the minds of many people the feeling that unionism was somehow un-American. In 1920 they began a great open-shop movement to break unions and reduce wages, under the alluring slogan, "The American Plan."

The paternalistic policies of welfare capitalism, combined with a continued crusade against the open shop, led to a decline in union membership during the 1920's. Many companies greatly improved working conditions by installing safety devices and improving sanitation. They raised their workers' morale by building attractive cafeterias and promoting athletic teams. Company welfare workers looked into the workers' family problems. By 1926, nearly 3,000,000 workers could look forward to pensions upon retirement. In other companies they could buy stock below market value. Altogether they owned less than 1 per cent, but it did much to change some workers' attitudes. Further, they could voice their grievances through company unions or workers' councils, which were often effective safety valves for the employer. Through devices like these, companies helped fend off unionism from the new mass-production industries like automobile manufacturing.

Within the skilled crafts, the A.F.L. continued quietly and conservatively under the presidency of William Green. Its leaders seemed more interested in maintaining labor monopolies, especially in the building trades, than in organizing industrial workers. Membership in the United Mine Workers dwindled after unsuccessful strikes in 1922. All together, union membership declined from over five million in 1920 to four and a third million in 1929.

In some industries, like coal mining and textiles in the South, hours were long and wages were pitiful. At Elizabethton, Tennessee, in 1929, mill girls were working 56 hours a week for 16 to 18 cents an hour. Behind the harried workers was always the threat of legal action if they sought recourse in unions. Federal courts were granting injunctions to break boycotts, or to enforce antiunion ("yellow dog") contracts. For most workingmen, however, conditions of labor had improved and living standards were up. Real wages increased about 26 per cent between 1919 and 1929. They still were far from adequate. The average was less than $1,500 at a time when it was estimated that $1,800 was required to maintain a minimum decent living standard.

Thunder from the Farm Belt

While the income of most Americans advanced during the 1920's, that of the farmers drastically declined. In 1920 they lost their price supports at the same time that the bloated wartime European market contracted. At home, as machines released men from heavy manual labor, consumption of starches sharply dropped.

Within agriculture there were great variations. Truck gardening more than doubled, and dairying and citrus growing increased a third, reflecting the shifts in eating habits. Many of such farmers enjoyed satisfactory incomes. At the same time, those on marginal or submarginal lands suffered so acutely that in the five years after 1919 thirteen million acres were abandoned. These farmers were unable to compete with new, expensive machinery, which especially helped contribute to the glut of wheat. The number of tractors in use increased from 230,000 in 1920 to 920,000 in 1930, displacing 7,450,-

000 horses and releasing an additional thirty-five million acres of land for crops. On the high plains, speculators bought the lands of bankrupt farmers, and grew wheat on it with improved tractors and combines. In the Texas panhandle alone, nearly three million new acres were ploughed. The success of the big operators made the desperation of small farmers the more acute. In the year ending June 30, 1927, the income of all the 6,300,000 farmers averaged only $548, and out of this farmers had to meet a variety of pressing obligations. Farm income in 1920 was 15 per cent of the national total; by 1929 it was only 9 per cent. It is not surprising that agricultural population dropped three million between 1921 and 1928. Those who remained on their farms began to agitate militantly for relief.

Even during the bonanza years of the war, agrarian agitation had stirred the Great Plains. In 1915 wheat growers of North Dakota had organized the Non-Partisan League, pledged to strict regulation of railroads and banks, and state ownership of grain elevators and farm credit agencies. It won control of the North Dakota government in 1916, then began to organize in adjacent states, and in 1920 joined with other radical groups to form the Farmer-Labor party. The new party had some success in the congressional election of 1922, but by 1924 even La Follette would not accept its support. It was too radical for farmers who were earning $1,000 to $4,000 a year.

These men, the middle 40 per cent of the farmers in terms of income, produced 46 per cent of the farm products, and were solid citizens in their communities. Acting often through the Farm Bureau Federation or the Grange, they sought government price supports. From the outset they had powerful strength in the Congress. During the special session of Congress in the spring of 1921, Midwestern congressional leaders from both parties, meeting in the offices of the Farm

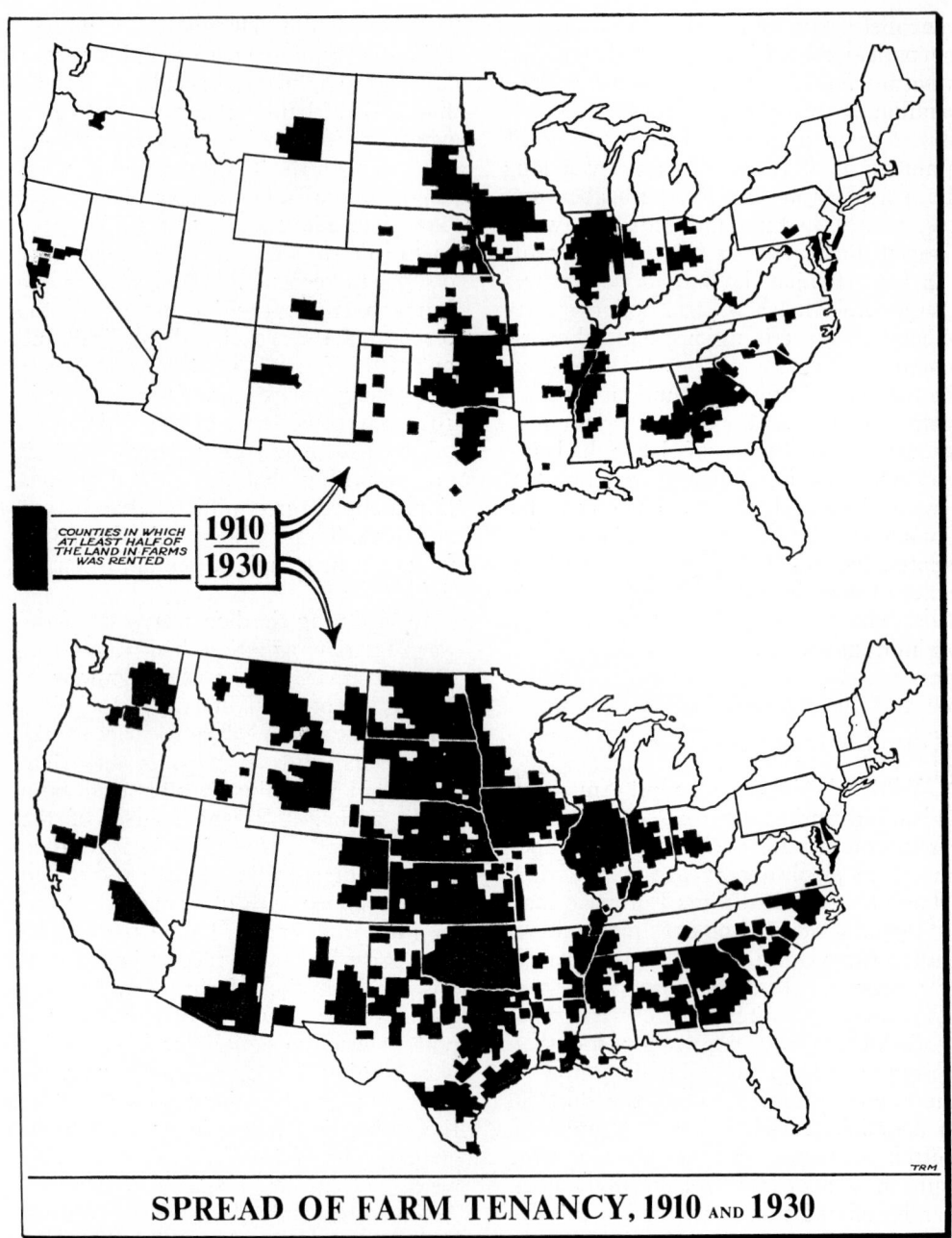

COUNTIES IN WHICH AT LEAST HALF OF THE LAND IN FARMS WAS RENTED

1910 / 1930

SPREAD OF FARM TENANCY, 1910 AND 1930

Bureau Federation, organized a farm bloc.

One price-raising scheme came to dominate the farmers' thinking. Behind the tariff barrier, the American protected price for crops should be raised to a "fair exchange value" based on the price of the crop during ten prewar years, compared with the general average of all prices during the same period. This price concept was called "parity." The means of obtaining parity prices for farmers within the country would be for a government corporation or farm board to buy up the surplus at the high American price, and sell it abroad at whatever it would bring on the world market. To make up for the loss, an equalization fee or tax would be charged the farmers on their entire crop.

Between 1924 and 1928 Senator Charles L. McNary of Oregon and Representative Gilbert Haugen of Iowa promoted this scheme in Congress. In 1924 the McNary-Haugen bill covered only grain, and was defeated in the House, but in 1926 the addition of cotton, tobacco, and rice brought Southern support. In 1927 Congress passed it, but President Coolidge coldly vetoed it as being preferential legislation contrary to the principles of laissez faire. (On the same day he signed an order raising the tariff on pig iron 50 per cent.) A year later, Congress again passed the McNary-Haugen bill, and Coolidge again vetoed it.

The U.S. and the World

The problem of developing Republican alternatives to the Wilsonian foreign policy fell largely on the shoulders of Secretary of State Charles Evans Hughes.

Hughes's policy involved first of all ending the war with Germany by an act of Congress, which was signed July 2, 1921. Hughes then negotiated separate peace treaties with the former Central Powers, to secure for the United States the benefits without the responsibilities of the Paris treaties. In time, Hughes permitted American delegations to participate in League conferences on minor matters as long as they did not make commitments. Throughout his years as Secretary of State he was chilly toward every European proposal for collective security. He did, in February, 1923, persuade President Harding to recommend that the United States join with reservations the World Court, an almost completely powerless body. But the World Court was an instrument of the League, and while internationally minded Americans ardently favored joining, the irreconcilables in the Senate violently fought it. Each succeeding President through Franklin D. Roosevelt advocated American adherence to the League; each time, through 1935, the Senate blocked it.

Through the Washington Arms Conference, Republicans made it appear that they were taking positive steps to preserve the peace. This was in effect a Republican substitute for entrance into the League. Senator Borah in May, 1921, had introduced a resolution calling for a conference to reduce armaments, but the basic impetus for the meeting came from the British, who feared a three-way naval race with the Americans and the Japanese. Japan had emerged from the war stronger than before in China and with troops still stationed in Siberia. It threatened to expand still further, to shut the "Open Door" in China, and to arm its new island possessions in the Pacific. American public opinion saw an even more serious threat in the Anglo-Japanese alliance. Hence the British, wishing to strengthen their amicable relations with the United States, proposed the conference. Hughes seized the initiative; President Harding issued invitations to a conference.

The arms conference opened on November 12, 1921, the day after burial rites for the Unknown Soldier at the Arlington Cemetery. Hughes in his opening speech startled the delegates and won enormous acclaim by dramatically presenting a concrete plan for the reduction in size of the fleets of the United States, Great Britain, and Japan. He proposed a ten-year moratorium on capital-ship construction (battleships, cruisers, and carriers) and the scrapping by the three powers of nearly 1,900,000 tons of ships already built or under construction. A British observer declared, "Secretary Hughes sunk in thirty-five minutes more ships than all the admirals of the world have sunk in a cycle of centuries."

In the negotiations that followed, Japan agreed to limit her capital ships to a total of approximately 300,000 tons compared with 500,000 tons each for the United States and Great Britain. In addition the United States pledged itself not to increase its fortifications in Guam and the Philippines. Japan and Great Britain made similar pledges. Thus the Five Power Pact of February 6, 1922, provided a ratio of 5:5:3, and of 1.75:1.75 for France and Italy, stopping what otherwise could have become a disastrous armaments race. Two other treaties aimed at guaranteeing the status quo in the Far East. The Nine Power Pact pledged a continuation of the "Open Door" in China. Afterwards Japan restored to China full sovereign rights in the Shantung Peninsula, and promised to withdraw her troops from Siberia. The Four Power Pact, among the United States, Great Britain, France, and Japan, was a mutual guarantee of insular rights in the Pacific. Upon its ratification, Japan relinquished her alliance with Great Britain.

These Washington treaties for nearly a decade lowered the tension between the United States and Japan. Their one unfortunate result was that the United States relinquished the physical force with which to impose its will in the Far East but retained its moral, economic, and political objectives in the area. The Senate came close to rejecting the Four Power Pact for fear it would commit the United States to some collective security arrangement in the Orient. On the other hand, the popularity of the Naval Limitation Treaty (Five Power Pact) is shown by the fact that only one Senator voted against its ratification.

In disarmament discussions the United States took an important part at Geneva and London, as well as Washington. What was of paramount political importance within the country was that the United States must at no time make any international commitment which could conceivably lead to the use of armed force.

This approach reached its peak in the Coolidge administration when millions of Americans (many of them isolationists) signed petitions urging the United States to promote a multilateral treaty outlawing war. The French foreign minister, Aristide Briand, had proposed a treaty of this sort between France and the United States. Secretary of State Frank B. Kellogg (who had succeeded Hughes) agreed, and at Paris in 1928 most civilized nations including the United States signed a treaty solemnly condemning war as an instrument of national policy, but providing no machinery whatever for enforcement. The treaty evoked much enthusiasm in the United States, for it seemed to offer collective security without any risks.

Toward Latin America, Hughes tried to extend the goodwill of the United States. During his first months in office, he was decidedly influenced by Sumner Welles, later one of the chief molders of the Good Neighbor policy. By 1924 Hughes had ended the marine occupation of Santo Domingo and prepared for its end in Nicaragua. He felt that the occupation was still necessary in Haiti.

Hughes moved away from the progressive policy of intervention and tried wherever possible to substitute the nonrecognition of undesirable governments for the landing of the marines. Neither he nor his successor in the Coolidge administration was ready to give up intervention entirely. For a time during the Coolidge administration, trouble with Mexico over the rights of American oil companies and renewed Marine intervention in Nicaragua seemed to indicate a retreat to the old policies. By 1928, however, Coolidge and Secretary Kellogg, were pursuing a more liberal policy in Latin America.

In European affairs the big issues were reparations and war debts. The failure of the United States to join the League had most serious repercussions on this problem, since the Reparations Commission, which was not under the chairmanship of an American as had been expected, set astronomically high sums for Germany to pay. Reparations payments depended to a considerable degree upon American private loans to Germany; war-debt payments from the Allies to the United States depended almost entirely upon reparations. The American public insisted which the United States was raising against their exports.

What kept the system going during the twenties was the huge total of private American loans pouring into German governmental units or corporations—about $2,500,000,000 between 1923 and 1930. Germany paid about $2,000,000,000 in reparations, and the former Allies about $2,600,000,000 in war-debt payments. It was an arrangement which the

PRIVATE LOANS AND WAR DEBTS AFTER WORLD WAR I

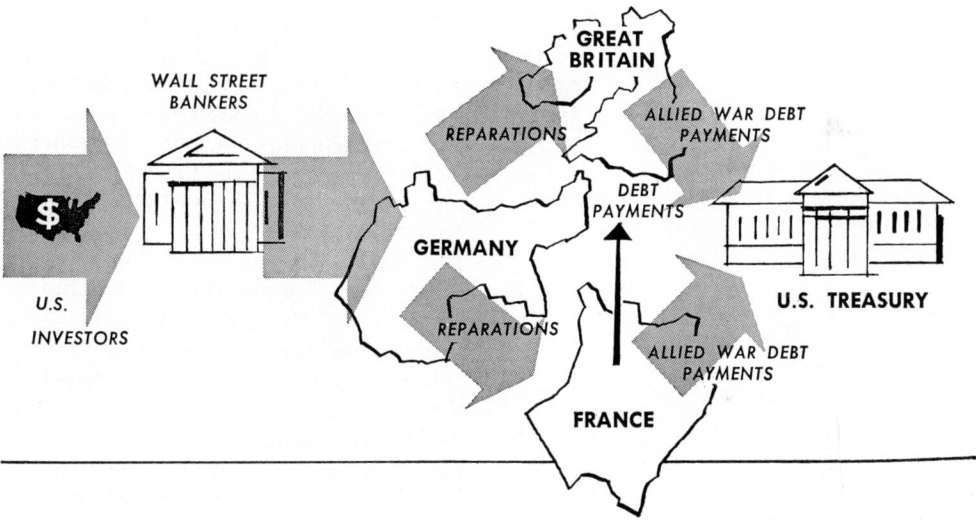

that the Allies should repay the $10 billion the United States had loaned during the war. Coolidge later epitomized the popular view when he remarked simply, "They hired the money, didn't they?"

The Congress pressured the former Allies, through a World War Foreign Debt Commission, to negotiate long-term schedules of debt payments. Between 1923 and 1926 the Commission reached agreements with the Allies (which the United States government insisted bore no relationship to German reparations payments). The administration did not worry as to how Germany, France, Italy, and the other debtors could make payments over the high tariff wall

United States government refused to recognize and which could work only as long as prosperity continued. It was part of a larger world system in which the United States was pouring out goods and building up huge investments abroad, yet through a protective tariff slowing down the reciprocal flow of goods into this country. It was a remarkable system while it worked, but it could not work for long.

As soon as the Republicans came into power in the spring of 1921, they enacted an emergency tariff measure to raise the low Underwood rates. In 1922 they passed the Fordney-McCumber Act providing protection especially for agriculture, the chemical industry, and manu-

EFFECT OF THE QUOTA ACTS ON SOURCES OF IMMIGRATION

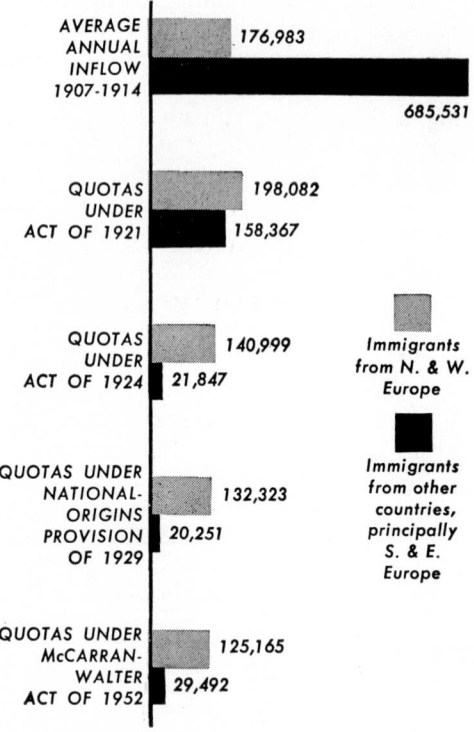

AVERAGE ANNUAL INFLOW 1907-1914 — 176,983 / 685,531

QUOTAS UNDER ACT OF 1921 — 198,082 / 158,367

QUOTAS UNDER ACT OF 1924 — 140,999 / 21,847

QUOTAS UNDER NATIONAL-ORIGINS PROVISION OF 1929 — 132,323 / 20,251

QUOTAS UNDER McCARRAN-WALTER ACT OF 1952 — 125,165 / 29,492

Immigrants from N. & W. Europe

Immigrants from other countries, principally S. & E. Europe

"new immigrants," and the unionists' fear that the newcomers were perpetuating a pool of cheap labor in the United States, were reinforced by the new allegation that some of them were radicals. This led employers who had previously favored immigration to switch to the restrictive side. In the spring of 1921, Congress passed an emergency immigration act, setting up a quota system: immigrants from any country could not exceed 3 per cent of the number of persons of their nationality who had been in the United States in 1910.

This cut the number of immigrants from 800,000 in the year ending June 30, 1921, to about 300,000 in the following twelve months. Racists still were not satisfied, so Congress in 1924 enacted the National Origins Act. This measure not only banned the people of East Asia entirely, but set a quota of 2 per cent for Europeans, and this on the basis of the 1890 census. It cut the yearly total to 164,000, heavily weighted in favor of those from northwestern Europe. On July 1, 1929, new smaller quotas based on the 1920 census went into effect, but during the entire depression decade of the thirties the total net immigration was less than 70,000. The great flood of so many decades had been cut to a few drops. In the decades that followed, the effects within the United States were profound.

Excluding all aliens ineligible to become citizens meant excluding the Japanese in particular. It was an unnecessary insult to the Japanese, since the Gentlemen's Agreement had worked well, and the application of a quota system to Japan would have allowed only a tiny trickle of immigrants. Indignation in Japan against the act of 1924 was so extreme that Hughes lamented privately, "It has undone the work of the Washington Conference and implanted the seeds of an antagonism which are sure to bear fruit in the future."

facturers threatened by Japanese and German competition. The tariff gave agriculture little real protection, but it did provide industrialists with several benefits. It accepted the principle that, when foreign firms had lower costs of production than their American competitors, the tariff should be high enough to offset the differential. It prohibited most competing imports and led to higher prices at home. Other nations followed the American lead in economic nationalism; by 1928 some sixty countries had raised their tariffs.

Along with high walls against competing goods, Congress finally succeeded in erecting barriers against incoming foreigners. The movement to curtail immigration came to a spectacularly successful climax with the beginning of the Harding administration. Racist objections to the

Life in the Jazz Age

For those who shared in the prosperity, and for those content to share in the frolics and foibles of the wealthy through tabloid newspaper accounts, it was a wonderful era. The national wealth of the United States was almost as great as that of all of Europe, and this was the impression newspaper readers and visitors received. It was the era when Florida realtors hired Bryan to lecture on the climate. Even though only an infinitesimal portion of Americans bought real estate in Florida during the land boom of 1924–5, the impression was that most people were dabbling in the speculation. So too with the stock market later in the decade. Millions shared in the national frenzies, but most of them did so only vicariously while living sober, quiet lives.

The average middle-class American family owned an automobile. There were 23,000,000 cars in use by 1929, and on Sundays it seemed as though they were all out on the new concrete highways. At home, people listened to the radio. The first commercial station, KDKA, broadcast the news of Harding's election in November, 1920; by 1924, the National Broadcasting Company had organized a nationwide network of stations; by 1930, over 12,000,000 American families had radios. Millions more had electric vacuum cleaners and washing machines; many were beginning to buy electric refrigerators. Household appliances were supplanting the housemaid and the hired girl. Food and clothing accounted for only 44 per cent of the family expenditures, compared with 58 per cent in 1899 —a clear indication of the rising living standards.

New ways of life, alarming to the older generation, swept America. Women seemed to have lost their modesty as they shortened their hair, applied lipstick, donned short skirts and silk stockings, and unblushingly began using words previously reserved for males. Younger people talked frankly and openly about sex. It was talk that frightened their elders, and was made doubly frightening by the disappearance of chaperons and the availability of automobiles. Compounding the evil in the eyes of elders were the many new road houses and speakeasies, where young people flaunted prohibition by drinking beer or cocktails. There too they listened to jazz and danced the new steps like the Charleston, which some preachers denounced to their flocks as lascivious. It seemed to many critics that Gertrude Stein had correctly labeled this the "lost generation"; these people could not believe that in time it too could mature into censorious middle age.

Motion pictures flamboyantly heralded the new moral code and together with tabloid papers helped fabricate false stereotypes of the period. An estimated 50,000,000 people a week went to theaters to see the "it" girl, Clara Bow, the glamorous Rudolph Valentino, the comedian Charlie Chaplin, gangster pictures, westerns, and great spectacles like *The Ten Commandments*. These helped standardize American habits, and not always in the most edifying way. Further, since nine tenths of the world's motion pictures were made in the United States, they brought to other countries curiously distorted notions of American culture. In 1927 a revolution struck the motion picture industry when the first important all-talking picture, *The Jazz Singer*, starring Al Jolson, was a phenomenal success. Motion pictures began to carry American speech also around the world.

In journalism, the twenties brought an even greater sensationalism than the nineties in some mass-circulation city papers. From England came the idea of the half-sized tabloid, which led to the founding of the *News, Mirror*, and *Graphic* in New York City, and similar papers throughout the country. Tabloid journalism came to mean what "yellow journal-

DETAIL FROM MURAL "CITY LIFE," BY THOMAS HART BENTON. Benton, one of the most vigorous young American painters of the twenties, at the close of the decade caught much of the drive and excitement and the froth and foibles of the era in a group of murals he painted for the New School for Social Research in New York City. Born in Indiana in 1889, the grandnephew of the first Senator from Missouri (whose name also was Thomas Hart Benton), he studied at the Chicago Art Institute and then in Paris, where he experimented with semi-abstract styles. He aspired to achieve a distinctively American art. (NEW SCHOOL FOR SOCIAL RESEARCH)

ism" had meant earlier, with the addition of a strong emphasis upon serial comic strips and sensational photographs. Millions of readers followed the gang wars in Chicago and murder trials in New York and elsewhere. Even the dignified New York *Times* had to capitulate to reader demands and lavish front-page space upon one spectacular murder trial. For the most part, however, the huge circulation of the sensational papers was largely among a new semiliterate audi-

ence; the older, less exciting, more responsible press went on much as before.

Among magazines, the *Saturday Evening Post*, with its conservative editorials and well-written stories, mirrored the era as faithfully as did President Coolidge. Close behind it in capturing the popular spirit was a reprint magazine founded in 1921, *Reader's Digest*, which filled its readers with inspiration and optimism, and guided them effortlessly through what they might consider difficult, serious subjects. It was the beginning of predigested reading. Much the same formula went into *Time*, the first of the news magazines, founded in 1925. In its cleverness, *Time* was one of the magazines tailored for the college graduates of the twenties. Another was the gay, sophisticated *New Yorker*, founded in 1925, which, with its clever cartoons and polished articles and stories, soon eclipsed the older *Life* and *Judge*. But the magazines which best typified the iconoclastic spirit of the intelligentsia and its rejection of middle-class values were *Smart Set* and the *American Mercury*. Their editors, Henry L. Mencken and George Jean Nathan, ridiculed the shibboleths of the decade, but more than that introduced to their readers many of the most vigorous writers of the era, from D. H. Lawrence and James Joyce to Theodore Dreiser and F. Scott Fitzgerald.

Arts and Ideas in the Twenties

Seldom before in American history has such a remarkable galaxy of new writers appeared. There was as much negativism from the expatriates in Paris as there had been before the war from Greenwich Village; many took perverse delight in damning the United States as a dollar-grubbing Philistine civilization. Despite this spirit, it was not a generation lost to letters, nor were the voices of protest ignored. Sherwood Anderson, giving up his paint factory, wrote tart Freudian sketches of small-town America in *Winesburg, Ohio* (1919). Sinclair Lewis more spectacularly exploited the same vein in his satiric *Main Street* (1920) and *Babbitt* (1922). His onslaught against business Philistinism, in a long series of novels, at times verged close to caricature, but in time brought Lewis a Nobel Prize. With far more pessimism, utilizing experimental episodic techniques, John Dos Passos dissected the life of the metropolis in *Manhattan Transfer* (1925). Theodore Dreiser came into his own in

THE SINCLAIR LEWISES GO CAMPING. In 1916, Lewis bought a Model-T Ford, and with his wife, Grace Hegger Lewis, embarked on a four-months trip from Sauk Center, Minnesota, to San Francisco. In the picture they are in Duluth. Lewis wanted to see first-hand more of the small-town America that he hoped to epitomize in a novel. Several years earlier he had drafted a book entitled *The Village Virus*, whose hero was a lawyer "who started practice in a prairie village and spiritually starved." By 1919, when Lewis was ready to write *Main Street*, he had, as he later wrote, "spent a good deal of time in Mid-Western villages and . . . I still felt that the ghetto-like confinement of small towns could be —not always was, but so easily could be—a respectable form of hell." (BROWN BROTHERS)

1925 with *An American Tragedy*, which analyzed with compassion both the psychological and environmental factors which led a young man to consider drowning his mistress. The novelist who best embodied the jazz age in both his personal life and his writing was F. Scott Fitzgerald, catapulted to success with *This Side of Paradise* (1920). Several of the older established novelists, such as Edith Wharton, Willa Cather, and Ellen Glasgow, continued to write excellent works. In contrast to them, young novelists appeared who helped set patterns for later decades. Above all, there were Ernest Hemingway and William Faulkner. The reaction against war was most vigorously stated in Hemingway's novel of disillusion, *A Farewell to Arms* (1929), which also helped set a new literary style. Faulkner, analyzing the South with morbid intensity in novels like *The Sound and the Fury* (1929) and *Sanctuary*

playwrights wrote for the experimental stage, which flourished at scores of colleges and cities, even while motion pictures were superseding the old legitimate-theater circuits. In poetry, two of the most significant writers were expatriates from the United States. These were T. S. Eliot in London, whose *Wasteland* appeared in 1922, and Ezra Pound, who settled in Italy where he wrote *Cantos* and

THEODORE DREISER

Dreiser's novel *Sister Carrie*, which chronicled the rise of Carrie Meeber from girlhood in a small town in Wisconsin to success as a Broadway actress, was such an affront to Victorian morality that it was virtually suppressed for seven years after its publication in 1900. But by 1925 Dreiser was an established and prosperous novelist—due in large part to the sponsorship of H. L. Mencken. Although Dreiser's works are studded with ill-chosen words and trite sentences, his best novels are well plotted and have firm structures. Dreiser was also able to convey the interplay of external surroundings and internal emotion, as in this passage telling how Carrie Meeber felt while seeking her first job in the booming city of Chicago: "These vast buildings, what were they? These strange energies and huge interests, for what purposes were they there? . . . The great streets were wall-lined mysteries to her; the vast offices, strange mazes which concerned far-off individuals of importance. She could only think of people connected with them as counting money, dressing magnificently, and riding in carriages. . . . It was all wonderful, all vast, all far removed, and she sank in spirit inwardly and fluttered feebly at heart as she thought of entering any one of these mighty concerns and asking for something to do —something that she could do—anything."

(1931), developed an abstruse stream-of-consciousness technique which profoundly influenced other writers.

In the drama these were the golden years of Eugene O'Neill, who drew from Ibsen, Strindberg, and Freud to develop American plays that were both critical and popular successes. *The Emperor Jones* (1920), *Anna Christie* (1922), *Strange Interlude* (1928), and other plays won O'Neill three Pulitzer Prizes in the decade, and helped maintain him in the forefront of American dramatists a decade later. A number of other young

embraced Fascism. At home, Edna St. Vincent Millay typified the twenties with her hedonistic love poetry, while Robinson Jeffers turned to dark naturalistic themes. Older poets like Edwin Arlington Robinson and Robert Frost continued to write in established veins, and numerous young poets experimented with innovations in techniques and topics.

In the arts and music, competent American artists and composers continued to produce along lines that in many cases had been pioneered before the war. Architects filled the great cities with skyscrapers and were active in city planning. Some of the surplus wealth of the twenties poured into European painting; Mellon matched his ingenuity in keeping taxes down with his lavish purchases of Old Masters, some of them from the dollar-hungry Soviet Union. By 1930 Amer-

from $24 in 1910 to $90 in 1930. Free elementary education had become established throughout the nation; illiteracy dropped from 7.7 per cent to 4.3 per cent. Enrollment in high schools increased 400 per cent, and universities grew nearly as rapidly.

WILLA CATHER

Although she wrote novels about areas as widely separated as French Canada and New Mexico, Willa Cather is notable particularly for her books about her native Nebraska. *My Antonia* (1918) was one of the first novels to describe the changes in a family of Bohemian immigrants as they struggled to establish themselves as farmers on the Great Plains. Miss Cather also advanced a theory of the novel that broke sharply with the loose, sprawling structure, crammed with detailed descriptions of physical objects, that had characterized most American fiction in the 19th century. In 1922 she wrote: "If the novel is a form of imaginative art, it cannot be at the same time a vivid and brilliant form of journalism. Out of the teeming, gleeming stream of the present it must select the eternal material of art. There are hopeful signs that some of the younger writers are trying to break away from mere verisimilitude, and, following the development of modern painting to interpret imaginatively the material and social investiture of their characters; to present their scene by suggestion rather than by enumeration. The higher processes of art are all processes of simplification. . . . Whatever is felt upon the page without being specifically named there—that, one might say, is created. It is the inexplicable presence of the thing not named, of the overtone divined by the ear but not heard by it, the verbal mood, the emotional aura of the fact or the thing or the deed, that gives high quality to the novel or the drama, as well as to poetry itself." (Willa Cather, *On Writing* [New York: Alfred A. Knopf, Inc., 1949].) Within four years after this passage was written, the viewpoint it expressed had found superb embodiment in two novels by younger Americans: F. Scott Fitzgerald's *The Great Gatsby* and Ernest Hemingway's *The Sun Also Rises*.

ican art galleries owned $2 billion worth of paintings. Along with this went a rapidly widening popular appreciation of fine art. Similarly, schools and colleges introduced muscial training and music appreciation courses. Innumerable Americans developed an interest in good art, fine music, and modern architecture.

The prosperity of the twenties spilled over into the educational system. The per-capita expenditure per pupil jumped

In letters, the arts, and learning, there was a seeking for values that would be something more than the advertising man's apotheosis of the mass-production culture, as expressed in the top nonfiction best seller of 1925–6, Bruce Barton's *The Man Nobody Knows*, a businessmen's life of Christ, who, according to Barton, "picked up twelve men from the bottom ranks of business and forged them into an organization that conquered the world." This seeking is why so many of the younger writers were rejecting the popular values of the United States for those of Europe, which did not seem to them as yet caught in the new commercial maelstrom. Others were trying to interpret the new society with the psychological tools suggested by Freud, forbidding the teaching of evolution. Ministers to the middle class who earlier had so exuberantly preached the Social Gospel or the great crusade in Europe, had been beaten down in 1919 when they took up the cause of the striking steel workers. Many businessmen were ready to adopt paternalistic policies and

---

H. L. MENCKEN

As columnist for the Baltimore *Sun*, and especially as editor of *The Smart Set* and *The American Mercury*, Mencken exercised great influence for the fifteen years following World War I. Often regarded as an iconoclast whose value was purely negative, Mencken actually used the grace and taste of the eighteenth-century aristocracy as a standard to condemn the "booboisie" he saw around him. Outstanding for his pioneering studies of the American language, for his opposition to censorship and prohibition, and for his championing of such writers as Joseph Conrad, Theodore Dreiser, and Ring Lardner, he wrote a virile and sinewy prose. His wit (and his scorn for American politicians) shows in his obituary for Calvin Coolidge, published in April, 1933: "In what manner he would have performed himself if the holy angels had shoved the Depression foreward a couple of years—this we can only guess, and one man's hazard is as good as another's. My own is that he would have responded to bad times precisely as he responded to good ones—that is, by pulling down the blinds, stretching his legs upon his desk, and snoozing away the lazy afternoons. . . . He slept more than any other President, whether by day or by night. Nero fiddled, but Coolidge only snored. . . . Counting out Harding as a cipher only, Dr. Coolidge was preceded by one World Saver and followed by two more. What enlightened American, having to choose between any of them and another Coolidge, would hesitate for an instant? There were no thrills while he reigned, but neither were there any headaches. He had no ideas, and he was not a nuisance."

---

or the economic determinism stemming from Marx.

Among ministers, publicists, philosophers, and economists seeking to interpret the new order, there was some confusion. The fundamentalist ministers went on much as before, although they became the butt of national ridicule in 1925 when their champion, William Jennings Bryan, matched wits with the agnostic Clarence Darrow in the famous Scopes trial involving a Tennessee law label them "Christian industrialism," but they denounced the militant Social Gospel as Bolshevism. Ministers further lost their hold on their following as middle-class reaction spread against two of the causes in which they had been so deeply involved, the war in Europe and prohibition. Many of them tended, consequently, to concentrate upon the building of fine churches and the development of a sophisticated theology embracing the new psychological concepts.

Many of the most popular publicists were negative in their view of government. Mencken and Irvin Babbitt launched some of their most scathing epigrams against the American democratic system. Walter Lippmann, who had been deeply involved in the New Nationalism and New Freedom, became aloof and brilliantly analytical in his observation of American society. The Socialist candidate for President in 1928, Norman Thomas, remarked, "The old reformer has become the Tired Radical and his sons and daughters drink at the fountain of the *American Mercury.*"

Nevertheless, many of the most influential philosophers and social scientists continued to write in modified progressive terms. John Dewey, at the peak of his influence, was expounding a socialized pragmatism: man through science and technology could develop an organized social intelligence which could plan a rational and fruitful future society. The aged Thorstein Veblen was placing a similar faith in science: the engineers in contrast to the businessmen could bring forth an economic utopia. This doctrine, carried to its ultimate conclusion, engen-

dered the technocracy movement of the early thirties. Other economists would not go this far, but some of them accepted Veblen's emphasis upon craftsmen and technicians, who, unlike businessmen, would not raise prices and restrict markets. Around them could develop an economy of still greater abundance. Agricultural economists, who were thinking in opposite terms of restriction, also looked forward to an age of social and economic planning. Among a wider group of readers, Charles A. Beard was disseminating some of these ideas. In his and Mary Beard's *Rise of American Civilization* (1927), expressing mild economic determinism and emphasizing social and cultural factors, he did much to perpetuate progressive thinking among the new generation of intellectuals. Vernon L. Parrington's *Main Currents of American Thought* (1927), tracing the same themes in literature, helped create a Jeffersonian cult. Writing on a popular level, Claude Bowers developed similar ideas. Franklin D. Roosevelt, reviewing Bowers's *Jefferson and Hamilton* in 1925, declared, "Hamiltons we have today. Is a Jefferson on the horizon?"

BIBLIOGRAPHY

The 1920's are approached from various points of view in the following: A. M. Schlesinger, Jr., *The Crisis of the Old Order* (1957); W. E. Leuchtenberg, *The Perils of Prosperity, 1914–32* (1958); Karl Schriftgiesser, *This Was Normalcy* (1948); F. L. Allen, *Only Yesterday* (1931); George Soule, *Prosperity Decade* (1947); H. U. Faulkner, *From Versailles to the New Deal* (1950); Lloyd Morris, *Postscript to Yesterday* (1947), and *Not So Long Ago* (1949); H. M. Robinson, *Fantastic Interim* (1943); Paul Sann, *The Lawless Decade* (1957); Mark Sullivan, *Our Times*, vols. 5–6; Preston Slosson, *The Great Crusade and After* (1930); The President's Research Committee on Social Trends, *Recent Social Trends in the United States* (1933); Robert and Helen Lynd, *Middletown* (1929); and

G. H. Knoles, *The Jazz Age Revisited* (1955).

On reconversion, see J. R. Mock and Evangeline Thurber, *Report on Demobilization* (1944). On the Red scare, Zechariah Chafee, Jr., *Free Speech in the United States* (1941); Robert Murray, *Red Scare* (1955); Theodore Draper, *The Roots of American Communism* (1957); and G. L. Joughin and E. M. Morgan, *The Legacy of Sacco and Vanzetti* (1948). The election of 1920 is covered in T. A. Bailey, *Wilson and the Great Betrayal*, and Frank Freidel, *Franklin D. Roosevelt: The Ordeal* (1954). S. H. Adams, *Incredible Era* (1939) is a popular account of Harding and his administration.

On foreign policy, see M. J. Pusey, *Charles Evans Hughes* (2 vols., 1951); Dexter Perkins, *Hughes and American Democratic Statesmanship* (1956); J. C. Vinson, *The Parchment Peace* (1955), on the Washington Conference; Vinson's *Borah and the Outlawry of War* (1957), and Robert Ferrell, *Peace in Their Time* (1952), on the Kellogg-Briand Pact. On the reaction against war, Selig Adler, *The Isolationist Impulse* (1957). On foreign economic policy, Herbert Feis, *The Diplomacy of the Dollar* (1950).

The most readable interpretation of Coolidge is W. A. White, *Puritan in Babylon* (1938). Claude Fuess, *Calvin Coolidge* (1940) is sympathetic and well documented. On the election of 1924, see Kenneth MacKay, *The Progressive Movement of 1924* (1947).

Among the economic analyses of the twenties are the following specialized works: Frederick Mills, *Economic Tendencies in the United States* (1932); Harald Barger, *Outlay and Income in the United States, 1921–1938* (1942); Joseph Schumpeter, *Business Cycles* (1939); Edwin Nourse and others, *America's Capacity to Produce* (1934); Maurice Leven and others, *America's Capacity to Consume* (1934); and Simon Kuznets, *National Income and Its Composition, 1919–1938* (1941). On technological innovations, see Siegfried Giedion, *Mechanization Takes Command* (1948). On agriculture, see J. H. Shideler, *Farm Crisis, 1919–1923* (1957); W. T. Hutchinson, *Lowden of Illinois* (2 vols., 1957); Robert Morlan, *Political Prairie Fire: The Nonpartisan League, 1915–1922* (1955); Theodore Saloutos and J. D. Hicks, *Agricultural Discontent in the Middle West, 1900–1939* (1951); Gilbert Fite, *George Peek and the Fight for Farm Parity* (1954); and Russell Lord, *The Wallaces of Iowa* (1947).

On the intellectual history of the twenties, see Alfred Kazin, *On Native Grounds* (1942); John Hutchens, *The American Twenties* (1952), a literary anthology; Edmund Wilson, *Shores of Light* (1952) and *The American Earthquake* (1958), contemporary essays; Malcolm Cowley, *Exile's Return* (1951 edition); Edgar Kemler, *The Irreverent Mr. Mencken* (1950); Walter Lippmann, *A Preface to Morals* (1929); Paul Carter, *The Decline and Revival of the Social Gospel* (1956); Frederick Hoffman, *Freudianism and the Literary Mind* (1945); Ray Ginger, *Six Days or Forever?* (1958), about the Scopes trial; N. F. Furniss, *The Fundamentalist Controversy, 1918–1931* (1954); and J. W. Prothro, *Dollar Decade* (1954).

33

THE GREAT DEPRESSION

A simple and effective way of perpetuating the Coolidge prosperity after 1928 seemed to be to put the "Great Engineer," Herbert Hoover, in the White House. His policies as Secretary of Commerce apparently guaranteed an indefinite continuation of businessmen's government, and of boom without bust. Hoover himself shared this faith. In his acceptance address in August, 1928, he proclaimed, "Given a chance to go forward with the policies of the last eight years, we shall soon with the help of God be in sight of the day when poverty will be banished from this nation." Yet fifteen months later the nation careened down into the blackest depression in its history. The depression brought to the fore new leadership and new policies—a New Deal.

Hoover in the White House

When President Coolidge announced, "I do not choose to run in 1928," a scramble began for the Republican nomination. Hoover was easily nominated on the first ballot to run on a platform emphasizing prosperity and straddling the troublesome issues of farm relief and prohibition.

Prosperity was also the decisive issue affecting the Democrats. The experienced politicians were still almost as badly divided as in 1924, but they saw no reason to turn their convention into another brawl when their candidate had no chance of winning against Republican prosperity. Even those who were ardently dry and Protestant raised no barrier against the wet, Catholic governor of New York, Alfred E. Smith. He was nominated on the first ballot to run on a platform not much more positive than that of the Republicans. It did, however, include a plank offering the farmers McNary-Haugenism.

More important, Smith promised, despite a compromise plan on prohibition, that he would favor relaxing the Volstead enforcement act. This forced prohibition into the forefront of the campaign. It probably would have been there anyway, since there was relatively little else except that and religion to campaign about.

Both Hoover and Smith were self-made men and proud of it. Hoover's path had been from an Iowa farm through Stanford University, and had been marked by a phenomenally successful rise as a business and government executive. Smith's had been from the East Side of

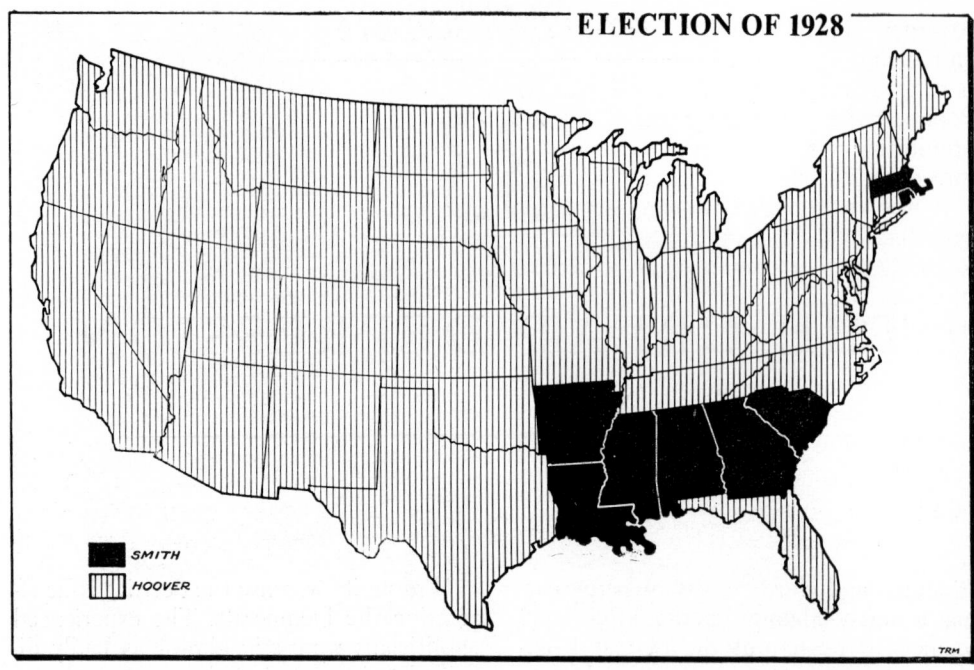

ELECTION OF 1928

SMITH
HOOVER

New York through the Fulton Fish Market and the Tammany hierarchy to the governorship of New York. There he had demonstrated a consummate political and administrative skill; he had reorganized the state government, fought to build schools, parks, and parkways, and struggled for public development of the great power sites. Both candidates were mild progressives dedicated to perpetuating the intimate ties between business and government.

This contest between two men of high character degenerated into one of the lowest mud-slinging campaigns in American history. Hoover himself campaigned on prosperity, popularly translated into the notion of a chicken in every pot and two cars in every garage. This left the political storms to sweep around Smith, who evoked more enthusiastic loyalty and venomous hatred than any candidate since Bryan. Millions of the urban masses, mostly themselves of immigrant and Catholic background, saw in Smith their spokesman, their great hero. In the Protestant South belief in prohibition

was still almost an act of faith, and the Ku Klux Klan was still boisterous in its anti-Catholicism. Fiery crosses greeted Smith near Oklahoma City, where he courageously denounced the Klan. Smith had no effective defense against the religious and prohibition issues; they overrode rural Americans' disgust with Hoover's coldness toward their demands.

The Hoover landslide far exceeded expectations. The popular vote was 21,391,-000 for Hoover, compared with 15,016,-000 for Smith; the electoral vote, 444 to 87.

Although, to some observers, the 1928 election seemed to be a great national referendum in favor of prohibition, this national restriction was not to last much longer than prosperity. During the campaign, Hoover had referred to prohibition as the "noble experiment," but enforcement was breaking down so badly that Congress stiffened the penalties for violating the Volstead Act, and authorized the new President to appoint a National Law Enforcement Commission. This commission, headed by a former

Attorney General, George Wickersham, and including such distinguished members as Newton D. Baker and Roscoe Pound, ultimately reported in 1931 that prohibition was not only not being enforced but was virtually unenforceable.

It was an opportunity ready-made for gangsters, who during the 1920's switched to the large-scale smuggling or manufacture and distribution of liquor, and the subverting of law enforcement officers. In Chicago, "Scarface" Al Capone built an underworld empire; based on beer and extending out into slot machines, laundries, and labor unions, it grossed about $60,000,000 per year. He guarded it against interlopers with an army of 700 to 1,000 gunmen. Between 1920 and 1927 over 250 gangsters were killed in Chicago warfare alone. Capone miraculously survived both his rivals and the forces of the law, until finally in 1931 he was convicted of federal income tax evasion.

Rampant gangsterism and the open flaunting of the law by millions of otherwise respectable citizens convinced many thoughtful Americans that prohibition was not worth its price in lawlessness. With the coming of the depression, some well-to-do people, already banded into organizations like the Crusaders, redoubled their efforts in the hope that repeal would bring lower income taxes and greater prosperity. By the time of the campaign of 1932, prohibition, compared with the depression, had evaporated as a serious issue and the Democrats bluntly advocated repeal. In February, 1933, Congress submitted to the states the Twenty-First Amendment repealing prohibition; by December it had been ratified, and the experiment was at an end.

No problems more serious than prohibition and farm relief were on President Hoover's agenda as he took office in March, 1929, presumably to bring the nation sane and scientific government.

Hoover's immediate positive step was to call Congress into special session in

PRESIDENT-ELECT HOOVER RIDING TO HIS INAUGURAL. Herbert Hoover, born in 1874, presented to the electorate of the 1920's the appealing spectacle of an orphaned Iowa farm boy who through intelligence, energy, and self-reliance had worked his way upward. He was the first student to enroll at Stanford University, where he studied mining engineering. He was so successful in managing mining enterprises in far parts of the world that by the time he was 40 in 1914, he was independently wealthy. Thereafter, he devoted himself to public service: organizing war relief in Europe, administering the wartime food program in the United States, and serving as Secretary of Commerce. At the time of his inauguration in 1929, Americans hailed him as a great humanitarian and engineer; he was at the height of his popularity. (NATIONAL ARCHIVES)

April, 1929, to enact farm-relief legislation and raise the tariff. Hoover's program, embodied in the Agricultural Marketing Act of 1929, established, for the first time in peacetime, large-scale government machinery to aid the farmer. The program was, as Hoover insisted, voluntary, and did not include any of the price-fixing schemes for which farm organizations were lobbying. In keeping with Hoover's long-established ideas, it encouraged the voluntary combination of farmers to help themselves under govern-

power to reduce production. When President Hoover later called for voluntary reduction of the wheat crop, acreage dropped only 1 per cent in Kansas, and that probably would have happened anyway. The Farm Board experiment thus underscored the futility of a voluntary crop-control program, and prepared the way for a more drastic measure.

Congress took advantage of President Hoover's proposal to raise agricultural tar-

THE TARIFF, 1920–1950

AVERAGE ANNUAL PERCENTAGE RATES ON DUTIABLE GOODS

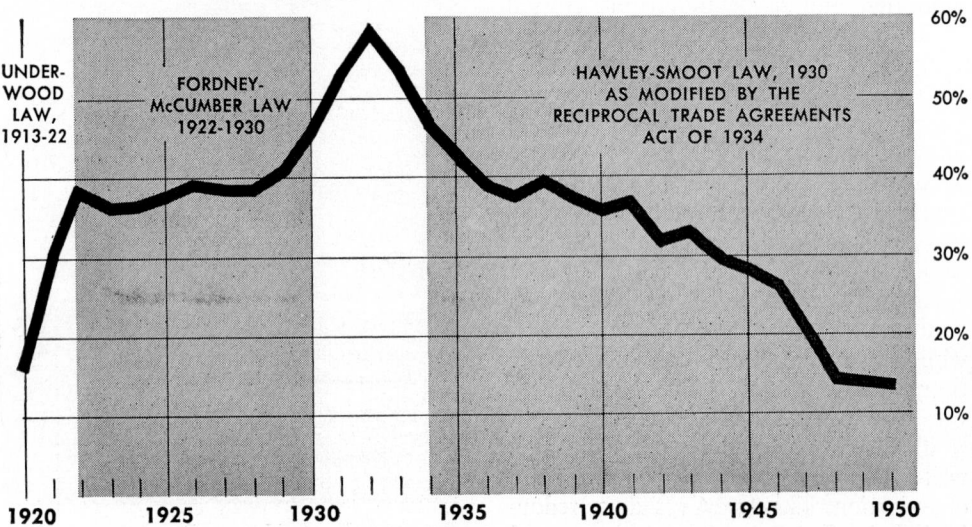

ment auspices. The machinery for this was a Farm Board of eight members to administer a revolving fund of $500,000,-000. It could loan this to national marketing cooperatives, or itself establish corporations to buy surpluses and thus raise prices. Within six months the depression precipitated farm prices toward new lows. Until the summer of 1931, the Wheat Stabilization Corporation and the Cotton Stabilization Corporation were able to keep prices a bit above world levels. By 1932 their funds were spent, their warehouses full, and grain prices at the lowest point since the reign of Queen Elizabeth I. The Farm Board had operated on too small a scale, and had no

iffs, and prepared an overall measure, the Hawley-Smoot bill, which contained 75 largely futile increases on farm products, and 925 on manufactured goods. It raised the average ad valorem duty from the 26 per cent of the Fordney-McCumber Act to a new high of 50 per cent. By the time it was ready for the President's signature in the spring of 1930, a thousand members of the American Economic Association had signed a petition urging him to veto it as an unwise piece of economic nationalism. He ignored such warnings and signed the measure. Other nations in reprisal placed high tariffs on American goods. In a time of world depression, rampant economic nationalism was perhaps inevitable, but it was unfortunate and unnecessary for the United States to lead the way.

The Wall Street Crash

As in the cases of farm relief and the tariff, almost every other action of the Hoover administration also revolved around the depression which was touched ers' garages; business inventories of all sorts were three times larger than a year before; freight carloadings, industrial production, and wholesale prices were all slipping downward.

On October 21, 1929, the stock market dropped sharply, and two days later the big crash began. Temporarily, J. P. Morgan and Company and other big bankers managed to stave off disaster, but on Oc-

PRICES OF COMMON STOCKS, 1920–1937

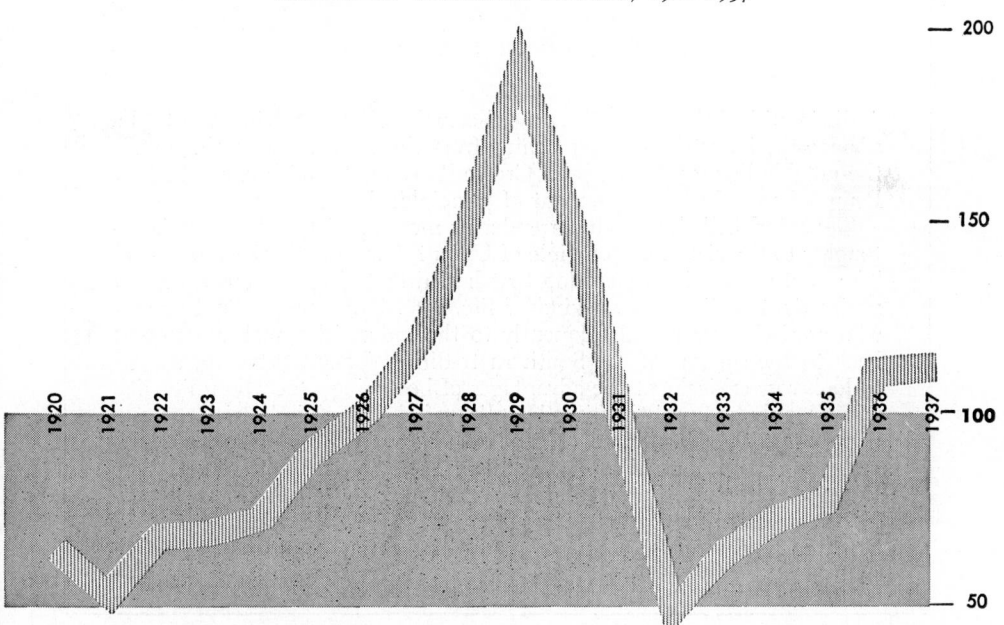

off by the collapse of the stock market in the fall of 1929. For several years stock prices had been rising so rapidly that they had little relation to the earning power of corporations; the New York Stock Exchange had become for many speculators a great national gambling casino, where everyone won almost all of the time.

During the summer of 1929, while speculators blithely pushed stock prices ever higher, there were many disquieting signs that the prosperity, so long gone for the farmers, was coming to an end for business. Construction had passed its peak in 1926, and by 1929 had declined drastically; automobiles were filling deal- tober 29 their efforts failed. Sixteen million shares were sold that day. Total losses for the month reached sixteen billion dollars. For two weeks more the market continued to drop until stocks had lost over 40 per cent in value.

The stock-market collapse was not the cause of the depression, but did precipitate it, through replacing the inflationary spiral with a deflationary one equally hard to stop. It brought to an end a decade of business optimism and opened one of almost unquenchable pessimism. Bewildered businessmen saw their only hope in retrenchment, and the more they retrenched, the worse conditions became.

For years afterward, economists, businessmen, and political leaders debated the causes of the depression. Something had gone shockingly wrong; just what it was they could not agree upon. The consensus of a later generation of economists, differently trained from their predecessors and having the advantage of hindsight, came to these conclusions: There were serious defects in the econ-

for even in 1929 only one family in six had an automobile, only one in five a fixed bathtub or electricity, and only one in ten a telephone.

Government had played the wrong role in the economic system. During the twenties the tax policies had helped increase the inequalities in incomes, whereas greater equality would have had the desirable effect of increasing con-

---

THE SOUTHERN AGRARIANS

A distinguished dozen Southern intellectuals collaborated in 1930 to denounce the industrialism encroaching from the North. Among them were the notable literary figures, John Crowe Ransom, Allen Tate, and Robert Penn Warren. In their statement of principles they declared:

"How far shall the South surrender its moral, social, and economic autonomy to the victorious principle of Union? That question remains open. The South is a minority section that has hitherto been jealous of its minority right to live its own kind of life. . . . The younger Southerners, who are being converted frequently to the industrial gospel, must come back to the support of the Southern tradition. They must be persuaded to look very critically at the advantages of becoming a 'new South' which will be only an undistinguished replica of the usual industrial community."—*I'll Take My Stand* (New York, Harper & Brothers, 1930).

A young Southern historian, William B. Hesseltine, retorted: "At no time in its history . . . has the American South been other than a horrible example of the spiritual failure of agrarianism."—"Look Away Dixie," *Sewanee Review* (1931).

---

omy which could not easily have been remedied. In the twenties, as production rose, too little of the profits went to farmers and other raw-materials producers, or to the workers. Too much went to the top 5 per cent of the income group, which received a third of all personal income, or into the building of new plants. As long as the expansion of capital facilities continued, it stimulated the economy, but it created more plant space than could be used. As a result, factories by 1929 were pouring out more goods than consumers could purchase. This did not mean Americans would not have consumed more had they had more income,

sumption. The tariff policies had meant that foreign trade could continue only as long as overseas loans were high. The economic policies encouraged concentration, and thus resulted in rigidly high prices. The government had done nothing to check speculation or regulate the securities market during the boom, and nothing effective to restore the buying power of farmers. In retrospect, critics of the government policies of the twenties asserted that it was not sufficient for the business of the government to be only business; it should have embraced all classes of the American people.

In facing the depression, the government, in the view of critics a generation later, continued to do the wrong things. It concentrated upon balancing the budget and keeping the nation upon the gold standard, both of which were deflationary when the country was suffering from too much deflation. Blame for these policies should not fall solely upon President Hoover; they were the ancient formulas for the conduct of government during a depression, and were urged upon the President by leaders of both parties and of business, and by experts in economics. Times had changed; these policies not only would not work but were destructive.

President Hoover was far more energetic and imaginative than any previous American President in trying to develop a program to combat the depression. His Secretary of the Treasury, Mellon, remembering the panic of 1873, was ready to see the economy go through the wringer in the old laissez-faire fashion; he was a "leave-it-alone liquidationist" who thought a thoroughgoing cycle of bankruptcy and deflation would be healthy. Hoover did not agree; he pointed out that only 30 per cent of the people lived on farms where they might weather such a depression by living on their own produce, compared with 75 per cent in the 1870's. He determined that the government should intervene positively but in a very limited way, seeking the voluntary cooperation of business and labor. His philosophy and techniques were the same as they had been when he was Secretary of Commerce.

First, to restore confidence, Hoover declared, "The fundamental business of this country, that is production and distribution of commodities, is on a sound and prosperous basis." Most of the business moguls echoed him. Next, he held a number of highly publicized meetings of business, farm, and labor leaders in Washington to try to rally the country into a voluntary program. Business participants pledged themselves not to cut payrolls or production; labor leaders, not to ask for better wages or hours. In addition, Hoover used the government to fight deflation. He announced a significant tax cut, and arranged for the Federal Reserve to provide liberal credit for business, and for the Farm Board to prop up farm prices. He asked Congress for an increase of $423 million in public works—a huge sum for the period—and called upon mayors and governors to engage in the "energetic yet prudent pursuit" of them. Beyond this, Hoover stood for a balanced budget and sound money.

During the first months after the stock crash it seemed as though these positive though mild steps might be sufficient. The pattern of the deflationary spiral became apparent only slowly as, with the gradual cancellation of orders, business leaders found they could no longer keep their full-employment pledges and began to lay off workers or put them on part time.

Democrats, finding in the growing depression the issue so conspicuously lacking two years earlier, campaigned vigorously in the fall of 1930. They barely won the House of Representatives, and with the aid of Republican progressives, took effective control of the Senate. From this point on, Congress began seriously to harass Hoover, demanding that he move from voluntary measures to large-scale federal relief and spending. Hoover would not budge, but it seemed in the spring of 1931 as though conditions were improving. The depression to this point had not been much more serious than that of 1921; perhaps it was nearly over.

Instead, the nation was dragged down into far worse conditions as the repercussions of European panic hit these shores. Since the flow of long-term American loans to central Europe had slackened several years previously, Germany and Austria had depended upon short-term credit. French bankers cut this off in March, 1931, and by May the largest bank in Austria had in effect collapsed. This disaster threatened to wreck the financial system of Germany and nations further west. Germany, appealing to the United States in June, obtained from President Hoover the proposal of a one-year moratorium on reparations and war debt payments, but France destroyed much of its good effect through its delay in accept-

and commodity prices continued to fall; bankruptcies and bank failures multiplied; unemployment soared. By December, 1931, when Congress met, conditions were so frightening that President Hoover abandoned his reliance upon voluntary measures, and proposed direct governmental action of an unprecedented

FOREIGN TRADE, 1900–1956

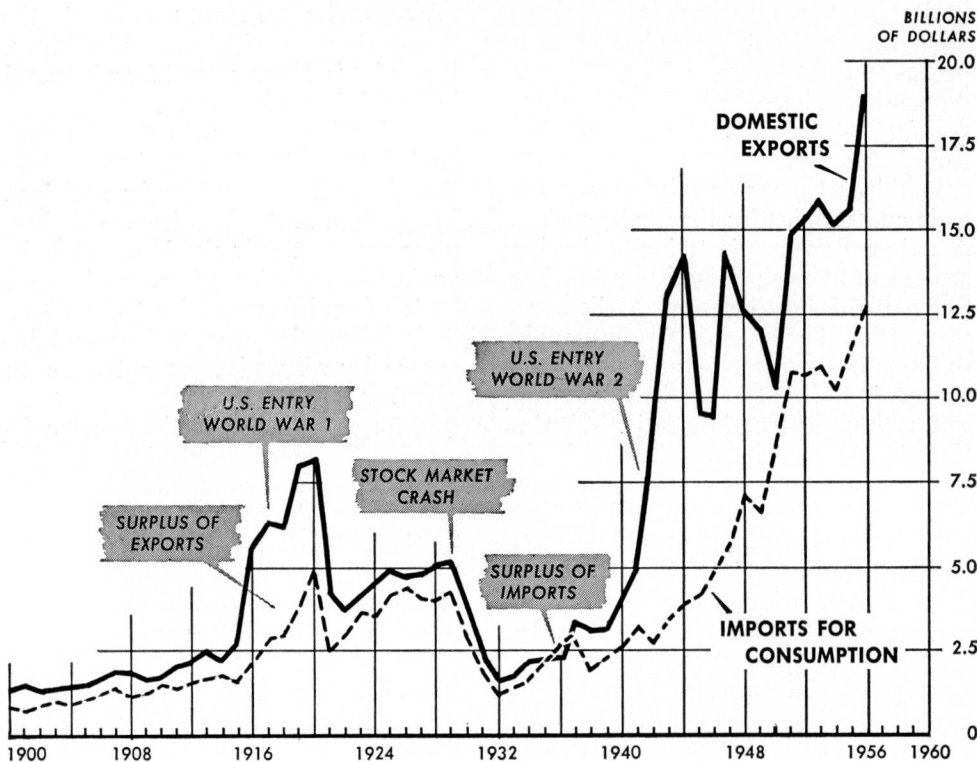

ing the plan. By September England and most other nations of the world went off the gold standard. The crisis in western Europe severely hit the United States in the spring of 1931, as European gold was withdrawn from American banks and European holdings of American securities were dumped on the market. As other nations devalued their currency in going off the gold standard, American trade with them declined disastrously.

From May, 1931, to July, 1932, the economy sank lower and lower. Security

sort to combat the depression. The Republican progressives and Democrats in Congress were so slow to act that Hoover felt they were deliberately sabotaging his program, that they did not want to bring about recovery before the election of 1932. Slowly they passed some of his measures.

In January, 1932, Congress created a giant loan agency, the Reconstruction Finance Corporation, which during 1932 loaned $1,500,000,000, mostly to banks, railroads, and businesses. Hoover, trying to parry criticism that he had set up a

HOOVER DAM. Conservationists for years urged the construction of a huge dam on the Colorado River, to utilize its large flow for irrigation and power production, and to prevent disastrous flooding of the Imperial Valley in California. Only the federal government was large enough to provide sufficient funds for the project. Through the 1920's, Hoover worked as chairman of the Colorado River Commission to reconcile conflicting claims of the seven states in the Colorado basin, and to obtain President Coolidge's reluctant approval of preliminary surveys. Hoover himself insisted that the power be sold as falling water to keep the government even out of the business of generating electricity. Work on the dam began in the Hoover administration. It was the first of the great self-liquidating public works to be constructed during the depression, directly employing 4,000 workers, and indirectly aiding thousands more. The dam and power houses cost $108 million; in addition the cities of southern California constructed a $220 million aqueduct to carry part of the water 259 miles to the Pacific coast. The dam, 726 feet high, created an artificial lake stretching 115 miles up the river, holding enough water to cover the state of Connecticut to a depth of ten feet. When the dam was finished in 1935, two years ahead of the contract date, it was dedicated by President Franklin D. Roosevelt. (NATIONAL ARCHIVES)

bread line for big business, asserted that its purpose was to stop deflation and thus increase employment, mainly by helping smaller businesses.

President Hoover also obtained some reform of the Federal Reserve system, and establishment of home loan banks, together with further capital for existing loan banks, to help prevent mortgage foreclosures. On the issues of very large-scale public works and direct relief, he clashed bitterly with progressives and Democrats in Congress. In July, 1932, he vetoed their bill as being impractical and dangerous; he felt that direct relief was a state and local responsibility. Subsequently, he signed a bill he had recommended, authorizing the R.F.C. to lend $300,000,000 for relief, and another $1,500,000,000 for self-liquidating public works.

Hoover believed that, while people must not go cold and hungry, feeding them was a voluntary and local responsibility. "If we start appropriations of this character," he had declared, "we have not only impaired something infinitely valu-

The chain reaction of unemployment slowly spread from 1930 into 1933. At first those in marginal or poorer jobs were hit hardest, as those who had been in better jobs moved downward. In time millions who had never been unemployed for any lengthy period of time in their lives were jobless and unable to find work of any sort. They were bewildered, for they had been brought up in the sturdy tradition of self-reliance, and dur-

---

RELIEF IN 1932

"The family of ―― was quarantined for scarlet fever four weeks and they were furnished with $9.65 worth of groceries, and when released the Welfare Board gave them one five cent loaf of bread, small sack of stale cookies, (donated by bakery), one pound of sugar, half pound of lard, two pounds of beans, half pound of pork, one bar of soap, and they were notified not to come back before Saturday. Today Mr. ―― applied again and was given one loaf of bread and a half pound of lard, this with what they got last Wednesday is supposed to last them a week. I believe this is a sample of the relief that is being given to several hundred families.

"The County Commissioners are distressed as their poor fund is $11,-000 overdrawn and the Welfare Board is out of funds."—Letter of October 15, 1932, from the Chamber of Commerce of a small city in Kansas to the Kansas Relief Committee, which forwarded it to the Reconstruction Finance Corporation.

---

able in the life of the American people but have struck at the roots of self-government." It was hard to impress the niceties of distinctions like this upon desperate people. Hoover, who for so many years had been one of the most popular of American heroes, became the scapegoat for the depression.

How People Faced the Depression

As the depression deepened, there were surprisingly few signs of social disorder or outbursts of violence within the United States. Communists agitated, won a few converts among intellectual leaders, and made almost no impact upon the masses.

ing the twenties had accepted the doctrine of rugged individualism—that opportunities were limitless if only one had the ambition and energy to take advantage of them. Now they were humiliated and baffled at not being able to provide for themselves and their families. As they remained idle for months and then years, they were in danger of losing their skills as well as their morale; physical and moral erosion threatened.

Care of the unemployed was a responsibility primarily of private charity, and for several years the President and governors exhorted citizens to contribute to the Red Cross or to emergency funds. But the task was far too great for private charity to handle. By 1931, the Red Cross

GENERAL MACARTHUR WATCHING BURNING OF BONUS ENCAMPMENT. During the summer of 1932 members of the Bonus Expeditionary Force in Washington agitated for immediate payment of a bonus for their services during the first World War. Only about half accepted rail fare home. President Hoover, contending that fewer than a third of the remainder were actually veterans, and that many were ex-convicts or Communists, ordered the army to evict them. Under the supervision of Chief of Staff Douglas MacArthur (left), with Dwight D. Eisenhower and George Patton as his aides, the soldiers drove out the bonus marchers and burned their encampment. (UNITED PRESS PHOTO)

could provide only 75¢ a week to feed each hungry family in southern Illinois.

Although several European nations had maintained unemployment insurance programs for decades, not a single state in the United States enacted such a law until January, 1932, when Wisconsin passed one. Even as the distress grew greater, many magazines and newspapers proclaimed that any permanent system of direct unemployment relief like the British dole would bankrupt the government and undermine the moral fiber of the recipients. It was not until September, 1931, that the New York legislature at the insistence of Governor Franklin D. Roosevelt established the first relief organization of any state, the Temporary Emergency Relief Administration, which became the model for other states and the prototype of the later federal relief agency.

To some of the unemployed who had recently moved to cities, the solution seemed to be to return to the farm; the migration away from farms was reversed. But farm prices fell so low that once again on parts of the plains farmers burned corn to keep warm. A rancher sold seven lambs in the Denver livestock market, and after paying commissions and fees received a check for 75¢. In a railroad diner, two lambchops cost the same amount. Prices of manufactured goods were relatively so high that it took ten bushels of wheat to buy a cheap pair of shoes. In drouth areas farmers lacked even sufficient food.

This is what had happened to farm prices:

	Cotton, per lb.	Corn and wheat, per bushel	
1919	35.3¢	$1.51	$2.16
1929	16.7	.79	1.03
1932	6.5	.31	.38

Some bewildered farmers around Sioux City, Iowa, in 1932 embargoed milk bound into the city, because they were receiving 2¢ a quart and it retailed for 8¢. Many more Iowa farmers participated in Milo Reno's militant Farmers' Holiday Association to block all farm products from the market until prices went higher. But this was a futile gesture. Most farmers waited for the election of 1932.

Through the summer of 1932, some twelve to fourteen thousand unemployed veterans began to congregate in Washington demonstrating for the immediate payments of their bonus for wartime service, not due until 1945. For weeks they lived in squalor in abandoned tenements, and in shanties on the mud flats of the Anacostia River. After Congress failed to pass a bonus bill, about half of them, discouraged, went home. The remainder, who ultimately would probably have left, alarmed Hoover and many Washingtonians. After a riot, the President called upon the army to oust them. Under the personal command of General Douglas MacArthur, with tanks, gas masks, and fixed bayonets, the army did so. "That was a bad looking mob," MacArthur declared. "It was animated by the essence of revolution."

The farmers' strike and the bonus march did not really threaten revolution. Even in this period of extreme despair, Americans were willing to depend upon the ballot box.

The Election of 1932

Republicans meeting in Chicago renominated Hoover in a spirit far from jubilant; they had little illusion what the outcome of the election would be. The Democrats, assembling later in an excited, expectant mood, saw almost certain victory after twelve years out of power. Almost anyone they nominated was sure to be elected.

Well over a majority of the candidates came pledged to vote for Governor Roosevelt of New York. Roosevelt, who astutely had been working for the nomination for years, to a considerable degree had bridged the gulf between the urban and rural Democrats. He was ready to emphasize economic issues and ignore the earlier divisions over prohibition and religion.

Roosevelt, breaking precedent, flew immediately to Chicago to deliver his acceptance address before the convention. He endorsed the Democratic platform, which except for a promise of prohibition repeal was not much bolder than that of the Republicans, and in his peroration declared, "I pledge you, I pledge myself, to a new deal for the American people." Thus the Roosevelt program acquired a name before the electorate had more than the haziest notion what it might embody.

Nor did they learn much during the campaign, for Roosevelt astutely confined himself to warm generalities which would offend few, yet suffice to bring him the enormous vote of protest against Hoover. Through Roosevelt's speeches ran many of the old progressive themes, together with the new suggestions of economic planning. An able team, largely of university professors under the leadership of Raymond Moley, helped devise policies and draft speeches for him. Newspapermen dubbed them the "Brain Trust." At the Commonwealth Club in San Francisco, Roosevelt broke furthest from the past by insisting that the government must assist business in developing an economic constitutional order. Everyone, he said, had a right to a comfortable living; the nation's industrial and agricultural mechanism could produce enough

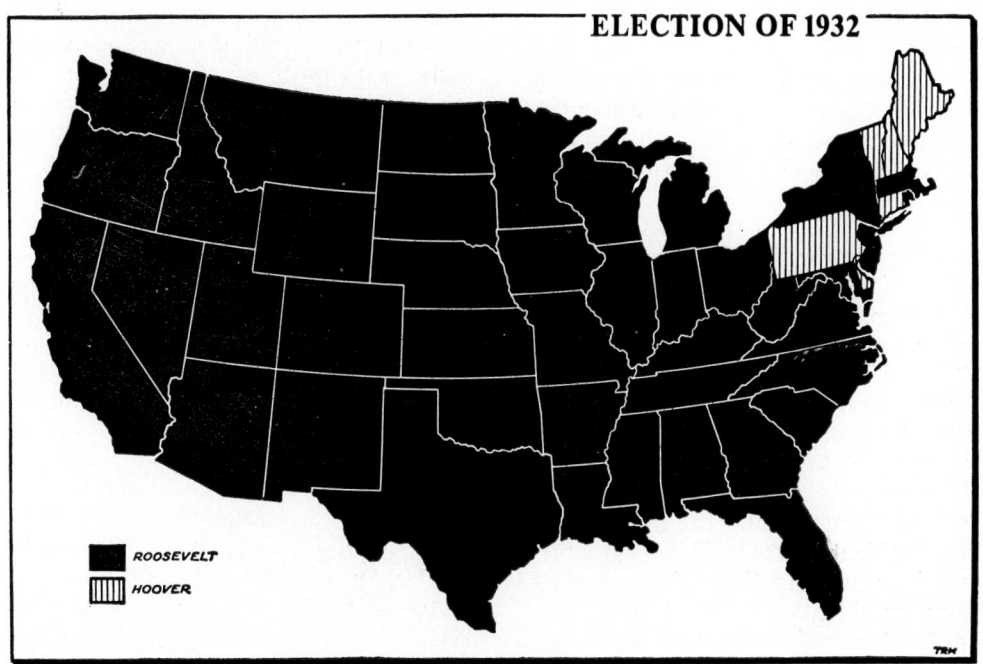

ROOSEVELT
HOOVER

and to spare. If need be, to achieve this end, government must police irresponsible economic power. Roosevelt felt he was doing no more than restate the objectives of Jefferson and Wilson in terms of the complexities of the thirties when he proposed that government should act as a regulator for the common good within the existing economic system. So far as Roosevelt explained the New Deal during the campaign, this was its essence.

President Hoover, tired and grim, took to the road in October to warn the populace that without his program things might be infinitely worse. His speeches were earnest, but dull and dreary in both style and delivery compared with Roosevelt's breezy, optimistic performances. Hoover was the last of the Presidents to scorn the aid of speechwriters.

Some voters, disappointed because they could detect little difference between Roosevelt's program and Hoover's turned to Norman Thomas and the Socialists or to William Z. Foster and the Communists. Yet, even in this year of despair, the

Socialists polled only 882,000 votes, and the Communists, 103,000. Roosevelt received 22,822,000 popular votes, or 57.4 per cent, to 15,762,000 (39.7 per cent) for Hoover, and carried the electoral college, 472 to 59. The Democrats carried both houses of Congress by top-heavy majorities. Roosevelt had won an overwhelming mandate—but for what?

Actually, there had been discernible differences between the two candidates and their programs other than the obvious one that Hoover was a worn, discredited President, and Roosevelt a buoyant candidate. Hoover had seen the depression as world-wide in origin and development; rather inconsistently he was ready to combat it internationally through currency stabilization, and nationally, through raising the tariff still higher if need be. Roosevelt chose to regard the depression as domestic, specifically Republican, in origin. During the campaign Hoover had forced him to equivocate on the old Democratic low-tariff position; Roosevelt was ready (as both his record as governor and his speeches indicated) to move toward economic nationalism. Like Hoover, he believed in economy and a balanced budget, although these would run contrary to his advocacy of social and economic planning. Unlike Hoover he was so far from being doctrinaire that inconsistencies in his program would bother him little.

President Hoover faced an agonizing four months before Roosevelt would take office on March 4: Norris's Twentieth ("lame duck") Amendment to end this long carry-over of a defeated President and Congress was not ratified until February, 1933. As the economy plummeted once again, Hoover ascribed the drop to lack of business confidence in the incoming President. There had been a brief economic upswing in the spring months of 1932, reaching a peak in July. (Economists later ascribed this to Hoover's own brief plunge into deficit financing through public-works spending and Reconstruction Finance Corporation loans.) Hoover felt he was bringing an end to the depression and that only the threat of unsettling measures from Roosevelt was preventing continued recovery. Hence, in a series of interchanges with Roosevelt during the winter of 1932–3, he tried to bind the President-elect to economic orthodoxy.

The first negotiations were over the question of European debts. Both Hoover and Roosevelt opposed cancellation, but Hoover wished to use the debts as a lever to re-establish an international gold standard. Tied in with this was the proposed International Economic and Monetary Conference, which Hoover hoped would restore financial stability. Roosevelt would make no commitments.

By February, 1933, an acute banking crisis had developed. Bank resources and deposits had been declining at an alarming rate. In the previous three years, 5,000 banks had failed, and one after another was collapsing as depositors lined up to withdraw their deposits. To prevent fail-

ures, governors began proclaiming banking holidays in their states, beginning with Michigan on February 14; by March 4 banking was at a halt or drastically restricted in all states but one.

President Hoover penned a lengthy longhand letter to Roosevelt, charging that the crisis was due to "steadily degenerating confidence" in the President-elect, and calling upon him to give prompt public assurance that there would be no tinkering with the currency, no heavy borrowing, and a balanced budget. Roosevelt did not even answer the President's letter for eleven days; he had not the slightest intention of adopting Hoover's views.

F. D. R. Takes Command

When Roosevelt was inaugurated, on March 4, 1933, most of the nation's banks were closed. At least thirteen million people were unemployed, some of them so close to starvation that they were scrabbling for food scraps on garbage dumps. Millions of farmers were on the brink of foreclosure; many others had fallen over the brink.

In his inaugural address, President Roosevelt spoke with vigor and confidence. "This great Nation will endure as it has endured, will revive and will prosper," he declared. "So, first of all, let me assert my firm belief that the only thing we have to fear is fear itself." Somehow these words, although they said nothing new, helped inspire the American people. From their depths of helplessness they were ready for the moment to be commanded, and in Roosevelt they saw someone ready to take strong leadership. Such leadership he promised. If Congress did not act, he announced, he would ask for "broad executive power to wage a war against the emergency, as great as the power that would be given to me if we were in fact invaded by a foreign foe."

Few Presidents have been better trained for the White House. Roosevelt

President and Mrs. Franklin D. Roosevelt Returning to the White House from the Inauguration, January 20, 1941. Long before he was inaugurated for his third term, President Roosevelt had become, for both those who loved and those who hated him, the symbol of dynamic presidential leadership. No one could have guessed in the black days before March 4, 1933, that he would set his mark on the age as have few Chief Executives. After his crippling polio attack in 1921, he had refused to surrender to his infirmity. He concealed it from the public so well that few realized he wore heavy leg-braces and regularly used a wheelchair. (FRANKLIN D. ROOSEVELT LIBRARY)

had served in the New York state senate, been wartime Assistant Secretary of the Navy, and had been twice elected governor of New York. He was skilled in both legislative and administrative techniques as well as in practical politics. As a youth he had spent much time in Europe, and maintained a continuing interest in foreign affairs. Roosevelt's ideology was progressive, molded by his wife's uncle, Theodore Roosevelt, whom he adored, and his former chief, Woodrow Wilson, whom he revered.

Neither he nor his advisors were clear-cut in their thinking. What was important was that Roosevelt, while basically rooted in the older economics and the social-justice tradition of the progressives, was ready to experiment. His program would be flexible, not doctrinaire; the new economic theories would grow from it, not it from the theories. When one of the brain trusters warned of perils ahead, Roosevelt declared, "There is nothing to do but meet every day's troubles as they come." This was Roosevelt's political pragmatism, and out of it grew the New Deal economic policies.

With the banking crisis at its height, he might well have taken drastic steps: nationalized the banks or even, as Alfred E. Smith had suggested, set aside the Constitution. The temper of the American people was such that they would not have long tolerated such drastic measures; the background of Roosevelt was such that he resorted to only the mildest of expedients.

During his first days as President, Roosevelt seemed bent above all upon restoring the confidence of businessmen. His initial program differed little from what they had been advocating. First he solved the banking crisis in a manner pleasing to the banking community. He issued a proclamation on March 6, 1933, closing all banks and stopping transactions or exports in gold for four days until Congress could meet in special session. On March 9, he sent it a conservative bill

which would bolster the stronger banks. It authorized the Federal Reserve system to issue notes against their assets, and the Reconstruction Finance Corporation to make them loans. The bill dealt a death blow to weaker banks; inspectors would deny them licenses to reopen. It stopped the ebb of gold from the Treasury and the country through prohibiting hoarding and exportation. In effect, the country went off the gold standard (officially it did so April 19, 1933). Congress passed the bill within four hours of its introduction. In the House, a rolled-up newspaper substituted for it, since there had not been time to print copies.

On March 12, in the first of his "fireside chats" over the radio, the President, speaking in a warm, intimate manner, told the American people that the crisis was over. "I can assure you," he declared, "that it is safer to keep your money in a reopened bank than under the mattress." And so indeed it was; by this simple legislation and his confident leadership, Roosevelt had averted the threat to banks and the capitalist system. Three fourths of the banks in the Federal Reserve system reopened within the next three days; a billion dollars in hoarded currency and gold flowed back into them within a month. During the next two years the R.F.C. loaned a billion dollars to shaky banks; the Treasury Department refused to license another 1,772 of them. Practically all unsafe banks were out of business; altogether the crisis had closed a total of 2,352. There were very few new failures in the years that followed.

On the morning after the passage of the Emergency Banking Act, Roosevelt further reassured business by sending Congress an economy bill, to balance the budget by cutting salaries of government employees and pensions of veterans as much as 15 per cent. It was, Roosevelt declared, the only way to avoid a billion-dollar deficit. This bill too passed almost instantly, although with such fierce opposition from veterans' organizations that it carried the House only with Republican votes. Pressure from veterans soon led Congress to rescind the pension cuts over Roosevelt's veto, but the President slashed drastically the regular expenditures of the government.

On March 13, 1933, Roosevelt proposed legalizing beer of 3.2 per cent alcoholic content, pending repeal of the prohibition amendment. This, he felt, would stimulate recovery and bring in needed taxes. (It also rescued millions of law vio-

pushed through it a remarkable array of legislation. Thus the New Deal took form.

Relief and Financial Reform

The first step was to feed the millions of hungry unemployed. While Roosevelt subscribed to his predecessor's maxim that relief was primarily the task of states and communities, he proposed that the federal government provide grants rather

---

THE HUNDRED DAYS

In the spring of 1933, President Roosevelt sent messages and draft bills to Congress proposing:

March 16—an agricultural recovery program

March 21—unemployment relief

March 29—federal supervision of investment securities

April 10 —creation of a Tennessee Valley Authority

April 13 —prevention of mortgage foreclosures on homes

May 4   —railroad recovery legislation

May 17 —an industiral recovery program

---

lators from the rigors of home brew and gangster-made beer.)

Thus far, except for the gold clause in the Emergency Banking Act, the program of the new administration might have been that of a Hoover with a smile. It restored the confidence of bankers and businessmen, the stock market going up 15 per cent. But this was anticipatory of real recovery to follow; for the moment nothing had been improved but the confidence of the American nation.

Roosevelt was expert enough in politics to know that this was the psychological moment to push through Congress a comprehensive program; he was clever enough in manipulating legislators to know how to maintain their support. He decided to keep Congress in special session, and in the next hundred-odd days

than loans to states. Congress established the Federal Emergency Relief Administration, and appropriated an initial half-billion dollars for it. Roosevelt appointed the director of the New York state relief agency, Harry Hopkins, whom he hardly knew as yet, to run the federal program. Hopkins was a dedicated social worker with a lively tongue and a keen sense of professional ethics. He ardently believed in work relief rather than direct relief, but in the spring of 1933 everyone hoped recovery was at hand so that relief would be needed only for a few months.

Congress also created an organization that reflected Roosevelt's keen interest in preserving natural as well as human resources, the Civilian Conservation Corps. It received a grant of $300 million to enroll 250,000 young men from relief families and 50,000 veterans and woodsmen, to work at reforestation and flood control. Ultimately the C.C.C. enrolled 500,000 young men, but this was only a fraction of the unemployed youths in the nation.

Mortgage relief was a pressing need of millions of farm owners and home owners. Roosevelt quickly consolidated all farm credit organizations into a new Farm Credit Administration. Congress voted such large additional funds for it that within two years it had refinanced a fifth of all farm mortgages in the United States. For farmers who had already lost their farms, the Frazier-Lemke Farm Bankruptcy Act of June, 1933, made possible recovery on reasonable terms. Unfortunately, these measures came too late to save all farmers; by 1934 a quarter of them for one reason or another had lost their property. A comparable Home Owners' Loan Corporation, established in June, 1933, in a three-year period loaned $3 billion to refinance the mortgages of over a million distressed householders. Altogether it carried about a sixth of the nation's urban mortgage burden. A year later, Congress established a Federal Housing Administration to insure mortgages for new construction and home repairs—more properly a recovery than a relief agency. All these mortgage agencies not only rescued mortgage holders, but also eased the burden on banks and insurance companies, thus filling a recovery function.

Under the New Deal, the Reconstruction Finance Corporation continued to function as the key loan agency. The Democratic Congress, which had inveighed against the R.F.C. policy of making large loans at the top which would provide aid to the individual only by trickling down, broadened its loaning powers. It could, and indeed did, lend to small businessmen. Under the conservative management of a shrewd Texan, Jesse Jones, it continued to make most of its loans to large enterprises and governmental units, on sound security and with

a high percentage of ultimate repayment. Between its establishment in 1932 and the defense crisis in 1941, it poured $15 billion into the American economy.

As cold weather approached in 1933 and the economy continued to edge downward, Roosevelt turned seriously toward managed currency as another device to bring recovery. Some of his advisers argued that producers of farm products and other commodities that had dropped drastically in price must receive more income. Only in this way could they pay their debts and buy durable goods like automobiles which had remained relatively high-priced.

By the summer of 1933 Roosevelt was ready to follow the reasoning of two Cornell University agricultural economists, that if the price of gold were increased, the prices of other commodities would rise in rough proportion. If the nation purchased quantities of gold, and cut the gold content of the dollar (as authorized by Congress), prices would automatically go up. When financially orthodox treasury officials refused to make the purchases, Roosevelt turned to the head of the Farm Credit Administration, Henry Morgenthau, Jr., who began purchasing gold every day along with wheat, corn, and oats. Soon he was made Secretary of the Treasury.

The silver-purchase program was of much the same purport and effect as the gold-purchase program. From the seven silver-producing states with their fourteen Senators came strong pressure, reminiscent of the Populist era, culminating in the Silver Purchase Act of 1934. This measure nearly tripled the price of silver at home. It also sent up the world silver price and wrought havoc in nations whose currency was on a silver standard. Secretary Morgenthau administered the measure as conservatively as possible, and it did little or nothing to bring inflation in the United States.

Roosevelt quickly stabilized the currency. He explained to a critical congressman, "I have always favored sound money, and do now, but it is 'too darned sound' when it takes so much of farm products to buy a dollar." In January, 1934, he obtained legislation and stabilized the gold content of the dollar at 59.06 per cent of the former amount. Altogether, the resort to managed currency did create new precedents for government action and thus, like the income tax a generation earlier, helped bring about in time an economic revolution. But it had little immediate effect upon recovery.

Some new way had to be found to care for the unemployed through the winter of 1933–4. Relief Administrator Hopkins persuaded the President to establish a temporary work relief program, the Civil Works Administration. Between November and April it put four million people to work at emergency projects. Sometimes it was made-work like leaf raking, to which critics applied an old Texas term, "boondoggling." Some of the projects, despite lack of funds for materials and tools, made substantial improvements. The output was of secondary importance; the work raised the morale of the unemployed, and increased their buying power by $950,000,000. The purchasing power thus injected into the economy was probably responsible for the wavering recovery, as the index of production rose once more from 71 in November, 1933, to 86 in May, 1934. But Roosevelt capitulated to fierce conservative criticism and liquidated the program in the spring of 1934.

After the passage of the emergency

banking measure at the outset of the New Deal, Roosevelt fostered, as he had pledged in his inaugural, measures to preserve the temple of American civilization from further malpractices by the moneychangers. In June, 1933, he signed the Glass-Steagall Act aimed at curbing speculation by banks, although it also established the Federal Deposit Insurance Corporation, which he had not favored. The F.D.I.C. guaranteed small deposits up to $2,500, and functioned so successfully that the guarantee was raised by successive stages to $10,000 by 1950. It was a longer task to work out a comprehensive overhauling and strengthening of the Federal Reserve system to remedy the defects that had appeared during the depression. This was accomplished through the Banking Act of 1935, which established a seven-man Board of Governors with firm, direct power over interest, or discount, rates and key functions of the Federal Reserve banks.

To protect investors further, Congress passed the so-called "Truth in Securities" Act of 1933, requiring corporations floating new securities to register them with the Federal Trade Commission, and provide full and accurate information on them. In June, 1934 Congress went further and established the Securities and Exchange Commission to police the stockmarkets. Wall Streeters protested, but their complaints lost some of their effect when the former head of the New York Stock Exchange was sentenced to Sing Sing for larceny.

BIBLIOGRAPHY

Most writings on President Hoover and his administration are adulatory or denunciatory. Among the defenses, see Hoover's Memoirs, vols. 2–3; W. S. Myers and W. H. Newton, The Hoover Administration (1936); and R. L. Wilbur and Arthur Hyde, The Hoover Policies (1937). R. Hofstadter's American Political Tradition contains a thoughtful critical essay.

On the election of 1928, see Edmund Moore, A Catholic Runs for President (1956), and Roy Peel and Thomas Donnelly, The 1928 Campaign: An Analysis (1931). Oscar Handlin, Al Smith and His America (1958), is a brief and sympathetic biography. On prohibition, three popular books are: Herbert Asbury, The Great Illusion (1950); Charles Merz, The Dry Dec-

ade (1931); and Virginius Dabney, *Dry Messiah: The Life of Bishop Cannon* (1949). On the crash and depression, see Broadus Mitchell, *Depression Decade* (1947); J. K. Galbraith, *The Great Crash* (1955); J. A. Morris, *What a Year!* (1956), a popular account of 1929; and Dixon Wecter, *Age of the Great Depression, 1929–1941* (1948), readable and sound social history. A contemporary economic analysis of considerable influence is A. A. Berle and G. C. Means, *The Modern Corporation and Private Property* (1932). Economic thinking of the period is described in Joseph Dorfman, *The Economic Mind in American Civilization*, vols. 4–5, 1918–1933 (1959).

On the early years of the New Deal, see A. M. Schlesinger, Jr., *The Age of Roosevelt: The Coming of the New Deal* (1958). Brief accounts of the New Deal are Dexter Perkins, *The New Age of Franklin Roosevelt* (1957), and D. W. Brogan, *The Era of Franklin D. Roosevelt* (1950). E. E. Robinson, *The Roosevelt Leadership* (1955) measures it against Hoover, and finds Roosevelt lacking at every point. Basil Rauch, *The History of the New Deal* (1944) is a pioneering work.

Among the biographies of Roosevelt, J. M. Burns, *Roosevelt: The Lion and the Fox* (1956) is a well-written Keynesian interpretation; R. G. Tugwell, *The Democratic Roosevelt* (1957), shrewdly interprets the effect of Roosevelt's early years upon his personality and policies; John Gunther's *Roosevelt in Retrospect* (1950) is an affectionate journalistic estimate; Frank Freidel's *Roosevelt* is a projected six-volume study, of which the three already in print carry Roosevelt through 1932. Bernard Bellush, *Roosevelt as Governor of New York* (1955) is a definitive monograph.

Some of the most useful and readable of the many memoirs are: Frances Perkins, *The Roosevelt I Knew* (1946), friendly but realistic; Raymond Moley, *After Seven Years* (1939), best of the hostile memoirs and indispensable on the early New Deal; J. A. Farley, *Behind the Ballots* (1938), on political maneuvering; S. I. Rosenman, *Working for Roosevelt* (1952), on speechwriting. H. L. Ickes, *Secret Diary* (3 vols., 1953–4), is a tart hodgepodge, not always reliable.

On the election of 1932, see R. V. Peel and T. C. Donnelly, *The 1932 Campaign* (1935); and Freidel, *Roosevelt*, vol. 3; and Harold F. Gosnell, *Champion Campaigner, Franklin D. Roosevelt* (1952).

34

DEVELOPMENT OF THE
NEW DEAL

Relief, Recovery, and Reform were the "three R's" of the New Deal. To achieve one or more of these general aims, Congress passed a number of specific measures regarding not only unemployment aid and currency and banking changes but also conservation, farm production, business regulation, labor organization, social security, and fiscal policies (taxing, borrowing, and spending). A series of "alphabetical agencies"—T.V.A., A.A.A., N.R.A., and so on—were set up to administer the various phases of the program.

Its critics, including former President Hoover, contended that it involved also a "fourth R," namely, Revolution. Certainly the program, which was rather cautious and conservative in 1933, became somewhat more radical and placed greater emphasis on reform in 1934 and 1935. Later on, however, the reform spirit declined, and by 1939 the whole emphasis of the administration had shifted from domestic to foreign problems. Moreover, the New Deal throughout had been directed toward patching up and preserving, not destroying, the political and eco-

nomic institutions that President Roosevelt and the American people had inherited.

T.V.A. and Conservation

Although recovery overshadowed it in the early New Deal, reform was there. Increasingly New Dealers turned their attention to measures which would remedy conditions they felt had helped bring the depression, and would make future depressions less likely. Their indignation burned especially hot against the private power interests, which they felt had gulled investors and overcharged consumers. The spectacular collapse of the great Insull utility empire in the Middle West lent credence to their charges. Thus the first and most spectacular of the New Deal reform measures was the creation of the Tennessee Valley Authority in May, 1933. It brought to fruition Senator Norris's dream that the Wilson dam at Muscle Shoals on the Tennessee River should bring greater abundance to the four and a half million people in an area rich in resources but subnormal in its living stand-

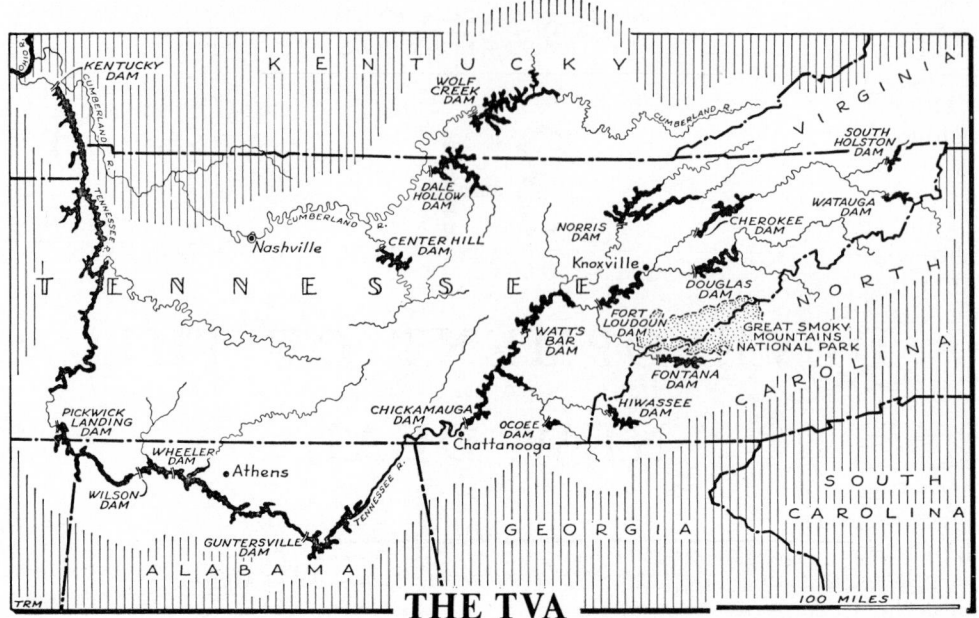

THE TVA

ards. Bascially, the T.V.A. was a project to prevent the devastating floods that all too frequently had rolled down the rivers of the area, and to provide cheap, plentiful electricity as a yardstick for the measurement of private rates. More than this, it became a great experiment in regional planning and rehabilitation.

Under a three-man board of directors with wide powers, the T.V.A. in the next twenty years improved five existing dams and constructed twenty new ones. It stopped floods in the largest heavy-rainfall region in the nation, and by holding back the water, provided an inland waterway system with a nine-foot channel 652 miles long, soon heavy with traffic. From water power, and increasingly from steam plants, it became the greatest producer of electricity in the United States. T.V.A. also manufactured low-cost phosphate fertilizers. It taught farmers how to use them, how to farm in order to restore the fertility of their soil, and how to contour-plow and reforest as a means of ending erosion. T.V.A. worked no miracles, but it did bring a higher living standard to the farmers of the area. It brought new

light industry and increased business. When the war came, it produced indispensable power for the production of munitions, aluminum, and plutonium.

In its "yardstick" function, T.V.A. drove down the price of power in the area from 10¢ a kilowatt hour to 3¢. Throughout the country, because of T.V.A. and other pressures, the average residential rate dropped from 5.52¢ in 1933 to 3.67¢ in 1942. While the power that was used increased 63 per cent throughout the country, it increased almost 100 per cent in the T.V.A. area. To private power companies the "yardstick" seemed grossly unfair, and they claimed the T.V.A. did not set its rates on the basis of true costs. T.V.A. officials claimed that they did, including payments to local and state governments in lieu of property taxes, comparable to those assessed against private power companies. The spokesman of private power was the vigorous, personable president of the Commonwealth and Southern Corporation, Wendell Willkie. After losing in the courts, in 1939 he sold his company's facilities in the area to T.V.A., and himself emerged as one of the most effective opponents of the New Deal.

Other great public power and irrigation developments were underway in the West during the same years. On the Colorado River, the Hoover Dam (begun during the Hoover administration) was finished in 1936, and on the Columbia River the Bonneville Dam in 1937 and the Grand Coulee Dam in 1942. Norris in 1937 proposed the creation of six additional regional authorities like the T.V.A.; Congress failed to act, and the decades-long debate over public versus private development of power continued.

To combat drouth conditions in the West, Roosevelt in 1934 by executive order set aside $15 million to build a "shelter belt" of trees on the Great Plains, to break the wind, collect moisture, and harbor wild life. Critics scoffed, but somehow the trees grew where no one had believed they would. A Soil Erosion Service (later Soil Conservation Service), using much Civilian Conservation Corps manpower, was active, especially in the West. Homesteading on the range, which meant dry-farming under almost insuperable difficulties, came to an end with the passage of the Taylor Grazing Act of 1934, which withdrew overgrazed land and set regulations for the use of public rangeland. Spoliation of Indian lands came to at least a temporary halt with the passage of the Indian Reorganization Act of 1934, intended to preserve the tribal domain, customs, and civil liberties of the Indians.

The "Triple A"

The Agricultural Adjustment Administration, created in May, 1933, marked the triumphant conclusion of the farmers' struggle for so many decades to obtain aid from the government. It was the logical climax to the Granger and Populist movements, and the drive for farm relief in the twenties. Henceforth, although the farmers formed a diminishing fraction of the population, they received preferential treatment from the government.

Among the farmers, Roosevelt looked especially to the relatively substantial ones, such as the 300,000 who even in 1933 were paying dues of $10 a year or more to the Farm Bureau Federation. These and the Grange wished a domestic-allotment program to limit crops. Poorer members of other farm organizations like the Farmers' Union and the National Farmers' Holiday Association opposed production cuts, seeking instead direct relief and, above all, inflation. Roosevelt could not ignore them altogether. He tried to develop a farm program which would fit the Farm Bureau formula, yet not drive poorer farmers into new revolt. In effect, Roosevelt let the farm organization leaders devise their own program. Fifty of them met in Washington early in March, 1933, and drafted an omnibus bill which contained scraps and reworkings of most of the old schemes. Primarily it provided for the "domestic-allotment" plan. Producers of seven basic commodities (wheat, cotton, corn, hogs, rice, tobacco, and milk and dairy products) were to receive benefit payments if they cut acreage or production. Funds for these payments would come from a processing tax upon the commodities. This meant taxing consumers to subsidize the farmer to grow less. In addition, the consumers would have to pay higher prices. For the farmer, prices were to be brought up to "parity," that is, a level that would provide the same price relationship of farm products to manufactured goods as during the period 1909–14.

Because the 1933 farm season was well under way when the A.A.A. began operations, large-scale destruction was necessary to cut surpluses. Six million pigs and 220,000 sows about to farrow were slaughtered. Nine tenths of their weight was inedible and processed into fertilizer, but they did provide 100 million pounds of pork for needy families. Opponents of the New Deal long cited this slaughter as one of its prime iniquities. To the relief of Agriculture Secretary Henry A. Wallace, bad weather so drastically cut the wheat crop that the A.A.A. did not have to intervene and then "explain the logic of plowing under wheat while millions lacked bread." Beginning in August, cotton farmers ploughed under a quarter of their crop—but it was the poorest quarter and they so intensively cultivated the

cuts in production. In this way cotton farmers received double the cash in 1933 that they had in 1931.

Farmers in other crop-reduction programs did not fare as well, although corn producers too could obtain commodity loans in the fall of 1933. The total income of all farmers went up only a fifth over 1932, and still lagged behind 1931. Rising prices of manufactured goods wiped away most of the farmers' gain in

FARM DEFAULTS AND FORECLOSURES, 1929–1945

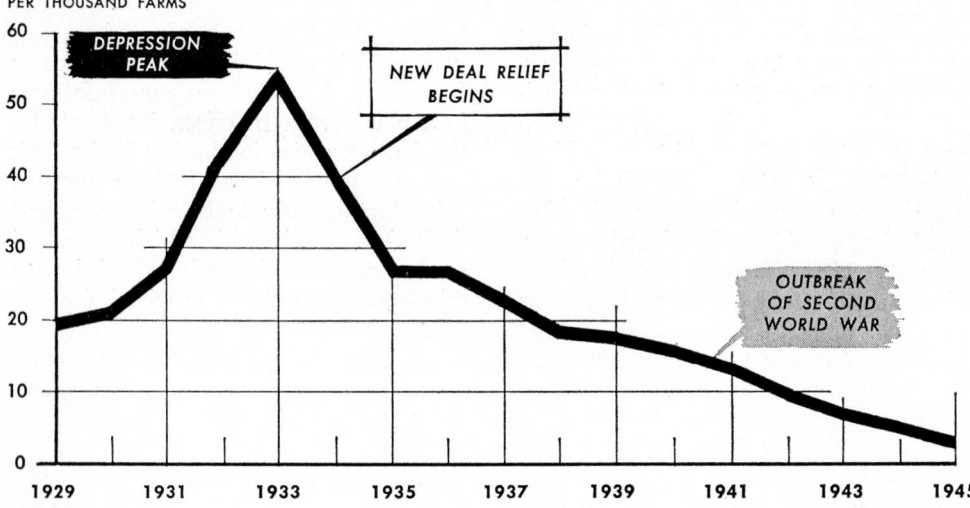

rest that 30 million acres produced somewhat more than 36 million had done the previous year.

Despite continued high cotton production, a short textile boom sent the price up from 5.5¢ per pound to 10.6¢ in the summer. Then it began to sag again, and was held to 9.6¢ in November only through another device. A subsidiary of the A.A.A., the Commodity Credit Corporation, loaned 10¢ per pound to cotton farmers who would agree to take additional land out of production the next year. Since the loan was in excess of the market value of cotton, the government in effect was buying the crop at a premium price upon the promise of drastic

real income. Through the marketing quotas set under the Bankhead Cotton Control Act of 1934, cotton production was cut from 13,000,000 bales to 9,600,000 in 1934 and 10,600,000 in 1935. After that, production began to soar again. Drought more than production quotas similarly reduced the output of wheat and corn and hogs. The cash income of farmers jumped from $4,700,000,000 in 1932 to $8,700,000,000 in 1936, and was even higher the following year. The relative position of the farmer improved. On the parity yardstick of 100 for the years 1909–14, the ratio of prices of farm products to those of manufactured goods increased from 61 in 1932 to 86 in 1935.

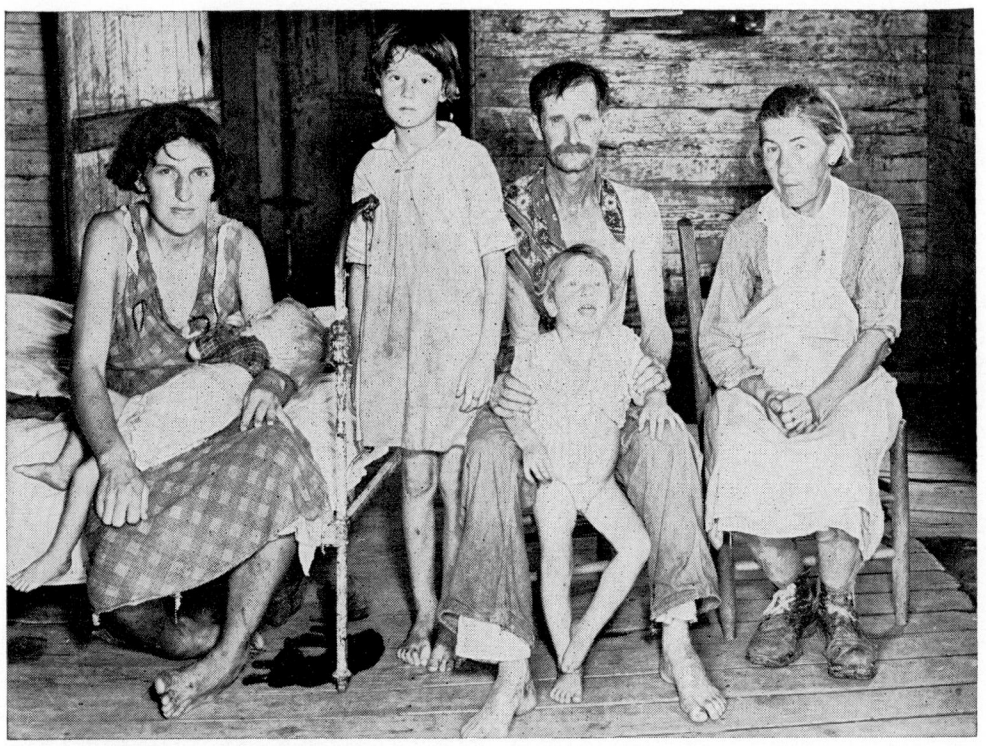

A SHARECROPPER'S FAMILY, 1936. "Total family incomes in a good year (1934 with a fair cotton crop at twelve cents a pound) averaged on the efficient plantations $312 for croppers and $417 for other share tenants. This included food raised and consumed by the family. . . . The 18,000,000 bale crop of 1937 so reduced the price that it is probable that the average cropper did not have more than $75 in net cash at the end of the year and the lowest fourth either came out in debt or did not have enough to replace the overalls and brogan shoes worn out in working the crop. Living standards as expressed in the miserable shacks that croppers and other share tenants occupy, the shoddy clothing they wear, and the inadequate diet they consume are indefensible. Here are over a million families who cannot in any real sense be considered a part of the American market. They live in a climate which will produce an amazing variety of sustenance. Yet they can barely exist in good years and know hunger in poor years."—T. J. Woofter, Jr. and Ellen Winston, *Seven Lean Years* (Chapel Hill: University of North Carolina Press, 1939). (LIBRARY OF CONGRESS)

Still, farm income did not exceed the quite inadequate 1929 amount until 1941.

The A.A.A. actually hurt many of the smaller marginal and submarginal farmers, especially in the cotton belt. One study of 500 sharecropper families indicated that their average income was $262 per year. At times the A.A.A. indirectly dispossessed them, because planters, in reducing their acreage to A.A.A. levels, sometimes evicted tenants and fired field hands. The A.A.A. tried unsuccessfully to stop evictions through prohibitory clauses in the acreage-reduction contracts. Thus the A.A.A. helped continue the great migration away from sharecropper cabins even though city jobs no longer awaited the migrants; rapid mechanization and the "Dust Bowl" on the Great Plains gave it impetus.

The Resettlement Administration, es-

FATHER AND SONS WALKING IN THE FACE OF A DUST STORM, CIMARRON COUNTY, OKLAHOMA. Beginning late in 1933, years of extreme drought and high winds further afflicted the depression-plagued farmers of the Great Plains. The worst-hit area, centering around the panhandles of Texas and Oklahoma, eastern Colorado and New Mexico, and western Kansas, came to be known as the "Dust Bowl." "Only those who have been caught out in a 'black blizzard' can have more than a faint conception of its terrors," Lawrence Svobida, a Kansas wheat farmer, has written. "The dust begins to blow with only a slight breeze. . . . The wind increases its velocity until it is blowing at forty to fifty miles an hour. Soon everything is moving—the land is blowing, both farm land and pasture alike. The fine dirt is sweeping along at express-train speed, and when the very sun is blotted out, visibility is reduced to some fifty feet; or perhaps you cannot see at all, because the dust has blinded you, and even goggles are useless to prevent the fine particles from sifting into your eyes."—Lawrence Svobida, *An Empire of Dust* (Caldwell, Idaho: The Caxton Printers, 1940). (LIBRARY OF CONGRESS)

tablished in 1935 to aid submarginal farmers, entered into a great variety of projects, which received spectacular adverse publicity and aided only a few farmers. In 1937, the Farm Security Administration, which replaced it, faced similar difficulties. The Resettlement Administration had planned to move 500,000 farm families; it actually resettled 4,441. However, by 1944 it and the F.S.A. had made 870,000 short-term rehabilitation loans and 41,000 long-range loans for the purchase of farms.

The Rural Electrification Administration was established in 1935 to extend power lines to farms through cooperatives. Since its activities stimulated private power companies also to extend into the country, it was effective both directly and indirectly. Power lines had reached only 4 per cent of the farms in 1925; they reached 25 per cent by 1940.

In January, 1936, the A.A.A. processing-tax scheme was declared unconstitutional by the Supreme Court, and the administration switched to a soil-conservation basis for the program. The new contracts provided that landlords must share payments for withdrawing land from production with their tenants and sharecroppers. Nevertheless in 1937, while the average plantation operator was grossing $8,328, of which $833 came from the soil conservation program, the average tenant family received only $385, of which $27 came from the government.

Agricultural interests pressed for a new A.A.A. to cope with an enormous threatened surplus. The end of the drought, increased mechanization, and other improvements like the rapid spread of hybrid corn in the Middle West outmoded the crop controls in the 1936 legislation. The Agricultural Adjustment Act of 1938 provided a number of devices to cut back production: soil-conservation payments, marketing quotas, export subsidies, and crop loans. Surpluses of five nonperishable commodities upon which farmers received loans would be stored under gov-

ernment seal until needed in lean years, thus creating what Secretary Wallace termed an "ever normal granary." The surpluses so stored were of vital aid in feeding allies during the war years. The 1938 act also established a Surplus Marketing Administration to channel surpluses to needy persons and provide food for school lunches.

The N. R. A. and Monopoly

Hard-pressed businessmen sought measures providing for government stabilization of business. Since 1931 leaders of the United States Chamber of Commerce and others had been urging an anti-deflation scheme which in effect meant price fixing through trade associations. This plan would have necessitated suspension of the antitrust laws. President Hoover, who earlier had given such strong impetus to the trade-association movement, indignantly opposed price-fixing schemes. His Attorney General forced five leading trade associations to dissolve, and the Federal Trade Commission forced revision of the trade-association codes for 62 industries.

In the spring of 1933, businessmen sought from Roosevelt what Hoover had refused them. Many of them also demanded government enforcement of their agreements in order to raise prices and stabilize production. The New Deal was ready to give them what they wanted if they would accept wages-and-hours regulation and other concessions for labor. As a consequence of such an arrangement, prices and wages would go up. Consumers' buying power might lag and thus defeat the scheme. Therefore the New Dealers drafting the great recovery bill added another ingredient for which there was much pressure: a large-scale public-works spending program to prime the economic pump. This was the genesis of the National Industrial Recovery Act, which passed Congress in June, 1933.

A new era of government alliance with

THE N.R.A. EAGLE. General Johnson chose a blue eagle as the N.R.A. emblem. "He is the Thunder Bird," Johnson explained, "—an Amerindian ideograph of unmeasured antiquity." In the summer of 1933 the blue eagle appeared in store windows all over America, and in hundreds of political cartoons. At that time Talburt in the New York *World Telegram* drew him jolting "Old Man Depression," but in May, 1935, after the Supreme Court decision invalidating the code system, Fitzpatrick in the St. Louis *Post-Dispatch* saw him as no more than a trussed dead bird.

business for the common good seemed to be opening. Roosevelt as he signed the act called it "the most important and far-reaching legislation ever enacted by the American Congress." On the same day the President appointed as Administrator the volatile, colorful General Hugh S. Johnson, who had pictured himself as a sort of benign Mussolini presiding over the economy.

The President turned over the $3,300,-000,000 for public works to Secretary of the Interior Harold L. Ickes, who slowly and methodically began to gather plans for projects, checking each carefully to make sure it would be really worthwhile. The need was for heavy spending in the next few months, but it was four years before Ickes' Public Works Administration pumped appreciable amounts of money into the economy.

President Roosevelt and N.R.A. administrator Johnson called upon an excited nation to accept an interim blanket code, providing minimum wages of 30¢ or 40¢ an hour, maximum working hours of thirty-five or forty per week, and the abolition of child labor. All employers who agreed with the code were to display the N.R.A. blue-eagle symbol; all consumers who cooperated were to sign pledges that they would buy only from blue-eagle establishments. In much the spirit of 1917, the nation participated in N.R.A. parades and rallies. The blue eagle with its slogan, "We Do Our Part," went up almost everywhere, and as Johnson began negotiating codes with big industries, recovery seemed really imminent.

By the beginning of September, 1933, specific codes for most of the big industries were in operation; by the following February, code making was complete, with 557 basic codes and 208 supplementary codes approved.

In the drafting of all the codes, Johnson had tried to serve as arbiter to balance the conflicting interests of business, labor, and the consumer. All three had been represented at the bargaining table, and to some degree received protection in the codes. Nevertheless, the real power in drafting the codes went to the businessmen themselves, and to the leaders within each industry. They flocked to Washington and in the urgency of the moment rewrote their old trade-association agreements into new N.R.A. codes. These codes often contained provisions that were difficult for small units in the industry to maintain. Basically most of them provided for limiting production and, although often in disguised form, for price fixing.

Production, after a sharp rise, skidded downward during the fall of 1933, from an index figure of 101 in July to 71 in November, even as prices began to creep upward. The brave words and great N.R.A. demonstrations of the spring and summer had not brought recovery. The New Deal honeymoon was over, and even as General Johnson had predicted, the dead cats began to fly.

In the spring of 1934 a National Recovery Review Board under the famous iconoclastic lawyer, Clarence Darrow, reported that the N.R.A. system was dominated by big business, and hinted that what was needed was socialism. In the ensuing storm of vituperation between Johnson and Darrow, the N.R.A. lost still further prestige. Johnson tried to make the N.R.A. more acceptable to small business, but was forced to resign in September, 1934. For some months thereafter, the N.R.A. limped along under a five-man board.

A case involving the National Recovery Administration finally reached the Supreme Court. The constitutional basis for the N.R.A. was the right of Congress to regulate commerce among the states, but the test case involved alleged code violations by the Schechter brothers, who were operating a wholesale poultry business in Brooklyn. Among the charges against them were the selling of poultry not in good condition and the unfair treatment of employees. The Court (1935) unanimously held that the Schechters were not engaged in interstate commerce, and that Congress had unconstitutionally delegated legislative power to the President to draft the codes.

The "sick chicken" decision outraged Roosevelt. Partly he saw in it a threat to the whole New Deal, and lashed out at

preme Court invalidation of legislation to prevent the overproduction of oil, Congress passed the Connally Act prohibiting the shipment of "hot oil" in interstate commerce. The Guffey Act of August, 1935, virtually re-enacted the N.R.A. bituminous-coal code, fixing prices, limiting production, and protecting labor. When the Supreme Court

ADJUSTMENT OF VARIOUS INDUSTRIES TO THE DEPRESSION

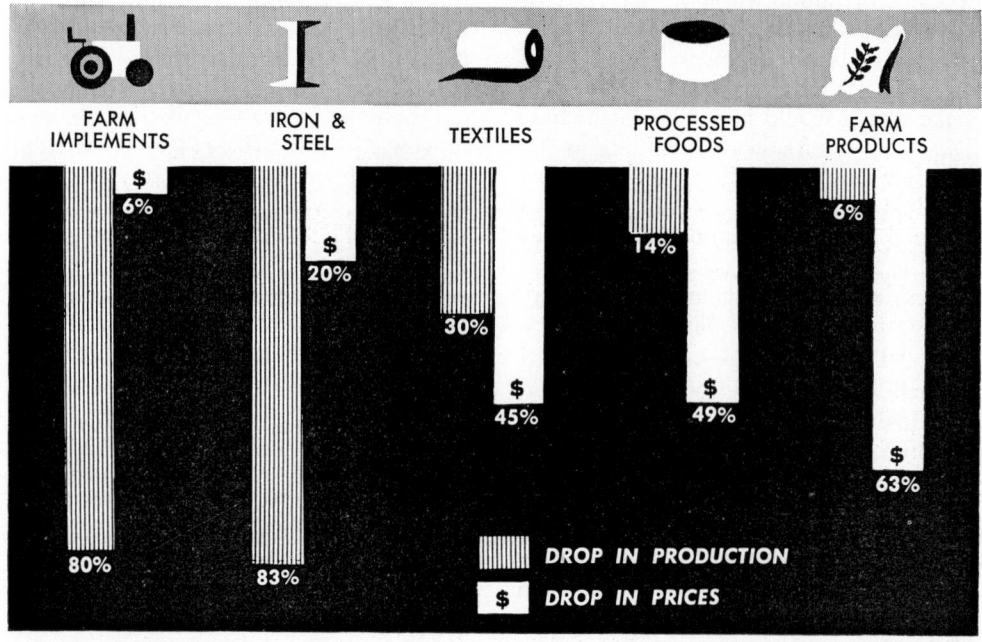

the judges for thinking in terms of the horse-and-buggy era. Further, he feared that little businessmen and laborers would suffer, as indeed they did, from unfair cutting of prices and wages. But the decision was more of a blessing than a catastrophe for the New Deal, since it ended the decrepit N.R.A. code system with its tacit suspension of the antitrust laws. "It has been an awful headache," Roosevelt confessed privately.

Much of the N.R.A. program that had benefited smaller business and overcompetitive producers was now enacted piecemeal to form a "little N.R.A." As early as February, 1935, in response to the Su-

threw out the new coal-control law in 1936, Congress passed the second Guffey Act of 1937. Roosevelt feared a wages-and-hours law would be unconstitutional, but did sign the Walsh-Healey Act of August, 1936, covering wages and hours on work done on federal contracts. In order to protect small retailers, the Robinson-Patman Act of 1936 prohibited wholesalers or manufacturers from giving preferential discounts or rebates to chain stores or other large buyers; the Miller-Tydings Act of 1937 fortified state "fair trade" price-fixing laws.

As yet Roosevelt did not resort to vigorous use of the antitrust laws, but he did advocate tightening the regulation of various segments of big business. In March, 1935, he recommended passage of an act to prohibit after five years the pyramiding of utility holding companies, which had led to such flagrant abuses in the 1920's. In the 1930's thirteen companies still controlled three fourths of the nation's electric power. They fought desperately through the summer of 1935 against what they viewed as a threatened "death sentence." One company alone spent $700,-000 lobbying against the measure. In the Holding Company Act of August, 1935, the companies gained a partial victory; it permitted two strata of holding companies above the operating companies.

In addition, Congress passed a series of other laws between 1935 and 1940 stiffening federal regulation. These strengthened the Federal Power Commission, brought trucks and carriers on inland waterways under the supervision of the Interstate Commerce Commission, created in 1936 a new Maritime Commission to subsidize and regulate a merchant fleet, and in 1938 set up a Civil Aeronautics Authority (later Board) to regulate airlines.

One of the most effective ways to regulate was to tax, and in June, 1935, Roosevelt proposed democratizing the federal tax structure by placing far higher levies upon big corporations and wealthy people. He pointed out that a person receiving $6,000 per year paid twice the tax levied upon one receiving $4,000, yet the tax upon a $5,000,000 income was at the same rate as on $1,000,000. Conservative newspapers immediately attacked his proposal as a "soak the rich" tax scheme, but it passed Congress in August, 1935. It wiped away the last vestiges of Secretary Mellon's influence on tax policy, as it established the highest rates in history at the top: a maximum 75 per cent income tax, 70 per cent estate tax, and 15 per cent corporate-income tax. It was an important step toward redistribution of American income.

Big business seemed to have grown bigger through New Deal inadvertence. The N.R.A. relaxation of the antitrust laws had given it an opportunity to thrive at the expense of smaller business. In the two years after the end of the codes, the Attorney-General initiated even fewer antitrust suits than during the N.R.A. period.

Then, in April, 1938, the President sent Congress a message vehemently denouncing the unjustifiable concentration of economic power. Less than 5 per cent of all corporations in 1935 owned 87 per cent of all the assets, he declared. This was leading to such a serious maldistribution of income, he pointed out, that in 1935-6 the upper 1.5 per cent of the population had a share of the national income as great as the 47 per cent at the bottom—and these had less than $1,000 per year per family. The remedy, Roosevelt proposed, was to study economic concentration and enact more modern antitrust laws to cope with the newer techniques of monopoly. In response, Congress established the Temporary National Economic Committee under the chairmanship of Senator O'Mahoney. It conducted lengthy public hearings and published 39 volumes of reports and 43 scientific monographs by the end of 1941. By that time the national attention was entirely engrossed elsewhere; legislation never followed.

Meanwhile, Roosevelt launched an immediate trust-busting program through Thurman Arnold, whom he appointed head of the Anti-Trust Division of the Department of Justice. Arnold, who felt there was nothing wrong with existing legislation, made new and sophisticated use of the Sherman and Clayton Acts as he undertook 215 major investigations and 92 test cases.

The Workers' Welfare

Frances Perkins, the first woman Cabinet member, had accepted the office of Labor Secretary only with Roosevelt's pledge that he would support a social-security program. For several years, she and a group of New Dealers sought to win converts in the cabinet, in Congress, and throughout the country to their view that social insurance would not only aid the unemployed but also help prevent future depressions.

The Social Security Act of August, 1935, provided two types of assistance for the aged. Those who were destitute could receive federal aid up to $15 per month, depending upon the matching sums states provided. Those who were working could receive upon retirement annuities provided from taxes upon their earnings and their employer's payroll. The 1935 law specified payments, to begin in 1942, ranging from $10 to $85 per month, and excluded wide categories of workers from the program—but it was a beginning. The act also provided for unemployment insurance, aid for the blind and crippled, and assistance for dependent mothers and children, all such funds to be administered by the states in keeping with minimum federal standards. A Social Security Board supervised the entire system.

Social Security could not immediately help those already unemployed in 1935; to aid them, Congress in April voted $5 billion to supplant direct relief with the Works Progress Administration. Work relief was more expensive, but was essential to prevent the moral erosion, and if possible to save the skills, of the unemployed.

The W.P.A. under Harry Hopkins did much to "help men keep their chins up and their hands in." It enrolled an average of 2,100,000 workers between 1935 and 1941 on a wide variety of projects. Since the W.P.A. workers were, theoretically at least, the less employable segment of the working force, and since almost all W.P.A. money went for wages rather than tools and materials, its undertakings could not compare in efficiency with private construction projects. Many people tended to forget this and regard W.P.A.

as a politically inspired paradise for loafers. Nevertheless, W.P.A. built nearly 600 airports and built or rebuilt 110,000 public buildings, more than a half-million miles of roads and streets, over 100,000 bridges, a half-million sewers, and over a million privies. In the realm of art, music, and the theater it gave opportunities to a remarkable proportion of the nation's talented people; its writers, for example, produced a useful set of state guidebooks.

The National Youth Administration, established in June, 1935, as a sort of "junior W.P.A.," aided young people between 16 and 25, seven eighths of whom received student aid in schools and colleges.

Meanwhile, improved living quarters were being provided for working-class families. From the outset in June, 1933, the Public Works Administration (P.W.A. —not the same as W.P.A.), through an Emergency Housing Division, began federal sponsorship of public housing. It cleared some of the nation's most notorious slum blocks, replacing them with some fifty developments containing almost 22,000 family units. The rent was an average of $26 per month, too high during these years for many previous slum dwellers to meet. Congress in 1937 finally passed Senator Wagner's bill creating the United States Housing Authority, which with $500,000,000 (later in 1941 increased to $1,600,000,000) took over and expanded the housing program to 511 projects with 161,000 units intended for the truly poor. Almost a third of the units went to Negroes—one of the largest pieces of federal aid they had ever received.

For those fortunate enough to be employed, Roosevelt preferred a paternalistic program of wages-and-hours guarantees, and social-security benefits. Union leaders wanted to use collective bargaining to gain these advantages for their workers, so they would look to the union, not to the government.

They had gained much of what they wanted just before the advent of the New Deal, with the passage in 1932 of the Norris-LaGuardia Act. This prohibited the courts from issuing injunctions against most ordinary collective-bargaining practices, and made unenforceable any "yellow-dog contracts"—pledges from employees that they would not join unions. The Norris-LaGuardia Act in effect stopped federal courts from interfering on behalf of employers in struggles with employees. It left management and the unions free to bring economic pressure upon each other as best they could in collective-bargaining procedures.

But in the depression years, employers were usually stronger than unions. Besides, strikes could interfere with economic recovery. Hence in 1933 section 7-(a) of the National Industrial Recovery Act affirmed the right of labor to bargain collectively, and led to a government agency, a National Labor Board, to settle disputes arising under section 7-(a). The result was a relatively weak board, tending at first to be favorable to employers.

While Roosevelt had always maintained cordial relations with labor leaders, he was little inclined to give them firm collective-bargaining guarantees in place of the weak section 7-(a) in the National Industrial Recovery Act. Congress, under the leadership of Senator Robert F. Wagner, felt differently; in May, 1935, the Senate passed his bill providing strong government protection for the unions. Roosevelt, bowing to the inevitable, signed the measure. What he had reluctantly accepted became one of the mainstays of the New Deal. The Wagner Act, passed at a time when unions were relatively weak, outlawed a number of the "unfair practices" by which management had been bludgeoning them, and created a powerful National Labor Relations Board to police the corporations. Militant labor thus obtained the governmental backing essential to its drive to unionize the great mass-production industries.

Even before the adoption of the Wagner Act, union membership had jumped from a depression low of less than 3,000,-

---

THE WAGNER ACT

The National Labor Relations Act of 1935 made it unlawful for employers to engage in the following unfair labor practices:

To interfere with employees in their right to self-organization, to form, join, or assist labor organizations, to bargain collectively through representatives of their own choosing, and to engage in concerted activities, for the purpose of collective bargaining or other mutual aid or protection.

To dominate or interfere with the formation or administration of any labor organization or contribute financial or other support to it.

By discrimination in regard to hire or tenure of employment or any term or condition of employment to encourage or discourage membership in any labor organization.

To discharge or otherwise discriminate against any employee because he has filed charges or given testimony under this Act.

To refuse to bargain collectively with the representatives of his employees duly chosen pursuant to other provisions in the Act.

ORGANIZED LABOR, 1900–1956

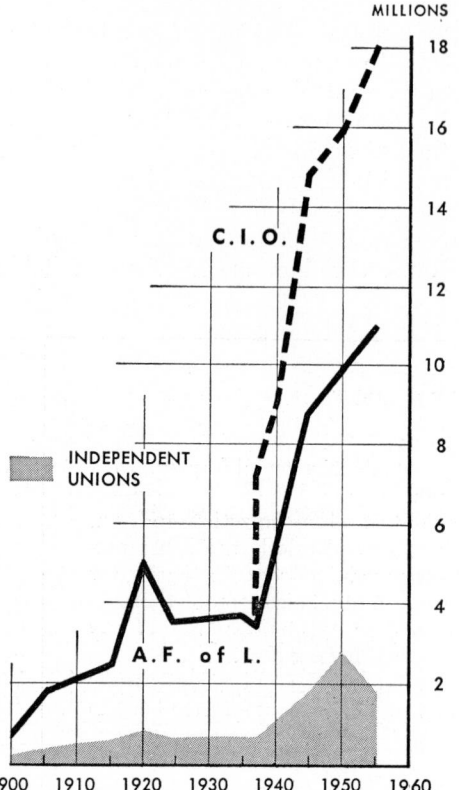

MILLIONS

new giant unions. Jurisdictional fights led to a schism between the A.F.L. and the industrial unionists, who formed a Committee for Industrial Organization in November, 1935. Industrial warfare followed, as both the A.F.L. and the C.I.O. mounted great rival organizational drives.

President Roosevelt and a few industrial leaders were inclined to be favorable toward industrial unionism. Gerald Swope of General Electric told Roosevelt that his company could not conceivably negotiate with a large number of craft unions but might find advantages in contracting with a single industrial union. Generally, however, in the spring of 1936 the point was still far off when big business could see advantages in big labor. Vigorous young organizers had to battle it out, often by physical force, with "loyal" strong-arm squads, occasionally with the police, and sometimes with rival organizers. The great difference between this and earlier periods of labor warfare was the aid the federal government provided unions through the National Labor Relations Board.

ooo to 4,200,000. A group of leaders of industrial unions (that is, those offering membership to everyone within an industry) had chafed over the conservatism of the craft unions (which took in only those working at a given trade). Men like the head of the United Mine Workers, John L. Lewis, and the leaders of the two great garment unions, Sidney Hillman of the Amalgamated Clothing Workers and David Dubinsky of the International Ladies' Garment Workers, in 1934 had forced President William Green of the A.F.L. and the craft unionists to agree to charter new industrial unions in the big unorganized industries.

In 1935 organization of these industries began. It led to violent opposition not only from the corporations but also from the A.F.L. craft unions, which feared they would be submerged by the

Through 1936 the United Automobile Workers gained recruits despite vigorous company opposition. There was good reason, for in 1934, at about the time the organizing drive began, 45 per cent of the auto workers were receiving less than $1,000 per year. General Motors alone, in an effort to keep down union organization, spent almost a million dollars on private detectives between 1934 and 1936. In the first two months of 1937 seventeen General Motors plants were struck through the device of the sit-down strike, as the workers stayed within the plants by their machinery. In February, General Motors recognized the U.A.W.; gradually in the following years, other automobile companies recognized the union. Rubber and other industries were similarly organized. Newspapers darkly saw in the sit-down strikes a menace to private property of a sort radicals had tried in Italy in 1919; courts outlawed sit-down

POLICE BATTLING STRIKERS. A newsreel man caught the first great onslaught of the police against the strikers at the South Chicago plant of the Republic Steel Company, May 30, 1937. Ten persons were killed. This picture was introduced as evidence at the Senate Civil Liberties Committee hearings on the strike. (UNITED PRESS PHOTO)

strikes, and much of the public became thoroughly alarmed.

Bloody warfare in the steel industry heightened their alarm. In 1936 the C.I.O. voted a half-million-dollar fund to organize the industry and began its great onslaught, winning tens of thousands of workers from company unions. United States Steel chose to capitulate rather than face a long strike just as prosperity seemed to be returning. In March, 1937, to the amazement of the nation, one of the company's subsidiaries signed a contract with the Steel Workers' Organizing Committee. For the first time, "Big Steel" was organized. The triumph was quickly blunted when three of the "Lit-tle Steel" companies, under the moral leadership of Tom Girdler of Republic Steel, who violently disapproved of unions, fought furiously. At the Republic plant in South Chicago on Memorial Day, 1937, the police killed ten strikers. Republic Steel, according to the prolabor La Follette committee, was the largest purchaser of tear gas and sickening gas in the United States; Youngstown Sheet and Tube Company owned an arsenal of over a thousand weapons. The Republic strikers lost completely, to the relief of middle-class Americans, who, like the newspapers they read, blamed the unions for the strife, and behind the unions, the New Deal.

Yet organized labor continued to grow. By 1941 union membership totaled about 9,500,000.

The Voters Approve

Though President Roosevelt originally wished to provide for the welfare of each of the main economic and political groups in the nation, realities forced him to become the champion of the new political coalition of farmers, laborers, and millions of underprivileged. In part Roosevelt shifted because he felt that large business had defected, that it had betrayed his recovery program and was fighting politically to destroy the New Deal. Aligned against him were some 70 per cent of the newspaper publishers and most of the large contributors of campaign funds. Roosevelt's quite human reaction was to regard this opposition as reckless and unprincipled, and to force reform upon it for its own good.

Far more important was the threat from the left, and it was this which was mainly responsible for the gradual change in emphasis of the New Deal. In undermining this threat, Roosevelt's political pragmatism combined with his humanitarian inclinations to carry him along the road to reform even further than the progressives had dared venture, toward positive government action on behalf of the general welfare.

Through 1934 the President was still trying to hold the support of businessmen and bankers. As late as October he told the American Bankers' Association, "The time is ripe for an alliance of all forces intent upon the business of recovery. In such an alliance will be found business and banking, agriculture and industry, and labor and capital. What an all-American team that would be!" There was little chance of it. In August, 1934, conservative businessmen and self-styled Jeffersonian Democrats founded the American Liberty League to fight for free enterprise, state rights, the open shop, and an end to New Deal bureaucracy.

As the congressional elections of 1934 approached, conservatives within the Liberty League and without campaigned against the New Deal on the grounds that it was destroying the Constitution and driving the country toward bankruptcy. All they succeeded in doing was to drive the dispossessed millions toward the New Deal. Instead of the shift back toward the Republican party which would have been normal in a mid-term election, the Democrats gained an additional ten seats each in the Senate and House.

Throughout the nation leaders arose who promised much to those despairing people whom the New Deal had not yet rescued. An elderly physician in California, Dr. Francis E. Townsend, attracted a following of five million destitute old people with his plan to obtain a federal pension of $200 per month for everyone over sixty. This would have cost nearly half the national income but, its proponents claimed, since the pensions would have had to be spent within the month, "the velocity of money" would have solved the depression. The immediate realities of the movement were that its promoters raised nearly a million dollars in two years and commanded a formidable block of votes.

Among restless people in northern cities, Father Charles Coughlin's politico-religious broadcasts attracted a wide following. Starting with a mixture of Papal encyclicals and Populism, he at first supported, then went far beyond, Roosevelt. Coughlin advocated silver inflation, and nationalization of banks, utilities, and natural resources. Ultimately in 1938 he founded the antidemocratic, anti-Semitic Christian Front. In January, 1935, he was able to demonstrate his power by inspiring an avalanche of letters and telegrams to Senators protesting against the World

Court. His program was vague, but the discontent he was able to tap was concrete.

From the South, Senator Huey P. Long of Louisiana succeeded in launching a far more telling assault upon the New Deal. He was a skillful politician who was able to build a powerful organization in Louisiana and a rapidly growing following that spilled out first into neighboring states, then by 1935 into the Middle West, the Pacific coast, and indeed, to at least a slight extent, into every part of the country. Within Louisiana, he had delighted his poverty-stricken supporters by immobilizing their traditional enemies through his strong-armed techniques. Within the state, he built bridges, roads, hospitals, and a modern educational system. It was an era of dictators in Europe, and it was easy to assail the self-styled Louisiana Kingfish with ambitions to be a Fuehrer, although his techniques were the time-honored ones of the American political boss. He was ambitious to become President and lured the masses by offering them more than Roosevelt. His "Share Our Wealth" program promised through confiscatory taxes on great fortunes to provide every family with what in those depression years seemed in itself a fortune: an income of $2,500 per year and a homestead worth $5,000. Even in Iowa, farmers guffawed when he called the Secretary of Agriculture, "Lord Corn Wallace." The New Dealers' political tactician, Postmaster-General James A. Farley, estimated in the spring of 1935 that Long could poll three or four million votes on a third-party ticket, and possibly even throw the 1936 election to the Republicans.

The "thunder from the left" was so ominous early in 1935 that many despairing New Dealers, chafing at Roosevelt's apparent inertia, predicted defeat in 1936. Roosevelt, who never liked to explain his tactics, remarked confidentially that he had no intention of engaging in public debate with the leaders of the "lunatic fringe." Rather, he quietly went about stealing their thunder with the reform programs the New Dealers had long been planning.

This vigorous reform program, enacted in its main outlines by 1936, left little doubt that Roosevelt would win re-election by a wide margin. Many millions felt that their personal lot had been improved by the New Deal. The violent attacks upon it from the right, and the cries of anguish over such measures as the "soak the rich" taxes, convinced them the more that Roosevelt was their friend. Despite the misgivings of many conservatives within the party, the Democratic convention in 1936 renominated him by acclamation. His control was so complete that he even obtained abrogation of the two-thirds rule through which minorities had so often hamstrung conventions.

As for the Republicans, they nominated their strongest candidate. Ignoring ex-President Hoover and the right wing, which was crying calamity, they chose a one-time Bull Mooser who had never strayed far from the 1912 Progressive position. This was the competent governor of Kansas, Alf M. Landon. His running mate was another Bull Mooser who had moved well to the right, the Chicago publisher Frank Knox. The Republican platform promised to do most of what the New Deal was undertaking—but more competently, constitutionally, and without running a deficit. Landon's dry voice could not match Roosevelt's radio pyrotechnics, and Landon had to fight to protect his moderate position from the militant Republican right.

The election demonstrated the extent to which the New Deal depended upon a coalition of farmers, union men, and the poor. The unions were the heaviest Democratic campaign contributors, providing a million dollars. Negroes switched *en masse* from the party of Lincoln to that of Roosevelt. The "lunatic fringe" coalition against Roosevelt stirred hardly a ripple. Huey Long had been assassinated the year before; the Union party candidate was "Liberty Bell" William Lemke—who was "cracked," said wiseacres. His ticket polled only 890,000 votes; the Socialists, 190,000; the Communists, under 80,000.

A pre-election postal card poll by the *Literary Digest* had indicated that Landon would win by a big margin. How could it be so wrong? The names and addresses of those polled were taken from old telephone directories. A majority of people who could afford telephones and had not been forced to move favored Landon. In the election he received 16,-680,000 popular votes compared with 27,477,000 for Roosevelt, and got the electoral votes of only Maine and Vermont.

Storm over the Supreme Court

President Roosevelt, when elected the second time, was at the zenith of his power. He had carried with him into the Congress many a freshman legislator pledged firmly to his support. These had reduced further the already small Republican minorities. By the close of the campaign, Roosevelt had boldly challenged those rightwing opponents whom he labeled "economic royalists."

It seemed to Roosevelt that, regardless of the outcome of the elections, these "economic royalists" would be in ultimate control as long as the Supreme Court continued to hold New Deal legislation unconstitutional. Foes of the Coal Act, the Holding Company Act, the National Labor Relations Act, and the Social Security Act were openly flouting them and resorting to the courts, confident that these measures would be destroyed like the N.R.A. and the first A.A.A. The Supreme Court, through its narrow interpretation of the federal power over commerce and taxation, and its broad interpretation of freedom of

contract in the Fourteenth Amendment, seemed to have created an economic no-man's land within which neither the federal nor the state governments could act.

Critics of the Court had been urging passage of some sort of constitutional amendment to provide the federal government with more extensive economic powers. Roosevelt's opinion (which subsequent Supreme Court decisions were to sustain) was that the Constitution granted adequate powers. All that was wrong was the Supreme Court's antiquated interpretation, he felt, but the four or five justices firmly opposed to the New Deal enjoyed excellent health and showed no signs of resigning. Consequently Roosevelt decided to propose adding to the Supreme Court, and to lower federal courts also hostile to the New Deal, new justices (presumably sharing his viewpoint) to match superannuated ones. At this point Roosevelt's political sixth sense deserted him and instead of presenting his proposal frankly and firmly in terms of its economic implications, he enclosed it in a larger scheme. Without informing congressional leaders in advance, in February, 1937, he sent a surprise message proposing a needed general overhauling of the federal court system, which would include the appointment of as many as six new Supreme Court justices. His nearest approach to frankness was a statement that the addition of younger blood would revitalize the courts and help them meet the needs and facts of an ever-changing world.

There was no real question about the constitutionality of Roosevelt's proposal, since Congress had from time to time changed the number of justices on the Supreme Court. But it aroused a great furore throughout the country. Many thoughtful people who had supported Roosevelt in 1936 heeded the warning of conservatives that it was through such constitutional shortcuts that dictators came into power. Roosevelt obviously had no such leanings, but it was feared that some successor of his might have. Besides, economic conditions had been improving steadily for several years and many people were well enough off to worry about constitutional principles as well as economic necessities. Within Congress, the controversy cut across party lines as some Democrats fought against the "packing" They joined with the bulk of the Republicans to form a new conservative coalition in Congress. Roosevelt fought back by openly proclaiming his reasons for wanting the measure, and by using every device of party discipline to round up votes in Congress. He might have succeeded in obtaining at least a compromise

---

PRESIDENT ROOSEVELT'S SECOND INAUGURAL ADDRESS

January 20, 1937

I see a great nation, upon a great continent, blessed with a great wealth of natural resources. . . . I see a United States which can demonstrate that, under democratic methods of government, national wealth can be translated into a spreading volume of human comforts hitherto unknown, and the lowest standard of living can be raised far above the level of mere subsistence.

"But here is the challenge to our democracy: In this nation I see tens of millions of its citizens—a substantial part of its whole population—who at this very moment are denied the greater part of what the lowest standards of today call the necessities of life.

"I see millions of families trying to live on incomes so meager that the pall of family disaster hangs over them day by day.

"I see millions whose daily lives in city and on farm continue under conditions labeled indecent by a so-called polite society half a century ago.

"I see millions denied education, recreation, and the opportunity to better their lot and the lot of their children.

"I see millions lacking the means to buy the products of farm and factory and by their poverty denying work and productiveness to many other millions.

"I see one-third of a nation ill-housed, ill-clad, ill-nourished."

---

of the court, while the Republican progressive Senator Robert M. La Follette, Jr., supported the President. La Follette declared the Court had already been "packed" for years "in the cause of Reaction and Laissez-Faire."

Since much of the electorate for the first time sided with the conservatives, some of the old-line Democratic leaders, especially from the South, who until now had gone along with the New Deal mainly because of party loyalty and pressure from their constituents, broke loose.

measure had not the Supreme Court itself eliminated the necessity for one.

The justices, including Brandeis, the oldest and most liberal, had been indignant over charges that they were too old to handle the business of the Court. Chief Justice Charles Evans Hughes even wrote a letter insisting that the Court was not falling behind in its work. Four of them, far to the right, were of no disposition to take a broader view of the Constitution. Three of them took a more progressive if not a New Deal view of the Constitution, and Chief Justice Hughes on occasion voted with them; on the other hand, Justice Owen J. Roberts more often voted with the conservative four. Just before the President sent his court plan to Congress, Roberts joined with Hughes and the three more liberal justices to validate, by a five-to-four decision in the case of *West Coast Hotel* v. *Parrish*, a state minimum-wage law. This reversed a five-to-four decision of the previous year invalidating a similar law. "You may have saved the country," Hughes jubilantly told Roberts. The decision was announced March 29, 1937. Two weeks later, the Court, again five to four, upheld the Wagner Act, and in May, the Social Security Act. Since there was no longer any need for a court plan, the new conservative alliance in Congress easily dealt Roosevelt a spectacular personal defeat. At the same time, the shift of the Supreme Court's interpretation of the Constitution was a significant victory for Roosevelt and the New Deal.

Amost at once the older justices began retiring, and Roosevelt replaced them one by one with his appointees. In the next decade the Roosevelt Court rewrote large sections of constitutional law. The new justices sharply divided among themselves, but usually upon technical matters. In the main they interpreted the commerce and tax clauses so broadly and the Fourteenth Amendment so narrowly that they laid few restrictions upon economic regulation by either the federal or the state governments. For several years they tended to restrict governments in their interference with organized labor, but by the end of a decade labor too was subject to firm restraints. Thus they removed almost all constitutional impediments to government regulation of the economic system.

Recession and Renewed Spending

A sharp recession developed in the fall of 1937. It came just as many economists were fearing an inflationary boom that might get out of hand. There had been a remarkable recovery by the summer of 1937. The national income, which had dropped from $82 billion in 1929 to $40 billion in 1932, was back up to nearly $72 billion.

Yet there were still 7,500,000 unemployed and nearly 4,500,000 families on relief. And there had been no upsurge of capital investment and business expansion as in the 1920's.

Recovery had come because the enormous sums spent on work relief, the gradual momentum of the public-works program, and the loans to farmers combined with the payment in 1936 (over Roosevelt's veto) of the veterans' bonus, powerfully stimulated the economy. Out of this experience emerged new economic theories, centering around the concept that the government could by liberal spending in hard times help pull the nation out of a depression. As a corollary, the government could help curb inflationary booms by means of restrictive policies. With all of their ramifications, these new economic theories came to be known as Keynesianism, after the famed British economist John Maynard Keynes.

In 1937 Roosevelt as much as his Republican opponents abhorred a deficit and worried about the mounting national debt, which had risen to $30 billion. He actually feared another disastrous boom like 1929. Acting therefore in terms of the older economics, he had the Federal Reserve tighten credit even though the upswing had been sound rather than speculative. More important still, he tried to balance the budget and drastically cut government spending. Between January and August, 1937, he cut the W.P.A. in half, sending a million and a half workers on unpaid "vacation."

And since, with the ending of the drought, a huge farm surplus was again imminent, produce prices fell drastically. The fragile new boom collapsed and sent the economy plummeting. The index of production dropped from 117 in August, 1937, to 76 in May, 1938; four million additional workers were thrown out of employment. It seemed like 1932 all over again.

In October, 1937, the President called Congress into special session to renew heavy public spending, and to reform the "selfish interests" he blamed for the recession. Congress passed an emergency appropriation of $5 billion; the public-works and work-relief programs once again poured these large sums into the economy, and by June, 1938, recovery was under way. The "spending school" had scored a point, and the government seemed to have assumed a new role in warding off threatened economic disaster.

So it was that the New Deal entered into its final stage of reform, combining what was as new as Keynesianism with what was as old as progressivism. The trend had seemed to be toward big government, big labor, and big business. Big government had come with the active intervention of the New Deal into so many aspects of the economy; the number of civilian government employees jumped from 588,000 in 1931 to 1,370,000 by 1941.

Since questions of constitutionality no longer seriously interfered, because of the changes in the Supreme Court, New Dealers fought through Congress in June, 1938, the Fair Labor Standards Act. This established a minimum wage of 25¢ an hour (to be raised gradually to 40¢ by 1945) and a maximum work week of forty-four hours (to be lowered to forty) for most labor, excepting agricultural, domestic, and maritime workers. It also forbade employment of children under 16 in most areas except agriculture. Low though these standards were, they raised the pay of 300,000 workers and shortened the work week for 1,300,000. In subsequent years they were raised repeatedly and broadened to include more categories of workers.

Roosevelt worried about the strong negative power the conservative coalition was developing in Congress. In many states, the Democratic party was under conservative leadership; Farley had done little to aid New Dealers who had tried to challenge this leadership, and indeed himself seemed strongly in sympathy with the conservatives. Roosevelt in the 1938 campaign intervened in several primaries, mostly in the South, to try to defeat powerful conservative Democrats who headed congressional committees. Since they had strong organizations behind them and his New Deal candidates were relatively unknown, they won in almost every contest. More important, the November election reflected the degree to which the prestige of Roosevelt and the New Deal were waning. The Republicans gained eighty seats in the House and seven in the Senate, and together with the conservative Democrats could dominate Congress.

By the end of 1938 the New Deal was close to its ideological limits. The threat of a second World War was beginning to overshadow even the most critical domestic problems. The President could drive Congress with its Southern committee chairmen in the direction of strong defense legislation and a vigorous foreign policy only if he compromised with them by abandoning reform.

Culture in New Deal America

To many intellectuals the New Deal was a stimulating challenge. They developed new concepts in economics, sociology, and political theory. Beyond this, they took an intense interest in a resurgence of American arts and culture.

Even before the establishment of the Federal Art Project, which came to enroll 5,000 persons, the government had aided artists through an earlier relief project and the commissioning of extensive murals for new public buildings. Some of these artists painted leftist themes comparable to those of the highly popular

"AMERICAN GOTHIC," BY GRANT WOOD. Wood brought back to Cedar Rapids, Iowa, the bright colors and stylized forms with which he had experimented during his art studies in Paris. His careful, sympathetic interpretation of the Iowa country-side and people was easy for his generation to understand, and won him wide ac-claim during the 1930's. "American Gothic" was the most popular painting at the Chicago Century of Progress Exposition of 1933. The art historian Oliver W. Larkin has written, "If his faces looked rather stony and his rounded hills monoto-nous and hard, Iowans explained that these qualities were indigenous ones in a country where a hen's shadow at noon fell sharp as a cut silhouette on the barn-yard." (THE ART INSTITUTE OF CHICAGO)

Mexican muralists. Many turned their attention, sometimes satirically, to the American scene. This was the heyday of Grant Wood, with his patterned Iowa landscapes and austere rural portraits, and of Thomas Hart Benton, who with dramatic sympathy portrayed sharecroppers and Negroes. In sculpture, typifying the new government aid and the resurgent nationalism, Gutzon Borglum finished the enormous heads of Washington, Jefferson, Lincoln, and Theodore Roosevelt spread across a mountainside in the Black Hills. Altogether, thousands of artists and sculptors worked during the depression years; never before had America possessed so many who were competent and promising.

Appreciation of the arts took a strong upturn, partly through art classes sponsored by the Federal Art Project, partly through the opening of new art museums. In 1941, the National Art Gallery in Washington opened, displaying collections of European art valued at $35 million, the gift of Andrew W. Mellon. Samuel H. Kress added four hundred Italian paintings. More people than ever before visited galleries, or bought reproductions of the old masters and of the French impressionists, especially Vincent Van Gogh.

Although jazz more than held its own, interest in classical music increased. The Federal Music Project employed 15,000 persons. They brought concerts to 100 million people, and gave free music lessons to over a half-million pupils, most of whom could have afforded neither concerts nor lessons. Much of the music they played was that of American composers, such as Roy Harris's Third Symphony, and Aaron Copland's "Music for the Theatre." Through new high quality radio receivers and recordings, many additional millions listened to fine music, especially the symphony broadcasts conducted by Arturo Toscanini and the Metropolitan Opera performances. In 1940 listeners contributed over $300,000 to

help "save the Met." Many millions more mourned the death in 1937 of young George Gershwin, composer of *Porgy and Bess* and *Rhapsody in Blue*. To the great mass of Americans, music still meant either sweet popular songs played by bands like Guy Lombardo's, or jazz like Benny Goodman's which came surging back into favor in 1934.

After depression and competition from motion pictures had thrown most actors and old vaudeville performers out of employment, the Federal Theater Project found employment for 12,500 of them. It brought performances to millions who had never previously seen a stage production. Some of these were highly successful as entertainment, some were of an advanced experimental nature, and some were so far to the left that they kindled the wrath of Congress. It killed the project in 1939. Many of the Broadway playwrights, impervious to Congress, also took a critical look at social problems, as did Lillian Hellman in *The Little Foxes*. Robert E. Sherwood, who illustrated another trend, stopped writing light comedies to dramatize the impotence of the intellectual (*The Petrified Forest*, 1936) and the menace of war (*Idiot's Delight*, 1936). Later, in the pressure of world events, he reversed themes, and glorified the intellectual fighting totalitarian aggression (*There Shall Be No Night*, 1940). Meanwhile, Thornton Wilder wrote *Our Town* (1938) and Eugene O'Neill, who in 1936 won a Nobel Prize, labored quietly on a lengthy cycle of plays.

Novelists likewise divided into those who, like Faulkner, seemed to be largely unaffected by the era, and others like Ernest Hemingway, who paralleled Sherwood's cycle from 1929 (*A Farewell to Arms*) to 1940 (*For Whom the Bell Tolls*). Thomas Wolfe richly and poetically portrayed the world swirling around him in these years in *Of Time and the River* (1935) and his posthumous *You Can't Go Home Again* (1940). Many other novelists turned out proletarian themes from Marxist molds. John Steinbeck sentimentalized his suffering protagonists in his best-selling novel on the Oklahoman trek to California, *The Grapes of Wrath* (1939). The lure of romantic escape and the bargain of the sheer bulk helped make spectacular best-sellers of Hervey Allen's *Anthony Adverse* (1933) and Margaret Mitchell's *Gone With the Wind* (1936).

Motion picture audiences dropped a third early in the depression, then by 1939 boomed to a yearly box-office average of $25 per family. Like radio serials, motion pictures dispensed mostly escape —because of the vigor of the Catholic-led Legion of Decency, founded in 1934, it was less sexy escape than in the twenties. Theaters also dispensed two movies rather than one, and offered give-aways of a wide variety in order to bolster the box-

---

OBJECTIVES OF THE FEDERAL THEATER PROJECT

"What part could art play in this program? Could we, through the power of the theatre, spotlight the tenements and thus help in the plan to build decent houses for all people? Could we, through actors and artists who had themselves known privation, carry music and plays to children in city parks, and art galleries to little towns? Were not happy people at work the greatest bulwark of democracy? . . .

"The Federal Theater at its best was working toward an art in which each region and eventually each state would have its unique, indigenous dramatic expression, its company housed in a building reflecting its own landscape and regional materials, producing plays of its past and present, in its own rhythm of speech and its native design, in an essentially American pattern."—Hallie Flanagan, *Arena* (New York: Duell, Pearce and Sloan, 1940).

Reading was one of the most inexpensive pursuits of the depression years, and although libraries suffered from slashed funds, book circulation increased 40 per cent by 1933. Depression likewise cut the cost of radios and enlarged the size of audiences. Twelve million families owned radios in 1929; twenty-eight million families, comprising 86 per cent of the population, had them by 1940. This fact in part explained why Roosevelt was able to campaign so successfully with at least 70 per cent of the metropolitan newspaper circulation opposing him. A radio serial, *Amos and Andy*, was so popular that Huey Long took the name of one of its characters, the Kingfish, as his sobriquet.

office. As yet, the coming threat to the movies, television, was still in the engineering laboratory, a curiosity exhibited at the World's Fairs of 1939. It was too expensive for commercial development during the depression.

The two depression factors of lack of funds and excess of leisure operated also in education. A third of the unemployed, it was estimated in 1935, were young people. Many went to school for lack of an alternative, and high school enrollment went up a third between 1929 and 1935. In spite of this, economy-minded chambers of commerce and citizens' committees led the drive for cuts so deep that they carved out educational sinew along

Drought Refugees Stalled on Highway, New Mexico, 1937. Between 1935 and 1939, drought and depression drove some 350,000 Dust Bowl farmers to California, to seek precarious seasonal employment in the fields and orchards. John Steinbeck in *The Grapes of Wrath* (1939) wrote a moving saga of their migration along Highway 66 across the plains, desert, and mountains, and their disappointing life in the great valley of California: "The people in flight streamed out on 66, sometimes a single car, sometimes a little caravan. All day they rolled slowly along the road, and at night they stopped near water. In the day ancient leaky radiators sent up columns of steam, loose connecting rods hammered and pounded. And the men driving the trucks and the overloaded cars listened apprehensively. How far between towns? It is a terror between towns. If something breaks—well, if something breaks we camp right here while Jim walks to town and gets a part and walks back and—how much food we got?" (New York: Viking Press, 1939). (LIBRARY OF CONGRESS)

with the fat. Colleges and universities dropped in enrollment until 1935, then more than recuperated, but continued to suffer budgetary crises. Vocational education was strongly emphasized on both levels, but serious students also explored social and economic questions so energetically that frightened civic and patriotic organizations warned that "pinks" were taking over the educational systems.

Alarmists feared "pinks" were taking over the churches also, for ministers responded as enthusiastically to the new demands for human welfare as they had once to the "social gospel." Of 20,000 ministers polled in 1934, nearly a third favored socialism, and three fifths, a "drastically reformed capitalism." The main intellectual current among ministers was toward neo-orthodoxy. Reinhold Niebuhr, without disavowing political and social liberalism, found powerful psychological pressures driving man toward sin, from which he could be rescued only by faith, that is, submission to God.

The depression seriously cut funds for medical research; in spite of this the thirties were another decade of advance. Ironically, by 1935, when the American Medical Association was warning that twenty million people were suffering malnutrition or were close to it, highly publicized discoveries in vitamin research were leading the well-fed to consume a variety of vitamin-fortified foods, and swallow vitamin pills in quantities second only to laxatives. Sulfa drugs, typhus vaccine, blood plasma, and the "artificial lung" all came into use. Life expectancy increased from 56 years in 1920 to 64 in 1940, but malnutrition, illness, and sometimes lack of good medical care wrought a heavy toll during the depression. Army medical examiners rejected almost half the first two million young men Selective Service called up in 1940–1. Yet doctors were ill-paid (even in 1929 half of them netted less than $3,000), and were idle much of the time. When some relief unit, and the Farm Security Administration offered medical aid to the destitute, the demand was overwhelming. Senator Wagner in 1938 introduced a national health bill, but it met stern opposition from the American Medical Association. Voluntary group health and hospitalization plans spread rapidly in some sixty cities and gained three million or more subscribers.

While scientists suffered serious cuts in research funds, university budgets and industrial research funds were back at a peak level by 1936; federal expenditures, by 1940. Thus the decade was one of increasing scientific research. The need for reorganization and reinvigoration of some of the government's scientific agencies led to the creation in 1933 of a Science Advisory Board, which futilely tried to obtain a New Deal for science. In 1935 the National Resources Committee (succeeding several similar planning agencies) took over the problem and prepared a study, *Research—A National Resource* (1940). The way was being prepared for centralized scientific planning and establishment of a scientific organization, but they were far from being a fact during the New Deal.

The thirties were years of marked scientific achievement in both basic and applied research in many fields. A chain of basic discoveries by men of many nationalities opened the way to the applications of nuclear fission. In 1931 Harold C. Urey of Columbia discovered a heavy isotope of hydrogen—deuterium—which, combined with oxygen atoms, formed "heavy water." Bombardment of deuterium atoms by various types of "atom smashers" brought new knowledge about the nature of the atom which could lead to revolutionary applications. Science, a neglected stepchild of the New Deal, was to become the salvation of a nation at war.

BIBLIOGRAPHY

The continuing poverty of millions of Americans is described in Dixon Wecter, *Age of the Great Depression* (1948); L. V. Armstrong, *We Too Are People* (1938); T. J. Woofter, Jr., and E. Winston, *Seven Lean Years* (1939); Vance Johnson, *Heaven's Tableland: The Dust Bowl Story* (1947); M. D. Lane and Francis Steegmuller, *America on Relief* (1938); and R. S. and H. M. Lynd, *Middletown in Transition* (1937).

On the N.R.A., see L. S. Lyon and others, *The National Recovery Administration* (1935), and H. S. Johnson, *The Blue Eagle from Egg to Earth* (1935). On A.A.A.: Russell Lord, *The Wallaces of Iowa* (1947); E. G. Nourse and others, *Three Years of the Agricultural Adjustment Administration* (1937); and J. D. Black, *Parity, Parity, Parity* (1942). On monetary policy: G. G. Johnson, Jr., *Treasury and Monetary Policy, 1933–1938* (1939), and A. S. Everest, *Morgenthau, New Deal and Silver* (1950). On the R.F.C.: Jesse Jones, *Fifty Billion Dollars* (1951). On the T.V.A.: David E. Lilienthal, *TVA: Democracy on the March* (1953 edition).

On the New Deal reform program, see Grace Abbott, *From Relief to Social Security* (1941); H. L. Hopkins, *Spending to Save* (1936); W. O. Douglas, *Democracy and Finance* (1940), concerning the Holding Company Act and the Securities and Exchange Commission; M. S. Eccles, *Beckoning Frontiers* (1951), regarding the Banking Act of 1935 and the Federal Reserve System; G. G. Johnson, Jr., *Public Works Expenditures 1933–1938* (1940); and Nathan Straus, *Seven Myths of Housing* (1944).

Milton Derber and others, *Labor under the New Deal* (1957) is a comprehensive group of excellent essays; see also Irving Bernstein, *New Deal Collective Bargaining Policy* (1950), essential on the background of the Wagner Act; Herbert Harris, *Labor's Civil War* (1940); Selig Perlman, *Labor in the New Deal Decade* (1945); and Philip Taft, *The A. F. of L. from the Death of Gompers to the Merger* (1959), which concludes a two-volume history of the A. F. of L.

On pressures from the left, see A. P. Sindler, *Huey Long's Louisiana* (1956); H. T. Kane, *Louisiana Hayride* (1941); and Twentieth Century Fund, *Townsend Crusade* (1936). On the Republican opposition to the New Deal, see Herbert Hoover, *Challenge to Liberty* (1934), and Alf M. Landon, *America at the Crossroads* (1936). On the Supreme Court controversy, see Joseph Alsop and Turner Catledge, *168 Days* (1938); R. H. Jackson, *The Struggle for Judicial Supremacy* (1941); and M. J. Pusey, *The Supreme Court Crisis* (1937). On the new Court, see C. H. Pritchett, *The Roosevelt Court* (1948).

On New Deal ideology, see Thurman Arnold, *Folklore of Capitalism* (1937), and on anti-trust policy, Arnold's *Bottlenecks of Business* (1940). Keynesian overviews of New Deal economics are: J. K. Galbraith and G. G. Johnson, Jr., *The Economic Effects of the Federal Public Works Expenditures* (1940); and Arthur Burns and Donald Watson, *Government Spending and Economic Expansion* (1940).

On the social and intellectual history of the 1930's, see Wecter, *Age of the Great Depression*; F. L. Allen, *Since Yesterday* (1940); Charles and Mary Beard, *America in Midpassage* (2 vols., 1939); Leo Gurko, *Angry Decade* (1947); and Milton Crane (ed.), *Roosevelt Era* (1947).

35

FROM ISOLATION TO INTERVENTION

Until the great depression struck, a second world war seemed to most Americans an impossibility. Then Japan under fanatical militarists, Germany under Hitler and the Nazis, and Italy under Mussolini and the Fascists launched upon their several programs of domestic tyranny and foreign conquest. It began to appear that the war to end war and make the world safe for democracy had accomplished neither aim.

Meanwhile the American government faced a choice of two broad lines of policy. On the one hand, the United States might join with Great Britain, France, and Russia in the hope that all together somehow could and would enforce peace —even at the risk of hastening a general war. On the other hand, this country might strengthen its position in the Western Hemisphere and concentrate upon keeping out of war instead of preventing it. Most of the American people favored the second of these alternatives.

After war came to Europe in September, 1939 (Japan being already at war with China), the foreign policy debate among Americans grew more and more

heated, and the alternatives less and less clear. Suddenly, on December 7, 1941, the debate was stilled.

Hoover-Stimson Policies

Toward Latin America, Hoover continued the movement which under his successor became the "Good Neighbor" policy. Before his inauguration he toured much of the hemisphere, promoting good will; during his administration he prepared for the removal of marines from Haiti, and did finally withdraw them from Nicaragua. He refused to intervene in Cuba, which was restless under a dictatorship. Throughout Latin America, as depression toppled about half the regimes, he recognized de facto rulers without questioning the means by which they had come into power. Even when several countries defaulted on their obligations in October, 1931, he did not press them to pay or threaten to seize their custom houses.

Toward Europe, American policies became increasingly important as economic conditions sagged. The moratorium on war-debt and reparations payments, begun in June, 1931, aided temporarily. Secretary of State Henry L. Stimson wished it to lead to a general cancellation of these hampering obligations but could not convince the President, who considered them sacred. Soon Germany ceased reparations payments, and nations owing the United States, except for Finland, began to default or make mere token payments.

Toward the Far East, policies were aimed at safeguarding American rights

sians and the Chinese Nationalists under Chiang Kai-shek, wrested the initiative from the Foreign Office in a manner little short of mutiny. In September, 1931, they launched a large-scale military campaign in Manchuria at a time when the United States and Great Britain were preoccupied with the monetary crisis. For several weeks Stimson was moderate, in the hope that the civilians in the Japanese cabinet could regain control; the British were even less disposed to pursue a strong policy. The Japanese Foreign

---

THE STIMSON DOCTRINE

"The American Government . . . can not admit the legality of any situation de facto nor does it intend to recognize any treaty or agreement entered into between those governments, or agents thereof, which may impair the treaty rights of the United States or its citizens in China, including those which relate to the sovereignty, the independence, or the territorial and administrative integrity of the Republic of China, or to the international policy relative to China, commonly known as the open-door policy; and that it does not intend to recognize any situation, treaty, or agreement which may be brought about by means contrary to the covenants and obligations of the pact of Paris of August 27, 1928, to which treaty both China and Japan, as well as the United States, are parties."— Identical notes sent to Japan and China, January 7, 1932.

---

while preserving peace. As unstable conditions in China continued throughout the 1920's, the United States could do little to protect China from the encroachments of strong nations. As Russia became stronger, she built up her forces in eastern Siberia, and in 1929, when China tried to oust her from Northern Manchuria, fought an undeclared war to retain her foothold. Stimson tried to invoke the Kellogg-Briand pact outlawing war, and to bring about mediation; he failed, demonstrating the weakness of the pact.

Japanese military leaders, feeling that their treaty rights in Southern Manchuria were being threatened both by the Rus-

Office engaged in conciliatory talk but was unable to alter events as the army plunged deeper into Southern Manchuria. By January 2, 1932, the conquest was complete.

As early as October, 1931, Stimson had felt the United States might have to cooperate with the League of Nations in imposing economic sanctions against Japan even though these might lead to war. Hoover strongly opposed such action, and in cabinet meetings discouraged Stimson by referring to the Washington treaties and the Kellogg-Briand pact as scraps of paper. He learned from the British that they too opposed sanctions. Hoover was willing to allow Stimson to exert moral suasion against the Japanese, and suggested that he apply the doctrine of nonrecognition against territorial changes brought by force of arms. Stimson did so on January 7, 1932.

The American people were eager to see the United States assume moral leadership against war, and nothing more. Their ideal was international disarmament, not policing. Hoover took strong leadership in trying to bring about this objective.

After the Geneva Conference of 1927 had failed to extend quotas to destroyers, cruisers, and submarines, the United States had threatened to begin a substantial building program. Hoover, fearing a naval race, called a conference that opened in London in January, 1930. There the United States, Great Britain, and Japan agreed not to build the capital ships authorized under the Washington treaty, and even to scrap some existing ships. They also agreed to ratios on smaller ships, to continue until 1936.

The United States participated vigorously in the World Disarmament Conference that opened under League sponsorship at Geneva in February, 1932. With the Japanese attacking Shanghai, and Hitler daily winning new converts to his militaristic Nazi movement in Germany, the French firmly demanded an international army and compulsory arbitration rather than disarmament. In June, 1932, Hoover tried to break the deadlock with a proposal to abolish immediately all offensive weapons such as bombing planes and tanks, and cut all land and naval forces approximately 30 per cent. Despite much enthusiasm for the proposal, it failed.

New Deal Diplomacy

President Roosevelt inherited from the Hoover administration the questions of war-debt settlements, disarmament, and economic stabilization. He failed to share Hoover's view that the proper settlement of these was a key to recovery. In April, 1934, he signed an act sponsored by Senator Hiram Johnson, forbidding private loans to any defaulting nations; thereupon all payments, except those of Finland, stopped altogether. Meanwhile, the United States continued to assert a strong moral position to try to bring about substantial disarmament. But Hitler was bent upon arming, and in October withdrew from both the Geneva conference and the League of Nations. The new arms race was underway.

In the same months that the hopes for an arms settlement collapsed, hopes for international economic stabilization went the same way, and the blame this time was assessed against Roosevelt. He had agreed to cooperate in a World Economic Conference which President Hoover had called to meet in London in June, 1933. He gave vague assurances to the representatives of eleven countries who visited him in advance that he favored currency stabilization, and announced May 16 that it was essential in order to "establish order in place of the present chaos." This was the policy under which Secretary of State Cordell Hull, a firm believer in international economic cooperation, and the American delegation went to London. After their arrival, President Roosevelt changed his mind, decided that currency stabilization would be disadvantageous until the dollar had fallen to a competitive position on the world market. Whatever chance of agreement there had been disappeared when Roosevelt on July 3, 1933, cabled Hull a "bombshell message" disavowing currency stabilization.

The hope of stimulating foreign trade led Roosevelt in November, 1933, to recognize Soviet Russia. Since the revolution of November, 1917, the Russian government had gone unrecognized while a number of irritating questions between the two nations continued to fester. Americans, hungry for what they unrealistically dreamed would be a substantial

Russian trade, were eager for recognition. The Russians had even stronger motives for obtaining recognition, for they were afraid of being attacked by Japan. Maxim Litvinov, the Russian Foreign Minister, after discussions with Roosevelt at the White House, agreed that Russia would end its propaganda activities in the United States, guarantee religious freedom and protection in the courts to Americans resident in Russia, and would negotiate a settlement of debts and claims.

By January, 1934, Roosevelt was ready to listen seriously to Hull's homilies on the necessity of lowering tariff barriers in order to improve foreign trade. With his support, Congress in June, 1934, passed Hull's cherished program, the Reciprocal Trade Agreements Act. It authorized the administration to negotiate three-year reciprocity agreements, lowering tariffs on specified goods coming in from individual nations by as much as 50 per cent in return for their arrangement to take certain American goods. Technically the new measure was an amendment to the Hawley-Smoot Tariff.

The immediate effect of the reciprocal trade agreements is difficult to estimate. During the depression years they were drafted carefully to cover only products not competitive with American industry and agriculture. By 1939 Hull had negotiated agreements with 21 countries, ranging from Cuba to the United Kingdom. These lowered the tariff an estimated 29 per cent, at the same time that they gained concessions for American exporters, especially growers of cotton and tobacco. By the end of 1938 American exports to the sixteen nations with which it then had trade agreements had increased nearly 40 per cent.

At the Inter-American Conference at Montevideo in December, 1933, Hull won such acclaim with his proposals for reciprocity that President Roosevelt gave him full support upon his return home. To small nations like Cuba, dependent

SECRETARY OF STATE CORDELL HULL. Secretary Hull (1871–1955), born in a log cabin in backwoods Tennessee, was first elected to Congress in 1907. Except for two years as Chairman of the Democratic National Committee, he served in one or the other house of Congress until 1933, strongly advocating lower tariffs. William L. Langer and S. Everett Gleason in *The Challenge to Isolation* have thus analyzed his policies: "Even earlier than Mr. Roosevelt, he had sensed the dangers in the world situation and had warned the country of them. As a man of great integrity and high principle he was especially disturbed by the rapidly progressing breakdown of international law and morality. His prescription against this menace was reaffirmation of traditional standards of justice and fair dealing, insistence on the value of peaceful methods to settle international differences, and return to more liberal trade relations as the only way to alleviate the existing world tension. His was a somewhat rigid, doctrinaire approach, criticized by those who felt that his constant harping on general principles revealed a disinclination to come to grips with concrete, practical problems. Mr. Hull was a man of the people and as such easily moved to that moral indignation characteristic of the American people when confronted by the iniquities of foreigners." W. L. Langer and S. Everett Gleason, *The Challenge to Isolation* (New York, Harper & Brothers, 1952). (Karsh, Ottawa)

upon exports to the United States, reciprocity seemed a way out of the depression. At the same time that Hull offered economic succor, he reiterated to the people of Latin America at Montevideo (while Roosevelt said the same thing in Washington), that the United States was opposed to armed intervention in Latin America. Most important of all, Hull signed a convention declaring, "No state has the right to intervene in the internal or external affairs of another." This, unlike American policy declarations, was a binding position.

Thus Hull took the United States a step further than the Hoover administration, which had unofficially disavowed the Theodore Roosevelt corollary to the Monroe Doctrine, but had reserved the right to intervene in self-defense. This seemed to be the American policy, as late as the summer of 1933, when revolution exploded in Cuba. Sumner Welles, one of the chief draftsmen of the new Latin American policy, was sent into Cuba rather than the Marines to offer the "good offices" of the United States. Welles helped bring pacification without intervention. In 1934, when a more conservative government came into power in Cuba, the United States gave up its right of intervention under the Platt Amendment. It also withdrew the last Marines from Haiti, and in 1936 negotiated a treaty (not ratified until 1939) relaxing the restrictions upon Panama.

The new Good Neighbor policy of nonintervention received a severe testing in 1938 when Mexico expropriated all foreign oil holdings, including property valued by its American owners at $200 million. The United States conceded the right of expropriation but at first contended that the price the Mexicans wished to pay was so trivial as to be confiscation. Nevertheless when, after years of involved controversy, in 1942 a commission evaluated the property at $24 million, the State Department told the protesting oil companies that they must

accept the settlement or receive nothing. This was a reversal of Dollar Diplomacy, a self-denial of the right to intervene to protect American property in Latin America. In terms of trade the new policy was of immediate benefit. As the threat of war in Europe increased, it came to mean also mutual defense, and this became paramount.

As for the Philippines, primarily the depression and secondarily isolationism brought them the long-sought but economically dubious blessing of independence. American producers of sugar, fats, and oils were determined to thrust their Filipino competitors outside the tariff wall; isolationists were eager to drop this dangerous Far Eastern military commitment. The Tydings-McDuffie Act of 1934 thrust upon the Philippines complete independence rather than the dominion status they sought. In 1935 the Philippines entered upon a transitional commonwealth period; on July 4, 1946, they became a fully independent republic. The United States was demonstrating that it was trying to rid itself of possessions rather than seize new ones.

At the London Naval Conference of 1935, the Japanese withdrew after they failed to obtain equality with the Americans and British in place of the 5:5:3 ratio, and thus opened the way for competitive naval building. So it was that in the isolationist years of the thirties, the United States built the fleet with which it was to fight the opening battles of a Pacific war.

The New Neutrality

The breakdown of the naval status quo and alarm over the threatened aggressions in both Asia and Europe convinced most Americans that at all costs they must stay out of impending wars. Many leaders of the peace movement who had been dedicated Wilsonians and advocates of the League had become disgusted with its inability to stop Japanese aggression. They reasoned that internationalism had failed, and that therefore they must fall back upon isolationism to maintain the peace. Others, taking an economic-determinist view of wars felt that Wall Streeters and munitions makers, combined with Wilson's legalistic insistence upon outmoded neutral rights on the high seas, had trapped the nation into World War I. Senate investigators, under the progressive Republican Gerald P. Nye of North Dakota, revealed exorbitant wartime profits and tax evasion, and claimed that bankers had sought war to rescue their loans to the Allies. President Roosevelt, himself impressed by the Nye investigation, wrote privately his regret than Bryan had left the State Department in 1915.

The Nye Committee findings and similar sensational popular writings convinced a large part of the public that entrance into World War I had been a frightful mistake. The way to avoid its repetition seemed to be to legislate these pitfalls out of existence. As Mussolini openly prepared to conquer Ethiopia in 1935, Americans feared that a general European war might develop. They felt the way to avoid involvement was not to participate in strong deterring pressure against Italy, since Mussolini might strike back. Rather it was to isolate the nation through neutrality legislation.

President Roosevelt also favored legislation, but he and Hull desired, as Hull had proposed in 1933, a law that would enable Roosevelt to embargo war supplies to the aggressor and allow their sale to the victim. He might thus have been able to cooperate with the League in coercing Mussolini to remain at peace. The line was this thin between collective security and isolation, but Congress did not dare risk even a mild gesture. Instead it passed a neutrality act providing a mandatory embargo against both aggressor and victim, and empowering the President to warn American citizens that they might travel on vessels of belligerents only at their own risk. This first Neutrality Act of August, 1935, was temporary legislation that expired at the end of February, 1936, and was then renewed, with even stronger isolationist provisions, to May, 1937.

When the attack upon Ethiopia came, in October, 1935, the League branded Italy an aggressor and voted sanctions against it. England and France made gestures against Italy, but showed no inclination toward determined action. Hull imposed a "moral embargo" upon oil. Mussolini easily conquered his African empire, then withdrew from the League, and in October, 1936, joined with Hitler to form a new Rome-Berlin axis.

The fiasco seemed to strengthen the determination of the American people to stay out of war. The new public opinion polls, based on samplings of only 1,500 to 3,500 people, with a probable error of 4 to 6 per cent, indicated top-heavy opinion against involvement. A typical poll in November, 1935, after the attack on Ethiopia, queried, "If one foreign nation insists upon attacking another, should the United States join with other nations to compel it to stop?" The answer: yes, 28 per cent; no, 67 per cent; no opinion, 5 per cent.

This anti-involvement sentiment continued to be the mood of the nation when a new danger arose in July, 1936, as General Francisco Franco and the Falangists (modeled after the Fascists) revolted against the Republican government in Spain. Hitler and Mussolini sided with Franco; Russia, France, and, to a lesser extent, Great Britain favored the Loyalists. To prevent the Spanish civil war from spreading into a general European conflict, England and France agreed to send no aid to either side. Roosevelt tried to cooperate, but could impose only another "moral embargo" since the second Neutrality Act did not cover insurrections. In January, 1937, Congress remedied this defect. The result was that the United States and other Western nations denied aid to Republican Spain. The Republican government came to depend increasingly upon Russia for what little aid it received. As for Franco, he received massive aid from Mussolini and Hitler, who ultimately crushed the Loyalists.

American feelings became inflamed over the invasion of Ethiopia and the Spanish civil war, but President Roosevelt voiced the majority attitude in August, 1936, a month after the outbreak of the war in Spain, when he asserted, "We shun political commitments which might entangle us in foreign wars; we avoid connection with the political activities of the League of Nations. . . . We are not isolationists except in so far as we seek to isolate ourselves completely from war." He emphasized, "I hate war."

In this spirit, Congress enacted the third Neutrality Act of May, 1937, which, while it gave the President larger discretion, tightened the previous laws and relinquished American claims to freedom of the seas in wartime.

Toward World War

A great Japanese drive into the five northern provinces of China began in the summer of 1937. At first the State Department pursued a "middle-of-the-road" policy, favoring neither country. Japan avoided declaring war, and President Roosevelt did not invoke the Neutrality Act. Private American ships at their own risk could carry arms and munitions to both belligerents. The administration's purpose was to help the Chinese, who needed American supplies more than the Japanese did.

By October, 1937, the administration was ready to take a firm position against Japan. The British proposed a joint arms embargo which seemed to involve no great risk. At this time and during the next four years, the consensus of the experts was that Japan was a mediocre military power. Hull persuaded Roosevelt to

make a statement to counteract isolationism. The President, speaking at Chicago facing the Chicago *Tribune* tower, went beyond his advisors and declared: "The peace-loving nations must make a concerted effort in opposition to those violations of treaties and those ignorings of humane instincts which today are creating a state of international anarchy, international instability from which there is no escape through mere isolation or neutrality." War, he asserted, was a contagion, which like a disease must be quarantined by the international community.

There is evidence that Roosevelt had in mind nothing more drastic than a collective breaking off of diplomatic relations, that he did not favor economic or military sanctions. Immediate press reaction and White House mail was favorable, but within a few days, as the Chicago *Tribune* and Hearst press continued to draw sinister implications from the "quarantine" speech, it plunged the nation, as the *Tribune* reported, into a "hurricane of war fright." This set back Roosevelt in his thinking. In November, 1937, he sent to Brussels a delegate to an international conference to consider the Japanese aggression, but instructed him not to take the lead, or be a tail to the British kite.

Japan had no need to fear economic or military reprisals from the United States. On December 12, 1937, young Japanese aviators bombed and sank the United States gunboat *Panay* on the Yangtze River. The aviators claimed they bombed it in error, but visibility was excellent and an American flag was painted on the deck. As at the sinking of the *Maine* in 1898, a wave of excitement swept the country, but this time it was fear that the nation might become involved in war. The United States quickly accepted the profuse Japanese apologies and offers of indemnity.

At the end of 1938, as she supplanted the Open Door with the New Order, Japan was making conditions almost untenable for Americans in China. But the threat of war in Europe overshadowed the Asian impasse.

The traditional American isolationism, as exemplified by Hearst editorials or the speeches of several Senators, involved strict nonintervention toward Europe but a considerably more active role in Asia—no sanctions, but an insistence upon the Open Door in China. Within the Western Hemisphere, toward both Canada and Latin America, these isolationists were ready to give the President almost a free hand. Indeed there were no more devout exponents of the Monroe Doctrine than they.

Roosevelt took full advantage of these feelings to inaugurate within the hemisphere policies which he could later apply across the Atlantic and Pacific. In December, 1936, he traveled all the way to Buenos Aires to put his personal prestige behind a pact to change the Monroe Doctrine into a mutual security agreement. Henceforth, if any outside power threatened the American republics, instead of the United States acting unilaterally they would all consult together for their own protection. The machinery also covered disputes among the republics themselves, but was specifically aimed at meeting the threat of the Axis. It provided that the members would consult "in the event of an international war outside America which might menace the peace of the American Republics." In December, 1938, with war in Europe imminent, the republics, at a meeting in Lima, Peru, established a means of consultation. Roosevelt also extended hemispheric security to the north in August, 1938, when he issued a declaration of solidarity with Canada.

By 1938, Hitler had rebuilt such a strong German army and air force that he was ready to embark upon a course of intimidation and conquest. In March, he proclaimed union with Austria and paraded triumphantly through Vienna. This union put western Czechoslovakia

into the jaws of a German vise. Hitler began tightening it with demands on behalf of the minority of 3,500,000 Germans in Czechoslovakia. In September, 1938, Hitler brought Europe to the brink of war with his demands for the cession of the Sudeten area in which the minority lived. The Czechs, who had a strong army, were ready to fight rather than submit, but the people of other Western nations, appalled at the threat of another world conflict, were eager for a settlement on almost any terms. Roosevelt joined in the pleas to Hitler for a peaceful solution. At Munich on September 29, the French and the British signed a pact with Hitler granting his demands in Czechoslovakia. "This is the last territorial claim I have to make in Europe," he declared.

Within a few weeks, the once strong Czechoslovakia was whittled down to impotence. In March, 1939, Hitler took over the remaining areas as German protectorates, thus demonstrating speedily the worthlessness of his Munich pledge. In April, he began harassing Poland. The British and French, seeing clearly that appeasement had failed, gave firm pledges to Poland and other threatened nations. They made half-hearted gestures toward Russia, which had been left out of the Munich settlement, but Stalin in August signed a nonaggression pact with Hitler. This freed Hitler to attack Poland if he could not frighten that country into submission. When Poland stood firm, Germany invaded it on September 1, 1939. Great Britain and France, true to their pledges, on September 3 declared war on Germany. World War II had begun.

Aiding the Allies

With the outbreak of war, Roosevelt issued a neutrality proclamation pointedly different from Wilson's 1914 plea for Americans to be neutral in thought as well as action. "This nation will remain a neutral nation," Roosevelt stated, "but I cannot ask that every American remain neutral in thought as well."

Promptly, Roosevelt called Congress into special session, and despite a heated debate was able to muster the votes for a revision of the Neutrality Act. The 1939 measure still prohibited American ships from entering the war zones, but it did allow belligerents to purchase arms on a "cash-and-carry" basis. Had Eng-

weakness turned into panic in the spring of 1940 when the Nazis invaded Denmark and Norway, then swept across Holland and Belgium deep into France. On May 16, Roosevelt asked Congress for an additional billion in defense expenditures and obtained it quickly. On the premise that the United States must build great air armadas to hold off the Nazis, he set a goal of at least 50,000 airplanes a year.

PUBLIC OPINION ABOUT INTERVENTION, 1939–1941 [1]

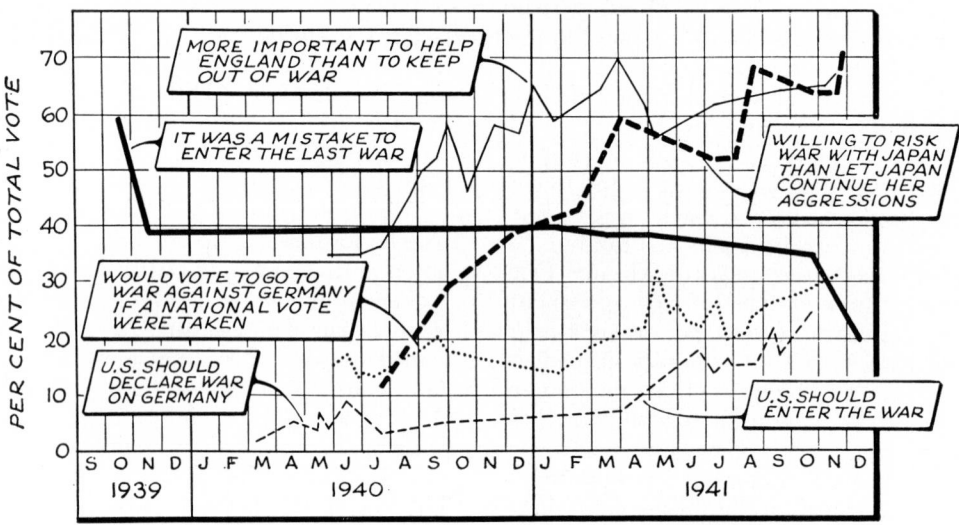

[1] Reproduced by permission of Professor Hadley Cantril and the Public Opinion Research Project of Princeton University

land and France been able to defeat Hitler with this limited assistance, Roosevelt probably would have been satisfied with it. Indeed, after the quick Nazi overrunning of Poland, during the quiet winter of 1939–40, overoptimistic American publicists asserted that the Allies were calling Hitler's bluff, and after a long and boring blockade on sea and land would triumph. During these months of the "phony war," American indignation flared hottest over the Russian invasion of Finland. The administration applied a tight "moral embargo" on shipments of munitions to Russia, but went no further.

Optimistic illusions about Hitler's

On June 10, 1940, Mussolini joined the Germans by attacking France. Roosevelt, speaking that evening, asserted, "The hand that held the dagger has struck it into the back of its neighbor." And, with France tottering from the German onslaught, he proclaimed that the United States would "extend to the opponents of force the material resources of this nation." He was taking the United States from a status of neutrality to one of nonbelligerency on the side of the democracies.

Twelve days later France fell, and in all western Europe only the shattered remnants of the British army that had been retrieved from Dunkirk opposed the Nazis. Already the new prime min ister, Winston Churchill, was showering Roosevelt with requests for destroyers and arms of all kinds to help the British man their bastion. The odds against the British were heavy, but Roosevelt made the bold and dangerous decision to "scrape the bottom of the barrel" and make it possible for the British to buy all available matériel of war. As the air soft-

In May, 1940, only 35 per cent favored aid to Britain at the risk of American in volvement; four months later, 60 per cent did. Yet as late as November, 1941, only 20 per cent of those polled favored a dec laration of war against Germany. Roose velt and the American public seemed to share incompatible aims. They wished to bring about the defeat of the Axis with out involving the United States in a shooting war. Some time in the next

---

"STOP HITLER NOW!"

"We Americans have naturally wished to keep out of this war—to take no steps which might lead us in But—

"We now know that every step the French and British fall back brings war and world revolution closer to US—our country, our institutions, our homes, our hopes for peace.

"Hitler is striking with all the terrible force at his command. His is a desperate gamble, and the stakes are nothing less than domination of the whole human race. . . .

"WE CAN HELP—IF WE ACT NOW—before it is forever too late.

"We can help by sending planes, guns, munitions, food. We can help to end the fear that American boys will fight and die in another Flanders, closer to home. . . .

"The United States of America is still the most powerful nation on earth—and the United States of America is YOU!"—Advertisement writ ten by Robert Sherwood for the Committee to Defend America by Aid ing the Allies, and widely published in June, 1940.

---

ening-up for the invasion of Britain be gan, Roosevelt gave fifty over-age destroy ers to the British in return for 99-year leases on eight bases from Newfoundland to British Guiana. It was, as Churchill later wrote, "a decidedly unneutral act."

Roosevelt threw the resources of the United States behind the British as com pletely as Congress would let him. He did so with the feeling that an Axis vic tory would mean disaster to the nation. A large part of the public seemed sud denly to agree. In March, 1940, only 43 per cent of those polled thought a Ger man victory would be a threat to the United States; by July, 69 per cent did.

eighteen months, Roosevelt probably came to feel that American entrance was desirable; the public never did.

The whole country was pulled into a great debate on the issue of neutrality ver sus all-out aid to the Allies. William Allen White, the Kansas editor, headed a Com mittee to Defend America by Aiding the Allies, often called the White Commit tee. White himself (like a large percent age of Americans) favored merely aid, but a minority wanted to go further and declare war. This group in April, 1941, founded the Fight for Freedom Commit tee. On the anti-involvement side, a Yale student, R. Douglas Stuart, Jr., organized an America First Committee under the chairmanship of a leading Chicago businessman, General Robert E. Wood. It drew upon the oratorical talent of the aviation hero, Charles Lindbergh, General Hugh Johnson, and Senators Nye and Wheeler. It won the editorial support of the Hearst and other large newspapers, and appealed to a considerable segment of patriotic Americans. Inevita-

tial candidate and sharp critic of the New Deal, Frank Knox, Secretary of the Navy.

The chagrined Republicans at Philadelphia promptly read Stimson and Knox out of the party but could not ignore the defense issue. They succumbed to the grassroots pressure, which had been built through a careful advertising campaign, and nominated a young internationalist,

---

LINDBERGH'S ISOLATIONIST ARGUMENT

"I know I will be severely criticized by the interventionists in America when I say we should not enter a war unless we have a reasonable chance of winning. . . . But I do not believe that our American ideals, and our way of life, will gain through an unsuccessful war. And I know that the United States is not prepared to wage war in Europe successfully at this time. . . .

"There is a policy open to this nation that will lead to success—a policy that leaves us free to follow our own way of life, and to develop our own civilization. It is not a new and untried idea. . . .

"It is based upon the belief that the security of a nation lies in the strength and character of its own people. It recommends the maintenance of armed forces sufficient to defend this hemisphere from attack by any combination of foreign powers. It demands faith in an independent American destiny. This is the policy of the America First Committee today. It is a policy not of isolation, but of independence; not of defeat, but of courage."—New York *Times*, April 24, 1941.

---

bly it also attracted a small fringe of pro-Nazi, anti-Semitic, and American fascist fanatics.

The debate was bitter, and through the summer and fall of 1940, it was complicated by a presidential election.

The Republicans met at Philadelphia in June, 1940, at the time of the collapse of France. National defense suddenly became the most important issue. Roosevelt underscored this, and stole headlines from the Republican convention, by appointing to his Cabinet two of the most distinguished Republicans. He made the elder statesman Henry L. Stimson Secretary of War, and the 1936 vice-presiden-

Wendell Willkie. It was a startling blow to the isolationist majority among the Republican politicians, but provided them with a tousle-haired, personable candidate who could win hysterical devotion from the amateur party workers. Both the platform and the candidate pledged that the nation would be kept out of war but would aid peoples fighting for liberty.

By the time the Democrats met in mid-July, it was a foregone conclusion that they would renominate Roosevelt. He was even able to force the Democratic politicians to swallow his choice for Vice President, Secretary of Agriculture

Henry A. Wallace, who was considered an advanced New Dealer.

Willkie embarked upon an appealing but slightly amateurish campaign, whistle-stopping so vigorously that he nearly lost his voice, denouncing the bad management of the New Deal rather than its basic program. Numerous right-wing Democrats and even some early New Dealers like Moley and General Johnson supported him. John L. Lewis threatened to resign as President of the C.I.O. if Willkie were not elected, a possibility that did not seem to frighten organized labor.

Roosevelt, a wily old campaigner, tried to give the appearance of not campaigning at all. Defense problems were so acute, he insisted, that he had to spend his time instead touring army bases, munitions plants, and shipyards, along routes which somehow took him through innumerable cities, where he cheerily greeted quantities of voters.

Foreign policy was paramount. On this, both Willkie and Roosevelt had much the same views: Willkie approved of the destroyers-bases agreement. Both made fervent antiwar statements to placate the isolationists. Willkie declared that if Roosevelt's promise to stay out of a foreign war was no better than his pledge to balance the budget, the boys were "already almost on the transports." This was an effective campaign issue which cut into Roosevelt's support. At Boston, Roosevelt (making the mental reservation that any attack upon the United States would not be a foreign war) picked up the challenge in words the isolationists were to mock incessantly:

"I have said this before, but I shall say it again and again and again:

"Your boys are not going to be sent into any foreign wars."

A large part of the vote of those opposing aid to the Allies went to Willkie. Those favoring vigorous aid or even intervention (including many who fer-

WENDELL L. WILLKIE. The son of a prosperous lawyer and landowner in Elwood, Indiana, Willkie (1892–1944) had been considered a red-sweatered campus radical at the University of Indiana. As a rising corporation lawyer in the 1920's, he remained a Democrat, but after 1933, when he became president of the Commonwealth and Southern utility company at a salary of $75,000 per year, he found it hard to retain his old party loyalties. As he challenged T.V.A. on behalf of private utilities, he managed to retain both the language and appearance of a rural radical. "It is an asset in my business to look like an Indiana farmer," he remarked, leading Secretary Ickes to sneer that Willkie was "a simple barefoot Wall Street lawyer." Willkie appealed enormously to many middle-class Americans as a liberal Republican who would retain the New Deal reforms, but encourage business and investment. One of the ablest Washington correspondents, Raymond Clapper, commented before the Republican convention that he was the only man the party could put up "who would have a ghost of a chance in the campaign." (NATIONAL ARCHIVES)

vently opposed New Deal domestic policies) voted for Roosevelt. They preferred Roosevelt's sure leadership to Willkie's inexperience. It was a relatively close vote: 27,244,000 for Roosevelt, and 22,-305,000 for Willkie; 449 electoral votes to 82. The combined third-party vote was less than 200,000. Within a few weeks, Willkie was on his way to England with a letter from Roosevelt to Churchill in his pocket.

Arsenal of Democracy

In addition to politicking, in the months after the fall of France, Roosevelt had to build makeshift defense machinery. With Willkie's aid, he pushed through the Burke-Wadsworth bill, passed in September, 1940, which inaugurated the first peacetime selective service in American history. This was the summer when he arranged to send destroyers to England, turned back new airplanes to the factory to be ferried across the Atlantic, and somehow ran the gauntlet of several anti-British, isolationist chairmen of Senate committees.

By mid-December, the British had so nearly exhausted their financial resources that they had practically stopped letting new contracts, yet Churchill warned Roosevelt that their needs would increase tenfold in the future. The Neutrality Act of 1939 and the Johnson Act of 1934 forbade American loans; a request for repeal would have reawakened the old furore about unpaid war debts. Roosevelt, cruising in the Caribbean af-

ter the election, thought of a formula. The United States should lend goods rather than money, "to eliminate the dollar sign" while serving as an "arsenal of democracy."

A "Lend-Lease" bill went into the congressional hopper at the right moment to bear a significant number: it became House Resolution of 1776. After fierce debate, the bill went through Congress by a wide margin, and in March, 1941, was signed by the President. It empowered him to spend an initial $7 billion—a sum as large as all the controversial loans of World War I.

Lend-Lease committed the United States formally to the policy the President had been following since the fall of France, pouring aid into Great Britain to help it withstand the German onslaught. Since Lend-Lease shipments had to cross the Atlantic to be of aid, the United States acquired a vital interest in keeping the Atlantic sea lanes open against the formidable wolf packs of German submarines, which in the spring of 1941 were destroying a half-million tons of shipping

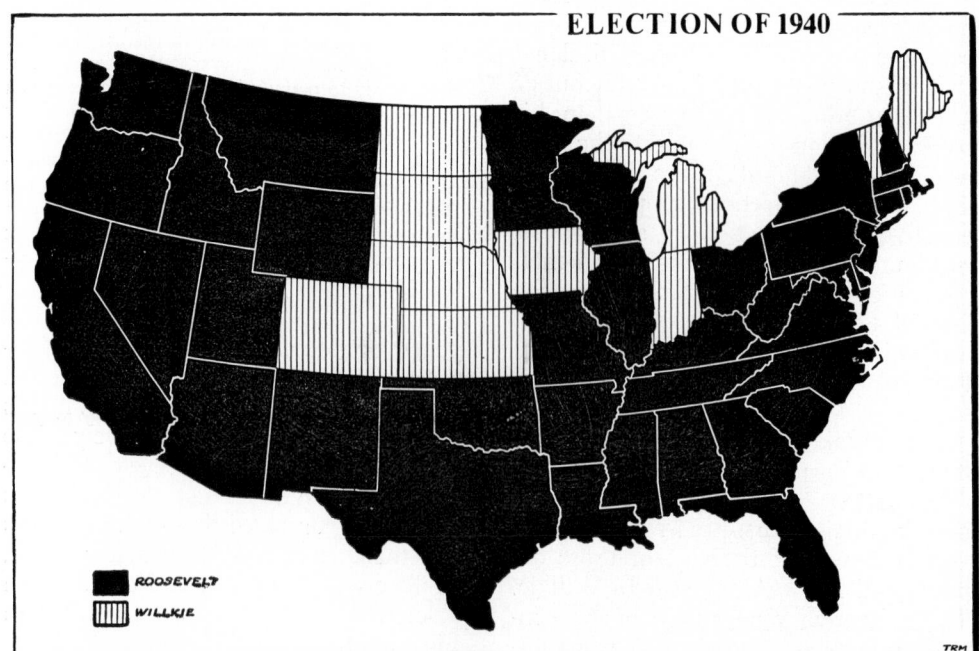

ELECTION OF 1940

ROOSEVELT
WILLKIE

TRM

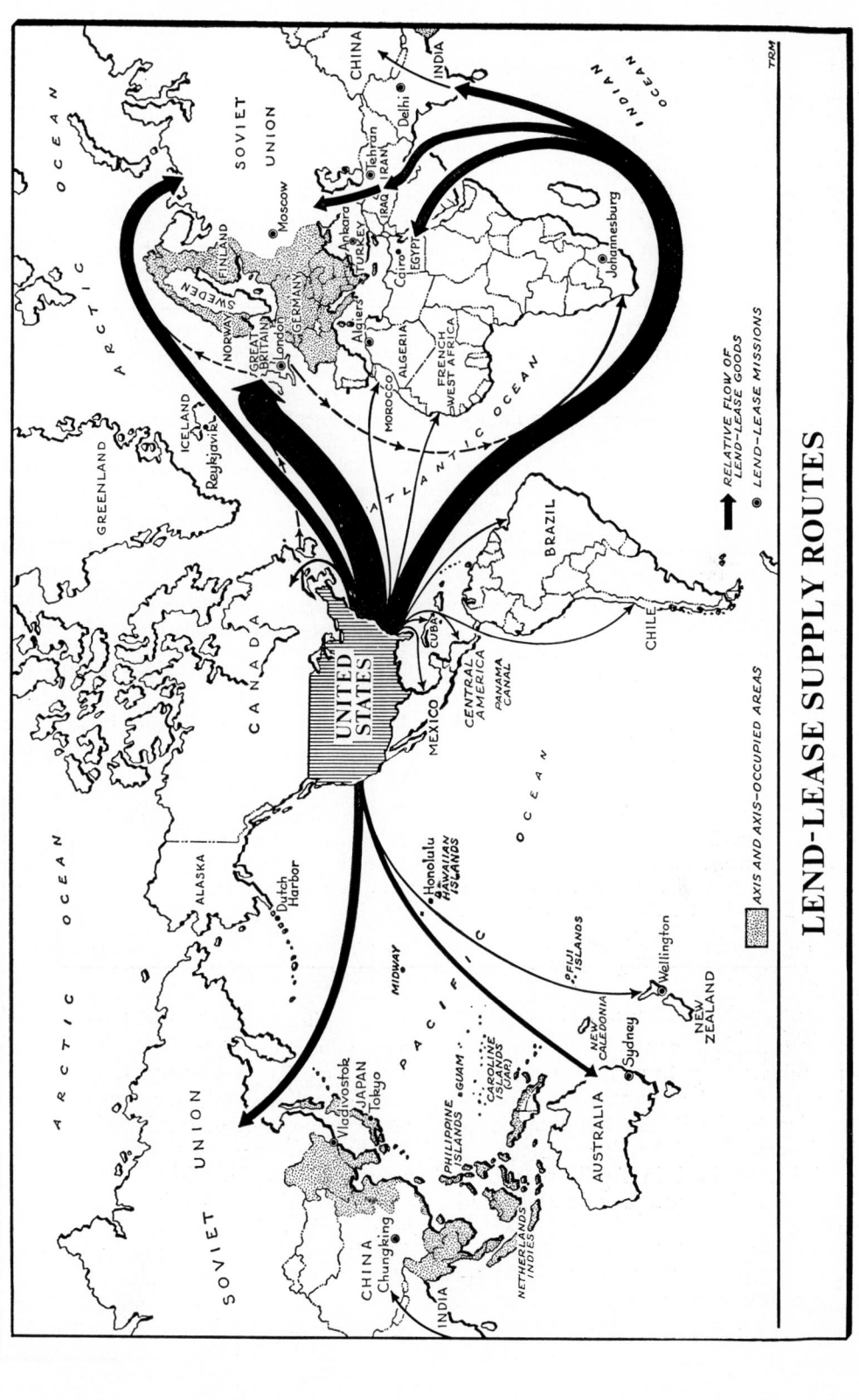

LEND-LEASE SUPPLY ROUTES

a month, twice as much as could be replaced. The President did not dare openly convoy vessels to England as Secretary Stimson urged; isolationists in Congress were too powerful. Instead he fell back upon the device of "hemispheric defense." The American republics had proclaimed an Atlantic neutrality to be followed if the United States entered the war. President Roosevelt demonstrated publicly in August, 1941, how close he had come to carrying the United States from nonbelligerency to cobelligerency with England when he met with Prime Minister Churchill off the coast of Newfoundland. Roosevelt refused to

---

SUMMARY OF ATLANTIC CHARTER

"Joint declaration of the President . . . and the Prime Minister. . . .
    "First, their countries seek no aggrandizement, territorial or other;
    "Second, they desire to see no territorial changes that do not accord with the freely expressed wishes of the people concerned;
    "Third, they respect the right of all peoples to choose the form of government under which they will live . . . ;
    "Fourth, . . . access on equal terms, to the trade and to the raw materials of the world . . . ;
    "Fifth, . . . fullest collaboration between all nations in the economic field with the object of securing, for all, improved labor standards, economic advancement, and social security;
    "Sixth, . . . a peace which will afford to all nations the means of dwelling in safety within their own boundaries, and which will afford assurance that all the men in all the lands may live out their lives in freedom from fear and want;
    "Seventh, such a peace should enable all men to traverse the high seas and oceans without hindrance;
    "Eighth, they believe that all of the nations of the world, for realistic as well as spiritual reasons, must come to the abandonment of the use of force. . . . Pending the establishment of a wider and permanent system of general security, . . . the disarmament of [aggressor] nations is essential. . . ."—August 14, 1941.

---

zone in 1939; Roosevelt in 1941 extended it far to the east, almost to Iceland, and ordered the Navy to patrol the area and give warning of aggressors. This meant radioing to the British the location of Nazi submarines. The United States occupied Greenland in April, 1941, and began escorting convoys as far as Iceland in July.

In secret, the United States had gone even further, for in the spring of 1941 American and British officers in Washington reached agreement on the strategy make military commitments but did sign with Churchill a press release on war aims, the Atlantic Charter. It called for national self-determination, greater economic opportunities, freedom from fear and want, freedom of the seas, and disarmament. As Churchill later pointed out, Roosevelt, representing a nation not at war, subscribed to a document that referred to "the final destruction of the Nazi tyranny" as a war aim.

In June, 1941, Hitler unleashed an enormous surprise attack against Russia, so powerful that American military leaders predicted that Russia would collapse in a few weeks or months. The Russians fell back before the deep Nazi incursions, but continued to fight, and in September Roosevelt, again gambling, extended Lend-Lease to them. This made it even more imperative to patrol the seas effectively.

The German answer was to strike back with submarines. In May, 1941, they sank the American ship *Robin Moor* off the coast of Brazil and replied to protests by saying, "Germany will continue to sink every ship with contraband for Britain whatever its name." In September, a submarine attacked but failed to hit the destroyer *Greer*, which was radioing the submarine's position to the British. President Roosevelt, who did not know, or at least did not reveal, what the *Greer* was doing, issued orders to the navy in the future to "shoot on sight." In October, another destroyer was hit, and the *Reuben James* was sunk. Congress voted legislation to arm merchantmen and allow them to sail to belligerent ports. Naval war with the Nazis was underway.

The Chief of Naval Operations, Admiral Harold R. Stark, wrote in his diary that fall that Hitler "has every excuse in the world to declare war on us now, if he were of a mind to." But Hitler did not, and war came from the Pacific, not the Atlantic.

Pearl Harbor

The Japanese saw in the European crisis an unparalleled opportunity to extend their empire. In the summer of 1939 they forced concessions from the British which demonstrated their intentions. The United States promptly took a most serious step and gave the requisite six months' notice to terminate its 1911 commercial treaty. Beginning in January, 1940, this country was free to cut off its shipments of oil, scrap iron, and other raw materials.

The United States was determined to restrain Japan, even at the risk of a war. More was at stake than tin, rubber, and other vital raw materials. In September, 1940, Japan signed a defensive alliance with Germany and Italy (the Tripartite Pact); any further Japanese thrusts would damage the world status quo to which the State Department was committed. The administration policy toward Japan was inseparably interrelated with that toward Germany, and subordinate to it.

Under the Export Control Act, by the fall of 1940 the United States had placed an embargo upon aviation gasoline and almost all raw materials with military potential, including scrap iron and steel. Already war was close. The Japanese government of Prince Konoye wished to conciliate the United States if it could do so without serious concessions. Negotiations began in the spring of 1941 and dragged on into December. At first the Japanese informally suggested rather generous proposals, but by May were making formal ones that were unacceptable: the United States should ask Chiang Kai-shek to make peace on Japan's terms, it should restore normal trade with Japan, and it should help Japan procure natural resources in Southeast Asia.

The German attack upon Russia relieved the Japanese of one of their greatest worries, since they thought they no longer needed to fear interference from Siberia. They decided to move into southern Indo-China and Thailand. The United States had broken the Japanese code, and through intercepted messages knew this was probably a prelude to attacks upon Singapore and the Dutch East Indies. At the end of July, 1941, when the Japanese occupied southern Indo-China, the United States, acting firmly with the British and the Dutch, froze Japanese assets and applied other tight economic sanctions. These put the Japanese into such a desperate plight that they would either have to abandon their aggressions or fight the United States.

Since the Japanese naval leaders wished to avoid a war they feared they might lose, the cabinet sought compromise. Prince Konoye requested a personal meeting with Roosevelt at which he was ready to make some concessions. (Simultaneously Japan prepared for war if agreement could not be reached.) Roosevelt was enthusiastic, since Konoye was ready to promise that Japan would not expand further southward and would not attack the United States in the event it fought a defensive war against Germany. Hull was discouraging because he feared Konoye could not bind the Supreme Command. On Hull's advice, Roosevelt refused to meet Konoye without specific advance commitments about China, and these Konoye would not give.

Roosevelt and Hull seemed to make the foolish error of thinking Japan was bluffing when she was not. Instead of making limited concessions which would have strengthened the Japanese moderates and postponed or avoided a war which the United States was in no position to fight in 1941, the American policy makers took an adamant moralistic position which played into the hands of the Japanese extremists. The Japanese made an even more grievous miscalculation by provoking a war few of their leaders were sure they could win.

Each nation refused to budge on the question of China. On November 20, 1941, Japan offered a modus vivendi (temporary settlement) highly favorable to herself. Hull rejected it and replied in the basic American terms, insisting that Japan get out of China. He not only knew Japan would not accept these but

knew also, through intercepted Japanese messages, that she had made her last offer and that after November 29 things automatically would happen. "I have washed my hands of the Japanese situation," Hull told Stimson on November 27, "and it is now in the hands of you and Knox, the Army and Navy."

The United States knew that Japan was on the move and that war was imminent. A large Japanese convoy was moving southward through the China Sea. The administration thought an attack upon American territory unlikely, and debated what to do. The commanders in Hawaii were routinely warned. Negligence there and in Washington, not diabolical plotting, as was later charged, led to the disaster ahead. Meanwhile, on November 25, a Japanese naval task force had sailed eastward from the Kuriles.

At 7:55 on Sunday morning, December 7, 1941, the first wave of Japanese airplanes hit the United States naval base at Pearl Harbor, Hawaii; a second wave came an hour later. The attacks were successful beyond Japan's greatest expectations. Within two hours the planes destroyed or severely damaged 8 battleships, 3 light cruisers, 4 miscellaneous vessels, 188 airplanes, and important shore installations. There were 3,435 casualties. The Japanese task force withdrew without being detected, having lost 29 airplanes, 5 midget submarines, and less than 100 persons. In this first strike, the United States was rendered almost impotent in the Pacific, but the bitterly wrangling nation was suddenly unified for the global war into which it had been precipitated.

THE MAGAZINE OF THE U.S.S. SHAW EXPLODING DURING THE JAPANESE RAID ON PEARL HARBOR. [OPPOSITE] The destroyer *Shaw*, in a new floating drydock, went through the first attack unscathed. One of the second wave of bombers at 9:12 a.m. hit her badly, and fire spread to her forward magazine, which about 9:30 went up spectacularly, blowing off her bow and sinking the dock. From the bridge aft the damage was so slight that the *Shaw* was refloated and a month later put in the same repaired dock to be fitted with a temporary bow. She steamed to the mainland to be rebuilt and later rejoined the fleet. (OFFICIAL U.S. NAVY PHOTO)

BIBLIOGRAPHY

On Hoover foreign policy, see R. N. Current, *Secretary Stimson* (1954), a critical evaluation; R. H. Ferrell, *American Diplomacy in the Great Depression* (1957); W. S. Myers, *The Foreign Policies of Herbert Hoover* (1940); Sara Smith, *The Manchurian Crisis, 1931–1932* (1948); H. L. Stimson and McGeorge Bundy, *On Active Service in Peace and War* (1948); and Alexander De Conde, *Herbert Hoover's Latin American Policy* (1951).

There is a compact survey of Roosevelt foreign policy in Allan Nevins, *The New Deal and World Affairs* (1950), and an even briefer one in Dexter Perkins, *The New Age of Franklin Roosevelt* (1957). The opening pages of W. L. Langer and S. E. Gleason, *The Challenge to Isolation, 1937–1940* (1952), contain a thoughtful evaluation of the techniques of Roosevelt and Hull. Hull's own account, with extensive quotation from documents, is in his *Memoirs* (2 vols., 1948); Robert Sherwood, *Roosevelt and Hopkins* (1948) is a readable account which takes Hopkins's viewpoint.

On the Good Neighbor policy, see E. O. Guerrant, *Roosevelt's Good Neighbor Policy* (1950), and H. F. Cline, *The United States and Mexico* (1953). On the recognition of Russia, R. P. Browder, *The Origins of Soviet-American Diplomacy* (1953), and W. A. Williams, *American-Russian Relations, 1781–1947* (1952). On neutrality legislation, E. M. Borchard and W. P. Lage, *Neutrality for the United States* (1940 ed.).

The most comprehensive account of the developing war crisis and American entrance is in Langer and Gleason's *Challenge to Isolation* (1952) and *Undeclared War* (1953). More specialized monographs are: F. Jay Taylor, *The United States and the Spanish Civil War, 1936–1939* (1956); Herbert Feis, *The Spanish Story* (1948), and *The Road to Pearl Harbor* (1950); and P. W. Schroeder, *The Axis Alliance and Japanese-American Relations, 1941* (1958).

Accounts highly critical of Roosevelt's policies are C. A. Beard, *American Foreign Policy, 1932–1940* (1946), and *President Roosevelt and the Coming of the War* (1948); and C. C. Tansill, *Back Door to War* (1952). Basil Rauch's *Roosevelt from Munich to Pearl Harbor* (1950) is a detailed refutation of Beard's charges. On the great debate over intervention, see Walter Johnson, *Battle Against Isolationism* (1944), and W. S. Cole, *America First* (1953). On the election of 1940, see M. E. Dillon, *Wendell L. Willkie* (1952). On the Japanese attack, see Walter Millis, *This is Pearl!* (1947).

36

THE

BATTLE FOR PRODUCTION

"Yesterday, December 7, 1941—a date which will live in infamy—the United States of America was suddenly and deliberately attacked by the naval and air forces of the Empire of Japan." Thus President Roosevelt addressed Congress on the Monday after the debacle at Pearl Harbor. Within four hours, the Senate unanimously, and the House 388 to 1, voted for a war resolution against Japan. Three days later Germany and Italy declared war, and on the same day, December 11, Congress reciprocated without a dissenting vote.

Mobilizing for Defense

Total war made the planning of industrial production as vital as military strategy. "War is no longer simply a battle between armed forces in the field," the Industrial Mobilization Plan of 1939 had stated, "—it is a struggle in which each side strives to bring to bear against the enemy the coordinated power of every individual and of every material resource at its command. The conflict extends from the soldier in the front line

to the citizen in the remotest hamlet in the rear." Recognizing this, Roosevelt, at the time of the Munich crisis in 1938, had ordered the armed forces to modernize their production plan. Just before the outbreak of war in Europe, in August, 1939, he authorized the War and Navy Departments to appoint a civilian advisory committee to survey the 1939 plan. This was the War Resources Board, made up of five leaders of big business together with the presidents of the Massachusetts Institute of Technology and Brookings Institution, and an army colonel. At this point politics began. The unfortunate use of the word "war" rather than "defense" in the title frightened the public, especially after the invasion of Poland when even the existence of such a body seemed a move toward involvement. The firmly anti-New-Deal attitude of the Board pained Roosevelt. He speedily disbanded the War Resources Board and submitted to the many pressures against substituting any new defense agencies.

With the collapse of France in the late spring of 1940, Roosevelt could delay no longer, even though he was embarking upon a new presidential campaign and wished to temper isolationist hostility. Rather than ask Congress to create defense agencies, he drew upon a 1916 statute for authority and re-established the Advisory Commission of the Council of National Defense. This time he used the word "defense" rather than "war," and carefully balanced all of the major national interests. He headed it with William Knudsen (General Motors) and Edward Stettinius (United States Steel) to conciliate business; Sidney Hillman (C.I.O.), labor; Chester Davis (A.A.A.), agriculture; Ralph Budd (who had been president of several railroads), transportation; Leon Henderson (a New Deal economist), prices; and Harriet Elliott (a dean at the Woman's College of the University of North Carolina), consumer protection. Closely associated with it as Coordinator of Purchasing was one of the nation's biggest buyers, Donald M. Nelson of Sears, Roebuck. At the first meeting, Chairman Knudsen asked Roosevelt, "Who's boss?" The President replied, "I am."

Out of this prototype grew the many defense agencies with their shifting or nebulous lines of authority and often ill-defined powers. Out of it came many of the heads of subsequent war agencies. Out of it too came one clear fact amid the many uncertainties: whatever war agencies developed, Roosevelt was of no disposition to abdicate or share his presidential powers.

In January, 1941, after the Advisory Commission had almost broken down and lost its control over priorities to the military, Roosevelt established a new Of-fice of Production Management under Knudsen and Hillman. In April, 1941, he created an Office of Price Administration and Civilian Supply under Leon Henderson. The new improvisations worked little better than the old in controlling priorities; in August, 1941, Roosevelt established a new priorities board for the O.P.M. Finally, after American entrance into the war, Roosevelt in January, 1942, organized a War Production Board under Donald Nelson. Although Nelson was personable and a good organizer, he was not strong enough to force civilian control over priorities, or a more equitable distribution of contracts among smaller manufacturers, or a well-balanced production plan. He remained head of the W.P.B. until August, 1944, but as early as October, 1942, lost much of his power when President Roosevelt persuaded Justice James F. Byrnes to resign from the Supreme Court to become in effect a sort of assistant president in charge of war production. Byrnes was head at first of the Office of Economic Stabilization, then after May, 1943, of the Office of War Mobilization. The O.W.M. developed into a workable war administration.

Materials for Victory

Meanwhile, with the awarding of the first large government contracts in the summer of 1940, industry began to boom.

Some manufacturers, still thinking in depression terms of an economy of scarcity, were at first reluctant to build new plants that they feared would lead to overproduction after the war. Still others

THE MUSHROOMING OF WAR PLANTS. [OPPOSITE] These two pictures of a West Virginia valley taken from the same spot, the one in 1941 and the other in 1942, indicate the remarkable speed with which the Morgantown Ordnance Plant was built and went into production. This was typical of the mushrooming construction all over the nation. The plant was one of 54 built by Du Pont in 32 locations for the government at a total cost of $1,034,000,000. Du Pont received a total fee, after taxes and all applicable charges, of $\frac{1}{15}$ of one per cent of the construction cost. (DU PONT)

would not accept contracts until they were sure of an adequate profit margin, or a speedy tax write-off on their new plants. It was the initial task of Knudsen, the production genius of General Motors, to persuade manufacturers that it was their patriotic duty to take contracts. As for the new war plants, even if later they should prove to be excess capacity, manufacturers need not worry about paying for them: the Reconstruction Finance Corporation received authorization from Congress in June, 1940, to finance the construction, expansion, and equipment of plants that it could then lease to contractors. Or, if manufacturers would put their own capital into defense construction, by act of Congress of October, 1940, they received a fast, five-year tax write-off. This meant that instead of deducting a normal 5 per cent for depreciation from their taxes on wartime profits, they could deduct 20 per cent of the cost of the plant. Manufacturers who turned to war production were not to suffer economically.

Neither were the war workers. The manufacturers, backed by the War and Navy Departments, wished to abrogate New Deal restrictions on government contracts in order to lengthen the hours of workers without paying overtime. Labor leaders, wishing to increase employment, fought bitterly for double shifts. Ultimately the government decreed a 40-hour week with time-and-a-half for overtime. Contractors had to comply with New Deal labor legislation—the Walsh-Healey, Fair Labor Standards, and Wagner Acts.

At the time of Pearl Harbor, the United States still had little armament because so much had been shipped to Great Britain and because so many of the plants had only recently begun production. The new productive capacity was remarkably large. Despite errors and chaotic conditions, the nation was producing more combat munitions than any of the belligerent nations—indeed almost

as much as Germany and Japan combined. Airplane production was up to a rate of almost 25,000 per year. The armed forces already had inducted and were training two million men. This mobilization was only a fraction of what was soon to come, for large scale construction of factories and training camps was underway. While the nation during the debate over neutrality had not built its defenses with the smoothness and speed that critics demanded, it had achieved a substantial degree of preparedness.

The Japanese attack on Pearl Harbor created almost as much chaos indirectly in American war production as it did directly in the fleet in the Pacific. The war agencies in Washington began ordering tremendous quantities—indeed far too much—of everything.

The problem of restoring some order to war production, then raising it to astronomical totals, was a joint one. The armed forces, the Maritime Commission, and other procurement agencies did the ordering. The War Production Board tried to control the size of the procurement program and to allocate materials between the armed forces and the civilians. The W.P.B. was thus trying to control the entire economy and inevitably coming into sharp clash with the armed forces over the size and nature of war orders as opposed to what was to be reserved for civilians. Internecine warfare among the agencies and personality clashes among the administrators were unavoidable.

Out of the confusion a pattern gradually emerged. The first step, singularly enough, was to cut back the building of plants, although at times this created a furor throughout a region, as when the Higgins Shipyards in New Orleans were abandoned. After the middle of 1942, the amount of new construction being begun declined sharply; in another six months, the larger part of the war plants and military facilities had been built.

The second step was to coordinate the

various phases of the war production program. As late as the summer of 1942, bottlenecks were halting some assembly lines. On July 4, the vital shipbuilding program had to be cut back because of scarcities of raw materials like steel plate and glass, and of components like valves, turbines, and engines. The W.P.B. eventually broke most of the bottlenecks through the Controlled Materials Plan, which established a balanced production of finished products and allocated precise quantities of raw materials to each manufacturer.

The shortage of rubber became so critical in 1942 that it required special attention. After the W.P.B. failed to solve the problem, Roosevelt in August, 1942, appointed a committee under Baruch to make a special report. It recommended sharp restrictions upon the use of motor vehicles, including a national speed limit of 35 miles per hour, and immediate construction of enormous synthetic rubber plants. Roosevelt ordered the restrictions, and appointed a Rubber Director in the W.P.B., William M. Jeffers, president of the Union Pacific Railroad, to construct the plants. By the end of 1943, the synthetic rubber industry was producing a third again as much rubber as the country had normally used before the war.

An indispensable adjunct of the war agencies was the Senate War Investigating Committee, headed by Harry S Truman, previously little known. The Senators consciously patterned it after the Committee on the Conduct of the War of the Civil War period, but avoided the pitfalls of their predecessors by ruling out questions of military policy. Instead they ferreted out incompetence and corruption in the war-production and military-construction programs: outrageous expense in building army camps, improper inspection of airplane engines, a quixotic scheme to build an Arctic pipeline, and the like. The Truman Committee not only uncovered and stopped hundreds of millions of dollars of waste, but by its

vigor led war administrators to be more diligent in preventing further waste. In the wartime expenditure of $400 billion there was amazingly little corruption.

By the beginning of 1944, war production reached such high levels that factories had substantially turned out what seemed to be needed to win the war. The output was double that of all Axis countries combined. Cutbacks began, but they were haphazard and ill-planned, and, when the armed forces met reverses, turned out in some instances to have been premature. With the cutbacks came pressure for a resumption of the manufacture of civilian durable goods. The military leaders stanchly opposed this. However, war needs even at their peak took only about a third of American production. While manufacture of such goods as automobiles, most electrical appliances, and nondefense housing had come to a halt in 1942, production of food, clothing, and repair and maintenance goods was continued or even slightly increased.

As war production grew, the problem of transporting the supplies within the country and overseas became acute. Inside the United States, the Office of Defense Transportation, established in December, 1941, coordinated all forms of transport—railroads, trucking, airlines, inland waterways, and pipelines. In contrast to the system in World War I, railroads remained under private control, but functioned effectively, carrying double the traffic of 1939 with only 10 per cent more locomotives and 20 per cent more freight cars. Since they could not, however, transport sufficient oil to the East when German submarines began attacking coastal tankers in 1942, the government authorized construction of the Big Inch pipeline from Texas to eastern Pennsylvania.

Transporting troops and supplies overseas required one of the most spectacular construction programs of all. The Germans had sunk more than twelve million tons of shipping by 1942. To replace it, the United States Maritime Commission had to abandon its program of building fast, efficient ships requiring scarce turbines, valves, and electrical equipment. As early as July, 1940, Admiral Emory S. Land, head of the Commission, and Knudsen recommended to the President mass production of a freighter that, while slow (sailing only 11 knots), would be simple to construct and not require scarce components. By using the existing designs for an old-fashioned British tramp steamer with a reciprocating engine and steam winches, they saved six months in starting production. This "Ugly Duckling" was the Liberty ship. After a slow beginning, builders substi-

Between the two wars, while the United States had neglected military research and development, Germany had sprinted far ahead, except in the field of radar. In the 1920's the Naval Research Laboratory in Washington had discovered the principle of radar by bouncing back a radio beam directed at a ship on the Potomac. The British had developed radar most highly, and it was their salvation during the air blitz of 1940–1941.

Other potential weapons were in the offing which, if the Germans developed them first, could mean Nazi victory in the war. (This was one of the reasons why the armed forces had decided to concentrate upon defeating Germany first.) The only way in which American scientists

---

UNITED STATES OUTPUT OF WAR MATÉRIEL

86,330 tanks	64,500 landing craft
296,400 airplanes	6,500 naval vessels
2,681,000 machine guns	5,400 cargo ships and transports

---

tuted welding for riveting and applied prefabrication and subassembly techniques in constructing it. In 1941, construction of Liberty ships required an average of 355 days; by the end of 1942, the time had been cut to 56 days, and one of Henry J. Kaiser's companies completed one in 14 days. During 1942 alone, 8 million tons of shipping were built; by 1945 the United States had over 36 million tons of ships afloat.

Scientists Against the Axis

The most revolutionary changes for the future came out of laboratories, as scientists pooled their skill in a race against those of the Axis—above all the Germans—to turn basic knowledge that was available to all into decisive weapons of war.

could catch up seemed to be through teamwork. The German threat brought creation of the government scientific agency that the New Deal had failed to produce. A leading scientist, Vannevar Bush, persuaded President Roosevelt to create a committee for scientific research in June, 1940. A year later, under the direction of Bush, it became the Office of Scientific Research and Development, which mobilized scientists with such effectiveness that in some areas they outstripped their German opponents.

The Americans and British developed superior radar, which not only detected enemy airplanes and ships, but helped direct shells against them. In these shells by 1943 they were using one of the most effective American inventions, radio-directed proximity fuses that detonated the shells as they neared their targets. American rocket research produced weapons enormously increasing the fire-power of airplanes, ships, and tanks, but lagged behind the progress made by the Germans, who before the end of the war were blasting London with enormous V-1 and V-2 rockets. The Germans also built the first jet airplanes and snorkel submarines, which would have been an even more serious menace if they had come into full production.

There was a danger, little publicized, that Germany might develop an atomic weapon. In the summer of 1939, a physicist, Enrico Fermi, and a mathematician, Albert Einstein, got word to President Roosevelt that German physicists had achieved atomic fission in uranium; what had long been theoretically possible had been accomplished. Next might come a bomb. The President authorized a small research project, and a race in the dark against the Nazis began. In December, 1942, physicists produced a controlled chain reaction in an atomic pile at the University of Chicago. The problem then became the enormous technical one of achieving this release of power in a bomb. Through the Manhattan District of the Army Engineer Corps, the government secretly poured nearly two billion dollars into plants to produce fissionable plutonium, and into another project under the supervision of J. Robert Oppenheimer which undertook to build a bomb. Here was an enormous and frightening gamble, against the hazards that the thing might not work and that the enemy might succeed first. Only after the war did the United States discover that the Germans were far from developing a usable atomic device. On July 16, 1945, after the end of the war in Europe, the first A-bomb was exploded, on a tower in New Mexico—producing the most blinding flash of light ever seen on earth, and a huge billowing mushroom cloud.

Manpower and American Society

Almost as complex as the scientific problems were the enigmas in integrating the domestic economy into the war machine: manpower, agriculture, production for civilian use, and finance.

The nation, after grappling for years with the problem of millions of unemployed, found itself hard pressed for sufficient people to swell the fighting forces, man the war plants, till the fields, and keep the domestic economy functioning. There were periodic demands for national service legislation or a labor draft, but unions were so vehemently opposed that no such measure ever passed the Senate. The relatively weak War Manpower Commission tried to coerce workers into remaining at defense jobs at the risk of being drafted, but the war came to an end without any tight allocation of manpower comparable to that of materials. The armed forces had first call upon men through Selective Service, which had been in operation since the fall of 1940. Altogether draft boards registered 31,000,000 men. Including volunteers, over 15,000,000 men and women served in the armed forces during the war. Nevertheless the working force jumped from 46,500,000 to over 53,000,000 as the 7,000,000 unemployed and many previously considered unemployable, the very young and the elderly, and several million women found jobs. The number of civilian employees of the federal government trebled.

This mobilization of manpower entailed the greatest reshuffling of population within such a short time in the entire history of the nation; altogether 27,300,000 people moved during the war. It meant also a heavy weight of wartime tension on American families. With the return of prosperity and the impending departure of soldiers, both marriage and birth rates jumped. In 1942 and 1943 about three million children were born each year, compared with two million a

UNEMPLOYMENT, 1929–1942

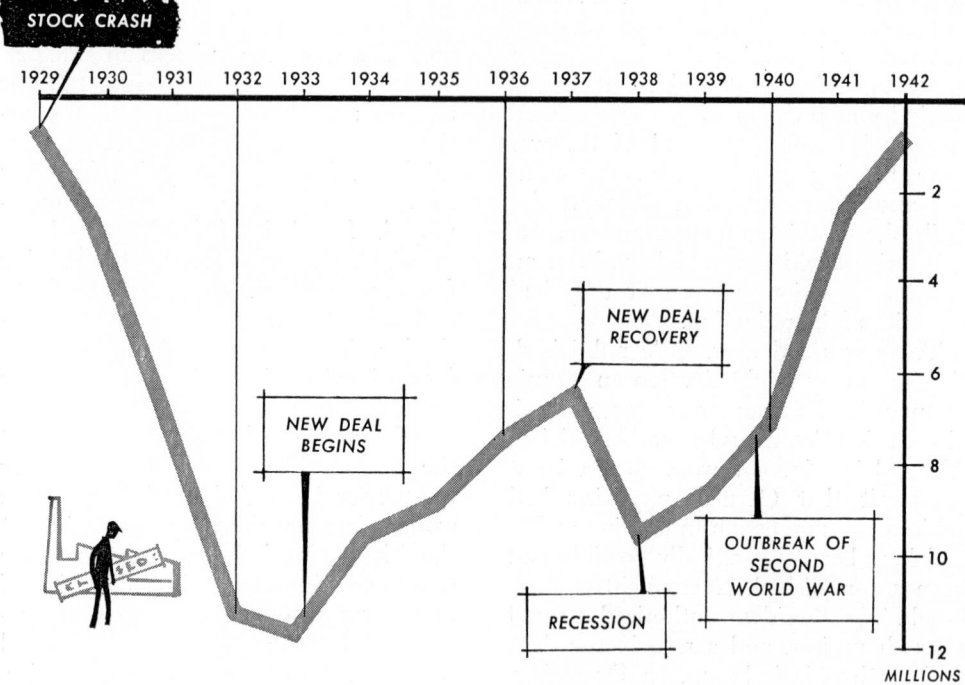

STOCK CRASH

1929 1930 1931 1932 1933 1934 1935 1936 1937 1938 1939 1940 1941 1942

NEW DEAL RECOVERY

NEW DEAL BEGINS

OUTBREAK OF SECOND WORLD WAR

RECESSION

2
4
6
8
10
12
MILLIONS

year before the war. But young wives and mothers fared badly in crowded housing near defense plants or army bases, or, after husbands had been shipped overseas, back home with parents. Draft boards deferred fathers as long as possible, but more than a million were ultimately inducted. More than two and a half million wives were separated from their husbands because of the war. The divorce rate increased slowly. Because men in the armed forces could in effect not be divorced without their consent, and many estranged wives stayed married in order to continue receiving allotment checks, a heavy backlog was built for postwar divorce courts.

When mothers were forced to work, children often suffered neglect, or were upset over the change. Court cases involving juvenile delinquency, especially among children from eight to fourteen, and among girls, the "bobby-soxers," increased 56 per cent. Even among the

nondelinquents, a serious price had to be paid at the time and later for the disruption of more American families for a longer period of time than ever before.

As adolescents found jobs, the percentage of those between 14 and 19 who attended school dropped from 62 in 1940 to 56 in 1944. Teachers also left for the armed forces or better-paying war jobs. Universities kept functioning through military research projects and training programs.

The great migration to war plants was stripping the agricultural South of underprivileged whites and Negroes alike, as 5,000,000 people moved within the South, and another 1,600,000 left the area completely. In the South this exodus led to the false rumor among outraged white housewives that the departing Negro domestics had formed "Eleanor Clubs," named after Mrs. Roosevelt, to "get a white woman in every kitchen by 1943." In the North, it led to explosive tension when Negroes, enjoying their new freedom, were jostled in crowded streetcars against indignant whites newly migrated from the South. A serious riot in which 25 Negroes and 9 whites were killed shook Detroit in June, 1943. New York narrowly averted a similar disaster. At the very time when the United States was fighting a war against the racist doctrines of Hitler, many whites became resentful over the rapid gains Negroes were making. In June, 1941, after the head of the Pullman porters' union, A. Philip Randolph, threatened a march on Washington, President Roosevelt established the Fair Employment Practices Committee. It worked diligently throughout the war against discrimination in employment. By 1944 two million Negroes were at work in war industry, and many previous barriers to economic opportunities for Negroes were permanently cracked.

Not everyone shared in the new prosperity. Government economists reported in 1943 that ten million families still received less than the $1675 per year requisite for a minimum standard of living. Most Americans, however, were relatively more affluent than they had been. The living standard of working people advanced rapidly; this was due less to wage increases than to payment of time-and-a-half for overtime beyond 40 hours. The average work week lengthened from 40.6 hours in 1941 to 45.2 in 1944. As living costs rose (on a 1935–1939 base of 100) from 100.4 in 1940 to 128.4 in 1945, gross weekly wages went up from $25.20 to $43.39. Working women and children created social problems, but they also brought additional prosperity to millions of families.

Restraining Labor Unions

Labor unions rapidly grew in strength during the war, and their unpopularity among Americans of the middle and upper classes increased. Union membership rose with the rise in the working force, from about ten and a half million workers in 1941 to over thirteen million in 1945. Keeping these workers satisfied was no easy matter. The administration was determined to prevent strikes and to restrain the formidable pressure of the la-

---

THE HOME FRONT IN 1942

"That was the spring when women took to wearing slacks in the streets (a great blow to the human race), old toothpaste tubes had to be turned in for new ones, men's trousers were commanded to be cuffless, and a radio comedian named Bob Hope began to play soldiers' camps around the country. . . .That was the spring we first heard about sugar rationing, with gasoline rationing to come. Ice cream was reduced to ten flavors, and civilian suffering really hit its stride when the War Production Board banned the use of metals for asparagus tongs, beer mugs, spittoons, bird cages, cocktail shakers, hair curlers, corn poppers, and lobster forks. New York blacked out, and for days we talked about how beautiful the great city looked stark and naked, silhouetted against the moon and the stars. . . . Sex reared its pretty head in factories as an occupational hazard. Girls were requested to quit wearing sweaters, peekaboo waists, halters, and other revealing garments. The boys were rubbernecking themselves into too many accidents."—Paul Gallico in Jack Goodman, ed., *While You Were Gone* (New York: Simon and Schuster, 1946).

bor unions from forcing wages, and thus all prices, upward. President Roosevelt followed the procedure of World War I by establishing a National Defense Mediation Board in March, 1941, made up of representatives of management, labor, and the public. In November, 1941, it broke down when the C.I.O members resigned over the refusal of the Board to recommend a union shop (i.e., one in which all new workers hired must join the union) in coal mines. In January, 1942, Roosevelt replaced it with the National War Labor Board, similarly constituted but much stronger. This Board could set wages, hours, and union conditions, and through the war powers of the President it could enforce these in a final extremity by government seizure and operation of plants.

On the union-shop question, which was creating such hostility between management and labor, the Board arrived at a compromise, the "maintenance of membership" clause. Nonmembers hired into a war plant did not have to join a union, but members had to remain in it, and the union remained the bargaining agent for the duration of the contract. Pressure for wage increases, which might contribute to inflation, was more serious. The Board hit upon a solution in ruling upon the Little Steel cases in July, 1942. Taking January 1, 1941, as the base date when workers had received a standard wage, it recognized a 15-per-cent rise in the cost-of-living index since then. Consequently, it felt that a proportionate increase for steel workers would be equitable. The Little Steel formula, except for those receiving substandard wages (like some textile workers), served thereafter as a wage ceiling.

Despite the no-strike pledges of the major unions, there were nearly 15,000 work stoppages during the war, involving the loss of more than 36 million mandays. These stoppages involved only one ninth of one per cent of the working time (though they indirectly caused more damage than this). When John L. Lewis's United Mine Workers defied the government in their strike against the Little Steel formula in May, 1943, Congress reacted by passing over Roosevelt's veto the Smith-Connally or War Labor Disputes Act of June, 1943, which required unions to wait thirty days before striking and empowered the President to seize a struck war plant.

Price Controls and War Finance

At the beginning of the war, with a two-year supply of wheat, cotton, and corn stored in Secretary Wallace's ever-normal granary, there seemed no danger of food shortages in the United States. But within six months after Pearl Harbor, scarcities of many sorts began to develop. The United States felt the increased demand of the armed forces and its allies, and the reduction of supplies due to the loss of fibers and oils from southeast Asia. By 1942 meat production was half again that of depression years, but American consumers with their increased buying power were eager to buy even more. Consumer income in 1943 was 65 per cent above depression levels, and much of it was in the pockets of people who had not eaten adequately for years.

A Food Administrator did exist, Chester Davis, but he resigned in protest when his views (and those of the American Farm Bureau Federation) did not prevail; his successor was Marvin Jones. Neither man had the dictatorial powers to provide for agriculture the scarce supplies and manpower that the dominant farm bloc in Congress would have liked to bestow upon agricultural producers. Rather, farmers had to depend upon whatever the War Production Board would allocate to them, and upon a generous draft-exemption program they obtained from Congress. They also received legislation raising the ceiling on com-

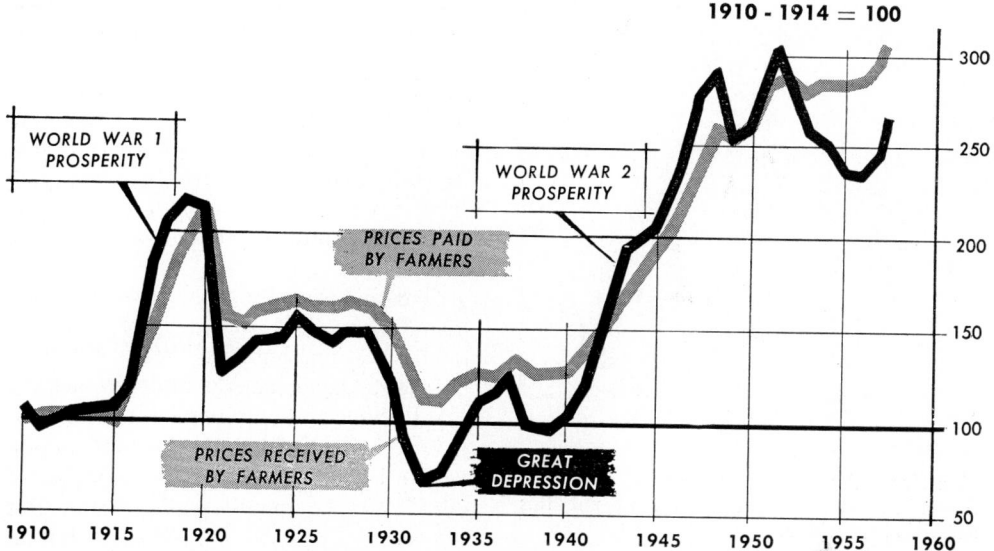

1910 - 1914 = 100

WORLD WAR 1
PROSPERITY

WORLD WAR 2
PROSPERITY

PRICES PAID
BY FARMERS

PRICES RECEIVED
BY FARMERS

GREAT
DEPRESSION

300

250

200

150

100

50

1910   1915   1920   1925   1930   1935   1940   1945   1950   1955   1960

modity prices to 110 per cent of parity. Since this came into conflict with the anti-inflation efforts of the administration, a dogged struggle developed between the President and the congressional farm bloc over farm prices. Neither side won entirely.

Pressures from business, farmers, and labor, combined with the scarcity of consumer goods and the burgeoning of buying power, created an almost irresistible trend toward inflation. During the defense period, the Office of Price Administration, under a vigorous New Dealer, Leon Henderson, lacked real coercive power and failed to halt inflation. Between the invasion of Poland and the attack on Pearl Harbor, prices of 28 basic commodities rose by nearly a fourth. Immediately thereafter, pressures became so acute that prices went up 2 per cent per month. Soon Congress hastily passed a bill authorizing only selective price-fixing and setting ceilings with a preferential trap door for agriculture.

The O.P.A. in April, 1942, issued a General Maximum Price Regulation that froze prices of consumer goods, and of rents in defense areas only, at their March, 1942, level. The greatest weakness was the rise of farm prices toward 110 per cent of parity which drove food prices —the most conspicuous item in any index—steadily upward. This gave ammunition to labor unions' barrage against fixed wages. In October 1942, Congress, grudgingly responding to the President's demand, passed the Anti-Inflation Act. Under its authority, Roosevelt immediately froze agricultural prices, wages, salaries, and rents throughout the country.

In July, 1943, Roosevelt appointed a former advertising executive with remarkable administrative talents, Chester Bowles, to head the O.P.A. With a small enforcement staff, Bowles braved general unpopularity to hold the increase in living costs during the next two years to 1.4 per cent. Altogether, the price level went up less than 29 per cent from 1939 to the end of the war, compared with 63 per cent between 1914 and the armistice.

Consumers nonetheless suffered numerous irritations and discomforts. The O.P.A., through unpaid local volunteers manning 5,600 price and rationing

THE HOME FRONT PLEDGE. The Office of Price Administration urged housewives to put this sticker in their windows.

boards, administered the rationing of canned goods, coffee, sugar, meat, butter and other fats, shoes, tires, gasoline, and fuel oil. The O.P.A. could not, however, control deterioration of quality. Black-marketing and overcharging grew in proportions far beyond O.P.A. policing capacity; in 1943 Congress slashed the funds of the enforcement division.

One of the most important inflationary controls was the sale of war bonds and stamps to channel off some of the excess purchasing power, which for the single year 1945 mounted to nearly $60 billion.

Throughout most of the war, personal incomes were at least a third greater than the available civilian goods and services. The Treasury Department, through eight war bond drives and its payroll deduction plans, but with few of the lurid or coercive touches of World War I, sold $40 billion worth of series "E" bonds to small investors, and $60 billion more to individuals and corporate entities other than banks.

Had this been the total of government loans, the effect would have been to quell inflation, but the Treasury had to borrow $87,500,000,000 more from Federal Reserve and commercial banks. Since in effect the banks created new credits which the government then spent, the effect was to inflate bank credits and money in circulation by over $100 billion.

Taxes did much more to drain off surplus purchasing power. The government raised 41 per cent of its war costs through taxation, compared with 33 per cent during World War I. The Revenue Act of 1942, which Roosevelt hailed as "the greatest tax bill in American history," levied a 94-per-cent tax on highest incomes; the President had suggested that no one should net more than $25,000 per year during the war. Also, for the first time, the income tax fell upon those in lower income brackets. To simplify payment for these new millions, Congress enacted a withholding system of

NUMBER OF PERSONS PAYING PERSONAL INCOME TAXES, 1939 and 1942

payroll deductions in 1943. Corporation taxes reached a maximum of 40 per cent on the largest incomes. In addition, excess profits were subject to a 90-per-cent tax, reclaiming for the government a large part of the return from war contracts. However, these taxes could be rebated to companies to aid them in reconversion, a provision of future significance. In effect, the government taxed away a large part of the profits of corporations, then returned it later when it was needed. A portfolio of heavy excise taxes on transportation, communication,

downward—had taken place. Despite the heavy taxation, by the end of the war consumers possessed an estimated $129 billion in liquid savings.

From 1941 to 1945 the federal government spent twice as much as the total appropriations from the creation of the government to 1941, and ten times as much as the cost of World War I—a total of $321 billion. The national debt rose from $49 billion in 1941 to $259 billion in 1945, yet the black warnings of national bankruptcy which had punctuated the New Deal years all but disappeared.

NATIONAL DEBT, 1910–1958

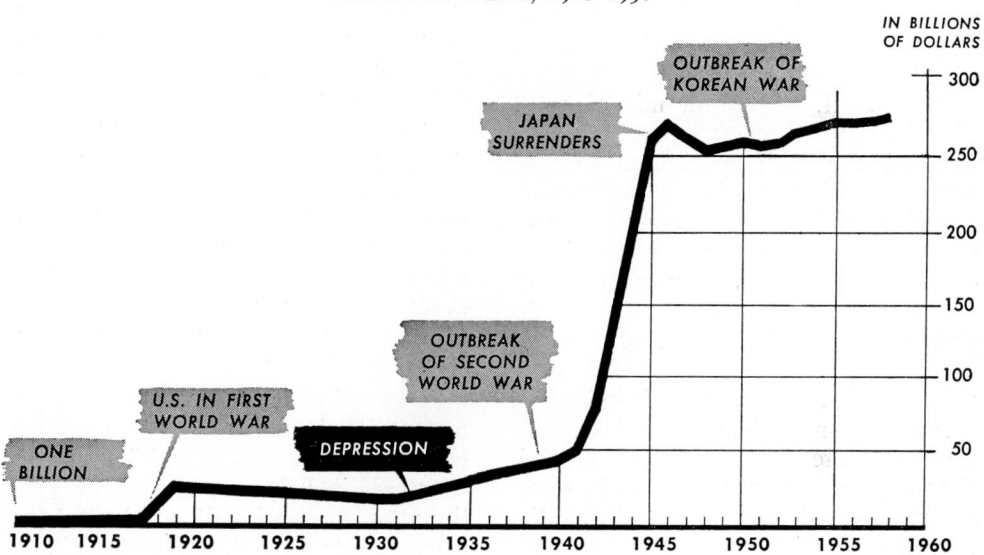

luxuries, and amusements completed the levies.

Between 1941 and 1945 the government raised $138 billion through taxation—nearly a $100 billion of it from income and excess profits taxes. Those in the top 5 per cent of the income scale suffered a serious relative economic loss, as their share of disposable income dropped from 26 per cent in 1940 to 16 per cent in 1944. Few persons or corporations were able to make fortunes out of the war, and a considerable amount of economic leveling—upward more than

Freedoms Abroad and at Home

In January, 1941, Roosevelt enunciated Four Freedoms as war aims—freedom of speech and worship and freedom from want and fear. But these never caught the public imagination as Wilson's Fourteen Points had done.

From Pearl Harbor on, there was the suspicion that through the Office of Censorship, almost immediately established under a competent Associated Press executive, Byron Price, the government was withholding information less because it was vital to the enemy than because it would be damaging to public opinion of the armed forces. Diligent newspapermen, aided by Price, exerted pressure on the armed forces to make censorship an instrument for security, not for the concealing of incompetence. Newspapers following Office of Censorship rules censored themselves to withhold local news that might be of value to the enemy.

The overlapping and conflict among government information agencies led to the establishment in June, 1942, of the Office of War Information under a shrewd news commentator, Elmer Davis. Although the O.W.I. consolidated four previous organizations, it coordinated rather than assumed the information function of domestic war agencies.

The O.W.I. aroused the misgivings of Congress, partly because of internal feuding and the mass resignation of the pamphlet writers, mainly because conservatives objected to several of the O.W.I. pamphlets: one opposing inflation, another on Negroes in the war, and another which was a tax primer. A fourth pamphlet intended only for overseas distribution, a cartoon biography of Roosevelt, especially worried antiadministration congressmen. They feared O.W.I. might promote New Dealish policies and the 1944 candidacy of Roosevelt. In 1943, Congress cut funds for the Domestic Branch so drastically that it had to stop producing propaganda.

Overseas, O.W.I. carried on a program employing 8,400 persons by VE day. Through "Voice of America" broadcasts begun in 1941 and propaganda of many sorts it presented an idealistic view of American war aims and aspirations for a peaceful postwar world. As the symbol of this idealism it dramatized President Roosevelt. By the end of the war, Roosevelt was more of a hero overseas than at home, and American aims appeared more idealistic abroad than in the United States.

The war produced less hatred and vindictiveness at home than had World War I. The energy that had gone into crude vigilantism in the earlier war went in the second World War into serving as air raid wardens and doing similar duties for the Office of Civilian Defense. People continued to eat hamburgers and sauerkraut and listen to Wagner. They demonstrated little animus toward Americans of German background and practically none toward Italians. A few Nazi agents and American fascists were jailed, but the most ambitious effort to punish them, a sedition trial of 28, ended in a mistrial after the defendants' lawyers had engaged in long weeks of delaying tactics. A few papers like Father Coughlin's *Social Justice* were barred from the mails. But socialists went unpunished, and religious conscientious objectors who were willing to register went to Civilian Public Service camps rather than prison.

In sad contrast to this moderation, the frenzy of public fury turned on the Japanese. The fighting in the Pacific developed a fierce savagery, reflected in the public anger within the United States. On the Pacific Coast, hatred of Americans of Japanese background became extreme. Wild stories circulated about sabotage at Pearl Harbor—later proven 100 per cent untrue. Under public pressure, Roosevelt in February, 1942, authorized the army to remove all people of Japanese ancestry from the West Coast. Some 117,000 people, two thirds of them United States citizens, were abruptly herded behind barbed wire, and later shipped into ten relocation centers in wild and disagreeable areas. They suffered the financial loss of at least 40 per cent of their possessions and for several years were barred from lucrative employment. Yet Japanese-Americans in Hawaii were left unmolested without incident throughout the war. There were 17,600 Japanese-Americans in the armed forces. Their units, especially in Italy, established outstanding records for bravery under fire.

JAPANESE-AMERICANS BEING EVACUATED FROM THE PACIFIC COAST. "Americans
. . . have held up to scorn the crudities of the Fascist regimes. Yet the history of
the evacuation policy could be an episode from the totalitarian handbook. The
resident Japanese minority became the scapegoat of military defeat at Hawaii. Racial prejudices, economic cupidity, and political fortune-hunting became inter-
twined with patriotic endeavor. In the face of exact knowledge to the contrary,
military officials propounded the theory that race determined allegiance. Civil administrators and the national legislature were content to rubber-stamp the military
fiat. . . .

"The American Civil Liberties Union has called the Japanese evacuation 'the
worst single wholesale violation of civil liberties of American citizens in our history.'
Later judgment will probably not lower that estimate, though it has already been
tempered in historical perspective as abrogated rights have been restored and most
Japanese in America have returned with full status to normal life."—Morton
Grodzins, *Americans Betrayed* (Chicago: University of Chicago Press, 1949). (NA-
TIONAL ARCHIVES)

This persecution of Japanese-Americans was the only major blemish in the
wartime civil liberties record, but it represented a serious erosion of civilian

rights, since the Supreme Court in 1944
validated the evacuation, and in other
decisions upheld military control over
civilians. In time of war or national emer-

gency, United States citizens could expect no court protection of their civil rights from military or executive authority. In this way the war had led to a threat to the civil rights of all Americans.

Wartime Politics

At times the sound and fury in Washington seemed almost to overshadow the struggle against the Axis. Despite all the platitudinous pleas to put aside politics in the interest of national unity, the struggles became if anything more virulent during the war. Conservatives saw in the war an opportunity to eradicate hated remnants of the New Deal; some liberals regarded it as an opportunity to bring Wilson's ideas to fruition, and even go beyond them to establish a global New Deal. Every one of the great pressure groups in the country fought to maintain or improve its relative position; spokesmen for large business and small, farmers and labor, jockeyed for position in Washington. The tenor of Congress continued to be conservative, and it was sensitive as always to the demands of organized constituents. Throughout the war, key committee chairmen who were leaders of the conservative coalition dominated Congress and forced their will upon President Roosevelt. Through the election of 1942, as the United States and its allies suffered unparalleled military disasters and the war administration in Washington seemed to compound confusion, the criticism rose to a crescendo. In the election, the Republicans gained 47 seats in the House and 10 in the Senate. Within both parties the trend was to the right.

President Roosevelt, in order to get crucial congressional support in prosecuting the war and planning the peace, continued to accept the sacrifice of New Deal measures. At a press conference he announced (1943) that "Dr. Win-the-War" had replaced "Dr. New Deal."

Dissatisfaction with wartime regimen-

tation and smoldering resentments still glowing from the prewar debate over intervention seemed to give the Republicans an opportunity in 1944. They had seen auguries of a national shift toward the right in the congressional election of 1942. In their vigorous young candidate, Governor Thomas E. Dewey of New York, who ran with Governor John W. Bricker of Ohio, they seemed to have an answer to Roosevelt and the aging New Dealers.

As for President Roosevelt, it was a foregone conclusion that he would be nominated for a fourth term if he so desired. There was none of the suspense that had preceded the third-term nomination. Rather, since he was visibly aging, and thinning so that his clothes ill fit him, there was much speculation over his choice for the Vice-Presidential nominee. Vice President Wallace was during the war the hero of most advanced New Dealers and much of the C.I.O. membership. But he was sneered at by party bosses and some Southern Democrats as a visionary who wished to extend the New Deal to the entire globe, to bring "a quart of milk for every Hottentot." They rallied behind James M. Byrnes of South Carolina, who had been functioning ably as unofficial assistant president —but Byrnes was unacceptable to organized labor. Out of the skirmishing among the rival factions within the Democratic party came Roosevelt's proposal of a compromise candidate acceptable to most of them, Senator Harry S Truman of Missouri. Truman had won newspaper approval as chairman of the Senate War Investigating Committee, was a consistent New Dealer in his voting record, and was from a border state. He was popular in the Senate.

Dewey was told that the United States had possessed the Japanese code at the time of Pearl Harbor, but an envoy from General Marshall persuaded him not to use this information, since it would hamper the war in the Pacific. Even without

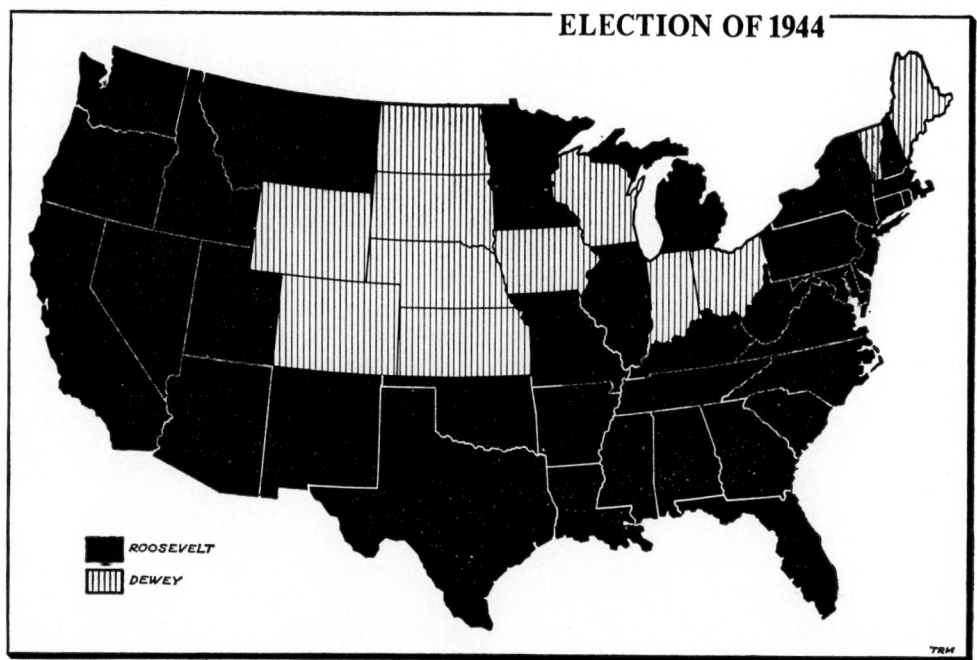

ELECTION OF 1944

ROOSEVELT
DEWEY

this issue, the election promised to be close—partly because the vote was likely to be small, and presumably a light vote would aid the Republicans.

The possibility was like an injection of adrenalin into Roosevelt. At the end of September, 1944, addressing a raucously appreciative audience of Teamsters Union members, he was at his sardonic best. He followed this triumph with a strenuous campaign in Chicago and throughout the East. This he climaxed with a day-long drive in an open car through New York City in a soaking rain. Everyone was drenched, and all but Roosevelt were exhausted.

This tour de force, seemingly proving Roosevelt's capacity to serve four more years, his international leadership, and his promise to return to the New Deal after the war, were a winning combination. Organized labor, working through the C.I.O. Political Action Committee, brought out the workers' votes. The President defeated Dewey by a margin of 432 electoral votes to 99, and a popular vote of 25,602,000 to 22,006,000. The Democrats lost one seat in the Senate, but gained twenty in the House. The Democratic victory seemed to mean a revival of the New Deal at home; and the campaign promises of both parties indicated that the United States would continue to take a lead in international affairs.

BIBLIOGRAPHY

Unfortunately there is no readable, dispassionate account of the battle for production. Eliot Janeway, *The Struggle for Survival* (1951), concentrates on conflicts in Washington; Donald M. Nelson's *Arsenal of Democracy* (1946) is his view of the War Production Board; Bruce Catton, *War Lords of Washington* (1948), emphasizes the influence of big business. The best overall survey is Bureau of the Budget, *The United States at War* (1946); an interesting compilation is Jack Goodman (ed.), *While*

You Were Gone: A Report on Wartime Life in the United States (1946).

More specialized studies are: James P. Baxter III, *Scientists Against Time* (1946); E. R. Stettinius, Jr., *Lend-Lease, Weapon of Victory* (1944); R. H. Connery, *The Navy and Industrial Mobilization in World War II* (1951); J. K. Galbraith, *Theory of Price Control* (1952); W. A. Nielander, *Wartime Food Rationing in the United States* (1947); W. W. Willcox, *The Farmer in the Second World War* (1947); Fred Witney, *Wartime Experiences of the National Labor Relations Board* (1949); Randolph E. Paul, *Taxation for Prosperity* (1947); E. S. Corwin, *Total War and the Constitution* (1947); M. Q. Sibley and P. E. Jacob, *Conscription of Conscience: The Conscientious Objector, 1940–1947* (1952); D. S. Thomas and others, *Salvage: Japanese American Evacuation and Resettlement* (1952); Morton Grodzins, *Americans Betrayed* (1949), on Japanese-Americans; J. tenBroek, E. N. Barnhart, and F. W. Matson, *Prejudice, War, and the Constitution* (1958), on the same subject; M. B. Clinard, *Black Market* (1952); Reuben Hill, *Families Under Stress* (1949); W. F. Ogburn (ed.), *American Society in Wartime* (1943); and J. S. Bruner, *Mandate from the People* (1944), on public opinion.

On politics, see Jonathan Daniels, *Frontier on the Potomac* (1946); Joseph Gaer, *First Round: The CIO Political Action Committee* (1944); and Roland Young, *Congressional Politics in the Second World War* (1955).

37

VICTORY WITHOUT PEACE

During World War II the United States was not, as it had been during World War I, a nation gingerly "associated" with the Allies. Rather, this country took the initiative in drafting and signing, on January 1, 1942, a Declaration by United Nations, setting forth the war aims of the Atlantic Charter, committing the nation's full resources, both military and economic, to the prosecution of the war, and pledging itself to cooperate with other signatories and not to make a separate peace. In effect, the United States was taking the lead in establishing a grand alliance, the United Nations, among the twenty-six signatory powers, and the twenty more that signed before the war was over. From this beginning, the United States, as it grew in military strength, took an ever more dominant lead in international diplomacy, as well as a determining part, very different from its 1917–18 experience, in war strategy.

The American War Machine

In December, 1941, neither the army nor the navy seemed very well prepared for the enormous tasks ahead, and the disaster at Pearl Harbor did not improve confidence in their commands. Enor-

mous industrial production alone could not win the war. The military must know what to order, and where and how to use it, on a scale they had not envisaged in their prewar establishments. At the outset, the navy possessed 300 combat ships —and it was a truism that navies usually fought wars with the ships they had when hostilities commenced—but at the close of the war it had 1,167 major ships and was employing only one of the prewar vessels in the final attacks on Japan.

The army in July, 1939, had in theory nine infantry divisions, but actually only the equivalent of about three and a half at half strength. Nor could it organize tactical units larger than a division. By mid-1941 it had twenty-nine infantry and cavalry divisions at nearly full strength, organized into four field armies —still less than half a million men. The army air force, nominally under the army but in practice almost independent, had only 22,000 officers and men and 2,400 aircraft in July, 1939.

There was little hint of what was to come. The most important of the war plans, Orange, devised to go into effect in case of conflict with Japan, had presumed primarily a naval war, with the army mobilizing over a million men. By

1940 the more comprehensive Rainbow plans superseded these; by December, 1941, a substantial mobilization was underway, though it was still far short of wartime totals.

Vast increases in personnel and equipment forced rapid changes in planning and organization. General George C. Marshall, Chief of Staff of the Army, reorganized the army high command in March, 1942. That same month, Admiral Ernest J. King, a clear-headed hard driver, became Chief of Naval Operations. Together with General H. H. Arnold of the army air force, these met with a personal representative of the President, Admiral

velt, who had always zealously guarded civilian control even in the Navy Department and the War Department, followed this course through the war. Conversely, he depended heavily upon the advice of the Joint Chiefs of Staff, and once major policy had been decided, seldom interfered with their strategy.

The first of the great policy decisions had come in 1940 when the Americans decided that even if Japan entered the war, their primary goal would be to defeat Germany with its superior military force, war production, and weapons development. The United States confirmed this priority in the initial wartime con-

EXPANSION OF U.S. ARMED FORCES, 1941–1945

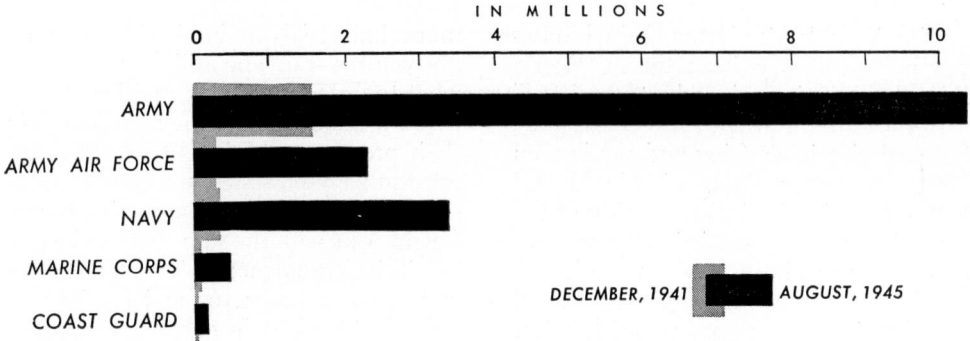

IN MILLIONS

ARMY

ARMY AIR FORCE

NAVY

MARINE CORPS

COAST GUARD

DECEMBER, 1941   AUGUST, 1945

William D. Leahy, to constitute the Joint Chiefs of Staff. They functioned as the overall command, and represented the United States in combined planning with the British or occasional negotiations with the Russians.

Over the Joint Chiefs of Staff was the Commander in Chief, President Roosevelt, who bore responsibility for the conduct of the war. Personally, and through assistants like Harry Hopkins and cabinet members, he coordinated the war planning of the Joint Chiefs with war production and manpower, and with foreign policy. In July, 1940, the War Plans Division of the Army General Staff had pointed out that civilians should decide the "what" of national policies, and the professional soldiers the "how." Roose-

ference with the British at the end of December, 1941. This decision did not mean neglecting the war against Japan. By August, 1941, when the buildup especially of airplanes was under way in the Philippines, and later when General MacArthur received orders to fight, the strategy was shifting to a two-front war. The war against Germany was to be offensive, while that against Japan was to be defensive. It was difficult to hold to this policy as the Japanese tide in the Pacific swelled far beyond the bounds the most pessimistic planners had anticipated. For the President, furious over Japanese treachery, and the navy, primarily responsible in the Pacific, it was not an easy decision to maintain. General MacArthur, the panic-stricken public on the Pacific Coast, and most Americans elsewhere clamored for prompt and stern action against the Japanese.

During the first chaotic months of shocking reverses, the armed forces allotted their men and supplies piecemeal to try to meet each new Axis threat. Top strategists emphatically warned that such dissipation of effort might lead to defeat. No one was more insistent than Dwight D. Eisenhower, who had been brought to Washington after Pearl Harbor as a Far Eastern expert, and by the spring of 1942 was head of the Operations Planning Division under General Marshall. In emphatic memoranda he hammered away at the need to build up men and supplies in Europe for the invasion of North Africa that Roosevelt and Churchill had decided upon in their December, 1941, meeting. Because of his vigor and his important role in developing an invasion plan, Eisenhower became the logical man to send to England in June, 1942, as Commanding General in the European theater.

On the Defensive, 1941–2

While the United States was building and equipping its fighting forces, it had to depend upon the Russians and the British to hold back the Germans as best they could. During the discouraging first six months of American participation it had to stand perilously on the defensive in both the Atlantic and the Pacific. There even seemed danger of a breakthrough in Egypt and the Caucasus which might enable the Germans and Japanese to join forces in the Middle East or India.

Ten hours after the strike at Pearl Harbor, Japanese airplanes hit the airfields at Manila, destroying half the American bombers and two thirds of the fighter planes. That same day the Japanese sank two British warships off Malaya, the only Allied warships in the Far East. Three days later Guam fell; then, in the weeks

that followed, Wake Island and Hong Kong. The great British fortress of Singapore in Malaya surrendered in February, 1942, the East Indies in March, and Burma in April. In the Philippines on May 6 the exhausted Philippine and American troops, having made brave withdrawals to the Bataan peninsula and the Island of Corregidor in Manila Bay, ran down the last American flag in the Far East.

Only one weak outpost, Port Moresby in southern New Guinea, stood as a bulwark against the invasion of Australia. It seemed likely to fall, but there containment began through the efforts on land of Australian and American troops, and on the sea, of American aircraft carriers. In the Battle of Coral Sea on May 6–7, 1942, the Americans turned back Japanese invasion forces threatening Port Moresby. Under General MacArthur, who had escaped from the Philippines, American and Australian troops began clearing the Japanese from New Guinea.

After the Battle of Coral Sea, the Navy, having intercepted Japanese messages, knew the next move and rushed every available plane and vessel into the central Pacific. Near Midway Island, June 3–6, 1942, these forces inflicted heavy damage on a Japanese invasion fleet and headed off a drive to capture the island and neutralize Hawaii. The United States had achieved its goal of containment in the Pacific, and as men and supplies could be spared from the operations against the Nazis, it could assume the offensive against Japan.

In the Atlantic during the early months of 1942, the Nazis tried by means of submarines to confine the Americans to the Western Hemisphere. By mid-January, the Germans had moved so many submarines to the Atlantic coast, where at night they torpedoed tankers silhouetted against the lights of cities, that they created a critical oil shortage. Against convoys bound for Europe they made attacks with devastating success. In the first eleven months, they sank over 8,000,000 tons of shipping—1,200,000 more than the United Nations had constructed—and threatened to delay indefinitely the large scale shipment of supplies and men to Europe. Gradually the United States countered by developing effective antisubmarine vessels, air patrols, detecting devices, and weapons.

The submarines made it difficult to send assistance to the British and Russians in the summer of 1942 when they needed it most. The German *Afrika Corps* raced to El Alamein, only seventy-five miles from Alexandria, Egypt, threatening the Suez Canal and the Middle East. At the same time, German armies in Russia were plunging toward the Caucasus. In May, the Russian foreign minister, Vyacheslav Molotov, visited Washington to demand an immediate second front that would divert at least forty German divisions from Russia; the alternative might be Russian collapse. Roosevelt promised to do everything possible to divert the Germans by invading France. But Churchill arrived the next month during the crisis when the Germans threatened Egypt, and strongly urged an invasion of North Africa instead.

The Mediterranean Offensive

The overwhelming losses in the August, 1942, raid on Dieppe, France, undertaken by experienced Canadian troops, indicated the wisdom of making the first American landing on a relatively unprotected flank. Through advance negotiations with officials of the Vichy government of defeated France, the Americans hoped to make a bloodless landing in French North Africa. At the end of October, 1942, the British opened a counteroffensive at El Alamein which sent the *Afrika Corps* reeling back. On November 8, Anglo-American forces landed at Oran, Algiers, and Casablanca, Morocco, with some bungling and grati-

fyingly few losses. They met determined French resistance only at Casablanca.

Admiral Jean Darlan, earlier one of the most notorious collaborators with the Nazis, signed an armistice with the Allies on November 12. He ordered a cease-fire and promised the aid of 50,000 French colonial troops. Outraged American liberals protested against the deal with the Vichyites as opposed to the French resistance forces under General Charles de Gaulle. They quieted somewhat a few weeks later when Darlan was assassinated. Unquestionably the Vichy gamble, unsavory though it was to idealists, saved lives and speeded the liberation of North Africa.

The Germans tried to counter the invasion by ferrying troops from Sicily into Tunisia at the rate of a thousand a day. Early in 1943 the *Afrika Corps*, which had retreated westward across Tripoli, joined them and threw the full weight of its armor against the green American troops. The Americans lost heavily, but with the aid of the British held onto their bases and gained in experience. Allied airpower and the British navy so seriously harassed the Axis supply line from Sicily that Germany decided not to make a major stand in Tunisia. From March into May, the British army in the east and the armies in the west under Eisenhower gradually closed a vise on the German and Italian troops. On May 12, 1943, the last Axis troops surrendered. The Mediterranean had been reopened and the Americans had learned lessons that would be useful in the successful invasion of France.

That invasion, despite the continued clamoring of the Russians, was not to take place immediately. The fighting in Tunisia had tied up too large a part of the Allied combat resources for too long. Nazi submarines were still taking too heavy a toll of the Allies' inadequate shipping. Some of the ships and production had to be diverted to the antisubmarine war, and others to the prosecution of the

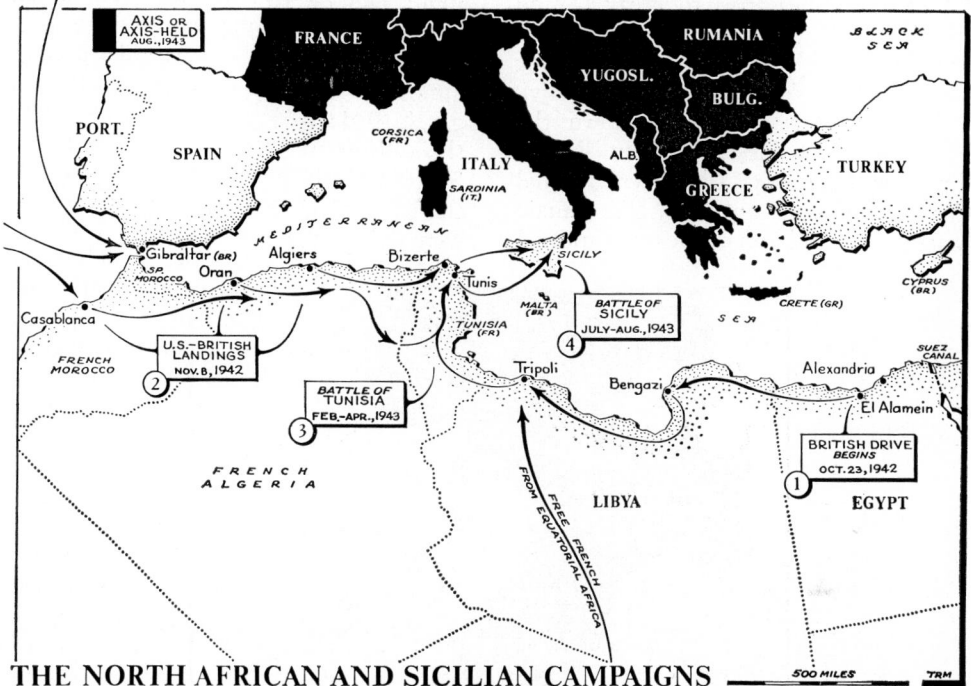

THE NORTH AFRICAN AND SICILIAN CAMPAIGNS

500 MILES   TRM

Pacific campaigns. Also, the planners in London had come to recognize that an enormous buildup was necessary for a successful cross-channel invasion. Fortunately for the Allies, the tide turned for the Russians also during the winter of 1943, when they had successfully held the Germans at Stalingrad in the Ukraine, eliminating an army of 250,000 men.

As early as mid-January, 1943, Roosevelt and Churchill and their staffs, while conferring at Casablanca, looked ahead to the next move. This was to be an invasion of Sicily, even though General Marshall feared it might delay the invasion of France. Churchill argued persuasively that the operation in Sicily might knock Italy out of the war and lead the Germans to tie up many divisions in defense of Italy and the Balkans.

On the night of July 9, 1943, American and British armies landed in the extreme southeast of Sicily, where defenses were comparatively light. The Americans made grievous errors, the worst being to shoot down 23 planeloads of their own paratroops, but learned from their mistakes. In 38 days the Allies conquered the island and looked toward the Italian mainland. Mussolini now fell from power, to be replaced by the pro-Allied Marshall Pietro Badoglio. At once Badoglio opened complicated negotiations to switch Italy to the side of the United Nations. As the negotiations went on, the Nazis moved eight strong divisions into northern Italy, concentrated other troops near Rome, and turned the country into an occupied defense bastion.

A limited but long and punishing campaign opened on the Italian peninsula on September 3, 1943. It started with the greatest optimism, for that same day the Italian government signed an armistice agreement and the Allies quickly seized bases and airfields in southern Italy. But the Nazi defenders fought so fiercely from hilly redoubts that by early 1944 they had stopped the slow and deliberately moving Allies at Monte Cassino.

When the Allies tried to break behind the line by landing at Anzio, also south of Rome, they were almost thrown back into the sea. With relatively few divisions, the Nazis were tying down the Allies and concentrating upon Russia. Finally in May, 1944, the Allies captured Cassino, pressed on from the Anzio beachhead, and on June 4 captured

night raid on Cologne. In August, the Americans made their first experimental daytime raids on the continent. Bombing almost around-the-clock began on a gigantic scale in February, 1944. One of the objects of these bombing raids was to draw German fighter planes into battle. By the end of the war, the Americans were flying over 7,000 bombers and 6,000

THE ITALIAN CAMPAIGN

Rome, just before the cross-channel invasion of France began.

The Liberation of Europe

In the fall of 1943 Germany was already reeling under the incessant blows from the growing Allied air power. Great Britain had begun its mass bombing of German industrial centers in the late spring of 1942 with a thousand-plane

fighters in Europe, had dropped nearly a million and a half tons of bombs, and had lost nearly 10,000 bombers. British figures were similar. Especially in the last year of the war, the bombing drastically cut production and impeded transportation, but as early as the winter of 1944 it so seriously demoralized the German people that 77 per cent of them regarded the war as lost.

The bombing attacks first upon the

THE INVASION OF NORMANDY. A Coast Guard combat photographer, climbing beyond the Nazi trench in the foreground to the top of the cliff, looked out at this panorama of channel waters crowded with ships, while landing craft were putting ashore men and supplies. The barrage balloons floated overhead to protect the ships from low-flying enemy strafers. One of them is resting on the deck of a LST (landing barge). Long lines of trucks were heading inland, carrying reinforcements for the battle for the Cotentin peninsula. (OFFICIAL COAST GUARD PHOTO)

aviation industry, then upon transportation, did much to clear the way for the invasion in the late spring. By May, 1944, the *Luftwaffe* was incapable of beating off the Allied air cover for an invasion. As D-day (invasion day) approached, the invasion was postponed from the beginning of May until early June despite the likelihood of worsening weather, in order to obtain an additional month's production of special landing craft. A sudden storm delayed the operation for a day, but on the morning of June 6, 1944, the invasion came, not at the narrowest part of the English Channel, where the Nazis expected it, but along sixty miles of the

Cotentin peninsula on the Normandy coast. While airplanes and battleships offshore incessantly bombarded the Nazi defenses, 4,000 vessels, stretching as far as the eye could see, brought in troops and supplies.

Within two weeks after the initial landings, the Allies had put ashore a million men and the equipment for them. They also had captured Cherbourg, only to find that the Germans had blocked its harbor so skillfully that it could not be used until August.

Well into July, the Allies fought mile by mile through the Norman hedgerows. The breakthrough came on July 25, 1944,

NORMANDY LANDINGS AND ALLIED OFFENSIVES TO THE RHINE

GREAT BRITAIN

NETH.

BELG.

GERMANY

FRANCE

SWITZ.

ITALY

SPAIN

NORTH SEA

ENGLISH CHANNEL

Norwich
Ipswich
London
Dover
Brighton
Portsmouth

Amsterdam
The Hague
Rotterdam
Arnhem
Münster

WAAL
MAAS

Dortmund
Essen
Düsseldorf
Cologne
Kassel

Dunkirk
Calais
Boulogne
Abbeville

Ghent
Antwerp
Brussels
Lille

Aachen
Bonn

REMAGEN BRIDGE MAR. 7, 1945

BATTLE LINE DECEMBER 15 1944

BATTLE OF THE BULGE DEC. 1944

Cherbourg
St. Lo
Caen
Falaise
Avranches
Le Havre
Rouen
Compiegne

Amiens
Cambrai
Dinant
Sedan

BREAKOUT AT ST. LO JULY 25, 1944

Bastogne
LUX.
SAAR

Coblenz
Frankfurt
Mainz
Mannheim
Karlsruhe

Reims
Verdun
Metz
Nancy
Strasbourg

MEUSE

Rennes
Laval
LeMans
Paris
Evreux
Chartres
Orléans

SEINE

Sens

Epinal
Colmar
Belfort
Freiburg
Basel

RHINE

Lorient

St. Nazaire
Nantes
Angers
Tours
Bourges

LOIRE

Sombernon
Dijon
Besançon

Nevers

Bern

La Rochelle
Rochefort
Limoges
Vichy
Clermont Farrand

Bourg
Lyon
Geneva

Grenoble
Turin

Bordeaux

GARONNE

Montélimar
Sisteron

Savona

RHONE

SAONE

Avignon
Nice
St. Raphaël

Bayonne
Toulouse
Montpellier
Narbonne
Marseille
Toulon
St. Tropez

Pamplona
Lérida
Barcelona
Perpignan

LANDINGS IN SOUTHERN FRANCE AUGUST 15, 1944

→ AMERICAN
⇒ BRITISH AND CANADIAN
⇢ FRENCH

TRM

100 MILES

when the Third Army under General George Patton, using its armor as cavalry had been used in earlier wars, smashed the German lines in an enormous sweep that moved southward into Brittany, then westward around the left flank of the German army. The invasion on the Mediterranean coast, beginning on August 15, quickly seized new ports (also seriously blocked) and opened new supply lines for the Allies. On August 25, French forces rode into Paris, jammed with cheering throngs. By mid-September, the Allied armies had driven the Germans from almost all of France and Belgium, including the port of Antwerp, and had come to a halt against a firm line of German defenses.

Cold weather, rain, and floods aided the Germans. In December, they struck with desperate fury along a seventy-five mile front in the Ardennes Forest, driving twenty miles toward Antwerp before they were stopped (in the "Battle of the Bulge") at Bastogne.

While the Allies were fighting their way through France to the Westwall (German defense line) and up the Italian peninsula, the Russian armies had been sweeping westward into central Europe and the Balkans. The Russian armies advanced more rapidly than had been expected and in late January, 1945, launched an offensive of over 150 divisions toward the Oder River, deep in Germany.

After liquidating the German thrust into the Ardennes, which had almost exhausted the Nazi fighting capacity, the Allied armies pushed on to the Rhine. The Americans captured Cologne on the west bank March 6, 1945, and on the next day, through remarkable luck, captured a bridge across the Rhine at Remagen. Troops poured across it. By the end of March the last great drives were underway as the British Montgomery with a million troops pushed across the north while Omar Bradley's army, sweeping through central Germany, completed the encirclement and trapping of 300,000 German soldiers in the Ruhr. Russian troops were about to mount a spring offensive only 35 miles from Berlin.

Although there were fears that the Nazis were preparing for a last stand in an Alpine redoubt centering around Berchtesgaden on the Austrian border, the German western front had in effect been demolished. The only question was where the Americans would next drive, and where they would join the Russians. The Americans were capable of moving much further eastward than had been anticipated, and could have beaten the Russians to Berlin and Prague. This would have cost American lives, but reaped political gain in Europe. General Eisenhower decided instead to send American troops to capture the Alpine redoubt, and to halt along the Elbe River in central Germany to meet the Russians.

President Roosevelt lived to see neither the final triumph nor the ultimate tragedy. Since the early months of 1944 his vigor had been gradually drained away. Suddenly, on the afternoon of April 12, 1945, he died of a cerebral hemorrhage, at Warm Springs, Georgia. The new President, Harry S Truman, who had been in no way briefed for his sudden enormous responsibilities, had to take over leadership of the war.

On May 8, 1945, the remaining German forces surrendered unconditionally. V-E (Victory in Europe) Day arrived amidst monster celebrations in western Europe and in the United States. The rejoicing was tempered only by knowledge of the continuing war against Japan.

The Pacific Offensive

The offensive strategy against the Japanese involved amphibious warfare of a type which the marine corps had been developing since the early 1920's. In the Pacific these new tactics came to be so perfected that troops were able to cross and seize vigorously defended beaches

ALLIED OFFENSIVES
IN THE PACIFIC

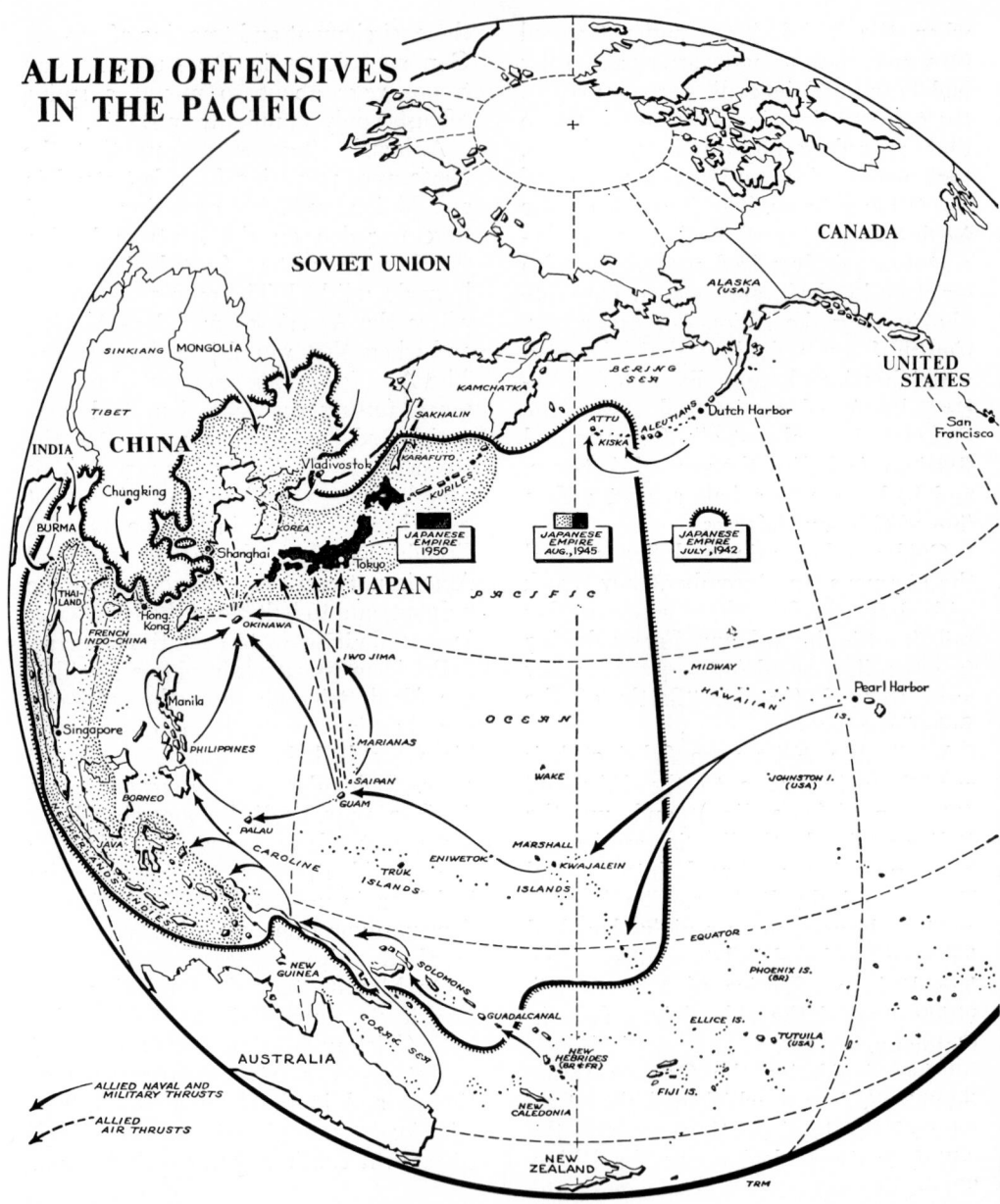

ALLIED NAVAL AND MILITARY THRUSTS

ALLIED AIR THRUSTS

when the United States could not by-pass and immobilize advanced Japanese strong points. The American strategy was, whenever feasible, "Hit 'em where they ain't."

The southern Solomon Islands to the east of New Guinea were being developed as a Japanese base for air raids

against American communications with Australia. In August, 1942, the navy and marines opened an offensive against three of these islands, Gavutu, Tulagi, and Guadalcanal. Around and on Guadalcanal a struggle of unprecedented fierceness developed as the United States and Japanese navies battled for control in a series of large-scale engagements. By the time the struggle was over, the United States and its allies had lost heavily in cruisers, carriers, and destroyers, but had sunk 47 Japanese vessels. The Japanese navy had lost its offensive strength and thereafter concentrated upon defensive operations.

During the months when the great naval battles had been going against the United States, the Americans had gained control of the air and thus were able to sustain the marines, and subsequently the army, in their precarious jungle onslaught. By February, 1943, Guadalcanal had been won. Through the year the island-hopping continued all around the enormous Japanese-held perimeter: in the South Pacific through the northern Solomons to New Georgia and in November to Bougainville; in the Central Pacific, also in November, the Marine landing on Makin and the bloody assault on Tarawa in the Gilberts; in the Northern Pacific, the inexpert reconquest of Kiska and Attu in the Aleutians.

Victories in the Marshall Islands in February, 1944, cracked the Japanese outer perimeter, and before the month was out the Navy had plunged far within it to wreck the bastion at Truk and raid Saipan in the Marianas. American submarines were increasingly harassing Japanese shipping, and thus hampering the economy. In 1943 they sank 284 ships; in 1944 they sank 492—necessitating by summer a cut of nearly a quarter in skimpy Japanese food rations and creating a crucial gasoline shortage. The inner empire of Japan was coming under relentless siege.

Meanwhile, in 1942, the Japanese forced General Joseph H. Stilwell out of Burma and brought their troops as far west as the mountains bordering on India. China was so isolated that the United States could send in meager supplies only through an aerial ferry over the "hump" of the Himalayas. On the return trip, the planes brought Chinese troops

for Stilwell to train and arm. Through 1943, Stilwell with Chinese, Indian, and a few American troops fought back through northern Burma, constructing a road and parallel pipeline across the rugged mountains into Yunnan province, China. The Ledo or Stilwell road was not open until the fall of 1944, but meanwhile the Air Transport Command managed to fly in sufficient supplies to enable the Fourteenth Air Force (before Pearl Harbor, the "Flying Tigers") to harass the Japanese. The Command undertook a still larger task, when, in June, 1944, from Chinese bases, B-29 bombers struck the Yawata steel mills in Japan. The Japanese retaliated in the next few months by overrunning the bases from which the bombers operated, and clearing the coastal area so they could bring supplies northward from southeast Asia by rail or road. They drove so far into the interior that they threatened the Chinese terminus of the Ledo Road, and perhaps even the center of government at Chungking.

The great Japanese offensive precipitated a long-simmering crisis in Chinese-American affairs, centering around the relations between General Stilwell and Chiang Kai-shek. Stilwell was indignant because Chiang was using many of his troops to maintain an armed frontier against the Chinese Communists and would not deploy them against the Japanese. In order to have bolstered Chiang adequately, the United States would have had to send such substantial immediate support that the campaigns against Germany and directly against Japan might have had to be slowed down or postponed.

During 1944 Japan came under heavy blockade from the sea and bombardment from the air. American submarines firing torpedoes and laying mines continued to make heavy inroads in the dwindling Japanese merchant marine.

In mid-June an enormous American armada struck the heavily fortified Mar-

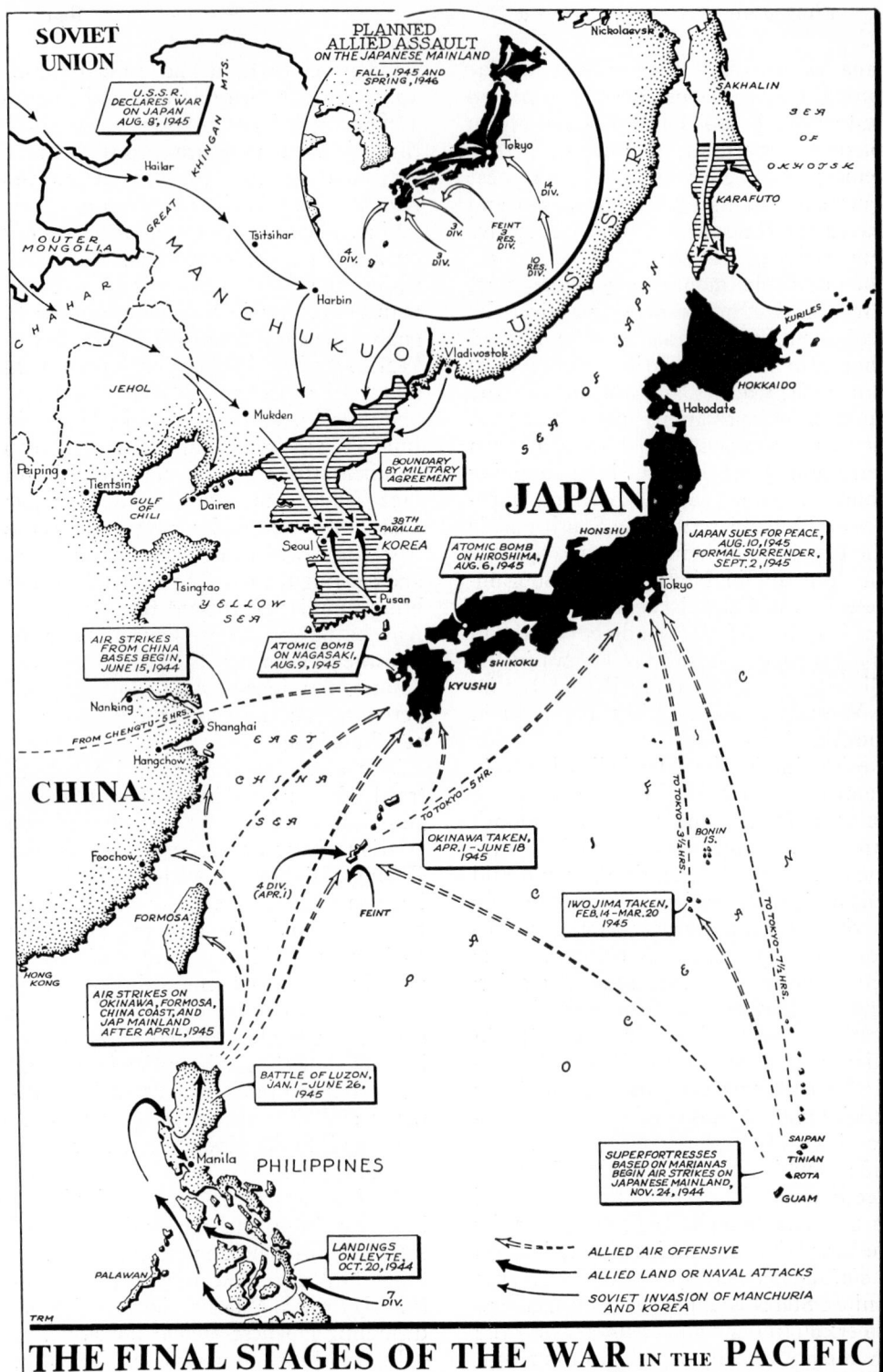

THE FINAL STAGES OF THE WAR IN THE PACIFIC

iana Islands, quickly but expensively capturing Tinian, Guam, and Saipan, 1350 miles from Tokyo. These were among the bloodiest operations of the war. In September the Americans landed on the Western Carolines. The way was being paved for the return to the Philippines. For weeks in advance Navy craft swept the central Pacific, and airplanes ranged over the Philippines and Formosa. Finally, on October 20 General MacArthur's troops landed on Leyte Island in the Philippines. The Japanese, threatened with being fatally cut off from their new empire in Southeast Asia, threw their remaining fleets against the invaders in three major encounters—together comprising the decisive Battle of Leyte Gulf, the largest naval engagement in history—and lost almost all their remaining sea power.

Atomic Triumph over Japan

With remarkable speed but grievous losses the American forces cut still deeper into the Japanese empire during the early months of 1945. While fighting continued in the Philippines, the marines landed in February on the tiny volcanic island of Iwo Jima, only 750 miles from Tokyo. The Americans needed Iwo Jima to provide fighter cover for Japan-bound bombers and a landing place for crippled ones. The Japanese defended it so grimly that the marines suffered over 20,000 casualties. It was the bloodiest battle in the history of the marine corps.

The battle for Okinawa, an island 65 miles long, beginning on April 1, 1945, was even bloodier. This island was 370 miles south of Japan, and its conquest clearly would be a prelude to an invasion of the main islands. On land and from the air, the Japanese fought with literally a suicidal fury. Week after week they sent *kamikaze* suicide planes against the American and British ships, losing 3,500 of them, but inflicting great damage. Ashore at night, Japanese troops launched

equally desperate attacks on the American lines. The United States and its allies suffered nearly 50,000 casualties on land and afloat before the battle came to an end in late June, 1945. The Japanese lost 110,000 killed and 7,800 prisoners.

This same sort of bitter fighting seemed to await the Americans when they invaded Japan—if indeed they had to invade. There were signs that the Japanese might instead surrender, for they had almost no ships and few airplanes with which to fight. In July, 1945, American warships stood offshore with impunity shelling industrial targets, most of which were already in ruins from the heavy bombing attacks. Long since, moderate Japanese leaders had regarded the war as lost. Upon the invasion of Okinawa, the Emperor appointed a new premier and charged him with suing for peace. The premier could not persuade the army leaders to lay down their arms, but nevertheless he, and in early summer the Emperor himself, tried to obtain mediation through Russia.

Apparently the Russians were determined, at their own time, to enter the war. But the atomic bomb rather than Russian intervention was to be decisive in ending it. At a meeting of Allied leaders in Potsdam, Germany, in mid-July, 1945, President Truman received word that the first atomic test was successful. He and Prime Minister Clement Attlee (who had succeeded Churchill) issued the Potsdam Declaration urging the Japanese to surrender or face utter devastation. The Premier wished to accept the ultimatum, but the army leaders would not surrender. President Truman had set August 3 as the deadline; when it passed and the Japanese fought on, he ordered an atomic bomb to be dropped on one of four previously selected Japanese cities.

On August 6, 1945, a B-29 dropped an atomic bomb on Hiroshima, completely destroying the hitherto undamaged city, and killing 80,000 people (according to American estimates) or 200,000 (accord-

ing to the Japanese). Even after the horror of Hiroshima, the Japanese army remained adamant. Russia declared war on Japan as of August 9. That same day, the Air Force dropped a second bomb on Nagasaki. This was the final blow. After frantic negotiations, on August 14 the Japanese government agreed to give up. On September 2, 1945, aboard the battleship *Missouri* in Tokyo bay, the articles of surrender were signed.

World War II was at an end. All together, some 14,000,000 men under arms had been killed, and countless millions of civilians had died. In comparison, about 322,000 Americans had been killed or were missing; total United States casualties were about 1,120,000. Despite this frightful expenditure in lives and an astronomical cost in material resources, the American people faced a future made uncertain and perilous by the tensions with the Russians and the threat of future atomic wars.

The Dangerous Alliance

Only the imminent threat of Axis victory had forced an uneasy and not too satisfactory unity between Russia and its Western allies, Great Britain and the United States. As the threat began to lift in 1943, it became an increasingly difficult and dangerous task to keep the alliance cemented until victory had been achieved, and to plan for a postwar world in which a decent peace could be maintained.

The difference between British and American strategy—the British opposing a cross-channel invasion and preferring campaigns in southern and eastern Europe—affected the two nations' dealings with the Russians. To a certain extent the United States seemed nearer to the Russian position in insisting with them upon an early invasion of France. Roosevelt personally tried hard to establish a warm relationship with Stalin, and in his efforts seemed at times to take a middle position between Stalin and Churchill.

As the Nazi tide began to recede, the postwar patterns would quickly emerge throughout eastern Europe, even as they were already appearing in Italy. Firm political agreements were necessary if these areas were not to fall entirely under Russian hegemony, just as firm military plans were essential to the achievement of final victory.

At Casablanca, Morocco, in January, 1943, after previous consultation with Churchill, Roosevelt announced the doctrine of unconditional surrender toward the Axis. What Roosevelt seemed to desire was to avoid the sort of negotiations that had marred the 1918 armistice, causing bickerings among the Allies at the time and German misunderstandings afterwards. As the war progressed, it became clear that "unconditional surrender" left the United Nations free to state to enemy nations the peace terms they might expect. Roosevelt and Churchill both emphasized in speeches through 1943 that it did not mean, as the Nazi propagandists charged, that extremely severe terms would be imposed. Yet, after the war, some historians charged that the "unconditional surrender" doctrine seri-

THE MUSHROOM CLOUD OVER NAGASAKI, JAPAN, AUGUST 9, 1945. [OPPOSITE] "When the atomic bomb exploded, an intense flash was observed first, as though a large amount of magnesium had been ignited, and the scene grew hazy with white smoke. At the same time at the center of the explosion, and a short while later in other areas, a tremendous roaring sound was heard and a crushing blast wave and intense heat were felt. The people of Nagasaki, even those who lived on the outer edge of the blast, all felt as though they had sustained a direct hit, and the whole city suffered damage such as would have resulted from direct hits every where by ordinary bombs."—Nagasaki prefectural report on the bombing. (OFFICIAL U.S. AIR FORCE PHOTO)

HIROSHIMA, JAPAN, LOOKING NORTHEAST, OCTOBER, 1945. "A single atomic bomb, the first weapon of its type ever used against a target, exploded over the city of Hiroshima at 0815 on the morning of 6 August 1945. Most of the industrial workers had already reported to work, but many workers were enroute and nearly all the school children and some industrial employees were at work in the open on the program of building-removal. . . . The explosion came as an almost complete surprise, and the people had not taken shelter. Many were caught in the open, and most of the rest in flimsily constructed homes or commercial establishments. The bomb exploded slightly northwest of the center of the city. Because of this accuracy and the flat terrain and circular shape of the city, Hiroshima was uniformly and extensively devastated. Practically the entire densely or moderately built-up portion of the city was leveled by blast and swept by fire. . . . The surprise, the collapse of many buildings, and the conflagration contributed to an unprecedented casualty rate. Seventy to eighty thousand people were killed, or missing and presumed dead, and an equal number were injured."—Report, United States Strategic Bombing Survey. (NATIONAL ARCHIVES)

ously discouraged the German underground, stiffened the Nazi will to fight, and thus lengthened the war.

In October, 1943, Secretary Hull, although he was 72 and in precarious health, flew to Moscow to confer with the British and Russian foreign ministers. His faith in Wilsonian idealism almost limitless, Hull returned from Moscow elated because the Russians had agreed to a Declaration of Four Nations on General Security. (China was the fourth nation.) This was a pledge to continue the united action of wartime "for the organization and maintenance of peace and security," and to create, as soon as practicable, a general international organization.

With an air of optimism Roosevelt and Churchill traveled eastward in November, 1943, for a long-awaited meeting with Stalin at Teheran, Iran. On the way they stopped at Cairo to confer with Chiang Kai-shek and to prepare a statement (released after the Teheran conference) drawing a map for the postwar

through an international organization of keeping Germany from ever again becoming a menace. Stalin wished Russia to retain the areas she had seized in her period of collaboration with Germany, including eastern Poland as far as the so-called Curzon line proposed in 1919. Roosevelt and Churchill agreed to the Polish boundary.

Roosevelt and Churchill seem not to have recognized realistically the nature of of the peace that was being foreshadowed at Teheran. In the general rejoicing over the apparent accord among the Big

---

UNCONDITIONAL SURRENDER

"Another point. I think we have all had it in our hearts and our heads before, but I don't think that it has ever been put down on paper by the Prime Minister and myself, and that is the determination that peace can come to the world only by the total elimination of German and Japanese war power. . . .

"The elimination of German, Japanese, and Italian war power means the unconditional surrender by Germany, Italy and Japan. That means a reasonable assurance of future world peace. It does not mean the destruction of the population of Germany, Italy or Japan, but it does mean the destruction of the philosophies in those countries which are based on conquest and the subjugation of other people."—Franklin D. Roosevelt, press conference at Casablanca, January 24, 1943.

Far East. They proposed stripping Japan of her empire in order to restore Manchuria, the Pescadores, and Formosa to China, and to create in due course a free and independent Korea. Japan was to lose, in addition, all other territory she had acquired since 1914.

At Teheran, Roosevelt undertook to establish a friendly, intimate relationship with Stalin of the sort he enjoyed with Churchill. Stalin reaffirmed his intention to bring Russia into the Pacific war as soon as hostilities ended in Europe, and expressed his satisfaction with the Cairo communiqué on Japan. In a cordial way the three leaders discussed means

Three, and in their assumption that Russia would be content within its new boundaries, they overlooked the appraisal one of the American participants at Teheran wrote a few days later: "The result would be that the Soviet Union would be the only important military and political force on the continent of Europe. The rest of Europe would be reduced to military and political impotence."

It was unrealistic to expect, as Roosevelt apparently did, that the Russians would forbear from exploiting the great European and Asian power vacuums that the defeat of Germany and Japan would create. This miscalculation led the United States into a tragic triumph—a victory without peace.

The Yalta Conference

Churchill's mood fluctuated with the ebb and flow of Russian good will. Upon leaving Moscow, he wrote Stalin, "This memorable meeting . . . has shown that there are no matters that cannot be adjusted between us when we meet together in frank and intimate discussion." By January, 1945, he was so badly disillusioned that he wrote Roosevelt concerning the forthcoming Yalta meeting, "This may well be a fateful Conference, coming at a moment when the Great Allies are so divided and the shadow of the war lengthens out before us. At the present time I think the end of this war may well prove to be more disappointing than was the last." Such was the bleak and unpromising setting for the great conference at Yalta in the Crimea in February, 1945.

At that time American forces were having to reduce Germany mile by mile;

there seemed no reason to think Japan would be different. General MacArthur insisted on the necessity for Russian aid, taking the position that otherwise the United States would have to fight a series of difficult and expensive campaigns to overcome the Japanese in Manchuria. Consequently the Joint Chiefs did not revise their timetable calling for the defeat of Japan eighteen months after German surrender, and they continued to regard Russian aid as desirable. Roosevelt expressed to Stalin his hope that Japan could be bombed into submission without invasion—but the Americans could not count upon it.

These were the limitations upon the Americans in their bargaining at Yalta. In return for Stalin's reiterated promise to enter the Far Eastern war two or three months after German surrender, Roosevelt and Churchill promised him the Kurile Islands north of Japan and the restoration of "the former rights of Russia" lost in the Russo-Japanese War. This meant the return of southern Sakhalin Island, the return of a lease on Port Arthur as a naval base and internationaliz-

---

PLANS FOR THE FAR EAST

"The Three Great Allies are fighting this war to restrain and punish the aggression of Japan. They covet no gain for themselves and have no thought of territorial expansion. It is their purpose that Japan shall be stripped of all the islands in the Pacific which she has seized or occupied since the beginning of the first World War in 1914, and that all the territories Japan has stolen from the Chinese, such as Manchuria, Formosa, and The Pescadores, shall be restored to the Republic of China. Japan will also be expelled from all other territories which she has taken by violence and greed. The aforesaid Three Great Powers, mindful of the enslavement of the people of Korea, are determined that in due course Korea shall become free and independent.

"With these objects in view the Three Allies, in harmony with those of the United Nations at war with Japan, will continue to persevere in the serious and prolonged operations necessary to procure the unconditional surrender of Japan."—Joint communiqué by Roosevelt, Chiang, and Churchill on the Cairo conference, December 1, 1943.

STALIN, ROOSEVELT, AND CHURCHILL AT TEHERAN. "We—The President of the United States, the Prime Minister of Great Britain, and the Premier of the Soviet Union, have met these four days past, in this, the Capital of our Ally, Iran, and have shaped and confirmed our common policy.

"We express our determination that our nations shall work together in war and in the peace that will follow. . . .

"Emerging from these cordial conferences we look with confidence to the day when all peoples of the world may live free lives, untouched by tyranny, and according to their varying desires and their own consciences.

"We came here with hope and determination. We leave here, friends in fact, in spirit and in purpose."—From joint statement issued December 1, 1943. (NATIONAL ARCHIVES)

ing of the port of Dairen, Manchuria (in both instances with recognition of Russia's pre-eminent interests), and joint operation with China of the Chinese Eastern and South Manchurian Railroads feeding into the ports. China was to retain sovereignty over Manchuria, but Roosevelt did not clarify what "pre-eminent interests" meant. (For many months these clauses remained secret because Russia was still at peace with Japan.)

In its disposition of central European questions, the Yalta conference for the most part ratified previous decisions. Germany was to be divided into zones of occupation previously agreed upon. Since Berlin was to be deep in the Russian zone, the Americans and British proposed an accord providing freedom of transit into Berlin. The Russians held back, and in the general spirit of amity at Yalta, the matter was postponed. At the time, the Russian demands for heavy reparations in the form of German factories, goods, and labor seemed far more important. The British tried to scale down the Russian demand for $20 billion in such reparations, of which Russia was to obtain half. This would so strip and starve the

Germans, Churchill pointed out, that the United States and Great Britain would have to feed them. Consequently they agreed to the Russian figure only as a basis for discussion by a reparations commission. Already, in the light of reality the West had left far behind the Morgenthau plan (initialed by Roosevelt and Churchill at Quebec in October, 1944) for the pastoralization of Germany.

One of the touchiest questions was to define a democratic government for Poland, a matter over which Russia and the West had negotiated for months. The Russians did not wish to allow the Polish government in exile in London or the Polish underground to assume any substantial share of power with a government the Russians established at Lublin. At the beginning of August, 1944, as the Red army drove within ten miles of Warsaw, the underground in the city arose against the Germans. The Russians halted, ignored the revolt, and despite the strong pleas of the United States and Great Britain, stood by while the Polish patriots in sixty-three days of fighting were annihilated. The Russian explanation was military exigency, but the situation seemed to show the sort of government Stalin was determined to establish in Poland.

At Yalta the West managed to obtain Stalin's agreement that the Lublin (Communist) government should be broadened to include democratic leaders from Poland and abroad. What the percentage should be was not specified. Subsequently the new government should hold "free and unfettered elections as soon as possible on the basis of universal suffrage and secret ballot." It would have been a satisfactory arrangement for the West had the terms been interpreted in their Western meaning. As for the Polish boundary, it was to follow the Curzon line in the east, and the Poles should receive territorial compensation in the north and west.

For the rest of liberated or defeated Europe, the Big Three agreed to establish interim governments "broadly representative of all democratic elements," to be followed by free elections which would create "governments responsible to the will of the people."

In years after the war, disappointed Americans harshly criticized the Yalta agreements, especially for their violations of the Atlantic Charter. The morality of the Far Eastern arrangements is open to challenge. Their purpose was to obtain Russian aid, which top military leaders thought would shorten the war against Japan and perhaps prevent a million American casualties. They promised nothing to Stalin that he could not have taken anyway. The morality of the European arrangements (except perhaps for the ethnic dislocations wrought by the new Polish boundaries) was defensible if the terms received their customary Western interpretation. Roosevelt may be most severely criticized for not insisting at every point upon absolutely clear, sharply defined agreements which could receive only one interpretation in Russia, and that the same as in the West. This was especially true of the question of entry into Berlin. Experience with the Russians long before Yalta pointed to the need of precise understandings.

Roosevelt was careless in this respect because he pinned his hopes upon the good faith of the Russians and their willingness to enter into and participate actively in an international organization for the preservation of the peace.

Founding the United Nations

A few months after war broke out in Europe, long before Pearl Harbor, Secretary Hull took the first step toward proposing a new international organization in which the United States would participate. In January, 1940, he appointed an Advisory Committee on Problems of Foreign Relations. On it served Congressmen from both parties and distinguished experts from within and without the State Department. Several private organizations like the Council on Foreign Relations also prepared numerous studies for the State Department.

President Roosevelt, firmly determined to avoid Wilson's failure, encouraged Hull to include Republicans in the planning for the peace. However, Roosevelt did not consult Congress before making his most famous statements of war aims; Senator Robert A. Taft asserted in Congress in November, 1943, that he did not believe "we went to war to establish the 'four freedoms' or any other freedom throughout the world," nor "for the purposes set forth in the Atlantic Charter." The administration, to counter this sort of resentment, included prominent Republicans in at least sketchy briefing on wartime diplomacy and let them participate more fully in postwar planning of many kinds. In this way it won their support. In March, 1943, four Senators, two Republican and two Democratic, none of whom were serving on the Foreign Relations Committee, introduced a resolution calling for American leadership in establishing a United Nations organization. Public opinion polls indicated a general enthusiasm for the resolution; the Senate passed a similar declaration 85 to 5. Senator Arthur H. Vandenberg of Michigan, previously one of the most forthright isolationists, assumed Republican leadership in helping mold a "bipartisan" foreign policy. He thus gained for himself and the Republican party new power and stature.

The Big Four powers, conferring in the summer and fall of 1944 at Dumbarton Oaks, a Harvard-owned estate in Washington, drafted tentative outlines for a new international organization. These were the starting points for the drafting of a United Nations charter at a conference of fifty nations in San Francisco, opening April 25, 1945. President Roosevelt before his death had appointed a bipartisan delegation headed by his new Secretary of State, Edward R. Stettinius, Jr. One of its most effective members was Senator Vandenberg, who helped to wrest concessions from the Russians at San Francisco and to win the votes of reluctant Republicans for ratification in the Senate.

Basically the charter of the United Nations was a refurbishing of the old Wilsonian League covenant with the former American objections removed through giving a veto to each of the five main powers. The Americans and British, as well as the Russians, had insisted upon the veto as a seemingly necessary protection of their sovereignty. The American delegates, led by Vandenberg, succeeded in obtaining for the small nations in the General Assembly freedom to discuss and make recommendations—in effect creating "a town meeting of the world."

The Senate quickly ratified the Charter on July 28, 1945, by a vote of 80 to 2, in remarkable contrast to the slow and painful death it had administered to American adherence in the League of Nations. But the great and growing gulf between Russia and the West destined the United Nations to be, like its predecessor, the League, a town meeting for international discussion or a sounding board for national views, rather than the forerunner of a world government.

BIBLIOGRAPHY

The best exposition of American wartime strategy is K. R. Greenfield (ed.), *Command Decisions* (1959). See also S. E. Morison, *Strategy and Compromise* (1958); more critical is Hanson W. Baldwin, *Great Mistakes of the War* (1950). A brief account of the war is Fletcher Pratt, *War for the World* (1950); a good pictorial account,

Life's Picture History of World War II (1950). A brilliant memoir and history is Winston S. Churchill, *Second World War* (6 vols., 1948–53); and a challenging account of the war in Europe from the British viewpoint is Chester Wilmot, *Struggle for Europe* (1952). Brief, clear reports are *General Marshall's Report: The Winning of the War in Europe and the Pacific* (1945), and *U.S. Navy at War, 1941–1945* (1946). The following multi-volume histories are well under way or completed: S. E. Morison, *History of United States Naval Operations in World War II* (14 vols., 1947–   ); *United States Army in World War II* (91 vols., 1947–   ); W. F. Craven and J. L. Cates (eds.), *Army Air Forces in World War II* (5 vols., 1948–53); and *Operational Narratives of the Marine Corps in World War II* (1947–   ). Among the memoirs are: Robert Sherwood, *Roosevelt and Hopkins;* H. L. Stimson and McGeorge Bundy, *On Active Service in Peace and War* (1948); Dwight D. Eisenhower, *Crusade in Europe* (1948); Omar N. Bradley, *A Soldier's Story* (1951); Henry H. Arnold, *Global Mission* (1949) and E. J. King and W. M. Whitehill, *Fleet Admiral King* (1952). On the organization and functioning of the military establishment, see R. S. Cline, *Washington Command Post* (1951); Mark S Watson, *Chief of Staff* (1950); and

S. M. Rosen, *Combined Boards of the Second World War* (1951).

A monumental account of wartime diplomacy is Herbert Feis, *Churchill, Roosevelt, Stalin* (1957). In addition to the memoirs of Churchill and Hull, and Sherwood's *Roosevelt and Hopkins,* see Sumner Welles, *Seven Decisions That Shaped History* (1951), and W. L. Langer, *Our Vichy Gamble* (1947).

See E. R. Stettinius, Jr., *Roosevelt and the Russians* (1949), on Yalta; J. F. Byrnes, *Speaking Frankly* (1947); H. S. Truman, *Memoirs* (2 vols., 1955); Arthur Vandenberg, Jr. (ed.), *The Private Papers of Senator Vandenberg* (1952), on foreign policy from Yalta to the Japanese surrender; and Herbert Feis, *The China Tangle* (1953), on wartime and postwar relations with China. A valuable compilation on Yalta is R. F. Fenno, Jr. (ed.), *The Yalta Conference* (1955). On the effects of the atomic bomb, see John Hersey, *Hiroshima* (1946).

On the United Nations, see L. M. Goodrich and Edvard Hambro, *Charter of the United Nations* (1949); E. P. Chase, *The United Nations in Action* (1950); and R. B. Russell, *A History of the United Nations Charter: The Role of the United States, 1940–1945* (1958). On atomic control, J. R. Newman and B. S. Miller, *The Control of Atomic Energy* (1948).

38

COLD WAR AND KOREA

After the Japanese surrender, a series of Russian thrusts into weak areas in Europe and Asia gave Americans rude shocks that halted each of the periodic drifts back toward relative isolation and united the nation in maintaining an armed peace—or "cold war." Again and again the normal desire of the American people to enjoy the high living standard and unprecedented prosperity of the postwar years was threatened by these crises; each time the people accepted heavier armaments, firmer international commitments, and even, if need be, the fighting of brushfire wars.

Delayed Peacemaking

Through no fault of his own, President Harry S Truman was ill prepared for the task of concluding the war and fabricating the peace. No one doubted his sincerity when he remarked to reporters the day after he had suddenly taken his oath of office, "I felt like the moon, the stars, and all the planets had fallen on me. I've got the most terribly responsible job a man ever had."

During the first phase of his relations with the Russians, into 1947, Truman

was moderately firm but tried to give the Soviet government no cause for protest. He was chagrined when in May, 1945, the Foreign Economic Administration enforced his order ending Lend-Lease so precipitately that it even called back some ships at sea. The British were the most hard-hit, but Stalin complained most bitterly.

At the Potsdam conference (July, 1945) Truman could secure few satisfactory agreements on questions involving occupied and liberated countries. Despite the failure at Potsdam, Truman's Secretary of State, James F. Byrnes, continued in a conciliatory fashion to seek accommodation with the Russians. The Potsdam conferees provided for a Council of Foreign Ministers to draft treaties with Italy and the former Axis satellites. During a tedious and depressing round of meetings of the Council in London, Moscow, Paris, and New York between September, 1945, and December, 1946, relations between the West and Russia steadily deteriorated, though five treaties were concluded. The one with Italy reflected Western demands; those with Finland, Hungary, Rumania, and Bulgaria in effect incorporated Soviet armistice

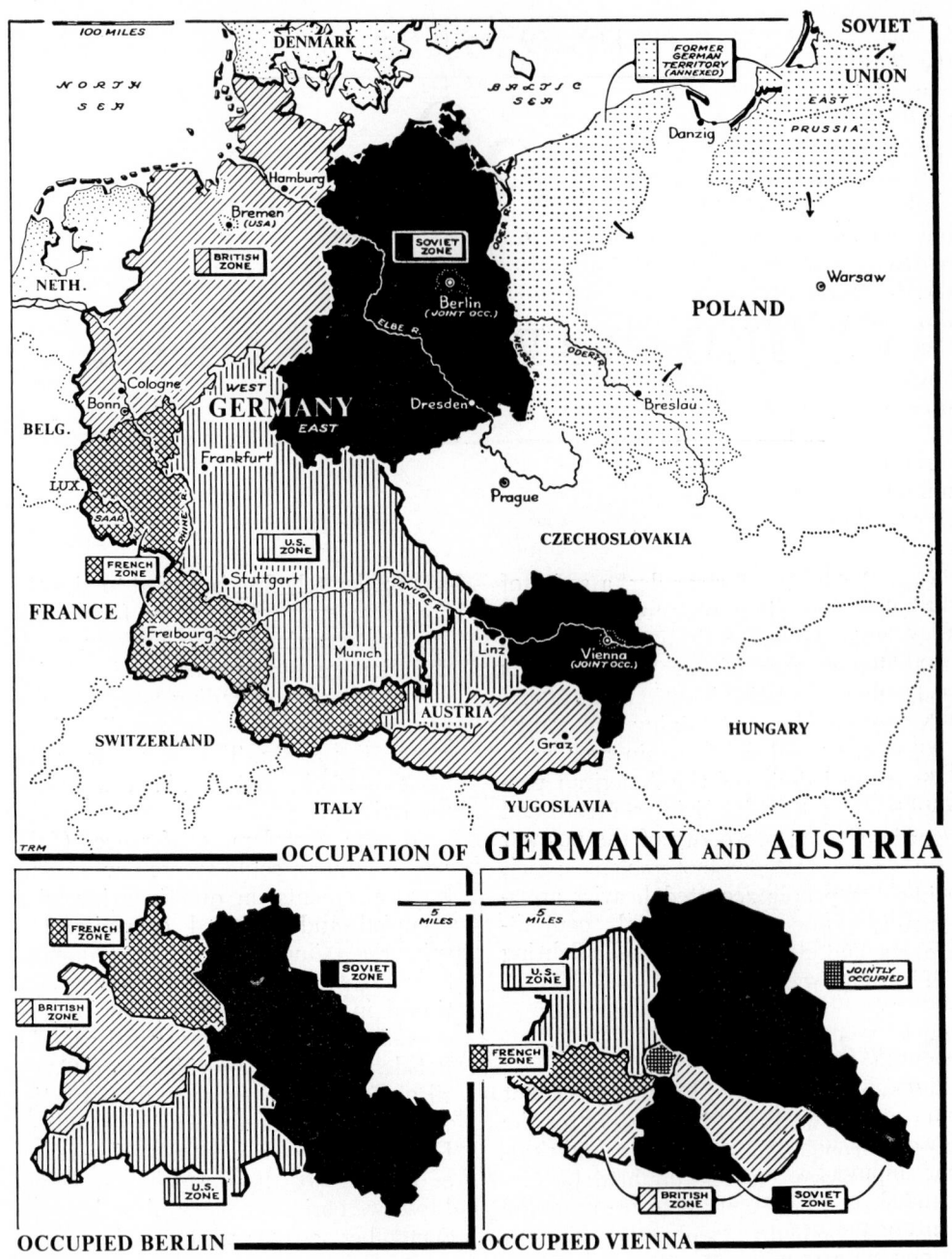

OCCUPATION OF GERMANY AND AUSTRIA

OCCUPIED BERLIN

OCCUPIED VIENNA

terms. The United States by ratifying the three latter treaties acquiesced in the Russian domination of these nations.

The greatest obstacle to a satisfactory settlement in Europe was Germany.

There a four-power Allied Control Council began sessions in Berlin marked by the same blocking and delaying tactics that made other joint conferences with the Russians so dismal. The Western nations had visualized unified controls for Germany to prevent its resurgence. But the Russians had no interest in a Germany reunified in a manner acceptable to the West; Germany was to remain split indefinitely.

In occupied Germany and Japan, meanwhile, the United States pursued firm but conflicting policies compounded of harshness and idealism. During the war the American people had come to hate the enemy leaders and were insistent that they be punished for their war crimes, especially those Nazis who were responsible for the maintenance of frightful concentration camps like Buchenwald and for the gas-chamber murder of millions of Jews. This led to the trials of thousands of Nazis and war criminals, capped by that of twenty-two key Nazi leaders before an International Military Tribunal at Nuremberg in 1945-6. Eleven were sentenced to death.

There was an equally sweeping purge of Japan, and a trial was held for twenty-five former top Japanese military and civil officials. Seven of them, including two premiers, were executed. The dangerous precedent seemed to be established, as Churchill pointed out, that "the leaders of a nation defeated in war shall be put to death by the victors."

At first the Americans seemed bent on the pastoralization as well as reform of conquered Germany. They banned all industry directly or indirectly contributing to German war potential, including even the construction of seagoing ships, drastically cut steel and chemical production, destroyed munition plants, and allowed the dismantling of some factories for shipment to the Russians. They disbanded cartels and encouraged only agriculture and peaceful domestic industries. Along with this, they wished to foster American-style democracy in place of the repudiated Nazism. These economic policies, coming at a time when so much of German housing and industry was rubble, and when several million exiles were making their way from the East or Czechoslovakia, reduced western Germany to a living standard not much better than that of a giant relief camp. The army undertook to feed the German people between 1945 and 1948 at a subsistence level of 950-1550 calories per day.

Even this near-starvation diet cost the British and Americans nearly half a billion dollars per year. The Russians were adding further to the economic burden by taking out of their zone (and from the western zones to the extent agreed at Potsdam) reparations totaling one and a half to three billion dollars per year. They were siphoning out of Germany more than the Americans and British could pump in.

In Japan American occupation policy suffered fewer obstacles, and profited from the initial errors in Germany. During the first critical weeks General MacArthur, the Supreme Commander for the Allied Powers (SCAP), set up an overwhelmingly American occupation, based on a directive radioed him from Washington, on August 29, 1945. Truman refused Stalin's demand that Russians occupy part of the northern Japanese island, Hokkaido. The irritated Russians had a voice, but no real power, on an eleven-country Far Eastern Commission in Washington and on a four-power Allied Council to advise MacArthur in Tokyo.

The American occupation of Japan acted rapidly to demilitarize and democratize the country. From the outset it recognized that Japan must be left with a healthy economy, but in practice—by limiting the nation's war potential—it reduced Japan like Germany to a relief state.

The Postwar Military Program

In the face of these growing menaces in Europe and Asia, the United States in the eighteen months after Japan's capitulation speedily dismantled its army, air force, and navy. At the end of the war, there was a popular demand to "bring the boys back." In April, 1945, President Truman announced that nearly 7,000,-000 men had been released from the army, "the most remarkable demobilization in the history of the world, or 'disintegration,' if you want to call it that." He proposed a system of universal military training, but Congress did no more between 1946 and 1948 than to pass limited Selective Service measures. The gradual whittling of the armed forces continued, until by the spring of 1950 the army was down to 600,000 men, and the ceiling on defense expenditures, to $13 billion. Lacking land armies, the United States sought to balance the Soviet power with atomic bombs and an air force that could deliver them.

Since September, 1945, the administration had been ready to negotiate an agreement with Russia which would "control and limit the use of the atomic bomb as an instrument of war" and "direct and encourage the development of atomic power for peaceful and humanitarian purposes." Great Britain and Canada joined with the United States in proposing international control of atomic energy. The United Nations Assembly responded by creating in January, 1946, the United Nations Atomic Energy Commission, to which the American member, Bernard Baruch, submitted a plan in June, 1946. This proposed a thoroughgoing system of control and inspection of atomic energy development through a United Nations agency. When the system became effective, the United States would liquidate its stockpile and join in an international ban on atomic bombs.

The Russians refused to accept the Baruch plan for international inspection and control of atomic development; instead they constantly and vociferously demanded that the United States unilaterally destroy its atom bombs. Through their wide propaganda they tried to marshal world indignation against the United States while they rushed ahead with their own research on atomic weapons. American scientists and military leaders, not aware as yet of the successful Russian espionage, and underrating Russian scientific and technical proficiency, predicted that it would be many years before the Soviet Union could produce a successful bomb.

Meanwhile, Congress lengthily debated the domestic control of American atomic energy. Democrats wished to vest control in civilians; Senator Vandenberg and the Republicans urged giving it to the heads of the armed forces. A compromise was reached in the Atomic Energy Act of August, 1946. This created a five-man civilian Atomic Energy Commission with complete control over research and development of fissionable materials; linked to it was a Military Liaison Committee.

Under the protection of an atomic umbrella, military leaders indulged in the luxury of a vigorous and prolonged controversy over unification of the various armed forces. This measure, proposed to bring greater efficiency and effectiveness, led instead to heightened rivalry, as the generals pushed for it, and the admirals feared for the loss of the marine corps and the relative weakening of the navy. Both sides brought the utmost pressure upon Congress. Finally in July, 1947, the National Security Act provided for a Secretary of Defense to preside over separate Departments of the Army, Navy, and Air Force, with the Joint Chiefs of Staff serving as advisers to him and to the President. To coordinate diplomacy and military planning, the 1947 act also provided for a National Security Council to consist of the President, certain cabinet members, and other advisers on foreign and military policy. This Council was to be served by two other new agencies, a National Security Resources Board and a Central Intelligence Agency.

Within the reorganized Pentagon Building the old rivalries continued. Indeed, through the creation of a separate air force there now appeared to be three separate services where there had been only two before. The first Secretary of Defense, Forrestal, exhausted by the struggle to make unification effective, resigned in March, 1949, and shortly committed suicide. His successor, Louis A. Johnson, became embroiled in a violent quarrel over cancellation of construction of a huge new aircraft carrier, culminating in the resignation of the Secretary of the Navy and replacement of the Chief

Secretary of State: "Unless Russia is faced with an iron fist and strong language another war is in the making."

Truman faced a peculiarly difficult task in trying to persuade the American public that a truly deep and serious rift was developing between Russia and the West. For too many war years they had listened to publicists ranging from that advanced New Dealer Henry Wallace to the Republican president of the United States Chamber of Commerce, Eric

---

KENNAN ON CONTAINMENT

"The Soviet pressure against the free institutions of the Western World is something that can be contained by the adroit and vigilant application of counter-force at a series of constantly shifting geographical and political points, corresponding to the shifts and maneuvers of Soviet policy, but which cannot be charmed or talked out of existence. The Russians look forward to a duel of infinite duration, and they see that already they have scored great successes. . . .

"But in actuality the possibilities for American policy are by no means limited to holding the line and hoping for the best. It is entirely possible for the United States to influence by its actions the internal developments, both within Russia and throughout the international Communist movement, by which Russian policy is largely determined. . . . It is . . . a question of the degree to which the United States can create among the peoples of the world generally the impression of a country which knows what it wants, which is coping successfully with the problems of its internal life and with the responsibilities of a World Power, and which has a spiritual vitality capable of holding its own among the major ideological currents of the time."—"X" [George F. Kennan] in *Foreign Affairs*, July, 1947.

---

of Naval Operations. This crisis led to amendments to the National Security Act in August, 1949, forcing greater unification, and formally establishing a Department of Defense.

Beginnings of Containment

As early as January, 1946, President Truman, upset over Russian delay in withdrawing troops from Iran and Russian threats toward Turkey, wrote his

Johnston, praising the Russians and picturing Stalin as a sympathetic figure. Many had come to imagine him as a benign, pipe-smoking sage, "good old Uncle Joe." In addition, idealists had too long placed all their hopes upon the "one world" which Wendell Willkie had preached so eloquently.

Not even the revered Winston Churchill could shift American opinion. In March, 1946, through Truman's arrangement, Churchill, speaking at Westminster

College in Fulton, Missouri, proclaimed a grim warning: "From Stettin in the Baltic to Trieste in the Adriatic an iron curtain has descended across the Continent. . . . I do not believe that Soviet Russia desires war. What they desire is the fruits of war and the indefinite expansion of their power and doctrines. . . . From what I have seen of our Russian friends and allies during the war, I am convinced that there is nothing they admire so much as strength, and there is nothing for which they have less respect than for weakness, especially military weakness."

A new Truman policy for countering Communist aggression began to unfold in the spring of 1947. Already George F. Kennan, counselor of the American embassy in Moscow, was warning the administration that it faced "a political force committed fanatically to the belief that with the U.S. there can be no permanent *modus vivendi*." The only answer, Kennan wrote anonymously in the July, 1947, number of *Foreign Affairs*, must be "a long-term, patient but firm and vigilant containment of Russian expansive tendencies." Russian pressure on Turkey and support of Communist guerilla forces in Greece emphasized the immediacy of the Soviet threat. The British had been aiding the Greek government, but could no longer carry the burden. Unless Stalin were contained quickly, he might achieve the centuries-old Russian prize of the straits leading from the Black Sea into the Mediterranean. Already Russia controlled Albania on the Adriatic.

On March 12, 1947, President Truman appeared before Congress to request $400 million to bolster the armed forces of Greece and Turkey, and to enunciate the doctrine that came to bear his name: "I believe that it must be the policy of the United States to support free peoples who are resisting attempted subjugation by armed minorities or by outside pressures." Senator Vandenberg again supported him, and the Republican Congress voted the Greek-Turkish Aid Act of May, 1947. The initial military aid and subsequent appropriations eased Russian pressure upon Turkey, and by the fall of 1949 brought to an end the long civil war against Communists in Greece.

Military aid was not enough. The Truman Doctrine logically led to a program of economic reconstruction to bolster the stability of Europe and help eradicate the misery out of which the Communist parties in western European countries were gaining recruits. Secretary of State George C. Marshall returned in April, 1947, from the Conference of Foreign Ministers in Moscow convinced that the Russians were interested only in profiting from the economic plight of Europe, not in ameliorating it. The solution, he and President Truman agreed, lay in State Department plans to aid European nations that were willing to cooperate with each other in rebuilding their economies. Speaking at the Harvard University commencement in June, 1947, Secretary Marshall offered aid to all those European nations (including Russia) who would join in drafting a program for recovery.

Russia denounced the Marshall Plan as American imperialism, and intimidated the satellites and Finland and Czechoslovakia into staying away from the planning conference. Germany had no government, and Spain was not invited. Sixteen other nations of Europe joined a Committee of European Economic Cooperation, which in September, 1947, presented specifications for reconstruction to create by 1951 a self-sufficient Europe. Opposition formed in Congress, but it was embarrassed from the start by possessing as unwelcome allies the American Communists, and in February, 1948, it was overwhelmed by a shocked and aroused public opinion when Czech Communists seized power in Prague. Congress in April established the Eco-

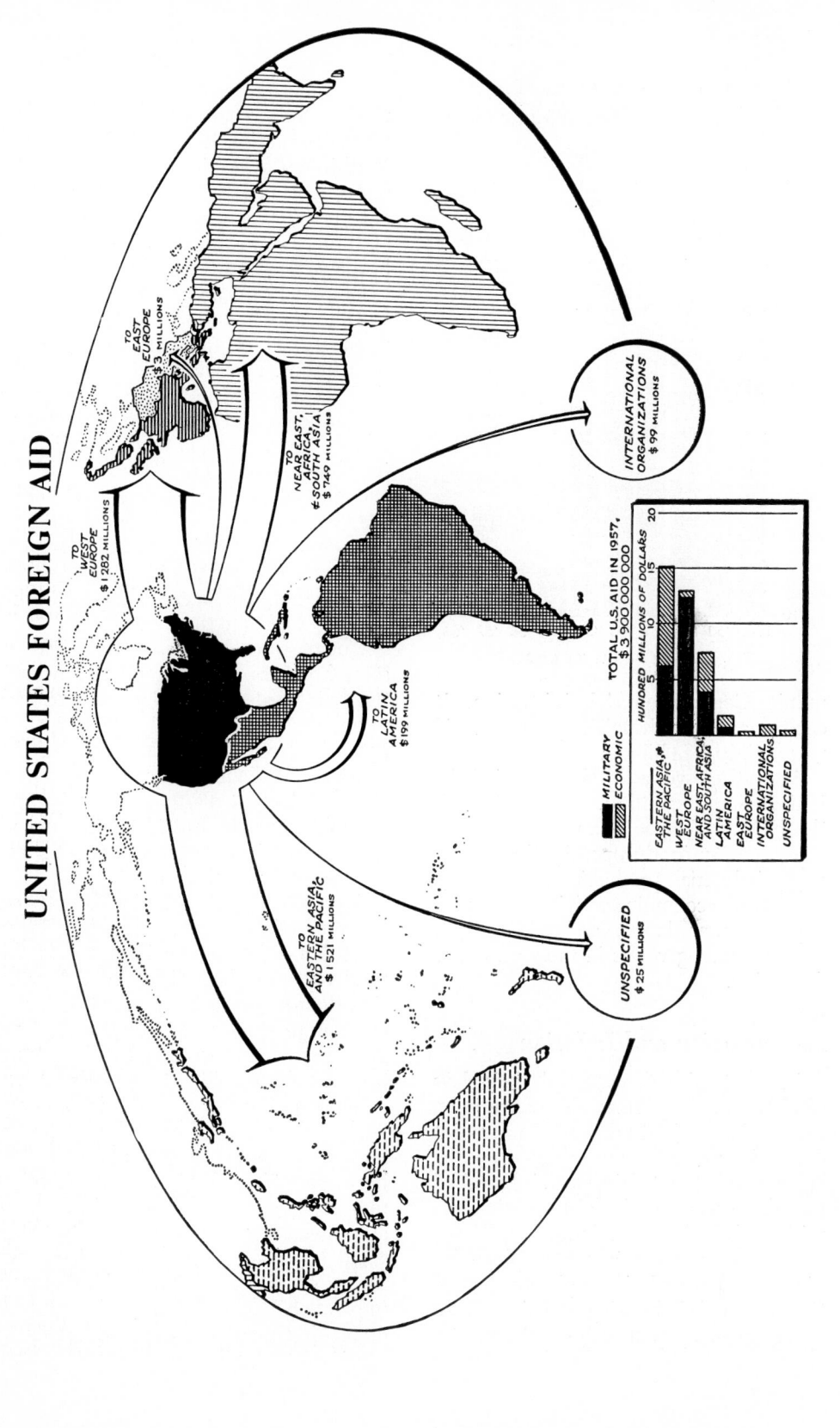

UNITED STATES FOREIGN AID

TO EAST EUROPE $3 MILLIONS

TO NEAR EAST, AFRICA, & SOUTH ASIA $749 MILLIONS

TO WEST EUROPE $1282 MILLIONS

INTERNATIONAL ORGANIZATIONS $99 MILLIONS

TO LATIN AMERICA $199 MILLIONS

TO EASTERN ASIA AND THE PACIFIC $1521 MILLIONS

UNSPECIFIED $25 MILLIONS

TOTAL U.S. AID IN 1957, $3 900 000 000

HUNDRED MILLIONS OF DOLLARS

MILITARY
ECONOMIC

EASTERN ASIA & THE PACIFIC
WEST EUROPE
NEAR EAST, AFRICA, AND SOUTH ASIA
LATIN AMERICA
EAST EUROPE
INTERNATIONAL ORGANIZATIONS
UNSPECIFIED

U.S. FOREIGN AID, 1949–1958

THE ANNUAL TREND

MILLIONS OF DOLLARS

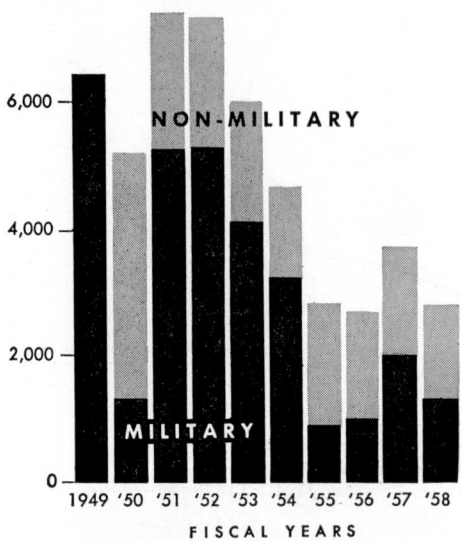

FISCAL YEARS

nomic Cooperation Administration. It cut the administration's request, but did vote an initial $4 billion.

Altogether over a three-year period the United States spent $12 billion through the ECA. It helped stimulate a remarkable recovery in Europe. By the end of 1950, industrial production was up 64 per cent, economic activity was well above prewar levels, and Communist strength among voters in most areas was dwindling.

Reconversion and Inflation

On September 6, 1945, only four days after the Japanese surrender ceremonies, the President sent to Congress a 21-point domestic program outlining what he later called the "Fair Deal." It called for the expansion of social security, the raising of the legal minimum wage from 40 to 65¢ an hour, a full employment bill, a permanent Fair Employment Practices Act, public housing and slum clearance, long-range planning for the protec-

tion of natural resources and building of public works (like TVA), and government promotion of scientific research. Within ten weeks, he sent additional recommendations to Congress for federal aid to education, for health insurance and prepaid medical care, and for the St. Lawrence seaway project.

Despite its preoccupation with reconversion and inflation, Congress acted upon several of the President's recommendations. The Maximum Employment Act became law in February, 1946. It established a three-man Council of Economic Advisers to aid the President and issue an annual economic report. Although the experts frequently disagreed, they became an integral part of the governmental machinery. They did much to accustom the public to the new economics that had been emerging during the New Deal and the war.

Congressional conservatives tried to steer Congress and the public away from the Fair Deal program by concentrating upon the reconversion of industry to peacetime production. Truman himself recommended, first, speedily removing all possible controls that would hamper reconversion, and second, preventing increases in prices, rents, and wages. The two aims could easily conflict.

After Germany surrendered, cutbacks in war orders began, and after Japan capitulated, $35 billion in contracts was suddenly cancelled. The War Production Board soon dropped controls, except on commodities still very scarce. Congress passed a new revenue bill cutting taxes nearly $6 billion. The War Assets Administration, established in January, 1946, sold several hundred war plants, mostly to the corporations which had been operating them, and disposed of mountains of surplus, some of which enabled veterans with priorities to start small businesses. Members of the armed forces, who were being demobilized at an unparalleled pace, found their problems of readjustment to civilian life eased by the Servicemen's Readjustment Act of 1944 (the "G.I. Bill of Rights") which provided them with further education and training, or aid while unemployed or starting in business or farming.

Industry changed back to civilian production with more speed and less economic dislocation than had been expected. The gloomy forecasts of eight million unemployed did not materialize. By the end of November, 1945, peacetime employment was up to the end-of-the-war total, and 93 per cent of the war plants had been reconverted.

The expected glut of surplus goods did not materialize either. Instead, acute problems of scarcity arose. Shortages ranged from automobiles and appliances to men's suits, nylon stockings, and beefsteak. Consumers commanded some $140 million in savings and billions more in credit with which to back their demands. Added to these were the needs of the rest of the world. Against such pressures, it was impossible for the Office of Price Administration to hold prices down to the 1941–2 level.

If prices were to be checked, wages must be also, and if wages were to be held down, so must prices be. It was a vicious circle. By January, 1946, workers had gone on strike in a number of the nation's critical industries: steel, automobiles, electrical manufacturing, and others. When Philip Murray demanded a 25¢-an-hour increase for the United Steelworkers to bring them up to their wartime take-home pay, President Benjamin F. Fairless of United States Steel, acting as spokesman for the industry, refused unless the government would allow a $7.00-per-ton increase in the price of steel. President Truman announced in February, 1946, that labor was entitled to the 33 per cent that living costs had gone up since January, 1941. The Wage Stabilization Board must approve the increase; but if it cut profits below the prewar level, the companies might obtain corresponding price increases. Ultimately

"WEATHER CLEAR, TRACK FAST." (BY D. R. FITZPATRICK IN ST. LOUIS *Post-Dispatch*)

there was a steel settlement allowing raises of 18½¢ an hour and $5.00 per ton. Throughout industry, the "bulge" led to a round of similar raises in wages and prices.

In April, 1946, John L. Lewis precipitated a fresh crisis. He demanded that the bituminous coal workers receive, even before wage increases, drastic improvement in safety rules and substantial contributions to a health and welfare fund. Refusing White House suggestions of compromise, he led out 400,000 miners on April 1, 1946. Within six weeks, as coal supplies dwindled, much of the nation's industrial production had to be cut back. In mid-May, Lewis allowed his workers back for twelve days' mining; in the interim a railroad strike threatened. The President, by broadcasting a warning that the army would run the railroads, managed to avert a new walk-out. The government took over the coal mines and provided the workers with most of what Lewis had demanded.

While unions were going on strike for higher wages, businessmen and farmers were exerting almost equal pressure upon Congress to obtain higher prices. Controls, they argued, were preventing full production, encouraging a black market, and robbing producers of a fair profit. After long debate, Congress passed a circumscribed price-control bill on June 27, 1946, just three days before the existing act was to expire. President Truman unexpectedly vetoed the bill as "a sure formula for inflation," and most price controls expired.

During the first sixteen days of July, 1946, the index of prices of 28 basic commodities jumped 25 per cent, compared with 13 per cent during the previous three years. On the first day of free trade at the Chicago stockyards, prime beef jumped from $18 to $22 per hundred weight. As prices soared, stock raisers, who had been holding back their cattle, rushed them to market. Congress rushed through a new price-control bill only slightly stronger than the vetoed one, and on July 25 President Truman signed it. The decontrol board it created studied meat prices, decided they were unreasonable, and ordered prices rolled back to the old levels. Stockmen once again held back cattle until they could force abandonment of controls; angry consumers chafed in near-empty butcher shops.

For several weeks, President Truman stood firm, but as public discontent focused on the Democratic party, politicians already fearful of the worst in the congressional elections of 1946 persuaded him to relent. On October 14, 1946, he announced the immediate ending of meat controls. Meat came back, but like many other commodities, with new price tags so high that the old black-market price seemed to have become the new legal standard. Millions of consumers on small, inflexible salaries or pensions were hurt, and felt little more tender toward the Democrats. Real earning dropped 12 per cent below July, 1945.

All that the Republicans needed in the fall of 1946 was the slogan, "Had Enough? Vote Republican." They captured both houses of Congress, controlling the House 246 to 188, and the Senate, 51 to 45.

President Truman, accepting the returns as a mandate to liquidate regulations, dropped almost all remaining controls on wages and prices and on the channeling of construction into low-cost homes. Congress continued rent control to March 1, 1948, but allowed rents to go up 15 per cent. Retail prices moved upward 3 per cent per month, canceling the gains organized labor had won in the spring of 1946. Unions fought for, and obtained, a second round of increases in 1947, and in 1948 as prices still went upward, a third round. The spiral of inflation was creeping upward relentlessly. Workers and others in modest circumstances began to notice that it was taking place under a Republican Congress whose spokesmen had asserted that laissez faire would cure the nation's ills.

The Chairman of the House Appropriations Committee, John Taber, proclaimed that he would apply a "meat-axe to government frills." He did so. Congress refused to appropriate funds for public housing, even of the moderate sort championed by Taft. It would not aid education, or extend social security; it slashed budget allowances for reclamation and power projects in the West. It passed a tax bill that, as President Truman pointed out in vetoing it, reduced the taxes of families receiving $2,400 or less by only 3 per cent, but of those receiving $100,-000 or more, from 48 to 65 per cent.

One of the few noncontroversial domestic achievements of this Congress was authorization of a commission on reorganization of the executive departments. President Truman appointed former President Hoover chairman of the commission. Congress already had voted to improve its own procedures and to reorganize its committees, cutting those in the House from 48 to 19, and in the Senate from 33 to 15.

The principal positive handiwork of

RESTRICTIONS ON UNIONS IN TAFT-HARTLEY ACT

Outlawed "closed shop" (which required that one must be a union member to be hired), but permitted "union shop" (which meant that, if the contract so provided, one had to join the union after being hired).

Provided "cooling off" periods and empowered the President to issue injunctions to prevent strikes imperiling national safety or health.

Prohibited as "unfair" union practices: jurisdictional strikes, refusal to bargain in good faith, secondary boycotts, exaction of pay for work not performed, and union contributions to political campaign funds.

Prohibited certification of unions as bargaining agents with employers until officers had filed affidavits that they were not Communists.

Required unions to register with the Secretary of Labor and submit annual financial reports to him.

Allowed employers to present their side during organizational campaigns, petition the National Labor Relations Board for elections to determine bargaining agents, and sue unions for breach of contract.

---

the Eightieth Congress was a new basic labor law to supplant the pro-labor Wagner Act of 1935. The Taft-Hartley Labor-Management Relations Act loosened some of the previous restrictions upon employers and added several prohibitions against the unions. It also provided for "cooling-off" periods before unions could strike. President Truman stingingly vetoed it on June 20, 1947. That same day Republicans and Southern Democrats in the House overrode his veto, 331 to 83; the Senate followed three days later, 68 to 25. In practice, the Taft-Hartley Act did not cripple organized labor, partly because of the skill of labor leaders and because of President Truman's appointment to the National Labor Relations Board of members sympathetic toward labor. But the law did emphatically turn most of organized labor against the Republicans and back to the support of President Truman.

Truman Beats Dewey

Significantly, when the Republicans met at Philadelphia in June, 1948, to nominate a presidential candidate, they rejected Senator Robert A. Taft, the vigorous leader of the Eightieth Congress, although he was the idol of many businessmen. Taft was hampered by his prewar isolationism and his lack of glamor as a campaigner. The Republicans again nominated Governor Thomas E. Dewey, who favored the new role of the United States in world affairs, and whose stand on domestic issues came closer to the Fair Deal than to the Republican record in Congress. His running mate was Governor Earl Warren of California, who was even more liberal. Their platform was a promise to continue all the things the Democrats had established, but do them more efficiently and cheaply.

It seemed a winning ticket and program, especially since the Democratic party suffered from two schisms. A faction to the left followed Henry A. Wallace out of the party. Wallace ran on a "Progressive" ticket to fight for thoroughgoing reform at home, and more friendly relations with Communists overseas. Around him rallied a sprinkling of Americans who felt the Truman domestic policies were too slow and ineffective, and above all, who feared the foreign policies would lead to a third World War. Around him also rallied the American Communists and fellow-travelers.

Despairing Democratic liberals, organized as Americans for Democratic Action, sought some more glamorous candidate than President Truman. The one candidate they could be sure would win votes by the million, General Eisenhower, rejected their overtures. At their convention in July, 1948, the Democrats gloomily accepted the inevitable, the nomination of President Truman. Certain of defeat, the liberals salvaged what they could by fighting through a platform containing a strong civil-rights plank that proposed federal legislation to prevent discrimination in employment, penalize lynching, and outlaw poll taxes. This platform was expected to help Northern and city Democrats in their local and state elections.

But it drove Southern Democrats, already angered by President Truman's espousal of a strong civil-rights program, into open revolt. Waving Confederate flags, a number of them met at Birmingham, Alabama, in July, 1948, to form the States Rights' Democratic Party and nominate Governor J. Strom Thurmond of South Carolina. They captured the party organization in Alabama, Louisiana, Mississippi, and South Carolina.

The revolts from both the left and the right seemed to leave President Truman in a pathetically hopeless position; all the public opinion polls showed him trailing far behind. Governor Dewey, campaigning in a cold and formal way, aroused as little animosity as possible, and seemed to be delivering previews of his inaugural. Instead of campaigning against the impeccable Governor Dewey, who stood for much the same in domestic and foreign policy, Truman launched his attack at the Republican Congress. Because he felt the press was giving a hostile impression of his administration, Truman embarked upon a strenuous personal tour of the United States, traveling

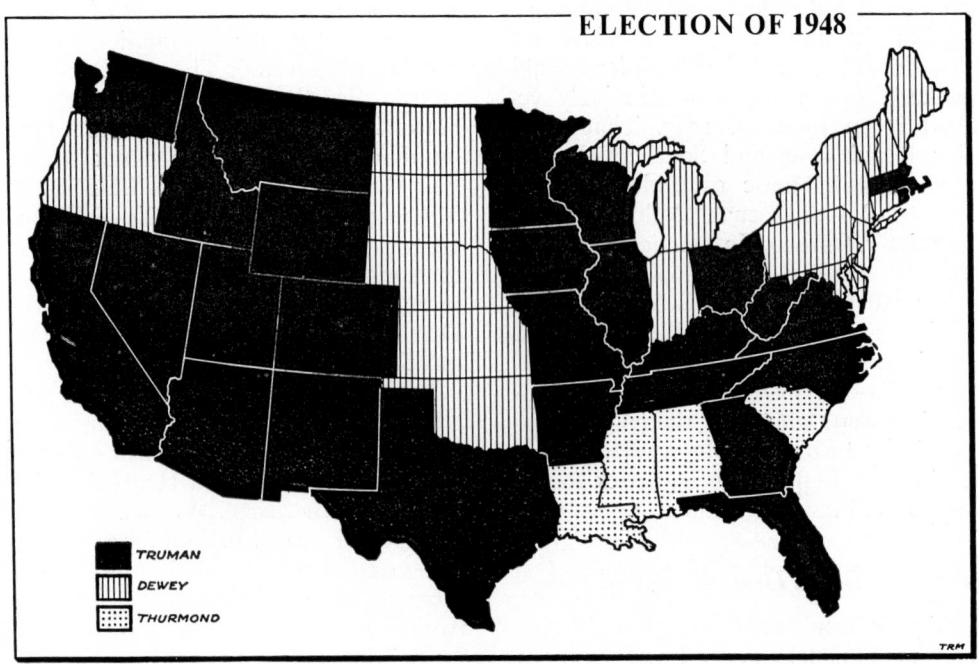

ELECTION OF 1948

TRUMAN
DEWEY
THURMOND

PRESIDENT TRUMAN—AN UNCOMMON MAN. During much of his nearly eight years in the White House, Harry S. Truman was an underrated President. He was of such unspectacular background and average appearance that it was easy to dismiss him as a person of no unusual qualifications or talents. Many people who had regarded President Roosevelt as the patron of the common man looked upon Truman as being himself the common man.

And so in some externals he was. He had been born in 1884 the son of a horse-trader in a small Missouri town and had grown up on a farm near Kansas City. He had not gone to college. During the first World War he acquitted himself well as an artillery officer, but after his return failed in the men's clothing business. In 1922 his fellow-veterans helped elect him a county commissioner (the title was Judge). Except for the 1924 term when the Ku Klux Klan defeated him, he remained in office until 1934. Although he allied himself with the notorious Kansas City boss, Tom Pendergast, he retained an impeccable reputation for honesty and sound administration. He was elected to the United States Senate in 1934, and without the support of the Roosevelt administration, re-elected in 1940. The chairmanship of a war investigating committee brought him favorable attention from the public and President Roosevelt. As a border-stater with a consistent New Deal voting record and warm friendships in the Congress, he was an ideal compromise candidate for the Vice Presidency in 1944.

As President, Truman retained many of the habits of thought and action growing out of his background, and in some minor ways made himself vulnerable to criticism. In facing problems, he studied diligently, read omniverously, and came firmly to decisions which set postwar policy. The Truman doctrine, Marshall plan, and Fair Deal domestic programs were his monuments.

As a campaigner, President Truman apparently had no chance in 1948, but he was remarkably successful in his extemporaneous speaking at whistle-stops, which together with his policies had rallied behind him much of the farm and labor vote. On the morning after the election he gleefully displayed a newspaper which had underestimated him—as indeed had much of the American public. (UNITED PRESS PHOTO)

31,700 miles to speak 356 times directly to the American people. In this "whistle stop" tour, he spoke only a few times from manuscripts, preferring his far more effective, rather blunt extemporaneous style. To all those groups who could be convinced they had a grievance against the Republican Congress, he appealed effectively, winning the strong support of organized labor, disgruntled farmers, and northern Negroes.

On election day, to the amazement of everyone but himself, President Truman defeated Dewey, 24,106,000 to 21,-969,000 in the popular vote, and 304 to 189 in the electoral vote. Thurmond's Dixiecrat ticket received 1,169,000 popular and 38 electoral votes. Wallace polled only 1,156,000. The Democrats also regained both houses of Congress by a margin of 93 seats in the House and 12 in the Senate.

The North Atlantic Alliance

In his inaugural address, January 20, 1949, President Truman challenged the nation to come to the succor of the "more than half the people of the world . . . living in conditions approaching misery." Point Four of his proposals for aiding them was technical assistance and the fostering of capital investment for their development. The Point Four or Technical Cooperation program began in 1950 with an appropriation of only $35 million, but spent $400 million in the next three years.

Soviet leaders reacted vigorously against the American efforts for world economic recovery. They had organized their own Warsaw Alliance of nine satellite nations in September, 1947, to combat "American imperialism." Through a new Cominform (Communist Information Bureau) they sought to eradicate traces of noncomformity throughout eastern Europe. Their greatest triumph was the successful coup in democratic Czechoslovakia in February, 1948. Be-

cause it was as horrifying to western Europeans as it was to Americans, it helped unify the Western world against the Communist countries. Later in the year, the pressure of Stalin and the Cominform on Marshal Tito provoked him to pull Communist Yugoslavia out of their orbit, and with American aid to embark upon an independent course between Russia and the West. In western Europe, Communist parties tried to thwart the Marshall Plan, especially by calling out on strike the unions they controlled in Italy and France. Despite the strikes, progress continued.

Meanwhile, the United States moved with the British and the rather reluctant French toward the creation of a self-governing, economically strong West Germany. The culmination came on June 7, 1948, when they announced plans for a new federal West German government with sovereignty over domestic matters and full membership in the European Recovery Program. They also reformed the currency to stop the inflationary flood of marks from the Soviet zone, which was hampering recovery.

The Russians retaliated. Taking advantage of the lack of a written guarantee of land transit across the Soviet zone, they clamped a tight blockade around the western sectors of Berlin. The object was to force the Western powers to abandon either Berlin or the proposed West German republic. President Truman, unwilling to risk war by ordering in armed convoys by land, ordered the supplying of Berlin by increasing on a massive scale the airlift begun in April. By the time bad weather hampered flights in the late fall, adequate stockpiles had been established in Berlin. Through the winter and into the spring of 1949, the airlift continued. It was a remarkable demonstration to Europeans—especially to the Germans—of what the Americans and British could achieve. Altogether they flew over 277,000 flights to bring in nearly 2,500,000 tons of food, fuel, and other supplies to maintain two million people. They carried in more than had previously been brought by train.

In the spring of 1949 the Russians backed down and ended the blockade. In October, 1949, the German Federal Republic came into existence at Bonn in West Germany, and the Soviets established a German Democratic Republic for East Germany.

Russian intransigence led to the consolidation of the Western countries into a new grand alliance. The North Atlantic Treaty was signed April 4, 1949, by twelve nations, and subsequently also by Greece and Turkey. It declared that an armed attack against one would be considered an attack upon all, and provided for the creation of joint millitary forces. Under it, the signatory powers established the North Atlantic Treaty Organization to construct a defense force that, while not equal to that of the Russians, would be large enough to make an attack highly costly.

The United States began to shift from economic to military aid as the Mutual Defense Act of 1949 appropriated an initial billion dollars for armaments for the signators. The governing body of NATO, the North Atlantic Council, established military headquarters near Paris early in 1951 under the supreme command of General Dwight Eisenhower. This was SHAPE (Supreme Headquarters, Allied Powers in Europe). The number of divisions and airplanes under NATO command began gradually to grow, but while its power was still relatively feeble, its chief significance was the commitment the United States had made with the nations of western Europe to stand firm against Russian threats.

That these threats were not to be taken lightly became even more clear on September 23, 1949, when President Truman issued a press statement: "We have evidence that within recent weeks an atomic explosion occurred in the U.S.S.R." The years of relative safety for the American people were already at an end.

China Turns Red

While the United States was struggling to contain Russia in Europe between 1947 and 1949, the Chinese Communists were destroying the armies of Chiang Kai-shek.

To prevent civil war and to effect a coalition government, the Truman administration in December, 1945, had sent General George C. Marshall to China. At first he obtained a cease-fire and encouraging signs of accommodation, but irreconcilable differences kept apart the two Chinese governments—the *Kuomintang* and the Communists. Finally in January, 1947, Marshall returned to Washington disgusted with both governments and all factions except a handful of powerless *Kuomintang* liberals.

Full-scale war broke out. Although the Nationalist (*Kuomintang*) armies were larger and better equipped, they soon began to fall back before the better trained, more vigorous Communist forces. As the inept Chiang Kai-Shek government failed both on the fighting front and at home, where inflation and inefficiency were rampant, by the middle of 1947 it was plunging toward defeat.

President Truman then sent General Wedemeyer, who had been Chiang's chief of staff, to investigate. Wedemeyer warned that Communist control of China would imperil American interests, since the Communists were in fact closely tied to the Soviet Union. He believed that the United States could rescue Chiang only by sending 10,000 army officers and other advisors to introduce reforms, together with massive material support.

President Truman did not request large-scale aid for Chiang, and for this omission critics subsequently castigated him. But to do so might have interfered with the program of containment in Europe; it would have been unpopular; and in any event, it probably would have been too late. Truman did ask Congress to provide $570 million; in April, 1948, it voted $400 million, of which China could spend only $125 million for military supplies. Basically the administration decided, as Secretary Marshall made clear, that the United States could not salvage the Nationalist government so that it would be "capable of reestablishing and then maintaining its control throughout all of China." The collapse was rapid, and it came through lack of morale rather than shortages of arms and supplies. In October, 1948, the Communists seized Mukden, Manchuria, and as Nationalist troops surrendered or defected, the Reds swept on with captured American arms into central and southern China. At the end of 1949, Chiang and the Nationalists fled to Formosa. All of China was under the new People's Republic, which ruthlessly consolidated its strength by liquidating several million dissidents, harrying out American businessmen, teachers, and missionaries, and proclaiming its propaganda to all of East Asia.

Though Great Britain and some of the western European nations recognized the new government of Red China, the United States refused to do so and blocked its entry into the United Nations. Also, beginning in 1947, the American government introduced new policies in Japan to strengthen that nation in a manner similar to the rebuilding of Germany.

The American occupation in Japan brought a democratization of the government, extension of rights to women and underprivileged groups, expansion of the educational system (from a starting point as high as the goal of educational reform in China), land reform as drastic as that in China, a curbing of the power of the monopolistic *zaibatsu* industrial system, and an improvement in the status of labor. In Japan, more than anywhere else in Asia, the United States helped develop a dynamic alternative to Communism. In 1949, to stimulate Japanese recovery, the United States ended its reparations and stopped the dismantling of industrial combinations.

Negotiation of a Japanese peace treaty began in 1950 through the skilled offices of a Republican, John Foster Dulles, whom President Truman appointed to undertake the task. Aside from the fact that it stripped Japan of all her conquests, including the Ryukyu Islands directly south of Japan (most notably Okinawa), it was a generous treaty. By recognizing the right of the sovereign Japanese nation to self-defense, it opened the way to re-armament. Thanks partly to its negotiation by a Republican, the treaty easily received Senate ratification, and went into effect April 28, 1952. A security treaty, signed at the same time, permitted the United States to maintain armed forces in Japan. Two years later, a mutual-defense-assistance pact provided for Japanese rearmament with American aid, but the building of armed forces proceeded slowly. Disarmament had been one of MacArthur's most cherished reforms, and the American-imposed Japanese constitution had banned war forever. This encouraged such a strong pacifist sentiment that as late as 1957 only 100,000 Japanese had joined the armed forces. The task of defending Japan continued to rest largely with the United States.

Several nations to the south which had suffered during the war either invasion or the threat of invasion viewed with some concern the rebuilding of Japan as a military power. To reassure them, the United States in 1951 signed a security treaty with the Philippines, and the ANZUS pact with Australia and New Zealand.

While rebuilding Japan, the Truman administration refused to capitulate to the demands of the so-called China Lobby for military and naval aid to Chiang on Formosa which might lead the nation into a war against Red China. On the contrary, the State Department issued a white paper (1949) charging the Nationalists with responsibility for their debacle. In January, 1950, Secretary of State Dean Acheson publicly outlined a Pacific defense perimeter which did not include Formosa or Korea. If these areas were attacked, he declared, the people invaded must rely upon themselves to resist, "and then upon the commitments of the entire civilized world under the charter of the United Nations."

Within a few months, East Asia became the focal point of American foreign policy as the cold war turned hot in Korea.

Conflict in Korea

During the hectic days at the end of the war in the Pacific, the United States had hastily proposed that Americans accept the surrender of the Japanese in the lower half of Korea, up to the 38th parallel, and that the Russians do the same in the northern half. At the moment the arrangement was useful to the United States. Afterwards, however, the Russians were willing to accept a reunited Korea only if it were Communist-dominated.

The 38th parallel became more and more an impenetrable barrier. To the north of it, the Communists developed a "peoples' government" with a strong aggressive army. To the south, the United Nations held elections that led to a government under the ardently nationalistic Dr. Syngman Rhee, long an exile in the United States. Rhee would have liked to extend his government to the north, but the United States provided the South Korean army only with relatively light defensive weapons. Consequently when the United States withdrew its forces from below the 38th parallel in June, 1949, South Korea was left militarily weaker than its even more aggressive northern twin.

The North Koreans acted swiftly, on June 24, 1950, launching a full-scale invasion that caught the South Koreans and

Americans completely by surprise. Almost immediately President Truman and Congress reversed the policy of withdrawal from the Asiatic mainland. The President brought the question of the invasion before the United Nations Security Council. It could act more quickly than the Assembly, and at the moment the Russians were boycotting it, and hence had no representative present to vote a paralyzing veto. The Council on June 25 passed an American resolution demanding that the North Koreans withdraw behind the 38th parallel, and two days later called upon members of the United Nations to "furnish such assistance to the Republic of Korea as may be necessary to repel the armed attack."

President Truman on June 27, sent United States air and sea forces to the aid of the South Koreans; on June 30 he ordered ground forces into Korea, and sent the Seventh Fleet to act as a barrier between the Chinese mainland and Formosa.

The Council of the United Nations on July 7, 1950, requested those nations providing troops to place them under a unified command headed by the United States. President Truman appointed General MacArthur commander-in-chief. Some fifteen nations besides the United States and the Republic of Korea provided troops, but these never comprised more than 9 per cent of the total fighting force. The United States sent about 48 per cent; South Korea mustered 43 per cent. What was officially a United Nations "police action" came to most Americans to seem a war on the part of the United States.

General MacArthur, who at first could draw upon only four understrength divisions in Japan, rushed in troop units piecemeal to slow the rapidly advancing North Koreans as they rushed southward past Seoul, threatening to envelope the entire tip of the peninsula. By thus sacrificing themselves, these forces gave MacArthur an opportunity to build stable

U.S.S. Missouri Bombarding North Korean Installations. Only five years after the Japanese capitulation had been signed on its decks, the Battleship *Missouri* was back in combat in the Korean War. On October 21, 1950, it fired salvos from its 16-inch guns at Chong-Jin, only thirty-nine miles from the Soviet border, in an effort to cut North Korean communications. (OFFICIAL U.S. NAVY PHOTO)

defenses around the port of Pusan in the extreme southeast. When the North Koreans struck there in force early in August, strong army and marine reinforcements fresh from the United States hurled them back at each point of assault. As men and supplies poured into Pusan, marine officers devised a bold plan of attack which General MacArthur reluctantly accepted. Rather than try to push the North Koreans back mile by mile, on September 15, 1950, while the United Nations troops around Pusan opened a sharp counteroffensive, he launched an amphibious assault far behind the North Korean lines at Inchon, near Seoul. It caught the Communists almost completely unprepared. The United Nations

troops quickly recaptured Seoul; within two weeks the North Korean armies, disrupted and demoralized, were fleeing as best they could to north of the 38th parallel.

Amid jubilation, the United States and the United Nations had to make new decisions. Should they capitalize upon their spectacular victory and move into North Korea? The premier of Red China on October 1 warned that the Chinese would "not allow seeing their neighbors being invaded by imperialists." A few days later, he announced the Chinese would send troops, and dispatched a warning to the United Nations through India. These threats worried American strategists, but there was a possibility that

China was bluffing, and there was the probability that the North Koreans, unless pursued, would recoup their strength and strike new blows.

The Joint Chiefs of Staff on September 27, 1950, ordered MacArthur to destroy the North Korean armed forces, but under no circumstances to cross the borders of China or Russia. The United Nations Assembly gave its sanction to the project on October 7, reiterating its aim to create "a unified, independent and democratic Korea." Two days later, the United Nations forces poured across the 38th parallel toward the Yalu River, which marked the boundary with Manchuria.

lessness in intervening without notice, and "massing a great concentration of possible reinforcing divisions with adequate supply behind the privileged sanctuary of the adjacent Manchurian border." Both in his private communications to the Joint Chiefs of Staff and in the encouragement he gave to pressure groups in the United States, MacArthur engaged in a vigorous campaign for permission to bomb this "privileged sanctuary." President Truman refused to allow all-out military action against China, because, he later explained, "if for no other reason . . . it was a gigantic booby trap."

In the two weeks after they first sighted

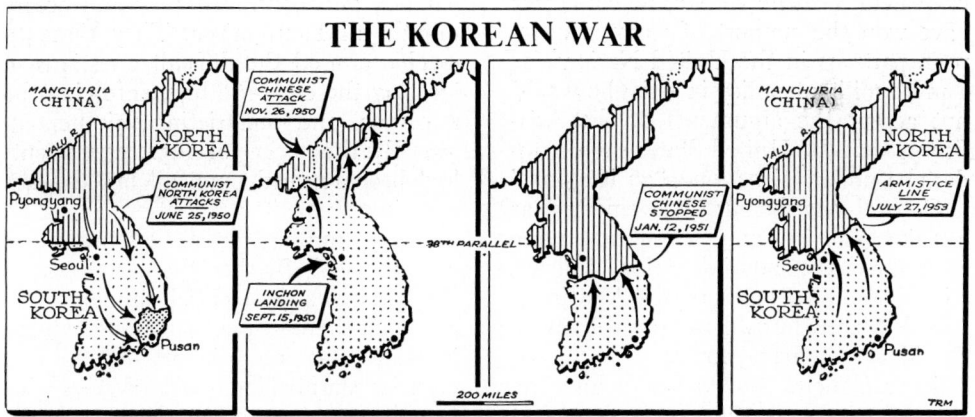

THE KOREAN WAR

For several weeks the advance into northern Korea went well. On October 19, the capital, Pyongyang, fell, and parachutists landed thirty miles beyond to trap much of the remaining North Korean army. Then, on October 26, a Chinese Communist soldier was captured; four days later, fourteen more were taken. By November 4, eight Chinese divisions had been identified, and Russian-made MIG fighter planes had briefly engaged the United Nations air force.

General MacArthur issued a special communiqué warning that "a new and fresh army now faces us," and excoriated the Chinese for their international law-

Chinese troops, the United Nations forces marched into a trap that was serious enough. The Chinese suddenly appeared in overwhelming numbers, stalled MacArthur's offensive, and hurled back advance units. Through December, 1950, in bitter weather, the outnumbered Eighth Army and X Corps fought a heroic withdrawal from North Korea. The United Nations tried to negotiate peace with the Chinese, but the Communists as they swept below the 38th parallel and recaptured Seoul set impossibly stiff terms. In March, 1951, the Eighth Army counterattacked, for a second and final time capturing Seoul and recrossing the 38th parallel. President Truman was ready again to seek a negotiated peace.

General MacArthur, far from ready to accept the position of his commander in chief, repeatedly made public his eagerness to win total victory in Korea at the risk of full involvement in war with China. On March 20, 1951, he communicated his views to the Republican minority leader in the House of Representatives, Joseph W. Martin, concluding: There is no substitute for victory."

President Truman clung to his thesis that, in the great struggle against Communism, western Europe with its concentration of heavy industry, not industrially weak Asia, was the main potential battlefield. Had he wished, he could not have won the support of western European partners in the United Nations for a more militant policy in Asia; he would not accept the arguments of the Asia-firsters that the United States should undertake unilateral action—"go it alone."

General MacArthur thus emerged as a major figure in American politics, trying to reverse the administration policies. Five days after Representative Martin released MacArthur's letter to the press, President Truman, on April 11, 1951, relieved General MacArthur of his commands. A groundswell of outrage swept the United States; a Gallup poll reported that 69 per cent of those interviewed favored the General, only 29 per cent the President. MacArthur upon his return was greeted hysterically wherever he appeared; millions watched their television sets as he addressed Congress.

Truman's policy of fighting a limited war of containment continued to baffle and exasperate a considerable part of the American people. It went too completely against the American tradition of total victory; it was too hard to explain to much of the public or even to many of the soldiers fighting endlessly through the rice paddies and on the hilltops of Korea.

In June, 1951, the Russian delegate to the United Nations hinted that settlement was possible. Armistice negotiations began on July 10, 1951, near the 38th parallel, and continued for many weary months at Panmunjom. They came to revolve around the difficult questions of locating the cease-fire line, enforcing the armistice, and repatriating prisoners of war. By the spring of 1952, agreements had been reached upon all but the last question; upon it, negotiations made no progress, and finally in October, 1952, were recessed. By then the nation was in the midst of a presidential campaign, and although there was no large-scale fighting in Korea, the interminable negotiations, endless skirmishing, and ever-growing casualties had worn out the patience of the American people.

BIBLIOGRAPHY

On postwar foreign policy, see William Reitzel and others, *United States Foreign Policy, 1945–1955* (1956), a scholarly analysis; the annual surveys by the Brookings Institution, beginning in 1947, *Major Problems of United States Foreign Policies*; and the surveys of the Council on Foreign Relations, *The United States in World Affairs*. On Truman's policies, see Truman, *Memoirs*; Byrnes, *Speaking Frankly*; Vandenberg, *Papers*; and Walter Millis (ed.), *The Forrestal Diaries* (1951). W. B. Smith, *My Three Years in Moscow* (1950), describes growing tensions with Russia; L. D. Clay, *Decision in Germany* (1950), depicts the struggle with Russia there. On occupation policy in Europe, see Hajo Holborn, *American Military Government* (1947); R. H. Jackson, *The Case Against Nazi War Criminals* (1946), and *The Nürnberg Case* (1947); and Drew Middleton, *The Struggle for Germany* (1949). On Japan, see Edward Reischauer, *The United States and Japan* (1957 ed.); and R. A. Fearey, *Occupation of Japan* (1950). Economic policy is described in S. E. Harris (ed.), *Foreign Economic Policy* (1948); R. F. Mikesell, *United States Economic Policy and International Relations* (1952); Department of State, *Point Four* (1950), and *Point Four Pioneers* (1951).

E. F. Goldman's *The Crucial Decade: America 1945–1955* (1956) is a colorful survey; Herbert Agar, *The Price of Power: America since 1945* (1957) is a very brief interpretation; F. L. Allen, *The Big Change* (1952), draws a contrast with the turn of the century. On the Truman administration, in addition to Truman's *Memoirs*, see Jonathan Daniels, *The Man from Independence* (1950), on Truman's background; and L. W. Koenig (ed.), *The Truman Administration* (1956). On domestic problems after 1945, see R. J. Havighurst and others, *The American Veteran Back Home* (1951); L. V. Chandler, *Inflation in the United States, 1940–1948* (1950); G. A Steiner, *The Government's Role in Economic Life*

(1953); H. A. Millis and E. C. Brown, *From the Wagner Act to Taft-Hartley* (1950); C. O. Gregory, *Labor and the Law* (1949); C. W. Mills, *The New Men of Power* (1948), on labor leaders; C. C. Taylor and others, *Rural Life in the United States* (1949); R. A. Dahl and R. S. Brown, *Domestic Control of Atomic Energy* (1951).

The most useful books on the Korean War and its background are G. M. McCune and A. L. Grey, Jr., *Korea Today* (1950); R. H. Rovere and A. M. Schlesinger, Jr., *The General and the President* (1951), a contemporary account of the war and especially the Truman-MacArthur controversy; R. M. Poats, *Decision in Korea* (1954); Carl Berger, *The Korea Knot: A Military-Political History* (1957); Department of the Army, *Korea—1950* (1952); and M. W. Cagle and F. A. Manson, *The Sea War in Korea* (1957). See also J. W. Spanier, *The Truman-MacArthur Controversy and the Korean War* (1959).

39

DOMESTIC AFFAIRS

OF THE 1950's

In the prosperous America of the 1950's a majority of the voters were more interested in preserving their economic gains than in adventuring toward new governmental programs or retreating toward earlier dogmas. They were moderates, enthusiastically supporting the moderate President, Dwight D. Eisenhower. As early as 1949 Eisenhower had stated his views when, as president of Columbia University, he addressed the American Bar Association. "The path to America's future," he declared, "lies down the middle of the road between the unfettered power of concentrated wealth . . . and the unbridled power of statism or partisan interests."

Trumanism and McCarthyism

In the disappointing months and years after World War II, as the warm feelings toward Russia turned into apprehension and even alarm, the public became increasingly afraid that traitors within the government were betraying it to the Russians.

During the period of the New Deal

and the war there had been some Communists and Communist sympathizers in the government. At a time when the Russians and the United States were allied this seemed of little consequence, but in 1942 and 1943 President Roosevelt established loyalty checks. By 1946 Russia seemed more a potential enemy than an ally. The Canadian government discovered that at least twenty-three of its employees in positions of trust had turned over secrets, some of them concerning nuclear fission, to Russian spies. Several of the spy rings had operated across the boundary in the United States.

The federal government began extensive efforts to ferret out Communists. President Truman in November, 1946, established a Temporary Commission on Employee Loyalty to recommend loyalty investigation systems and safeguards of fair hearings. This led in March, 1947, to the establishment of loyalty boards to undertake a sweeping investigation of all federal employees. In August, 1950, the President authorized the dismissal in sensitive departments of even those deemed no more than "bad security risks." By

1951 more than 3,000,000 government employees had been cleared, over 2,000 had resigned, and 212 had been dismissed.

Against the recommendations of the Departments of Defense and Justice and of the Central Intelligence Agency, Congress passed over the President's veto the McCarran Internal Security Act of September, 1950. This did not outlaw Communist organizations but required them to publish their records. It barred Communists from employment in defense plants, and denied them passports.

Already, in 1948, the Attorney General had obtained indictments against eleven key Communist leaders for violation of the Smith Act of 1940 which prohibited conspiring to teach the violent overthrow of the government. During their nine-month trial in 1949, the Communists engaged in elaborate harassing tactics which further aroused the public against them. They were convicted. In June, 1951, in the case of *Dennis v. United States*, the Supreme Court in a 6-to-2 decision rejected their appeal. Chief Justice Fred Vinson held that advocating or teaching revolution in the existing state of the world or even conspiring to do so, fell within Justice Holmes's earlier definition of what was punishable—that it constituted a "clear and present danger." Justice Hugo Black in dissenting remarked, "There is hope that in calmer times, when the present pressures, passions, and fears subside, this or some later court will restore the First Amendment liberties to the high preferred place where they belong in a free society."

While the Supreme Court was solemnly deciding that civil liberties must be circumscribed to protect the modern state, some less careful politicians were capitalizing upon the growing public hysteria over several spectacular cases. Above all there was the case of Alger Hiss, in which these politicians seemed to put on trial and condemn a whole generation of liberal intellectuals. Hiss, a handsome

VICE PRESIDENT RICHARD M. NIXON. Nixon, born in California in 1913, educated at Whittier College and Duke Law School, served as a Lieutenant-Commander in the Navy during the war. A committee of 100 Republicans chose him to run in 1946 against a leading New Deal congressman, endorsed by the C.I.O. Nixon won. In Congress, he helped draft the Taft-Hartley Act, and the Mundt-Nixon bill, much of which was later incorporated in the McCarran Internal Security Act. As a member of the House Un-American Affairs Committee, he became famous through his persistence in keeping the Alger Hiss affair alive. In 1948 he ran for the Senate from California on the anti-Communist issue, and won by a huge plurality. At the age of 39, in 1952, he was elected Vice President. (NATIONAL ARCHIVES)

and ambitious young man, had risen rapidly in the government during the 1930's to become a high-ranking member of the State Department. He was present as a clerk at the Yalta conference, but in no way influenced policy there. In 1947 he resigned to head the Carnegie Endowment for International Peace. A self-avowed former Communist agent, Whittaker Chambers, had denounced Hiss as early as 1939, but because he provided no details and no supporting evidence, Chambers was ignored. In 1948 he repeated his accusations before the House Un-American Activities Committee. When Hiss sued him for slander, Chambers produced microfilms of classified State Department documents Hiss allegedly had given him in 1937 and 1938.

Hiss was brought to trial for perjury (the statute of limitations prevented indictment for espionage). He called upon a number of the nation's most distinguished liberals to bear witness to his character. The first trial ended with a hung jury in July, 1949; the second ended with conviction in January, 1950.

More important in convincing Americans that a real Communist menace existed was the revelation that a young British scientist, Dr. Klaus Fuchs, had turned over to Russian agents full details on the manufacture of atomic bombs. His confession led to the trial and ultimate execution of Julius and Ethel Rosenberg, Americans who were alleged to have been his accomplices—and who were hailed as martyrs by Communists throughout the world.

Among the politicians who capitalized upon the public's fears, none was more sensational in his rise than Senator Joseph McCarthy of Wisconsin. Already some other politicians were winning fame through crusading against Communism. Representative Richard Nixon, who had helped keep the Hiss affair alive until Chambers produced the incriminating microfilms, was on his way to the Senate and a national reputation. McCarthy decided to exploit the same issue, and did so in February, 1950, by charging that there were a large number of Communists and men loyal to the Communist party still shaping foreign policy in the State Department. When a subcommit-

tee of the Senate Foreign Relations Committee took up his charges, they found not a single Communist or fellow-traveler.

An excited public numbering many millions eagerly swallowed McCarthy's new claims as he went on from sensation to sensation more rapidly than his detractors could refute his earlier, unsubstantiated charges. Millions wanted to believe McCarthy when he attacked as Communists the "whole group of twisted-thinking New Dealers [who] have led America near to ruin at home and abroad." McCarthy was providing a troubled nation with a scapegoat, and the Republican party with a winning issue.

In 1950 a troubled electorate was upset over the charges of subversion at home and the involvement of the United States in the Korean War, which many of them regarded as the result of a conspiracy in the State Department. When Hiss was convicted in January, his former acquaintance Secretary of State Dean Acheson declared he would not turn his back on him, meaning, Acheson later explained, that he was following "Christ's words setting forth compassion as the highest of Christian duties." But Acheson's remark, together with President Truman's early reference to the Hiss case as a red herring, served as Republican campaign texts. Representative Nixon declared, "Traitors in the high councils of our own government have made sure that the deck is stacked on the Soviet side of the diplomatic tables."

Bipartisanship in foreign policy disappeared as the Republicans pressed their issue. They did not capture Congress in November, 1950, but they gained 28 seats in the House and 5 in the Senate. Neo-isolationists in December, heartened by the election results, and no longer restrained by Senator Vandenberg, who was fatally ill, opened a "great debate" in the Senate over foreign policy. They succeeded in passing a resolution in

April, 1951, restraining the President from sending troops to western Europe without congressional authorization.

Meanwhile, President Truman made but little headway with his Fair Deal. Congress did vote the Displaced Persons Act of 1950 liberalizing the 1948 legislation which the President had denounced as discriminatory against Catholics and Jews because its quotas were unfavorable to people from southern and eastern Europe. It increased the number of persons to be admitted from 205,000 to 415,000 —but even this latter figure was a total, not a yearly number. Congress also implemented some of Truman's proposed reforms. The National Housing Act of 1949 provided for the construction over the succeeding six years of 810,000 housing units for lower-income families, together with a subsidy for forty years to bridge the gap between costs and the rents the tenants could afford to pay. It also provided grants for slum clearance and rural housing. Congress voted increased appropriations for power development and reclamation in the West, for T.V.A. and for the Farmers Home Administration (which carried on the rehabilitation work of the earlier Resettlement Administration and Farm Security Administration). In contrast, the Fair Deal health-insurance program went down to crashing defeat under the vigorous opposition of the American Medical Association, which raised a $3 million fund to combat it. Federal aid for education failed because of dissension over whether aid should go to parochial schools.

Republicans undermined the Truman administration with charges of favor-peddling and corruption, which, while they did not involve the President personally, did implicate men in the White House. The President's military aide had received as a gift a $520 deep-freeze unit; the wife of an examiner of loans for the Reconstruction Finance Corporation had acquired a $9,540 mink coat. These be-

came the symbols of a moral malaise in Washington, of those who could obtain contracts in return for a 5-per-cent fee, others who could arrange R.F.C. loans, and still others who could take care of tax difficulties in the Bureau of Internal Revenue. President Truman reorganized the R.F.C. and reformed the Bureau of Internal Revenue and the Department of Justice, but much too slowly to satisfy his Republican critics.

As the election of 1952 approached there was no indication that the majority of voters wished to reverse either Truman's foreign policy or his domestic program. They did want to "clean up the mess in Washington," and above all they wanted to see an end to the drawn-out, wearying Korean War.

Eisenhower Elected

It was not surprising that in times so troubled the voters overwhelmingly turned to a popular American general who they felt could lead them to a new security in a frightening world. It was significant that they turned not to MacArthur but to Dwight D. Eisenhower, so closely linked to the military and foreign policies of the Roosevelt and Truman administrations.

Partly this was the logic of politics. The wing of the Republican party holding to the views of MacArthur was committed to Senator Robert A. Taft—but it was a minority within the party, even though it controlled the Republican National Committee. The majority (knowing they could count upon the votes of most of the minority) sought a candidate who could pull strong support from many who had favored the Democratic foreign and domestic policy. Consequently, they looked to General Eisenhower—whom some liberal Democrats had sought to draft in 1948.

In the struggle for delegates, Eisenhower easily carried the East, and Taft the Middle West. Later, in a violent

EISENHOWER V. TAFT. Two factions in the Republican party, the more internationalist and the more isolationist, polarized around General Dwight D. Eisenhower and Senator Robert A. Taft in the early months of 1952.

General Eisenhower, born in 1890 in Texas and raised in Kansas, had graduated from West Point and risen steadily in the army, mainly through staff positions.
After serving as Supreme Commander in the second World War, he was briefly
President of Columbia University, then returned to uniform as head of the new
NATO command. He was the symbol both of victory during the war and collective
security through the United Nations afterwards. The only inkling of his political
views lay in his speeches while a civilian, which were little homilies remniscent of
his roots in the rural life of a simpler era. They appealed to the yearnings of his
listeners without giving them much idea how he could cope with the complexities
of the 1950's. Politically this was all to the good.

Eisenhower said privately that he was willing to run only in order to prevent the
nomination of Taft and a resurgence of isolationism. Yet in September, 1952, he
had to invite Taft to confer with him at the President's house on the Columbia
University campus. Taft promised to do everything possible, short of sacrificing
friends and principles, to help Eisenhower win. (UNITED PRESS PHOTO)

struggle on the floor of the convention,
the Eisenhower forces won contested
delegations, and with them, the nomination on the first ballot. Senator Richard M. Nixon of California, who was acceptable to conservative Republicans, was
nominated for the Vice Presidency. The
platform was ambiguous enough to cover

disagreements between the two wings of
the party. Early in September, Eisenhower went still further to mollify the
Midwestern Republicans by conferring
with Taft. He promised patronage to the
Taft followers, and avowed that the main
issue of the campaign was "liberty against
creeping socialization"—but he did not

compromise on foreign policy. Later in Wisconsin he was conciliatory toward Senator McCarthy. Thus he was able to campaign with the diverse factions of the party unified behind him.

As for the Democrats, the Northern wing of the party was in control at the convention. President Truman had announced on March 30 that he would not run again; the most vigorous campaigner in the primaries, Senator Estes Kefauver

Taft-Hartley Act, and high price supports for farmers.

To the delight of most intellectuals, Governor Stevenson began delivering speeches brilliant in their phraseology and eloquence, clever in their wit, and startling in their candor. He drew the hearty support of a group that came to be known derisively by their opposition as "the eggheads" as he promised to "talk sense to the American people." But Gen-

---

THE TASK IN MID-CENTURY

"The Ordeal of the Twentieth Century—the bloodiest, most turbulent era of the Christian age—is far from over. Sacrifice, patience, understanding and implacable purpose may be our lot for years to come.

"Let's face it. Let's talk sense to the American people. Let's tell them the truth, that there are no gains without pains, that we are now on the eve of great decisions, not easy decisions, like resistance when you're attacked, but a long, patient, costly struggle which alone can assure triumph over the great enemies of man—war, poverty and tyranny—and the assaults upon human dignity which are the most grievous consequences of each.

"Let's tell them that the victory to be won in the Twentieth Century, this portal to the golden age, mocks the pretensions of individual acumen and ingenuity. For it is a citadel guarded by thick walls of ignorance and mistrust which do not fall before the trumpets' blast or the politicians' imprecations or even a general's baton. They are, my friends, walls that must be directly stormed by the hosts of courage, morality and of vision, standing shoulder to shoulder, unafraid of ugly truth, contemptuous of lies, half-truths, circuses and demagoguery."—From Adlai E. Stevenson's speech of acceptance at the Democratic National Convention, July 26, 1952.

---

of Tennessee, won little support among party leaders; Vice President Alben Barkley was deserted by labor spokesmen, who declared he was too old. Instead the Northern leaders drafted Governor Adlai E. Stevenson of Illinois, who had earlier declared he would not run. His running mate was the liberal Senator John J. Sparkman of Alabama. The platform stated the positions of the Northern Democrats: endorsement of the Truman foreign policies, civil rights, repeal of the

eral Eisenhower appealed much more effectively to businessmen and the masses by promising to end their various frustrations.

Republican campaigners played upon the triple theme of "Communism, corruption, and Korea." Speaking in Detroit on October 24, 1952, Eisenhower promised to bring the war to "an early and honorable end." To help do so, he promised he would make a personal trip to Korea. The response at the polls was

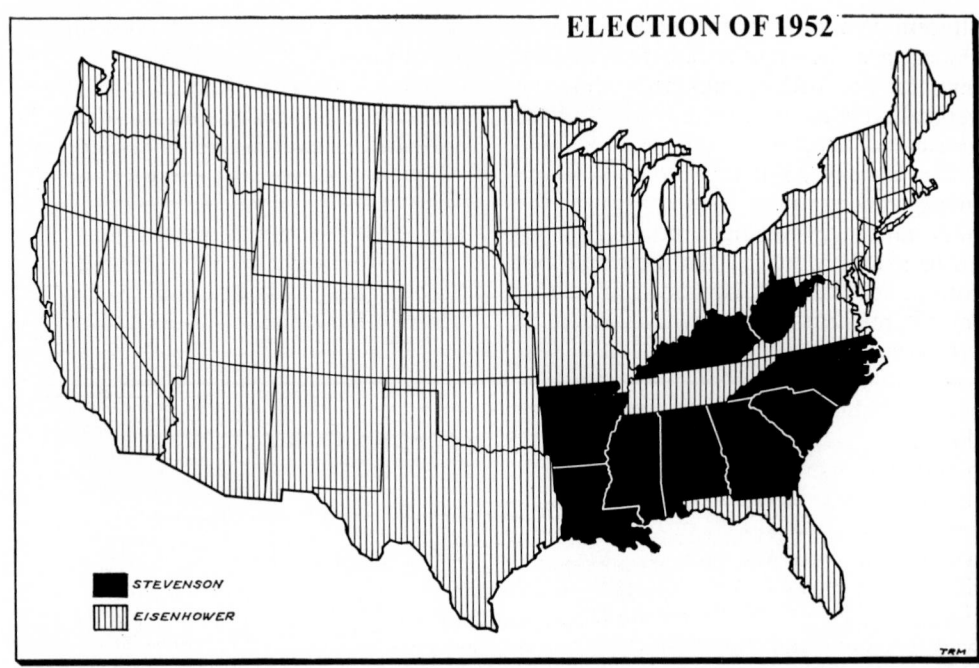

STEVENSON

EISENHOWER

overwhelming. Eisenhower polled 33,-824,000 votes to 27,315,000 for Stevenson; the electoral vote was 442 to 89. The Republicans carried both houses of Congress, but surprisingly, despite Eisenhower's sweeping victory, only by narrow margins: eight seats in the House, and an even split in the Senate. The Republican candidate was far more popular than his party.

Businessmen Go to Washington

President Eisenhower established a businessmen's administration in Washington. He appointed the president of General Motors, Charles E. Wilson, to be Secretary of Defense; George Humphrey, president of M. A. Hanna and Co. (once Mark Hanna's firm) to be Secretary of the Treasury; a New England manufacturer, Sinclair Weeks, to be Secretary of Commerce; and two automobile distributors, Douglas McKay and Arthur E. Summerfield, to be Secretary of the Interior and Postmaster Gen-

eral. The new Secretary of State, John Foster Dulles, had been one of the highest-paid corporation lawyers in the country. The Secretary of Agriculture was Ezra T. Benson, a conservative specialist in farm marketing; the Secretary of Health, Education and Welfare (when that department came into existence in April, 1953) was Mrs. Oveta Culp Hobby, wartime commander of the WAC's and wife of a wealthy Texas publisher; the Attorney General was Herbert Brownell, who had been legal aide to Governor Dewey; the Secretary of Labor, who resigned before the year was out, was Martin Durkin, the pro-Stevenson president of the plumbers' union. "Eight millionaires and a plumber," the *New Republic* disrespectfully remarked. Wilson at the hearing on his appointment played into the hands of Democratic critics by testifying that he had long assumed that "what was good for our country was good for General Motors, and vice versa." A few days later, Stevenson declared in a speech, "While the New Dealers have all left Washington to make way for the car dealers, I hasten to say that I, for one, do not believe the story that the general welfare has become a subsidiary of General Motors."

President Eisenhower's system of administering the government gave special importance to this cabinet preponderantly made up of businessmen. In the techniques that he developed, he borrowed from earlier army experience. He established his assistant, Sherman Adams, former Governor of New Hampshire, as a sort of chief of staff, and from Adams down, he established a chain of command. Through the cabinet, and through numerous new committees, administrators arrived at important policy decisions which they referred to the President. Since many of the men who formulated them, in addition to the cabinet officers, were business leaders the President had brought to Washington, over-all policies came to bear strongly the stamp of business.

Eisenhower Prosperity

When the administration came into power, although the Korean War was continuing, almost all price controls were dropped. Secretary Humphrey instead substituted sound-money policies to restrict credit, and thus try to prevent inflation. By the fall of 1953 the threat was of deflation. When the economy slackened, Secretary Humphrey and the Federal Reserve Board reversed the scarce-money policies and eased credit. The Republican administration's first venture with the built-in stabilizers of social security and the expedients of Keynesian economics was a success. By the summer of 1955 the American economy was again booming.

In order to avoid strikes which might unsettle economic conditions, several large industries, led by the automobile manufacturers, made new concessions to organized labor. As early as 1948 Walter

Reuther, the president of the United Automobile Workers, had obtained from General Motors, and later from other manufacturers, an "escalator clause" in contracts, providing for automatic increases or decreases in wages every three months as the consumers' price index rose or fell. In 1955 he demanded from the Ford Motor Company a guaranteed annual wage. Ford compromised by agreeing that workers should receive 65 per cent of their net weekly wages for the first four weeks they were unemployed, and 60 per cent for the next twenty-two weeks. General Motors followed. A few months later, steel workers received from the American Can Company and the Continental Can Company the first genuine guarantee of an annual wage.

The round of wage increases continued through 1956. After a five-week strike, steel workers won a substantial increase; the United Mine Workers without a strike obtained a 30¢-an-hour increase. Factory workers' wages went up to approximately $80.00 per week. These wage increases, together with other factors, led to widespread wholesale price increases and a renewed threat of inflation.

In December, 1955, the American Federation of Labor and the Congress of Industrial Organizations merged at the top into a new giant federation, the AFL-CIO. The powerful Teamsters' Brotherhood in 1957 became the focal point of a congressional investigation into labor racketeering. A Senate committee charged the president of the Teamsters, David Beck, with the possible misappropriation of over $320,000 in union funds. When Beck appeared before the committee, he refused to answer questions, invoking the constitutional protection of the Fifth Amendment against self-incrimination. Ultimately the committee brought forth so much evidence against Beck that he did not stand for re-election as President of the Teamsters. But the Teamsters, at their convention, defiantly elected, as their new President, James Hoffa, also under attack by the committee. His election led to the eviction of the Teamsters, the largest union in the United States, from the AFL-CIO. The congressional investigation led to the Labor Reform Act of 1959, which was intended to promote honest elections of union officials, safeguard union funds, ban Communist leaders, and restrict boycotting and picketing.

The great staples piled up in surplus, and from 1948 to 1956, farm prices dropped a third while the national income went up by half. In 1948 farmers received 8.9 per cent of the national income; in 1956, only 4.1 per cent. Farm population declined steadily, to 22,300,-000 in 1956—only a ninth of the nation. In that single year, one out of every eleven of the farm population either moved to a city or was absorbed in an expanding city.

While farm produce prices fell, consumer food prices continued to rise. Mainly this was because distribution costs were steadily going up. The farmer was caught in a squeeze, as prices for his produce slipped while prices of what he bought gradually increased.

As surpluses of such agricultural staples as wheat and cotton piled up, the government sought to bolster the prices through $8 billion worth of purchases. In 1954 President Eisenhower and Secretary of Agriculture Benson proposed a shift away from rigid price supports to a flexible sliding-scale program. The purpose was to cut government losses and end artificiality in production and distribution. The 1955 harvest was the first to be grown under the new flexible system, but already Democratic politicians were denouncing flexible supports as ones that could only "flex" downward. Seeking to win the farm vote, in 1956 they wrote a bill providing for high price supports and a subsidy for farmers who let land lie fallow. They thought they had put President Eisenhower in an impos-

sible position, and as they expected, he vetoed the bill. But in May, 1956, he pulled out of the vetoed bill the provision for a "soil bank" of fallow land, and threw it back at the congressional Democrats. In this form, Congress passed the bill and it became law. Under the 1956 program, farmers took 12,300,000 acres out of production in return for payments of over a quarter billion dollars. In the realm of public power development, the administration demonstrated its friendliness toward private enterprise. The President in 1953 referred to expansion of the Tennessee Valley Authority as "creeping socialism." The administration sought to circumvent the T.V.A. by contracting with the Dixon-Yates syndicate in 1954 to build a huge steam power plant on the banks of the Mississippi. The administration declared the contract would save taxpayers an immediate $100 million in construction costs, but opponents pointed to the large profits the syndicate would collect over many years. The power would cost the government $3.5 million per year more than T.V.A. power. Ultimately in 1955, when the city of Memphis, Tennessee, offered to build the plant, the President retreated to the principle of decentralization and canceled the Dixon-Yates contract.

The Eisenhower administration departed from its predecessors in power development policy through proposing federal "partnership" with local public or private enterprise in power construction, when the projects were too large for them to undertake alone. Secretary of the Interior McKay thus permitted a private power company to plan three smaller power dams in Hell's Canyon on the Snake River, rather than obtain appropriations for one large federal multipurpose dam. In keeping with his feeling that development of resources should be decentralized, President Eisenhower signed a bill turning over to states offshore oil lands along the Gulf of Mexico and the Pacific Coast.

To the satisfaction of bankers, the Reconstruction Finance Corporation was liquidated, rather than kept inoperative for a future emergency. While business taxes were cut, to encourage corporate initiative, spending was reduced so as to keep a more nearly balanced budget.

President Eisenhower took a firm stand against so-called "socialized medicine." Congress passed no health-insurance legislation, but in 1954 did extend social security to ten million more people, and unemployment compensation to an additional four million.

The public housing program, as Congress finally enacted it in July, 1955, involved building only 45,000 units a year for four years in a nation of 160,000,000 people. The nation, burgeoning with 32,-800,000 school children already, with a 50-per-cent increase likely within a decade, was short some quarter million schoolrooms. Local authorities were running out of building funds and reaching their debt limits. The President rushed to Congress in February, 1955, a message urging a federal expenditure of $1,100,-000,000 over a period of years. The same month, the President also proposed a highway building program. In 1955 Congress did not act on either proposal; in 1956 it did authorize a ten-year highway building program for which it would allocate $24,825,000,000.

This concept of the limited role of the federal government in providing for the general welfare was an integral part of the Eisenhower policies, to which he sometimes referred as "dynamic conservatism." It appealed to many members of Congress. During his first two years in office, when Congress was narrowly Republican, the President was supported more often than not by a coalition of liberal Republicans and Democrats.

The voters in 1954 veered slightly toward the Democrats, who thereafter controlled the House of Representatives, 232 to 203, and the Senate, 49 to 47. Although they thus took over committee chairmanships, congressional policy changed little as a result of the election.

Civil Liberties and Civil Rights

The hunt for subversives in the government was intensified early in the Eisenhower administration. Large numbers of employees resigned or were dismissed; the administration at one point gave their total as 2,200. But most of the serious security risks had already been ousted in the Truman administration. A study of some four hundred of the Eisenhower administration cases by the Fund for the Republic of the Ford Foundation indicated that in a majority of them the charges had been insupportable, and often reinstatement ultimately followed. In July, 1955, the Congress established a bipartisan Commission on Government Security to re-evaluate the security program.

Senator Joseph McCarthy himself plummeted from the national limelight to relative obscurity. His downfall followed his serious blunder in obliquely attacking President Eisenhower and directly assailing Secretary of the Army Robert Stevens, in January, 1954. The attacks led to congressional hearings, which turned into a great national spectacle viewed by millions over television. Many people for the first time saw McCarthy in action, as for thirteen days he bullied and harried Secretary Stevens, evading issues through irrelevant countercharges and insinuations, and interrupting to object at every point. As the public watched, McCarthy seemed to change from a national hero into something of a villain, then into a low buffoon. In December, 1954, the Senate voted 67 to 22 to condemn McCarthy, but his hold over the American public had already largely disintegrated. He died in May, 1957, a has-been, symbolic of the degree to which the nation had left behind the era of McCarthyism.

Remnants of the attitudes that had

made possible the rise of McCarthy remained. There was, for example, the case of a consultant to the Atomic Energy Commission, J. Robert Oppenheimer, who had directed the wartime laboratory at Los Alamos which made the first atomic bomb. In 1950 he had opposed

three-man board voted two to one against granting him security clearance; the A.E.C. ratified the decision four to one. Scientists were bitterly split over the wisdom of the decision.

The Supreme Court, as a result of the appointments of the Republican Presi

---

BROWN ET AL. V. BOARD OF EDUCATION OF TOPEKA ET AL.

"In approaching this problem, we cannot turn the clock back to 1868 when the [Fourteenth] Amendment was adopted, or even to 1896 when *Plessy* v. *Ferguson* was written. We must consider public education in the light of its full development and its present place in American life throughout the Nation. Only in this way can it be determined if segregation in public schools deprives these plaintiffs of the equal protection of the laws.

"Today, education is perhaps the most important function of state and local governments. Compulsory school attendance laws and the great expenditures for education both demonstrate our recognition of the importance of education to our democratic society. It is required in the performance of our most basic public responsibilities, even service in the armed forces. It is the very foundation of good citizenship. Today it is a principal instrument in awakening the child to cultural values, in preparing him for later professional training, and in helping him to adjust normally to his environment. In these days it is doubtful that any child may reasonably be expected to succeed in life if he is denied the opportunity of an education. Such an opportunity where the state has undertaken to provide it, is a right which must be made available to all on equal terms.

"We come then to the question presented: Does segregation of children in public schools solely on the basis of race, even though the physical facilities and other 'tangible' factors may be equal, deprive the children of the minority group of equal educational opportunities? We believe that it does."—Excerpt of opinion of the Supreme Court delivered by Chief Justice Earl Warren.

---

the development of a hydrogen bomb. The F.B.I. in November, 1953, distributed to the White House and several government departments a report on Oppenheimer detailing his prewar associations with Communists. On order from President Eisenhower, a "blank wall" was placed between Oppenheimer and government secrets, pending hearings. A

dent, seemed to be moving toward a more liberal rather than conservative policy. In one case in 1957 it ruled that the government could not use secret F.B.I. evidence against a defendant unless it was made available to his lawyers. Congress quickly passed legislation safeguarding F.B.I. files. In four other cases the Court protected individuals who were suspected of being subversive against undue encroachment by federal or state power. In 1958 the Court ruled five to four that the State Department, in the absence of an act of Congress, was exceeding its authority in refusing passports to persons who failed to file affidavits "with respect to present or past membership in the Communist party." These decisions attracted relatively little attention compared with the Supreme Court rulings on desegregation.

versed this doctrine in the case of *Brown v. Board of Education of Topeka* in May, 1954. Chief Justice Earl Warren (who had been appointed by President Eisenhower in September, 1953, after the death of Chief Justice Vinson) delivered the unanimous opinion of the Court: "We conclude that in the field of public education the doctrine of 'separate but equal' has no place. Separate educational facilities are inherently unequal." The Court granted that South-

---

STATE OF SOUTH CAROLINA, RESOLUTION ON DESEGREGATION

"For almost sixty years, beginning in 1896, an unbroken line of decisions of the [Supreme] Court interpreted the Fourteenth Amendment as recognizing the right of the States to maintain racially separate public facilities for their people. If the Court in the interpretation of the Constitution is to depart from the sanctity of past decisions and to rely on the current political and social philosophy of its members to unsettle the great constitutional principles so clearly established, the rights of individuals are not secure and government under a written Constitution has no stability. . . .

"The educational opportunities of white and colored children in the public schools of South Carolina have been substantially improved during recent years and highly satisfactory results are being obtained in our segregated schools. If enforced, the decision of the Court will seriously impair and retard the education of the children of both races, will nullify these recent advances and will cause untold friction between the races."— Excerpt from Joint Resolution, February 14, 1956.

A series of cases before the Supreme Court breaking down bit by bit racial segregation in public education had been pressed by the National Association for the Advancement of Colored People since the late 1930's. Their target was a Supreme Court decision of 1896, *Plessy v. Ferguson*, which had interpreted the requirement of the Fourteenth Amendment that states give "equal protection of the laws" to mean that separate but equal facilities could be furnished to Negroes. Finally, the Supreme Court re-

ern states might move gradually toward desegregation.

States in the deep South and several border states resorted to every possible legal device to avoid mixed schools. Each September, mob action against integration in a few communities within the South attracted widespread attention throughout the world. By the fall of 1957, of some 3,000 biracial school districts in the South, a total of 684 had already been integrated. Schools within these districts in large cities in the upper South or the border area, like Washington, Baltimore, Louisville, and St. Louis, opened quietly on a desegregated basis. But 2,300 districts, including all those in the deep South and Virginia, remained segregated. Some districts attempted desegregation on a very slow, token basis. One of these was Little Rock, Arkansas, where intervention by the governor and

District of Columbia. "There must be no second-class citizens in this country," he wrote the Negro Representative Adam Clayton Powell. Representative Powell, ironically, was instrumental in killing President Eisenhower's school-aid program of 1956, which provided for grants of a quarter-billion dollars a year for five years to match state funds. Powell suc-

INTEGRATION IN SOUTHERN SCHOOLS

1960

	Total Negro Enrollment	Negroes in Public Schools with Whites
Alabama	267,259	0
Arkansas	104,205	98
Delaware	14,063	6,196
District of Columbia	89,451	73,290
Florida	201,091	512
Georgia	306,158	0
Kentucky	42,778	12,000
Louisiana	261,491	0
Maryland	130,076	28,072
Mississippi	271,761	0
Missouri	82,000	35,000
North Carolina	302,060	34
Oklahoma	39,405	10,246
South Carolina	255,616	0
Tennessee	146,700	169
Texas	279,374	3,300
Virginia	203,229	103
West Virginia	24,010	12,000
Totals	3,020,727	181,020

mob threats led President Eisenhower to send federal troops to maintain order.

Pressure from growing blocs of Negro voters in the North, and from Negroes rising in economic status in the South and their supporters, helped bring other changes. President Eisenhower completed the desegregation of the armed forces, and tried to bring about greater integration in the government and the

ceeded in amending the bill to ban racial segregation; Southern segregationists aligned themselves with Northern conservatives to defeat it.

Congress in August, 1957, after debating 63 days, passed a new civil rights law —the first since Reconstruction—to give federal protection to Negroes wanting to vote. In eight Southern states with an adult Negro population of over 3,750,-

ooo, only 850,000 or 23 per cent were even registered, and still fewer went to the polls. In a 1955 election in Mississippi, only about 1 per cent of the adult Negroes voted. The civil-rights act empowered the federal government to remove some of the obstacles that state and local officials were allegedly placing in the way of Negro registration and voting. Federal judges were empowered to enjoin state officials from refusing to register qualified persons, and might fine recalcitrant officials up to $300 and sentence them to 45 days in jail without jury trial.

Eisenhower's Second Term

In September, 1955, President Eisenhower was at the height of his popularity. Only the anti-third-term Twenty-second Amendment, ratified in 1951 as a belated slap at Roosevelt, seemed to bar him from staying in the White House as long as he chose. Apparently his health was excellent, but while vacationing in Colorado, on the morning of September 24, he suffered a heart attack.

The President began to make a promising recovery, but no one expected he could possibly run for another term. During his long hospitalization in Denver and his convalescence in Gettysburg, he began to "ease" rather than "bulldoze" his way back into his presidential duties.

A panel of doctors met with the press in February, 1956, to state that the scar on the President's heart muscle had healed. It was almost an anticlimax when Eisenhower stated that he would run again. In June, stricken a second time, he was operated upon for ileitis. Although the operation was serious, Eisenhower's advisers never let the question arise whether or not he would continue as a candidate—and except among some Democrats it seemed a matter above debate. At the Republican convention in San Francisco at the end of August, he and Vice President Nixon were renominated by acclamation. The proceedings seemed to some observers to reflect more the atmosphere of a coronation than a party convention. Even while the President was recuperating from his heart attack, public-opinion polls attested to his overwhelming popularity. Regardless of this, Stevenson and Estes Kefauver fought vigorously for the Democratic nomination in state primary after primary. In the end, Stevenson triumphed at the Democratic convention and Kefauver became the vice-presidential nominee.

It was a rather dull campaign. Stevenson sought an issue by proposing that the United States agree to end hydrogen bomb tests. The average voter, relieved because the stalemate in nuclear weapons seemed to rule out a third world war, refused to worry about international affairs until actual shooting in the Suez area just before election day sent him to seek refuge with Eisenhower as commander in chief. Altogether, about 58 per cent of the voters marked their ballots for Eisenhower, although he was 66, the oldest man ever to be re-elected to the Presidency, and had suffered two serious illnesses in little more than a year past. He received 35,582,000 votes to 26,029,000 for Stevenson, and carried 41 states.

It was not much of a triumph for the Republican party. The prestige of the President pulled some Republican Congressmen to narrow victories, but as in 1954 the Democrats won control over both houses of Congress.

During President Eisenhower's second administration, domestic policies were little changed. In 1957 Congress occupied itself largely with trying to slash the President's $71,800,000,000 budget, the largest in peacetime history. Even Secretary of the Treasury Humphrey (who resigned a few months later) joined in the onslaught against the "terrific" expenditures.

At the close of 1957 the nation skidded into the most serious recession since the

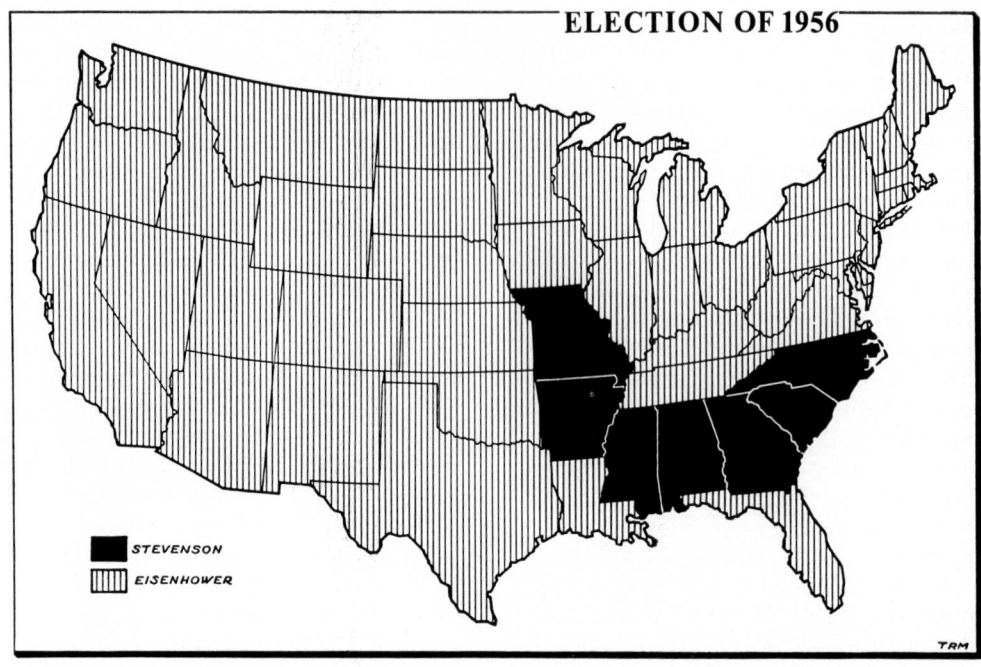

STEVENSON

EISENHOWER

TRM

war. By the late spring of 1958 industrial production had dropped 14 per cent below the level of a year earlier, and approximately five million workers were unemployed. Again the so-called "built-in stabilizers" of the economy, such as unemployment insurance payments to those out of work, somewhat softened the blow of the recession.

As Republicans prepared for the congressional campaign of 1958, they were handicapped by the persistence of economic trouble. Some of the more conservative Republican candidates, most notably Senate Minority Leader William Knowland, running for governor of California, centered their campaigns around attacks on organized labor. In some states they sought "right-to-work" laws to outlaw union shops (plants in which every employee hired must join the union). This sort of onslaught in most states succeeded only in insuring a large labor vote for Democratic candidates. The Republican party was also weakened by the revelation in the spring of 1958 that Sherman Adams, in effect

the President's chief of staff, had received gifts from a New England textile manufacturer. Adams resigned in September, too late to benefit the party.

The result on November 4, 1958, was a Democratic landslide of impressive proportions. The Democrats won 13 additional seats in the Senate, giving them a 62 to 34 majority. They gained an added 47 seats in the House of Representatives, providing a majority of 282 to 153—the largest margin since Roosevelt's 1936 victory.

The voter reaction in 1958 had slight effect upon the national administration in the two years that followed. President Eisenhower presented Congress in January 1959 with a $77,000,000,000 budget, which he promised would be in balance —a budget which northern Democrats decried as not sufficiently large in an expanding economy and not providing the services the nation needed. At first the Democrats in Congress gave promise of pushing far beyond the President's limited requests. But as a renewed sweep of prosperity wiped out the recession in the spring of 1959, public opinion began to react to the incessant warnings of the President and of conservative publicists that budget balancing was the only way to avoid another ruinous round of inflation. Eisenhower, acting more vigorously than in previous years, was able to marshal much public suppor and congressional voting strength for his conservative course. Speaker Sam Rayburn and Senate Majority Leader Lyndon Johnson were more disposed to compromise than to throw their large Democratic majorities against him. Again and again he vetoed measures, and with one exception (an omnibus public works "pork barrel" bill) sufficient northern Republicans and southern Democrats coalesced to uphold his vetoes.

Among the more notable steps taken by Congress was the passage of an enabling act for Alaska, which was admitted as the forty-ninth state in January, 1959, and for Hawaii, which was admitted as the fiftieth, in August, 1959.

Mid-Century America

In the 1950's the American people were enjoying a living standard far beyond any they had previously known. The output of goods and services, measured in dollars of equal purchasing power, had doubled since the 1920's. Even allowing for inflation and heavy taxation, the average American had 16 per cent more income by 1956 than in 1947, and 53 per cent more than in 1929. Family income had more than tripled since the boom year 1918. A remarkable redistribution of the wealth had taken place also. In 1929 the top 5 per cent of the population received a third of the income; by 1956 they received only 18 per cent. Among city families, in 1929 only 15 per cent earned the equivalent of $4,000 to $7,500 per year (in dollars of the fifties); in 1956 43 per cent did.

Labor's share of the national income rose from 18 per cent in 1929 to 29 per cent in 1956, while the average work week decreased from 44 hours to 40 hours. The industrial worker enjoyed 15 or 20 hours a week more free time than had his father or grandfather at the turn of the century. Unlike them, upon retirement he could look forward to a pension; welfare and pension plans had increased twentyfold since 1929.

Because of their higher income, workers in the fifties were spending a smaller percentage of their wages for food, clothing, and housing, and more for automobiles, medical care, recreation, and vacations. The statistics on national consumption in 1956 were staggering: food, $71,300,000,000; housing, $48,100,000,000; automobile transportation, $27,000,000,000. More than nine out of ten families had refrigerators; four out of five, a television set; three out of four, at least one car; three out of five owned their own home; and one in ten even had air conditioning. In 1945 there were only 9,000 swimming pools in use; in the single year 1957, 55,000 were installed.

But the picture was not entirely cheerful. As late as 1951 one family in six was living on only $1,500 per year or less. This meant existence in dwellings little better than shacks in the country, or slums in the cities. For many millions more, adequate housing was either a dream or an extravagance. The National Housing Conference estimated in 1957 that only one city family in six was earning enough to buy satisfactory housing without spending over one-fifth of its income.

Since the turn of the century, women had entered the working force in increasing numbers. In 1900, half the adult women had never in their lives held jobs; by the 1950's, one third of the women over 14 were working, and nine tenths had worked at one time or another. The oldfashioned "career woman," refusing marriage, was nearly gone; only 7 per cent of women failed to marry. The modern counterpart of the girls who had

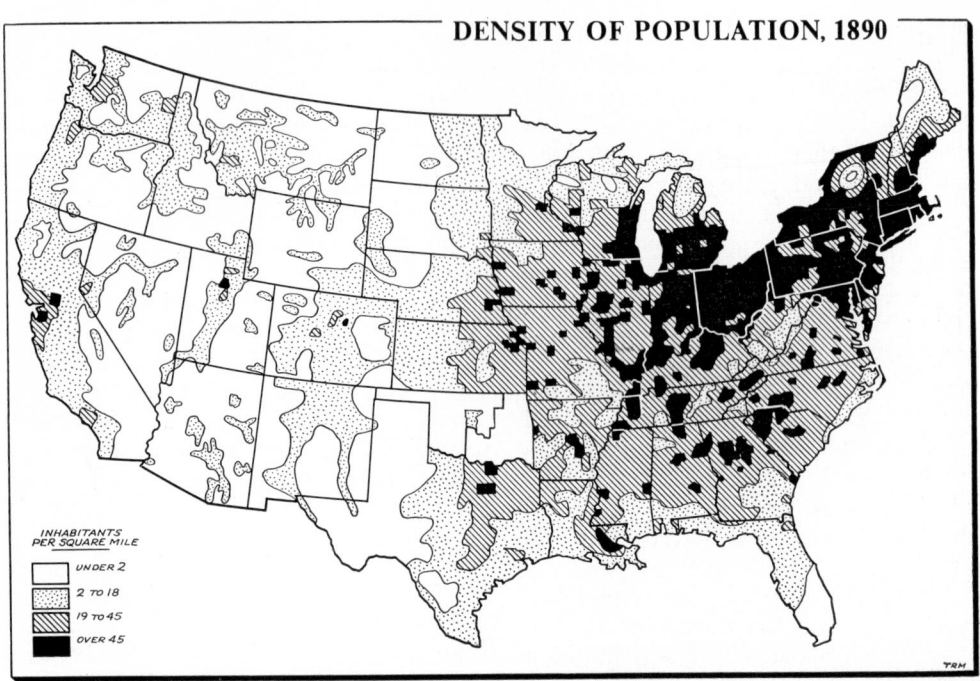

DENSITY OF POPULATION, 1890

INHABITANTS
PER SQUARE MILE

UNDER 2
2 TO 18
19 TO 45
OVER 45

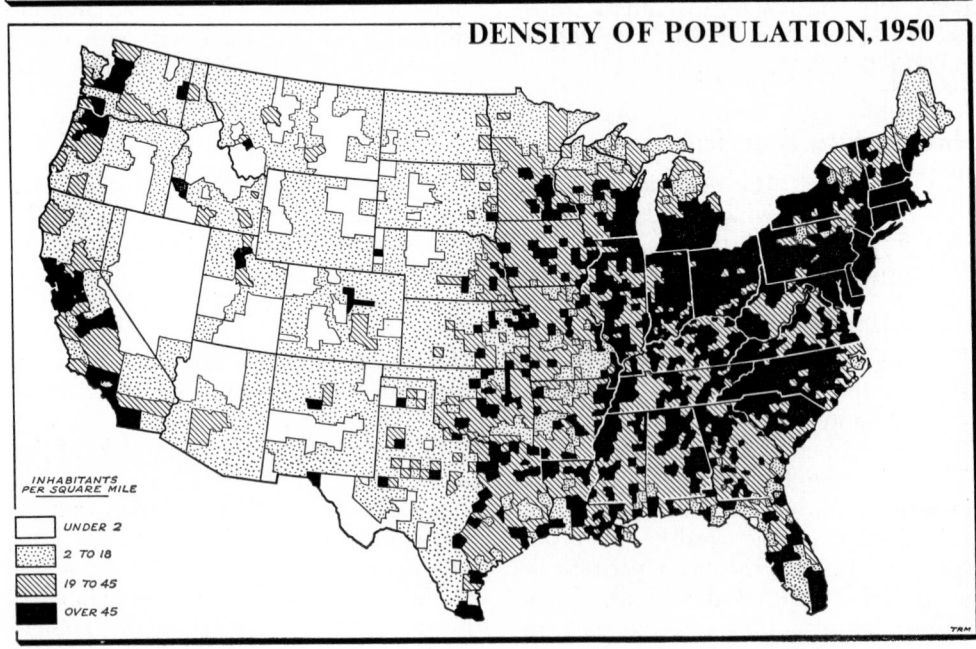

DENSITY OF POPULATION, 1950

INHABITANTS
PER SQUARE MILE

UNDER 2
2 TO 18
19 TO 45
OVER 45

worked in the Lowell textile mills in the
1830's were the airline hostesses; on one
of the largest airlines they stayed an average of only 26 months, and 85 per cent
of them left to be married. Women were

filling an increasing number of professional positions, but still were not being
trained in keeping with their potentiali-
ties. Only a quarter of those capable of
finishing college were doing so; only 1

in 300 of those qualified was earning a Ph.D. degree.

Negroes rapidly were improving their working and economic status. By 1957, the average Negro wage-earner was receiving four and a half times as much as in 1940; professional men had increased 103 per cent; skilled workers, 181 per cent, and clerical and sales people, 223 per cent. More than 98 per cent of Negro children between 7 and 13 were attending school, and Negro college enrollment was increasing six times as fast as white enrollment. A third of the Negroes owned their own homes. Compared with the population of Italy, which was about the same size as the American Negro population, they were opulent, but their incomes still averaged far below those of white Americans.

The key to continued future prosperity seemed to be a rapidly expanding population and increased productivity. In the 1930's the expectation was that the population would be 140 million in 1960; actually it was well past 170 million before that date. A tidal wave of children was hitting schools and colleges in the late fifties. They would soon be marrying, raising their own families, and buying ever-increasing quantities of consumer goods. The way to increase production to supply them seemed to lie in more and more automation. The precision machinery being installed in Detroit and elsewhere could turn out high-quality products far more rapidly than ever before. The problem was one of keeping costs down. In Detroit the cost of tooling—preparing the machines and dies to turn out the models of a single year—went up from $1,400,000,000 for 1954 to nearly $2,000,000,000 for the year 1956. The reason for the increase was almost entirely automation.

During the increase in production, the United States began to change from a "have" to a "have-not" nation in natural resources. Between 1900 and 1950 the production of bituminous coal rose two and a half times, of copper three times, of iron ore three and a half times, and of crude oil thirty times. Now the largest importer of copper, lead, and zinc, the United States was becoming dependent upon other nations for its raw materials, leading to a flow of dollars overseas. Within the United States, producers were having to learn methods of conservation or were turning to the development of synthetics. As the rich iron deposits began to dwindle, steel companies developed processes to make use of lower-grade ore, and opened new ore deposits in Labrador and elsewhere.

Already, the United States was begin-

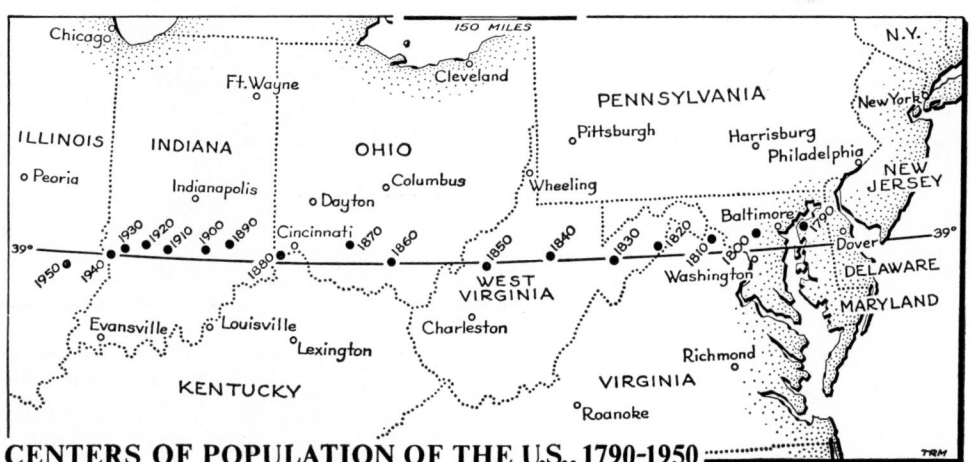

CENTERS OF POPULATION OF THE U.S., 1790-1950

TEENAGE OPINIONS

"Only 45 per cent of the nation's young adults believe that newspapers should be allowed to print anything they want except military secrets. . . .

"Twenty-six per cent believe that the police should be allowed to search a person or his home without a warrant. . . .

"Twenty-five per cent agree that some groups should not be allowed to hold public meetings.

"Seventeen per cent say that it may be right for police to jail people without naming the charges against them.

"Thirty-three per cent say that people who refuse to testify against themselves should be made to talk or should be severely punished. An additional 20 per cent are uncertain about this point. . . .

"Fourteen per cent think there is something evil about scientists. . . .

"Thirty per cent declare that one can't raise a normal family and become a scientist.

"Thirty-five cent believe that it's necessary to be a genius to become a good scientist and 45 per cent think their own school backgrounds are too poor to permit them to choose science as a career.

"Thirty-seven per cent say that immigration of foreigners into this country should be greatly restricted since it may mean 'lowering national standards.'

"Thirty-eight per cent feel that the greatest threat to democracy in the United States comes from foreign ideas and foreign groups."—H. H. Remmers and D. H. Radler, *The American Teenager* (1957).

---

ning to develop electric power from atomic energy. Two small power plants were completed in 1957, and fourteen more were planned or under construction. Altogether they had a capacity of more than 1,000,000 kilowatts of electric power—compared with the 900,000 kilowatts comprising the United States share from the great St. Lawrence water-power project being constructed at the same time. Economical nuclear reactors had yet to be developed, but with few major hydroelectric sites remaining in the United States, atomic energy seemed to be the key to future expansion of electric power.

Applications of scientific knowledge, both civilian and military, were being developed at such a rapid pace that they created a sharp pressure for addi-

LEVER HOUSE. [OPPOSITE] After World War II, the development of the tall office building culminated in structures in which nearly the entire area of the external walls was glass. An outstanding example is Lever House on Park Avenue in midtown New York, designed by the firm of Skidmore, Owings & Merrill. Almost all of the first floor is an open arcade with a delightful garden. The second floor covers almost the entire site. The tower begins at the third floor, and is 22 stories high. The 1,404 windows, rhythmically separated by thin strips of stainless steel, are of blue glass, which appears colorless from within the building, and which admits light while filtering out 35 per cent of the heat in sunlight. This permits better control of the temperature within the sealed, air-conditioned structure. Nearly all of the 900 persons working in the building have their desks within 25 feet of a window. (LEVER BROTHERS COMPANY)

TIME NEEDED TO CROSS THE ATLANTIC, 1620–1950

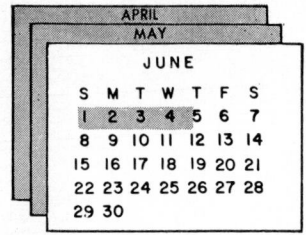

1620   *MAYFLOWER ... 65 days*

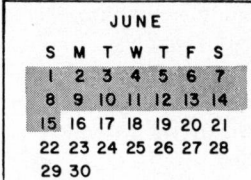

1838   *FIRST STEAMSHIP ... 15 days*

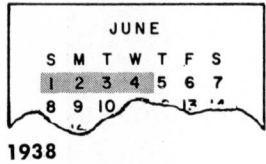

1938

QUEEN MARY ... 4 days

1943

FERRY COMMAND ... 7 hours

NEW YORK TO SAN FRANCISCO 1848–1960
(COMMERCIAL OR REGULAR TRANSPORTATION)

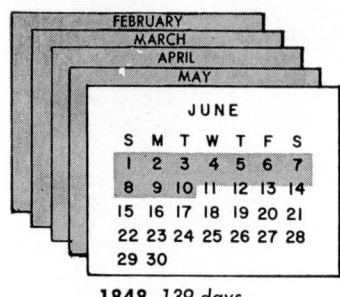

1848 *139 days*

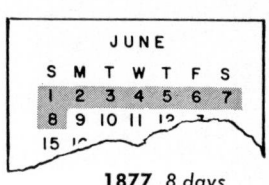

1877 *8 days*

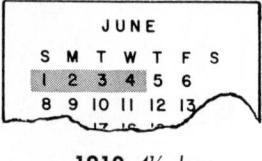

1910 *4½ days*

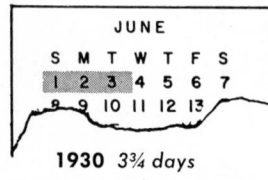

1930 *3¾ days*

1950 *10 hours*

1960 *4 hours, 15 minutes*

---

tional basic research. Congress in 1950 established the National Science Foundation, and by 1957 was spending $3,-377,000,000 for research and development.

The most comprehensive and spec-tacular of basic research enterprises, in which the United States cooperated with 62 other countries including Russia, was the International Geophysical Year, run-ning from July 1, 1957 to the end of 1958. It involved exploring the globe from pole to pole, and from ionosphere to core, and included the launching of earth satellites and the establishment of an American base at the South Pole.

In medical research, the most important advance was the development of an effective polio vaccine by Dr. Jonas Salk of the University of Pittsburgh. The vaccine was first used on a large scale in 1955, and within two years the polio rate in the United States dropped 80 per cent. Advances in medical research, extensive public health programs, private health insurance plans covering 73 per cent of the people—all these contributed to a lengthening life span. In 1900 life expectancy had been 49 years; by 1955 it was 70 years.

Improved technology made air travel, a luxury before World War II, a commonplace in the decade afterward. Travelers abandoned passenger trains for private automobiles and buses for short distances, and for airplanes for long distances. While railroads cut back their passenger service, airlines rapidly expanded. By 1954 they were carrying 32,-000,000 passengers a year, the airlanes were already so crowded, despite a safety interval of ten minutes between airplanes, that near-collisions were frequent. One spectacular collision over the Grand Canyon killed 128 persons. Airlines rushed to install more electronic safety equipment as they switched to faster airplanes to carry far more passengers.

The postwar decade marked the advent of television, as the twenties did that

THE PERFECTION OF TELEVISION, 1947. By the time of the campaign of 1948, hundreds of thousands of Americans were watching the candidates for the first time on television, a new and important political factor. They were following endless hours of entertainment also on the new medium. But as Dahl satirically suggested in his 1947 cartoon, pioneering television was already a vehicle for seemingly endless "commercials." (BY FRANCIS W. DAHL IN THE BOSTON Herald)

WILLIAM FAULKNER. Born in 1897, the grandson of a Confederate colonel, Faulkner was brought up in Oxford, Mississippi. During the 1920's he supported himself badly at a number of odd jobs. In 1929 he won acclaim with his third novel, *Sartoris*, the story of a decaying Southern family—a recurring theme with Faulkner. That same year he published *The Sound and the Fury*, the first of more than a dozen interconnected novels with a setting in imaginary Yaknapatawpha County. (BROWN BROTHERS)

of radio. In 1947 fewer than 10,000 people owned television sets, with which they could view programs a few hours a day from a handful of stations. A decade later over 40,000,000 sets in American homes, hotels, and bars were tuned in to 467 stations. Motion-picture attendance dropped from a wartime high of 90,000,000 a week to about 40,000,000. Television even more than radio meant mass communication to nationwide audience. One musical show presented over 245 stations one night in March, 1957, reached an estimated audience of 100,000,000—enough people to fill a Broadway theater every night for 165 years. In the 1952 campaign, television seemed to have remade presidential elections as both candidates made extensive and expensive use of the new medium. By 1956 the effect had somewhat worn off. President Eisenhower received an audience rating one night of only 17.9 compared with 27.6 for his TV adviser, Robert Montgomery, appearing on another network.

While television served as the great outlet for the new leisure of many people, more persons than ever before were engaging in outdoor recreation and do-it-yourself home crafts. Patronage of the arts flourished—attendance at the theater, concerts, and exhibitions, and participation in theatrical and musical groups and "Sunday painting." Sales of good books as well as trash in paper covers, and of inexpensive phonograph records, both classics and rock-and-roll, mounted astronomically. Never had so many people participated so deeply and enthusiastically in the arts.

Pioneers in the arts of the twenties and thirties became the accepted pillars of the fifties. Frank Lloyd Wright appeared on TV, and modern architecture became commonplace. Eugene O'Neill's plays enjoyed long runs on Broadway after his death. Ernest Hemingway and William Faulkner became two of the patriarchs of writing for the Western world as well

SCHOOL ENROLLMENT, 1900–1960

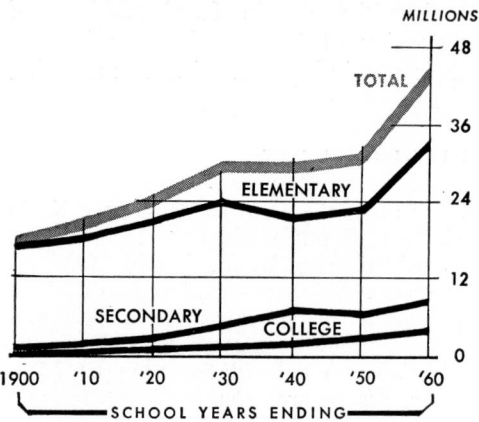

as the United States. Hemingway at times seemed to be parodying his earlier virile, trenchant style; Faulkner retained his master's touch in portraying the deep South he knew so well, and through it seeing the world. New novelists created temporary sensations and achieved best-selling success with their interpretations of the war and the postwar world, but to their contemporaries in the 50's, none seemed to approach the talent of the leaders of the "lost generation." Faulkner, when he received the Nobel Prize in 1950, set forth what he considered to be the novelist's task: "It is [his] privilege to help man endure by lifting his heart, by reminding him of the courage and honor and pride and compassion and pity and sacrifice which have been the glory of his past. The poet's voice need not merely be the record of man, it can be one of the props, the pillars to help him endure and prevail."

One task of all responsible citizens in the fifties was to improve the schools of the nation. A serious teacher shortage existed as the nation prepared for an influx of students well beyond the existing teaching and classroom capacity. State and local school authorities, spending approximately $2 billion a year on new schools, were doing no more than stay even, not eliminating the accumulated shortages or preparing for future needs. Universities likewise faced problems of expansion of their student bodies and their physical plants without sacrificing the level of their teaching. Men and women of high quality were needed as instructors in institutions ranging from kindergarten through graduate schools.

BIBLIOGRAPHY

Concerning the 1952 campaign, see Kevin McCann, *The Man From Abilene* (1952), on Eisenhower; N. F. Busch, *Adlai E. Stevenson* (1952); and Stevenson's *Major Campaign Speeches* (1953). On the Eisenhower administration, see R. J. Donovan, *Eisenhower, The Inside Story* (1956); M. J. Pusey, *Eisenhower the President* (1956); R. H. Rovere, *Affairs of State: The Eisenhower Years* (1956); and M. W. Childs, *Eisenhower: Captive Hero* (1958).

An indispensable interpretation of the political revolution of the era is Samuel Lubell, *The Future of American Politics* (1952). See also Lubell's *The Revolt of the Moderates* (1956). On corruption, see Blair Bolles, *How to Get Rich in Washington* (1952), and P. H. Douglas, *Ethics in Government* (1952). A. M. Rose, *The Negro in Postwar America* (1950), is a competent survey. Significant regional economic studies are: C. B. Hoover and B. U. Ratchford, *Economic Resources and Policies of the South* (1951); Wendell Berge, *Economic Freedom for the West* (1946); and S. E. Harris, *The Economics of New England.*

On questions of individual rights and loyalty, see The President's Committee on Civil Rights, *To Secure These Rights* (1947); Alan Barth, *The Loyalty of Free Men* (1951); Clair Wilcox (ed.), *Civil Liberties under Attack* (1951); H. D. Lasswell, *National Security and Individual Freedom* (1950); C. H. Pritchett, *Civil Liberties and the Vinson Court* (1954); Joseph R. McCarthy, *McCarthyism* (1952); and Jack Anderson and R. W. May, *McCarthy* (1952). A survey of the erosion of civil liberties, carrying into the post-McCarthy period, is J. W. Caughey, *In Clear and Present Danger* (1958). Michael Straight, *Trial by Television* (1954), details the Army-McCarthy hearings. J. L. O'Brian, *National Security and Individual Freedom* (1955), analyzes the Eisenhower program; C. P. Curtis, *The Oppenheimer Case* (1955), deals with a *cause célèbre.* An historical setting for the loyalty issue of the 1950's is provided by H. M. Hyman, *To Try Men's Souls: Loyalty Tests in American History* (1959).

Aspects of the Negro's place in American society are treated in the following: Richard Bardolph, *The Negro Vanguard* (1959); F. L. Broderick, *W. E. B. DuBois: Negro Leader in a Time of Crisis* (1959); Jack Greenberg, *Race Relations and American Law* (1959); L. D. Reddick, *Crusader Without Violence: A Biography of Martin Luther King* (1959); and Southern Education Reporting Service, *Southern Schools: Progress and Problems* (1959).

Important social and economic analyses of mid-century America are C. W. Mills, *White Collar* (1951), and *Power Elite* (1956); David Riesman, *The Lonely Crowd* (1950); W. H. Whyte, *The Organization Man* (1956); D. M. Potter, *People of Plenty: Economic Abundance and the American Character* (1954); and J. K. Galbraith, *The Affluent Society* (1958). Thomas C. Cochran provides historical perspective in *The American Business System* (1957). The cultural scene is well covered by Max Lerner, *America as Civilization: Thought and Life in the United States Today* (1957). Domestic issues of the 1950's are related to their historical background in Carl N. Degler, *Out of Our Past: The Forces That Shaped Modern America* (1959).

40

A BALANCE OF TERROR

In the 1950's, with the basic policies of the United States toward Russia well established, the perils and challenge of the clash between the two great power blocs overshadowed all else, and seemed even to imperial the very survival of mankind. Diplomacy between the two great nations centered in a race for superiority in nuclear weapons. Although by 1949 the Russians had exploded an atomic bomb, the United States continued to hold a lead sufficiently impressive to deter the Communist bloc from launching a full-scale war, despite its preponderance of manpower and conventional implements of war. But year by year the Russians narrowed the American lead in nuclear weapons. By 1957 the Soviet Union appeared to assume the lead in some categories.

Negotiating a Korean Armistice

Before his first inauguration President-elect Eisenhower flew to Korea to talk to commanders about means of obtaining an honorable truce. He issued a press statement there asserting, "We have no panaceas, no trick ways of settling any problems." In his inaugural he committed himself to a firm policy in Korea and elsewhere in the struggle against Communists. "In the final choice," he declared, "a soldier's pack is not so heavy a burden as a prisoner's chains." He informed Congress that the United States would encourage the strengthening of the South Korean armed forces, and would no longer use the Seventh Fleet to shield Red China from Chiang Kai-shek.

Less than two months after President Eisenhower took office, Stalin died. This opened the possibility of an end to the Korean war and perhaps some moderation of the cold war. When the new Soviet premier, Georgi Malenkov, inaugurated more conciliatory policies, the President called upon Russia to show its good faith by signing an Austrian peace treaty and supporting an armistice in Korea. Through the spring of 1953 negotiations for an armistice proceeded rather smoothly. By June, when they were almost completed, President Rhee disrupted them by freeing unilaterally 27,-ooo North Korean troops who did not wish to be repatriated. Nevertheless, on July 27, 1953, a final armistice agreement was signed at Panmunjom. It provided for a cease-fire and withdrawal of both armies two kilometers back of the existing battle line, which ran from coast to coast, from just below the 38th parallel in the west to thirty miles north of it in the east.

In succeeding months the United Nations sent northward more than 70,000 North Korean and Chinese Communist prisoners, and received in return only 3,597 Americans, 7,848 South Koreans, and 1,315 prisoners of other nationalities. Within three months a political conference to seek peaceful unification of Korea was to be held, but it never took place. Instead, the armistice turned into an uneasy and indefinite armed truce. In 1957, after the Communists had long been violating armistice prohibitions against introducing new armaments, the United States announced it also was sending more modern weapons into Korea. The United States not only continued to face a threat from North Korea, but had to restrain President Rhee, who bitterly threatened to unify Korea by force. The Senate ratified a mutual defense treaty in 1954, but warned that the United States would not support South Korean military aggression.

The Korean war (officially only a police action) had lasted more than three years and cost the United States alone 25,000 dead, 115,000 other casualties, and $22 billion. For Americans who liked to think in terms of total victory, it seemed painfully inconclusive. The fighting had settled no problems in the Far East except to prevent the Communist conquest of South Korea.

Dulles and "Massive Retaliation"

A real threat to peace in Asia continued to come from Communist China. Serious trouble arose in Indo-China, where the French, who had been slow and reluctant in giving firm guarantees of independence, for eight years had been fighting the Indochinese Communist leader, Ho Chi Minh. Against the Communists in Indo-China, Secretary

of State John Foster Dulles tried to use a new policy.

As Secretary of State from 1953 to 1959, Dulles gave the impression of formulating policy decisions out of his own head. A sturdy moralist, a skilled and stubborn advocate, and a tireless worker, he seemed to feel that he must participate personally in innumerable top-level negotiations all over the globe. Since as Secretary he flew 479,286 miles outside of the United States, his detractors liked to wisecrack that he was demonstrating an infinite capacity for taking planes. Assuming much of the normal functions of State Department officials, diplomats, and even the President, he dominated the making of foreign policy. President Eisenhower was said to have remarked once, "If anything happened to Foster, where could I find a man able to replace him?"

The Eisenhower administration had come into office firmly committed to existing collective-security arrangements and a Europe-first priority. Nevertheless it maintained a tenuous compromise with the ardently nationalistic Asia-first wing of the party. This group was exploiting at home the thesis that setbacks in Asia were due to internal subversion in the Truman administration, that Communist aggression in Asia must be met with military force, and that economic aid to remove the grievances the Communists were exploiting was a waste of money. Their hero was Chiang Kai-shek, and their special villain, Red China, which must be curbed or destroyed at all costs. Concurring with this group at some points were the business leaders dominant in the Eisenhower administration, who were determined that defense expenditures must fit within a balanced budget.

The pressures of these groups helped lead to crucial decisions in 1953. Again, as before the Korean war, a movement began to reduce the military establishment. At the same time, the Eisenhower

SECRETARY OF STATE JOHN FOSTER DULLES REPORTING TO PRESIDENT EISENHOWER, MAY 17, 1955. The Eisenhower administration made extensive use of television to dramatize its actions among the American people. For the first time the President's press conferences were televised, and on several occasions like this, Secretary Dulles reported to the President in front of the television cameras. He had just returned from Europe, where he had signed the treaty restoring sovereignty to Austria. (DEPARTMENT OF STATE)

administration wished to meet the Communist challenge in Indo-China and elsewhere. The solution seemed to lie in a "new look" in defense policy, equally pleasing to the Secretaries of Defense, the Treasury, and State. This meant a cutting of the expensive army ground forces, and low expenditures on unproven missiles research and basic scientific research. Secretary of Defense Charles E. Wilson, an expert on practical matters of automobile production, defined basic research as "when you don't know what you are doing." The United States would depend especially upon its thermonuclear weapons and their delivery by the air force. Popularized, this was the policy of "more bang for a buck."

A new foreign policy was necessary to make the "new look" in defense operate

adequately. Secretary of the Treasury George M. Humphrey, looking at it from a standpoint of cost, asserted that the United States had "no business getting into little wars." If the nation had to intervene, he declared, "let's intervene decisively with all we have got or stay out." This was the economic basis for Secretary of State Dulles's policy of "massive retaliation." The United States would depend less on local defense, he declared in an address on January 12, 1954, and depend more on "the deterrent of massive retaliatory power . . . a great capacity to retaliate instantly, by means and at times of our own choosing."

Upon occasion, so Dulles declared two years later, this policy brought the United States close to war, but he said it produced the desired results. In Jan-

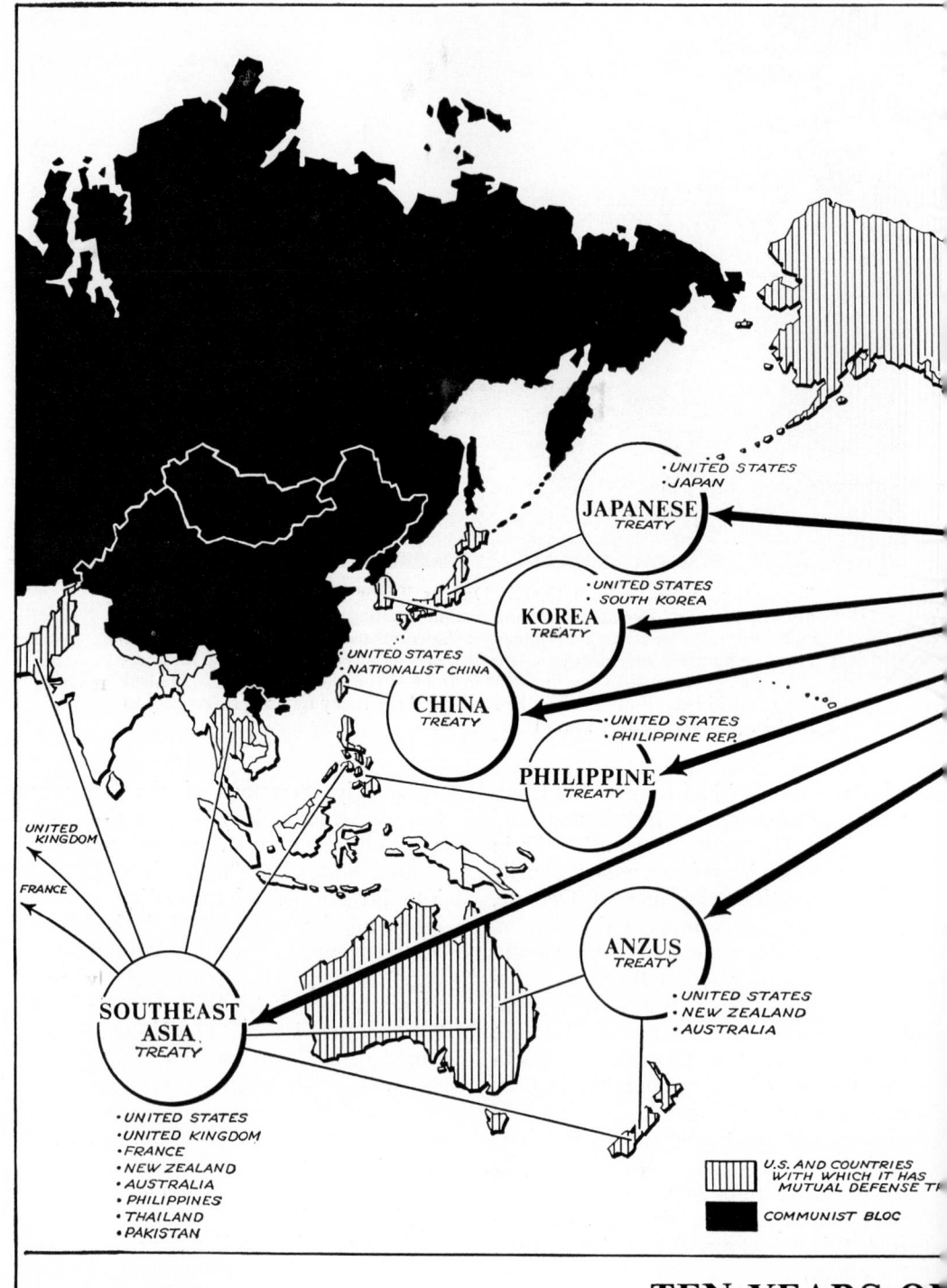

JAPANESE TREATY
• UNITED STATES
• JAPAN

KOREA TREATY
• UNITED STATES
• SOUTH KOREA

CHINA TREATY
• UNITED STATES
• NATIONALIST CHINA

PHILIPPINE TREATY
• UNITED STATES
• PHILIPPINE REP.

ANZUS TREATY
• UNITED STATES
• NEW ZEALAND
• AUSTRALIA

UNITED KINGDOM

FRANCE

SOUTHEAST ASIA TREATY
• UNITED STATES
• UNITED KINGDOM
• FRANCE
• NEW ZEALAND
• AUSTRALIA
• PHILIPPINES
• THAILAND
• PAKISTAN

▦ U.S. AND COUNTRIES WITH WHICH IT HAS MUTUAL DEFENSE TR

■ COMMUNIST BLOC

TEN YEARS OF

TRM

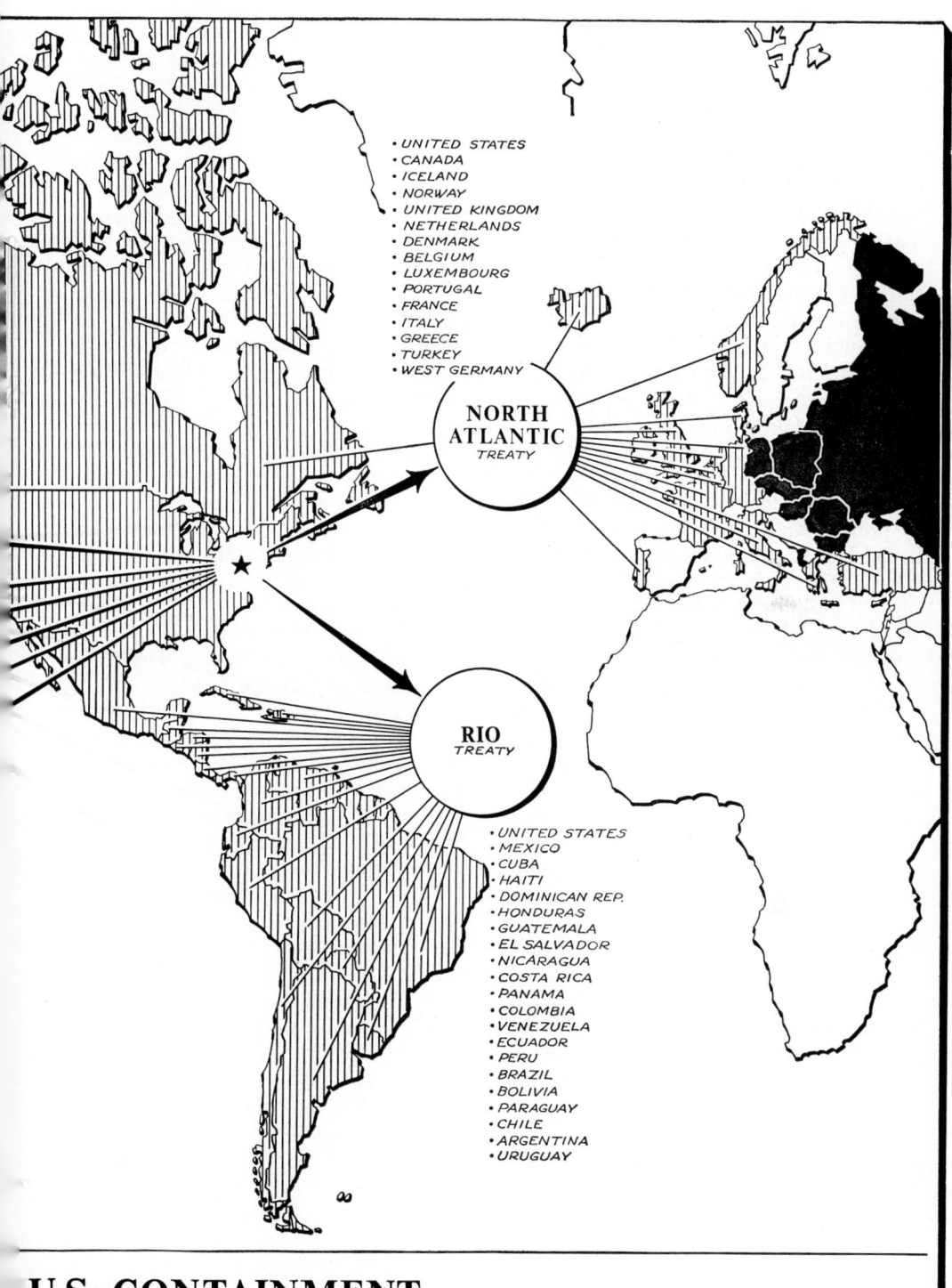

NORTH
ATLANTIC
TREATY

- UNITED STATES
- CANADA
- ICELAND
- NORWAY
- UNITED KINGDOM
- NETHERLANDS
- DENMARK
- BELGIUM
- LUXEMBOURG
- PORTUGAL
- FRANCE
- ITALY
- GREECE
- TURKEY
- WEST GERMANY

RIO
TREATY

- UNITED STATES
- MEXICO
- CUBA
- HAITI
- DOMINICAN REP.
- HONDURAS
- GUATEMALA
- EL SALVADOR
- NICARAGUA
- COSTA RICA
- PANAMA
- COLOMBIA
- VENEZUELA
- ECUADOR
- PERU
- BRAZIL
- BOLIVIA
- PARAGUAY
- CHILE
- ARGENTINA
- URUGUAY

U.S. CONTAINMENT

uary, 1956, *Life* magazine quoted him: "The ability to get to the verge without getting into the war is the necessary art. If you cannot master it, you inevitably get into war. If you try to run away from it, if you are scared to go to the brink, you are lost." Critics of Dulles, within the United States and abroad, suggested that "brinkmanship" had not worked in this salutary fashion. Rather, they suggested, war-weariness on both sides and mutual fear of atomic retaliation led to compromise solutions in Korea and Indo-China and to a continued modus vivendi over Formosa.

The Indo-China crisis offered the first test of the new Eisenhower-Dulles policies. Undoubtedly the end of the Korean war had enabled the Chinese Reds to provide at least indirect aid to the Indo-Chinese Communist at a time when the French were tottering on the edge of military disaster. In the spring of 1954, the Communist forces besieged a French and Vietnamese army of 12,000 in the frontier fortress of Dienbienphu. Already the United States was underwriting 70 per cent of the French financial cost of the war, but without direct military aid, Dienbienphu and perhaps all of Indo-China would be lost.

At a press conference, President Eisenhower likened the nations in Southeast Asia to a row of dominoes. The moral was implicit; the first domino must not be allowed to fall. Many of the President's advisers favored at least bombing the besieging army with carrier-based planes, but Dulles failed to gain support among allied nations. Congressional leaders had no stomach for an intervention which might soon involve more ground troops than the Korean war, and in which the United States might have to fight alone. The United States did not intervene; there was no "massive retaliation." Dienbienphu fell on May 7, 1954. At a conference in Geneva, the United States, stripped of bargaining power (except for the threat of unilateral inter-vention) had to stand by, neither associating itself with negotiations with Red China, nor approving of agreements in July, 1954, which provided for a cease-fire and partitioning of Indo-China.

After the Geneva Conference, Secretary Dulles succeeded in building a Southeast Asia Treaty Organization (SEATO) in September, 1954, to serve as a counterpart of NATO and help contain Communism. It was far less impressive, since the terms of the Geneva conference kept the nations of Indo-China (Vietnam, Laos, and Cambodia) from participating. Nationalist China, no longer recognized by Great Britain, could not join for that reason; several of the most important Asian states (India, Ceylon, Burma, and Indonesia) refused to join because they were committed to neutralism. This left only three nations of Southeast Asia—Pakistan, Thailand, and the Philippines—to join with the United States, Great Britain, France, Australia, and New Zealand. They drew up a pact, weaker than the North Atlantic Treaty, providing only that an attack upon one would be regarded as a threat to the others. SEATO opened the way for economic and military aid, but without the key nations of Southeast Asia participating, it remained a relatively ineffective organization.

The United States continued to function in Asia as best it could on a virtually unilateral basis. Trouble with Communist China developed over some islands immediately off the mainland which Chiang continued to garrison—Quemoy, and the Matsu and Tachen Islands. Occasionally Chiang's air force attacked the Communists from them. Since the Mutual Defense Treaty with Chiang, signed at the end of 1954, did not include these islands, Red China in January, 1955, began air attacks upon the Tachens and bombardment of Quemoy. Before invasion could follow, Congress granted President Eisenhower rather indefinite emergency powers to aid Chiang. These sufficed to maintain a precarious status quo.

Intermittently, the Chinese Communists renewed their pressure upon Quemoy and Matsu. In August, 1958, they began a serious bombardment. Secretary Dulles, although not always clear in what he said, implied repeatedly that the United States would help Chiang defend the islands. But the United States could not count upon the support of other Western nations if a large-scale struggle with Red China developed. The militant Chinese Communists in 1959 pressed on other borders. After crushing a revolt in Tibet, they pushed troops across several ill-defined frontiers into areas claimed by India. Of much more serious concern to the United States, they backed a Communist penetration deep into Laos, one of the nations of Indo-China.

In the involved and unending struggle with Communist China, the American arsenal of atomic weapons was of relatively little effect even against a nation which as yet did not possess any. Against Russia, with its rapidly expanding nuclear strength, the threat of massive thermonuclear retaliation was still less effective.

Our German Ally

Fortunately, the United States and its allies did not depend upon nuclear superiority alone. The concept of the North Atlantic Treaty Organization was embodied in its emblem of a sword and a shield. The sword stood for atomic weapons, the striking force, and the shield for conventional ground forces, to deter or withstand attack. During the Korean War the United States began to rebuild its military establishment at home and gradually to pour funds into NATO, to strengthen its defenses in terms of ground forces as well as atomic weapons.

Europeans worried over the slowness of the United States to provide arms and men, its failure (partly because of constitutional limitations) to commit itself clearly in advance to resist any armed attack on western European nations, and its desire to rearm Germany.

While the French were still afraid of the Germans, the Germans themselves were so war-weary that it was difficult to persuade them to arm again. Between 1950 and 1954 they were able to win back step by step almost all their sovereignty in return for rearming. During these years the vexing problem was how the new western European defense force would be constituted. The French proposed a European Defense Community consisting of France, Italy, the Benelux countries (Belgium, The Netherlands, and Luxemburg) and West Germany. It would build a supranational army in which no division would have more than 12,000 men from the same country. It would be under the NATO supreme command. This fragmentation of national forces would circumvent the building of a large German army. But the United States and Germany favored larger national army units, and succeeded in obtaining a provision that integration would be at the level of army corps made up of several divisions. The specter of a resurgent German army led the French Communist deputies and the right wing nationalists in the French Assembly to unite in August, 1954, to defeat ratification of the European Defense Community treaty.

Some new way had to be found to make the rearming of Germany acceptable to France. Great Britain in October, 1954, placated the French by promising to keep four divisions and a tactical air force on the Continent as long as its allies wanted them. With this reassurance, France agreed to a treaty that same month restoring full sovereignty to Germany (except for the stationing of allied troops in West Berlin until Germany was reunified). To take the place of the European Defense Community a weak and limited treaty organization, created earlier, was expanded and strengthened into the Western European Union, including all the European Defense Community nations plus Great Britain. National armies were not to be scrambled as had been earlier planned, but the West German army was to be limited to twelve divisions, which would be supplied to NATO. Germany promised not to seek reunification or extension of her boundaries through force, and was prohibited from manufacturing atomic, biological, or chemical weapons. Germany joined NATO and thus directly became a military ally of the United States. In 1957 it contributed its first forces, five divisions totaling 120,000 men.

The Summit Conference, 1955

After the death of Stalin in 1953, there were increasing signs that new policies were developing in the Kremlin which might lead to more freedom behind the Iron Curtain and some relaxation of tensions with the Western powers. Russia extended an olive branch to Tito of Yugoslavia, returned a key base to Finland, recognized the Federal Republic of West Germany, and signed a peace treaty with Japan. Above all, it joined with Western powers in signing a peace treaty with Austria, making it a neutral state, and terminating the long military occupation.

The softening of Soviet policy and the increase in international exchanges brought pressure from western Europe, Asia, and even within the United States for a conference among the heads of state—a "summit conference" to consider means of easing international tensions. But the greatest single motive for such a meeting was the knowledge that both the United States and Russia were manufacturing hydrogen bombs of staggering destructive power.

In August, 1953, the Russians had set off a hydrogen explosive. President Ei-

senhower warned a few weeks later that the physical security of the United States had "almost totally disappeared before the long-range bomber and the destructive power of a single bomb." The meaning of this became dramatically clear in the spring of 1954 when the United States announced that it had exploded in the Pacific a bomb powerful enough to destroy or put out of commission all of New York City.

Against this background, the American people, after an initial wariness, became enthusiastic about the meeting of the heads of the United States, Great Britain, France, and Russia at Geneva in July, 1955. President Eisenhower, hopeful that he could wage "a war for peace," proposed at the meetings that the Russians and the United States exchange blueprints of their armed forces and permit inspection of their military installations from the air. He declared to Premier Nicolai A. Bulganin, "The United States will never take part in an aggressive war." Bulganin replied, "Mr. President, we believe that statement."

The affability of the Russians at Geneva immensely relieved the American people, who were hopeful for the moment that a real change of policy had come about. This "Geneva spirit," as newspapermen called it, led to a general feeling on the part of most Western nations that a nuclear war between Russia and the United States would not develop. Secretary Dulles declared that the conference had avoided "creating an illusion that all was now so well that we could safely relax our efforts to build individual and collective self-defense." All proposals from both sides had been referred to a foreign ministers' conference that met at the end of October, 1955; even before it met, several nations began to scale down their NATO contributions.

President Eisenhower upon his return from Geneva warned, "We must never be deluded into believing that one week of friendly, even fruitful negotiations can wholly eliminate a problem arising out of the wide gulf that separates East and West." The American public, less inclined to caution, greeted the President with unrestrained acclaim.

The subsequent foreign ministers' conference failed dismally to agree upon German unification, disarmament, or lowering of trade barriers. Even before it adjourned, the "Geneva spirit" rapidly evaporated throughout the West.

Menace in the Middle East

Soon a new Russian drive was launched toward the Middle East, where the United States had long been deeply involved because of its conflicting interests in the populace of the new state of Israel, and in the oil of the Arabs.

During World War II, the British, in order not to offend the Arabs, had continued restrictions upon immigration to Palestine; both political parties in the United States favored lifting these restrictions and creating a Jewish state. After the war, the British brought the problem to the United Nations, which recommended partitioning Palestine between Jews and Arabs. The Jews successfully fought off military attacks from the Arabs, and on the day the British mandate ended, May 14, 1948, proclaimed a new government. President Truman recognized it within a few minutes, thus ending United Nations proposals to put Palestine under a temporary trusteeship. The new nation, Israel, fought off armies from surrounding Arab nations until the United Nations established an unstable truce in 1949. Although the United States tried to promote amity, relations between Israel and its neighbors continued close to the point of explosion, and other quarrels in the Middle East persisted.

Gradually the United States won over some of the Arab nations to the Western defense system. This country leased air bases from Saudi Arabia; and through the Baghdad Pact of February, 1955, Secretary Dulles managed to bring the northern bloc of Arab states, Iraq, Iran, and Pakistan, into the defense arrangement.

Dulles's diplomacy was less successful with Egypt, which for years had quarreled with the British over the Sudan and British bases along the Suez Canal. The United States tried to mediate; in 1954 the British agreed to remove their troops from the Suez area. After Gamal Abdel Nasser came to power, the State Department tried to woo him, although he proclaimed emphatic neutralist and Arab nationalist policies, and strove for leadership of the entire Arab world. Secretary Dulles tried to win him with offers of economic aid—even the sum needed to construct an enormous dam on the Nile. The Russians offered aid also, and, to the dismay of Western people filled with the "Geneva spirit," won. Russia concluded a deal, made public in September, 1955, trading large quantities of armaments in exchange for cotton.

With sufficient Communist arms, Nasser might destroy Israel. He could also threaten the security system the United States was trying to build in the Middle East, since with the arms that went to Nassar and his close ally, Syria, would also go Russian experts to show Egyptians how to use them. Secretary Dulles met the challenge. Instead of continuing to be conciliatory toward Egypt, in July, 1956, he suddenly withdrew his promise to provide funds for a dam. A week later, Nasser retaliated by seizing the Suez Canal, purportedly to obtain money for the dam. This action gave him a stranglehold on the main oil line to Europe, since two thirds of the proven oil reserves of the world were in the Middle East, and four fifths of the oil for western Europe was flowing from there.

During the tedious months of negotiations with Nasser which followed, Great Britain, France, and Israel all came to feel that they were not obtaining as much support as they should from the United States. Meanwhile, the armed strength of Egypt was growing rapidly. On October 29, 1956, Israeli forces struck a preventive blow at Egypt; the next day the British and French intervened to drive the Egyptian forces from the Suez Canal zone. They were militarily successful, but not before the Egyptians had thoroughly blocked the canal. The United States led the United Nations in denouncing the military intervention; the Western alliances seemed in danger of dissolving; Russia threatened to send "volunteers" to the aid of Egypt. Under these pressures, the British and French issued a cease-fire order on November 6. Another prolonged truce between Egypt and Israel began under the supervision of the United Nations.

The power vacuum in the Middle East in the weeks after the Suez cease-fire created new opportunities for the spread of Communism. Once again the American public was alarmed and incensed, since coincident with the Suez crisis came brutal Soviet suppression of an uprising in Hungary. Because of the nuclear stalemate, the United States could not intervene in Hungary. It limited itself to fostering United Nations resolutions of censure and to admitting tens of thousands of refugees.

In the Middle East more positive action afterward seemed possible. The public was receptive when the President appeared before Congress January 5, 1957, to enunciate what came to be called the "Eisenhower Doctrine." He asked Congress to authorize military and economic aid "to secure and protect the territorial independence" of Middle Eastern nations "against overt armed aggression from any nation controlled by international communism." Congress authorized the President to use armed force as he deemed necessary, and to spend $200 million (without the restrictions of the Mutual Security Act) on economic aid in the area.

As an instrument of pressure upon Egypt, the Eisenhower Doctrine was of little effect. Nasser reopened the Suez Canal on his own terms, and with Soviet aid continued penetration of his neighbors. In April, 1957, American policy seemed more successful when the United States rushed its Sixth Fleet to the eastern Mediterranean to bolster the government of Jordan. Three other states, Saudi Arabia, Iraq, and Lebanon, seemed to give at least tacit support to the Eisenhower Doctrine.

Soviet penetration in the next few months, both through feeding Arab nationalism and through providing arms to Egypt, Syria, and Yemen, effectively countered the American policy. In August, 1957, the Russians negotiated a $500 million arms-and-aid pact with Syria. In its aftermath, a pro-Soviet army clique seized power. Since the clique of course did not ask for American aid, the Eisenhower Doctrine was inoperative in Syria, but the State Department, declaring that Syria's neighbors were alarmed, sent them weapons. The strong tone of the United States led to an unfavorable reaction among the Arab nations, and they reaffirmed their solidarity.

Egypt and Syria, combining to form the United Arab Republic, continued to exert pressure on their neighbors. When in July, 1958, a pro-Nasser clique took over Iraq, it appeared that Lebanon and Jordan might also come under Nasser's domination. The pro-Western government of Lebanon requested aid against rebels, and the United States rushed in troops. At the same time Great Britain sent forces into Jordan. In the fall of 1958, when conditions became stabilized in Lebanon, the United States withdrew its troops. Iraq continued to be a serious problem. Secretary Dulles, in order to balance its loss from the Baghdad Pact mutual defense organization, announced that the United States would assume full partnership in the alliance. But the withdrawal of Iraq from the alliance did

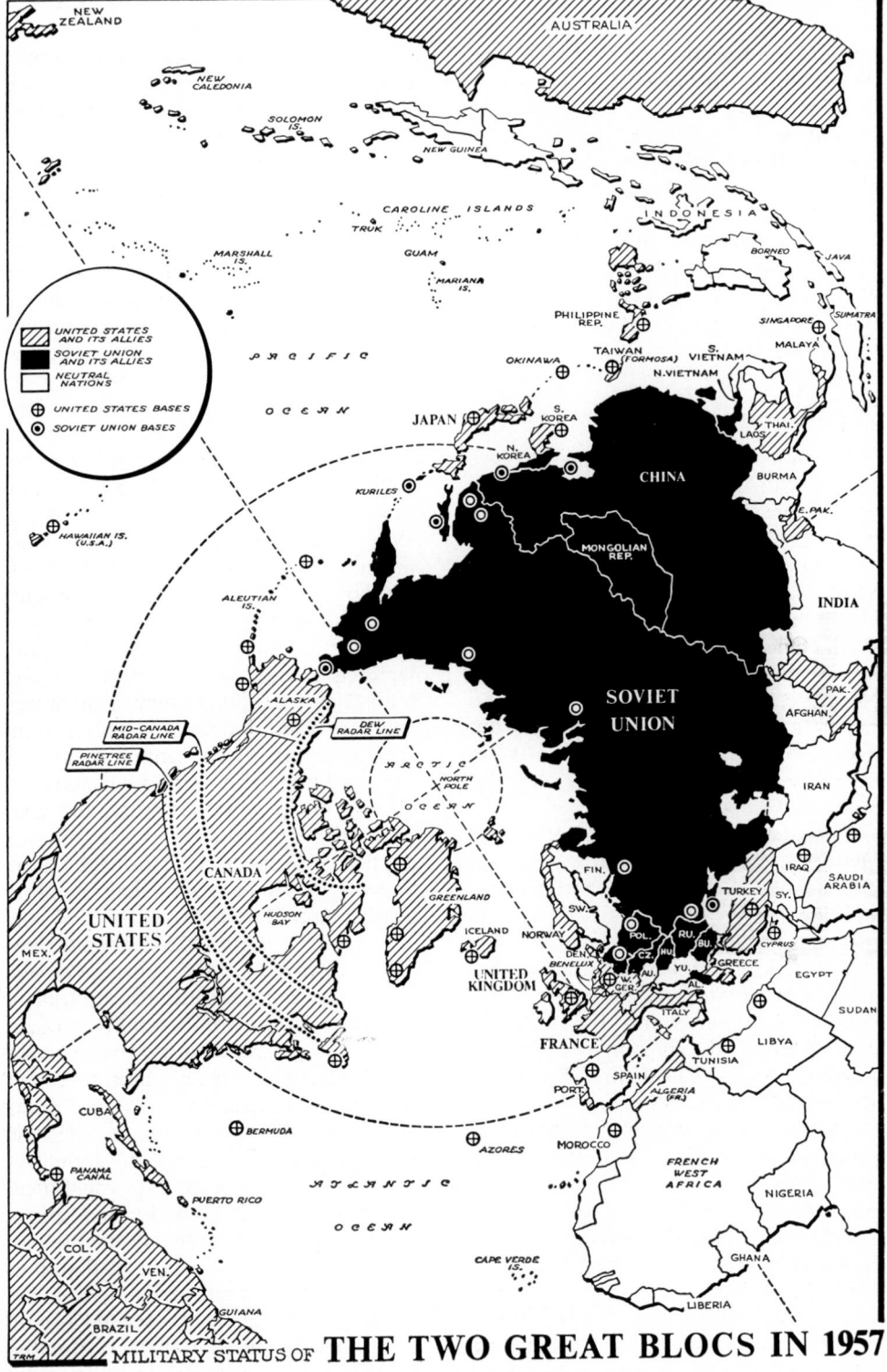

MILITARY STATUS OF **THE TWO GREAT BLOCS IN 1957**

not lead the country into Nasser's United Arab Republic as expected. The elements favoring this course soon fell from power in Iraq, and the danger in 1959 and after seemed to be that the country would swing into the Communist bloc. Reacting against the Communist trend in Iraq, Nasser veered back more toward the West, and the United States began again plying him with favors. Conditions were thus unstable and uncertain in much of the Middle East.

The Disgruntled Neighbors

The incessant threats against areas close to the Communist perimeter so occupied the American government and people that they paid scant attention to an area of vital worth to the United Sates and of growing vulnerability to Communist influence, the nations to the south. One of the minor ironies of this hectic age was the erosion of the Good Neighbor feeling between Latin American nations and the United States during the very years when this country was extending much of the Good Neighbor policy to Europe and Asia.

On paper there was no deterioration. Quite the contrary; the Latin American nations signed new pacts and received additional forms of aid. They all became members of the United Nations. In 1947, at a conference at Rio de Janeiro, they drafted an Inter-American Treaty of Reciprocal Assistance, and the following year established an Organization of American States. The United States had abandoned the old unilateral Monroe Doctrine by entering into pacts and organizations providing for mutual action whether in defense, settlement of disputes, or economic cooperation.

Yet the overwhelming military and economic power of the "colossus of the North" remained. Latin Americans were not pleased when the United States brought its prestige to bear against the totalitarian dictator of Argentina,

Juan D. Perón, in 1946-7, even though the pressure failed. They were not much more pleased when the United States successfully brought pressure against a pro-Communist regime in Guatemala in 1954. But in the late fifties, when many of the nations overthrew dictators, the more common complaint was that the United States had been too friendly toward despots, as in Venezuela, and not enthusiastic enough about rebels like Fidel Castro, who came into power in Cuba in 1959, and who thereafter devoted himself to denunciations of "Yankee imperialism."

Above all, the problems from which Latin American peoples were suffering were economic. After the close of World War II, they could no longer sell raw materials from their farms and mines to the United States in such large quantities or at such favorable prices as before. The soaring costs of the American manufactured goods they imported further hurt them. At home they were undergoing a rapid industrial revolution, an accompanying social evolution, and an explosive population increase at the highest rate in the world, as much as 2.5 per cent per year. Already their combined population had passed that of the United States. All these factors helped create acute internal problems.

Inevitably the United States would have to be involved in the solution of economic questions because the hostility of neighbors to the south would be potentially ruinous, and because the two areas had become increasingly interdependent economically. Trade with Latin America exceeded eight billion dollars a year by the end of the fifties, and accounted for a third of the imports and a quarter of the exports of the United States. Eighty per cent of the foreign capital in Latin America was American; it had a book value of about nine and a half billion dollars. (This figure was second only to the thirteen billion dollars invested in Canada, which was also unhappy about its economic relations with the United States.)

It seemed to Latin Americans that, despite these close economic ties, the United States was doing little specific to help them solve their problems—to provide adequate capital for large-scale development, to stabilize raw materials at a profitable level, and to conquer inflation. They felt neglected as the American government poured billions into Europe and Asia while giving Latin America only a comparative pittance. Secretary Dulles was occupied elsewhere, and the Eisenhower administration, under the influence of two successive conservative Secretaries of the Treasury, was cold to requests for government loans for development. The festering economic ills and other grievances which could easily be focused against the United States were ready-made for the Communists. Exercising an influence out of proportion to their small numbers, they were active from Cuba to Guatemala and Argentina.

Despite riots and disorders, the Latin American discontent received little notice in the United States until May, 1958, when Vice President Nixon was mobbed in Lima and Caracas. In the aftermath of the national shock, the State Department speeded changes in policy which were already slowly under way. This country helped Latin American nations negotiate export quota pacts among themselves to raise the price of coffee and some metals, and it expedited negotiations toward the establishment of a regional common market among the republics. When in June, 1958, the President of Brazil called for an Operation Pan-America to speed economic development, the American government agreed to furnish nearly half the capital for a new billion-dollar Inter-American Bank to make development loans. It also tried to improve public relations in a way Nixon had suggested by giving no more than a correct handshake to dictators but offering a warm embrace to democratic leaders.

The administration was increasing its attention to Latin America none too soon, since it was obvious that the well-disciplined, widely pervasive Communist activities throughout the area were receiving direction from Russia. Latin American Communist leaders returned early in 1959 from attending the twenty-first party congress in Moscow to begin the systematic denunciation of the new program of the United States. Before long the Russians concluded a trade pact with the Castro government of Cuba, and in 1960 Castro invited the Russian prime minister for a visit. So far as the United States was concerned, the long arm of international Communism seemed to be reaching uncomfortably close to home.

The Rocket Race

What made the onslaught of Communist ideology and power especially frightening was the seeming failure of the United States to keep pace with the Soviet Union in the development of intercontinental ballistic missiles, a weakness which Russia tried to exploit throughout the world. In early 1957 the United States appeared to be abreast or ahead of Soviet Russia in the development of guided missiles with nuclear warheads. Because of the potential horror of these weapons, both nations seemed ready to reach disarmament agreements during seven months of discussions in 1957 at a meeting of the United Nations subcommittee in London. Both sides apparently wanted to stop experiments with nuclear weapons, establish controls over them, cut conventional armaments, and regulate long-range missiles and satellites. Then trouble ensued. As an integral part of any disarmament plan, the United States and the West insisted upon schemes of strict inspection, including proposals for aerial photography over strips of each other's territory. To this the Soviet Union would not agree. By the fall, the optimism of spring had changed to a melancholy recognition that because of rapid Russian advances in weapons development, the world was reaching what the *New York Times* called a "balance of terror."

Through the summer of 1957 American experts had complacently held that the United States was ahead of Russia in missile development. Then, in August, Russia announced that she had successfully tested an intercontinental ballistic missile. In contrast, the United States had successfully tested only intermediate-range missiles that had traveled from 1,500 to 3,000 miles. The Russian claims received sobering confirmation in October when Soviet scientists, using a rocket booster engine more powerful than any yet developed in the United States, launched the first successful satellite, the "sputnik."

In the weeks following the launching of the satellite, Nikita S. Khrushchev, who in a series of bold moves had just consolidated his power in the Kremlin, issued a series of strong statements. The intent of his "sputnik diplomacy" was clearly to shake the Western alliance and impress neutral nations. The reaction within the United States, especially when the first American attempt to launch a much smaller satellite failed, was more one of angry fear than of congratulations to the Russian scientists. Three months later the United States began launching its own, smaller satellites. Moves began to overhaul the teaching of science and to provide greater financial support for basic scientific research. The public insisted, and the President agreed, that dis-

sensions and interservice rivalries in the Department of Defense must come to an end. Congress in 1958 debated a measure to overhaul the defense organization.

As an indication of his concern, President Eisenhower, although he was just recuperating from a mild stroke, flew to Paris in December 1957 to lend strong moral support at a NATO conference. In January, 1958, he devoted almost the entirety of his annual message to Congress to the armaments crisis and to the need to surpass Russia in providing aid for underdeveloped countries. He called upon an acquiescent Congress for heavy additional expenditures to rush development and construction of long-range missiles and of submarines and cruisers that could launch missiles. The first task confronting the nation was "to ensure our safety through strength," he pointed out, "But we could make no more tragic mistake than merely to concentrate on military strength. For if we did only this, the future would hold nothing for the world but an age of terror."

As a means of ameliorating the tension, lengthy negotiations went on with Russia over arrangements for another summit conference. In December, 1957, Soviet Premier Bulganin asked for a meeting to sign a nonaggression pact between the two power blocs, prohibit nuclear tests and the use of nuclear weapons, and establish a zone in Central Europe in which production of nuclear weapons and stockpiles would be banned. In ensuing correspondence, the Russians insisted upon a meeting upon terms favorable to them; the Americans insisted upon American terms. There seemed to be little common ground.

Meanwhile, extensive nuclear testing

LAUNCHING THE FIRST AMERICAN SATELLITE. [OPPOSITE] On January 31, 1958, four months after the Russians launched the first satellite—three months after they sent up one so big that it contained a dog—the United States, using a Jupiter-C launching vehicle, put into orbit the first American satellite, called Explorer I. It was 80 inches long, 6 inches in diameter, and weighed 30.8 pounds. In it were devices for measuring temperature, cosmic rays, and the frequency of meteorite particles, and radios for transmitting the measurements. (U.S. ARMY PHOTOGRAPH)

after 1954 by both the United States and Russia, climaxed by the Russian explosion of several "dirty" bombs, greatly increased the fallout of radioactive isotopes. Even though as yet exposure of populations was relatively slight compared to the radiation to which human beings were normally exposed, throughout the world there was a fear of the harmful effects from radioactive fallout. "Any dose, however small, produces some biological effect and . . . this effect is harmful," the Joint Congressional Committee on Atomic Energy granted in a 1959 report. If testing were to continue at the same rate as that of the previous five years over the next two generations, the report warned, the predicted average concentration of radioactive strontium in bone would be close to what scientists had estimated would be the maximum permissible body burden. This threat, well before 1959, was bringing popular pressure for the curtailing of nuclear tests.

In the spring of 1958, Khrushchev announced a unilateral suspension of nuclear tests in Russia. This left Eisenhower faced with the choice of two courses: He could follow the reasoning of most officials in the Defense Department who held that nuclear weapons were the only way in which the United States could counter the enormous land armies of Russia and China—and continue tests. Or he could promise to stop tests provided Russia would agree to adequate inspection, and perhaps an end to production of nuclear components of weapons.

He decided upon the latter course, and announced that the United States and its allies would suspend tests for one year beginning October 31, 1958. The suspension would continue on a year-to-year basis, provided a proper system of control could be developed and substantial progress could be made on disarmament negotiations. Russia, proclaiming that this was a Western trick, announced that it would resume testing. Neverthe-

less, President Eisenhower declared that the United States for the time being would continue its suspension of tests as it sought some workable agreement with the Soviet Union. Representatives of the United States, Great Britain, and Russia met in Geneva and slowly, laboriously, tried to construct a regulatory treaty.

In 1959 Khrushchev made much propaganda use of the failure of the United States to catch up with Russia in astronautical feats. "You send up oranges while we send up tons," he characteristically boasted, calling attention to the difference in the sizes of warheads that could be mounted on Soviet rockets and American ones. Actually, the missiles gap between the two nations was not as great as had been feared two years earlier. Russia was, as its shots into outer space continued to prove, well ahead in rocketry, but apparently the number of intercontinental ballistic missiles it possessed was not large enough to destroy the growing retaliatory arsenal of American missiles. The United States was successfully producing and testing its own missiles, and developing plans for hiding and spreading the launching sites so that it would require ten times as many Russian missiles to destroy them. The success of the Navy in constructing atomic-powered submarines which could launch missiles, and in bringing the submarines up through the ice at the North Pole, was a dramatic example of American achievement. The naval development of "Project Tepee," a radio-monitoring system which could detect any missile launchings anywhere in the world, was an indication of the technical advance of American defense.

If the Russians were to attack the United States they could not expect their own cities to remain unscathed. The reverse held equally true, that American nuclear power would be incapable of destroying all the sites from which the Russians could launch missiles. An attack upon the United States, if it came, the

Congressional Joint Committee on Atomic Energy reported in August, 1959, might kill fifty million people, seriously injure twenty million more, and destroy or render unusable for months half of the dwellings in the country. Crops would be contaminated and swept by fire. The only hopeful note was that bomb shelters for the entire population could reduce casualties by 25 or 30 per cent.

Top-Level Diplomacy

Suddenly, in November, 1958, Khrushchev precipitated a new crisis over Berlin, where the West's position was, as always, vulnerable. He asserted that conditions had changed so markedly in Berlin since the end of the war that the occupation agreements no longer applied. In six months he proposed to sign a separate peace treaty with the government of East Germany, turning over to it all the Russian occupation functions in Berlin including control over the access routes stretching 110 miles to West Germany.

The United States insisted that its treaty rights still held, and undertook the twofold task of trying to maintain unity regarding Berlin among its Western allies, and of insisting upon concessions from the Soviet government corresponding to any it might make. Neither task was easy. Russia made alternate proposals as unacceptable as the first demand had been, and Khrushchev manipulated the issue to try to force a summit meeting. The United States was not willing to go further than a foreign ministers' meeting unless the Russians became more conciliatory; but the Geneva sessions beginning in May, 1959, were discouragingly unfruitful.

Meanwhile, the burden of conducting American foreign policy had shifted to a new Secretary of State, Christian Herter, when Dulles, dying of cancer, resigned in April, 1959. Herter was a strong successor. He had capped his foreign service record as a young man with a successful career in politics. But he by no means perpetuated the one-man determination of foreign policy that had distinguished Dulles. President Eisenhower seemed to assume a larger measure of responsibility, and this also pointed toward new interchanges at the top with the Russians.

SECRETARY DULLES ON UNITED STATES FOREIGN POLICY

"I think that our foreign policy must constantly be adapted to new and changing situations. It is nothing new that there are trouble spots in the world. . . . I have constantly said that we need to keep our foreign policy flexible and adaptable to changing situations. But I do not believe that there is anything basically different that we can do. . . .

"If there are differences in the free world this is nothing that should surprise us. We need to take them into account, particularly when fomented by hostile forces, and we should do so. But I do not think it calls for any basic change in the American policies which are based upon our own traditions and our own faith as to how we conduct our affairs with the other countries of the world."—Statement at a news conference, May 20, 1958.

Exchanges at lower levels had been going on at an increasing rate since the Geneva thaw of 1955. One of its few positive effects had been personal and cultural interchanges of musicians, dancers, students, and delegations of all kinds, climaxed in the summer of 1959 by a visit to the United States of Anastas Mikoyan, a Soviet deputy premier, and to Russia of Vice President Nixon. The Russians demonstrated their wares at a fair in New York City, and the Americans at a corresponding fair in Moscow showed crowds of Russians the components of the high standard of living in the United States. While Nixon was at the fair, he engaged in informal debate with Khrushchev. The Russian press was for the most part hostile, but the crowds were friendly, and Khrushchev himself, while holding dogmatically to Soviet positions, seemed to demonstrate a keen interest in things American.

In August, 1959, President Eisenhower announced he would exchange visits with the Russian leader. The purpose in inviting Khrushchev, Eisenhower explained, was "to give him the opportunity to see what Americans are like" and "to give him, face to face, the basic convictions of our people on the major issues of the day." Khrushchev, during his travels in the United States, received on the whole a hearty welcome, despite the coldness of most American officials and the hostile demonstrations of certain groups, especially those sympathizing with the Hungarian rebels of 1956. He impressed Americans with his energy, toughness, and—except for a few petulant outbursts—good humor. Eisenhower, postponing his return visit, made tours of Western Europe, Southern Asia, and Latin America, to the cheers of enthusiastic crowds at almost every stop.

A second "summit" conference, to meet in Paris, was scheduled for May, 1960. On May 1 an unarmed American "U-2" plane was downed inside the Soviet Union. The American government at first denied, then acknowledged and attempted to justify, the fact that the plane had been engaged in aerial reconnaissance of a kind the United States had been carrying on, systematically but secretly, for some time. At the Paris meeting, unsatisfied by Eisenhower's belated promise to discontinue flights over Russian territory, Khrushchev made the U-2 incident an occasion for denouncing Eisenhower and breaking up the conference.

Khrushchev also took back his invitation for Eisenhower to go to the Soviet Union. Eisenhower, having planned to stop in Japan on the way home from Russia, went ahead with arrangements for a Far Eastern trip, in June. A new security pact, authorizing continued American bases in Japan, awaited ratification. Communist agitators now played upon the pacifism of the Japanese people, a pacifism which American occupation policies earlier had stimulated. In Tokyo, mobs began wild demonstrations against the pact, against Premier Nobusuke Kishi, who sponsored it, and against the Eisenhower visit. At the last minute, after the President had got as far as Manila, his Japan appearance was called off. The Kishi government managed to put the unpopular treaty into effect, but the Eisenhower administration could scarcely avoid a serious loss, throughout the world, to American prestige, which already had been weakened by the administration's handling of the spy-plane affair.

Dilemmas of the 1960's

For the American government and people, a whole series of dilemmas remained to be faced in the decade of the sixties.

How, for instance, could we get along with colonial powers like France, which was desperately trying to put down a revolt of Arabs in Algeria, and at the same time build friendship with newly independent peoples like the Arabs of Tunisia and Morocco? How could we maintain friendly relations with both Israel and the United Arab Republic, deadly foes of one another that these two were? How could we, in view of anti-American movements in Cuba and Panama, protect our interests in the Panama Canal and its approaches without jeopardizing the friendship of our Good Neighbors elsewhere in Latin America? How could we reconcile the need for economic aid abroad with the demands for tax reduction at home? How could we gain the support of the "uncommitted" nations of Asia and Africa—nations of colored peoples—while discriminating against colored people in our own country? How could we insure the freedom of outposts such as Taiwan and West Berlin without the horrors of a thermonuclear war? How could we meet the Communist danger in all its forms and still preserve our traditional rights and liberties as a democracy?

The dilemmas of the sixties were more difficult to solve, and yet more demanding of solutions, than any the American people had ever been called upon to face. Still, the entire history of the United States had been largely a story of dilemmas met and more or less successfully disposed of. The past gave reason for hope rather than despair.

BIBLIOGRAPHY

For a fairly comprehensive general treatment, see Jules Davids, *America and the World of Our Time: U.S. Diplomacy in the Twentieth Century* (1960). Aspects of the subject are discussed from different points of view in W. A. Williams, *The Tragedy of American Diplomacy* (1959); T. K. Finletter, *Foreign Policy: The Next Phase* (1958); Alexander DeConde (ed.), *Isolation and Security* (1957); Norman Graebner, *The New Isolationism* (1956); H. L. Roberts, *Russia and America: Dangers and Prospects* (1956); and Walter Millis, *Arms and Men* (1956). A good brief analysis is W. G. Carleton, *The Revolution in American Foreign Policy* (rev. ed., 1957). See also L. J. Halle, *Dream and Reality: Aspects of American Foreign Policy* (1959); Dean Acheson, *Power and Diplomacy* (1958); C. W. Mills, *The Causes of World War Three* (1958); and Drew Pearson and Jack Anderson, *U.S.A.—Second-Class Power?* (1958).

On the Dulles diplomacy, see J. F. Dulles, *War or Peace* (1950), and J. R. Beal, *John Foster Dulles* (1957). On the effects of nuclear explosives, see H. A. Kissinger, *Nuclear Weapons and Foreign Policy* (1957), and T. K. Finletter, *U.S. Foreign Policy and Military Power in the Hydrogen Age* (1954).

Among the important area studies are the following: E. O. Reischauer, *Wanted: An Asian Policy* (1955); Geraldine Fitch, *Formosa Beachhead* (1953); R. H. Fifield, *The Diplomacy of Southeast Asia, 1945–1958* (1958); J. C. Campbell, *Defense of the Middle East* (1958); H. B. Ellis, *Israel and the Middle East* (1957); F. E. Manuel, *Realities of American-Palestine Relations* (1949); E. A. Speiser, *The United States and the Near East* (1949); L. V. Thomas and R. N. Frye, *The United States and Turkey and Iran* (1951); and B. T. Moore, *NATO and the Future of Europe* (1958).

APPENDICES

THE

DECLARATION OF INDEPENDENCE

In Congress, July 4, 1776,

THE UNANIMOUS DECLARATION OF THE THIRTEEN UNITED STATES OF AMERICA

When, in the course of human events, it becomes necessary for one people to dissolve the political bands which have connected them with another, and to assume, among the powers of the earth, the separate and equal station to which the laws of nature and of nature's God entitle them, a decent respect to the opinions of mankind requires that they should declare the causes which impel them to the separation.

We hold these truths to be self-evident, that all men are created equal; that they are endowed by their Creator with certain unalienable rights; that among these, are life, liberty, and the pursuit of happiness. That, to secure these rights, governments are instituted among men, deriving their just powers from the consent of the governed; that, whenever any form of government becomes destructive of these ends, it is the right of the people to alter or to abolish it, and to institute a new government, laying its foundation on such principles, and organizing its powers in such form, as to them shall seem most likely to effect their safety and happiness. Prudence, indeed, will dictate that governments long established, should not be changed for light and transient causes; and, accordingly, all experience hath shown, that mankind are more disposed to suffer, while evils are sufferable, than to right themselves by abolishing the forms to which they are accustomed. But, when a long train of abuses and usurpations, pursuing invariably the same object, evinces a design to reduce them under absolute despotism, it is their right, it is their duty, to throw off such government and to provide new guards for their future security. Such has been the patient sufferance of these colonies, and such is now the necessity which constrains them to alter their former systems of government. The history of the present King of Great Britain is a history of repeated injuries and usurpations, all having, in direct object, the establishment of an absolute tyranny over these States. To prove this, let facts be submitted to a candid world:—

He has refused his assent to laws the most wholesome and necessary for the public good.

He has forbidden his governors to pass laws of immediate and pressing importance, unless suspended in their operation till his assent should be obtained;

and, when so suspended, he has utterly neglected to attend to them.

He has refused to pass other laws for the accommodation of large districts of people, unless those people would relinquish the right of representation in the legislature; a right inestimable to them, and formidable to tyrants only.

He has called together legislative bodies at places unusual, uncomfortable, and distant from the depository of their public records, for the sole purpose of fatiguing them into compliance with his measures.

He has dissolved representative houses repeatedly for opposing, with manly firmness, his invasions on the rights of the people.

He has refused, for a long time after such dissolutions, to cause others to be elected; whereby the legislative powers, incapable of annihilation, have returned to the people at large for their exercise; the state remaining, in the meantime, exposed to all the danger of invasion from without, and convulsions within.

He has endeavored to prevent the population of these States; for that purpose, obstructing the laws for naturalization of foreigners, refusing to pass others to encourage their migration hither, and raising the conditions of new appropriations of lands.

He has obstructed the administration of justice, by refusing his assent to laws for establishing judiciary powers.

He has made judges dependent on his will alone, for the tenure of their offices, and the amount and payment of their salaries.

He has erected a multitude of new offices, and sent hither swarms of officers to harass our people, and eat out their substance.

He has kept among us, in time of peace, standing armies, without the consent of our legislatures.

He has affected to render the military independent of, and superior to, the civil power.

He has combined, with others, to subject us to a jurisdiction foreign to our Constitution, and unacknowledged by our laws; giving his assent to their acts of pretended legislation:

For quartering large bodies of armed troops among us:

For protecting them by a mock trial, from punishment, for any murders which they should commit on the inhabitants of these States:

For cutting off our trade with all parts of the world:

For imposing taxes on us without our consent:

For depriving us, in many cases, of the benefit of trial by jury:

For transporting us beyond seas to be tried for pretended offenses:

For abolishing the free system of English laws in a neighboring province, establishing therein an arbitrary government, and enlarging its boundaries, so as to render it at once an example and fit instrument for introducing the same absolute rule into these colonies:

For taking away our charters, abolishing our most valuable laws, and altering, fundamentally, the powers of our governments:

For suspending our own legislatures, and declaring themselves invested with power to legislate for us in all cases whatsoever.

He has abdicated government here, by declaring us out of his protection, and waging war against us.

He has plundered our seas, ravaged our coasts, burnt our towns, and destroyed the lives of our people.

He is, at this time, transporting large armies of foreign mercenaries to complete the works of death, desolation, and tyranny, already begun, with circumstances of cruelty and perfidy scarcely paralleled in the most barbarous ages, and totally unworthy the head of a civilized nation.

He has constrained our fellow citizens, taken captive on the high seas, to bear arms against their country, to become the executioners of their friends, and brethren, or to fall themselves by their hands.

He has excited domestic insurrections amongst us, and has endeavored to bring on the inhabitants of our frontiers, the merciless Indian savages, whose known rule of warfare is an undistinguished destruction of all ages, sexes, and conditions.

In every stage of these oppressions, we have petitioned for redress, in the most humble terms; our repeated petitions have been answered only by repeated injury. A prince, whose character is thus marked by every act which may define a tyrant, is unfit to be the ruler of a free people.

Nor have we been wanting in attention to our British brethren. We have warned them, from time to time, of attempts made by their legislature to extend an unwarrantable jurisdiction over us. We have reminded them of the circumstances of our emigration and settlement here. We have appealed to their native justice and magnanimity, and we have conjured them, by the ties of our common kindred, to disavow these usurpations, which would inevitably interrupt our connections and correspondence. They, too, have been deaf to the voice of justice and consanguinity. We must, therefore, acquiesce in the necessity which denounces our separation, and hold them, as we hold the rest of mankind, enemies in war, in peace, friends.

We, therefore, the representatives of the United States of America, in general Congress assembled, appealing to the Supreme Judge of the world for the rectitude of our intentions, do, in the name, and by the authority of the good people of these colonies, solemnly publish and declare, that these united colonies are, and of right ought to be, free and independent states: that they are absolved from all allegiance to the British Crown, and that all political connection between them and the state of Great Britain is, and ought to be, totally dissolved; and that, as free and independent states, they have full power to levy war, conclude peace, contract alliances, establish commerce, and to do all other acts and things which independent states may of right do. And, for the support of this declaration, with a firm reliance on the protection of Divine Providence, we mutually pledge to each other our lives, our fortunes, and our sacred honor.

The foregoing Declaration was, by order of Congress, engrossed, and signed by the following members:

John Hancock

NEW HAMPSHIRE
Josiah Bartlett
William Whipple
Matthew Thornton

MASSACHUSETTS BAY
Samuel Adams
John Adams
Robert Treat Paine
Elbridge Gerry

RHODE ISLAND
Stephen Hopkins
William Ellery

CONNECTICUT
Roger Sherman
Samuel Huntington
William Williams
Oliver Wolcott

NEW YORK
William Floyd
Philip Livingston
Francis Lewis
Lewis Morris

NEW JERSEY
Richard Stockton
John Witherspoon
Francis Hopkinson
John Hart
Abraham Clark

PENNSYLVANIA
Robert Morris
Benjamin Rush
Benjamin Franklin
John Morton
George Clymer
James Smith
George Taylor
James Wilson
George Ross

DELAWARE
Caesar Rodney
George Read
Thomas M'Kean

MARYLAND
Samuel Chase
William Paca
Thomas Stone
Charles Carroll,
    of Carrollton

VIRGINIA
George Wythe
Richard Henry Lee
Thomas Jefferson
Benjamin Harrison
Thomas Nelson, Jr.
Francis Lightfoot Lee
Carter Braxton

NORTH CAROLINA
William Hooper
Joseph Hewes
John Penn

SOUTH CAROLINA
Edward Rutledge
Thomas Heyward, Jr.
Thomas Lynch, Jr.
Arthur Middleton

GEORGIA
Button Gwinnett
Lyman Hall
George Walton

Resolved, That copies of the Declaration be sent to the several assemblies, conventions, and committees, or councils of safety, and to the several commanding officers of the continental troops; that it be proclaimed in each of the United States, at the head of the army.

THE CONSTITUTION OF THE
UNITED STATES OF AMERICA [1]

We the People of the United States, in Order to form a more perfect Union, establish Justice, insure domestic Tranquility, provide for the common defence, promote the general Welfare, and secure the Blessings of Liberty to ourselves and our Posterity, do ordain and establish this CONSTITUTION for the United States of America.

ARTICLE I

SECTION 1. All legislative Powers herein granted shall be vested in a Congress of the United States, which shall

[1] This version, which follows the original Constitution in capitalization and spelling, was published by the United States Department of the Interior, Office of Education, in 1935.

consist of a Senate and House of Representatives.

SECTION 2.   The House of Representatives shall be composed of Members chosen every second Year by the People of the several States, and the Electors in each State shall have the Qualifications requisite for Electors of the most numerous Branch of the State Legislature.

No Person shall be a Representative who shall not have attained to the Age of twenty-five Years, and been seven Years a Citizen of the United States, and who shall not, when elected, be an Inhabitant of that State in which he shall be chosen.

[Representatives and direct Taxes [2] shall be apportioned among the several States which may be included within this Union, according to their respective Numbers, which shall be determined by adding to the whole Number of free Persons, including those bound to Service for a Term of Years, and excluding Indians not taxed, three fifths of all other Persons.] [3] The actual Enumeration shall be made within three Years after the first Meeting of the Congress of the United States, and within every subsequent Term of ten Years, in such Manner as they shall by Law direct. The Number of Representatives shall not exceed one for every thirty Thousand, but each State shall have at Least one Representative; and until such enumeration shall be made, the State of New Hampshire shall be entitled to chuse three, Massachusetts eight, Rhode-Island and Providence Plantations one, Connecticut five, New York six, New Jersey four, Pennsylvania eight, Delaware one, Maryland six, Virginia ten, North Carolina five, South Carolina five, and Georgia three.

When vacancies happen in the Representation from any State, the Executive Authority thereof shall issue Writs of Election to fill such Vacancies.

[2] Altered by 16th Amendment.
[3] Negated by 14th Amendment.

The House of Representatives shall chuse their Speaker and other Officers; and shall have the sole Power of Impeachment.

SECTION 3.   The Senate of the United States shall be composed of two Senators from each State, chosen by the Legislature thereof, for six Years; and each Senator shall have one Vote.

Immediately after they shall be assembled in Consequence of the first Election, they shall be divided as equally as may be into three Classes. The Seats of the Senators of the first Class shall be vacated at the Expiration of the second Year, of the second Class at the Expiration of the fourth Year, and of the third Class at the Expiration of the sixth Year, so that one-third may be chosen every second Year; and if Vacancies happen by Resignation, or otherwise, during the Recess of the Legislature of any State, the Executive thereof may make temporary Appointments until the next Meeting of the Legislature, which shall then fill such Vacancies.

No Person shall be a Senator who shall not have attained to the Age of thirty Years, and been nine Years a Citizen of the United States, and who shall not, when elected, be an Inhabitant of that State for which he shall be chosen.

The Vice President of the United States shall be President of the Senate, but shall have no vote, unless they be equally divided.

The Senate shall chuse their other Officers, and also a President pro tempore, in the absence of the Vice President, or when he shall exercise the Office of President of the United States.

The Senate shall have the sole Power to try all Impeachments. When sitting for that purpose, they shall be on Oath or Affirmation. When the President of the United States is tried, the Chief Justice shall preside: And no person shall be convicted without the Concurrence of two thirds of the Members present.

Judgment in Cases of Impeachment

shall not extend further than to removal from Office, and disqualification to hold and enjoy any Office of honor, Trust, or Profit under the United States: but the Party convicted shall nevertheless be liable and subject to Indictment, Trial, Judgment, and Punishment, according to Law.

SECTION 4. The Times, Places and Manner of holding Elections for Senators and Representatives, shall be prescribed in each State by the Legislature thereof; but the Congress may at any time by Law make or alter such Regulations, except as to the Places of Chusing Senators.

The Congress shall assemble at least once in every Year, and such Meeting shall be on the first Monday in December, unless they shall by Law appoint a different Day.

SECTION 5. Each House shall be the Judge of the Elections, Returns and Qualifications of its own Members, and a Majority of each shall constitute a Quorum to do Business; but a smaller number may adjourn from day to day, and may be authorized to compel the Attendance of absent Members, in such Manner, and under such Penalties, as each House may provide.

Each House may determine the Rules of its Proceedings, punish its Members for disorderly Behavior, and, with the Concurrence of two thirds, expel a Member.

Each House shall keep a Journal of its Proceedings, and from time to time publish the same, excepting such Parts as may in their Judgment require Secrecy; and the Yeas and Nays of the Members of either House on any question shall, at the Desire of one fifth of those Present, be entered on the Journal.

Neither House, during the Session of Congress, shall, without the Consent of the other, adjourn for more than three days, nor to any other Place than that in which the two Houses shall be sitting.

SECTION 6. The Senators and Representatives shall receive a Compensation for their Services, to be ascertained by Law, and paid out of the Treasury of the United States. They shall in all Cases, except Treason, Felony, and Breach of the Peace, be privileged from Arrest during their Attendance at the Session of their respective Houses, and in going to and returning from the same; and for any Speech or Debate in either House, they shall not be questioned in any other Place.

No Senator or Representative shall, during the Time for which he was elected, be appointed to any civil Office under the Authority of the United States, which shall have been created, or the Emoluments whereof shall have been increased, during such time; and no Person holding any Office under the United States shall be a Member of either House during his continuance in Office.

SECTION 7. All Bills for raising Revenue shall originate in the House of Representatives; but the Senate may propose or concur with Amendments as on other bills.

Every Bill which shall have passed the House of Representatives and the Senate, shall, before it become a Law, be presented to the President of the United States; If he approve he shall sign it, but if not he shall return it, with his Objections, to that House in which it shall have originated, who shall enter the Objections at large on their Journal, and proceed to reconsider it. If after such Reconsideration two thirds of that House shall agree to pass the bill, it shall be sent, together with the objections, to the other House, by which it shall likewise be reconsidered, and if approved by two thirds of that House, it shall become a Law. But in all such Cases the Votes of both Houses shall be determined by Yeas and Nays, and the Names of the Persons voting for and against the Bill shall be entered on the Journal of each House respectively. If any Bill shall not be returned by the President within ten Days (Sundays excepted) after it shall have been presented to him, the Same shall be a Law, in like Manner as if he had signed it, unless the Congress by their Adjournment prevents its Return, in which Case it shall not be a Law.

Every Order, Resolution, or Vote to which the Concurrence of the Senate and House of Representatives may be necessary (except on a question of Adjournment) shall be presented to the President of the United States; and before the Same shall take Effect, shall be approved by him, or being disapproved by him, shall be repassed by two thirds of the Senate and House of Representatives, according to the Rules and Limitations prescribed in the Case of a Bill.

SECTION 8. The Congress shall have Power To lay and collect Taxes, Duties, Imposts and Excises, to pay the Debts and provide for the common Defence and general Welfare of the United States; but all Duties, Imposts and Excises shall be uniform throughout the United States;

To borrow money on the credit of the United States;

To regulate Commerce with foreign Nations, and among the several States, and with the Indian Tribes;

To establish an uniform Rule of Naturalization, and uniform Laws on the subject of Bankruptcies throughout the United States;

To coin Money, regulate the Value thereof, and of foreign Coin, and fix the Standard of Weights and Measures;

To provide for the Punishment of counterfeiting the Securities and current Coin of the United States;

To establish Post Offices and post Roads;

To promote the Progress of Science and useful Arts, by securing for limited Times to Authors and Inventors the exclusive Right to their respective Writings and Discoveries;

To constitute Tribunals inferior to the Supreme Court;

To define and punish Piracies and Fel-

onies committed on the high Seas, and Offenses against the Law of Nations;

To declare War, grant Letters of Marque and Reprisal, and make Rules concerning Captures on Land and Water;

To raise and support Armies, but no Appropriation of Money to that Use shall be for a longer Term than two Years;

To provide and maintain a Navy;

To make Rules for the Government and Regulation of the land and naval forces;

To provide for calling forth the Militia to execute the Laws of the Union, suppress Insurrections and repel Invasions;

To provide for organizing, arming, and disciplining the Militia, and for governing such Part of them as may be employed in the Service of the United States, reserving to the States respectively, the Appointment of the Officers, and the Authority of training the Militia according to the discipline prescribed by Congress;

To exercise exclusive Legislation in all Cases whatsoever, over such District (not exceeding ten Miles square) as may, by Cession of particular States, and the acceptance of Congress, become the Seat of the Government of the United States, and to exercise like Authority over all Places purchased by the Consent of the Legislature of the State in which the Same shall be, for the Erection of Forts, Magazines, Arsenals, dock-Yards, and other needful Buildings;—And

To make all Laws which shall be necessary and proper for carrying into Execution the foregoing Powers, and all other Powers vested by this Constitution in the Government of the United States, or in any Department or Officer thereof.

SECTION 9. The Migration or Importation of such Persons as any of the States now existing shall think proper to admit, shall not be prohibited by the Congress prior to the Year one thousand eight hundred and eight, but a tax or duty may be imposed on such Importation, not exceeding ten dollars for each Person.

The privilege of the Writ of Habeas Corpus shall not be suspended, unless when in Cases of Rebellion or Invasion the public Safety may require it.

No Bill of Attainder or ex post facto Law shall be passed.

No capitation, or other direct, Tax shall be laid unless in Proportion to the Census or Enumeration herein before directed to be taken.

No Tax or Duty shall be laid on Articles exported from any State.

No Preference shall be given by any Regulation of Commerce or Revenue to the Ports of one State over those of another: nor shall Vessels bound to, or from, one State, be obliged to enter, clear, or pay Duties in another.

No Money shall be drawn from the Treasury, but in Consequence of Appropriations made by Law; and a regular Statement and Account of the Receipts and Expenditures of all public Money shall be published from time to time.

No Title of Nobility shall be granted by the United States: And no Person holding any Office of Profit or Trust under them, shall, without the Consent of the Congress, accept of any present, Emolument, Office, or Title, of any kind whatever, from any King, Prince, or foreign State.

Section 10. No State shall enter into any Treaty, Alliance, or Confederation; grant Letters of Marque and Reprisal; coin Money; emit Bills of Credit; make any Thing but gold and silver Coin a Tender in Payment of Debts; pass any Bill of Attainder, ex post facto Law, or Law impairing the Obligation of Contracts, or grant any Title of Nobility.

No State shall, without the Consent of the Congress, lay any Imposts or Duties on Imports or Exports, except what may be absolutely necessary for executing its inspection Laws: and the net Produce of all Duties and Imposts, laid by any State on Imports or Exports, shall be for the Use of the Treasury of the United States; and all such Laws shall be subject to the Revision and Control of the Congress.

No State shall, without the Consent of Congress, lay any duty of Tonnage, keep Troops, or Ships of War in time of Peace, enter into any Agreement or Compact with another State, or with a foreign Power, or engage in War, unless actually invaded, or in such imminent Danger as will not admit of delay.

ARTICLE II

Section 1. The executive Power shall be vested in a President of the United States of America. He shall hold his Office during the Term of four years, and, together with the Vice President, chosen for the same Term, be elected, as follows:

Each State shall appoint, in such Manner as the Legislature thereof may direct, a Number of Electors, equal to the whole Number of Senators and Representatives to which the State may be entitled in the Congress: but no Senator or Representative, or Person holding an Office of Trust or Profit under the United States, shall be appointed an Elector.

[The Electors shall meet in their respective States, and vote by Ballot for two persons, of whom one at least shall not be an Inhabitant of the same State with themselves. And they shall make a List of all the Persons voted for, and of the Number of Votes for each; which List they shall sign and certify, and transmit sealed to the Seat of the Government of the United States, directed to the President of the Senate. The President of the Senate shall, in the Presence of the Senate and House of Representatives, open all the Certificates, and the Votes shall then be counted. The Person having the greatest Number of Votes shall be the President, if such Number be a Majority of the whole Number of Electors appointed; and if there be more than one who have such Majority, and have an equal Number of Votes, then the House of Representatives shall immediately chuse by Ballot one of them for President; and if no Person have a Majority, then from the five highest on the List the said House shall in like Manner chuse the President. But in chusing the President, the Votes shall be taken by States, the Representation from each State having one Vote; a quorum for this Purpose shall consist of a Member or Members from two-thirds of the States, and a Majority of all the States shall be necessary to a Choice. In every Case, after the Choice of the President, the Person having the greatest Number of Votes of the Electors shall be the Vice President. But if there should remain two or more who have equal votes, the Senate shall chuse from them by Ballot the Vice President.] [4]

The Congress may determine the Time of chusing the Electors, and the Day on which they shall give their Votes; which Day shall be the same throughout the United States.

No person except a natural-born Citizen, or a Citizen of the United States, at the time of the Adoption of this Constitution, shall be eligible to the Office of President; neither shall any Person be eligible to that Office who shall not have attained to the Age of thirty-five years, and been fourteen Years a Resident within the United States.

In Case of the Removal of the President from Office, or of his Death, Resignation, or Inability to discharge the Powers and Duties of the said Office, the same shall devolve on the Vice President, and the Congress may by Law provide for the Case of Removal, Death, Resignation, or Inability, both of the President and Vice President, declaring what Officer shall then act as President, and such Officer shall act accordingly, until the disability be removed, or a President shall be elected.

The President shall, at stated Times,

[4] Revised by 12th Amendment.

receive for his Services a Compensation, which shall neither be increased nor diminished during the Period for which he shall have been elected, and he shall not receive within that Period any other Emolument from the United States, or any of them.

Before he enter on the execution of his Office, he shall take the following Oath or Affirmation:—"I do solemnly swear (or affirm) that I will faithfully execute the Office of President of the United States, and will, to the best of my Ability, preserve, protect, and defend the Constitution of the United States."

SECTION 2. The President shall be Commander in Chief of the Army and Navy of the United States, and of the Militia of the several States, when called into the actual Service of the United States; he may require the Opinion, in writing, of the principal Officer in each of the executive Departments, upon any subject relating to the Duties of their respective Offices, and he shall have Power to Grant Reprieves and Pardons for Offenses against the United States, except in Cases of Impeachment.

He shall have Power, by and with the Advice and Consent of the Senate, to make Treaties, provided two thirds of the Senators present concur; and he shall nominate, and by and with the Advice and Consent of the Senate, shall appoint Ambassadors, other public Ministers and Consuls, Judges of the supreme Court, and all other Officers of the United States, whose Appointments are not herein otherwise provided for, and which shall be established by Law: but the Congress may by Law vest the Appointment of such inferior Officers, as they think proper, in the President alone, in the Courts of Law, or in the Heads of Departments.

The President shall have Power to fill up all Vacancies that may happen during the Recess of the Senate, by granting Commissions which shall expire at the End of their next Session.

SECTION 3. He shall from time to time give to the Congress Information of the State of the Union, and recommend to their Consideration such Measures as he shall judge necessary and expedient; he may, on extraordinary occasions, convene both Houses, or either of them, and in Case of Disagreement between them, with respect to the Time of Adjournment, he may adjourn them to such Time as he shall think proper; he shall receive Ambassadors and other public Ministers; he shall take Care that the Laws be faithfully executed, and shall Commission all the Officers of the United States.

SECTION 4. The President, Vice President and all civil Officers of the United States, shall be removed from Office on Impeachment for, and Conviction of, Treason, Bribery, or other high Crimes and Misdemeanors.

ARTICLE III

SECTION 1. The judicial Power of the United States, shall be vested in one supreme Court, and in such inferior Courts as the Congress may from time to time ordain and establish. The Judges, both of the supreme and inferior Courts, shall hold their Offices during good Behaviour, and shall, at stated Times, receive for their Services, a Compensation, which shall not be diminished during their Continuance in Office.

SECTION 2. The judicial Power shall extend to all Cases, in Law and Equity, arising under this Constitution, the Laws of the United States, and Treaties made, or which shall be made, under their Authority;—to all Cases affecting ambassadors, other public ministers and consuls;—to all cases of admiralty and maritime Jurisdiction;—to Controversies to which the United States shall be a Party;—to Controversies between two or more States;—between a State and Citizens of another State; [5]—between Citizens of different States,—between Citizens of the same State claiming Lands under Grants of different States, and between a State, or the Citizens thereof, and foreign States, Citizens or Subjects.

In all Cases affecting Ambassadors, other public Ministers and Consuls, and those in which a State shall be Party, the supreme Court shall have original Jurisdiction. In all the other Cases before mentioned, the supreme Court shall have appellate Jurisdiction, both as to Law and Fact, with such Exceptions, and under such Regulations as the Congress shall make.

The trial of all Crimes, except in Cases of Impeachment, shall be by Jury; and such Trial shall be held in the State where the said Crimes shall have been committed; but when not committed within any State, the Trial shall be at such Place or Places as the Congress may by Law have directed.

SECTION 3. Treason against the United States, shall consist only in levying War against them, or in adhering to their Enemies, giving them Aid and Comfort. No Person shall be convicted of Treason unless on the Testimony of two Witnesses to the same overt Act, or on Confession in open Court.

The Congress shall have power to declare the Punishment of Treason, but no Attainder of Treason shall work Corruption of Blood, or Forfeiture except during the Life of the Person attainted.

ARTICLE IV

SECTION 1. Full Faith and Credit shall be given in each State to the public Acts, Records, and judicial Proceedings of every other State. And the Congress may by general Laws prescribe the Manner in which such Acts, Records and Proceedings shall be proved, and the Effect thereof.

SECTION 2. The Citizens of each State shall be entitled to all Privileges and Immunities of Citizens in the several States.

A Person charged in any State with Treason, Felony, or other Crime, who

---

[5] Qualified by 11th Amendment.

shall flee from Justice, and be found in another State, shall on demand of the executive Authority of the State from which he fled, be delivered up, to be removed to the State having Jurisdiction of the crime.

No Person held to Service or Labour in one State, under the Laws thereof, escaping into another, shall, in Consequence of any Law or Regulation therein, be discharged from such Service or Labour, but shall be delivered up on Claim of the Party to whom such Service or Labour may be due.

Section 3.   New States may be admitted by the Congress into this Union; but no new State shall be formed or erected within the Jurisdiction of any other State; nor any State be formed by the Junction of two or more States, or parts of States, without the Consent of the Legislatures of the States concerned as well as of the Congress.

The Congress shall have Power to dispose of and make all needful Rules and Regulations respecting the Territory or other Property belonging to the United States; and nothing in this Constitution shall be so construed as to Prejudice any Claims of the United States, or of any particular State.

Section 4.   The United States shall guarantee to every State in this Union a Republican Form of Government, and shall protect each of them against Invasion; and on Application of the Legislature, or of the Executive (when the Legislature cannot be convened) against domestic Violence.

ARTICLE V

The Congress, whenever two-thirds of both Houses shall deem it necessary, shall propose Amendments to this Constitution, or, on the Application of the Legislatures of two-thirds of the several States, shall call a Convention for proposing Amendments, which, in either Case, shall be valid to all Intents and Purposes, as part of this Constitution, when ratified by the Legislatures of three-fourths of the several States, or by Conventions in three-fourths thereof, as the one or the other Mode of Ratification may be proposed by the Congress; Provided that no Amendment which may be made prior to the Year One thousand eight hundred and eight shall in any Manner affect the first and fourth Clauses in the Ninth Section of the first Article; and that no State, without its Consent, shall be deprived of its equal Suffrage in the Senate.

ARTICLE VI

All Debts contracted and Engagements entered into, before the Adoption of this Constitution, shall be as valid against the United States under this Constitution, as under the Confederation.

This Constitution, and the Laws of the United States which shall be made in Pursuance thereof; and all Treaties made, or which shall be made, under the Authority of the United States, shall be the supreme Law of the Land; and the Judges in every State shall be bound thereby, any Thing in the Constitution or Laws of any State to the Contrary notwithstanding.

The Senators and Representatives before mentioned, and the Members of the several State Legislatures, and all executive and judicial Officers, both of the United States and of the several States, shall be bound by Oath or Affirmation to support this Constitution; but no religious Test shall ever be required as a qualification to any Office or public Trust under the United States.

ARTICLE VII

The Ratification of the Conventions of nine States shall be sufficient for the Establishment of this Constitution between the States so ratifying the same.

Done in Convention by the Unanimous Consent of the States present the Seventeenth Day of September in the Year of our Lord one thousand seven hundred and Eighty seven, and of the Independence of the United States of America the Twelfth. In Witness whereof We have hereunto subscribed our Names.[6]

George Washington
PRESIDENT AND DEPUTY FROM VIRGINIA

NEW HAMPSHIRE
John Langdon
Nicholas Gilman

MASSACHUSETTS
Nathaniel Gorham
Rufus King

CONNECTICUT
William Samuel Johnson
Roger Sherman

NEW YORK
Alexander Hamilton

NEW JERSEY
William Livingston
David Brearley
William Paterson
Jonathan Dayton

PENNSYLVANIA
Benjamin Franklin
Thomas Mifflin
Robert Morris
George Clymer
Thomas FitzSimons
Jared Ingersoll
James Wilson
Gouverneur Morris

DELAWARE
George Read
Gunning Bedford, Jr.
John Dickinson
Richard Bassett
Jacob Broom

MARYLAND
James McHenry
Daniel of St. Thomas Jenifer
Daniel Carroll

[6] These are the full names of the signers, which in some cases are not the signatures on the document.

VIRGINIA
John Blair
James Madison, Jr.

NORTH CAROLINA
William Blount
Richard Dobbs Spaight
Hugh Williamson

SOUTH CAROLINA
John Rutledge
Charles Cotesworth Pinckney
Charles Pinckney
Pierce Butler

GEORGIA
William Few
Abraham Baldwin

ARTICLES IN ADDITION TO, AND AMENDMENT OF, THE CONSTITUTION OF THE UNITED STATES OF AMERICA, PROPOSED BY CONGRESS, AND RATIFIED BY THE LEGISLATURES OF THE SEVERAL STATES, PURSUANT TO THE FIFTH ARTICLE OF THE ORIGINAL CONSTITUTION [7]

[ARTICLE I]

Congress shall make no law respecting an establishment of religion, or prohibiting the free exercise thereof; or abridging the freedom of speech, or of the press; or the right of the people peaceably to assemble, and to petition the Government for a redress of grievances.

[ARTICLE II]

A well regulated Militia, being necessary to the security of a free State, the right of the people to keep and bear Arms shall not be infringed.

[ARTICLE III]

No Soldier shall, in time of peace, be quartered in any house, without the consent of the Owner, nor in time of war, but in a manner to be prescribed by law.

[7] This heading appears only in the joint resolution submitting the first ten amendments.

[ARTICLE IV]

The right of the people to be secure in their persons, houses, papers, and effects, against unreasonable searches and seizures, shall not be violated, and no Warrants shall issue, but upon probable cause, supported by Oath or affirmation, and particularly describing the place to be searched, and the persons or things to be seized.

[ARTICLE V]

No person shall be held to answer for a capital or otherwise infamous crime, unless on a presentment or indictment of a Grand Jury, except in cases arising in the land or naval forces, or in the Militia, when in actual service in time of War or public danger; nor shall any person be subject for the same offense to be twice put in jeopardy of life or limb; nor shall be compelled in any criminal case to be a witness against himself, nor be deprived of life, liberty, or property, without due process of law; nor shall private property be taken for public use, without just compensation.

[ARTICLE VI]

In all criminal prosecutions, the accused shall enjoy the right to a speedy and public trial, by an impartial jury of the State and district wherein the crime shall have been committed, which district shall have been previously ascertained by law, and to be informed of the nature and cause of the accusation; to be confronted with the witnesses against him; to have compulsory process for obtaining witnesses in his favor, and to have the Assistance of Counsel for his defense.

[ARTICLE VII]

In suits at common law, where the value in controversy shall exceed twenty dollars, the right of trial by jury shall be preserved, and no fact tried by a jury, shall be otherwise reexamined in any Court of the United States, than according to the rules of the common law.

[ARTICLE VIII]

Excessive bail shall not be required, nor excessive fines imposed, nor cruel and unusual punishments inflicted.

[ARTICLE IX]

The enumeration in the Constitution, of certain rights, shall not be construed to deny or disparage others retained by the people.

[ARTICLE X]

The powers not delegated to the United States by the Constitution, nor prohibited by it to the States, are reserved to the States respectively, or to the people.

[Amendments I-X, in force 1791.]

[ARTICLE XI] [8]

The Judicial power of the United States shall not be construed to extend to any suit in law or equity, commenced or prosecuted against one of the United States by Citizens of another State, or by Citizens or Subjects of any Foreign State.

[ARTICLE XII] [9]

The Electors shall meet in their respective States and vote by ballot for President and Vice-President, one of whom, at least, shall not be an inhabitant of the same State with themselves; they shall name in their ballots the person voted for as President, and in distinct ballots the person voted for as Vice-President, and they shall make distinct lists of all persons voted for as President, and of all persons voted for as Vice-President, and of the number of votes for each, which lists they shall sign and certify, and transmit sealed to the seat of the government of the United States, directed to the President of the Senate;—The President of the Senate shall, in the presence of the Senate and House of Representatives, open all the certificates and the votes shall then

[8] Adopted in 1798.
[9] Adopted in 1804.

be counted;—The person having the greatest number of votes for President, shall be the President, if such number be a majority of the whole number of Electors appointed; and if no person have such majority, then from the persons having the highest numbers not exceeding three on the list of those voted for as President, the House of Representatives shall choose immediately, by ballot, the President. But in choosing the President, the votes shall be taken by states, the representation from each state having one vote; a quorum for this purpose shall consist of a member or members from two-thirds of the states, and a majority of all the states shall be necessary to a choice. And if the House of Representatives shall not choose a President whenever the right of choice shall devolve upon them, before the fourth day of March next following, then the Vice-President shall act as President, as in the case of the death or other constitutional disability of the President.—The person having the greatest number of votes as Vice-President, shall be the Vice-President, if such number be a majority of the whole number of Electors appointed, and if no person have a majority, then from the two highest numbers on the list, the Senate shall choose the Vice-President; a quorum for the purpose shall consist of two-thirds of the whole number of Senators, and a majority of the whole number shall be necessary to a choice. But no person constitutionally ineligible to the office of President shall be eligible to that of Vice-President of the United States.

ARTICLE XIII [10]

SECTION 1. Neither slavery nor involuntary servitude, except as a punishment for crime whereof the party shall have been duly convicted, shall exist within the United States, or any place subject to their jurisdiction.

SECTION 2. Congress shall have power to enforce this article by appropriate legislation.

ARTICLE XIV [11]

SECTION 1. All persons born or naturalized in the United States, and subject to the jurisdiction thereof, are citizens of the United States and of the State wherein they reside. No State shall make or enforce any law which shall abridge the privileges or immunities of citizens of the United States; nor shall any State deprive any person of life, liberty, or property, without due process of law; nor deny to any person within its jurisdiction the equal protection of the laws.

SECTION 2. Representatives shall be apportioned among the several States according to their respective numbers, counting the whole number of persons in each State, excluding Indians not taxed. But when the right to vote at any election for the choice of electors for President and Vice-President of the United States, Representatives in Congress, the Executive and Judicial officers of a State, or the members of the Legislature thereof, is denied to any of the male inhabitants of such State, being twenty-one years of age, and citizens of the United States, or in any way abridged, except for participation in rebellion, or other crime, the basis of representation therein shall be reduced in the proportion which the number of such male citizens shall bear to the whole number of male citizens twenty-one years of age in such State.

SECTION 3. No person shall be a Senator or Representative in Congress, or elector of President and Vice-President, or hold any office, civil or military, under the United States, or under any State, who, having previously taken an oath, as a member of Congress, or as an officer of the United States, or as a member of any State legislature, or as an executive or judicial officer of any State, to support the Constitution of the United States,

---

[10] Adopted in 1865.

[11] Adopted in 1868.

shall have engaged in insurrection or rebellion against the same, or given aid or comfort to the enemies thereof. But Congress may by a vote of two-thirds of each House, remove such disability.

SECTION 4. The validity of the public debt of the United States, authorized by law, including debts incurred for payment of pensions and bounties for services in suppressing insurrection or rebellion, shall not be questioned. But neither the United States nor any State shall assume or pay any debt or obligation incurred in aid of insurrection or rebellion against the United States, or any claim for the loss or emancipation of any slave; but all such debts, obligations, and claims shall be held illegal and void.

SECTION 5. The Congress shall have the power to enforce, by appropriate legislation, the provisions of this article.

ARTICLE XV [12]

SECTION 1. The right of citizens of the United States to vote shall not be denied or abridged by the United States or by any State on account of race, color, or previous condition of servitude—

SECTION 2. The Congress shall have power to enforce this article by appropriate legislation.

ARTICLE XVI [13]

The Congress shall have power to lay and collect taxes on incomes, from whatever source derived, without apportionment among the several States, and without regard to any census or enumeration.

ARTICLE XVII [14]

The Senate of the United States shall be composed of two Senators from each State, elected by the people thereof, for six years; and each Senator shall have one vote. The electors in each State shall have the qualifications requisite for electors of the most numerous branch of the State legislatures.

When vacancies happen in the representation of any State in the Senate, the executive authority of such State shall issue writs of election to fill such vacancies: *Provided,* That the legislature of any State may empower the executive thereof to make temporary appointments until the people fill the vancancies by election as the legislature may direct.

This amendment shall not be so construed as to affect the election or term of any Senator chosen before it becomes valid as part of the Constitution.

ARTICLE XVIII [15]

SECTION 1. After one year from the ratification of this article the manufacture, sale, or transportation of intoxicating liquors within, the importation thereof into, or the exportation thereof from the United States and all territory subject to the jurisdiction thereof for beverage purposes is hereby prohibited.

SECTION 2. The Congress and the several States shall have concurrent power to enforce this article by appropriate legislation.

SECTION 3. This article shall be inoperative unless it shall have been ratified as an amendment to the Constitution by the legislatures of the several States, as provided in the Constitution, within seven years from the date of the submission hereof to the States by the Congress.

ARTICLE XIX [16]

The right of citizens of the United States to vote shall not be denied or abridged by the United States or by any State on account of sex.

[12] Proclaimed March 30, 1870.
[13] Passed July, 1909.
[14] Passed May, 1912, in place of Article I, Section 3, clause I, of the Constitution and that part of clause 2 of the same Section which pertains to the filling of vacancies.

[15] Passed December 3, 1917.
[16] Adopted in 1920.

Congress shall have power to enforce this article by appropriate legislation.

ARTICLE XX [17]

SECTION 1. The terms of the President and Vice-President shall end at noon on the 20th day of January, and the terms of Senators and Representatives at noon on the 3d day of January, of the years in which such terms would have ended if this article had not been ratified; and the terms of their successors shall then begin.

SECTION 2. The Congress shall assemble at least once in every year, and such meeting shall begin at noon on the 3d day of January, unless they shall by law appoint a different day.

SECTION 3. If, at the time fixed for the beginning of the term of the President, the President elect shall have died, the Vice-President elect shall become President. If a President shall not have been chosen before the time fixed for the beginning of his term, or if the President elect shall have failed to qualify, then the Vice-President elect shall act as President until a President shall have qualified; and the Congress may by law provide for the case wherein neither a President elect nor a Vice-President elect shall have qualified, declaring who shall then act as President, or the manner in which one who is to act shall be selected, and such person shall act accordingly until a President or Vice-President shall have qualified.

SECTION 4. The Congress may by law provide for the case of the death of any of the persons from whom the House of Representatives may choose a President whenever the right of choice shall have devolved upon them, and for the case of the death of any of the persons from whom the Senate may choose a Vice-President whenever the right of choice shall have devolved upon them.

SECTION 5. Sections 1 and 2 shall take effect on the 15th day of October following the ratification of this article.

SECTION 6. This article shall be inoperative unless it shall have been ratified as an amendment to the Constitution by the legislatures of three-fourths of the several States within seven years from the date of its submission.

ARTICLE XXI [18]

SECTION 1. The eighteenth article of amendment to the Constitution of the United States is hereby repealed.

SECTION 2. The transportation or importation into any State, Territory, or possession of the United States for delivery or use therein of intoxicating liquors, in violation of the laws thereof, is hereby prohibited.

SECTION 3. This article shall be inoperative unless it shall have been ratified as an amendment to the Constitution by conventions in the several States, as provided in the Constitution, within seven years from the date of the submission hereof to the States by the Congress.

ARTICLE XXII [19]

No person shall be elected to the office of the President more than twice, and no person who has held the office of President, or acted as President, for more than two years of a term to which some other person was elected President shall be elected to the office of the President more than once.

But this Article shall not apply to any person holding the office of President when this Article was proposed by the Congress, and shall not prevent any person who may be holding the office of President, or acting as President, during the term within which this Article becomes operative from holding the office of President or acting as President during the remainder of such term.

[17] Adopted in 1933.

[18] Adopted in 1933.
[19] Adopted in 1951.

Sovereigns of England and Great Britain, 1485–1820

The ruler was King (or Queen) of England until 1707, except for the interregnum of 1649–1660, during which Oliver Cromwell made himself Lord Protector. The ruler was King (or Queen) of Great Britain after the union of England and Scotland in 1707, and King (or Queen) of Great Britain and Ireland after 1800.

HENRY VII, 1485–1509
HENRY VIII, 1509–1547
EDWARD VI, 1547–1553
MARY, 1553–1558

ELIZABETH, 1558–1603
JAMES I (VI OF SCOTLAND), 1603–1625
CHARLES I, 1625–1649
   OLIVER CROMWELL, 1650–1658
   RICHARD CROMWELL, 1658–1659
CHARLES II, 1660–1685
JAMES II, 1685–1688
WILLIAM III AND MARY II, 1689–1694
WILLIAM III, 1694–1702
ANNE, 1702–1714
GEORGE I, 1714–1727
GEORGE II, 1727–1760
GEORGE III, 1760–1820

Admission of States to the Union

(For the first thirteen, the date given is that of ratification of the Constitution.)

1	Delaware	Dec. 7, 1787	26.	Michigan	Jan.	26, 1837
2.	Pennsylvania	Dec. 12, 1787	27.	Florida	Mar.	3, 1845
3.	New Jersey	Dec. 18, 1787	28.	Texas	Dec.	29, 1845
4.	Georgia	Jan. 2, 1788	29.	Iowa	Dec.	28, 1846
5.	Connecticut	Jan. 9, 1788	30.	Wisconsin	May	29, 1848
6.	Massachusetts	Feb. 6, 1788	31.	California	Sept.	9, 1850
7.	Maryland	Apr. 28, 1788	32.	Minnesota	May	11, 1858
8.	South Carolina	May 23, 1788	33.	Oregon	Feb.	14, 1859
9.	New Hampshire	June 21, 1788	34.	Kansas	Jan.	29, 1861
10.	Virginia	June 25, 1788	35.	West Virginia	June	19, 1863
11.	New York	July 26, 1788	36.	Nevada	Oct.	31, 1864
12.	North Carolina	Nov. 21, 1789	37.	Nebraska	Mar.	1, 1867
13.	Rhode Island	May 29, 1790	38.	Colorado	Aug.	1, 1876
14.	Vermont	Mar. 4, 1791	39.	North Dakota	Nov.	2, 1889
15.	Kentucky	June 1, 1792	40.	South Dakota	Nov.	2, 1889
16.	Tennessee	June 1, 1796	41.	Montana	Nov.	8, 1889
17.	Ohio	Mar. 1, 1803	42.	Washington	Nov.	11, 1889
18.	Louisiana	Apr. 30, 1812	43.	Idaho	July	3, 1890
19.	Indiana	Dec. 11, 1816	44.	Wyoming	July	10, 1890
20.	Mississippi	Dec. 10, 1817	45.	Utah	Jan.	4, 1896
21.	Illinois	Dec. 3, 1818	46.	Oklahoma	Nov.	16, 1907
22.	Alabama	Dec. 14, 1819	47.	New Mexico	Jan.	6, 1912
23.	Maine	Mar. 15, 1820	48.	Arizona	Feb.	14, 1912
24.	Missouri	Aug. 10, 1821	49.	Alaska	Jan.	3, 1959
25.	Arkansas	June 15, 1836	50.	Hawaii	Aug.	21, 1959

Presidential Elections

YEAR	CANDIDATES	PARTIES	POPULAR VOTE	ELECTORAL VOTE
1789	GEORGE WASHINGTON (*Va.*)			69
	John Adams			34
	Others			35
1792	GEORGE WASHINGTON (*Va.*)			132
	John Adams			77
	George Clinton			50
	Others			5
1796	JOHN ADAMS (*Mass.*)	Federalist		71
	Thomas Jefferson	Democratic-Republican		68
	Thomas Pinckney	Fed.		59
	Aaron Burr	Dem.-Rep.		30
	Others			48
1800	THOMAS JEFFERSON (*Va.*)	Dem.-Rep.		73
	Aaron Burr	Dem.-Rep.		73
	John Adams	Fed.		65
	C. C. Pinckney	Fed.		64
	John Jay	Fed.		1
1804	THOMAS JEFFERSON (*Va.*)	Dem.-Rep.		162
	C. C. Pinckney	Fed.		14
1808	JAMES MADISON (*Va.*)	Dem.-Rep.		122
	C. C. Pinckney	Fed.		47
	George Clinton	Dem.-Rep.		6
1812	JAMES MADISON (*Va.*)	Dem.-Rep.		128
	De Witt Clinton	Fed.		89
1816	JAMES MONROE (*Va.*)	Dem.-Rep.		183
	Rufus King	Fed.		34
1820	JAMES MONROE (*Va.*)	Dem.-Rep.		231
	John Quincy Adams	Dem.-Rep.		1
1824	JOHN Q. ADAMS (*Mass.*)	Dem.-Rep.	108,740	84
	Andrew Jackson	Dem.-Rep.	153,544	99
	William H. Crawford	Dem.-Rep.	46,618	41
	Henry Clay	Dem.-Rep.	47,136	37
1828	ANDREW JACKSON (*Tenn.*)	Democrat	647,286	178
	John Quincy Adams	National Republican	508,064	83
1832	ANDREW JACKSON (*Tenn.*)	Democrat	687,502	219
	Henry Clay	Whig	530,189	49
	John Floyd	Whig		11
	William Wirt	Anti-Mason	33,108	7
1836	MARTIN VAN BUREN (*N.Y.*)	Democrat	762,678	170
	W. H. Harrison	Whig		73
	Hugh L. White	Whig	735,651	26
	Daniel Webster	Whig		14
	W. P. Mangum	Whig		11

Presidential Elections (continued)

YEAR	CANDIDATES	PARTIES	POPULAR VOTE	ELECTORAL VOTE
1840	WILLIAM H. HARRISON (*Ohio*)	Whig	1,275,016	234
	Martin Van Buren	Democrat	1,129,102	60
	J. G. Birney	Liberty	7,069	
1844	JAMES K. POLK (*Tenn.*)	Democrat	1,337,243	170
	Henry Clay	Whig	1,299,062	105
	J. G. Birney	Liberty	62,300	
1848	ZACHARY TAYLOR (*La.*)	Whig	1,360,099	163
	Lewis Cass	Democrat	1,220,544	127
	Martin Van Buren	Free Soil	291,263	
1852	FRANKLIN PIERCE (*N.H.*)	Democrat	1,601,274	254
	Winfield Scott	Whig	1,386,580	42
	John P. Hale	Free Soil	155,825	
1856	JAMES BUCHANAN (*Pa.*)	Democrat	1,838,169	174
	John C. Frémont	Republican	1,341,264	114
	Millard Fillmore	American	874,534	8
1860	ABRAHAM LINCOLN (*Ill.*)	Republican	1,866,452	180
	Stephen A. Douglas	Democrat	1,375,157	12
	John C. Breckinridge	Democrat	847,953	72
	John Bell	Union	590,631	39
1864	ABRAHAM LINCOLN (*Ill.*)	Republican	2,213,655	212
	George B. McClelan	Democrat	1,805,237	21
1868	ULYSSES S. GRANT (*Ill.*)	Republican	3,012,833	214
	Horatio Seymour	Democrat	2,703,249	80
1872	ULYSSES S. GRANT (*Ill.*)	Republican	3,597,132	286
	Horace Greeley	Democrat-Liberal Republican	2,834,125	66
1876	RUTHERFORD B. HAYES (*Ohio*)	Republican	4,036,298	185
	Samuel J. Tilden	Democrat	4,300,590	184
1880	JAMES A. GARFIELD (*Ohio*)	Republican	4,454,416	214
	Winfield S. Hancock	Democrat	4,444,952	155
1884	GROVER CLEVELAND (*N.Y.*)	Democrat	4,874,986	219
	James G. Blaine	Republican	4,851,981	182
1888	BENJAMIN HARRISON (*Ind.*)	Republican	5,439,853	233
	Grover Cleveland	Democrat	5,540,309	168
1892	GROVER CLEVELAND (*N.Y.*)	Democrat	5,556,918	277
	Benjamin Harrison	Republican	5,176,108	145
	James B. Weaver	People's	1,041,028	22
1896	WILLIAM MC KINLEY (*Ohio*)	Republican	7,104,779	271
	William J. Bryan	Democrat-People's	6,502,925	176
1900	WILLIAM MC KINLEY (*Ohio*)	Republican	7,207,923	292
	William J. Bryan	Democrat-Populist	6,358,133	155
1904	THEODORE ROOSEVELT (*N.Y.*)	Republican	7,623,486	336
	Alton B. Parker	Democrat	5,077,911	140
	Eugene V. Debs	Socialist	402,283	—

Presidential Elections (continued)

YEAR	CANDIDATES	PARTIES	POPULAR VOTE	ELECTORAL VOTE
1908	WILLIAM H. TAFT (*Ohio*)	Republican	7,678,908	321
	William J. Bryan	Democrat	6,409,104	162
	Eugene V. Debs	Socialist	420,793	—
1912	WOODROW WILSON (*N.J.*)	Democrat	6,293,454	435
	William H. Taft	Republican	3,484,980	8
	Theodore Roosevelt	Progressive	4,119,538	88
	Eugene V. Debs	Socialist	900,672	—
1916	WOODROW WILSON (*N.J.*)	Democrat	9,129,606	277
	Charles E. Hughes	Republican	8,538,221	254
	A. L. Benson	Socialist	585,113	—
1920	WARREN G. HARDING (*Ohio*)	Republican	16,152,200	404
	James M. Cox	Democrat	9,147,353	127
	Eugene V. Debs	Socialist	919,799	—
1924	CALVIN COOLIDGE (*Mass.*)	Republican	15,725,016	382
	John W. Davis	Democrat	8,386,503	136
	Robert M. LaFollette	Progressive	4,822,856	13
1928	HERBERT HOOVER (*Cal.*)	Republican	21,391,381	444
	Alfred E. Smith	Democrat	15,016,443	87
	Norman Thomas	Socialist	267,835	—
1932	FRANKLIN D. ROOSEVELT (*N.Y.*)	Democrat	22,821,857	472
	Herbert Hoover	Republican	15,761,841	59
	Norman Thomas	Socialist	881,951	—
1936	FRANKLIN D. ROOSEVELT (*N.Y.*)	Democrat	27,751,597	523
	Alfred M. Landon	Republican	16,679,583	8
	William Lemke	Union and others	882,479	—
1940	FRANKLIN D. ROOSEVELT (*N.Y.*)	Democrat	27,244,160	449
	Wendell L. Willkie	Republican	22,305,198	82
1944	FRANKLIN D. ROOSEVELT (*N.Y.*)	Democrat	25,602,504	432
	Thomas E. Dewey	Republican	22,006,285	99
1948	HARRY S. TRUMAN (*Mo.*)	Democrat	24,105,695	303
	Thomas E. Dewey	Republican	21,969,170	189
	J. Strom Thurmond	State-Rights Democrat	1,169,021	39
	Henry A. Wallace	Progressive	1,156,103	—
1952	DWIGHT D. EISENHOWER (*Kan.*)	Republican	33,936,252	442
	Adlai E. Stevenson	Democrat	27,314,992	89
1956	DWIGHT D. EISENHOWER (*Kan.*)	Republican	35,575,420	457
	Adlai E. Stevenson	Democrat	26,033,066	74

President	Vice President	Secretary of State	Secretary of Treasury
1. George Washington, Federalist 1789	John Adams, Federalist 1789	T. Jefferson 1789 E. Randolph 1794 T. Pickering 1795	Alex. Hamilton 1789 Oliver Wolcott 1795
2. John Adams, Federalist 1797	Thomas Jefferson, Republican 1797	T. Pickering 1797 John Marshall 1800	Oliver Wolcott 1797 Samuel Dexter 1801
3. Thomas Jefferson, Republican 1801	Aaron Burr, Republican 1801 George Clinton, Republican 1805	James Madison 1801	Samuel Dexter 1801 Albert Gallatin 1801
4. James Madison, Republican 1809	George Clinton, Republican 1809 Elbridge Gerry, Republican 1813	Robert Smith 1809 James Monroe 1811	Albert Gallatin 1809 G. W. Campbell 1814 A. J. Dallas 1814 W. H. Crawford 1816
5. James Monroe, Republican 1817	D. D. Tompkins, Republican 1817	J. Q. Adams 1817	W. H. Crawford 1817
6. John Quincy Adams, Nat'l Rep. 1825	John C. Calhoun, Republican 1825	Henry Clay 1825	Richard Rush 1825
7. Andrew Jackson, Democratic 1829	John C. Calhoun, Democratic 1829 Martin Van Buren, Democratic 1833	M. Van Buren 1829 E. Livingston 1831 Louis McLane 1833 John Forsyth 1834	Sam. D. Ingham 1829 Louis McLane 1831 W. J. Duane 1833 Roger B. Taney 1833 Levi Woodbury 1834
8. Martin Van Buren, Democratic 1837	Richard M. Johnson, Democratic 1837	John Forsyth 1837	Levi Woodbury 1837
9. William H. Harrison, Whig 1841	John Tyler, Whig 1841	Daniel Webster 1841	Thos. Ewing 1841
10. John Tyler, Whig and Democratic 1841		Daniel Webster 1841 Hugh S. Legare 1843 Abel P. Upshur 1843 John C. Calhoun 1844	Thos. Ewing 1841 Walter Forward 1841 John C. Spencer 1843 Geo. M. Bibb 1844
11. James K. Polk, Democratic 1845	George M. Dallas, Democratic 1845	James Buchanan 1845	Robt. J. Walker 1845
12. Zachary Taylor, Whig 1849	Millard Fillmore, Whig 1849	John M. Clayton 1849	Wm. M. Meredith 1849
13. Millard Fillmore, Whig 1850		Daniel Webster 1850 Edward Everett 1852	Thomas Corwin 1850
14. Franklin Pierce, Democratic 1853	William R. D. King, Democratic 1853	W. L. Marcy 1853	James Guthrie 1853
15. James Buchanan, Democratic 1857	John C. Breckinridge, Democratic 1857	Lewis Cass 1857 J. S. Black 1860	Howell Cobb 1857 Philip F. Thomas 1860 John A. Dix 1861
16. Abraham Lincoln, Republican 1861	Hannibal Hamlin, Republican 1861 Andrew Johnson, Unionist 1865	W. H. Seward 1861	Salmon P. Chase 1861 W. P. Fessenden 1864 Hugh McCulloch 1865

and Cabinet Members, 1789–1865

Secretary of War		Attorney-General		Postmaster-General *		Secretary of Navy		Secretary of Interior	
Henry Knox	1789	E. Randolph	1789	Samuel Osgood	1789	Established		Established	
T. Pickering	1795	Wm. Bradford	1794	Tim Pickering	1791	April 30, 1798.		March 3, 1849.	
Jas. McHenry	1796	Charles Lee	1795	Jos. Habersham	1795				
Jas. McHenry	1797	Charles Lee	1797	Jos. Habersham	1797	Benj. Stoddert	1798		
John Marshall	1800	Theo. Parsons	1801						
Sam'l Dexter	1800								
R. Griswold	1801								
H. Dearborn	1801	Levi Lincoln	1801	Jos. Habersham	1801	Benj. Stoddert	1801		
		Robert Smith	1805	Gideon Granger	1801	Robert Smith	1801		
		J. Breckinridge	1805			J. Crowninshield	1805		
		C. A. Rodney	1807						
Wm. Eustis	1809	C. A. Rodney	1809	Gideon Granger	1809	Paul Hamilton	1809		
J. Armstrong	1813	Wm. Pinkney	1811	R. J. Meigs, Jr.	1814	William Jones	1813		
James Monroe	1814	Richard Rush	1814			B. W. Crownin-			
W. H. Crawford	1815					shield	1814		
Isaac Shelby	1817	Richard Rush	1817	R. J. Meigs, Jr.	1817	B. W. Crownin-			
						shield	1817		
Geo. Graham	1817	William Wirt	1817	John McLean	1823	Smith Thompson	1818		
J. C. Calhoun	1817					S. L. Southard	1823		
Jas. Barbour	1825	William Wirt	1825	John McLean	1825	S. L. Southard	1825		
Peter B. Porter	1828								
John H. Eaton	1829	John M. Berrien	1829	Wm. T. Barry	1829	John Branch	1829		
Lewis Cass	1831	Roger B. Taney	1831	Amos Kendall	1835	Levi Woodbury	1831		
B. F. Butler	1837	B. F. Butler	1833			Mahlon Dickerson	1834		
Joel R. Poinsett	1837	B. F. Butler	1837	Amos Kendall	1837	Mahlon Dickerson	1837		
		Felix Grundy	1838	John M. Niles	1840	Jas. K. Paulding	1838		
		H. D. Gilpin	1840						
John Bell	1841	J. J. Crittenden	1841	Francis Granger	1841	George E. Badger	1841		
John Bell	1841	J. J. Crittenden	1841	Francis Granger	1841	George E. Badger	1841		
John McLean	1841	Hugh S. Legare	1841	C. A. Wickliffe	1841	Abel P. Upshur	1841		
J. C. Spencer	1841	John Nelson	1843			David Henshaw	1843		
Jas. M. Porter	1843					Thomas W. Gilmer	1844		
Wm. Wilkins	1844					John Y. Mason	1844		
Wm. L. Marcy	1845	John Y. Mason	1845	Cave Johnson	1845	George Bancroft	1845		
		Nathan Clifford	1846			John Y. Mason	1846		
		Isaac Toucey	1848						
G. W. Crawford	1849	Reverdy Johnson	1849	Jacob Collamer	1849	Wm. B. Preston	1849	Thomas Ewing	1849
C. M. Conrad	1850	J. J. Crittenden	1850	Nathan K. Hall	1850	Wm. A. Graham	1850	A. H. Stuart	1850
				Sam D. Hubbard	1852	John P. Kennedy	1852		
Jefferson Davis	1853	Caleb Cushing	1853	James Campbell	1853	James C. Dobbin	1853	R'bt. McClelland	1853
John B. Floyd	1857	J. S. Black	1857	Aaron V. Brown	1857	Issac Toucey	1857	Jacob Thompson	1857
Joseph Holt	1861	Edw. M. Stanton	1860	Joseph Holt	1859				
S. Cameron	1861	Edward Bates	1861	Horatio King	1861	Gideon Welles	1861	Caleb B. Smith	1861
E. M. Stanton	1862	Titian J. Coffey	1863	M'tgomery Blair	1861			John P. Usher	1863
		James Speed	1864	Wm. Dennison	1864				

Presidents, Vice Presidents,

President	Vice President	Secretary of State	Secretary of Treasury	Secretary of War
17. Andrew Johnson 1865 Unionist		Wm. H. Seward 1865	Hugh McCulloch 1865	E. M. Stanton 1865 U. S. Grant 1867 L. Thomas 1868 J. M. Schofield 1868
18. Ulysses S. Grant 1869 Republican	Schuyler Colfax 1869 Republican Henry Wilson 1873 Republican	E. B. Washburne 1869 Hamilton Fish 1869	Geo. S. Boutwell 1869 W. A. Richardson 1873 Benj. H. Bristow 1874 Lot M. Morrill 1876	J. A. Rawlins 1869 W. T. Sherman 1869 W. W. Belknap 1869 Alphonso Taft 1876 J. D. Cameron 1876
19. Rutherford B. Hayes 1877 Republican	William A. Wheeler 1877 Republican	W. M. Evarts 1877	John Sherman 1877	G. W. McCrary 1877 Alex. Ramsey 1879
20. James A. Garfield 1881 Republican	Chester A. Arthur 1881 Republican	James G. Blaine 1881	Wm. Windom 1881	R. T. Lincoln 1881
21. Chester A. Arthur 1881 Republican		F. T. Frelinghuysen 1881	Chas. J. Folger 1881 W. Q. Gresham 1884 Hugh McCulloch 1884	R. T. Lincoln 1881
22. Grover Cleveland 1885 Democratic	T. A. Hendricks 1885 Democratic	Thos. F. Bayard 1885	Daniel Manning 1885 Chas. S. Fairchild 1887	W. C. Endicott 1885
23. Benjamin Harrison 1889 Republican	Levi P. Morton 1889 Republican	James G. Blaine 1889 John W. Foster 1892	Wm. Windom 1889 Charles Foster 1891	R. Proctor 1889 S. B. Elkins 1891
24. Grover Cleveland 1893 Democratic	Adlai E. Stevenson 1893 Democratic	W. Q. Gresham 1893 Richard Olney 1895	John G. Carlisle 1893	D. S. Lamont 1893
25. William McKinley 1897 Republican	Garret A. Hobart 1897 Republican Theodore Roosevelt 1901 Republican	John Sherman 1897 Wm. R. Day 1897 John Hay 1898	Lyman J. Gage 1897	R. A. Alger 1897 Elihu Root 1899
26. Theodore Roosevelt 1901 Republican	Chas. W. Fairbanks 1905 Republican	John Hay 1901 Elihu Root 1905 Robert Bacon 1909	Lyman J. Gage 1901 Leslie M. Shaw 1902 G. B. Cortelyou 1907	Elihu Root 1901 Wm. H. Taft 1904 Luke E. Wright 1908
27. William H. Taft 1909 Republican	James S. Sherman 1909 Republican	P. C. Knox 1909	F. MacVeagh 1909	J. M. Dickinson 1909 H. L. Stimson 1911
28. Woodrow Wilson 1913 Democratic	Thomas R. Marshall 1913 Democratic	Wm. J. Bryan 1913 Robert Lansing 1915 Bainbridge Colby 1920	W. G. McAdoo 1913 Carter Glass 1918 D. F. Houston 1920	L. M. Garrison 1913 N. D. Baker 1916
29. Warren G. Harding 1921 Republican	Calvin Coolidge 1921 Republican	Chas. E. Hughes 1921	Andrew W. Mellon 1921	John W. Weeks 1921
30. Calvin Coolidge 1923 Republican	Charles G. Dawes 1925 Republican	Chas. E. Hughes 1923 Frank B. Kellogg 1925	Andrew W. Mellon 1923	John W. Weeks 1923 Dwight F. Davis 1925
31. Herbert Hoover 1929 Republican	Charles Curtis 1929 Republican	H. L. Stimson 1929	Andrew W. Mellon 1929 Ogden L. Mills 1932	James W. Good 1929 P. J. Hurley 1929
32. Franklin D. Roosevelt 1933 Democratic	John Nance Garner 1933 Democratic Henry A. Wallace 1941 Democratic Harry S. Truman 1945 Democratic	Cordell Hull 1933 E. R. Stettinius, Jr. 1944	Wm. H. Woodin 1933 Henry Morgenthau, Jr. 1934	Geo. H. Dern 1933 H. A. Woodring 1936 H. L. Stimson 1940
33. Harry S. Truman 1945 Democratic	Alben W. Barkley 1949 Democratic	James F. Byrnes 1945 Geo. C. Marshall 1947 Dean G. Acheson 1949	Fred M. Vinson 1945 John W. Snyder 1946	Robt. H. Patterson 1945 K. C. Royall 1947 **
34. Dwight D. Eisenhower 1953 Republican	Richard M. Nixon 1953 Republican	John Foster Dulles 1953 Christian Herter 1959	George C. Humphrey 1953 Robert B. Anderson 1957	

** Lost cabinet status in 1947.

and Cabinet Members Since 1865

Attorney-General	Postmaster-General	Secretary of Navy	Secretary of Interior	Secretary of Agriculture	Other Members
James Speed 1865 Henry Stanbery 1866 Wm. M. Evarts 1868	Wm. Dennison 1865 A. W. Randall 1866	Gideon Welles 1865	John P. Usher 1865 James Harlan 1865 O. H. Browning 1866	Cabinet status since 1889.	*Secretary of Commerce and Labor* Established Feb. 14, 1903.
E. R. Hoar 1869 A. T. Ackerman 1870 Geo. H. Williams 1871 Edw. Pierrepont 1875 Alphonso Taft 1876	J. A. J. Creswell 1869 Jas. W. Marshall 1874 Marshall Jewell 1874 Jas. N. Tyner 1876	Adolph E. Borie 1869 Geo. M Robeson 1869	Jacob D. Cox 1869 C. Delano 1870 Zach. Chandler 1875		G. B. Cortelyou 1903 Victor H. Metcalf 1904 O. S. Straus 1907 Chas. Nagel 1909
Chas. Devens 1877	David M. Key 1877 Horace May- nard 1880	R. W. Thompson 1877 Nathan Goff, Jr. 1881	Carl Schurz 1877		(Department divided, 1913)
W. MacVeagh 1881	T. L. James 1881	W. H. Hunt 1881	S. J. Kirkwood 1881		*Secretary of Commerce*
B. H. Brewster 1881	T. O. Howe 1881 W. Q. Gresham 1883 Frank Hatton 1884	W. E. Chandlr 1881	Henry M. Teller 1881		W. C. Redfield 1913 Joshua W. Alexander 1919 H. C. Hoover 1921
A. H. Garland 1885	Wm. F. Vilas 1885 D. M. Dickinson 1888	W. C. Whitney 1885	L. Q. C. Lamar 1885 Wm. F. Vilas 1888	N. J. Colman 1889	H. C. Hoover 1925 W. F. Whiting 1928
W. H. H. Miller 1889	J. Wanamaker 1889	Benj. F. Tracy 1889	John W. Noble 1889	J. M. Rusk 1889	R. P. Lamont 1929 R. D. Chapin 1932
R. Olney 1893 J. Harmon 1895	W. S. Bissell 1893 W. L. Wilson 1895	Hilary A. Herbert 1893	Hoke Smith 1893 D. R. Francis 1896	J. S. Morton 1893	D. C. Roper 1933 H. L. Hopkins 1939
J. McKenna 1897 J. W. Griggs 1897 P. C. Knox 1901	James A. Gary 1897 Chas. E. Smith 1898	John D. Long 1897	C. N. Bliss 1897 E. A. Hitchcock 1899	James Wilson 1897	Jesse Jones 1940 Henry A. Wallace 1945 W. Averell Harriman 1946 Charles W. Sawyer 1948
P. C. Knox 1091 W. H. Moody 1904 C. J. Bonaparte 1907	Chas. E. Smith 1901 Henry C. Payne 1902 Robt. J. Wynne 1904 G. B. Cortelyou 1905 G. von L. Meyer 1907	John D. Long 1901 Wm. H. Moody 1902 Paul Morton 1904 C. J. Bonaparte 1905 Victor H. Metcalf 1907 T. H. Newberry 1908	E. A. Hitchcock 1901 J. R. Garfield 1907	James Wilson 1901	Sinclair Weeks 1953 Lewis L. Strauss 1958 Frederick H. Mueller 1959
G. W. Wicker- sham 1909	F. H. Hitchcock 1909	G. von L. Meyer 1909	R. A. Ballinger 1909 W. L. Fisher 1911	James Wilson 1909	*Secretary of Labor* Established March 4, 1913 W. B. Wilson 1913 J. J. Davis 1921
J. C. Mc- Reynolds 1913 Thos. W. Gregory 1914 A. M. Palmer 1919	A. S. Burleson 1913	Josephus Daniels 1913	F. K. Lane 1913 J. B. Payne 1920	D. F. Houston 1913 E. T. Meredith 1920	W. N. Doak 1930 Frances Perkins 1933 L. B. Schwellen-bach 1945 M. J. Tobin 1948
H. M. Daugherty 1921	Will H. Hays 1921 Hubert Work 1922 Harry S. New 1923	Edwin Denby 1921	Albert B. Fall 1921 Hubert Work 1923	H. C. Wallace 1921	M. P. Durkin 1953 James P. Mitchell 1953
H. M. Daugherty 1923 Harlan F. Stone 1924 John G. Sargent 1925	Harry S. New 1923	Edwin Denby 1923 Curtis D. Wilbur 1924	Hubert Work 1923 Roy O. West 1928	H. M. Gore 1924 W. M. Jardine 1925	*Secretary of Defense* Established July 26, 1947. James V. Forrestal 1947
Wm. D. Mitchell 1929	Walter F. Brown 1929	Chas. F. Adams 1929	Ray L. Wilbur 1929	Arthur M. Hyde 1929	Louis A. Johnson 1949 George C. Marshall 1950
H. S. Cummings 1933 Frank Murphy 1939 Robt. H. Jackson 1940 Francis Biddle 1941	James A. Farley 1933 Frank C. Walker 1940	Claude A. Swanson 1933 Chas. Edison 1940 Frank Knox 1940 James V. Forrestal 1944	Harold L. Ickes 1933	H. A. Wallace 1933 C. R. Wickard 1940	Robert A. Lovett 1951 Charles E. Wilson 1953 Neil McElroy 1957 Thomas Gates 1960
Tom C. Clark 1945 J. H. McGrath 1949 James P. McGranery 1952	Robt. E. Hannegan 1945 Jesse L. Donaldson 1947	James V. Forrestal 1945 ††	Harold L. Ickes 1945 Julius A. Krug 1946 O. L. Chapman 1951	C. P. Anderson 1945 C. F. Brannan 1948	*Secretary of Health, Education, and Welfare* Established April 1, 1953. Oveta Culp Hobby 1953
Herbert Brownell, Jr. 1953 William P. Rogers 1957	Arthur E. Summerfield 1953		Douglas McKay 1953 Fred Seaton 1956	Ezra T. Benson 1953	Marion B. Folsom 1955 Arthur S. Flemming 1958

†† Lost cabinet status in 1947.

Division and State	1790	1800	1810	1820	1830	1840	1850	1860
UNITED STATES	3,929,214	5,308,483	7,239,881	9,638,453	12,866,020	17,069,453	23,191,876	31,443,321
GEOGRAPHIC DIVISIONS								
New England	1,009,408	1,233,011	1,471,973	1,660,071	1,954,717	2,234,822	2,728,116	3,135,283
Middle Atlantic	952,632	1,402,565	2,014,702	2,699,845	3,587,664	4,526,260	5,898,735	7,458,985
South Atlantic	1,851,806	2,286,494	2,674,891	3,061,063	3,645,752	3,925,299	4,679,090	5,364,703
East South Central	109,368	335,407	708,590	1,190,489	1,815,969	2,575,445	3,363,271	4,020,901
West South Central			77,618	167,680	246,127	449,985	940,251	1,747,667
East North Central		51,006	272,324	792,719	1,470,018	2,924,728	4,523,260	6,926,884
West North Central			19,783	66,586	140,455	426,814	880,335	2,169,832
Mountain							72,927	174,923
Pacific							105,871	444,053
NEW ENGLAND								
Maine	96,540	151,719	228,705	298,335	399,455	501,793	583,169	628,279
New Hampshire	141,885	183,858	214,460	244,161	269,328	284,574	317,976	326,073
Vermont	85,425	154,465	217,895	235,081	280,652	291,948	314,120	315,098
Massachusetts	378,787	422,845	472,040	523,287	610,408	737,699	994,514	1,231,066
Rhode Island	68,825	69,122	76,931	83,059	97,199	108,830	147,545	174,620
Connecticut	237,946	251,002	261,942	275,248	297,675	309,978	370,792	460,147
MIDDLE ATLANTIC								
New York	340,120	589,051	959,049	1,372,812	1,918,608	2,428,921	3,097,394	3,880,735
New Jersey	184,139	211,149	245,562	277,575	320,823	373,306	489,555	672,035
Pennsylvania	434,373	602,365	810,091	1,049,458	1,348,233	1,724,033	2,311,786	2,906,215
SOUTH ATLANTIC								
Delaware	59,096	64,273	72,674	72,749	76,748	78,085	91,532	112,216
Maryland	319,728	341,548	380,546	407,350	447,040	470,019	583,034	687,049
Dist. of Columbia		14,093	24,023	33,039	39,834	43,712	51,687	75,080
Virginia	747,610	880,200	974,600	1,065,366	1,211,405	1,239,797	1,421,661	1,596,318
West Virginia								
North Carolina	393,751	478,103	555,500	638,829	737,987	753,419	869,039	992,622
South Carolina	249,073	345,591	415,115	502,741	581,185	594,398	668,507	703,708
Georgia	82,548	162,686	252,433	340,989	516,823	691,392	906,185	1,057,286
Florida					34,730	54,477	87,445	140,424
EAST SOUTH CENTRAL								
Kentucky	73,677	220,955	406,511	564,317	687,917	779,828	982,405	1,155,684
Tennessee	35,691	105,602	261,727	422,823	681,904	829,210	1,002,717	1,109,801
Alabama				127,901	309,527	590,756	771,623	964,201
Mississippi		8,850	40,352	75,448	136,621	375,651	606,526	791,305
WEST SOUTH CENTRAL								
Arkansas			1,062	14,273	30,388	97,574	209,897	435,450
Louisiana			76,556	153,407	215,739	352,411	517,762	708,002
Oklahoma								
Texas							212,592	604,215
EAST NORTH CENTRAL								
Ohio		45,365	230,760	581,434	937,903	1,519,467	1,980,329	2,339,511
Indiana		5,641	24,520	147,178	343,031	685,866	988,416	1,350,428
Illinois			12,282	55,211	157,445	476,183	851,470	1,711,951
Michigan			4,762	8,896	31,639	212,267	397,654	749,113
Wisconsin						30,945	305,391	775,881
WEST NORTH CENTRAL								
Minnesota							6,077	172,023
Iowa						43,112	192,214	674,913
Missouri			19,783	66,586	140,455	383,702	682,044	1,182,012
North Dakota								
South Dakota								
Nebraska								28,841
Kansas								107,206
MOUNTAIN								
Montana								
Idaho								
Wyoming								
Colorado								34,277
New Mexico							61,547	93,516
Arizona								
Utah							11,380	40,273
Nevada								6,857
PACIFIC								
Washington								11,594
Oregon							13,294	52,465
California							92,597	379,994

United States, 1790–1950

	1870	1880	1890	1900	1910	1920	1930	1940	1950
	39,818,449	50,155,783	62,947,714	75,994,575	91,972,266	105,710,620	122,775,046	131,669,275	150,697,361
N.E.	3,487,924	4,010,529	4,700,749	5,592,017	6,552,681	7,400,909	8,166,341	8,437,290	9,314,453
M.A.	8,810,806	10,496,878	12,706,220	15,454,678	19,315,892	22,261,144	26,260,750	27,539,487	30,163,533
S.A.	5,853,610	7,597,197	8,857,922	10,443,480	12,194,895	13,990,272	15,793,589	17,823,151	21,182,335
E.S.C.	4,404,445	5,585,151	6,429,154	7,547,757	8,409,901	8,893,307	9,887,214	10,778,225	11,477,181
W.S.C.	2,029,965	3,334,220	4,740,983	6,532,290	8,784,534	10,242,224	12,176,830	13,064,525	14,537,572
E.N.C.	9,124,517	11,206,668	13,478,305	15,985,581	18,250,621	21,475,543	25,297,185	26,626,342	30,399,368
W.N.C.	3,856,594	6,157,443	8,932,112	10,347,423	11,637,921	12,544,249	13,296,915	13,516,990	14,061,394
Mtn.	315,385	653,119	1,213,935	1,674,657	2,633,517	3,336,101	3,701,789	4,150,003	5,074,998
Pac.	675,125	1,114,578	1,888,334	2,416,692	4,192,304	5,566,871	8,194,433	9,733,262	14,486,527
Me.	626,915	648,936	661,086	694,466	742,371	768,014	797,423	847,226	913,774
N.H.	318,300	346,991	376,530	411,588	430,572	443,083	465,293	491,524	533,242
Vt.	330,551	332,286	332,422	343,641	355,956	352,428	359,611	359,231	377,747
Mass.	1,457,351	1,783,085	2,238,947	1,805,346	3,366,416	3,852,356	4,249,614	4,316,721	4,690,514
R.I.	217,353	276,531	345,506	428,556	542,610	604,397	687,497	713,346	791,896
Conn.	537,454	622,700	746,258	908,420	1,114,756	1,380,631	1,606,903	1,709,242	2,007,280
N.Y.	4,382,759	5,082,871	6,003,174	7,268,894	9,113,614	10,385,227	12,588,066	13,479,142	14,830,192
N.J.	906,096	1,131,116	1,444,933	1,883,669	2,537,167	3,155,900	4,041,334	4,160,165	4,835,329
Pa.	3,521,951	4,282,891	5,258,113	6,302,115	7,665,111	8,720,017	9,631,350	9,900,180	10,498,012
Del.	125,015	146,608	168,493	184,735	202,322	223,003	238,380	266,505	318,085
Md.	780,894	934,943	1,042,390	1,188,044	1,295,346	1,449,661	1,631,526	1,821,244	2,343,001
D.C.	131,700	177,624	230,392	278,718	331,069	437,571	486,869	663,091	802,178
Va.	1,225,163	1,512,565	1,655,980	1,854,184	2,061,612	2,309,187	2,421,851	2,677,773	3,318,680
W.Va.	442,014	618,457	762,794	958,800	1,221,119	1,463,701	1,729,205	1,901,974	2,005,552
N.C.	1,071,361	1,399,750	1,617,949	1,893,810	2,206,287	2,559,123	3,170,276	3,571,623	4,061,929
S.C.	705,606	995,577	1,151,149	1,340,316	1,515,400	1,683,724	1,738,765	1,899,804	2,117,027
Ga.	1,184,109	1,542,180	1,837,353	2,216,331	2,609,121	2,895,832	2,908,506	3,123,723	3,444,578
Fla.	187,748	269,493	391,422	528,542	752,619	968,470	1,468,211	1,897,414	2,771,305
Ky.	1,321,011	1,648,690	1,858,635	2,147,174	2,289,905	2,416,630	2,614,589	2,845,627	2,944,806
Tenn.	1,258,520	1,542,359	1,767,518	2,020,616	2,184,789	2,337,885	2,616,556	2,915,841	3,291,718
Ala.	996,992	1,262,505	1,513,401	1,828,697	2,138,093	2,348,174	2,646,248	2,832,961	3,061,743
Miss.	827,922	1,131,597	1,289,600	1,551,270	1,797,114	1,790,618	2,009,821	2,183,796	2,178,914
Ark.	484,471	802,525	1,128,211	1,311,564	1,574,449	1,752,204	1,854,482	1,949,387	1,909,511
La.	726,915	939,946	1,118,588	1,381,625	1,656,388	1,798,509	2,101,593	2,363,880	2,683,516
Okla.			258,657	790,391	1,657,155	2,028,283	2,396,040	2,336,434	2,233,351
Tex.	818,579	1,591,749	2,235,527	3,048,710	3,896,542	4,663,228	5,824,715	6,414,824	7,711,194
Ohio	2,665,260	3,198,062	3,672,329	4,157,545	4,767,121	5,759,394	6,646,697	6,907,612	7,946,627
Ind.	1,680,637	1,978,301	2,192,404	2,516,462	2,700,876	2,930,390	3,238,503	3,427,796	3,934,224
Ill.	2,539,891	3,077,871	3,826,352	4,821,550	5,638,591	6,485,280	7,630,654	7,897,241	8,712,176
Mich.	1,184,059	1,636,937	2,093,890	2,420,982	2,810,173	3,668,412	4,842,325	5,256,106	6,371,766
Wis.	1,054,670	1,315,497	1,693,330	2,069,042	2,333,860	2,632,067	2,939,006	3,137,587	3,434,576
Minn.	439,706	780,773	1,310,283	1,751,394	2,075,708	2,387,125	2,563,953	2,792,300	2,982,483
Iowa	1,194,020	1,624,615	1,912,297	2,231,853	2,224,771	2,404,021	2,470,939	2,538,268	2,621,073
Mo.	1,721,295	2,168,380	2,679,185	3,106,665	3,293,335	3,404,055	3,629,367	3,784,664	3,954,653
N.D.	2,405	36,909	190,983	319,146	577,056	646,872	680,845	641,935	619,636
S.D.	11,776	98,268	348,600	401,570	585,888	636,547	692,849	642,961	652,740
Neb.	122,993	452,402	1,062,656	1,066,300	1,192,214	1,296,372	1,377,963	1,315,834	1,325,510
Kan.	364,399	996,096	1,428,108	1,470,495	1,690,949	1,769,257	1,880,999	1,801,028	1,905,299
Mont.	20,595	39,159	142,924	243,329	376,053	548,889	537,606	559,456	591,024
Ida.	14,999	42,610	88,548	161,772	325,594	431,866	445,032	524,873	588,637
Wyo.	9,118	20,789	62,555	92,531	145,965	194,402	225,565	250,742	290,529
Col.	39,864	194,327	413,249	539,700	799,024	939,629	1,035,791	1,123,296	1,325,089
N.M.	91,874	119,565	160,282	195,310	327,301	360,350	423,317	531,818	681,187
Ariz.	9,658	40,440	88,243	122,931	204,354	334,162	435,573	499,261	749,587
Utah	86,786	143,963	210,779	276,749	373,351	449,396	507,847	550,310	688,862
Nev.	42,491	62,266	47,355	42,335	81,875	77,407	91,058	110,247	160,083
Wash.	23,955	75,116	357,232	518,103	1,141,990	1,356,621	1,563,396	1,736,191	2,378,963
Or.	90,923	174,768	317,704	413,536	672,765	783,389	953,786	1,089,684	1,521,341
Cal.	560,247	864,694	1,213,398	1,485,053	2,377,549	3,426,861	5,677,251	6,907,387	10,586,223

Chief Justices of the Supreme Court

John Jay, *New York*	1789–1795		Melville W. Fuller, *Illinois*	1888–1910
John Rutledge, *South Carolina*	1795		Edward D. White, *Louisiana*	1910–1921
Oliver Ellsworth, *Connecticut*	1795–1799		William H. Taft, *Ohio*	1921–1930
John Marshall, *Virginia*	1801–1835		Charles E. Hughes, *New York*	1930–1941
Roger B. Taney, *Maryland*	1836–1864		Harlan F. Stone, *New York*	1941–1946
Salmon P. Chase, *Ohio*	1864–1873		Fred M. Vinson, *Kentucky*	1946–1953
Morrison R. Waite, *Ohio*	1874–1888		Earl Warren, *California*	1953–

Speakers of the House of Representatives

F. A. C. Muhlenberg, *Pennsylvania*	1789–1791		Galusha A. Grow, *Pennsylvania*	1861–1863
Jonathan Trumbull, *Connecticut*	1791–1793		Schuyler Colfax, *Indiana*	1863–1869
F. A. C. Muhlenberg, *Pennsylvania*	1793–1795		James G. Blaine, *Maine*	1869–1875
Jonathan Dayton, *New Jersey*	1795–1799		Michael C. Kerr, *Indiana*	1875–1876
Theodore Sedgwick, *Massachusetts*	1799–1801		Samuel J. Randall, *Pennsylvania*	1876–1881
Nathaniel Macon, *North Carolina*	1801–1807		Joseph W. Keifer, *Ohio*	1881–1883
Joseph B. Varnum, *Massachusetts*	1807–1811		John G. Carlisle, *Kentucky*	1883–1889
Henry Clay, *Kentucky*	1811–1814		Thomas B. Reed, *Maine*	1889–1891
Langdon Cheves, *South Carolina*	1814–1815		Charles F. Crisp, *Georgia*	1891–1895
Henry Clay, *Kentucky*	1815–1820		Thomas B. Reed, *Maine*	1895–1899
John W. Taylor, *New York*	1820–1821		David B. Henderson, *Iowa*	1899–1903
Philip P. Barbour, *Virginia*	1821–1823		Joseph G. Cannon, *Illinois*	1903–1910
Henry Clay, *Kentucky*	1823–1825		Champ Clark, *Missouri*	1911–1919
John W. Taylor, *New York*	1825–1827		Frederick H. Gillett, *Massachusetts*	1919–1925
Andrew Stevenson, *Virginia*	1827–1834		Nicholas Longworth, *Ohio*	1925–1931
John Bell, *Tennessee*	1834–1835		John Nance Garner, *Texas*	1931–1933
James K. Polk, *Tennessee*	1835–1839		Henry T. Rainey, *Illinois*	1933–1934
R. M. T. Hunter, *Virginia*	1839–1841		Joseph W. Byrns, *Tennessee*	1934–1936
John White, *Kentucky*	1841–1843		William B. Bankhead, *Alabama*	1936–1940
John W. Jones, *Virginia*	1843–1845		Sam Rayburn, *Texas*	1940–1947
John W. Davis, *Indiana*	1845–1847		Joseph W. Martin, Jr.,	
R. C. Winthrop, *Massachusetts*	1847–1849		*Massachusetts*	1947–1949
Howell Cobb, *Georgia*	1845–1851		Sam Rayburn, *Texas*	1949–1953
Linn Boyd, *Kentucky*	1851–1855		Joseph W. Martin, Jr.,	
N. P. Banks, *Massachusetts*	1856–1857		*Massachusetts*	1953–1955
James L. Orr, *South Carolina*	1857–1859		Sam Rayburn, *Texas*	1955–
William Pennington, *New Jersey*	1860–1861			

GENERAL BIBLIOGRAPHY

BOOK LISTS The chapter bibliographies in this volume provide references to selected books bearing upon the subjects of the particular chapters. This general bibliography includes certain of the more important books dealing with American history as a whole or with some fairly long period or broad phase of it. Most of the books listed here and on previous pages contain bibliographies of their own, and these are useful for the further pursuit of any topic the student may be interested in. The most recent and inclusive bibliographical volume is the *Harvard Guide to American History*, edited by Oscar Handlin and associates at Harvard University (1954). The student should bear in mind, however, that any list of books becomes "dated" the moment it is published; it remains useful only for finding items already in print at that time. For finding more recently published books—together with appraisals of them—the student is referred to the *American Historical Review* and the *Mississippi Valley Historical Review*, both of which appear quarterly.

MAPS AND STATISTICS The standard map collection for American history is C. O. Paullin's *Atlas of the Historical Geography of the United States* (1932). Briefer collections, designed for the student, are the *American History Atlas*, edited by A. B. Hart, D. M. Matteson, and H. E. Bolton (1942), which embodies a traditional approach to map-making; and the *Historical Atlas of the United States*, edited by C. L. Lord and E. H. Lord (rev. ed., 1953), which contains more variety and a more modern touch. Well chosen census data is given in *Historical Statistics of the United States, 1789–1945*, prepared by the Bureau of the Census with the co-operation of the Social Science Research Council (1949).

ORIGINAL SOURCES The kinds of records that history is made from are copiously illustrated in *American History Told by Contemporaries* edited by A. B. Hart (5 vols., 1897–1929). A standard compilation, especially valuable for official records and court decisions, is H. S. Commanger's *Documents of American History* (rev. ed., 1949). Less extensive but more varied in their selections are *Readings in American History*, edited by Oscar Handlin (1957); *The Shaping of the American Tradition*, edited by L. Hacker and H. Zahler (1947); and *The People Shall Judge*, edited by the staff in Social Sciences I at the University of Chicago (2 vols., 1949). Great issues and dilemmas of the past are presented with both contemporary documents and subsequent historical interpretations in *Problems in American Civilization*, sponsored by the Department of American Studies at Amherst College (29 vols., 1949–1957); and in *Problems in American History*, edited by R. W. Leopold and A. S. Link (rev. ed., 1957).

THE PICTORIAL RECORD Pictures, which give a sense of reality to the past as nothing else can, are to be found abundantly in *The Pageant of America*, edited by R. H. Gabriel (15 vols., 1925–1929); the *Album of American History*, edited by J. T. Adams (4 vols., 1944–1948); and *Life in America*, edited by M. B. Davidson (2 vols., 1951).

GEOGRAPHICAL INFLUENCES E. C. Semple, *American History and Its Geographic Conditions* (rev. ed., 1933), though originally published more than half a century ago, is still useful as a general introduction. H. R. Brown, *Historical Geography of the United States* (1948), traces in fascinating detail the interplay of environment and settlement, region by region. A special kind of geographical interpretation is that of Frederick Jackson Turner, who influenced the thinking of a whole generation of historians with his essays, gathered together in *The Frontier in American History* (1920) and *The Significance of Sections in American History* (1932). What happened to the "free land," which Turner believed had determined the course of American history, is told by R. E. Robbins in *Our Landed Heritage* (1942). The most recent and thorough volume tracing the frontier movement is R. A. Billington's *Westward Expansion* (1949).

HISTORIES: COMPREHENSIVE American history is told in brief lives of men who made it in the *Dictionary of American Biography*, edited by Allen Johnson and Dumas Malone (21 vols., 1928–1944). A handy reference is the *Dictionary of American History*, edited by J. T. Adams and R. V. Coleman (5 vols., 1940). *The American Nation: A History*, edited by A. B. Hart (28 vols., 1904–1916), each volume written by a leading authority, was for many years a standard set. As is usual with such co-operative histories, the individual volumes vary in quality; some are still valuable, others obsolete. *The New American Nation Series*, edited by H. S. Commager and R. B. Morris (40-odd volumes projected, 1954–   ), undertakes to incorporate the latest scholarship and will largely replace the old series. The *Chronicles of America* (50 vols. edited by Allen Johnson, 1918–1921; 6 additional vols. edited by Allan Nevins, 1950–1951) are written in a popular vein by well informed authors. A *History of the South*, edited by W. H. Stephenson and E. M. Coulter (12 vols. projected, 1947–   ), is detailed and authoritative for the part of the country it treats.

POLITICAL AND CONSTITUTIONAL R. H. Gabriel, *The Course of American Democratic Thought* (rev. ed., 1956), interprets political philosophy. W. E. Binkley,

American Political Parties (rev. ed., 1945), surveys the externals of politics. Richard Hofstadter, *The American Political Tradition* (1948), probes the thinking and motivation of political leaders. Two general accounts of constitutional history are A. H. Kelly and W. A. Harbison, *The American Constitution* (1948), and C. B. Swisher, *American Constitutional Development* (1943). H. C. Hockett, *The Constitutional History of the United States, 1776–1826* (2 vols., 1939), is a detailed treatment of the first half century. Charles Warren, *The Supreme Court and the Constitution* (2 vols. 1937), is the most comprehensive general work.

DIPLOMATIC Documents illustrating the history of foreign relations are contained in *The Record of American Diplomacy*, edited by R. J. Bartlett (rev. ed., 1954), and in *The Shaping of American Diplomacy*, edited by W. A. Williams (1956); the Williams book also gives selections from the writings of diplomatic historians. Textbooks are J. W. Pratt, *A History of the United States Foreign Policy* (1955); S. F. Bemis, *A Diplomatic History of the United States* (rev. ed., 1955); and T. A. Bailey, *A Diplomatic History of the American People* (rev. ed., 1958), which pursues the thesis that public opinion determines foreign policy. Area studies include Dexter Perkins, *History of the Monroe Doctrine* (rev. ed., 1955); S. F. Bemis, *The Latin American Policy of the United States* (1943); and A. W. Griswold, *The Far Eastern Policy of the United States* (1938). The ideas and arguments justifying American expansion are analyzed by A. J. Weinberg, *Manifest Destiny* (1935).

MILITARY AND NAVAL G. T. Davis gives a somewhat critical account of naval development in *A Navy Second to None* (1940). Harold and Margaret Sprout treat the same subject more enthusiastically in *The Rise of American Naval Power* (1942) and *Toward a New Order of Sea Power* (1943). In *Military Heritage of America* (1956) R. E. and T. N. Dupuy provide an able introduction to the study of the military history of the United States. In *Arms and Men* (1956) Walter Millis puts the development of American strategy into the broad setting of technological and other changes. A. A. Ekirch, Jr., tells the story of the changing problems of civil and military relationships in *The Civilian and the Military* (1956).

ECONOMIC *The Economic History of the United States* is told by experts in a series edited by Henry David and others (9 vols. projected, 1945–   ). Convenient summaries are H. U. Faulkner, *American Economic History* (rev. ed., 1954); and E. C. Kirkland, *A History of American Economic Life* (rev. ed., 1951). Aspects of the subject are treated with thoroughness by B. H. Meyer and others, *History of Transportation in the United States before 1860* (1917); E. R. Johnson and others, *History of Domestic and Foreign Commerce of the United States* (2 vols., 1915); V. S. Clark, *History of Manufactures in the United States* (3 vols., 1929); L. C. Gray, *History of Agriculture in the Southern United States to 1860* (2 vols., 1925); and P. W. Bidwell and J. I. Falconer, *History of Agriculture in the Northern United States, 1620–1860* (1925). The first three hundred years of American farming are well summarized by E. E. Edwards in the Department of Agriculture's *Yearbook of Agriculture* for 1940. Financial history is surveyed in W. J. Schultz and M. B. Caine, *Financial Development of the United States* (1937). Seymour Dunbar's *History of Travel in America* (4 vols., 1915) is both readable and authoritative. Sidney Ratner's *American Taxation: Its History* (1942) is comprehensive.

TECHNOLOGICAL J. W. Oliver, *History of American Technology* (1956) is a fairly detailed and factual treatment, without illustrations. A *Popular History of American Invention*, edited by Waldemar Kaempffert (2 vols., 1924), is a useful introduction to the subject, though neither complete nor entirely accurate. Roger Burlingame relates technological invention to political and social history in *March of the Iron Men* (1938) and *Engines of Democracy* (1940). Siegfried Giedion, *Mechanization Takes Command* (1948), provocatively interprets the influence of technology upon the American home.

BUSINESS AND LABOR The role of business in American history as a whole is emphasized by T. C. Cochran and William Miller in *The Age of Enterprise* (1942). Business thinking, as well as general economic thought, is set forth in Joseph Dorfman's *The Economic Mind in American Civilization* (3 vols., 1946–1949). L. M. Hacker presents one interpretation of the stages of business development in *The Triumph of American Capitalism* (1940), and N. S. B. Gras presents another interpretation in *Business and Capitalism* (1946). The worker's place in history is revealed through original records in the *Documentary History of American Industrial Society*, edited by J. R. Commons and others (10 vols., 1910–1911). Commons and his associates also are authors of the comprehensive *History of Labor in the United States* (4 vols., 1918–1935), which is based mainly on the documents cited above. An interpretive account of labor organization is Selig Perlman's *History of Trade Unionism in the United States* (1922). A useful bibliography is Henrietta M. Larson's *Guide to Business History* (1948).

SOCIAL A pioneering co-operative work is *A History of American Life*, edited by A. M. Schlesinger and D. R. Fox (13 vols., 1927–1948). General accounts of church history are W. W. Sweet, *The Story of Religion in America* (rev. ed., 1939); and W. L. Sperry, *Religion in America* (1946). A. W. Calhoun's *A Social History of the American Family* (3 vols., 1917–1919) is the only thing of its kind, as is Dixon Wecter's *The Saga of American Society* (1936), which is a history of "high society." Aspects of the use of leisure are recounted in F. R. Dulles, *America Learns to Play* (1940), and J. A. Krout, *Annals of American Sport* (1940). Other phases of social history are treated in F. R. Packard, *History of Medicine in the United States* (2 vols., 1931); and J. H. Franklin, *From Slavery to Freedom: A History of American Negroes* (1948).

IMMIGRATION This phase of social history receives a broad, general treatment in Carl Wittke, *We Who Built America* (1940), which stresses the immigrant contribution. M. L. Hansen, *The Immigrant in*

American History (1940), is a collection of essays reinterpreting the subject. The same author's *The Atlantic Migration, 1607–1860* (1940) was projected as the first volume of a comprehensive history, which Hansen's untimely death left uncompleted. Oscar Handlin, *The Uprooted* (1951), reveals the heart and soul of the immigrants, especially those from Eastern Europe in the twentieth century. The reaction of natives to immigrant arrivals is told by R. A. Billington, *The Protestant Crusade, 1800–1860* (1938); and John Higham, *Strangers in the Land* (1938), which takes up where Billington's book leaves off.

INTELLECTUAL Charles and Mary Beard, in *The Rise of American Civilization* (2 vols., rev. ed., 1933), make a brilliant effort to integrate the history of ideas with history in general. In *The American Spirit* (1942) the same authors elaborate upon their conception of what is distinctive in American ideas. Merle Curti, *The Growth of American Thought* (rev. ed., 1951), is a thorough, inclusive account. V. L. Parrington, *Main Currents in American Thought* (3 vols., 1927–1930), organizes the story biographically and presents it from the point of view of a Jeffersonian liberal. The history of schools is summarized by E. W. Knight, *Education in the United States* (rev. ed., 1951). Higher education is treated by Merle Curti, *Social Ideals of American Educators* (1935); and by Richard Hofstadter and

W. P. Metzger, *The Development of Academic Freedom in the United States* (1955). Both of these books are considerably broader than their titles indicate. Americans do not have the reputation of being a philosophical people, yet they have had their philosophers, as H. W. Schneider shows in *A History of American Philosophy* (1946).

LITERARY AND ARTISTIC H. L. Mencken, *The American Language* (3 vols., 1936–1948), deals lovingly and entertainingly with words and their history. See also M. M. Mathews (ed.), *A Dictionary of Americanisms on Historical Principles* (2 vols., 1951), which embodies a great deal of political as well as social and cultural history. Standard works on their respective subjects are F. L. Mott's *A History of American Magazines* (5 vols., 1930–1959) and his *American Journalism* (rev. ed., 1950). The history of literature and the fine arts may be traced in the following: R. E. Spiller and others, *Literary History of the United States* (3 vols., 1943); A. H. Quinn, *A History of the American Drama* (rev. ed., 1943); J. T. Howard, *Our American Music* (rev. ed., 1946); O. W. Larkin, *Art and Life in America* (1949); Alexander Eliot, *Three Hundred Years of American Painting* (1957); Edgar P. Richardson, *History of American Painting* (1956); and T. E. Tallmadge, *The Story of Architecture in America* (rev. ed., 1936).

PAPERBACK EDITIONS

Numerous books on American history may be purchased in soft-cover editions at comparatively moderate prices. Those available are listed, along with titles on various other subjects, in the catalog 6500 *Paperbound Books in Print*, which is published quarterly by R. R. Bowker Company, 62 West 45th Street, New York 36, N.Y. The interested student should consult his librarian or his book dealer for further information. If desired books are not available locally, they may be ordered directly from Book Mail Service, Box 363, Jamaica, New York. A sampling of the titles in American history follows:

Adams, Henry, *The United States in 1800* (Cornell)
American Heritage Reader (Dell)
Angle, Paul (ed.), *The Lincoln Reader* (Pocket Books)

Baldwin, Joseph, *Flush Times of Alabama and Mississippi* (Sagamore)
Becker, C. L., *The Declaration of Independence* (Vintage)

Bemis, S. F., *The Diplomacy of the American Revolution* (Indiana University)

Bowen, C. D., *John Adams and the American Revolution* (Universal Library)

Brebner, J. B., *The Explorers of North America, 1492–1806* (Anchor)

Brockway, T. P., *Basic Documents in United States Foreign Policy* (Anvil)

Bryce, James, edited and abridged by L. M. Hacker, *The American Commonwealth* (Sagamore)

Burlingame, Roger, *Benjamin Franklin* (New American Library)

Butcher, M. J., *The Negro in American Culture* (New American Library)

Canby, Courtlandt (ed.), *Lincoln and the Civil War: A Profile and a History* (Dell)

Cash, W. J., *The Mind of the South* (Anchor)

Charnwood, Lord, *Abraham Lincoln* (Pocket Books)

Chinard, Gilbert, *Thomas Jefferson: The Apostle of Americanism* (Ann Arbor)

Commager, H. S., *America in Perspective* (New American Library)

Crane, V. W., *The Southern Frontier, 1670–1732* (Ann Arbor)

Crèvecoeur, J. H. St. J. de, *Letters from an American Farmer* (Dutton)

Ellis, J. T., *American Catholicism* (Chicago)

Franklin, Benjamin, *Autobiography of Benjamin Franklin* (Pocket Books)

Glazer, Nathan, *American Judaism* (Chicago)

Handlin, Oscar, *Race and Nationality in American Life* (Anchor)

Heffner, R. D., *A Documentary History of the United States* (New American Library)

Hofstadter, Richard, *The American Political Tradition* (Vintage)

Hofstadter, Richard (ed.), *Great Issues in American History: A Documentary Record*, Vol. I (Vintage)

Jameson, J. F., *The American Revolution Considered as a Social Movement* (Beacon)

Johnson, Gerald, *Andrew Jackson* (Bantam)

Kemmerer, D. L., and Hunter, M. H., *Economic History of the United States* (Littlefield, Adams & Co.)

Kraus, Michael, *The North Atlantic Civilization* (Anvil)

Leech, Margaret, *Reveille in Washington* (Universal Library)

Logan, R. W., *The Negro in the United States* (Anvil)

Miller, Perry (ed.), *The American Puritans: Their Prose and Poetry* (Anchor)

Miller, Perry, *The American Transcendentalists* (Anchor)

Millis, Walter, *Arms and Men* (New American Library)

Morgan, E. S., *The Birth of the Republic: 1763–89* (Chicago)

Morison, S. E., *Christopher Columbus, Mariner* (New American Library)

Morris, R. B., *The American Revolution: A Short History* (Anvil)

Morris, R. B., *Basic Documents in American History* (Anvil)

Morris, Richard (ed.), *Basic Ideas of Alexander Hamilton* (Pocket Books)

Padover, S. K., *Jefferson* (New American Library)

Parkman, Francis, *The Oregon Trail* (New American Library)

Pratt, Fletcher, *Short History of the Civil War* (Pocket Books)

Rose, Arnold, *The Negro in America* (Beacon)

Rossiter, Clinton, *American Presidency* (New American Library)

Rossiter, Clinton, *The First American Revolution* (Harvest)

Rourke, Constance, *American Humor: A Study of the National Character* (Anchor)

Schlesinger, A. M., Jr., *The Age of Jackson*, abridged (New American Library)

Shannon, Fred, *American Farmers' Movements* (Anvil)

Small, Major A. R., *The Road to Richmond* (University of California)

Smith, H. N., *Virgin Land* (Vintage)

Swisher, C. B., *Historic Decisions of the Supreme Court* (Anvil)

Tate, Allen, *Stonewall Jackson* (Ann Arbor)

Tocqueville, Alexis de, *Democracy in America*, abridged (Vintage)

Wertenbaker, T. J., *The Puritan Oligarchy* (Universal Library)

Williams, T. Harry (ed.), *Abraham Lincoln, Selected Speeches, Messages and Letters* (Rinehart)

Woodward, C. Vann, *Reunion and Reaction* (Anchor)

INDEX

AAA, *see* Agricultural Adjustment Administration

Abbey, Edwin A., 102

Abilene (Kansas), 476

Ableman v. Booth, 363

abolitionists, 306, 313–15, 333, 337; 1848 election, 352; intensified propaganda, 361–2; Dred Scott case, 371–3; and John Brown, 376; *see also* antislavery

abominations, tariff of, 237, 241, 248, 250

academies, 155–6, 308, 331

Acadia, 64, 68

accidents, industrial, 508, 599

Acheson, Dean (b. 1893), 830, 838

Adams, Abigail (Mrs. John; 1744–1818), 174

Adams, Charles Francis, 453

Adams, Charles Francis, Jr. (1835–1915), *quoted*, 407

Adams, Henry (1893–1918), 569, 574

Adams, John (1735–1826), 235, 400; illus., 146; as Patriot leader, 82, 87, 91, 94; and Declaration of Independence, 94; as diplomat, 105, 110, 111–12, 116; Vice President, 128–9, 130, 143; "midnight" appointments, 132–3, 181; Presidential candidate, 145; elected President, 145; advisers to, 146, 147; as President, 146–53, 174, 179, 184; X.Y.Z. affair, 146–7; election of 1800, 151–2; ideal of university, 157; *quoted* on Jefferson, 231; Jefferson *quoted* on, 231; death, 231

Adams, John Quincy (1767–1848), 400; illus., 236; Treaty of Ghent, 208; election of 1820 and, 214; as Secretary of State, 214, 215, 216, 227, 228, 229, 233–4, 235; Florida and, 215; as Presidential candidate, 234, 235; as President, 235–7; "corrupt bargain," 235, 237; cabinet, 235; background, 235; as Congressman, 235; foreign affairs, 236; internal improvements, 236; Panama fiasco, 236; states' rights, 236; Indians and, 236; tariff of 1828 and, 236–7; election of 1828, 237–8; defeat for re-election, 238; and "gag rule," 333

Adams, Samuel (1722–1803), 80, 82, 89, 91; illus., 80; Boston "massacre," 82; Boston "tea party," 84; Shays's Rebellion, 121

Adams, Sherman, 843, 850

Adamsites, *see* National Republican party

Adamson Act (1916), 637

Addams, Jane (1860–1935), 507, 604

adding machine, invention of the, 492

Addyston Pipe and Steel Co. v. U.S., 615

advertising, 489, 504, 605, 686

Advisory Commission of the Council of National Defense, 776

aeronautics regulation, 690

AFL-CIO, 843; eviction of Teamsters', 844

Africa, 5, 541; slave trade, 37–8; *see also* North Africa; names of countries

Agassiz, Louis (1807–1885), 305, 309

Age of Reason, The (Paine), 163

Agricultural Adjustment Act (1938), 735

Agricultural Adjustment Administration, 729, 731–5

agricultural equipment and machines, 293–4, 513

agricultural experiment stations, 514

Agricultural Marketing Act (1929), 712

agriculture: colonial, 32–4; regional differences, 32; farm life (1800), illus., 162–3; export, 290; improved methods, 293–5; in 1800's, 293–6; specialization, 295; soil depletion, 295; West, 295; South, 325–7, 444–5; Civil War and, 386–7; Southern rehabilitation, 444–5; share-crop and crop-lien system, 444–5; farming frontier, 484–6; mechanization of, 513; subsistence *vs.* commercial farming, 513; improved techniques, 513; exports, 514; expansion of facilities, 514; scientific, 514; Hatch Act, 514; farm population, 515; farm problems and grievances, 515–16; National Grange and, 518–21, 695, 731; Smith-Lever Act, 637; during 1920's, 695–7, 712; Hoover Administration and, 712; New Deal and, 731–5; farm defaults and foreclosures, 1929–1945 (chart), 732; World War II, 784–5; "soil bank" plan, 844; *see also* farmers; irrigation; parity prices

Agriculture, Department of, 622

Aguinaldo, Emilio (b. 1870?), 558

air brake, Westinghouse, 497

Air Commerce Act (1926), 690

A NOTE ON THE TYPE

THIS BOOK *is set in* ELECTRA, *a Linotype face designed by* W. A. DWIGGINS (1880–1956), *who was responsible for so much that is good in contemporary book design. Electra cannot be classified as either modern or old-style. It is not based on any historical model, nor does it echo a particular period or style.*

This book was printed and bound by The Book Press, Brattleboro, Vermont. The paper was manufactured by S. D. Warren Co., Boston. Typography and binding design by VINCENT TORRE.